ITALY

Where to Stay and Eat
for All Budgets

Must-See Sights
and Local Secrets

Ratings You Can Trust

Fodor's Travel Publications   New York, Toronto, London, Sydney, Auckland
www.fodors.com

FODOR'S ITALY 2005
Editor: Matthew Lombardi

Editorial Production: Tom Holton
Editorial Contributors: David Allan, Peter Blackman, Ryan Bradley, Nick Bruno, Linda Cabasin, Lisa Dunford, Elaine Eliah, Robin S. Goldstein, David Graham, Dana Klitzberg, Aaron Maines, Francesca Marretta, Julie Mazur, Clare Pedrick, Chris Rose, Patricia Rucidlo, Mark Walters, Amy Wang
Maps: David Lindroth, *cartographer;* Bob Blake and Rebecca Baer, *map editors*
Design: Fabrizio La Rocca, *creative director;* Guido Caroti, *art director;* Moon Sun Kim, *cover designer;* Melanie Marin, *senior picture editor*
Production/Manufacturing: Colleen Ziemba
Cover Photo: (Country road and house, Tuscany): Simon Des Rochers/Masterfile

ISBN 1-4000-1410-7

ISSN 0361-977X

SPECIAL SALES
This book is available for special discounts for bulk purchases for sales promotions or premiums. Special editions, including personalized covers, excerpts of existing books, and corporate imprints, can be created in large quantities for special needs. For more information, write to Special Markets/Premium Sales, 1745 Broadway, MD 6-2, New York, New York 10019, or e-mail specialmarkets@randomhouse.com.

AN IMPORTANT TIP & AN INVITATION
Although all prices, opening times, and other details in this book are based on information supplied to us at press time, changes occur all the time in the travel world, and Fodor's cannot accept responsibility for facts that become outdated or for inadvertent errors or omissions. So **always confirm information when it matters,** especially if you're making a detour to visit a specific place. Your experiences—positive and negative—matter to us. If we have missed or misstated something, **please write to us.** We follow up on all suggestions. Contact the Italy editor at editors@fodors.com or c/o Fodor's at 1745 Broadway, New York, New York 10019.

PRINTED IN THE UNITED STATES OF AMERICA

10 9 8 7 6 5 4 3 2 1

DESTINATION ITALY

No less an observer of life than Goethe once recorded in the now-famous diaries he kept of his 18th-century journey through Italy, "I can honestly say I've never been as happy in my life as now." The great German poet was neither the first nor the last visitor to fall blissfully under the spell of this fabled land, with its stunning landscapes, stupendous contributions to Western civilization, and unabashed enthusiasm for life's pleasures. You may be enchanted by the impossible brushstrokes forming Michelangelo's Adam on the ceiling of the Sistine Chapel, or by the afternoon light cascading across the blazing red rooftops of Florence, viewed from Brunelleschi's dome. You may be taken in by the melodious frenzy amid the mountains of sardines and cured olives in Palermo's Vucciria market, or bewitched by a gondola gliding along a Venetian canal, its passage silently watched by Gothic palaces with delicately arched eyebrows. Be prepared to be swept away. Buon viaggio!

Tim Jarrell, Publisher

CONTENTS

Maps

CloseUps

ON THE ROAD WITH FODOR'S

A trip takes you out of yourself. Concerns of life at home disappear, driven away by more immediate thoughts—about, say, what marvels will beguile the next day, or where you'll have dinner. That's where Fodor's comes in. We make sure that you know all your options, so that you don't miss something that's just around the next bend. Because the best memories of your trip might well have nothing to do with what you came to Italy to see, we guide you to sights large and small all over the country. You might set out to immerse yourself in Florence's Renaissance treasures, but back at home you find yourself unable to forget a perfect afternoon spent strolling in an Umbrian hill town. With Fodor's at your side, serendipitous discoveries are never far away.

Our success in showing you every corner of Italy is a credit to our extraordinary writers. Although there's no substitute for travel advice from a good friend who knows your style, our contributors are the next best thing—the kind of people you would poll for travel advice if you knew them.

After completing his master's degree in art history, Peter Blackman settled permanently in Italy in 1986. Since then he's worked as a biking and walking tour guide, managing to see more of Italy than most of his Italian friends. When he's not leading a trip, you'll find Peter at his home in Chianti, listening to opera and planning his next journey.

Disinclined to stray far from superb wine and spectacular skiing, travel writer Ryan Bradley divides his time between northern Italy and northern California. Although his professional wine training and habitual alpinism have drawn him to the Dolomites, he never feels quite prepared for the existential challenge of a face-to-face encounter with Bolzano's iceman.

Freelance writer, photographer, and Italian-to-English translator Nick Bruno divides his time between Dundee, Scotland, and southern Italy, where his family roots lie. While in Puglia and Campania he divides his time between guidebook research and olive eating.

From African war zones to Asian mountaintops, writer and journalist Elaine Eliah has captured pieces of the world in words. Since settling in Venice in 1999, she's rowed nearly every canal and sailed many of the Venetian Republic's Adriatic trade routes. She currently writes, teaches English, and helps travelers discover the magic of her adopted home.

Although Robin S. Goldstein is trained in philosophy at Harvard and law at Yale, his heart has always been in his travel writing. His credits include not only his home base of Italy but also Spain, Mexico, Ecuador, and the Galapagos Islands. Once a resident of Genoa, he now spends most of his time in the *mezzogiorno* and along the Sicilian coast.

David Graham was a tour guide in Europe, Southeast Asia, and the Middle East before moving to Vicenza in the 1980s. During his years in the Venetian Arc region he's been particularly inspired by the hand-tended vineyards, the spectacular mountains, and Trieste's sparkling coastline. David now lives in Venice, where he is a translator specializing in art and architecture.

Originally a fashion, food, and wine publicist in New York, Dana Klitzberg went on to study at the Institute of Culinary Education and work as a chef at the renowned Manhattan restaurant San Domenico. After a stint cooking in a restaurant in Rome, she decided to make the Eternal City her home. Now she runs her own company, through which she caters, gives cooking classes, and conducts culinary tours of the city.

A. H. Maines is a freelance writer, editor, and translator based in Milan. He has written for a number of newspapers and magazines, including the *International Herald Tribune,* the *New York Times,* and *The Guardian.*

A native Neapolitan, Francesca Marretta has left a trail of ink on 1,000 kilometers of Italy's southern coastline in the process of working on several guidebooks. An English-language interpreter, she's traveled to Russia, the Czech Republic, and the United Kingdom, but is always exhilarated (and exasperated) upon her return to the high-heeled boot.

British journalist Clare Pedrick studied Italian at Cambridge University, and soon afterward she settled in Italy, restoring a ruined house in the Umbrian mountains before transplanting to Rome. She has served as a reporter for the Associated Press, special correspondent for the *Washington Post,* and European editor for World News Link. Clare and her family have recently returned to the simpler life in Umbria, from where she writes a column for the Rome-based English-language magazine *The American.*

Chris Rose arrived in Naples from Manchester, England, planning to stay for three months. Twelve years later, he's still there, writing guidebooks, teaching English, and organizing events with writers and artists visiting from Britain. You can read his short story "The Shoemaker General of Naples" in *New Writing 10,* published by Picador.

Florence resident Patricia Rucidlo holds master's degrees in Italian Renaissance history and art history. When she's not extolling the virtues of a Pontormo masterpiece or angrily defending the Medici, she's leading wine tours in Chianti, catering private dinner parties, or working on a cookbook.

An editor, travel writer, and naturalist, British-born Mark Walters first settled in Naples as a British Council lecturer in the 1980s. He completed his graduate studies in classics and now, when not hiking or playing field hockey, he leads study tours around the Mediterranean.

ABOUT THIS BOOK

There's no doubt that the best source for travel advice is a like-minded friend who's just been where you're headed. But with or without that friend, you'll have a better trip with a Fodor's guide in hand. Once you've learned to find your way around its pages, you'll be in great shape to find your way around your destination.

SELECTION

Our goal is to cover the best properties, sights, and activities in their category, as well as the most interesting communities to visit. We make a point of including local food lovers' hot spots as well as neighborhood options, and we avoid all that's touristy unless it's really worth your time. You can go on the assumption that everything you read about in this book is recommended wholeheartedly by our writers and editors. Flip to On the Road with Fodor's to learn more about who they are. It goes without saying that no property mentioned in the book has paid to be included.

RATINGS

Orange stars ★ denote sights and properties that our editors and writers consider the very best in the area covered by the entire book. These, the best of the best, are listed in the Fodor's Choice section in the front of the book. Use the index to find complete descriptions. Black stars ★ highlight the sights and properties we deem Highly Recommended, the don't-miss sights within any region. In cities, sights pinpointed with numbered map bullets ❶ in the margins tend to be more important than those without bullets.

SPECIAL SPOTS

Pleasures & Pastimes focuses on types of experiences that reveal the spirit of the destination. Watch for Off the Beaten Path sights. Some are out of the way, some are quirky, and all are worth your while. If the munchies hit while you're exploring, look for Need a Break? suggestions.

TIME IT RIGHT

Wondering when to go? Check On the Calendar up front and chapters' Timing sections for weather and crowd overviews and best times to visit.

SEE IT ALL

Use Fodor's exclusive Great Itineraries as a model for your trip. (For a good overview of the entire destination, follow those that begin the book, or mix regional itineraries from several chapters.) In cities, Good Walks guide you to important sights in each neighborhood; ☞ indicates the starting points of walks and itineraries in the text and on the map.

BUDGET WELL

Hotel and restaurant price categories from ¢ to $$$$ are defined in the opening pages of each chapter—expect to find a balanced selection for every budget. For attractions, we always give standard adult admission fees; reductions are sometimes available for children, students, and senior citizens.

BASIC INFO	Smart Travel Tips lists travel essentials for the entire area covered by the book; city- and region-specific basics end each chapter. To find the best way to get around, see the transportation section; see individual modes of travel ("By Car," "By Train") for details. We assume you'll check Web sites or call for particulars.
ON THE MAPS	Maps throughout the book show you what's where and help you find your way around. Black and orange numbered bullets **①** **①** in the text correlate to bullets on maps.
BACKGROUND	In general, we give background information within the chapters in the course of explaining sights as well as in CloseUp boxes and in Understanding Italy at the end of the book. To get in the mood, review the suggestions in Books & Movies.
FIND IT FAST	Within the book, chapters are arranged in a roughly north-to-south direction starting with Venice. Chapters are divided into smaller regions, within which towns are covered in logical geographical order; attractive routes and interesting places between towns are flagged as En Route.
DON'T FORGET	Restaurants are open for lunch and dinner daily unless we state otherwise; we mention dress only when there's a specific requirement and reservations only when they're essential or not accepted—it's always best to book ahead. Hotels have private baths, phones, TVs, and air-conditioning unless otherwise indicated. We always list facilities but not whether you'll be charged extra to use them, so when pricing accommodations, find out what's included.
SYMBOLS	

Many Listings

★ Fodor's Choice
★ Highly recommended
⊠ Physical address
✛ Directions
🕮 Mailing address
☎ Telephone
🖶 Fax
⊕ On the Web
✎ E-mail
🎟 Admission fee
☉ Open/closed times
▶ Start of walk/itinerary
Ⓜ Metro stations
▭ Credit cards

Outdoors

⅄ Golf
⚠ Camping

Hotels & Restaurants

🏨 Hotel
🛏 Number of rooms
⚐ Facilities
⦿| Meal plans
✕ Restaurant
🖀 Reservations
👔 Dress code
↘ Smoking
🍺 BYOB
✕🏨 Hotel with restaurant that warrants a visit

Other

🐾 Family-friendly
🔋 Contact information
⇨ See also
⊠ Branch address
☞ Take note

1 Venice

A maze of waterways, bridges, alleys, and tiny squares, Venice is a magical place apart. In this city of Marco Polo, Titian, and Vivaldi, a vaporetto ride down the Grand Canal—Venice's own 5th Avenue—is a fairy-tale journey past the city's shimmering, sometimes decaying palaces. "Venice is like eating an entire box of chocolate liqueurs in one go," Truman Capote once remarked, and the city will indeed stuff you with spectacular art and a distinctive, primarily fish-based cuisine. During February's Carnivale you'll find even the pigeons are pressed for space in Piazza San Marco, the city's heart.

2 The Venetian Arc

Green plains, reaching inland from Venice's lagoon until they touch the Alpine foothills, hold several of Italy's art cities. Elegant Vicenza bears the signature of the great 16th-century architect Andrea Palladio. Farther west, Verona is famed for the tombs of the Della Scala lords, the romantic settings associated with Shakespeare's *Romeo and Juliet,* and an ancient arena, still packing in the crowds for everything from opera to rock and roll. Art lovers head to Padua for Giotto's Scrovegni Chapel and carvings by Donatello and Lombardo in the Basilica Sant'Antonio. In the east, the region of Friuli-Venezia Giulia has for centuries been coveted and conquered by warring powers; you can sense their influence in the cafés of Trieste and the castle of Miramare.

3 The Dolomites

Northern Italy's Dolomite Mountains are known for stupefying cliffs and curiously shaped peaks, charming meadows and crystal-clear lakes, and splintered crags—it's little wonder that Leonardo da Vinci depicted them in the haunting background of his *Mona Lisa.* The region is Italy's year-round sports playground, with seeing just as important as skiing in jet-set Cortina d'Ampezzo and Madonna di Campiglio. You can explore the Strada del Vino (Wine Route) between Italian-speaking Trento and Germanic Bolzano (home to a celebrated iceman); zip along the 48 hairpin turns of Stelvio Pass, and marvel at the mountain vistas from the *Grande Strada delle Dolomiti* (Great Dolomites Road).

4 Milan, Lombardy & the Lakes

Poets, royals, Roman emperors, and mere mortals have long swooned over Lakes Como, Garda, and Maggiore, where deep-blue waters and hillsides clad with voluptuous gardens surround Europe's toniest resorts. Other sophisticated pleasures are found in Milan, Italy's urbane commercial capital, where next season's fashions can be had for a price. Ringing Milan on the Po plain are the walled outposts of Cremona, Pavia, and Mantua, where Renaissance dukes built towering palaces and intricate churches. Majestic landscapes surround Riva del Garda, huddled under soaring cliffs on the northern tip of Lake Garda, and Bergamo, whose walls rise over a breathtaking Alpine vista.

5 Piedmont/Valle d'Aosta

Piedmont has always felt the influence of nearby France, so don't be surprised if Paris comes to mind while you stroll down Turin's tree-lined boulevards or sample the region's rich, elaborate food. But this is also Alpine territory, and the rigors that nature has imposed have created a hardworking and fiercely independent spirit that perfectly balances the cultured sophistication of the city. Tucked away in their own corner of northwestern Italy, Piedmont and the Valle d'Aosta are often neglected by international tourists—though that status will change, at least temporarily, when Turin hosts the 2006 Winter Olympics.

6 The Italian Riviera

Hemmed in by the Alps on one side and the Ligurian Sea on the other, the towns in this swath of northwestern Italy are either fishing villages, tiny harbors, seaside resorts, or major ports—most notable of the latter being Genoa. That the region is intimately linked to the sea, as both friend and foe, is symbolized by the rows of buildings, called *palazzate,* that face the sea in practically every coastal town. Painted in earthy ochre, yellow, red, or brown, they attach together as though to form a defensive wall, but with windows looking out toward the open sea. It's not surprising to learn that Christopher Columbus was a Ligurian.

7 Emilia-Romagna

Emilia-Romagna owes its beginnings to the Romans, who built the Via Aemilia in 187 BC. Today the road spans the flat, foggy region, traversing a landscape of medieval castles and crumbling farmhouses from Piacenza to the murky Adriatic beaches of Rimini. Mosaics in nearby Ravenna are glittering treasures left from Byzantine rule. Bologna is the region's principal cultural and intellectual center. Rows of street arcades wind through grandiose towers and conceal some of the best restaurants in Italy. Emilia-Romagna is Italy's pasta heartland, and its formidable gastronomic inventions include tortellini, the balsamic vinegar of Modena, buttery prosciutto, and the complex Parmigiano Reggiano cheese from the Parma area, now sprinkled all over the world.

8 Florence

Florence, the "Athens of Italy" and the key to the Renaissance, hugs the banks of the Arno River, where it lies folded among the cypress-studded hills of north-central Tuscany. Elegant and somewhat aloof, this historic center of European civilization still shares with Rome the honor of first place among Italian cities for the magnitude of its artistic works, among them Botticelli's *Birth of Venus* and Michelangelo's *David.* Down every street you'll make new discoveries of Romanesque, Gothic, or Renaissance architecture, sheltering masterful paintings and sculpture. Equally as splendid are the magnificent palaces of the Medici, whose patronage rocketed Florence to the forefront of the Renaissance.

9 Tuscany

Nature outdid herself in Tuscany, the region on the Ligurian and Tyrrhenian seas that has Florence as its principal city. Punctuated by thickly wooded slopes, sun-warmed vineyards, olive groves, and dramatic hill towns, Tuscany's milk-and-honey vistas have changed little since Renaissance artists first beheld them. Not surprisingly, you'll find some of Italy's greatest art treasures here, including the 13th-century Leaning Tower of Pisa and Piero della Francesca's *Legend of the True Cross* frescoes in Arezzo. The time traveler will be entranced by medieval Siena, and the Chianti region has seduced many an expatriate who couldn't summon the will to return home. There are also miles of sandy and rocky beaches and a few gorgeous islands, Elba being the largest.

10 Umbria & the Marches

Umbria, dubbed "Italy's green heart," has a rich artistic inheritance that includes the frescoes of Assisi's Basilica di San Francesco, the brooding Palazzo dei Consoli in Gubbio, and the Gothic glory of Orvieto's cathedral. Umbria bears the stamp of its Roman past close to the surface; most of the region's important towns lie either along the ancient Via Flaminia (opened in 219 BC to connect Rome to the Adriatic coast) or close to one of its many branch roads—so expect to see Roman villas, aqueducts, theaters, walls, and temples. Eastward, in the region of the Marches on the Adriatic, is Urbino, where the Ducal Palace reveals more about the artistic energy of the Renaissance than a shelf of history books.

11 Rome

It's hard to imagine another city in the world that offers so much pleasure for the senses. Rome's moderate weather may frustrate Italians dying to display their furs, but for travelers from less clement lands the warm breeze with just a whiff of the sea is a delight. So, too, are the endless visual surprises: round any corner and be greeted by a dazzling fountain, a quiet Renaissance carving, or the green spray of a palm tree or maritime pine. Food is to the palette what the city's vistas are to the eye: luscious and ubiquitous. Climb almost any one of Rome's famous seven hills or take a walk in one of the huge, majestic parks and you're likely to find striking tranquillity in the midst of the urban bustle.

12 Lazio, Abruzzo & Molise

There are many worthwhile, generally undervisited sights in the regions that surround Rome. Lazio has papal palaces, landscaped gardens, medieval hill towns, and antiquities both Etruscan and Roman. Trips farther afield in the mainly mountainous regions of Abruzzo and Molise will give you a chance to appreciate fine archaeological sites, the unadulterated culture of age-old hill towns, and the natural beauty of Italy's finest national park, Parco Nazionale d'Abruzzo.

13 Naples & Campania

A happy combination of spectacular geology, rich cultural heritage, and excellent standards of hospitality, Campania is the Italy many travelers dream about. At Pompeii you can see how Romans once defined the good life before heading to the pint-size island of Capri for a present-day dose of sybaritic pleasures. Among the almost clichéd list of names—Amalfi, Positano, Vesuvius, Ravello—the crowds seemingly dissipate and you can still "discover" pockets of undiluted beauty. In pole position, emerging from decades of decline and urban neglect, is the vibrant, heritage-rich Naples, the most operatic of cities.

⑭ Puglia

Linger awhile on the fertile farmland and rocky coast that make up Italy's heel, and you'll discover that the sunbaked landscape yields more than olives and grapes. Greeks, Romans, Holy Roman Emperors, and other conquerors stayed long enough to leave their mark on such places as the Casbah-like fishing port of Gallipoli, and Lecce, where baroque palaces dominate a youthful nerve center. Even more exotic are the eye-catching *trulli*—mysterious, conical-roof dwellings built from blocks of limestone; there are more than 1,000 of them in the town of Alberobello. One of the greatest appeals of the region is what still isn't here: large-scale development along the seductive coastline, at its most alluring on the cove-studded Gargano Promontory.

⑮ Basilicata & Calabria

The southernmost regions of the peninsula are known informally as the *mezzogiorno*—literally "midday" for the blazing sun that presides over medieval villages, shimmering seas, and immensely varied landscapes. The pleasure of traveling here is stumbling upon places far off the beaten path—the simple *sassi,* dwellings partially hewn from caves, in the Basilicata village of Matera, perhaps, or the churches perched upon rocky promontories all along the Tyrrhenian coast of Calabria. Reggio di Calabria's national museum has a dazzling collection of antiquities.

⑯ Sicily

The architecture of Sicily reflects the island's centuries of changing dominion by the Greeks, Byzantines, Arabs, Normans, and Spaniards. Baroque church–hopping could be a sport in the cacophonous streets of Palermo and seafaring Siracusa. The breezes are sultry, and everyday life is without pretense, as witnessed in the workaday stalls of the fish markets all along the ports of the Tyrrhenian and Ionian coasts, bursting with tuna, swordfish, and sardines. Greek ruins stand sentinel in Agrigento's Valley of the Temples, blanketed in almond, oleander, and juniper blossoms. All over the island the ins and outs of life are celebrated each day as they have been for centuries—over a morning coffee, at the family lunch table, and in the magical evening *passeggiata*.

⑰ Sardinia

Too distant from imperial and papal Rome to be influenced by the character of the mainland, Sardinia is as unique as its weather-worn landscape. Although the indigenous culture is one of Italy's most interesting, many travelers opt to explore the high-profile Costa Smeralda, a chic resort developed by the Aga Khan, who discovered its charms when his yacht took shelter from a storm. Intrepid travelers head for the *nuraghi,* cyclopean stone defensive structures that are among prehistory's enigmas. Severely beautiful Sardinia is a prime destination if you're looking for a vacation getaway—whether of the chic or rugged variety.

GREAT ITINERARIES

Italian Gardens
7 to 9 days

Using the living materials and elements of nature to achieve studied aesthetic effects, Italians are masters at creating gardens, and have been from the Renaissance and baroque ages until well into the 19th century. Usually framing country villas or grand city palaces, the most spectacular gardens are laid out with an artist's eye for perspective and color; many are studded with statuary and fanciful fountains. A tour of some of Italy's most beautiful gardens begins in Milan, gateway to the Lake District—ideally in spring, when azaleas and rhododendrons are in glorious bloom. Note that some gardens are not open in winter or in inclement weather; always call ahead.

STRESA
3 days. Spend the better part of one day on an excursion from the stately Lake Maggiore resort town of Stresa, exploring the Borromean Islands, from the decorative baroque palace and terraced gardens on Isola Bella to the Renaissance-style villa on Isola Madre, surrounded by a lush park where peacocks strut amid banks of azaleas, rhododendrons, and camellias. To plant the elaborately tiered gardens of Isola Bella and Isola Madre, a 16th-century count had laborers haul soil to the islands in boats. The next day hop on a ferry to Verbania and get off at the embarcadero of the Villa Taranto. Adorned with terraces, cascades, and fountains, its vast garden was laid out in the 20th century and remains one of Europe's finest. Some 20,000 plant species—many rare and exotic—grow here. (⇨ Chapter 4, Lake Maggiore and Lake Orta.)

BELLAGIO
2 or 3 days. Settle into this beauty spot on Lake Como surrounded by romantic vistas. At Villa Melzi, which some regard as the most serendipitous site in the entire Lake District, a fabulous staircase blooms with azaleas in spring and is topped by a neoclassic palace. Just across the lake in Tremezzo, one stop away on the ferry, is Villa Carlotta, a wedding present to Charlotte of Russia in 1843. The luxuriant gardens and park are known for their spectacular rhododendrons and azaleas. From Tremezzo, take the ferry to Sala Comacina, where, during visiting hours, there is regular ferry service to Villa Balbaniello, one of the most romantic sites of all. Check opening times with the Bellagio or Tremezzo tourist offices. Afterward, if you have time, take the leisurely ferry trip around the Maggiore or Como lakes to get glimpses of many more villa gardens from the boat. (⇨ Chapter 4, Lake Como.)

FLORENCE
2 or 3 days. Make Florence your base for a series of visits to the gardens of the Medici villas on the city's outskirts. These gardens feel somewhat austere, their beauty lying in the artful arrangements of evergreens. Roam through the Giardini Boboli, behind Palazzo Pitti, laid out for Eleanor of Toledo, wife of Medici Grand Duke Cosimo I, noting how the plan was ingeniously adapted to a very irregular site. Then, together with some city sightseeing to help you focus on the Medici influence in Florence, continue your villa touring in half-day excursions. Villa Gamberaia, a legacy of the wealthy Capponi family, is an elegant Italian garden set in olive groves in the hills of Settignano. North of Florence, toward Sesto Fiorentino, the vast Medici gardens of Villa di Castello are festooned with more than 500 lemon trees. At the Medici Villa La Petraia, sculptures by Renaissance masters adorn the 16th-century Italian garden, and a park is landscaped in 19th-century style. (⇨ Chapter 8, Side Trips from Florence.)

By Public Transportation
Trains make frequent runs between Milan and Stresa (about 60 minutes), Como (30 minutes), and Lecco (30 minutes). The good lake ferry service makes it easy to explore villages on the Maggiore and Como lakes (ferry trips are no more than 30 minutes). Travel by bus from Como to Bellagio and between Lecco and Bellagio (both trips about 75 minutes, depending on traffic). By train it takes about 3½ hours to travel between Milan and Florence. To reach Villa Gamberaia from Florence, take Bus 10, marked Settignano. To reach Villa La Petraia take Bus 28; Villa di Castello is within walking distance.

Turin

Asti

60 km
(37 mi)

Alba

San Remo

A Food Lover's Tour
10 to 14 days

Sampling Italy's best food and wines in the very places they are produced will enrich your understanding of the country and its people. On this itinerary through a country where good eating and drinking is the rule, you'll take in the birthplace of some wonderful wines, a gracious city renowned for exquisite chocolates and its grand fin de siècle cafés, truffle country, and, last but not least, Emilia-Romagna's Parma, which is as rich in history and art as in its culinary delights. In northern Italy, near the Dolomites, you'll see how irresistible cooking mixes Italian and Austrian accents.

MAP KEY	
Italian Gardens	
A Food Lover's Tour	

TURIN

1 or 2 days. Dine on as many as 30 antipasti followed by a creamy risotto, and top off your meal with a delectable dessert. Then head for one of the city's historic cafés to savor the wonderful pastries along with your espresso. And don't forget to pick up some of the city's celebrated hazelnut chocolates, called *gianduiotti*. Southeast of Turin in the Monferrato and Langhe districts, rolling hills are blanketed with the vineyards that produce Barolo, "king of the wines and wine of kings," in addition to Barbaresco and others. (⇨ Chapter 5, Turin and Fortified Cities of the Po Plain.)

ASTI, ALBA & PARMA

2 days. Spend a day exploring the wineries in the area. Asti has lent its name to Spumante, a sparkling white that brings bubbles of gaiety to every kind of celebration in

Italy. Some like it sweet, especially as a dessert wine, but many choose the brut version, much like champagne and made by the same method. Spend another day in Alba, stopping at the Castello di Barolo to sample the wine and visit the wine museum. While in the area, let the aroma of white truffles tickle your senses, and treat your taste buds to a range of culinary specialties that exalt this regal tuber. Alba is the capital of the Langhe wine country; its October wine and truffle fair features a rousing medieval-style tournament. En route to Verona, make a detour to Parma for a quintessential Italian meal. (⇨ Chapter 5, Fortified Cities of the Po Plain and Chapter 7, Emilia.)

VERONA

1 or 2 days. This could be your base for an excursion north to Trento, where some of Italy's best Spumanti are produced. Verona's ancient Roman Arena, medieval buildings, and characteristic restaurants deserve some attention, too. (⇨ Chapter 2, Padua, Verona, Vicenza and Chapter 3, Trentino.)

BOLZANO

1 or 2 days. If you spend the night here, you'll have time to enjoy the area's distinctive Austrian-Italian cuisine and to follow the Strada del Vino (Wine Road) that starts at Caldaro, 15 km (9 mi) south of Bolzano. (⇨ Chapter 3, Alto Adige & Cortina and Heart of the Dolomites.)

TREVISO

2 days. Medieval buildings, canals, mill wheels, and an abundance of inns where you can savor local dishes and wines make this a good base for exploring the area. Spend a day on an excursion to Udine, or follow the Strada del Vino Rosso (Red Wine Road) through cabernet and merlot country along the Piave River from Conegliano, where sparkling, fruity Prosecco is made. A bowl of *pasta e fagioli*–the hearty bean-and-pasta soup, a specialty of the Veneto region–will sustain you. (⇨ Chapter 2, Treviso & the Hillside Towns and Friuli-Venezia Giulia.)

UDINE

1 day. Another optional overnight stop, this attractive city was ruled by Venice and shows it, with stone Venetian lions rampant on graceful buildings and columns in pretty piazzas. The Collio wine district nearby is known for its amazing and utterly distinctive local cheeses. (⇨ Chapter 2, Friuli-Venezia Giulia.)

CHIANTI

2 or 3 days. Spend at least two days roaming through the Chianti district between Florence and Siena, where you can delve into the subtle differences in vintages and perhaps swerve out of the district's official confines into the realm of Brunello di Montalcino. Here, it seems that even the tiniest village harbors a precious artwork or two by Tuscan masters. Many wineries offer guided tours of their cellars, often part of historic estates belonging to families that can trace their origins back to the Middle Ages or the Renaissance. (⇨ Chapter 9, Chianti and Southern Tuscany.)

By Public Transportation

Local trains and buses make the 45-minute run from Turin to Asti and Alba. Parma is on the Milan line; switch at Piacenza (30 minutes). Return to Turin to get a train on the main east–west line to Verona (three hours from Turin). In Verona you'll find frequent service on another main line to Trento (one hour) and Bolzano (a two-hour trip). Return to Verona for a

train to Padua, 60 minutes away. Treviso can be reached by train (60 minutes) or bus (70 minutes) from Padua. Udine is on a main line that passes through Padua; journey time is 2½ hours. There is fast service on the same line to Florence (2¾ hours from Venice), where you can get a local train or bus to make the 90-minute trip to Siena. Local buses serve the Chianti district.

Classical Highlights
8 to 12 days

Well colonized by the ancient Greeks, then epicenter of the Roman Empire, Italy has a wealth of classical sites, many of them in an excellent state of preservation. Rome was, of course, the capital of the Roman Empire, and a number of ancient sites remain here today, seemingly plunked down in the middle of the modern metropolis. Campania, too, is full of important classical landmarks, from both the Roman and the Greek eras, and Pompeii is not the only vestige of the eruption of nearby Mt. Vesuvius. If you have more time and a more intense interest in ancient history, you'll want to travel all the way to Sicily, the large island just off the toe of Italy's boot. Settled by the Greeks, it was a center of trade and culture in the Hellenic world, and it still is richly endowed with remarkable sites.

ROME

2 or 3 days. Spend at least a day exploring Ancient Rome–the Capitoline Hill, the Roman Forum, the Circus Maximus, the Colosseum, the Pantheon–and on subsequent days, venture out to the Via Appia and the Catacombs, or study classical sculptures in the Vatican Museums and antiquities in the Museo Nazionale Romano in

Palazzo Altemps. It is quite an experience to turn a corner and see a famous building, such as the Colosseum, across the street, with traffic whizzing blithely past its crumbling arches. (⇨ Chapter 11, Exploring Rome.)

NAPLES AND CAMPANIA

2 or 3 days. After arriving in Naples from Rome, spend the afternoon at the Museo Archeologico Nazionale. Herculaneum and Pompeii can be visited in one day from Naples, but it would be a very full day, and it is best to break it into two separate excursions. The relics being unearthed from the lava at Herculaneum are even better preserved than the once-buried ruins at Pompeii. On another day, enjoy an excursion down the Amalfi Coast or take the A3 to Paestum, with its still-intact Greek temples. Take an optional day to tour the area just west of Naples–the Roman amphitheater at Pozzuoli, spooky Lake Avernus, the Roman resort town at Baia, with its excavated baths, and the Sibyl's Cave at Cumae, perhaps the oldest Greek colony in Italy. (⇨ Chapter 13, Naples; the Phlegrean Fields; Herculaneum, Vesuvius, Pompeii; and the Amalfi Coast.)

PALERMO, SICILY

1 day. Visit the Museo Archeologico Regionale and nearby Segesta, with its fine Doric Greek temple. (⇨ Chapter 16, Palermo and Western Coast to Agrigento.)

MAP KEY
══════
Classical Highlights

By Public Transportation

Train service between Rome and Naples is fast and frequent, taking less than two hours on express trains. The Circumvesuviana train line can take you conveniently from Naples to Pompeii (a 35-minute trip) and Herculaneum (about 20 minutes' travel time). There's a train station right in Paestum (1½ hours from Naples). A ferry operates from Naples to Palermo, Sicily (it's a four- to nine-hour trip), and a main train line makes the five-hour run between Palermo and Siracusa, which is also reached from Messina (a three-hour trip) and Catania (1½ hours). Taormina is a one-hour train ride from Messina. Other sites on Sicily—such as Agrigento (two hours from Palermo)—are better reached by bus than by the unreliable local train service.

AGRIGENTO

1 or 2 days. Explore the Valley of the Temples, an extensive Greek site, and if you have time, make your way up the coast to see the spectacular Greek temple complex at Selinunte. (⇨ Chapter 16, Western Coast to Agrigento.)

SIRACUSA

1 or 2 days. Visit the Parco Archeologico in town, the splendid Museo Archeologico, and, if there's time, take an excursion to see the mosaics at the Imperial Roman Villa at Casale, just south of Piazza Armerina. (⇨ Chapter 16, Siracusa and Eastern Sicily.)

TAORMINA

1 day. Get a fine view of Mt. Etna and see the town's Greek theater, its backdrop the shimmering Mediterranean; the theater is still used for a summer arts festival. (⇨ Chapter 16, Eastern Sicily.)

Civitavecchia

Rome
A1 (219 km (136 mi)

LATIUM

MOLISE

CAMPANIA

A1

Cumae
Lake Avernus
Pozzuoli
Baie
Pompeii
Naples
Herculaneum
A3
Salerno
Amalfi
S18
A3
Paestum

BASILICATA

488 km (303 mi)

TYRRHENIAN SEA

CALABRIA

A3

Messina
A20
A18

Palermo
A20
235 km (146 mi)
S113

S189
128 km (80 mi)

Etna
111 km (69 mi)
Taormina

Selinunte
S115
102 km (63 mi)

SICILY

Catania
S114

Agrigento
212 km (132 mi)
S115
A18
Siracusa

WHEN TO GO

The main tourist season runs from April to mid-October. The so-called low season from fall to early spring may be cooler and rainier, but it has its rewards: less time waiting in line and more time for unhurried views of what you want to see. Tourists crowd the major art cities at Easter, when Italians flock to resorts and to the country. From March through May, busloads of schoolchildren take cities of artistic and historical interest by storm. You don't want to be on an Italian beach in August because of the crowds. June and September are best; July can be crowded at the major resorts.

Climate

The best months for sightseeing are April, May, June, September, and October, when the weather is mild. The hottest months, July and August, can be unpleasant. Winters are relatively mild in most places on the main tourist circuit but always include some rainy spells. In general, the northern half of the peninsula and the Adriatic Coast down to Puglia are rainier than elsewhere. Except for Taormina and some towns on the Italian Riviera, coastal resorts usually close up tight from October through Easter.

🏴 Forecasts **Weather Channel Connection** ☎ 900/932-8437 95¢ per minute from a Touch-Tone phone ⊕ www.weather.com.

ROME

Jan.	52F	11C	May	74F	23C	Sept.	79F	26C
	40	5		56	13		62	17
Feb.	55F	13C	June	82F	28C	Oct.	71F	22C
	42	6		63	17		55	13
Mar.	59F	15C	July	87F	30C	Nov.	61F	16C
	45	7		67	20		49	10
Apr.	66F	19C	Aug.	86F	30C	Dec.	55F	13C
	50	10		67	20		44	6

FLORENCE

Jan.	48F	9C	May	73F	23C	Sept.	79F	26C
	36	2		54	12		59	15
Feb.	52F	11C	June	81F	27C	Oct.	68F	20C
	37	3		59	15		52	11
Mar.	57F	14C	July	86F	30C	Nov.	57F	14C
	41	5		64	18		45	7
Apr.	66F	19C	Aug.	86F	30C	Dec.	52F	11C
	46	8		63	17		39	10

VENICE

Jan.	42F	6C	May	70F	21C	Sept.	75F	24C
	33	1		56	13		61	16
Feb.	46F	8C	June	76F	25C	Oct.	65F	19C
	35	2		63	17		53	12
Mar.	53F	12C	July	81F	27C	Nov.	53F	12C
	41	5		66	19		44	7
Apr.	62F	17C	Aug.	80F	27C	Dec.	46F	8C
	49	10		65	19		37	3

Italy's top seasonal events are listed below, and any one of them could provide the stuff of lasting memories. It is revealing that the Italian "festa" can be translated either as "festival" or "holiday" or "feast"—food is usually fundamental to Italian celebrations. Contact the **Italian Government Travel Office** (⇨ Visitor Information) for exact dates and further information.

ONGOING	
Dec.–June	The Stagione Operistica (Opera Season) is in full swing, notably in Milan, Turin, Florence, Rome, Naples, Parma, Venice, and Genoa.
WINTER	
Early Dec.	The Festa di Sant'Ambrogio (Feast of St. Ambrose) in Milan officially opens La Scala's opera season.
Dec. 31	Rome stages a rousing Capo D'Anno (New Year's Eve) celebration, dubbed the Festa di San Silvestro, with fireworks in Piazza del Popolo.
Jan. 5–6	Roman Catholic Epifania (Epiphany Celebrations) and decorations are evident throughout Italy. Notable is the Epiphany Fair at Piazza Navona in Rome.
Early Feb.	The Festa del Fiore di Mandorlo (Almond Blossom Festival) in Agrigento is a week of folk music and dancing, with groups from many countries, in the Valley of the Temples.
Jan. 30–Feb. 8	A big do in the 18th century and revived in the latter part of the 20th century, Carnevale in Venice includes concerts, plays, masked balls, fireworks, and indoor and outdoor happenings of every sort. It is probably Italy's most famous festival, bringing in hundreds of thousands. During Carnivale di Viareggio, in the Tuscan beach town Viareggio, masked pageants, fireworks, a flower show, and parades are among the festivities. The Carnivale d'Ivrea, near Turin, includes three days of folklore, costumes, parades, and cooking in the streets. The party culminates with the Battle of the Oranges, which features real fruit flying through the air.
SPRING	
Mar. 20–27	Settimana Santa (Holy Week) features parades and outdoor events in every major city and most small towns in Italy, but Rome, Naples, Assisi, and Florence have particularly notable festivities.
Mar. 25	In Rome, a torchlight nighttime Venerdì Santo (Good Friday Procession) led by the pope winds from the Colosseum past the Roman Forum and up the Palatine Hill.
Mar. 27	The Easter Sunday Scoppio del Carro (Explosion of the Cart) in Florence is the eruption of a cartful of fireworks in the Piazza del Duomo, set off by a mechanical dove released from the altar dur-

	ing High Mass. Needless to say, Messa di Pasqua al Vaticana (Easter Mass at the Vatican) in Rome is long, intense, and packed, with many people attending in elaborate holiday costumes.
Late Apr.– Early July	Maggio Musicale Fiorentino (Florence May Music Festival) is the oldest and most prestigious Italian festival of the performing arts.
May 1	The Festa di Sant'Efisio in Cagliari sees a procession of marchers and others in splendid Sardinian costume.
May 9	The Sagra del Pesce (Feast of the Fish), in Camogli on the Italian Riviera, is a high-spirited—and free—community-wide fish fry.
Mid-May	During the Corsa dei Ceri (Race of the Candles) in Gubbio, a procession to the top of Mt. Ingino features young men in local costume carrying huge wooden pillars.
May 22	The Cavalcata Sarda (Sardinian Cavalcade) is a traditional procession of more than 3,000 people in Sardinian costume winding through Sassari.
Late May– Early June	The Regata delle Quattro Repubbliche Marinare (Regatta of the Great Maritime Republics) sees keen competition among the four former maritime republics—Amalfi, Genoa, Pisa, and Venice.
May 29	The Palio della Balestra (Palio of the Archers) is a medieval crossbow contest in Gubbio, dating back to 1461.

SUMMER

June	On three consecutive days in June, usually on the third week of the month, the Infiorata (Flower Festival), in Genzano (Rome), is a religious procession along streets carpeted with flowers in splendid designs.
June 2	The Festa della Republic, formerly the royal national holiday, is celebrated with a flurry of Italian flags.
June 24	Calcio Storico (Soccer Games in 16th-Century Costume), in Florence, commemorate a match played in 1530. Festivities include fireworks displays.
June 24	Florence grinds to a halt to celebrate the Festa di San Giovanni (Feast of St. John the Baptist) in honor of its patron saint. Many shops and bars close, and at night a fireworks display along the Arno attracts thousands.
June 26	The Gioco del Ponte (Battle of the Bridge), in Pisa, is a medieval parade and contest.
Late June– Mid-July	The Festival dei Due Mondi (Festival of Two Worlds), in Spoleto, is perhaps Italy's most famous performing arts festival, bringing in a worldwide audience for concerts, operas, ballets, film screenings, and crafts fairs. Plan well in advance.

June–Early Aug.	The Festival Internazionale dell'Operetta (Summer Operetta Festival) is held in Trieste.
July 2 & Aug. 16	The world-famous Palio in Siena is a bareback horse race with ancient Sienese factions showing their colors and participants competing for a prized *palio* (banner).
Early July–Late Aug.	The L'Arena di Verona Stagione Lirica (Arena of Verona Outdoor Opera Season) heralds spectacular productions in the 22,000-seat Roman amphitheater of Verona.
July	The Umbria Jazz Festival, in Perugia, brings in many of the biggest names in jazz each summer.
July 16	The Festa del Redentore (Feast of the Redeemer) is a procession of gondolas and other craft commemorating the end of the plague of 1575 in Venice. The fireworks over the lagoon are spectacular.
Late July–Mid-Sept.	Settimane Musicali di Stresa (Stresa Musical Weeks) comprise a series of concerts and recitals in Stresa.
Late Aug.–Early Sept.	The Festival di Venezia (Venice Film Festival), the oldest of the international film festivals, takes place mostly on the Lido.
FALL	
Sept. 4	The Regata Storica (Historic Regatta) includes a traditional competition between two-oar gondolas in Venice.
Sept. 4	The Giostra del Saracino (Joust of the Saracen) is a tilting contest with knights in 13th-century armor in Arezzo.
Sept. 16	The Giostra della Quintana (Joust of the Quintana) is a 17th-century-style joust and historical procession in the Umbrian town of Foligno.
Oct. 2	Alba's Giostra delle Cento Torri (100 Towers Tournament) features costumes and races and is held a week before the opening of the Fiera del Tartufo (Truffle Fair), a food fair centered on the white truffle.
Oct. 4	The Festa di San Francesco (Feast of St. Francis) is celebrated in Assisi, his birthplace.

PLEASURES & PASTIMES

The Art of Enjoying Art Travel veterans will tell you that the seemingly countless masterpieces of Italian art can cause first-time visitors—eyes glazed over from a heavy downpour of images, dates, and names—to lean, Pisa-like, on their companions for support. After a surfeit of Botticellis and Bronzinos and the 14th Raphael, even the miracle of the High Renaissance may begin to pall. The secret is to act like a turtle—not a hare—and take your sweet time. Instead of trotting after briskly efficient tour guides, allow the splendors of the age to unfold—slowly. Museums are only the most obvious places to view the treasures. Get out and explore the actual settings—medieval chapels, Rococo palaces, and Romanesque town squares—for which Italy's marvelous art was conceived centuries ago and where much of it remains. Instead of studying a Gothic statue in Florence's Bargello, spend an hour in the medieval cloisters of the nearby convent of San Marco; by all means, take in Michelangelo's *David* in Florence's Accademia, but then meander down the 15th-century street, a short bus ride away, where he was born. You'll find that after three days of trotting through museums, a walk through a quiet neighborhood will help restore your sense of perspective.

Of course, there may be many art treasures that will not quicken your pulse, but one morning you may see a Caravaggio so perfect, so beautiful, that your knees will buckle.

The Great Outdoors Italy's magnificent art is a logical complement to the gorgeous terrain from which it was born. Here you can climb and ski in the Dolomites and the Alps, lounge on beaches from Venice's Lido to Sicily's Aeolian Islands, and walk the sun-washed coastlines of the Riviera and Amalfi. The best thing about Italy's natural beauty may be that so much of it is so accessible: from the seat of your car or bicycle you have the privilege of watching the lakes of Lombardy or the hills of Tuscany pass before you. The landscape throughout the country achieves a remarkable harmony between man and nature. Architectural masterpieces sprout from hilltops and cliffs, and vineyards and olive groves add perfect Italian accents to the countryside.

Il Caffè The Italian day begins and ends with coffee, and more cups of coffee punctuate the time in between. To live like the Italians do, drink as they drink, standing at the counter or sitting at an outdoor table of the corner bar. (In Italy, the term *bar* means coffee bar.) A primer: *Caffè* means coffee, and Italian standard issue is what Americans call espresso—short, strong, and usually taken very sweet. *Cappuccino* is a foamy half-and-half of espresso and steamed milk; cocoa powder (*cacao*) on top is acceptable, cinnamon not. If you're thinking of having a cappuccino for dessert, think again—Italians drink only caffè or *caffè macchiato* (with a spot of steamed milk) after lunchtime. Confused? Homesick? Order *caffè americano* for a reasonable facsimile of good old filtered joe.

The Italian Table

You'll find the merits of Italian cooking sung throughout this book, from the "On the Menu" boxes near the beginning of each chapter to the often-glowing restaurant reviews to the "Understanding Italy" section in the back. Believe what you read. Each region of Italy has its own distinct, time-tested cuisine that's a source of pride equally felt in family kitchens, modest trattorias, and sophisticated restaurants. What Italians of every region hold in common is a respect for the pleasures of the table. They take the utmost care in creating staples—bread, wine, cheese, and olive oil are just the beginning of the list—and build their cuisine from there. Another shared characteristic of Italian food is a tendency to revere the most humble ingredients; chefs will devote the same attention to day-old bread that they do to priceless truffles.

If you're a connoisseur of sophisticated cuisine, you should be prepared to journey off the beaten path. Many of Italy's most heralded (and most expensive) restaurants are located in the countryside and in small, otherwise unexceptional towns. For Italian foodies, such places are pilgrimage sites, where they can escape the city and indulge in a long, opulent meal free from outside distractions.

La Passeggiata

A favorite Italian pastime is the *passeggiata*, literally, the promenade. In the late afternoon and early evening, especially on weekends, couples, families, and packs of teenagers stroll the main streets and piazzas of Italy's towns. It's a ritual of exchanged news and gossip, window-shopping, flirting, and gelato eating that adds up to a uniquely Italian experience. To join in, simply hit the streets for a bit of wandering. You may feel more like an observer than a participant, until you realize that observing is what la passeggiata is all about.

Shopping

"Made in Italy" is synonymous with style, quality, and craftsmanship, whether it refers to high fashion or Maserati automobiles. The best buys are leather goods of all kinds—from gloves to bags to jackets—silk goods, knitwear, gold jewelry, ceramics, and local handicrafts. Keep in mind that every region has its specialties. Venice is known for glassware, lace, and velvet; Milan and Como for silk; the Dolomites and the mountainous regions of Calabria and Sicily for hand-carved wooden objects; Florence for straw goods, gold jewelry, leather, and paper products; Naples for coral and cameos; Assisi for embroidery; and Deruta, Gubbio, Vietri, and many towns in Puglia and Sicily for ceramics.

FODOR'S CHOICE

The sights, restaurants, hotels, and other travel experiences on these pages are our writers' top picks—our Fodor's Choices. They're the best of their type in Italy—not to be missed and always worth your time. In the destination chapters that follow, you will find all the details.

LODGING

$$$$ De la Poste, Cortina D'Ampezzo, Dolomites. The owners make you feel like old friends at this chalet in the heart of one of Italy's poshest ski resorts.

$$$$ Punta Tragara, Capri, Campania. Perched over the landmark I Faraglioni rock formation, this hotel has baronial guest rooms and a poolside restaurant so beautiful it stops conversation.

$$$$ San Domenico Palace, Taormina, Sicily. A former convent is now a pleasure palace with ultramodern facilities, excellent service, and timeless views.

$$$$ Villa d'Este, Cernobbio, Lombardy. The choice of Napoléon and the Duchess of Windsor is as grand as ever.

$$$ Britannia, Rome. A central location and an attentive staff are just the beginning of what makes this small hotel a find.

$$$ Castello di Petrata, Assisi, Umbria. Peace and tranquillity reign in this splendidly converted fortress; the view from the pool will take your breath away.

$$$ Fonte de' Medici, Greve in Chianti, Tuscany. Country living doesn't get much better than at this Antinori-owned *agriturismo* in the heart of Chianti.

$$$ Hotel Ripagrande, Ferrara, Emilia-Romagna. Everything feels just right in this immaculate 15th-century palazzo.

$$$ Villa Novecento, Courmayeur, Valle d'Aosta. Recuperate at this charming, cozy retreat after a day of hiking or skiing on the slopes of Monte Bianco.

$$–$$$ Castello Formentini, Friuli-Venezia Giulia, Venetian Arc. Be the king of the castle—if only for a night—feasting with your fingers and sleeping in modernized medieval splendor.

$$–$$$ Pensione Accademia Villa Maravege, Venice. A garden with a view of the Grand Canal is just one of the pleasures at this Venetian villa.

$$ Grotta Palazzese, Polignano a Mare, Puglia. Here's your chance to stay in a cavelike nook carved into an Adriatic cliff.

$$	Hotel San Luca, Spoleto, Umbria. Stroll through a rose garden, sip afternoon tea, and rest your head on a firm, elegant bed—who could ask for more?
$$	La Riserva, Ventimiglia, Italian Riviera. Tucked in the hills near the French-Italian border, this is frontier living at its very best and a great place for a romantic getaway.
$$	Morandi alla Crocetta, Florence. A former Benedictine convent, carefully reappointed, provides a soothing place to rest your head.

BUDGET LODGING

$	Locanda di Mirandolina, Tuscania, Lazio. The rooms are small but immaculate at this courteously run guesthouse; the restaurant is also topflight.
$	Locanda di San Martino, Matera, Basilicata. The rooms are delightfully renovated former cave dwellings in the heart of Matera's old town.
$	Lorelei et Londres, Sorrento, Campania. Step back in time at this quintessential pensione. The facilities are spare, but the views of the Bay of Naples are the envy of hotels charging twice the price.
¢	Airone, Siracusa, Sicily. If you're a backpacker, or traveling on a backpacker's budget, you'll appreciate the spacious rooms and reasonable rates here.
¢	La Pallotta, Assisi, Umbria. Ask for a room with a view at this family-run Assisi bargain with a fine restaurant.
¢	Residenza Johanna I, Florence. Simple but appealing rooms in a good location make this the savvy budget traveler's residence of choice in Florence.

RESTAURANTS

$$$$	Cibrèo, Florence. Chef/owner Fabio Pichi creates terrific Tuscan food with flair.
$$$$	Il Convivio, Rome. Tucked behind Piazza Navona, this favorite of in-the-know gourmands and Roman professionals is one of the capital's brightest gastronomic gems.
$$$$	San Domenico, Imola, Emilia-Romagna. In the Italian region most dedicated to food worship, this is a gourmet's temple.
$$$–$$$$	Il Poeta Contadino, Alberobello, Puglia. Innovative *pugliesi*-style cuisine is served in an evocative space containing old stone walls, vaulted ceilings, and mellow lighting.
$$$–$$$$	S'Apposentu, Cagliari, Sardinia. Chef Roberto Petzi has taken creative island cooking to a new level at this cutting-edge restaurant dramatically set in Cagliari's Teatro Lirico.

$$$ | **Su Gologone,** Nuoro, Sardinia. Sample recipes that date back hundreds of years at this country inn set among the olive groves. You can also spend the night here in supremely relaxing rustic comfort.

$$$ | **Gener Neuv,** Asti, Piedmont. Watch the River Tanaro drift by as you sip Asti Spumante and dine on first-rate local *cucina.*

$$–$$$ | **Il Mulinazzo,** Palermo, Sicily. Palermo food lovers happily drive 45 minutes out of town to indulge in chef Nino Graziano's sophisticated Sicilian cuisine. For what may be the island's finest restaurant, the prices are strikingly reasonable.

$$–$$$ | **La Cacciatore,** near Cividale, Venetian Arc. Have a cross-cultural dining experience at this rustic trattoria where Italy meets Slovenia.

$$–$$$ | **Trattoria Montina,** Milan, Lombardy. The best cosmopolitan Italy has to offer: fine food, fair prices, and even an entertaining host.

$$–$$$ | **U' Giancu,** near Rapallo, Italian Riviera. Original cartoons, including Beetle Bailey and Peanuts, all with dedications to the restaurant from the artists, cover the walls of this delightful shrine to good food and good humor.

$–$$$ | **Il Ritrovo,** Positano, Campania. Perched high up above the beautiful village of Positano, this is not only a fine place to eat but also one where you can enjoy breathtaking views.

$$ | **Bucadisantantonio,** Lucca, Tuscany. The Tuscan cuisine here is handled with grace and aplomb.

$–$$ | **Grappolo D'Oro Zampanò,** Rome. Off of historic Campo de' Fiori, this is both pizzeria and civilized restaurant, featuring a seasonal menu of inventive regional fare.

$–$$ | **Taverna Kerkira,** Bagnara Calabra, Calabria. This friendly, unpretentious eatery serves inspired creations with a distinctly Greek air.

BUDGET RESTAURANTS

$ | **Al Donizetti,** Bergamo, Lombardy. Choose from among the region's best hams and cheeses or order a full meal to complement this wine bar's selection of more than 800 bottles.

$ | **Bancogiro,** Venice. This *bacaro* with contemporary flair takes full advantage of its location next to the Rialto markets.

¢–$ | **Cantina Palazzo dei Mercanti,** Viterbo, Lazio. This casual spot shares a kitchen with one of Lazio's most sophisticated restaurants. The result is great food for pocket change.

¢ | **Sorbillo,** Naples, Campania. As simple as the best things in life, this is one of Naples's oldest pizzerias. It hasn't changed its winning formula since opening nearly 100 years ago.

ANTIQUITIES

Imperial Roman Villa, Piazza Armerina, Sicily. More than 12,000 square feet of Roman mosaics fill what's thought to have been a hunting lodge of the emperor Maximianus Heraclius.

Mausoleo di Galla Placidia, Ravenna, Emilia-Romagna. Some of the most dazzling Byzantine mosaics in the Western world are hidden inside a humble brick tomb.

Ostia Antica, Lazio. Ancient Rome's port city is now a remarkably well-preserved archaeological site in a pretty, parklike setting.

Pompeii, Campania. When Mt. Vesuvius erupted in AD 79, covering Pompeii in volcanic ash and mud, it created a museum of daily life in the ancient world.

Pantheon, Rome. Sit in a café in the car-free piazza that overlooks this Roman architectural masterpiece and take pleasure in watching today's elegant Romans stroll by.

Sassi, Matera, Basilicata. This spooky network of ancient cave dwellings is one of the most striking sights in all Italy.

Su Nuraxi, Sardinia. Dating back to the 16th century BC, the *nuraghi*—stone fortresses of prehistoric civilizations—are Sardinia's most mysterious archaeological feature, and this one is the island's most impressive.

Valle dei Templi, Agrigento, Sicily. These are some of the world's best-preserved remains from classical Greece.

CHURCHES

Basilica di San Francesco, Arezzo, Tuscany. Piero della Francesca's *Legend of the True Cross,* executed on three walls of the choir in this 14th-century church, has been said to exhibit "the most perfect morning light in all Renaissance painting."

Basilica di San Francesco, Assisi, Umbria. The fresco cycle here illustrating the life of St. Francis is counted among the masterpieces of the Renaissance, and the soaring double basilica makes them an appropriately majestic home.

Cappella degli Scrovegni, Padua, Venetian Arc. Brilliant frescoes by Giotto, impeccably restored and preserved, decorate Italy's second-most famous chapel.

Duomo, Siracusa, Sicily. One of Italy's great monuments to the passing of time: a baroque cathedral built on top of still-visible Greek columns from the 6th century BC.

Santa Croce, Florence. The resting place of Michelangelo, Galileo, and Machiavelli also contains the most important art of any church in Florence.

Santa Maria Gloriosa dei Frari, Venice. The blazing colors of two of Titian's most spectacular altarpieces illuminate this monumental Venetian Gothic church.

Santo Stefano, Bologna, Emilia-Romagna. This splendid basilica stands on what's been the site of numerous churches through the ages.

MUSEUMS

Galleria degli Uffizi, Florence. Simply one of the world's great art collections.

Museo Archeologico dell'Alto Adige, Bolzano, Dolomites. The impossibly well-preserved body of the iceman Ötzi, the star attraction here, was unearthed in 1991 after 5,300 very cold years.

Museo e Galleria Borghese, Rome. With the setting as exquisite as the art, this small, supremely elegant museum showcases some of the best baroque and Renaissance art in Italy.

Museo Egizio, Turin, Piedmont. A surprising treasure: one of the world's richest collections of Egyptian art outside Cairo.

Musei Vaticani, Rome. The sheer size of the Vatican Museums is daunting, but the Sistine Chapel, the Raphael Rooms, and scores of masterpieces reward your effort.

ONLY IN ITALY

Festa di Sant'Efisio, Cagliari, Sardinia. Tradition isn't a cliché in Sardinia's tourist-trade lexicon, and of the island's time-honored festivals none has greater exuberance than Cagliari's annual binge.

Gondola Ride, Venice. Whether at midday or midnight, it's magical plying these surreal waterways, where fairy-tale palazzos waltz by, veiled in silvery mist.

Mount Etna, Sicily. Sicily's greatest natural attraction is also Europe's highest active volcano at 10,902 feet—and a ski destination to boot.

A Night at the Opera, Arena di Verona, Venetian Arc. Even if you're not an opera lover, you're likely to get a kick from the starlit spectacles held at this ancient Roman arena, where sopranos and baritones might share the stage with horses or elephants.

Piazza del Campo, Siena, Tuscany. Perhaps it's the unique shell-shape design that makes this one of Italy's most pleasing piazzas. Have a coffee or a gelato, then climb the Torre del Mangia for unparalleled views of Siena's red roofs and the surrounding countryside.

Piazza del Duomo, Parma, Emilia-Romagna. The medieval meets the baroque at this tranquil square in the heart of Parma.

Promenades, Merano, Dolomites. Ambling along the pleasant walkways of this famed spa town, you'll understand its year-round appeal.

Sagra del Pesce, festival, Camogli, Italian Riviera. Every year on the second Sunday in May, the normally quiet town of Camogli springs to life for what is certainly one of the world's most fun and festive (and free) outdoor fish fries—the feast day of San Fortunato.

PALACES

Palazzo Ducale, Urbino, the Marches. If the Renaissance was, in ideal form, a celebration of the nobility of man and his works, of the light and purity of the soul, then in no other palace in Italy are its tenets better illustrated.

Palazzo Reale, Genoa, Italian Riviera. The vast wealth of Genoa's 17th-century merchant princes is on impressive display at this magnificent palace.

Villa La Rotonda, Vicenza, Venetian Arc. A kind of Renaissance update of the Pantheon in Rome, Palladio's most famous villa was the inspiration for Thomas Jefferson's Monticello, as well as numerous capitol buildings.

TOWNS

Bellagio, Lombardy. Once called "Italy's prettiest town," it still seems to be more of an operetta set than a resort.

Cortina d'Ampezzo, Dolomites. For the classic Italian skiing experience, this old-school resort remains without peer.

Lecce, Puglia. Extravagant baroque churches are the showpieces of this town in Italy's deep south, a stomping ground of the ancient Greeks, bold Crusaders, and a landed aristocracy. All left their marks.

Ravello, Campania. This town on the Amalfi coast has two spectacular villas that compete for the title of most beautiful spot in southern Italy.

SMART TRAVEL TIPS

Finding out about your destination before you leave home means you won't squander time once you've arrived organizing the everyday minutiae of your vacation. You'll be more streetwise when you hit the ground as well, better prepared to explore the aspects of Italy that drew you here in the first place. The organizations in this section can provide information to supplement this guide; contact them for up-to-the-minute details, and consult the A to Z sections that end each chapter for facts on the various topics as they relate to Italy's many regions. Happy landings!

ADDRESSES

Addresses in Italy are fairly straightforward: the street is followed by the street number. However, you might see an address with a number plus "bis" or "A"; for instance, "Via Verdi 3/bis" or "Via Mazzini 8/A." This indicates that 3/bis and 8/A are the next doors down from Via Verdi 3 and Via Mazzini 8. In Rome, street numbers flow down one side of a street and back up the other. In central Florence, the letter "r" following an address (e.g., Via Santo Spirito 35/r) refers to "rosso" (red), the color of the number painted on the wall. Red addresses are commercial; blue or black numbers are residential.

Venice addresses consist of the name of one of the city's six neighborhoods and a number. The hitch is that the numbers don't go in any sequential order, so San Marco 3672 and 3673 might well be several narrow winding streets away from each other. When helpful, the Venetian addresses in this book include the nearest *campo*, bridge, or *calle*.

In rural areas some addresses give only the route name or the distance in kilometers along a major road (e.g., Via Fabbri, km 4.3), or sometimes only the name of the small village in which the site is located.

AIR TRAVEL

The price of flying within Italy is often comparable to the cost of train travel, although be sure to factor in the expense of getting to and from the airport. When flying out of Italian airports, always check with the airport or tourist agency about up-coming strikes, which are frequent in Italy and often affect air travel.

BOOKING

When you book, look for nonstop flights and remember that "direct" flights stop at least once. Try to avoid connecting flights, which require a change of plane. Two airlines may operate a connecting flight jointly, so ask whether your airline operates every segment of the trip; you may find that the carrier you prefer flies you only part of the way. To find more booking tips and to check prices and make online flight reservations, log on to www.fodors.com.

CARRIERS

When flying internationally, you must usually choose between a domestic carrier, the national flag carrier of the country you are visiting (Alitalia for Italy), and a foreign carrier from a third country. National flag carriers have the greatest number of non-stops. Domestic carriers may have better connections to your hometown and serve a greater number of gateway cities. Third-party carriers may have a price advantage.

On international flights, Alitalia serves Rome, Milan, and Venice. The major international hubs in Italy are Milan and Rome, served by Continental Airlines and Delta Air Lines. American Airlines and United Airlines fly into just Milan. US Airways serves only Rome.

Direct service from Heathrow and Gatwick is provided by Alitalia and British Airways (BA). From Manchester, there are two direct BA flights daily to Milan, and daily flights to Rome. Smaller, no-frills airlines also provide service between Great Britain and Italy. EasyJet connects London with Bologna, Virgin Express London and Rome (via Brussels), and British Midland London and Milan. Ryanair, departing from London Stansted, has daily flights to a number of cities in Italy. Privately run Meridiana has two or three direct flights between London and Olbia on Sardinia weekly in summer, and flights daily to Florence throughout the year. Meridiana also connects London with Catania.

Alitalia also connects Canada and Italy. Qantas flies from various cities in Australia

via Bangkok, arriving in Rome. Alitalia and New Zealand Air fly from Auckland to Rome with a stop in London. Another option if you're coming from Australia or New Zealand is Thai Airlines, landing in Rome via Bangkok.

Alitalia—in addition to other major European airlines and smaller, privately run companies such as Meridiana and Air One—offers an extensive network of flights within Italy. Ask your domestic or Italian travel agent about discounts.

Tickets for intra-Italy flights cost less when purchased from agents within Italy. Tickets are frequently sold at discounted prices, so check the cost of flights, even one-way, as an alternative to train travel.

To & From Italy Air New Zealand ☎ 800/262-1234 in U.S., 800/663-5494 in Canada, 0800/028 4149 in U.K., 13-24-76 in Australia, 0800/737 000 in New Zealand ⊕ www.airnz.com. **Alitalia** ☎ 800/223-5730 in U.S., 0870/544 in U.K., 61/292-44-2222 in Australia, 06/65641 in Rome, 848/865641 elsewhere in Italy ⊕ www.alitalia.it. **American Airlines** ☎ 800/433-7300 in U.S., 02/69682464 in Milan ⊕ www.aa.com. **British Airways** ☎ 800/403-0882 in U.S. and Canada, 0870/850-9850 in U.K., 1300/767-177 in Australia, 0800/274 847 in New Zealand, 06/52492800 in Italy ⊕ www.britishairways.com. **Continental Airlines** ☎ 800/231-0856 in U.S., 02/69633256 in Milan, 800/296230 elsewhere in Italy ⊕ www.flycontinental.com. **Delta Air Lines** ☎ 800/241-4141 in U.S., 06/65954406 in Italy ⊕ www.deltaairlines.com. **Lufthansa** ☎ 800/399-5838 in U.S., 800/563-5954 in Canada, 0870/8377 747 in U.K., 1300-655-727 in Australia, 0800 945 220 in New Zealand ⊕ www.lufthansa.com. **Qantas,** ☎ 800/227-4500 in U.S., 06/52482725 in Rome ⊕ www.qantas.com. **Thai Airlines** ☎ 800/426-5204 in U.S., 61-1300-651-960 in Australia, 64-9-377-3886 in New Zealand ⊕ www.thaiair.com. **United Airlines** ☎ 800/241-6522 in U.S., 02/69633707 in Milan ⊕ www.ual.com. **US Airways** ☎ 800/428-4322 in U.S., 848/813177 in Italy ⊕ www.usairways.com.

Smaller Airlines Air One ☎ 06/488800 in Rome, 800/900966 elsewhere in Italy, 06/48880066 from cell phones ⊕ www.flyairone.it. **EasyJet** ☎ 0870/6076543 in U.K. ⊕ www.go-fly.com. **Meridiana** ☎ 199/111333 in Italy ⊕ www.meridiana.it. **Ryanair** ☎ 08701/569569 in U.K., 199/114114 in Italy ⊕ www.ryanair.com. **Virgin Express** ☎ 32/70353637 in U.S., Canada, Australia, and New Zealand, 0207/

744-0004 in U.K., 02/48296000 in Milan, 800/097097 elsewhere in Italy.

CHECK-IN & BOARDING

Always **find out your carrier's check-in policy.** Plan to arrive at the airport about two hours before your scheduled departure time for domestic flights and 2½ to 3 hours before international flights. You may need to arrive earlier if you're flying from one of the busier airports or during peak air-traffic times. When flying within Italy, allow at least two hours before scheduled departure time.

To avoid delays at airport-security checkpoints, try not to wear any metal. Jewelry, belt and other buckles, steel-toe shoes, barrettes, and underwire bras are among the items that can set off detectors.

Assuming that not everyone with a ticket will show up, airlines routinely overbook planes. When everyone does, airlines ask for volunteers to give up their seats. In return, these volunteers usually get a several-hundred-dollar flight voucher, which can be used toward the purchase of another ticket, and are rebooked on the next flight out. If there are not enough volunteers, the airline must choose who will be denied boarding. The first to get bumped are passengers who checked in late and those flying on discounted tickets, so get to the gate and check in as early as possible, especially during peak periods.

Always **bring a government-issued photo ID** to the airport; even when it's not required, a passport is best.

CUTTING COSTS

The least expensive airfares to Italy are priced for round-trip travel and must usually be purchased in advance. Airlines generally allow you to change your return date for a fee; most low-fare tickets, however, are nonrefundable. It's smart to call a number of airlines and check the Internet; when you are quoted a good price, book it on the spot—the same fare may not be available the next day, or even the next hour. Always check different routings and look into using alternate airports. Also, price off-peak flights, which may be significantly less expensive than others. Travel agents, especially low-fare specialists (⇨ Discounts & Deals), are helpful.

Consolidators are another good source. They buy tickets for scheduled flights at reduced rates from the airlines, then sell them at prices that beat the best fare available directly from the airlines. (Many also offer reduced car-rental and hotel rates.) Sometimes you can even get your money back if you need to return the ticket. Carefully read the fine print detailing penalties for changes and cancellations, purchase the ticket with a credit card, and confirm your consolidator reservation with the airline.

When you fly as a courier, you trade your checked-luggage space for a ticket deeply subsidized by a courier service. There are restrictions on when you can book and how long you can stay. Some courier companies list with membership organizations, such as the Air Courier Association and the International Association of Air Travel Couriers; these require you to become a member before you can book a flight.

🔁 Consolidators **AirlineConsolidator.com** ☎ 888/468-5385 ⊕ www.airlineconsolidator.com. **Best Fares** ☎ 800/880-1234 or 800/576-8255 ⊕ www.bestfares.com; $59.90 annual membership. **Cheap Tickets** ☎ 800/377-1000 or 800/652-4327 ⊕ www.cheaptickets.com. **Expedia** ☎ 800/397-3342 or 404/728-8787 ⊕ www.expedia.com. **Hotwire** ☎ 866/468-9473 or 920/330-9418 ⊕ www.hotwire.com. **Now Voyager Travel** ✉ 45 W. 21st St., Suite 5A New York, NY 10010 ☎ 212/459-1616 🖷 212/243-2711 ⊕ www.nowvoyagertravel. com. **Onetravel.com** ⊕ www.onetravel.com. **Orbitz** ☎ 888/656-4546 ⊕ www.orbitz.com. **Priceline. com** ⊕ www.priceline.com. **Travelocity** ☎ 888/709-5983, 877/282-2925 in Canada, 0870/876-3876 in U.K. ⊕ www.travelocity.com.

🔁 Courier Resources **Air Courier Association/ Cheaptrips.com** ☎ 800/280-5973 ⊕ www. aircourier.org or www.cheaptrips.com. **International Association of Air Travel Couriers** ☎ 308/632-3273 ⊕ www.courier.org.

🔁 Discount Passes **Boomerang Pass,** Qantas ☎ 800/227-4500, 0845/774-7767 in U.K., 131-313 in Australia, 0800/808-767 in New Zealand ⊕ www. qantas.com. **FlightPass** ☎ 888/387-2479 Europe-byAir ⊕ www.europebyair.com.

ENJOYING THE FLIGHT

All flights within Italy are smoke-free. State your seat preference when purchasing your ticket, and then repeat it when you confirm and when you check in. For more legroom you can request one of the few emergency-aisle seats at check-in, if you're capable of moving obstacles comparable in weight to an airplane exit door (usually between 35 pounds and 60 pounds)—a Federal Aviation Administration requirement of passengers in these seats. Seats behind a bulkhead also offer more legroom, but they don't have underseat storage. Don't sit in the row in front of the emergency aisle or in front of a bulkhead, where seats may not recline.

Ask the airline whether a snack or meal is served on the flight. If you have dietary concerns, request special meals when booking. These can be vegetarian, low-cholesterol, or kosher, for example. It's a good idea to pack some healthful snacks and a small (plastic) bottle of water in your carry-on bag. On long flights try to maintain a normal routine to help fight jet lag. At night get some sleep. By day eat light meals, drink water (not alcohol), and **move around the cabin** to stretch your legs. For additional jet-lag tips consult *Fodor's FYI: Travel Fit & Healthy* (available at bookstores everywhere).

FLYING TIMES

Flying time to Milan and Rome is approximately 8½ hours from New York, 10–11 hours from Chicago, 11½ hours from Dallas (via New York), 11½ hours from Los Angeles, 2 hours from London (to Milan), and 23½ hours from Sydney.

HOW TO COMPLAIN

If your baggage goes astray or your flight goes awry, complain right away. Most carriers require that you **file a claim immediately.** The Aviation Consumer Protection Division of the Department of Transportation publishes *Fly-Rights,* which discusses airlines and consumer issues and is available online. You can also find articles and information on mytravelrights.com, the Web site of the nonprofit Consumer Travel Rights Center.

𝄜 Airline Complaints Aviation Consumer Protection Division ⊠ U.S. Department of Transportation, Office of Aviation Enforcement and Proceedings, C-75, Room 4107, 400 7th St. SW, Washington, DC 20590 ☎ 202/366-2220 ⊕ airconsumer.ost.dot.gov. **Federal Aviation Administration Consumer Hotline** ⊠ for inquiries: FAA, 800 Independence Ave. SW, Washington, DC 20591 ☎ 800/322-7873 ⊕ www.faa.gov.

RECONFIRMING

Check the status of your flight before you leave for the airport. You can do this on your carrier's Web site, by linking to a flight-status checker (many Web booking services offer these), or by calling your carrier or travel agent. Always confirm international flights at least 72 hours ahead of the scheduled departure time. Confirm flights within Italy the day before travel.

AIRPORTS

The major gateways to Italy are Rome's **Aeroporto Leonardo da Vinci,** better known as **Fiumicino** (FCO), and Milan's **Aeroporto Malpensa 2000** (MXP). There are direct connections from both airports to Florence. For information about regional airports, *see* the A to Z sections at the end of each chapter.

𝄜 Airport Information Aeroporto Leonardo da Vinci, known as Fiumicino ⊠ 35 km [20 mi] southeast of Rome ☎ 06/5951 ⊕ www.adr.it. **Aeroporto Malpensa** ⊠ 45 km [28 mi] north of Milan ☎ 02/7485-2200 ⊕ www.sea-aeroportimilano.it.

DUTY-FREE SHOPPING

Duty-free shopping in airports has been eliminated in Italy (and other EU [European Union] countries) when you are traveling within member nations; when flying out of or in to Italy, however, duty-free shopping is still an option.

BEACHES

With 7,420 km (4,610 mi) of coastline facing three seas—the Adriatic to the northeast, the Ionian to the southeast, and the Tyrrhenian to the west—Italy offers every type of beach scene. Italy has several world-famous beaches, like those along the Costa Smeralda in Sardinia and the town of Portofino in Liguria, and great stretches of deserted and untouched coastline, many found in eastern Calabria, Sardinia, and the islands around Sicily. In

Emilia-Romagna, Riccione and Rimini are famous for their nightlife and seaside fitness programs (Spinning classes to weight lifting, water gymnastics to Latin dance classes). The Tremiti Islands (off the Adriatic coast, between Molise and Puglia), the Gargano Peninsula (in Puglia), Tropea (in Calabria), Taormina (in Sicily), the islands of Capri and Ischia (in the Gulf of Naples), the Amalfi Coast (in Campania), Ponza (off the coast of Lazio), and the island of Elba (off the coast of Livorno in Tuscany) bring together a natural beauty with a low-key worldliness.

Note the difference between private and public beaches. Public ones are free but offer no services. On the most popular ones it's sometimes possible to buy sandwiches and soft drinks from kiosks or roaming vendors, but don't depend on them, or upon the presence of pay telephones, toilets, or showers. Private beaches charge admission and range from downright spartan (cold showers and portable toilets) to luxurious (with gardens, stylish bars, fish restaurants, and private guest huts). Admission policies and prices vary accordingly. Most establishments offer a chaise longue, chair, and umbrella for between €15 and €40 a day, with extra chaises rented out for an additional fee. Some of the most exclusive places cater only to patrons who pay by the week or month. Inquire at local tourist offices for details.

Don't underestimate the scorching power of the Italian sun. The "tanning season" begins in early May, and beach life starts in earnest in early June, with the opening of beach concessionaires, called *stabilimenti*. During weekends and holidays and in August, most sea resorts and beaches tend to be very crowded, some posting "no vacancy" (*completo*) signs by 10 AM, so an early start is essential. In northern and central Italy, sunbathing topless is common practice; in the south it could lead to undesired attention from local men. Nowhere in Italy, except at the rare nudist beach, is it common practice to walk around topless, and wearing beach attire (bare chests and thighs) in town is frowned upon. The summer season ends in early September.

BIKE TRAVEL

Italians are great bicycling enthusiasts, and biking in Italy is a terrific way to see the country, particularly in places such as Tuscany, where two-lane roads wind through startlingly beautiful countryside. The best times to bike are in spring and fall; July and August are unbearably hot in most places. Rentals are easily obtained in most cities. Given the generally hilly terrain, it's essential to have a good map with elevations, distances, and the various types of roads clearly marked. An excellent map choice is the green regional series issued by the Italian Touring Club, available at major bookstores. Road conditions are generally good throughout Italy, but, as you move along it's always a good idea to ask local tourist information offices about bike-friendly routes. Especially in smaller towns and villages cyclists do not go unnoticed, and if you speak a little Italian you'll be likely to meet sympathetic native cyclists eager to give valuable tips about the region. Always park (and lock) your bike inside your hotel for the night. And an important related note: laundry facilities are rare in Italy and can be found only in the bigger cities.

🚲 Local Resources **FIAB** ⊠ Viale Col Moschin 1, 30171 Mestre, Veneto 🕾🖷 041/921515 ⊕ www.fiab-onlus.it.

🚲 Rentals **Happy Rent** ⊠ Via Farini 3, Rome 🕾 06/481-8185. **I Bike Italy** ⊠ Viale Galoppatoio 33, Rome 🕾 06/3225240.

🚲 Bike Tours **Backroads** ⊠ 801 Cedar St., Berkeley, CA 94710 🕾 510/527-1555 or 800/462-2848 🖷 510/527-1444 ⊕ www.backroads.com. **Bike Riders** ⌁ Box 130254, Boston, MA 02113 🕾 617/723-2354 or 800/473-7040 🖷 617/723-2355 ⊕ www.bikeriderstours.com. **Butterfield & Robinson** ⊠ 70 Bond St., Suite 300, Toronto, Ontario, Canada M5B 1X3 🕾 416/864-1354 or 800/678-1147 🖷 416/864-0541 ⊕ www.butterfield.com. **Ciclismo Classico** ⊠ 30 Marathon St., Arlington, MA 02474 🕾 781/646-3377 or 800/866-7314 🖷 781/641-1512 ⊕ ciclismoclassico.com. **EEI Travel,** ⊠ 19021 120th Ave., Suite 102, Bothell, WA 98011 🕾 425/487-6711 or 800/927-3876 🖷 425/487-3750 or 800/270-0509 ⊕ www.europeexpress.com). **Euro-Bike Tours** ⌁ Box 990, De Kalb, IL 60115 🕾 800/321-6060 🖷 815/758-8851 ⊕ www.eurobike.com. **Europeds** ⊠ 761 Lighthouse Ave., Monterey, CA 93940 🕾 831/646-4920 🖷 831/655-4501. **Naturequest** ⊠ 30872 South Coast Hwy.,

Suite 185, Laguna Beach, CA 92651 ☎ 949/499-9561 or 800/369-3033 📠 949/499-0812 ⊕ www. naturequesttours.com.

BIKES IN FLIGHT

Most airlines accommodate bikes as luggage, provided they are dismantled and boxed; check with individual airlines about packing requirements. Some airlines sell bike boxes, which are often free at bike shops, for about $20 (bike bags can be considerably more expensive). International travelers often can substitute a bike for a piece of checked luggage at no charge; otherwise the cost is about $100. Most U.S. and Canadian airlines charge $40–$80 each way.

BOAT & FERRY TRAVEL

Ferries connect the mainland with all major islands. To many destinations there is also *aliscafo* (hydrofoil) service, which is generally twice as fast as ferries and double the price. Service is considerably more frequent in summer. Car ferries go to Sicily and Sardinia and many islands, including Elba, Ponza, Capri, Ischia, and the Lido near Venice. A ferry to Capri from Naples will cost about €7 one-way; via hydrofoil, €12. If you are traveling in July or August, try to make reservations at least a month ahead for Sicily or Sardinia. (Same-day ticket purchase is available for shorter trips.)

Tirrenia operates ferries to Liguria, Naples, Sicily, Sardinia, and Tunisia. SNAV operates ferries between Naples and Palermo (high-speed ferries only from April to early October), and hydrofoils between Naples and Capri. Alilauro has hydrofoils and car ferries between Naples and Ischia and Ischia and Capri to the Amalfi coast in summer. Capri is reached by Caremar, from Naples and Sorrento. Adriatica connects Italy with Greece. Trenitalia ferries sail from Civitavecchia to Golfo Aranci, near Olbia. Toremar serves Elba from Piombino. For the Lake District, contact Navigazione Laghi.

FARES & SCHEDULES

You can pick up schedules and buy tickets from any local Italian travel agent, most of whom speak English. Major credit cards are generally accepted, but cash is always

the preferred form of payment. Costs vary depending on car size and the type of accommodation on the ferry. Travel between Naples and Palermo, for instance, costs from €90 for a small-size car and no sleeping quarters to €290 for a large car and a sleeping cabin for two.

🚢 Adriatic Coast Ferries **Adriatica** ✉ Via San Nicola da Tolentino 27, Rome ☎ 06/4818341 ⊕ www. adriatica.it.

🚢 Mediterranean Ferries **Alilauro** ✉ Molo Beverello, Napoli, ☎ 081/7611004 ⊕ www.alilauro.it. **Caremar** ✉ Molo Beverello, Napoli ☎ 081/5513882 ⊕ www.caremar.it. **SNAV** ✉ Stazione Marittima Terminal Napoli, Naples ☎ 081/7612348 ⊕ www. snavali.com. **Tirrenia** ✉ Rione Sirignano 2, Napoli ☎ 199/123199 within Italy, 081/3172999 from abroad and on cell phones ⊕ www.tirrenia.it. **Toremar** ✉ Piazzale Premuda 13/14, Piombino ☎ 0565/31100 ⊕ www.toremar.it. **Trenitalia** ☎ 892021 www. trenitalia.com.

🚢 Northern Lakes Ferries **Navigazione Laghi** ✉ Via Ludovico Ariosto 21, Milan ☎ 02/4676101, 800/ 551801 within Italy ⊕ www.navlaghi.it.

BUSINESS HOURS

Religious and civic holidays are frequent in Italy. Depending on their local importance, businesses may close for the day (businesses do not close on a Friday or Monday if the holiday falls on the weekend).

BANKS & POST OFFICES

Banks are open weekdays 8:30 to 1:30 and for an hour in the afternoon, depending on the bank. Post offices are open Monday–Saturday 9–2; central and main district post offices stay open until 6:30 PM weekdays, 9–2 on Saturday. On the last day of the month all post offices close at midday.

MUSEUMS & SIGHTS

Most churches are open from early morning until noon or 12:30, when they close for three hours or more; they open again in the afternoon, closing about 6 PM. A few major churches, such as St. Peter's in Rome and San Marco in Venice, are open all day. Note that sightseeing in churches during religious rites is discouraged. Museum hours vary and often change with the seasons. Many museums are closed one day a week, often on Monday. During low season, hours are often abbreviated; during high season, many places stay open until late at night. Always check locally.

PHARMACIES

Pharmacies are generally open weekdays from 8:30 to 1 and from 4 to 8, and Saturday mornings 9 to 1. Local pharmacies cover the off-hours in shifts: on the door of every pharmacy is a list of which pharmacies in the vicinity will be open on Saturday afternoon, Sunday, or 24 hours.

SHOPS

Most shops are open Monday–Saturday from 9 to 1 and from 3:30 or 4 to 7:30. Clothing shops are generally closed on Monday mornings. Barbers and hairdressers, with some exceptions, are closed Sunday and Monday. Some bookstores and fashion and tourist-oriented shops in places such as Rome and Venice are open all day, as well as Sunday. Chain supermarkets such as Standa have continuous hours and are open on Sunday; smaller *alimentari* (delicatessens) and other food shops are usually closed one evening during the week (it varies according to the town) and almost always on Sunday.

BUS TRAVEL

Italy's bus network is extensive, although buses are not as attractive an option as in other European countries, partly because of the comparative low cost and convenience of train travel. However, in some areas buses can be faster and more direct than local trains, so it's a good idea to **compare bus and train schedules.** To reach some smaller towns, the bus is likely to be your only option. Bus service outside cities is organized on a regional level and often operated by private companies. Strikes can sometimes affect bus travel. For further information about bus travel within Italy, see the A to Z sections at the end of the regional chapters in this guide.

If you're traveling by bus from the United Kingdom, **have some euros on hand to spend en route.** And be sure to consider the train, as bus fares are quite high, especially when you take the long and tiring overnight journey into account. Eurolines runs bus service to Rome once a week from London, three times a week between June and September.

CUTTING COSTS

Because there's no national bus line in Italy, all bus service is run by regional companies, some of which provide day excursions from their base of operations. Generally children under two ride for free, and children ages two to eight travel at half price. Contact the local tourist office for information. If you need a car seat for your child, it's best to bring your own; bassinets are not provided.

FARES & SCHEDULES

Unlike city buses, for which you must buy your ticket from a machine, newsstand, or tobacconist and stamp it after you board, private bus lines usually have a ticket office in town or allow you to pay when you board.

🚌 Bus Information **Eurolines** ✉ 52 Grosvenor Gardens, London SW1W 0AU ☎ 020/7730-8235 or 020/7730-3499 ⊕ www.eurolines.com.

CAMERAS & PHOTOGRAPHY

Be on the lookout for signs indicating that photographs are not allowed; some museums and other institutions retain the sole right to photograph their works. Do not use a flash in museums or when photographing paintings or sculptures. The *Kodak Guide to Shooting Great Travel Pictures* (available at bookstores everywhere) is loaded with tips.

🎞 Photo Help **Kodak Information Center** ☎ 800/ 242-2424 ⊕ www.kodak.com.

EQUIPMENT PRECAUTIONS

Don't pack film or equipment in checked luggage, where it is much more susceptible to damage. X-ray machines used to view checked luggage are extremely powerful and therefore are likely to ruin your film. Try to ask for hand inspection of film, which becomes clouded after repeated exposure to airport X-ray machines, and keep videotapes and computer disks away from metal detectors. Always keep film, tape, and computer disks out of the sun. Carry an extra supply of batteries, and be prepared to turn on your camera, camcorder, or laptop to prove to airport security personnel that the device is real.

FILM & DEVELOPING

In Rome and most major cities you'll see scores of photo developing shops, many with service in one hour (or less). In smaller cities look for a shop with a Kodak sign outside its door. Developing film in Italy costs around €12 per 36-exposure roll, and film is €9 for a color 36-exposure roll. Because costs are higher in Italy, it's a good idea to **stock up on film before you leave.**

VIDEOS

Although VHS videotapes and players are common, be forewarned that Italy, like other countries in Europe, uses a different video system than the one used in North America. This means you won't be able to play the videotapes you bring from home on Italian equipment, and tapes purchased in Italy won't work in an American VCR. This is also the case with DVDs: European players aren't compatible with American disks.

CAR RENTAL

Renting a car in Italy is essential for exploring the countryside, but not if you plan to stick to city travel. Signage on country roads is usually good, but be prepared for fast and impatient fellow drivers.

Hiring a car with a driver can come in handy, particularly if you plan to do some wine tasting or drive along the Amalfi Coast. Ask at your hotel for recommended drivers, or inquire at the local tourist information office. Typically, drivers are paid by the day, and are usually rewarded with a tip of about 15% on completion of the journey.

Fiats in a variety of sizes are the most typical rental cars. Remember that most Italian cars have standard transmissions. If you want to rent an automatic, you must be specific when you reserve the car. Higher rates will apply.

🚗 Major Agencies **Alamo** ☎ 800/522-9696 ⊕ www.alamo.com. **Avis** ☎ 800/331-1084, 800/879-2847 in Canada, 0870/606-0100 in U.K., 02/9353-9000 in Australia, 09/526-2847 in New Zealand ⊕ www.avis.com. **Budget** ☎ 800/527-0700, 0870/156-5656 in U.K. ⊕ www.budget.com. **Dollar** ☎ 800/800-6000, 0800/085-4578 in U.K. ⊕ www.dollar.com. **Hertz** ☎ 800/654-3001, 800/263-0600 in Canada, 0870/844-8844 in U.K., 02/9669-2444 in Australia, 09/256-8690 in New Zealand ⊕ www.hertz.com. **National Car Rental** ☎ 800/227-7368, 0870/600-6666 in U.K. ⊕ www.nationalcar.com.

CUTTING COSTS

Most major American car-rental companies have offices or affiliates in Italy, but the rates are generally better if you make a reservation from abroad rather than from within Italy. The price of rentals is uniform for each company throughout the country: you will not save money, for example, if you pick up a vehicle at a city rental office rather than at an airport. For a good deal, **book through a travel agent who will shop around.** Weekend rates with limited mileage are usually good deals.

Do look into wholesalers, companies that do not own fleets but rent in bulk from those that do and often offer better rates than traditional car-rental operations. Prices are best during off-peak periods. Rentals booked through wholesalers often must be paid for before you leave home.

🚗 🚗 Wholesalers **Auto Europe** ☎ 207/842-2000 or 800/223-5555 🖷 207/842-2222 ⊕ www.autoeurope.com. **Destination Europe Resources** (DER) ✉ 9501 W. Devon Ave., Rosemont, IL 60018 ☎ 800/782-2424 🖷 800/282-7474 ⊕ www.der.com. **Europe by Car** ☎ 212/581-3040 or 800/223-1516 🖷 212/246-1458 ⊕ www.europebycar.com. **Kemwel** ☎ 877/820-0668 or 800/678-0678 🖷 207/842-2147 ⊕ www.kemwel.com.

INSURANCE

When driving a rented car you are generally responsible for any damage to or loss of the vehicle. Collision policies that car-rental companies sell for European rentals typically don't cover stolen vehicles. Indeed, all car-rental agencies operating in Italy require that you buy a theft-protection policy. Before you rent—and purchase collision coverage—see what coverage you already have under the terms of your personal auto-insurance policy and credit cards.

REQUIREMENTS & RESTRICTIONS

In Italy your own country's driver's license is acceptable. An International Driver's Permit is nonetheless not a bad idea; it's available from the American or Canadian Automobile Association and, in the United

Kingdom, from the Automobile Association or Royal Automobile Club. These international permits are universally recognized, and having one may save you a problem with the local authorities. In Italy you must be 21 years of age to rent an economy or subcompact car, and most companies require customers under the age of 23 to pay by credit card. Upon rental, all companies require credit cards as a warranty; to rent bigger cars (2,000 cc or more) you must often show two credit cards. Call local agents for details. There are no special restrictions on senior-citizen drivers.

Car seats are required for children under three and must be booked in advance. The cost ranges from €26 to €40 for the duration of the rental.

SURCHARGES

Before you pick up a car in one city and leave it in another, ask about drop-off charges or one-way service fees, which can be substantial. Also inquire about early-return policies; some rental agencies charge extra if you return the car before the time specified in your contract, whereas others give you a refund for the days not used. To avoid a hefty refueling fee, fill the tank just before you turn in the car, but be aware that gas stations near the rental outlet may overcharge. It's almost never a deal to buy the tank of gas that's in the car when you rent it; the understanding is that you'll return it empty, but some fuel usually remains.

The cost for an additional driver is about €5 per day.

CAR TRAVEL

There is an extensive network of *autostrade* (toll highways), complemented by equally well-maintained but free *superstrade* (expressways). The ticket you are issued upon entering an autostrada must be returned when you exit and pay the toll; on some shorter autostrade, mainly connecting highways, the toll is paid upon entering. Viacard cards, on sale at many autostrada locations, or any major credit card make paying tolls easier and faster. *Uscita* means "exit." A *raccordo* is a ring road surrounding a city. *Strade statali* (state highways, de-

noted by *S* or *SS* numbers) may be two-lane roads, as are all secondary roads; directions and turnoffs are not always clearly marked.

EMERGENCY SERVICES

Automobil Club Italiano (ACI) offers 24-hour road service. Dial 803/116 from any phone 24 hours a day to reach the ACI dispatch operator. Also, your rental car company may have an emergency tow service that can be reached with a toll-free call. Check your paperwork or ask when renting.

When you're on the road, always carry a good road map, a flashlight, and, if possible, a cellular phone so that in case of a breakdown you can call for help. When speaking to ACI, ask and you will be transferred to an English-speaking operator. Be prepared to tell the operator which road you're on, the direction you're going, e.g., "*verso* (in the direction of) Pizzo," and the *targa* (license plate number) of your car.

⬛ ACI Emergency Service ☎ 803/116.

GASOLINE

Gas stations (*benzinai*) are generally open Monday–Saturday 7–7 with a break at lunchtime. Many stations have automatic self-service pumps that accept only bills of 5, 10, 20, and 50 euros; some, but not all, also take credit cards. Gas stations on autostrade are open 24 hours. Gas costs about €1.05 per liter.

PARKING

Parking space is at a premium in most towns, especially in the *centri storici* (historic centers), which are filled with narrow streets and restricted circulation zones. Fines for parking violations are high, and rules are strictly enforced. Towing is common, and often the places where the cars are towed are difficult to get to, so it's simply not worth the risk. It is often a good idea (if not the only option) to park your car in a designated (preferably attended) lot. Parking in an area signposted ZONA DISCO (disk zone) is allowed for limited periods (from 30 minutes to two hours or more—the limit is posted); if you don't have the cardboard disk (inquire at the local tourist office or car rental agency) to show what time you parked, you can use a piece of paper. The *parcometro,* the Italian version of metered parking in which you put coins into a machine for a stamped ticket that you leave on the dashboard, has been introduced in some cities. It's advisable to **leave your car only in guarded parking areas.**

ROAD CONDITIONS

Autostrade are generally well maintained, well marked, and easy to follow, as are most interregional highways. The condition of provincial (county) roads varies, but road maintenance at this level is generally good in Italy.

ROAD MAPS

Street and road signs are often challenging—a good map and patience are essential. Local road maps can be obtained at the point of rental pickup. Alternatively, most bookstores such as Feltrinelli sell them as do most highway gas stations. In major cities look for the Touring Club Italiano's shop. They sell maps (road, bicycle, and hiking maps, among others). Probably the best road maps are those produced by Michelin.

RULES OF THE ROAD

Driving is on the right. Regulations are largely as in Britain and the United States, except that the police have the power to levy on-the-spot fines. Using handheld mobile phones while driving is illegal; fines can exceed €100. In most Italian towns the use of the horn is forbidden in certain, if not all, areas; a large sign, ZONA DI SILENZIO, indicates where. Speed limits are 130 kph (80 mph) on autostrade and 110 kph (70 mph) on state and provincial roads, unless otherwise marked.

The blood-alcohol content limit for driving is 0.5 gr (stricter than U.S. limits) with fines up to €5,000 for surpassing the limit and the possibility of six months' imprisonment. Though enforcement of laws varies depending on region, fines for speeding are uniformly stiff: 10 kph over the speed limit can warrant a fine of up to €500; over 10 kph, and your license could be taken away from you.

Nonetheless, Italians drive fast and are impatient with those who don't. Tailgating is

the norm here—the only way to avoid it is to get out of the way. Drivers also honk a lot, often to alert other drivers of their moves. Right turns on red lights are forbidden. Headlights are not compulsory in cities when it rains or snows, but it's a good idea to turn them on. However, they are mandatory when driving on all roads outside city limits at all hours. Seat belts (front and back) and children's car seats are compulsory.

CHILDREN IN ITALY

Although Italians love children and are generally very tolerant and patient with them, they provide few amenities for them. Some discounts do exist. Always ask about a *sconto bambino* (child's discount) before purchasing tickets. Children under a certain height ride free on municipal buses and trams. Children under 18 who are EU citizens are admitted free to state-run museums and galleries, and there are similar privileges in many municipal or private museums. *Fodor's Around Rome with Kids* (available in bookstores everywhere) can help you plan your days together.

If you are renting a car, don't forget to arrange for a car seat when you reserve. For general advice about traveling with children, consult *Fodor's FYI: Travel with Your Baby* (available in bookstores everywhere).

FLYING

If your children are two or older, ask about children's airfares. As a general rule, infants under two not occupying a seat fly at greatly reduced fares or even for free. But if you want to guarantee a seat for an infant, you have to pay full fare. Consider flying during off-peak days and times; most airlines will grant an infant a seat without a ticket if there are available seats. When booking, confirm carry-on allowances if you're traveling with infants. In general, for babies charged 10% to 50% of the adult fare you are allowed one carry-on bag and a collapsible stroller; if the flight is full, the stroller may have to be checked or you may be limited to less.

Experts agree that it's a good idea to use safety seats aloft for children weighing less than 40 pounds. Airlines set their own policies: if you use a safety seat, U.S. carriers usually require that the child be ticketed, even if he or she is young enough to ride free, because the seats must be strapped into regular seats. And even if you pay the full adult fare for the seat, it may be worth it, especially on longer trips. Do **check your airline's policy about using safety seats during takeoff and landing.** Safety seats are not allowed everywhere in the plane, so get your seat assignments as early as possible.

When reserving, request children's meals or a freestanding bassinet (not available at all airlines) if you need them. But note that bulkhead seats, where you must sit to use the bassinet, may lack an overhead bin or storage space on the floor.

FOOD

In restaurants and trattorias you may find a high chair or a cushion for the child to sit on, but rarely do they offer a children's menu. **Order a *mezza porzione*** (half portion) of any dish, or **ask the waiter for a *porzione da bambino*** (child's portion) or ***pasta in bianca*** (pasta with butter), Italian children's favorite. Though spaghetti and meatballs are not found on menus, approximations to it, such as spaghetti *al pomodoro* (spaghetti with tomato sauce) are suitable substitutions. Italian children are fond of spaghetti with Parmesan, and even if it's not on the menu, most chefs will be happy to prepare it. Pizza, either in a pizzeria or at stand-up shops, offers a familiar treat for children. Generally, children are best taken to casual establishments such as trattorias. Only exceptionally well-behaved children should go to higher-end restaurants; indeed, it's rare to see Italian children in them.

LODGING

Most hotels will provide cots or cribs with prior arrangement; four- and five-star hotels normally have these on hand. The same holds true with babysitting; budget hotels will most likely be unable to provide the service. Some five-star hotels and *agriturismi* (farm stays) do not allow children, so inquire beforehand. Pools in city hotels are a rarity, and video games virtually unheard of. If you're staying at a hotel with satellite TV, you will have access to some English-language news programs, but little more. Even *The Simpsons* is dubbed into Italian.

Most hotels in Italy allow children under a certain age to stay in their parents' room at no extra charge, but others charge for them as extra adults; be sure to **find out the cut-off age for children's discounts.** The Luxury Collection of Sheraton Hotels has 15 properties in Italy, all of which welcome families. Club Med has a "Mini Club" (for ages 4–10) and a "Kids Club" at its ski village in Sestriere. There are also kids' programs at summer resort villages in Metaponto (Basilicata) and on the islands of Sicily and Sardinia, marketed mainly to Europeans. Some of the Valtur vacation villages also have special facilities and activities for children.

🗗 Best Choices **Club Med** ⊠ 7001 N. Scottsdale Rd., Suite 1010, Scottsdale, AZ 85253 ☎ 800/258–2633 or 888/WEBCLUB ⊕ www.clubmed.com. **Sheraton Hotels** ⊠ 1111 Westchester Ave., White Plains, NY 10604 ☎ 800/221–2340 ⊕ www.starwood.com. **Valtur** ⊠ Piazza della Repubblica 59, Rome 00185 ☎ 06/471061 🖷 06/4706321 ⊕ www.valtur.it.

PRECAUTIONS

Italian tap water is heavily chlorinated, which is one reason why most Italians drink bottled water. Apple juice (*succo di mele*) is readily available in most bars and supermarkets, as are other fruit juices and popular soft drinks.

Mosquitoes can be pesky once the weather warms. Travel with your usual brand of children's insect repellant. There are several Italian brands—Autun, for instance—that also do the trick. They are available in pharmacies and supermarkets.

SIGHTS & ATTRACTIONS

Places that are especially appealing to children are indicated by a rubber-duckie icon (🐥) in the margin.

SUPPLIES & EQUIPMENT

The cost of diapers in Italy is similar to that in other places, though American brands such as Pampers and Huggies are slightly higher than in the United States. COOP is a reliable brand; you'll pay about €10 for 50 diapers.

Italian formula (both in premixed and powder forms) generally contains more vitamins than its American counterparts; Plasmon is a good brand. Italian bottles are identical to American ones, but it is difficult to find no-spill glasses for toddlers; it's best to bring a couple along with you.

COMPUTERS ON THE ROAD

Getting online in Italian cities isn't difficult: public Internet stations and Internet cafés, some open 24 hours a day, are becoming more and more common. Prices differ from place to place, so **spend some time to find the best deal.** This isn't always readily apparent: a place might have higher rates, but because it belongs to a chain you won't be charged an initial flat fee again when you move to a different city that has the same chain. Some hotels have in-room modem lines, but, as with phones, using the hotel's line is relatively expensive. Always check modem rates before plugging in, and set your computer to ignore the dial tone. You may need an adapter for your computer for the European-style plugs. As always, if you are traveling with a laptop carry a spare battery and an adapter. Never plug your computer into any socket before asking about surge protection. IBM sells a pea-size modem tester that plugs into a telephone jack to check whether the line is safe to use.

CONSUMER PROTECTION

Most stores in Italy do not allow customers to return or exchange merchandise, even if there is a minor flaw in the product. Clothing stores are particularly inflexible, and will often not permit shoppers to try on shirts or blouses.

Whether you're shopping for gifts or purchasing travel services, **pay with a major credit card** whenever possible, so you can cancel payment or get reimbursed if there's a problem (and you can provide documentation). If you're buying a package or tour, always consider travel insurance that includes default coverage (⇨ Insurance).

CRUISE TRAVEL

Several major cruise lines offer Mediterranean cruises that feature stops in Italy as well as Italy-only cruises. Cunard cruises in the Mediterranean call at Genoa,

Livorno, Rome, and Lipari. Festival Cruises has a "Carnevale" cruise that sails from Venice to Malta, Tunisia, Sicily, and Croatia, returning to Venice in time for the Carnevale celebration. Mediterranean Shipping Cruises (MSC) sails in Sicily, Tunisia, the Balearic Islands, Spain, and France. Royal Olympic Cruises has multiple departures leaving from Venice with ports of call in Dubrovnik, Istanbul, Corfu, Mykonos, and Santorini.

To learn how to plan, choose, and book a cruise-ship voyage, consult *Fodor's FYI: Plan & Enjoy Your Cruise* (available in bookstores everywhere).

🚢 Cruise Lines **Cunard** ⊠ 6100 Blue Lagoon Dr., Miami, FL 33126 ☎ 800/728–6273 in U.S. and Canada, 0800/0523840 in U.K., 612/92506666 in Australia and New Zealand ⊕ www.cunardline.com. **Festival Cruises** ⊠ via XX Settembre 28, 16121 Genoa ☎ 010/5490700 ⊕ www.festivalcruises.com. **Mediterranean Shipping Cruises** ⊠ Via A. Depretis 31, 80133 Naples ☎ 081/7942400 or 081/794211 ⊕ www.msccruises.com. **Royal Olympia Cruises** ⊠ 805 3rd Ave., New York, NY 10022–7513 ☎ 800/ 872–6400 in U.S. and Canada 🖷 888/662–6237 ⊕ www.royalolympiacruises.com.

CUSTOMS & DUTIES

When shopping abroad, keep receipts for all purchases. Upon reentering the country, **be ready to show customs officials what you've bought.** Pack purchases together in an easily accessible place. If you think a duty is incorrect, appeal the assessment. If you object to the way your clearance was handled, note the inspector's badge number. In either case, first ask to see a supervisor. If the problem isn't resolved, write to the appropriate authorities, beginning with the port director at your point of entry.

IN AUSTRALIA

Australian residents who are 18 or older may bring home A$400 worth of souvenirs and gifts (including jewelry), 250 cigarettes or 250 grams of cigars or other tobacco products, and 1,125 ml of alcohol (including wine, beer, and spirits). Residents under 18 may bring back A$200 worth of goods. Members of the same family traveling together may pool their allowances. Prohibited items include meat products. Seeds, plants, and fruits need to be declared upon arrival.

🛈 **Australian Customs Service** 🗗 Regional Director, Box 8, Sydney, NSW 2001 ☎ 02/9213–2000 or 1300/363263, 02/9364–7222 or 1800/020–504 quarantine-inquiry line 🖷 02/9213–4043 ⊕ www.customs.gov.au.

IN CANADA

Canadian residents who have been out of Canada for at least seven days may bring in C$750 worth of goods duty-free. If you've been away fewer than seven days but more than 48 hours, the duty-free allowance drops to C$200. If your trip lasts 24 to 48 hours, the allowance is C$50. You may not pool allowances with family members. Goods claimed under the C$750 exemption may follow you by mail; those claimed under the lesser exemptions must accompany you. Alcohol and tobacco products may be included in the seven-day and 48-hour exemptions but not in the 24-hour exemption. If you meet the age requirements of the province or territory through which you reenter Canada, you may bring in, duty-free, 1.5 liters of wine *or* 1.14 liters (40 imperial ounces) of liquor *or* 24 12-ounce cans or bottles of beer or ale. Also, if you meet the local age requirement for tobacco products, you may bring in, duty-free, 200 cigarettes and 50 cigars. Check ahead of time with the Canada Customs and Revenue Agency or the Department of Agriculture for policies regarding meat products, seeds, plants, and fruits.

You may send an unlimited number of gifts (only one gift per recipient, however) worth up to C$60 each duty-free to Canada. Label the package UNSOLICITED GIFT—VALUE UNDER $60. Alcohol and tobacco are excluded.

🛈 **Canada Customs and Revenue Agency** ✉ 2265 St. Laurent Blvd., Ottawa, Ontario K1G 4K3 ☎ 800/461-9999 in Canada, 204/983-3500, 506/636-5064 ⊕ www.ccra.gc.ca.

IN ITALY

Of goods obtained anywhere outside the EU, the allowances are (1) 200 cigarettes or 100 cigarillos (under 3 grams) or 50 cigars or 250 grams of tobacco; (2) 2 liters of still table wine or 1 liter of spirits over 22% volume; and (3) 50 milliliters of perfume and 250 milliliters of toilet water.

Of goods obtained (duty and tax paid) within another EU country, the allowances are (1) 800 cigarettes or 400 cigarillos (under 3 grams) or 200 cigars or 1 kilogram of tobacco; (2) 90 liters of still table wine or 10 liters of spirits over 22% volume or 20 liters of spirits under 22% volume or 110 liters of beer.

There is no quarantine period in Italy, so if you want to travel with Fido or Tiger, it's possible. Contact your nearest Italian consulate to find out what paperwork is needed for entry into Italy with a pet; generally, it is a certificate noting that the animal is healthy and up-to-date on its vaccinations. Keep in mind, however, that the United States has some stringent laws about reentry: pets must be free of all disease, especially those communicable to humans, and they must be vaccinated against rabies at least 30 days before returning. This means that if you are in Italy for a short-term stay, you must find a veterinarian or have your pet vaccinated before departure. (This law does not apply to puppies less than three months old.) Pets should arrive at the point of entry with a statement, in English, attesting to this fact.

🛈 **Ministero delle Finanze, Direzione Centrale dei Servizi Doganali, Divisione I** ✉ Via Carucci 71, 00143 Rome, Italy ☎ 06/50242117. **Dogana Sezione Viaggiatori** ✉ Customs, Aeroporto Leonardo da Vinci, Fiumicino 00054 Rome ☎ 06/65954343.

IN NEW ZEALAND

All homeward-bound residents may bring back NZ$700 worth of souvenirs and gifts; passengers may not pool their allowances, and children can claim only the concession on goods intended for their own use. For those 17 or older, the duty-free allowance also includes 4.5 liters of wine or beer; one 1,125-ml bottle of spirits; and either 200 cigarettes, 250 grams of tobacco, 50 cigars, *or* a combination of the three up to 250 grams. Meat products, seeds, plants, and fruits must be declared upon arrival to the Agricultural Services Department.

🛈 **New Zealand Customs** ✉ Head office: The Customhouse, 17–21 Whitmore St., Box 2218, Wellington

☎ 09/300-5399 or 0800/428-786 ⊕ www.customs. govt.nz.

IN THE U.K.

If you are a U.K. resident and your journey was wholly within the European Union, you probably won't have to pass through customs when you return to the United Kingdom. If you plan to bring back large quantities of alcohol or tobacco, check EU limits beforehand. In most cases, if you bring back more than 200 cigars, 3,200 cigarettes, 400 cigarillos, 10 liters of spirits, 110 liters of beer, 20 liters of fortified wine, and/or 90 liters of wine, you have to declare the goods upon return. Prohibited items include unpasteurized milk, regardless of country of origin.

🗐 **HM Customs and Excise** ⊠ Portcullis House, 21 Cowbridge Rd. E, Cardiff CF11 9SS ☎ 0845/010-9000 or 0208/929-0152 advice service, 0208/929-6731 or 0208/910-3602 complaints ⊕ www.hmce.gov.uk.

IN THE U.S.

U.S. residents who have been out of the country for at least 48 hours may bring home, for personal use, $800 worth of foreign goods duty-free, as long as they haven't used the $800 allowance or any part of it in the past 30 days. This exemption may include 1 liter of alcohol (for travelers 21 and older), 200 cigarettes, and 100 non-Cuban cigars. Family members from the same household who are traveling together may pool their $800 personal exemptions. For fewer than 48 hours, the duty-free allowance drops to $200, which may include 50 cigarettes, 10 non-Cuban cigars, and 150 ml of alcohol (or 150 ml of perfume containing alcohol). The $200 allowance cannot be combined with other individuals' exemptions, and if you exceed it, the full value of all the goods will be taxed. Antiques, which U.S. Customs and Border Protection define as objects more than 100 years old, enter duty-free, as do original works of art done entirely by hand, including paintings, drawings, and sculptures. This doesn't apply to folk art or handicrafts, which are in general dutiable.

You may also send packages home duty-free, with a limit of one parcel per addressee per day (except alcohol or tobacco products or perfume worth more than $5). You can mail up to $200 worth of goods for personal use; label the package PERSONAL USE and attach a list of its contents and their retail value. If the package contains your used personal belongings, mark it AMERICAN GOODS RETURNED to avoid paying duties. You may send up to $100 worth of goods as a gift; mark the package UNSOLICITED GIFT. Mailed items do not affect your duty-free allowance on your return.

To avoid paying duty on foreign-made high-ticket items you already own and will take on your trip, register them with Customs before you leave the country. Consider filing a Certificate of Registration for laptops, cameras, watches, and other digital devices identified with serial numbers or other permanent markings; you can keep the certificate for other trips. Otherwise, bring a sales receipt or insurance form to show that you owned the item before you left the United States.

For more about duties, restricted items, and other information about international travel, check out U.S. Customs and Border Protection's online brochure, *Know Before You Go.*

🗐 **U.S. Customs and Border Protection** ⊠ For inquiries and equipment registration, 1300 Pennsylvania Ave. NW, Washington, DC 20229 ⊕ www.cbp.gov ☎ 877/287-8667, 202/354-1000 ⊠ For complaints, Customer Satisfaction Unit, 1300 Pennsylvania Ave. NW, Room 5.2C, Washington, DC 20229.

DISABILITIES & ACCESSIBILITY

Italy has only recently begun to provide facilities such as ramps, telephones, and restrooms for people with disabilities; such things are still the exception, not the rule. Travelers' wheelchairs must be transported free of charge, according to Italian law, but the logistics of getting a wheelchair on and off trains and buses can make this requirement irrelevant. Seats are reserved for people with disabilities on public transportation, but few buses have lifts for wheelchairs. High, narrow steps for boarding trains create additional problems. At many monuments and museums, and even in some hotels and restaurants, architectural barriers make access difficult. Wheelchair access to bathrooms in restaurants is nearly nonexistent. Capdarco or Roma per Tutti can provide information about events and services for disabled people.

Contact the nearest Italian consulate about bringing a guide dog into Italy. This requires an import license, a current certificate detailing the dog's inoculations, and a letter from your veterinarian certifying the dog's good health.

◪ Local Resources Capdarco ⌖ C/o Co.In Cooperative Integrate, Via Enrico Giglioli 54/a, Rome, 00169 ☎ 06/71290123 🖷 06/71290125. **Roma per Tutti** ✉ Via di Torricola 87, 00178 Rome 🖷 06/71623919 🖷 06/71290125 ⊕ www.romapertutti.it.

LODGING

The Italian Government Travel Office (ENIT: ⇨ Visitor Information) can give you a list of hotels that provide access and addresses of Italian associations for travelers with disabilities.

Because Italian lodgings are often in buildings that are several hundred years old, many are not equipped with elevators. Many of them have steps at the entrance. When booking a hotel, inquire about entranceways: ramps are still rare.

In Rome the five-star Hotel de Russie has four rooms available for people who use wheelchairs. The Locarno, also near Piazza del Popolo, has one accessible room. A budget option is the Alimandi, near the Vatican.

The Hotel Excelsior in Florence is wheelchair accessible.

In Venice the San Zulian and the luxurious Danieli both have two rooms that are wheelchair accessible.

In Milan the Grand Hotel Duomo has a junior suite available for people who use wheelchairs. The equally luxurious and modern Westin Palace has two wheelchair-friendly rooms.

RESERVATIONS

When discussing accessibility with an operator or reservations agent, ask hard questions. Are there any stairs, inside *or* out? Are there grab bars next to the toilet *and* in the shower/tub? How wide is the doorway to the room? To the bathroom? For the most extensive facilities meeting the latest legal specifications, opt for newer accommodations. If you reserve through a toll-free number, consider also calling the hotel's local number to confirm the information from the central reservations office. Get confirmation in writing when you can.

SIGHTS & ATTRACTIONS

Getting around in Italy with a wheelchair is difficult but not impossible. In Rome, for example, the Musei Vaticani and the Museo Nazionale di Castel Sant'Angelo are accessible (but the Colosseum and Forum are not). In Florence the Uffizi, Palazzo Pitti, Duomo, Baptistery, and Accademia are all accessible. Local tourist offices provide maps and lists, rated on degrees of ease and difficulty, of banks, supermarkets, sites, hotels, and restaurants.

TRANSPORTATION

Most buses in Italy cannot accommodate wheelchairs; only a few have special ramps. A handful of subway stops in the Rome subway system are accessible to people who use wheelchairs. Local tourist offices are sometimes helpful with information about mass transit.

Getting around in Venice on the vaporetti is relatively easy; however, when *acqua alta* (high water) floods pedestrian areas, as it does sporadically between October and April, movement for people who use wheelchairs becomes virtually impossible.

More than 150 railroad stations throughout the country have a reception service to assist people who use wheelchairs; this service must be booked 24 hours in advance. To do so, consult a travel agency or go to www.trenitalia.com, select the Italian-language version, and click on "servizi per i disabili." The ferry line Tirrenia has two wheelchair-accessible cabins on their routes to Sardinia.

◪ Complaints Aviation Consumer Protection Division (⇨ Air Travel) for airline-related problems. **Departmental Office of Civil Rights** ✉ For general inquiries, U.S. Department of Transportation, S-30, 400 7th St. SW, Room 10215, Washington, DC 20590 ☎ 202/366-4648 🖷 202/366-9371 ⊕ www.dot.gov/ost/docr/index.htm. **Disability Rights Section** ✉ NYAV, U.S. Department of Justice, Civil Rights Division, 950 Pennsylvania Ave. NW, Washington, DC

20530 ⌨ ADA information line 202/514–0301, 800/ 514–0301, 202/514–0383 TTY, 800/514–0383 TTY ⊕ www.ada.gov. **U.S. Department of Transportation Hotline** ☎ For disability-related air-travel problems, 800/778–4838 or 800/455–9880 TTY.

TRAVEL AGENCIES
In the United States, the Americans with Disabilities Act requires that travel firms serve the needs of all travelers. Some agencies specialize in working with people with disabilities.

🛈 Travelers with Mobility Problems **Access Adventures/B. Roberts Travel** ✉ 206 Chestnut Ridge Rd., Scottsville, NY 14624 ☎ 585/889–9096 ⊕ www. brobertstravel.com 🖉 dltravel@prodigy.net, run by a former physical-rehabilitation counselor. **CareVacations** ✉ No. 5, 5110–50 Ave., Leduc, Alberta, Canada, T9E 6V4 ☎ 780/986–6404 or 877/478–7827 🖶 780/ 986–8332 ⊕ www.carevacations.com, for group tours and cruise vacations. **Flying Wheels Travel** ✉ 143 W. Bridge St., Box 382, Owatonna, MN 55060 ☎ 507/ 451–5005 🖶 507/451–1685 ⊕ www. flyingwheelstravel.com.

🛈 Travelers with Developmental Disabilities **Sprout** ✉ 893 Amsterdam Ave., New York, NY 10025 ☎ 212/222–9575 or 888/222–9575 🖶 212/222–9768 ⊕ www.gosprout.org.

DISCOUNTS & DEALS
Be a smart shopper and compare all your options before making decisions. A plane ticket bought with a promotional coupon from travel clubs, coupon books, and direct-mail offers or purchased on the Internet may not be cheaper than the least expensive fare from a discount ticket agency. And always keep in mind that what you get is just as important as what you save.

DISCOUNT RESERVATIONS
To save money, look into discount reservations services with Web sites and toll-free numbers, which use their buying power to get a better price on hotels, airline tickets (⇨ Air Travel), even car rentals. When booking a room always **call the hotel's local toll-free number** (if one is available) rather than the central reservations number—you'll often get a better price. Always ask about special packages or corporate rates.

When shopping for the best deal on hotels and car rentals, look for guaranteed exchange rates, which protect you against a falling dollar. With your rate locked in you won't pay more, even if the price goes up in the local currency.

🛈 Airline Tickets **Air 4 Less** ☎ 800/AIR4LESS; low-fare specialist.

🛈 Hotel Rooms **Accommodations Express** ☎ 800/ 444–7666 or 800/277–1064 ⊕ www.acex.net. **Hotels. com** ☎ 800/246–8357 ⊕ www.hotels.com. **International Marketing & Travel Concepts** ☎ 800/790– 4682 ⊕ www.imtc-travel.com. **Steigenberger Reservation Service** ☎ 800/223–5652 ⊕ www.srs-worldhotels.com. **Turbotrip.com** ☎ 800/473–7829 ⊕ www.turbotrip.com.

PACKAGE DEALS
Don't confuse packages and guided tours. When you buy a package you travel on your own, just as though you had planned the trip yourself. Fly/drive packages, which combine airfare and car rental, are often a good deal. In cities ask the local visitor's bureau about hotel and local transportation packages that include tickets to major museum exhibits or other special events. If you **buy a rail/drive pass** you may save on train tickets and car rentals. All Eurailpass holders get a discount on Eurostar fares through the Channel Tunnel and often receive reduced rates for buses, hotels, ferries, sightseeing cruises, and car rentals.

EATING & DRINKING
The restaurants we list are the cream of the crop in each price category. Properties indicated by an ✕🏨 are lodging establishments whose restaurant warrants a special trip.

CATEGORY	COST
$$$$	over €22
$$$	€16–€22
$$	€11–€16
$	€7–€11
¢	under €7

*Prices are for a second course (*secondo piatto*) and are given in euros.*

A few pointers on Italian dining etiquette: menus are posted outside most restaurants (in English in tourist areas); if not, you might step inside and ask to take a look at the menu, but don't ask for a table unless you intend to stay. Italians take their food as it is listed on the menu, seldom making special requests such as "dressing on the side" or "hold the olive oil." If you have special dietary needs, though, make them known, and they can usually be accommodated. Although mineral water makes its way to almost every table, you can always order a carafe of tap water (acqua di rubinetto or acqua semplice) instead, but keep in mind that such water is highly chlorinated. Doing this, however, will mark you distinctly as a tourist.

Spaghetti should be eaten with a fork rolled against the side of the dish, although a little help from a spoon will not horrify the locals the way cutting spaghetti into little pieces might. Wiping your bowl clean with a (small) piece of bread is fine in less formal eateries. Order your espresso (Italians almost never drink a cappuccino after breakfast) after dessert, not with it. When you are ready for it, ask for the check (il conto): unless it's well past closing time, no waiter will put a bill on your table without your having asked first. Don't ask for a doggy bag.

MEALS & SPECIALTIES

What's the difference between a ristorante and a trattoria? Can you order food at an enoteca? Can you go to a restaurant just for a snack, or order just a salad at a pizzeria? The following definitions should help.

Not too long ago, restaurants tended to be more elegant and expensive than trattorie and osterie, which served more traditional, home-style fare in an atmosphere to match. But the distinction has blurred considerably, and an osteria in the center of town might be far fancier (and pricier) than a ristorante across the street. In all these types of places you are generally expected to order at least a two-course meal, such as: a *primo* (first course) and a *secondo* (main course) or a *contorno* (vegetable side dish); an antipasto (starter) followed by either primo or secondo; or a secondo and a *dolce* (dessert).

In an *enoteca* (wine bar) or pizzeria it's common to order just one dish. An enoteca menu is often limited to a selection of cheese, cured meats, salads, and desserts, but if there's a kitchen you'll also find veg-etable soups, pasta, meat, and fish. Most pizzerias don't offer just pizza, and although the other dishes on the menu are supposed to be starters there's no harm in skipping the pizza. The typical pizzeria fare includes *affettati misti* (selection of cured pork), simple salads, various kinds of bruschetta and crostini (similar to bruschetta, sometimes topped with cheese and broiled) and, in Rome, *fritti* (deep-fried finger food) such as *olive ascolane* (green olives with a meat stuffing) and *supplì* (rice balls stuffed with mozzarella). All pizzerias serve fresh fruit, ice cream, and simple desserts.

Throughout the country the handiest and least expensive places for a quick snack between sights are probably bars, cafés, and pizza *al taglio* (by the slice) spots. Bars in Italy are primarily places to get a coffee and a bite to eat rather than drinking establishments. Most have a selection of *panini* (sandwiches, often warmed up on the griddle—*piastra*) and *tramezzini* (sandwiches made of untoasted white bread triangles). In larger cities, bars also serve prepared salads, fruit salads, cold pasta dishes, and yogurt around lunchtime. Most bars offer beer and a variety of alcohol as well as wines by the glass (sometimes good but more often mediocre). A café (*caffè* in Italian) is like a bar but usually with more tables. Pizza at a café is to be avoided—it's usually frozen and reheated in a microwave. If you place your order at the counter, ask if you can sit down: some places charge considerably more for table service, others do not. In self-service bars and cafés it's good manners to clean up your table before you leave. Note that in some places you have to pay a cashier, then place your order and show your *scontrino* (receipt) at the counter. Pizza al taglio shops sell pizza by weight: just point out which kind you want and how much. Very few pizza al taglio shops have seating.

Italian cuisine is still largely regional. Ask what the local specialties are: by all means, have spaghetti *alla carbonara* (with bacon and egg) in Rome, pizza in Rome or Naples, *crespelle* (savory crepes) in Florence and in Tuscany, truffles in the Piedmont, and risotto *alla milanese* in Milan.

MEALTIMES

Breakfast (*la colazione*) is usually served from 7 to 10:30, lunch (*il pranzo*) from 12:30 to 2:30, dinner (*la cena*) from 7:30 to 10. Peak times are usually 1:30 for lunch and 9 for dinner. Enoteche and bacari (wine bars) are open also in the morning and late afternoon for a snack at the counter. Most pizzerias open at 8 PM and close around midnight–1 AM, or later in summer and on weekends. Most bars and cafés are open from 7 AM until 8–9 PM; a few stay open until midnight or so.

Unless otherwise noted, the restaurants listed in this guide are open daily for lunch and dinner.

PAYING

Prices for goods and services in Italy include tax. Restaurant menu prices usually include service (*servizio*) unless otherwise indicated on the menu (in which case it is added on to the prices listed on the menu). It is customary to leave a small tip (one euro to 10%) in appreciation of good service. Tips are always given in cash. Most restaurants charge a separate "cover" charge per person, usually listed on the menu as "*pane e coperto.*" It should be a modest charge (€1–€2.50 per person), except at the most expensive restaurants. Whenever in doubt, ask about the servizio and pane e coperto policy upon ordering, so as to avoid unpleasant discussions about payment later. The price of fish dishes is often given by weight (before cooking), so the price you see on the menu is for 100 grams of fish, not for the whole dish. An average fish portion is about 350 grams. Tuscan *bistecca fiorentina* (florentine steak) is also often priced by weight.

Major credit cards are widely accepted in Italian eating establishments, though cash is usually the preferred, and sometimes the only, means of payment. More restaurants take Visa and MasterCard than American Express. Remember that there's no line on which to write a tip on the receipt; you will be presented with a slip that includes only the cost of the meal.

RESERVATIONS & DRESS

Reservations are always a good idea; we mention them only when they're essential

or not accepted. Book as far ahead as you can, and reconfirm as soon as you arrive. (Large parties should always call ahead to check the reservations policy.) Pizzerias and enoteche usually accept reservations only for large groups.

We mention dress only when men are required to wear a jacket or a jacket and tie. But unless they are at a sea resort eating outdoors and perfectly tanned, Italian men never wear shorts or running shoes in a restaurant—no matter how humble—or in an enoteca. The same "rules" apply to ladies' casual shorts, running shoes, and plastic sandals. Shorts are acceptable in pizzerias and cafés.

WINE, BEER & SPIRITS

The grape has been cultivated in Italy since the time of the Etruscans, and Italians justifiably take pride in their local product. Though almost every region produces good-quality wine, the two most renowned areas are Piedmont and Tuscany.

If you're in a restaurant or trattoria, ask your waiter about the house wine; sometimes it's very good indeed, sometimes it isn't. Wine in Italy is considerably less expensive than almost anywhere else. Beer, oddly, is more expensive than a glass of wine, and though Italy does produce beer it's not nearly as notable as its wine.

Beer, wine, and spirits can be purchased in any bar, grocery store, or enoteca, any day of the week. There's no minimum drinking age in Italy. Italian children begin drinking wine mixed with water at mealtimes when they are teens or even younger.

Many bars have their own *aperitivo della casa* (house aperitif). Italians are most imaginative with their mixed drinks—always shaken, never blended.

ELECTRICITY

To use electric-powered equipment purchased in the United States or Canada, **bring a converter and adapter.** The electrical current in Italy is 220 volts, 50 cycles alternating current (AC); wall outlets take Continental-type plugs, with two or three round prongs.

If your appliances are dual-voltage, you'll need only an adapter. Don't use 110-volt outlets marked FOR SHAVERS ONLY for high-wattage appliances such as blow-dryers. Most laptops operate equally well on 110 and 220 volts and so require only an adapter.

EMBASSIES

🛂 Australia **Australian Embassy** ✉ Via Alessandria 215, 00198 Rome ☎ 06/852721 ⊕ www.australian-embassy.it.

🛂 Canada **Canadian Embassy** ✉ Via G. B. de Rossi 27, 00161 Rome ☎ 06/445981 ⊕ www.dfait-maeci.gc.ca/canadaeuropa/italy.

🛂 New Zealand **New Zealand Embassy** ✉ Via Zara 28, 00198 Rome ☎ 06/4417171.

🛂 United Kingdom **British Embassy** ✉ Via XX Settembre 80A, 00187 Rome ☎ 06/42200001 ⊕ www.britain.it.

🛂 United States **U.S. Embassy** ✉ Via Veneto 121 00187 Rome ☎ 06/46741 ⊕ www.usembassy.it.

EMERGENCIES

No matter where you are in Italy, **dial 113 for all emergency services,** including the police, or find somebody (your concierge, a passerby) who will call for you, as not all 113 operators speak English; the Italian word to use to draw people's attention in an emergency is *"Aiuto!"* (Help!, pronounced "ah-YOU-toh"). *"Pronto soccorso"* means "first aid" and when said to an operator will get you an *ambulanza* (ambulance). If you just need a doctor you should ask for *"un medico"*; most hotels will be able to refer you to a local doctor. Don't forget to ask the doctor for *una ricevuta* (an invoice) to show to your insurance company in order to get a reimbursement. Other useful Italian words to use in an emergency are *"Al fuoco!"* (Fire!, pronounced "ahl fuh-WOE-co"), and *"Al ladro!"* (Follow the thief!, pronounced "ahl LAH-droh").

Italy has a national police force *(carabinieri)* as well as local police force *(polizia)*. Both are armed and have the power to arrest and investigate crimes. **Always report the loss of your passport to either the carabinieri or the police,** as well as to your embassy. Local traffic officers are known as *vigili* (though their official name is *polizia municipale*)—they are responsible for, among other things, giving out parking

tickets and clamping cars. They wear white (in summer) or black uniforms and many are women. Should you find yourself involved in a minor car accident in town, you should contact the vigili. A country-wide toll-free number is used to call the carabinieri in case of emergency.

🛂 **Carabinieri** ☎ 112. **Emergencies** ☎ 113.

ENGLISH-LANGUAGE MEDIA

BOOKS

Most major cities have bookstores that cater to an English-reading clientele. The nationwide chain Feltrinelli International, for example, has a large selection of English-language books (pricier than at home since they are all imported). Rome has several independent English-language bookstores, as do several other cities, including Florence.

NEWSPAPERS & MAGAZINES

The best source for news in English is the *New York Times*–owned *International Herald Tribune,* which is sold at most newsagents in the major cities and major tourist towns. *USA Today* and most of the London newspapers are also available. You can find the Sunday *New York Times* in some places, but be prepared to pay €12 for it. Various national versions of *Vogue* are obtainable, as are *Time, Newsweek, Elle, The Economist, InStyle, The New Yorker, Vanity Fair, The Tatler,* and *People,* among others. But they don't come cheap: *Vanity Fair,* for example, costs more than €8.

Rome's English-language bimonthly *Wanted in Rome* lists events.

RADIO & TELEVISION

Radio broadcasts are almost completely in Italian. Unless you have satellite TV (with access to CNN or SkyNews), or unless you speak Italian, Italian television is completely inaccessible, as everything is either spoken in Italian or dubbed into Italian. MTV is sometimes broadcast in English with Italian subtitles—but that's the exception, not the rule. Vatican Radio broadcasts world news in English three times a day throughout Italy, with Vatican news included.

ETIQUETTE & BEHAVIOR

Italy is filled with churches, and many of them have significant works of art in them. Because they are places of worship, care should be taken with appropriate dress. Shorts, spaghetti straps, sleeveless garments: these are taboo at St. Peter's in Rome and in many other churches throughout Italy. So, too, are short shorts anywhere. When touring churches—especially in the summer when it's hot and no sleeves are desirable— it's wise to carry a sweater, or scarf, to wrap around your shoulders before entering the church. **Do not enter a church with food,** and do not drink from your water bottle while inside. **Do not go in if a service is in progress.** And if you have a cellular phone **turn it off before entering.**

Italians who are friends greet each other with a kiss, usually first on the right cheek, and then on the left. When you meet a new person, shake hands.

BUSINESS ETIQUETTE

Showing up on time for business appointments is expected in Italy, especially in Milan. Business lunches are more common than business dinners. Business cards are used throughout Italy, and business suits are the norm for both men and women.

GAY & LESBIAN TRAVEL

Same-sex couples traveling in major cities and beach resorts should meet with no raised eyebrows on the part of the locals. However, overt displays of affection in public are rare. Gay bars, mostly catering to men (and some of which ban women), can be found in all major cities. Some mainstream bars and nightclubs have a gay night during the week; inquire at the local tourist office.

🖪 Local Contacts & Community Centers **Azione Gay e Lesbica** ⊕ C/o Andrea del Sarto, Via Manara 12, Florence ☎ 055/671298 ⊕ www. azionegayelesbica.it. **Circolo di Cultura Omosessuale Mario Mieli** ✉ Via Corinto 5, Rome ☎ 06/59604622 ⊕ www.mariomieli.org.
🖪 Gay- & Lesbian-Friendly Travel Agencies **Different Roads Travel** ✉ 8383 Wilshire Blvd., Suite 520, Beverly Hills, CA 90211 ☎ 323/651-5557 or 800/429-8747 (Ext. 14 for both) 🖷 323/651-5454 ✍ lgernert@tzell.com. **Kennedy Travel** ✉ 130 W. 42nd St., Suite 401, New York, NY 10036 ☎ 212/840-

8659, 800/237-7433 🖷 212/730-2269 ⊕ www. kennedytravel.com. **Now, Voyager** ✉ 4406 18th St., San Francisco, CA 94114 ☎ 415/626-1169 or 800/255-6951 🖷 415/626-8626 ⊕ www.nowvoyager.com. **Skylink Travel and Tour/Flying Dutchmen Travel** ✉ 1455 N. Dutton Ave., Suite A, Santa Rosa, CA 95401 ☎ 707/546-9888 or 800/225-5759 🖷 707/636-0951; serving lesbian travelers.

HEALTH

The Centers for Disease Control and Prevention (CDC) in Atlanta caution that most of Southern Europe is in the "intermediate" range for risk of contracting traveler's diarrhea. Part of this risk may be attributed to an increased consumption of olive oil and wine, which can have a laxative effect on stomachs used to a different diet. The CDC also advises all international travelers to swim only in chlorinated swimming pools unless they are absolutely certain the local beaches and freshwater lakes are not contaminated. Italy's private beaches are very clean, public ones less so.

OVER-THE-COUNTER REMEDIES

It's always best to **travel with your own tried and true medicines.** The regulations regarding what medicines require a prescription are not likely to be exactly the same in Italy and in your home country— all the more reason to bring what you need with you. Aspirin (*l'aspirina*) can be purchased at any pharmacy, but Tylenol and Advil are unavailable.

HIKING & WALKING

Italy has many good places to hike and an extensive network of long trails. The Sentiero Italia is a national trail running from Reggio Calabria on the toe of Italy's boot to the central section of the Apennine mountains. There are plans to lengthen it farther north and to the western Alps, and from there to the Dolomites and Udine in the Friuli region. For detailed information on the Sentiero Italia contact the CAI (Club Alpino Italiano) headquarters or local offices. Local tourist information offices can also be helpful.

🖪 Hiking Organizations **CAI** ✉ Via Petrella 19, 20124 Milan ☎ 02/2057231 🖷 02/205723201.
🖪 Hiking & Walking Tours **Abercrombie & Kent** (⇨ Group Tours, Super-Deluxe). **Above the Clouds**

Trekking ⌖ Box 388, Hinesburg, VT 05461 ☎ 802/ 482-4848 or 800/233-4499 🖷 802/482-5011 www. aboveclouds.com. **Backroads** (⇨ Bike Travel). **Butterfield & Robinson** (⇨ Bike Travel). **Ciclismo Classico** (⇨ Bike Travel). **Country Walkers** ⌖ Box 180, Waterbury, VT 05676-0180 ☎ 802/464-9255 or 800/ 464-9255 ⊕ www.countrywalkers.com. **EEI Travel** (⇨ Bike Travel). **Italian Connection, Walking & Culinary Tours** ✉ 11 Fairway Dr., Suite 210, Edmonton, Alberta, Canada ☎ 800/462-7911 ⊕ www. italian-connection.com. **Mountain Travel-Sobek** ✉ 6420 Fairmount Ave., El Cerrito, CA, 94530 ☎ 510/ 527-8100 or 888/687-6235 🖷 510/525-7710 ⊕ www. mtsobek.com. **Wilderness Travel** ✉ 1102 9th St., Berkeley, CA 94710 ☎ 510/558-2488 or 800/368-2794 🖷 510/558-2489 ⊕ www.wildernesstravel.com.

HOLIDAYS

If you can avoid it, don't travel at all in Italy in August, when much of the population is on the move, especially around Ferragosto, the August 15 national holiday, when cities such as Rome and Milan are deserted and many restaurants and shops are closed. (Of course, with residents away on vacation, this makes crowds less of a bother for tourists.)

National holidays in 2005 include January 1 (New Year's Day); January 6 (Epiphany); March 27 and March 28 (Easter Sun. and Mon.); April 25 (Liberation Day); May 1 (Labor Day or May Day); June 2 (Festival of the Republic); August 15 (Assumption, better known as Ferragosto); November 1 (All Saints' Day); December 8 (Immaculate Conception); December 25 and 26 (Christmas Day and the feast of St. Stephen).

Feast days of patron saints are observed locally. Many businesses and shops may be closed in Florence, Genoa, and Turin on June 24 (St. John the Baptist); in Rome on June 29 (Sts. Peter and Paul); in Palermo on July 15 (St. Rosalia); in Naples on September 19 (San Gennaro); in Bologna on October 4 (San Petronio); in Trieste on November 3 (San Giusto); and in Milan on December 7 (St. Ambrose). Venice's feast of St. Mark is April 25, the same as Liberation Day, so the Madonna della Salute on November 21 makes up for the lost holiday. (*Also see* Festivals and Seasonal Events *under* When to Go.)

INSURANCE

The most useful travel-insurance plan is a comprehensive policy that includes coverage for trip cancellation and interruption, default, trip delay, and medical expenses (with a waiver for preexisting conditions).

Without insurance you'll lose all or most of your money if you cancel your trip, regardless of the reason. Default insurance covers you if your tour operator, airline, or cruise line goes out of business—the chances of which have been increasing. Trip-delay covers expenses that arise because of bad weather or mechanical delays. Study the fine print when comparing policies.

If you're traveling internationally, a key component of travel insurance is coverage for medical bills incurred if you get sick on the road. Such expenses aren't generally covered by Medicare or private policies. U.K. residents can buy a travel-insurance policy valid for most vacations taken during the year in which it's purchased (but check preexisting-condition coverage). British and Australian citizens need extra medical coverage when traveling overseas.

Always **buy travel policies directly from the insurance company**; if you buy them from a cruise line, airline, or tour operator that goes out of business you probably won't be covered for the agency or operator's default, a major risk. Before making any purchase, review your existing health and home-owner's policies to find what they cover away from home.

🛈 Travel Insurers In the U.S.: **Access America** ✉ 2805 N. Parham Rd., Richmond, VA 23294 ☎ 800/284-8300 🖷 804/673-1491 or 800/346-9265 ⊕ www.accessamerica.com. **Travel Guard International** ✉ 1145 Clark St., Stevens Point, WI 54481 ☎ 715/345-0505 or 800/826-1300 🖷 800/955-8785 ⊕ www.travelguard.com.

🛈 In the U.K.: **Association of British Insurers** ✉ 51 Gresham St., London EC2V 7HQ ☎ 020/ 7600-3333 🖷 020/7696-8999 ⊕ www.abi.org.uk. In Canada: **RBC Insurance** ✉ 6880 Financial Dr., Mississauga, Ontario L5N 7Y5 ☎ 800/668-4342 or 905/ 816-2400 🖷 905/813-4704 ⊕ www.rbcinsurance. com. In Australia: **Insurance Council of Australia** ✉ Insurance Enquiries and Complaints, Level 12, Box 561, Collins St. W, Melbourne, VIC 8007 ☎ 1300/ 780808 or 03/9629-4109 🖷 03/9621-2060 ⊕ www.

iecltd.com.au. In New Zealand: **Insurance Council of New Zealand** ✉ Level 7, 111–115 Customhouse Quay, Box 474, Wellington ☎ 04/472-5230 🖷 04/473-3011 ⊕ www.icnz.org.nz.

LANGUAGE

In the main tourist cities the language barrier is not a big problem. Most hotels have English speakers at their reception desks, and you can always find someone who speaks at least a little English. Remember that the Italian language is pronounced as it is written (many Italians try to speak English by enunciating every syllable, with disconcerting results). You may run into a language barrier in the countryside, but a phrase book and close attention to the Italians' astonishing use of pantomime and expressive gestures will go a long way. Try to **master a few phrases for daily use;** see the back of this book for a list of rudimentary terms.

LANGUAGES FOR TRAVELERS

A phrase book and language-tape set can help get you started. *Fodor's Italian for Travelers* (available at bookstores everywhere) is excellent.

LODGING

The lodgings we list are the cream of the crop in each price category. We always list the facilities that are available, but we don't specify whether they cost extra; when pricing accommodations, always ask what's included and what costs extra. Properties are assigned price categories based on the range between their least and most expensive standard double room at high season (excluding holidays). Properties marked ✕⌷ are lodging establishments whose restaurants warrant a special trip. Hotels with the designation **BP** (for Breakfast Plan) at the end of their listing include breakfast in their rate, though in some cases the offerings may be little more than coffee and a roll. Those designated **EP** (European Plan) have no meals included; **MAP** (Modified American Plan) means you get breakfast and dinner; **FAP** (Full American Plan) includes all meals.

CATEGORY	MAIN CITIES	ELSEWHERE
$$$$	over € 290	over €220
$$$	€210–€290	€160–€220
$$	€140–€210	€110–€160
$	€80–€140	€70–€110
¢	under €80	under €70

Prices are for two people in a standard double room in high season, including tax and service, and are given in euros. "Main cities" are Florence, Milan, Rome, and Venice.

APARTMENT & VILLA RENTALS

If you want a home base that's roomy enough for a family and comes with cooking facilities, consider a furnished rental. These can save you money, especially if you're traveling with a group. Home-exchange directories sometimes list rentals as well as exchanges.

🏠 International Agents **At Home Abroad** ⌂ 163 Third Ave., No. 319, New York, NY 10003 ☎ 212/421-9165 🖷 212/533-0095 ⊕ www.athomeabroadinc.com. **Drawbridge to Europe** ✉ 98 Granite St., Ashland, OR 97520 ☎ 541/482-7778 or 888/268-1148 🖷 541/482-7779 ⊕ www.drawbridgetoeurope.com. **Hideaways International** ✉ 767 Islington St., Portsmouth, NH 03801 ☎ 603/430-4433 or 800/843-4433 🖷 603/430-4444 ⊕ www.hideaways.com, annual membership $145. **Hometours International** ✉ 1108 Scottie La., Knoxville, TN 37919 ☎ 865/690-8484 or 866/367-4668 ⊕ thor.he.net/~hometour/. **Interhome** ✉ 1990 N.E. 163rd St., Suite 110, North Miami Beach, FL 33162 ☎ 305/940-2299 or 800/882-6864 🖷 305/940-2911 ⊕ www.interhome.us. **Solemar** ✉ 1990 N.E. 163rd St., Suite 110, North Miami Beach, FL 33162 ☎ 305/940-2299 or 800/882-6864 🖷 305/940-2911 ⊕ www.visit-toscana.com. **Vacation Home Rentals Worldwide** ✉ 235 Kensington Ave., Norwood, NJ 07648 ☎ 201/767-9393 or 800/633-3284 🖷 201/767-5510 ⊕ www.vhrww.com. **Villanet** ✉ 1251 N.W. 116th St., Seattle, WA 98177 ☎ 206/417-3444 or 800/964-1891 🖷 206/417-1832 ⊕ www.rentavilla.com. **Villas and Apartments Abroad** ✉ 183 Madison Ave., Suite 201, New York, NY 10016 ☎ 212/213-6435 or 800/433-3020 🖷 212/213-8252 ⊕ www.vaanyc.com. **Villas International** ✉ 4340 Redwood Hwy., Suite D309, San Rafael, CA 94903 ☎ 415/499-9490 or 800/221-2260 🖷 415/499-9491 ⊕ www.villasintl.com.

🏠 Local Agents **Homes International** ✉ Via Bissolati 20, Rome 00187 ☎ 06/4881800 🖷 06/4881808 ✍ homesint@tin.it. **Property International**

✉ Viale Aventino 79, Rome 00153 📠 06/5743170 🖨 06/5743182 ✍ Property.rm@flashnet.it.

🎦 Rental Listings *Wanted in Rome* is a bimonthly magazine with extensive listings for short-term rentals in Italy. Another good source for rentals is *EYP*, the English yellow pages for Italy, available at English bookstores.

🎦 In Rome *EYP* ⊕ www.intoitaly.it. *Wanted in Rome* ✉ Via dei Delfini 17, Rome 00186 Italy 📠 06/6790190 🖨 06/6783798 ⊕ www.wantedinrome.com. **🎦 In the U.K.** **CV Travel** ✉ 43 Cadogan St., London SW3 2PR, England 📠 020/7581–0851. **Magic of Italy** ✉ 227 Shepherds Bush Rd., London W6 7AS, England 📠 020/8748–7575.

CAMPING

Camping is particularly common in beach towns (and Italy has many of them) and in the mountains. Campgrounds are generally crowded in summer and vary in their amenities: some have showers, toilets, sinks, bars, restaurants, pools, and shade trees.

Sleeping on the beach is illegal in Italy, as is camping in farmers' fields or in the woods, which is not to say that people don't do it. Sicily and its satellite islands have excellent summer camping facilities. The two best are El Bahira in San Vito Lo Capo, and Bazia in Furnari Marina, west of Milazzo.

FARM HOLIDAYS & AGRITOURISM

Rural accommodations in *agriturismo* (agritourism) are working farms or vineyards, often with stone farmhouses that accommodate a number of guests. Contact local APT tourist offices or buy *Agriturism,* compiled by Agriturist, which includes more than 1,600 farms in Italy. Although it's available in Italian only from major bookstores, pictures and the use of international symbols describing facilities make the guide a good tool to use.

🎦 Agencies **Italy Farm Holidays** ✉ 547 Martling Ave., Tarrytown, NY 10591 📠 914/631–7880 🖨 914/631–8831 ⊕ www.italyfarmholidays.com.

HOME EXCHANGES

If you would like to exchange your home for someone else's, join a home-exchange organization, which will send you its updated listings of available exchanges for a year and will include your own listing in at least one of them. It's up to you to make specific arrangements.

🎦 Exchange Clubs **HomeLink International** 📩 Box 47747, Tampa, FL 33647 📠 813/975–9825 or 800/638–3841 🖨 813/910–8144 ⊕ www.homelink.org; $110 yearly for a listing, online access, and catalog; $70 without catalog. **Intervac U.S.** ✉ 30 Corte San Fernando, Tiburon, CA 94920 📠 800/756–4663 🖨 415/435–7440 ⊕ www.intervacus.com; $125 yearly for a listing, online access, and a catalog; $65 without catalog.

HOSTELS

No matter what your age, you can save on lodging costs by staying at hostels. Hostels in Italy are found both in remote towns and large cities, the latter offering dozens. Although usually very clean, they range from the bare-bones (no linen) to near bed-and-breakfasts. Many offer rooms for couples or families. When booking, inquire about lights-out time and the noise level—some hostels with a young clientele are lax in enforcing evening quiet hours.

In some 4,500 locations in more than 70 countries around the world, Hostelling International (HI), the umbrella group for a number of national youth-hostel associations, offers single-sex, dorm-style beds and, at many hostels, rooms for couples and family accommodations. Membership in any HI national hostel association, open to travelers of all ages, allows you to stay in HI-affiliated hostels at member rates; one-year membership is about $28 for adults (C$35 for a two-year minimum membership in Canada, £14 in the U.K., A$52 in Australia, and NZ$40 in New Zealand); hostels charge about $10–$30 per night. Members have priority if the hostel is full; they're also eligible for discounts around the world, even on rail and bus travel in some countries.

🎦 Organizations **Hostelling International–USA** ✉ 8401 Colesville Rd., Suite 600, Silver Spring, MD 20910 📠 301/495–1240 🖨 301/495–6697 ⊕ www.hiusa.org. **Hostelling International–Canada** ✉ 205 Catherine St., Suite 400, Ottawa, Ontario K2P 1C3 📠 613/237–7884 or 800/663–5777 🖨 613/237–7868 ⊕ www.hihostels.ca. **YHA England and Wales** ✉ Trevelyan House, Dimple Rd., Matlock, Derbyshire DE4 3YH, U.K. 📠 0870/870–8808, 0870/770–8868, 0162/959–2600 🖨 0870/770–6127 ⊕ www.yha.org.uk. **YHA Australia** ✉ 422 Kent St., Sydney, NSW 2001 📠 02/9261–1111 🖨 02/9261–1969

⊕ www.yha.com.au. **YHA New Zealand** ⊠ Level 1, Moorhouse City, 166 Moorhouse Ave., Box 436, Christchurch ☎ 03/379–9970 or 0800/278–299 🖷 03/365–4476 ⊕ www.yha.org.nz.

HOTELS

All Italian hotels are graded on a star scale, from five stars for the most deluxe hotels to one star for the most modest. This system has no relation to the stars you'll find in this book denoting highly recommended properties; it is administered by local boards on the basis of a complicated evaluation of facilities and services, and it can be misleading—it reflects the facilities available, but not necessarily how well they are maintained. No matter the hotel, **ask for one of the better rooms,** since less desirable rooms—and there usually are some—don't give you what you're paying for. Except in five-star and some four-star hotels, rooms may be very small by U.S. standards.

In all hotels there's a rate card inside the door of your room or inside the closet door; it tells you exactly what you will pay for that particular room (rates in a given hotel may vary according to the location and type of room). On this card, breakfast and any other optionals must be listed separately. Any discrepancy between the basic room rate and that charged on your bill is cause for complaint to the manager and to the police.

By law, breakfast is supposed to be optional, but most hotels quote room rates including breakfast. When you book a room, **ask whether the rate includes breakfast** (*colazione*). You are under no obligation to take breakfast at your hotel, but in practice most hotels expect you to do so. The trick is to "offer" guests "complimentary" breakfast and have its cost built into the rate. However, it's encouraging to note that many of the hotels we recommend provide generous buffet breakfasts instead of simple, even skimpy "Continental breakfasts." Remember, if the latter is the case, you can eat for less at the nearest coffee bar.

The quality of rooms in older hotels may be very uneven; if you don't like the room you're given, request another. A front room may be larger or have a view, but it also may have a lot of street noise. If you're a light sleeper, **request a quiet room when making reservations.**

Rooms in lodgings listed in this guide have a shower and/or bath unless noted otherwise. (Hotels with three or more stars always have private bathrooms). Remember to **specify whether you prefer to have a bathtub or shower.** Rooms in the three-star category and under often have only showers.

Sheraton/The Luxury Collection has 15 Italian properties, almost all five-star deluxe. Jolly has 32 four-star hotels in Italy. Atahotels has 20 mostly four- and five-star hotels. Starhotels has 14 mainly four-star hotels. Space Hotels has 80 independently owned four- and three-star hotels. Leading Hotels of the World has about 20 independently owned four- and five-star hotels. AGIP Motels is a chain of about 50, mostly four-star motels on main highways; the motels are commercial, functional accommodations for business travelers and tourists needing 40 winks, but they—and the Jolly hotels—can be the best choice in many out-of-the-way places.

Best Western, an international association of independently owned hotels, has some 75 mainly three- and four-star hotels in Italy; call to request the *Europe and Middle East Atlas* that lists them. The Sun Rays Pool comprises four- and five-star hotels, as well as several agriturismi with horseback riding.

RESERVING A ROOM

High season in Italy generally runs from Easter through the beginning of November, and then for two weeks at Christmastime. During low season and whenever a hotel is not full, it's often possible to negotiate a discounted rate. Major cities such as Rome and Milan have no official off-season as far as hotel rates go, though some hotels do offer substantial discounts during the slower parts of the year and on weekends. Always **inquire about special rates.** Major cities have hotel-reservation service booths in train stations.

Useful terms to know when booking a room are *aria condizionata* (air-conditioning), *bagno in stanza* (private bath), *letto matrimoniale* (double bed), *letti singoli* (twin beds), and *letti singoli uniti* (twin beds pushed together). Italy does not really have queen- or king-size beds, though some beds, particularly in four- and five-star accommodations, can be larger than standard. Phrases that could come in handy include the following:

Vi prego di fornire informazioni riguardo il vostro albergo/pensione. Vorrei una camera doppia/camera matrimoniale con bagno in camera. (Please supply me with information regarding your hotel/pension. I would like a room with two single beds/a double bed with private bath).

Una camera su un piano alto e con vista. (A room on a high floor with a view.)

Una camera a un piano basso. (A room on a low floor.)

Una camera silenziosa. (A quiet room.)

It's always a good idea to have your reservation, dates, and rate confirmed by fax or e-mail. If you need to cancel your reservation, be sure to do so by fax or e-mail and keep a record of the transmission, particularly if dealing directly with an Italian hotel.

🏢 Hotel Chain Numbers **Atahotels** 🕾 02/895261 in Milan ⊕ www.atahotels.it. **Best Western** 🕾 800/528-1234 ⊕ www.bestwestern.com. **Choice** 🕾 800/424-6423 ⊕ www.choicehotels.com. **Clarion** 🕾 800/424-6423 ⊕ www.choicehotels.com. **Comfort Inn** 🕾 800/424-6423 ⊕ www.choicehotels.com. **Four Seasons** 🕾 800/332-3442 ⊕ www.fourseasons.com. **Holiday Inn** 🕾 800/465-4329 ⊕ www.ichotelsgroup.com. **Hyatt Hotels & Resorts** 🕾 800/233-1234 ⊕ www.hyatt.com. **Inter-Continental** 🕾 800/327-0200 ⊕ www.ichotelsgroup.com. **Jolly** 🕾 800/221-2626 in U.S. (except New York), 800/237-0319 in Canada, 0800/1827798 in U.K., 800/017703 in Italy ⊕ www.jollyhotels.it. **Leading Hotels of the World** 🕾 800/745-8883 in U.S. and Canada, 0800/2888 8882 in U.K., 800/222 033 or 61-2 9377-84444 in Australia, 0 800 44 1016 in New Zealand ⊕ www.lhw.com. **Marriott** 🕾 800/228-9290 ⊕ www.marriott.com. **Le Meridien** 🕾 800/543-4300 ⊕ www.lemeridien.com. **Quality Inn** 🕾 800/424-6423 ⊕ www.choicehotels.com. **Radisson** 🕾 800/333-3333 ⊕ www.radisson.com. **Ramada** 🕾 800/228-2828, 800/854-7854 international reservations ⊕ www.ramada.com or www.ramadahotels.com. **Sheraton** 🕾 800/325-3535 ⊕ www.starwood.com/sheraton. **Space Hotels** 🕾 800/813013 or 06/4457346 in Italy ⊕ www.spacehotels.it. **Starhotels** 🕾 055/

36921 in Florence ⊕ www.starhotels.com. **Westin Hotels & Resorts** 🕾 800/228-3000 ⊕ www.starwood.com/westin.

MAIL & SHIPPING

The Italian mail system is notoriously slow. Allow up to 15 days for mail to and from the United States, Canada, Australia, and New Zealand. It takes about a week to and from the United Kingdom and within Italy.

OVERNIGHT SERVICES

Overnight mail is generally available in all major cities and at resort hotels. Pickups are daily, excluding Saturday and Sunday. Service is reliable; a Federal Express letter to the United States costs about €30, to the United Kingdom, €51, and to Australia and New Zealand €33. Overnight delivery usually means 24–36 hours.

If your hotel can't assist you, try an Internet shop, many of which also offer overnight mail services using major carriers at reasonable rates.

🏢 Major Services **DHL** 🕾 199-199-345, 24 hrs a day. **Federal Express** 🕾 800/123800, weekdays 8–7. **SDA** 🕾 800/016027, weekdays 8:30–7:30, Sat. 9–noon.

POSTAL RATES

Airmail letters (lightweight stationery) and postcards cost €0.52 for the first 20 grams to the United States and Canada and €0.62 to Australia and New Zealand; for heavier stationery you should go to the post office. Always stick the blue airmail tag on your mail, or write "Airmail" in big, clear characters to the side of the address. Postcards and letters to the United Kingdom and other EU countries, including Italy, cost €0.52 for the first 20 grams. Do not be fooled by the "airmail," however, as mail sent this way can often take weeks to arrive at its destination.

Posta Prioritaria (stationery and small packages up to 2 kilograms) is a much more effective means of mailing postcards and letters. Mail to Italian addresses and the United Kingdom costs €0.60, to the United States and Canada €0.80, and to Australia and New Zealand €1. Delivery from Italy to the United States generally takes about one week. *Postacelere* (up to 20 kilograms) is a special-delivery service from the post office that guarantees delivery within 24 hours in Italy and three to five days abroad. As regular stamps are not valid for this service, make sure you buy the special golden Posta Prioritaria stamps. Postacelere rates to the United States and Canada are between €28.35 (€28.15 to the United Kingdom and the rest of Europe) for parcels up to 500 grams (a little more than a pound) and €141.90 (€111.75 to the United Kingdom and Europe) for packages weighing 20 kilos (44 pounds).

You can buy stamps at tobacconists and post offices.

RECEIVING MAIL

Correspondence can be addressed to you in care of the Italian post office. Letters should be addressed to your name, "c/o Ufficio Postale Centrale," followed by "Fermo Posta" on the next line, and the name of the city (preceded by its postal code) on the next. You can **collect it at the central post office** by showing your passport or photo-bearing ID and paying a small fee. American Express also has a general-delivery service. There's no charge for cardholders, holders of American Express traveler's checks, or anyone who booked a vacation with American Express.

SHIPPING PARCELS

You can ship parcels via air or surface. Air takes about two weeks, and surface anywhere up to three months to most countries. If you have purchased antiques, ceramics, or other objects, ask if the vendor will do the shipping for you; in most cases, this is a possibility.

MONEY MATTERS

Prices vary from region to region and are substantially lower in the countryside than in touristy cities. Good value for the money can be had in the scenic Trentino–Alto Adige region and the Dolomites and in Umbria and the Marches. With a few exceptions, southern Italy, Sicily, and Sardinia also offer good values, but hotels are not always up to par. Of Italy's major cities, Venice and Milan are the most expensive. Resorts such as the Costa Smeralda, Portofino, and Cortina d'Ampezzo cater to the rich and famous and charge top prices.

Admission to the Vatican Museums is €9.30; to the Galleria degli Uffizi, €11.50 (including reservation fee). The cheapest seat at Rome's Teatro dell'Opera runs €16.55. Getting into a Milan nightclub will set you back about €20. A daily English-language newspaper is €2. A Rome taxi ride (1⅓ km [1 mi]) costs €5.15. An inexpensive hotel room for two, including breakfast, in Rome is about €100; an inexpensive dinner in Rome is €40, and a ½-liter carafe of house wine €3.50. A simple pasta dish runs about €10, a cup of coffee €0.80, and lunch from a *rosticceria* (pre-pared-food shop) about €8.50. A Coca-Cola (taken standing at a café counter) is €2, and a pint of beer is €3.70. Prices are slightly higher in major cities and ski and beach resorts.

Prices throughout this guide are given for adults. Substantially reduced fees are al-most always available for children, stu-dents, and senior citizens from the EU; citizens of non-EU countries rarely get discounts. For information on taxes, *see* Taxes.

ATMS

Fairly common in cities and towns as well as in airports and train stations, ATMs are the easiest way to get euros in Italy. Don't, however, count on finding ATMs in small towns and rural areas. Italian ATMs are commonly attached to a bank—you won't find one, for example, in a supermarket—although they are at times out of service. Do **check with your bank** to confirm you have an international PIN number, to find out your maximum daily withdrawal al-lowance, and to learn what the bank fee is for withdrawing money. The word for ATM in Italian is *bancomat,* for PIN, *codice segreto.* Both four- and five-digit PINs work for ATMs in Italy; keypads have only numbers, no letters.

CREDIT CARDS

Throughout this guide, the following ab-breviations are used: **AE,** American Ex-press; **DC,** Diners Club; **MC,** MasterCard; and **V,** Visa.

🔟 Reporting Lost Cards **American Express** ☏ 800/874 333 international collect. **Diners Club** ☏ 702/797–5532 collect. **MasterCard** ☏ 800/870866 toll-free within Italy. **Visa** ☎ 800/877232 toll-free within Italy.

CURRENCY

The euro is the main unit of currency in Italy, as well as in 11 other European countries. Under the euro system there are eight coins: 1, 2, 5, 10, 20, and 50 *centesimi* (at 100 centesimi to the euro), and 1 and 2 euros. There are seven notes: 5, 10, 20, 50, 100, 200, and 500 euros.

CURRENCY EXCHANGE

At this writing, the exchange rate was about 0.71 euros to the U.S. dollar; 0.53 euros to the Canadian dollar; 1.29 euros to the pound sterling; 0.57 euros to the Australian dollar; and 0.47 euros to the New Zealand dollar.

For the most favorable rates, **change money through banks.** Although ATM transaction fees may be higher abroad than at home, ATM rates are excellent because they're based on wholesale rates offered only by major banks. You won't do as well at exchange booths in airports or rail and bus stations, in hotels, in restaurants, or in stores. To avoid lines at airport exchange booths, get a bit of local currency before you leave home.

🖪 Exchange Services **International Currency Express** ✉ 427 N. Camden Dr., Suite F, Beverly Hills, CA 90210 ☎ 888/278–6628 orders 🖷 310/278–6410 ⊕ www.foreignmoney.com. **Travel Ex Currency Services** ☎ 800/287–7362 orders and retail locations ⊕ www.travelex.com.

TRAVELER'S CHECKS

Do you need traveler's checks? It depends on where you're headed. If you're going to rural areas and small towns, go with cash; traveler's checks are best used in cities. Lost or stolen checks can usually be replaced within 24 hours. To ensure a speedy refund, buy your own traveler's checks—don't let someone else pay for them: irregularities like this can cause delays. The person who bought the checks should make the call to request a refund. Make sure to **get traveler's checks in euros,** not U.S. dollars.

PACKING

The weather is considerably milder, in the winter at least, in Italy than in the north

and central United States or Great Britain. At the height of summer stick with very light clothing, as it can get steamy; even during summer months a sweater may be necessary for cool evenings, especially in the mountains and on islands. Sunglasses, a hat, and sunblock are essential. Brief summer afternoon thunderstorms are common in Rome and inland cities, so an umbrella will come in handy. In winter bring a medium-weight coat and a raincoat for Rome and farther south. Northern Italy calls for heavier clothes, gloves, hats, scarves, and boots. Even in Rome and other milder areas, central heating may not be up to your standards, and interiors can be cold and damp; take wool or flannel rather than sheer fabrics. Bring sturdy shoes for winter and comfortable walking shoes in any season.

Italians dress exceptionally well. They do not usually wear shorts. Men aren't required to wear ties or jackets anywhere, except in some of the grander hotel dining rooms and top-level restaurants, but are expected to look reasonably sharp—and they do. Formal wear is the exception rather than the rule at the opera nowadays, though people in expensive seats usually do get dressed up.

A certain modesty of dress (no bare shoulders or knees) is expected in churches, and strictly enforced in many, especially in Rome at St. Peter's and the Vatican Museums and in Venice at the Basilica di San Marco.

For sightseeing **pack a pair of binoculars;** they will help you get a good look at painted ceilings and domes. If you stay in budget hotels **take your own soap and towel.** Many such hotels either do not provide soap or give guests only one tiny bar per room, and towels often look like what you'd use to dry dishes.

In your carry-on luggage, pack an extra pair of eyeglasses or contact lenses and enough of any medication you take to last a few days longer than the entire trip. You may also ask your doctor to write a spare prescription using the drug's generic name, as brand names may vary from country to country. In luggage to be checked, **never**

pack prescription drugs, valuables, or un-developed film. And don't forget to carry with you the addresses of offices that handle refunds of lost traveler's checks. Check *Fodor's How to Pack* (available at online retailers and bookstores everywhere) for more tips.

To avoid customs and security delays, carry medications in their original packaging. Don't pack any sharp objects in your carry-on luggage, including knives of any size or material, scissors, nail clippers, and corkscrews, or anything else that might arouse suspicion.

To avoid having your checked luggage chosen for hand inspection, don't cram bags full. The U.S. Transportation Security Administration suggests packing shoes on top and placing personal items you don't want touched in clear plastic bags.

CHECKING LUGGAGE

You're allowed to carry aboard one bag and one personal article, such as a purse or a laptop computer. Make sure what you carry on fits under your seat or in the overhead bin. Get to the gate early, so you can board as soon as possible, before the overhead bins fill up.

Baggage allowances vary by carrier, destination, and ticket class. On international flights you're usually allowed to check two bags weighing up to 70 pounds (32 kilograms) each, although a few airlines allow checked bags of up to 88 pounds (40 kilograms) in first class. Some international carriers don't allow more than 66 pounds (30 kilograms) per bag in business class and 44 pounds (20 kilograms) in economy. On domestic flights the limit is usually 50 to 70 pounds (23 to 32 kilograms) per bag. In general, carry-on bags shouldn't exceed 40 pounds (18 kilograms). Most airlines won't accept bags that weigh more than 100 pounds (45 kilograms) on domestic or international flights. Expect to pay a fee for baggage that exceeds weight limits. Check baggage restrictions with your carrier before you pack.

Airline liability for baggage is limited to $2,500 per person on flights within the United States. On international flights it amounts to $9.07 per pound or $20 per kilogram for checked baggage (roughly $640 per 70-pound bag), with a maximum of $634.90 per piece, and $400 per passenger for unchecked baggage. You can buy additional coverage at check-in for about $10 per $1,000 of coverage, but it often excludes a rather extensive list of items, shown on your airline ticket.

Before departure, itemize your bags' contents and their worth, and label the bags with your name, address, and phone number. (If you use your home address, cover it so potential thieves can't see it readily.) Include a label inside each bag and **pack a copy of your itinerary.** At check-in make sure each bag is correctly tagged with the destination airport's three-letter code. Because some checked bags will be opened for hand inspection, the U.S. Transportation Security Administration recommends that you leave luggage unlocked or use the plastic locks offered at check-in. TSA screeners place an inspection notice inside searched bags, which are re-sealed with a special lock.

If your bag has been searched and contents are missing or damaged, file a claim with the TSA Consumer Response Center as soon as possible. If your bags arrive damaged or fail to arrive at all, file a written report with the airline before leaving the airport.

🔊 Complaints **U.S. Transportation Security Administration Contact Center** ☎ 866/289–9673 ⊕ www.tsa.gov.

PASSPORTS & VISAS

When traveling internationally, carry your passport even if you don't need one (it's always the best form of ID) and **make two photocopies of the data page** (one for someone at home and another for you, carried separately from your passport). If you lose your passport, promptly call the nearest embassy or consulate and the local police.

U.S. passport applications for children under age 14 require consent from both parents or legal guardians; both parents must appear together to sign the application. If only one parent appears, he or she must submit a written statement from the other parent authorizing the application for a passport for the child. A parent with sole authority must present evidence of it when applying; acceptable documentation includes the child's certified birth certificate listing only the applying parent, a court order specifically permitting this parent's travel with the child, or a death certificate for the nonapplying parent. Application forms and instructions are available on the Web site of the U.S. State Department's Bureau of Consular Affairs (⊕ travel.state.gov).

ENTERING ITALY

Citizens of Australia, Canada, New Zealand, and the United States need only a valid passport to enter Italy for stays of up to 90 days. Citizens of the United Kingdom need only a valid passport to enter Italy for an unlimited stay.

PASSPORT OFFICES

The best time to apply for a passport or to renew is in fall and winter. Before any trip, check your passport's expiration date, and, if necessary, renew it as soon as possible.

🔃 Australian Citizens **Passports Australia** Australian Department of Foreign Affairs and Trade ☎131-232 ⊕ www.passports.gov.au.

🔃 Canadian Citizens **Passport Office** ⊠ To mail in applications: 200 Promenade du Portage, Hull, Québec J8X 4B7 ☎ 819/994-3500 or 800/567-6868 ⊕ www.ppt.gc.ca.

🔃 New Zealand Citizens **New Zealand Passports Office** ☎ 0800/22-5050 or 04/474-8100 ⊕ www. passports.govt.nz.

🔃 U.K. Citizens **U.K. Passport Service** ☎ 0870/ 521-0410 ⊕ www.passport.gov.uk.

🔃 U.S. Citizens **National Passport Information Center** ☎ 877/487-2778, 888/874-7793 TDD/TTY ⊕ travel.state.gov.

RESTROOMS

Public restrooms are rather rare in Italy; the locals seem to make do with well-timed pit stops and rely on local bars. Although private businesses can refuse to make their toilets available to the passing public, some bars will allow you to use the restroom if you ask politely. Alternatively, it is not uncommon to pay for a little something—a few cents for a mineral water or coffee—to get access to the facilities. Standards of cleanliness and comfort vary greatly. In cities, restaurants, hotel lobbies, department stores such as La Rinascente and Coin, and McDonald's restaurants tend to have the cleanest restrooms. Pubs and bars rank among the worst. In general it's in your interest to carry some toilet paper with you. There are bathrooms in all airports and train stations (in major train stations you'll also find well-kept pay toilets for €0.25–0.50) and in most museums. There are also bathrooms at highway rest stops and gas stations: a small tip (€.25–€.50) to the attendant is always appreciated. There are no bathrooms in churches, post offices, or subway stations or at public beaches. Pay toilets in the centers of Italian towns are the exception, not the rule. In Venice, however, pay toilets are well posted and strategically located along the main drags that link Piazzale Roma and the train station with the city center; the cost is €0.50.

SAFETY

Don't wear a money belt or a waist pack, both of which peg you as a tourist. Distribute your cash and any valuables (including your credit cards and passport) between a deep front pocket, an inside jacket or vest pocket, and a hidden money pouch. Do not reach for the money pouch once you're in public.

If you carry a bag or camera, use one with straps; you should sling it across your body bandolier-style, adjusting the height to hip level or higher. Don't hold your bag on the street side of your body. Always be on the lookout for pickpockets, especially when in city buses and subways, when making your way through train corridors, and in busy piazzas or tourist spots.

LOCAL SCAMS

A word of caution: "gypsy" children are plentiful in Rome and other major cities, and are adept pickpockets. One tactic is to approach a tourist and proffer a piece of cardboard with writing on it. While you attempt to read the message *on* it, the children's hands are busy *under* it, trying to make off with purses or valuables. If you see such a group, avoid them—they are quick and know more tricks than you do. If traveling in a rental car, it's a good idea when making stops at rest areas and autogrills (a chain of highway cafeterias) to have someone remain near the car, as such cars are easily recognized by professional thieves.

WOMEN IN ITALY

Purse-snatching is not uncommon, and thieves operate on *motorini* (mopeds) as well as on foot. If you carry a purse, choose one with a zipper and a thick strap that you can drape across your body. Store only enough money in the purse to cover casual spending. Distribute the rest of your cash and any valuables between deep front pockets, inside jacket or vest pockets, and a concealed money pouch.

The difficulties encountered by women traveling alone in Italy are often overstated. Younger women have to put up with much male attention, but it is rarely dangerous or hostile. Ignoring whistling and questions is the best response.

SENIOR-CITIZEN TRAVEL

To qualify for age-related discounts, mention your senior-citizen status up front when booking hotel reservations (not when checking out) and before you're seated in restaurants (not when paying the bill). Be sure to have identification on hand. When renting a car ask about promotional car-rental discounts, which can be cheaper than senior-citizen rates.

🎓 Educational Programs **Elderhostel** ✉ 11 Ave. de Lafayette, Boston, MA 02111-1746 ☎ 877/426-8056, 978/323-4141 international callers, 877/426-2167 TTY 🖶 877/426-2166 ⊕ www.elderhostel.org.

SHOPPING

Italy produces fine wines, clothes, leatherwork, and jewelry, among other things. The notice PREZZI FISSI (fixed prices) means just that—it's a waste of time to bargain unless you're buying a sizable quantity of goods or a particularly costly object. Always try to bargain, however, at outdoor markets (except food markets) and when buying from street vendors. For information on V.A.T. refunds, *see* Taxes.

KEY DESTINATIONS

Perhaps the best shopping of all can be had in Rome, which is teeming with stores to suit all tastes. Savvy shoppers should visit during the *saldi* (sales), which happen just after the New Year and run as late as March, and then again in July through early September. Serious bargains in shoes and clothing can be found.

Factory outlets have only recently begun to appear in Italy. Prada has an outlet in Montevarchi, Fendi has one in Rignano sull'Arno, and there's a mall featuring Armani and Gucci in Leccio—all between Florence and Arezzo. The McArthur Glen designer outlet near Asti has bargains on Italian and international labels.

SMART SOUVENIRS

From sacred to kitsch, Rome has no shortage of keepsakes. For rosary beads made of anything from glow-in-the-dark plastic to semiprecious stones, head for the shops that line Borgo Pio, near St. Peter's. The least expensive will cost about €5; the more expensive, several hundred. For centerpiece fruit made of painted marble, look in shops near the Trevi fountain. Pieces costs about €15. The Porta Portese market has plenty of souvenirs. Aprons emblazoned with naked Davids (€5) and other figures are sold widely, along with historic prints of Rome, which can cost up to €50.

WATCH OUT

If you have purchased any work of art (painting, sculpture, miniature, cameo, etc.), make sure that the piece is certified as being less than 50 years old. Any art deemed older than that must receive clearance from the Italian government to leave the country.

If you have purchased an antique, the dealer will provide you with a certificate attesting to the integrity of the piece and the price paid. Some dealers will ship the object for you; others leave it to you to arrange shipping.

SIGHTSEEING GUIDES

Every province in Italy has licensed tour guides who are allowed by Italian law to take groups and individuals to selected sites. Some of them are eminently qualified in relevant fields such as history and art history; others have simply managed to pass the test. Inquire at any tourist office for a licensed, English-speaking guide. When you speak to the guide, ask about his or her qualifications and specialties. Also check to make sure that the guide's English is understandable. The rates are fixed; find out what they are before hiring the guide. It is illegal for the guide to charge you more than the fixed fee. Tipping is appreciated but not obligatory.

Some places, such as the Duomo in Florence, offer free guided tours in English by a volunteer. Such guides may be longer on enthusiasm than knowledge.

SMOKING

In 2002, laws were enacted banning smoking in many public places, including bars and restaurants, but Italians are unrepentant smokers and compliance is arbitrary in many cases. Fortunately, many restaurants now have no-smoking rooms, and some insist that smoking is allowed only at the bar. Smokers should check to see if there's a VIETATO FUMARE (No Smoking) sign before lighting up. Best bets for smoke-free environments are large establishments and, weather permitting, eating outside. All FS trains have no-smoking cars: always specify when you make reservations.

STUDENTS IN ITALY

In the major art cities there are plenty of sources of information and lodging geared to students' needs. Students from member nations in the EU with valid ID cards may sometimes receive discounts at museums, galleries, exhibitions, and entertainment venues, and on some transportation. Students who aren't EU citizens generally pay the usual entrance fees.

🚩 IDs & Services **STA Travel** ✉ 10 Downing St., New York, NY 10014 ☎ 212/627-3111, 800/777-0112 24-hr service center 🖨 212/627-3387 ⊕ www.sta.com. **Travel Cuts** ✉ 187 College St., Toronto, Ontario M5T 1P7, Canada ☎ 800/592-2887 in U.S., 416/979-2406 or 866/246-9762 in Canada 🖨 416/979-8167 ⊕ www. travelcuts.com.

LOCAL RESOURCES

The Centro Turistico Studentesco (CTS) is a student and youth travel agency with offices in major Italian cities. CTS helps its clients find low-cost accommodations and bargain fares for travel in Italy and else-

where. CTS is also the Rome representative for EuroTrain International.

TAXES

HOTELS

The service charge and the 9% IVA, or V. A.T. (value-added tax), are included in the rate except in five-star deluxe hotels, where the IVA (12% on luxury hotels) may be a separate item added to the bill upon departure.

RESTAURANTS

No tax is added to restaurant bills. Sometimes you will find a service charge of approximately 10–15% added to your check; in some cases the menu may say that the service charge is already included in the menu prices.

VALUE-ADDED TAX

The IVA is 20% on clothing, wine, and luxury goods. On consumer goods it's already included in the amount shown on the price tag, whereas on services it may not be. If a store you shop in has a EURO TAX FREE sign outside and you make a purchase above €155, present your passport and request a "Tax Free Shopping Check" when paying.

In general, when making a purchase **ask for a V.A.T. refund form** and find out whether the merchant gives refunds—not all stores do, nor are they required to. Have the form stamped like any customs form by customs officials when you leave the country or, if you're visiting several European Union countries, when you leave the EU. Be ready to show customs officials what you've bought (pack purchases together, in your carry-on luggage); budget extra time for this. After you're through passport control, take the form to a refund-service counter for an on-the-spot refund, or mail it to the address on the form (or on the envelope with it) after you arrive home.

A service processes refunds for most shops. You receive the total refund stated on the form. Global Refund is a Europe-wide service with 210,000 affiliated stores and more than 700 refund counters at major airports and border crossings. Its refund form is called a Tax Free Check. The service issues refunds in the form of cash, check, or credit-card adjustment. If you don't have time to wait at the refund counter, you can mail in the form instead.

V.A.T. Refunds Global Refund ✉ 99 Main St., Suite 307, Nyack, NY 10960 ☎ 800/566-9828 🖷 845/348-1549 ⊕ www.globalrefund.com.

TELEPHONES

Italy's telephone system is quite reliable whether you use landlines, phone booths, or cell phones. Direct dialing is easy to do; just remember Italian telephone numbers do not have a standard number of digits (they can range anywhere from four digits to seven), and the city code (comparable to an area code) must be dialed whenever placing a call—even if you are within the same city.

You can use hotel telephone lines, but you will pay dearly for it. If you want to make telephone calls from public phones, it is best to buy a telephone card (available at any tobacconist's). There are national cards (to be used only within Italy) and international cards. Make sure to specify when purchasing.

AREA & COUNTRY CODES

The country code for Italy is 39. When dialing an Italian number from abroad, **do not drop the initial 0** from the local area code (as was formerly the procedure). Here are area codes for major cities: Bologna 051; Brindisi 0831; Florence 055; Genoa 010; Milan 02; Naples 081; Palermo 091; Perugia 075; Pisa 050; Rome 06; Siena 0577; Turin 011; Venice 041; Verona 045. For example, a call from the United States to Rome would be dialed as 011 + 39 + 06 + phone number.

The country code is 1 for the United States and Canada, 61 for Australia, 64 for New Zealand, and 44 for the United Kingdom.

DIRECTORY & OPERATOR ASSISTANCE

For general information in English, dial 4176. To place international telephone calls through an operator dial 170 or long-distance access numbers (⇨ International Calls).

INTERNATIONAL CALLS

Since hotels tend to overcharge for long-distance and international calls, it's best to make such calls from public phones using telephone cards.

You can **make collect calls from any phone by dialing 172,** which will get you an English-speaking operator. Rates to the United States are lowest on Sundays and 10 PM–8 AM (Italian time) the rest of the week.

You can place a direct call to the United States by reversing the charges or using your calling card. When calling from pay telephones insert a coin, which will be returned upon completion of your call. You automatically reach an operator in the country of destination and thereby avoid all language difficulties.

LOCAL & LONG-DISTANCE CALLS

For all calls within Italy—local and long-distance—you must dial the regional area code (*prefisso*), which begins with a 0, such as 06 for Rome, 041 for Venice. If you are calling from a public phone you must deposit a coin or use a calling card to get a dial tone. Rates vary according to the time of day; it's cheaper to call within Italy during nonworking hours (before 9 AM and after 7 or 8 PM), and it's cheaper to dial internationally at these times.

LONG-DISTANCE SERVICES

AT&T, MCI, and Sprint access codes make calling long-distance relatively convenient, but you may find the local access number blocked in many hotel rooms. First ask the hotel operator to connect you. If the hotel operator balks, ask for an international operator or dial the international operator yourself. One way to improve your odds of getting connected to your long-distance carrier is to travel with more than one company's calling card (a hotel may block Sprint, for example, but not MCI). If all else fails, call from a pay phone.

Access Codes AT&T Direct ☎ 800/172-444. **MCI WorldPhone** ☎ 800/172-401/404. **Sprint International Access** ☎ 800/172-405.

PHONE CARDS

Prepaid *carte telefoniche* (phone cards) are available throughout Italy and more convenient than coins. Cards in different denominations are sold at post offices, tobacconists, most newsstands, and bars, and may be used in almost every public pay phone. Tear off the corner of the card and insert it in the slot. When you dial, its value appears in the window. After you hang up, the card is returned. The best card to use when calling North America or Europe is the €5 or €10 Europa card, which gives you a local number to dial and roughly 180 minutes and 360 minutes, respectively, of calling time.

PUBLIC PHONES

Public pay phones are scarce, though they can be found at train and subway stations, post offices, in hotel lobbies, and in some bars. In rural areas, town squares usually have a pay phone. Some pay phones accept only euro coins, others only *carte telefoniche*, so it's smart to have both ready (⇨ Phone Cards).

TIME

Italy is six hours ahead of Eastern Standard Time, one hour ahead of Great Britain, 10 hours behind Sydney, and 12 hours behind Auckland. Like the rest of Europe, Italy uses the 24-hour (or "military") clock, which means that after noon you continue counting forward: 13:00 is 1 PM, 23:30 is 11:30 PM.

TIPPING

The following guidelines apply in major cities, but Italians tip smaller amounts in smaller cities and towns. In restaurants a service charge of about 10% (but as high at 15%) sometimes appears as a separate item on your check. Some restaurants say on the menu that cover and service charge are included. Either way, it's customary to leave an additional 5%–10% tip for the waiter, depending on the service. Tip checkroom attendants €1 per person and rest-room attendants €0.50 (more in expensive hotels and restaurants). In major cities tip €0.05 for whatever you drink standing up at a coffee bar, €0.25 or more for table service in cafés. At a hotel bar tip €1 and up for a round or two of cocktails.

Italians rarely tip taxi drivers, which is not to say that you shouldn't do it. A euro or two, depending on the length of the journey, is appreciated—particularly if the driver helps with luggage. Railway and airport porters charge a fixed rate per bag. Tip an additional €0.25 per person, more if the porter is helpful. Give a barber €1–€1.50 and a hairdresser's assistant €1.50–€4.15 for a shampoo or cut, depending on the type of establishment.

On sightseeing tours, tip guides about €1.50 per person for a half-day group tour, more if they are very good. In monasteries and other sights where admission is free, a contribution (€0.50–€1) is expected. Service-station attendants are tipped only for special services, for example, €1 for checking your tires.

In hotels give the *portiere* (concierge) about 15% of his bill for services, or €2.50–€5 if he has been generally helpful with dinner reservations and such. For two people in a double room leave the chambermaid about €0.75 per day, or about €4.50–€5 a week in a moderately priced hotel; tip a minimum of €1 for valet or room service. Double amounts in an expensive hotel. In expensive hotels tip doormen €0.50 for calling a cab and €1.50 for carrying bags to the check-in desk, bellhops €1.50–€2.50 for carrying your bags to the room, and €2–€2.50 for room service.

TOURS & PACKAGES

Because everything is prearranged on a prepackaged tour or independent vacation, you spend less time planning—and often get it all at a good price.

BOOKING WITH AN AGENT

Travel agents are excellent resources. But it's a good idea to collect brochures from several agencies, as some agents' suggestions may be influenced by relationships with tour and package firms that reward them for volume sales. If you have a special interest, find an agent with expertise in that area; the American Society of Travel Agents (ASTA; ⇨ Travel Agencies) has a database of specialists worldwide. You can log on to the group's Web site to find an ASTA travel agent in your neighborhood.

Make sure your travel agent knows the accommodations and other services of the place being recommended. Ask about the hotel's location, room size, beds, and whether it has a pool, room service, or programs for children if you care about these.

Has your agent been there in person or sent others whom you can contact?

Do some homework on your own, too: local tourism boards can provide information about lesser-known and small-niche operators, some of which may sell only direct.

BUYER BEWARE

Each year consumers are stranded or lose their money when tour operators—even large ones with excellent reputations—go out of business. So check out the operator. Ask several travel agents about its reputation, and try to **book with a company that has a consumer-protection program.** (Look for information in the company's brochure.) In the United States, members of the United States Tour Operators Association are required to set aside funds ($1 million) to help eligible customers cover payments and travel arrangements in the event that the company defaults. It's also a good idea to choose a company that participates in the American Society of Travel Agents' Tour Operator Program; ASTA will act as mediator in any disputes between you and your tour operator.

Remember that the more your package or tour includes, the better you can predict the ultimate cost of your vacation. Make sure you know exactly what is covered, and beware of hidden costs. Are taxes, tips, and transfers included? Entertainment and excursions? These can add up.

▣ Tour-Operator Recommendations American Society of Travel Agents (⇨ Travel Agencies). National Tour Association (NTA) ⊠ 546 E. Main St., Lexington, KY 40508 ☎ 859/226–4444 or 800/682–8886 ⎕ 859/226–4404 ⊕ www.ntaonline.com. **United States Tour Operators Association** (USTOA) ⊠ 275 Madison Ave., Suite 2014, New York, NY 10016 ☎ 212/599–6599 ⎕ 212/599–6744 ⊕ www.ustoa.com.

TRAIN TRAVEL

Traveling by train in Italy is simple and efficient. Major cities are connected by rail, and it's easy to navigate the Italian rail system. Though no trains in the system go directly to the airports, there are connecting commuter lines that will get you from the airport to the main train stations.

You can either purchase your tickets in advance or upon arrival in Italy (where tickets are sold at every train station and at travel agencies). If you plan to arrive in Rome and go directly to Florence, it would make the most sense to have your train ticket with you rather than to endure the hassle of waiting in often long lines at the station. If you have Internet access, you can consult train schedules at ⊕ www.trenitali.it; otherwise your travel agent will have to make the arrangements for you.

You can order tickets directly online at ⊕ www.raileurope.com, where all major credit cards are accepted. Generally tickets arrive within two to three mailing days. If you're in a hurry, you can pay an additional $30 for overnight delivery.

If you are considering using a Eurail Pass or any of its variations you must buy the pass **before** leaving your home country, as they are not sold in Italy.

The fastest trains on the *Trenitalia*, the Italian State Railways, are the Eurostar trains that operate on several main lines, including Rome–Milan via Florence and Bologna. Seat reservations are mandatory at all times. There are smoking and no-smoking cars on all trains. Nonsmokers should ask for seats some distance from the smoking car, as the poorly designed partitions are not smokeproof. Some Eurostar trains (the ETR 460 trains) have little aisle and luggage space (though there is a space near the door where you can put large bags). To avoid having to squeeze through narrow aisles, board only at your car (look for the number on the reservation ticket). Car numbers are displayed outside next to the door. Next-fastest trains are the *Intercity* (IC) trains, for which you pay a supplement and for which seat reservations may be required and are always advisable. *Diretto* and *Interregionale* trains usually make more stops and are a little slower. *Regionale* and *locale* trains are the slowest; many serve commuters.

Note that in some Italian cities—Milan, Turin, Genoa, Naples, and Rome included—there are two or more main-line stations, although one is usually the principal terminal or through-station. Be sure of the name of the station your train arrives in or departs from.

There is refreshment service on all long-distance trains, with mobile carts and a cafeteria or dining car. Tap water on trains is not drinkable.

Traveling by night is inexpensive (since you pay by distance and not extra for a bed), but never leave your belongings unattended (even for a minute!) and make sure the door of your compartment is locked. More comfortable trains run on the longer routes (Sicily–Rome, Sicily–Milan, Sicily–Venice, Rome–Turin, Lecce–Milan); ask for the good-value T3, Intercity Notte, and Carrozza Comfort. The Vagone Letto Excelsior has private bathrooms, coffee machines, microwave ovens, refrigerators, and a suite with a double bed and TV.

Train service between Milan, Florence, Rome, and Naples is frequent throughout the day. For the most part, trains stick to schedule, although during peak tourist season delays may occur. Train strikes of various kinds are also common, so it's a good idea to make sure the train you want to take is in fact running.

CLASSES

Most Italian trains have first and second classes. On local trains the first-class fare gets you little more than a clean doily on the headrest of your seat, but on long-distance trains you get wider seats, more legroom, and better ventilation and lighting. At peak travel times first-class train travel is worth the difference. Remember **always to make seat reservations in advance,** for either class. One advantage of traveling first class is that the cars are almost always not crowded—or at the very least less crowded than the second-class compartments. A first-class ticket, in Italian, is *prima classe*; second is *seconda classe.*

CUTTING COSTS

To save money **look into rail passes.** But be aware that if you don't plan to cover many miles you may come out ahead by buying individual tickets. If Italy is your only destination in Europe **consider purchasing an Italian Flexi Rail Card Saver** (sold only outside Italy), which allows a limited number

of travel days within one month: for four days of travel ($239 first class, $191 second class) and eight days of travel ($261 first class, $210 second class). These tickets are cheaper if you travel in groups of two or more or are under age 26.

Once in Italy, **ask about the Cartaverde (Green Card)** if you're under 26 (€30 for one year), which entitles you to a 15% discount on first- and second-class tickets. Those under 26 should also inquire about discount travel fares under the Billet International Jeune (BIJ) and Euro Domino Junior schemes. In Italy you can also **purchase the Carta d'Argento (Silver Card)** if you're over 60 (€30 for one year), which allows a 15% discount on first- and second-class travel. **Comitive Ordinarie** (Ordinary Group Travel) entitle parties of at least six people traveling together to a 20% discount on all tickets except from the Friday before April 25 to the Sunday after May 1, July–August, and December 15–January 10. For further information check out the Trenitalia Web site (⊕ www.trenitalia.com).

Italy is one of 17 countries in which you can **use Eurailpasses,** which provide unlimited first-class travel in all the participating countries. If you plan to rack up the miles, get a standard pass. Passes are available for 15 days ($588), 21 days ($762), one month ($946), two months ($1,338), and three months ($1,654). You can also receive free or discounted fares on some ferry lines.

The Eurail Selectpass allows for travel from three to five contiguous countries on one pass, and can be used in eighteen European countries. The Eurail Selectpass Saver allows travel in any three, four, or five contiguous countries. Five days of first-class travel in two months within three countries is $304; four countries $340; five countries $374.In addition to standard Eurailpasses, **ask about special rail-pass plans.** Among these are the Eurail Youthpass (for those under age 26), the Eurail Saverpass and Eurail Saver Flexipass (which give a discount for two or more people traveling together), the Eurail Flexipass (which allows a certain number of travel days within a set period), and the EurailDrive Pass (which combines travel by train and rental car).

Whichever pass you choose, remember that you must **purchase your Eurailpass or Eurail Selectpass before you leave** for Europe. You can get further information and order tickets at the Rail Europe Web site (⊕ www.raileurope.com).

Many travelers assume that rail passes guarantee them seats on the trains they wish to ride. Not so. You need to **book seats ahead even if you are using a rail pass.** Seat reservations are required on some European trains, particularly high-speed trains, and are a good idea on trains that may be crowded—particularly in summer on popular routes. You will also need a reservation if you purchase sleeping accommodations.

🚄 Information & Passes **CIT Rail** ⊠ 15 W. 44th St., New York, NY 10036 ☎ 800/248-7245. **DER Tours** ☎ 800/782-2424 🖷 800/282-7474. **Rail Europe** ⊠ 44 S. Broadway, White Plains, NY 10601 ☎ 800/438-7245 or 877/257-2887 ⊕ www.raileurope.com.

FARES & SCHEDULES

Trains can be very crowded; it's always a good idea to make a reservation. To avoid long lines at station windows **buy tickets and make seat reservations up to two months in advance** at travel agencies displaying the FS emblem. Tickets can be purchased at the last minute, but seat reservations must be made at agencies (or the train station) up until about three hours before the train departs from its originating city. For trains that require a reservation (all Eurostar and some Intercity trains), you may be able to get a seat assignment just before boarding the train; look for the conductor on the platform.

Tickets are good for two months after the date of issue, but right before departure **you must validate tickets in the yellow machines located in the departure area.** Once stamped, tickets are valid for 6 hours on distances of less than 200 km (124 mi) or for 24 hours on distances of 200 km or more. If you wish to stop along the way and your final destination is more than 200 km away, you can stamp the ticket a second time before it expires so as to extend its validity to a maximum of 48 hours from the time it was first stamped. If you forget to stamp your ticket in the machine or you

didn't make it to the station in time to buy the ticket, you must seek out a conductor and pay a minimum €8 fine. At the discretion of the conductor, fines can be as high as twice the cost of the ticket. Don't wait for the conductor to find out that you are without a valid ticket (unless the train is overcrowded and walking becomes impossible), as he might charge you a much heavier fine. You can buy train tickets for nearby destinations (within a 200-km [124-mi] range) at tobacconists and at ticket machines in stations.

🚄 Train Information **Trentalia** ☎ 892021 in Italy ⊕ www.trenitalia.com.
🚄 From the U.K. **British Rail** ☎ 020/7834-2345 ⊕ www.rail.co.uk. **French Railways** ☎ 02/7254 4350 or 02/6747 9349 ⊕ www.sncf.com.

PAYING

You can pay for your train tickets in cash or with a major credit card such as American Express, Diner's Club, MasterCard, and Visa.

RESERVATIONS

Though reservations are not mandatory (except on Eurostar trains), it's wise to reserve in advance through a travel agent or at a station sales office. It costs only an additional euro or so, and you are guaranteed a seat. Simply holding a train ticket does not guarantee a seat on any Eurostar, Intercity, or regional train. In summer it's fairly common to stand for a good part of the journey, as trains are crowded.

TRANSPORTATION AROUND ITALY

Italy has an extensive network of train connections, though with the exception of the rapid Eurostar trains, don't expect efficient service: delays due to technical problems and frequent strikes will put you behind schedule. Buses may offer a more direct alternative for destinations reached by several train transfers. Always check the cost of flying between cities; plane tickets can cost less than train fare. If you plan on venturing into the countryside, renting a car is the best option.

TRAVEL AGENCIES

A good travel agent puts your needs first. Look for an agency that has been in business at least five years, emphasizes customer service, and has someone on staff who specializes in your destination. In addition, **make sure the agency belongs to a professional trade organization.** The American Society of Travel Agents (ASTA)—the largest and most influential in the field with more than 20,000 members in some 140 countries—maintains and enforces a strict code of ethics and will step in to help mediate any agent-client disputes involving ASTA members if necessary. ASTA (whose motto is "Without a travel agent, you're on your own") also maintains a Web site that includes a directory of agents. (If a travel agency is also acting as your tour operator, *see* Buyer Beware *in* Tours & Packages.)

🔢 Local Agent Referrals **Centro Turistico Studentesco (CTS)** ✉ Corso Vittorio Emanuele II 297, Rome, 00186 ☎ 06/6872672 🖷 06/6872562 🌐 www.cts.it. **American Society of Travel Agents (ASTA)** ✉ 1101 King St., Suite 200, Alexandria, VA 22314 ☎ 703/739-2782 or 800/965-2782 24-hr hotline 🖷 703/684-8319 🌐 www.astanet.com. **Association of British Travel Agents** ✉ 68-71 Newman St., London W1T 3AH ☎ 020/7637-2444 🖷 020/7637-0713 🌐 www.abta. com. **Association of Canadian Travel Agencies** ✉ 130 Albert St., Suite 1705, Ottawa, Ontario K1P 5G4 ☎ 613/237-3657 🖷 613/237-7052 🌐 www.acta.ca. **Australian Federation of Travel Agents** ✉ Level 3, 309 Pitt St., Sydney, NSW 2000 ☎ 02/9264-3299 or 1300/363-416 🖷 02/9264-1085 🌐 www.afta.com.au. **Travel Agents' Association of New Zealand** ✉ Level 5, Tourism and Travel House, 79 Boulcott St., Box 1888, Wellington 6001 ☎ 04/499-0104 🖷 04/499-0786 🌐 www.taanz.org.nz.

VISITOR INFORMATION

Learn more about foreign destinations by checking government-issued travel advisories and country information. For a broader picture consider information from more than one country.

🔢 Tourist Information **Italian Government Tourist Board (ENIT)** ✉ 630 5th Ave., Suite 1565, New York, NY 10111 ☎ 212/245-4822 🖷 212/586-9249 ✉ 500 N. Michigan Ave., Chicago, IL 60611 ☎ 312/644-0996 🖷 312/644-3019 ✉ 12400 Wilshire Blvd., Suite 550,

Los Angeles, CA 90025 ☎ 310/820-1898 🖷 310/820-6357 ✉ 175 Bloor St. E, Suite 907, South Tower, Toronto, Ontario M4W 3R8 ☎ 416/925-4882 🖷 416/925-4799 ✉ 1 Princes St., London W1B 2.8AY ☎ 020/7408-1254 🖷 020/73993567 🌐 www.italiantourism.com.

🔢 Regional Offices **Florence** ✉ Via Cavour 1/r, next to Palazzo Medici-Riccardi, 50129 ☎ 055/290832 🌐 www.firenze.toscana.it. **Milan** ✉ Stazione Centrale, 20121 ☎ 02/72524370 🌐 www.milaninfotourist. com. **Naples** ✉ Piazza fel Gesù, 80135 ☎ 081/5523328 🌐 www.ept.napoli.it. **Palermo** ✉ Piazza Castelnuovo 35, 90141 ☎ 091/583847 🌐 www.palermoturismo.com. **Rome** ✉ Via Parigi 5, 00185 ☎ 06/36004399 🌐 www.romaturismo.it. **Venice** ✉ Train Station Cannaregio ☎ 041/5298727 🌐 www.turismovenezia.it.

🔢 Government Advisories **U.S. Department of State** ✉ Overseas Citizens Services Office, 2100 Pennsylvania Ave. NW, 4th floor, Washington, DC 20520 ☎ 202/647-5225 interactive hotline or 888/407-4747 🌐 www.travel.state.gov. **Consular Affairs Bureau of Canada** ☎ 800/267-6788 or 613/944-6788 🌐 www.voyage.gc.ca. **U.K. Foreign and Commonwealth Office** ✉ Travel Advice Unit, Consular Division, Old Admiralty Building, London SW1A 2PA ☎ 0870/606-0290 or 020/7008-1500 🌐 www.fco. gov.uk/travel. **Australian Department of Foreign Affairs and Trade** ☎ 300/139-281 travel advice, 02/6261-1299 Consular Travel Advice Faxback Service 🌐 www.dfat.gov.au. **New Zealand Ministry of Foreign Affairs and Trade** ☎ 04/439-8000 🌐 www.mft.govt.nz.

WEB SITES

Do check out the World Wide Web when planning your trip. You'll find everything from weather forecasts to virtual tours of famous cities. Be sure to visit Fodors.com (🌐 www.fodors.com), a complete travel-planning site. You can research prices and book plane tickets, hotel rooms, rental cars, vacation packages, and more. In addition, you can post your pressing questions in the Travel Talk section. Other planning tools include a currency converter and weather reports, and there are loads of links to travel resources.

VENICE

1

Updated by
David Graham

IT IS CALLED LA SERENISSIMA, or "the most serene," a reference to the monstrous power, majesty, and wisdom of this city that was for centuries the unrivaled mistress of trade between Europe and the Orient and the staunch bulwark of Christendom against the tides of Turkish expansion. "The most serene" also refers to the way in which those visiting have looked upon Venice, a miraculous city imperturbably floating on its calm blue lagoon.

Built entirely on water by men who dared defy the sea, Venice is unlike any other town. No matter how many times you have seen it in movies or TV commercials, the real thing is more surreal and dreamlike than you could ever imagine. Its landmarks, the Basilica di San Marco and the Palazzo Ducale, seem hardly Italian: delightfully idiosyncratic, they are exotic mélanges of Byzantine, Gothic, and Renaissance styles. Shimmering sunlight and silvery mist soften every perspective here, and you understand how the city became renowned in the Renaissance for its artists' rendering of color. It's full of secrets, inexpressibly romantic, and at times given over entirely to pleasure.

Founded in the 5th century by refugee Veneti, mainlanders escaping barbarian invasion, Venice rose from the marshes to dominate the Adriatic and hold the gorgeous East in fee. Early in its history the city called in Byzantine artists to decorate its churches with brilliant mosaics, still glittering today. In the 13th through 15th century the influence of Gothic architecture produced the characteristic type of palace in the Florid Gothic style, with the finely wrought facades for which the town is famous. The Renaissance arrived in Venice relatively late, at a time when the city had reached its peak in power and prosperity. In its early phase the style is referred to as Lombardesque, after the Lombardo family of architects, famed for rendering colored marble decoration in intertwined discs, roundels, and crosses. Early Renaissance artists—Carpaccio, Giorgione, and the Bellini brothers, Giovanni and Gentile—were active in Venice between the late 15th and early 16th century. Along with the stars of the next generation—Veronese, Titian, and Tintoretto—they played a decisive role in the development of Western art, and their work still covers walls and ceilings all over the city.

Venice's height of political and economic importance came in the 15th and 16th centuries, when it extended its domain inland to include all of what is now known as the Veneto region and part of Lombardy. For 400 years the great maritime city-republic had been growing in power, but after the 16th century the tide changed. The Ottoman Empire blocked Venice's Mediterranean trade routes, and newly emerging sea powers such as Britain and the Netherlands broke Venice's monopoly by opening oceanic trading routes. Like its steadily dwindling fortunes, Venice's art and culture began a prolonged decline, leaving only the splendid monuments to recall a fabled past, with the 18th-century paintings of Canaletto and frescoes of Giambattista Tiepolo striking a glorious swan song.

You must walk almost everywhere in Venice (Venezia in Italian), and where you can't walk, you must go by water. Occasionally you walk *in* water, when normally higher fall and spring tides are exacerbated by falling barometers and southeasterly winds. The result is *acqua alta*—flooding in the lowest parts of town, especially Piazza San Marco, which lasts a few hours,

If you have 2 days

Greet Venice with a morning cruise along the Grand Canal from Ferrovia to San Zaccaria. You'll treasure seeing Piazza San Marco for the first time from the water, as centuries of travelers have done before you. Visit the Basilica, Palazzo Ducale, and Museo Correr, and allow time to enjoy the view from atop the Campanile. Meander out Salizada San Moisè, shopping and lunching along the way. Take the traghetto in Campo Santa Maria del Giglio or cross the Grand Canal via Accademia Bridge. Bear left to reach Santa Maria della Salute, with more than a dozen Titian paintings, and Punta della Dogana, one of the best panoramas in town. Top off your afternoon with Peggy Guggenheim's 20th-century collection, or let centuries of Venetian art at the Gallerie dell'Accademia show you how this city has changed through the ages. Stretch your legs at sunset with a walk along the Zattere, accompanied by a gelato. After dinner, splurge on a romantic gondola ride. On Day 2 start early to beat the crowds at the Rialto Bridge and market. Don't miss the lively pescheria, where fish have been sold for more than 1,000 years. Follow the main drag to Campo San Polo and the Basilica dei Frari, with two important works by Titian, then see more than 60 Tintoretto works at the Scuola Grande di San Rocco. After lunch choose between 18th-century art at Ca' Rezzonico and modern art at Ca' Pesaro. After dinner, if you're not yet out of money and energy, head to the Casinò, where composer Richard Wagner once lived.

If you have 4 days

Follow the itinerary above for days 1 and 2. Choose one of your remaining days—let the weather be your guide—to cruise the lagoon islands: Murano with its glassworks; Burano with its lace making; romantic Torcello, one of the first islands settled by the Venetians; and San Michele, with what must be the best views of any cemetery in the world. Lunch at Murano or Burano, or carry along a picnic. On your other morning, let the Naval Museum and Arsenale show you the source of this maritime republic's power. Visit the Scuola di San Giorgio degli Schiavoni for the city's finest selection of Vittore Carpaccio's works. Wind your way to Campo Santa Maria Formosa and the Querini-Stampalia gallery of Venetian art. Don't miss nearby Santa Maria dei Miracoli, a tiny jewel box of a church, and massive Santi Giovanni e Paolo, the final resting place of several doges. Meander through Cannaregio, visiting Ca' d'Oro, a building as beautiful as the art collection it houses. End your day in the synagogues of the Jewish Ghetto, and learn how that name, from Venetian dialect, became known worldwide.

If you have 7 days

If you're fortunate enough to have a full week in Venice, you'll be able to not only see the sights, but relax and really enjoy the subtle charms of the great city. Rather than running out of time before you've run out of sights along the jam-packed itineraries listed above, you can cut any of the day's tours in half, leaving time in your sightseeing for more lingering in cafés and losing yourself along the canals less traveled. If you need a break from the sights, rent a bicycle for a trip along the beaches of Lido and Pellestrina.

until the tide recedes. Work has begun on the Moses Project, a plan that would close off the lagoon when high tides threaten, but it's a much-debated response to an emotionally charged problem. Protecting Venice and its lagoon from high tides, high use, and the damaging wave action caused by powerboats is among the city's most contentious issues.

In spite of these drawbacks, Venetians have mastered the art of living well. You'll see them going about their daily affairs in *vaporetti* (water buses), aboard the *traghetti* (traditional gondola ferries) that carry them across the Grand Canal, in the *campi* (squares), and along the *calli* (narrow streets). They are nothing if not skilled—and remarkably tolerant—in dealing with the veritable armies of tourists from all over the world that inundate the city almost year-round.

EXPLORING VENICE

Piazza San Marco is unquestionably the heart of Venice. The city is made up of six *sestieri*, or neighborhoods: San Marco, west of Piazza San Marco; Castello, east of San Marco; Cannaregio, to the northwest; Santa Croce and San Polo, roughly between the station and the Grand Canal; and Dorsoduro, diagonally across the Grand Canal from San Marco. Canals, called *rii* (singular *rio*), have frequent bridges, but the Grand Canal has only three—Ponte degli Scalzi (near the train station), Ponte di Rialto, and Ponte dell'Accademia—a fact that can complicate getting around. If you find yourself on the wrong bank with no bridge in sight, look for signs that say *traghetto* (gondola ferry) and hop across in style, saving your legs and your mood.

A street is called a *calle,* unless it runs along a canal, in which case it's a *riva* or a *fondamenta.* Only San Marco is called a *piazza*; any other Venetian square is a *campo.* Winding backstreets can confuse anyone's sense of direction, and spotting reference points (such as bell towers) above rooftops is difficult. Even streets that seem familiar can be deceptive, and shops that were your landmarks can suddenly close their shutters for the night. Taking a vaporetto along the Grand Canal is a wonderful way to get an overview, but the city should really be explored on foot; sestieri are best savored by strolling from a Renaissance church to a chatty *bacaro* (wine shop), stopping on the way to admire the boats moored along a canal or sitting at a café for cappuccino and pastry while you watch Venice's dolce vita unfold before your eyes.

Fifteen Venetian churches, known as the **Chorus churches** (☎ 041/2750462 ⊕ www.chorus-ve.org), have been singled out for their artistic merit; Santa Maria del Giglio, Santo Stefano, Santa Maria Formosa, Santa Maria dei Miracoli, Santa Maria Gloriosa dei Frari, San Polo, San Giacomo dell'Orio, San Stae, Sant'Alvise, Madonna dell'Orto, San Pietro di Castello, Santissimo Redentore, San Sebastiano, Gesuati, and San Giovanni Elemosinario. They're open to visitors all day except Sunday morning, and usually someone there can provide information and a free leaflet in English. Postcards and booklets about the sights are on sale. Single church entry costs €2.50, or you can visit them all with an €8 Chorus pass. The price of the pass includes audio guides except in the Frari, where they

Carnevale

". . . All the world repaire to Venice to see the folly and madnesse of the Carnevall . . .'tis impossible to recount the universal madnesses of this place during this time of licence." So commented traveler John Evelyn in 1646, and indeed, Carnevale (Carnival) was once an excuse for all manner of carnal indulgence. In its 18th-century heyday, festivities began on December 26 and lasted two months; the festival has since traded some of its more outlandish flavor for vast commercialization and lasts only the 10 days preceding Ash Wednesday.

Getting Lost

There's no escaping the fact that Venice is a difficult place to navigate. Narrow, winding streets, meaningless building numbers, and a shortage of easily visible landmarks by which to orient yourself all add to the confusion. Fortunately, getting lost in Venice can be a pleasure. You may not find the Titian masterpiece you'd set out to see, but instead you might come across an ageless bacaro or a charming shop that makes your afternoon; opportunities for such serendipity abound. And the city is nothing if not self-contained—sooner or later, perhaps with the help of a patient native, you can rest assured that you'll regain your bearings.

Shopping

Alluring shops abound in Venice. You'll find countless vendors of trademark Venetian wares such as glass and lace; the authenticity of some goods can be suspect, but they're often pleasing to the eye regardless of their place of origin. For more sophisticated tastes (and deeper pockets), there are jewelers, antiques dealers, and high-fashion boutiques on a par with those in Italy's larger cities but often maintaining a uniquely Venetian flair. There are also some interesting craft and art studios, where you can find high-quality, one-of-a-kind articles, from handmade shoes to decorative lamps and mirrors.

Traveling by Boat

There's something special about using boats to get around a city. You can start as soon as you get off the plane by taking the Alilaguna ferry right to the heart of town. The vaporetti (water buses) not only get you from point to point but provide an excellent sightseeing platform: you can stand outside in the sun—or take a seat up front on some of the older boats—and watch the Grand Canal's extraordinary Gothic and Renaissance architecture pass by. Out on the lagoon, a cruise on the big *motonave* steamer from St. Marks to Burano and Torcello is a cooling option in the midsummer heat, with plenty of shady outdoor seats from which to enjoy the view and the breeze. Back in town, don't be reluctant to use the *traghetti*, the gondola-style boats that cross the Grand Canal at strategic points, providing a brief, but affordable, gondola ride.

---

cost €0.50. The artwork in Chorus churches is labeled and the staff can show you where to switch on lighting for selected paintings.

Eleven museums currently make up Venice's **Musei Civici** (☎ 041/2715911 ⊕ www.museiciviciveneziani.it). A Museum Pass costing €15.50 and valid for three months lets you make one visit to each museum. A Mu-

Venice

TRE ARCHI

Rio del Battello · Rio di S. Girolamo · Rio d. Madonna dell'Orto · Rio di S. Sensa · Sacc. delle Miseric

Canale di Cannaregio · CANNAREGIO · Campo del Ghetto Nuovo · F. della Misericordia · Rio della Misericordia

35

Bridge to Mainland

GUGLIE · C. Riello · Ponte Guglie · R. t. S. Leonardo · Rio d.S. Fosca di Noal · Rio d. Rac

34

Stazione Ferroviaria Santa Lucia · Lista di Spagna · R.D. BIASIO · S. MARCUOLA · Grand Canal (Canalazzo) · Rio d.S. Fosca

33

FERROVIA · Ponte degli Scalzi · Riva d.Biasio · Lista d. Bari · Zuan Degola · S. STAE · **21** · **22** · **32** · CA' D'ORO · Strada Nuova

Piccolo · Rio d. S. Tintor · C. d. Tintor · C. Larga · **20** · Campo d. Pescheria

PIAZZALE ROMA · Corte Canal · Rio Marin · Gradisca · SANTA CROCE · R. di S. Cassiano · C. dei Botteri · Erberia

C.d.S. Andrea · Piazzale Roma · C. della Lana · C. d. Lacca · C. d. Fonderia · C. d. Chiovere · SAN POLO · **17** · Campo S. Polo · R. di S. Silvestro · **16** · Rio del Vin · **15** · RIALTO

19 · **18** · R. Terrà · S. SILVESTRO · Riva · del Carbon

Rio Nuovo · F. Minotto · Rio della Frescada · S. TOMÀ · Grand Canal (Canalazzo) · S. Luca · Campo Manin

Rio Terà dei Pensieri · Rio Foscari · Campo di S. Margherita · S. ANGELO · C. d. Mandola · Barcaroli · Piscina · Frezzeria

Fond. dei Cereri · Fond. Rossa · Rio terà Canal · **12** · Rio d.S. Margherita · C. d. Carrozze · Campo S. Angelo · SAN MARCO

Calle dei Guardiani · Rio d.S. Barnaba · **13** · **14** · Campo S. Stefano · C. Lga · 22 Marzo

Rio di S. Nicola · Calle Avogaria · Campo S. Barnaba · CA' · REZZONICO · S. SAMUELE · **6** · VALLA

11 · Saliz. San Basegio · Calle della Toletta · ACCADEMIA · Ponte dell' Accademia · C. Lga 22 Marzo · S. Moisè

Fondamenta delle Zattere · Rio di Ognissanti · Campo della Carità · **7** · S.M. DEL GIGLIO · **8** · SALUTE

S. BASILIO · C.po S. Agnese · **10** · ZATTERE · **9** · Chiesa · Fond. Venier · R. Terà di Catecumeni · DORSODURO

SACCA FISOLA · Beata Giuliana · C. della Sacca · Lavraneri · Canale della Giudecca

Fondamenta della Scuola · Calle Rimini · Sacca Fisola · Fond. S. Biagio · Fond. S. Biagio · PALANCA · CHIESA DEL REDENTORE

Rio d.S. Biagio · R. d. Convertiti · Fond. S. Eufemia · **37** · REDENTORE · GIUDECCA

Venetian Lagoon 38 - 41 see detail map

CIMITERO Cimitero San Michele

ITALY

0   440 yards
0   400 meters

FOND. NUOVE

31

Canale delle Fondamente Nuove

OSPEDALE CIVILE

CELESTIA

San Francesco della Vigna

30   28   29

Ponte di Rialto

Campo S. Marina   Campo S. Maria

26   27

25

Darsena Grande

Rio d. Vergini

San Pietro di Castello   San Pietro

SAN ZACCARIA

CASTELLO

23

5   1   2   3   4

Piazza San Marco

Rio della Tana

SAN MARCO GIARDINETTI

S. ZACCARIA
S. ZACCARIA JOLANDA
S. ZACCARIA DANIELI

24

V. Garibaldi   Rio d.S.Anna

ARSENALE

Riva dei Sette Martiri

Bacino San Marco

S. GIORGIO

36

S. Giorgio Maggiore

GIARDINI

LIDO

ZITELLE

Fond. delle Zitelle

Calle Michelangelo

KEY

▲ Vaporetto stop

🛈 Tourist information

⚑ Start of tour

seum Card, good only at the Piazza San Marco museums—Palazzo
Ducale, Museo Correr, Museo Archeologico, and Biblioteca Nazionale
Marciana—costs €11.

Note that Gallerie dell'Accademia and other Venetian museums have
no cafés inside and don't permit you to bring in food or drink. The staff
might allow you to run to the nearest bar and return without paying a
second admission, but this is left to their discretion. There are, however,
refreshments available in Palazzo Ducale, Museo Correr, Ca' Rezzonico, Querini-Stampalia, and the Peggy Guggenheim Collection.

*Numbers in the text correspond to numbers in the margin and on the
Venice and Venetian Lagoon maps.*

Piazza San Marco

One of the world's most evocative squares, Piazza San Marco is the heart
of Venice, a vast open space bordered by an orderly procession of arcades marching toward the fairy-tale cupolas and marble lacework of
the Basilica di San Marco. Perpetually packed by day with people and
fluttering pigeons, it can be magical at night, especially in winter, when
mists swirl around the lampposts and the Campanile.

**a good
walk**

Start your tour of **Piazza San Marco** ❶ ☛ at the **Basilica di San Marco** ❷,
with its Pala d'Oro and Museo Marciano. Next get a bird's-eye view of
the piazza and city from the **Campanile** ❸. Move on to the Piazzetta San
Marco to visit the glorious **Palazzo Ducale** ❹ and its Ponte dei Sospiri.
Return to Piazza San Marco and cross to the side opposite the Basilica,
where you'll find the **Museo Correr** ❺ in the Ala Napoleonica—so named
because Napoléon built this wing enclosing the square.

TIMING   It takes a full day to really see everything, so if time is limited you'll have
to prioritize. Plan on 1½ hours for the Basilica and its Pala d'Oro, Galleria, and Museo Marciano. You'll want at least two hours to appreciate the Palazzo Ducale. Do take time to enjoy the piazza itself from a
café table, or on a clear day, from atop the Campanile.

What to See

★ ❷ **Basilica di San Marco.** An opulent synthesis of Byzantine and Romanesque styles, Venice's gem is laid out in a Greek-cross floor plan
and topped with five plump domes. It didn't become the cathedral of
Venice until 1807, but its role as the Chiesa Ducale (doge's private chapel)
gave it immense power and wealth. The original church was built in
828 to house the body of St. Mark the Evangelist. His remains, filched
from Alexandria by the doge's agents, were supposedly hidden in a barrel under layers of pickled pork to sneak them past Muslim guards. The
escapade is depicted in the 13th-century mosaic above the door farthest
left of the front entrance, one of the earliest mosaics on the heavily decorated facade; look closely to see the church as it appeared at that time.

A 976 fire destroyed most of the original church. It was rebuilt and reopened in 1094, and for centuries it would serve as a symbol of Venetian wealth and power, endowed with all the riches admirals and
merchants could carry off from the Orient, to the point where it earned

the nickname Chiesa d'Oro (Golden Church). The four bronze horses that prance and snort over the doorway are copies of sculptures that victorious Venetians took from Constantinople in 1204 after the fourth crusade (the originals are in the Museo di San Marco). The rich, colorful exterior decorations, including the numerous different marble columns, all came from the same source. Look for a medallion of red porphyry in the floor of the porch inside the main door. It marks the spot where, in 1177, Doge Sebastiano Ziani orchestrated the reconciliation between Barbarossa—the Holy Roman Emperor—and Pope Alexander III. Dim lighting, galleries high above the naves—they served as the *matroneum* (women's gallery)—the *iconostasis* (altar screen) and the single massive Byzantine chandelier all seem to wed Christianity with the Orient, giving San Marco its exotic blend of majesty and mystery.

The basilica is famous for its 43,055 square feet of stunning mosaics, which run from floor to ceiling thanks to an innovative roof of brick vaulting. Many of the original windows were filled in to make room for even more artwork. At midday, when the interior is fully illuminated, the mosaics truly come alive, the shimmer of their tiny gold tiles becoming nothing short of magical. The earliest mosaics are from the 11th and 12th centuries, and the last were added in the early 1700s. One of the most recent is the *Last Judgment,* believed to have been designed by Tintoretto (1518–94), on the arch between the porch and the nave. Inside the main entrance, turn right on the porch to see the Book of Genesis depicted on the ceiling. Ahead through a glass door, 13th-century mosaics depict St. Mark's life in the **Cappella Zen** (Zen Chapel). The **Cappella della Madonna di Nicopeia,** in the left transept, holds the altar icon that many consider Venice's most powerful protector. In nearby **Cappella della Madonna dei Mascoli** the life of the Virgin Mary is depicted in fine 15th-century mosaics, believed to be based on drawings by Jacopo Bellini and Andrea Mantegna.

In the **Santuario** (Sanctuary), the main altar is built over the tomb of St. Mark, its green marble canopy lifted high on carved alabaster columns. Perhaps even more impressive is the **Pala d'Oro,** a dazzling gilt silver screen encrusted with 1,927 precious gems and 255 enameled panels. Originally commissioned in Constantinople by Doge Orseolo I (976–978), it was enlarged and embellished over four centuries by master craftsmen and wealthy merchants. The bronze door leading from the sanctuary into the sacristy is by Jacopo Sansovino (1486–1570). In the top left corner the artist included a self-portrait, and above that, he pictured friend and fellow artist Titian. The **Tesoro** (Treasury), entered from the right transept, contains many treasures carried home from conquests abroad.

Climb the steep stairway to the **Galleria** and the **Museo di San Marco** for the best overview of the basilica's interior. From here you can step outdoors for a sweeping panorama of Piazza San Marco and and out over the lagoon to San Giorgio. The museum was completely renovated and reopened in 2003. The displays focus mainly on the types of mosaic and how they have been restored over the years. But the highlight is a close-up view of the original gilt bronze horses that were once on the outer gallery. The four were most probably cast in Rome and taken to Constantinople, where the Venetians pillaged them after sacking that city. When Napoléon (1769–1821) sacked Venice in 1797, he took them to Paris. They were returned after the fall of the French Empire, but came home "blind"—their big ruby eyes had been sold.

Be aware that guards at the door turn away anyone with bare shoulders or knees; no shorts, short skirts, or tank tops are allowed. If you want a free guided tour in English during summer months (less certain in winter, as the guides are volunteers), look for groups forming on the porch inside the main door. You may also arrange tours by appointment. ☒ *Piazza San Marco* 🕾 *Basilica 041/5225205, tours 041/5225697* 📠 *Basilica free, Tesoro € 2, Santuario and Pala d'Oro €1.50, Galleria and Museo di San Marco € 3* ☉ *May–Oct., Mon.–Sat. 9:45–5, Sun. 2–5; Nov.–Apr., Mon.–Sat. 9:45–4, Sun. 2–4; last entry ½ hr before closing* Ⓥ *Vallaresso/San Zaccaria.*

🕭 ❸ **Campanile.** Venice's famous brick bell tower (325 feet tall, plus the angel) had been standing nearly 1,000 years when in 1902, practically without warning, it collapsed, taking with it Jacopo Sansovino's 16th-century marble loggia at the base. The crushed loggia was promptly restored, and the new tower, rebuilt to the old plan, reopened in 1912. In the 15th century, clerics found guilty of immoral behavior were suspended in wooden cages from the tower. Some were forced to subsist on bread and water for as long as a year, and others were left to starve. The stunning view from the tower on a clear day includes the Lido, the lagoon, and the mainland as far as the Alps but, strangely enough, none of the myriad canals that snake through the city. ☒ *Piazza San Marco* 🕾 *041/5224064* 📠 *€6* ☉ *June–Sept., 9 AM–sunset but not later than 9 PM; Oct.–May, 9–4; last entry ½ hr before closing. Closed 2–3 wks in Jan.* Ⓥ *Vallaresso/San Zaccaria.*

❺ **Museo Correr.** Exhibits in this museum of Venetian art and history range from the absurdly high-soled shoes worn by 16th-century Venetian ladies (who walked with the aid of a servant) to the huge *Grande Pianta Prospettica* by Jacopo de' Barbari (circa 1440–1515), which details in carved wood every nook and cranny of 16th-century Venice. The city's proud naval history is evoked in several rooms through highly descriptive paintings and a numerous maritime objects, including ships' cannon and some surprisingly large iron mast-top navigation lights. The Correr has a room devoted entirely to antique games, and its second-floor **Quadreria** (Picture Gallery) has works by Venetian, Greek, and Flemish painters. The Correr exhibition rooms lead directly into the **Museo Archeologico** and the **Stanza del Sansovino,** the only part of the **Biblioteca Marciana** open to visitors. ☒ *Piazza San Marco, Ala Napoleonica* 🕾 *041/5225625* 📠 *€11 Piazza San Marco museum card, €15.50 Musei Civici pass* ☉ *Apr.–Oct., daily 9–7; Nov.–Mar., daily 9–5; last tickets sold 1½ hrs before closing* Ⓥ *Vallaresso/San Zaccaria.*

★ ❹ **Palazzo Ducale** (Doge's Palace). Rising above the Piazzetta San Marco, this Gothic-Renaissance fantasia of pink-and-white marble is a majestic expression of the prosperity and power attained during Venice's most glorious period. Some architectural purists find the building top-heavy, its hulking upper floors resting upon a graceful ground-floor colonnade, but one can hardly imagine the palace with any other design. Always much more than a residence, it was White House, Senate, torture chamber, and prison rolled into one. Venice's participatory democracy began around 700 and had an elected doge who ruled for life. In practice he was little more than a figurehead; real power rested with the Great Council, which once had more than 2,000 members. Although originally an elected body, in the 13th century it became an aristocratic stronghold, members inheriting seats from noble ancestors. The Senate, a group of 200 elected from the Great Council, passed laws, but executive powers belonged to the College, a committee of 25. In the 14th century the Council of Ten was formed to protect state security and soon became the most powerful and most feared branch of government.

Though a fortress for the doge existed here in the early 9th century, the building you see today was begun in the 12th century, and like the basilica next door was continually remodeled over the centuries. Near the basilica you'll see the ornately Gothic **Porta della Carta** (Gate of the Paper), where official decrees were traditionally posted, but visitors enter under the portico facing the water. You'll find yourself in an immense courtyard with the **Scala dei Giganti** (Stairway of the Giants) directly ahead, guarded by Sansovino's huge statues of Mars and Neptune. Though ordinary mortals must use the central interior staircase, its upper flight is the lavishly gilded **Scala d'Oro** (Golden Staircase), also by Sansovino. It may seem odd that you have to climb so many steps to reach the government's main council rooms and reception halls, but imagine how this extraordinary climb must have impressed, and perhaps intimidated, foreign emissaries.

The palace's sumptuous chambers are awe-inspiring in themselves, their walls and ceilings covered with works by Venice's greatest artists. Visit the **Anticollegio,** a waiting room outside the Collegio's chamber, where you'll see the *Rape of Europa* by Veronese (1528–88) and Tintoretto's *Bacchus and Ariadne Crowned by Venus.* Veronese also painted the ceiling of the adjacent **Sala del Collegio.** The ceiling of the **Sala del Senato** (Senate Chamber) features *The Triumph of Venice* by Tintoretto, magnificent surely, but dwarfed by his masterpiece *Paradise* in the **Sala del Maggiore Consiglio** (Great Council Hall). A vast work commissioned for a vast hall, this dark, dynamic piece is the world's largest oil painting (23 by 75 feet). The room's carved, gilt ceiling is breathtaking, especially with Veronese's majestic *Apotheosis of Venice* filling one of the center panels. Around the upper walls, study the portraits of the first 76 doges, and you'll notice one picture is missing near the left corner of the wall opposite *Paradise.* A black painted curtain, rather than a portrait, marks Doge Marin Falier's fall from grace; he was beheaded for treason in 1355, which the Latin inscription bluntly explains.

A narrow canal separates the Palace's east side from the cramped cell blocks of the **Prigioni Nuove** (New Prisons). High above the water arches the enclosed marble **Ponte dei Sospiri** (Bridge of Sighs), which earned its name from the sighs of those being led to their fate. Look out its windows to see the last earthly view these prisoners had.

The palazzo's "Secret Itinerary" tour takes you to the doge's private apartments, through hidden passageways to the interrogation (torture) chambers, and into the rooftop *piombi* (lead) prison, named for its lead roofing. Venetian-born writer and libertine Giacomo Casanova (1725–98), along with an accomplice, managed to escape from the piombi in 1756, the only men ever to do so. ⊠ *Piazzetta San Marco* ☎ *041/2715911* 🔲 *€11 Piazza San Marco museum card, €15.50 Musei Civici pass* ☉ *Apr.–Oct., daily 9–7; Nov.–Mar., daily 9–5; last tickets sold 1 hr before closing* 🔲 *€6 English guided tours* ☉ *Tues.–Thurs., Sat. 11:30* 🔲 *€12.50 "Secret Itinerary" tour* ☉ *English tours in morning; reservations advisable* Ⓥ *Vallaresso/San Zaccaria.*

▶ ❶ **Piazza San Marco** (St. Mark's Square). If you face the basilica from in front of the Correr Museum, you'll notice that rather than being a strict rectangle, this square opens wider at the basilica end, creating the illusion that it's even larger than it is. On your left, the long, arcaded building is the **Procuratie Vecchie,** built in the early 16th century as offices and residences for the powerful procurators (magistrates) of San Marco. On your right is the **Procuratie Nuove,** built half a century later in a more grandiose classical style. It was originally planned by Venice's great Renaissance architect, Sansovino, to carry on the look of his **Libreria Sansoviniana** (Sansovinian Library), but he died before construction on the Nuove had begun. Vincenzo Scamozzi (circa 1552–1616), a neoclassicist pupil of Andrea Palladio (1508–80), completed the design and construction. Still later, the Procuratie Nuove was modified by architect Baldassare Longhena (1598–1682), one of Venice's baroque masters.

When Napoléon entered Venice with his troops in 1797, he called Piazza San Marco "the world's most beautiful drawing room"—and promptly gave orders to redecorate it. His architects demolished a 16th-century church with a Sansovino facade in order to build the **Ala Napoleonica** (Napoleonic Wing), or Fabbrica Nuova (New Building), which linked the two 16th-century procuratie and effectively enclosed the piazza.

> **need a break?**
>
> **Caffè Florian** (☎ 041/5205641), located in the Procuratie Nuove, has served coffee to the likes of Casanova, Charles Dickens, and Marcel Proust. It's Venice's oldest café, continuously open since 1720 (though you'll find it closed on winter Wednesdays). Counter seating is less expensive than taking a table, especially when there's live music. In the Procuratie Vecchie, **Caffè Quadri** (☎ 041/5289299) exudes almost as much history as Florian across the way, and is similarly pricey. It was shunned by 19th-century Venetians when the occupying Austrians made it their gathering place. During winter season it closes on Mondays. If you'd like to happy hour with ghosts of Ernest Hemingway, Aristotle Onassis, and Orson Welles, head to **Harry's Bar** (☎ 041/5285777). Walk out Piazza San Marco near the Correr Museum and turn left at Calle Vallaresso; you'll find the legendary hangout right at the vaporetto landing. Harry's still boasts Venice's driest martinis and freshest Bellinis (white peach juice and sparkling Prosecco wine).

Piazzetta San Marco. This "little square" leads from Piazza San Marco to the waters of Bacino San Marco (St. Mark's Basin). The *molo* (land-

CRUISING THE GRAND CANAL

VENETIANS CALL IT CANALAZZO, *but to the rest of the world it's the Grand Canal. The shallow ribbon of water (average depth 9 feet) winds 4 km (2½ mi) from the Ferrovia (train station) to Piazza San Marco, in its course passing 200 opulent palazzos born of a culture obsessed with luxury and fantasy. Though the canal may be more romantic viewed by gondola, sightseeing is more flexible (you can get on and off at any stop) and less expensive by vaporetto, the Venetian water bus. If you board Line 1 at Ferrovia and take it straight through to San Marco, here are some of the sights to look for. (Those in bold have full listings in this chapter.)*

*To your left as you leave the Ferrovia is Santa Maria di Nazareth, whose barefoot friars earned it the nickname Scalzi (barefoot) Church. Pass beneath Ponte di Scalzi, the first of three bridges, and where Canal di Cannaregio branches, a corner of **Palazzo Labia** towers behind the church. Opposite the San Marcuola stop is Fondaco dei Turchi, Venice's natural-history museum. **Palazzo Vendramin-Calergi,** the city's casino, stands just past the dock. Next stop on the right is at the richly decorated **San Stae** church; leaving it, you'll pass Longhena's **Ca' Pesaro** and the equally classical Ca' Corner della Regina. The vaporetto recrosses to stop at lovely, pink-and-white **Ca' d'Oro;** opposite, you'll see the fruit and vegetable market and covered market next door, where Venetians have bartered for fish since the 1300s. With bridge number two, **Ponte di Rialto,** looming ahead, Fondaco dei Tedeschi (today the main post office) lies to the left, and opposite is Ca' dei Camerlenghi, 16th-century home of the State Treasury.*

The vaporetto stops in front of Ca' Loredan and Ca' Farsetti, 12th- and 13th-century buildings that make up Venice's city hall.

*Ahead is Palazzo Grimani, Michele Sanmicheli's Renaissance masterpiece, now an appeals court. At the San Angelo stop is another massive Renaissance piece, Ca' Corner Spinelli, this the work of Mauro Codussi. Opposite is large, salmon-color Palazzo Pisani Moretta, faithfully restored down to candlelit chandeliers. The boat stops at San Tomà; straight ahead, past a sharp bend, is Ca' Foscari, once a doge's home and now site of the city's largest university. Veering left, the boat pulls up beside Longhena's baroque **Ca' Rezzonico.** Directly opposite is **Palazzo Grassi,** one of the canal's newest properties. Approaching the canal's final bridge, you stop at a former church and monastery complex that houses the world-renowned **Gallerie dell'Accademia.***

*Under Accademia Bridge the boat seems to move more quickly as you enter the home stretch, but it's hard to miss the patch of green ahead. A garden cradles Casetta Rossa (small red house), which has sheltered painters, poets, and princes; it stands in the shadow of Palazzo Corner Ca' Grande next door. Opposite is Palazzo Venier dei Leoni, which holds the **Peggy Guggenheim Collection** of contemporary art. The boat again stops on the left near the Gritti Palace Hotel; now you can see the canal begin to widen out. The last stop on the right is at **Santa Maria della Salute,** another Longhena creation. At the tip of Punta della Dogana (a former customhouse), the golden goddess of fortune acts as weather vane. At the Vallaresso stop you've left the Grand Canal, but don't disembark yet: stay on board for a view of the **Palazzo Ducale** and **Basilica di San Marco** behind it, then get off at San Zaccaria.*

ing), once the grand entrance to the Republic, has two columns towering above the waterfront. One is topped by the winged lion, a traditional emblem of St. Mark that became the symbol of Venice itself; the other supports St. Theodore, the city's first patron, along with his dragon. Between these columns the Republic traditionally executed convicts.

Torre dell'Orologio. Five hundred years ago, when this enameled clock was built, twin Moors would strike the hour, and three wise men with an angel would walk out and bow to the Virgin Mary on Epiphany (January 6) and during Ascension Week (40 days after Easter). An inscription on the tower reads HORAS NON NUMERO NISI SERENAS ("I only count happy hours"); if that's true, perhaps happy hours will return to Venice when they finally fix the clock. It's been under restoration for years, but you can visit the three wise men in the Palazzo Ducale, where they are on display. ⊠ *North side of Piazza San Marco.*

Dorsoduro

The long, narrow sestiere across the Grand Canal to the south of San Marco is a place of monumental churches, meandering canals, the city's finest art museums, and a sunny boardwalk.

a good walk

Start out across the Grand Canal from Dorsoduro in **Campo Santo Stefano** ⑥ ☛ and visit its 14th-century church. Then take Ponte dell'Accademia over the canal to sestiere Dorsoduro (named for its "hard back" solid clay foundation) and the **Gallerie dell'Accademia** ⑦, where you'll see an unparalleled collection of Venetian painting. Head toward the eastern point of the peninsula, Punta della Dogana, for one of the best views in town. **Santa Maria della Salute** ⑧ certainly deserves attention inside and out before you backtrack to the 20th-century **Peggy Guggenheim Collection** ⑨. Next stop is the Zattere, a wide boardwalk where on sunny days you'll swear half the city is out for a *passeggiata,* or stroll. Visit the church of the **Gesuati** ⑩ if only to peek at the Tiepolo ceiling, and don't miss the *bocca di leoni* (lion's mouth) between this church and its older sibling, Santa Maria della Visitazione.

Past the lion's mouth, take a right to see the Squero di San Trovaso, where gondolas have been built and repaired for centuries. Returning to the Zattere, continue to the San Basilio vaporetto stop. Ahead lies Stazione Marittima, where in summer cruise ships line the dock; instead of crossing that bridge, turn right on Calle del Vento alongside the canal. Opposite the next bridge is the church of **San Sebastiano** ⑪, filled with Veronese's paintings and site of his grave. Calle del Vento angles right and opens into the small campo of Chiesa dei Carmini. Around the corner is the beautiful **Scuola Grande dei Carmini** ⑫, and just beyond is lively Campo Santa Margarita, packed with markets and kids, students and tourists. Stop here for a well-deserved coffee or glass of wine.

Leave the campo at Rio San Barnaba to see the most photographed vegetable vendor in town. You'll cross Ponte dei Pugni (Bridge of Fists), former battleground of the Nicolotti (Westsiders) and Castellani (Eastenders), Venice's Hatfields and McCoys. The calle alongside San Barnaba church leads to **Ca' Rezzonico** ⑬ and the Museo del Settecento

Veneziano. If you've had your fill of history, and **Palazzo Grassi** ⑭ has a show that catches your eye, hop across on a traghetto.

TIMING This walk takes about two hours without stops, but it's a full day, or more, if you want to see all the sights. The Gallerie dell'Accademia demand a few hours by themselves, but if time is short an audio guide can help you cover the highlights in about an hour. Give yourself at least 1½ hours for the Guggenheim Collection. The churches and Scuola Grande dei Carmini are not large, and unless something grabs your attention a half hour should be enough for each one. Ca' Rezzonico deserves a couple of hours.

What to See

★ ⑬ **Ca' Rezzonico.** Designed by Baldassare Longhena in the 17th century, this palace was completed nearly 100 years later by Giorgio Massari and became the last home of English poet Robert Browning (1812–89). Elizabeth Taylor and Richard Burton danced in the baroque ballroom in the 1960s. Today Ca' Rezzonico is the home of the **Museo del Settecento** (Museum of Venice in the 1700s). Its main floor is packed with period furniture and tapestries in gilded salons (note the four Tiepolo ceiling frescoes) and successfully retains the feel of an old Venetian palazzo. Upper floors contain hundreds of paintings, most from Venetian schools of artists. There's even a restored apothecary, complete with powders and potions. ⊠ *Fondamenta Rezzonico, Dorsoduro 3136* ☎ *041/2410100* 🎟 *€6.50, €15.50 Musei Civici pass* ☉ *Apr.–Oct., Wed.–Mon. 10–6; Nov.–Mar., Wed.–Mon. 10–5; last entry 1 hr before closing* Ⓥ *Ca' Rezzonico.*

▶ ❻ **Campo Santo Stefano.** In Venice's most prestigious residential neighborhood, you'll find one of the city's busiest crossroads; it's hard to believe this square once hosted bullfights, with bulls (or oxen) tied to a stake and baited by dogs. For centuries the campo was grass except for a stone avenue called the *liston*. It was so popular for strolling that in Venetian dialect *"andare al liston"* still means "go for a walk." A sunny meeting spot popular with Venetians and visitors alike, the campo also hosts outdoor fairs during Christmas and Carnevale seasons. Check out the 14th-century **Chiesa di Santo Stefano** and its ship's-keel roof, created by shipbuilders. You'll see works by Tintoretto and the tipsiest bell tower in town—best appreciated from nearby Campo San Angelo. ⊠ *Campo Santo Stefano, San Marco* ☎ *041/2750462 Chorus* 🎟 *€2, €8 Chorus pass* ☉ *Mon.–Sat. 10–5, Sun. 1–5* Ⓥ *Accademia.*

★ ❼ **Gallerie dell'Accademia.** Napoléon founded these galleries in 1807 on the site of a religious complex he'd suppressed, and what he initiated amounts to the world's most extraordinary collection of Venetian art. Jacopo Bellini (1400–71) is considered the father of the Venetian Renaissance, and in Room 2 you can compare his *Madonna and Child with Saints* with such later works as *Madonna of the Orange Tree* by Cima da Conegliano (circa 1459–1517) and *Ten Thousand Martyrs of Mt. Ararat* by Vittore Carpaccio (1450–1526). Jacopo's son Giovanni (circa 1430–1516) draws your eye not with his subjects but with his rich color. Rooms 4 and 5 are full of his Madonnas; note the contrast between the young Madonna and child and the neighboring older Madonna after the crucifixion—you'll see the colors of dawn and dusk in Venice. Room 5 contains *Tempest* by Giorgione (1477–1510), a work that was revolutionary in its time and has continued to intrigue viewers and critics over the centuries. It depicts a storm approaching as a nude woman nurses her child and a soldier looks on. The overall atmosphere that Giorgione creates is as important as any of his figures.

In Room 10, *Feast in the House of Levi,* commissioned as a Last Supper, got Veronese dragged before the Inquisition over its depiction of dogs, jesters, and German (therefore Protestant) soldiers. The artist saved his neck by simply changing the title, so that the painting represented a different biblical feast. Titian's *Presentation of the Virgin* (Room 24) is the collection's only work originally created for the building in which it hangs. Don't miss Rooms 20 and 21, with views of 15th- and 16th-century Venice by Carpaccio and Gentile Bellini (1429–1507), Giovanni's brother—you'll see how little the city has changed.

Booking tickets in advance isn't essential but helps during busy seasons and costs only an additional €1. Booking is necessary to see the **Quadreria,** where additional works cover every inch of a wide hallway. A free map names art and artists, and the bookshop sells a more informative English-language booklet. In the main galleries a €4 audio guide saves reading but adds little to each room's excellent annotation; audio/video guides (€6) are more exhaustive and also ease navigating. ⊠ *Campo della Carità, Dorsoduro 1050* ☏ *041/5222247, 041/5200345 reservations* ⊕ *www. gallerieaccademia.org* 🎫 *€6.50, €11 includes Ca' d'Oro and Museo Orientale* ⊙ *Tues.–Sun. 8:15–7:15, Mon. 8:15–2* Ⓥ *Accademia.*

❿ **Gesuati.** When the Dominicans took over the church of Santa Maria della Visitazione from the suppressed order of Gesuati laymen in 1668, Giorgio Massari was commissioned to build this church. It has a score of works by Giambattista Tiepolo (1696–1770), Giambattista Piazzetta (1683–1754), and Sebastiano Ricci (1659–1734). ⊠ *Zattere Dorsoduro* ☏ *041/2750462 Chorus* 🎫 *€2, €8 Chorus pass* ⊙ *Mon.–Sat. 10–5, Sun. 1–5* Ⓥ *Zattere.*

⎧ need a ⎫
⎩ break? ⎭

There's no sunnier spot in Venice than **Fondamenta delle Zattere,** along the southern edge of Dorsoduro. It's the city's gigantic public terrace, with bustling bars and gelato shops; come here to stroll, read in the open air, and play hooky from sightseeing. The Zattere's most decadent treat is found at **Gelateria Nico** (⊠ Dorsoduro 922 ☏ 041/ 5225293)—order their famous *gianduiotto,* a nutty slab of chocolate ice cream floating on a cloud of whipped cream, and relax on the big, welcoming deck.

⓮ **Palazzo Grassi.** The Grassi family from Bologna bought their way into aristocracy in 1718, then bought into the Grand Canal 30 years later, when Giorgio Massari designed their neoclassical palace; it was to become the canal's last grand addition. The automotive giant Fiat acquired the property in 1985 and turned it into a venue for art and history exhibitions. It is open only during special exhibitions. ⊠ *Campo San*

Samuele, San Marco 3231 ☎ *041/5231680* ⊕ *www.palazzograssi.it* Ⓥ *San Samuele.*

❾ **Peggy Guggenheim Collection.** A small but choice selection of 20th-century painting and sculpture is on display at this gallery in the heiress Guggenheim's former Grand Canal home. Through wealth and social connections, Guggenheim (1898–1979) became a serious art patron, and her collection here in Palazzo Venier dei Leoni includes works by Picasso, Kandinsky, Pollock, Motherwell, and Ernst (at one time her husband). The museum serves beverages, snacks, and light meals in its refreshingly shady, artistically sophisticated garden. ⊠ *Calle San Cristoforo, Dorsoduro 701* ☎ *041/2405411* ⊕ *www.guggenheim-venice.it* 🎟 *€10* 🕐 *Mid-May–Feb., Wed.–Mon. 10–6; Mar.–mid-May, daily 10–6* Ⓥ *Accademia.*

⓫ **San Sebastiano.** Paolo Veronese (1528–88) established his reputation while still in his twenties with the frescoes at this, his parish church, and for decades he continued to embellish them with amazing trompe-l'oeil scenes. Don't miss his altarpiece *Madonna in Glory with Saints.* Veronese is buried beneath his bust near the organ. ⊠ *Campo San Sebastiano, Dorsoduro* ☎ *041/2750462 Chorus* 🎟 *€2, €8 Chorus pass* 🕐 *Mon.–Sat. 10–5, Sun. 1–5* Ⓥ *San Basilio.*

❽ **Santa Maria della Salute.** The view of La Salute (as this church is commonly called) from the Riva degli Schiavoni at sunset or from the Accademia Bridge by moonlight is unforgettable. Baldassare Longhena was 32 years old when he won a competition to design a shrine honoring the Virgin Mary for saving Venice from a plague that killed 47,000 residents. Outside, this simple white octagon is adorned with a colossal cupola lined with snail-like buttresses and a Palladian-style facade; inside are a polychrome marble floor and six chapels. The Byzantine icon above the main altar has been venerated as the Madonna della Salute (of health) since 1670, when Francesco Morosini brought it here from Crete. Above it is a sculpture showing Venice (left) on her knees while the plague (right) is driven from the city. The **Sacrestia Maggiore** contains a dozen works by Titian, including his *San Marco Enthroned with Saints* altarpiece. You'll also see Tintoretto's *The Wedding at Canaan*, and on special occasions the altar displays a 15th-century tapestry depicting the Pentecost. For the Festa della Salute, held November 21, Venetians make a pilgrimage here and light candles in thanksgiving for another year's health. ⊠ *Punta della Dogana, Dorsoduro* ☎ *041/5225558* 🎟 *Church free, sacristy €1.50* 🕐 *June–Sept., daily 9–noon and 3–6; Oct.–May, daily 9–noon and 3–5:30* Ⓥ *Salute.*

⓬ **Scuola Grande dei Carmini.** Venice's *scuole* were not schools, though that's how the word today translates. These secular institutions were established by different social groups—foreigners, tradesmen, followers of a particular saint—and concentrated on supporting their own members or helping society's neediest citizens. The tradesmen's or servants' scuole formed social security nets for their elderly and disabled members. Wealthier scuole assisted orphans and provided dowries so poor girls could marry.

When the order of Santa Maria del Carmelo commissioned Longhena to build Scuola Grande dei Carmini in the late 1600s, their brotherhood of 75,000 members was the largest in Venice and one of the wealthiest. Little expense was spared in the decorating of stuccoed ceilings and carved ebony paneling, and the artwork was choice, even before 1739, when Tiepolo painted the **Sala Capitolare.** In what many consider his best work, Tiepolo's nine great canvases vividly transform some rather unpromising religious themes into flamboyant displays of color and movement. ⊠ *Campo dei Carmini, Dorsoduro 2617* ☎ *041/ 5289420* 🖾 *€5* ☉ *Nov.–Mar., daily 9–4; Apr.–Oct., Mon.–Sat. 9–6, Sun. 9–4* Ⓥ *Ca' Rezzonico.*

> **need a break?** Filled with cafés and restaurants, **Campo Santa Margarita** also has produce vendors, pizza by the slice, and benches where you can sit and eat. For more than a portable munch, bask in the sunshine at popular **il Caffé** (☎ 041/5287998), commonly called Caffé Rossa for its bright red exterior. It's open past midnight, serving drinks and light refreshment every day except Sunday.

San Polo & Santa Croce

The smallest of Venice's six sestieri, San Polo and Santa Croce were named after their main churches, though the Chiesa di Santa Croce was demolished in 1810. This walk includes some big attractions, such as Santa Maria Gloriosa dei Frari and the Scuola Grande San Rocco, as well as some worthwhile but lesser-known churches.

> **a good walk** Begin your tour at Venice's most famous bridge, the **Ponte di Rialto** ⑮ ▶, which unites sestiere San Marco (west) with San Polo (east). Shops abound here; on the San Marco side of the bridge they sell everything that's hip, on the San Polo side everything edible. Chiesa di San Giacometto, where you see the first fruit vendors as you descend on the San Polo side, was probably built in the 11th and 12th centuries, about the time the surrounding market came into being. Public announcements were traditionally read in the church's campo; its 24-hour clock, though lovely, has rarely worked. If you want to take part in the food shopping, come early to beat the crowds and bear in mind that a *metà kilo* is about a pound and an *etto* is a few ounces.

Heading south away from Rialto on Ruga Vechia San Giovanni, look for a gate on your left. It marks the entrance to **San Giovanni Elemosinario** ⑯, which is completely devoid of a facade because it always leased the outdoor space to vendors. This street continues to **Campo San Polo** ⑰ and **Santa Maria Gloriosa dei Frari** ⑱; you can save your feet by hopping a vaporetto from San Silvestro to San Tomà, where a short walk brings you to the Frari. Two of Titian's finest works hang there, and the nearby **Scuola Grande di San Rocco** ⑲ is a treasury of works by Tintoretto.

Cross the bridge in front of the Frari and turn left. After another bridge you'll enter Campo San Stin. Turn right from here into Calle de Ca' Donà and continue to Campo San Agostin. Take the first left after the campo (Rio Terá Primo) and go straight ahead to the **San Giacomo dell'Orio** ⑳ campo and church, a peaceful place for a drink, a rest, and a chance to glimpse daily life. Leave from the corner that narrows into Calle Larga, cross over the bridge to your right, and turn left then right into Ramo del Tentor, which leads to Salizada San Stae. A left here brings you to the Grand Canal at the whimsically baroque **San Stae** ㉑. From here signs direct you over a bridge and down a narrow alley to **Ca' Pesaro** ㉒, the site of both the Museum of Modern Art and the Oriental Museum.

TIMING The walk itself takes only about an hour, but there's a lot to see. If you do any shopping, or even pop in at a few churches along the way, you'll easily stretch it into a half day. You'll want at least two hours to see both collections at Ca' Pesaro.

What to See

㉒ **Ca' Pesaro.** Longhena's grand baroque palace is the beautifully restored home of two impressive collections. The **Galleria Internazionale d'Arte Moderna** has works by 19th- and 20th-century artists such as Klimt, Kandinsky, Matisse, and Miró. It also has a collection of representative works from Venice's Biennale art show that amounts to a panorama of 20th-century art. The **Museo Orientale** has a small but striking collection of oriental porcelains, musical instruments, arms, and armor. ⊠ *San Stae, Santa Croce 2076* ☎ *041/5240662 Galleria, 041/5241173 Museo Orientale* ⊗ *Apr.–Oct., Tues.–Sun. 10–6; Nov.–Mar., Tues.–Sun. 10–5* 🎫 *€5.50 includes both museums* Ⅴ *San Stae.*

⑰ **Campo San Polo.** Only Piazza San Marco is larger than this square, where not even the pigeons manage to look cozy, and the echo of children's voices bouncing off the surrounding palaces makes the space seem even more cavernous. Not long ago Campo San Polo hosted bull races, fairs, military parades, and packed markets, but now it only really comes alive on summer nights, when it hosts the city's outdoor cinema. The **Chiesa di San Polo** has been restored so many times that little remains of the original 9th-century church, and sadly, 19th-century alterations were so costly that the friars sold off many great paintings to pay bills. Though Giambattista Tiepolo is represented here, his work is outdone by 16 paintings of his son Giandomenico (1727–1804), including the *Stations of the Cross* in the oratory to the left of the entrance. The younger Tiepolo also created a series of expressive and theatrical renderings of the saints. Look for altarpieces by Tintoretto and Veronese that managed to escape auction. San Polo's bell tower remained unchanged through the centuries—don't miss the two lions guarding it, playing with a disembodied human head and a serpent. ⊠ *Campo San Polo* ☎ *041/ 2750462 Chorus* 🎫 *€2, €8 Chorus pass* ⊗ *Mon.–Sat. 10–5, Sun. 1–5* Ⅴ *San Tomà.*

★ ▶ ⑮ **Ponte di Rialto** (Rialto Bridge). The competition to design a stone bridge across the Grand Canal (replacing earlier wooden versions) attracted the late 1500s' best architects, including Michelangelo, Palladio, and Sansovino, but the job went to the less famous but appropriately named Antonio da Ponte. His pragmatic design featured shop space and was high enough for galleys to pass beneath; it kept decoration and cost to a minimum at a time when the republic's coffers were low due to continual wars against the Turks and the opening of oceanic trade routes.

Along the railing you'll enjoy one of the city's most famous views: the Grand Canal vibrant with boat traffic. Ⓥ *Rialto.*

⓴ **San Giacomo dell'Orio.** It was named after a laurel tree *(orio),* and today trees give character to the square. Add benches and a fountain (with drinking bowl for dogs), and this pleasantly odd-shape campo becomes a welcoming place for friendly conversation, picnics, and neighborhood kids at play. Legend has it the **Chiesa di San Giacomo dell'Orio** was founded in the 9th century on an island still populated by wolves. The current church dates from 1225; its short unmatched Byzantine columns survived renovation during the Renaissance, and the church never lost the feel of an ancient temple sheltering beneath its 15th-century ship's-keel roof. In the sanctuary, large marble crosses are surrounded by a bevy of small medieval Madonnas. The altarpiece is *Madonna with Child and Saints* (1546) by Lorenzo Lotto (1480–1556), and the sacristies contain works by Palma il Giovane (circa 1544–1628). ⊠ *Campo San Giacomo dell'Orio, Santa Croce* ☎ *041/2750462 Chorus* ▨ *€2, €8 Chorus pass* ⊗ *Mon.–Sat. 10–5, Sun. 1–5* Ⓥ *San Stae.*

⓰ **San Giovanni Elemosinario.** Storefronts make up the facade, and the altars were built by market guilds—poulterers, messengers, and fodder merchants—at this church intimately bound to the Rialto Market. It's as rich inside as it is simple outside. During San Giovanni Elemosinario's restoration, workers stumbled upon a frescoed cupola by Pordenone (1484–1539) that had been painted over centuries earlier. Don't miss Titian's *St. John the Almsgiver* and Pordenone's *Sts. Catherine, Sebastian, and Roch,* which in 2002 were returned after 30 years by the Gallerie dell'Accademia, a rarity for Italian museums. ⊠ *Rialto Ruga Vechia S. Giovanni* ☎ *041/2750462 Chorus* ▨ *€2, €8 Chorus pass* ⊗ *Mon.–Sat. 10–5, Sun. 1–5* Ⓥ *San Silvestro or Rialto.*

⓴ **San Stae.** The most renowned Venetian painters and sculptors of the early 18th century—known as the Moderns—decorated this church with the legacy left by Doge Alvise Mocenigo II, who's buried in the center aisle. A broad sampling of these masters includes works by Tiepolo, Ricci, Piazzetta, and Lazzarini. ⊠ *Campo San Stae, Santa Croce* ☎ *041/ 2750462 Chorus* ▨ *€2, €8 Chorus pass* ⊗ *Mon.–Sat. 9–5, Sun. 1–5* Ⓥ *San Stae.*

⓲ **Santa Maria Gloriosa dei Frari.** This immense Gothic church of russet-color brick, completed in the 1400s after more than a century of work, is deliberately austere, befitting the Franciscan brothers' insistence on spirituality and poverty. However, *I Frari* (as it's known locally) contains some of the most brilliant paintings in any Venetian church. Visit the sacristy first, to see Giovanni Bellini's 1488 triptych *Madonna and Child with Saints* in all its mellow luminosity, painted for precisely this spot. The Corner Chapel on the other side of the chancel is graced by Bartolomeo Vivarini's 1474 altarpiece *St. Mark Enthroned and Saints John the Baptist, Jerome, Peter, and Nicholas,* of similar exquisite detail and color. There is also a fine sculpture of St. John the Baptist here by Jacopo Sansovino. You'll appreciate the rapid development of Venetian Renaissance painting by contrasting Bellini

Fodor$Choice
★

and Vivarini with the heroic energy of Titian's *Assumption,* over the main altar, painted some 30 years later. Unveiled in 1518, this work was not initially accepted by the church, precisely because of the innovative style and bright colors, especially Titian's trademark red, which would make it famous.

Titian's beautiful *Madonna di Ca' Pesaro,* in the left aisle, was modeled after his wife, who died in childbirth. The painting took almost 10 years to complete, and in it Titian totally disregarded the conventions of his time by moving the Virgin out of center frame and making the saints active participants. On the same side of the church look at the spooky, pyramid-shape monument to the sculptor Antonio Canova (1757–1822). Across the nave is a neoclassical 19th-century monument to Titian, executed by two of Canova's pupils. ⊠ *Campo dei Frari, San Polo* ☎ *041/ 2728618, 041/2750462 Chorus* ✆ *€2, €8 Chorus pass* ☉ *Mon.–Sat. 9–6, Sun. 1–6* Ⓥ *San Tomà.*

> **need a break?**
> On a narrow passage between the Frari and San Rocco, **Gelateria Millevoglie** (a Thousand Desires; ☎ 041/5244667) has pizza slices, calzones, and gelato so popular it backs up traffic. It's closed in December and January, but the rest of the year it's open 10 AM to midnight, seven days a week.

⑲ Scuola Grande di San Rocco. St. Rocco's popularity stemmed from his miraculous recovery from the plague and his care for fellow sufferers. Throughout the plague-filled Middle Ages, followers and donations abounded, and this elegant example of Venetian Renaissance architecture was the result. Although it is bold and dramatic outside, its contents are even more stunning—a series of more than 60 paintings by Tintoretto. In 1564 Tintoretto edged out competition for a commission to decorate a ceiling by submitting not a sketch, but a finished work, which he moreover offered free of charge. *Moses Striking Water from the Rock, The Brazen Serpent,* and *The Fall of Manna* represent three bodily sufferings—thirst, disease, and hunger—that San Rocco and later his brotherhood strived to counteract. ⊠ *Campo San Rocco, San Polo 3052* ☎ *041/5234864* ✆ *€5.50; students up to 26 €4; children up to 18 free if accompanied by parent* ☉ *Mar. 28–Nov. 2, daily 9–5:30; Nov. 3–Mar. 27, daily 10–4; last entrance ½ hr before closing* Ⓥ *San Tomà.*

> **need a break?**
> The bridge behind Scuola Grande di San Rocco leads to a bustling little student area of bars and restaurants. **Café Noir** (⊠ Calle Crosera, Dorsoduro 3805 ☎ 041/710925) has a good selection of sandwiches, and buying food gives you discounts on Web-surfing. It's open until 2 AM but is closed Sunday. **Pasticceria Tonolo** (⊠ Calle Crosera Dorsoduro 3764 ☎ 041/5237209) has been fattening Venetians since 1886. During Carnevale it's still the best place in town for *fritelle,* fried doughnuts (traditional raisin or cream-filled); during acqua alta, the staff dons rubber boots and keeps working. The place is closed on Monday, and there's no seating anytime.

Castello & Cannaregio

Twice the size of tiny San Polo and Santa Croce, Castello and Cannaregio combined spread east to west from one end of Venice to the other. From working-class shipbuilding neighborhoods to the world's first ghetto, you'll see a cross section of city life that's always existed beyond the palace walls. Churches that could make a Renaissance pope jealous await you, as does one of the Grand Canal's prettiest palaces, Ca' d'Oro, but you'll also find detour options for leaving the crowds behind.

a good
walk

Wake up with the lions, the ones guarding the awesome gates of the **Arsenale** ㉓ ⌐, and see where the Republic forged its mighty sea power. The **Museo Storico Navale** ㉔, just a bridge away, has ships and models from Venice and around the world. See some of Carpaccio's best paintings at the **Scuola di San Giorgio degli Schiavoni** ㉕ before navigating the maze that leads to the square of **Santa Maria Formosa** ㉖. It has a fountain, vegetable market, church, and canal—all the prerequisites for a perfect Venetian campo—and the **Querini-Stampalia** ㉗, a library and art collection housed in an elegantly restored palace. Signs direct you north toward **Santi Giovanni e Paolo** ㉘ campo and church. With all its entombed VIPs, it's Venice's answer to Westminster Abbey.

If you're here in the afternoon, stop by the former foundling home called the **Ospedaletto** ㉙, a short walk down Babaria de le Tole. Otherwise head west from Santi Giovanni e Paolo's main door, where three bridges lead to **Santa Maria dei Miracoli** ㉚, a stop you won't want to miss. Around the back of the church, recross the bridge to Campo Santa Maria Nova and walk ahead to Campo San Canzian, where another bridge leads to Calle Muazzo. If you take a right turn here, after two bridges and five minutes you'll arrive at the church of the **Gesuiti** ㉛, a baroque masterpiece of inlaid marble. A left turn at Calle Muazzo leads through Campo Santi Apostoli and then to Strada Nova, the main thoroughfare to the train station. Following the bold yellow signs toward the station, you'll see a small calle leading left to the Ca' d'Oro vaporetto landing, where you can visit the beautiful marble palace of **Ca' d'Oro** ㉜. Farther along the road to the station, signs leading to the San Marcuola vaporetto landing will put you near Venice's casino in **Palazzo Vendramin-Calergi** ㉝, a fine Renaissance palace with a wonderful garden alongside—both looking directly onto the Grand Canal. Continue on toward the station to the Ponte de le Guglie, from which you can admire the **Palazzo Labia** ㉞ out to the left. Walk back down the bridge and left beside the Cannaregio canal to a small gateway on the right leading into the **Jewish Ghetto** ㉟, for centuries the heart of Jewish culture in Venice.

TIMING   This tour requires time and energy: it involves a couple of hours of walking, even if you never enter a building, and offers little chance to hop a boat and save your legs. Some sights have restricted hours, making it virtually impossible to see everything even in a full day. Your best bet is to choose a few sights to make your priorities, time your tour around their open hours, and then drop in at whatever others happen to be open as you're passing by. If you're touring on Friday, keep in mind that synagogues close at sunset.

What to See

☝ ☞ **㉓ Arsenale.** The Venetian Republic never could have thrived without the Arsenale shipyard, which is said to have been founded in 1104 on twin islands. The immense facility that evolved was given the old Venetian dialect name *arzanà,* borrowed from the Arabic *darsina'a,* meaning "workshop." At times it employed as many as 16,000 *arsenalotti,* workers who were among the most respected shipbuilders in the world. (Dante immortalized these sweating men armed with pitch and boiling tar in his *Inferno.*) Their diligence was confirmed time and again—whether building 100 ships in 60 days to battle the Turks in Cyprus (1597) or completing one perfectly armed warship—start to finish—while King Henry III of France attended a banquet. The Arsenale's impressive Renaissance **gateway** (1460) is guarded by four lions, war booty of Francesco Morosini, who took the Peloponnese from the Turks in 1687. The 10-foot-tall lion on the left stood sentinel more than 2,000 years ago near Athens, and experts say its mysterious inscription is runic "graffiti" left by Viking mercenaries hired to suppress 11th-century revolts in Piraeus. If you look at the winged lion above the doorway, you'll notice that the Gospel at his paws is open but lacks the customary *Pax* inscription; praying for peace perhaps seemed inappropriate above a factory that manufactured weapons. The zone belongs to the Italian Navy and isn't regularly open to the public, but it opens for the Biennale and for Venice's festival of traditional boats, held every May. If you're here during those times, don't miss the chance for a look inside. ⊠ *Campo dell'Arsenale, Castello* Ⓥ *Arsenale.*

★ **㉜ Ca' d'Oro.** This exquisite Venetian Gothic palace was once literally a "Golden House," when its marble traceries and ornaments were embellished with pure gold. Created in 1434 by the enamored patrician Marino Contarini for his wife, Ca' d'Oro became a love offering a second time when a 19th-century Russian prince gave it to Maria Taglioni, a celebrated classical dancer who collected palaces along the Grand Canal. The last proprietor, perhaps more taken with Venice than with any of his lovers, left Ca' d'Oro to the city, after having had it carefully restored and filled with antiquities, sculptures, and paintings that today make up the **Galleria Franchetti.** Besides Mantegna's celebrated *St. Sebastian* and other first-rate Venetian works, the Galleria Franchetti contains the type of fresco that once adorned the exteriors of Venetian buildings (commissioned by those who could not afford a marble facade). One such detached fresco displayed here was made by a young Titian for the (now grayish-white) facade of the Fondaco dei Tedeschi, now the main post office. ⊠ *Calle Ca' d'Oro, Cannaregio 3933* ☎ *041/5222349* ☞ *€5, €11 includes Gallerie dell'Accademia and Museo Orientale* ☉ *Tues.–Sun. 8:15–7:15, Mon. 8:15–2; last entry ½ hr before closing* Ⓥ *Ca' d'Oro.*

㉛ Gesuiti. Extravagantly baroque, this 18th-century church completely abandons classical Renaissance straight lines in favor of flowing, twisting forms. Its interior walls resemble brocade drapery, and only touching will convince skeptics that rather than paint, the green-and-white walls are inlaid marble. Over the first altar on the left the *Martyrdom of St. Lawrence* is a dramatic example of Titian's feeling for light and movement. ⊠ *Campo dei Gesuiti, Cannaregio* ☎ *041/5286579* ☉ *Daily 10–noon and 3–5* Ⓥ *Fondamente Nuove.*

③⑤ Jewish Ghetto. The neighborhood that gave the world the word *ghetto* is today a quiet warren of backstreets that is still home to Jewish institutions, a kosher restaurant, a rabbinical school, and five synagogues. Though Jews may have arrived earlier, the first synagogues weren't built and a cemetery wasn't founded until the Askenazim, or Eastern European Jews, came in the late 1300s. Dwindling coffers may have prompted the Republic to sell temporary visas to Jews, but over the centuries they were alternately tolerated and expelled. The Rialto commercial district, as vividly recounted in Shakespeare's *The Merchant of Venice,* depended on Jewish merchants and moneylenders for trade, and to help cover ever-increasing war expenses.

In 1516 relentless local opposition forced the Senate to confine Jews to an island in Cannaregio, named for its *geto* (foundry), which produced cannon. Gates at the entrance were locked at night, and boats patrolled the surrounding canals. The German accents of early residents changed "geto" into "ghetto." Jews were allowed only to lend money at low interest, operate pawnshops controlled by the government, trade in textiles, or practice medicine. Jewish doctors were highly respected and could leave the ghetto at any hour when on duty. Though ostracized, Jews were nonetheless safe in Venice, and in the 16th century the community grew considerably, with refugees from the Near East, southern and central Italy, Spain, and Portugal. The ghetto was allowed to expand twice, but it still had the city's densest population and consequently ended up with the city's tallest buildings (nine stories); notice the slanting apartment blocks on Campo del Ghetto Nuovo. Although the gates were pulled down after Napoléon's 1797 arrival, the Jews realized full freedom only in the late 19th century with the founding of the Italian state. On the eve of World War II there were about 1,500 Jews left in the ghetto: 247 were deported by the Nazis; eight returned.

The area has Europe's highest density of Renaissance-era synagogues, and visiting them is a unique cross-cultural experience. Though each is marked by the tastes of its individual builders, Venetian influence is evident throughout. Women's galleries resemble those of theaters from the same era, and some synagogues were decorated by artisans who were simultaneously active in local churches.

The small but well-arranged **Museo Ebraico** highlights centuries of Jewish culture with splendid silver Hanukkah lamps and torahs, and handwritten, beautifully decorated wedding contracts in Hebrew. Tours of the ghetto in Italian and English leave hourly from the museum. ⊠ *Campo del Ghetto Nuovo, Cannaregio 2902/b* ☎ *041/715359* ⊕ *www. museoebraico.it* ⊠ *Museum €3; museum and synagogues €8* ⊙ *June–Sept., Sun.–Fri. 10–6:45; last tour 5:30; Oct.–May, Sun.–Fri. 10–5:45; last tour 4:30* Ⓥ *San Marcuola or Guglie.*

You might complete your circuit of Jewish Venice with a visit to the **Antico Cimitero Ebraico** (Ancient Jewish Cemetery) on the Lido, full of fascinating old tombstones half hidden by ivy and grass. The earliest grave dates from 1389; the cemetery remained in use until the late 18th century. ⊠ *Via Cipro, Lido* ☎ *041/715359* ⊠ *€8* ⊙ *Tours Fri. 10:30, Sun. 2:30; call for arrangements* Ⓥ *Lido–S.M.E.*

🔄 ㉔ **Museo Storico Navale** (Museum of Naval History). The boat collection here includes scale models such as the doges' ceremonial *Bucintoro,* and full-size boats such as Peggy Guggenheim's private gondola complete with romantic *felze* (cabin). There's a range of old galley and military pieces, and also a large collection of seashells. ⊠ *Campo San Biagio, Castello 2148* ☎ *041/5200276* 💶 *€1.55* 🕐 *Weekdays 8:45–1:30, Sat. 8:45–1* Ⓥ *Arsenale.*

㉙ **Ospedaletto.** This 16th-century "little hospital" was one of four church foundling homes that each had an orchestra and choir of orphans. Entering through **Santa Maria dei Derelitti** (St. Mary of the Destitute) you'll see a large gallery built for the young musicians. The orphanage is now a home for the elderly; its beautiful 18th-century **Sala della Musica** (Music Room) is the only one of its kind to survive. On the far wall the fresco by Jacopo Guarana (1720–1808) depicts Apollo, god of music, surrounded by the orphan musicians and their maestro, Pasquale Anfossi. ⊠ *Calle Barbaria delle Tole, Castello 6691* ☎ *041/2719012* 💶 *€2* 🕐 *Thurs.–Sat. 3:30–6:30* Ⓥ *Fondamente Nuove or Rialto.*

㉞ **Palazzo Labia.** Once the home of 18th-century Venice's showiest family, this palace is now the Venetian headquarters of the Italian media giant RAI—modern broadcasting goes baroque. In the **Tiepolo Room,** the Labia's gorgeous ballroom, the final flowering of Venetian painting is seen in Giambattista Tiepolo's playful frescoes of Antony and Cleopatra set among dwarfs and Barbary pirates. You have to call ahead to arrange a visit here. ⊠ *Campo San Geremia, Cannaregio 275* ☎ *041/781277* 💶 *Free* 🕐 *Wed.–Fri. 3–4* Ⓥ *Ferrovia.*

㉝ **Palazzo Vendramin-Calergi.** This Renaissance classic with an imposing carved frieze is the work of Mauro Codussi (1440–1504). You can see some of its interior by dropping into the **Casinò di Venezia.** Fans of Richard Wagner (1813–83) might enjoy visiting the **Sala di Wagner,** the room (separate from the casino) in which the composer died. Though rather plain, it's loaded with music memorabilia. ⊠ *Cannaregio 2040* ☎ *041/5297111, 041/5232544 Fri. AM to reserve Wagner Room tours* 💶 *€5, free to gamblers, Sala di Wagner free* 🕐 *Slots 2:45 PM–2:30 AM, tables 3:30 PM–2:30 AM Wagner Room Sat. AM by appointment* Ⓥ *San Marcuola.*

㉗ **Querini-Stampalia.** The art collection at this Renaissance palace includes Giovanni Bellini's *Presentation in the Temple* and Sebastiano Ricci's triptych *Dawn, Afternoon, and Evening.* Portraits of newlywed Francesco Querini and Paola Priuli were left unfinished on the death of Giacomo Palma il Vecchio (1480–1528); note the groom's hand and the bride's dress. Original 18th-century furniture and stuccowork are a fitting background for Pietro Longhi's portraits. Nearly 70 works by Gabriele Bella (1730–99) capture scenes of Venetian street life. Admission Friday and Saturday includes concerts with antique instruments at 5 and 8:30. ⊠ *Campo Santa Maria Formosa, Castello 5252* ☎ *041/2711411* ⊕ *www.querinistampalia.it* 💶 *€6* 🕐 *Tues.–Thurs. and Sun. 10–6, Fri. and Sat. 10–10* Ⓥ *San Zaccaria.*

need a break?   **Florian Art e Caffè** (☎ 041/5206675), inside the Querini-Stampalia, is an offshoot of the famed San Marco café and offers a way to enjoy Florian hospitality without paying uptown prices. Drinks, specialty pastries, and full lunches are available daily except Monday.

㉖ Santa Maria Formosa. Guided by his vision of a beautiful Madonna, 7th-century St. Magno is said to have followed a small white cloud and built a church where it settled. Gracefully white, the marble building you see today dates from 1492, built by Mauro Codussi on an older foundation. The interior is a blend of Renaissance decoration, a Byzantine cupola, barrel vaults, and narrow-columned screens. Of interest are two fine paintings: *Our Lady of Mercy* by Bartolomeo Vivarini (1415–84) and *Santa Barbara* by Palma il Vecchio. The surrounding square bustles with sidewalk cafés and a produce market on weekday mornings. ⊠ *Campo Santa Maria Formosa, Castello* ☎ *041/5234645, 041/2750462 Chorus* ▨ *€2, €8 Chorus pass* ☉ *Mon.–Sat. 10–5, Sun. 1–5* Ⓥ *Rialto.*

★ ㉚ Santa Maria dei Miracoli. Tiny yet perfectly proportioned, this early Renaissance gem is sheathed in marble and decorated inside with exquisite marble reliefs. Architect Pietro Lombardo (circa 1435–1515) miraculously compressed the building into its confined space, then created the illusion of greater size by varying the color of the exterior, adding extra pilasters on the building's canal side, and offsetting the arcade windows to make the arches appear deeper. The church was built in the 1480s to house *I Miracoli,* an image of the Virgin Mary that is said to perform miracles—look for it on the high altar. ⊠ *Campo Santa Maria Nova, Cannaregio* ☎ *041/2750462 Chorus* ▨ *€2, €8 Chorus pass* ☉ *Mon.–Sat. 10–5, Sun. 1–5* Ⓥ *Rialto.*

★ ㉘ Santi Giovanni e Paolo. This massive Dominican church, commonly called San Zanipolo, contains a wealth of art. The 15th-century stained-glass window near the side entrance is breathtaking for its brilliant colors and beautiful figures, made from drawings by Bartolomeo Vivarini and Gerolamo Mocetto. The second official church of the Republic after San Marco, San Zanipolo is the Venetian equivalent of London's Westminster Abbey, with a great number of important people, including 25 doges, buried here. Artistic highlights include an outstanding polyptych by Giovanni Bellini (right aisle, second altar); Alvise Vivarini's *Christ Carrying the Cross* (sacrestia); and Lorenzo Lotto's *Charity of St. Antonino* (right transept). Don't miss the *Cappella del Rosario* (Rosary Chapel), off the left transept, built in the 16th century to commemorate the 1571 victory of Lepanto, in western Greece, when Venice led a combined European fleet to defeat the Turkish navy. The chapel was devastated by a fire in 1867 and restored in the early years of the 20th century with works from other churches, among them the sumptuous Veronese ceiling paintings. However quick your visit, don't miss the Pietro Mocenigo tomb to the right of the main entrance, a monument built by the ubiquitous Pietro Lombardo and his sons. ⊠ *Campo dei Santi Giovanni e Paolo, Castello* ☎ *041/5235913* ▨ *Free* ☉ *Mon.–Sat. 7:30–12:30 and 3:30–6, Sun. 3–6* Ⓥ *Fondamente Nuove or Rialto.*

②⑤ Scuola di San Giorgio degli Schiavoni. Founded in 1451 by the Dalmatian community, this small scuola was, and still is, a social and cultural center for migrants from what is now Croatia. It's dominated by one of Italy's most beautiful rooms, lavishly yet harmoniously decorated with the *teleri* (large canvases) of Vittore Carpaccio (circa 1465–1525). A lifelong Venice resident, Carpaccio painted legendary and religious figures against backgrounds of Venetian architecture. Here he focused on saints especially venerated in Dalmatia: St. George, St. Tryphone, and St. Jerome. He combined observation with fantasy, a sense of warm color with a sense of humor (don't miss the priests fleeing St. Jerome's lion, or the body parts in the dragon's lair). ⊠ *Calle dei Furlani, Castello 3259/a* ☎ *041/5228828* ⌸ *€3* ☽ *Apr.–Oct., Tues.–Sat. 9:30–12:30 and 3:30–6:30, Sun. 9:30–12:30; Nov.–Mar., Tues.–Sat. 10–12:30 and 3–6, Sun. 10–12:30* Ⓥ *Arsenale/San Zaccaria.*

need a break? Baking and catering since 1879, the **Rosa Salva** family today has several outposts scattered around Venice. Visit their **bar** (☎ 041/5227949) in Campo SS. Giovanni e Paolo for pastries and coffee or for some of their homemade gelato. Grab an outdoor table at **Bar ai Miracoli** (☎ 041/5231515) and gaze across the canal at Maria dei Miracoli, Lombardo's miracle in marble.

off the beaten path **SAN FRANCESCO DELLA VIGNA** (St. Francis of the Vineyard) – Legend says this is where an angel awakened St. Mark the Evangelist with the famous words, "Pax tibi Marce Evangelista meus" (Peace to you, Mark, my Evangelist), which became the motto of the Venetian Republic. The land was given in 1253 to the Franciscans, who kept the vineyard but replaced the ancient church. Bring some €.20 coins to light up the Antonio Vivarini (circa 1415–84) triptych of Sts. Girolamo, Bernardino da Siena, and Ludovico, which hangs to your right as you enter the main door, and Giovanni Bellini's *Madonna with Saints* inside the Cappella Santa. Antonio da Negroponte's glittering gold *Madonna Adoring the Child*, near the side door, is an inspiring work of the late 15th century. Here you'll see the transition from formal Gothic rigidity to naturalistic Renaissance composition and detailed decoration. Two cloisters open out from the left aisle, paved entirely with VIP tombstones. ⊠ *Campo San Francesco della Vigna, Castello* ☎ *041/5206102* ⌸ *Free* ☽ *Daily 8:30–12:30 and 3–7* Ⓥ *Celestia.*

SAN PIETRO DI CASTELLO – This church's stark campanile, the first in Venice built from marblelike Istrian stone, stands out against the picturesque, workaday slips along the Canale di San Pietro and the Renaissance cloister, which for years was a squatters colony. The Veneti settled on the island where the church is located years before Venice was officially founded, but today it's a sleepy, almost forgotten place, with little to suggest that for 1,000 years the church was Venice's cathedral—until the Basilica di San Marco superseded it in 1807. The interior has some minor 17th-century art and San Pietro's ancient *cattedra* (throne). ⊠ *Campo San Pietro, Castello* ☎ *041/2750462 Chorus* ⌸ *€2, €8 Chorus pass* ☽ *Mon.–Sat. 10–5, Sun. 1–5* Ⓥ *San Pietro di Castello or Giardini.*

San Giorgio Maggiore & the Giudecca

Beckoning travelers across St. Mark's Basin, sparkling white through the mist, is the island of San Giorgio Maggiore, separated by a small channel from the Giudecca. A tall brick campanile on that distant bank perfectly complements the Campanile of San Marco. Beneath it looms the stately dome of one of Venice's greatest churches, San Giorgio Maggiore. The Giudecca's history may be shrouded in mystery, but today the island is about as down to earth as you can get and one of the city's few remaining neighborhoods that feels truly Venetian.

a good boat trip

Take vaporetto Line 82 from San Zaccaria across St. Mark's Basin to the island of San Giorgio to visit Palladio's church of **San Giorgio Maggiore** �36 ☞. In the adjacent monastery the Fondazione Cini operates a music institute and a school of art restoration. It's only open to the public for exhibitions, conferences, and performances at its lovely outdoor amphitheater, Teatro Verde. The next three vaporetto stops are on the **Giudecca** �37.

TIMING   A half day should be plenty of time to enjoy the sights. Allow about a half hour to see each of the churches, and an hour or two to visit the Giudecca neighborhood.

What to See

�37 **Giudecca.** The island's name is something of a mystery. It may come from a possible 14th-century Jewish settlement, or because 9th-century nobles condemned to *giudicato* (exile) were sent here. It became a pleasure garden for wealthy Venetians during the Republic's long and luxurious decline, but today, like Cannaregio, it's largely working class. The Giudecca provides spectacular views of Venice and is becoming increasingly gentrified. While here, visit the **Santissimo Redentore** church, designed by Palladio and built to commemorate a plague. The third weekend in July it's the site of Venetians' favorite festival, Redentore, featuring boats, fireworks, and outdoor feasting. Thanks to several bridges, you can walk the entire length of the Giudecca's promenade, relaxing at one of several restaurants or just taking in the lively atmosphere. Accommodations run the gamut from youth hostels to the city's most exclusive hotel, Cipriani. ⊠ *Fondamenta San Giacomo, Giudecca* ☎ 041/ 5231415, 041/2750462 *Chorus* 🖃 €2, €8 *Chorus pass* ☉ *Mon.–Sat. 10–5, Sun. 1–5* Ⓥ *Redentore.*

☞ �36 **San Giorgio Maggiore.** There's been a church on this island since the 8th century, with a Benedictine monastery added in the 10th century (closed to the public). Today's refreshingly airy and simply decorated church of brick and white marble was begun in 1566 by Palladio and displays his architectural hallmarks of mathematical harmony and classical influence. *The Last Supper* and the *Gathering of Manna,* two of Tintoretto's later works, line the chancel. To the right of the entrance hangs *The Adoration of the Shepherds* by Jacopo Bassano (1517–92); his foothills home, Bassano del Grappa, is evident in the natural subjects, country life, and terra-firma colors he chooses. The monks are happy to show Carpaccio's *St. George and the Dragon,* hanging in a private room, if they have time. The campanile is so tall that it was struck by lightning in 1993. Take the elevator to the top for some of the finest views in town. ⊠ *Isola di San Giorgio Maggiore* ☎ *041/5227827* ✉ *Church free, campanile €3* ⊗ *June–Sept., daily 9:30–12:30 and 2–6:30; Oct.–May, daily 9:30–12:30 and 2–5* Ⓥ *San Giorgio.*

Islands of the Lagoon

The perfect vacation from your Venetian vacation is an escape to Murano, Burano, and Torcello, the islands of the northern lagoon. Torcello offers greenery, breathing space, and picnic opportunities (remember to pack lunch). Burano is a toy town of houses painted in a riot of colors—blue, yellow, pink, ochre, and dark red. Visitors still love to shop here for "Venetian" lace, even though the vast majority of it is machine-made in Taiwan. Murano is renowned for its glass, but also notorious for the high-pressure sales on its factory tours, even those organized by top hotels. Vaporetto connections to Murano aren't difficult, and for the price of a boat ticket you'll buy your freedom and more time to explore. The Murano "guides" herding new arrivals follow a rotation so that factories take turns giving tours, but you can avoid the hustle by just walking away.

a good boat trip

Line 41 leaves San Zaccaria (front of the Savoia e Jolanda hotel) every 20 minutes, circling the east end of Venice and stopping at Fondamente Nuove before making the five-minute hop to the **San Michele** ㊳ ☛ island cemetery and then heading on to **Murano** ㊴. To see glassblowing, get off at Colonna; the Museo stop will put you near the Museo Vetrario, with a fascinating display of glass dating from the 1st century AD to the 19th. A bit farther down Fondamenta Giustinian you'll see the Basilica di Santi Maria e Donato, with its mosaic floor complete with Murano glass. Make your way to the island's Faro, a lighthouse that still guides boats into the lagoon. From the Faro stop, Line LN runs to **Burano** ㊵, where you can see traditional lace-making at the Scuola di Merletto di Burano. Line LN continues to the sleepy island of **Torcello** ㊶, only five minutes away. A paved lane from the landing follows the canal across the island. You'll pass elegantly reclusive Locanda Cipriani before reaching a grassy square and the beautifully eerie cathedral of Santa Maria Assunta.

TIMING   In summer San Zaccaria is connected to Murano by express vaporetto Line 5; the trip takes 25 minutes. In winter the local Line 41 takes about 45 minutes. From Fondamente Nuove, boats leave every 10 minutes. Line LN goes from Fondamente Nuove direct to Murano, Burano, and Torcello every 30 minutes, and the full trip takes 45 minutes each way. Hitting all the sights on all the islands takes a full day. If you limit yourself to Murano and San Michele, a half day will suffice.

What to See

★ ㊵ **Burano.** Cheerfully painted houses line the canals of this quiet village where lace making rescued a faltering fishing economy centuries ago. As you walk the 100 yards from the dock to Piazza Galuppi, the main square, you pass stall after stall of lace vendors. These good-natured ladies won't press you with a hard sell, but don't expect precise product information or great bargains—real handmade Burano lace costs $1,000 to $2,000 for a 10-inch doily.

The **Museo del Merletto** (Lace Museum) lets you marvel at the intricacies of Burano's lace making. It's also a skills center—more sewing circle than school—where on weekdays you'll usually find women carrying on the tradition. They sometimes have authentic pieces for sale privately. ⊠ *Piazza Galuppi 187* ☎ *041/730034* ☑ *€4, €6 with Museo Vetrario, €15.50 Musei Civici pass* ۞ *Apr.–Oct., Wed.–Mon. 10–5; Nov.–Mar., Wed.–Mon. 10–4* Ⓥ *Burano.*

☾ ❸❾   **Murano.** As in Venice, bridges here link a number of small islands, which are dotted with houses that once were workmen's cottages. In the 13th century the Republic, concerned about fire hazard, moved its glassworks to Murano, and today you can visit the factories and watch glass being made. Many of them line the Fondamenta dei Vetrai, the canal-side walkway leading from the Colonna vaporetto landing. Before you reach Murano's Grand Canal (250 yards from the landing) you'll pass the **Chiesa di San Pietro Martire.** Reconstructed in the 16th century, it houses Giovanni Bellini's *Madonna and Child* and Veronese's *St. Jerome.* ⊠ *Fondamenta dei Vetrai* ☎ *041/739704* ۞ *Mon.–Sat. 9–12:30 and 2–5* Ⓥ *Colonna.*

The collection at the **Museo Vetrario** (Glass Museum) ranges from priceless antiques to only slightly less expensive modern pieces. You'll see authentic Venetian styles and patterns, including the famous Barovier wedding cup (1470–80). ⊠ *Fondamenta Giustinian 8* ☎ *041/739586* 🖾 *€4, €6 with Museo del Merletto, €15.50 Musei Civici pass* ☉ *Apr.–Oct., Thurs.–Tues. 10–5; Nov.–Mar., Thurs.–Tues. 10–4; last tickets sold ½ hr before closing.* Ⓥ *Museo.*

The **Basilica dei Santi Maria e Donato,** just past the glass museum, is among the first churches founded by the lagoon's original inhabitants. The elaborate mosaic pavement includes the date 1140; its ship's-keel roof and Veneto-Byzantine columns add to the semblance of an ancient temple. ⊠ *Fondamenta Giustinian* ☎ *041/739056* 🖾 *Free* ☉ *Daily 8–noon and 4–7* Ⓥ *Museo.*

► ❸❽ **San Michele.** This cypress-lined island is home to the pretty Renaissance church of **San Michele in Isola**—and to some of Venice's most illustrious deceased. The church was designed by Codussi; the graves include those of poet Ezra Pound (1885–1972), impresario and art critic Sergey Diaghilev (1872–1929), and composer Igor Stravinsky (1882–1971). Surrounded by the living sounds of Venice's lagoon, this would seem the perfect final resting place. However, these days newcomers are exhumed after 10 years and transferred to a less grandiose location. ☎ *041/2730111* 🖾 *Free* ☉ *Apr.–Sept., daily 7:30–6; Oct.–Mar., daily 7:30–4* Ⓥ *San Michele.*

★ ❹❶ **Torcello.** In their flight from barbarians 1,500 years ago, the first Venetians landed here, prospering even after many left to found the city of Venice. As malaria took its toll and the island's wool manufacturing was priced out of the market, Torcello became a ghost town. In the 16th century there were 10 churches and 20,000 inhabitants; today you'll be lucky to see one of the island's 16 permanent residents.

Santa Maria Assunta was built in the 11th century, and Torcello's wealth at the time is evident in the church's high-quality Byzantine mosaics. The massive *Last Judgment* shows sinners writhing in pain, while opposite, above the altar, the Madonna looks calmly down from her field of gold. Ask to see the inscription dated 639 and a sample of mosaic pavement from the original church. The adjacent **Santa Fosca** church, added when the body of the saint arrived in 1011, is still used for religious services. It's worth making the climb up the adjacent **Campanile** for an incomparable view of the lagoon wetlands. ⊠ *Torcello* ☎ *041/730119* 🖾 *Santa Maria Assunta €3; Campanile €3* ☉ *Mar.–Oct., daily 10:30–6; Nov.–Feb., daily 10–5* Ⓥ *Torcello.*

need a break?

Locanda Cipriani (☎ 041/730150), closed Tuesday and January and February, is famous for good food and Ernest Hemingway, who often came to Torcello seeking solitude. Today the restaurant (not to be confused with the Giudecca's Cipriani hotel) is busy, with well-heeled customers speeding in for lunch (dinner also on weekends). Dining is pricey, but you can relax in the garden with just a glass of Prosecco.

WHERE TO EAT

The general standard of Venetian restaurants suffers from the effects of mass tourism, but it is still possible to eat well in Venice at moderate prices. It's always a good idea to reserve your table or have your hotel concierge do it for you. Dining hours are limited, starting at 12:30 or 1 for lunch and ending at 2:30 or 3, when restaurants close for the afternoon, opening up again to start serving about 7:30 and closing again at 11 or midnight on weekend nights and earlier (10–11) on weekdays and in the low season. Most close one day a week and are also likely to close without notice for vacation or renovation. Few have signs on the outside, so when the metal blinds are shut tight you can't tell a closed restaurant from a closed TV-repair shop.

Restaurants usually display a menu in the window so you can check out what's available before committing yourself. Also check the (very) fine print: most places add a cover charge of €1.50–€2 per person. Some also add a service charge of 10%–15%. In such cases tipping is unwarranted.

A great Venetian tradition revolves around *bacari,* the local name for the little watering holes where locals have gone for centuries to have a glass of wine, *cicheti* (little savory snacks, usually cold), and a chat.

WHAT IT COSTS In euros				
	$$$$	**$$$**	**$$**	**$**	**¢**
AT DINNER	over €22	€16–€22	€11–€16	€7–€11	under €7

Prices are for a second course *(secondo piatto).*

Cannaregio

$$$ ✕ **Il Sole sulla Vecia Cavana.** Owner Stefano Monti opened this spot in 2001, and it immediately became a star of the Venice dining scene. The young, talented kitchen staff create winning Italian and Venetian dishes such as *filetti di pesce a cottura differenziata* (fish fillet, cooked on one side and quickly seared on the other), tender baby cuttlefish, and, among desserts, *gelato al basilico* (basil ice cream). The 18th-century *cavana* (boathouse) maintains its original low columns, arches, and brick walls, but has been decorated with contemporary flair. ✉ *Rio Terà SS. Apostoli, Cannaregio 4624* ☎ *041/5287106* ▭ *AE, DC, MC, V* ✪ *Closed Mon., 2 wks in Jan., and Aug.* Ⓥ *Rialto/Ca' d'Oro.*

★ **$$–$$$**   ✕ **Vini da Gigio.** A quaint, friendly, family-run trattoria on the quay side of a canal just off the Strada Nova, da Gigio is very popular with Venetians and other visiting Italians, who appreciate the affable service, the well-prepared homemade pasta, fish, and meat dishes, the imaginative and varied cellar, and the high-quality draft wine. It's good for a simple lunch at tables in the barroom. ✉ *Fondamenta de la Chiesa, Cannaregio 3628/a* ☎ *041/5285140* ▭ *AE, DC, MC, V* ✪ *Closed Mon., 3 wks Jan. and Feb., 1 wk in June, and 3 wks Aug. and Sept.* Ⓥ *Ca' d'Oro.*

$–$$ ✕**Algiubagiò.** A waterfront table is more affordable here on Venice's largely forgotten northern Fondamente Nuove. Enjoy the summer shade and breeze off the water as you gaze over toward San Michele and Murano, and even the Dolomites on a clear day. It's an excellent lunch choice, with big, creative salads—such as lettuce, arugula, tuna, prawns, capers, and onions—that are meals in themselves. There are also pasta dishes with freshly made seasonal sauces, pizzas, and main courses. The young, friendly staff serves ice cream, drinks, and snacks all day. A table here is worth the walk. ⊠ *Fondamente Nuove Cannaregio 5039* ☎ *041/ 5236084* ⊟ *AE, DC, MC, V* Ⓜ *Fondamenta Nuove.*

$–$$ ✕**Anice Stellato.** Hidden away on one of the most romantic fondamente of Cannaregio, this family-run bacaro-trattoria is the place to stop for fairly priced, great-tasting food in a part of town that doesn't teem with restaurants. The space has plenty of character: narrow columns rise from the colorful mosaiclike floor, dividing the room into cozy booths. Traditional Venetian fare is enriched with such offerings as *carpacci di pesce* (thin slices of raw tuna, swordfish, or salmon dressed with olive oil and fragrant herbs), tagliatelle with king prawns and zucchini flowers, and several tasty fish stews. Meat dishes are also served, including a tender beef fillet stewed in Barolo wine with potatoes. ⊠ *Fondamenta de la Sensa, Cannaregio 3272* ☎ *041/720744* ⊟ *AE, DC, MC, V* ✆ *Closed Mon. and Tues., and Aug.* Ⓥ *S. Alvise.*

★ **$** ✕**Trattoria Ca′ d′Oro.** Known commonly as La Vedova (the Widow), this warm trattoria not far from the Ca' d'Oro was opened as a low-key bacaro by the owner's great-grandparents. A Venetian terrazzo floor, old marble counter, and rustic furnishings lend a pleasant authenticity that's matched by the food and service. Cicheti include tender *seppie roste* (grilled cuttlefish), *polpette* (meatballs), and baccalà mantecato. The house winter pasta is the *pastisso de radicio rosso* (lasagna with sausage, radicchio, and béchamel sauce). In spring the chef switches to pastisso *de asparagi* (with asparagus). ⊠ *Calle del Pistor, Cannaregio 3912* ☎ *041/ 5285324* ⊟*No credit cards* ✆ *Closed Thurs. No lunch Sun.* Ⓥ *Ca' d'Oro.*

Castello

$$$$ ✕**Do Leoni.** The Two Lions, in the Hotel Londra Palace, is a sumptuous candlelit setting in which to sample Venetian and other Italian cuisine. Young Sicilian chef Stefano Mazzone is a veteran of stints in luxury hotels throughout Italy; his seasonal menu is inventive and indulges in savory flights of fantasy. He elevates such earthy soups as zuppa di fagioli to new levels; his seven-course tasting menu utilizes such non-Italian ingredients as vanilla and ginger. The summer terrace occupies a good portion of the Riva. ⊠ *Riva degli Schiavoni, Castello 4171* ☎ *041/ 5200533* ⌖ *Reservations essential* ⊟ *AE, DC, MC, V* Ⓥ *San Zaccaria.*

★ **$$$** ✕**Alle Testiere.** A strong local following can make it tough to get one of the five tables at this tiny trattoria near Campo Santa Maria Formosa. With its decidedly unglamorous ceiling fans, the place feels as informal as a bistro (or a saloon); the food, however, is much more sophisticated. Chef Bruno Gavagnin's dishes stand out for lightness and balance: try the *gnocchetti con moscardini* (little gnocchi with tender baby octopus) or the linguine with *coda di rospo* (monkfish), or inquire about the carpac-

ON THE MENU

VENETIAN CUISINE is based on seafood—granseola (crab), moeche (soft-shell crab), and seppie or seppioline (cuttlefish) are all prominently featured, and trademark dishes include sarde in saor (fried sardines with olive oil, onions, pine nuts, and raisins) and baccalà mantecato (cod creamed with milk and olive oil). When served whole, fish is usually priced by the etto (100 grams, about ¼ pound) and can be quite expensive. Antipasti may take the form of a seafood salad, prosciutto, or pickled vegetables. As a first course, Venetians favor risotto, the creamy rice dish, prepared with vegetables or shellfish. Pasta, too, is paired with seafood sauces: pasticcio di pesce is pasta baked with fish, usually baccalà, and bigoli is a strictly local pasta shaped like short, thick spaghetti, usually served with nero di seppia (squid-ink sauce). A classic first course is pasta e fagioli (thick bean soup with pasta). Polenta (creamy cornmeal) is another pillar of regional cooking; it's often served with fegato alla veneziana (calves' liver and onions).

Though it originated on the mainland, tiramisu is Venice's favorite dessert, a heavenly concoction of mascarpone (a rich, soft double-cream cheese), espresso, chocolate, and savoiardi (ladyfingers). Local wines are the dry white Tocai and Pinot from the Friuli region and bubbly white Prosecco, a naturally fermented sparkling wine that is a shade less dry. Popular red wines include merlot, cabernet, raboso, and refosco. You can sample all of these in Venice's bacari (local watering holes), where wine is served by the glass (known as an ombra in Venetian dialect) and accompanied by cicheti (snacks such as marinated fish, deep-fried vegetables, and meatballs), often substantial enough for a light meal.

cio of the day. The well-assembled wine list is particularly strong on local whites. The dining room is strictly no-smoking. ✉ Calle del Mondo Novo, Castello 5801 ☎ 041/5227220 ⚑ Reservations essential ▤ MC, V ⊘ Closed Sun. and Mon. Ⓥ Rialto/San Zaccaria.

★ $–$$$ ✕ **Corte Sconta.** You're close to seafood heaven at this firm favorite on the Venetian dining scene. Simple wooden tables are arranged around an open courtyard with outdoor seating in summer. You could make a meal of the seafood antipasti alone, but you'd miss out on such delights as spaghetti *neri alle capesante e zucchine* (cuttlefish-ink pasta with scallops and zucchini) and *vongole veraci spadellate allo zenzero* (clams sauteed in ginger). The house dessert is a warm zabaglione with Venetian cookies, and the house wine is a smooth, still Prosecco, backed up by a good range of bottled wines. ✉ Calle del Pestrin, Castello 3886 ☎ 041/5227024 ⚑ Reservations essential ▤ AE, DC, MC, V ⊘ Closed Sun. and Mon., 4 wks Jan. and Feb., 4 wks July and Aug. Ⓥ Arsenale.

¢–$ ✕ **Da Remigio.** Local Venetian residents almost fill this place, especially on the weekend (you'll need to book ahead), and it's easy to see why: the food is good, the service prompt, and the atmosphere lively. The *canocchio bollite* (boiled, then chilled, shredded mantis shrimp) is a perfect starter, particularly when paired with an effervescent local white wine. Though seconds are strong on fish, Da Remigio also turns out respectable non-fish dishes such as the spaghetti *con porcini* (with mushrooms) and grilled meats. ⊠ *Salizzada dei Greci, Castello 3416* ☎ *041/5230089* ⌂ *Reservations essential* ▤ *AE, DC, MC, V* ✆ *Closed Tues., 2 wks July and Aug., and 4 wks Dec. and Jan. No dinner Mon.* Ⓥ *Arsenale.*

Dorsoduro

★ **$$$–$$$$** ✕ **Ai Gondolieri.** If you're somewhat sick of fish, this is the place to come, as meat and food of the mainland are menu mainstays. Despite the tourist-trap name, it's a favorite with Venetians. Feast on *filetto di maiale con castraure* (pork fillet with baby artichokes), duck breast with apple and sweet onion, or more traditional dishes from the Veneto hills such as horse meat and game, gnocchi, and polenta. The wine list is above average in quality and variety. ⊠ *Fondamenta dell'Ospedaletto, Dorsoduro 366* ☎ *041/5286396* ▤ *AE, DC, MC, V* ✆ *Closed Tues. No lunch July and Aug.* Ⓥ *Accademia.*

★ **$$** ✕ **La Bitta.** The decor is more discreet, the dining hours longer, and the service friendlier and more efficient here than in many small restaurants in Venice—and the creative nonfish menu is a temptation at every course. You can start with a light salad of Treviso radicchio and crispy bacon, followed by smoked-beef carpaccio or *gnocchetti ubriachi al Montasio* (small marinated gnocchi with Montasio cheese). Then choose from secondi such as lamb chops with thyme, *anatra in pevarada* (duck in a pepper sauce), or Irish Angus fillet steak. Secondi are served with vegetables, which helps bring down the price. The restaurant is open only for dinner, but serves much later than most, continuously from 6:30 to 11. ⊠ *Calle Lunga San Barnaba Dorsoduro 2753/A* ☎ *041/5230531* ▤ *No credit cards* ✆ *No lunch. Closed Sun.* Ⓥ *Ca' Rezzonico.*

$ ✕ **Ai 4 Feri.** The paper tablecloths and cozy, laid-back ambience are all part of this small restaurant's charm. The menu varies according to what's fresh that day; imaginative combinations of ingredients in the *primi* (first courses)—herring and sweet peppers, salmon and radicchio, giant shrimp and broccoli (with pumpkin gnocchi)—are the norm. A meal here followed by after-dinner drinks at Campo Santa Margherita, a five-minute walk away, makes for a lovely evening. The kitchen closes early on weekdays. ⊠ *Calle Lunga San Barnaba, Dorsoduro 2754/a* ☎ *041/5206978* ▤ *No credit cards* ✆ *Closed Sun. and June* Ⓥ *Ca' Rezzonico.*

San Marco

$$$$ ✕ **Al Graspo de Ua.** Opened in the 19th century as a small osteria, the "Bunch of Grapes" became the meeting place of artists and movie stars back in the 1960s. Today it serves a faithful clientele of wealthy Italians. The decor is a miscellany of plants, sculpture, candlelight, and paintings set against brick and white-stucco walls. The owner, Lucio Zanon, speaks fluent English and will introduce you to a wide-ranging menu of fresh pastas, seasonal risottos, and meat and seafood. A treat in late spring is the thick white asparagus from Bassano, which, with a couple of fried eggs, is eaten as a main course. Desserts are all homemade. ⊠ *Calle dei Bombaseri, San Marco 5094* ☎ *041/5223647* ▤ *AE, DC, MC, V* ✆ *Closed Mon. and 1 wk in Jan.* Ⓥ *Rialto.*

Where to Stay & Eat in Venice

¢ ✕ **Enoteca al Volto.** Just steps away from the Rialto Bridge, this bar has been around since 1936; the fine cicheti and primi have a lot to do with its staying power. Two small, dark rooms with wooden tables and chairs provide the backdrop to the enjoyment of simple fare. The place prides itself on its considerable wine list of both Italian and foreign vintages; if you stick to the *panini* (sandwiches) and a cicheto or two, you'll eat very well for very little. If you opt for one of the primi of the day, the price category goes up a notch. ⊠ *Calle Cavalli, San Marco 4081* ☎ *041/5228945* ▭ *No credit cards* ⊙ *Closed Sun.* Ⓥ *Rialto.*

San Polo

★ $$$$ ✕ **Osteria da Fiore.** Tucked away on a little calle off the top of Campo San Polo, Da Fiore is a favorite among high-end diners for its superbly prepared Venetian cuisine and refined yet relaxed atmosphere. A superlative seafood lunch or dinner here might include delicate hors d'oeuvres of moeche, scallops, and tiny octopus, followed by a succulent risotto or pasta *con scampi e radicchio* (with shrimp and radicchio), and a perfectly cooked main course of *rombo* (turbot) or *tagliata di tonno* (tuna steak). ⊠ *Calle del Scaleter, San Polo 2202* ☎ *041/721308* ⌁ *Reservations essential* ▭ *AE, DC, MC, V* ⊙ *Closed Sun. and Mon., Aug., and Dec. 24–Jan. 15* Ⓥ *San Silvestro/San Stae.*

$–$$ ✕ **Alla Madonna.** It's true that many hotels in town send their guests here, and that sometimes there are more foreigners present than locals, but for quality and price this osteria is hard to beat. In short, it's a rare Venetian bargain. The ubiquitous copper pots line the ceilings, walls are covered with paintings and prints, and bow-tied waiters in white jackets rush among tables delivering plates filled with hefty portions. The *granseola* (crab) is particularly winning here; make sure to ask for some extra-virgin olive oil. If possible, try to save room for the tiramisu. ⊠ *Calle della Madonna, San Polo 594* ☎ *041/5223824* ▭ *AE, MC, V* ⊙ *Closed Wed. and part of Aug.* Ⓥ *Rialto/San Silvestro.*

Santa Croce

$$–$$$ ✕ **Vecio Fritolin.** Until not so long ago, fish was fried and sold "to go" throughout Venice just as in London, except that it was paired with polenta rather than chips. A sign advertising fish to go still hangs outside the "Old Fry Shop," but nowadays you can only dine in. A second sign, announcing cicheti available to go, still holds true. At this tidy bacaro *con cucina* you can have a traditional meal featuring such dishes as bigoli in salsa, baked fish with herbs, and non-Venetian lamb chops. ⊠ *Calle della Regina, Santa Croce 2262* ☎ *041/5222881* ▭ *AE, DC, MC, V* ⊙ *Closed Mon., 2 wks in Jan., and 2 wks in Aug. No lunch Tues.* Ⓥ *San Stae.*

$–$$ ✕ **La Zucca.** The simple place settings, latticed-wood walls, a canal window, and mélange of languages make this place feel as much like a typical vegetarian restaurant as you could expect to find in Venice. Though the menu does have superb meat dishes such as the *piccata di pollo ai caperi e limone con riso* (sliced chicken with capers and lemon served with rice), more attention is paid to dishes from the garden: try the *radicchio di Treviso con funghi e scaglie di Montasio* (Treviso radicchio with mushrooms and shavings of Montasio cheese) or the *finocchi piccanti* *con olive* (fennel in a spicy tomato-olive sauce). ⊠ *Calle del Tintor, Santa Croce 1762* ☎ *041/5241570* ⌕ *Reservations essential* ⊟ *AE, DC, MC, V* ⊙ *Closed Sun., 1 wk in Aug.* Ⓥ *San Stae.*

$ ✕ **Bancogiro.** Come to this casual spot for a change from standard Venetian food. Yes, fish is on the menu, but offerings such as mousse *di gamberoni con salsa di avocado* (shrimp mousse with an avocado sauce) and Sicilian-style *sarde incinte* (stuffed, or "pregnant," sardines) are far from typical fare. The wine list and cheese plate are both divine. The location is in the heart of the Rialto market in a 15th-century *loggia*. There are tables upstairs in a carefully restored, no-smoking room with a partial view of the Grand Canal; when it's warm you can sit outdoors and get the full canal view. ⊠ *Campo San Giacometto, Santa Croce 122 (under the porch)* ☎ *041/5232061* ⊟ *No credit cards* ⊙ *Closed Mon. No dinner Sun.* Ⓥ *Rialto.*

FodorśChoice
★

¢–$ ✕ **Al Prosecco.** Locals stream into this place, order the "spritzer bitter" (a combination of white wine, Campari, and seltzer water), and continue on their way. Or they linger over a glass of one of the numerous wines on offer, perhaps also tucking into a tasty panino, such as the *porchetta romane verdure* (roasted pig, Roman style, with greens). Proprietors Davide and Stefano preside over a young and friendly staff who reel off the day's specials with ease. There are a few tables in the enticing back room, and when the weather's warm you can eat outside on the beautiful campo. ⊠ *Campo S. Giacomo da l'Orlo, Santa Croce 1503* ☎ *041/5240222* ⊟ *No credit cards* ⊙ *Closed Sun.* Ⓥ *San Stae.*

WHERE TO STAY

Most of Venice's hotels are in renovated palaces, but space is at a premium—and comes for a price—with all Venice lodging. The most exclusive hotels are indeed palatial, although even they may have some small, dowdy rooms. In lower price categories rooms may be cramped, and not all hotels have lounge areas. Because of preservation laws, some hotels are not allowed to have elevators. Air-conditioning can be essential if you suffer in summer heat; some hotels charge a supplement for it. Although the city has no cars, it does have boats plying the canals and pedestrians chattering in the streets, even late at night, so ask for a quiet room if noise bothers you. In summer don't leave your room lights on at night *and* your window wide open: mosquitoes can descend en masse. If you find that these creatures are a problem, ask at your hotel's desk for a Vape, a plug-in antimosquito device.

It is *essential* to know how to get to your hotel when you arrive, as transport can range from arriving in a very expensive water taxi or gondola to wandering alleys and side streets—luggage in hand—with relapses of déjà vu. Many hotels accept reservations online; the handy Web site ⊕ www.veniceinfo.it offers free information (with photographs) about most hotels in town. It's advisable to book well in advance. If you don't have reservations, try **Venezia Sì** (☎ 800/843006 toll-free in Italy Mon.–Sat. 9–7, 0039/0415222264 from abroad 🖷 0039/0415221242 from abroad), which offers a free reservation service over the phone. It's the public relations arm of **AVA** (Venetian Hoteliers Association) and has booths where you can make same-day reservations at **Piazzale Roma** (☎ 041/5231397 ⊘ Daily 9 AM–10 PM), **Santa Lucia train station** (☎ 041/715288 or 041/715016 ⊘ Daily 8 AM–9 PM), and **Marco Polo Airport** (☎ 041/5415133 ⊘ Daily 9 AM–10 PM).

Prices

Venetian hotels cater to all tastes and come in all price ranges. Rates are about 20% higher than in Rome and Milan, but can be reduced by as much as half off-season (November–March, excluding Christmas and Carnevale, and also to some degree in August).

WHAT IT COSTS In euros					
	$$$$	**$$$**	**$$**	**$**	**¢**
FOR 2 PEOPLE	over €290	€210–€290	€140–€210	€80–€140	under €80

Prices are for two people in a standard double room in high season.

Cannaregio

★ **$$** 🏨 **Hotel Antico Doge.** If you're looking for a small, intimate hotel in a quiet yet central location, look no farther. This delightful palazzo was once home to Doge Marino Falier. It has been completely modernized in elegant Venetian style, with a wealth of textiles and some fine original furnishings. Some rooms have *baldacchini* (canopied beds) and views; all have fabric walls and hardwood floors. Situated on a small canal and only minutes away from San Marco and the Rialto Bridge, this is an oasis of tranquillity. An ample buffet breakfast is served in a room with a frescoed ceiling and a Murano chandelier. ⊠ *Campo SS. Apostoli, Cannaregio 5643, 30131* ☎ *041/2411570* 🖷 *041/2443660* ⊕ *www.anticodoge.com* 🛏 *13 rooms, 2 suites* 🔧 *In-room safes, minibars, cable TV, bar, Internet* 🗏 *AE, DC, MC, V* ⴶ❘ *BP* Ⅴ *Ca' D'oro.*

$ 🏨 **Bernardi Semenzato.** This is a particularly inviting little place just off Strada Nova and near the gondola ferry to the Rialto market. Some rooms have exposed ceiling beams, and some have rooftop or garden views. All rooms are very basic, but those in the nearby *dipendenza* (annex) are larger with newer amenities. ⊠ *Calle dell'Oca, Cannaregio 4366, 30121* ☎ *041/5211052* 🖷 *041/5222424* ⊕ *www.hotelbernardi.com* 🛏 *24 rooms, 14 with bath* 🔧 *Cable TV, some pets allowed, no-smoking rooms* 🗏 *AE, MC, V* ⊘ *Closed Jan. and 2 wks Nov. and Dec.* ⴶ❘ *BP* Ⅴ *Ca' d'Oro.*

Castello

$$$$ 🏨 **Danieli.** You'll feel like a doge in Venice's largest luxury hotel, a complex of newer buildings and a 14th-century palazzo. Sumptuous Venetian decor prevails from the moment you set foot in the soaring atrium with its sweeping staircase. Long favored by world leaders and movie stars, it's predictably expensive and very elegant. The rooftop terrace restaurant has a heavenly view but unexceptional food. May through October, you have access to the pool, tennis courts, and beach of the Hotel Excelsior on the Lido via a private (free) launch running on the hour. ⊠ *Riva degli Schiavoni, Castello 4196, 30122* ☏ *041/5226480, 041/2961222 reservations in English* 🖷 *041/5200208* ⊕ *www. luxurycollection.com/danieli* ➷ *221 rooms, 12 suites* ♧ *Restaurant, room service, in-room data ports, in-room safes, minibars, cable TV, bar, babysitting, dry cleaning, laundry service, concierge, Internet, business services, meeting rooms, some pets allowed, no-smoking rooms* ▭ *AE, DC, MC, V* ⭐ *EP* Ⓥ *San Zaccaria.*

$$$$ 🏨 **Hotel Londra Palace.** A wall of windows overlooking the lagoon and the island of San Giorgio makes this the hotel of choice for soaking up that extraordinary lagoon view—sweeping all the way from the Salute to the Lido. The downstairs restaurant is all glass, light, and water views, and 34 rooms offer the same spectacle. The view must have been pleasing to Tchaikovsky, who wrote his 4th Symphony here in 1877. Neoclassical public rooms, with splashes of blue-and-green glass suggesting the sea, play nicely off guest rooms, which have fine fabric, damask drapes, Biedermeier furniture, and Venetian glass. A change in management in 2003 has brought a breath of fresh air to the place; the staff is top-notch, as are the restaurant and bar. ⊠ *Riva degli Schiavoni, Castello 4171, 30122* ☏ *041/5200533* 🖷 *041/5225032* ⊕ *www.hotelondra.it* ➷ *36 rooms, 17 suites* ♧ *Restaurant, room service, in-room data ports, in-room fax, in-room safes, minibars, cable TV, piano bar, wine bar, babysitting, dry cleaning, laundry service, concierge, Internet, business services, meeting room* ▭ *AE, DC, MC, V* ⭐ *BP* Ⓥ *San Zaccaria.*

★ **$$$–$$$$** 🏨 **Savoia e Jolanda.** Here you'll get the best deal from among the high-end hotels along this fabulous waterfront. Fifteen of the guest rooms open directly onto the splendid lagoon panorama, and all are decorated with sumptuous tapestries, fine fabric curtains, and Murano glass chandeliers; they have high ceilings—some are coffered—and many get a great deal of light. There's a copious buffet breakfast, and the restaurant stays open all day. ⊠ *Riva degli Schiavoni, Castello 4187, 30122* ☏ *041/5206644* 🖷 *041/5207494* ⊕ *www.hotelsavoiajolanda.com* ➷ *36 rooms, 15 suites* ♧ *Restaurant, room service, in-room data ports, in-room safes, some in-room hot tubs, minibars, cable TV, bar, babysitting, dry cleaning, laundry service, concierge, Internet, some pets allowed, no-smoking rooms* ▭ *AE, DC, MC, V* ⭐ *BP* Ⓥ *San Zaccaria.*

$$ 🏨 **Ca' Formenta.** You're in residential rather than tourist Venice here, but the front rooms still have a wonderful lagoon view. The simple building dates from the 15th century, but after a complete makeover it opened as a new hotel in 2003 with high-quality services, an elevator, and a canalside entrance for guests arriving by water taxi. The daily 15-minute stroll along the waterfront between Piazzo San Marco and this friendly gem of a hotel is through a genuinely "local" part of the city, with plenty of cafés and restaurants. One of the rear rooms has direct access to a pleasant rooftop terrace with tables. ⊠ *Via Garibaldi, Castello 1650, 30122* ☏ *041/5285494* 🖷 *041/5204633* ⊕ *www.hotelcaformenta.it* ➷ *14 rooms* ♧ *In-room data ports, in-room safes, minibars, cable TV, laundry service* ▭ *AE, DC, MC, V* ⭐ *BP* Ⓥ *Arsenale/Giardini.*

$–$$ 🏨 **La Residenza.** The word *residenza* in Italian suggests a good deal of aristocratic elegance, and this hotel, with more the feeling of a private noble mansion than a hotel, does not disappoint. The grand hall on the *piano nobile* (main floor) of this 15th-century building looks almost disproportionately opulent. Well-preserved 18th-century stuccowork adorns the ceilings and walls, along with precious oil paintings. Oriental carpets partially hide the beautiful Venetian terrazzo floor. The rooms are spacious—some with lordly views over the campo in front—and were all upgraded in late 2000, and stucco decorations and frescoes were carefully restored in 2003/04. ⊠ *Campo Bandiera e Moro, Castello 3608, 30122* ☎ *041/5285315* 🖷 *041/5238859* ⊕ *www.venicelaresidenza. com* 🛏 *14 rooms* ⚲ *In-room safes, minibars, lounge; no smoking* ▤ *MC, V* ⦿ *BP* Ⓥ *Arsenale.*

$ 🏠 **Santa Maria della Pietà.** There's more space—both public and private— in this *casa per ferie* (vacation house) than in many four-star hotels in Venice. It occupies two historic palaces and was opened as new by the owners (a nonreligious charitable society) in 1999. Completely restored with Venetian terrazzo floors throughout, it has big windows and a huge rooftop terrace with coffee shop, bar, and unobstructed lagoon views. On top of all this, it is excellently situated—just 100 yards from the main waterfront and about 10 minutes' walk from St. Mark's—meaning you'll have to book early to stay here. The spartan rooms have only beds and wardrobes, but the shared bathrooms are plentiful, spacious, and scrupulously clean. Some family rooms with up to six beds are available. ⊠ *Calle della Pietà, Castello 3701, 30122* ☎ *041/2443639* 🖷 *041/ 2411561* 🛏 *15 rooms* ⚲ *Coffee shop, bar, lounge; no room phones, no room TVs* ▤ *No credit cards* ⦿ *BP* Ⓥ *San Zaccaria/Arsenale.*

Dorsoduro

$$$$ 🏠 **Ca' Pisani.** Here's a breath of fresh air: a Venetian hotel with no brocades and chandeliers to be found. Instead there's a tasteful mix of modern design and well-chosen antique pieces. The entrance hall has marble floors and an interesting play of colors and lights; the rooms contain original art deco pieces from the '30s and '40s (every bed is different). The no-smoking wine bar La Rivista serves light meals all day, and upstairs are a Turkish bath and a wooden rooftop terrace where you can take the sun. ⊠ *Rio Terà Antonio Foscarini, Dorsoduro 979/a, 30123* ☎ *041/2401411* 🖷 *041/2771061* ⊕ *www.capisanihotel.it* 🛏 *25 rooms, 4 suites* ⚲ *Restaurant, room service, in-room data ports, in-room safes, minibars, cable TV with movies, Turkish bath, wine bar, dry cleaning, laundry service, concierge, Internet, some pets allowed, no-smoking floor* ▤ *AE, DC, MC, V* ⦿ *BP* Ⓥ *Accademia.*

★ $$$–$$$$ 🏠 **American.** It's hard to pick out this quiet, family-run hotel from the houses along the fondamenta: there are no lights, flags, or large signs on the yellow stucco facade. A hall decorated with reproduction antiques and Oriental rugs leads to a breakfast room reminiscent of a theater foyer, with red velvet chairs and gilt wall lamps. A 2002 overhaul has made the place sparkle, though the four-story building still has no elevator. Rooms are spacious and tastefully furnished in sage-green and delicate pink fabrics, with lacquered Venetian-style furniture throughout. Some front rooms have terraces with canal views. ⊠ *San Vio, Dorsoduro 628, 30123* ☎ *041/5204733* 🖷 *041/5204048* ⊕ *www.hotelamerican.com* 🛏 *28 rooms, 2 suites* ⚲ *In-room data ports, in-room safes, minibars,* *cable TV, babysitting, Internet, no-smoking rooms* ⊟ *AE, DC, MC, V* ⫼⊙⫼ *BP* Ⓥ *Accademia.*

$$$ ⊞ **Hotel Pausania.** From the moment you ascend the grand staircase rising above the fountain of this 14th-century palazzo, you sense the combination of good taste and modern comforts that characterizes Hotel Pausania. Light-colored rooms are spacious, with comfortable furniture and carpets with rugs thrown over them. Some rooms face the small canal (which can become a bit noisy early in the morning) in front of the hotel, whereas others look out over the large garden courtyard. ⊠ *Fondamenta Gherardini, Dorsoduro 2824, 30123* ☎ *041/5222083* 🖷 *041/5222989* ⊕ *www.hotelpausania.it* ⟿ *26 rooms* ⚭ *Minibars, cable TV, bar, babysitting, dry cleaning, concierge, some pets allowed* ⊟ *AE, MC, V* ⫼⊙⫼ *BP* Ⓥ *Ca' Rezzonico.*

$$–$$$ ⊞ **Pensione Accademia Villa Maravege.** A secret garden awaits just beyond an iron gate, complete with a mini Palladian-style villa, flower beds, stone cupids, and verdant trees—all rarities in Venice. Aptly nicknamed "Villa of the Wonders," this patrician retreat once served as the Russian embassy and was the residence of Katharine Hepburn in the movie *Summertime*. Conservative rooms are outfitted with Victorian-era antiques and fine tapestry. The location is on a promontory where two side canals converge with the Grand Canal, which can be seen from the garden. Book well in advance. ⊠ *Fondamenta Bollani, Dorsoduro 1058, 30123* ☎ *041/5210188* 🖷 *041/5239152* ⊕ *www.pensioneaccademia. it* ⟿ *27 rooms* ⚭ *In-room safes, minibars, cable TV, bar, babysitting, dry cleaning, laundry service* ⊟ *AE, DC, MC, V* ⫼⊙⫼ *BP* Ⓥ *Accademia.*

Fodor'sChoice
★

$$ ⊞ **Agli Alboretti.** The Alboretti is one of the many hotels clustered at the foot of the Ponte dell'Accademia. Its unpretentious, rather small rooms are blessed with plenty of light. Their nautical decor, with original pieces taken from old ships' cabins, goes well with the cries of seagulls living along the nearby Giudecca Canal. The newly installed elevator is a welcome addition. In warm weather, breakfast is served in an inner courtyard under a rose bower; a small terrace with potted plants is open during the warmer months. ⊠ *Rio Terrà Foscarini, Dorsoduro 884, 30123* ☎ *041/5230058* 🖷 *041/5210158* ⊕ *www.aglialboretti.com* ⟿ *20 rooms* ⚭ *Restaurant, in-room data ports, cable TV, bar, dry cleaning, laundry service, concierge, some pets allowed, no-smoking rooms* ⊟ *AE, DC, MC, V* ⫼⊙⫼ *BP* Ⓥ *Accademia.*

★ **$–$$** ⊞ **La Calcina.** The Calcina sits in an enviable position along the sunny Zattere, with views across the wide Giudecca Canal. You can sunbathe on the *altana* (wooden roof terrace) or enjoy an afternoon tea in one of the reading corners of the shadowy, intimate hall with flickering candlelight and barely perceptible classical music. A stone staircase (no elevator) leads to the rooms upstairs, with parquet floors, original art deco furniture and lamps, and firm beds. The Piscina bar and restaurant offers drinks and freshly made snacks or full meals all day in the elegant dining room or on the wooden waterside terrace out front. ⊠ *Zattere, Dorsoduro 780, 30123* ☎ *041/5206466* 🖷 *041/ 5227045* ⊕ *www.lacalcina.com* ⟿ *29 rooms, 26 with bath, 5 suites* ⚭ *Restaurant, in-room safes; no room TVs* ⊟ *AE, DC, MC, V* ⫼⊙⫼ *BP* Ⓥ *Zattere.*

Giudecca

$$$$ 🏨 **Cipriani.** It's impossible to feel stressed in this oasis of stunning rooms and suites, some with garden patios. The hotel launch whisks you to Giudecca from San Marco and back at any hour; those dining at the exceptional Ristorante Harry Cipriani can use it as well. The restored 17th-century-style Palazzo Vendramin is the premium choice, with views across to Piazza San Marco, but the main hotel and Palazzetto, a modern annex facing the Canale della Giudecca, also offer extraordinary luxury. Prices are high even by Venetian standards, but this is the only place in town with such extensive facilities and services, from an Olympic-size pool and tennis courts to cooking courses, fitness programs, and even a vineyard. ⊠ *Giudecca 10, 30133* ☎ *041/5207744* 🖷 *041/5207745* ⊕ *www.hotelcipriani.it* ⮫ *54 rooms, 50 suites* ♨ *2 restaurants, room service, in-room safes, minibars, cable TV, tennis court, saltwater pool, health club, massage, sauna, spa, bar, babysitting, dry cleaning, laundry service, concierge, Internet, meeting room, no-smoking rooms* ▤ *AE, DC, MC, V* ⊘ *Main hotel closed Nov.–Mar.; Palazzo Vendramin closed 2–3 wks in Jan.* ⑩ *BP* Ⓥ *Zitelle.*

Lagoon

$$$$ 🏨 **San Clemente Palace.** If you prefer wide-open spaces to the intimacy of Venice, this is your hotel. It occupies an entire island, about 15 minutes from Piazza San Marco by (free) shuttle launch, with acres of parkland, a swimming pool, tennis courts, wellness center, and four restaurants. The 19th-century buildings are on the site of a 12th-century monastery, of which only the chapel remains. They form a large quadrangle and contain spacious, modern rooms. The view back to Venice with the Dolomites behind on a clear day is stunning. This brand new hotel (opened 2003), offers all the five-star comforts: it even has three holes of golf. ⊠ *Isola di San Clemente 1, San Marco, 30124* ☎ *041/2445001* 🖷 *041/2445800* ⊕ *www.sanclemente.thi.it* ⮫ *107 rooms, 96 suites* ♨ *Restaurants, coffee shop, in-room data ports, in-roof safes, minibars, cable TV, 3-hole golf course, tennis courts, pool, exercise equipment, health club, hair salon, hot tub, massage, sauna, spa, bars, shop, laundry service, convention center, meeting rooms, some pets allowed, no-smoking rooms* ▤ *AE, DC, MC, V* ⑩ *BP.*

Lido

$$–$$$$ 🏨 **Quattro Fontane.** This fine hotel in a well-maintained mansion run by Danish sisters Bente and Pia Bevilacqua offers the serenity of the Lido in a location that's a 15-minute walk and 20-minute boat ride from Piazza San Marco. Well-decorated rooms with period furniture and tasteful tapestries overlook the lush surrounding garden of mature trees and shrubs, with clearings for dining tables in summer. Common areas contain an odd collection of masons' aprons, pipes, ex-votos, masks from Jakarta, Roman seals, and seashells. A huge fireplace adds warmth and character in the colder months. After a full day you can relax in the library, stocked with books in many languages. ⊠ *Via delle Quattro Fontane 16, Lido, 30126* ☎ *041/5260227* 🖷 *041/5260726* ⊕ *www.*

quattrofontane.com ➥ *54 rooms, 4 apartments* ⚐ *Restaurant, in-room safes, minibars, cable TV, tennis court, bar, library, babysitting, dry cleaning, laundry service, meeting room* ▤ *AE, DC, MC, V* ⊘ *Closed Nov.–Mar.* ⦿| *BP* Ⓥ *Lido.*

San Marco

$$$$ ▦ **Gritti Palace.** Queen Elizabeth, Greta Garbo, and Winston Churchill all made this their Venetian address. The feeling of being in an aristocratic private home pervades this legendary hotel replete with fresh flowers, fine antiques, sumptuous appointments, and old-fashion service. The dining terrace on the Grand Canal is best enjoyed in the evening, when the boat traffic dies down. May through October, you have access to the pool, tennis courts, and beach of the Hotel Excelsior on the Lido via a private (free) launch. ⊠ *Campo Santa Maria del Giglio, San Marco 2467, 30124* ☎ *041/794611* ⊟ *041/5200942* ⊕ *www.luxurycollection.com* ➥ *87 rooms, 6 suites* ⚐ *Restaurant, room service, in-room data ports, in-room safes, minibars, cable TV with movies, bar, babysitting, dry cleaning, laundry service, concierge, Internet, business services, meeting rooms, some pets allowed, no-smoking rooms* ▤ *AE, DC, MC, V* ⦿| *BP* Ⓥ *Giglio.*

$$$$ ▦ **Il Palazzo at the Bauer.** Il Palazzo, under the same management as the larger Bauer Hotel, is the ultimate word in luxury. Bevilacqua and Rubelli fabrics cover the walls, and no two rooms are decorated the same. What they have in common, however, are high ceilings, Murano glass, marbled bathrooms, and damask drapes. Many have sweeping views. Breakfast is served on Venice's highest terrace, appropriately named il Settimo Cielo (Seventh Heaven). The outdoor hot tub, also on the 7th floor, offers views of La Serenissima that won't quit. ⊠ *Campo San Moisè, San Marco 1459, 30124* ☎ *041/5207022* ⊟ *041/5207557* ⊕ *www.bauervenezia.it* ➥ *35 rooms, 40 suites* ⚐ *Restaurant, room service, in-room data ports, in-room fax, in-room safes, some in-room hot tubs, minibars, cable TV with movies, golf privileges, health club, outdoor hot tub, massage, sauna, Turkish bath, dock, bar, babysitting, dry cleaning, laundry service, concierge, Internet, some pets allowed, no-smoking rooms* ▤ *AE, DC, MC, V* ⦿| *EP* Ⓥ *Vallaresso.*

★ $$$$ ▦ **Monaco & Grand Canal.** Major upgrading and expansion of this landmark canal-side hotel have resulted in a blend of Venetian elegance and contemporary design. The centerpiece of the restored original section is the convivial waterfront restaurant; many guest rooms share the same panoramic lagoon views. A big, bright reception area, created by roofing an inner courtyard with glass, leads to the new rear section, which was once the Sala del Ridotto, a luxurious gambling house. It's almost worth staying here just to spend time in the sumptuous lounge with adjoining bar. Rooms in both sections are in modern Italian style, with spacious bathrooms in a warm, beige marble. ⊠ *Calle Vallaresso, San Marco 1332, 30124* ☎ *041/5200211* ⊟ *041/5200501* ⊕ *www.hotelmonaco.it* ➥ *87 rooms, 12 suites* ⚐ *Two restaurants, room service, in-room data ports, in-room safes, some in-room hot tubs, minibars, cable TV, dock, bar, piano bar, babysitting, dry cleaning, laundry* *service, concierge, meeting rooms, some pets allowed, no-smoking rooms* = *AE, DC, MC, V* |O| *BP* V *Vallaresso.*

★ **$$–$$$** 🏠 **San Zulian.** A minimalist entrance hall leads to rooms that are a refined variation on the Venetian theme, with lacquered 18th-century-style furniture and parquet floors. Room 304 is on two levels and has its own delightful covered veranda. Two ground-floor rooms have bathrooms equipped for people with disabilities. The handy location near San Marco and the Rialto and the top-notch staff make a stay here eminently enjoyable. ⊠ *Campo della Guerra, San Marco 534/535, 30124* 🕾 *041/ 5225872 or 041/5226598* 🖷 *041/5232265* ⊕ *www.hotelsanzulian. com* 🛌 *25 rooms* ♿ *In-room safes, minibars, some pets allowed* = *AE, DC, MC, V* |O| *BP* V *Vallaresso / San Zaccaria.*

$ 🏠 **Albergo San Samuele.** Near the Grand Canal and Palazzo Grassi, this friendly hotel has clean, sunny rooms in surprisingly good shape for the price. Five of the bathrooms are relatively new, with white-and-gray-blue tiles, and the walls are painted in crisp, pleasant shades of pale pink or blue. Curtains and bedspreads are made from antique-looking fabrics, and although the furniture is of the boxy modern kind, the owners are gradually adding more interesting-looking pieces. ⊠ *Salizzada San Samuele, San Marco 3358, 30124* 🕾🖷 *041/5228045* 🛌 *10 rooms, 7 with bath* ♿ *Fans, some pets allowed, no-smoking rooms; no a/c, no room TVs* = *No credit cards* |O| *EP* V *San Samuele.*

San Polo

$$$ 🏠 **Sturion.** At the end of the 13th century this building housed foreign merchants selling their wares at the Rialto, and Carpaccio depicted it in his 1494 *Miracle of the Cross* (on view at the Accademia). Now it's decorated in 18th-century Venetian style and run with great care by a Venetian family. Rooms are done in red-and-gold brocade (two with views of the Grand Canal); there's also a small but inviting breakfast room. Two rooms comfortably sleep four and are perfect for families. All rooms have coffee- and tea-making facilities, an uncommon feature for Italy. Be warned that the stairs are steep here (the hotel is on the 4th and 5th floors), and there's no elevator. ⊠ *Calle del Sturion, San Polo 679, 30125* 🕾 *041/5236243* 🖷 *041/5228378* ⊕ *www.locandasturion. com* 🛌 *11 rooms* ♿ *In-room safes, minibars, Internet, some pets allowed, no-smoking rooms* = *AE, MC, V* |O| *BP* V *S. Silvestro/Rialto.*

NIGHTLIFE & THE ARTS

The Arts

A Guest in Venice, a monthly bilingual booklet free at most hotels, is your most accessible, up-to-date guide to Venice happenings. It also includes information about pharmacies, vaporetto and bus lines, and the main trains and flights. You can visit their Web site, ⊕ www. aguestinvenice.com, for a preview of musical, artistic, and sporting events. *Venezia News,* available at newsstands, has similar information but also includes in-depth articles about noteworthy events. The tourist office publishes *Leo* and *Bussola,* bimonthly brochures in Italian and English listing events and updated museum hours. *Venezia da Vivere* is a seasonal guide listing nightspots and live music. Several Venice Web sites allow you to scan the cultural horizon before you arrive; try ⊕ www.ombra.net, ⊕ www.veniceonline.it, and ⊕ www.venicebanana.com.

The **Biennale** cultural institution organizes events year-round, including the film festival, which begins the last week of August. The Biennale international exhibition of contemporary art is held in odd-numbered years, usually from mid-June to early November, at the Giardini della Biennale, and in the impressive Arsenale. Visit ⊕ www.labiennale.org for information. Last but not least, don't ignore the posters you see everywhere in the streets. They're often the most up-to-date information you can find.

Festivals

Carnevale (⊕ www.aguestinvenice.com) takes place on 10 (or more) days leading up to Ash Wednesday; if you're not planning on joining in the revelry, it's wise to choose another time to visit, as prices skyrocket and sightseeing becomes almost impossible. For information about the various costume balls and parties, try the related **Web site** (⊕ www.meetingeurope.com) or call the **Venice tourist office** (☎ 041/5298711).

The third weekend of July, the **Festa del Redentore** (Feast of the Redeemer) commemorates the end of a 16th-century plague that killed about 47,000 city residents. Just as doges have done annually for centuries, you too can make a pilgrimage across the temporary bridge connecting Zattere to the Giudecca. Venetians take to the water to watch fireworks at midnight, but if you can't find a boat the Giudecca is the best place to be. Young folks traditionally greet sunrise on the Lido beach while their elders attend church.

Music

Although there are occasional jazz and Italian pop concerts in clubs around town, the vast majority of music you'll hear is classical, with Venice's famed Vivaldi the composer frequently featured. A number of churches and palazzos regularly host concerts, as do the Ca' Rezzonico and Querini Stampalia museums. You'll find these events listed in publications such as *A Guest in Venice*; also try asking the tourist information office or your concierge. The **Vela Call Center** (☎ 041/2424 ☉ Daily 8–8) has information about musical events, and you can buy tickets at Vela sales offices in Piazzale Roma, Ferrovia, and Calle dei Fuseri (a 10-minute walk from San Marco). (When busy, the Vela Call Center number doesn't give a signal, but instead is silent.) The travel agency **Kele & Teo** (✉ Ponte dei Bareteri, San Marco 4930 ☎ 041/5208722) has tickets for a number of venues and is conveniently located midway between Rialto and San Marco.

Opera

Teatro La Fenice (✉ Campo San Fantin, San Marco ☎ 041/786511 ⊕ www.teatrolafenice.it), one of Italy's oldest opera houses, has witnessed many memorable premieres, including the 1853 first-night flop of Verdi's *La Traviata*. It's also had its share of disasters, the most recent being a terrible fire, deliberately set in January 1996. It has been completely restored, with opera scheduled to recommence in November 2004. Visit the Fenice Web site for a schedule of performances and to buy tickets.

Nightlife

Piazza San Marco is a popular meeting place in nice weather, when the cafés stay open late and all seem to be competing to offer the best live music. The younger crowd of Venetians and visitors tends to gravitate toward Rialto Bridge, with Campi San Bartolomeo and San Luca on one side and Campo Rialto Nuovo on the other. Especially popular with university students are Cannaregio's Fondamenta della Misericordia and the area around Campo Santa Margarita and San Pantalon.

Bars

L'Olandese Volante (⊠ Campo San Lio, near Rialto ☎ 041/5289349) is a popular hangout for many young Venetians. Nothing special by day, **Bar Torino** (⊠ Campo San Luca ☎ 041/5223914) is one of Venice's liveliest nightspots, open late and spilling out onto the campo in summer. **Bácaro Jazz** (⊠ Across from Rialto Post Office ☎ 041/5285249) has music and meals until 2 AM, and its gregarious staff is unlikely to let you feel lonely. The **Martini Scala Club** (⊠ Campo San Fantin, San Marco 1983 ☎ 041/5224121), the Antico Martini restaurant's elegant bar, has live music from 10 to 3:30. Full meals are served until 2. One of the original late-night Venetian nightspots, **Paradiso Perduto** (⊠ Fondamenta della Misericordia, Cannaregio 2540 ☎ 041/720581) serves up inexpensive fish dishes and sometimes has live music on weekends; it's closed on Tuesday and Wednesday.

Campo Santa Margarita is a student hangout all day and late into the night. Try **Margaret Duchamp** (⊠ Campo Santa Margarita, Dorsoduro 3019 ☎ 041/5286255) for reasonably priced snacks and drinks. The bohemian **Il Caffè** (⊠ Campo Santa Margarita, Dorsoduro 2963 ☎ 041/5287998), also known as Caffè Rosso for its red exterior, is especially popular in nice weather.

Casinos

The city-run gambling casino in the splendid **Palazzo Vendramin-Calergi** is a classic scene of well-dressed high-rollers playing French roulette, Caribbean poker, chemin de fer, 30–40, and slots. You must be 18 to enter, and men must wear jackets. ⊠ *Cannaregio 2040* ☎ *041/5297111* ◰ *€10 entry includes €10 in chips* ◷ *Slots 2:45 PM–2:30 AM; tables 3:30 PM–2:30 AM* **Ⓥ** *San Marcuola.*

Mestre's **Ca' Noghera** casino, near the airport, has slots, blackjack, craps, poker, and roulette. Minimum age is 18. There's a free shuttle bus from Piazzale Roma from 4:05 PM until closing. ⊠ *Via Triestina 222, Tessera, Mestre* ☎ *041/5297111* ◰ *€10 entry includes €10 in chips* ◷ *Slots 11 AM–3:30 AM; tables 3:30 PM–3:30 AM.*

Nightclubs

Just a vaporetto hop from Venice is **Discoteca Acropolis** (⊠ Lungomare Guglielmo Marconi 22, Lido ☎ 041/5260466). It's a trendy summer spot, open March–October, with disco, live performances, and a terrace bar.

An artistic blend of iron beams with silver candlesticks and old brick with white tablecloths has transformed a vintage refrigerated warehouse into casually sophisticated **Frigo** (⊠ Viale Ancona, 18 Mestre ☎ 041/5319293). Flashback to the old supper-club days, when diners got up and danced any time during their meal, as Frigo's DJ varies the music with the night's clientele. (The well-designed sound system means dancing and dinner conversation aren't mutually exclusive.) A menu from pizza to pepper steak is available from 7:30 PM to 1:30 AM, and though it's a five-minute taxi ride from Piazzale Roma (or buses 80 and N2 drop you within a 10-minute walk), your dining dollars go lots farther at the inland town of Mestre, where Frigo is located.

For dancing in Venice, try tiny **Piccolo Mondo** (⊠ Dorsoduro 1056/a ☎ 041/5200371), near the Accademia Galleries, which charges no cover and has disco until 4 AM.

SPORTS

Running

The most scenic running route (6–7 km [4–4½ mi] long) heads east from Piazza San Marco and skirts the lagoon along the Riva degli Schiavoni to the pine wood of Sant'Elena. You can return by way of the picturesque neighborhood of Castello and the island of San Pietro di Castello. This route can get packed with pedestrians from spring through fall, so if you don't want to run a slalom course, try Lido Beach or the area around Zattere.

Swimming

Those looking for a cooling break in summer should head for the **Lido** (Ⓥ S.M. Elizabetta). Large sections of the long, narrow beach are private, renting chairs and umbrellas, and offering toilets, showers, and restaurants. If your hotel has no beach rights, you can pay for entry. The free beach areas, with no facilities, are generally crowded unless you head south by bus toward Malamocca and Alberoni.

Venice's two public pools are open some hours for *nuoto libero* (free swim). Both close in July and August and charge €4.50 per visit. Though neither has lockers, receptionists will usually keep valuables for you. Venice's larger pool is the eight-lane, 26-meter **Piscina Comunale** (⊠ Island of Sacca Fisola, Giudecca ☎ 041/5285430 Ⓥ Sacca Fisola line 82). Four-lane, 25-meter **Piscina di Sant'Alvise** (⊠ Cannaregio 3161 ☎ 041/713567 Ⓥ Sant'Alvise) is in a building that was once the community laundry.

Tennis

Some hotels have access to tennis courts at private clubs; if you're looking to play, the first step is to check with your concierge. The **Lido Tennis Club** (⊠ Via Sandro Gallo 163, Lido ☎ 041/5260954) offers court time to nonmembers year-round. **Club Ca' del Moro** (⊠ Via F. Parri 6, Alberoni, Lido ☎ 041/770965) has courts available for nonmembers. The **Hotel des Bains** (✉ Lungomare Guglielmo Marconi 17, Lido ☎ 041/5265921) rents tennis courts to nonguests from March through November.

SHOPPING

In Venice there are plenty of elegant shops and boutiques representing famous brands and celebrity designers, but there is also a growing number of local artists and craftspeople selling high-quality jewelery, lamps, shoes, and pottery direct from their studios; look for them dotted around the San Polo and Santa Croce districts. Most Venetian paintings are just sophisticated postcards, but some interesting works can be found in galleries near La Fenice and Campo Santo Stefano.

It's always a good idea to mark the location of a shop that interests you on your map; otherwise you may not be able to find it again in the maze of tiny streets. Regular store hours are usually 9–12:30 and 3:30 or 4–7:30; some stores are closed on Saturday afternoon or Monday morning. Food shops are open 8–1 and 5–7:30, and are closed Wednesday afternoon and all day Sunday. Many tourist-oriented shops are open all day, every day. Some shops close for both a summer and a winter vacation.

Food Markets

The morning open-air fruit and vegetable market at **Rialto** offers animated local color and commerce. On Tuesday through Saturday mornings the **fish market** (adjacent to the Rialto produce market) provides an impressive lesson in ichthyology, with species you've probably never seen before. In the Castello district you'll find a lively food market weekday mornings on **Via Garibaldi.**

Shopping Districts

The **San Marco** area is full of shops and couture boutiques such as Armani, Missoni, Valentino, Fendi, and Versace. **Le Mercerie,** along with the Frezzeria and Calle dei Fabbri, leading from Piazza San Marco, are some of Venice's busiest shopping streets. Other good shopping areas surround Calle del Teatro and Campi San Salvador, Manin, San Fantin, and San Bartolomeo. Less-expensive shops are between the Rialto Bridge and San Polo.

Specialty Stores

Glassware
Glass, most of it made in Murano, is Venice's number one product, and you'll be confronted by mind-boggling displays of traditional and contemporary glassware, much of it kitsch. Take your time and be selective. You will probably find that prices in Venice's shops and the showrooms of Murano's factories are pretty much the same. However, because of competition, shops in Venice with wares from various glassworks may charge slightly less.

Domus (✉ Fondamenta dei Vetrai, Murano 82 ☎ 041/739215) has a selection of smaller objects and jewelry from the best glassworks. For chic, contemporary glassware, Carlo Moretti is a good choice; his designs are on display at **L'Isola** (✉ Campo San Moisè, San Marco 1468 ☎ 041/5231973). **Marina Barovier** (✉ Calle delle Botteghe, off Campo Santo Stefano, San Marco 3216 ☎ 041/5236748 ⊕ www.barovier.it) has an excellent selection of contemporary collectors' glass.

Go to Michel Paciello's **Paropàmiso** (✉ Frezzeria, San Marco 1701 ☎ 041/5227120) for stunning Venetian glass beads and traditional jewelry from all over the world. **Pauly** (✉ Piazza San Marco 73, 77, and 316; Ponte dei Consorzi ☎ 041/5209899) has four centrally located shops with an impressive selection of glassware at better prices than on Murano. **Venini** (✉ Piazzetta dei Leoncini 314, San Marco ☎ 041/5224045 ⊕ www.venini.com) has been an institution since the 1930s, attracting some of the foremost names in glass design.

Lace & Fabrics

Much of the lace and embroidered linen sold in Venice and on Burano is really made in China or Taiwan. However, at **Il Merletto** (✉ Sotoportego del Cavalletto, under the Procuratie Vecchie, Piazza San Marco 95 ☎ 041/5208406), you can ask for the authentic, handmade lace kept in the drawers behind the counter. This is the only place in Venice connected with the students of the Scuola del Merletto in Burano, who, officially, do not sell to the public. Hours of operation are 10–5. A top address for linen is **Jesurum** (✉ Procuratie Nuove, San Marco 60–61 ☎ 041/5229864 ✉ Merceria del Capitello, San Marco 4857 ☎ 041/5206177 ⊕ www.jesurum.it). Go to **Lorenzo Rubelli** (✉ Palazzo Corner Spinelli, San Marco 3877 ☎ 041/5236110 ⊕ www.rubelli.it) for the same brocades, damasks, and cut velvets used by the world's most prestigious decorators. **Venetia Studium** (✉ Calle Larga XXII Marzo, San Marco 2403 ☎ 041/5229281 ✉ Calle Larga XXII Marzo, San Marco 723 ☎ 041/5229859 ⊕ www.venetiastudium.com) sells silk scarves, bags, and cushion covers, as well as the famous Fortuny lamps.

Lamps

The studio **A Mano** (✉ Rio Terà, San Polo 2616 ☎ 041/715742), near the Frari, is worth hunting down. Alessandro Savadori makes imaginative table, wall, and ceiling lamps that may well cross the boundary from craft into art.

Masks

Mondonovo (✉ Rio Terà Canal, Dorsoduro 3063 ☎ 041/5287344) is a cut above most of Venice's many mask stores.

Shoes

Fine shoes and boots are handmade to order at **Daniela Ghezzo, Segalin a Venezia** (✉ Calle dei Fuseri San Marco 4365 ☎ 041/5222115), operated by one of the world's few female shoemakers.

CloseUp

VENETIAN MASKS REVEALED

N THE TIME OF THE REPUBLIC, *the mask trade was vibrant—Venetians wore masks all year to go about town incognito. Napoléon suppressed their use, a by-product of his effort to end Carnevale, and when Carnevale was revived in the late 1970s, mask making returned as well. Though many workshops use centuries-old techniques, none have been in business for more than 30 years.*

A landmark date in the history of Venetian masks is 1436, when the mascareri (mask makers) founded their guild, but masks were popular well before then. Laws regulating their use appeared as early as 1268, intended to prevent wearers from carrying weapons and masked men disguised as women from entering convents to seduce nuns.

In the 18th century, masks started being used by actors playing the traditional roles of the commedia dell'arte. Inexpensive papier-mâché versions of these masks can be found everywhere. The character Arlecchino has the round face and surprised expression, Pantalone is the one with the curved nose and long mustache, and Pulcinella has the protruding nose.

The least expensive mask is the white Bauta, smooth and plain with a short, pointed nose intended to disguise the wearer's voice; in the 18th century it was commonly accompanied by a black three-cornered hat and a black cloak. The pretty Gnaga, which resembles a cat's face, was used by gay men to "meow" proposals to good-looking boys. The basic Moretta is a black oval with eyeholes. The Medico della Peste (the Plague Doctor) has a beaklike nose and glasses; during the plague of 1630 and 1631, doctors wore masks with herbs inside the nose intended to filter infected air and glasses to protect the eyes.

VENICE A TO Z

To research prices, get advice from other travelers, and book travel arrangements, visit www.fodors.com.

AIRPORTS & TRANSFERS

Venice's Aeroporto Marco Polo is served by domestic and international flights, including connections from 21 European cities, plus direct flights from Moscow and New York's JFK. In addition, Treviso Airport, some 20 mi (32 km) north of Venice, receives daily arrivals from London's Stansted Airport.

A shuttle bus or 10-minute walk takes you from Marco Polo's terminal to a dock where public and private boats are available to deliver you direct to Venice's historic center. For €10 per person, including bags, Alilaguna operates regularly scheduled service from predawn until nearly midnight. It takes about an hour to reach the landing near Piazza San Marco, stopping at the Lido on the way. A *motoscafo* (water taxi) carries up to four people and four bags to the city center in a sleek, modern powerboat. The base cost is €80, and the trip takes about 25 minutes. Each additional person, bag, and stop costs extra, so it's essential to agree on a fare before boarding.

Blue ATVO buses take 20 minutes to make the nonstop trip from airport to Piazzale Roma; from here you can get a vaporetto to the landing nearest your hotel. The ATVO fare is €3, and tickets are available on the bus when the airport ticket booth (open 9–7:30) is closed. Orange ACTV local buses (Line 5) leave for Venice at 10 and 40 minutes past every hour (hourly service after 11:10 PM) and take 30 minutes; before boarding, you must buy a €1 ticket at the airport tobacconist-newsstand, open 6:30 AM–9 PM, or from the ATVO/ACTV booth in the arrivals hall on the ground floor. During rush hour, luggage can be a hassle on the local bus. A land taxi from the airport to Piazzale Roma costs about €40.

🚩 Airport Information **Aeroporto Marco Polo** ✉ Tessera, 10 km (6 mi) north of the city on the mainland ☎ 041/2609260 ⊕ www.veniceairport.it.

🚩 Taxis & Shuttles **Alilaguna** ☎ 041/5235775. **ATVO** ☎ 041/929500. **Motoscafo** ☎ 041/5222303 airport transfers. **Radio Taxi** ☎ 041/936222.

BOAT & FERRY TRAVEL

BY GONDOLA · It's hard to believe that Venice could get any more beautiful, but as your gondola glides away from the fondamenta, a magical transformation takes place—you've left the huddled masses behind to marvel at the city as visitors have for centuries before you. To some it feels like a Disney ride, and some complain about flotsam, jetsam, and less than pleasant odors, but if you insist that your gondolier take you winding through the tiny side canals, you'll get out of the city's main salon and into her intimate chambers, where only private boats can go. San Marco is loaded with gondola stations, but to get off the circuit, and maybe even have a canal to yourself, try the San Tomà or Santa Sofia (near Ca' d'Oro) stations. The price of a 50-minute ride is supposed to be fixed at €62 for up to six passengers, rising to €77.50 between 8 PM and 8 AM, but these are minimums and you may have difficulty finding a gondolier who will work for that unless the city is empty. Bargaining can help, but in any case come to terms on cost and duration before you start, and make it clear that you want to see more than just the Grand Canal.

BY MOTOSCAFO · Water taxis aren't cheap; you'll spend about €50 for a short trip in town, €60 to the Lido, and €80 per hour to visit the outer islands. The fare system is convoluted, with luggage handling, waiting time, early or late hours, and even ordering a taxi from your hotel adding expense. Always agree on the price first.

BY TRAGHETTO · Few tourists know about the two-man gondola ferries that cross the Grand Canal at various fixed points. At €.40, they're the cheapest and shortest gondola ride in Venice, and they can save a lot of walking. Look for TRAGHETTO signs and hand your fare to the gondolier when you board.

BY VAPORETTO · ACTV water buses serve several routes daily and after 11 PM provide limited service through the night. Some routes cover the length of the Grand Canal, and others circle the city and connect Venice with the lagoon islands. Landing stages are clearly marked with name and line number, but check before boarding to make sure the boat is going in your direction.

Line 1 is the Grand Canal local, calling at every stop and continuing via San Marco to the Lido. The trip takes about 35 minutes from Ferrovia to Vallaresso, San Marco. Circular Line 41 (the odd number indicates it goes counterclockwise) will take you from San Zaccaria to Murano, and Line 42 (clockwise) makes the return trip. Likewise, take Line 42 from San Zaccaria to Giudecca's Redentore, but Line 41 to return. Line 51 (counterclockwise) runs from the station to San Zaccaria via Piazzale Roma, then continues to the Lido. From the Lido, Line 52 circles clockwise, stopping at San Zaccaria, Zattere, Piazzale Roma, the station, Fondamente Nuove (connect to northern lagoon islands), San Pietro di Castello, and back to the Lido. From San Zaccaria, Line 82 (same number both directions) loops past Giudecca and Zattere, then stops at Tronchetto (parking garage) on the way to Piazzale Roma and the station. From the station, Line 82 becomes the Grand Canal express to Rialto, with some boats continuing to Vallaresso (San Marco) and in summer going all the way to the Lido beaches. Line N runs from roughly midnight to 6 AM, stopping at the Lido, Vallaresso, Accademia, Rialto, the train station, Piazzale Roma, Giudecca, and San Zaccaria, then returning in the opposite direction.

FARES & SCHEDULES An ACTV water bus ticket for all lines except the Grand Canal costs €3.50, or €6 round-trip (valid for 24 hours); a single ride on the Grand Canal line costs €5. (Children under four ride free.) Another option is Travel Cards: €10.50 buys 24 hours and €22 buys 72 hours of unlimited travel on ACTV boats and buses. A shuttle ticket allows you to cross a canal, one stop only, for €1.80

Line information is posted at each landing, and complete timetables for all lines are available for €.50 at ACTV/Vela ticket booths, located at most major stops. Buy tickets before getting on the boat and remember to validate them in the yellow time-stamp machines. Tickets are also sold on the boat; you must ask to buy one immediately upon boarding, which can be a hassle. When inspectors come aboard, ticketless riders are fined, as are those who didn't validate tickets. Ignorance will not spare you; the fine is €23, and getting fined can be embarrassing. The law says you must also buy tickets for dogs, baby strollers left unfolded, and bags over 28 inches long (there's no charge for your bag if you have a Travel Card), but this is generally enforced only for very bulky bags. The telephone number for ferry information listed below is poorly manned and offers only a disconcerting silence when busy. It's probably easier to ask one of the ticket-office staff for information (most speak English).

🚢 **Boat & Ferry Information** **ACTV** ☎ 041/2424 ⊕ www.actv.it; www.velaspa.com. **Water taxi** ☎ 041/723112 or 041/5222303.

BUS TRAVEL TO & FROM VENICE
From Venice's Piazzale Roma terminal, buses connect with Mestre, the Brenta Riviera, Padua, Treviso, Cortina d'Ampezzo, and other regional destinations as well as many major European cities.

FARES & SCHEDULES ACTV buses to Mestre (€1) are frequent, and there's night service; ACTV buses to Padua (€3.30) leave at 25 and 55 minutes past each hour and stop along the Brenta River. ATVO has daily buses to Cortina (€10.40) June–September and throughout the Christmas–New Year holidays. Buses leave Venice at 7:50 AM and depart from Cortina at 3:15 PM. Service is available only on weekends September–May.

🚌 Bus Information **ACTV** ☎ 041/2424. **ATVO** ☎ 041/5205530 ⊕ www.atvo.it. **Bus Terminal** ✉ Piazzale Roma, across the Grand Canal from the train station, Santa Croce.

CAR RENTAL

🚗 Local Agencies **Avis** ✉ Piazzale Roma, Santa Croce ☎ 041/5225825 ✉ Aeroporto Marco Polo ☎ 041/5415030 ⊕ www.avis.com. **Easy Car** ✉ Aeroporto Marco Polo ☎ 041/5416557 ⊕ www.easycarspa.com. **Hertz** ✉ Piazzale Roma, Santa Croce ☎ 041/5284091 ✉ Aeroporto Marco Polo ☎ 041/5416075 ⊕ www.hertz.com. **Sixt Rent-a-Car** ✉ Aeroporto Marco Polo ☎ 041/5415032 ⊕ www.sixt.com.

CAR TRAVEL

Venice is on the east–west A4 autostrada, which connects with Padua, Verona, Brescia, Milan, and Turin. If you bring a car to Venice, you will have to pay for a garage or parking space. Warning: don't be waylaid by illegal touts, often wearing fake uniforms, who may try to flag you down and offer to arrange parking and hotels; drive directly to one of the parking garages and do not leave valuables in the car. There's a luggage-check office, open daily 6 AM–9 PM, next to the Pullman Bar on the ground floor of the municipal garage at Piazzale Roma. You can take your car to the Lido; the car ferry (Line 17) makes the half-hour trip about every 50 minutes from a landing at Tronchetto, but in summer there can be long lines. It costs €8.78–18.08, depending on the size of the car.

PARKING Parking at Autorimessa Comunale costs €19 for 24 hours. The private Garage San Marco costs €19 for up to 12 hours and €26 for 12–24 hours plus a €1 supplement Sunday, nights, and holidays. You can reserve a space in advance at either of these garages; you'll come upon both immediately after crossing the bridge from the mainland. Another alternative is Tronchetto parking (€18 for 1–24 hours); watch for signs for it coming over the bridge—you'll have to turn right before you get to Piazzale Roma. Many hotels have negotiated guest discounts with San Marco or Tronchetto garages; get a voucher when you check in at your hotel and present it when you pay the garage. Line 82 connects Tronchetto with Piazzale Roma and Piazza San Marco and also goes to the Lido in summer. When there's thick fog or extreme tides, a bus runs to Piazzale Roma instead. Avoid private boats—they're a rip-off.

🅿 **Autorimessa Comunale** ✉ Piazzale Roma, Santa Croce, end of S11 road ☎ 041/2727301 ⊕ www.asmvenezia.it. **Garage San Marco** ✉ Piazzale Roma 467/f, Santa Croce, turn right into bus park ☎ 041/5232213 ⊕ www.garagesanmarco.it. **Tronchetto** ☎ 041/5207555.

DISABILITIES & ACCESSIBILITY

In Venice, bridges, historic buildings that cannot be modernized, and traveling by boat complicate matters for people with mobility concerns. Don't rely on tourist maps that indicate lifts on certain bridges around town; these rarely if ever work. Vaporetto Lines 1 and 82 have the most deck space, but boarding water taxis can sometimes be hazardous.

Kiosks in the airport, train station, and parking areas that book hotels can dispense only information member hotels provide; there are no set criteria for designating a hotel as accessible. InformaHandicap's Web site has helpful information for chair users, and questions e-mailed in English are answered. Palazzo Ducale, Museo Correr, the Campanile di San Marco, Ca' Rezzonico, Palazzo Grassi, Ca' d'Oro, and the Scuola di San Rocco have either lifts or ramps. Most churches, including the Basilica di San Marco, have one or two low steps to overcome.

🚺 **InformaHandicap** ✉ Viale Giuseppe Garibaldi 155, 30174 Mestre ☎ 041/5341700 🖷 041/5342257 ⊕ www.comune.venezia.it/handicap.

EMBASSIES & CONSULATES

There is no U.S. or Canadian consular service.

🚺 United Kingdom **U.K. Consulate** ✉ Campo della Carità [near Gallerie dell'Accademia], Dorsoduro 1051 ☎ 041/5227207.

EMERGENCIES

The U.K. Consulate can recommend doctors and dentists, as can your hotel or any pharmacy. The nearest pharmacy is never far, and they take turns staying open nights, Saturday afternoons, and Sundays; the list of after-hours pharmacies is posted on the front of every pharmacy and appears in daily newspapers.

🚺 Emergency Services **General Emergencies** ☎ 113. **Ambulance** ☎ 118. **Carabinieri** ☎ 112.

ENGLISH-LANGUAGE MEDIA

BOOKS   Cafoscarina, close to Università Ca' Foscari, has a large selection of English literature, mainly classics. Emiliana and Studium stock books about Venice and Italian food, with a few fiction paperbacks. The Venice Pavilion, off Piazza San Marco near the Giardini Reali, has a good selection of books and novels featuring the city. For books about Venice's maritime culture, lagoon, and environment, try Maredicarta.

NEWSPAPERS &   You can find English-language newspapers at a stall beside the San Marco post office
MAGAZINES   (behind Museo Correr), at the train station, and in Campo SS. Apostoli, between Rialto and Ca' d'Oro.

🚺 **Cafoscarina** ✉ Campiello Squellini, Dorsoduro 3259 ☎ 041/5229602. **Emiliana** ✉ Calle Goldoni, San Marco 4487, between Piazza San Marco and Campo San Luca ☎ 041/5220793. **Maredicarta** ✉ Fondamenta dei Tolentini, Santa Croce 222, across from train station ☎ 041/716304. **Studium** ✉ Calle de la Canonica, San Marco 337/c, off Piazzetta dei Leoncini ☎ 041/5222382. **Venice Pavilion** ✉ San Marco 2 ☎ 041/5225150.

MAIL & SHIPPING

Venice's main post office (Monday–Saturday 8–6) is housed in the Fondaco dei Tedeschi, near the Rialto bridge. You'll find a Federal Express office just outside Piazza San Marco, opposite Hotel Luna.

TOURS

BOAT TOURS   Boat tours to the islands of Murano, Burano, and Torcello, organized by Serenissima Motoscafi and Consorzio San Marco, leave from various docks around Piazza San Marco daily. These 3½-hour trips cost €18 and can be annoyingly commercial, often emphasizing glass-factory showrooms and pressuring you to buy at prices even higher than normal. Trips depart at 9:30 and 2:30 April–October, at 2:30 November–March.

More than a dozen major travel agents in Venice have grouped together to provide frequent, good-quality tours of the city. Serenaded gondola trips, with or without dinner (€70/32), can be purchased at any of their offices or at American Express. Nightly tours leave at 7:30 and 8:30 May–September, at 7:30 only in April and October, and at 3:30 November–March.

🔂 **American Express** ✉ Salizada San Moisè, San Marco 1471 ☎ 041/5200844 📠 041/5229937. **Serenissima Motoscafi** ☎ 041/5224281. **Consorzio San Marco** ☎ 041/2406712.

PRIVATE GUIDES Cooperativa Guide Turistiche Autorizzate has a list of more than 100 licensed guides. Tours lasting about two hours with an English-speaking guide start at €113 for up to 30 people. Agree on a total price before you begin, as there can be some hidden extras. Guides are of variable quality.

🔂 **Cooperativa Guide Turistiche Autorizzate** ✉ San Marco 750, near San Zulian ☎ 041/5209038 📠 041/5210762.

TOURS OF THE REGION American Express and other agencies also offer several excursions in the Veneto region of the Venetian Arc. A boat trip to Padua along the Brenta River makes stops at three Palladian villas, and you return to Venice by bus. The tours run three times a week (Tuesday, Thursday, and Saturday) from March to October and cost €62 per person (€86 with lunch); bookings need to be made a few days in advance.

The Palladio Villa Tour (by minibus, maximum eight people) includes villas plus a walking tour of Vicenza (Wednesdays; €104 per person, optional lunch extra).

The Hills of the Veneto tour (by minibus, maximum eight people) visits the picturesque hill towns of Marostica, Bassano del Grappa, and Asolo, with stops at Villa Barbaro at Maser and at a vineyard along Strada del Prosecco for Prosecco wine tasting (Tuesday, Thursday, and weekends; €104 per person, optional lunch extra).

For a break from the heat, consider the Dolomite Tour (by minibus, maximum eight people) through the stupendous scenery in the Dolomite mountains; stops include Titian's birthplace Pieve di Cadore, Lakes Santa Caterina and Misurina, the famous Cime di Lavaredo peaks, and Cortina d'Ampezzo (Monday and Friday, €113 per person, including a packed lunch). For these last three tours it is essential to make reservations at least a week in advance in high season.

🔂 Fees & Schedules **American Express** ✉ Salizada San Moisè, San Marco 1471, ☎ 041/5200844 📠 041/5229937.

WALKING TOURS More than a dozen major travel agents offer a two-hour walking tour of the San Marco area (€27), which ends with a glassblowing demonstration daily (no Sunday tour in winter). From April to October there's also an afternoon walking tour that ends with a gondola ride (€30). Venicescapes, an Italo-American cultural association, offers several themed itineraries focusing on history and culture as well as tourist sights. Their three- to seven-hour tours are private, and groups are small (generally six to eight people). Reservations are recommended during busy seasons, and prices start at €200 for two people. Walks inside Venice also does several themed tours for small groups starting at €65 per hour and lasting up to three hours.

🚩 Fees & Schedules **Alba Travel** ✉ Calle dei Fabbri, San Marco 4538 ☎ 041/2770164 🖨 041/5200781 ⊕ www.albatravel.it. **Oltrex Viaggi** ✉ Castello 4192 ☎ 041/5242840 🖨 041/5221986 ⊕ www. oltrex.it. **Venicescapes** ✉ Campo San Provolo, Castello 4954 🖨🖨 041/5206361 ⊕ www.venicescapes.org. **Walks inside Venice** 🖨🖨 041/5241706 or 041/5202434 ⊕ www.walksinsidevenice.com.

TRAIN TRAVEL

Venice has rail connections with every major city in Italy and Europe. Some continental trains do not enter Venice but stop only at the mainland Mestre station. All trains traveling to and from Venice Santa Lucia stop at Mestre, and it's just a 10-minute hop on the next passing train. If you change from a regional train to an Intercity or Eurostar, you'll need to upgrade with a *supplemento* (extra charge) or be liable for a hefty fine. You'll also be fined if before boarding you forget to validate your train ticket in one of the yellow machines found on or near platforms.

FARES & SCHEDULES   🚩 Train Information **Stazione Ferroviaria Santa Lucia** ✉ Grand Canal, northwest corner of the city, Cannaregio ☎ 892021 Trenitalia train information ⊕ www.trenitalia.com. **Stazione Ferroviaria Venezia-Mestre** ✉ Mestre, 12 km [7 mi] northwest of Venice ☎ 892021 ⊕ www.trenitalia.com.

TRANSPORTATION AROUND VENICE

Getting around Venice presents some unusual problems: the city's layout has few straight lines; house numbering seems nonsensical; and the *sestieri* (six districts) of San Marco, Cannaregio, Castello, Dorsoduro, Santa Croce, and San Polo all duplicate each other's street names. Traveling by vaporetto can be bewildering, and too often you're forced to walk. Yellow signs, posted on many busy corners, point toward the major landmarks—San Marco, Rialto, Accademia, etc.—but don't count on finding these once you're deep into residential neighborhoods. Even buying a good map at a newsstand—the kind showing all street names and vaporetto routes—won't necessarily keep you from getting lost. However, getting lost in Venice may mean you've also lost most of the other tourists; patience with yourself and the Venetians you ask for help can go a long way toward making the experience part of the adventure.

TRAVEL AGENCIES

🚩 Local Agent Referrals **Gran Canal** ✉ Ponte del Ovo, near Rialto Bridge, San Marco 4759 ☎ 041/2712111 🖨 041/5223380. **Kele & Teo** ✉ Ponte dei Bareteri, San Marco 4930 between San Marco and Rialto ☎ 041/5208722 🖨 041/5208913.

VISITOR INFORMATION

The train-station branch of the Venice Tourist Office is open daily 8–6:30; other branches generally open at 9:30.

The "Rolling Venice" pass, costing €3 and valid throughout a calendar year, buys visitors ages 14–29 discounts on 72-hour vaporetto passes and admission to lots of museums, and at assorted hotels, restaurants, and shops. Just show your passport or ID at Vela ticket offices (major vaporetto stops), at the Assessorato alla Gioventù (weekdays 9:30–1, plus Tuesday and Thursday afternoons 3–5), or at the Associazione Italiana Alberghi per la Gioventù (Monday through Saturday 8–2). A Venice Card allows you to avoid lines at city museums and prepays for vaporetti and municipal toilets. Order online (www.venicecard.it) or by phone (041/2424) and pay cash when you pick up the card. Price depends on how many days you're staying; though convenient, it's not a significant discount.

🏢 **Assessorato alla Gioventù** ✉ Corte Contarina, San Marco 1529, behind Piazza San Marco post office ☎ 041/2747651. **Associazione Italiana Alberghi per la Gioventù** ✉ Calle Castelforte, San Polo 3101, near San Rocco ☎ 041/5204414. **Rolling Venice** ☎ 041/2714747 ⊕ www.comune.venezia.it.

Venice Tourist Offices ☎ 041/5298711 ⊕ www.turismovenezia.it ✉ Marco Polo Airport ✉ Train Station, Cannaregio ✉ Procuratie Nuove, San Marco 71/f, near Museo Correr ✉ Venice Pavilion, San Marco, near Giardini Reali ✉ Garage Comunale, Piazzale Roma ✉ S. Maria Elisabetta 6/a, Lido ☉ Summer only ☎ 041/5265711.

THE VENETIAN ARC

2

Updated by
Elaine Eliah

THE ARC AROUND VENICE—encompassing the Veneto and Friuli–Venezia Giulia regions and stretching from Verona to Trieste—falls under the historical and spiritual influence of its namesake city. Whether seaside or inland, the emblem of Venice, St. Mark's winged lion, is emblazoned on palazzos or poised on pedestals, and the art, architecture, and way of life all reflect the splendor of La Serenissima.

Long before Venetians had made their presence felt, Ezzelino III da Romano (1194–1259), a larger-than-life scourge who was excommunicated by Pope Innocent IV, laid claim to Verona, Padua, and the surrounding lands and towns. After he was ousted, powerful families such as Padua's Carrara and Verona's della Scala (Scaligeri) vied throughout the 14th century to annex these territories. With the rise of Venetian rule came a time of relative peace, when noble families from the lagoon and the mainland commissioned Palladio to design their palazzos and enlisted the three *T*s—Titian, Tintoretto, and Tiepolo—to decorate their interiors. This opulent legacy, superimposed upon medieval castles and fortifications, is central to the identities of present-day Padua, Vicenza, and Verona.

Tucked into Italy's northeastern corner—Adriatic to the south, a ring of mountains to the north, and Slovene and Austrian borders to the northeast—is Friuli–Venezia Giulia, with a varied landscape and even more diverse cultural history that's reflected in its architecture, language, and cuisine. It's been marched through, fought over, hymned by patriots, and romanticized by James Joyce, Rainer Maria Rilke, and Jan Morris. It's seen Fascists and Communists, Romans, Habsburgs, and Huns. It survived by forging sheltering alliances—Udine beneath the wings of San Marco (1420), Trieste choosing Duke Leopold of Austria (1382) over Venetian domination.

Some of World War I's fiercest fighting took place in Friuli–Venezia Giulia, where memorials and cemeteries commemorate hundreds of thousands who died before the arrival of Italian troops in 1918 finally liberated Trieste from Austrian rule. During World War II one of Italy's two concentration camps, still visitable, was in Trieste. Thousands of ethnic Slav residents bore the brunt of Fascist persecution, and in Istria Italian residents suffered Yugoslavia's retaliation. When peace was declared in other parts of Europe, Trieste became a subject of Cold War conflict between Zone A and Zone B—the free-world Allies versus Tito's socialism. Only in 1976 was the "Trieste question" finally resolved: Italy retained the city but surrendered the entire Istrian Peninsula, now part of Croatia. With Slovenia's 1991 declaration of independence from Yugoslavia, confrontation again flared along the border, but the admission of Slovenia to the European Union (May 2004) may finally end the area's bloody legacy.

Exploring the Venetian Arc

The Venetian Arc encompasses the coastal crescent and the inland plain that stretches from the mouths of the Po and Adige rivers southwest of Venice to Trieste and the Slovenian border east of Venice. It bridges two

Italian regions—the Veneto and Friuli–Venezia Giulia—and is mainly flat green farmland spotted with low hills that swell and rise steeply inland in a succession of plateaus and high meadows to the snow-tipped Alps.

Much of the pleasure of exploring this area comes from discovering the individual variations on the overall Venetian theme that confer special charm on each of the towns. Some, such as Verona, Treviso, and Udine, have a solid medieval look; Asolo, the Town of a Hundred Horizons, has an idyllic setting; Bassano combines a bit of both. Padua is ennobled by Giotto's frescos, Vicenza by the villas of Palladio. Udine, often overlooked, is home to the first important frescoes by Giambattista Tiepolo (1696–1770), and is a small and pleasantly bourgeois base from which to explore the rest of the Friuli area. In Trieste, after a climb to the hill of San Giusto with its cathedral and castle, the aroma of freshly roasted coffee that fills the city center is hard to resist. Most of all, you'll find artistic jewels everywhere, from the great Venetian masters in Verona to Veronese's lighthearted frescoes in Villa Barbaro at Maser.

About the Restaurants & Hotels

Eating out in Veneto and Friuli–Venezia Giulia is a major social event, especially Sunday lunch, when restaurants are often noisy and tables at a premium. (Conversely, you'll encounter little traffic on country roads from midmorning to midafternoon on Sunday, making it a pleasant time to tour.) Throughout the week, restaurants stick to fairly rigid dining hours—you'll be lucky to find much more than a bar snack from 2:30 until 7 in the evening. The best restaurants change their menus regularly—even daily—so it's not uncommon to get a recited list of offerings rather than a printed menu. Don't be daunted if your Italian doesn't go beyond *sì* and *no:* waiters and waitresses can usually offer passable translations.

The area around Venice has been hosting visitors for centuries, resulting in a wide range of accommodations and prices; as you'd expect, smaller, slightly out-of-the-way places cost less than their posh Adriatic resort counterparts. It's a trend in the region for hotels to renovate and subsequently hike their prices, but good low-cost options can still be found. Look for weekend bargains at hotels catering to business clients. Expect to pay more as you approach Venice, since mainland towns absorb the overflow when Venice is most crowded, during Carnevale (Carnival, held two weeks preceding Lent) and from spring through autumn. *Agriturismo* (farm stay) information is available at local tourist information offices and sometimes on the offices' Web sites.

WHAT IT COSTS In euros					
	$$$$	**$$$**	**$$**	**$**	**¢**
RESTAURANTS	over €22	€16–€22	€11–€16	€7–€11	under €7
HOTELS	over €220	€160–€220	€110–€160	€70–€110	under €70

Restaurant prices are for a second course (*secondo piatto*). Hotel prices are for two people in a standard double room in high season, including tax and service.

Hard as it may be to leave the unique beauty of Venice behind, the Venetian Arc is a perfect complement to a Venetian stay. Beneath the gaze of St. Mark's lion, grandiose architecture and touches of medieval culture blend flawlessly through the cities, hills, and plains. You can ponder whether Romeo and Juliet really met their tragic fate in Verona, and whether Attila actually had his Huns build a hill in Udine just to watch a city burn; meanwhile, you'll have a chance to delight in some of the best food and wine Italy has to offer.

2

You can visit many cities on one- or two-day excursions from Venice itself. A three-day itinerary will restrict you to the principal sights, excluding Trieste. Five days' exploring will give you plenty to savor and remember, but you'll need discipline to keep up a swift pace. A seven-day trip will give you time to really experience the architecture, history, and culture of this beautiful region.

Numbers in the text correspond to numbers in the margin and on the Venetian Arc and Verona maps.

If you have 3 days

Begin your drive at **Villa Pisani** ❶ ➤, a spectacular palace on splendid grounds. Continue into **Padua** ❷ to visit the Cappella degli Scrovegni. Farther west is ▦ **Verona** ❹–⓱, where you should spend your first night. The following day, see Palladio's architecture in **Vicenza** ❸ and head for **Marostica** ⓲, ▦ **Bassano del Grappa** ⓳, and **Asolo** ⓴. Your last day, sip wine along the Prosecco Road to **Conegliano** ㉓, then stop in **Treviso** ㉒ or **Udine** ㉔ before taking the autostrada back to Venice.

If you have 5 days

Follow the three-day itinerary until Asolo, but at a slower pace. Stop in ▦ **Verona** ❹–⓱ for the first two nights; then, after visiting **Asolo** ⓴ on the third day, stop at Villa Barbaro in **Maser** ㉑ before heading to ▦ **Treviso** ㉒ or ▦ **Conegliano** ㉓ for the night. On the fourth day, visit **Udine** ㉔ and **Cividale** ㉕; drive south through **Cormòns** ㉖ wine country to ▦ **Trieste** ㉗. Spend the evening and the following morning here before visiting **Castello di Miramare** ㉘ and taking the A4 back to Venice.

If you have 7 days

Follow the above itinerary but spend a night in ▦ **Bassano del Grappa** ⓳ or ▦ **Asolo** ⓴. The following day, sip Prosecco as you head to ▦ **Treviso** ㉒, for sightseeing, shopping, and your fourth night. On the fifth day, visit **Conegliano** ㉓ and **Cividale** ㉕; choose to spend the fifth night in ▦ **Udine** ㉔ for further sightseeing, or drive to ▦ **Cormòns** ㉖ and savor Italy's "great whites" of the Collio wine region. Head to ▦ **Trieste** ㉗ and enjoy a day and night in this cosmopolitan city. Get a leisurely start to your last day, maybe having a picnic in the **Castello di Miramare** ㉘ park before taking the A4 back to Venice.

Timing

If you want to get the most out of your stay, come in late spring and early summer (May and June) or in September and October. Winter is a good time to avoid travel to the region; foggy conditions and wet, bone-chilling cold are not unusual from November through March. Opera and theater buffs should come in spring and summer, when outdoor performances are held.

THE ROAD TO PADUA & VICENZA

Foremost among the treasures of the Veneto region are the beautiful villas of Andrea Palladio (1508–80) built to render *la vita* all the more *dolce* for 16th-century aristocrats. Other important sights include Giotto's 14th-century frescoes in Padua's Cappella degli Scrovegni and many of Donatello's greatest sculptures.

Villa Pisani

❶ *10 km (6 mi) southeast of Padua.*

Extensive grounds with rare trees, ornamental fountains, and garden follies surround this extraordinary 18th-century palace in Stra. It was one of the last of many stately residences constructed along the Brenta River from the 16th to 18th century by wealthy Venetians for their *villeggiatura*—vacation and escape from the midsummer humidity. Tiepolo's trompe-l'oeil frescoes on the ballroom ceiling alone are worth the visit. If you have youngsters in tow surfeited with old masters, explore the gorgeous **park** and **maze** (open March–November). ⊠ *Stra* ☎ *049/ 502074* ☞ *€5, maze and grounds €2.50* ☼ *Apr.–Sept., Tues.–Sun. 9–7; Oct.–Mar., Tues.–Sun. 9–4; last entry 1 hr before closing.*

Padua

❷ *37 km (23 mi) west of Venice, 92 km (57 mi) east of Verona.*

Bustling Padua (Padova in Italian) has long been one of northern Italy's major cultural centers. It's home to the peninsula's second-oldest university, founded in 1222, which attracted the likes of Dante (1265–1321), Petrarch (1304–74), and Galileo Galilei (1564–1642). The artists Giotto (circa 1266–1337), Donatello (circa 1386–1466), and Mantegna (1431–1506) left great works here. If you plan to visit many of the local sights, invest in the **Padova Card** (€15), valid for 48 hours, or an entire weekend from Friday to Sunday evening. You'll get free access to Padua city buses, entrance to some of the principal museums (including the Cappella degli Scrovegni and the Museo Civico), and discounts for many other attractions, including boat trips on the Brenta River. Cards are available at **tourist information offices** (☎ 049/8767927), near Galleria Pedrocchi, in Padova railway station, and in many of the surrounding towns.

Fodor'sChoice **Cappella degli Scrovegni** (Scrovegni Chapel), perhaps the most famous
★ chapel in Italy after the Sistine, was erected by wealthy Paduan Enrico Scrovegno to atone for the usury practiced by his deceased father, Regi-

Concerts & Opera

Verona and Vicenza offer some of Italy's most spectacular opportunities for indulging in the passions of open-air operas and concerts. You can take your place in Verona's ancient Roman amphitheater and watch the grand spectacle of *Aïda* or just take in a free jazz or folk concert on a warm summer evening. Alternatively, sit back like a true-born aristocrat and listen to a concert in the regal setting of a Vicenzo villa. You can also treat yourself to an unforgettable performance in Palladio's Teatro Olimpico. Smaller towns run concert seasons, too.

Villas & Palazzos

The countless villas and palaces sprinkled throughout the Venetian hinterland and the Palladian villas along the Brenta River should not be missed. These gracious country homes give insight into the way wealthy Venetians used to—and still do—spend leisure time. Many of the villas are privately owned but open to the public at certain times or by special request. Local tourist offices can be helpful in providing information on visiting these jewels.

---

naldo. Commissioned to decorate its interior, Giotto and his assistants worked from 1303 to 1305 on a magnificent fresco cycle illustrating the lives of Mary and Christ. In typical medieval comic-strip fashion, the 38 panels are arranged in tiers intended to be read from left to right. Opposite the alter is a powerful *Last Judgment,* where Enrico offers his chapel to the Virgin. The depth and perspective in these frescoes—which include the first blue skies in Western painting—were revolutionary. Mandatory reservations, available by Web or phone, are for a specific time and are nonrefundable. In order to preserve the artwork, doors are opened only every 15 minutes. A maximum of 25 visitors at a time must spend 15 minutes in an acclimatization room before making a 15-minute chapel visit. Note that in summer the chapel may stay open as late as 10 PM to accommodate the abundance of viewers. You can see fresco details as part of a virtual tour at Museo Civico Eremitani. ⊠ *Piazza Eremitani, 8* ☎ *049/8204551 information, 049/2010020 reservations* ⊕ *www.cappelladegliscrovegni.it* ⊠ *€12 (includes Museo Civico Eremitani) or Padova Card* ☉ *Daily 9–7.*

The **Museo Civico Eremitani** (Civic Museum), housed in what was once a monastery, has its quota of works by Venetian masters, as well as fine collections of archaeological pieces and ancient coins. ⊠ *Piazza Eremitani, 8* ☎ *049/8204551* ⊠ *€10 or Padova Card* ☉ *Tues.–Sun. 9–7.*

The 16th-century **Palazzo del Bo'** houses the **Università di Padova,** founded in 1222. The building, which now features an 18th-century facade, is named after the Osteria del Bo' (*bo'* means "ox"), an Đinn that once stood on the site. This is worth a visit to see the exquisite and perfectly proportioned anatomy theater and a hall with a lectern used by Galileo. You can enter only as part of a guided tour. Most guides speak English, but it is worth checking ahead by phone.

Venetian Arc

KEY

Ferry

▲ Start of itinerary

ITALY

SLOVENIA

CROATIA

Adriatic Sea

Golfo di Venezia

Laguna Veneta

Golfo di Trieste

FRIULI-VENEZIA GIULIA

VENETO

TO SPLIT, DUBROVNIK AND ISTANBUL

Trieste ⑳

Cormòns ㉖

Nova Gorica

Gorizia

Monfalcone

Aquileia

Castello di Miramare

Koper

Portorož

Piran

Umag

Cividale del Friuli ㉕

Udine ㉔

Portogruaro

Caorle

Lido di Jesolo

Lido

Venice

Alberoni

Chioggia

Tagliamento

Livenza

Piave

Sile

Meduna

Conegliano ㉓

Pordenone

Oderzo

Treviso ㉒

Dolo

Villa Pisani ①

Stra

Brenta

Padua ②

Plove di Sacco

Vittório Veneto

Sella di Fadalto

Valdobbiadene

Montebelluna

MONTELLO

Maser ㉑

Asolo ⑳

Bassano del Grappa

Marostica ⑱

⑲

Vicenza ③

Feltre

Schio

Valdagno

TO PEDEMONTE DI SAN PIETRO IN CARIANO

Verona ④ - ⑰

see detail map

TO SOMMACAMPAGNA

Valpolicella

S. Bonifacio

Praglia

Abano Terme

Montegrotto Terme

Monselice

Este

Montagnana

Legnago

Montagnana

Trento

Rovereto

Adige

Adige

Po

20 miles

30 km

⊠ *Via VIII Febbraio* ☎ *049/8273047* 🖃 €3 🕙 *Apr.–Oct., Mon., Wed., and Fri. at 3, 4, and 5, Tues., Thurs., and Sat. at 9, 10, and 11; Nov.–Mar., Mon., Wed., and Fri. at 3 and 4, Tues., Thurs., and Sat. at 10 and 11.*

Palazzo della Ragione, also called Il Salone, was built in the Middle Ages as the seat of Padua's government. Today its street-level arcades shelter shops and cafés. Art shows are often held upstairs in the frescoed **Salone** (Hall), where there's an enormous 15th-century wooden replica of Gattamelata's bronze steed sculpted by Donatello. ⊠ *Piazza della Ragione* ☎ *049/8205006* 🖃 *Salone €4 or Padova Card; shows €8 or €4 with Padova Card* 🕙 *Tues.–Sun. 9–7.*

The huge **Basilica di Sant'Antonio** is a cluster of Byzantine domes and slender, minaretlike towers that gives the church an Asian-inspired style reminiscent of San Marco in Venice. The interior is sumptuous, too, with marble reliefs by Tullio Lombardo (circa 1455–1532), the greatest in a talented family of marble carvers who decorated many churches in the area, among them Santa Maria dei Miracoli in Venice. The artistic highlights here, however, all bear Donatello's name: the 15th-century Florentine master did the remarkable series of bronze reliefs illustrating the life of St. Anthony—whose feast day, Festa di Sant'Antonio on June 13, draws pilgrims from all over Europe—as well as the bronze statues of the Madonna and saints on the high altar. Standing in front of the church is Donatello's powerful statue of the *condottiere* (mercenary general) Erasmo da Narni, known by the nickname Gattamelata. It was cast in bronze—a monumental technical achievement—in 1453 and had an enormous influence on the development of Italian Renaissance sculpture. ⊠ *Piazza del Santo* ☎ *049/8242811* ⊕ *www.santantonio.org* 🕙 *Daily 6:20 AM–7 PM.*

The often overlooked 12th-century **Battistero del Duomo** (Cathedral Baptistery) contains mid-1370s frescoes depicting scenes from the Book of Genesis. They're the greatest work of Giusto de' Menabuoi, who further developed Giotto's style of depicting human figures naturally, using perspective and realistic lighting. The baptistery is a refreshingly cool retreat from the city. ⊠ *Piazza Duomo* ☎ *049/656914* 🖃 *€2.50, or €1.50 with Padova Card* 🕙 *Daily 10–6.*

The **Orto Botanico** (Botanic Garden) was founded in 1545 by order of the Venetian Republic to supply the university with medicinal plants. You can stroll the arboretum and wander through hothouses and beds of plants that were first introduced to Italy in this Renaissance garden, which still maintains its original layout. A St. Peter's palm, planted in 1585, stands protected in its own private greenhouse. ⊠ *Via Orto Botanico, 15* ☎ *049/8272119* 🖃 *€4* 🕙 *Apr.–Oct., daily 9–1 and 3–6; Nov.–Mar., Mon.–Sat. 9–1.*

The **Piazza dei Signori** has some fine examples of 15th- and 16th-century buildings. On the west side, the **Palazzo del Capitanio** has an impressive **Torre dell'Orologio,** with an astronomical clock dating from 1344. The **Duomo** is just a few steps away.

ON THE MENU

CloseUp

WITH THE DECISIVE seasonal changes of the Venetian Arc, it's little wonder so many restaurants shun printed menus. Some of the region's defining culinary elements are from the field and the forest, and are only available at certain times of year: in spring, white asparagus and wild herbs; in autumn, chestnuts, radicchio, and wild mushrooms.

The catch of the day, whether from the Adriatic or Lake Garda, is always a good bet. Inland, meat prevails: pork and veal standards are supplemented with lamb and rabbit, and goose, duck, and guinea fowl are all common poultry options. North around Asolo, snails are popular. In Verona, a tradition of eating horse meat dates to a bloody 19th-century skirmish, when a starving populace ate the animals killed in battle. Pastisada (stewed horse meat) remains popular. In Friuli–Venezia Giulia, menus show the influences of

Austria, Hungary, Slovenia, and Croatia. You may find wild deer and hare on the menu, along with renowned San Daniele del Friuli prosciutto.

For starches, the Veneto dines on bigoli (thick, whole-wheat pasta), and risotto is wine-saturated with Amarone in Verona and Prosecco in Conigliano. You'll encounter gnocchi made with pumpkin or plums in Udine, strudel filled with bruscandoli (wild greens) in Cormòns. Polenta is everywhere, varying from a stiff porridge topped with Gorgonzola or stews, to a patty grilled alongside meat or fish.

Austrian-style pastries will sweeten your stay in Trieste, and Verona scoops some of the best gelato. Treviso claims to have invented the area's signature dessert, tiramisu, but chefs in virtually every kitchen believe they hold the secret to making the best version.

> off the beaten path

ABANO TERME AND MONTEGROTTO TERME – These two hot-spring spas, about 12 km (7 mi) south of Padua, lie at the foot of the Euganean Hills, whose rustic villages and hand-tilled vineyards are also well worth a visit. If a bit of pampering sounds better than traipsing yet another church or castle, indulge yourself with massage, stone therapy, skin peeling, or a series of mud treatments, especially recommended for joint aches. Who knows, you might even get back to work feeling like you've really had a vacation. You can schedule individual health and beauty treatments, or book accommodation and treatments at a number of hotels operated by **GB Terme Hotels.** ✉ Via Pietro d'Abano, 1 ☎ 049/8665100 🖷 049/8669779 ⊕ www.gbhotels.it.

If you'd just like to test the waters, have a thermal swim at **Columbus Garden.** ✉ Via Martiri D'Ungheria, 22 ☎ 049/8601555 🖾 €8 Mon.–Sat., €9 Sun. ⊙ June–mid-Sept., daily 9 AM–11 PM; mid-Sept.–May, weekdays 12:30–11, weekends 9 AM–11 PM.

PRAGLIA – You can tour the evocative halls and cloisters of this 15th-century Benedictine monastery hidden in the hills, where resident monks make and sell honey, skin-care products, and herbal teas. Head 12 km (7 mi) southwest of Padua, following signs for Abano Terme on the south side of the city. The monastery closes to the public on special occasions such as funerals, as well as on holy days, so it's advisable to call ahead before making a visit. Note that the monks who show you around speak Italian only. ☎ *049/ 9999300 🖼 Free, donations welcome � Apr.–Oct., Tues.–Sun. 3:30–5:30; Nov. and Dec., and Feb. and Mar., Tues.–Sun. 2:30–4:30.*

MONTAGNANA – The walls surrounding this medieval town 50 km (30 mi) southwest of Padua are remarkably well preserved, enclosing a market square, a 500-year-old cathedral, and several tempting restaurants. Its former rivals, Este and Monselice, are 20 km (12 mi) east on the same road.

Where to Stay & Eat

$$–$$$ ✕ **La Vecchia Enoteca.** The ceiling is mirrored, the shelves are filled with books and wine, and the silverware once belonged to a cruise line. It's a luxurious setting for enjoying *branzino in crosta di patate* (sea bass with a potato crust) or beef with rosemary and balsamic vinegar, followed by a homemade dessert such as *crema catalana* (creme caramel). ⊠ *Via Santi Martino e Solferino 32* ☎ *049/8752856* 🖃 *MC, V* ☉ *Closed Sun., 4 wks July and Aug.* No lunch Mon.

$ ✕ **Osteria L'Anfora.** At this loud and lively spot the unlikely decor of old wine bottles alongside framed rugby shirts actually seems to make sense. Padua's older-than-students crowd comes for wine and jazz, especially at happy hour, to see what's going on around town and to sample the extensive wine list. The simple, reasonably priced menu of pastas, salads, and a couple of daily specials make return clients of many. ⊠ *Via Dei Soncin 13* ☎ *049/656629* 🖃 *AE, MC, V* ☉ *Closed Sun.*

¢–$ ✕ **Gigi Bar.** Yellow walls and tablecloths brighten this restaurant where high ceilings open up a 2nd-floor seating area. The central kitchen is behind a counter just low enough for the convivial owner to supervise the equally friendly dining-room staff. His popular fish soup is one of the affordable seafood dishes that keep locals queuing up. There are also steaks, salads, vegetable plates, and pizzas with a surprisingly light crust. ⊠ *Via Verdi 18/20* ☎ *049/8760028* 🖃 *V, MC, DC* ☉ *Closed Tues., 2 wks in July.*

¢ ✕ **Brek.** Workers in northern Italy flock to this modern chain of self-service restaurants for fast food Italian style. Browse the hot and cold buffet islands, make your choices, and watch your pasta or pizza created before your eyes; while your steak is grilled, select some vegetable side dishes. Brek won't take much time out of your touring schedule or much cash out of your wallet. ⊠ *Piazza Cavour 54* ☎ *049/8753788* 🖃 *AE, DC, MC, V.*

★ $$$ 🏨 **Villa Pisani, Vescovana.** The spacious high-ceilinged rooms in this enormous 16th-century villa are furnished entirely with period pieces—some units even have fully frescoed walls. All rooms look out over stunning formal gardens and beyond to a 15-acre park with rare trees, a chapel, a theater, and a concealed swimming pool. You'll also have access to three big *sale* (lounges), where you can chat with the few other lucky guests and Signora Scalabrin, who shares her patrician living areas, music, and books. With breakfast served on silver platters, this is a bed-and-breakfast that outstrips almost all the hotel competition. ⊠ *Via Roma 19, 35040 Vescovana, 30 km (19 mi) south of Padua, off highway A13* 🏨 *0425/920016* ⊕ *www.villapisani.it* ⤳ *7 rooms, 1 suite* ♨ *Pool, horseback riding, Internet, convention center, free parking, some pets allowed; no a/c in some rooms, no room phones, no TV in some rooms, no smoking* ⊟ *AE, DC, MC, V* ¶◯| *BP.*

$$–$$$ 🏨 **Majestic Toscanelli.** The elegant entrance with potted evergreens flanking the steps sets the tone in this stylish, central hotel close to the Piazza della Frutta. Plants figure strongly in the breakfast room as well, and the charming bedrooms are furnished in different styles, from 19th-century mahogany and brass to French Empire. ⊠ *Via dell'Arco 2, 35122* ☎ *049/663244* 🖷 *049/8760025* ⊕ *www.toscanelli.com* ⤳ *28 rooms, 6 suites* ♨ *In-room data ports, some in-room safes, minibars, cable TV with movies, bar, meeting room, parking (fee), some pets allowed (fee), no-smoking floor* ⊟ *AE, DC, MC, V* ¶◯| *BP.*

$$–$$$ 🏨 **Methis.** At strikingly modern Methis, which takes its name from the Greek words for style and spirit, the four floors of guest rooms are designed to reflect the elements: from gentle earth tones on the 1st floor to fiery red, to cool blue, to airy whiteness in the top-floor suites. Minimalist rooms have Japanese-style tubs; four are equipped for guests with disabilities. The lobby bathroom is worth a visit just to wash your hands in the fountain. ⊠ *Riviera Paleocapa 70, 35141* ☎ *049/8725555* 🖷 *049/8725135* ⊕ *www.methishotel.com* ⤳ *52 rooms, 7 suites* ♨ *In-room data ports, in-room safes, minibars, cable TV with movies and video games, gym, bar, Internet, meeting room, free parking, no-smoking floor* ⊟ *AE, DC, MC, V* ¶◯| *BP.*

$ 🏨 **Al Fagiano.** Some rooms in this peaceful hotel have views of the Basilica di Sant'Antonio's spires and cupolas. Facilities are modest, but an amiable staff and central location make this a convenient, pleasant place to stay. ⊠ *Via Locatelli 45, 35100* ☎ *049/8750073* 🖷 *049/8753396* ⊕ *www.alfagiano.it* ⤳ *29 rooms* ♨ *In-room data ports, cable TV, bar, parking (fee)* ⊟ *AE, DC, MC, V* ¶◯| *EP.*

¢ 🏨 **Casa del Pellegrino.** Sharing the piazza with the Basilica di Sant'Antonio, this rather austere hotel has simple rooms arranged hospital-fashion along polished corridors. The newer annex 100 yards behind the main building has modern hotel amenities, including air-conditioning. A cavernous restaurant downstairs serves cheap, simple fare. ⊠ *Via Cesarotti 21, 35123* ☎ *049/8239711* 🖷 *049/8239780* ⊕ *www.casadelpellegrino.com* ⤳ *157 rooms, 124 with bath* ♨ *Restaurant, cable TV, bar, parking (fee); no a/c in some rooms* ⊟ *AE, MC, V* ⊘ *Closed last wk Dec.–Jan.* ¶◯| *EP.*

Nightlife & the Arts

CAFÉS Nineteenth-century **Caffè Pedrocchi** (⊠ Piazzetta Pedrocchi ☎ 049/8781231) serves 150-year-old-recipe zabaglione and minted espresso in a neoclassical cross between museum and stage set. The café is open daily from 9 to 9, and until midnight Thursday–Saturday, when there may be jazz or tango music. The upstairs rooms, with frescoed ceilings, are open Tuesday–Sunday 10–1 and 3–6. When art shows are on display there, admission is €3.

Victoria (✉ Via Savonarola 149 ☎ 049/8721530) is a *birreria* (bar serving primarily beer) that occasionally has live music; it's closed on Monday. **Limbo** (✉ Via San Fermo 44 ☎ 049/656882), closed on Monday and Tuesday, is a restaurant-pizzeria open late, with live music and a disco downstairs.

Shopping

On the ground floor of the **Palazzo della Ragione** (✉ Piazza della Ragione) you'll find a mouthwatering food market where shops sell choice salami and cured meats, local cheeses, wines, coffee, and tea. With the fruit and vegetable market in the piazza outside, you can pick up all the makings of a fine picnic.

Surrounded by a canal and 78 statues, parklike **Prato della Valle** hosts a market where on Saturdays you can buy everything from clothes to kitchenware, and antiques on the third Sunday of every month. Heaven awaits your sweet tooth at **Dolciaria** (✉ Via Santi Martino e Solferino 35 ☎ 049/663463), a specialist at fulfilling chocoholic dreams with products from all over the world.

Vicenza

❸ *60 km (37 mi) east of Verona, 32 km (19 mi) west of Padua.*

Vicenza bears the distinctive signature of the 16th-century architect Andrea Palladio, whose name has been given to the "Palladian" style of architecture. He gracefully incorporated elements of classical architecture—columns, porticoes, and domes—into a style that reflected the Renaissance celebration of order and harmony. His elegant villas and palaces were influential in propagating classical architecture in Europe, especially Britain, and later in America—most notably at Thomas Jefferson's Monticello.

In the mid-16th century Palladio was commissioned to rebuild much of Vicenza, which had been greatly damaged during wars waged against Venice by the League of Cambrai, an alliance of the papacy, France, the Holy Roman Empire, and several neighboring city-states. Palladio made his name with the basilica, begun in 1549 in the heart of Vicenza, then embarked on a series of lordly buildings, all of which adhere to the same classicism. Many of his works join the Venetian Gothic and baroque palaces that line **Corso Palladio,** an elegant shopping thoroughfare where Vicenza's status as one of Italy's wealthiest cities is evident.

At the heart of Vicenza is **Piazza dei Signori,** the site of **Palazzo della Ragione,** commonly known as Palladio's basilica, though it's not a church at all but originally a courthouse and public meeting hall. Palladio made his name by successfully modernizing the medieval building, grafting a graceful two-story exterior loggia onto the existing Gothic structure. Take a look also at the **Loggia del Capitaniato,** opposite, which Palladio designed but never completed. Note that the palazzo and its loggia are open to the public only when there's an exhibition. ☒ *Piazza dei Signori* ☎ *0444/32368.*

★ The **Teatro Olimpico,** Palladio's last and perhaps most exciting work, was completed after his death by Vincenzo Scamozzi (1552–1616). Based closely on the model of an ancient Roman theater, it represents an important development in theater and stage design and is noteworthy for its acoustics and the cunning use of perspective in Scamozzi's permanent backdrop. The anterooms are frescoed with images of important figures in Venetian history. ☒ *Piazza Matteotti* ☎ *0444/222800* ☒ *€8 includes admission to Palazzo Chiericati and Museo Naturalistico e Archeologico* ☉ *Sept.–June, Tues.–Sun. 9–5; July and Aug., Tues.–Sun. 9–7.*

The exquisite and unmistakably Palladian **Palazzo Chiericati** houses Vicenza's **Museo Civico.** The museum's Venetian collection includes paintings by Tiepolo (1696–1770) and Tintoretto (1519–94). ☒ *Piazza Matteotti* ☎ *0444/321348* ☒ *€8 includes admission to Teatro Olimpico and Museo Naturalistico e Archeologico* ☉ *Sept.–June, Tues.–Sun. 9–5; July and Aug., Tues.–Sun. 9–7.*

In a city dominated by Palladio, the distinctly baroque **Palazzo Leoni Montanari** is often overlooked, as are its galleries. On display are more than 500 Orthodox icons dating back to the 13th century, making this one of the most significant such collections outside Russia. A second gallery of Veneto art includes paintings by Longhi (1702–1785), Canaletto (1697–1768), and Francesco Guardi (1712–1793). ☒ *Contrà Santa Corona 25* ☎ *800/578875* ⊕ *www.palazzomontanari.com* ☒ *€3.50* ☉ *Fri.–Sun. 10–6, Wed. and Thurs. variable hours for special shows.*

★ Palladio's most famous work, **Villa La Rotonda,** seems less a villa than a Roman-style temple, which is precisely what the architect intended. Take time to admire it from all sides; it's easy to detect that this building was the inspiration for Monticello and many state capitols in the United States. The interior is typical of Palladio's grand style, with a distinctive use of open space. Getting to the villa is a pleasant 20- to 30-minute walk from Vicenza's city center, or take Bus 8 from Viale Roma. The villa is privately owned; note the limited hours that it's open to the public. ☒ *Via della Rotonda 29* ☎ *0444/321793* ☒ *€6, grounds €3* ☉ *Villa: mid-Mar.–Oct., Wed. 10–noon and 3–6. Grounds: mid-Mar.–Oct., Tues.–Sun. 10–noon and 3–6; Nov.–mid-Mar., Tues.–Sun. 10–noon and 3–5.*

Villa Valmarana ai Nani, an 18th-century country house, is decorated with a series of frescoes by Giambattista Tiepolo depicting fantastic visions of a mythological world, including one of his most stunning works, the *Sacrifice of Iphigenia.* The neighboring Foresteria, or guesthouse, holds more frescoes showing 18th-century Veneto life at its most charming by Tiepolo's son Giandomenico (1727–1804). You can reach the villa on foot by following the same path that leads to Palladio's Villa la Rotonda. ☒ *Via dei Nani 2/8* ☎ *0444/54386, 0444/ 321803 Foresteria* ☒ *€6* ☉ *Mid-Mar.–Oct., Wed., Thurs., and weekends 10–noon, also Tues.–Sun. 3–6.*

Where to Stay & Eat

$–$$ ✕ **Antico Ristorante agli Schioppi.** Veneto country-style decor matches simple yet imaginative cuisine in this family-run restaurant established in 1897. Begin with the Parma ham served with eggplant mousse and Parmesan. The *baccalà* (salt cod) is a must, as are the *petto d'anitra all'uva moscata e indivia* (duck breast with muscat grapes and endive) and *coniglio alle olive nere* (rabbit with black olives). Desserts include ever-so-light fruit mousse and a pear cake with red-wine sauce. ⊠ *Contrà del Castello 26* ☎ *0444/543701* ⊟ *AE, DC, MC, V* ⊗ *Closed Sun., last wk of July–mid-Aug., and Jan. 1–6. No dinner Sat.*

★ $ ✕ **Ponte delle Bele.** With all the pine furniture and lacy lamps, you feel like you've stumbled into a Alpine cabin, so it's no surprise when your homemade pasta resembles dumplings or spaetzle, or has a name like *strangolapreti* (priest choker). At this friendly Italian/Tyrolean restaurant, your prosciutto might be made from wild deer or boar. Try guinea fowl roasted with white grapes, or the local cheese plate served with honey and preserves (but take care with the tough rye cracker-bread, which only a dentist could love). ⊠ *Contrà Ponte delle Bele 5* ☎ *0444/320647* ⊟ *AE, DC, MC, V* ⊗ *Closed Sun.*

¢–$ ✕ **Antica Casa Della Malvasia.** The fireplace beckons across this large hall with arched ceilings and heavy wooden tables. Choose from a large selection of salads, pastas, and local meat and fish dishes, including the local specialty *baccalà Vicentina* (codfish). The adjacent bar, where you can also order food, is especially popular with a lively university crowd. ⊠ *Contrà delle Morette 5* ☎☎ *0444/543704* ⊟ *AE, DC, MC, V* ⊗ *Closed Mon. and Aug.*

¢   ✕ **Brek.** See review under Where to Stay & Eat in Padua, above. ⊠ *Corso Palladio 10/12* ☎ *0444/327829* ⊟ *AE, DC, MC, V* ⊗ *Closed Mon.*

¢   ✕ **Righetti.** Simple, reasonable fare ensures a regular clientele at this self-service restaurant, especially for lunch. There's always a pasta, risotto, and a hearty soup like *orzo e fagioli* on the menu. Grilled meats and vegetables, salads, and baccalà are available daily. After staking out a table with paper place mats and cutlery, line up (with elbows ready) at the food counters. Then help yourself to bread, wine, and water. After you've dined, tell the cashier what you've had and he'll total your (very reasonable) bill. ⊠ *Piazza Duomo 3* ☎ *0444/543135* ⊟ *No credit cards* ⊗ *Closed weekends and Aug.*

$ 🔲 **Giardini.** You're in good company in this central piazza, flanked by Palladio's Teatro Olimpico and Palazzo Chiericati, while the town center itself is just a few steps away. The hotel is tastefully furnished in modern Italian style with two rooms equipped for guests with disabilities. ⊠ *Viale Giurioli 10, 36100* ☎☎ *0444/326458* ⊕ *www.hotelgiardini. com* ⤿ *17 rooms* ⌂ *In-room safes, minibars, cable TV, bar, meeting room, free parking* ⊟ *AE, DC, MC, V* ⊗ *Closed Dec. 23–Jan. 2* ⍟❘ *BP.*

¢   🔲 **Due Mori.** In the heart of Vicenza off Piazza dei Signori, this hotel, dating from 1883, was one of the first in town. It's a favorite with regular visitors, light and airy, yet at the same time cozy. All rooms are furnished with antiques and detailed in wood, and two are equipped for guests with disabilities. ⊠ *Contrà Do Rode 24, 36100* ☎ *0444/321886* 🖷 *0444/326127* ✑ *hotelduemori@inwind.it* ⤿ *30 rooms* ⌂ *Bar, some* *parking, some pets allowed; no a/c, no room TVs* 🖃 *MC, V* ⊙ *Closed last 2 wks July* ⦿| *EP.*

Nightlife & the Arts

MUSIC & THEATER The **Teatro Olimpico** (🖃 Piazza Matteotti ☎ 0444/222801 ⊕ www. comune.vicenza.it) hosts a jazz festival in May, classical concerts in June, and classical drama performances in September. Even if your Italian is dismal, it's thrilling to see a performance in Palladio's magnificent theater.

VERONA

On the banks of the fast-flowing Adige River 60 km (37 mi) west of Vicenza, enchanting Verona boasts timeless monuments, a picturesque town center, and a romantic reputation as the setting of Shakespeare's *Romeo and Juliet*. With its lively Venetian air and proximity to Lake Garda, it attracts hordes of tourists, especially during summer's renowned opera season and spring's Vinitaly, one of the world's most important wine expos, where for five days you can sample the wines of more than 3,000 wineries from dozens of countries.

Verona grew to power and prosperity within the Roman Empire as a result of its key commercial and military position in northern Italy. After the fall of the Empire, the city continued to flourish under the guidance of Barbarian kings such as Theodoric, Alboin, Pepin, and Berenger I, reaching its cultural and artistic peak in the 13th and 14th centuries under the della Scala dynasty. (You'll see the *scala*, or ladder, emblem all over town.) In 1404 Verona traded its independence for security and placed itself under the control of Venice. (The other recurring architectural motif is the lion of St. Mark, symbol of Venetian rule.) Verona remained under Venetian protection until 1797, when Napoléon invaded. In 1814 the entire Veneto region was won by the Austrians, and it was finally united with the rest of Italy in 1866.

Exploring Verona

If you're going to visit more than a sight or two, it's worthwhile to purchase a Verona Card, available at museums, churches, and tobacconists for €8 (one day) or €12 (three days). You'll get a single admission to most of the city's significant museums and churches, and you can ride free on city buses. Alternatively, you can visit Verona's five major churches with a €5 combined ticket, available at the churches. Do note that Verona's churches strictly enforce their dress code: no tanks, sleeveless shirts, shorts, or short skirts.

a good walk

Start in Piazza Brà, the vast and airy square at the center of the city. The **Arena di Verona** ❹ ► on the east side of the square, built in the 1st century AD, is one of the largest and best-preserved Roman amphitheaters anywhere. Take Via Leoncino westward to Via San Cosimo, where a right will bring you to the church of **San Fermo Maggiore** ❺. From there, head northwest on Via del Cappello to reach the **Casa di Giulietta** ❻, with the most famous balcony in Italy. Continue up Via San Cappello to Piazza delle Erbe, a busy square with an open-air market; just to the northeast is the **Piazza dei Signori** ❼, surrounding which are the **Palazzo della Ragione** ❽, **Loggia del Consiglio** ❾, and **Palazzo degli Scaligeri** ❿. It's a short walk through Piazza Indipendenza to Ponte Nuova and across the river to the **Giardino Giusti** ⓫ and the church of **Santa Maria in Organo** ⓬. Follow Via Santa Maria in Organo up to the Teatro Romano and **Museo Archeologico** ⓭. The **Duomo** ⓮ is just over Ponte Pietra. From here either take Via Duomo and Corso Sant'Anastasia to **Sant'Anastasia** ⓯, or take a riverside stroll (or Bus 76) to 14th-century **Castelvecchio** ⓰, guarding the old brick footbridge over the Adige. The stunning Romanesque church **San Zeno Maggiore** ⓱ is another few minutes' walk downriver.

TIMING It takes about an hour to walk the route and three hours to see all the sights.

What to See

▶ ❹ **Arena di Verona.** Only four arches remain of the arena's outer rings, but
Fodor'sChoice otherwise the structure is so complete that it's easy to imagine the days
★ when the cruel deaths of countless gladiators, wild beasts, and Christians passed as entertainment here. Today the arena hosts Verona's summer opera, famous for spectacular productions before audiences of up to 16,000. The best operas are the big, splashy ones that demand huge choruses, Cinerama sets, lots of color and movement, and, if possible, camels, horses, or elephants. The music can be excellent, and the acoustics are fine, too. If you book a place on the cheaper terraces, be sure to take or rent a cushion—four hours on a 2,000-year-old stone bench can be an ordeal. ✉ *Piazza Brà 5* ☎ *045/8003204* 💰 *€3.10 or Verona Card, €1 1st Sun. of month* ☉ *Mon. 1:45–7:15, Tues.–Sun. 8:30–7:15, on performance days 8:30–3; last entry 45 mins before closing.*

❻ **Casa di Giulietta** (Juliet's House). The small courtyard balcony will help bring Shakespeare's play to life, even if it is part of a 20th-century remodeling. Despite historians' claims that the famous lovers had no real-life counterparts, thousands of visitors refuse to let truth get in the way of a good story. ✉ *Via Cappello 23* ☎ *045/8034303* 💰 *€3.10 or Verona Card* ☉ *Mon. 1:30–7:30, Tues.–Sun. 8:30–7:30; last entry 6:45.*

⓰ **Castelvecchio** (Old Castle). This crenellated, russet brick building with massive walls, towers, turrets, and a vast courtyard was built for Cangrande II della Scala in 1354. It presides over a street lined with attractive old buildings and palaces of the nobility. To really appreciate the massive castle complex, you need to enter the **Museo di Castelvecchio**, which gives you a good look at the vaulted halls and the collections of Venetian art and medieval weapons and jewelry. For the benefit of sightless visitors, some paintings have been rendered in plastic relief and have recorded explanations. ✉ *Corso Castelvecchio 2* ☎ *045/592985* 💰 *€3.10 or Verona Card, free 1st Sun. of month* ☉ *Mon. 1:30–7:30, Tues.–Sun. 8:30–7:30; last entry 6:45.*

⓮ **Duomo.** Verona's cathedral is an amalgamation of religious buildings, the earliest dating back to 380; it's ornately Romanesque but also shows Venetian and even Byzantine influences. Noteworthy inside are carvings of Oliver and Roland, two of Charlemagne's knights, guarding the

Verona

300 meters
300 yards

KEY

▲ Start of walk

main entrance, and Titian's *Assumption* gracing the first chapel on the left. ✉ *Via Duomo* ☎ *045/8008813* 💶 *€2, €5 for combined churches ticket, or Verona Card* ✆ *Nov.–Feb., Tues.–Sat. 10–1 and 1:30–4, Sun. 1–5; Mar.–Oct., Mon.–Sat. 10–5:30, Sun. 1–5:30.*

⓫ **Giardino Giusti.** In 1570 Agostino Giusti designed these formal gardens on the hillside behind his villa. Though the toothy mask halfway up the hill no longer breathes flames, little has been changed of Giusti's maze, fountains, or stalactite grotto. And though Verona might no longer be recognizable to Johann Wolfgang von Goethe (1749–1832), you can still enjoy the terrace views that inspired this German poet and dramatist to record his impressions. ✉ *Via Giardino Giusti 2* ☎ *045/8034029* 💶 *€5* ✆ *Apr.–Sept., daily 9–8; Oct.–Mar., daily 9–7.*

❾ **Loggia del Consiglio.** This graceful structure, built in the 12th century as a site for city council meetings, still serves as seat of the provincial government. ✉ *Piazza dei Signori* ✆ *Closed to the public.*

⓭ **Museo Archeologico.** The views of the city from this museum housed in an old monastery high above the **Teatro Romano** are even better than its archaeological exhibits. The Roman Theater, built in the same era as the Arena di Verona, is sometimes used in summer for dramatic productions. ✉ *Rigaste del Redentore 2* ☎ *045/8000360* 💶 *€2.60 or Verona Card, free 1st Sun. of month* ✆ *Mon. 1:30–7:30, Tues.–Sun. 8:30–7:30; last entry 6:45.*

❿ **Palazzo degli Scaligeri.** The iron-fisted della Scalas ruled Verona from this medieval stronghold. Though the palazzo is closed to the public, you can gaze into the adjacent **Arche Scaligere,** site of the suitably impressive marbled Gothic tombs of family members Cangrande I ("Big Dog"), Mastino II ("Mastiff"), and Cansignorio ("Top Dog"). ✉ *Piazza dei Signori.*

❽ **Palazzo della Ragione.** An elegant pink marble staircase leads up from the *mercato vecchio* (old market) courtyard to the magistrates' chambers. Though this 12th-century palace, also known as the Palazzo del Comune, is closed to the public, you can get the highest view in town from atop its 270-foot-tall **Torre dei Lamberti.** Would-be endurance athletes can save €0.60 by climbing the stairs; for everyone else there's an elevator. (✉ *Piazza dei Signori* ☎ *045/8032726* 💶 *€1.50, €2.10 with elevator, or Verona Card* ✆ *Mon. 1:30–7:30, Tues.–Sun. 8:30–7:30; last entry 6:45.*

❼ **Piazza dei Signori.** Verona's most impressive piazza, the center of things for more than 1,000 years, is today lorded over by a pensive statue of Dante, often as not with a pigeon on his head. His back is toward the Loggia del Consiglio and his left hand points toward the Palazzo degli Scaligeri. He faces Palazzo del Capitanio (to his left) and Palazzo della Ragione (to his right). All these buildings are closed to the public except those on government business.

❺ **San Fermo Maggiore.** From its humble Benedictine beginnings, San Fermo grew through the centuries, in part as a result of rebuilding after floods from the nearby Adige river. The tomblike lower church, dating from the 8th century, became usable again when the Adige was reengineered to stay within its banks. The mammoth upper church completed in the 14th century has the Veneto's oldest and perhaps finest ship's-keel ceiling, decorated with paintings of 400 saints. ⊠ *Stradone S. Fermo* ☎ *045/8007287* ▣ *€2, €5 for combined churches ticket, or Verona Card* ⊙ *Nov.–Feb., Tues.–Sat. 10–1 and 1:30–4, Sun. 1–5; Mar.–Oct., Mon.–Sat. 10–6, Sun. 1–6.*

★ ⑰ **San Zeno Maggiore.** Possibly Italy's finest Romanesque church, San Zeno stands between two medieval bell towers. A 13th-century rose window depicts the wheel of fortune, and bronze doors from the 11th and 12th centuries are decorated with scenes from the Bible and from the life of Verona's patron saint, Zeno, who's buried in the crypt. Look for the statue of *San Zeno Laughing* to the left of the main altar—the unknown artist, or perhaps the saint himself, must have had a sense of humor. A *Madonna and Saints* triptych by Andrea Mantegna (1431–1506) hangs over the main altar, and a peaceful cloister lies to the north (left) of the nave. ⊠ *Piazza San Zeno* ☎ *045/8006120* ▣ *€2, €5 for combined churches ticket, or Verona Card* ⊙ *Nov.–Feb., Tues.–Sat. 10–1 and 1:30–4, Sun. 1–5; Mar.–Oct., Mon.–Sat. 8:30–6, Sun. 1–6.*

⑫ **Santa Maria in Organo.** The choir and sacristy of this 15th-century church are masterpieces of inlaid wood created by Benedictine Fra Giovanni (1458–1525). With remarkable perspective and shading, the series of panels depicts local buildings, an idealized Renaissance town, wildlife, and fruits radiant with the monk's love of life and eye for detail. ⊠ *Piazzetta Santa Maria in Organo* ☎ *045/591440* ⊙ *Daily 7:30–noon and 2:30–6:30.*

⑮ **Sant'Anastasia.** Verona's largest church, completed in 1481, is a fine example of Gothic brickwork and has a grand doorway with elaborately carved biblical scenes. The finest of its numerous frescoes is the pastel *St. George and the Princess* by Pisanello (1377–1455) above the Pellegrini Chapel right off the main altar, where the saint appears more gentleman than warrior. As you come in, look for the *gobbi* (hunchbacks) supporting holy-water stoups. ⊠ *Vicolo Sotto Riva 4* ☎ *045/8004325* ▣ *€2, €5 for combined churches ticket, or Verona Card* ⊙ *Nov.–Feb., Tues.–Sat. 10–1 and 1:30–4, Sun. 1–5; Mar.–Oct., Mon.–Sat. 9–6, Sun. 1–6.*

off the beaten path

TOMBA DI GIULIETTA – If you find compelling the myth that Juliet is buried in this old chapel near the river, a few minutes' walk south from the arena, and that she wed her Romeo here, then ignore the fact that the structure is a former orphanage and Franciscan monastery. In the crypt there's an open sarcophagus labeled as Juliet's tomb, and the city of Verona helps perpetuate the fantasy by conducting civil weddings in the chapel. ⊠ *Via del Pontiere, 35* ☎ *045/8000361* ▣ *€2.60 or Verona Card, free 1st Sun. of month* ⊙ *Mon. 1:30–7:30, Tues.–Sun. 8:30–7:30; last entry 6:45.*

Where to Stay & Eat

$$$$ ✕ **Il Desco.** *Cucina dell' anima* (soul food) is how Chef Elia Rizzo describes his contemporary cuisine in which natural flavors are preserved through quick cooking and limiting the number of ingredients per dish to three. He spares no expense in selecting those ingredients, and you pay accordingly to sample them: suckling pig in black truffle sauce and guinea fowl in chocolate and balsamic vinegar sauce are two of the typically elegant options. For a real splurge, order the tasting menu (€108), which includes appetizers, two first courses, two second courses, and dessert. The fine food is complemented by the dining room's tapestries and paintings. ☒ *Via Dietro S. Sebastiano 7* ☎ *045/595358* ⌂ *Reservations essential* ☰ *DC, MC, V* ⊗ *Closed Sun. and Mon. (dinner served Mon. in July, Aug., and Dec.), Dec. 25–Jan. 10, and June 15–30.*

★ **$–$$$** ✗ **Bottega Del Vino.** The prayer on the wall *(Dio mi guardi do chi non beve vino)* asks for protection from non–wine drinkers; a good-luck gobbo hovers above, holding a lantern and the key to a wine cellar with more than 100,000 bottles. Through the lively crowd of locals, elbow your way to the bar for a sandwich and a glass of wine from the wall-size list. Or make it a full bottle and a full meal—try the Amarone wine risotto or prizewinning *brasato Amarone* (marinated pork cutlet). ☒ *Via Scudo di Francia 3* ☎ *045/8004535* ☰ *AE, DC, MC, V* ⊗ *Closed Tues.*

¢ ✗ **Brek.** See review under Where to Stay & Eat in Padua, above. ☒ *Piazza Brà, 20* ☎ *045/8004561* ☰ *AE, DC, MC, V.*

¢ ✗ **Osteria al Duca.** Folks jam this place at lunchtime, sharing tables, wine, and conversation in a building legend claims to have been Romeo's birthplace. Beneath low-slung ceilings, generous portions of local specialties are served with a wine list that belies the simplicity of the surroundings. Try Gorgonzola served with polenta, vegetarian eggplant with mozzarella, or homemade *bigoli al torchio,* a thick spaghetti forced through a press. ☒ *Arche Scaligere 2* ☎ *045/594474* ☰ *MC, V* ⊗ *Closed Sun. and mid-Dec.–mid-Jan.*

★ **$$$$** ✗▥ **Villa del Quar.** This 16th-century villa surrounded by gardens and vineyards is 15 minutes by car from Verona's city center. Leopoldo and Evelina Montresor spared no expense converting part of their villa home into a sophisticated luxury hotel with antiques and marble bathrooms. Service is attentive but relaxed, whether at the poolside bar or in the acclaimed Arquade restaurant. Chef Bruno Barbieri's creative menu might include baked scallops with radicchio and *speck* (prosciutto-like ham) or chocolate mousse served with crisp, caramelized eggplant. Sommelier Alberto Besco can help select wines for your meal or help organize a visit to some of Valpolicella's best wineries. ☒ *Via Quar 12, 37020 Pedemonte di San Pietro in Cariano, 10 km (6 mi) northwest of Verona* ☎ *045/6800681* 🖷 *045/6800604* ⊕ *www.hotelvilladelquar.it* ▭ *18 rooms, 9 suites* ⌂ *Restaurant, in-room data ports, in-room safes, minibars, cable TV, pool, gym, massage, bar, Internet, meeting room, helipad, free parking, some pets allowed, no-smoking rooms* ☰ *AE, DC, MC, V* ⊗ *Closed Jan.–mid-Mar. Restaurant closed Mon. Oct.–May. No lunch Tues.* ▯◎▯ *BP.*

$$$$ ▥ **Gabbia d'Oro.** Set in a historic building off Piazza delle Erbe in the ancient heart of Verona, this hotel is a tasteful fantasia of romantic ornamentation, exquisite fabrics, and gorgeous period furniture. Guest rooms, each different, have frescoes, beamed ceilings, and canopy beds, some festooned with rosy-cheeked cherubs. You can relax outdoors in the medieval courtyard, in the comfortable orangerie, or on the roof terrace. The breakfast spread (not included during opera season) is to die for. ☒ *Corso Porta Borsari 4/a, 37121* ☎ *045/8003060* 📠 *045/590293* ⊕ *www.hotelgabbiadoro.it* ⤳ *8 rooms, 19 suites* ♿ *In-room safes, minibars, bar, parking (fee), some pets allowed, no-smoking rooms* ▭ *AE, DC, MC, V* ☉ *BP.*

$ ▥ **Armando.** A few minutes' walk from the Arena, this contemporary hotel in a residential area offers respite from the busy city, as well as easier parking. Rooms are decorated with light, modern furniture, and some family rooms sleep up to five. In the airy breakfast room downstairs Signora Diana serves a hearty breakfast (not included in the price) of yogurt, fresh fruit, cheese, rolls, and coffee, with melon and prosciutto in summer. ☒ *Via Dietro Pallone 1, 37120* ☎ *045/8000206* 📠 *045/8036015* ⤳ *19 rooms* ♿ *No-smoking rooms* ▭ *MC, V* ☉ *EP* ⊘ *Closed late Dec.*

$ ▥ **Torcolo.** The warm welcome extended by owners Diana and Silvia, the pleasant, unfussily decorated rooms, and the central location on a peaceful street close to Piazza Brà and the Arena all make the Torcolo a good value. Breakfast, which costs an extra €7–€11, is served outside on the terrace in front of the hotel in summer. ☒ *Vicolo Listone 3, 37121* ☎ *045/8007512* 📠 *045/8004058* ⊕ *www.hoteltorcolo.it* ⤳ *19 rooms* ♿ *In-room safes, minibars, cable TV, parking (fee), some pets allowed* ▭ *AE, DC, MC, V* ☉ *EP* ⊘ *Closed mid-Jan.–mid-Feb.*

Nightlife & the Arts

Nightclubs

Alter Ego (☒ Via Torricelle 9 ☎ 045/915130) packs in a hip, thirty-ish crowd for disco and drinks Friday and Saturday nights from 11 PM to 4 AM. **Berfi's** (☒ Via Lussemburgo 1 ☎ 045/508024) is a popular and pricey nightspot with a restaurant and piano bar, open from 8:30 PM to 4 AM Friday to Sunday. You'll need to take a taxi, as it's in Verona's *zona industriale* (industrial area).

Opera

Of all the venues for enjoying opera in the region, pride of place must go to the **Arena di Verona.** During its summer opera season (July–September), audiences of as many as 16,000 sit on the original stone terraces, dating from the time when gladiators fought to the death, or in the modern cushioned stalls. The huge stage is wonderful for grand productions such as *Aïda,* but the experience is memorable no matter what's playing. Sometimes you can even listen from **Piazza Brà** cafés. Order tickets by phone or online. ☒ *Piazza Brà 28* ☒ *Box office* ☒ *Via Dietro Anfiteatro 6/b* ☎ *045/8005151* ⊕ *www.arena.it.*

FodorśChoice
★

Shopping

Antiques & Housewares

The area around the Gothic church of **Sant'Anastasia** is full of antiques shops, most catering to serious collectors. You can picnic on the Piazza dei Signori in the cool breeze after a strenuous day of antiques hunting. The perfect place to splurge on a modern decorative piece is **Alternative**

(✉ Vicolo San Marco in Foro 2, ☎ 045/8010910), with trendy glass artwork and design objects.

Markets

Verona's two markets, on **Piazza delle Erbe** and **Piazza Cittadella,** both open Monday–Saturday 8–1 and 3:30–sundown, have a selection of food, wine, clothing, antiques, and even pets.

Wine

Vinitaly (☎ 045/8298170 ⊕ www.vinitaly.com), the famous international wine show, takes place for five days in early April each year at the Fiera di Verona on Viale del Lavoro 8. It claims to make Verona the "world capital of quality wines" for the week, attracting more than 3,000 exhibitors from dozens of countries. The show runs 9–7 daily, with an admission charge of €30 per day.

TREVISO & THE HILLSIDE TOWNS

In this area directly north of Venice, market towns cling to the steep foothills of the Alps and the Dolomites alongside streams raging down from the mountains. Villa Barbaro, one of Palladio's most graceful country villas, is here, as are the arcaded streets of Treviso and the graceful Venetian Gothic structures of smaller hill towns.

Marostica

⓲ *7 km (4½ mi) west of Bassano del Grappa, 26 km (16 mi) northeast of Vicenza.*

From the 14th-century Castello Inferiore, where the town council still meets, an ancient stone wall snakes up the hill to enclose the Castello Superiore, with its commanding views. Marostica's most celebrated feature is Piazza Castello, checkerboarded in colored stone, the site of chess games using human pieces.

Where to Stay

★ **$–$$** 🏨 **Due Mori.** Recessed lighting adds to the modern, minimalist design at this historic inn, which has been this medieval town's only refuge for travelers since the 18th century. Warm wooden floors and soft-beige marble bathrooms are all made of local materials. Some rooms have magical views of the olive-studded terraces behind the town, the upper castle, and the ancient city wall. Two rooms are wheelchair accessible. There's a chic restaurant downstairs. Due Mori makes a comfortable base for touring the surrounding hills and towns of the northern Veneto. ✉ *Corso Mazzini 73, 36063* ☎ *0424/471777* 🖷 *0424/476920* ⊕ *www. duemori.com* 🛏 *11 rooms* ⚐ *Restaurant, in-room data ports, minibars, cable TV, free parking, some pets allowed, no-smoking rooms* 🗎 *MC, V* ⊙ *Closed 1st wk Jan., 1 wk mid-Aug.* ⑩⑴ *BP.*

Sports & the Outdoors

A game of human-scale chess known as **Partita a Scacchi** is acted out in Piazza Castello by players in medieval costume on the second weekend in September in even-numbered years. The game lasts three evenings. Tickets go on sale in April; for information and bookings, contact Marostica's **tourist office** (☎ 0424/72127 ⊕ www.marosticascacchi.it).

Bassano del Grappa

⑲ *7 km (4½ mi) east of Marostica, 37 km (23 mi) north of Venice.*

Nestled at the base of the Mt. Grappa massif (5,880 feet), with the mountain-fresh Brenta River sluicing through, this town seems to be higher in the mountains than it actually is. Bassano has old streets lined with low-slung buildings adorned with wooden balconies and pretty flowerpots. Bright ceramic wares produced in the area are displayed in shops along byways that curve uphill toward a centuries-old square and, even higher, to a belvedere with a good view of Mt. Grappa and the beginning of the Val Sugana.

Bassano's most famous landmark is the **Ponte degli Alpini,** a covered bridge named for Italy's Alpine soldiers. There's been a bridge spanning the Brenta here since 1209, but floods and wars have required repeated rebuilding. The present version was constructed by Alpine soldiers following World War II. They used Andrea Palladio's 16th-century design, which astutely calls for easily replaceable wood as the building material.

Bassano is home to the famous **Nardini** distillery, where grappa has been distilled for more than a century. Stop in for a sniff or a snifter at any of the local cafés or at their very own *bottega* (shop), which has an excellent view of the Ponte degli Alpini.

Where to Stay & Eat

$-$$ ✕ **Osteria Terraglio.** The creative modern menu here focuses on absolute freshness, from the wonderful array of savory snacks to the big, crisp *insalatone* (main-course salads with tuna or various cheeses) to the steak fillet, cut to order. Special tasting sessions of local delicacies such as asparagus, cold-pressed olive oil, and fine wines are a regular feature. October through May there's live jazz on Tuesday evening. ⊠ *Piazza Terraglio 28* ☎ *0424/521064* ▭ *AE, DC, MC, V* ☉ *Closed Mon.*

$-$$ ✕ **Ristorante Birreria Ottone.** Proprietor Otto Wipflinger's Austrian ancestors might not recognize the beer hall they opened a century ago, but they would taste the same recipes—such as goulash with cumin—that have kept locals coming back for simple lunches and more elaborate dinners. With the addition of starched tablecloths and innovative drop-down lighting, the atmosphere now is more that of a comfortable restaurant than a beer hall. ⊠ *Via Matteotti 48/50* ☎ *0424/522206* ▭ *AE, DC, MC, V* ☉ *Closed Tues. and first 3 wks in Aug. No dinner Mon.*

$$ ✕▥ **Ca' Sette.** Were it not for an engraving showing Napoléon's troops massed in the courtyard, you'd never guess the vintage of this hotel, which has an ultramodern interior. Each room is unique, but all have in common tasteful designs in local wood and marble. Light sleepers might have difficulty with a rather busy road. With the town center just 2 km (1 mi) away, you can use one of the hotel's bicycles and save the hassle of driving or parking. The restaurant **Ca' 7** ($$–$$$) is among the best in the area. ⊠ *Via Cunizza da Romano 4, 36061* ☎ *0424/383350* ▭ *0424/393287* ⊕ *www.ca-sette.it* ⇥ *17 rooms, 2 suites* ⌂ *Restaurant, in-*

room data ports, in-room safes, minibars, parking, some pets allowed, no-smoking rooms ☰ *AE, DC, MC, V* ☉ *Restaurant closed Mon., 1st wk in Jan., and 2 wks mid-Aug. No dinner Sun.* ⫶◎⫶ *BP.*

$–$$ ⊞ **Bonotto Belvedere.** This historic hotel has richly decorated public rooms with period furnishings and Oriental rugs; the lounge has an open fireplace and a piano. Guest rooms are decorated in traditional Venetian or contemporary style. There are two rooms equipped for people with disabilities. The elegant restaurant has classic Italian seafood and meat dishes. ⊠ *Piazzale G. Giardino 14, 36061* ☎ *0424/529845* 🖷 *0424/529849* ⊕ *www.bonotto.it* 🛏 *83 rooms, 4 suites* ⚑ *Restaurant, some in-room data ports, cable TV with movies, piano bar, Internet, meeting rooms, parking (fee), some pets allowed (fee), no-smoking rooms* ☰ *AE, DC, MC, V* ☉ *Restaurant closed Sun.* ⫶◎⫶ *BP.*

$ ⊞ **Al Castello.** In a restored town house at the foot of the medieval Torre Civica, the Cattapan family's Castello is a reasonably priced, attractive choice. The simply furnished rooms all differ in shape and size. The best ones, at the front, have a small balcony offering a view of the charming square below. ⊠ *Piazza Terraglio 19, 36061* 🖷🖷 *0424/228665* ⊕ *www. hotelalcastello.it* 🛏 *11 rooms* ⚑ *Bar, Internet* ☰ *AE, MC, V* ⫶◎⫶ *EP.*

Shopping

The Bassano del Grappa region is famous for ceramics. At **L'arte della Ceramica,** (⊠ Via Angarano 21 ☎ 0424/503901) you'll find handmade reproductions of timeless designs, a step above some of the imported kitsch sold in some shops around town.

Preserved foods are another Bassano specialty. **Il Melario** (⊠ Via Angarano, 13 ☎ 0424/502168) has one of the best selections in town, including dried wild mushrooms and myriad liqueurs, honeys, and jams. If the friendly proprietor neglects to offer, ask to taste his roasted fava beans, a wholesome snack.

Asolo

㉒ *11 km (7 mi) east of Bassano del Grappa, 33 km (20½ mi) northwest of Treviso.*

The romantic, charming hillside hamlet of Asolo was the consolation prize of an exiled queen. At the end of the 15th century, Venetian-born Caterina Cornaro was sent here by Venice's doge to keep her from interfering with Venetian administration of her former kingdom of Cyprus, which she had inherited from her husband. To soothe the pain of exile she established a lively and brilliant court in Asolo. Over the centuries, Venetian aristocrats continued to build gracious villas on the hillside, and in the 19th century Asolo once again became the idyllic haunt of musicians, poets, and painters. From the outside, you can explore villas once inhabited by Robert Browning and the actress Eleonora Duse. Be warned that the town's charm vaporizes on holiday weekends when the crowds pour in. At the center of town is the **Piazza Maggiore,** with Renaissance palaces and fin-de-siècle cafés. The empty **Rocca** (🎟 €1.50 ☉ 10–12:30 and 3–7), uphill from the Piazza Maggiore and past Caterina's ruined castle, is a medieval fortress from which you get a view of Asolo's 100 horizons. It closes when the weather turns bad.

Where to Stay & Eat

$–$$$ ✕ **Ca' Derton.** Just behind the main square you can choose between the formality of a restaurant's white-lace tablecloths or the rustic tables (and lower prices) of an *enoteca* (wine bar) at Ca' Derton. Either way, you order from the same menu, which includes such dishes as venison with pomegranate, pasta with partridge and radicchio, and vanilla ice cream with pure Modena basalmic vinegar. ⊠ *Piazza D'Annunzio 11* ☎ *0423/ 529648* ⊟ *AE, DC, MC, V* ⊘ *Closed Mon. and 2 wks in midsummer. No dinner Sun.*

¢–$ ✕ **Al Bacaro.** Since 1892 this osteria has been a second home to Asolani laborers and craftsmen. Whether you eat downstairs in the bar with copper kettles or upstairs in the dining room with lacy lamps, you'll get affordable wines and home-style food that includes stewed game, tripe, and snails, but rarely pasta. ⊠ *Via R. Browning 165* ☎ *0423/55150* ⊟ *AE, DC, MC, V* ⊘ *Closed Wed. and 2 wks in Aug.*

$$$$ ✕⌂ **Villa Cipriani.** A romantic hillside garden surrounded by country homes is the setting for this historic villa. Its 19th-century antiques are complemented by modern creature comforts and discreet service. The superb restaurant ($$–$$$$) has a terrace overlooking the garden, a perfect place for a meal or an aperitif. The Asolo Golf Club is close by. ⊠ *Via Canova 298, 31011* ☎ *0423/523411* ⊟ *0423/952095* ⊕ *www. villacipriani.hotelinvenice.com* ⇨ *31 rooms* ⌂ *Restaurant, in-room safes, minibars, cable TV with movies, bar, Internet, meeting room, parking (fee), some pets allowed (fee), no-smoking floor* ⊟ *AE, DC, MC, V* ⏀ *BP.*

★ **$$$–$$$$** ⌂ **Al Sole.** Al Sole's terrace is a welcoming sight, elegantly perched over the town of Asolo. Overstuffed chairs fill the lobby, and all rooms are richly furnished in antiques. The hotel was once actress Eleonora Duse's favorite haunt, and her favorite room has been preserved. The restaurant, closed Wednesday, serves modest single-course meals. Two rooms are equipped for guests with disabilities. ⊠ *Via Collegio 33, 31011* ☎ *0423/528111* ⊟ *0423/528399* ⊕ *www.albergoalsole.com* ⇨ *22 rooms, 1 suite* ⌂ *Restaurant, in-room data ports, in-room safes, minibars, cable TV with movies, gym, bar, Internet, meeting room, free parking, no-smoking rooms* ⊟ *AE, DC, MC, V* ⏀ *BP.*

Shopping

Asolo hosts a two-day antiques market on the second weekend of every month except July and August.

Maser

㉑ *7 km (4½ mi) northeast of Asolo, 33 km (20½ mi) northwest of Treviso.*

★ One of Palladio's most gracious Renaissance creations, **Villa Barbaro** was built just outside the town of Maser for two brothers opening a winery, and today it remains in the same family's hands. Inside, Paolo Veronese's opulent frescoes bring the 16th century to life, but they may have been a source of conflict. Story has it that Palladio believed

Veronese's false doors and trompe-l'oeil scenes distorted the architectural design; the pair never again collaborated. A World Heritage Site, Villa Barbaro is worth going out of your way to see, but because it continues to be privately owned and occupied, visiting hours are limited. ☒ *Via Cornuda 7* ☎ *0423/923004* ☞ *€5* ⊙ *Mar.–Oct., Tues. and weekends 3–6; Nov.–Feb., weekends 2:30–5. Closed Dec. 24–Jan. 6.*

Where to Eat

¢–$ ✕ **Da Bastian.** Fifteen minutes' walk from Villa Barbaro, this fine restaurant with a pleasant garden is a good lunch stop. There's always homemade pasta, but the main menu is seasonal; you might find grilled mushrooms, pumpkin tortellini, chicken cacciatore, or *trippa alla Veneta* (tripe in tomato and white wine). One popular risotto is made with *ortiche* (nettles). The dessert trolley is laden with homemade cakes and fruit tarts. ☒ *Via Cornuda, follow signs* ☎ *0423/565400* ☷ *No credit cards* ⊙ *Closed Thurs. and Aug. No dinner Wed.*

Treviso

㉒ *35 km (22 mi) southeast of Maser, 30 km (19 mi) north of Venice.*

Treviso is a busy commercial center with fashionable shops and boutiques. The nickname "Little Venice" is a somewhat inflated claim for the town, though it does have canals and a Venetian air. "The Painted City" is a more appropriate title: you'll come across frescoes practically everywhere you look.

The most important church in Treviso is **San Nicolò**, an impressive Gothic structure with an ornate vaulted ceiling and frescoes of the saints by Tommaso da Modena (circa 1325–1379); the depiction of *St. Agnes* on the north side is particularly charming. More remarkable are Tommaso's astoundingly realistic portraits of 40 Dominican friars in the seminary next door. They include one of the earliest-known paintings of a subject wearing glasses. ☒ *Seminario Vescovile, Via San Nicolò* ☎ *0422/ 3247* ⊙ *Church: Mon.–Sat. 8–noon and 4–6:30, Sun. 4–6:30. Seminary: Sept.–June, daily 7 AM–9 PM; July and Aug., Mon.–Sat. 7 AM–8:30 PM, Sun. 7–1.*

Inside Treviso's seven-domed **Duomo,** the Malchiostro Chapel contains an *Annunciation* by Titian and frescoes by Pordenone (1484–1539), including an *Adoration of the Magi.* The crypt is worth a visit for its 12th-century columns. ☒ *Piazza del Duomo* ⊙ *Daily 7:30–12:30 and 3–7.*

The **Piazza dei Signori** is the heart of medieval Treviso and still the town's social center, with outdoor cafés and some impressive public buildings. One of these, the Palazzo dei Trecento, has a small alley behind it that leads to the *pescheria* (fish market), on an island in one of the small rivers that flow through town.

Restored and operated by a private foundation, **Casa dei Carraresi** (☒ *Via Palestro, 33-35* ☎ *0438/513151* ⊕ *www.lineadombra.it*) hosts significant international art exhibitions that generally run from October to March.

Where to Stay & Eat

★ **$–$$** ✗ **Toni del Spin.** Wood-paneled with '30s decor, this place oozes delightful, old-fashion character. Locals love the friendly and bustling feel as well as the wholesome food. The menu is chalked on a hanging wooden board for immediate updating. Soups might include the filling *zuppa d'orzo e fagioli* (barley and bean soup). *Faraona* (guinea fowl) is a specialty, and autumn brings roast goose to the menu. Don't leave without quaffing a glass or two of Prosecco. ⊠ *Via Inferiore 7* ☎ *0422/543829* ▤ *AE, MC, V* ⊘ *Closed Sun. and Aug. No lunch Mon.*

¢–$ ✗ **Osteria Muscoli's.** The bar is always busy with locals popping in for an *ombra* (glass of wine), but there are rough-hewn tables in back where you can sit and enjoy traditional osteria fare. Open-face *crostini* (grilled bread) sandwiches, sliced meats, and quichelike pies arrive on wood cutting boards. The daily menu might include soup with radicchio and chestnuts, polenta with cheese, or catch of the day from the fish market across the bridge. ⊠ *Via Pescheria 23* ☎ *0422/583390* ▤ *No credit cards* ⊘ *Closed Sun. Apr.–Aug., Wed. Oct.–Mar., and 3 wks in Sept.*

¢ ✗ **Brek.** See review under Where to Stay & Eat in Padua, above. ⊠ *Corso del Popolo 25/27* ☎ *0422/590012* ▤ *AE, DC, MC, V.*

$ ▦ **Hotel Campeol.** For more than 40 years travelers have found a quiet, cozy stay at this small family-run hotel in the heart of Treviso. Rooms are simple but more than adequate, and bathrooms are nostalgically avocado. Breakfast is available for €6 in a brightly painted common room. The Campeol is situated within a pedestrian area, and though cars can pull in to unload, street parking is scarce. ⊠ *Piazza G. Ancilotto 4, 31100* ☎ *0422/56601* ✍ *info@albergocampeol.it* ➯ *14 rooms* ☖ *No a/c* ▤ *AE, DC, MC, V* ⊘ *Closed last 2 wks in July* ⎮◯⎮ *EP.*

$ ✗▦ **Locanda La Colonna.** Centrally located on a vine-covered, 15th-century courtyard, this small no-smoking hotel is worth booking ahead. Rich wood floors and decorative marble make the modestly furnished rooms seem lush. Flower-frescoed ceilings and old-fashion washstands add to the charm. You'll feel history seeping through the walls in Locanda's restaurant ($$), where you can sit amid pillars, frescoes, and arches. The chef favors fish, and beef with rosemary is a perfumey delight. The same menu is available in the adjacent wine bar, formerly the carriage house. ⊠ *Via Campana 27, 31100* ☎ *0422/544804* ▤ *0422/419177* ⊕ *www.ristorantelacolonna.it* ➯ *7 rooms* ☖ *Restaurant, bar, some pets allowed; no smoking* ▤ *AE, DC, MC, V* ⊘ *Restaurant closed Mon. and 2 wks in mid-Aug. No dinner Sun.* ⎮◯⎮ *EP.*

Conegliano

㉓ *23 km (14 mi) north of Treviso, 60 km (37 mi) north of Venice.*

Conegliano is in the heart of wine-producing country. The town itself is attractive, with Venetian-style villas and frescoed houses, but the real draw is the wine, particularly the effervescent Prosecco di Conegliano.

Where to Stay

$ ▦ **Canon d'Oro.** The centrally located Canon d'Oro occupies a 16th-century building with a frescoed facade and a terraced garden in the back.

TRAVELING THE WINE ROADS

YOU'D BE HARD-PRESSED to find a more stimulating and varied wine region than northeastern Italy. From the Valpolicella, Bardolino, and Soave produced near Verona to the superlative whites of the Collio region, wines from the Veneto and Friuli–Venezia Giulia earn more Denominazione di Origine Controllata (DOC) seals for uniqueness and quality than those of any other area of Italy.

You can travel on foot, by car, or by bicycle over hillsides covered with vineyards, each field nurturing subtly different grape varieties. On a casual trip through the countryside you're likely to come across wineries that will welcome you for a visit; for a more organized tour, check at local tourist information offices, which have maps of roads, wineries, and vendors. (If you find yourself in Bassano del Grappa, stop by Nardini distillery to pick up some grappa, the potent liqueur made from grape husks.) Be advised that Italy has become more stringent about its driving regulations; seat belts and designated drivers can save fines, embarrassment, or worse.

One of the most hospitable areas in the Veneto for wine enthusiasts is the stretch of country north of Treviso, where you can follow designated wine roads—tours that blend a beautiful rural setting with the delights of the grape. Authorized wine shops where you can stop and sample are marked with a sign showing a triangular arrangement of red and yellow grapes. There are three routes to choose from, and they're managable enough that you can do them all comfortably over the course of a day or two.

Montello & Asolo Hills
This route provides a good balance of vineyards and non-wine-related sights. It winds its way from Nervesa della Battaglia, a couple of miles south of Conegliano, past two prime destinations in the area, the lovely village of Asolo and the Villa Barbaro at Maser. Asolo produces good Prosecco, whereas Montello favors merlot and cabernet. Both areas also yield pinot and chardonnay.

Piave River
The circular route starts and ends in Conegliano, home of Italy's first Wine Institute. It follows the river Piave and runs through orchards, woods, and hills. Among the area's gems are the DOC Torchiato di Fregona and Refrontolo Passito, both made according to traditional methods. Raboso del Piave, renowned since Roman times, ages well and complements local dishes such as beans and pasta or goose stuffed with chestnuts. The other reds are cabernet, merlot, and cabernet sauvignon. As an accompaniment to fish, choose a Verduzzo del Piave or, for an aperitif, the lovely warm-yellow Pinot Grigio del Piave.

Prosecco
This route runs for 47 km (29 mi) between Valdobbiadene and Conegliano, winding between knobby hills covered in grapevines. These hang in festoons on row after row of pergolas to create a thick, luxuriant mantle of green. Turn off the main route to explore the narrower country lanes, most of which eventually join up. They meander through tiny hamlets and past numerous family wineries where you can taste and purchase the wines. Spring is an excellent time to visit, with no fewer than 15 local wine festivals held between March and early June.

The comfortable, modern rooms are popular with business travelers, and the friendly staff makes foreign visitors feel at home. ⊠ *Via XX Settembre 131, 31015* ☎ *0438/34246* 🖷 *0438/34249* ⊕ *www. hotelcanondoro.it* ⤴ *51 rooms* ⚭ *Restaurant, in-room data ports, in-room safes, minibars, cable TV, bar, free parking, some pets allowed, no-smoking rooms* ⊟ *AE, DC, MC, V* ¶⊙¶ *BP.*

FRIULI–VENEZIA GIULIA

The peripheral location of the Friuli–Venezia Giulia region in Italy's northeastern corner makes it easy to overlook, but with its ethnic mix of Italian, Slavic, and central European cultures, it's a fascinating area to explore. The old Austrian port of Trieste—once an important symbol of Italian nationalism—and the medieval city of Udine are perfect bases for regional excursions.

Udine

㉔ *71 km (44 mi) east of Conegliano, 127 km (79 mi) northeast of Venice.*

Udine commands a view from the Alpine foothills to the Adriatic Sea; it stands on a mound that, according to legend, was erected so Attila the Hun could watch the burning of Aquileia, the important Roman center to the south. In the Middle Ages Udine flourished, thanks to its favorable trade location and the right granted by the local patriarch to hold regular markets. There is a distinctly Venetian feel to the city, noticeable in the architecture of Piazza della Libertà under the stern gaze of the lion of St. Mark, symbol of Venetian power.

From the hilltop **Castello** panoramic views extend to Monte Nero (7,360 feet) in neighboring Slovenia. Here Udine's civic museums of art and archaeology are centralized under one roof. Particularly worth seeing is the national and regional art collection in the **Galleria d'Arte Antica**, which has canvases by Friulian Nicola Grassi (1682–1745), and Venetians Vittore Carpaccio (circa 1460–1525) and Giambattista Tiepolo. ⊠ *Castello di Udine* ☎ *0432/502872* 🖾 *€2.50, free Sun.* ⊙ *Tues.–Sat. 9:30–12:30 and 3–6, Sun. 9:30–12:30.*

Where to Stay & Eat

$$–$$$ ✕ **Vitello d'Oro.** On the terrace al fresco, or beneath a stained-glass ceiling, Udine's landmark restaurant, popular among locals for special occasions, serves regional classics and *nouveau* creations. Try *carrè di cinghiale* (saddle of wild boar) or fish roasted with *ristretto al porto*, a port wine reduction. If you haven't left room for a rich sweet, at least try a taste of homemade chestnut ice cream. ⊠ *Via Valvason 4* ☎ *0432/ 508982* ⊟ *AE, DC, MC, V* ⊙ *Closed Sun. June–Aug., Wed. Sept.–May. No lunch Mon.*

★ ¢ ✕ **Al Cappello.** Hats cram the ceiling of this whimsical osteria, which is completely painted orange except for the black wall that lists 100 wines available by the glass. Appetizer-size sandwiches, *frico* (a potato and cheese bake), and meats grilled with a splash of vinegar are served at the counter; linger over wine and the day's pasta special at one of the shared tables. Tables outside are served through an open window. ⊠ *Via Paolo Sarpi 5* ☎ *0432/299327* ☐ *No credit cards* ☉ *Closed Mon., 3 wks in Jan. and 3 wks in midsummer. No dinner Sun.*

$$ ⊡ **Clocchiatti.** Large double doors open into rooms with canopy beds and flowers hanging from the terraces. The upper floor of this 19th-century villa has Alpine-style wooden ceilings and paneling. On a quiet street, not far from the train station, Clocchiatti has plenty of space for gardens and parking. ⊠ *Via Cividale 29, 33100* ☎☎ *0432/505047* ⊕ *www. hotelclocchiatti.it* ⇦ *13 rooms* ♤ *In-room safes, minibars, cable TV, bar, free parking, some pets allowed* ◎I *BP.*

Cividale del Friuli

㉕ *17 km (11 mi) east of Udine, 144 km (89 mi) northeast of Venice.*

Cividale was founded in AD 53 by Julius Caesar, then commander of Roman legions in the area. Locals say their Ponte del Diavolo, bridging the Natisone River, is supported by rocks the devil tossed down during a tantrum. Here you'll find Celtic and Roman ruins alongside Venetian Gothic buildings, including the Palazzo Comunale. Cividale's Renaissance **Duomo** contains a magnificent 12th-century silver gilt altarpiece. ⊠ *Piazza Duomo* ☎ *0432/731144* ☉ *Apr.–Oct., Mon.–Sat. 9:30–noon and 3–7, Sun. 3–7; Nov.–Mar., Mon.–Sat. 9:30–noon and 3–6, Sun. 3–6.*

You can trace the area's history at the **Museo Archeologico,** and learn about the importance of Cividale and Udine in the period following the collapse of the Roman Empire. The collection includes weapons and jewelry from 6th-century Lombard warriors, who swept through much of what is now Italy. ⊠ *Piazza Duomo 13* ☎ *0432/700700* ☒ *€2* ☉ *Mon. 9–2, Tues.–Sun. 8:30–7:30.*

The **Tempietto Longobardo,** perched above the meandering river, is a little gem of a Lombard church. It has an archway with a vine motif, guarded by an 8th-century procession of female figures. The fine carved wooden stalls date from the 14th century. ⊠ *Via Monastero Maggiore* ☎ *0432/ 700867* ☒ *€2* ☉ *Apr.–Sept., Mon.–Sat. 9:30–12:30 and 3–6:30, Sun. 9:30–1 and 3–7:30; Oct.–Mar., Mon.–Sat. 9:30–12:30 and 3–5, Sun. 9:30–12:30 and 2:30–6.*

Where to Eat

¢–$ ✕ **Ai Tre Re.** Here, legend says, three kings once divided up the countryside, and since the 1500s The Three Kings has refreshed travelers within its stone-walled garden or beside its 6-ft-square woodstove. Beneath the beamed ceiling everything is homemade, including the bread of wheat and *maize* (corn). Try pumpkin gnocchi with smoked ricotta, followed by sausage in cream sauce or cheese grilled with wild herbs. ⊠ *Via Stretta San Valentino 31* ☎ *0432/700416* ☐ *MC, V* ☉ *Closed Tues., June, and Oct.*

Cormòns

㉖ *18 km (11 mi) south of Cividale del Friuli.*

Southeast of Udine, in the rolling hills of Friuli–Venezia Giulia, Cormòns is the epicenter of the Collio region, a producer of exceptional white wine. Route 356, just west of the Slovenian border, winds through miles of vineyard-covered hills. Residents boast that Ribolla grapes have grown here for 1,000 years, and that a 1632 document proves the region's Tocai grapes are the source of Hungary's famous Tokay wine. Local Picolit grapes are said to have been the source of papal communion wine for centuries, and it is still made here by the Sovereign Military Order of Malta.

The region has changed hands in bloody battles since the days of imperial Rome. Following World War II, international arbitrators determined whose farms would be part of Italy and whose would end up within Tito's Yugoslavia. It's no surprise that many residents here speak Slovenian in their homes and have relatives or cultivate fields across the border. In May 2004 the border effectively dissolved when Slovenia was welcomed into the European Union.

Where to Stay & Eat

$$ ✕ **Trattoria Al Giardinetto.** The wrought-iron gate and wide front porch make it feel like you're entering a family home, and indeed this restaurant is run by three brothers. Though they call their cuisine Friulian, they've come up with creative techniques imitated throughout Europe, such as cooking *in conserva,* steaming food with wine inside canning jars; you open your jar at the table, unlocking delightful aromas. All Giardinetto's ingredients are fresh, seasonal, and local, except for the cocoa in their desserts, such as *fondente di Araguani 72%,* which uses designer chocolate so rich it could substitute for a main course. For dinner, reservations are a must. ⊠ *Via Matteotti 54/56* ☎ *0481/60257* ▤ *AE, DC, MC, V* ⊘ *Closed Mon. and Tues.*

$$–$$$ ✕▦ **La Cacciatore.** Set among the Collio's vineyards, La Cacciatore
Fodor'sChoice serves food that reflects the region's Slovenian-Austrian-Italian cultural
★ blend: tortellini become *zlikrofi,* and gnocchi are made with plums instead of potatoes and served with butter and cinnamon. You'll even find wild *sambuco* (elderflowers) and *dragoncello* (taragon) in the desserts. The prix-fixe menu (€48–€55) provides a consistently delicious meal. The restaurant is the centerpiece of La Subida, Josko and Loredana Sirk's painstakingly created country refuge, which also includes the less formal (and less expensive) Osteria La Subida and rustic yet modern cabins ($$) for overnight stays. ⊠ *Loc. Monte 22, 34071* ☎ *0481/60531* ⚎ *0481/61616* ⊕ *www.lasubida.it* ⊅ *13 apartments* ⚴ *Restaurant, refrigerators, cable TV, tennis, pool, bicycles, horseback riding, bar, some pets allowed; no a/c* ▤ *MC, V* ⊘ *Restaurant closed Tues. and Wed., 3 wks in Feb., and Aug 1–10. No lunch Mon., Thurs., or Fri. Osteria closed Thurs. and Nov. Apartments closed 3 wks in Feb.* ﴾❂﴿ *EP.*

$$–$$$ ▦ **Castello Formentini.** Count Formentini's castle has been ancestral prop-
Fodor'sChoice erty for five centuries. The restored complex today includes a winery, sports
★ facilities, and superb accommodations that blend antique furnishings with modern conveniences. Not only is breakfast included, but a complimentary buffet/bar is available throughout the day. About once a month the massive hall hosts medieval banquets complete with sword fights, fireeaters, 15th-century recipes, and no forks. Though such events can feel contrived and tacky, here they pull it off with style. ⊠ *Via Oslavia 2,*

*San Floriano del Collio, just outside Gorizia 34070 ☎ 0481/884051
🖷 0481/884052 ⊕ www.golfhotelcastelloformentini.it 🛏 14 rooms, 1
suite ⚘ Snack bar, minibars, cable TV, 9-hole golf course, tennis, pool,
bar, meeting room, some pets allowed, no-smoking rooms; no a/c in some
rooms ▤ AE, DC, MC, V ⊗ Closed Dec. 20–Jan. ⅋ BP.*

Trieste

㉗ *64 km (40 mi) southeast of Udine, 163 km (101 mi) east of Venice.*

Surrounded by rugged countryside and a beautiful coastline, Trieste is
built on a hillside above what was once the chief port of the Austro-
Hungarian Empire. Typical of Trieste are its belle-epoque cafés. Like Vienna's coffeehouses, these are social and cultural centers and much-beloved
refuges from winter's bitter *bora* (wind from the north).

The sidewalk cafés on the vast seaside **Piazza dell'Unità d'Italia** are popular meeting places in the summer months. The square is similar to Piazzetta San Marco in Venice; both are focal points of architectural
interest and command fine views of the water. On the inland side of Piazza dell'Unità d'Italia, steps behind the **Palazzo Comunale** (Town Hall)
lead uphill, tracing Trieste's upward expansion from its roots as a
Roman fishing port.

The **Civico Museo Revoltella e Galleria d'Arte Moderna** (Revoltella Museum and Gallery of Modern Art) was founded in 1872, when the city
inherited the palazzo, library, and art collection of shipping magnate Baron
Pasquale Revoltella, vice president of the consortium that built the Suez
Canal. An adjacent building holds one of the country's most important
collections of 19th- and 20th-century art, with Italian artists particularly well represented. Hours vary for special exhibits, but don't miss a
summer evening at the museum's rooftop café, where the view rivals
the artwork. ⊠ *Via Armando Diaz 27* ☎ *040/6754158* 🖅 *€5* ⊗ *Mon.
and Wed.–Sat. 10–2 and 4–7, Sun. 10-7; July 15–Aug., Thurs.–Sat. 10
AM–midnight.*

In the 14th-century **Cattedrale di San Giusto** there are remnants of two
previous churches built on the same ground, the earlier dating from the
5th century. The exterior includes fragments of Roman tombs and temples, adding to the jumble of styles: the pillars of the main doorway are
the most conspicuous Roman element. Inside, don't miss the 12th-cen-
tury gold mosaic behind the main altar. ⊠ *Piazza Cattedrale 2* ☎ *040/
309666* ⊗ *Apr.–Sept., daily 8–7:30; Oct.–Mar., daily 8–6:30.*

The hilltop **Castello di San Giusto** was built on the ruins of the Roman
town of Tergeste. Given the excellent view, it's no surprise that 15th-
century Venetians turned the castle into a shipping observation point;
the structure was further enlarged by Trieste's subsequent rulers, the Habsburgs. Some of the best exhibits in the **Museo Civico del Castello di
San Giusto** are the displays of weaponry and armor. ⊠ *Piazza Cattedrale 3* ☎ *040/309362 castle, 040/313636 museum* 🖅 *€2* ⊗ *Museum
Tues.–Sun. 9–1. Castle Apr.–Sept., daily 9–7; Oct.–Mar., daily 9–5.*

CloseUp

TRIESTE'S CAFFÈ CULTURE

TRIESTE IS JUSTLY FAMOUS for its coffee, and so it is perhaps no coincidence that its former mayor Riccardo Illy is patriarch of Illycaffè, supplier of top-quality caffeine fixes throughout Italy and the world. The elegant civility of Trieste plays out beautifully in a caffè culture rivaling that of Vienna. In Trieste, as elsewhere in Italy, ask for a caffè and you'll get a thimbleful of high-octane espresso. Your cappuccino here will also come in an espresso cup, with only half as much frothy milk as you'll find elsewhere and a dollop of whipped cream. Many cafés are part of a torrefazione (roasting shop), so you can sample a cup and then buy beans to take with you.

Few cafés in Italy—or in the world—can rival **Antico Caffè San Marco** (⊠ Via Cesare Battisti 18 ☎ 040/363538) for its art deco style and bohemian atmosphere. After being destroyed in World War I, it was rebuilt in the 1920s and became a meeting place for local intellectuals. **Cremcaffè** (⊠ Piazza Carlo Goldoni 10, ☎ 040/636555) isn't the place to sit and read the paper, but its downtown location and selection of 20 coffee blends make it one of the busiest cafés in town. Founded in 1830, classic **Caffè Tommaseo** (⊠ Piazza Tommaseo 4/c ☎ 040/362666) is a comfortable place to linger, especially on weekend evenings and Sunday morning when there's live music. For a great view of the great piazza, you couldn't do better than **Caffè Degli Specchi** (⊠ Piazza dell'Unità d'Italia 7 ☎ 040/365777), where the many mirrors heighten the opportunities for people-watching. The atmosphere is more modern than old-world at **I Paesi del Caffè** (⊠ Via Einaudi 1 ☎ 040/633897), which brews and sells beans of top international varieties, including Jamaica Blue Mountain.

🕭 At Trieste's **Museo del Mare** you'll learn how Venetian galley rowers managed to sit three abreast and not smash one another with their oars. Displays include lots of boat models and a diorama with *casoni* (fishermen's grass huts) and submerged *seragi* (fishnet traps). Outside is a park area with giant anchors and shady benches. ⊠ *Via di Campo Marzio 5* ☎ *040/304987* 🎫 *€3* 🕐 *Tues.–Sun. 8:30–1:30.*

A statue of Habsburg emperor Leopold I looks out over **Piazza della Borsa**, which contains Trieste's original stock exchange, the **Borsa Vecchia**, a neoclassical building now serving as the chamber of commerce.

off the beaten path

GROTTA GIGANTE – More than 300 feet high, 900 feet long, and 200 feet wide, this gigantic cave is filled with spectacular stalactites and stalagmites. Allow 50 minutes for the tour (which is required). The location is about 10 km (6 mi) north of Trieste; Bus 42 takes you there from Piazza Oberdan about every 30 minutes. It's cool inside year-round, so bring a sweater, and be prepared for a 500-step climb. ☎ *040/327312* ⊕ *www.grottagigante.it* 🎫 *€7.50* 🕐 *Apr.–June and Sept., Tues.–Sun.10–6; July and Aug., daily 10–6; Mar. and Oct., Tues.–Sun. 10–4; Nov.–Feb., Tues.–Sun. 10–noon and 2–4. Apr.–Sept., tours leave every 30 mins; other months, every hr.*

Where to Stay & Eat

$$ ✕ **Suban.** It's worth a taxi ride into the hills to visit this landmark trattoria. The rustic decor is rich in dark wood, stone, and wrought iron; the Italian fare shows Slovenian, Hungarian, and Austrian influences. Among the specialties are *jota carsolina* (cabbage, potato, and bean soup) and duck breast in Tocai wine sauce. Some dishes can be heavy; plan accordingly if you want to have room left for the delicious Hungarian-influenced *rigo janci* (a mousselike chocolate pudding). ⊠ *Via Emilio Comici 2/d,* ☎ *040/54368* ▭ *AE, DC, MC, V* ⊘ *Closed Tues., 3 wks in Aug., and 1 wk in early Jan. No lunch Mon.*

$$ ✕ **Trattoria ai Fiori.** Fish are delivered fresh off the boat by fishermen still in their gum boots. Other draws at this small restaurant are the homemade bread, the roasted coffee, the wine cellar's 12,000-plus bottles, and 150 varieties of grappa on display as you enter the restaurant. Have your fish grilled simply, or try a seasonal variation such as steamed on a bed of wild mushrooms and truffles. ⊠ *Piazza Attilio Hortis 7* ☎☎ *040/300633* ▭ *AE, DC, MC, V* ⊘ *Closed Sun. and Mon.*

★ **¢–$** ✕ **Antipastoteca di Mare.** Nautical kitsch and Little Mermaid curtains add to the charm of Roberto Surian's homey little restaurant hidden away near Castello di San Giusto. The menu is exclusively seafood, accompanied only by a simple salad, potatoes, polenta, and house wine. Among the outstanding dishes are calamari and barley salad, and scallops, mussels, and sardines with basil. The fish soup of sardines, mackerel, and tuna topped with diced garlic bread won first prize in Trieste's prestigious Sarde Day competition. ⊠ *Via della Fornace 1* ☎ *040/ 309606* ▭ *No credit cards* ⊘ *Closed Mon. No dinner Sun.*

¢ ✕ **Brek.** See review under Where to Stay & Eat in Padua, above. ⊠ *Via S. Francesco, 10* ☎ *040/371331* ▭ *AE, DC, MC, V.*

$$$$ ✕▦ **Duchi d'Aosta.** Since the 1400s, hotels on this spot have hosted everyone from sailors and merchants to Austrian emperors. Continuously reincarnated like the city of Trieste itself, Duchi d'Aosta today welcomes guests with valet parking, Oriental carpets, and rich brocade. Rooms are furnished in dark-wood antiques; some have terraces, and one is equipped for wheelchair users. On the ground floor is one of the city's most elegant restaurants, Harry's Grill ($$$), a spinoff of Harry's Bar in Venice. Now under separate ownership, it serves food far superior to that of the more famous original. ⊠ *Piazza dell'Unità d'Italia 2, 34121* ☎ *040/7600011* 🖷 *040/366092* ⊕ *www.grandhotelduchidaosta.com* ⇆ *53 rooms, 2 suites* ⟲ *Restaurant, minibars, cable TV with movies, some in-room hot tubs, bar, meeting rooms, parking (fee), some pets allowed, no-smoking rooms* ▭ *AE, DC, MC, V* ⌦ *BP.*

★ **$$–$$$** ✕▦ **Riviera & Maximilian's.** Travel just 7 km (4 mi) north of Trieste and you've left the city behind. There are stunning views across the Golfo di Trieste, and you can take an elevator down to a private beach, pool, and children's area. Rooms vary from modern design to vintage wood, and some have balconies and kitchenettes. The restaurant, Le Terrazze, ($–$$), looks out on a lovely panorama and serves fine regional cuisine. ⊠ *Strada Costiera 22, 34010* ☎ *040/224551* 🖷 *040/224300* ⊕ *www. hotelrivieraemaximilian.com* ⇆ *56 rooms, 2 suites, 9 apartments* ⟲ *Restaurant, in-room data ports, minibars, cable TV with movies, beach,* *bar, Internet, meeting rooms, parking, some pets allowed; no a/c in some rooms* ▭ *AE, DC, MC, V* ⏐⚬⏐ *BP.*

$$ ▦ **Alla Posta.** A roaring fire in the lobby reading lounge and Italian marble bathrooms make this a popular midrange choice. It's well located for bus and train connections; soundproof windows let you enjoy a piazza view without the piazza noise. Rooms are outfitted with high-tech controls for heating, air-conditioning, and wake-up calls. ⊠ *Piazza Oberdan 1* ☏ *040/365208* 🖶 *040/633720* ⊕ *www.albergopostatrieste. it* 🛏 *47 rooms* ⚴ *In-room data ports, in-room safes, minibars, cable TV with movies, some pets allowed* ▭ *AE, DC, MC, V* ⏐⚬⏐ *BP.*

¢ ▦ **Alabarda.** Bright, spacious rooms make this family-operated hotel the best deal in central Trieste. It's only a 10-minute walk from the train station, and the staff is happy to help you with local services, maps, and city bus tickets. Some front rooms are noisy. ⊠ *Via Valdirivo 22,* ☏ *040/ 630269* 🖶 *040/639284* ⊕ *www.hotelalabarda.it* 🛏 *17 rooms, 7 with bath* ⚴ *In-room data ports, cable TV, Internet, some pets allowed; no a/c in some rooms* ▭ *AE, DC, MC, V* ⏐⚬⏐ *BP.*

Nightlife & the Arts

The **opera** season in Trieste runs from October through May, with a brief operetta festival in July and August. Contact the **tourist information office** (⊠ Piazza dell'Unità d'Italia 4/b ☏ 040/3478312) or the **opera house** (⊠ Piazza Verdi 1 ☏ 040/6722111 ⊕ www.teatroverdi-trieste. com) for details on events.

Shopping

Trieste's busy shopping street, **Corso Italia,** is reached from Piazza della Borsa. There are antiques markets on the streets of the city's old center on the third Sunday of each month. Trieste has some 60 antiques dealers, jewelers, and secondhand shops, and a large antiques fair is held in the city at the end of October.

Castello di Miramare

★ ☾ ❷ *7 km (4½ mi) northwest of Trieste.*

Archduke Maximilian of Habsburg, brother of Emperor Franz Josef and retired commander of the Austrian navy, built this seafront extravaganza in the 19th century. It features ship's-keel wooden ceilings, marine-blue furnishings, and windows onto the Adriatic. His peaceful retirement was interrupted in 1864 when he reluctantly became Emperor of Mexico; he was killed three years later by a Mexican firing squad. The castle was later owned by the Duke of Aosta, who installed modern plumbing in his art deco bathroom. Within the 54-acre garden surrounding the castle is **Tropical Park** greenhouse, which is populated by butterflies and birds. Bus 36 from Piazza Oberdan in Trieste leaves for here every half hour. ⊠ *Miramare* ☏ *040/224143 castello, 040/224406 greenhouse* ⊕ *www.castello-miramare.it* 🎫 *Castle €4; guided tour by reservation €3; greenhouse €6.50* ☉ *Castle daily 9–7, last entry 30 mins before closing. Park daily Apr.–Sept., 8–7; Nov.–Feb., 8–5; Mar. and Oct., 8–6. Greenhouse daily Apr.–Oct., 9–6; Nov.–Mar., 10–5.*

THE VENETIAN ARC A TO Z

To research prices, get advice from other travelers, and book travel arrangements, visit www.fodors.com.

AIRPORTS

The main airport serving the Venetian Arc is Aeroporto Marco Polo, 10 km (6 mi) north of Venice, which handles international and domestic flights to the region. A few European airlines schedule flights to Aeroporto Valerio Catullo, southwest of Verona; it's also served by a number of charter flights. A regular bus service connects the airport with Verona's Porta Nuova railway station.

Aeroporto di Treviso, 5 km (3 mi) southeast of Treviso, 32 km (19 mi) north of Venice, is also served by charter flights (check ⊕ www.ryanair. com for flights to and from London's Stansted airport). Flights to Treviso sometimes include transportation from the airport to Venice or other destinations; otherwise there is an ACTT local bus service to Treviso every 30 minutes during the day (until 9 PM), or a taxi will come to the airport to pick you up from Treviso. There are domestic and some European flights (including a daily Ryanair London service) to Aeroporto Ronchi dei Legionari, 35 km (22 mi) northwest of Trieste, linked with the Trieste's Piazza della Libertà bus terminal (beside the railway station) by regular APT bus service, or you can take a convenient *servizio navetta* (shuttle).

🚩 Airport Information **Aeroporto Marco Polo** ⊠ Tessera, 10 km (6 mi) north of Venice ☎ 041/2609260 or 041/2609240 automated system ⊕ www.veniceairport.it. **Aeroporto Valerio Catullo di Verona Villafranca** ⊠ 11 km (7 mi) southwest of Verona ☎ 045/8095666 ⊕ www.aeroportoverona.it. **Aeroporto Ronchi dei Legionari** ☎ 0481/ 773224 ⊕ www.aeroporto.fvg.it. **Aeroporto di Treviso** ☎ 0422/315131.

🚩 Taxis & Shuttles **APT** ☎ 0481/593511 ⊕ www.aptgorizia.it. **Servizio Navetta** ☎ 340/ 2306444 ⊕ www.aeroporto.fvg.it. **Taxi** ☎ 0422/431515 automated system in Italian.

BUS TRAVEL

There are interurban and interregional connections throughout the Veneto and Friuli. Local tourist offices may be able to provide details of timetables and routes; otherwise contact the local bus station or, in some cases, the individual bus companies operating from the station, listed below.

🚩 Bus Information **ACTT buses** ⊠ Piazzale Duca D'Aosta 25, Treviso ☎ 0422/327253. **ACTV buses** ⊠ Piazzale Roma, Venice ☎ 041/24240 buses to Brenta Riviera ⊕ www. actv.it. **APTV buses** ⊠ Autostazione di Verona Porta Nuova, Piazzale XXV Aprile, Verona ☎ 045/8057911 ⊕ www.aptv.it. **ATVO buses** ⊠ Piazzale Roma, Venice ☎ 041/ 5205530 ⊕ www.atvo.it. **FTV buses** ⊠ Piazzale della Stazione near Campo Marzio, Vicenza ☎ 0444/223115 ⊕ www.ftv.vi.it. **SITA buses** ⊠ Piazzale Boschetti, Padua ☎ 049/8206844 ⊕ www.sita-on-line.it. **TT buses** ⊠ Piazza della Libertà, Trieste ☎ 800/016675 ⊕ www.triestetrasporti.it.

CAR RENTAL

🚩 Local Agencies **Avis** ☎ nationwide reservations/information 199/100133 toll-free, ⊠ Piazza Stazione 1, Padua ☎ 049/664198 ⊠ Piazzale Duca D'Aosta 1, Treviso

☎ 0422/542287 ✉ Stazione Marittima, Molo dei Bersaglieri 3, Trieste ☎ 040/300820 ✉ Aeroporto Ronchi dei Legionari, Trieste ☎ 0481/777085 ✉ Viale Giacomo Leopard 5/a, Udine ☎ 0432/501149 ✉ Stazione Ferroviaria Verona Porta Nuova, Verona ☎ 045/8006636 ✉ Viale Milano 88, Vicenza ☎ 0444/321622. **Europcar** ✉ Piazzale della Stazione 6, Padua ☎ 049/657877. **Hertz** ☎ Nationwide reservations/information 199/112211 toll-free ✉ Molo dei Bersaglieri 3, Trieste ☎ 040/3220098 ✉ Aeroporto Ronchi dei Legionari, Trieste ☎ 0481/777025 ✉ Via Francesco Crispi 17, Udine ☎ 0432/ 511211 ✉ Piazzale della Stazione 1 Padua ☎ 049/8752202 ✉ Porta Nuova Railway Station, Verona ☎ 045/8000832 ✉ Railway Station, Vicenza ☎ 0444/231728

CAR TRAVEL

The main access roads to the Venetian Arc from southern Italy are both linked to the A1 (Autostrada del Sole), which connects Bologna, Florence, and Rome. They are the A13, which culminates in Padua, and the A22, which passes through Verona running north–south. The road linking the region from east to west is the A4, the primary route from Milan to as far as Trieste, skirting Verona, Padua, and Venice along the way. The distance from Verona, in the west, to Trieste is 263 km (163 mi). Branches link the A4 with Treviso (A27), Pordenone (A28), and Udine (A23).

EMERGENCY ACI Emergency Service offers 24-hour roadside assistance.
SERVICES 🚗 **ACI dispatchers** ☎ 803/116.

EMERGENCIES

For first aid, dial the general emergency number (113) and ask for *pronto soccorso* (first aid). Be prepared to give your address. (If you can find a concierge or some other Italian-speaker to call on your behalf, do so, as not all 113 operators speak English.) All pharmacies post signs on the door with addresses of pharmacies that stay open at night, on Saturday afternoon, and on Sunday.
🚗 **Police, Ambulance, Fire** ☎ 113.

TOURS

Many of the best tours begin and end in Venice, because so much of the region is accessible from there. The Burchiello excursion boat makes an all-day villa tour along the Brenta River Canal; contact American Express for information. For those who prefer to go it alone, the most practical way is to hire a car for the day. Local tourist offices will be able to put you in contact with the Tourist Guides Association or provide you with a list of authorized guides, for whom there is an official tariff rate.
🚗 **American Express** ✉ Salizada San Moisè 1471, San Marco, Venice ☎ 041/5200844 🖶 041/5229937. **Association of Trieste Authorized Guides** ☎ 040/365248. **Padua Authorized Guides** ⊕ www.guidepadova.it

TRAIN TRAVEL

Trains on the main routes from the south stop almost hourly in Verona, Padua, and Venice. From northern Italy and the rest of Europe, trains usually enter via Milan or through Porta Nuova station in Verona. To the west of Venice, on the main line running across the north of Italy, are Padua (30 minutes from Venice), Vicenza (1 hour), and Verona (1½ hours); to the east is Trieste (2 hours). Local trains link Venice to Bassano del Grappa (1 hour), Padua to Bassano del Grappa (1 hour), Vicenza to Treviso (1 hour), and Udine to Trieste (1 hour). Treviso and Udine both lie on the main line from Venice to Tarvisio, on which Eurocity trains continue to Vienna and Prague. Call Trenitalia for information, or check out their Web site.

🖪 Train Information **Trenitalia** ☎ 892021 ⊕ www.trenitalia.com.

TRAVEL AGENCIES

🖪 Local Agent Referrals **American Express** ✉ Fabretto Viaggi/American Express, Via Risorgimento 20, Padua ☎ 049/666133 ✉ Uvet American Express, Via Francia 5, Verona ☎ 045/505200

VISITOR INFORMATION

🖪 Tourist Information **Asolo** ✉ Piazza Garibaldi, 31011 ☎ 0423/529046. **Bassano del Grappa** ✉ Lago Corona d'Italia 35, 36061 ☎ 0424/524351 ⊕ www.vicenzae.org. **Marostica** ✉ Piazza Castello 1, 36063 ☎ 0424/72127 ⊕ www.marosticaonline.it. **Padua** ✉ Padova Railway Station ☎ 049/8752077 ✉ Vicolo Pedrocchi ☎ 049/8767927 ⊕ www.apt.padova.it. **Treviso** ✉ Piazza Monte di Pietà 8, 31100 ☎ 0422/547632. **Trieste** ✉ Piazza dell Unità d'Italia 4/b, 34100 ☎ 040/3478312 ⊕ www.triestetourism.it. **Udine** ✉ Piazza I Maggio 7, 33100 ☎ 0432/295972 ⊕ www.turismo/fvg.it. **Verona** ✉ Piazza Brà, 37100 ☎ 045/8068680 ✉ Porta Nuova Railway Station, ☎ 045/8000861 ⊕ www.tourism.verona.it. **Vicenza** ✉ Piazza Giacomo Matteotti 12, 36100 ☎ 0444/320854 ✉ Piazza dei Signori 8 ☎ 0444/544122 ⊕ www.ascom.vi.it/aptvicenza.

THE DOLOMITES: TRENTINO–ALTO ADIGE

3

Updated by
Ryan Bradley

THE VAST, MOUNTAINOUS DOMAIN of northeastern Italy, unlike other famous Alpine ranges, has remained relatively undeveloped. The virginal landscape is a playground for outdoor sports: ski fanatics travel across the world to take on the same steep slopes that have tested Olympic champions; mountaineers scale the sheer rock faces; and hikers trek between local way stations known as *rifugi*. In the lowland valleys you'll find prosperous towns, secluded villages, picture-book castles, and rustic bridges.

The Dolomites, sprawling over the Trentino–Alto Adige region and into parts of Lombardy (by the Swiss border) and the Veneto (along the Austrian border), became internationally known as a winter sports center when Cortina d'Ampezzo hosted the 1956 Winter Olympics. Today scores of funiculars and chairlifts provide access to 1,200 km (750 mi) of ski runs, as well as ski jumps and bobsled runs.

Less accessible are the strange, rocky pinnacles themselves—which jut straight up like chimneys and in places look more like Utah's Monument Valley than any European range—looming over scattered, isolated mountain lakes. From plateaus atop the highest mountains, in the "untouchable zones" reached only after arduous hours of climbing beyond the lifts' end, you can see Italy on one side and Austria or Switzerland on the other.

Straddling the Brenner Pass—the main access point between Italy and central Europe—the Dolomites play host to a mixture of cultures. Too often overlooked by travelers going through the Brenner Pass are the picturesque and prosperous mountain towns of Trento, Bolzano, and Merano. All three are marked by a departure in architectural style, with surrounding mountains serving as a backdrop for onion-bulb roofs and jutting spires uncharacteristic of the rest of Italy.

Whereas Trentino is largely Italian-speaking, Alto Adige is predominantly Germanic: until World War I, the area was Austria's South Tirol. The persistence of Austro-German influence can be seen in the profusion of pastry shops, lively beer halls, rustic restaurants serving hearty meat-and-dumpling fare, and in an earlier daily schedule. Reflecting this diversity, the area has enjoyed special status since 1948 as the Autonomous Region of Trentino–Alto Adige, made up of the independent provinces of Trento and Bolzano. There is also a third language to be heard in the area: Ladin, an offshoot of Latin still spoken by a small community primarily in the Val Gardena. The language can credit centuries of isolation in mountain strongholds for its survival. Signs throughout much of the Dolomites are bilingual. Where useful, place names in this chapter are given in Italian with German equivalents in parentheses.

Exploring the Dolomites

The only way to get around in this mountainous region is by following the river valleys as they carve their courses through the Dolomite massifs. Two of the most heavily traveled paths are formed by the Isarco and Adige rivers: the Isarco begins at the Brenner Pass and runs due south to Bolzano, where it joins the Adige (which originates near the Swiss border and passes Verona on its way to the Adriatic Sea). Italy's main road and rail connections to central Europe follow these rivers northward en route to the Brenner Pass. Note that it's difficult to reach the ski areas—or any town outside of Rovereto, Trento, Bolzano, and Merano—without a car.

About the Hotels & Restaurants

Accommodations in the Dolomites range from restored castles to spic-and-span chalet guesthouses, from stately 19th-century hotels to chic modern ski resorts. Even a small village may have scores of places to stay, many of them very inexpensive. Hotel information offices at train stations and tourist offices can help you sidestep the language problem if you arrive without reservations. The Bolzano train station has a 24-hour hotel service, and tourist offices will give you a list of all the hotels in the area, arranged by location and price.

Many hotels at ski resorts cater primarily to longer stays at full or half board: it's wise to book ski vacations as packages in advance. Outside the ski season, accommodations are easier to find, but reservations are still recommended. Nearly all rural accommodations close from early November to mid- or late December, as well as for a month or two after Easter.

Everything in South Tirol (Alto Adige) has more than a tinge of the Teutonic. Even when given change for your morning cappuccino, you'll be thanked with *"danke, grazie."* Heavier, more rustic food is served in dining rooms designed in the style of traditional Tirolean *Stuben* (drinking halls), with warm wood paneling. Although the early dining schedule you'll find in Germany or Austria is somewhat tempered here, your options for late-night dining will be more limited than in southern Italy, where *la dolce vita* has a much firmer grip.

Not to be missed are the outdoor *Wurst* carts, even (or perhaps especially) in colder weather. After placing your order at these movable sausage stands you'll get a sheet of wax paper, followed by a dollop of mustard, a hard Kaiser roll, and your chosen Wurst. You can sometimes make your selection by pointing to whatever picture seems most appealing; if not, pass on the familiar-sounding *Frankfurter* and try the local *Meraner*. The carts can reliably be found in Bolzano (Piazza delle Erbe, or in front of the archaeological museum) and Merano (Piazza del Grano, or along the river).

WHAT IT COSTS In euros				
$$$$	**$$$**	**$$**	**$**	**¢**
RESTAURANTS over €22	€16–€22	€11–€16	€7–€11	under €7
HOTELS over €220	€160–€220	€110–€160	€70–€110	under €70

Restaurant prices are for a second course (*secondo piatto*). Hotel prices are for two people in a standard double room in high season, including tax and service.

Timing

Skiers should plan their trip between mid-December and April, when most resorts are open. But powder hounds, beware: snowfall in early

Mountain roads are generally of excellent quality and well maintained, but in winter are often covered in snow and buffeted by high winds. Closures can begin as early as November and continue until May, in particular on the high mountain passes such as Passo di Gavia and Passo dello Stelvio.

Numbers in the text correspond to numbers in the margin and on the Dolomites: Trentino–Alto Adige and Bolzano maps.

3

If you have
3 days

Book three nights in 🗺 **Bolzano** ❼–⓬ ⌐; explore the town on your first day, and on your second, start off early to tour **Trento** ❶. If time permits, add a stop in **Rovereto** ❷ or **Caldaro** ㉔ before returning to Bolzano. On your last day, you'll have a choice: a relaxing visit to the spa town of **Merano** ⓮ or an exhilarating drive through the Heart of the Dolomites by heading north to **Chiusa** ⓰, east through the Val Gardena and past **Ortisei** ㉒, south to **Canazei** ㉑ via the spectacular Passo di Sella, then west onto the Great Dolomites Road leading back to Bolzano, passing **Lago di Carezza** ㉕ en route.

If you have
5 days

Start with the three-day itinerary, choosing the **Merano** ⓮ option on Day 3. Your next day will be heavy on driving: head through **Cornedo** ⓯, **Fiè allo Sciliar** ㉓, and **Chiusa** ⓰ to **Bressanone** ⓱, where you'll turn east for **Brunico** ⓲ and **Dobbiaco** ⓳. Your destination for the night is the historic resort of 🗺 **Cortina d'Ampezzo** ⓴. Spend the morning exploring Cortina before returning along the Great Dolomites Road through the Passo di Falzarego to **Canazei** ㉑, then north via the Passo di Sella to 🗺 **Ortisei** ㉒, in the heart of the Val Gardena, for your last night.

If you have
8 days

Book two nights in 🗺 **Bolzano** ❼–⓬ ⌐; explore the town on your first day, and on your second, start off early to **Trento** ❶. After a short tour continue south to **Rovereto** ❷ and **Riva del Garda** on the tip of Lake Garda, then on to **Pinzolo** ❸ and the chic resort 🗺 **Madonna di Campiglio** ❹. On your next day, you'll get a bird's-eye view of the Dolomites as you head north over Campo Carlo Magno; at Dimaro, swing west and head for the dizzyingly high Passo di Gavia and 🗺 **Bormio** ❺. On your fourth day drive the breathtaking **Passo dello Stelvio** ❻ on the way to sleepy **Naturno** ⓭ and, finally, lovely 🗺 **Merano** ⓮. For your last three days, pick up the five-day itinerary at Merano, but spend a night in **Brunico** ⓲ and **Dobbiaco** ⓳, or a second night in 🗺 **Cortina d'Ampezzo** ⓴.

winter is unreliable; scrutinize snow reports if you're planning to visit before mid- to late February. The Dolomites do not receive as much consistent snow as the Alps, and some years there is little snow all season. With the exception of the main bargain period known as *settimane bianche* (white weeks) in January and February, the slopes are relatively crowd-free. Booking well in advance of your ski holiday is highly recommended, as lack of snow in the early part of the season can sometimes cause overcrowding later on.

Summer is the season for hiking in the Dolomites: mountain temperatures drop sharply in September, and trails can remain icy well into June. Spring and autumn are delightfully tourist-free in the valley towns, and if you're in South Tirol in the fall, a tour of its cozy wine taverns to taste the new wine (and hot roasted chestnuts) is not to be missed.

TRENTINO

The areas east and west of Trento are collectively known as Trentino, a region shaped roughly like a butterfly. Some of the passes in this region close during the winter months, so if you're traveling during this period you will not be able to follow the entire "Great Itineraries" outlined above in their entirety.

Trento

❶ *51 km (32 mi) south of Bolzano, 24 km (15 mi) north of Rovereto.*

Capital of the autonomous Trentino province, Trento is a fashionable university town that retains an architectural charm befitting its historical importance. Its Piazza del Duomo remains splendid, and its enormous medieval palazzo dominates the city landscape in virtually its original form. It was here, from 1545 to 1563, that the structure of the Catholic Church was redefined at the Council of Trent. This was the starting point of the Counter-Reformation, which brought half of Europe back to Catholicism. You'll see the word *consiglio* (council) everywhere in Trento—in hotel, restaurant, and street names, and even on wine labels.

Free guided tours of Trento are offered every Saturday, leaving from the **tourist office** (✉ Via Manci 2 ☎ 0461/983880). You can meet at 10 AM for a visit to the Castello del Buonconsiglio and a wine tasting, or 3 PM for a tour of the city center. Reservations are not required.

The massive Romanesque **Duomo,** also known as the Cathedral of San Virgilio, forms the southern edge of the Piazza del Duomo. Locals refer to this square as the city's *salotto* (sitting room), as in fine weather it's always filled with students and residents drinking coffee, enjoying an aperitif, or reading the newspaper. A baroque **Fontana del Nettuno** presides over it all. When skies are clear, pause here to savor the view of the mountaintops enveloping the city.

Within the Duomo, unusual arcaded stone stairways border the austere nave. Ahead is the *baldacchino* (altar canopy), a clear copy of Bernini's masterpiece in St. Peter's in Rome. In the small Cappella del Crocifisso (Chapel of the Crucifix) to the right is a mournful 15th-century crucifixion, with the Virgin Mary and John the Apostle. This crucifix, by German artist Sixtus Frei, was a focal point of the Council of Trent: each decree agreed on during the two decades of deliberations was solemnly read out in front of it. Outside, walk around to the back of the cathedral to see an exquisite display of the 14th-century stonemason's art, from

Enrosadira

The Dolomites, the inimitable craggy peaks Le Corbusier called "the most beautiful work of architecture ever seen," are never so arresting as at dusk, when the last rays of sun create a pink hue that languishes into purple. In the Ladin language, spoken only in the isolated valleys below, this magnificent transformation has its own word—the *enrosadira*. You can certainly enjoy this phenomenon from a distance, but what makes the Dolomites such an appealing year-round destination is the multitude of options for getting onto the mountains themselves. Whether you come for a pleasant stroll or a technical ascent in summer, to plunge down sheer faces or glide across peaceful valleys in winter, or to brave narrow switchbacks in a rented Fiat, your perspective, like the peaks themselves, can only become more rose-colored.

Hiking & Climbing

The Dolomites are a major draw for serious climbers—it's not surprising that Reinhold Messner, the first climber to reach the summit of Everest without oxygen, is a lifelong resident. For those interested in subtler thrills, the hiking options are abundant and beautiful. If you're in between—wanting to get off the trails but lacking extensive mountaineering experience—a guided trip along the Vie Ferrate (Iron Ways) may be for you. These mountain routes have fixed climbing aids (steps, ladders, bridges, safety cables), which were originally left by the Alpine divisions of the Italian and Austro-Hungarian armies and have since been converted for recreational use. However you travel through the mountains, you can take advantage of a well-maintained network of *rifugi*, cozy shelters that are destinations in themselves. And if none of this seems your speed, you can simply set out on one of the foothill strolls—Merano's Passeggiata Tappeiner, or the Passeggiata del Guncina in Bolzano—without leaving the valley towns.

Skiing

The Dolomites offer some of the most spectacular downhill skiing in Europe, with the facilities to match. The most comprehensive centers are the unabashedly upscale resorts of Cortina d'Ampezzo and Madonna di Campiglio, which draw an international clientele with their impressive terrain, expansive interconnected lift systems, tradition of warm hospitality, and lively après-ski. If you seek authentic Tirolean *Gemütlichkeit,* move on from Cortina and Madonna and visit one of the numerous more rustic resorts throughout the region: at Val Gardena or Alta Badia your lift-mate is more likely to be a German-speaking schoolteacher from a neighboring town than a businessman from Milan (or Tokyo). Both major resorts and out-of-the-way villages have well-marked trails for *sci di fondo* (cross-country skiing), and you can also usually get permission to blaze trails across virgin snowfields by inquiring at the local tourist office (or just asking at the nearest farmhouse). The winter season generally runs from December to April, but the early season often suffers from light snowfall, and the best conditions often aren't seen until late February.

The Dolomites: Trentino–Alto Adige

KEY
▲ Start of itinerary

ON THE MENU

THE DOLOMITE REGION *combines Italian cuisine with local Tirolean specialties, which are much like the dishes of Austria and central Europe. Alimentari (food shops) stock a bounty of regional cheeses, pickles, salami, and smoked meats—perfect for picnics—and bakeries turn out a wide selection of crusty dark rolls and caraway-studded rye breads. The best of the cheeses are the mild Asiago and fontal and the more pungent puzzone di Moena (literally, "stinkpot").*

Local dishes vary from one isolated mountain valley to the next. Don't miss Speck tirolese (smoked ham). Other specialties include Canederli, also known as Knoedel, a type of dumpling with many variations, served either in broth or with a sauce; Würste (sausages) and sauerkraut; ravioli made from rye flour, stuffed with spinach, and fried; and apple or pear strudel. The local wine vintages (and fruit brandies) are delicious.

the small porch to the intriguing knotted columns on the graceful apse. ✉ *Piazza del Duomo* ☎ *0461/980132* ◷ *Daily 7:30–noon and 2:30–7:30.*

★ The crenellated **Palazzo Pretorio,** situated so as to seem like a wing of the Duomo, was built in the 13th century as the fortified residence of the prince-bishops, who enjoyed considerable power and autonomy within the medieval hierarchy. The remarkable palazzo has lost none of its original splendor. The crenellations are not merely decorative: the square pattern represents ancient allegiance to the Guelphs (the triangular crenellations seen elsewhere in town represent Ghibelline loyalty). The Palazzo now houses the **Museo Diocesano Tridentino,** where you can see paintings showing the seating plan of the prelates during the Council of Trent; early-16th-century tapestries by Pieter van Aelst, the Belgian artist who carried out Raphael's 15th-century designs for the Vatican tapestries; carved wood altars and statues; and an 11th-century sacramentary, or book of services. These and other precious objects all come from the cathedral's treasury. Accessible through the museum, a subterranean **archaeological area** reveals ancient ruins of a 6th-century Christian basilica and a gate dating from the 9th century. ✉ *Piazza del Duomo 18* ☎ *0461/234419* ✉ €*3, includes archaeological area* ◷ *Wed.–Mon. 9:30–12:30 and 2–5:30.*

Many sessions of the Council of Trent met at the Renaissance church **Santa Maria Maggiore.** Limited light enters through the simple rose window over the main door, so you'll have to strain to see the magnificent ceiling, an intricate combination of stucco and frescoes. The church is off the northwest side of the Piazza del Duomo, about 200 yards down Via Cavour. ✉ *Via Cavour* ◷ *Daily 8:30–noon and 2:30–8.*

Locals refer to **Via Belenzani** as Trento's outdoor gallery because of the frescoed facades of the hallmark Renaissance palazzi. It's an easy 50-yard walk up the lane behind the church of Santa Maria Maggiore.

★ The **Castello del Buonconsiglio** (Castle of Good Counsel) was once the stronghold of the prince-bishops; its position and size made it easier to defend than the Palazzo Pretorio. As you face it, you can see the evolution of architectural styles, starting with the medieval fortifications of the Castelvecchio section on the far left, down to the more decorative Renaissance **Magno Palazzo,** built three centuries later in 1530. The Castello now houses the **Museo Provinciale d'Arte** (Provincial Art Museum), where permanent and visiting exhibits of art and archaeology are displayed in frescoed medieval halls or under Renaissance coffered ceilings. The 13th-century **Torre dell'Aquila** (Eagle's Tower) holds the highlight of the museum, a 15th-century *ciclo dei mesi* (cycle of the months). This four-walled fresco is full of charming and detailed scenes of medieval life in both court and countryside. An escorted walk through the castle walls is required to visit the tower. You'll need to follow signs to a small office, and wait for a guide to take you up. ✉ *Via Bernardo Clesio 5* ☎ *0461/233770* ⊕ *www.buonconsiglio.it* 🎫 *€5 Torre dell'Aquila €1* ☉ *Tues.–Sun. 9–noon and 2–5* ☞ *Admission and hrs vary when exhibitions are held.*

The **Museo Storico in Trento** (Trento Historical Museum), housed in the former joiner's shop inside the castle walls, has been undergoing restoration and is scheduled to reopen sometime in 2005. The focus is modern Trentino history, with dioramas and displays about the region from the unification of Italy in 1861 through World War II. ✉ *Via Bernardo Clesio 3* ☎ *0461/230482.*

The **Torre Verde** (Green Tower; ✉ Piazza Raffaello Sanzio, near the castle), is part of Trento's 13th-century fortifications, standing alongside other fragments of the city walls. The **Torre Vanga** (✉ Via Torre Vanga, near the river) also dates from the 13th century and guards the medieval bridge Ponte San Lorenzo, which crosses the Adige River. A cable car (€2 round-trip) leaves from the bridge to the lookout point **Belvedere di Sardagna,** 1,200 feet above Trento.

The **Museo d'Arte Moderna e Contemporanea di Trento** is installed in the Palazzo delle Albere, a Renaissance villa on the Adige River. Works in the permanent collection date from the 19th and 20th centuries, but the real focus here is a rotating exhibition of contemporary artists. ✉ *Palazzo delle Albere, Via Ruggero da Sanseverino 45* ☎ *0461/234860* ⊕ *www. mart.tn.it* 🎫 *€8* ☉ *Tues.–Sun. 10–6.*

From late June to late September a regional **Superfestival** (⊕ superfestatrento.it) highlights historic castles as venues for performances and evocations of fact and legend. The festival includes music, costumes, banquets, and train excursions to the castles. A summer bonus is the weeklong **Festive Vigiliane,** a spectacular pageant in the Piazza del Duomo, culminating on June 26, when townspeople don medieval clothing in honor of their patron saint. Since 1936 the June wine festival **Mostra dei Vini** (☎ 0461/983880) has attracted would-be Bacchuses of every stripe; farmers from surrounding hillside towns bend elbows with sommeliers from all over Italy. The weeklong festival includes tastings, tours, and prizes.

> **off the beaten path**
>
> **LEVICO TERME** – About 20 km (12 mi) southeast of Trento and just east of the summer resorts of Lago di Caldonazzo is a medieval *terme* (thermal bath) town in the Val Sugana. This valley enclave was inhabited by the Celts and then conquered by the Romans; the Latin-derived Ladin is still spoken today. Spa therapies must be booked two weeks in advance at **Palazzo delle Terme** (⊠ Viale Vittorio Emanuele, Levico Terme 38056 ☎ 0461/706481 🖶 0461/707722 ⊘ May–Oct., Mon.–Sat. 7–12:30)

Where to Stay & Eat

★ **$$$** ✕ **Le Due Spade.** This Tirolean tavern near the Duomo offers superb local dishes, able service, and the warmth of wood paneling and an antique stove. You can sample traditional *gnocchetti di ricotta* (ricotta cheese dumplings) and such savory second courses as *tagliata di Angus alla griglia* (grilled slivers of beef) served with an aromatic herb sauce. Given the restaurant's deserved popularity with locals and the limited seating, reservations are a must. ⊠ *Via Rizzi 11* ☎ *0461/234343* ⚐ *Reservations essential* ☰ *AE, DC, MC, V* ⊘ *Closed Sun. No lunch Mon.*

$$ ✕ **Chiesa.** Near the castle, a 15th-century building conceals a bright, modern restaurant that attracts romancing couples and power lunchers alike. Ubiquitous apple imagery and excellent risotto *alle mele* (with apples) celebrate the local produce—there's even a set meal featuring apples in every course. Otherwise, the food is traditional: specialties are *maccheroncini con salsiccia e verze* (short, narrow pasta tubes with sausage and cabbage), and *tonco de Pontesel* (a stew of mixed meat made according to a 15th-century recipe). ⊠ *Via San Marco 64* ☎ *0461/238766* ☰ *AE, DC, MC, V* ⊘ *Closed Sun.*

¢ ✕ **Pizzeria Laste.** Owner Guido Rizzi invented pizza Calabrese, a white pizza with garlic, mozzarella, and hot red-pepper flakes. He's a deserving national pizza-making champion; each of his 35 pies—including the *sedano* (mozzarella, celery root, *grana* cheese, oregano)—is delectable. Save room for dessert: pizza *dolce* is made with bananas, strawberries, kiwi, and caramel. The pizzeria is housed in a pleasant villa in the hills above the city center—a bit hard to reach, but worth it. ⊠ *Via alle Laste 39, Cognola* ☎ *0461/231570* ☰ *MC, V* ⊘ *Closed Tues.*

$–$$ ✕▦ **Castel Pergine.** This hilltop 13th-century castle, appropriated by Trento's prince-bishops in the 16th century and now skillfully managed by the Austrian-Swiss Schneider-Neffs, is 12 km (7½ mi) east of Trento. Amid the labyrinth of stone and brick chambers, prisons, and chapels you'll find sparse, rustic rooms with carved-wood trim, lace curtains, and heavy wooden beds, some canopied. The grounds host a different modern-art installation each year. The popular candlelit restaurant serves ages-old seasonal recipes from Trento in lighter guises. ⊠ *Pergine Val Sugana 38057* ☎ *0461/531158* 🖶 *0461/531329* ⊕ *www.castelpergine.it* ⇥ *21 rooms, 14 with bath* ⚐ *Restaurant, horseback riding, bar, library; no a/c, no room TVs* ☰ *AE, DC, MC, V* ⊘ *Closed Nov.–Mar. No lunch Mon.* ❢❢ *MAP.*

$$$ ▦ **Boscolo Grand Hotel Trento.** Its contemporary rounded facade amid ancient palaces makes this hotel on Piazza Dante an anomaly. Inside it has lush modern appointments, from the marble and woodwork in the lobby and lounges to the Clesio restaurant's rich drapery. Rooms are ample, with thick carpets and clubby, wood-trim furniture. ⊠ *Via Alfieri 1, 38100* ☏ *0461/271000* 🖷 *0461/271001* ⊕ *www.grandtrento. boscolohotels.com* 🖢 *126 rooms, 10 suites* ⚐ *Restaurant, in-room safes, minibars, cable TV, sauna, bar, laundry service, meeting rooms, parking (fee)* ▤ *AE, DC, MC, V* ❢⊙❢ *BP.*

$$$ ⊞ **Imperial Grand Hotel Terme.** For spa treatment and modern comforts, choose this graciously restored estate—formerly home to Austrian nobility—in the nearby spa town of Levico Terme (20 km [12 mi] east of Trento). It has a beautiful indoor pool, a garden, and a fine Tuscan restaurant. ⊠ *Via Silva Domini 1, 38056 Levico Terme* ☏ *0461/706104* 🖷 *0461/706350* ⊕ *www.imperialhotel.it* 🖢 *81 rooms* ⚐ *Restaurant, minibars, cable TV, 2 pools (1 indoor), gym, spa, meeting rooms, free parking* ▤ *AE, DC, MC, V* ⊙ *Closed Nov.–Mar.* ❢⊙❢ *BP.*

★ $$ ⊞ **Accademia.** This friendly, character-filled hotel occupies an ancient house in the historic center of Trento, close to Piazza del Duomo. Framed by a beautiful arched entryway, the public rooms retain the ancient vaulting, but the bedrooms are modern and comfortably equipped. There's a courtyard garden. ⊠ *Vicolo Colico 4/6, 38100* ☏ *0461/ 233600* 🖷 *0461/230174* ⊕ *www.accademiahotel.it* 🖢 *41 rooms, 2 suites* ⚐ *Restaurant, minibars, meeting rooms* ▤ *AE, DC, MC, V* ⊙ *Closed Dec. 24–Jan. 6* ❢⊙❢ *BP.*

$$ ⊞ **Buonconsiglio.** Near the train station, this elegant hotel offers well-kept, sizable rooms and efficient service, perfect for the business traveler. The public spaces are decorated with modern art. ⊠ *Via Romagnosi 18, 38100* ☏ *0461/272888* 🖷 *0461/272889* ⊕ *www.hotelbuonconsiglio. it* 🖢 *46 rooms, 1 suite* ⚐ *In-room safes, minibars, cable TV, bar, meeting rooms, parking (fee)* ▤ *AE, DC, MC, V* ⊙ *Closed 2 wks mid-Aug.* ❢⊙❢ *BP.*

$ ⊞ **Aquila d'Oro.** This small hotel offers comfort, efficiency, and a prime location steps from Piazza del Duomo. Most rooms have nondescript contemporary furniture in somber colors. The friendly owner can offer good suggestions about what to see, do, and eat while in town. ⊠ *Via Belenzani 76, 38100* ☏☏ *0461/986282* ⊕ *www.aquiladoro.it* 🖢 *20 rooms* ⚐ *Minibars, bar* ▤ *AE, DC, MC, V* ⊙ *Closed late Dec.–mid.-Feb.* ❢⊙❢ *BP.*

The Arts

The **Festivale di Musica Sacra** (Sacred Music Festival; ☏ 0462/983880) is a monthlong series of concerts in May and June held in Trentino's churches. **I Suoni delle Dolomiti,** held in June and July, offer the idyllic experience of chamber music played in grassy meadows, echoing through the mountain air. This series of free concerts is held at refuges high in the hills of Trentino. For more information, contact the **Trento APT** (☏ 0461/983880).

In July and August, wine buffs can take part in the **Vinum Bonum** (☏ 0461/ 822820) program offering music and wine tastings for €8 at different cellars in Trentino each Tuesday, Thursday, and Friday from 4:30 to 7.

Shopping

MARKETS The **Enoteca di Corso** (⊠ Corso 3 Novembre 54) is an extraordinary shop laden with local products, including cheese, salami, and wine. The small morning **Mercato di Piazza Lodron** is held in Piazza Alessandro Vittoria, where you can pick up meats, cheeses, produce, local truffles, and porcini mushrooms. A number of pleasant souvenir shops and glassware outlets line **Via Manci,** near the church of Santa Maria Maggiore. A flea market is held in **Piazza Garzetti** on the second Sunday of every month except January and August.

WOODEN CRAFTS **Il Pozzo** (⊠ Piazza Pasi 14/l) sells excellent handcrafted wooden objects.
& CERAMICS **Il Laboratorio** (⊠ Via Roma 12) specializes in terra-cotta pieces molded by local artists. **Galleria Trentino Art** (⊠ Via Belenzani 43/45) offers traditional Trentino handicrafts.

Rovereto

❷ *24 km (15 mi) south of Trento, 75 km (47 mi) south of Bolzano.*

Some of the fiercest fighting of World War I took place in the wooded hills around the medieval town of Rovereto, with Italian and Austrian troops bogged down in prolonged and costly conflict. Every evening at nightfall you're reminded of the thousands who died by the ringing of the Campana dei Caduti (Bell of the Fallen). Today, Rovereto is Trentino's peaceful second city. Its 15th-century castle looks down on winding streets, long-shadowed piazzas, and crumbling pastel-color villas.

need a break? Weathered wine barrels serve as tables at **Bacchus** (⊠ Via Garibaldi 29 ☎ No phone), where you can enjoy an excellent selection of local wines by the glass. Better yet, find a spot at the bar and ask for a bitter *negroni sbagliato* to be ladled out of the largest wine glass you've ever laid eyes upon (in addition to the usual Campari, gin, and vermouth, this "mistaken" negroni also employs vodka, oranges, and a few undisclosed ingredients).

The **Museo Storico Italiano della Guerra** (Italian Historical War Museum) was founded after World War I to commemorate the conflict—and to warn against repeating its atrocities. An authoritative exhibition of military artifacts is displayed in the medieval castle perched above Rovereto; the views alone warrant a visit. In warmer weather you can also see a collection of artillery from the Great War housed in a former air-raid shelter. ⊠ *Via Castelbarco 7* ☎ *0464/438100* ⊕ *www.museodellaguerra. it* 🎫 *€4* ⊗ *Tues.–Sun. 10–6. Artillery collection closed Dec.–Apr.*

The paintings of native son Fortunato Depero (1892–1960), a prominent futurist, can be found throughout town. You'll also see a good selection of his work at the **Museo D'Arte Moderna e Contemporanea.** ⊠ *Corso Bettini 43* ☎ *0464/438887* ⊕ *www.mart.tn.it* 🎫 *€8* ⊗ *Tues.–Thurs. 10–6, Fri.–Sun. 10–9.*

Where to Stay & Eat

$$$–$$$$ ✕ **Ristorante Al Borgo.** Renowned throughout Italy for its creative cuisine, Al Borgo has a modernist take on classics, even on the simple *tagliolini ai frutti di mare* (long ribbons of pasta with shellfish). Trentino specialties on the menu might include *strangola preti* (literally "priest-chokers," a heavy pasta dish). In fall, you might find *polentina* (soft,

creamy polenta) with a fondue of Trentino cheeses and truffle. The restaurant's interior is elegant and calm, with attractive art adorning the walls. ⊠ *Via Garibaldi 13* ☎ *0464/436300* ⌂ *Reservations essential* ⊟ *AE, DC, MC, V* ⊘ *Closed Mon., 1 wk in late Jan., 3 wks in July, and Sun. in Aug. No dinner Sun.*

$$ ✕▦ **Hotel Rovereto.** This modern, central hotel capably hosts international travelers—brothers Marco and Fausto Zani preside over welcoming public spaces and warm-color guest rooms, while their mother, Wanda, cooks in the kitchen. The airy, candlelit Ristorante Novecento ($$) is one of the city's most appealing restaurants: luscious dishes, paired with local wines, include *tortelli con fonduta di formaggi* (pasta squares with spinach and ricotta in a butter sauce) and *quaglia con finferli e polenta* (quail with wild mushrooms and polenta). ⊠ *Corso Rosmini 82/d, 38068* ☎ *0464/435222* 📠 *0464/439644* ⊕ *www.hotelrovereto.it* 🛏 *49 rooms* ⌂ *Restaurant, in-room safes, minibars, meeting rooms, parking (fee)* ⊟ *AE, DC, MC, V* ⊘ *Closed mid-Jan.–Feb. Restaurant closed Sun. and Aug.* ⍑◎ *BP.*

Nightlife & the Arts

The **Rovereto Oriente Occidente Festival** (☎ 0464/431660 ⊕ www.orienteoccidente.it) in early September offers exhibitions of contemporary dance, theater, and cuisine. Late September brings the **Festival Internazionale W. A. Mozart** (☎ 0464/439988), with classical performances at the exquisite 18th-century **Teatro Zandonai** (⊠ Corso Bettini 82 ☎ 0464/452159).

en route Traveling south from Rovereto, head west on S240 until you reach the lovely town of Riva del Garda in Lombardy. Turn north on S45bis in Riva del Garda, then west onto S237 until you reach Tione, a small farming community. From here, head north on S239 to reach Pinzolo.

Pinzolo

❸ *75 km (47 mi) northwest of Rovereto, 59 km (37 mi) northwest of Trento.*

Just north of the small mountain village of Pinzolo (on S239), stop at the church of **San Virgilio** to see the remarkable 16th-century fresco on the exterior south wall. Painted in 1539 by the artist Simone Baschenis, the painting describes the Dance of Death: a macabre parade of 40 sinners from all walks of life (in roughly descending order of worldly importance), each guided to his end by a ghoulish escort. Unfortunately, the church's interior is closed to the public.

Madonna di Campiglio

❹ *14 km (9 mi) north of Pinzolo, 88 km (55 mi) southwest of Bolzano.*

The chichi winter resort of Madonna di Campiglio has surpassed Cortina d'Ampezzo as the most fashionable place for young Italians to ski and be seen in the Dolomites. Madonna's popularity is well deserved, with more than 130 km (80 mi) of well-groomed ski runs served by 39 lifts. The resort itself is a modest 5,000 feet above sea level, but the downhill runs, summer hiking paths, and mountain-biking trails venture high up into the surrounding peaks (including Pietra Grande at 9,700 feet). An excursion to the Punta Spinale (Spinale Peak) on the year-round cable car affords magnificent views of the Brenta Dolomites.

Where to Stay

$$$$ ⊞ **Golf Hotel.** You'll need to make your way north to the Campo Carlo Magno pass to reach this grand hotel, the former summer residence of Habsburg emperor Franz Josef. A modern wing has been added, but old-world charm persists: rooms 114 and 214 retain the lavish imperial style, and the rest of the resort is replete with verandas, Persian rugs, and bay windows. In summer the golf course attracts a tony crowd. Note that the hotel offers only half- or full-board packages. ⊠ *Via Cima Tosa 3, 38084* ☎ *0465/441003* 🖷 *0465/440294* ⊕ *www.golfhotelcampiglio. it* ➔ *107 rooms, 8 suites* ⚷ *Restaurant, minibars, cable TV, 9-hole golf course, bar, convention center, free parking* ⊟ *AE, DC, MC, V* ⊗ *Closed mid-Apr.–mid-June and mid-Sept.–Nov.* ⊺⊙⊺ *MAP.*

$$$$ ⊞ **Grifone.** A comfortable Alpine lodge that catches the sun, the Grifone has a distinctive wood facade, flower-decorated balconies, and rooms with views of the forested slopes. The restaurant serves home cooking as well as international dishes. The hotel is south of the lake, a bit out of town, but the Spinale cable car is nearby. Half or full board is required. ⊠ *Via Vallesinella 7, 38084* ☎ *0465/442002* 🖷 *0465/440540* ⊕ *www.hotelgrifone.it* ➔ *40 rooms* ⚷ *Restaurant, in-room safes, cable TV, bar, free parking; no a/c* ⊟ *AE, DC, MC, V* ⊗ *Closed May and June and Sept.–Nov.* ⊺⊙⊺ *MAP.*

★ **$$$$** ⊞ **Savoia Palace.** This central hotel is also Madonna's most traditional, full of carved-wood and mountain-style furnishings. Two fireplaces blaze away in the bar, where you can relax as you recall the day's exploits on the ski slopes. The elegant restaurant serves a mixture of local specialties and rich dishes combining Italian and Austrian influences. Full or half board is required. ⊠ *Viale Dolomiti di Brenta 18, 38084* ☎ *0465/441004* 🖷 *0465/440549* ⊕ *www.savoiapalace.com* ➔ *55 rooms* ⚷ *Restaurant, in-room safes, minibars, cable TV, bar; no a/c* ⊟ *AE, DC, MC, V* ⊗ *Closed Apr.–June and mid-Sept.–mid-Dec.* ⊺⊙⊺ *MAP.*

Sports & the Outdoors

GOLF   The 9-hole course on **Campo Carlo Magno** (☎ 0465/441003 🖷 0465/440298) is open July through mid-September.

HIKING   The local **tourist office** (⊠ Via Pradalago 4 ☎ 0465/442000) supplies maps of a dozen treks leading to waterfalls, lakes, and stupefying views.

SKIING   **Madonna di Campiglio** offers some of the best skiing in the Dolomites, with kilometers of interconnecting runs linked by cable cars and lifts, an impressive vertical drop, and plenty of off-piste opportunities. Advanced skiers will delight in the extremely difficult terrain found on certain mountain faces, but there are also many intermediate and beginner runs, all accessible from town. Madonna's cachet as the ski resort of choice among young Italians is evident in its increasingly well-organized lodging, skiing, and trekking facilities. One-day ski passes (€35) can be purchased at the *funivia* (cable car) in town. ☎ *0465/447744* ⊕ *www.campiglio.to.*

en route Just a couple of miles north of Madonna di Campiglio is a stunning pass in the Dolomites, **Campo Carlo Magno** (5,500 feet). This is where Charlemagne is said to have stopped in AD 800 on his way to Rome to be crowned emperor. Stop here to glance over the whole of northern Italy. Resume your descent with caution (in the space of a mile or so, you will descend more than 2,000 feet via hairpin turns and switchbacks). Turn left at Dimaro and continue 37 km (23 mi) west through another high pass, **Passo del Tonale** (6,200 feet). At Ponte di Legno, turn north on S300 and, passing the **Lago Nero** (Black Lake) on your left just before the summit, head for Bormio through the **Passo di Gavia** (8,600 feet).

Bormio

❺ *20 km (12 mi) south of Passo dello Stelvio, 100 km (60 mi) southwest of Merano.*

At the foot of Stelvio Pass, Bormio is the most famous ski resort on the western side of the Dolomites, with 38 km (24 mi) of long pistes and a 5,000-plus-foot vertical drop. In summer its cool temperatures and clean air entice Italians away from cities in the humid Lombard plain. This dual-season popularity supports the plentiful shops, restaurants, and hotels in town. Bormio has been known for the therapeutic qualities of its waters since the Roman era, so you'll also find numerous spas.

Bormio makes a good base for exploring the Alps' biggest national park, the **Parco Nazionale dello Stelvio,** spread over 1,350 square km (520 square mi) and four provinces. Opened in 1935 with the express intent to preserve flora and protect fauna, today it thrives, with more than 1,200 types of plants, 600 different mushrooms, and more than 160 species of animals, including the chamois, ibex, and roe deer. ⊠ *S38* ☎ *0342/ 910100* ⊕ *www.parks.it/parco.nazionale.stelvio* ☜ *Free.*

Where to Stay

$$$ 🏨 **Posta.** Ostelli della Posta hotels, stagecoach inns of days gone by, are a time-honored tradition in northern Italy. The reception and atmosphere of this town-center hotel, with its warm wood detail in the low-vaulted areas, help to temper the cold. Rooms are cozy and comfortable, with heavy drapery and bed linens. Perks include a small health club with a pool, sauna, gym, and Turkish bath—and a shuttle bus to the slopes. ⊠ *Via Roma 66, 23032* ☎ *0342/904753* 🖷 *0342/904484* ⊕ *www. hotelposta.bormio.it* ↪ *50 rooms* ⟡ *Restaurant, in-room safes, cable TV, indoor pool, health club, sauna, Turkish bath, pub; no a/c* ▤ *AE, DC, MC, V* ☉ *Closed May and June and Sept.–Nov.* ⑩ *BP.*

$$ 🏨 **Nazionale.** Bordering the Stelvio National Park, this central hotel caters to the winter and summer crowds. Behind the wooden exterior, rooms are small but well equipped, with balconies on all floors except the top one. The hotel operates a shuttle bus to the cable cars. ⊠ *Via al Forte 28, 23032* ☎ *0342/903361* 🖷 *0342/905294* ⊕ *www.hotelnazionale. info* ↪ *48 rooms* ⟡ *2 restaurants, in-room safes, minibars, sauna, bar, recreation room, shops; no a/c* ▤ *AE, DC, MC, V* ☉ *Closed mid-Sept.–Nov. and mid-Apr.–May* ⑩ *BP.*

Sports

SKIING The main mountain above the town is **Vallecetta,** and the secondary ski area is called San Colombano. The **base funivia** (☎ 0342/901451) is in the center of Bormio and connects you to a network of lifts. You can buy a one-day ski pass (€31) and pick up a trail map at the base. From there, the funivia takes you to the Bormio 2000 station, from which you can either ski down intermediate trails or get another funivia up to the Cima Bianca station. Terrain is mostly intermediate. The most reliable time to ski at Bormio is late February or after, as early season snowfall is not guaranteed.

Passo dello Stelvio

★ ❻ *20 km (12 mi) north of Bormio, 80 km (48 mi) west of Merano.*

At just over 9,000 feet, the Passo dello Stelvio is the second-highest pass in Europe, connecting the Valtellina in Lombardy with the Val Venosta in Alto Adige. The view from the top is well worth the drive; looking north you can see Switzerland. The pass is open from May or June to October, depending on weather conditions. Stelvio itself is a year-round skiing center, with many of its runs open in summer.

en route Between the Stelvio Pass and the town of Spondigna, 30 km (19 mi) of road wind down 48 hair-raising hairpin turns. The views are spectacular, but this descent is not for the faint of heart. In Spondigna keep to the right for the road to Naturno.

BOLZANO (BOZEN)

▶ *32 km (19 mi) south of Merano, 50 km (31 mi) north of Trento.*

Bolzano (Bozen), the capital of the autonomous province of Alto Adige, is tucked in among craggy peaks in a Dolomite valley just 77 km (48 mi) from the Brenner Pass and Austria. Protected by mountains to the north and the east, this bustling town lies along the main north–south artery connecting Italy with central Europe (the A22 autostrada and the well-traveled rail route to Innsbruck now ply this ancient route). Tirolean culture dominates Bolzano's language, food, architecture, and people. It may be hard to remember that you're in Italy when walking the city's colorful cobblestone streets and visiting its lantern-lighted cafés, where you may enjoy sauerkraut and a beer among a lively crowd of blue-eyed German-speakers. However, fine Italian espresso, fashionable boutiques, and reasonable prices will help remind you where you are. With castles and steeples topping the landscape, this quiet city at the confluence of the Isarco (Eisack) and Talvera rivers has retained a provincial appeal. Proximity to fabulous skiing and mountain climbing—not to mention the world's oldest preserved mummy—make it a worthwhile, if undis-covered, tourist destination. And its streets are immaculate: with the high-est per capita earnings of any city in Italy Bolzano's residents enjoy a standard of living that is second to none.

Exploring Bolzano

Begin in **Piazza Walther** ⑦ ↦, Bolzano's geographic and cultural center, and head to the striking **Duomo** ⑧. Exit the cathedral to the west, heading away from Piazza Walther, and continue to the **Chiesa dei Domenicani** ⑨ and the connected Cappella di San Giovanni, where you can see Bolzano's best collection of frescoes. Cross Piazza Domenicani (to the northeast), and head up Via Goethe to the market square, **Piazza delle Erbe** ⑩. Next, turn east onto Via dei Portici, Bolzano's busiest shopping street. After making your way to Casa della Pesa (on the right), the site of public weighings of goods until 1780, turn south into Piazza del Grano, Bolzano's medieval center and grain market. Exit onto Via Argentieri, another *vicolo* (ancient street), to the west. When you return to Piazza delle Erbe, head west on Via Museo, which will take you to the **Museo Civico** ⑪ and **Museo Archeologico** ⑫, with its 5,300-year-old iceman. Spend the rest of your day at these two museums.

TIMING   Allow at least half a day for this walk.

What to See

Castel Mareccio (Schloss Maretsch). This castle, tucked below mountains and enveloped by vineyards, dates from the 13th century. You may have to view it from the outside, unfortunately, as it is closed (indefinitely) for restoration. ⊠ *Lungotalvera, Bolzano, head north along the river* ☎ *0471/976615.*

Castel Roncolo (Schloss Runkelstein). This red-roof, meticulously kept castle sits among green hills and farmhouses north of town. It was built in 1237, destroyed half a century later, and then rebuilt soon thereafter. A beautifully preserved cycle of medieval frescoes can be viewed inside. A tavern (☎ *0471/324073*) in the courtyard serves excellent local food and wines. ⊠ *Via San Antonio, from Piazza delle Erbe, head north along Via Francescani and continue through Piazza Madonna, connecting to Via Castel Roncolo* ☎ *0471/329808* ⊕ *www.comune.bolzano.it/roncolo/ ie* ⊠ *€8* ☽ *Tues.–Sun. 10–6.*

⑨ **Chiesa dei Domenicani** (Dominican Church). This 13th-century church in Piazza dei Domenicani is renowned as Bolzano's main repository for paintings, especially frescoes. In the adjoining **Cappella di San Giovanni** you can see works from the Giotto school, one of which is a *Triumph of Death* (circa 1340). Despite its macabre subject, this fresco shows the birth of a pre-Renaissance sense of depth and individuality. ⊠ *Piazza Domenicani* ☎ *0471/973133* ☽ *Church and chapel Mon.–Sat. 9:45–5:30* ⊠ *Free.*

⑧ **Duomo.** The city's Gothic cathedral was built between the 12th and 14th century; its lacy spire looks down on the mosaiclike tiles covering its pitched roof. Inside are 14th- and 15th-century frescoes and an intricately carved stone pulpit dating from 1514. Outside, don't miss the **Porta del Vino** (Wine Gate) on the northeast side; decorative carvings of grapes and harvest workers attest to the long-standing importance of wine to this region. ⊠ *Piazza Walther* ☎ *0471/978676* ☽ *Weekdays 9:45–noon and 2–5, Sat. 9:45–noon.*

⑫ Museo Archeologico dell'Alto Adige (South Tirol Museum of Archeology).
Fodor's Choice This museum has gained international fame for Ötzi, its 5,300-year-old
★ iceman, discovered in 1991 and the world's oldest naturally preserved
body. In 1998 Italy acquired it from Austria after it was determined that
the body lay 100 yards inside Italy. The iceman's leathery remains are
displayed in a freezer, preserved along with his longbow, ax, and clothing. The rest of the museum relies on models and artifacts from nearby
archaeological sites (with the help of an eloquent acoustic guide) to lead
visitors not only through Ötzi's Copper Age, but also into the preceding Paleolithic and Neolithic eras, and the Bronze and Iron ages that
followed. An audio guide costs €2. ⊠ *Via Museo 43* ☎ *0471/982098*
⊕*www.iceman.it* ☎ *€8* ⊙ *Tues., Wed., and Fri.–Sun. 10–6, Thurs. 10–8;
last admission 1 hr before closing.*

⑪ Museo Civico (Civic Museum). Bolzano's municipal museum is a rich collection of traditional costumes, wood carvings, and archaeological exhibits. It's scheduled to reopen following renovations by the end of 2004.
⊠ *Via Cassa di Risparmio 14* ☎ *0471/974625* ☎ *€5* ⊙ *Tues. 10–6,
Wed. 10–8, Thurs.–Sun. 10–6.*

Passeggiata del Guncina. An 8-km (5-mi) botanical promenade dating from 1892 ends with a panoramic view of Bolzano. ⊹ *Entrance near Vecchia Parrocchiale, in Gries, across the river and up Corso Libertà.*

🔟 Piazza delle Erbe. A bronze statue of Neptune, which dates back to 1745, presides over a bountiful fruit and vegetable market in this square. The stalls spill over with colorful displays of local produce; bakeries and grocery stores showcase hot breads, pastries, cheeses, and delicatessen meats—a complete range of picnic supplies. Try the *speck tirolese* (smoked ham, thinly sliced) and the apple strudel.

▶ **❼ Piazza Walther.** This pedestrian-only square is Bolzano's heart; in warmer weather it serves as an open-air living room where locals and tourists alike can be found at all hours sipping a drink (such as a glass of chilled Riesling). In the center stands Heinrich Natter's white-marble, neo-Romanesque **Monument to Walther,** built in 1889. The piazza's namesake was the 12th-century German wandering minstrel Walther von der Vogelweide, whose songs lampooned the papacy and praised the Holy Roman Emperor.

Vecchia Parrocchiale (Old Parish Church). Said to have been built in 1141, this church is worth a visit, if only for the elaborately carved 15th-century wooden altar of Michael Pacher, a masterpiece of the Gothic style. The 11th-century Romanesque crucifix was probably brought here from France. ⊠ *Via Martin Knoller, in Gries, across the river and up Corso Libertà* ⊙ *Apr.–Oct., weekdays 10:30–noon and 2:30–4.*

off the beaten path

RENON (RITTEN) PLATEAU – The Earth Pyramids of Renon Plateau make up a bizarre geological formation where erosion has left a forest of tall, thin, needlelike spires of rock, each topped with a boulder. The **Soprabolzano funicular** (🎫 €7 round-trip) leaves from Via Renon, about 300 yards left of the Bolzano train station. At the top, an electric train takes you to the site, which is at Collalbo, just above Bolzano.

Where to Stay & Eat

★ **$$$** ✕ **Zür Kaiserkron.** Traditional Tirolean opulence and attentive service set the stage for some of the best food in town. Appetizers might include potato blini with salmon caviar, and marinated artichokes with butter (not to be missed if available). Main dishes, such as veal with black truffle–and–spinach *canederli* (dumplings) make use of ingredients from the local valleys. This place is popular with dignified local businesspeople. ⊠ *Piazzetta Mostra* ☎ *0471/970770* ⊟ *AE, DC, MC, V* ⊙ *Closed Sun. No dinner Sat.*

★ **$–$$** ✕ **Batzenhausl.** A medieval building in the center of town houses this smart, modern take on the traditional Stube. It's a popular meeting place for locals, who hold animated conversations over glasses of local wine and tasty South Tirolean specialties such as speck tirolese and *mezzelune casarecce ripiene* (house-made stuffed half-moons of pasta). If you're seeking a quiet meal, ask for a table on the second floor, near the handsome stained-glass windows. ⊠ *Via Andreas Hofer 30* ☎ *0471/050950* ⊟ *MC, V.*

$ ✕ **Alexander.** Typical Tirolean dishes are served up in a convivial atmosphere at this city-center restaurant. The venison ham and the lamb cutlets *al timo con salsa all'aglio* (with thyme and garlic sauce) are particularly good, but make sure to leave room for the rich chocolate cake. ⊠ *Via Aosta 37* ☎ *0471/918608* ⊟ *MC, V* ⊗ *Closed Sat.*

$ ✕ **Cavallino Bianco.** Ask a local for a restaurant recommendation in Bolzano, and you're likely to be pointed toward this dependable favorite near Via dei Portici. A wide selection of Italian and German dishes is served in a spacious, comfortable dining room; you'll see lots of extended families enjoying a meal together. ⊠ *Via Bottai 6* ☎ *0471/973267* ⊟ *No credit cards* ⊗ *Closed Sun. No dinner Sat.*

$ ✕ **Hopfen & Co. (Bozner Bier).** Authentic, tasty Tirolean specialties such as fried white Würstel, sauerkraut, and grilled ribs complement the excellent home-brewed Austrian-style pilsner and wheat beer at this lively pub-restaurant. On some nights there's live music. ⊠ *Piazza delle Erbe 17* ☎ *0471/300788* ⊟ *MC, V.*

★ $$$–$$$$ ▦ **Hotel Greif.** Even in a hospitable region, the Greif is a rare gem. This small central hotel has been a Bolzano landmark for centuries, and a beautiful renovation has set a standard for modern amenities in Alto Adige. In-room workstations with ISDN Internet connections and private whirlpool baths are just a few of the perks. Public spaces are light, airy, and immaculate, and each unique room was designed by a different local artist. ⊠ *Piazza Walther 1, 39100* ☎ *0471/318000* ⊟ *0471/318148* ⊕ *www.greif.it* ⤳ *33 rooms* ⟁ *In-room data ports, in-room safes, minibars, cable TV, hot tubs, Internet, parking (fee)* ⊟ *AE, DC, MC, V* ⧦ *BP.*

$$$–$$$$ ▦ **Park Hotel Laurin.** An exercise in art nouveau opulence, this hotel presides over a large park in the middle of town. Its history is speckled with visits from Europe's grand nobility, including Archduke Franz Ferdinand (whose murder in Sarajevo sparked World War I) and King Leopold of Belgium, and Field Marshal Montgomery. Today it's considered the finest hotel in all of Alto Adige, offering art-filled modern guest rooms and handsome public spaces (the frescoes in the bar tell the legend of the Dwarf King Laurin). ⊠ *Via Laurin 4, 39100* ☎ *0471/311000* ⊟ *0471/311148* ⊕ *www.laurin.it* ⤳ *88 rooms, 8 suites* ⟁ *Restaurant, in-room safes, minibars, cable TV, pool, bar, convention center, parking (fee), nosmoking rooms* ⊟ *AE, DC, MC, V* ⧦ *BP.*

★ $$$–$$$$ ▦ **Schloss Korb.** It's worth the 5-km (3-mi) drive west from Bolzano to reach this romantic 13th-century castle with crenellations and a massive tower, perched in a park amid vine-covered hills. Much of the ancient decor is preserved, and the public rooms are filled with antiques, elaborate wood carvings, paintings, and attractive plants. The rooms are comfortably furnished, and some in the tower have striking Romanesque arched windows. ⊠ *Missiano, Via Castel d'Appiano 5, 39050* ☎ *0471/636000* ⊟ *0471/636033* ⊕ *www.highlight-hotels.com/korb* ⤳ *57 rooms, 5 suites* ⟁ *Restaurant, 2 tennis courts, 2 pools (1 indoor), sauna, bar, parking (fee); no a/c* ⊟ *No credit cards* ⊗ *Closed Nov.–Mar.* ⧦ *BP.*

$$ ⌂ **Luna-Mondschein.** This central yet secluded hotel in a tranquil garden dates from 1798. The comfortable rooms have wood paneling throughout; those overlooking the garden have balconies, others offer good views of the mountains. First-rate dining is available in both the cozy, convivial Tirolean Weinstube and the art nouveau Ristorante Van Gogh, one of the city's best. ⌂ *Via Piave 15, 39100* ☎ *0471/975642* 🖶 *0471/975577* ⊕ *www.hotel-luna.it* ⤶ *85 rooms* ⌂ *Restaurant, Weinstube, meeting rooms, parking (fee); no a/c* ▭ *AE, DC, MC, V* ⦿❘ *BP.*

Nightlife & the Arts

Fairs
Spring is heralded each May with large **flower markets** as well as other events, including concerts and folklore and art exhibits. On August 24 the **Bartolomeo Horse Fair** takes place on Renon Mountain northeast of the town. Hundreds of farmers converge for a day of serious trading and merriment.

Nightlife
A centuries-old tradition of late-night merriment carries on at **Hopfen & Co.** (⌂ Piazza delle Erbe 17 ☎ 0471/300788). **Batzenhausl** (⌂ Via Andreas Hofer 30 ☎ 0471/050950) is another traditional favorite among locals. The bar at **Vögele** stays open until 1 AM, offering an outstanding selection of wines by the glass in a relaxed setting (⌂ Via Goethe 3 ☎ 0471/973938). If only a properly poured pint of Guinness will do, **Pogue Mahone's** (⌂ Vicolo Erbe 10 ☎ 0471/978339) is your place.

Music
There's a lively music scene in town. Information is available at the tourist office. For opera information and schedules, call **Friends of Opera** (☎ 0471/913223). Orchestral concerts are held at **Haus der Kultur** (⌂ Via Sciliar 1 ☎ 0471/977520). The **Park Hotel Laurin Bar** (⌂ Via Laurin 4 ☎ 0471/311000) hosts jazz combos on Fridays and a jazz pianist all other nights.

Theater
Theater is popular in Bolzano—contact the tourist office for a weekly schedule. A frequently used venue is the imposing **Nuovo Teatro Comunale** (⌂ Piazza Verdi 40 ☎ 0471/304130 ⊕ www.ntbz.net). **Cortile Theater im Hof** (⌂ Piazza delle Erbe 37 ☎ 0471/980756) specializes in children's theater. Note that performances may be in German.

Sports & the Outdoors

Biking
If you're in decent shape, a great way to see some of the surrounding castles, lakes, and forested valleys of the Dolomites is by bike. **Alp Bike** (☎ 0471/280795 ⊕ www.alpbike.it) offers different guided excursions almost every day, at all levels, but you must reserve a week or more ahead for the more ambitious trips.

Hiking
Club Alpino Italiano (⌂ Piazza delle Erbe 46 ☎ 0471/981391 ⊕ www. cai.it) provides helpful information for hiking and rock climbing. It's important to follow safety procedures and to have all the latest information on trails and conditions.

CloseUp

LODEN & LEDERHOSEN

SHOPPING IS TRULY AN EVENT *in the Alto Adige; in larger towns stores are clustered in a small clutch of arcaded streets, keeping shoppers dry on rainy and snowy days. The strong Tirolean influence makes for local products that are quite different from those elsewhere in Italy.*

Traditional clothes—loden goods, lederhosen, dirndls, and linen suits with horn buttons—are a good buy, costing less than in neighboring Austria. Local crafts such as embroidered goods, wood carvings, and figures for nativity scenes also make excellent gifts. Of course there is no shortage of boutiques supplying the under-35 Italian dress code: jet-black and icy-gray designer clothes and accessories. Although store hours are not subject to the draconian store-closing laws that limit shopping across the northern border, neither are they immune from the midafternoon closure so fervently embraced to the south.

Shopping

Local Crafts

The long, narrow arcades of **Via dei Portici** house shops that specialize in Tirolean crafts and clothing—lederhosen, loden goods, linen suits, and dirndls. The largest store for locally made handcrafted goods is **Artigiani Atesini** (⊠ Via Portici 39 ☎ 0471/978590).

Markets

From the end of November to Christmas Eve there's a traditional **Christkindlmarkt** (Christmas market) in Piazza Walther, with stalls selling all kinds of Christmas decorations and local handcrafted goods. An outdoor fruit and vegetable market takes over the central **Piazza delle Erbe** Monday through Saturday from 8 to 1. A weekly flea market takes place Saturday morning in **Piazza della Vittoria.**

Wine

Walk down a small alleyway near Piazza delle Erbe to discover **Il Baccaro,** a tiny *enoteca* (wine bar) and wine shop. It's invariably filled with older men engrossed in animated conversation—you can't go wrong buying a bottle of whatever they're drinking. (⊠ Via Argentieri 17 ☎ 0471/971421). On Saturdays in October the **Bacchus Urbanus** program leads guided excursions to vineyards near Bolzano; contact the tourist office (☎ 0471/307000) for details.

ALTO ADIGE & CORTINA

Alto Adige (Südtirol), the northern half of the region and for centuries part of the Austro-Hungarian Empire, was ceded to Italy at the end of World War I. Ethnic differences led to inevitable tensions in the 1960s and again in the '80s, though a large measure of autonomy has, for the most part, kept the lid on nationalist ambitions.

Naturno (Naturns)

⓭ *61 km (38 mi) east of Passo dello Stelvio, 44 km (27 mi) northwest of Bolzano.*

Colorful houses with painted murals on their walls line the streets of Naturno (Naturns), a major horticultural center. Art lovers will appreciate the church of **San Procolo**, which is frescoed inside and out and has wall paintings that are the oldest in the German-speaking world, dating from the 8th century. It's northeast of the town center, just off S38. ⌧ *Via San Procolo* ⊙ *Tues.–Sun. 9:30–noon and 2:30–5:30.*

A five-minute drive west of Naturno, in the hills above the hamlet of Stava, is the 13th-century **Castel Juval,** since 1983 the home of the South Tirolese climber and polar adventurer Reinhold Messner—the first man to conquer Everest solo and the first to reach its summit without oxygen. Part of the castle has been turned into a museum, showing Messner's collection of Tibetan art, mountaineering illustrations, and masks from around the world. ⌧ *Viale Europa 2* ☎ *348/4433871 or 0473/ 221852* ⌧ *€6* ⊙ *Palm Sunday–June, Sept., and Oct., Thurs.–Tues. 10–4.*

Where to Eat

$$ ✕ **Juval Inn.** Just below Castel Juval, Reinhold Messner's Juval Inn is an old-style hostelry in a restored farmhouse, serving traditional local dishes and wines provisioned from his own farm. ⌧ *Schlosswirt-Juval* ☎ *0473/668238* ⊟ *No credit cards* ⊙ *Closed Wed., July and Aug., and Nov.–Palm Sunday.*

need a break? The source of the full-flavored beer served throughout the region is the striking **Forst Brewery** (⌧ Via Venosta 8, Lagundo ☎ 0473/260270), on the road connecting Naturno and Merano. Tours are offered in the summer, 2–4, but you'll need to call ahead for reservations. You can turn up anytime to sample the product line; in summer cross the covered, flower-lined bridge to reach a delightful beer garden.

Merano (Meran)

★ ⓮ *24 km (15 mi) north of Bolzano, 100 km (62 mi) northeast of Bormio.*

The second-largest town in Alto Adige, Merano (Meran) was once the capital of the Austrian region of Tirol. When the town and surrounding area were ceded to Italy as part of the 1919 Treaty of Versailles, Innsbruck became the capital. Merano, however, continued to be known as a spa town, attracting European nobility for its therapeutic waters and its peculiar grape cure, which consists simply of eating the grapes grown on the surrounding hillsides. Sheltered by mountains, Merano has an unusually mild climate, with summer temperatures rarely exceeding 80°F and winters that usually stay above freezing, despite the skiing that is within easy reach. Along the narrow streets of Merano's old town, houses have little towers and huge wooden doors, and the pointed arches of the Gothic cathedral sit next to neoclassical and art nouveau buildings. Merano serves as a good respite from mountain adventures, or from the bustle of nearby Trento and Bolzano.

The 14th-century Gothic **Duomo,** with a crenellated facade and an ornate campanile, sits in the heart of the old town. The Capella di Santa Barbara, just behind the cathedral, is an octagonal church containing a 15th-century pietà. ⊠ *Piazza del Duomo* ☉ *Easter–Sept., daily 8–noon and 2:30–8; Oct.–Easter, daily 8–noon and 2:30–7.*

Overlooking the town atop Mt. Tappeinerweg is a castle that was the home of poet Ezra Pound from 1958 to 1964. Still in the Pound family, the castle now houses the **Brunnenburg Agricultural Museum,** devoted to Tirolean country life. Among its exhibits are a blacksmith's shop and, not surprisingly, a room with Pound memorabilia. To get there, take Bus 3, which departs every hour on the hour, from Merano to Dorf Tirol. ⊠ *Ezra Pound Weg 6* ☎ *0473/923533* ⊡ *€2.50* ☉ *Apr.–Nov., Wed.–Mon. 10–5.*

The **Terme di Merano** (thermal baths) are closed for a extensive renovation and expansion, to include a luxury hotel. Until this huge complex of spa facilities reopens in 2005, the spas operated by individual hotels are your best option. ⊠ *Via Piave 6* ☎ *0473/237724* ⊕ *www. termemerano.it.*

Fodor'sChoice ★
A stroll along one of Merano's well-marked, impossibly pleasant **Promenades** may yield better relaxation than even a spa treatment. **Passeggiata Tappeiner** is a 3-km (2-mi) path offering panoramic views from the hills north of the Duomo, and the exceptionally mild climate gives way to diverse botanical pleasures along the walk. **Passeggiata d'Estate** (Summer Promenade) runs along the shaded south bank of the Passirio River, and the **Passeggiata d'Inverno** (Winter Promenade), on the exposed north bank, provides more warmth and the Wandelhalle—a sun-trap decorated with idyllic paintings of surrounding villages. **Sentierro di Sissi** (Sisi's Walk) follows a path from Trauttmansdorff Castle 2 km (1 mi) southeast of town, to the heart of Merano. Sisi, the popular Austrian Empress Elisabeth, who put Merano on the map as a spa destination, was an inveterate ambler.

need a break?
Cafe Saxifraga (⊠ Passeggiata Tappeiner ☎ 0473/237249) occupies an enviable position overlooking Merano and the peaks enveloping the town; an extensive selection of teas and other beverages can be enjoyed in the wooden Stube or on the patio offering panoramic views. You can enjoy a rich hot chocolate or a cold beer above a gurgling waterfall at **Cafe Glif** (⊠ Passeggiata Glif 51 ☎ 0473/234701), at the northeast edge of the Passeggiata d'Inverno.

Where to Stay & Eat

★ $$$–$$$$ ✕ **Sissi.** In this relaxed leafy restaurant just off Via dei Portici, rustic regional dishes are prepared with the precision of haute Italian cooking. Menu choices may include risotto *alle erbe* (with herbs) and *filetto di vitello con salsa di alloro* (veal fillet with bay-leaf sauce); a set menu (about €50) provides a complete five-course dinner. ⊠ *Via Galilei 44* ☎ *0473/231062* ⌨ *Reservations essential* ▭ *MC, V* ☉ *Closed Mon. and Jan.–mid-Mar.*

$$ ✕ **Seiben.** Young Meraners crowd the hip bar on the ground floor of this modern bistro, centrally located in the town's main arcade. Upstairs, a more mature crowd enjoys the contemporary cooking and attentive service in the jazz-themed dining room. Don't miss the Blues Brothers, poised over the staircase. ⊠ *Via dei Portici 232* ☎ *0473/210636* ▤ *MC, V* ⊘ *Closed Tues. No lunch Sun.*

$-$$ ✕ **Haisrainer.** Among the rustic Stuben lining Via dei Portici, this one is most popular with locals and tourists alike; a menu in English is available for the latter. Warm wooden walls provide a comfortable setting for Tirolean and Italian standards: try the *zuppa al vino bianco* (stew with white wine) or the seasonal risottos (with asparagus in spring, or Barolo in chillier months). ⊠ *Via dei Portici 100* ☎ *0473/237944* ▤ *MC, V* ⊘ *Closed Sun.*

¢-$ ✕ **Vinoteca-Pizzeria Relax.** You may have difficulty choosing from the long list of appetizing pizzas at this casual spot directly opposite the Grand Hotel Palace. Ask the friendly English-speaking staff for help. If a glass of locally produced wine inspires you to bring a bottle or two home, you're unlikely to find a better selection, or a more pleasant environment for browsing. ⊠ *Via Cavour 31* ☎ *0473/236735* ▤ *AE, MC, V* ⊘ *Closed Sun. and 2 wks in late Feb.*

★ $$$$ ▦ **Grand Hotel Palace.** Merano's finest hotel is an old-world institution set in an extensive garden. The public spaces are attractive and comfortable, with art nouveau touches, Tiffany glass, marble pillars, and high ceilings; the guest rooms are spacious. The renowned spa—offering baths, massages, mud treatments, and other cures—attracts fatigued soccer stars and others in search of renewal. Rooftop suites have balconies with stunning views of Merano's steeples and the surrounding mountains. ⊠ *Via Cavour 2, 39012* ☎ *0473/271000* 🖷 *0473/271100* ⊕ *www.palace.it* ⇌ *125 rooms, 12 suites* ⌂ *2 restaurants, minibars, cable TV, pool, spa, bar, wine shop, meeting rooms, free parking* ▤ *AE, DC, MC, V* ⦿❙ *BP.*

$$$ ▦ **Castello Labers.** On a hilltop amid forested slopes about 3 km (2 mi) northeast of Merano's center, this castle hotel with red-tile gables, towers, and turrets is unmistakably Tirolean in style. Ceiling beams, painted fresco decorations, and crossed halberds on the walls complete the look. The hospitable Stapf-Neubert family owns the hotel and takes an active part in its management. ⊠ *Via Labers 25, 39012* ☎ *0473/234484* 🖷 *0473/234146* ⊕ *www.castellolabers.it* ⇌ *32 rooms* ⌂ *Restaurant, in-room safes, tennis court, pool; no a/c* ▤ *AE, DC, MC, V* ⊘ *Closed Nov.–Mar.* ⦿❙ *BP.*

$-$$ ▦ **Conte di Merano.** If you don't feel like paying for one of Merano's resort hotels, this simple central hotel is a good alternative. Steps away from Via dei Portici and open year-round, it's an efficient base for exploring the town. Rooms are spartan, but clean, comfortable, and well equipped. ⊠ *Via delle Corse 78, 39012* ☎ *0473/232181* 🖷 *0473/ 211874* ⇌ *23 rooms* ⌂ *Restaurant, in-room safes, cable TV, bar, free parking* ▤ *AE, DC, MC, V* ⦿❙ *BP.*

Nightlife & the Arts

Merano is a quiet town after dark, but there is no shortage of pleasant watering holes. Younger Meraners favor **Bar Piccolo** (⊠ Corso Libertà 5 ☎ 0473/236765). Alternatively, mellow cafés such as **Cafe Darling** (✉ Passegiata Inverno 5 ☎ 0473/237221) line the promenade along the river.

The **Grape Festival** on the third Sunday of October has parades and wine tastings in Piazza del Duomo. Farmers test indigenous Haflinger horses in the highly charged **horse race** on Easter Monday.

Shopping

Merano's main shopping street, the narrow arcaded **Via dei Portici** (Laubengasse), runs west from the cathedral. You'll find regional products—wood carvings, Tirolean-style clothing, embroidery, cheeses, salami, and fruit schnapps—along with more standard clothing-boutique shopping. You can taste a selection of locally grown varietals at the retail outlet of winemaker **Burggräfler** (✉ Via dei Portici 218 ☎ 0473/237147). From the end of November until Christmas Eve, Merano holds a traditional **Christkindlmarkt** in the main square.

Cornedo

🔟 *6 km (4 mi) east of Bolzano.*

At dusk, the craggy peaks of the Catinaccio Mountains become the canvas for a dramatic pink-and-purple lighting display; Cornedo is the place to savor this spectacle. A local legend describes the origin of the light: Laurin, King of the Dwarfs, became infatuated with the daughter of the neighboring (human) king, and captured her with the aid of a magic hood that made him invisible. As he spirited her back to the mountains, the dwarf king was pursued by many knights, who were able to track the kidnapper after spotting his beloved rose garden. Laurin was captured and imprisoned, but when he finally managed to escape and return home, he cast a spell turning the betraying roses into rocks, so they could be seen neither by day nor night. Laurin forgot about dusk, however, which is why the spectacular pinkish-red display is at its best just before twilight. (This legend is the subject of the frescos in the bar of the Park Hotel Laurin, in Bolzano.)

Chiusa (Klausen)

🔟 *24 km (15 mi) north of Cornedo, 30 km (19 mi) northeast of Bolzano.*

Beautiful narrow streets are lined with houses built in the 15th and 16th centuries in Chiusa (Klausen), the main town in the Val Isarco. Geraniums and begonias fill window boxes beneath the carved wooden shutters. From here you can catch a bus east to Val di Funes, where the church of **Santa Maddalena** is spectacularly hemmed in by the Geisler Peaks.

Above the town of Chiusa is the Benedictine monastery of **Saviona** (Saeben), built as a castle in the 10th century but occupying a site that was fortified in Roman times. The monastery buildings date from the late Middle Ages and are a mixture of Romanesque and Gothic architecture surrounded by walls and turrets. Guided visits are organized by the Tourist Association in Chiusa; contact the local **tourist office** (✉ Piazza Tinne 6 ☎ 0472/847424).

Bressanone (Brixen)

17 *14 km (9 mi) north of Chiusa, 40 km (25 mi) northeast of Bolzano.*

Bressanone (Brixen) is an important artistic center and was the seat of prince-bishops for centuries. Like their counterparts in Trento, these medieval administrators had the delicate task of serving two masters—the pope (the ultimate spiritual authority) and the Holy Roman Emperor (the civil and military power). Since the papacy and the Holy Roman Empire were virtually at war throughout the Middle Ages, Bressanone's prince-bishops became experts at tact and diplomacy. The imposing **Duomo** was built in the 13th century but acquired a baroque facade 500 years later; its 14th-century cloister is decorated with medieval frescoes. ⊠ *Piazza Duomo* ☉ *Daily 8–noon and 3–6.*

The Bishop's Palace, which now houses the **Museo Diocesano** (Diocesan Museum), holds an abundance of local medieval art, particularly Gothic wood carvings. The wooden statues and liturgical objects were all collected from the cathedral treasury. During the Christmas season, curators arrange the museum's large collection of antique nativity scenes; look for the shepherds wearing Tirolean hats. ⊠*Palazzo Vescovile 2* ☎*0472/830505* ⊕ *www.dioezesanmuseum.bz.it* ☑ *€5, nativity scenes €3.50* ☉ *Mar. 15–Oct., Tues.–Sun. 10–5, nativity scenes Dec. and Jan., daily 2–5.*

> **off the beaten path**
>
> **Abbazia di Novacella,** near Bressanone, has been making wine for at least nine centuries. You can wander the delightful grounds of the Augustinian abbey, where a progression of Romanesque, Gothic, and baroque styles can be seen, dating from its founding in 1142. In the tasting room you can sample all varietals produced in the Isarco valley; Novacella is most famous for its Sylvaner. ⊠ *Località Novacella 1, Varna 39040, 3 km (2 mi) north of Bressanone* ☎☎ *0472/836189* ⊟ *AE, MC, V* ☉ *Mon.–Sat. 10–7, tasting room Mon.–Sat. 9–noon and 2–6.*

Where to Stay & Eat

$$–$$$ ✕ **Fink.** This restaurant under the arcades in the pedestrian-only town center offers friendly service and an affordable daily set menu. The rustic wood-paneled dining room upstairs serves international dishes and hearty Tirolean specialties. Try the *carré di maiale gratinato* (pork roasted with cheese and served with cabbage and potatoes) or the *castrato alla paesana* (a lamb stew). ⊠ *Via Portici Minori 4* ☎ *0472/834883* ⊟ *MC, V* ☉ *Closed Wed., July 1–14, and Feb. 1–14. No dinner Tues.*

★ $$$ ▥ **Elephant.** This cozy inn, one of the region's best, takes its name from the 1550 visit of King John III of Portugal, who stopped here while leading an elephant (a present for Austria's Emperor Ferdinand) over the Alps. Each room is unique, many with antiques and paintings. Housed on the park property is the separate Villa Marzari, with 14 rooms. Some of the best food in town is served in the hotel restaurant, a rustic three-room Stube. ⊠ *Via Rio Bianco 4, 39042* ☎ *0472/832750* ⊟ *0472/ 836579* ⊕ *www.hotelelephant.com* ⤴ *44 rooms* ⚹ *Restaurant, minibars, cable TV, 2 tennis courts, pool, gym, sauna, free parking* ⊟ *DC, MC, V* ☉ *Closed early Jan.–Mar. and Nov.* ❍ *BP.*

$ ▣ **Croce d'Oro** (Goldenes Kreuz). A five-century-old tradition of hospitality is still practiced by the Reiserer family at this central, pink hotel. Interior styles range from a modern reception area to a tavern-style bar; guest rooms are spacious, with sturdy wood appointments. The hotel is open year-round. ⊠ *Bastioni Minori 8, 39042* ☎ *0472/836155* 🖷 *0472/834255* ⊕ *www.goldeneskreuz.it* ⇥ *75 rooms* ⌂ *Restaurant, in-room safes, cable TV, spa, bar; no a/c* ⊟ *No credit cards* ¶⊘∣ *BP.*

Shopping

From the end of November until January 6, there is a traditional **Christkindlmarkt** in the Piazza Duomo, with stalls selling Christmas decorations and local handcrafted goods.

Brunico (Bruneck)

★ ⑱ *33 km (20 mi) east of Bressanone, 65 km (40 mi) northwest of Cortina d'Ampezzo.*

With its medieval quarter nestling below the 13th-century bishop's castle, Brunico (Bruneck) is in the heart of the Val Pusteria. This quiet, picturesque town is divided by the Rienza River, with the old quarter on one side and the modern quarter on the other.

The **Museo Etnografico dell'Alto Adige** (Alto Adige Ethnographic Museum) re-creates a Middle Ages farming village, built around a more modern 300-year-old mansion. The wood-carving displays are the most interesting. The museum is in the district of Teodone, just outside the town. ⊠ *Via Duca Diet 24, Teodone* ☎ *0474/552087* ⊕ *www.provincia.bz. it/volkskundemuseen* ▦ *€3.60* ☉ *Mid-Apr.–Oct., Tues.–Sat. 9:30–5:30, Sun. 2–6.*

Where to Stay

$$ ▣ **Andreas Hofer.** There's a Tirolean feel to this bright, comfortable hotel set in a large garden outside the center of town. Rooms are modern, with chalet-style balconies overlooking the Val Pusteria. ⊠ *Via Campo Tures 1, 39031* ☎ *0474/551469* 🖷 *0474/551283* ⊕ *www.andreashofer.it* ⇥ *54 rooms* ⌂ *Restaurant, pool, sauna, bar, Weinstube; no a/c* ⊟ *MC, V* ¶⊘∣ *BP.*

Sports

The **Alta Badia ski area** (⊕ www.altabadia.org) can be reached by heading south on S244 from Brunico. It's less expensive—and more Austrian in character—than other, more famous ski destinations in this region.

Dobbiaco (Toblach)

⑲ *25 km (16 mi) east of Brunico, 34 km (21 mi) north of Cortina d'Ampezzo.*

In Dobbiaco (Toblach), Italian is spoken grudgingly, and the atmosphere is more Austrian than that of much of Austria itself. It's not surprising that Gustav Mahler (1860–1911), the great Austrian composer, came here often for inspiration.

Where to Stay

$$$ ☒ **Cristallo.** Wood beams and paneling lend an Old Tirolean patina to this small hotel in a garden outside town. The architecture and furnishings reflect the local preference for combining traditional chalet design with functional, comfortable modern furniture. You can relax in the cozy and informal Stube. ⊠ *Viale S. Giovanni 37, 39034* ☎ *0474/972138* 🖷 *0474/972755* ⊕ *www.hotelcristallo.com* ⟿ *30 rooms* ⬩ *Restaurant, in-room safes, cable TV, indoor pool, sauna, bar, free parking; no a/c* ⊟ *MC, V* ⊘ *Closed mid-Mar.–mid-June and mid-Oct.–mid-Dec.* ⍟ *MAP.*

★ $$ ☒ **Alpenhotel Ratsberg.** To reach this traditional chalet you can take the 10-minute cable-car ride to Monte Rota or drive up by car. Front rooms have stunning mountain views from balconies, and those in the back look out over the dense mountain forest. You needn't take the cable car back down for sustenance: the hotel has a good restaurant, a bar, and a Tirolean-style Stube. ⊠ *Monte Rota 10, 39034* ☎ *0474/972913* 🖷 *0474/972216* ⊕ *www.alpenhotel-ratsberg.com* ⟿ *30 rooms* ⬩ *Restaurant, cable TV, tennis court, indoor pool, sauna, bar, free parking; no a/c* ⊟ *No credit cards* ⊘ *Closed Apr. and May and Nov.–late Dec.* ⍟ *BP.*

Sports

SKIING Groomed trails for **cross-country skiing** (usually loops marked off by the kilometer) accommodate differing degrees of ability. Inquire at the local tourist office. Downhill skiing can be found at the modest **Monte Elmo** (⊕ www.helmbahnen.com).

Cortina d'Ampezzo

㉒ *30 km (19 mi) south of Dobbiaco.*

Fodor'sChoice
★ Cortina d'Ampezzo has been the Dolomites' mountain resort of choice for more than 100 years; the Winter Olympics were held here in 1956. Although its glamorous appeal to younger Italians may have been eclipsed by steeper, sleeker Madonna di Campiglio, Cortina remains, for many, Italy's most idyllic incarnation of an Alpine ski town.

Surrounded by mountains and dense forests, the "The Pearl of the Dolomites" is in a lush meadow 4,000 feet above sea level. The town hugs the slopes beside a fast-moving stream, and a public park extends along one bank. Higher in the valley, luxury hotels and the villas of the rich are identifiable by their attempts to hide behind stands of firs and spruces. The bustling center of Cortina d'Ampezzo has little nostalgia for old-time atmosphere, despite its Alpine appearance. The tone is set by smart shops and cafés as chic as their well-dressed patrons, whose corduroy knickerbockers may well have been tailored by Armani. Cortina is the place to go for a whiff of the heady aroma of wealth and sophistication. Unlike the neighboring resorts, the feeling here is distinctly fashionable, unapologetically Italian.

On Via Cantore, a winding road heading up out of town to the northeast (becoming S48), you can stop and see the **Pista Olimpica di Bob** (Olympic Bobsled Course), a leftover from the 1956 Winter Games. The course is open to the public, but at unpredictable times.

Where to Stay & Eat

$$ ✕ **Tavernetta.** Near the Olympic ice-skating rink, this popular restaurant has Tirolean-style, wood-paneled dining rooms and a local clientele. Here you can try Cortina specialties such as *zuppa di porcini* (porcini mushroom soup), ravioli *di cervo* (stuffed with venison), and game. ⊠ *Via dello Stadio 27/a* ☎ *0436/867494* ▭ *AE, DC, MC, V* ☉ *Closed Wed., mid-June–mid-July, and Nov.*

$$$$ ✕▥ **De la Poste.** Loyal skiers return year after year to this lively hotel;

Fodor$Choice   its main terrace bar is one of Cortina's social centers. De la Poste has
★   been under the careful management of the Manaìgo family since 1936. Each unique room has antiques in characteristic Dolomite style; almost all have wooden balconies. A refined main dining room—with high ceilings and large chandeliers—serves nouvelle cuisine and superb soufflés; there's also a more informal grill room with wood paneling and the family's pewter collection. ⊠ *Piazza Roma 14, 32043* ☎ *0436/4271* ▦ *0436/868435* ⊕ *www.delaposte.it* ▭ *83 rooms* ♨ *2 restaurants, minibars, cable TV, bar, free parking; no a/c* ▭ *AE, DC, MC, V* ☉ *Closed Apr.–mid-June and Oct.–mid-Dec.* ⦿ *MAP.*

$$$$ ▥ **Corona.** This cozy Alpine lodge is run by Luciano Rimoldi, a noted ski instructor who has coached such luminaries as Alberto Tomba. Modern art adorns small but comfortable pine-paneled rooms; the convivial bar is a pleasant place to relax. The hotel is a five-minute walk—across the river—from the center of town, and a 10-minute ride from the lifts (a ski bus stops out front). ⊠ *Via Val di Sotto 12, 32040* ☎ *0436/3251* ▦ *0436/867339* ⊕ *www.sunrise.it/cortina/link/hcorona. html* ▭ *44 rooms* ♨ *Restaurant, cable TV, bar, free parking; no a/c* ▭ *AE, DC, MC, V* ☉ *Closed Apr.–June and Sept.–Nov.* ⦿ *MAP.*

$$$$ ▥ **Miramonti Majestic.** This imposing and luxe hotel, more than a century old, has a magnificent mountain-valley position about 1 km (½ mi) south of town. A touch of formality comes through in the imperial Austrian design, and the interior reflects the period style throughout. There's always a roaring fire in the splendid bar, and the hotel's recreation rooms are lined with windows overlooking mountain vistas. The history of Cortina is intricately tied to the Miramonti, and you'll feel a part of it all here. ⊠ *Località Peziè 103, 32043* ☎ *0436/4201* ▦ *0436/867019* ⊕ *www.cortina.dolomiti.org/hmiramonti* ▭ *105 rooms* ♨ *Restaurant, minibars, cable TV, 9-hole golf course, 2 tennis courts, indoor pool, gym, sauna, bar, meeting rooms, free parking; no a/c* ▭ *AE, DC, MC, V* ☉ *Closed Apr.–June and Sept.–mid-Dec.* ⦿ *MAP.*

Nightlife & the Arts

At the **Europa** (⊠ Corso Italia 207 ☎ 0436/3221) hotel you can mingle with the couture set at the VIP disco; nonguests are welcome, but don't expect to spend less than €30.

Sports

SKIING   Cortina's long and picturesque ski runs will delight intermediates, but advanced skiers might lust for steeper terrain, which can be found only off-piste. The most impressive views (and steepest slopes) are on **Monte Cristallo,** based at **Misurina.** The **Faloria** gondola runs from the center of town. From its top you can get up to most of the other central mountains. Farther out of town, don't miss the **Cinque Torri** and **Passo Falzarego** runs. All runs are covered by the **Dolomiti Superski pass** (☎ 0471/795397 ✉ €37 ⊕ www.dolomitisuperski.com), good for the entire region.

en route As you enter the Crepa Tunnel on the S48 from Cortina d'Ampezzo, the ascent for the Passo di Falzarego begins. The **Passo Pordoi** leads to the so-called Heart of the Dolomites. The roads around this region of the Sella mountains are among the most spectacular in Europe. At a fork in the road farther ahead the road to the left leads to Canazei, the one to the right into Val Gardena.

HEART OF THE DOLOMITES

The area between Bolzano and the mountain resort Cortina d'Ampezzo is dominated by two major valleys, Val di Fassa and Val Gardena. Both share the spectacular panorama of the Sella mountain range, known as the Heart of the Dolomites. Val di Fassa cradles the beginning of the Grande Strada delle Dolomiti (Great Dolomites Road—S48 and S241), which runs from Bolzano as far as Cortina d'Ampezzo. This route, opened in 1909, comprises 110 km (68 mi) of relatively easy grades and smooth driving between the two towns—a slower, more scenic alternative to traveling by way of Brunico and Dobbiaco along the S49.

With some of the best views of the Dolomites, Val Gardena is famous as a ski resort, freckled with well-equipped, picturesque towns overlooked by the oblong Sasso Lungo (Long Rock), which is more than 10,000 feet above sea level. It's also home to the Ladins, descendants of soldiers sent by the Roman emperor Tiberius to conquer the Celtic population of the area in the 1st century AD. Forgotten in the narrow cul-de-sacs of isolated mountain valleys, the Ladins have developed their own folk traditions and speak an ancient dialect that is derived from Latin and similar to the Romansch spoken in some high valleys in Switzerland.

In both Val di Fassa and Val Gardena, recreational options are less comprehensive, but less expensive than in better-known resorts like Cortina. The culture and language here are firmly Germanic.

Canazei

㉑ *60 km (37 mi) west of Cortina d'Ampezzo, 52 km (32 mi) east of Bolzano.*

Of the year-round resort towns in the Val di Fassa, Canazei is the most popular. The mountains around this small town are threaded with hiking trails and ski slopes, surrounded by large clutches of conifers. Four kilometers (2½ mi) west of Canazei, an excursion from Campitello di Fassa to the vantage point at **Col Rodella** is a must. A cable car rises some 3,000 feet to a full-circle vista of the Heart of the Dolomites, including the Sasso Lungo and the rest of the Sella range.

Where to Stay

$$ 🏨 **Alla Rosa.** The view of the imposing Dolomites is the real attraction at this central hotel; ask for a room with a balcony. The reception area is spacious and welcoming, and guest rooms pleasantly blend rustic and modern elements. There's a modest restaurant serving local and international cuisine, and a cozy bar. Half board is required. ✉ *Via del Faure 18, 38032* 📞 *0462/601107* 📠 *0462/601481* 🌐 *www.hotelallarosa. com* 🛏 *49 rooms* ♿ *Restaurant, minibars, cable TV, sauna, bar, recreation room, parking (fee); no a/c* ▭ *MC, V* 🍴 *MAP.*

---

en route The **Passo di Sella** is a famous mountain pass in the Dolomites. It can be approached from the S48 and continues into Val Gardena through the most panoramic mountain scenery in Europe. The road descends to Ortisei, passing the smaller resorts of Selva Gardina and Santa Cristina.

Ortisei (St. Ulrich)

㉒ *28 km (17 mi) north of Canazei, 35 km (22 mi) northeast of Bolzano.*

Ortisei (St. Ulrich), the jewel in the crown of Val Gardena's resorts, is a hub of activity both summer and winter. There are hundreds of miles of hiking trails and accessible ski slopes, including the Siusi slopes to the south. Hotels are everywhere and facilities are excellent, with swimming pools, ice rinks, health spas, tennis courts, and bowling. Most impressive of all is the location, a valley surrounded by formidable views in all directions. The Val Gardena comes alive with a parade of horse-drawn sleighs on January 1.

For centuries Ortisei has also been famous for the expertise of its woodcarvers, and there are still numerous workshops. Apart from making religious sculptures—particularly the wayside Calvaries you come upon everywhere in the Dolomites—Ortisei's carvers were long known for producing wooden dolls, horses, and other toys. As itinerant peddlers they traveled every spring on foot with their loaded packs as far as Paris, London, and St. Petersburg. Fine historic and contemporary examples of local woodworking can be seen at the **Museo della Val Gardena** (Val Gardena Local Heritage Museum). ✉ *Via Rezia 83, Ortisei* 📞 *0471/797554* 🌐 *www.val-gardena.com* 🎫 *€3* 🕐 *Feb.–mid-Mar., Tues.–Fri. 2:30–5:30; June and Sept.–mid-Oct., Tues.–Fri. 2–6; July and Aug., Tues.–Sat. 10–noon and 2–6, Sun. 2–6.*

Where to Stay

★ $$$$ 🏨 **Adler.** This hotel, the best in the valley, has been under the same family management since 1810. The original building has been enlarged several times, yielding spacious guest rooms and an expansive spa complex but retaining much of the old turreted-castle appeal. Most guests stay for a full week, picking up the busy schedule of activities (such as guided ski tours and snowshoe walks) when they arrive on Saturday evening. Half board is required. ✉ *Via Rezia 7, 39046* 📞 *0471/775000* 📠 *0471/ 775555* 🌐 *www.hotel-adler.com* 🛏 *123 rooms* ♿ *Restaurant, in-room safes, minibars, cable TV, pool, health club, hair salon, sauna, bar, chil-*

dren's programs, free parking ⊟ *MC, V* ⊗ *Closed mid-Apr.–mid-May and Nov.* ⦿ *MAP.*

$$$$ ⌨ **Cavallino Bianco.** In the town center and only a five-minute walk from the main ski facilities, this hotel looks like a gigantic dollhouse, with delicate wooden balconies and an eye-catching wooden gable. Beyond this facade lies a sprawling, all-inclusive modern resort, but the cozy bar— with its large, handcrafted fireplace—retains some of the charm of the old postal hotel. ⊠ *Via Rezia 22, 39046* ☎*0471/783333* 📠*0471/797517* ⊕ *www.cavallino-bianco.com* ↘ *184 rooms* ⚭ *Restaurant, coffee shop, minibars, cable TV, pool, sauna, spa, bar, dance club, free parking; no a/c* ⊟ *AE, DC, MC, V* ⊗ *Closed mid-Apr.–mid-May and mid-Oct.–mid-Dec.* ⦿ *MAP.*

Sports

With almost 600 km (370 mi) of accessible downhill slopes, Ortisei is one of the most popular ski resorts in the Dolomites. Prices are good and facilities are among the most modern. An immensely popular route, the **Sella Ronda** relies on well-placed chairlifts to connect 26 km (16 mi) of downhill skiing around the colossal Sella massif, passing through several towns along the way. You can ski the loop, which requires intermediate ability and a full day's effort, either clockwise or counterclockwise. Going with a guide is highly advised; consult the tourist office in **Selva Gardena** (☎ 0471/795122) or **Ortisei** (☎ 0471/796328) for more information.

There are more than 90 km (56 mi) of cross-country skiing trails. The **Val Gardena Ski cooperative** (☎ 0471/792092 ⊕ www.val-gardena.com) has snow reports and information on seasonal events.

Fiè allo Sciliar (Völs am Schlern)

㉓ *26 km (16 mi) southwest of Ortisei, 18 km (11 mi) east of Bolzano.*

Fiè (Völs) is in a valley with the Renon Mountains on one side, the Siusi Mountains on the other, and acres of green coniferous forest in every direction. In the town is the parish church of **Santa Maria Assunta,** built in the 16th century in the late Gothic style.

Where to Stay

★ **$$$** ⌨ **Turm.** The *turm* (tower) that houses this welcoming hotel on the edge of Sciliar National Park dates from the 13th century and has been used as a courthouse, dungeon, and tavern. Now owned and run by the Pramstrahler family, it's furnished with their charming collection of paintings and antiques. The onion-dome hostelry also has an excellent restaurant and extensive spa offerings. ⊠ *Piazza della Chiesa 9, 39050* ☎ *0471/725014* 📠 *0471/725474* ⊕ *www.hotelturm.it* ↘ *35 rooms* ⚭ *Restaurant, in-room safes, 2 pools (1 indoor), spa, free parking* ⊟ *MC, V* ⊗ *Closed 2 wks mid-Jan. and mid-Nov.–mid-Dec.* ⦿ *BP.*

Sports

The **Oswald von Wolkenstein Cavalcade,** named after the medieval South Tirolese knight and troubadour, is held every year on the first or second weekend of June. After a colorful procession, teams of local equestrians compete in fast-paced events.

Caldaro (Kaltern)

㉔ *22 km (14 mi) south of Fiè allo Sciliar, 15 km (9 mi) south of Bolzano.*

Caldaro (Kaltern) is a vineyard village with clear views of castles high up on the surrounding mountains, a backdrop that reflects the centuries of division that forged the unique character of the area. Caldaro architecture is famous for the way it blends Italian Renaissance elements of balance and harmony with the soaring windows and peaked arches of the local Gothic tradition. The church of **Santa Caterina**, on the main square, is a good example.

Close to Caldaro's main square is the **Museo Provinciale del Vino** (South Tirolean Museum of Wine), with exhibits on how local wine has historically been made, stored, served, and worshipped. You can call ahead to reserve a wine tasting (€4.60) in the museum's cellar. ⊠ *Via dell'Oro 1* ☎ *0471/963168* ⊕ *www.provinz.bz.it/volkskundemuseen* ⊠ *€2.10* ⊘ *Apr.–mid.-Nov., Tues.–Sat. 9:30–noon and 2–6, Sun. 10–noon.*

Lago di Carezza

㉕ *35 km (22 mi) east of Caldaro, 29 km (18 mi) east of Bolzano.*

Glacial Lake Carezza is some 5,000 feet above sea level. The azure blue of the waters can at times change to magical greens and purples, reflections of the dense surrounding forest and rosy peaks of the Dolomites. You can hike down to this most quintessential of mountain lakes from the nearby village of the same name; there's a fountain with two marmots in the center of town.

THE DOLOMITES: TRENTINO–ALTO ADIGE A TO Z

To research prices, get advice from other travelers, and book travel arrangements, visit www.fodors.com.

AIRPORTS

The nearest airport, but the least well connected, is Aeroporto Bolzano Dolomiti (BZO), with scheduled service to Rome (FCO) and Innsbruck (INN). A bit farther to the south, Verona (VRN) is well connected by road and rail with the Dolomite area. Direct intercontinental flights are available into Milan Malpensa (MXP) to the southwest or Munich (MUC) to the north, both about a four-hour drive from Bolzano.

🏴 Airport Information **Aeroporto Bolzano Dolomiti** ☎ 0471/255255 ⊕ www.abd-airport.it. **Aeroporto Valerio Catullo di Verona Villafranca** ☎ 045/8095666 ⊕ www.aeroportoverona.it. **Aeroporto Milan Malpensa** ☎ 02/74852200 ⊕ www.sea-aeroportimilano.it. **Munich International Airport** ☎ 049/8997500 ⊕ www.munich-airport.de.

BUS TRAVEL

Only a handful of buses link Bolzano with Milan and Venice; the service between these cities and Trento is more frequent (for instance, there's hourly bus service between Riva del Garda and Trento), but if you want to get to Merano or Cortina d'Ampezzo you will have to change in either Trento or Bolzano. For information, call SASA.

Local buses connect the train stations at Trento, Bolzano, and Merano with the mountain resorts. The service is fairly frequent between most main towns during the day. Though some parts of the region remain out of the reach of public transportation, it's possible to visit even the remotest villages without a car if you are equipped with the local bus timetables, available from regional and local tourist offices, and lots of time. Still, most towns are designed for people with cars, and getting between your hotel, ski lifts, and après-ski locales without a vehicle can be very tricky.

🚌 Bus Information **SASA** (Società Autobus Servizi d'Area) ☎ 0471/974292.

CAR RENTAL

A car is highly recommended for exploring this region. Several international chains have local offices.

🚗 Local Agencies **Avis** ✉ Piazza Verdi 18, Bolzano ☎ 0471/971467 ⊕ www.avis.com ✉ Via Brennero 127, Trento ☎ 0461/420276. **Europcar** ✉ Via Galvani 28, Bolzano ☎ 0471/935231 ⊕ www.europcar.com ✉ Via Ragazzi del 99 25/a, Trento ☎ 0461/390747. **Hertz** ✉ Piazza Verdi 42, Bolzano ☎ 0471/981411 ⊕ www.hertz.com ✉ Via Roma 276, Merano ☎ 0473/234313 ✉ Via Lungadige Apuleio 20, Trento ☎ 0461/421555. **Sixt** ✉ Piazza Leonardo da Vinci 3, Trento ☎ 0461/261532 ⊕ www.sixt.com.

CAR TRAVEL

The most important route in the region is autostrada A22, the main north–south highway linking Italy with central Europe by way of the Brenner Pass. It connects Bressanone, Bolzano, Trento, and Rovereto, and near Verona joins the A4, running east–west across northern Italy from Trieste to Milan and Turin.

Roads in the broad mountain valleys are usually wide two-lane routes, but the roads up into the highest passes can be narrow, winding, and, especially in winter, subject to sudden closure. (Some are closed to traffic entirely in winter.) Call Autostrada Weather Information Service in Bolzano for information on weather-related closures. Even under the best conditions, expect to negotiate mountain roads at speeds no greater than 50 kph (30 mph).

EMERGENCY   ACI Emergency Service offers 24-hour roadside assistance.
SERVICES   🚗 **ACI dispatchers** ☎ 803/116. **Autostrada Weather Information Service** ☎ 0471/413810.

EMERGENCIES

For first aid, ask for *pronto soccorso,* and be prepared to give your address. Pharmacies take turns staying open late and on Sunday; for the latest information, consult the current list posted on the front door of each pharmacy or ask at the local tourist office.

🚑 **Ambulance** ☎ 118. **Polizia** (local police) ☎ 113.

LANGUAGE

Alto Adige is the only region in Italy with two official languages: Italian and German. In Bolzano, Merano, and environs, street signs, menus, city names, and street chatter are completely bilingual, and depending on your features you may be spoken to in a local dialect of German rather than Italian when you're at a shop or café. Meanwhile, all of Trentino and the ski resorts of Madonna di Campiglio and Cortina d'Ampezzo are strictly Italian-speaking, but the regional accent—most noticeable in the "r," which is guttural rather than rolled—is still quite distinctive.

MAIL & SHIPPING

Post offices are generally open on weekdays 8–6:30 and Saturday 8–12:30. The office in Bolzano's old town closes midafternoon; later hours can be found at the branch on Via Duca D'Aosta, across the Talvera River from the main branch.

🖪 Post Offices **Bolzano** ✉ Piazza Parrocchia 13 ☎ 0471/322260 ✉ Via Duca D'Aosta 104 ☎ 0471/473711. **Bressanone** ✉ Via San Cassiano 2 ☎ 0472/836193. **Cortina d'Ampezzo** ✉ Largo Poste 18/a ☎ 0436/882411. **Madonna di Campilgio** ✉ Pradalago 10/k ☎ 0465/441028. **Merano** ✉ Via Roma 120 ☎ 0473/237116. **Rovereto** ✉ Largo Poste 7 ☎ 0464/402249. **Trento** ✉ Piazza Vittoria 20 ☎ 0461/984714.

SPORTS & THE OUTDOORS

HIKING & CLIMBING   Local tourist offices can provide information on less-demanding trails.
🖪 Hiking & Climbing **Associazione Rifugi del Trentino** ✉ Piazza Centa 13/7, 38100 Trento ☎☎ 0461/826066. **Club Alpino Italiano** ✉ Piazza delle Erbe 46, Bolzano ☎ 0471/981391 ✉ Corso della Libertà 188, Merano ☎ 0473/448944 ✉ Via Manci 57, Trento ☎ 0461/981871 ⊕ www.cai.it. **Società degli Alpinisti Tridentini** ✉ Via Manci 57, 38100 Trento ☎ 0461/981871.

TOURS

If you are without a car or if you don't care to drive over mountain roads, guided tours from Bolzano or Trento can show you the Dolomites the easy way. However, the sudden and frequent snowfalls mean that tours are offered in summer only.

BUS TOURS   In Bolzano city sightseeing and local excursions are organized by the SAD bus company, near the train station. In Trento city sightseeing can be arranged through the city tourist office.
🖪 Fees & Schedules **SAD** ✉ Via Conciapelli 60 ☎ 167/846047.

SINGLE-DAY TOURS   In July and August, the SAD bus company's full-day mountain tours include a "Great Dolomites Tour" from Bolzano to Cortina and a tour of the Val Venosta that climbs over the Stelvio Pass into Switzerland. A tour of the Val Gardena and the Siusi Alps is available from April to October.

From June through September the Calderari e Moggioli travel agency offers a full-day guided bus tour of the Brenta Dolomites and its own "Great Dolomites Tour," a full-day drive over the Pordoi and Falzarego passes to Cortina d'Ampezzo and Lake Misurina. The Trentino tourist office also organizes guided tours and excursions by train to castles in the region.
🖪 Fees & Schedules **Calderari e Moggioli** ✉ Via Manci 46 ☎ 0461/980275.

TRAIN TRAVEL

The express train line that links the towns of Bolzano, Trento, and Rovereto connects with other main lines at Verona, just south of the region. Eurocity trains on the Dortmund–Venice and Munich–Innsbruck–Rome routes also stop at these stations. An express train line follows the course of the Adige Valley from Munich and Innsbruck to the Brenner Pass southward past Bolzano, Trento, and Rovereto. Branch lines from Trento and Bolzano go to some of the smaller valleys, but most of the mountain attractions are beyond the reach of trains. Contact Ferrovie dello Stato, the national train operator, for more information.

🚆 Train Information **FS–Trenitalia** ☎ 892021 ⊕ www.trenitalia.com.

VISITOR INFORMATION

🚆 Tourist Information **Alto Adige Tourism** ☎ 0471/999999 🖷 0471/999900 ⊕ www. hallo.com. **Bolzano** ✉ Piazza Walther 8 ☎ 0471/307000 🖷 0471/980128 ⊕ www. bolzano-bozen.it. **Bormio** ✉ Via Roma 131/b ☎ 0342/903300 🖷 0342/904696 ⊕ www. valtellinaonline.com. **Bressanone** ✉ Via Stazione 9 ☎ 0472/836401 🖷 0472/836067. **Brunico** ✉ Via Europa 26 ☎ 0474/555722 🖷 0474/555544. **Caldaro** ✉ Piazza Mercato 8 ☎ 0471/963169 🖷 0471/963469. **Canazei** ✉ Piazza Marconi 5 ☎ 0462/601113 🖷 0462/602502. **Chiusa** ✉ Piazza Tinne 6 ☎ 0472/847424 🖷 0472/847244. **Cortina d'Ampezzo** ✉ Piazzetta San Francesco 8 ☎ 0436/3231 🖷 0436/3235 ⊕ www.cortina. dolomiti.com. **Dobbiaco** ✉ Via Dolomiti 3 ☎ 0474/972132 🖷 0474/972730. **Dolomites Tourism** ☎ 0437/941148 🖷 0437/944202 ⊕ www.dolomiti.org. **Fiè allo Sciliar** ✉ Via Bolzano 4 ☎ 0471/725047 🖷 0471/725488. **Madonna di Campiglio** ✉ Via Pradalago 4 ☎ 0465/442000 🖷 0465/440404 ⊕ www.campiglio.to. **Merano** ✉ Corso Libertà 45 ☎ 0473/27200 🖷 0473/235524 ⊕ www.meraninfo.it. **Naturno** ✉ Piazza Municipio 1 ☎ 0473/666077 🖷 0473/666369. **Ortisei** ✉ Via Rezia 1 ☎ 0471/796328 🖷 0471/ 796749. **Rovereto** ✉ Corso Rosmini 6 ☎ 0464/430363 🖷 0464/435528. **Santa Cristina** ✉ Via Chemun 9 ☎ 0471/793046 🖷 0471/793198. **Selva Gardena** ✉ Via Mëisules 213 ☎ 0471/795122 🖷 0471/794245. **Trentino Tourism** ☎ 0461/839000 🖷 0461/260245 ⊕ www.trentino.to. **Trento** ✉ Via Manci 2 ☎ 0461/983880 🖷 0461/232426.

MILAN, LOMBARDY & THE LAKES

4

Updated by
A. H. Maines

ONE IS TEMPTED TO DESCRIBE LOMBARDY as a place with something for everyone—Milan, capital of all that is new in Italy; the great Renaissance cities of the Po plain, Pavia, Cremona, and Mantua, where even the height of summer can be comparatively peaceful; and the lakes, where glacial waters framed by the Alps have been praised as the closest thing to paradise by writers throughout the ages, from Virgil to Ernest Hemingway.

"Nothing in the world," wrote Stendhal in 1817, "can be compared to the fascination of those burning summer days passed on the Milanese lakes, in the middle of those chestnut groves so green that they immerse their branches in the waves." Millions of travelers have since agreed that for sheer beauty the lakes of northern Italy—Como, Maggiore, Garda, and Orta—have few equals. Adding to their unspoiled beauty are the Alpine foothills, 18th- and 19th-century villas and exotic formal gardens, toy villages, and dozens of resorts that were once Europe's most fashionable. Still, one cannot imagine Catullus returning to his "jewel" Sirmione, on Lago di Garda, without being a little daunted by its development as a resort town. Milan can be disappointingly modern—rather too much like the place you have come here to escape—but its historic buildings and art collections rival those of Florence and Rome.

More than 3,000 years ago, explorers from the highly civilized realm of Etruria in central Italy wandered northward beyond the River Po. The Etruscans extended their dominance into this region for hundreds of years but left little of their culture. They were succeeded by the Cenomani Gauls, who were conquered in turn by the legions of Rome in the later days of the Republic. The region became known as Cisalpine Gaul ("Gaul this side of the Alps"). Under the rule of Augustus it became a Roman province, and its warlike, independent people citizens of Rome. Virgil, Catullus, and both Plinys were born in the region during the relatively tranquil era known to its victors as the Pax Romana.

The decline of the Roman Empire was followed by invasion by Attila of the Huns and Theodoric of the Goths. These conquerors in turn gave way to the Lombards, who then ceded to Charlemagne their iron crown, which became the emblem of his vast but unstable empire. Even before the fragile bonds that held this empire together had begun to snap, the cities of Lombardy were erecting walls in defense against the Hungarians and against each other. These city-states formed the Lombard League, which, in the 12th century, finally defeated the German Frederick Barbarossa.

Once the northern invaders had been defeated, new and even bloodier strife began. In each city the Guelphs (bourgeois supporters of the popes) and the Ghibellines (noblemen loyal to the so-called emperors) clashed with each other. The city-states declined, and each fell under the yoke of powerful local rulers. The Republic of Venice dominated Brescia and Bergamo. Mantua was ruled by the Gonzaga, and the Visconti and Sforza families took over Como, Cremona, Milan, and Pavia.

The Battle of Pavia in 1525, in which the generals of Holy Roman Emperor Charles V (1500–58) defeated the French, brought on 200 years of Spanish occupation. It was then that the routed Francis I famously declaimed, "All is lost, save honor." The Spaniards were, on the whole, less cruel than the local tyrants, and were hardly resisted by the Lombards. The War of the Spanish Succession, in the early years of the 18th century, threw out the Spaniards and brought in the Austrians instead, whose dominion was "neither liked nor loathed" during the nearly 100 years of its existence.

Napoléon and his generals defeated the Austrians at the turn of the 19th century. The Treaty of Campoformio resulted in the proclamation of the Cisalpine Republic, which quickly became the Republic of Italy and, just as rapidly, the Kingdom of Italy, which in turn lasted only until Napoléon's defeat brought back the Austrians. But Milan, as the capital of Napoléon's Republic, had enjoyed a taste of glory, and the city's independent citizens, along with those of the other Lombard cities, were not slow to resent the loss of a new national identity. From 1820 on, the Lombards joined the Piedmontese and the house of Savoy in a long struggle against the Habsburgs and, in 1859, finally defeated Austria and brought about the re-creation of the Kingdom of Italy two years later.

Milan and other cities of Lombardy have not lost their independence and their hatred of domination. Nowhere in Italy was the eventual partisan insurrection against Benito Mussolini—to whom they had first given power—and the German regime better organized or more successful. It was in the city's Piazza Loreto that the dead bodies of Mussolini and his lover, Claretta Petacci, were put on display, in the same spot where a group of partisans had been shot a few weeks before. Milan was liberated from the Germans by its own partisan organization before the entrance of Allied troops; escaping Allied prisoners could find sanctuary there when fighting was still going on to the south. In the 1990s this independent spirit was expressed through popular support for the right-wing political movement known as the Lega Nord (Northern League). Today the ever-sensible Milanese have turned their attention back to business, making Lombardy the Internet capital of Italy and a region that single-handedly accounts for one-fifth of Italy's economy.

Exploring Milan, Lombardy & the Lakes

Lombardy's greatest merit may be its diversity. Jagged Alpine vistas and deep glacial lakes stretch from the Swiss border down to Milan's outskirts, where they meet the flat, fertile plain that extends from the banks of the River Po. The A4 autostrada connects Milan to Italy's industrial belt, which extends west to Turin and east through Brescia, Lombardy's second-biggest city. Scattered across the plains to the south are the Renaissance city-states of Pavia, Cremona, and Mantua.

Most international travelers arrive at Malpensa airport, some 50 km (31 mi) northwest of Milan. As the airport is closer to Lakes Como and Maggiore than to Milan itself, you can skip the city and head straight for the hills if you like; Lake Garda is a two-hour drive east of Milan. The best way to see the lake country is to rent a car in fall or spring and

A week is enough to see the area thoroughly; five days will give you time to see all the sights, but you'll have to keep on the move. Three days will give you a taste of the major sights in the area, but time will be precious and morning starts will have to be early.

Numbers in the text correspond to numbers in the margin and on the Milan and Lombardy & the Lakes maps.

4

If you have
3 days

Spend the first day walking around ▦ **Milan** ❶–⓰ ▶. The next morning, head east on the A4 autostrada and stop in the Alpine, medieval town of **Bergamo** ㉙ before continuing on to ▦ **Sirmione** ㉗ on Lake Garda. If you arrive early enough, you may wish to drive around the lake a bit before bedding down for the night. On Day 3 take the A4 west past Bergamo, switch to the S432, and drive around the southern shore of Lake Como, stopping in **Bellagio** ㉚ for lunch and spending the night in ▦ **Como** ㉞.

If you have
5 days

Follow the three-day itinerary, but after Bergamo continue east and take the A22 south to ▦ **Mantua** ⑳, where you can enjoy Mantegna's masterpieces. On Day 3 drive around Lake Garda, stopping at any gorgeous lakeside spot that catches your fancy, and spend the night in ▦ **Riva del Garda** ㉔ on the north side of the lake, or ▦ **Sirmione** ㉗ on the south. The next morning, take the A4 back west to Lake Como, visiting Madonna del Ghisallo and **Bellagio** ㉚ and taking ferries to the lake towns of **Varenna** ㉛ and **Tremezzo** ㉜, where you'll find the magnificent Villa Carlotta. On the final day, head west to **Orta San Giulio** ㉟ on Lake Orta. It's only a short hop from there to Lake Maggiore, which you can explore by steamer.

If you have
7 days

Spend two days in ▦ **Milan** ❶–⓰ ▶, then start south along the A7 to **Pavia** ⑰ and **Cremona** ⑱ before continuing on to ▦ **Mantua** ⑳. From there follow the five-day plan above; make sure to stop in **Gargnano** ㉕ and **Gardone Riviera** ㉖ on Lake Garda, where you should visit Gabriele d'Annunzio's former home, Il Vittoriale.

---

thread a leisurely path along the small mountain roads that link the lakes' least-spoiled northern tips. This is splendid mountain-driving country, with some of the most beautiful and challenging roads in the world. Without a car, however, it's still possible to see many of the region's sights, thanks to extensive bus routes and the many vaporetti (water taxis) that thread across the lakes. The throngs that descend upon the lakes in July and August, particularly on weekends, make reservations absolutely necessary—especially at Lake Como, the quintessential Italian lake resort.

About the Restaurants & Hotels

Milan is by far the most cosmopolitan city in Italy. A burgeoning immigrant population has led to the appearance of inexpensive South American, African, Asian, and Middle Eastern restaurants along with the traditional Italian establishments. The Lake District is in full swing only from late spring through early fall; many restaurants and hotels cut back on operations during the winter.

The hotels in Italy's richest region generally cater to a clientele willing to pay for extra comfort. Many are converted from handsome old villas and have well-landscaped grounds—try to visit one or two, even if you don't stay the night. Most of the famous lake resorts are expensive; more reasonably priced accommodations can be found in the smaller towns and villages. Local tourism offices can be an excellent source of information about affordable and attractive out-of-the-way accommodations. In Milan, trade fairs and business bookings generate constant competition for rooms. Reservations are recommended year-round and essential in spring and summer.

WHAT IT COSTS In euros				
$$$$	**$$$**	**$$**	**$**	**¢**
RESTAURANTS				
over €22	€16–€22	€11–€16	€7–€11	under €7
HOTELS				
IN MILAN over €290	€210–€290	€140–€210	€80–€140	under €80
ELSEWHERE over €220	€160–€220	€110–€160	€70–€110	under €70

Restaurant prices are for a second course (*secondo piatto*). Hotel prices are for two people in a standard double room in high season, including tax and service.

Timing

Lake roads can become congested in July and August, especially on evenings and weekends. Fewer people visit in spring and fall, and in winter the lakeside towns are positively deserted. Note that many of the ferry services stop running in October and recommence in May. Early summer and early fall are the best times to see the area, though October can be chilly for swimming.

MILAN

Italy's business hub and crucible of chic is the country's most populous and prosperous city, serving as the capital of commerce, finance, fashion, and media. It's also Italy's transport hub, with the biggest international airport, most rail connections, and best subway system. Leonardo Da Vinci's *Last Supper* and other great works of art are here, as well as a spectacular Gothic Duomo, the finest of its kind. Milan even reigns supreme where it really counts (in the minds of many Italians), routinely trouncing the rest of the nation with its two premier soccer teams.

And yet, Milan hasn't won the battle for hearts and minds. Most tourists prefer Tuscany's hills and Venice's canals to Milan's hectic efficiency and wealthy indifference, and it's no surprise that in a country of medieval hilltop villages and skilled artisans, a city of grand boulevards and global corporations leaves visitors asking the real Italy to please stand

Shopping

Milan is one of the clothing capitals of the world, home to global fashion giants such as Armani, Prada, and Trussardi. Behind these famous names stands a host of smaller, less renowned tailors, stylists, and designers who help make this cosmopolitan city a shopper's paradise. Milan truly offers a shop for every taste, from its broad Corso Buenos Aires, which has the highest ratio of shops per square foot of anywhere in Europe, to the bourgeois Via Montenapoleone, where a cuff link can cost more than a four-course meal. "Oh bej, oh bej," murmur the Milanese in dialect as they wander from one store window to the next, and for shoppers it truly can be "beautiful, beautiful."

4

Water Sports

There are schools for sailing, scuba diving, waterskiing, and windsurfing in Riva del Garda, on the northern tip of Lake Garda. Torbole, 5 km (3 mi) east of Riva del Garda on S240, is a prime spot for windsurfing. Lake Como also has well-equipped sailing and windsurfing schools as well as waterskiing.

---

up. They're right, of course. Milan is more European than Italian, a new buckle on an old boot, and although its old city can stand cobblestone for cobblestone against the best of them, seekers of Roman ruins and fairy-tale towns may pass. But Milan's new faces are hidden behind splendid beaux-arts facades and in luxurious 19th-century palazzos, and those lured by its world-class shopping and European sophistication enjoy the city's lively, cosmopolitan feel.

For their part, most Italians consider the Milanese an affront to their ideal of *la dolce vita,* and they, too, are right. The Milanese don't conform to the Italian stereotypes. Whereas Florentines boast about its past and politicians in Rome bicker about its present, the Milanese are too busy building Italy's future to live the slow, sensual lifestyle preferred by their countrymen. This is part choice and part necessity. Milan never had it easy. To turn their landlocked outpost into a regional power, they had to dig an extensive network of deep canals, eventually linking the city to the Po, Ticino, and Adda rivers. Lacking natural defenses, they built strong walls to keep the marauding hordes at bay. For income, local merchants took advantage of nearby Alpine trade routes to build a great trading center. Even talent was imported when needed; from St. Ambrose and Leonardo da Vinci to the waves of migrants who fueled its growth in the second half of the 20th century, outsiders have been drawn to Milan for its open, freewheeling commercial culture and acceptance of new ideas. The result has been an ever-expanding power, and a juicy target for conquest.

Virtually every invader in European history—Gaul, Roman, Goth, Longobard, and Frank—as well as a long series of rulers from France, Spain, and Austria, took a turn at ruling the city. After being completely sacked by the Goths in AD 539 and by the Holy Roman Empire under

Lombardy
& the Lakes

SWITZERLAND

Locarno
Ascona
Brissago

Cannobio
Cannero
Riv.

Lugano
Menaggio
Cadenabbia
Verbania 37
**Villa
Pallavicino**
*Isola
San Moltarone*
Giulio
ISOLE
BORROMEE
Laveno
Tremezzo 32
Sala
Comacina
Ossucio
Villa Carlotta
Villa Melzi
Bellagio

Omegna
Gignese
Stresa 36
Belgirate

Armeno

Lago
Varese
Varese
Cernobbio 33
34 **Como**

Orta San Giulio 35
Arona
Angera

*Lago
di
Orta*

PIEDMONT

Bellano
Varenna 31

Lago di Como

SS38

**Villa
Balbianello**
**Chiesa della
Madonna del Ghisallo**

Lecco
San Pellegrino
Terme

LOMBARDY
Bergamo 29
Capriate
San Gervasio

TO
QUARNA
SOTTO

TO
TURIN
Novara

Aeroporto
Malpensa ✈

Milan
1 - 16
see detail
map

Aeroporto
Milano Linate ✈

Cassano d'Ad
Trevigli

Abbiategrasso
Vigevano

Certosa
di Pavia

Pavia 17

Lodi

ITALY

Po

KEY
▶ Start of itinerary

CloseUp

ON THE MENU

Unlike most other Italian regions, Lombardy traditionally exhibits a northern European preference for butter rather than oil as its cooking medium, which imparts a rich and distinctive flavor to the cuisine. Alla milanese—Milanese-style cooking—usually means the food is dipped in egg and bread crumbs mixed with grated Parmesan, then sautéed in butter. One of the most popular specialties here, osso buco, is almost always paired with risotto, which the alla milanese preparation enriches with chicken broth and saffron.

The lakes are a good source of fish, particularly trout and pike. Gorgonzola—a strong, creamy, veined cheese—and panettone—a sweet yeast bread with raisins, citron, and anise—both hail from the Milan area and can be found throughout Lombardy. The most rewarding wines of the region, worth searching wine lists for, are the red Valtellina Superiore and Oltrepò Pavese, as well as the delicious light sparkling whites from the Franciacorta area.

Frederick Barbarossa in 1157, Milan became one of the first independent city-states of the Renaissance. Its heyday of self-rule proved comparatively brief. From 1277 until 1500 it was ruled by the Visconti and subsequently the Sforza dynasties. These families were known, justly or not, for a peculiarly aristocratic mixture of refinement, classical learning, and cruelty, and much of the surviving grandeur of Gothic and Renaissance art and architecture is their doing. Be on the lookout in your wanderings for the Visconti family emblem—a viper, its jaws straining wide, devouring a child.

Exploring Milan

The city center is compact and walkable, although it's faster to use the efficient Metropolitana (subway) to reach locations farther afield. Driving the streets of Milan is difficult at best, and parking can be downright miserable, so leave the car behind.

Milan's main sites and arteries radiate out from the massive Duomo. Corso Vittorio Emanuele leads northeast into the *quadrilatero* (fashion district), lined with elegant window displays from Milan's celebrated designers. Beyond La Scala, north of the Duomo, are the winding streets of the Brera section, the traditional bohemian quarter. To the northwest, past Milan's most exclusive residential district, is the imposing Renaissance Castello Sforzesco. Banks cluster in the ancient financial district just west of the Duomo, and bookshops and cafés can be found in the university quarter to the southeast. The **tourist office** (⊠ Via Marconi 1 ☎ 02/72524301 ⊕ www.milaninfotourist. com ⊙ Mon.–Sat. 9–1 and 2–6, Sun. 9–1 and 2–6) in Piazza Duomo is an excellent place to begin your visit. Free maps are available, but the pocket-size MiniCity® version may be the best €3 you can spend in Milan.

The Duomo & Points North

a good walk

Start at the **Duomo** ❶ ☞ and visit its roof, museum, and the **Battistero Paleocristiano** ❷. Then move on to **Galleria Vittorio Emanuele** ❸, just beyond the northern tip of the cathedral's facade. Continue across the transepts of the Galleria and head north to **Teatro alla Scala** ❹, where Verdi found fame. Head northeast on Via Manzoni, stopping in the **Museo Poldi-Pezzoli** ❺ to view its collection of Renaissance paintings. Continue on Via Manzoni, then turn right on Via Monte Napoleone, plunging into the *quadrilatero d'oro* (golden quadrangle), Milan's high-fashion district. Turn left on Via Sant'Andrea, then left again on Via della Spiga to return to Via Manzoni. From here you can make a detour to the Giardini Pubblici (great for kids) and the **Museo Civico di Storia Naturale** ❻ on the eastern side of the park. Backtrack south on Via Manzoni and return to the Montenapoleone metro station; take a right onto the short Via Croce Rosa, then an immediate left onto Via Monte di Pietà. At Via di Brera, turn right into the bohemian district anchored by the **Pinacoteca di Brera** ❼. After exploring the gallery (and the outdoor cafés), head west on Via Fiori Chiari, which tapers to a tiny *vicolo* (alleyway) before hitting busy Via Mercato. Turn left, then right on Via Arco and cross a small piazza with intersecting tram tracks. You'll see the imposing stone towers of **Castello Sforzesco** ❽ rising straight ahead—make your way to the entrance in the central, square tower. After viewing the castle's collections, walk back past the fountain, past the statue of Garibaldi, and onto the pedestrian-only boulevard Via Dante, which leads back toward the Duomo.

TIMING   The walk itself will take about two hours; allow a full day to roam the museums, shop for gifts, and sip caffè. Note that most museums and some churches are closed Monday.

What to See

❷ **Battistero Paleocristiano.** Beneath the Duomo's piazza lies this baptistery ruin dating from the 4th century. Although opinion remains divided, it is widely believed to be where Ambrose, Milan's first bishop and patron saint, baptized Augustine. Tickets are available at the kiosk inside the cathedral. ⊠ *Piazza del Duomo, enter through Duomo* ☎ *02/86463456* 🎟 *€1.50* ☉ *Daily 9:30–5:15* Ⓜ *Duomo.*

❽ **Castello Sforzesco.** For the serious student of Renaissance military engineering, the Castello must be something of a travesty, so often has it been remodeled or rebuilt since it was begun in 1450 by the *condottiere* (hired mercenary) who founded the city's second dynastic family, Francesco Sforza, fourth duke of Milan. Though today the word "mercenary" has a pejorative ring, during the Renaissance all Italy's great soldier-heroes were professionals hired by the cities and principalities that they served. Of them—and there were thousands—Francesco Sforza (1401–66) is considered one of the greatest, most honest, and most organized. It is said he could remember the names not only of all his men but of their horses as well. His rule signaled the enlightened age of the Renaissance, but preceded the next foreign rule by a scant 50 years.

Milan

Since the turn of the last century, the Castello has housed municipal museums devoted variously to Egyptian and other antiquities, musical instruments, paintings, and sculpture. Highlights are the **Sala delle Asse,** a frescoed room still sometimes attributed to Leonardo da Vinci (1452–1519). Michelangelo's unfinished *Rondanini Pietà* is believed to be his last work—an astounding achievement for a man nearly 90, and a moving coda to his life. ⊠ *Piazza Castello, Brera* ☏ *02/88463700* ⊕ *www.milanocastello.it* ⊠ *Free* ⊙ *Tues.–Sun. 9–5:30* Ⓜ *Cairoli.*

★ ⌐ ❶ **Duomo.** This intricate Gothic structure—Italy's largest—has been fascinating and exasperating visitors and conquerors alike since it was begun by Galeazzo Visconti III (1351–1402), first duke of Milan, in 1386. Consecrated in the 15th or 16th century, it was not completed until just before the coronation of Napoléon as king of Italy in 1809. Whether or not you concur with travel writer H. V. Morton's 1964 assessment that the cathedral is "one of the mightiest Gothic buildings ever created," there is no denying that for sheer size and complexity it is unrivaled; its look is more Gotham than Milan. The capacity is reckoned to be 40,000. Usually it is empty, a sanctuary from the frenetic pace of life outside and the perfect place for solitary contemplation. The poet Percy Bysshe Shelley swore by it—claiming it was the only place to read Dante.

The building is adorned with 135 marble spires and 2,245 marble statues. The oldest part is the **apse.** Its three colossal bays of curving and counter-curved tracery, especially the bay adorning the exterior of the stained-glass windows, should not be missed. At the end of the southern transept down the right aisle lies the **tomb of Gian Giacomo Medici.** The tomb owes some of its design to Michelangelo but was executed by Leone Leoni (1509–90) and is generally considered to be his masterpiece; it dates from the 1560s. Directly ahead is the Duomo's most famous sculpture, the gruesome but anatomically instructive figure of **San Bartolomeo** (St. Bartholomew), whose glorious martyrdom consisted of being flayed alive. It is usually said the saint stands "holding" his skin, but this is not quite accurate. It would appear more that he is luxuriating in it, much as a 1950s matron might have shown off a new fur stole.

As you enter the apse to admire those splendid windows, glance at the **sacristy doors** to the right and left of the altar. The lunette on the right dates from 1393 and was decorated by Hans von Fernach. The one on the left also dates from the 14th century and is ascribed jointly to Giacomo da Campione and Giovanni dei Grassi. Don't miss the view from the Duomo's **roof;** walk out the left (north) transept to the stairs and elevator. Sadly, air pollution drastically reduces the view on all but the rarest days. As you stand among the forest of marble pinnacles, remember that virtually every inch of this gargantuan edifice, including the roof itself, is decorated with precious white marble dragged from quarries near Lake Maggiore by Duke Visconti's team along road laid fresh for the purpose and through the newly dredged canals.

Inspection and possible repair of 12 of the northern spires means the facade facing the piazza may be shrouded in scaffolding through most of 2005, although as individual sections are restored, some scaffolding comes down. The rest of the Duomo's intricate masonry and statuary, including the gleaming, emblematic **Madonnina** perched on the highest spire, remain unencumbered. ⊠ *Piazza del Duomo* ☎ *02/86463456* 🖼 *Stairs to roof €3.50, elevator €5* 🕙 *Mid-Feb.–mid-Nov., daily 9–5:45; mid-Nov.–mid-Feb., daily 9–4:15* Ⓜ *Duomo.*

Exhibits at the **Museo del Duomo** shed light on the cathedral's history and include some of the treasures removed from the exterior for preservation purposes. ⊠ *Piazza del Duomo 14* ☎ *02/860358* 🖼 *€6, €7 including ticket for the Duomo's elevator* 🕙 *Daily 10–1:15 and 3–6.*

★ ❸ **Galleria Vittorio Emanuele.** This spectacularly extravagant, late-19th-century glass-topped, barrel-vaulted tunnel is essentially one of the planet's earliest and most select shopping malls. It's rivaled perhaps only by GUM, off Red Square in Moscow, for sheer belle-epoque splendor. Its architect, Giuseppe Mengoni, is the only mall designer known to have died for his cause—he lost his footing on the roof and tumbled to his death on the floor below just days before the Galleria's opening in 1877.

Like its suburban American cousins, the Galleria fulfills numerous social functions. This is the city's heart, midway between the Duomo and La Scala, and it is sometimes called Il Salotto (the Living Room). It teems with life, inviting people-watching from the tables that spill from the Galleria's bars and restaurants, where you can enjoy a ridiculously overpriced coffee. Books, records, clothing, food, wine, pens, jewelry, and myriad other goods are all for sale in the Galleria, and you'll also find here Savini, one of Milan's classic restaurants.

Like the cathedral, the Galleria is cruciform in shape. Even in poor weather the great glass dome above the octagonal center is a splendid sight. And the floor mosaics are a vastly underrated source of pleasure, even if they are not to be taken too seriously. They represent Europe, Asia, Africa, and the United States; those at the entrance arch are devoted to science, industry, art, and agriculture. Be sure to follow tradition and spin your heels once or twice on the more "delicate" parts of the bull beneath your feet in the northern apse; the Milanese believe it brings good luck. ⊠ *Piazza del Duomo* 🕙 *Most shops daily 9:30–1 and 3:30–7, others later or all day* Ⓜ *Duomo.*

🄲🄱 ❻ **Museo Civico di Storia Naturale** (Municipal Natural History Museum). Exhibits here appeal to animal and nature lovers, and anyone else who can appreciate stilted arrangements of narwhals, elephant seals, and bug-besieged hippopotami. It's on the eastern edge of the **Giardini Pubblici** (Public Gardens), an outlet for active young children. ⊠ *Corso Venezia 55, Porta Venezia* ☎ *02/88463337* ⊕ *www.assodidatticamuseale.it* 🖼 *€3* 🕙 *Tues.–Fri. 9–6, weekends 9:30–6:30; last entry 30 mins before closing* Ⓜ *Palestro.*

❺ **Museo Poldi-Pezzoli.** This exceptional museum opened in 1881 was once a private residence and collection, and contains not only pedigreed paintings but also porcelain, textiles, and a cabinet with scenes from Dante's life. The gem is undoubtedly the *Portrait of a Lady* by Antonio Pollaiolo (1431–98), one of the city's most prized treasures and the source of the museum's logo. The collection also includes masterpieces by Botticelli (1445–1510), Andrea Mantegna (1431–1506), Giovanni Bellini (1430–1516), and Fra Filippo Lippi (1406–69), whose uncomplicated, heartrending style won him the favor and patronage of Florence's Piero de' Medici (1416–69), son of Cosimo and father of Lorenzo il Magnifico (1449–92). ⊠ *Via Manzoni 12, Brera* ☎ *02/794889* ⊕ *www. museopoldipezzoli.it* ⊠ *€6* ⊙ *Tues.–Sun. 10–6* Ⓜ *Montenapoleone.*

★ ❼ **Pinacoteca di Brera** (Brera Gallery). The collection here is star-studded even by Italian standards. The entrance hall (Room I) displays 20th-century sculpture and painting, including Carlo Carrà's (1881–1966) confident, stylish response to the schools of cubism and surrealism. After that, the museum's 38 other rooms are arranged in chronological order—pace yourself.

The somber, moving *Cristo Morto* (*Dead Christ*) by Mantegna (1430–1506) dominates Room VI, with its sparse palette of umber and its foreshortened perspective. Mantegna's shocking, almost surgical precision—in the rendering of Christ's wounds, the face propped up on a pillow, the day's growth of beard—tells of an all-too-human agony. It is one of Renaissance painting's most quietly wondrous achievements, finding an unsuspected middle ground between the excesses of conventional gore and beauty in representing the Passion's saddest moment.

Room XXIV offers two additional highlights of the gallery. Raphael's (1483–1520) *Sposalizio della Vergine,* with its mathematical composition and precise, alternating colors, portrays the betrothal of Mary and Joseph (who, though older than the other men gathered, wins her hand when the rod he is holding miraculously blossoms). *La Vergine con il Bambino e Santi* (*Madonna with Child and Saints*), by Piero della Francesca (1420–92), is an altarpiece commissioned by Federico da Montefeltro (shown kneeling, in full armor, before the Virgin); it was intended for a church to house the Duke's tomb. The ostrich egg hanging from the apse, depending on whom you ask, either commemorates the miracle of his fertility—Federico's wife died months after giving birth to a long-awaited male heir—or alludes to his appeal for posthumous mercy, the egg symbolizing the saving power of grace. ⊠ *Via Brera 28* ☎ *02/722631* ⊕ *www.brera.beniculturali.it* ⊠ *€5* ⊙ *Tues.–Sun. 8:30–7:15; last admission 45 mins before closing* Ⓜ *Cairoli, Lanza, or Montenapoleone.*

off the beaten path	**LATIN QUARTER** – Take time to wander around the lively quarter surrounding the Pinacoteca di Brera. The narrow streets lined with boutiques, crafts shops, cafés, restaurants, and music clubs make up what's often referred to as Milan's Greenwich Village. A longtime haunt of artists and musicians, it has a number of clubs and cafés presenting live music late into the night.

❹ **Teatro alla Scala.** You need know nothing of opera to sense that, like Carnegie Hall, La Scala is closer to a cathedral than an auditorium. Here Verdi established his reputation and Maria Callas sang her way into opera lore. It looms as a symbol—both for the performer who dreams of singing here and for the opera buff who knows every note of *Rigoletto* by heart. Audiences are notoriously fickle and have been known to jeer performers who do not do appropriate justice to their beloved *opera lirica.* The opera house was closed after destruction by Allied bombs in 1943, reopened at a performance led by Arturo Toscanini in 1946, and closed again in 2002 for long-overdue renovations. The massive modern reconstruction project, which left only the exterior shell standing, is officially completed as of the December 7, 2004, reopening, though final touches may extend into 2005. ☒ *Piazza della Scala* ☎ *02/86077 box office* ⊕ *www.teatroallascala.org* Ⓜ *Duomo.*

At **Museo Teatrale alla Scala** you can admire librettos, posters, costumes, instruments, and design sketches for the theater, curtains, and viewing box decorations, along with an explanation of the reconstruction project and several interactive exhibits. A highlight is the collection of antique gramophones and phonographs. ☒ *Piazza della Scala* ☎ *02/ 4691249* ▣ *€5* ⊙ *Daily 9–6; last admission at 5:15.*

South & West of the Duomo

a good walk

From the Duomo, head southwest on Via Torino, pausing to admire Bramante's Renaissance masterpiece, the church of **San Satiro** ❾ ▶. Backtrack a bit toward the Duomo, turning left on Via Spadari, then left again on Via Cantù to reach Piazza Pio XI—and the beautiful **Pinacoteca Ambrosiana** ❿ gallery and attached library. Find your way south to Via Fulcorina, then turn right, walking northwest until you hit Corso Magenta. Turn left, visiting the city's **Museo Civico Archeologico** ⓫ before continuing on to admire Milan's most precious painting: the *Last Supper,* in the monastery of **Santa Maria delle Grazie** ⓬. Backtrack on Corso Magenta, turning right onto Via Carducci. At the intersection of Via Carducci and Via San Vittore you will find the medieval **Basilica di Sant'Ambrogio** ⓭; walking a block west on Via San Vittore will take you to the **Museo Nazionale della Scienza e Tecnica** ⓮. When finished in the Sant'Ambrogio neighborhood, head east on Via de Amicis, then (after about a five-minute walk) turn left on Corso Porta Ticinese to reach the church of **San Lorenzo Maggiore** ⓯. South on Corso Porta Ticinese, just outside the limits of the old city, is the bustling **Navigli district** ⓰. You can hike back toward the Duomo, or hop on the subway to return to the city center.

TIMING   Allow a full day for this walk. Note that most museums and some churches are closed on Monday. Your itinerary should be adapted to accommodate the time of your reservation to view the *Last Supper.*

What to See

⓭ **Basilica di Sant'Ambrogio** (Basilica of St. Ambrose). Noted for its medieval architecture, the church was consecrated by St. Ambrose in AD 387, and is the model for all Lombard Romanesque churches. ☒ *Piazza Sant'Ambrogio 15* ☎ *02/86450895* ⊙ *Mon.–Sat. 7–noon and 2:30–7, Sun. 3–8* Ⓜ *Sant'Ambrogio.*

⓫ **Museo Civico Archeologico** (Municipal Archaeological Museum). Housed in a former monastery, this museum has some enlightening relics from Milan's Roman past—from everyday utensils and jewelry to several fine examples of mosaic pavement. ⊠ *Corso Magenta 15, Sant'Ambrogio* ☎ *02/86450011* 🎟 *Free* ⊙ *Tues.–Sun. 9–5:30* Ⓜ *Cadorna.*

> **need a break?** A bit overcrowded at night, the **Bar Magenta** (⊠ Via Carducci 13, at Corso Magenta, Sant'Ambrogio ☎ 02/8053808) can be a good stop en route during the day. Beyond lunch, beer, or coffee, the real attraction is its casual but civilized, quintessentially Milanese ambience.

🐾 ⑭ **Museo Nazionale della Scienza e Tecnica** (National Museum of Science and Technology). This museum houses an extensive, eccentric collection of engineering achievements, from metal-processing equipment to full-size locomotives. But the highlights are undoubtedly the exhibits based on the inventive technical drawings of Leonardo da Vinci. On the 2nd floor a collection of models based on these sketches is artfully displayed, with Leonardo's paintings offering striking counterpoint overhead. Explanations are not offered in English, leaving you to ponder possible purposes for the contraptions. On the ground level—in the hallway between the courtyards—is a "workshop" featuring interactive, moving models of the famous *vite aerea* (aerial screw) and *ala battente* (beating wing), thought to be forerunners of the modern helicopter and airplane, respectively. ⊠ *Via San Vittore 21, Sant'Ambrogio* ☎ *02/ 48555200* ⊕ *www.museoscienza.org* 🎟 *€7* ⊙ *Tues.–Fri. 9:30–4:50, weekends 9:30–6:20* Ⓜ *Sant'Ambrogio.*

⑯ **Navigli district.** In medieval times a network of navigable canals, called *navigli*, crisscrossed Milan. Almost all have been covered over, but in this romantic, bohemian neighborhood two long canals—Naviglio Grande and Naviglio Pavese—and part of a third—Darsena—survive. They're lined with quaint shops, art galleries, cafés, restaurants, and clubs. ⊠ *South of Corso Porta Ticinese, Porta Genova* Ⓜ *Porta Genova.*

⑩ **Pinacoteca Ambrosiana.** This museum, founded in the 17th century by Cardinal Federico Borromeo, is one of the city's treasures. Here you can contemplate works of art such as Caravaggio's *Basket of Fruit*, prescient in its realism, and Raphael's awesome preparatory drawing for *The School of Athens* in the Vatican, as well as paintings by Leonardo, Botticelli, Luini, Titian, and Brueghel. The adjoining library, the Biblioteca Ambrosiana, also sometimes hosts exhibits and is considered to be the oldest Italian public library, dating from 1609. ⊠ *Piazza Pio XI 2, near Duomo* ☎ *02/806921* ⊕ *www.ambrosiana.it* 🎟 *€7.50* ⊙ *Museum Tues.–Sun. 10–5:30. Library weekdays 9:30–5.*

⑮ **San Lorenzo Maggiore.** Sixteen ancient Roman columns line the front of this sanctuary; 4th-century paleochristian mosaics survive in the Cappella di Sant'Aquilino (Chapel of St. Aquilinus). ⊠ *Corso di Porta Ticinese 39, Porta Ticinese* ☎ *02/89404129* 🎟 *Mosaics €2* ⊙ *Daily 8:30–12:30 and 2:30–6:30.*

▶ ⑨ **San Satiro.** First built in 876, this architectural gem was later perfected by Bramante (1444–1514), demonstrating his command of proportion and perspective, keynotes of Renaissance architecture. Bramante tricks the eye with a famous optical illusion that makes a small interior seem extraordinarily spacious and airy, while accommodating a beloved 13th-century fresco. ⊠ *Via Torino 9, near Duomo* ⊙ *Weekdays 7:30–11:30 and 3:30–6:30, weekends 9–noon and 3:30–7.*

★ ⑫ **Santa Maria delle Grazie.** Leonardo da Vinci's *The Last Supper*, housed in the church and former Dominican monastery of Santa Maria delle Grazie, has had an almost unbelievable history of bad luck and neglect—its near destruction in an American bombing raid in August 1943 was only the latest chapter in a series of misadventures, including, if one 19th-century source is to be believed, being whitewashed over by monks. Well-meant but disastrous attempts at restoration have done little to rectify the problem of the work's placement: it was executed on a wall unusually vulnerable to climatic dampness. Yet Leonardo chose to work slowly and patiently in oil pigments—which demand dry plaster—instead of proceeding hastily on wet plaster according to the conventional fresco technique. Novelist Aldous Huxley (1894–1963) called it "the saddest work of art in the world." After years of restorers' patiently shifting from one square centimeter to another, Leonardo's masterpiece is free of the shroud of scaffolding—and centuries of retouching, grime, and dust. Astonishing clarity and luminosity have been regained. *Reservations are required* to view the work; call several days ahead for weekday visits and several *weeks* in advance for a weekend visit. The reservations office is open 9 AM–6 PM weekdays and 9 AM–2 PM on Saturday. Viewings are in 15-minute slots.

Despite Leonardo's carefully preserved preparatory sketches in which the apostles are clearly labeled by name, there still remains some small debate about a few identities in the final arrangement. But there can be no mistaking Judas, small and dark, his hand calmly reaching forward to the bread, isolated from the terrible confusion that has taken the hearts of the others. One critic, Frederick Hartt, offers an elegantly terse explanation for why the composition works: it combines "dramatic confusion" with "mathematical order." Certainly, the amazingly skillful and unobtrusive repetition of threes—in the windows, in the grouping of the figures, and in their placement—adds a mystical aspect to what at first seems simply the perfect observation of spontaneous human gesture.

The painting was executed in what was the order's refectory, now called the **Cenacolo Vinciano.** Take a moment to visit Santa Maria delle Grazie itself. It's a handsome church, with a fine dome, which Bramante added along with a cloister about the time that Leonardo was commissioned to paint *The Last Supper.* If you're wondering how two such giants came to be employed decorating and remodeling the refectory and church of a comparatively modest religious order, and not, say, the Duomo, the answer lies in the ambitious but largely unrealized plan to turn Santa Maria delle Grazie into a magnificent Sforza family mausoleum. Though Ludovico il Moro Sforza (1452–1508), seventh duke of Milan, was but one generation away from the founding of the Sforza dynasty, he was its last ruler. Two years after Leonardo finished *The Last Supper* Ludovico was defeated and imprisoned in a French dungeon for the remaining eight years of his life. ⊠ *Piazza Santa Maria delle Grazie 2,* *off Corso Magenta, Sant'Ambrogio* ☎ *02/89421146* 💳 *€6.50 plus €1.50 reservation fee* ☺ *Tues.–Sun. 8–7:30, last entry 6:45* Ⓜ *Cadorna.*

off the beaten path

LEONARDO'S HORSE – In 1482 Leonardo da Vinci proposed and undertook a daunting project: building the largest equestrian statue in the world to honor the father of Ludovico Sforza. To Leonardo's great regret he never got farther than a full-scale (at 24 feet high) clay model—with the French army threatening Milan, bronze became too scarce. The project lost momentum for almost five centuries, until an article in *National Geographic* inspired retired United Airlines pilot Charles Dent to begin fund-raising for the horse's belated bronze incarnation (based on drawings that had been found in Madrid in 1965). His improbable quest yielded Japanese-American sculptor Nina Akamu's *Il Cavallo*, which was presented as a gift to the people of Italy at San Siro on September 30, 1999, 500 years to the day after French archers used Leonardo's original model for target practice. ✉ *Via Piccolomini, between the racetrack and the soccer stadium, San Siro* 🌐 *www.leonardoshorse.org.*

FANTASY WORLD MINITALIA – Between Milan and Bergamo, this theme park has a relief model of Italy, with about 200 models of the country's most important monuments. ✉ *A4 autostrada toward Bergamo, Capriate San Gervasio, 35 km (22 mi) east of Milan* ☎ *02/9090169* 🌐 *www.fantasyworld.it* 💳 *€16* ☺ *Mar.–Sept., Tues.–Fri. 9:30–6, weekends 9:30–7:30.*

Where to Eat

★ **$$$$** ╳ **Cracco-Peck.** A famous local chef (Carlo Cracco) joins forces with Milan's premier gourmet foods store (Peck) to push the bar for Milan restaurants a notch higher. The dining room is done in an elegant style that favors cool earth tones. Specialties include Milanese classics such as saffron risotto and breaded veal cutlet, and be sure to save room for light, steam-cooked tiramisu. ✉ *Via Victor Hugo 4, near Duomo* ☎ *02/ 866774* 🍴 *Reservations essential* 🖃 *AE, DC, MC, V* ☺ *No lunch Sat. Closed Sun., 10 days in Jan., and 2 wks in Aug.; no dinner Sat. in July and Aug.* Ⓜ *Duomo.*

★ **$$$$** ╳ **Don Carlos.** This restaurant near La Scala is nothing like its indecisive operatic namesake (whose betrothed was stolen by his father). Flavors are bold, their presentation precise and full of flair: broiled red mullet floats on a lacy layer of crispy leek. Walls are saturated with sketches of the theater, and the aria recordings are every bit as well chosen as the wine list, setting the perfect stage for discreet business negotiation or, better yet, refined romance. ✉ *Grand Hotel et de Milan, Via Manzoni 29, Duomo* ☎ *02/723141* 🍴 *Reservations essential* 🖃 *AE, DC, MC, V* ☺ *Closed Aug. No lunch* Ⓜ *Montenapoleone.*

★ **$$$$** ╳ **L'Antica Osteria del Ponte.** Rich, imaginative seasonal cuisine composed according to the inspired whims of chef Ezio Santin is reason enough to make your way 20 km (12 mi) southwest of Milan to one of Italy's finest restaurants. The setting is a traditional country inn, where a wood fire warms the rustic interior in winter. The menu changes regularly; in fall, wild porcini mushrooms are among the favored ingredients. ⊠ *Cassinetta di Lugagnano, 3 km (2 mi) north of Abbiategrasso* ☎ *02/ 9420034* ⚐ *Reservations essential* ▭ *AE, DC, MC, V* ⊗ *Closed Sun., Mon., Dec. 25–Jan. 12, and Aug.*

$$$$ ✕ **Nobu.** From a minimalist corner of the Armani mini-mall, Milan's Nobu serves the same delicious Japanese-Peruvian fusion as its siblings in the world's other culinary capitals. Cocktails, appetizers, and beautiful people can be found at the ground-floor bar, well worth a visit even if you're not dining upstairs. ⊠ *Via Pisoni, 1, corner of Via Manzoni 31, Quadrilatero* ☎ *02/72318645* ⚐ *Reservations essential* ▭ *AE, DC, MC, V* ⊗ *Closed Sun.* Ⓜ *Montenapoleone.*

$$$$ ✕ **Savini.** Classic, classy Savini, in the east wing of Galleria Vittorio Emanuele, is a Milanese institution, with red carpets and cut-glass chandeliers characteristic of its late-19th-century roots. Stick with the standards: the Milanese specialty risotto *al salto* (cooked as a pancake, grilled in the pan) is excellent here, as are the *cotoletta di vitello* (veal cutlet) and osso buco. ⊠ *Galleria Vittorio Emanuele, Duomo* ☎ *02/ 72003433* ▭ *AE, DC, MC, V* ⊗ *Closed Sun., Jan. 1–6, and Aug. 6–31* Ⓜ *Duomo.*

$$$–$$$$ ✕ **Antica Trattoria della Pesa.** Fin-de-siècle furnishings, dark-wood paneling, and old-fashion lamps still look much as they must have when this eatery opened 100 years ago. It's authentic Old Milan, and the menu is right in line, offering risotto, minestrone, and osso buco. ⊠ *Viale Pasubio 10, Porta Volta* ☎ *02/6555741* ▭ *AE, DC, MC, V* ⊗ *Closed Sun., Aug., and Dec. 24–Jan. 6* Ⓜ *Porta Garibaldi.*

$$$–$$$$ ✕ **Boeucc.** Milan's oldest restaurant, opened in 1696, is on the same square as novelist Alessandro Manzoni's house, not far from La Scala. With fluted columns, chandeliers, thick carpets, and a garden, it has come a long way from its basement origins (*boeucc,* pronounced "butch," is old Milanese for *buco,* or "hole"). You'll savor such dishes as penne *al branzino e zucchini* (with sea bass and zucchini) and *gelato di castagne con zabaglione caldo* (chestnut ice cream with hot zabaglione). ⊠ *Piazza Belgioioso 2, near Scala* ☎ *02/76020224* ⚐ *Reservations essential* ▭ *AE* ⊗ *Closed Sat., Aug., and Dec. 24–Jan. 4. No lunch Sun.* Ⓜ *Montenapoleone, Duomo.*

$$$–$$$$ ✕ **Joia.** At this haute-cuisine vegetarian restaurant near Piazza della Repubblica delicious dishes are artistically prepared by chef Pietro Leemann. The ever-changing menu offers dishes such as ravioli with basil, potatoes, pine nuts, and crisp green beans. A fish menu is also available. ⊠ *Via Panfilo Castaldi 18, Porta Venezia* ☎ *02/29522124* ▭ *AE, DC, MC, V* ⊗ *Closed Sun., 3 wks in Aug., and Dec. 24–Jan. 7. No lunch Sat.* Ⓜ *Repubblica.*

$$–$$$$ ✕ **La Terrazza.** An office building at the edge of the fashion district is home to this stylish eatery where contemporary design dominates both food and decor. Well-dressed businessmen seem to underappreciate the inventive "Mediterannean sushi," which might use sunflower seeds, pesto, blood oranges, or olive tapenade. Orzo and even barley are used instead of rice; a nine-piece sampler is about €20. In warmer weather the namesake terrace provides a calm view over the Giardini Publici. ⊠ *Via*

Palestro 2, Quadrilatero ☎ *02/76002277* ═ *AE, DC, MC, V* ⊗ *Closed weekends and last 3 wks in Aug.* Ⓜ *Turati.*

$$–$$$
FodorʼsChoice
★

✕ **Trattoria Montina.** Twin brothers Maurizio and Roberto Montina have turned this restaurant into a local favorite. Don't be fooled by the "trattoria" name—Chef Roberto creates exquisite modern Italian dishes such as warmed bruschetta with brie and prosciutto, while Maurizio moves around the restaurant chatting and taking orders. Their warm chocolate and pear pie is alone worth the trip. ⊠ *Via Procaccini 54, Procaccini* ☎ *02/3490498* ═ *DC, MC, V* ⊗ *Closed Sun. and 2 wks in Jan. and Aug. No lunch Mon.* Ⓜ *Trams 1, 19, 29, 33.*

★ **$$**
✕ **Da Abele.** The superb risotto dishes at this neighborhood trattoria change with the season, and there may be just two or three on the menu at any one time. Try them all. The setting is relaxed, the service informal, the prices strikingly reasonable. Outside the touristy center of town but quite convenient by subway, this trattoria is invariably packed with locals. ⊠ *Via Temperanza 5, Loreto* ☎ *02/2613855* ═ *AE, DC, MC, V* ⊗ *Closed Mon., late July–late Aug., and Dec. 15–Jan. 7. No lunch* Ⓜ *Pasteur.*

$$
✕ **La Libera.** Although this establishment in the heart of Brera calls itself a *birreria con cucina* (beer cellar with kitchen), its young clientele comes here for the excellent food and relaxed surroundings. A soft current of jazz and sylvan decor soothe the ripple of conversation. The creative cooking varies with the season, but could include *insalata esotica* (avocado, chicken, rice, and papaya salad) or *rognone di vitello con broccoletti e ginepro* (veal kidneys with broccoli and juniper berries). ⊠ *Via Palermo 21, Brera* ☎ *02/8053603* ═ *AE, DC, MC, V* ⊗ *No lunch* Ⓜ *Moscova.*

$–$$
✕ **Trattoria Milanese.** Between the Duomo and the Basilica di Sant'Ambrogio, this small, popular trattoria has been run by the same family in the same location since 1933. It's invariably crowded, especially at dinner, when the regulars love to linger. Food is classic regional in approach; good choices include risotto and cotoletta alla Milanese. ⊠ *Via Santa Marta 11, near Duomo* ☎ *02/86451991* ═ *AE, DC, MC, V* ⊗ *Closed Tues., July 15–Sept. 1, and Dec. 24–Jan. 6* Ⓜ *Duomo, Cordusio, Missori.*

$
✕ **La Bruschetta.** This tiny, bustling first-class pizzeria near the Duomo serves specialties from Tuscany and other parts of Italy. The wood oven is in full view, so you can see your pizza cooking in front of you, although there are plenty of nonpizza dishes available, too, such as spaghetti *alle cozze e vongole* (with clam and mussel sauce) and grilled and skewered meats. ⊠ *Piazza Beccaria 12, Duomo* ☎ *02/8692494* ═ *AE, MC, V* ⊗ *Closed Mon., 3 wks in Aug., and late Dec.–early Jan.* Ⓜ *Duomo.*

$
✕ **La Capanna.** Signora cooks and her husband pours wine at this popular trattoria near the Piola Metro stop (and the university). The food is predominantly Tuscan—Tuscan salami, pappardelle, fish, and steak—but some Milanese specialties are also on the menu. It's possible to dine on the restaurant's veranda year-round. ⊠ *Via Donatello 9, University District* ☎ *02/29400884* ═ *AE, DC, MC, V* ⊗ *Closed Wed. No lunch Sat.* Ⓜ *Lima.*

¢–$
✕ **Al Tempio d'Oro.** It may be noisy, it may have the ambience of an Italian pub, but the food is very good, filling, and—for Milan—surprisingly

cheap. This comfort-food spot is also near the train station, which makes it a great place to eat before embarking on a journey or, indeed, before beginning your visit to Milan. The menu is hardly haute cuisine, but you'll find an excellent selection of Mediterranean dishes ranging from a plain pasta to a more exotic Maghrebin couscous. The paella is delicious. ⊠ *Via delle Leghe 23, Stazione Centrale* ☎ *02/26145709* ▤ *DC, MC, V* ☾ *Closed Sun. and 2 wks in Aug.* Ⓜ *Pasteur.*

¢–$ ✕ **Taverna Morigi.** This dusky, wood-paneled wine bar near the stock exchange is the perfect spot to enjoy a glass of wine with cheese and cold cuts. At lunch, pasta dishes and select entrées are available; pasta is the only hot dish served in the evening. You can drop in any time for a bite, but if you're coming for a meal a reservation is a good idea. ⊠ *Via Morigi 8, Sant'Ambrogio* ☎ *02/86450880* ▤ *AE, DC, MC, V* ☾ *Closed Sun. and Aug. No lunch Sat.* Ⓜ *Cordusio, Cairoli.*

¢ ✕ **Pizza Ok.** Pizza is almost the only item on the menu at this popular spot near Corso Buenos Aires, but it's very good and the dining experience will be easy on your pocketbook. Possibilities for toppings seem endless. ⊠ *Via Lambro 15, Porta Venezia* ☎ *02/29401272* ▤ *No credit cards* ☾ *Closed Mon., Aug., and Dec. 24–Jan. 7* Ⓜ *Porta Venezia.*

Where to Stay

$$$$ ▥ **Four Seasons.** The elegant restoration of a 15th-century monastery in the middle of Milan's most exclusive shopping district has produced a precious gem—for which you'll pay dearly. The hotel blends European sophistication with American comfort. In addition to opulent marble bathrooms, the rooms are individually decorated to maintain the complex's classic feel. Modern amenities are juxtaposed with antique furniture: you'll find Internet access alongside your four-poster bed. Most rooms face a quiet central courtyard. ⊠ *Via Gesù 8, Quadrilatero, 20121* ☎ *02/77088* ☎ *02/77085000* ⊕ *www.fourseasons.com* ⇝ *93 rooms, 25 suites* ◇ *2 restaurants, room service, minibars, cable TV, health club, bar, laundry service, Internet, business services, meeting rooms, parking (fee), no-smoking rooms* ▤ *AE, DC, MC, V* ¶Ⓞ| *EP* Ⓜ *Montenapoleone, Cavour.*

$$$$ ▥ **Grand Hotel et de Milan.** This elegant hotel near La Scala opened its doors in 1863 and has served as a home away from home for everyone from old-world nobility to modern glitterati. (Giuseppe Verdi commandeered a suite for 20 years.) The rooms are named for the famous people who have stayed in them, and decorated tastefully with corresponding period furniture. The hotel's bar and lounge offer late-19th-century charm, with marble, tapestries, and verdant palms. ⊠ *Via Manzoni 29, Scala, 20121* ☎ *02/723141* ☎ *02/86460861* ⊕ *www.grandhoteletdemilan.it* ⇝ *87 rooms, 8 suites* ◇ *Restaurant, room service, minibars, cable TV, bar, laundry service, parking (fee), no-smoking rooms* ▤ *AE, DC, MC, V* ¶Ⓞ| *EP* Ⓜ *Montenapoleone.*

★ $$$$ ▥ **The Gray.** At this small luxury hotel you get the best of everything, from location to amenities—all for a price. The interiors are decorated by famed Italian designer Guido Ciompi (who handles Gucci boutiques the world over). The atmosphere is trendy chic, from bottom-lighted tables in the hotel restaurant to patterns of laser light that play across the walls of the lobby. Rooms come equipped with everything from plasma TVs to specially designed oversize toiletries. The entire facility is equipped for high-speed wireless Internet. ⊠ *Via San Raffaele 6, near Duomo, 20121* ☎ *02/7208951* ⌂ *02/866526* ⊕ *www.hotelthegray.com* ⇨ *21 rooms* ♿ *Restaurant, room service, minibars, cable TV, bar, laundry service, Internet, business services, no-smoking rooms* ▭ *AE, DC, MC, V* ⭐ *EP* Ⓜ *Duomo.*

★ **$$$$** Ⓣ **Park Hyatt Milano.** This hotel provides every luxury Hyatt prides itself in, all smack in the city's historic center. Rooms have high ceilings, spacious bathrooms, and pleasant light colors that brighten even the darkest Milan days. Although the original 19th-century building's facade is intact, the interiors have been completely renovated, including a skylit internal lounge, created from what was once the courtyard, that's a marvel. The staff is courteous to the point of clairvoyance, and the hotel restaurant serves excellent Italian as well as Continental fare. ⊠ *Via Tommaso Grossi 1, near Duomo, 20121* ☎ *02/88211234* ⌂ *02/88211235* ⊕ *www.milan.park.hyatt.com* ⇨ *117 rooms* ♿ *Restaurant, room service, minibars, cable TV, health club, bar, laundry service, business services, meeting rooms, no-smoking rooms* ▭ *AE, DC, MC, V* ⭐ *EP* Ⓜ *Duomo.*

★ **$$$$** Ⓣ **Principe di Savoia.** Here you'll find all the trappings of an exquisite hotel: lavish mirrors, drapes, and carpets, and gracious bedrooms with eclectic fin-de-siècle furnishings. Newer rooms, added when the Principe took over the neighboring Duca di Milan, are done in an English style. The hotel's restaurant serves excellent contemporary Italian cuisine. The presidential suite comes with a marbled pool. ⊠ *Piazza della Repubblica 17, Porta Nuova, 20124* ☎ *02/62301* ⌂ *02/6595838* ⊕ *www.principedisavoia.com* ⇨ *399 rooms, 5 suites* ♿ *2 restaurants, room service, minibars, cable TV, health club, bar, laundry service, business services, convention center, meeting room, no-smoking rooms* ▭ *AE, DC, MC, V* ⭐ *EP* Ⓜ *Repubblica.*

$$$–$$$$ Ⓣ **Grand Hotel Duomo.** The location of this elegant, modern hotel is so central that if you look out of a front-facing window you'll find a Duomo gargoyle staring back at you. The comfortable, spacious rooms and duplex suites are done in swatches of golds, creams, and browns. ⊠ *Via San Raffaele 1, near Duomo, 20121* ☎ *02/8833* ⌂ *02/86462027* ⊕ *www.grandhotelduomo.com* ⇨ *162 rooms* ♿ *3 restaurants, room service, minibars, cable TV, bar, laundry service, business services, meeting rooms, parking (fee), no-smoking rooms* ▭ *AE, DC, MC, V* ⭐ *EP* Ⓜ *Duomo.*

$$$–$$$$ Ⓣ **Pierre Milano.** No expense was spared to furnish each room of this intimate luxury hotel in a different style, with color-coordinated fabrics and both modern and antique furniture. Everything is electronic: you can open the curtains, turn off the lights, get personal messages on your TV screen—all at the touch of a button. It's on the inner beltway, near the medieval basilica of Sant'Ambrogio. ⊠ *Via de Amicis 32, Sant'Ambrogio, 20123* ☎ *02/72000581* ⌂ *02/8052157* ⊕ *www.hotelpierremilano.it* ⇨ *51 rooms* ♿ *Restaurant, room service, in-room safes, minibars, cable TV, bar, laundry service, parking (fee), no-smoking rooms* ▭ *AE, DC, MC, V* ⭐ *BP* Ⓜ *Sant'Ambrogio.*

$$$–$$$$ 🏨 **Westin Palace.** Milan's premier business hotel offers comfort and connectivity, with high-speed Internet access in every room. Don't be fooled by the functional 1950s-era exterior: rooms are decorated with precious Empire-style antiques, and bathrooms are lined with Issoire green and Portugal pink marble. ⊠ *Piazza della Repubblica 20, Porta Nuova, 20124* ☎ *02/63361* 🖷 *02/654485* ⊕ *www.westin.com* 🛏 *244 rooms* ⚒ *2 restaurants, room service, in-room data ports, in-room safes, minibars, cable TV, bar, laundry service, Internet, business services, meeting rooms, parking (fee), no-smoking rooms* ⊟ *AE, DC, MC, V* ⵏⵔⵉ *EP* Ⓜ *Repubblica.*

$$$ 🏨 **Hotel Spadari al Duomo.** This intimate boutique hotel near the Duomo and the Pinacoteca Ambrosiana has its own private art collection. Rooms are elegantly furnished; junior suites on the 7th floor have views of the cathedral. Simple fare is served in the bar. ⊠ *Via Spadari 11, near Duomo, 20123* ☎ *02/72002371* 🖷 *02/861184* ⊕ *www.spadarihotel. com* 🛏 *40 rooms, 3 suites* ⚒ *Minibars, cable TV, bar, no-smoking rooms.* ⊟ *AE, DC, MC, V* ⵏⵔⵉ *BP* Ⓜ *Duomo.*

$$ 🏨 **Antica Locanda Leonardo.** Convenient to *The Last Supper* and near the city center, this small hotel opens onto an inner courtyard, making it one step removed from the city traffic outside. It's been owned and run by the same family for more than 40 years, and the staff is welcoming and helpful. Many rooms look out onto the courtyard or the garden in back. ⊠ *Corso Magenta 78, Sant'Ambrogio, 20123* ☎ *02/463317* 🖷 *02/48019012* ⊕ *www.leoloc.com* 🛏 *20 rooms* ⚒ *Cable TV, bar, laundry service* ⊟ *AE, DC, MC, V* ☷ *Closed Dec. 27–Jan. 5 and 3 wks in Aug.* ⵏⵔⵉ *BP* Ⓜ *Sant'Ambrogio.*

$$ 🏨 **Ariston.** "Bio-architectural" principles prevail at this hotel near the Duomo, which was built using natural materials and has ionized air circulating throughout. As you might expect from such a progressive-minded place, the attitude and ambience are warm and informal. The buffet breakfast includes organic foods, free Internet access is available in the lobby, and bicycles are available in summer. ⊠ *Largo Carrobbio 2, near Duomo, 20123* ☎ *02/72000556* 🖷 *02/72000914* ⊕ *www. brerahotels.com/ariston* 🛏 *46 rooms* ⚒ *Minibars, cable TV, bicycles, bar, laundry service, Internet, parking (fee), no-smoking rooms* ⊟ *AE, DC, MC, V* ☷ *Closed late July–early Aug.* ⵏⵔⵉ *BP.*

$–$$ 🏨 **Canada.** You get good value at this friendly, small hotel close to Piazza del Duomo and on the edge of a district full of shops and restaurants. Rooms are furnished in a nondescript fashion but have the usual modern trappings. ⊠ *Via Santa Sofia 16, near Duomo, 20122* ☎ *02/58304844* 🖷 *02/58300282* ⊕ *www.canadahotel.it* 🛏 *35 rooms* ⚒ *Cable TV, bar, laundry, Internet, parking (fee)* ⊟ *AE, DC, MC, V* ⵏⵔⵉ *BP* Ⓜ *Crocetta.*

$–$$ 🏨 **Hotel Gran Duca di York.** Priests once occupied this 1890s art nouveau building, but the atmosphere these days is less austere, with a welcoming lobby and open public spaces. Peaceful rooms done in muted colors open onto a small elevated courtyard. With an ideal location a few steps west of the Duomo, it offers good value by Milan standards. Call ahead to reserve a private terrace at no extra cost. ⊠ *Via Moneta 1/a, near Duomo, 20123* ☎ *02/874863* 🖷 *02/8690344* 🛏 *33* *rooms* ⓒ *Minibars, cable TV, bar, laundry service, meeting rooms, parking (fee)* ⊟ *AE, MC, V* ⊘ *Closed Aug.* ⦿| *EP* Ⓜ *Cordusio.*

$–$$ 🖼 **Hotel Vittoria.** This family-owned hotel is on a quiet residential street minutes from the Galleria Vittorio Emanuele and the Duomo. The guest rooms are tiny but in pristine condition, and the courteous staff is eager to ensure your comfort. In summer, breakfast is served in the small garden at the back. ✉ *Via Pietro Calvi 32, East Central Milan, 20129* ☎ *02/ 5456520* 🖷 *02/55190246* ⌗ *20 rooms* ⓒ *In-room safes, minibars, cable TV, no-smoking rooms* ⊟ *AE, DC, MC, V* ⦿| *EP* Ⓜ *San Babila.*

$ 🖼 **Gritti.** The Gritti is a bright, cheerful hotel with adequate rooms and good views (from the inside upper floor) of tiled roofs and the gold Madonnina statue on top of the Duomo, a few hundred yards away. ✉ *Piazza Santa Maria Beltrade 4, north end of Via Torino, Duomo, 20123* ☎ *02/ 801056* 🖷 *02/89010999* ⊕ *www.hotelgritti.com* ⌗ *48 rooms* ⓒ *Minibars, cable TV, bar, laundry service, meeting room, parking (fee), some pets allowed* ⊟ *AE, MC, V* ⦿| *BP* Ⓜ *Duomo.*

★ $ 🖼 **London.** On a quiet side street off Via Dante, the London's polite, efficient staff hosts its many Anglophone patrons in clean, well-appointed rooms. It's a comfortable choice, with good value and convenient access to Milan's main sights. ✉ *Via Rovello 3, Castello, 20121* ☎ *02/ 72020166* 🖷 *02/8057037* ⊕ *www.hotellondonmilano.com* ⌗ *29 rooms* ⓒ *Cable TV, bar, laundry service, Internet* ⊟ *MC, V* ⊘ *Closed Aug. and Dec. 23–Jan. 3* ⦿| *EP* Ⓜ *Cairoli, Cordusio.*

$ 🖼 **San Francisco.** In a residential area between the central station and the university, this midsize hotel is handy to Metro stations on two lines (Loreto or Piola stop). The management is friendly, the rooms are bright and clean, and there's a charming garden. ✉ *Viale Lombardia 55, University District, 20131* ☎ *02/2361009* 🖷 *02/26680377* ⊕ *www.hotelsanfrancisco.it* ⌗ *31 rooms* ⓒ *Bar, Internet, meeting room* ⊟ *AE, DC, MC, V* ⦿| *BP* Ⓜ *Loreto, Piola.*

Nightlife & the Arts

The Arts

For listings, consult the monthly *Milano Mese,* which has English content and is free at APT (tourist board) offices, or the weekly *ViviMilano,* in Italian, sold with the Wednesday edition of the newspaper *Corriere della Sera* (⊕ www.vivimilano.corriere.it).

MUSIC The **Conservatorio** (✉ Via del Conservatorio 12, near Duomo ☎ 02/ 7621101) is the best place in the city for classical concerts and is a popular year-round venue for the well-heeled. The modern **Auditorium di Milano** (✉ Corso San Gottardo, corner with Via Torricelli, Conchetta ☎ 02/83389201) houses the **Orchestra Verdi** during its concert season (September–June).

OPERA Milan's hallowed **Teatro alla Scala** (✉ Piazza della Scala ☎ 02/86077 reservations ⊕ www.teatroallascala.org) has undergone a complete renovation, with everything replaced save the building's exterior walls. Special attention was paid to modernizing the acoustics and stage system. You can find out information about performances and purchase tickets at the Scala Web site or by using the automated phone reservation system. Note that there is a last-minute box office in Via Filodrammatici that often provides excellent deals for those who haven't planned ahead. Get in line early.

THEATER Milan's **Piccolo Teatro** (☎ 02/72333222 ⊕ www.piccoloteatro.org) is made up of three separate venues, each of which is noted for its excellent productions. The intimate **Teatro Paolo Grassi** (✉ Via Rovello 2, Castello) is the historical headquarters of the theater, named after its founder. The spacious, modern **Teatro Giorgio Strehler** (✉ Largo Greppi 1, east of the Piazzo Castello, Brera) takes its name from a famous Italian theater director and holds dance and musical performances as well as plays. The horseshoe-shape **Teatro Studio** (✉ Via Rivoli 6, Castello) is a popular venue for experimental theater and music concerts.

Nightlife

BARS Milan has a bar somewhere to suit any style; those in the nicer hotels are respectably chic. **El Brellin** (✉ Vicolo Lavandai at Alzaia Naviglio Grande, Navigli ☎ 02/58101351) is one of the many bars in this arty district. It also serves Sunday brunch, fast becoming a Milanese tradition; it's closed Sunday evening. In the Brera quarter, check out the **Giamaica** (✉ Via Brera 32, Brera ☎ 02/876723), a traditional hangout for artists from the nearby Brera art school. On summer nights this neighborhood pulses with life; street vendors and fortune-tellers jostle for space alongside the outdoor tables. For a break from the traditional, try trendy **SHU** (✉ Via Molina delle Armi, Ticinese ☎ 02/58315720), whose gleaming interior looks like a cross between *Star Trek* and Cocteau's *Sleeping Beauty*. The techno-style **Trussardi Bar** (✉ Piazza della Scala 5 ☎ 02/80688295) has an enormous plasma screen that keeps hip barflies entertained with video art.

NIGHTCLUBS For an evening of live music—predominantly rock to jazz—head to perennial favorite **Le Scimmie** (✉ Via Ascanio Sforza 49, Navigli ☎ 02/89402874). **Blue Note** (✉ Via Borsieri 37, Garibaldi ☎ 02/69016888 ⊕ www.bluenotemilano.com) is a European branch of the famous New York nightclub, and features regular performances by some of the most famous names in jazz, as well as blues and rock concerts. Evening performances are occasionally accompanied by wine tastings. **Hollywood** (✉ Corso Como 15/c, Centro Direzionale ☎ 02/6598996) continues to be one of the most popular places for the sunglasses set.

La Banque (✉ Via Bassano Porrone 6, near Scala ☎ 02/86996565) is an exclusive and expensive bar, dance club, and restaurant popular for anything from an *aperitivo* to a night on the town. **Magazzini Generali** (✉ Via Pietrasanta 14, Porta Vigentina ☎ 02/55211313), in what was an old warehouse, is a fun, futuristic venue for dancing and concerts. It's closed on Sunday. **Propaganda** (✉ Via Castelbarco 11, Porta Romana ☎ 02/58310682), near the Bocconi University, has a spacious dance floor. Music varies but includes Latin American and revival nights. The hip **Café l'Atlantique** (✉ Viale Umbria 42, Porta Romana ☎ 02/55193906) is a popular place for dancing the night away and enjoying a generous buffet brunch on a lazy Sunday afternoon; it's closed Monday.

Sports

Car Racing

Lombardy Formula I fans are passionate, living and dying with the fortunes of their beloved team Ferrari. All converge on the second Sunday in September for the **Italian Grand Prix,** held 15 km (9 mi) northeast of Milan in Monza. The track was built in 1922 in the **Parco di Monza** (⊕ www.monzanet.it), which also has a hippodrome, a golf course, and other facilities.

Soccer

AC Milan and Inter Milan, two of the oldest and most successful teams in Europe, vie for the heart of soccer-mad Lombardy. For residents, the city is *Milano* but the teams are *Milan,* a vestige of their common founding as the Milan Cricket and Football Club in 1899. When an Italian-led faction broke off in 1908, the new club was dubbed Internazionale (or "Inter"), to distinguish it from the bastion of English exclusivity that would become AC Milan (or simply "Milan"). Since then, the picture has become more clouded: although Milan prides itself as the true team of the city and of its working class, and Inter can more persuasively claim pan-Italian support, there is little of the social tension that defines—and inflames—other often-violent intracity rivalries, like the one between Rome's two soccer powers. Milan is too busy, and too sensible, for all that.

AC Milan and Inter Milan share the use of **San Siro Stadium (Stadio Meazza)** (⊠ Via Piccolomini) during their August–May season. With more than 60,000 of the 85,000 seats appropriated by season-ticket holders and another couple of thousand allocated to visiting fans, tickets to the Sunday games can be difficult to come by, especially for high-profile matches. You can purchase advance AC Milan tickets at Cariplo bank branches, including one at Via Verdi 8, or at the club's **Web site** (⊕ www.acmilan.com). Inter tickets are available at Banca Popolare di Milano branches, including one at Piazza Meda 4, or **online** (⊕ www.inter.it). To reach San Siro, take subway Line 1 (red) toward Molino Dorino, exit at the Lotto station, and board a bus for the stadium. Alcohol—save tasty little bottles of Borghetti coffee liqueur—is not sold inside, but beer poured into plastic cups by vendors outside is allowed past the gates. If you're a soccer fan but can't get in to see a game, you might settle for a **stadium tour** (☎ 02/4042432 ⊕ www.sansirotour.com), which includes a visit to the Milan-Inter museum. Tours are available every half hour from Gate 21 from 10 AM to 5 PM, except on game Sundays; they cost €12.50.

Shopping

Milan's *fortissimo* occurs twice a year, at the end of February and October (for women) and June and January (for men), when the world's fashion elite descend on the city for the famous ready-to-wear designer shows that invariably set next season's international styles. Bargain-hunting seasons are in mid-January and again in mid-July, when everything, steeply discounted, flies off the shelves.

Department Stores

La Rinascente (⊠ Piazza del Duomo ☎ 02/88521) is Milan's most important department store, stocking everything from Armani to Zegna over eight floors. While there, check out the terrace bar on the top floor. **Coin** (⊠ Piazza Cinque Giornate, Porta Vittoria ☎ 02/55192083) has an impressive selection at midrange prices.

Markets

Food and innumerable other goods, new and old, are available in open-air stalls all over Milan. In many markets bargaining is no longer the custom. You can try to haggle, but if you fear getting ripped off go to the stalls where prices are clearly marked. Bargains can be found at the huge **Mercato Papiniano** (⊠ Viale Papiniano, and the Fiera di Senigallia, on Via Calatafimi, Porta Genova) on Saturday and Tuesday mornings. If you collect coins, stamps, or telephone cards (collected in Italy like baseball cards in the United States), go on Sunday morning to the market at **Via Armorari** (⊠ Off Piazza Cordusio, near Duomo). Milan's most comprehensive antiques market is the **Mercatone dell'Antiquario**, held on the last Sunday of each month along the Naviglio Grande. The third Saturday of every month there's a major antiques and flea market on **Via Fiori Chiari**, near Via Brera.

Shopping Districts

Via Manzoni, at the northern end of Piazza della Scala, leads into the
★ **quadrilatero**, Milan's most luxurious shopping district, perhaps the most luxurious in Italy. In a few small streets laid out like a game of hopscotch—Via Monte Napoleone, Via Sant'Andrea, Via della Spiga—are the shops of the great Italian designers, such as Armani, Versace, and Gianfranco Ferré. Don't come here looking for affordable fashion—that has been relegated to the other side of the Duomo. Shops are usually open 9–1 (except Monday morning) and 4–7:30; many are closed in August. A good locator map of the best boutiques in the area is mounted on a pole at the corner of Via della Spiga and Via Borgospesso.

Wander around the **Brera** to find stores with personality. The densest concentration of wares is along Via Brera, Via Solferino, Corso Garibaldi, and Via Paolo Sarpi. **Corso Buenos Aires**, which runs northeast from the Giardini Pubblici, is a wide boulevard dense with shops catering to locals, and as such often having better prices than those in the city center. **Corso Vittorio Emanuele** has clothing, leather goods, and shoe shops, some with goods at reasonable prices. **Via Monte Napoleone** has several top-notch jewelers and a profusion of antiques stores and designer fashion boutiques.

Specialty Stores

CLOTHING   For the constant redefinition of red-carpet style, **Giorgio Armani** (⊠ Via Sant'Andrea 9, near Duomo ☎ 02/76003234) is the fashion temple. The flashy Armani megastore **Armani/Via Manzoni 31** (⊠ Via Manzoni 31, Brera ☎ 02/72318600) encompasses a number of shops and restaurants, including **Emporio Armani**. **Cerruti 1881** (⊠ Via della Spiga 20, near Duomo ☎ 02/76009777) has elegant styles with an edge for men and women. Head to **Prada** (⊠ Galleria Vittorio Emanuele 63/65, near

CLOTHES MAKE THE CITY

WHEN MARIUCCIA MANDELLI decided in 1954 to stamp her collection with the name "Krizia," she anticipated fashion-mad Milan with an uncanny foresight. The name adopted by the former teacher is derived from a character in one of Plato's dialogues who spends all of his money on clothes and jewelry for fatuous and vain women. Several billion dollars of revenue are earned each year in Milan's Golden Triangle, the approximately 1-square-km (½ square mi) area spanning Via della Spiga, Via Monte Napoleone, and Via Sant'Andrea that's home to most of Italy's high-fashion houses.

Milan's designers, Mandelli among them, are known for a subversive attitude. Legends abound: Missoni's famous 1967 show, in which the black silk dresses of bra-less models became transparent on the catwalk; Moschino's 1980s-era anti-fashion Minnie Mouse dresses and fried-egg buttons; the late Gianni Versace's rock-and-roll aesthetic that put chains and leather on the catwalk. One notable exception is Armani, whose fluid, elegant designs have stood the test of time and continue to be synonymous with elegance.

It's all but impossible to get in to see the shows, held at the start of January (men's spring-summer), the end of February (women's spring-summer), the beginning of October (women's fall-winter), and the end of June (men's fall-winter). Houses hold lavish, celebrity-studded presentations, and admission is by invitation only. The trade organization, Camera Nazionale della Moda Italiana, suggests giving it a go anyway. If you contact houses directly before the shows, you may be able to wheedle your way in among the glitterati.

Duomo ☎ 02/876979) for Miuccia's bewitching minimalist designs, smart leather goods, and a famous series of fin-de-siècle murals. **Etro** (✉ Via Spartaco 3, near Duomo ☎ 02/57931) offers funky, cutting-edge clothing for both men and women. **Gucci** (✉ Via Monte Napoleone 5, near Duomo ☎ 02/771271) offers the fashion house's best for both men and women, from clothing to handbags and accessories. **Gianfranco Ferré** (✉ Via Sant'Andrea 15, near Duomo ☎ 02/794864) concentrates on swank, ready-to-wear apparel, with great ties. Daring design is the fashion at **Versace** (✉ Via Monte Napoleone 11, near Duomo ☎ 02/76008528). **Moschino** (✉ Via Sant'Andrea 12, near Duomo ☎ 02/76000832) endlessly challenges convention. **Roberto Cavalli** (✉ Via della Spiga 42, near Duomo ☎ 02/76020900) is the place for zebra stripes and sexy prints. **Fendi** (✉ Via Sant'Andrea 16, near Duomo ☎ 02/799544) is known for smart purses, fur, and leather. Designer duo **Dolce & Gabbana** (Women's: ✉ Via della Spiga 2; Men's: Corso Venezia 15, near Duomo ☎ 02/76001155 ✉ Men's: ✉ Corso Venezia 15, near Duomo ☎ 02/76028485) favor shrink-wrap lines and strappy shoes. If you want the look without designer prices, **Salvagente** (✉ Via F. Bronzetti 16, Porta Vittoria ☎ 02/76110328) has brand names at about a third of retail.

HOUSEWARES **L'Utile e il Dilettevole** (✉ 46 Via della Spiga, near Duomo ☎ 02/795044) sells enchanting Italian country-style items for the home. **Alessi** (✉ Corso Matteotti 9, near Duomo ☎ 02/795726) specializes in kitchenware by famous Italian and international designers. **High-Tech** (✉ Piazza XXV Aprile 12, Porta Garibaldi ☎ 02/6241101) has everything you can think of for the house, from kitchen utensils to televisions to imported ottomans.

SHOES For top-quality, classic men's and women's shoes, choose **Ferragamo** (✉ Via Monte Napoleone 3, near Duomo ☎ 02/76000054 ✉ Men's shoes ✉ Via Monte Napoleone 20/5, Duomo ☎ 02/76006660). For a mix of style and tradition, try **Fratelli Rossetti** (✉ Via Monte Napoleone 1, near Duomo ☎ 02/76021650). Shoe addicts will want a gorgeous pair from **La Vetrina di Beryil** (✉ Via Statuto 4, Brera ☎ 02/654278) to add to their collection. Comfortable but stylish shoes are found at **Casadei** (✉ Via Sant'Andrea 17, near Duomo ☎ 02/76318293). Python shoes are a trademark of **Sergio Rossi** (✉ Via Monte Napoleone 6a, near Duomo ☎ 02/76006140).

PAVIA, CREMONA & MANTUA

Once proud medieval fortress towns rivaling Milan in power, these centers of industry and commerce on the Po plain still play a key role in Italy's wealthiest, most populous region. Pavia is celebrated for its extravagant Carthusian monastery, Cremona for its incomparable violin-making tradition. A diminutive utopian Renaissance city, Sabbioneta was the fruit of one man's obsession, and Mantua—the most picturesque of them all—was the home of the fantastically wealthy Gonzaga dynasty for almost 300 years.

Pavia

⑰ *41 km (25 mi) south of Milan.*

Pavia was once Milan's chief regional rival. The city dates from at least the Roman era and was the capital of the Lombard kings for two centuries (572–774). It was once known as "the city of a hundred towers," but only a handful have survived the passing of time. Its prestigious university was founded in 1361 on the site of a 10th-century law school, but has roots dating back to antiquity.

The 14th-century **Castello Visconteo** now houses the local **Museo Civico** (Municipal Museum), with an archaeological collection and a picture gallery featuring works by Correggio. ✉ *Viale 11 Febbraio, near Piazza Castello* ☎ *0382/33853* ✑ *€6* ☽ *Feb.–June and Sept.–Nov., Tues.–Sun. 10–5:30 (last entry 5:10); Dec. and Jan., and July and Aug., Tues.–Sun. 9–1:30 (last entry 12:45). Hours frequently revised.*

In the Romanesque church of **San Pietro in Ciel d'Oro** you can visit the tomb of Christianity's most celebrated convert, St. Augustine, housed in a Gothic marble ark on the high altar. ✉ *Via Matteotti* ☽ *Mon.–Sat. 9–noon and 3–5, Sun. mass.*

The main draw in Pavia is the **Certosa** (Carthusian monastery), 8 km (5 mi) north of the city center. Its elaborate facade shows the same relish for ornamentation as the Duomo in Milan. The Certosa's extravagant grandeur was due in part to the plan to have it house the tombs of the family of the first duke of Milan, Galeazzo Visconti III (who died during a plague, at age 49, in 1402). And extravagant it was—almost unimaginable—in an age before modern transport. The very best marble was used, taken undoubtedly by barge from the quarries of Carrara, roughly 240 km (150 mi) away. Though the floor plan may be Gothic— a cross shape divided into a series of squares—the gorgeous fabric that rises above it is triumphantly Renaissance. On the facade, in the lower frieze, are medallions of Roman emperors and Eastern monarchs; above them are low reliefs of scenes from the life of Christ and from the career of Galeazzo Visconti III.

The first duke was the only Visconti to be interred here, and then only some 75 years after his death, in a tomb designed by Gian Cristoforo Romano. Look for it in the right transept. In the left transept is a more appealing tomb—that of a rather stern middle-aged man and a beautiful young woman. The man is Ludovico il Moro Sforza (1452–1508), seventh duke of Milan, who commissioned Leonardo to paint *The Last Supper*. The woman is Ludovico's wife, Beatrice d'Este (1475–97), one of the most celebrated women of her day, the embodiment of brains, culture, birth, and beauty. Married when he was 40 and she was 16, they had enjoyed six years together when she died while giving birth to a stillborn child. Ludovico commissioned the sculptor Cristoforo Solari to design a joint tomb for the high altar of Santa Maria delle Grazie in Milan. Originally much larger, the tomb for some years occupied the honored place as planned. Then for reasons that are still mysterious the Dominican monks, who seemed to care no more for their former patron than they did for their faded Leonardo fresco, sold the tomb to their Carthusian brothers to the south. Sadly, part of the tomb and its remains were lost. ☒ *Certosa, 8 km (5 mi) north of Pavia* ☎ *0382/925613* ⊕ *www.comune.pv.it/certosadipavia* ☒ *Free, donation requested* ⊙ *Open Tues.–Sun. 9–11:30 and 2:30–4:30.*

Where to Eat

$$$$ ✕**Locanda Vecchia Pavia al Mulino.** At this sophisticated art nouveau restaurant 150 yards from the Certosa you'll find creative versions of traditional regional cuisine, including *rane* (frogs), the local specialty, in risotto or cooked on a spit. *Casoncelli* (stuffed pasta), *petto d'anatra* (duck breast), and veal cutlet alla milanese are done with style, as are the imaginative seafood dishes. For dessert, consider the hot chocolate pudding with white-chocolate sauce. ☒ *Via al Monumento 5, Certosa* ☎ *0382/925894* ⚑ *Reservations essential* ▭ *AE, DC, MC, V* ⊙ *Closed Mon., 3 wks in Aug., and 2 wks in Jan. No lunch Wed.*

Nightlife & the Arts

During the first half of September, Pavia's **Settembre Pavese** festival presents street processions, displays, and concerts.

Cremona

🔞 *104 km (65 mi) east of Pavia, 106 km (66 mi) southeast of Milan.*

Cremona is the world's premier place to buy a violin—as true today as when Andrea Amati (1510–80) invented the modern instrument here in the 16th century. Though cognoscenti continue to revere the Amati name, it was an apprentice of Amati's nephew for whom the fates had reserved wide and lasting fame. In a career that spanned an incredible 68 years, Antonio Stradivari (1644–1737) made more than 1,200 instruments—including violas, cellos, harps, guitars, and mandolins, in addition to his fabled violins. Labeled simply with a small printed slip reading ANTONIUS STRADIVARIUS CREMONENSIS. FACIEBAT ANNO . . .— the date inserted in a neat italic hand—they remain the most coveted, most expensive stringed instruments in the world.

Strolling about this quiet, medium-size city, you will notice that violin making continues to flourish. There are, in fact, more than 50 *liutai*, many of them graduates of the Scuola Internazionale di Liuteria (International School of Violin Making), who continue to work by traditional methods in shops scattered throughout Cremona. You are usually welcome to these ateliers, especially if contemplating the acquisition of your own instrument; the tourist office has addresses.

Cremona's other claim to fame is its native *torrone* (nougat), which is said to have been invented here on the evening of October 25, 1441, in honor of the marriage of Bianca Maria Visconti and Francesco Sforza. Visconti's dowry included not only the usual jewels and riches, but also the city of Cremona itself. A new confection, originally prepared by heating almonds, egg whites, and honey over low heat and shaped and named after the city's tower, was created in symbolic celebration. The annual Festa del Torrone is held in the main piazza on the third Sunday in October

The **Piazza del Comune,** surrounded by the Duomo, tower, baptistery, and city hall, is distinctive and harmonious: the combination of old brick, rose- and cream-color marble, terra-cotta, and old copper roofs brings Romanesque, Gothic, and Renaissance together with unusual success. Dominating Piazza del Comune is the **Torrazzo** (Big Tower), the city's symbol and perhaps the tallest campanile in Italy, visible for a considerable distance across the Po plain. It's open to visitors, but in winter hours fluctuate depending on the weather. The tower's astronomical clock is the 1583 original. ⊠ *Piazza del Comune* ▧ €6 ⊗ *Daily 9–6.*

Cremona's Romanesque **Duomo** was consecrated in 1190. Here you'll find the beautiful *Story of the Virgin Mary and the Passion of Christ,* the central fresco of an extraordinary cycle commissioned in 1514 and featuring the work of local artists, including Boccacio Boccancino, Giovan Francesco Bembo, and Altobello Melone. ⊠ *Piazza del Comune* ⊗ *Daily 7:30–noon and 3:30–7.*

Legendary violin maker Antonio Stradivari lived, worked, and died near the verdant square at No. 1 **Piazza Roma.** According to local lore,

Stradivari kept each instrument in his bedroom for a month before varnishing, imparting part of his soul before sealing and sending it out into the world. In the center of the park is **Stradivari's grave,** marked by a simple tombstone.

The **Museo Stradivariano** (Stradivarius Museum) in Palazzo Affaitati houses the city's collection of stringed treasures: a viola and five violins, including the golden-orange "Il Cremonese 1715" Stradivarius. Informative exhibits display Stradivari's paper patterns, wooden models, and various tools. ⊠ *Via Ugolani Dati 4* ☎ *0372/407770* ⊠ €7 ☻ *Tues.–Sat. 9–6, Sun. 10–6.*

Where to Stay & Eat

$$ ✕ **La Sosta.** This traditional Cremonese restaurant looks to the 16th century for culinary inspiration, following a time-tested recipe for a favored first course, gnocchi *Vecchia Cremona.* The homemade salamis are also excellent. To finish off the evening, try the *semifreddo al torroncino* (chilled almond cake) and a dessert wine. ⊠ *Via Sicardo 9* ☎ *0372/456656* ▤ *AE, DC, MC, V* ☻ *Closed Mon. and 3 wks in Aug. No dinner Sun.*

★ $ ✕ **Centrale.** Close to the cathedral, this old-style trattoria is a favorite among locals for traditional Cremonese fare, such as succulent *cotechino* (pork sausage) and *tortelli di zucca* (a small pasta with pumpkin filling), at moderate prices. ⊠ *Vicolo Pertusio 4* ☎ *0372/28701* ▤ *AE, DC, MC, V* ☻ *Closed Thurs. and July.*

$$ ▥ **Delle Arti Design Hotel.** The name fits at this central hotel with elegant modern interiors and eclectic designer furniture. The contemporary feel provides a nice contrast to the surrounding historic center. ⊠ *Via Bonomelli 8, 26100* ☎ *0372/23131* ⊟ *0372/21654* ⊕ *www.dellearti.com* ⇆ *33 rooms* ⚙ *Minibars, cable TV, bar, gym, sauna, meeting rooms, Internet, parking (fee), no-smoking rooms* ▤ *AE, DC, MC, V* ⍢ *BP.*

$–$$ ▥ **Hotel Continental.** This comfortable modern hotel is well equipped to satisfy its international business clientele. At the end of the road to the autostrade, on the periphery of the historic center, it makes a convenient base for those wisely disinclined to navigate old Cremona by car. ⊠ *Piazza Libertà 26, 26100* ☎ *0372/434141* ⊟ *0372/454873* ⊕ *www. hotelcontinentalcremona.it* ⇆ *62 rooms* ⚙ *Minibars, cable TV, bar, meeting rooms, parking (fee), Internet* ▤ *AE, DC, MC, V* ⍢ *BP.*

Nightlife & the Arts

At the end of May and the beginning of June, Cremona hosts an annual festival in honor of native composer Claudio Monteverdi, the great baroque pioneer of modern opera. Contact the **Teatro Ponchielli** (☎ 0372/ 022010 ⊕ www.teatroponchielli.it) for details.

Shopping

For sweet, tooth-crunching nougat, visit the famed **Sperlari store** (⊠ Via Solferino 25 ☎ 0372/22346 ⊕ www.fieschi1867.com). Cremona's best nougat and *mostarda* (a soft sweet made from preserved fruit) have been sold from this handsome shop since 1836; Sperlari and parent company Fieschi have grown into a confection empire. Look for the historical product display in the back.

Sabbioneta

⑲ *45 km (28 mi) southeast of Cremona, 34 km (21 mi) southwest of Mantua.*

Sleepy Sabbioneta is an unremarkable agricultural town, where nothing of note happened before—or since—an explosion of planning and building in the 16th century. It was conceived, designed, and built by Vespasiano Gonzaga (1531–91), whose glorious attainments in public service were exceeded in fame only by his ignominious treatment of his three wives. Upon retiring from military life at 47, he resolved to turn an old castle and a few squalid cottages into the perfect city—a tiny, urbane metropolis where the most gifted artists and greatest writers would live in perfect harmony with a perfect patron. After some five years of planning and another five of work, the village was transformed into an elegant, star-shape, walled fortress dubbed Little Athens, with a rational grid of streets, two palaces, two squares, two churches, an exquisite theater (said to be the first in Europe with a roof) designed by Vincenzo Scamozzi (1552–1616), and a noble gallery of antiquities (a forerunner of today's art galleries). Gonzaga died four years later; with him Sabbioneta's aspirations to greatness faded, turning this earliest of planned cities into a surreal ghost-utopia.

The **Ufficio Turistico del Comune di Sabbioneta** (⊠ Piazza d'Armi 1 ☎ 0375/221044 ⊕ www.comune.sabbioneta.mn.it ⊙ Apr.–Sept., Tues.–Sun. 10–1 and 2–5:30; Oct.–Mar., Tues.–Sun. 10–1 and 2–5) organizes tours to the Palazzo Ducale, the Teatro Olimpico, and the Palazzo del Giardino. Tours begin whenever enough people have assembled. In the majestic **Palazzo Ducale** (Ducal Palace) are four fine equestrian figures of Vespasiano Gonzaga and his forebears. The **Teatro Olimpico** (an adaptation of Palladio's theater at Vicenza by the man who helped him build it) has been restored, and its frescoes, once whitewashed, have been uncovered. The **Palazzo del Giardino** has a dusty but impressive gallery of antique sculptures.

Sabbioneta's **synagogue,** now a shuttered and derelict building, is the sole trace of the city's prosperous 16th-century Jewish community. You'll have to ask someone to point it out. The **tourist promotion office** (APT; ⊠ Via Vespasiano Gonzaga 27 ☎ 0375/52039) leads tours to religious sites, including the synagogue.

Where to Stay & Eat

¢ ✕▥ **Al Duca.** In Sabbioneta's historical center, Al Duca serves local specialties such as risotto *alla mantovana* (with sausage), *stracotto di asino con polenta* (donkey roast with polenta), and tortelli di zucca. It also has comfortable, reasonably priced guest rooms. ⊠ *Via della Stamperia 18, 46018* ☎ *0375/52474* 🖶 *0375/220021* 🛏 *10 rooms* ▤ *MC, V* ⅁ *Restaurant* ⊙ *Restaurant closed Mon.* ⏐⊙⏐ *BP.*

Mantua

 34 km (21 mi) northeast of Sabbioneta, 192 km (119 mi) southeast of Milan.

Mantua stands tallest among the ancient walled cities of the Po plain. Its fortifications are circled on three sides by the passing Mincio River, which long provided Mantua with protection, fish, and a steady stream of river tolls as it meandered from Lake Garda to join the Po. It may not be flashy or dramatic, but Mantua's beauty is subtle and deep, hiding a rich trove of artistic, architectural, and cultural gems beneath its slightly somber facade. Winters are foggy and summers are soggy; you'll get the most out of the city in the delightful fall or spring.

Although Mantua first came to prominence in Roman times as the home of Virgil, its grand monuments date from the glory years of the Gonzaga dynasty. From 1328 until the Austrian Habsburgs sacked the city in 1708, the dukes and marquesses of the Gonzaga clan reigned over a wealthy independent *commune,* and the arts thrived in the relative peace of that period. Andrea Mantegna (1431–1506), who served as court painter for 50 years, was the best known of a succession of artists and architects who served Mantua through the years, and some of his finest work, including his only surviving fresco cycle, can be seen here. Leon Battista Alberti (1404–72), who designed two impressive churches in Mantua, was widely emulated later in the Renaissance.

The 500-room **Palazzo Ducale** gives the impression that it took centuries to build. From a distance, the group of buildings dominates the skyline, and the effect is fascinating. The **Appartamento del Paradiso** is praised for its view, but its greatest interest may be that its decorator and first resident was Isabella d'Este (1474–1539). Not only was she married at 16, like her younger sister Beatrice (of the tomb in the Certosa at Pavia), but she was apparently also Ludovico il Moro Sforza's first choice for a wife—until he learned she was already engaged to a Gonzaga rival. Isabella was one of the great patrons of the Renaissance. She survived her sister by more than 40 years, and the archives of her correspondence, totaling more than 2,000 letters, are considered some of the most valuable records of the era.

The high point of all 500 rooms is the **Camera degli Sposi**—literally, "Chamber of the Wedded Couple," where Duke Ludovico and his wife held court. Mantegna painted it over a nine-year period at the height of his power, finishing at age 44. He made a startling advance in painting by organizing the picture plane in a way that systematically mimics the experience of human vision. Even now, more than five centuries later, you can sense the excitement of a mature artist, fully aware of the great importance of his painting, expressing his vision with a masterly, joyous confidence. Don't miss the celebrated trompe l'oeil (overhead), the image of Mantegna himself (in purple, on the right side of the western fresco), or the dwarf peering out from behind the dress of Ludovico's wife (in the northern fresco). Dwarf collecting was one of the more bizarre pastimes of Renaissance princes—according to historians, the dwarfs were considered to be something between celebrity comics and members of the ducal family.

Walk-up visitors to Mantua's Palazzo Ducale must take part in a fast-paced guided tour conducted in Italian; signs in each room provide explanations in English. Alternatively, call the **tourist office** (⊠ Piazza Mantegna 6 ☎ 0376/328253) to arrange for English-language tours. ⊠ *Piazza Sordello* ☎ *0376/224832* ⊠ *€6.50* ⊗ *Tues.–Sun. 8:45–7:15, last entry 6:30.*

Serious Mantegna aficionados will want to visit the **Casa di Andrea Mantegna,** designed by the artist himself and built around an intriguing circular courtyard, which is usually open to view. The interior can be seen only by appointment or during occasional art exhibitions. ⊠ *Via Acerbi 47* ☎ *0376/360506* ⊠ *€3* ⊗ *Tues.–Sun. 10–12:30; also 3–6 during exhibitions.*

Mantegna's tomb is in the first chapel to the left in the basilica of **Sant' Andrea** (1472, some sections earlier or later). The current structure, a masterwork by the architect Alberti, is the third built on this spot to house the relic of the Precious Blood. The crypt holds two reliquaries containing earth believed to be soaked in the blood of Christ, brought to Mantua by Longinus, the soldier who pierced his side. They are displayed only on Good Friday. ⊠ *Piazza delle Erbe* ⊗ *Daily 8–12:30 and 3–6.*

> **need a break?**   **Caravatti** (⊠ Portico Broletto 16, on Piazza delle Erbe ☎ 0376/321653) is Mantua's oldest café, having served aperitivi since 1865. As its name suggests, **Bar Sociale** (⊠ Piazza Cavallotta 16 ☎ 0376/322122) is a favored meeting place for locals.

Palazzo Te is one of the greatest of all Renaissance palaces, built between 1525 and 1535 by Isabella d'Este's son, Federigo II Gonzaga (1500–40), for his mistress. It is the singular mannerist creation of artist-architect Giulio Romano, decorated with extravagant mythological paintings not to every critic's taste. Nevertheless, as the magnificently frescoed **Sala dei Giganti** (Room of Giants) proves, the palace does not skimp on pictorial drama. The depiction of Jupiter's rage against the Titans, whom he cast down from Mount Olympus, may have served as a warning to ambitious aristocrats contemplating a less-celestial coup. ⊠ *Viale Te* ☎ *0376/323266* ⊕ *www.centropalazzote.it, www.palazzote.it* ⊠ *€8* ⊗ *Mon. 1–6, Tues.–Sun. 9–5:30.*

Where to Stay & Eat

★ **$$$$** ✕ **Al Bersagliere.** One of Lombardy's best restaurants is this rustic four-room tavern in the tiny riverside hamlet of Goito, 16 km (10 mi) north of Mantua on Route 236. It has been run by a single family for more than 150 years. The fish in particular is excellent, as is a Mantuan classic, frog soup. ⊠ *Via Goitese 260, Goito* ☎ *0376/60007* ⚑ *Reservations essential* ⊟ *AE, DC, MC, V* ⊗ *Closed Mon., Tues., and 3 wks in Aug.*

★ **$$$$** ✕ **Ambasciata.** Heralded by food critics the world over as one of Italy's finest restaurants, Ambasciata (Italian for "embassy") takes elegance and service to extremes rarely, if ever, achieved outside Europe. Chef Romano

Tamani makes frequent appearances abroad (at New York's Le Cirque 2000, for one) but is at home in tiny Quistello, 20 km (12 mi) southeast of Mantua, where he offers to those willing to make the trek (and pay the bill) an ever-changing array of superlative creations such as *timballo di lasagne verdi con petto di piccione sauté alla crème de Cassis* (green lasagna with breast of pigeon and red currant). ⊠ *Via Martiri di Belfiore 33, Quistello* ☎ *0376/619169* ⌘ *Reservations essential* ⊟ *AE, DC, MC, V* ⊘ *Closed Mon., Jan. 1–20, and Aug. 5–25. No dinner Sun.*

$$$–$$$$ ✕ **L'Aquila Nigra.** Down a small side street opposite the Palazzo Ducale, this popular restaurant is set in a former medieval convent, where frescoes grace the walls. Diners choose from such local dishes as *medaglione di anguilla all'aceto balsamico* (medallion of eel with balsamic vinegar), *saltarelli e frittata di zucchine* (lightly fried freshwater shrimp and zucchini), and *petto di faraona in pane grattinata con rosmarino* (breaded guinea fowl with rosemary). Reservations are recommended. ⊠ *Vicolo Bonacolsi 4* ☎ *0376/327180* ⊟ *AE, DC, MC, V* ⊘ *Closed 3 wks in Aug., Sun. (except for Sun. lunch in Apr. and May, and Sept. and Oct.), and Mon.*

$$ ✕ **Ristorante Pavesi.** Locals have been coming to this central restaurant for delicious food at reasonable prices since 1918. The menu changes every two months; homemade pasta is always a good bet. In warmer months you can dine on Mantua's handsome main square. ⊠ *Piazza Erbe 13* ☎ *0376/323627* ⊟ *AE, DC, MC, V* ⊘ *Closed Feb.*

$$ ✕ **Trattoria dei Martini–Il Cigno.** Set in a romantic 16th-century palazzo with period frescoes, this restaurant scores well for atmosphere. The menu has such local specialties as tortelli di zucca, *insalata di cappone* (chicken salad), *luccio in salsa di verdura all'aceto* (pike with vegetable and vinegar sauce), and variations on the Lombard favorite, risotto. Reservations are recommended. ⊠ *Piazza d'Arco 1* ☎ *0376/327101* ⊟ *AE, DC, MC, V* ⊘ *Closed Mon., Tues., Aug., and 1 wk in Jan.*

$$$ ▦ **San Lorenzo.** As if spacious, comfortable rooms, authentic early-19th-century furnishings, and a prime location weren't enough, many rooms here have wonderful views overlooking Piazza Concordia, and some have private terraces. In summer, breakfast is served on the roof. ⊠ *Piazza Concordia 14, 46100* ☎ *0376/220500* ⊟ *0376/327194* ⊕ *www.hotelsanlorenzo.it* ⊅ *32 rooms* ⌂ *Minibars, cable TV, bar, meeting rooms, Internet, free parking* ⊟ *AE, DC, MC, V* �’❘ *BP.*

$$ ▦ **Hotel Broletto.** Here you'll get comfortable, clean digs in a perfect location. The furniture was new in the '60s and has stuck around long enough to come back in style. ⊠ *Via Accademia 1, 46100* ☎ *0376/223678* ⊟ *0376/221297* ⊕ *http://space.tin.it/viaggi/fsmirnov* ⊅ *16 rooms* ⌂ *Minibars, cable TV* ⊟ *AE, DC, MC, V* ⊘ *Closed for a period in July and late Dec.* ❘❘ *BP.*

The Arts

Each year on the **Feast of the Assumption** (August 15) a contest is held in Mantua to determine who is the best *madonnaro* (street artist). Some of the painters can re-create masterpieces in a matter of minutes.

Free concerts are held on Sunday afternoons, December through February, at the opulent **Teatro Bibiena** (⊠ Via Academia 47 ☎ 0376/327653); a 14-year-old Mozart performed at the inaugural concert in 1770.

LAKE GARDA, BRESCIA & BERGAMO

Lake Garda has had a perennial attraction for travelers and writers alike; even essayist Michel de Montaigne (1533–92), whose 15 months of travel journals contain not a single other reference to nature, paused to admire the view down the lake from Torbole, which he called "boundless."

Lake Garda is 50 km (31 mi) long, ranges roughly 1 km–16 km (½ mi–10 mi) wide, and is as much as 1,135 feet deep. The terrain is flat at the lake's southern base and mountainous at its northern tip. As a consequence, its character varies from stormy inland sea to crystalline Nordic-style fjord. It's the biggest lake in the region and by most accounts the cleanest. Drivers should take care on the hazardous hairpin turns on the lake road.

Bardolino

㉑ *24 km (15 mi) northeast of Sirmione, 157 km (97 mi) east of Milan.*

Bardolino, which makes unremarkable but famous red wine, is one of the biggest summer resorts on the lake. It stands on the eastern shore at the wider end of the lake. Here there are two handsome Romanesque churches: **San Severo,** from the 11th century, and **San Zeno,** from the 9th. Both are in the center of the small town. Bardolino has the lake's most active nightlife. Of its several festivals, the best one is the **Cura dell'Uva** (Grape Cure Festival) in late September–early October. It's a great excuse to indulge in the local vino, which is light, dry, and often slightly sparkling. (Bring aspirin, just in case the cure turns out to be worse than the disease.)

Punta di San Vigilio

㉒ *6 km (4 mi) north of Bardolino, 163 km (101 mi) east of Milan.*

Just about everyone agrees that this is the prettiest spot on Garda's eastern shore. Punta di San Vigilio is full of cypresses from the gardens of the 15th-century **Villa Guarienti di Brenzone** (✉ Frazione Punta San Vigilio 1); the villa itself is closed to the public.

Malcesine

㉓ *28 km (17 mi) north of Punta di San Vigilio, 190 km (118 mi) east of Milan.*

One of the loveliest areas along the upper eastern shore of Lake Garda, Malcesine is principally known as a summer resort with sailing and windsurfing schools. Its 13 campsites and tourist villages tend to make the town crowded in season, but there are nice walks from the town toward the mountains. Six ski lifts and more than 11 km (7 mi) of runs of varying degrees of difficulty serve skiers. Dominating the town is the 12th-century **Castello Scaligero,** built by the Della Scalas.

The futuristic *funivia* (cable car) zipping visitors to the top of **Monte Baldo** (5,791 feet) is unique in the world: it rotates. After a 10-minute ride you're high in the Veneto, where you can stroll while enjoying spectacular views of the lake. You can ride the cable car down or bring along a mountain bike (or hang glider) for the descent. ⊠ *Via Navene Vecchia 12* ☎ *0457/ 7400206* 🖅 *€13 round-trip* ☉ *Daily 8–4.*

Riva del Garda

㉔ *18 km (11 mi) north of Malcesine, 180 km (112 mi) east of Milan.*

Set on the northern tip of Lake Garda against a dramatic backdrop of jagged cliffs and miles of beaches, Riva del Garda is the lake's quintessential resort town. The old city, set around a pretty harbor, was built up during the 15th century, when it was a strategic outpost of the Venetian Republic.

The heart of Riva del Garda, the lakeside **Piazza 3 Novembre,** is surrounded by medieval palazzos. Standing in the piazza and looking out onto the lake you can understand why Riva del Garda has become a windsurfing mecca: mountain air currents ensure good breezes on even the sultriest midsummer days.

The **Torre Apponale,** predating the Venetian period by three centuries, looms above the medieval residences of the main square; its crenellations recall its defensive purpose.

Where to Stay & Eat

$$$ ✕ **Castel Toblino.** A lovely stop for a lakeside drink or a romantic dinner, this castle is right on a lake in Sarche, about 20 km (12 mi) north of Riva toward Trento. The compound is said to have been a prehistoric, then Roman, village, and was later associated with the Church of Trento. Bernardo Clesio had it rebuilt in the 16th century in the Renaissance style. It's now a sanctuary of fine food, serving such local specialties as lake fish and guinea fowl. ⊠ *Via Caffaro 1, Sarche* ☎ *0461/ 864036* ▤ *MC, V* ☉ *Closed Tues., mid-Nov.–Feb. No dinner some Mon.*

$$$–$$$$ 🏨 **Hotel du Lac et du Parc.** Riva's most splendid hotel has elegance befitting its cosmopolitan name, with personalized service rarely found on Lake Garda since its aristocratic heyday. The airy public spaces include a dining room, bar, and beautifully manicured private garden leading to the public beach. The rooms are well appointed and comfortable; be sure to ask for air-conditioning. ⊠ *Viale Rovereto 44, 38066* ☎ *0464/ 551500* 🖷 *0464/555200* ⊕ *www.hoteldulac-riva.it* 🛏 *164 rooms, 5 suites* ᐧ *2 restaurants, minibars, cable TV, 2 tennis courts, indoor pool, gym, hair salon, sauna, Turkish bath, beach, bar, free parking; no a/c in some rooms* ▤ *AE, DC, MC, V* ☉ *Closed Nov.–Mar.* ᵀⓄᴵ *BP.*

$$$ 🏨 **Hotel Sole.** Within a lakeside 15th-century palazzo in the center of town, this lovely, understated hotel offers comfortable, affordable rooms. The terraced front rooms open to breathtaking views of the lake, and a secluded rooftop terrace is a perfect retreat from crowded beaches in summer. ⊠ *Piazza 3 Novembre 35, 38066* ☎ *0464/552686* 🖷 *0464/ 552811* ⊕ *www.hotelsole.net* 🛏 *52 rooms* ᐧ *Restaurant, room service, in-room safes, refrigerators, cable TV, sauna, bicycles, bar, free parking* ▤ *AE, DC, MC, V* ᵀⓄᴵ *BP.*

$$–$$$ 🏨 **Luise.** This cozy, reasonably priced hotel has great amenities, including a big garden and a large swimming pool. Luise's restaurant, La

Limonaia, is recommended for its Trentino specialties. ✉ *Viale Rovereto 9, 38066* ☎ *0464/550858* 🖨 *0464/554250* ⊕ *www.hotelluise.com* 🛏 *67 rooms* ⚙ *Restaurant, minibars, cable TV, tennis court, pool, laundry, no-smoking rooms* ⊟ *AE, DC, MC, V* ⦿ *BP.*

Sports
Contact **Circolo Surf Torbole** (✉ Colonia Pavese ☎ 0464/505385) for news on windsurfing in the area.

en route

After passing the town of Limone—where it is said the first lemon trees in Europe were planted—take the fork to the right about 5 km (3 mi) north of Gargnano and head to Tignale. The view from the Madonna di Monte Castello church, some 2,000 feet above the lake, is spectacular. Adventurous travelers will want to follow this pretty inland mountain road to Tremosine; be warned that the road winds its way up the mountain through hairpin turns and blind corners that can test even the most experienced drivers.

Gargnano

㉕ *30 km (19 mi) south of Riva del Garda, 144 km (89 mi) east of Milan.*

This small port town was an important Franciscan center in the 13th century, and now comes alive in the summer months when German tourists, many of whom have villas here, crowd the small pebble beach. An Austrian flotilla bombarded the town in 1866, and some of the houses still bear marks of cannon fire. Mussolini owned two houses in Gargnano: one is now a language school and the other, Villa Feltrinelli, has been restored and reopened as a luxury hotel.

Where to Stay & Eat

$$$$ ✕ **La Tortuga.** This rustic trattoria is more sophisticated than it first appears, with an extensive wine cellar and nouvelle-style twists on local dishes. Specialties include *agnello con rosmarino e timo* (lamb with rosemary and thyme), *persico con rosmarino* (perch with rosemary), and *carpaccio d'anatra all'aceto balsamico* (goose carpaccio with balsamic vinegar). ✉ *Via XXIV Maggio, at the small harbor* ☎ 0365/71251 ⊟ *AE, DC, MC, V* ⊗ *Closed Tues. No lunch Nov.–Mar.*

$$$$ 🏨 **Villa Feltrinelli.** This 1892 art nouveau villa hotel, named for the Italian publishing family that used to vacation here, is immersed in private gardens and faces the lake. Meticulously restored in 2002, it has frescoed ceilings, wood paneling, and original tile floors. The rooms are spacious and equipped with every luxury (as befits the final bill). If you can afford it, take the tower room. There's an extensive library open to guests. ✉ *Via Rimembranza 38/40, 25084* ☎ *0365/798000* 🖨 *0365/798001* ⊕ *www.villafeltrinelli.com* 🛏 *20 rooms* ⚙ *Restaurant, room service, minibars, cable TV, health club, bar, laundry service, business services, no-smoking rooms* ⊟ *AE, DC, MC, V* ⊗ *Closed late Oct.–Easter* ⦿ *BP.*

¢ 🏨 **Hotel Bartabel.** This cozy hotel on the main street offers comfortable accommodations at a rock-bottom price. The restaurant has an elegant terrace overlooking the lake. ⊠ *Via Roma 39, 25084* ☎ *0365/71330* 🖷 *0365/790009* 🛏 *10 rooms* 🍴 *Restaurant; no a/c* ▭ *AE, DC, V* ⊘ *Closed mid–late Nov. Restaurant closed Mon.* ❍| *EP.*

Sports & the Outdoors

The **Upper Brescian Garda Park** stretches over nine municipalities on the western side of the lake, from Salò to Limone (the northernmost town in the park), covering 147 square mi. Call the **Limone Hotel Owners Association** (⊠ Via Quattro Novembre 2/C ☎ 0365/954720) for trail and bicycle-rental information. They're also the people to contact if you'd like to take part in one of the free treks led by the Gruppo Alpini Limone every Sunday from June to September.

Gardone Riviera

㉖ *12 km (7 mi) south of Gargnano, 139 km (86 mi) east of Milan.*

Gardone Riviera, a once-fashionable 19th-century resort now delight-fully faded, is the former home of the flamboyant Gabriele d'Annunzio (1863–1938), one of Italy's greatest modern poets. D'Annunzio's estate, **Il Vittoriale,** perched on the hills above the town, is an elaborate memo-rial to himself, filled with the trappings of conquests in art, love, and war (of which the largest is a ship's prow in the garden), and complete with an imposing mausoleum. ⊠ *Gardone Riviera* ☎ *0365/296511* ⊕ *www.vittoriale.it* 🎟 *€16 tour of house and museum, €11 for either house or museum, €6 for grounds alone* ⊘ *Grounds Apr.–Sept., daily 8:30–8; Oct.–Mar., daily 9–5. House and museum Apr.–Sept., Tues.–Sun. 9:30–7; Oct.–Mar., Tues.–Sun. 9–1 and 2–5.*

More than 2,000 Alpine, subtropical, and Mediterranean species thrive at the **Giardino Botanico Hruska.** ⊠ *Via Roma* ☎ *0365/20347* 🎟 *€7* ⊘ *Mar. 15–Oct. 15, daily 9:30–6:30.*

off the beaten path

SALÒ MARKET – Four kilometers (2½ mi) south of Gardone Riviera is the enchanting lakeside town of Salò, which history buffs may recognize as the capital of the ill-fated Social Republic set up in 1943 by the Germans after they liberated Mussolini from the Gran Sasso. Every Saturday morning an enormous market is held in the Piazza dei Martiri della Libertà, with great bargains on everything from household goods to clothing to foodstuffs. In August or September a lone vendor often sells locally unearthed *tartufi neri* (black truffles) at affordable prices.

Where to Stay & Eat

★ **$$$$** ▦ **Villa del Sogno.** A narrow winding road takes you from town to this imposing villa, which surveys the valley and the lake below it. The large hotel terrace and the quiet surrounding grounds create a sense of escape. You may think twice about a busy sightseeing itinerary once you've set-tled into position in the sun, cool drink in hand. ⊠ *Corso Zanardelli 107* ☎ *0365/290181* 🖷 *0365/290230* ⊕ *www.villadelsogno.it* 🛏 *28 rooms, 5 suites* 🍴 *Restaurant, tennis court, pool, gym* ▭ *AE, DC, MC, V* ⊘ *Closed late Oct.–late Mar.* ❍| *BP.*

$$$–$$$$ 🏨 **Grand Hotel Fasano.** A former 19th-century hunting lodge between Gardone and Maderno, the Fasano has matured into a seasonal hotel of a high standard. To one side you face the deep waters of Lake Garda; on the others you're surrounded by a 12,000-square-mi private park where the original Austrian owners no doubt spent their days chasing game. Besides myriad activities on the water, there are two golf courses in the vicinity. Rooms with a view—and a balcony—are worth the extra cost. ⊠ *Corso Zanardelli 190* 🕾 *0365/290220* 🖷 *0365/290221* ⊕ *www.grand-hotel-fasano.it* 🛏 *68 rooms* ♨ *Restaurant, minibars, cable TV, tennis court, pool, beach, waterskiing, free parking* ▤ *No credit cards* ⊗ *Closed mid-Oct.–mid-May* ⦿l *BP.*

★ **$$$–$$$$**   ✕🏨 **Villa Fiordaliso.** The pink-and-white lakeside Villa Fiordaliso—once home to Claretta Petacci, given to her by Benito Mussolini—is a high-quality restaurant, but it also has seven tastefully furnished rooms, some overlooking the lake. The Claretta Suite is where Mussolini and Petacci were said to have carried on an affair. The art nouveau restaurant features seasonal ingredients such as zucchini flowers and porcini mushrooms, paramount in salads and soups. ⊠ *Corso Zanardelli 150* 🕾 *0365/20158* 🖷 *0365/290011* ⊕ *www.villafiordaliso.it* 🛏 *6 rooms, 1 suite* ♨ *Restaurant, cable TV, free parking* ▤ *AE, DC, MC, V* ⊗ *Closed mid-Nov.–mid-Feb. Restaurant closed Mon. No lunch Tues.* ⦿l *BP.*

★ **$$$**   ✕🏨 **Gran Hotel Gardone.** Directly facing the lake, this majestic 1800s villa is surrounded by an attractive landscaped garden. Many rooms look out over the lake, and the ground-floor Winnie's Bar, named after Winston Churchill, a frequent guest, envelopes you in charming art nouveau furniture and decorations. ⊠ *Corso Zanardelli 84* 🕾 *0365/20261* 🖷 *0365/22695* ⊕ *www.grangardone.it* 🛏 *180 rooms* ♨ *Minibars, cable TV, pool, sauna, laundry service, meeting rooms, parking (fee)* ▤ *AE, DC, MC, V* ⊗ *Closed mid-Oct.–Mar.* ⦿l *BP.*

¢   🏨 **Villa Maria Elisabetta.** Many of the rooms in this charming hotel run by a group of hospitable nuns have views of Lago di Garda. You can sit in the hotel's garden or take one of the ground's trails down for a dip in the lake or a bask in the sun. ⊠ *Corso Zanardelli 180* 🕾 *0365/20206* 🖷 *0365/2020818* 🛏 *42 rooms* ♨ *Restaurant, bar; no a/c, no room TVs* ▤ *No credit cards* ⊗ *Closed Oct. 18–Dec. 18* ⦿l *BP.*

Nightlife & the Arts

Gardone's tranquillity is its greatest attraction, but that doesn't inhibit conviviality. Visitors and locals alike relish a *passeggiata* (stroll) along the lakefront, stopping perhaps to enjoy an ice cream or aperitif. **La Terrazza** (⊠ Via Zanardelli 190 🕾 0365/290220), in the Grand Hotel Fasano, is particularly elegant. Winston Churchill reputedly enjoyed more than a few brandies in the belle-epoque surroundings.

Il Vittoriale (🕾 0365/296511) holds a series of concerts and other performing arts in its outdoor theater in July and August.

Sirmione

★ ㉗   *138 km (86 mi) east of Milan.*

Dramatically rising out of Lake Garda is the enchanting town of Sirmione. *"Paene insularum, Sirmio, insularumque ocelle,"* sang Catullus in a homecoming poem: "it is the jewel of peninsulas and islands, both." The forbidding Castello Scaligera stands guard behind the small bridge connecting Sirmione to the mainland; beyond, cobbled streets wind their way through medieval arches past lush gardens, stunning lake views, and gawking crowds. Originally a Roman resort town, Sirmione served under the dukes of Verona and later Venice as Garda's main point of defense. It has now reclaimed its original function, bustling with visitors in the summer. Cars aren't allowed into town; parking is available by the tourist office at the entrance.

Locals will almost certainly tell you that the so-called **Grotte di Catullo** (Grottoes of Catullus) were once the site of the villa of Catullus (87–54 BC), one of the greatest pleasure-seeking poets of all time. Present archaeological wisdom, however, does not concur, and there is some consensus that this was the site of two villas of slightly different periods, dating from about the 1st century AD. But never mind—the view through the cypresses and olive trees is lovely, and even if Catullus didn't have a villa here he is closely associated with the area and undoubtedly did have a villa nearby. The ruins are at the top of the isthmus and are poorly signposted: walk through the historic center and past the various villas to the top of the spit; the entrance is on the right. A small museum offers a brief overview of the ruins (on the far wall); for guided tours in English, call 02/20421469. ⊠ *Grotte di Catullo* ☎ *030/916157* ✇ *€4* ⏱ *Mar.–mid-Oct., Tues.–Sun. 8:30–7; mid-Oct.–Feb., Tues.–Sun. 8:30–5.*

The **Castello Scaligero** was built, along with almost all the other castles on the lake, by the Della Scala family. As hereditary rulers of Verona for more than a century before control of the city was seized by the Visconti in 1402, they counted Garda among their possessions. You can go inside to take in the nice view of the lake from the tower, and you can swim at the nearby beach. ⊠ *Piazza Castello, Sirmione* ☎ *030/916468* ✇ *€4* ⏱ *Tues.–Sun 8:30–7.*

off the beaten path

GARDALAND AMUSEMENT PARK – This park has more than 40 different rides and water slides, making it Italy's largest amusement park. It's 12 km (8 mi) east of Sirmione. ⊠ *Castelnuovo del Garda* ☎ *045/6449777* ⊕ *www.gardaland.it* ✇ *€23* ⏱ *July and Aug., daily 9 AM–midnight; Apr.–June and Sept., daily 9–6:30; Oct., weekends 9–6:30.*

Where to Stay & Eat

$$$$ ✕ **La Rucola.** Next to Sirmione's castle, this elegant, intimate restaurant has a creative menu, with seafood and meat dishes accompanied by a good choice of wines. Three fixed-price menus are available. ⊠ *Via Strentelle 3* ☎ *030/916326* ▤ *AE, DC, MC, V* ⏱ *Closed Thurs. and Jan.–mid-Feb. No lunch Fri.*

★ **$$** ✕ **Vecchia Lugana.** This elegant, if slightly stuffy, restaurant outside of town at the base of the peninsula serves surprisingly inventive cuisine. Try the river shrimp sauteed with orange and dressed with honey, or any of the local fish dishes. In warm months, you can dine in the garden. ⊠ *Piazzale Vecchia Lugana 1, Lugana di Sirmione* ☎ *030/919012*

⊟ *AE, DC, MC, V* ⊘ *Closed Mon., Tues., and Jan.–mid-Feb. No lunch in Nov.*

$–$$ ✕ **Ristorante Al Pescatore.** Lake fish is the specialty at this simple, popular restaurant in Sirmione's historical center. Try grilled trout with a bottle of local white wine and settle your meal with a walk in the nearby public park. ⊠ *Via Piana 20* ☎ *030/916216* ⊟ *AE, DC, MC, V* ⊘ *Closed Wed. and 1 wk in Nov.*

★ **$$$$** ▦ **Villa Cortine.** This former private villa in a secluded park risks being just plain ostentatious, but it's saved by the sheer luxury of its setting and the extraordinary professionalism of its staff. The hotel dominates a low hill, and the grounds—a colorful mixture of lawns, trees, statues, and fountains—go down to the lake. The villa itself dates from the early part of the 19th century, although a wing was added in 1952: the trade-off is between the more charming decor in the older rooms and the better lake views from the newer ones. In summer a three-night minimum stay and half board are required. The hotel also has relaxing private thermal baths. ⊠ *Via Grotte 6* ☎ *030/9905890* 🖷 *030/916390* ⊕ *www. hotelvillacortine.com* ⇥ *48 rooms, 6 suites* ⚷ *Restaurant, minibars, cable TV, tennis court, pool, beach, bar, meeting rooms, free parking* ⊟ *AE, DC, MC, V* ⊘ *Closed late Oct.–mid-Apr.* �ION *MAP.*

$$$–$$$$ ▦ **Hotel Sirmione.** Just inside the city walls, near the Castello, this hotel and spa sits amid lakeside gardens and terraces. Rooms are furnished with comfortable Scandinavian slat beds, matching floral draperies and wall coverings, and built-in white furniture. Many guests have been returning for years, due largely to the homespun feel and the attentiveness of the staff. ⊠ *Piazza Castello 19* ☎ *030/916192* 🖷 *030/916558* ⊕ *www. termedisirmione.com* ⇥ *101 rooms* ⚷ *Restaurant, minibars, cable TV, pool, spa, 2 bars, Internet, parking (fee)* ⊟ *AE, DC, MC, V* ION *BP.*

Brescia

㉘ *40 km (25 mi) west of Sirmione, 100 km (62 mi) east of Milan.*

Modern, industrial, and thoroughly nondescript, Lombardy's second-largest city is a fine place to do business. Hard-core art hunters may find the few remnants from its storied past a rewarding counterbalance to Brescia's current fascist-era design; otherwise you should skip the town.

The ruins of the **Capitolino,** a temple built by the Emperor Vespasian in AD 73, testify to Brescia's Roman origins. The adjoining Museo Romano is closed indefinitely for restoration, but its outstanding exhibits—including the famed 1st-century bronze *Winged Victory*—can be viewed in the **Santa Giulia Museo della Città** down the street. ⊠ *Via Musei 81/ a* ☎ *030/2977834* ⊕ *www.comune.brescia.it/musei* 🎫 *€8* ⊘ *June–Sept., Tues.–Sun. 10–6; Oct.–Mar., Tues.–Sun. 9:30–5:30.*

Works by Raphael (1483–1520), Tintoretto (1518–94), Tiepolo (1727–1804), and Jean Clouet (1485–1540) hang in the **Pinacoteca Civica Tosio Martinengo.** ⊠ *Piazza Moretto 4* ☎ *030/3774999* 🎫 *€3* ⊘ *June–Sept., Tues.–Sun. 10–5; Oct.–May, Tues.–Sun. 9:30–1 and 2:30–5.*

Palladio (1508–80) and Sansovino (1486–1570) contributed to the splendid **Palazzo della Loggia,** the Lombard-Venetian palace of marble overlooking the Piazza della Loggia.

Where to Stay & Eat

★ **$$$$** ✕ **Gualtiero Marchesi.** Never afraid to try something new, owner-chef Gualtiero Marchesi is celebrated as one of the first practitioners of *la cucina nuova* (nouvelle cuisine). Tiny lake fish are served in paper folded in origami fashion; soups are garnished with caviar; and ravioli are served *aperto* (unsealed at the edges) or *fazzoletto* (folded handkerchief style). The desserts—and prices—are stellar. ⊠ *Albereta Hotel, Via Vittorio Emanuele 11, Erbusco, 24 km (15 mi) west of Brescia* ☎ *030/7760562* ⚐ *Reservations essential* ⚎ *Jacket and tie* ⊟ *AE, DC, MC, V* ⊘ *Closed Mon. and 2 wks in Jan. No dinner Sun.*

$$$$ ⚏ **Vittoria.** Centrally located among 16th-century buildings, Vittoria is done in the Venetian style, with a hint of Byzantium and the spice routes in its pointed arches and windows. Many of the rooms are adorned with antiques, and the service is on a high level. ⊠ *Via delle X Giornate 20, 25100* ☎ *030/280061* ⚏ *030/280065* ⊕ *www.hotelvittoria.com* ⚐ *66 rooms* ⚐ *Restaurant, minibars, cable TV, bar, meeting rooms* ⊟ *AE, DC, MC, V* ⊚ *BP.*

Bergamo

㉙ *55 km (34 mi) west of Brescia, 52 km (32 mi) east of Milan.*

From behind a set of battered Venetian walls high on an Alpine hilltop, medieval Bergamo majestically surveys the countryside. Behind are the snowcapped Bergamese Alps, and two funiculars connect the ancient **Bergamo Alta** (Upper Bergamo) to the modern **Bergamo Bassa** (Lower Bergamo) below. A worthwhile destination in its own right, Bergamo Bassa's long arteries and ornate piazzas speak to its centuries of prosperity, but it's nonetheless overshadowed by Bergamo Alta's magnificence. The massive **Torre Civica** offers a great view of the two cities. ⊠ *Piazza Vecchia* ☎ *035/247116* ⚏ *€3* ⊘ *Apr.–Oct., Sun.–Tues. 9:30–7, Sat. 9:30–9:30; Nov.–Mar., Sat. 9:30–4:30, Tues.–Fri. by appointment only.*

Bergamo's **Duomo** and **Battistero** are the most substantial buildings in Piazza Duomo. But the most impressive is the **Cappella Colleoni,** with stunning marble decoration. ⊠ *Piazza Duomo* ⚏ *Free* ⊘ *Daily 10–12:30 and 2:30–5:30.*

In the **Accademia Carrara** you will find an art collection that is surprisingly rewarding given the Accademia's size and remote location. Many of the Venetian masters are represented—Mantegna, Bellini, Carpaccio (circa 1460–1525/26), Tiepolo, Francesco Guardi (1712–93), Canaletto (1697–1768)—as well as Botticelli (1445–1510). ⊠ *Bergamo Bassa, Piazza Carrara 82* ☎ *035/247149* ⊕ *www.accademiacarrara.bergamo.it* ⚏ *€2.58, free Sun.* ⊘ *Apr.–Sept., Tues.–Sun. 10–12:45 and 3–6:30; Oct.–Mar., Tues.–Sun. 9:30–12:30 and 2:30–5:30.*

Where to Stay & Eat

★ **$$–$$$** ✕ **Taverna Colleoni dell'Angelo.** Angelo Cornaro is the name behind the Taverna del Colleoni, on the Piazza Vecchia right behind the Duomo. He serves imaginative fish and meat dishes, both regional and international, all expertly prepared. ✉ *Piazza Vecchia 7* ☎ *035/232596* ▭ *AE, DC, MC, V* ☾ *Closed Mon. and 1 wk in Aug.*

$$ ✕ **Da Ornella.** The vaulted ceilings of this popular trattoria on the main street in the upper town are marked with ancient graffiti, created by (patiently) holding candles to the stone overhead. Ornella herself is in the kitchen, turning out *casoncelli* (stuffed pasta) in butter and sage and platters of assorted roast meats. Three prix-fixe menus are available during the week, two on the weekend. Reservations are recommended. ✉ *Via Gombito 15* ☎ *035/232736* ▭ *AE, DC, MC, V* ☾ *Closed Thurs.*

$$ ✕ **La Trattoria del Teatro.** Traditional regional food tops the bill at this good-value restaurant in the upper town. The polenta is a silky delight, and game is recommended in season. Fettuccine *con funghi* (with mushrooms) is deceptively simple but a rich and memorable specialty. ✉ *Piazza Mascheroni 3* ☎ *035/238862* ▭ *No credit cards* ☾ *Closed Mon. and 2 wks mid-July.*

$ ✕ **Al Donizetti.** Find a table in the back of this central, cheerful *enoteca*
FodorsChoice (wine bar) before choosing local hams and cheeses to accompany your
★ wine (more than 800 bottles available, with many offerings by the glass). Heartier meals are also available, such as eggplant stuffed with cheese and salami, but save room for the desserts, which are well paired with dessert wines. ✉ *Via Gombito 17/a* ☎ *035/242661* ▭ *AE, MC, V* ☾ *Closed Tues.*

$$ ✕🖭 **Agnello d'Oro.** A 17th-century tavern on the main street in Upper Bergamo, with wooden booths and walls hung with copper utensils and ceramic plates, Agnello d'Oro is a good place to imbibe the atmosphere as well as the good local wine. Specialties are typical Bergamese risotto and varieties of polenta served with game and mushrooms. The same establishment has 20 modestly priced rooms ($). ✉ *Via Gombito 22,* ☎ *035/249883* 🖷 *035/235612* ⤶ *20 rooms* ⚒ *Restaurant; no a/c* ▭ *AE, DC, MC, V* ☾ *Restaurant closed Mon. and Jan. 7–Feb. 5. No dinner Sun.* ⦿❘ *EP.*

$$–$$$$ 🖭 **Excelsior San Marco.** The most comfortable hotel in Lower Bergamo, the Excelsior San Marco is only a short walk from the walls of the upper town. The rooms are surprisingly quiet considering the central location. You can breakfast on the rooftop terrace. ✉ *Piazza della Repubblica 6, 24122* ☎ *035/366111* 🖷 *035/223201* ⊕ *www.hotelsanmarco.com* ⤶ *155 rooms* ⚒ *Restaurant, in-room safes, minibars, cable TV, bar, laundry service, Internet, free parking, no-smoking rooms* ▭ *AE, DC, MC, V* ⦿❘ *BP.*

Nightlife & the Arts

The annual summer **Festival Internazionale del Pianoforte** (International Piano Festival) is held in Bergamo's **Teatro Donizetti** (✉ Piazza Cavour 15 ☎ 035/4160602 ⊕ www.teatrodonizetti.it). Call the theater for information about drama, opera, and ballet events throughout the year.

en route The Chiesa della Madonna del Ghisallo (Church of the Patroness of
Bicyclists), open daily from March through November, is not far
from the shores of Lake Como and affords a fine view. You will often
see cyclists parked outside taking a breather after their uphill
struggle, but many come simply in homage to this unique Madonna.
It's located 48 km (30 mi) northwest of Bergamo, on the road to
Bellagio.

LAKE COMO

For those whose idea of heaven is palatial villas, rose-laden belvederes,
hanging wisteria and bougainvillea, lanterns casting a glow over lakeshore
restaurants, and majestic Alpine vistas, heaven is Lake Como. In his *Charterhouse of Parma,* Stendhal described it as an "enchanting spot, un-
equaled on earth in its loveliness." Virgil called it simply "our greatest"
lake. Though summer crowds do their best to vanquish the lake's
dreamy mystery and slightly faded old-money gentility, they fail. Como
remains a consummate pairing of natural and man-made beauty. The
villa gardens, like so many in Italy, are a union of two landscape traditions: that of Renaissance Italy, which values order, and of Victorian England, which strives to create the illusion of natural wildness. Such
gardens are often framed by vast areas of picturesque farmland—fruit
trees, olive groves, and vineyards.

Lake Como is some 47 km (30 mi) long north to south and is Europe's
deepest lake (almost 1,350 feet). If not driving, you arrive at the lake
by pulling into the railway station at Como, a leading textile center famous for its silks. Many travelers hasten to the vaporetti waiting to take
them to Bellagio and the *centro di lago,* the center region of the lake's
three branches, and its most beautiful section. From Bellagio, vaporetti
and car ferries traverse the lake, making it easy for travelers to get to
the other main towns, Cernobbio, Tremezzo, and Varenna.

Bellagio

30 *30 km (19 mi) northeast of Como, 56 km (35 mi) northwest of Berg-*
FodorsChoice *amo.*
★

Sometimes called the prettiest town in Europe, Bellagio always seems
to be flag-bedecked, with geraniums ablaze in every window and
bougainvillea veiling the staircases, or *montées,* that thread through the
town. At dusk Bellagio's nightspots—including the wharf, where an orchestra serenades dancers under the stars—beckon you to come and
make merry. It's an impossibly enchanting location, one that inspired French
composer Gabriel Faure to call Bellagio "a diamond contrasting brilliantly with the sapphires of the three lakes in which it is set."

Boats ply the lake to Tremezzo, where Napoléon's worst Italian enemy,
Count Sommariva, resided at Villa Carlotta; and a bit farther south of
Tremezzo, to Villa Balbianello. Check with the **Bellagio tourist office**
(✉ Piazza Mazzini (Pontile Imbarcadero) ☎ 031/950204 ⊕ www.
bellagiolakecomo.com) for the hours of the launch to Tremezzo.

★ **Villa Serbelloni,** a property of the Rockefeller Foundation, has celebrated gardens on the site of Pliny the Elder's villa overlooking Bellagio. There are only two guided visits per day, restricted to 30 people each, and in May these tend to be commandeered by group bookings. ⊠ *Near Palazza della Chiesa* ☎ *031/950204* ⊠ *€5* ⊘ *Guided visits Apr.–Oct., Tues.–Sun. at 11 and 4; tours gather 15 mins before start.*

The famous gardens of the **Villa Melzi** were once a favorite picnic spot for Franz Lizst, who advised author Louis de Ronchaud in 1837: "When you write the story of two happy lovers, place them on the shores of Lake Como. I do not know of any land so conspicuously blessed by heaven." The gardens are open to the public, and though you can't get into the 19th-century villa, don't miss the lavish Empire-style family chapel. The Melzi were Napoléon's greatest allies in Italy (the family has passed down the name "Josephine" to the present day). ⊠ *Via Lungolago Marconi* ☎ *031/951281* ⊠ *€5* ⊘ *Apr.–Oct., daily 9–6.*

Where to Stay & Eat

$–$$ ✕⌂ **La Pergola.** Try to reserve a table on the terrace at this popular lakeside restaurant about 1 km (½ mi) from Bellagio, on the other side of the peninsula. The best dining option is the freshly caught fish. You can also stay in one of the inn's 11 rooms, all of which have baths. ⊠ *Pescallo, Piazza del Porte, 22021* ☎ *031/950263* 🖶 *031/950253* ⊕ *www.lapergolabellagio.it* 🛏 *11 rooms* ⚭ *Restaurant* ⊟ *AE, MC, V* ⊘ *Restaurant closed Tues.* ⍾ *BP.*

$ ✕⌂ **Silvio.** At the edge of town, this family-owned trattoria with a lakeshore terrace specializes in fresh fish. Served cooked or marinated, with risotto or as a ravioli stuffing, the fish is caught by Silvio's family—it's local cooking at its best. Many of the modestly priced guest rooms have balconies and lake views. ⊠ *Lòppia di Bellagio, Via Carcano 10, 22021* ☎ *031/950322* ⊕ *www.bellagiosilvio.com* 🛏 *21 rooms* ⚭ *Restaurant, cable TV* ⊟ *MC, V* ⊘ *Closed Jan. and Feb.* ⍾ *BP.*

★ **$$$$** ⌂ **Grand Hotel Villa Serbelloni.** Designed to cradle nobility in high style, this hotel is a refined haven for the discreetly wealthy, set within a pretty park down the road from the Punta di Bellagio. The sense of 19th-century luxury has not so much faded as mellowed: the rooms are immaculate and plush; public areas are gilt and marble with thick, colorful carpets. Staff is unobtrusive and very knowledgeable about lake transportation. Churchill's and John Kennedy's former rooms face the Tremezzina, a group of towns across the lake. ⊠ *Via Roma 1, 22021* ☎ *031/950216* 🖶 *031/951529* ⊕ *www.villaserbelloni.it* 🛏 *83 rooms* ⚭ *2 restaurants, room service, minibars, cable TV, tennis court, 2 pools, health club, hair salon, sauna, Turkish bath, laundry service, Internet, free parking, no-smoking rooms* ⊟ *AE, DC, MC, V* ⊘ *Closed mid-Nov.–early Apr.* ⍾ *BP.*

$$$ ⌂ **Du Lac.** In the center of Bellagio, by the landing dock, this comfortable, medium-size hotel owned by an Anglo-Italian family has a relaxed and congenial feel. Most rooms have views of the lake and mountains, and there's a rooftop terrace garden for drinks or dozing. ⊠ *Piazza Mazzini 32, 22021* ☎ *031/950320* 🖶 *031/951624* ⊕ *www.bellagiohoteldulac. com* 🛏 *48 rooms* ⚭ *Restaurant, minibars, cable TV, bar, free parking* ⊟ *MC, V* ⊘ *Closed Nov.–Mar.* ⍾ *BP.*

$$–$$$ ⌂ **Hotel Florence.** This villa dating from the 1880s has an impressive lobby with vaulted ceiling and an imposing Florentine fireplace. Most of the rooms, furnished with interesting antiques, are large and comfortable and have splendid views of the lake. The restaurant and bar draw locals and visitors; there's live music on weekends. ⊠ *Piazza Mazzini 46, 22021* ☎ *031/950342* 🖷 *031/951722* ⇌ *30 rooms* △ *Restaurant, cable TV, bar; no a/c* ⊟ *AE, DC, MC, V* |○| *MAP* ⊘ *Closed Nov.–Mar.*

$–$$$ ⌂ **Belvedere.** In Italian, Belvedere means "beautiful view," an apt description of this enchanting spot. The hotel has been in the Martinelli-Manoni family since 1880, and the unbroken tradition of service makes it one of the best places to stay in town. Antique chairs and eye-catching rugs complement the modern, understated rooms. The bathrooms are expertly designed for maximum comfort. Outstanding terraced gardens have replaced the vineyards that once surrounded the house. The restaurant is very good. ⊠ *Via Valassina 31, 22021* ☎ *031/950410* 🖷 *031/950102* ⊕ *www.belvederebellagio.com* ⇌ *68 rooms* △ *Restaurant, cable TV, pool, bar, meeting rooms, free parking, no-smoking rooms; no a/c* ⊟ *AE, DC, MC, V* ⊘ *Closed Nov.–Mar.* |○| *BP.*

Varenna

㉛ *6 km (4 mi) northeast of Bellagio, 56 km (35 mi) northwest of Bergamo.*

You can reach Varenna by ferry from Bellagio. The principal sight here is the spellbinding garden of the **Villa Monastero,** which, as its name suggests, was originally a monastery. Now it's an international science and convention center. ⊠ *Varenna* ☎ *0341/295459* 🖭 *€2* ⊘ *Apr.–Oct., daily 9–7.*

Tremezzo

㉜ *34 km (21 mi) north of Cernobbio, 78 km (48 mi) north of Milan.*

If you're lucky enough to visit the small lakeside town of Tremezzo in late spring or very early summer, you will find the magnificent **Villa Carlotta** a riot of color, with more than 14 acres of azaleas and dozens of varieties of rhododendrons in full bloom. The villa was built between 1690 and 1743 for the luxury-loving marquis Giorgio Clerici. The garden's collection is remarkable, particularly considering the difficulties of transporting delicate plants before the age of aircraft. Palms, banana trees, cacti, eucalyptus, a sequoia, orchids, and camellias are counted among the more than 500 species.

According to local lore, one reason for the Villa Carlotta's magnificence was a competition between the marquis's son-in-law, who inherited the estate, and the son-in-law's archrival, who built *his* summer palace directly across the lake (Villa Melzi, in Bellagio). Whenever either added to his villa and garden, it was tantamount to taunting the other in public. Eventually the son-in-law's insatiable taste for self-aggrandizement prevailed. The villa's last (and final) owners were Prussian royalty (including the "Carlotta" of the villa's name); the property was confiscated during World War I.

The villa's interior is worth a visit, particularly if you have a taste for the romantic sculptures of Antonio Canova (1757–1822). The best-known is his *Cupid and Psyche,* which depicts the lovers locked in an odd but graceful embrace, with the young god above and behind, his wings extended, while Psyche awaits a kiss that will never come. The villa can be reached by boats from Bellagio. ☎ *0344/40405* ⊕ *www.villacarlotta. it* 🚊 *€7* ⊘ *Apr.–Sept., daily 9–6; Mar. and Oct., daily 9–11:30 and 2–4:30.*

off the beaten path

VILLA BALBIANELLO – This may be the most magical house in all of Italy. It sits on its own little promontory, Il Dosso d'Avedo—separating the bays of Venus and Diana—around the bend from the tiny fishing village of Ossuccio. Relentlessly picturesque, the villa is composed of loggias, terraces, and *palazzini* (tiny palaces), all spilling down verdant slopes to the lakeshore, where you'll find an old Franciscan church, a magnificent stone staircase, and a statue of San Carlo Borromeo blessing the waters. Don't be surprised if the lakeside location looks as familiar as it does cinematic: the intergalactic romance of *Star Wars: Episode II* was shot here. The villa is most frequently reached by launch from Como and Bellagio. Check with the **Como tourist office** (☎ 031/269712) for hours. Visits are usually restricted to the gardens, but if you plan in advance it's also possible to tour the villa itself. You pay €30 for a guide—regardless of how many are in your party—and an additional €5 entrance fee. Send a fax to reserve an **English-speaking guide** (🖷 0344/55575). ⊠ *Il Dosso di l'Avedo* ☎ *0344/56110* 🚊 *Gardens €5* ⊘ *Apr.–Oct., Tues., Thurs., and Fri. 10–1 and 2-6, weekends 10–6.*

Where to Stay

$$$$ 🏨 **Grand Hotel Tremezzo.** One hundred windows of this turn-of-the-20th-century building face the lake. The hotel, in the middle of a private park stretching over 12½ acres, has many creature comforts, from a heated swimming pool and private landing on the lake to a hillside for jogging. All rooms have a view of the lake or the park. The 18-hole Menaggio & Cadenabbia golf course is about five minutes away by car. ⊠ *Via Regina 8, 22019* ☎ *0344/42491* 🖷 *0344/40201* ⊕ *www.grandhoteltremezzo. com* 🛏 *98 rooms, 2 suites* 🖧 *3 restaurants, room service, minibars, cable TV, tennis court, 2 pools, gym, hair salon, sauna, billiards, Ping-Pong, 3 bars, Internet, meeting room, no-smoking rooms, helipad, free parking* ⊟ *AE, DC, MC, V* ⊘ *Closed mid-Nov.–Feb.* ⑩ *BP.*

$ 🏨 **Rusall.** Situated on the hillside above Tremezzo in the midst of a large garden, this small and reasonably priced hotel offers quiet and privacy. You can lie out on the terrace and enjoy a nice view. Rooms are simple and comfortable. ⊠ *Via S. Martino, 2, Rogaro, 22019* ☎ *0344/40408* 🖷 *0344/40447* ⊕ *www.rusallhotel.com* 🛏 *19 rooms* 🖧 *Restaurant, tennis court, bar, Internet; no a/c* ⊟ *AE, DC, MC, V* ⑩ *EP.*

Cernobbio

33 *5 km (3 mi) north of Como, 53 km (34 mi) north of Milan.*

The legendary resort of Villa d'Este is perhaps the only reason to visit Cernobbio (which is otherwise overrun with private villas)—but it's reason enough. If you're planning to say "budget be damned" in only one place, this just might be it. Built over the course of roughly 45 years for fisherman-turned-cardinal Tolomeo Gallio, the **Villa d'Este** has had a colorful and somewhat checkered history since its completion in 1615, swinging wildly between extremes of grandeur and dereliction. Its tenants have included the Jesuits, two generals, a ballerina, Caroline of Brunswick—the disgraced and estranged wife of the future king of England, George IV—a family of ordinary Italian nobles, and, finally, a czarina of Russia. Its life as a private summer residence ended in 1873, when it was turned into the fashionable hotel it has remained ever since.

Where to Stay & Eat

$$ ✕ **Il Gatto Nero.** This restaurant in the hills above Cernobbio has a splendid view of the lake. Specialties include risotto *ai funghi porcini* (with porcini mushrooms), *pappardelle al ragù di selvaggini* (pasta with wild game sauce), wild game, and lake fish. ⊠ *Via Monte Santo 69, Rovenna* 🕾 *031/512042* ▤ *AE, DC, V* ☉ *Closed Mon. No lunch Tues.*

$$$$ ▦ **Villa d'Este.** One of the grandest hotels in Italy, the 17th-century Villa
Fodor's Choice   d'Este has long welcomed Europe's rich and famous, from Napoléon
★   to the Duchess of Windsor. The chandeliers in the vast lobby illuminate marble staircases leading to guest rooms furnished in the Empire style: walnut paneling, sofas in striped silk, and gorgeous antiques. A broad veranda sweeps out to the lakefront, where a swimming pool extends above the water. The fanciful pavilions, temples, miniature forts, and mock ruins make for an afternoon's walk of quietly whimsical surprises. ⊠ *Via Regina 40, 22012* 🕾 *031/3481* 🖷 *031/348844* ⊕ *www.villadeste. it* ⊷ *148 rooms, 13 suites* ♢ *3 restaurants, room service, minibars, cable TV, 8 tennis courts, indoor pool, sauna, squash, bar, nightclub, laundry service, Internet, free parking, no-smoking rooms* ▤ *AE, DC, MC, V* ☉ *Closed mid-Nov.–Feb.* ⅋⊙⅋ *FAP.*

Como

➌➍ *5 km (3 mi) south of Cernobbio, 30 km (19 mi) southwest of Bellagio, 49 km (30 mi) north of Milan.*

Como, on the south shore of the lake, is only part elegant resort, where cobbled pedestrian streets wind their way past parks and bustling cafés. The other part is an industrial town renowned for its silk production. If you're traveling by car, leave it outside the town center, as traffic can be mayhem, and streets are often closed.

The splendid 15th-century Renaissance-Gothic **Duomo** was begun in 1396, the facade was added in 1455, and the transepts were completed in the mid-18th century. The dome was designed in 1744 by Filippo Juvara (1678–1736), chief architect of many of the sumptuous palaces of the royal house of Savoy. The facade has statues of two of Como's most famous sons, Pliny the Elder and Pliny the Younger, whose writings are among the most important documents from antiquity. Inside, the works of art include Luini's *Holy Conversation*, a fresco cycle by Morazzone, and the *Marriage of the Virgin Mary* by Ferrari. ⊠ *Piazza del Duomo* ☉ *Daily 7–noon and 3–7.*

need a break?

Directly across from the Duomo, **Bar Argentino** (⊠ Via Pretorio 1 ☎ 031/304455) is a hip local hangout with an extensive list of grappas, substantial snacks at aperitivo hour (usually from 5:30 to 7:30), and tables that look out onto a well-traveled piazza.

At the heart of Como's medieval quarter, the city's first cathedral, **San Fedele**, is worth a peek, if only because it is one of the oldest churches in the region. ⊠ Piazza San Fedele ☉ Daily 7–noon and 3–7.

If you brave Como's industrial quarter, you will find the beautiful church of **Sant'Abbondio**, a gem of Romanesque architecture begun by Benedictine monks in 1013 and consecrated by Pope Urban II in 1095. Inside, the five aisles of the church converge on a presbytery with a semi-circular apse decorated with a cycle of 14th-century frescoes—now restored to their original magnificence—by Lombard artists heavily influenced by the Sienese school. In the nave the cubical capitals are the earliest example of this style in Italy. ⊠ Via Sant'Abbondio ☉ Daily 7–6.

Exhibiting the path of production from silkworm litters to *moiré*-finishing machinery, the **Museo Didattico della Seta** (Silk Museum) is small but complete. Within the compound of the Como *Setificio* (textile school), the museum preserves the history of a manufacturing region that continues to supply almost three-fourths of Europe's silk. The friendly staff will give you an overview of the museum; they are also happy to provide brochures and information about local retail shops. The museum's location isn't well marked: follow the textile school's driveway around to the low-rise concrete building on the left, and follow the shallow ramp down to the entrance. ⊠ Via Velleggio 3 ☎ 031/303180 ⊕ www.museosetacomo.com ☒ €8 ☉ Tues.–Fri. 9–noon and 3–6. *Tours in English available by reservation.*

off the beaten path

CASTIGLIONE OLONA – This Gothic *collegiata* (collegiate church) and baptistery with superlative frescoes by Giotto's pupil Masolino da Panicale is 18 km (11 mi) west of Como. ☎ 0331/858903 ☒ €5 ☉ Apr.–Sept., Tues.–Sat. 9:30–noon and 2–5:30; Oct.–Mar., Tues.–Sat. 10–noon and 2:30–5:30.

Where to Stay & Eat

$$$$ ✗ **La Locanda dell'Isola.** Isola Comacina, Lake Como's only island and five minutes by boat from Sala Comacina, is rustic and restful but at times crowded. The same could be said for the Locanda. Forget any notions of choosing from a menu, because here the deal is a set price for a set meal, with drinks included. The good news is that the food is delicious, the service is friendly, and the setting is magnificent. You'll have to pace yourself through a mixed antipasto, salmon, trout, chicken, salad, cheese, coffee, and dessert. ⊠ Isola Comacina, Sala Comacina ☎ 0344/55083 ☲ No credit cards ☉ Closed Tues. and Nov.–Mar.

$$ ✗ **Raimondi.** This elegant restaurant in the Hotel Villa Flori (2 km [1 mi] toward Cernobbio) offers good value and a superb location, with a large terrace poised over the lake. The local freshwater fish is your best option, but a wide range of Italian dishes are capably prepared. The restaurant's season is longer than most, owing to its popularity with local residents. ⊠ *Via Cernobbio 12* ☎ *031/338233* ▣ *AE, DC, MC, V* ☾ *Closed Mon. and Dec.–Feb. 14. No lunch Sat.*

$$–$$$ 🏠 **Barchetta Excelsior.** Though it has a rather unprepossessing exterior, this central, modern hotel is comfortable, with many rooms looking directly across Piazza Cavour to Lake Como. The rooms are airy and spacious, with those on the upper floors commanding the best views. Ask for a lake view, though the noise of the piazza can be a distraction. The Barchetta is run by the group that owns Villa d'Este. ⊠ *Piazza Cavour 1, 22100* ☎ *031/3221* 🖨 *031/302622* ⊕ *www.hotelbarchetta.com* 🛏 *84 rooms ⚲ 2 restaurants, minibars, cable TV, bar, Internet, no-smoking rooms* ▣ *AE, DC, MC, V* ⦿ *BP.*

★ **$$–$$$** 🏠 **Terminus.** Commanding a panoramic view over Lake Como, this early-20th-century art nouveau building is the city's finest hotel. The marbled public spaces have an understated elegance, and the guest rooms are done in floral patterns and furnished with large walnut wardrobes and silk-covered sofas. In summer, the garden terrace is perfect for relaxing over a drink. ⊠ *Lungolario Trieste 14, 22100* ☎ *031/329111* 🖨 *031/302550* ⊕ *www.albergoterminus.com* 🛏 *40 rooms ⚲ Restaurant, in-room data ports, in-room safes, minibars, cable TV, massage, sauna, meeting room, free parking, no-smoking rooms* ▣ *AE, DC, MC, V* ⦿ *EP.*

$$–$$$ 🏠 **Villa Flori.** Italian patriot Garibaldi spent his wedding night here, in a suite that now bears his name. The hotel enjoys a panoramic view and has a highly acclaimed restaurant, Raimondi. ⊠ *Via Cernobbio 12, 22100* ☎ *031/33820* 🖨 *031/570379* ⊕ *www.hotelvillaflori.com* 🛏 *45 rooms ⚲ Restaurant, minibars, cable TV, meeting room* ▣ *AE, DC, MC, V* ⦿ *EP.*

$ 🏠 **Tre Re.** This clean, spacious, welcoming hotel is a few steps west of the cathedral and convenient to the lake. Although the exterior gives away the age of this 16th-century former convent, the rooms are airy, comfortable, and modern. The moderately priced restaurant shares an ample terrace with the hotel. ⊠ *Via Boldoni 20, 22100* ☎ *031/265374* 🖨 *031/241349* ⊕ *www.hoteltrere.com* 🛏 *41 rooms ⚲ Restaurant, cable TV, bar, Internet, free parking* ▣ *MC, V* ☾ *Closed mid-Dec.–mid-Jan.* ⦿ *BP.*

Sports

Various facilities for waterskiing and all water sports can be found on the lake; contact the **Tourist Office** (⊠ Piazza Cavour 17 ☎ 031/269712) in Como.

Shopping

While in Como, seize the opportunity to shop for fine European silk directly from its source. One of the biggest names is **Mantero** (⊠ Via San Abbondio 8 ☎ 031/321510), which supplies major design houses like Yves Saint Laurent, Nina Ricci, and Trussardi. Not far from the lake, good deals on ties, scarves, and shirts can be found at the factory store of **Binda** (⊠ Viale Geno 6 ☎ 031/3861629). **Frey** (⊠ Via Garibaldi 10 ☎ 031/267012) has a factory outlet on the western edge of the old town selling silk clothes and accessories. Every Saturday (except the first Saturday of every month), Piazza San Fedele holds a **local crafts market** from 9 to 7.

LAKE MAGGIORE & LAKE ORTA

Magnificently scenic, Lake Maggiore has its mountainous western shore in Piedmont, its lower eastern shore in Lombardy, and its northern tip in Switzerland. The lake stretches nearly 50 km (30 mi), and is up to 5 km (3 mi) wide. The better-known resorts are on the western shore, particularly Stresa, a tourist town that provided a setting for Hemingway's *A Farewell to Arms*. A mountainous strip of land separates Lake Maggiore from Lake Orta, its smaller neighbor to the west, in Piedmont. Orta attracts fewer visitors than the three larger lakes, and can be a pleasant alternative in the summer.

Orta San Giulio

35 *76 km (47 mi) northwest of Milan.*

At the end of a small peninsula jutting out into Lake Orta, this charming town is full of 18th-century buildings adorned with wrought-iron balustrades and balconies. The shady main square looks out across the lake to the small island of San Giulio. There is nothing more relaxing than sitting at one of the piazza cafés and watching the languid waters, where sailboats catch mountain breezes.

Rising up behind Orta, **Sacro Monte** (Sacred Mountain) is an interesting hike. Pass the Church of the Assumption at the edge of the old town, and just ahead is a gateway marked Sacro Monte. This leads to a comfortable climb that takes about 40 minutes round-trip. As you approach the top, you pass no fewer than 20 17th-century chapels, all devoted to St. Francis of Assisi. Within them, frescoes and striking, life-size terracotta statue groups (a total of almost 400 figures) illustrate incidents from the saint's life. The campanile of the last chapel provides a view over the lake and the town, about 350 feet below.

The island of **San Giulio** is accessible by hired boat for about €6 round-trip per boatload of up to four people. The island takes its name from the 4th-century St. Julius, who—like St. Patrick in Ireland—is said to have banished snakes from the island. Julius is also said to have founded the **Basilica** in AD 390, although the present building shows more signs of its renovations in the 10th and 15th centuries. Inside, there's a black-marble pulpit (12th century) with elaborate carvings, and a crypt containing relics of the saint. In the sacristy of the church is a large bone said to be from one of the beasts destroyed by the saint, but it actually resembles a whalebone.

Much of the area is occupied by private villas; it takes only a few minutes to walk around the parts of the island open to the public. The view to Orta, with Sacro Monte behind it, is memorable, particularly in the late afternoon when the light picks up the glint of the wrought-iron traceries. Signs laud the virtues of silence and contemplation, and the island's quiet is broken only by the pealing of the basilica's bells.

Where to Stay & Eat

$$–$$$ ✕▥ **Hotel San Rocco.** Half the rooms in this converted 17th-century lake-side convent on the edge of town have views of the water, garden, and surrounding mountains; many also have balconies. The restaurant ($$$) serves international cuisine and has beautiful views of the lake. ✉ *Via Gippini 11, 28016* ☎ *0322/911977* 📠 *0322/911964* ⊕ *www. hotelsanrocco.it* 🛏 *74 rooms* ⚭ *Restaurant, minibars, cable TV, pool, bar, parking (fee)* ▤ *AE, DC, MC, V* ⧉| *BP.*

---

en route

Follow the shore drive from Orta San Giulio north to Omegna, at the head of Lake Orta. A mile or so west of Omegna, in the village of Quarna Sotto, there's a musical-instrument factory that's worth a stop. The shore drive continues around the rest of the lake, and at the southern end you can pick up S229, which will take you back to the A4 autostrada.

If you're going to Stresa from Orta San Giulio, you'll first pass through the town of Armeno, where in late summer and early fall you're likely to see whole families out in the woods, crouched down in their hunt for wild mushrooms, or—if they're lucky—truffles. Oaks blend into evergreens as you climb La Borromea, a 9-km (5½-mi) twisting, panoramic mountain road toward Mottarone (at 4,900 feet, the tallest peak between the lakes). The road continues through Gignese, which offers a last dramatic view of Maggiore before descending to Stresa on its western shore.

Stresa

🔢 *16 km (10 mi) east of Orta San Giulio, 80 km (50 mi) northwest of Milan.*

Stresa, which has capitalized on its central lakeside position and its good connections to the Isole Borromee (Borromean Islands) in Lake Maggiore, has to some extent become a victim of its own success. The luxurious elegance that distinguished its heyday has faded; the grand hotels are still grand, but traffic now encroaches upon their parks and gardens. Even the undeniable loveliness of the lakeshore drive has been threatened by the roar of diesel trucks and BMW traffic. One way to escape is to head for the Isole Borromee.

As you wander around the palms and semitropical shrubs of **Villa Pallavicino,** don't be surprised if you're followed by a peacock or even an ostrich: they're part of the zoological garden and are allowed to roam almost at will. From the top of the hill on which the villa stands you can see the gentle hills of the Lombardy shore of Lake Maggiore and, nearer and to the left, the jewel-like Borromean Islands. In addition to a bar and restaurant, the grounds also have picnic spots. ✉ *Via Sempione 8* ☎ *0323/31533* 🎫 *€6.70* ⊘ *Early Mar.–Oct., daily 9–6.*

Boats to the **Isole Borromee** leave every 15–30 minutes from the dock at Stresa's Piazza Marconi. Although you can hire a private boatman, it's cheaper and just as convenient to use the regular service. Make sure you buy a ticket allowing you to visit all the islands—Bella, Dei Pescatori, and Madre. The islands take their name from the Borromeo family, which has owned them since the 12th century.

Isola Bella (Beautiful Island) is the most famous of the three, and the first that you'll visit. It is named after Isabella, whose husband, Carlo III Borromeo (1538–84), built the palace and terraced gardens for her as a wedding present. Wander up the 10 terraces of the gardens, where peacocks roam among the scented shrubs, statues, and fountains, for a splendid view of the lake. Before Count Carlo began his project, the island was rocky and almost devoid of vegetation; the soil for the garden had to be transported from the mainland. Visit the palazzo to see the rooms where famous guests—including Napoléon and Mussolini—stayed in 18th-century splendor. ☎ *0323/30556* 🖾 *Garden and palazzo €9* ☉ *Late Mar.–Sept., daily 9–5:30.*

Stop for a while at the tiny **Isola dei Pescatori** (Island of the Fishermen), less than 100 yards wide and only about ½ km (¼ mi) long. Of the three islands, this one has remained closest to the way it was before the Borromeos began building. The island's little lanes strung with fishing nets and dotted with shrines to the Madonna are the definition of picturesque; little wonder that in high season the village is crowded with postcard stands.

Isola Madre (Mother Island) is the largest of the three and, like Isola Bella, has a large botanical garden. Even dedicated nongardeners should take time to see the profusion of exotic trees and shrubs running down to the shore in every direction. Two special times to visit are April (for the camellias) and May (when azaleas and rhododendrons are in bloom). Also on the island is a 16th-century palazzo, where an antique puppet theater is on display, complete with string puppets, prompt books, and elaborate scenery designed by Alessandro Sanquirico, who was a scenographer at La Scala in Milan. ☎ *0323/31261* 🖾 *€8.50* ☉ *Late Mar.–Sept., daily 9–5:30.*

For more information about the islands and how to get there, contact the **Stresa tourist office** (✉ Piazza Marconi 16 ☎ 0323/30150) or ask at the landing stages (look for Navigazione Lago Maggiore signs). There's also a **Web site** (⊕ www.borromeoturismo.it) dedicated to the islands.

Where to Stay

$$$$ 🏨 **Grand Hotel des Iles Borromées.** This palatial establishment has catered to a demanding European clientele since 1863. And though it still has the spacious salons and lavish furnishings of the turn of the 20th century, it has been discreetly modernized. The bathrooms are luxurious. ✉ *Corso Umberto I 67, 28838* ☎ *0323/938938* 🖶 *0323/32405* ⊕ *www.borromees.it* ➡ *161 rooms, 11 suites* ♨ *Restaurant, room service, minibars, cable TV, tennis court, indoor pool, spa, bar, laundry service, Internet, convention center, helipad, free parking* ➡ *AE, DC, MC, V* ⊠ *BP.*

$ 🏨 **Primavera.** A few blocks up from the lake, Primavera has compact, simply furnished rooms in a 1950s building hung with flower boxes. Most rooms have balconies overlooking the streets of Stresa's old center. ☒ *Via Cavour 39, 28838* ☎ *0323/31286* 🖷 *0323/33458* 🛏 *31 rooms* ⅄ *Cable TV, bar, Internet, meeting rooms, parking (fee); no a/c* ➟ *AE, DC, V* ☺ *Closed mid-Nov.–mid-Mar.* ⅠⓄⅠ *BP.*

Verbania

㊲ *16 km (10 mi) north of Stresa, 95 km (59 mi) northwest of Milan.*

Verbania, across the Gulf of Pallanza from Stresa, is known for the **Villa Taranto,** which has magnificent botanical gardens. The villa was acquired in 1931 by Scottish captain Neil McEachern, who expanded the gardens considerably, adding terraces, waterfalls, more than 3,000 plant species from all over the world, and broad meadows sloping gently down to the lake. In 1938 McEachern donated the entire complex to the Italian people. ☒ *Via Vittorio Veneto 111* ☎ *0323/404555* ⊕ *www. villataranto.it* 🖾 *€8* ☺ *Late Mar.–Oct., daily 8:30–7:30; last admission 1 hr before closing.*

Where to Stay & Eat

$–$$ ✕ **Da Cesare.** Off Piazza Cadorna and close to the embarcadero, this hotel restaurant serves tasty risotto *con filetti di persico* (with perch fillets) and typical Piedmontese meat dishes, such as beef braised in Barolo wine. ☒ *Da Cesare, Via Mazzini 14* ☎ *0323/31386* ➟ *AE, DC, MC, V* ☺ *Closed Tues. and mid-Dec.–late Feb.*

$$$$ ✕🏚 **Il Sole di Ranco.** The same family has run this lakeside inn for more than 150 years. The present chefs, Davide Brovelli and his father, Carlo, do the family proud. Lake trout and perch find their way onto the menu, as do artichoke dishes in spring and eggplant in summer. Guest rooms ($$$–$$$$) are in two late-19th-century villas surrounded by a garden and overlooking the lake. ☒ *Piazza Venezia 5, Ranco, near Angera* ☎ *0331/976507* 🖷 *0331/976620* 🖉 *ivanett@tin.it* ⅄ *Restaurant reservations essential* 🛏 *14 rooms* ⅄ *Restaurant, minibars* ➟ *AE, DC, MC, V* ☺ *Closed Dec. and Jan. Restaurant closed Tues. No lunch Mon.* ⅠⓄⅠ *BP.*

$ 🏚 **Il Chiostro.** Originally a 17th-century convent, this hotel expanded into the adjoining 19th-century textile factory, adding some conference facilities. Rooms are clean and functional. ☒ *Via Fratelli Cervi 14, 28900* ☎ *0323/404077* 🖷 *0323/401231* ⊕ *www.chiostrovb.it* 🛏 *100 rooms* ⅄ *Restaurant, cable TV, meeting rooms* ➟ *AE, DC, MC, V* ⅠⓄⅠ *BP.*

MILAN, LOMBARDY & THE LAKES A TO Z

To research prices, get advice from other travelers, and book travel arrangements, visit www.fodors.com.

AIRPORTS & TRANSFERS

Aeroporto Malpensa (MXP), 50 km (31 mi) northwest of Milan, services all intercontinental flights, as well as many European and domestic flights. Aeroporto Milano Linate (LIN), 10 km (6 mi) east of Milan, handles the remainder of European and domestic traffic. Malpensa Shuttle Buses (€8) run every 90 minutes between the two airports.

The Malpensa Express Train connects Malpensa airport with the Cadorna train station near downtown Milan. The 40-minute train ride costs €9 (€12 round-trip), leaving Cadorna every half hour from 5:50 AM to 8:20 PM and Malpensa every half hour 6:45 AM to 9:45 PM. Malpensa Express Buses run on the same route outside of these hours. In addition, Malpensa Shuttle Buses (€5) go to and from Milan's central train station (Stazione Centrale). STAR FLY buses (€2.50) run between Milano Linate and the central train station every half hour, and municipal Bus 73 (€1) runs to Piazza San Babila.

Driving from Malpensa to Milan takes about an hour; take Route S336 east to the A8 autostrada southeast. From Milano Linate, follow the signage west into the central downtown area.

Taxis wait directly outside the arrival building doors at Malpensa, and will take you downtown for about €70. The fare from Milano Linate is about €20.

🛈 Airport Information **Aeroporto Malpensa** ☎ 02/74852200 ⊕ www.sea-aeroportimilano.it. **Aeroporto Milano Linate** ☎ 02/74852200.

🛈 Taxis & Shuttles **Malpensa Express Train** ☎ 02/27763 automated system, 02/20222 desk. **Malpensa Shuttle Buses** ☎ 02/58583185. **STAR FLY** ☎ 02/717106.

BOAT & FERRY TRAVEL

There's frequent daily ferry and hydrofoil service between towns on the lakes and a range of round-trip excursions with dining service (optional) on board.

FARES & SCHEDULES

🛈 Boat & Ferry Information **Navigazione Laghi** ✉ Via Ariosto 21, Milan ☎ 02/4676101 ⊕ www.navigazionelaghi.it. **Navigazione Lago di Como** ✉ Via per Cernobbio 18, Tavernola, near Como ☎ 031/579211. **Navigazione Lago di Garda** ✉ Piazza Matteotti 2, Desenzano ☎ 030/9149511. **Navigazione Lago Maggiore** ✉ Viale Baracca 1, Arona ☎ 800/551801.

BUS TRAVEL

Bus service is best avoided on intercity routes, since it is neither faster, cheaper, nor more convenient than the railways; trains are generally better than buses for getting around the cities of the plain. If you are determined to travel by bus, Autostradale serves several destinations from its hub at Autostazione Garibaldi, north of Milan's city center.

There's regular bus service between the small towns on the lakes, and it tends to be a cheaper way of getting around than ferry or hydrofoil service. The bus service around Lake Garda serves mostly towns on the western shore. Call SIA for information.

🛈 Bus Information **Autostradale** ☎ 02/637901. **SIA** ☎ 030/3774237.

CAR RENTAL

International car-rental companies serve Milan's airports and city locations throughout Lombardy. The city of Brescia rents electric cars for €3 per hour, €15 per day—pick one up at the station and float silently through the city.

🛈 Local Agencies **Avis** ✉ Piazza Diaz 6, Milan ☎ 02/863494 ⊕ www.avisautonoleggio.it ✉ Aeroporto Milano Linate, Milan ☎ 02/715123 ✉ Aeroporto Malpensa, Milan ☎ 02/

5858481. **Europcar** ⊠ Via Galvani 12, Milan ☎ 02/66710491 ⊕ www.europcar.it ⊠ Aeroporto Milano Linate, Milan ☎ 02/76110258 ⊠ Aeroporto Malpensa, Milan ☎ 02/ 5858621. **Hertz** ⊠ Aeroporto Milano Linate, Milan ☎ 02/70200256 ⊠ Aeroporto Malpensa, Milan ☎ 02/58581137 ⊕ www.hertz.it.

🎫 Municipal Services **Brescia electric car rental** ☎ 030/2053022.

CAR TRAVEL

Although trains are often more convenient for intercity travel, renting a car is the best way to appreciate Lombardy's varied landscape—and the only way to explore its winding lake roads. Several major autostrada routes intersect at Milan, all connected by the circular *tangenziale*, which rings the city. The A4 runs west to Turin and east to Venice; A1 leads south to Bologna, Florence, and Rome; A7 angles southwest down to Genoa. To reach the lakes, take A8 northwest to Lago Maggiore, or A9 north, which runs past Lake Como and over the St. Gotthard Pass into Switzerland.

Although these major highways will allow you to make good time between the cities of the plain, you'll have to follow secondary roads—often of great beauty—around the lakes. S572 follows the southern and western shores of Lake Garda, S45b edges the northernmost section of the western shore, and S249 runs along the eastern shore. Around Lake Como, follow S340 along the western shore, S36 on the eastern shore, and S583 on the lower arms. S33 and S34 trace the western shore of Lago Maggiore.

EMERGENCY SERVICES ACI, the Italian auto club, offers 24-hour roadside assistance (free to members, for a fee to nonmembers). Regularly spaced roadside service phones are available on the autostrade.

🎫 **ACI dispatchers** ☎ 803/116.

EMBASSIES & CONSULATES

🎫 Australia **Australian Consulate** ⊠ Via Borgogna 2, Milan ☎ 02/777041.
🎫 Canada **Canadian Consulate** ⊠ Via Vittor Pisani 19, Milan ☎ 02/67581.
🎫 New Zealand **New Zealand Consulate** ⊠ Via Guido d'Arezzo 6, Milan ☎ 02/48012544.
🎫 United Kingdom **U.K. Consulate** ⊠ Via San Paolo 7, Milan ☎ 02/723001.
🎫 United States **U.S. Consulate** ⊠ Via Principe Amedeo 2, Milan ☎ 02/290351.

EMERGENCIES

English-speaking officers with the *carabinieri* (the national police) are available 24 hours a day. You can dial the nationwide ambulance number wherever you are, and it will connect you to the nearest local emergency service. For first aid, ask for *pronto soccorso,* and be prepared to give your address.

There are a number of pharmacies open 24 hours a day, including one on the upper level of Stazione Centrale in Milan. Others take turns staying open late and on weekends; to find the nearest one, check the roster outside any pharmacy or the list published in the *Corriere della Sera* newspaper.

🎫 **Ambulance** ☎ 118. **Carabinieri** ☎ 112. **Police** ☎ 113.
🎫 24-Hour Pharmacies **Stazione Centrale** ⊠ Piazza Duca D'Aosta, Milan ☎ 02/6690735.

ENGLISH-LANGUAGE MEDIA

BOOKS **American Bookstore** (⊠ Via Camperio at Via Dante, Castello, Milan ☎ 02/878920). **English Bookshop** (⊠ Via Ariosto at Via Mascheroni, Porta Magenta, Milan ☎ 02/4694468 ⊕ www.englishbookshop.it). **Feltrinelli Bookstore** (⊠ Piazza del Duomo, Milan ☎ 02/86996897). **FNAC** (⊠ Via Torino, corner of Via della Palla, Duomo, Milan ☎ 02/869541). **Hoepli** (⊠ Via Hoepli 5, Duomo, Milan ☎ 02/864871).

MAIL & SHIPPING

🖪 Overnight Services **DHL** ⊠ Via Agnello 15, Duomo, Milan ☎ 199199345. **United Parcel Service** ⊠ Via Albricci 10, Missori, Milan ☎ 800/877877.

🖪 Internet Access **Internet Enjoy** ⊠ Via Medici 6, Sant'Ambrogio, Milan ☎ 02/866800 ⊠ Piazza 24 Maggio, Naviglio, Milan ☎ 02/8357225. **Virgin** ⊠ Piazza Duomo 8, Milan ☎ 02/88001200.

🖪 Post Offices **Milan** ⊠ Via Cordusio 4, Duomo, Milan ☎ 02/8690460.

SAFETY

Milan is a fairly safe city, but it always pays to keep a close eye on your purse or wallet. Outside the city, you're far more likely to be invited to dinner by friendly strangers than to be robbed or harassed.

TAXIS

Taxi fares in Milan are expensive compared with those in American cities, but drivers are honest. A short downtown hop averages €10. Taxis wait at stands or can be called; they are difficult (but not impossible) to flag down on the street.

🖪 Taxi Companies **Autoradiotaxi** ☎ 02/8585. **Taxiblu** ☎ 02/4040. **Amicotaxi** ☎ 02/4000. **Radiotaxi** ☎ 02/6969.

TOURS

For tours in Milan, contact the tourist office, which organizes three-hour walking tours of the city Monday mornings at 10 (€15) as well as guided tours to city museums (many of which do not have their own guides). In the lakes, private launches can often be arranged through your hotel. There are also convenient tram tours that take tourists around the city in a refurbished 1930s tram car. Tickets (€10) are valid all day, and can be purchased at the **Milan tourist office** (⊠ Via Marconi 1 ☎ 02/72524300 ⊕ www.milanoinfotourist.com).

TRAIN TRAVEL

Although Milan has a bewildering number of railway stations, only one is of concern, Stazione Centrale, unless you travel on local routes at peculiar hours—in which case service can begin or terminate in suburban stations (most notably Milano Lambrate for Bergamo, and Stazione Nord for Como). From Stazione Centrale, there's frequent direct service to Como, Bergamo, Brescia, Sirmione, Pavia, Cremona, and Mantua. Premium international (EC) service and premium (IC) domestic service connect Milan with major European cities. For general information on trains and schedules, contact the FS–Trenitalia (it is easier to use the Web site). Metro Line 3 (yellow) links Milano Centrale with Piazza Duomo.

🖪 Train Information **FS–Trenitalia** ☎ 892021 ⊕ www.trenitalia.com. **Milano Centrale** ⊠ About 3 km [2 mi] northwest of the Duomo ☎ 892021.

TRANSPORTATION AROUND MILAN

Milan has an excellent system of public transport, consisting of three subway lines and 120 tram and bus routes. Tickets are valid for one trip on the Metropolitana (subway) or 75 minutes on buses and trams, and must be purchased before you board and then stamped at station entrances or poles inside trolleys and buses. Standard tickets cost €1 and can be purchased from news vendors, tobacconists, and—at larger stops—machines (some of which require exact change). All-inclusive subway, bus, and tram tickets cost €3 for 24 hours or €5.50 for 48 hours; they're available at Duomo Metro and Stazione Centrale Metro stations. Trains run from 6 AM to 12:30 AM every five minutes; for more information, call the ATM or visit the information office in the Duomo stop.

There's no free street parking unless you have a special resident's permit, but there are garages and parking meters. Parking in the city center is possible 7 AM–8 PM for a fee. For car service with a driver, call Autonoleggio Pini.

🚩 **ATM (Azienda Trasporti Milanesi)** ☎ 800/808181 ⊕ www.atm-mi.it. **Autonoleggio Pini** ☎ 02/29400555 🖷 02/2047843 ⊕ www.pini.it.

TRAVEL AGENCIES

🚩 Local Agent Referrals **Compagnia Italiana Turismo (CIT)** ⊠ Via Dante 6, Castello, Milan ☎ 02/863701. **American Express Travel Agency** ⊠ Via Larga 4, Duomo, Milan ☎ 02/721041.

VISITOR INFORMATION

🚩 Tourist Information **Bellagio** ⊠ Piazza Mazzini (Pontile Imbarcadero) ☎🖷 031/950204 ⊕ www.bellagiolakecomo.com. **Bergamo** ⊠ Vicolo Aquila Nera at Piazza Vecchia, Upper Bergamo ☎035/242226 🖷035/232730 ⊠Viale Vittorio Emanuele 20, Bergamo Bassa ☎ 035/210204 🖷 035/230184 ⊕ www.apt.bergamo.it. **Brescia** ⊠ Corso Zanardelli 34 ☎ 030/43418 🖷 030/3756450 ⊕ www.bresciaholiday.com. **Cernobbio** ⊠ Via Regina ☎🖷 031/510198. **Como** ⊠ Piazza Cavour 17 ☎ 031/269712 🖷 031/240111 ⊕ www.lakecomo.org. **Cremona** ⊠ Piazza del Comune 5 ☎ 0372/23233 🖷 0372/534080 ⊕ www.aptcremona.it. **Malcesine** ⊠ Via Capitanato 6/8 ☎ 045/7400044 🖷 045/7401633 ⊕ www.aptgardaveneto.com. **Mantua** ⊠ Piazza A. Mantegna 6 ☎ 0376/328253 🖷 0376/363292 ⊕ www.aptmantova.it. **Milan** ⊠ Via Marconi 1 (Piazza Duomo) ☎02/72524301 🖷02/72524350 ⊕www.milanoinfotourist.com. **Pavia** ⊠Via Fabio Filzi 2 ☎ 0382/22156 🖷 0382/32221 ⊕ www.apt.pavia.it. **Riva del Garda** ⊠ Giardini di Porta Orientale 8 ☎0464/554444 🖷0464/520308 ⊕www.gardaqui.com. **Sabbioneta** ⊠ Via Vespasiano Gonzaga 27 ☎🖷 0375/52039 ⊠ Piazza D'Armi 1 ☎ 0375/221044 🖷 0375/222119 ⊕ www.comune.sabbioneta.mn.it. **Sirmione** ⊠ Viale Marconi 2 ☎ 030/916114 🖷 030/916222. **Stresa** ⊠ Piazza Marconi 16 ☎ 0323/30150 🖷 0323/32561 ⊕ www.distrettolaghi.it. **Tremezzo** ⊠ Piazzale Trieste ☎ 0344/40493.

PIEDMONT/ VALLE D'AOSTA

5

FIND YOUR FAVORITE MUMMY
at Turin's world-class Museo Egizio ⇨*p.207*

ASCEND TO A MEDIEVAL ABBEY
at the Sacra di San Michele ⇨*p.218*

SCHUSS DOWN OLYMPIC SLOPES
at the Sestriere ski resort ⇨*p.219*

TAKE A CABLE CAR INTO THE CLOUDS
on towering Monte Bianco ⇨*p.227*

DISCOVER UNBEATABLE BARGAINS
at McArthur Glen designer outlet ⇨*p.233*

SAMPLE THE KING OF ITALIAN WINES
at Castello di Barolo, near Alba ⇨*p.233*

Updated by
Peter Blackman

FROM ALPINE VALLEYS hemming the highest mountains in Europe to the mist-shrouded lowlands skirting the Po River; from pulsating industrial centers turning out the best of Italian design to tiny stone villages isolated above the clouds; from hearty peasant cooking in farmhouse kitchens to French-accented delicacies accompanied by some of Italy's finest wines—the Piedmont and the spectacular Valle d'Aosta regions, tucked away in the country's northwest corner, present delightful surprises even in a land famed for its natural beauty.

Valle d'Aosta's Italian Alps afford excellent skiing and climbing at renowned resort towns such as Courmayeur and Breuil-Cervinia. In the Piedmontese lowlands, Turin, the regional capital, is a historical center that today also serves as the heart of Italy's auto industry. Don't be put off by Turin's industrial reputation—it also has elegant piazzas, high fashion, fine chocolate, and worthwhile museums. Currently the city is busy highlighting its attractions in preparation for hosting the Winter Olympics of 2006. Near Turin are Alba, home of fragrant Italian white truffles, seasonal delicacies that sell for more than $1,000 per pound; Asti, Barolo, and Barbaresco, all famous wine centers; and the modern business hubs Ivrea, Novara, and Alessandria.

Napoléon's regime controlled both regions in the 19th century, and French influence remains evident in everything from traditional recipes redolent of mountain cheeses, truffles, and cream to Versailles-style gardens and wide, tree-lined boulevards. Well-dressed women in the refined cafés of Turin are addressed more often as *madama* than *signora,* and French is often used in the more remote mountain hamlets.

Piedmont (Piemonte in Italian, meaning "foot of the mountains") was originally inhabited by Celtic tribes who were absorbed by the conquering Romans. As allies of Rome, the Celts held off Hannibal when he came down through the Alpine passes with his elephants, but they were eventually defeated, and their capital—Taurasia, the present Turin—was destroyed. The Romans rebuilt the city, giving its streets the grid pattern that survives today. (Roman ruins can be found throughout both regions and are particularly conspicuous in the town of Aosta.) With the fall of the Roman Empire, Piedmont suffered the fate of the rest of Italy and was successively occupied and ravaged by barbarians from the east and the north. In the 11th century, the feudal French Savoy family ruled Turin briefly; toward the end of the 13th century it returned to the area, where it would remain, almost continuously, for 500 years. In 1798 the French republican armies invaded Italy, but when Napoléon's empire fell, the house of Savoy returned to power.

Beginning in 1848, Piedmont was one of the principal centers of the Risorgimento, the movement for Italian unity. In 1861 the Chamber of Deputies of Turin declared Italy a united kingdom. Rome became the capital in 1870, marking the end of Piedmont's importance in the political sphere. Nevertheless, the architectural splendors of Turin, together with some unheralded but excellent museums, continue to draw visitors.

Piedmont became one of the first industrialized regions in Italy, and the automotive giant FIAT—the Fabbrica Italiana Automobili Torino—was established here in 1899. Today the region is the center of Italy's automobile, metalworking, chemical, and candy industries, having attracted thousands of workers from Italy's south. The FIAT company, led by the Agnelli family—Italy's equivalent of the Kennedys—has been perhaps the most important player in the region's rise to power and affluence.

Valle d'Aosta to the north is famous for its Alpine beauty and fortified castles. It was settled in the 3rd millennium BC by people from the Mediterranean and later by a Celtic tribe known as the Salassi, who eventually fell to the Romans. By the 12th century the Savoy family had established itself, and the region's feudal nobles moved into the countryside, building the massive castles that you still see there today. Valle d'Aosta enjoyed relative autonomy as part of the Savoy kingdom and was briefly ruled by the French four separate times. The region is still officially bilingual; though Italian is the mother tongue of most locals, you're likely to encounter French as well.

Exploring Piedmont/Valle d'Aosta

The vast Po plain, which stretches eastward in a wide belt across the top of the Italian peninsula, begins in Piedmont, where the Po River has its source in the Coolidge Glacier on 11,000-foot-high Monviso. But Piedmont is primarily a mountainous region. The Maritime Alps lie to the south of Turin, and the rolling hills of the Monferrato and Langhe districts make up the landscape to the city's southeast. High Alpine crests of Valle d'Aosta rise to the north and west of the plain. As you wind your way northeast into Valle d'Aosta, you are in the Italian Loire, where solid, imposing castles sit in the shadow of Europe's most impressive peaks, Monte Bianco and Monte Cervino. Nature has endowed Piedmont and Valle d'Aosta with some of the most striking scenery in Italy.

Like any rugged, mountainous region, the Italian Alps can be tricky to navigate. Roads that look like superhighways on the map can be narrow and twisting, with steep slopes and cliff-side drops. Generally, roads are well maintained, but the sheer distance covered by all of those curves tends to take longer than you might expect, so it's best to figure in extra time for getting around. This is especially true in winter, when weather conditions can cause slow traffic and road closings. Be sure to check with local tourist offices and police before venturing off the beaten path, and find out whether you may need tire chains for snowy and icy roads. Train routes, on the other hand, are more or less reliable in the region.

About the Restaurants & Hotels

The Piedmontese take their food and their wine very seriously, and although you will find a similar range of eating establishments here as in other regions of Italy, the number of formal restaurants, with elaborate service and extraordinary wine lists, most certainly exceeds the national average. This holds true both in cities and in the country, where even simply named trattorias may offer a *menu di degustazione* (a multicourse tasting menu) accompanied by wines appropriate to each dish. In Turin the ritual of the *aperitivo* has been finely tuned, and most cafés from

Numbers in the text correspond to numbers in the margin and on the Piedmont/ Valle d'Aosta and Turin maps.

If you have
3 days

If you have limited time, you should concentrate first on 🔀 **Turin** ❶–❶ ▶, including the **Duomo di San Giovanni** ❶, where the famous shroud is housed; the 17th-century **Palazzo Reale** ❷, former residence of the Savoy royal family; and the churches of **San Carlo** ❺ and **Santa Cristina** ❻, which flank the impressive **Piazza San Carlo** ❼. Take time to enjoy one or more of the city's authentic old-world cafés and walk by the striking **Mole Antonelliana** ⓫, an odd structure that was once the world's tallest building and now houses an extensive cinema museum. On the second day head north along the A5 motorway to 🔀 **Aosta** ㉙ to see its large and well-preserved Roman ruins and enjoy some regional French-influenced cooking. If you have a couple of hours to spare on your way to Aosta, see **Castello Fénis** ㉘, well worth the detour. On the third day continue on to 🔀 **Courmayeur** ㉚ for magnificent views of Monte Bianco. Alternatively, you can catch a glimpse of one or the other and then double back through Aosta to **Cogne and the Parco Nazionale del Gran Paradiso** ㉛. Alternatively, return to Turin on the third day and head southeast into the vineyard-blanketed hills around medieval 🔀 **Asti** ㉜.

If you have
5 days

For your first three days, follow the plan outlined above. On the fourth day double back to Turin and make an excursion to **Saluzzo** ㉒, an old town steeped in 15th-century atmosphere—or, if the Alps are your primary interest, spend the fourth day in the mountains, at the **Parco Nazionale del Gran Paradiso** ㉛. On the fifth day travel to 🔀 **Asti** ㉜ and the surrounding hills, where great wine and good food attract gastronomic adventurers.

If you have
7 days

Make 🔀 **Turin** ❶–❶ ▶ your base for three days, exploring the city and making one or two day trips, to **Saluzzo** ㉒, with its picturesque hilltop center and castles; the castle at **Rivoli** ⓲ and the medieval abbeys of **Abbazia di Sant'Antonio di Ranverso** ⓳ and **Sacra di San Michele** ㉑ (Umberto Eco's inspiration); or the resorts of **Sestriere** ㉓ and **Bardonecchia** ㉔, in Piedmont's mountains close to the French border. On the third day head for the mountains of Valle d'Aosta; visit the **Castello Fénis** ㉘ on the way to 🔀 **Aosta** ㉙, a good base for excursions into the mountains that will keep you moving on the fourth and fifth days to **Courmayeur** ㉚, **Breuil-Cervinia** ㉗, and **Cogne and the Parco Nazionale del Gran Paradiso** ㉛; devote the better part of a day to the stunning national park. Head south on the sixth day to 🔀 **Asti** ㉜ and follow the provincial roads through the vineyards of the hilly Monferrato and Langhe districts of south-central Piedmont, delving into their culinary and enological delights. On the seventh day head east across the fertile Po plain toward the rice-growing capital of **Vercelli** ㉟, making sure you see the Duomo, then continue on your way to Milan, only 75 km (45 mi) away.

the early evening onward provide lavish buffets that are included in the price of a cocktail—a respectable substitute for dinner if you are traveling on a limited budget. As a result, restaurants in Turin tend to fill only after 9 PM.

High standards and opulence are characteristic of Turin's better hotels, and the same is true, translated into the Alpine idiom, at the top mountain resort hotels. The less-expensive hotels in cities and towns are generally geared to business travelers; make sure to ask if lower weekend rates are available. The **Turin Tourist Board** (✉ Via Bogino 8, Centro ☎ 011/8185011 🖷 011/883426 ⊕ www.turismotorino.org) provides a booking service for hotels and bed-and-breakfast–style accommodation in the city. In order to use the service, you must book hotels 48 hours in advance and B&Bs seven days in advance.

You can usually count on a measure of charm and comfort at even the more modest resort hotels. Summer vacationers and winter skiers keep occupancy rates and prices high at the resorts during these peak seasons. Many mountain resort hotels accept half- or full-board guests only, occasionally for stays of at least a week; some have off-season rates that can reduce the cost by a full price category. If you're a skier, ask about package deals that can give you a break on the price of lift tickets.

In anticipation of the 2006 Winter Olympics, legislation governing alternative (usually inexpensive) types of lodging, such as bed-and-breakfasts, has been relaxed. Whatever style of accommodations you choose, if you decide to attend the Olympics expect rates and availability to be at a premium—start your planning well in advance. The travel agency **Montagnedoc** (✉ Viale Giolitti 7/9, Pinerolo ☎ 0121/794003 🖷 0121/794932 ⊕ www.montagnedoc.it), which operates in conjunction with the tourist offices in the towns hosting the 2006 Winter Olympics, provides help with locating and booking accommodations, and is a good source for information about all-inclusive Olympics packages.

WHAT IT COSTS In euros				
$$$$	**$$$**	**$$**	**$**	**¢**
RESTAURANTS over €22	€16–€22	€11–€16	€7–€11	under €7
HOTELS over €220	€160–€220	€110–€160	€70–€110	under €70

Restaurant prices are for a second course (*secondo piatto*). Hotel prices are for two people in a standard double room in high season, including tax and service.

Timing
Unless you are dead set on skiing, the region can be visited in either summer or winter (and for that matter, there's summer skiing at Monte Cervino). In winter, road conditions can be treacherous, especially higher up in the mountains. The ski resorts of Valle d'Aosta are popular with Italians and non-Italians alike, so book your accommodations in advance. Snow conditions for skiing vary drastically year to year—there is nothing approaching the consistency of, say, the Colorado and Utah Rockies—so keep apprised of weather conditions. If you are vis-

Skiing Skiing is the major sport in both the Piedmont and Valle d'Aosta. Resorts with excellent facilities abound near the highest mountains in Europe—Monte Bianco (Mont Blanc), Monte Rosa, Monte Cervino (the Matterhorn), and the Gran Paradiso. The so-called Via Lattea (Milky Way)—five skiing areas near Sestriere with 400 km (almost 250 mi) of linked runs and 90 ski lifts—provides practically unlimited skiing. And it's not unusual to find yourself skiing portions of the same day in Italy and then in France. Best of all, the lift tickets, running around €35 for a day's pass, are significantly less expensive than at major U.S. resorts.

5

Climbing & Hiking The Torinese will tell you how reassured they feel when the mountains appear on clear days. At the head of the completely flat Po Valley, these regions are almost completely surrounded by mountains, and it's here that some of the Italy's best hiking and climbing is to be found. For beginners, the beautiful and well-marked trails that wind through Italy's first national park, the Gran Paradiso, are breathtaking, whereas experienced climbers, accompanied by professional guides, might want to try their hands on Monte Bianco (Mont Blanc).

iting in summer, try to avoid coming in August, the holiday month for the vast majority of Italians, many of whom will head to the mountains for a vacation of walking, hiking, and relaxing.

TURIN

Turin—Torino, in Italian—is roughly in the center of Piedmont/Valle d'Aosta and 128 km (80 mi) west of Milan; it's on the Po River, on the edge of the Po plain, which stretches eastward all the way to the Adriatic. Turin's flatness and wide, angular, tree-lined boulevards are a far cry from Italian *metropoli* to the south; the region's decidedly northern European bent is quite evident in its nerve center. Apart from its role as northwest Italy's major industrial, cultural, intellectual, and administrative hub, Turin also has a reputation as Italy's capital of black magic and the supernatural. This distinction is enhanced by the presence of Turin's most famous, and controversial, relic, the Sacra Sindone (Holy Shroud), still believed by many Catholics to be the cloth in which Christ's body was wrapped when he was taken down from the cross.

Downtown Turin

Many of Turin's major sights are clustered around Piazza Castello, and others are on or just off the porticoed Via Roma, one of the city's main thoroughfares, which leads 1 km (½ mi) from Piazza Castello south to Piazza Carlo Felice, a landscaped park in front of the train station. First opened in 1615, Via Roma was largely rebuilt in the 1930s, during the Mussolini era.

Piedmont/
Valle d'Aosta

CloseUp

ON THE MENU

THESE TWO REGIONS *offer rustic specialties from farmhouse hearths, fine cuisine with a French accent— and everything in between. The area's best-known dish is probably polenta, creamy cornmeal served with carbonada (veal stew), melted cheese, or wild mushrooms. Also at the top of the favorites list are agnolotti dal plin, crescent-shape stuffed pasta, served with the pan juices of roast veal or with melted butter and shaved tartufi bianchi (white truffles) from Alba. Another regional specialty is fonduta, a local version of fondue, made with melted cheese, eggs, and sometimes grated truffles. Fontina and ham also often deck out the ubiquitous French-style crepes alla valdostana, served casserole style.*

Throughout the region, though especially in Turin, you will find that most meals are accompanied by grissini (bread sticks). Invented in Turin in the 17th century to ease the digestive problems of little Prince

Vittorio Amedeo II (1675–1730), these, when freshly made and hand-rolled, are a far cry from the thin and dry, plastic-wrapped versions available elsewhere. Napoléon called them petits batons and was, it seems, addicted to them.

Though desserts here are less sweet than in some other Italian regions, treats like panna cotta (a cooked milk custard), torta di nocciole (hazelnut torte), and bonet (a pudding made with hazelnuts, cocoa, milk, and macaroons) still delight. Turin is renowned for its delicate pastries and fine chocolates, especially for the hazelnut gianduiotti.

Piedmont is one of Italy's most important wine regions, producing full-bodied reds, such as Barolo, Barbaresco, Freisa, Barbera, and the lighter Dolcetto. Asti Spumante, a sweet sparkling wine, comes from the region, and Valle d'Aosta is famous for schnappslike brandies made from fruits or herbs.

---

a good walk

Start on Piazza San Giovanni at the **Duomo di San Giovanni ❶ ▶**, the hushed and shadowy repository of the city's famed relic. To the right of the Duomo is a passage that leads to the Piazzetta Reale and the imposing **Palazzo Reale ❷**, where you can visit the sumptuous rococo interiors and, in a separate wing to the east, the Armeria Reale. The massive building occupying an entire block at the center of Piazza Castello is **Palazzo Madama ❸**, parts of which are open to the public. In the northwest corner of the same square take time to observe Guarini's lively architectural vision in the church of **San Lorenzo ❹**. Go southwest on Via Roma, a street rebuilt with arcades in the 1930s. Continuing a few blocks, you come to the twin churches of **San Carlo ❺** and **Santa Cristina ❻** on the **Piazza San Carlo ❼**. Just off the northeast end of Piazza San Carlo is the imposing Palazzo dell'Accademia delle Scienze, where you may devote an hour or two to the collections housed inside, the **Galleria Sabauda ❽** and the **Museo Egizio ❾**. To the east, across the street, is the graceful **Palazzo Carignano ❿**, an important building in Italian history and a good example of Piedmontese baroque. The east facade of the palace faces Piazza Carlo Alberto, from which you head north for one block to reach Via Po. Turn right and then continue east to Via Montebello, where you turn left to reach the **Mole Antonelliana** ⑪, Turin's oddest and most conspicuous building and the site of a cinema museum.

TIMING This walk takes the better part of a day if you plan to linger in the museums. It includes the most important of Turin's sights, so it's a suitable plan to follow if you're trying to "do" the town in one day.

What to See

▶ ❶ **Duomo di San Giovanni.** The most impressive part of Turin's 15th-century cathedral is the shadowy, black marble–walled **Cappella della Sacra Sindone** (Chapel of the Holy Shroud), where the famous relic was housed before a fire in 1997. The chapel was designed by the priest and architect Guarino Guarini (1604–83), a genius of the baroque style who was official engineer and mathematician to the court of Duke Carlo Emanuele II of Savoy. The fire caused severe structural damage, and the chapel is closed indefinitely while restoration work proceeds.

The Sacra Sindone (Holy Shroud) is a 4-yard-long sheet of linen, thought by millions to be the burial shroud of Christ, bearing the light imprint of his crucified body. The shroud first made an appearance around the middle of the 15th century, when it was presented to Ludovico of Savoy in Chambéry. In 1578 it was brought to Turin by another member of the Savoy royal family, Duke Emanuele Filiberto. It was only in the 1990s that the Catholic Church began allowing rigorous scientific study of the shroud. Not surprisingly, results have bolstered both sides of the argument. On the one hand, three separate university teams—in Switzerland, Britain, and the United States—have concluded, as a result of carbon 14 dating, that the cloth is a forgery dating from between 1260 and 1390. On the other hand, they are unable to explain how medieval forgers could have created the shroud's image, which resembles a photographic negative, and how they could have had the knowledge or means to incorporate traces of Roman coins covering the eyelids and endemic Middle Eastern pollen woven into the cloth. Either way, the shroud continues to be revered as a holy relic, exhibited to the public on very rare occasions—the next official display is planned for 2025. In lieu of the real thing, a photocopy is on permanent display near the altar of the Duomo. ✉ *Piazza San Giovanni, Centro* ☎ *011/4361540* ☉ *Mon.–Sat. 6:30–noon and 3–7, Sun. 8–noon and 3–7.*

❽ **Galleria Sabauda.** Some of the most important paintings from the vast collections of the house of Savoy are displayed here. The collection is particularly rich in 16th- and 17th-century Dutch and Flemish paintings: note the *St. Francis with Stigmata* by Jan Van Eyck (1395–1441), in which the saint receives the marks of Christ's wounds while a companion cringes beside him. Other Dutch masterpieces include paintings by Anthony Van Dyck (1599–1641) and Rembrandt (1606–69). *Tobias and the Angel* by Piero del Pollaiuolo (circa 1443–96) is showcased, and other featured Italian artists include Fra Angelico (circa 1400–55), Andrea Mantegna (1431–1506), and Paolo Veronese (1528–88). Along with the Egyptian Museum, the gallery is housed in the **Palazzo dell'Accademia delle Scienze,** a baroque tour de force designed by priest-architect Guarino Guarini. ✉ *Via Accademia delle Scienze 6, Centro*

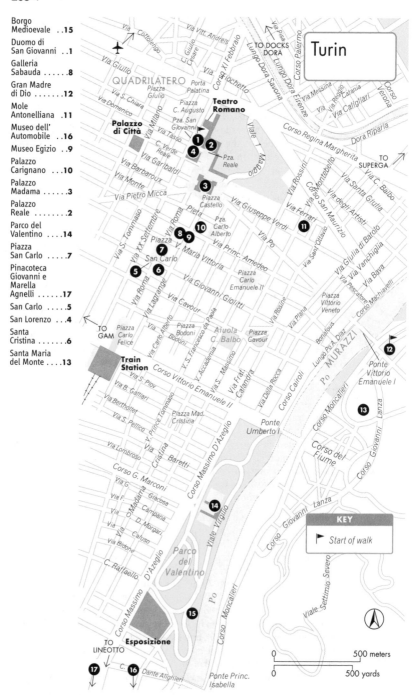

Turin

☎ *011/547440* 🎟 *€4, €8 combined ticket includes Museo Egizio* ⊙ *Fri.–Tues. 8:30–2, Wed. and Thurs. 2–7:30.*

★ ⓫ **Mole Antonelliana.** You can't miss the unusual square dome and thin, elaborate spire of this Turin landmark above the city's rooftops. This odd structure, built between 1863 and 1889, was originally intended to be a synagogue, but costs escalated and eventually it was bought by the city of Turin. In its time it was the tallest brick building in the world. You can take the crystal elevator to reach the terrace at the top of the dome for an excellent view of the city, the plain, and the Alps beyond. Also worth a visit is the Mole's **Museo Nazionale del Cinema** (National Cinema Museum), which embraces more than 34,000 square feet and houses many items of film memorabilia as well as a film library with some 7,000 titles. ⊠ *Via Montebello 20, Centro* ☎ *011/8125658* ⊕ *www.museonazionaledelcinema.it* 🎟 *Museum €5.20, elevator €3.62, combination ticket €6.80* ⊙ *Museum Tues.–Fri. and Sun. 9–8, Sat. 9 AM–11 PM; ticket sales end 75 mins before closing; elevator Tues.–Fri. and Sun. 10–8, Sat. 10 AM–11 PM.*

❾ **Museo Egizio.** The Egyptian Museum's superb collection includes statues of pharaohs and mummies and entire frescoes taken from royal tombs—all in all, it's one of the world's finest and largest museums of its kind. Look for the magnificent 13th-century BC statue of Ramses II and the fascinating Tomb of Kha. The latter was found intact with furniture, supplies of food and clothing, writing instruments, and a complete set of personal cosmetics and toiletries. Unfortunately, the museum's objects are not always displayed according to modern standards. Along with carefully constructed exhibits with detailed information in English and Italian you will also find rooms that resemble warehouses filled with objects, with little or no information identifying what they are. ⊠ *Via Accademia delle Scienze 6, Centro* ☎ *011/5617776* ⊕ *www.museoegizio. it* 🎟 *€6.50, €8 combined ticket includes Galleria Sabauda* ⊙ *Tues.–Sun. 8:30–7:30; ticket sales end 1 hr before closing.*

Fodor's Choice ★

❿ **Palazzo Carignano.** A baroque triumph by Guarino Guarini (the priest who designed several of Turin's most noteworthy structures), this redbrick palace was built between 1679 and 1685 and would play an important role in the 19th-century unification of Italy. Vittorio Emanuele II of Savoy (1820–78), united Italy's first king, was born within its walls, and Italy's first parliament met here from 1860 to 1865. The palace now houses the **Museo del Risorgimento,** a museum honoring the 19th-century movement for Italian unity. ⊠ *Via Accademia delle Scienze 5, Centro* ☎ *011/5621147* ⊕ *www.regione.piemonte.it/cultura/risorgimento* 🎟 *€5* ⊙ *Tues.–Sun. 9–7; ticket sales end 1 hr before closing.*

❸ **Palazzo Madama.** In the center of Piazza Castello, this castle was named for the Savoy queen Maria Cristina, who made it her home in the 17th century. The building incorporates the remains of a Roman gate with later medieval and Renaissance additions. Filippo Juvarra (1678–1736) designed the castle's monumental baroque facade. Open to the public are the atrium; the large central room known as Il Voltone, where a glass floor reveals the castle's Roman foundations; Juvarra's splendid baroque staircase; and the Salone del Senato, where you'll find temporary art exhibitions. ✉ *Piazza Castello, Centro* ☎ *011/4429912* ⊕ *www.comune. torino.it/palazzomadama* ✉ *Free, exhibitions €3.50* ☉ *Tues.–Fri. and Sun. 10–8, Sat. 10 AM–11 PM.*

➋ **Palazzo Reale.** This 17th-century palace, the former Savoy royal residence, is an imposing work of brick, stone, and marble that stands on the site of one of Turin's ancient Roman city gates. In contrast to its sober exterior, the palace's interior is swathed in luxurious, mostly rococo trappings, including tapestries, gilt ceilings, and sumptuous 17th- to 19th-century furniture. Behind the palace you can relax in the royal gardens. ✉ *Piazza Castello, Centro* ☎ *011/4361455* ✉ *Palace €5.50, gardens free* ☉ *Palace, Tues.–Sun. 8:30–6:15; accompanied visits leave every 40 mins; gardens, 9–1 hr before sunset.*

The **Armeria Reale** (Royal Armory), in a wing of the Royal Palace, holds one of Europe's most extensive collections of arms and armor. It's a must-see for connoisseurs. ✉ *Entrance at Piazza Castello 191, Centro* ☎ *011/ 543889* ✉ *€2.07* ☉ *Tues.–Sun. 10:30–7:30.*

➐ **Piazza San Carlo.** Surrounded by shops, arcades, fashionable cafés, and elegant baroque palaces, this is one of the most beautiful squares in Turin. In the center stands a statue of Duke Emanuele Filiberto of Savoy, victor at the battle of San Quintino in 1557. The melee heralded the peaceful resurgence of Turin under the Savoy after years of bloody dynastic fighting. The fine bronze statue erected in the 19th century is one of Turin's symbols.

> **need a break?**
>
> A chocolate lover's pilgrimage to Turin inevitably leads to **Al Bicerin** (✉ Piazza della Consolata 5, Centro ☎ 011/4369325 ☉ Closed Wed.), which first opened its doors in 1763. Cavour, Nietzsche, Puccini, and Dumas have all sipped here, and if you order the house specialty, the *bicerin* (a hot drink with layers of chocolate, coffee, and cream), you'll understand why. Don't be surprised if the friendly and energetic owner, Marité Costa, also tries to tempt you with one of her flavored *zabajoni* (warm eggnogs). Chocolate goodies, including chocolate-flavored pasta, are on sale in the café store. The historic **Caffè San Carlo** (✉ Piazza San Carlo 156, Centro ☎ 011/532586) is usually lively with locals gathered at the marble-top tables under the huge crystal chandelier.

➎ **San Carlo.** The ornate baroque facade of this 17th-century church was enhanced in the latter part of the 19th century to harmonize with the facade of the neighboring Santa Cristina. ✉ *Piazza San Carlo, south end of square, right corner Centro* ☎ *011/5620922* ☉ *Weekdays 8–noon and 4–6:30, Sat. 8–noon and 4–6, Sun. 9–12:45 and 4–6.*

➍ **San Lorenzo.** Architect Guarino Guarini was in his mid-60s when he began this church in 1668. The masterful use of geometric forms and the theatrical control of light and shadow show him working at his mature and confident best. Stand in the center of the church and look up into the cupola to enjoy the full effect. ✉ *Piazza Castello, Centro* ☎ *011/ 4361527* ☉ *Daily 8:30–noon and 4–7.*

need a
break?

The tiny café **Mulassano** (✉ Piazza Castello 15, Centro ☎ 011/ 547990), decorated with marble and finely carved wood panels, is famous for its *tramezzini* (small triangular sandwiches made with lightly toasted white bread), invented here in the 1920s. Popular with the pre- and post-theater crowd, the café also offers a unique roulette system for clients trying to decide on who pays the bill—ask the cashier for an explanation.

❻ Santa Cristina. Built in the mid-17th century, this church received a baroque-style face-lift by Juvarra in 1715. ✉ *Piazza San Carlo, south end of square, left corner Centro* ☎ *011/539281* ☉ *Daily 7–noon and 3–7.*

off the
beaten
path

GALLERIA CIVICA D'ARTE MODERNA E CONTEMPORANEA (GAM) – In 1863 Turin was the first Italian city to begin a public collection devoted to contemporary art. Housed in a modern building on the edge of downtown, a permanent display of more than 600 paintings, sculptures, and installation pieces provides an exceptional glimpse of how Italian contemporary art has evolved since the late 1800s. The Futurist, Pop, Neo Dada, and Arte Povera movements are particularly well represented, and the gallery has a fine video and art film collection. ✉ *Via Magenta 31, Centro* ☎ *011/5629911* ⊕ *www.gamtorino.it* ✉ *€5.50* ☉ *Tues.–Sun. 9–7.*

Along the Po

The Po River is narrow and unprepossessing here in Turin, only a hint of the broad waterway that it becomes as it flows eastward toward the Adriatic. It's flanked, however, by formidable edifices, a park, and a lovely pedestrian path.

a good
tour

Start on the east side of Piazza Vittorio Veneto, at the end of Via Po. Cross the river on Ponte Vittorio Emanuele I, the bridge leading to the church of **Gran Madre di Dio** ⑫ ▶, a replica of Rome's Pantheon. To reach the church of **Santa Maria del Monte** ⑬, follow Corso Moncalieri south and then wend your way upward to the top of the hill. Return to Corso Moncalieri and cross the next bridge downstream, Ponte Umberto I, to the **Parco del Valentino** ⑭, opened in 1856. One of the city's many pretty pedestrian paths, Viale Virgilio, runs parallel to the river and leads to the Castello del Valentino, reminiscent of castles on the Loire. Go south on Viale Virgilio to the **Borgo Medioevale** ⑮, a replica of a medieval hamlet and castle. From the park, catch a bus or taxi or just keep on walking south on Corso Massimo d'Azeglio for about 25 minutes to the **Museo dell'Automobile** ⑯, a low, modern building filled with the sleek, glamorous cars of yesteryear. Heading east, a short walk brings you to Via Nizza and the Lingotto, the location of the small but excellent collection of the **Pinacoteca Giovanni e Marella Agnelli** ⑰.

TIMING Four hours should be enough to allow you to cover the ground with ease, but if you are an automobile buff, allow more time for the Museo dell'Automobile.

CloseUp

THE OLYMPICS COME TO TURIN

TURIN PLAYS HOST to the 20th Winter Olympics in 2006, and the impact of the event will linger long after the international spotlight has moved on. With the Olympics as an impetus (and further spurred by recent crises in the auto industry—FIAT is one of the city's principal employers), Turin hopes to transcend its image as a city of industry to become identified as a dynamic cultural and recreational tourist destination.

The Olympic events themselves will take place between February 10 and 26 at several locations in the region. Turin will be the site for ice hockey, figure skating, and speed skating. Curling will be in nearby Pinerolo, and the remaining events will take place in mountain resorts to the west: Bardonecchia (snowboarding), Cesana–San Sicario (biathlon, women's downhill trials, bobsled, luge, and skeleton), Pregelato (ski-jumping, Nordic combination, and cross-country skiing), Sestriere (downhill skiing), and Sauze d'Oulx (freestyle skiing). Three Olympic Villages—in Turin, Sestriere, and Bardonecchia—will house 5,000 athletes, coaches, and national officials, while the 10,000 members of the media will stay in six media centers. One and a half million spectators are expected to attend the Games. If you want to be one of them, contact the Organizing Committee (TOROC, see Sports, below) to find out about event tickets, and Montagnedoc (see About the Restaurants& Hotels, above) for help with lodging and package deals.

The Olympics will have a significant long-term impact on Turin, bringing about nothing less than a fundamental reorientation of the city. The central train station, Porta Nuova, and the nearby historical center have long been the focal points of activity, but the Olympics have helped foster development both to the west and along the city's north—south axis. The Olympic Village and Olympic skating rink are being built near a former FIAT factory, the Lingotto, to the south of the city core. Once entirely an industrial zone, the area is being transformed into a residential and commercial center: new hotels and restaurants are sprouting up everywhere, and the Lingotto train station, little used after the closure of the FIAT factory, is being enlarged. After the Games, the Olympic Village will be turned into a university residence, and the skating arena will become part of Lingotto's convention center, which opened in 2003.

With the Olympics in mind, construction is under way on the city's first subway system—a section linking the Lingotto Olympic area with downtown Turin should be finished by late 2005. From the Porta Nuova station, the subway will head toward the now secondary Porta Susa station and then continue toward Turin's rapidly expanding western limits, with the first stage scheduled for completion in 2006. The intention is to transform Porta Susa into Turin's principal train station, making it a hub in Europe's high-speed train network, with fast links to Milan, Venice, Lyon, and the rest of Europe. Eventually the Porta Nuova station will close; although rumors circulate about turning it into a museum, like the d'Orsay train station in Paris, much water will flow under the political bridge before a final decision is made.

The impact of the Olympics will spread beyond the city limits. The most important developments in the mountain centers affect the range of skiing and hospitality services available: new runs and lifts are being added, new facilities are being built, and many of the existing hotels are receiving facelifts. All in all, you can expect the Piedmont to be a busy place through 2006.

What to See

☾ ⓯ **Borgo Medioevale.** Along the banks of the Po, this complex, built for a General Exhibition in 1884, is a faithful reproduction of a typical Piedmont village in the Middle Ages: craft shops, houses, a church, and stores cluster the narrow lanes, and in the center of the village the **Rocca Medioevale,** a medieval castle, provides the town's main attraction. ⊠ *Southern end of Parco del Valentino, San Salvario* ☎ *011/4431701* 🎫 *Village free, Rocca Medioevale €3* ⊘ *Village Apr.–Oct., daily 9–8; Nov.–Mar., daily 9–7; Rocca Medioevale Tues.–Sun. 9–7; groups of no more than 25 enter the castle every ½ hr; ticket counter closes at 6:15.*

▶ ⓬ **Gran Madre di Dio.** On the east bank of the Po, this neoclassical church is modeled after the Pantheon in Rome. It was built between 1827 and 1831 to commemorate the return of the house of Savoy to Turin after the fall of Napoléon's empire. ⊠ *Piazza Gran Madre di Dio, Borgo Po* ☎ *011/8193572* ⊘ *Mon.–Sat. 7:30–noon and 3:30–7, Sun. 7:30–1 and 3:30–7.*

★ ⓰ **Museo dell'Automobile.** No visit to car-manufacturing Turin would be complete without a pilgrimage to see perfectly conserved Bugattis, Ferraris, and Isotta Fraschinis. Here you'll get an idea of the importance of FIAT—and automobiles in general—to Turin's economy. There's a collection of antique cars from as early as 1896, and displays show how the city has changed over the years as a result of its premier industry. For the true automobile fan, there's even a section devoted to the history of car tires. (During 2004 and 2005, a yearlong closure for restoration is planned. At time of writing, the dates of this closure were as yet undetermined—call ahead before visiting.) ⊠ *Corso Unità d'Italia 40, Millefonti* ☎ *011/677666* ⊕ *www.museoauto.org* 🎫 *€5.50* ⊘ *Tues. and Wed., and Fri. and Sat. 10–6:30, Thurs. 10–8, and Sun. 10–8:30.*

⓮ **Parco del Valentino.** This pleasant riverside park is a great place to stroll, bike, or jog. Originally the grounds of a relatively simple hunting lodge, the park owes its present arrangement to Madama Maria Cristina of France, who received the land and lodge as a wedding present after her marriage to Vittorio Amedeo I of Savoy. With memories of 16th-century French châteaux in mind, she began work in 1620 and converted the lodge into a magnificent palace, the **Castello del Valentino.** The building, now home to the University of Turin's Faculty of Architecture, is not open to the general public. Next to the palace are botanical gardens, established in 1729, where local and exotic flora can be seen in a hothouse, herbarium, and arboretum. ⊠ *Parco del Valentino, San Salvario* ☎ *011/6707446 botanical gardens* 🎫 *Botanical gardens €3* ⊘ *Botanical gardens Apr.–Sept., weekends 9–1 and 3–7.*

⓱ **Pinacoteca Giovanni e Marella Agnelli.** This gallery was opened by Gianni Agnelli (1921–2003), the head of FIAT and patriarch of one of Italy's most powerful families, just four months before his death. The emphasis here is on quality rather than quantity: 25 works of art from the Agnelli private collection are on permanent display, along with temporary exhibitions. There are four magnificent scenes of Venice by Canaletto (1697–1768), two splendid views of Dresden by Canaletto's nephew,

Bernardo Bellotto (1720–1780), several works by Manet (1832–1883), Renoir (1841–1919), Matisse (1869–1954), and Picasso (1881–1973), and fine examples of the work of Italian Futurist painters Balla (1871–1958) and Severini (1883–1966). The gallery is located on the top floor of the **Lingotto,** a former FIAT factory that was completely transformed between 1982 and 2002 by architect Renzo Piano. The multilevel complex now contains two hotels, a shopping mall, several movie theaters, restaurants, and an auditorium. ⊠ *Via Nizza 230, Lingotto* ☎ *011/0062008* ⊕ *www. pinacoteca-agnelli.it* ⊠ *€4* ⊙ *Tues.–Sun. 9–7.*

⑬ Santa Maria del Monte. The church and convent standing on top of 150-foot Monte dei Cappuccini date from 1583. Don't be surprised if you find yourself in the middle of a wedding party: local couples often come here to have their pictures taken. Next to the church is the tiny **Museo Nazionale della Montagna,** a museum dedicated to mountains and to mountain climbing. ⊠ *Monte dei Cappuccini, above Corso Moncalieri, Borgo Po* ☎ *011/6604414 church, 011/6604104 museum* ⊕ *Museum, www.museomontagna.org* ⊠ *Church free; museum €5* ⊙ *Church, daily 9–noon, and 2:30–6; museum, daily 9–7.*

> **off the beaten path**

SASSI–SUPERGA COG TRAIN – The 18-minute ride from Sassi up the Superga hill is an absolute treat on a clear day. The view of Torino and the Alps from the top is magnificent, and the hill is crowned by the **Parco Naturale Collina Torinese,** a tranquil retreat from the bustle of the city. If you feel like a little exercise, you can walk back down to Sassi (approximately two hours) on one of the well-marked, wooded trails that start from the upper station. Other circular trails lead through the park and back to Superga, where mountain bikes are also available for rent. ⊠ *Piazza G. Modena, Sassi* ☎ *Cog train 011/5764733, bike rentals 011/8903667* ⊕ *www.gtt.to.it* ⊠ *Weekdays €1.55 one-way, €3.10 round-trip; weekends €2.58 one-way, €4.13 round-trip* ⊙ *Hourly service Mon. and Wed.–Fri. 9–noon and 2–8; hourly service Tues. 7 PM–midnight; hourly service weekends 9–8.*

BASILICA DI SUPERGA – Since 1731, Superga has been the burial place of kings. Visible from miles around, the thoroughly baroque church was designed by Juvarra in the early 18th century, and no less than 58 monuments of members of the Savoia family are to be found in the crypt. ⊠ *Strada della Basilica di Superga 73* ☎ *Basilica, 011/ 8980083, crypt and royal tombs, 011/8997456* ⊙ *Basilica: Apr.–Oct., daily 9–noon and 3–6; Nov.–Mar., daily 9–noon and 3–5. Crypt and royal tombs: Apr.–Oct., Mon.–Thurs. 9:30–1:30 and 2:30–6:30, Fri. 2:30–6:30, weekends 9:30–7:30; Nov.–Mar., weekends 9:30–1:30 and 2:30–6:30.*

Where to Stay & Eat

★ $$$–$$$$ ✕ **Al Garamond.** The ochre-color walls and the ancient brick vaulting set the stage in this small and brightly decorated restaurant. Traditional and innovative dishes of both meat and seafood are prepared with creative flair; you might try the tantalizing *rombo in crosta di patate al barbera* (turbot wrapped in sliced potatoes and baked with Barbera wine). For dessert, the mousse *di liquirizia e salsa di cioccolato bianco* (licorice mousse with white chocolate sauce) is a must, even if you don't usually like licorice. The level of service here is high, even by demanding Turin standards. ⊠ *Via G. Pomba 14, Centro* ☎ *011/8122781* ▤ *AE, MC, V* ⊙ *Closed Sun., Jan. 1–6, and 3 wks in Aug. No lunch Sat.*

$$$–$$$$ ✕ **Del Cambio.** Set in a palace dating from 1757, this is one of Europe's most beautiful and historic restaurants, with decorative moldings, mirrors, and hanging lamps that look just as they did when Italian national hero Cavour dined here more than a century ago. The cuisine draws heavily on Piedmontese tradition and is paired with fine wines of the region. Agnolotti with *sugo d'arrosto* (roast veal sauce) is a recommended first course. ⊠ *Piazza Carignano 2, Centro* ☎ *011/546690* 🎩 *Jacket and tie* ⌂ *Reservations essential* ▤ *AE, DC, MC, V* ⊙ *Closed Sun., Jan. 1–6, and 3 wks in Aug.*

$$$–$$$$ ✕ **Vintage 1997.** The first floor of an elegant town house in the center of Turin makes a fitting site for this sophisticated restaurant. You might try such specialties as *vitello tonnato alla nostra maniera* (roast veal with a light tuna sauce) or *code di scampi con costolette di coniglio su crema di scalogno* (prawn tails and rabbit in a scallion sauce). For the especially hungry gourmet there's the *menu del Vintage,* a 13-course feast that covers the full range of the restaurant's cuisine. There's an excellent wine list, with regional, national, and international vintages well represented. ⊠ *Piazza Solferino 16/h, Centro* ☎ *011/535948* ▤ *AE, DC, MC, V* ⊙ *Closed Sun. and 3 wks in Aug. No lunch Sat.*

$$–$$$ ✕ **Hosteria La Vallée.** Small and romantic, with elegant tableware and linens, select pieces of antique furniture, and carefully designed lighting, this restaurant tucked away in a quiet section of central Turin has developed a devoted clientele. Recommended are *agnello scottato all'aglio e rosmarino* (lamb grilled with garlic and rosemary) followed by *sformato di cacao con cuore di fondente* (warm chocolate pudding). ⊠ *Via Provana 3b, Centro* ☎ *011/8121788* ▤ *AE, MC, V* ⊙ *Closed Sun., Jan. 1–7, and Aug. No lunch.*

$$–$$$ ✕ **L'Agrifoglio.** This intimate local favorite has just 10 tables. Specialties change with the seasons, but you might find such delicacies as risotto *al Barbaresco* (with Barbaresco wine) and *agnolotti dal plin al sugo d'arrosto* on the menu. L'Agrifoglio stays open late for the after-theater and after-cinema crowd. ⊠ *Via Accademia Albertina 38, Centro* ☎ *011/837064* ▤ *AE, DC, MC, V* ⊙ *Closed Sun. and Mon. No lunch.*

$–$$ ✕ **Savoia.** The enthusiasm of chef and owner Mario Ferrero permeates three small rooms decorated with a few choice pictures and antique furniture. His kitchen turns out creative takes on Piedmontese specialties that change with the seasons. The bread and pasta are homemade, and the wine cellar is tended with equal care. ⊠ *Via Corta d'Appello 13, Centro* ☎ *011/4362288* ▤ *AE, DC, MC, V* ⊙ *Closed Sun. No lunch Sat.*

$ ✕ **Porto di Savona.** Look for this centuries-old tavern under the arcades of vast Piazza Vittorio Veneto, where it once served as a terminal for the Turin–Savona stagecoach line. The small street-level and upstairs dining rooms have a decidedly old-fashion air; the marble stairs are well worn, and the walls are decked with photos of Old Turin. Customers sit at long wooden tables to eat home-style Piedmontese cooking, including gnocchi with Gorgonzola and *bollito misto* (mixed boiled meats, appropriately served only in winter). The Barbera house wine is good. ⊠ *Piazza Vittorio Veneto 2, Centro* ☎ *011/8173500* ⊟ *MC, V* ⊘ *Closed Mon., 1st 2 wks in Jan., and last 2 wks in Aug. No lunch Tues.*

¢–$ ✕ **Locanda da Betty.** At this small and homey trattoria in the center of Turin traditional Piedmont cuisine is served to a usually packed house. The inexpensive four-course menu di degustazione is an especially good deal. ⊠ *Via Bogino 17/e, Centro* ☎ *011/8170583* ⊟ *No credit cards* ⊘ *Closed Sun.*

$$$$ ▥ **Grand Hotel Sitea.** The finest of Turin's four-star hotels, the Sitea is ideally located in the city's historic center. Decorated in a warmly classical style, the public areas and guest rooms are elegant and comfortable. As might be expected from a first-rate hotel, the level of service is a top-notch combination of courtesy and thoughtful efficiency. Weekend rates are available. ⊠ *Via Carlo Alberto 35, Centro 10123* ☎ *011/5170171* 🖶 *011/548090* ⊕ *www.thi.it* 🛏 *112 rooms, 2 suites* ⟂ *Restaurant, in-room data ports, minibars, cable TV with movies, bar, meeting rooms, parking (fee), some pets allowed* ⊟ *AE, DC, MC, V* ⦿ *BP.*

$$$$ ▥ **Le Meridien Art+Tech.** Designed by architect Renzo Piano, this luxury hotel is part of the renovation, begun in 1982, of the former Lingotto FIAT factory. Cherrywood paneling continues the style of the rest of the building, and the approach throughout is typically minimalist, with ultramodern fixtures and designer furniture decorating the rooms. The track on the roof, once used by FIAT to test its cars, is available to clients for jogging. ⊠ *Via Nizza 262, Lingotto 10126* ☎ *011/6642000* 🖶 *011/6642001* ⊕ *www.lemeridien.com* 🛏 *141 rooms, 1 suite* ⟂ *Restaurant, in-room data ports, in-room safes, minibars, cable TV with movies, bar, Internet, meeting rooms* ⊟ *AE, DC, MC, V* ⦿ *BP.*

$$ ▥ **Genio.** The Genio, like many hotels in Turin, has undergone a complete transformation in preparation for the Winter Olympics in 2006. Though steps away from the main train station, spacious and tastefully decorated rooms provide a quiet haven from the bustle of the city beyond. Best of all is the service, which resembles that of a friendly family-run inn rather than a big-city, business hotel. ⊠ *Corso Vittorio Emanuele II 47, Centro 10125* ☎ *011/6505771* 🖶 *011/6508264* ⊕ *www.hotelgenio.it* 🛏 *120 rooms, 3 suites* ⟂ *Minibars, meeting rooms, parking (fee)* ⊟ *AE, DC, MC, V* ⦿ *BP.*

$$ ▥ **La Maddalena.** It may be difficult to book a stay at this small bed-and-breakfast hotel (there are only three bedrooms), but it's worth a try. You'll be made to feel instantly at home by the proprietor, Maddalena Vitale, in this delightfully decorated and comfortably cluttered apartment not far from Turin's main train station. One room has a double bed and ensuite bathroom; the other two rooms have twin beds and private bathrooms across the hall. ⊠ *Via San Secondo 31, Centro 10128* 🖶🖶 *011/591267* ⊕ *www.iam-maddalena.com* 🛏 *3 rooms* ⟂ *In-room data ports; no a/c* ⊟ *No credit cards* ⦿ *BP.*

$$ ▥ **Liberty.** *Liberty* is a term used by Italians to refer to the art nouveau style, and this small, conveniently located hotel is true to its name, with

period-style furnishings and an ambience to match. It's a favorite of academics, artists, and others who appreciate its solid, old-fashion comfort enhanced by the Anfossi family's attentive courtesy. The hotel is on the upper floor of an otherwise poorly maintained building, so don't be put off by by the shabby entrance and the rickety elevator. ⊠ *Via Pietro Micca 15, Centro, 10121* ☎ *011/5628801* 🖶 *011/5628163* ⊕ *www.hotelliberty-torino.it* ↪ *35 rooms* ⚫ *Restaurant, bar* ☰ *AE, DC, MC, V* |◎| *BP.*

★ $$ ▦ **Victoria.** Rare style, attention to detail, and comfort are the hallmarks of this boutique hotel furnished and managed to create the feeling of a refined town house. The newer wing has a grand marble staircase and individually decorated guest rooms. The same attention to detail is found in the older rooms, and the sitting room and breakfast room are particularly attractive. ⊠ *Via Nino Costa 4, Centro, 10123* ☎ *011/5611909* 🖶 *011/5611806* ⊕ *www.hotelvictoria-torino.com* ↪ *94 rooms, 6 suites* ⚫ *Pool, bicycles, bar, parking (fee), no-smoking rooms; no a/c in some rooms* ☰ *AE, DC, MC, V* |◎| *BP.*

Nightlife & the Arts

The Arts

MUSIC Classical music concerts are held in the famous **Conservatorio Giuseppe Verdi** (⊠ Via Mazzini 11, Centro ☎ 011/8121268 ⊠ Piazza Bodoni, Centro ☎ 011/888470) throughout the year but primarily in winter. The **Settembre Musica Festival** (☎ 011/4424703), held for three weeks in September, highlights classical music; call for specifics. Traditional sacred music and some modern religious pieces are performed in the **Duomo** (⊠ Via Montebello 20, Centro ☎ 011/8154230) on Sunday evening; performances are usually advertised in the vestibule or in the local edition of Turin's nationally distributed newspaper, *La Stampa*. The Thursday edition comes with a supplement on music and other entertainment possibilities.

OPERA The **Teatro Regio** (⊠ Piazza Castello 215, Centro ☎ 011/8815557 🖶 011/8815214 ⊕ www.teatroregio.torino.it), one of Italy's leading opera houses, has its season from October to June. You can buy tickets for most performances (premieres sell well in advance) at the box office or on the Web site, where discounts are offered on the day of the show. It's also possible to book tickets via mail or fax. Payment for reservations must be made by credit card, international postal order, or eurocheque within 20 days of confirmation.

Nightlife

Two areas of Turin are enormously popular nightlife destinations: the Docks Dora, to the north of city center, and the Murazzi embankment, near the Ponte Vittorio Emanuele I, which is especially popular in summer.

The **Docks Dora** (⊠ Via Valprato 68, Madonna di Campagna ☎ 011/280251 ☉ Mon.–Sat. 9 PM–4 AM) is a complex of old warehouses that have been converted into artists' studios, gallery spaces, bars, cafés, and theaters. Live music and performances keep the area hopping, and the disco **Café Blue** serves up dance music all night long. Take the 51 bus from the Porta Susa train station or catch it heading north past the Duomo.

On the Murazzi, near the Ponte Vittorio Emanuele I, is **Jammin's** (⊠ Murazzi del Po 17, Centro ☎ 011/882869 ⊘ May–Sept., Mon.–Sat. 9 PM–4 AM), a popular disco with a mixed crowd; there's live music on Friday. A trendy meeting place for an aperitif or a pre-disco drink in the piazza at the end of Via Po is the wine bar **Caffè Elena** (⊠ Piazza Vittorio Veneto 5, Centro ☎ 011/8123341 ⊘ Thurs.–Tues. 9 AM–2 AM). Popular with Turin's younger crowd, **Hennessy** (⊠ Strada Traforo del Pino 23, Pino Torinese ☎ 011/8998733 ⊕ www.hennessyclub.com ⊘ Mon.–Sat. 10 PM–3 AM) is a large disco in an upscale residential district on the eastern side of the Po, with commercial and techno music. With music, often live, that ranges from British pop and rock to punk, crossover, soul, and reggae, **Barrumba** (⊠ Via San Massimo 1, Centro ☎ 011/883322 ⊕ www.barrumba.it ⊘ Thurs.–Sat. 10:30 PM–4:30 AM) is usually packed with a mix of young Turinese, university students, and visitors. South of the main train station is **Rockcity** (⊠ Via Bertini 2, San Salvario ☎ 011/3184737 ⊘ Thurs.–Sat. 10:30 PM–4 AM), where you'll find a smart crowd in their mid-twenties to mid-thirties listening to rock, techno, and commercial music.

Sports

Soccer

Turin's two professional soccer clubs, Juventus and Torino, play their games in the **Stadio delle Alpi** (⊠ 6 km [4 mi] northwest of city, Venaria). Juventus is one of Italy's most successful and most popular teams. There is fierce rivalry between its supporters and those of visiting clubs, especially Inter Milan and AC Milan. Home matches are usually played on Sunday afternoon during the season, which runs from late August to mid-May. It's possible to purchase tickets for Juventus and Torino games in any *tabaccheria* (tobacco shop) with a sign bearing a capital "T."

Winter Olympics

The **Organizing Committee for the Winter Olympics in Torino** (TOROC; ⊠ Corso Novara 96 Centro ☎ 011/6310511 🖷 011/6310500 ⊕ www. torino2006.org) is responsible for managing the sports events for the 2006 Games, as well as the opening and closing ceremonies. They have detailed schedules of the events and information about how to obtain tickets. Their comprehensive Web site, which includes an online ticket service, is the first place to check for games-related information.

Shopping

Chocolate

The tradition of chocolate making began in Turin in the early 17th century. Chocolate at that time was an aristocratic drink, but in the 19th century a Piedmontese invention made it possible to further refine cocoa, which could then be used to create solid bars and candies. The most famous of all Turin chocolates is the gianduiotto (with cocoa, sugar, and hazelnuts), first concocted in 1867. The tradition of making these delicious treats has been continued at the small, family-run **Peyrano** (⊠ Corso Moncalieri 47, Centro ☎ 011/6602202 ⊕ www.peyrano.it), where more than 80 types of chocolate confections are made and sold. **Stratta**

(✉ Piazza San Carlo 191, Centro ☎ 011/547920), one of Turin's most famous chocolate shops, has been around since 1836 and sells confections of all kinds—not just the chocolates in the lavish window displays but also fancy cookies, rum-laced fudges, and magnificent cakes.

Markets

Go to the famous **Balon Flea Market** (✉ Piazza Repubblica, Centro) on Saturday morning for excellent bargains on secondhand books and clothing and good browsing among stalls selling local specialties such as gianduiotti. (Be aware, however, that the market is also famous for its pickpockets.) The second Sunday of every month a special antiques market, appropriately called the **Gran Balon,** sets up shop in Piazza Repubblica.

Specialty Stores

Most people know that Turin produces more than 75% of Italy's cars, but they are often unaware that it's also a clothing manufacturing city. Top-quality boutiques stocking local, national, and international lines are clustered along Via Roma and Via Garibaldi. Piazza San Carlo, Via Po, and Via Maria Vittoria are lined with antiques shops, some—but not all—specializing in 18th-century furniture and domestic items.

Specialty food stores and delicatessens abound in central Turin. For a truly spectacular array of cheeses and other delicacies, try Turin's famous **Borgiattino** (✉ Via Accademia Albertina 38/a, Centro ☎ 011/8394686). For hand-rolled grissini—some as long as 4 feet—the bakery **Bersano** (✉ Via Barbaroux 5, Centro ☎ 011/5627579) is the best place in town. **Tabernalibraria** (✉ Via Bogino 5, Centro ☎ 011/836515) is a delightful combination of *enoteca* (wine bar), delicatessen, and bookstore.

THE COLLINE & SAVOY PALACES

As you head west from Turin into the Colline ("little hills"), castles and medieval fortifications begin to pepper the former dominion of the house of Savoy and the Alps come into better and better view. In the region lie the storybook medieval towns of Avigliana, Rivoli, and Saluzzo; 12th-century abbeys; and, farther west in the mountains, the ski resorts of Bardonecchia and Sestriere, two of the venues chosen for the 2006 Winter Olympics.

Stupinigi

⑱ *8 km (5 mi) southwest of Turin.*

The **Palazzina di Caccia,** in the town of Stupinigi, was built by Juvarra in 1729 as a hunting lodge for the house of Savoy. More like a sumptuous royal villa, its many wings, landscaped gardens, and surrounding forests give a clear idea of the level of style to which the Savoy were accustomed. This regal aspect was not lost on Paolina Buonaparte, who briefly held court here during her brother Napoléon's reign over Italy. Today the Palazzina houses the **Museo d'Arte e Ammobiliamento** (Museum of Art and Decoration), a vast collection of paintings and furniture gathered from numerous Savoy palaces in the Turin area. You can get there by taking Bus 41 from Turin's Porta Nuova train station.

⊠ *Via Principe Amedeo 7* ☎ *011/3581220* ☒ *€6.20* ⊗ *Apr.–Oct., Tues.–Sun. 10–7:30, last entrance at 6:50; Nov.–Mar., Tues.–Sun. 10–6, last entrance at 5:20.*

Rivoli

🔟 *16 km (10 mi) northwest of Stupinigi, 13 km (8 mi) west of Turin.*

The Savoy court was based in Rivoli in the Middle Ages. The 14th- to 15th-century **Casa del Conte Verde** (House of the Green Count) sits right in the center of town, and the richness of its decorations hints at the wealth and importance of the owner (and of Rivoli) during the period. Inside, a small gallery hosts temporary exhibitions. ⊠ *Via Fratelli Piol 8* ☎ *011/9563020* ☒ *Changes with exhibits* ⊗ *Changes with exhibits.*

The castle of Rivoli now houses the **Museo d'Arte Contemporaneo** (Museum of Contemporary Art). The building was begun in the 17th century and then redesigned but never finished by Juvarra in the 18th century; it was finally completed in the late 20th century by minimalist Turin architect Andrea Bruno. On display are changing international exhibitions and a permanent collection of 20th-century Italian art. To get to Rivoli from downtown Turin, take Tram 1 and then Bus 36. ⊠ *Piazzale Mafalda di Savoia* ☎ *011/9565222* ⊕ *www.castellodirivoli.org* ☒ *€6.50* ⊗ *Tues.–Thurs. 10–5, Fri.–Sun. 10–7.*

Abbazia di Sant'Antonio di Ranverso

🔟 *6 km (3½ mi) west of Rivoli, 23 km (14 mi) west of Turin.*

This abbey was originally a hospital, founded in the 12th century by the Hospitallers of St. Anthony to care for victims of St. Anthony's Fire, a painful medical condition brought on by consuming contaminated rye. Pilgrims came here over the centuries for cures and to offer thanks for a miraculous recovery. The 15th-century frescoes with their lifelike depictions of pilgrims and saints retain their original colors. ⊠ *Buttigliera Alta west of Rivoli, off SS25* ☎ *011/9367450* ☒ *€2.58* ⊗ *Nov.–Mar., Tues.–Sun. 9–12:30; Apr.–Oct., Tues.–Sun. 9–12:30 and 2–6; last entrance ½ hr before closing.*

Sacra di San Michele

★ 🔟 *20 km (13 mi) west of Abbazia di Sant'Antonio di Ranverso, 43 km (27 mi) west of Turin.*

Unless you plan a 14-km (9-mi) hike from the town of Avigliana, a car is essential for an excursion to the Abbey of St. Michael, perhaps best known as inspiration for the setting of Umberto Eco's novel *The Name of the Rose.* San Michele was built on Monte Pirchiriano in the 11th century to stand out: it occupies the most prominent location for miles around, hanging over a 3,280-foot bluff. When monks came to enlarge the abbey they had to build part of the structure on supports more than 90 feet high—an engineering feat that was famous in medieval Europe and is still impressive today. By the 12th century this important abbey controlled 176 churches in Italy, France, and Spain; one of the abbeys under its influence was Mont-Saint-Michel in France. Because of its strategic position it came under frequent attacks over the next five centuries and was eventually abandoned in 1622. It was restored in the late 19th and early 20th centuries.

From **Porta dello Zodiaco,** a splendid Romanesque doorway decorated with the signs of the zodiac, you climb 150 steps, past 12th-century sculptures, to reach the church. On the left side of the interior are 16th-century frescoes representing New Testament themes; on the right are depictions of the founding of the church. Go down to the crypt to see the 9th- to 12th-century chapels. ☎ *011/939130* ⊕ *www.sacradisanmichele.com* ✉ *€2.50* ◷ *Mar. 16–Oct. 15, Tues.–Sat. 9:30–12:30 and 3–6, Sun. 9:30–noon and 2:40–6; Oct. 16–Mar. 15, Tues.–Sat. 9:30–12:30 and 3–5, Sun. 9:30–noon and 2:40–5; mandatory accompanied visits leave every 30 mins.*

Saluzzo

㉒ *58 km (36 mi) southwest of Turin.*

The russet-brick town of Saluzzo—a flourishing medieval center and later seat of a Renaissance ducal court—is a well-preserved gem with narrow, winding streets, frescoed houses, Gothic churches, and elegant Renaissance palaces. A map with instructions for a walking tour of the town's sights is available from the local **tourist information office** (⊠ Via Griselda 6 ☎ 0175/46710 ⊕ www.comune.saluzzo.cn.it). The older and more interesting part of the town hugs a hilltop in the Po Valley and is crowned by **La Castiglia,** a 13th-century castle that has served as a prison since the 1820s.

The exterior of the **Castello di Manta,** 4 km (2½ mi) south of Saluzzo, is austere, but inside are frescoes and other decorations of the period. Knights and damsels from an allegorical poem written by Marquis Tommaso III of Saluzzo, humanist lord of the castle, parade in full costume in the 15th-century frescoes of the **Sala del Barone.** The castle sometimes hosts exhibits, at which time higher admission is charged. ⊠ *Via al Castello 14, Manta* ☎ *0175/87822* ✉ *€4.50* ◷ *Mar.–mid-Dec., Tues.–Sun. 10–1 and 2–6.*

Sestriere

㉓ *32 km (20 mi) east of Briançon, 93 km (58 mi) west of Turin.*

In the early 1930s, before skiing became a sport for commoners, the patriarch of the FIAT automobile dynasty had this resort built, with two distinctive tower hotels and ski facilities that have been developed into some of the best in the Alps. The resort lacks the charm of older Alpine centers, overdevelopment has added some eyesores, and the mountains don't have the striking beauty of those in Valle d'Aosta. But skiers have an excellent choice of trails, some of them crossing the border into France.

Where to Stay

$$$ 🏨 **Principi di Piemonte.** Large and elegant, this luxurious hotel sits on the slopes above the town, near the lifts and the town's golf course. Its

CloseUp

ALPINE SKIING AT A DISCOUNT

TO ITALIAN SKIERS, *a weeklong holiday on the slopes is known as a settimana bianca (white week). Ski resort hotels in the Piedmont and Valle d'Aosta* encourage these getaways by offering six- and seven-day packages, and though they're designed with the domestic market in mind, you can save some money by taking advantage of the offers.

Prices depend on location and the number of mints you want on your pillow; they are usually, though not always, based on half- or full-board packages. A week in Sestriere or Bardonecchia starts at around €300 per person for six nights with breakfast in a relatively simple hotel and can reach more than €1,200 per person for a week, full board, in deluxe accommodations. In Courmayeur you can expect to pay from around €250 to more than €1,350 per person for the same range of accommodations, and a similar package in Cogne will cost from €200 to

€1,000 per person. You can inquire about packages at any of the ski-destination hotels listed in this chapter; further listings are available from the towns' tourist offices (contact information is at the end of the chapter).

As an alternative, many skiing areas also offer apartment-rental services. With kitchens and room for two to six people (or more), these apartments can be a great way to cut your overall costs. Wherever you go, you should budget at least an additional €175 for a six-day ski pass, which is a minimal savings over the daily rate. Prices can vary considerably during the season; contact the local tourist offices or visit their Web sites for details.

---

secluded location heightens the sense of exclusivity, and though showing signs of age the hotel still attracts a stylish clientele. The restaurant and a cozy bar invite après-ski relaxation. ⊠ *Via Sauze 3/B, 10058* ☎ *0122/7941* 🖷 *0122/755411* ⊕ *www.framon-hotels.com* 🛏 *96 rooms, 4 suites* ⅗ *Restaurant, indoor pool, hot tub, sauna, Turkish bath, bar, meeting rooms, some pets allowed* ⊟ *AE, DC, MC, V* ⊗ *Closed early Apr.–June and Sept.–Nov.* ⅼ⊙⅃ *BP.*

$$-$$$ 🏨 **Hotel Cristallo.** Half of the rooms at this hotel opened in 2003 face the ski slopes of Sestriere, and the ski-lift base is just across the road. You'll find all the facilities you need for a stay in the mountains either in the hotel or just steps away from the lobby entrance. Rooms are elegantly and warmly furnished in the style of a modern ski lodge; ask for one with a terrace facing the view. ⊠ *Via Pinerolo 5, 10058* ☎ *0122/750707* 🖷 *0122/755152* ⊕ *www.newlinehotels.com* 🛏 *40 rooms* ⅗ *Restaurant, minibars, gym, sauna, Turkish bath, bar, Internet, parking (fee)* ⊟ *AE, DC, MC, V* ⅼ⊙⅃ *BP.*

$ 🏨 **Miramonti.** Nearly every room has a terrace at this pleasant, central, modern chalet. The ample, comfortable rooms are done in traditional mountain style, with lots of exposed wood and coordinated floral-print fabrics. ⊠ *Via Cesana 3, 10058* ☎ *0122/755333* 🖷 *0122/755375* *h.miramonti@tiscalinet.it* ⤳ *30 rooms* ☖ *Restaurant, minibars, exercise equipment, bar, meeting rooms, some pets allowed* ▤ *AE, DC, MC, V* ⦿ *BP.*

Sports & the Outdoors

SKIING At 6,670 feet, the **Sestiere ski resort** (☎ 0122/799411 for conditions) was built in the late 1920s under the auspices of Turin's Agnelli family. The slopes get good snow some years from November through May, other years from February through May. The **tourist office** (☎ 0175/46710 ⊕ www.comune.sestriere.to.it) in Sestriere provides complete information about lift tickets, ski runs, mountain guides, and equipment rentals, here and in neighboring towns such as Bardonecchia and Claviere. Its excellent Web site is also navigable in English. A quaint village with slate-roof houses, **Claviere** (⊠ 17 km [11 mi] west of Sestriere) is one of Italy's oldest ski resorts. Its slopes overlap with those of the French resort of Montgenèvre.

Bardonecchia

㉔ *36 km (22 mi) northwest of Sestriere, 89 km (55 mi) west of Turin.*

This sunny town is one of Italy's oldest winter ski resorts, attracting hardy sports enthusiasts from Turin since the 1920s. It's near the entrance to the Fréjus train and automobile tunnels.

Where to Stay

$$ 🏨 **Des Geneys-Splendid.** One of the best hotels in the area sits in a pine-filled private park near the town center. The 1930s style is evident in the arched windows on the ground floor, the stucco walls, and the long wrought-iron balconies. The public rooms are spacious and comfortable, and there's a playroom for children. ⊠ *Via Einaudi 21, 10052* ☎ *0122/99001* 📠 *0122/999295* ⊕ *www.desgeneys.com* ⤳ *53 rooms, 4 suites* ☖ *Restaurant, gym, piano bar, meeting rooms* ▤ *AE, DC, MC, V* ⊗ *Closed mid-Apr.–mid-June and mid-Sept.–Nov.* ⦿ *BP.*

$ 🏨 **Bucaneve.** Just a short walk from the ski lift, this small family-owned hotel is popular with the ski crowd. A cozy reading room and restaurant add to the allure of these affordable lodgings. ⊠ *Viale della Vecchia 2, 10052* ☎ *0122/999332* 📠 *0122/999980* ⊕ *www.hotelbucanevebardonecchia.it* ⤳ *20 rooms, 4 suites* ☖ *Restaurant, bar, Internet, some pets allowed; no a/c* ▤ *AE, MC, V* ⊗ *Closed Oct. and Nov.* ⦿ *BP.*

★ ¢ 🏨 **Asplenia.** Skiers love this small, modern version of a mountain chalet near the town center and the ski lifts. The ample rooms are comfortably furnished, with a small entryway and a balcony affording beautiful views. ⊠ *Viale della Vittoria 31, 10052* ☎ *0122/999870* 📠 *0122/901968* ⊕ *www.asplenia.it* ⤳ *17 rooms, 4 suites* ☖ *Restaurant, some pets allowed* ▤ *AE, DC, MC, V* ⦿ *BP.*

VALLE D'AOSTA

The unspoiled beauty of the highest peaks in the Alps, the Matterhorn and Monte Bianco, competes with the magnificent scenery of Italy's oldest national park in Valle d'Aosta, a semiautonomous, bilingual region tucked away at the border with France and Switzerland. Luckily, you don't have to choose—the region is small, so you can fit skiing, après-ski, and wild ibex into one memorable trip. The main Aosta Valley, largely on an east–west axis, is hemmed in by high mountains where glaciers have gouged out 14 tributary valleys, six to the north and eight to the south. A car is very helpful here, but take care: though distances are relatively short as the crow flies, steep slopes and winding roads add to your mileage and travel time.

Coming up from Turin, beyond Ivrea the road takes you through countryside that becomes hillier and hillier, passing through steep ravines guarded by brooding, romantic castles. Pont St. Martin, about 18 km (11 mi) north of Ivrea, is the beginning of bilingual (Italian and French) territory.

Bard

㉕ *65 km (40 mi) north of Turin.*

A few minutes beyond the French-speaking village of Pont St. Martin you pass through the narrow Gorge de Bard and reach the **Forte di Bard** (closed to the public), a 19th-century reconstruction of a fort that stood for eight centuries, serving the Savoys for six of them. In 1800 Napoléon entered Italy through this valley and used the cover of darkness to get his artillery units past the castle unnoticed. Ten years later he remembered this inconvenience and had the fortress destroyed.

St. Vincent

㉖ *28 km (17 mi) north of Bard, 93 km (58 mi) north of Turin.*

The town of St. Vincent has been a popular spa resort since the late 18th century. Its main draw these days is the **Casinò de la Vallée**, one of Europe's largest gambling casinos. You must present identification and be at least 18 years old to enter. Dress is elegant, with jacket and tie requested at the French gaming tables. ⊠ *Via Italo Mus 1* ☎ *0166/5221* ⊕ *www.casinodelavallee.it* ⊠ *Sun.–Fri. €5, Sat. €10* ⊘ *Mon.–Thurs. 2 PM–2:30 AM, Fri. 2 PM–3 AM, Sat. 2 PM–3:30 AM, Sun. 10:30 AM–2:30 AM.*

Where to Stay & Eat

★ **$$$** ✕ **Nuovo Batezar—da Renato.** This tiny restaurant of only eight tables ranks among the best in all of Italy. The ambience is rustic yet elegant, with arches and beamed ceilings enhanced by local antiques and fine crystal. The menu, which changes with the seasons, is Valdostana and Piemontese, with creative variations. Mushrooms, fish, fresh game, and truffles often play prominent roles. As a starter, try the homemade pasta or the *pazzarella* (a small pizza with porcini mushrooms, mozzarella, and truffles). ⊠ *Via Marconi 1, steps from casino* ☎ *0166/513164* ⊜ *Reservations essential* ▤ *AE, DC, MC, V* ⊘ *Closed Wed., 3 wks in June, and Nov. 15–30. No lunch weekdays.*

$$$$ ▦ **Billia.** A luxury belle-epoque hotel with faux-Gothic touches, the Billia is in a park in the middle of town and connects directly to the casino by a passageway. Half the rooms are done in modern and half in period decor, replete with all creature comforts. The hotel has extensive facilities, including a conference center and a health club. ⊠ *Viale Piemonte 72, 11027* ☎ *0166/5231* 🖷 *0166/523799* ⊕ *www.grandhotelbillia.com* ➲ *233 rooms, 7 suites* ♨ *Restaurant, tennis court, pool, health club, sauna, bar, convention center* ⊟ *AE, DC, MC, V* ⍥ *BP.*

$ 🖼 **Elena.** The central location is the selling point of this hotel near the casino. The spacious rooms, some with balconies and/or king-size beds, are decorated with color-coordinated fabrics in a comfortable modern style. ⊠ *Via Biavaz 2 (Piazza Zerbion), 11027* ☎ *0166/512140* 🖷 *0166/537459* ✉ *hotel.elena@libero.it* ➲ *46 rooms, 2 suites* ♨ *Restaurant, minibars, gym, sauna, Turkish bath, bar, meeting rooms, parking (fee), no-smoking rooms; no a/c in some rooms* ⊟ *AE, DC, MC, V* ⍥ *BP.*

Breuil-Cervinia/The Matterhorn

㉗ *30 km (18 mi) north of St. Vincent, 116 km (72 mi) north of Turin.*

Breuil-Cervinia is a village at the base of the **Matterhorn** (Monte Cervino in Italian; Mont Cervin in French). Like the village, the famous peak straddles the border between Italy and Switzerland, and all sightseeing and skiing facilities are operated jointly. Splendid views of the peak can be seen from **Plateau Rosa** and the **Cresta del Furggen,** both of which can be reached by cable car from the center of Breuil-Cervinia. Although many locals complain that the tourist facilities and condominiums in the village have changed the face of their beloved Breuil, most would agree that the cable car has given them access to climbing and off-trail skiing in ridges that were once inaccessible.

Where to Stay & Eat

★ $$$$ ✕🖼 **Les Neiges d'Antan.** In a pine wood at Perrères, just outside Cervinia, this small, rustic, family-run inn is quiet and cozy, with three big fireplaces and a nice view of the Matterhorn. An excellent restaurant ($$$–$$$$) serves French dishes and local specialties such as *zuppa Valpellinentze* (a hearty soup of bread, cabbage, and Fontina cheese) and an opulent antipasto (local salami, country pâté, *tomino* cheese, and much more). ⊠ *Località Perrères, 3½ km (2 mi) outside Cervinia, 11021* ☎ *0166/948775* 🖷 *0166/948852* ⊕ *www.lesneigesdantan.it* ➲ *21 rooms, 3 suites* ♨ *Restaurant, room TVs with movies, sauna, bar; no a/c* ⊟ *MC, V* ☾ *Closed May and June, and mid-Sept.–Nov.* ⍥ *BP.*

$–$$ ✕🖼 **Cime Bianche.** This calm, quiet mountain-lodge restaurant is one of the few dining spots in town to offer regional Valdostana cuisine, serving fonduta, polenta, and wild game as well as pastas in a rustic setting. The wood beams and tables are typical of a ski resort, but meals are produced with greater care than your average après-ski affairs. The commanding view covers the Matterhorn and Grandes Murailles. Reservations are highly recommended. There are also 15 guest rooms, all with balconies. ⊠ *Località La Vieille 44, toward the ski area, near the base lift* ☎ *0166/949046* 🖷 *0166/948061* ✉ *le.cime.bianche@galactica.it* ➲ *15 rooms* ♨ *Restaurant, bar; no a/c* ⊟ *MC, V* ☾ *Closed Mon., and May and June* ⍥ *BP.*

★ $$$$ 🖼 **Hermitage.** A marble relief of St. Theodolus at the entrance reminds you that this was the site of a hermitage, but asceticism has given way to comfort and elegance at what is now one of the most exclusive hotels in the region. It has the look of a relaxed but posh family chalet, with rustic antiques, petit-point upholstery, a fire always glowing in the enormous hearth, and a candlelit dining room. The bright bedrooms have balconies; suites have antique fireplaces and 18th-century furnishings. While here you can make use of the extensive health and beauty facilities and play golf (for half price) at the Cervinia Golf Club. ⊠ *Via Piolet 1, Località Chapellette, 11021* ☎ *0166/948998* 🖷 *0166/949032* ⊕ *www. hotelhermitage.com* ⤳ *30 rooms, 6 suites* ⅃ *Restaurant, golf privileges, indoor pool, health club, massage, sauna, bar, Internet, meeting rooms* ▤ *AE, DC, MC, V* ☉ *Closed May and June, and Sept. and Oct.* ¶Ol *BP.*

$$$ 🏨 **Bucaneve.** This small central hotel catering to longer stays is decorated in typical mountain style, with lots of wood paneling, cheery floral upholstery in spacious lounges, and terraces dripping with geraniums. Après-ski, there's a restaurant (half board is required) and a cozy bar with a big fireplace and pianist in the evening. ⊠ *Piazza Jumeaux 10, 11021* ☎ *0166/949119* 🖷 *0166/948308* ⊕ *www.hotel-bucaneve.it* ⤳ *20 rooms, 6 suites* ⅃ *Restaurant, gym, hot tub, sauna, piano bar, meeting rooms* ▤ *AE, MC, V* ☉ *Closed May–late June and Sept.–Nov., depending on weather* ¶Ol *MAP.*

$$$ 🏨 **Chalet Valdotain.** About 2 km (1 mi) outside of town on the road to Châtillon, this Alpine chalet has wooden balconies and snug rooms with terrific views of the Matterhorn. It's known for good food and a friendly atmosphere. ⊠ *Località Lago Bleu 2, 11021* ☎ *0166/949428* 🖷 *0166/ 948874* ⊕ *www.chaletvaldotain.it* ⤳ *35 rooms* ⅃ *Restaurant, pool, gym, sauna, Turkish bath, bar* ▤ *AE, DC, MC, V* ☉ *Closed May–mid-June and mid-Sept.–early Dec.* ¶Ol *BP.*

Sports & the Outdoors

CLIMBING Serious climbers can make the ascent of the **Matterhorn** from Breuil-Cervinia after registering with the local mountaineering officials at the **tourist office** (⊠ Via Carrel 29 ☎ 0166/949136). This climb is for skilled and experienced climbers only. Less demanding hikes follow the lower slopes of the valley of the River Marmore, to the south of town.

SKIING Because its slopes border the Cervino glacier, this resort at the foot of the Matterhorn offers year-round skiing. Sixty lifts and a total of almost 200 mi of ski runs ranging from beginner to expert make the area one of the best and most popular in Italy. Contact the **Breuil-Cervinia tourist office** (☎ 0166/949136) for information.

Castello Fénis

★ ㉘ *11 km (7 mi) west of St. Vincent, 104 km (65 mi) north of Turin.*

The best-preserved medieval fortress in Valle d'Aosta, the many-turreted Castello Fénis was built in the mid-14th century by Aimone di Challant, a member of a prolific family related to the Savoys. The castle, which used a double ring of walls for its defense, is the sort imagined by schoolchildren, with pointed towers, portcullises, and spiral staircases. The 15th-century courtyard surrounded by wooden balconies is elegantly decorated with well-preserved frescoes. Inside you can see the kitchen, with an enormous fireplace that provided central heat in winter, the armory, and the spacious, well-lighted rooms used by the lord and lady of the manor. If you have time to visit only one castle in Valle d'Aosta, this should be it. ☎ 0165/764263 ⬜ €5 ☉ Mar.–June, daily 9–6:30; July and Aug., daily 9–7:30; Sept., daily 9–6:30; Oct.–Feb., Wed.–Mon. 10–5; maximum of 25 people allowed to enter every ½ hr.

| en route | The highway continues climbing through Valle d'Aosta to the town of Aosta itself. The road at this point is heading almost due west, with rivulets from the wilderness reserve Parco Nazionale del Gran Paradiso streaming down from the left to join the Dora Baltea River, one of the major tributaries of the Po and an increasingly popular spot for rafting. Be careful driving here in late spring, when melting snow can turn some of these streams into torrents. |

Aosta

❷❾ 12 km (7 mi) west of Castello Fénis, 113 km (70 mi) north of Turin.

Aosta stands at the junction of two of the important trade routes that connect France and Italy—the valleys of the Rhône and the Isère. Its significance as a trading post was recognized by the Romans, who built a garrison here in the 1st century BC. At the eastern entrance to town, in the Piazza Arco d'Augusto and commanding a fine view over Aosta and the mountains, is the **Arco di Augusto** (Arch of Augustus), built in 25 BC to mark Rome's victory over the Celtic Salassi tribe. (The sloping roof was added in 1716 in an attempt to keep rain from seeping between the stones.) The present-day layout of streets in this small city tucked away in the Alps more than 644 km (400 mi) from Rome is the clearest example of Roman street planning in Italy. Well-preserved Roman walls form a perfect rectangle around the center of Aosta, and the regular pattern of streets reflects its role as a military stronghold. St. Anselm, born in Aosta, later became archbishop of Canterbury in England.

The **Collegiata di Sant'Orso** is the sort of church that has layers of history in its architecture. Originally there was a 6th-century chapel on this site founded by the Archdeacon Orso, a local saint. Most of this structure was destroyed or hidden when an 11th-century church was erected over it. This church, in turn, was encrusted with Gothic, and later baroque, features, resulting in a jigsaw puzzle of styles, but, surprisingly, not a chaotic jumble. The 11th-century features are almost untouched in the crypt, and if you go up the stairs on the left from the main church you can see the 11th-century frescoes (ask the sacristan for entrance). These restored frescoes depict the life of Christ and the Apostles: although only the tops are visible, you can see the expressions on the faces of the disciples. Take the outside doorway to the right of the main entrance to see the church's crowning glory, its 12th-century **cloister.** Next to the church, it's enclosed by some 40 stone columns with masterfully carved capitals depicting scenes from the Old and New Testaments and the life of St. Orso. The turrets and spires of Aosta peek out above. ⊠ Via Sant'Orso ☎ 0165/40614 ☉ Apr.–Sept., daily 9–5; Oct.–Mar., daily 10–5.

The huge **Roman Porta Pretoria,** regally guarding the city, is a remarkable relic from the Roman era. The area between the massive inner and outer gates was used as a small parade ground for the changing of the guard. ⊠ *West end of Via Sant'Anselmo.*

The 72-foot-high ruin of the facade of the **Teatro Romano** guards the remains of the 1st-century BC amphitheater, which once held 20,000 spectators. Only a bit of the outside wall and seven of the amphitheater's original 60 arches remain, and these are built into the facade of the adjacent convent of the sisters of San Giuseppe. The convent will usually allow you in to see these arches (ask at the entrance). ⊠ *Via Anfiteatro 4.*

Aosta's **Duomo** dates from the 10th century, but all that remains from that period are the bell towers. The decoration inside is primarily Gothic, but the main attraction of the cathedral predates that era by 1,000 years: a carved ivory diptych portraying the Roman Emperor Honorius and dating from AD 406 is among the many ornate objects housed in the treasury. ⊠ *Via Monsignor de Sales* ☎ *0165/40251* ☽ *Treasury Apr.–Sept., Tues.–Sun. 9–11:30 and 3–5:30; Oct.–Mar., Sun. 3–5:30.*

Where to Stay & Eat

$$$ ✕ **Vecchio Ristoro.** At this centrally located converted mill furnished with antiques and a large ceramic stove the chef-proprietor takes pride in creative versions of regional favorites. Among them may be *marbrè di bollito misto con bagnet verde* (terrine of mixed boiled meats with a parsley and anchovy sauce) and *carrè d'agnello gratinato alle erbe* (grilled loin of lamb in a pastry and herb crust). ⊠ *Via Tourneuve 4* ☎ *0165/33238* ▭ *AE, DC, MC, V* ☽ *Closed Sun., June, and 1 wk in Nov. No lunch Mon.*

$$–$$$ ✕ **Taverna Nando.** A wine cellar with wooden floors and vaulted ceilings, this family-run tavern is in the center of Aosta, and it has a terrace for outdoor dining. Try regional specialties such as fonduta, carbonada, and *cervo* (venison) with mushrooms. ⊠ *Via de Tillier 41* ☎ *0165/44455* ▭ *AE, DC, MC, V* ☽ *Closed Mon. and June 20–July 10.*

$–$$ ✕ **La Brasserie du Commerce.** Small, lively, and informal, this place is in the heart of Aosta, near central Piazza E. Chanoux. On a sunny summer day try to get a table on the terrace. Typical valley dishes such as fonduta are on the menu, as well as many vegetable dishes and salads. ⊠ *Via de Tillier 10* ☎ *0165/35613* ⟑ *Reservations not accepted* ▭ *AE, DC, MC, V* ☽ *Closed Sun.*

$ ✕ **Praetoria.** Just outside the Porta Pretoria, this simple and unpretentious restaurant serves hearty local food. The pasta is homemade, and all of the menu offerings, such as *crespelle alla valdostana* (crepes with cheese and ham), are strictly traditional. ⊠ *Via S. Anselmo 9* ☎ *0165/44356* ▭ *AE, DC, MC, V* ☽ *Closed Thurs.*

$$–$$$ ⊡ **Holiday Inn Aosta.** This modern, comfortable hotel has the advantages of a central location and rooms with the chain's predictable amenities. There's local color, however, in the attractive Provençal fabrics and the views of the mountains. Rooms equipped for people with disabilities are available. ⊠ *Corso Battaglione Aosta 30, 11100* ☎ *0165/236356* ⊟ *0165/236837* ⊕ *www.sixcontinentshotels.com* ⇔ *45 rooms, 5 suites*

⛴ *Restaurant, room TVs with movies, bar, business services, some pets allowed (fee), no-smoking rooms* ☱ *AE, DC, MC, V* ⑩ *BP.*

★ **$$** ⊡ **Milleluci.** This small and inviting family-run hotel sits on a hillside overlooking Aosta, 1 km (½ mi) north of town. A huge brick hearth and rustic wooden beams highlight the lounge. Bedrooms, some with balconies, are bright and pleasantly decorated and have good views of the city and mountains. Ten rooms are reserved for nonsmokers and some rooms are equipped for people with disabilities. The hotel provides breakfast only. ⊠ *Località Porossan Roppoz 15, 11100* ☏ *0165/235278* ⎙ *0165/235284* ⊕ *www.hotelmilleluci.com* ⟿ *26 rooms, 5 suites* ⛴ *Tennis court, pool, sauna, bar, Internet, no-smoking rooms; no a/c* ☱ *AE, DC, MC, V* ⑩ *BP.*

¢ ⊡ **Casa Ospitaliera del Gran San Bernardo.** In a castle given as a gift to the Order of St. Bernard by Amedeo of Savoy in 1137, this simple pension 15 km (8 mi) north of Aosta, still part of a monastery and run by monks, is a good base for cross-country skiing or hiking. The no-frills accommodation, the hearty food included in the full meal plan, and the chance to sleep in a 12th-century castle at bargain prices all add to the charm of this place from another time. ⊠ *Rue de Flassin 3, 11010 Saint-Oyen* ☏ *0165/78247* ⎙ *0165/789512* ⟿ *15 rooms* ⛴ *No a/c, no room phones, no room TVs* ☱ *No credit cards* ⊘ *Closed May* ⑩ *FAP.*

Nightlife & the Arts

Each summer a series of **concerts** is held in different venues around the city. Organ recitals in July and August attract performers of world renown. Call the **tourist board** (⊠ Piazza E. Chanoux 8 ☏ 0165/236627) for information.

Shopping

Aosta and the surrounding countryside are famous for wood carvings and wrought iron. There's a permanent **crafts exhibition** in the arcades of Piazza E. Chanoux, in the heart of Aosta; it's a good place to pick up a bargain. Each year on the last two days of January all of Aosta turns out for the **Sant'Orso Fair,** where all sorts of crafts are on sale, including handmade lace from nearby Cogne, carved wood and stonework, and brightly colored woolens.

Courmayeur/Monte Bianco

★ ㉚ *35 km (21 mi) northwest of Aosta, 150 km (93 mi) northwest of Turin.*

The main attraction of Courmayeur is a knock-'em-dead view of Europe's tallest peak, **Monte Bianco** (Mont Blanc). Jet-set celebrities flock here, following a tradition that dates from the late 17th century, when Courmayeur's natural springs first began to draw visitors. The spectacle of the Alps gradually surpassed the springs as the biggest draw (the Alpine letters of the English poet Percy Bysshe Shelley were almost advertisements for the region), but the biggest change came in 1965 with the opening of the Mont Blanc tunnel. Since then, ever increasing numbers of travelers have passed through the area.

Luckily, planners have managed to keep some restrictions on wholesale development within the town, and its angled rooftops and immaculate cobblestone streets maintain a cozy (if prepackaged) feeling. There is no train directly into Courmayeur, so if you don't have a car you'll need to bus it from nearby Pré-Saint-Didier, which is accessible by train from Aosta.

From La Palud, a small town 4 km (3½ mi) north of Courmayeur, you can catch the cable car up to the top of Monte Bianco. In summer, if you get the inclination, once up top you can switch cable cars and descend into Chamonix, in France. In winter you can ski parts of the route off-piste. The Funivie La Palud whisks you up first to the Pavillon du Mont Fréty—a starting point for many beautiful hikes—and then to the Rifugio di Torino, before arriving at the viewing platform at **Punta (Pointe) Helbronner** (more than 11,000 feet), which is also the border post with France. Monte Bianco's attraction is not so much its shape (much less distinctive than that of the Matterhorn) as its expanse and the vistas from the top.

The next stage up—only in summer—is on the **Télépherique de L'Aiguille du Midi,** as you pass into French territory. The trip is particularly impressive: you dangle over a huge glacial snowfield (more than 2,000 feet below) and make your way slowly to the viewing station above Chamonix. It's one of the most dramatic rides in Europe. From this point you're looking down into France, and if you change cable cars at the Aiguille du Midi station you can make your way down to Chamonix itself. The return trip covers the same route. Schedules are unpredictable, depending on weather conditions and demand; you can get information by sending an e-mail to **cable car operators** (info@montebianco.com) or calling the **Courmayeur tourist office** (☏ 0165/842060). ✉ *Fraz. La Palud 22* ☏ *0165/89925 Italian side (La Palud), 00/33450536210 French side (Aiguille du Midi)* ⊕ *www.montebianco.com* 🖆 *€11 round-trip to Pavillon du Mont Fréty, €32 round-trip to Helbronner, €48 round-trip to Aiguille du Midi, €75 round-trip to Chamonix* ☼ *Call for hrs. Closed mid-Oct.–mid-Dec., depending on demand and weather.*

Where to Stay & Eat

★ $$–$$$$ ✕ **Cadran Solaire.** This warm and inviting restaurant is in the town center, in what was the oldest tavern in Courmayeur. It's been renovated by the Garin family in such a way as to highlight the 17th-century stone vault, the old wooden floor, and the huge fireplace. The menu offers seasonal specialties and innovative interpretations of regional dishes, and the restaurant's bar is a cozy and popular place for a before-dinner drink. ✉ *Via Roma 122* ☏ *0165/844609* ⌲ *Reservations essential* 🟰 *AE, MC, V* ☼ *Closed Tues., May, and Oct.*

★ $$ ✕ **Maison de Filippo.** Here you'll find country-style home cooking in a mountain house with lots of atmosphere, furnished with antiques, farm tools, and bric-a-brac of all kinds. There's a set menu only, which includes an abundance of antipasti and a tempting choice of local soups and pasta dishes, followed by a wide range of second courses. Cheese, dessert, and fresh fruit complete the meal. Reserve in advance, for it's one of the most popular restaurants in Valle d'Aosta. ✉ *Entrèves* ☏ *0165/869797* ⌲ *Reservations essential* 🟰 *MC, V* ☼ *Closed Tues., mid-May–June, and Oct. and Nov.*

$$$$ ✕▥ **Royal e Golf.** A grand Courmayeur landmark in the town center, the Royal rises high above the surrounding town. Decorated with terraces, flowers, and wood paneling, it is the most elegant, upscale spot in town, with modern rooms and an evening piano bar. The hotel caters to longer stays with half- or full-board service. The main restaurant, Grill Royal e Golf, is a sight in itself, locally renowned for such culinary creations as frogs' legs in a basil fish broth. Reservations (and jacket and tie) are required at the Grill, which is open for dinner only and is closed Monday. ✉ *Via Roma 87, 11013* ☎ *0165/831611* 🖷 *0165/842093* ✐ *hotelroyalgolf@ventaglio.com* ↱ *80 rooms, 6 suites* ⚬ *2 restaurants, minibars, pool, health club, sauna, Turkish bath, bar, piano bar, Internet, meeting rooms, some pets allowed, no-smoking rooms; no a/c* ▤ *AE, DC, MC, V* ☾ *Closed wk after Easter–mid-June and mid-Sept.–Nov.* ⏍ *MAP.*

$$$$ ▥ **Pavillon.** This elegant modern version of a rustic chalet comes complete with warm golden-tone wood paneling, stylish furnishings, and a clubby bar. Some stunning contemporary stained glass decorates the public areas and the well-equipped health center. ✉ *Strada Regionale 62, 11013* ☎ *0165/846120* 🖷 *0165/846122* ⊕ *www.pavillon.it* ↱ *40 rooms, 10 suites* ⚬ *Restaurant, indoor pool, health club, hot tub, massage, sauna, steam room, bar, meeting room, some pets allowed; no a/c* ▤ *AE, DC, MC, V* ☾ *Closed end Apr.–June 15, Oct. and Nov.* ⏍ *FAP.*

$$$ ▥ **Auberge de la Maison.** All the rooms at this cozy and modern hotel have views of Monte Bianco. A massage here can be the perfect ending to a day of hiking or skiing. ✉ *Via Passerin d'Entrèves, 11013* ☎ *0165/ 869811* 🖷 *0165/869759* ⊕ *www.aubergemaison.it* ↱ *30 rooms, 3 suites* ⚬ *Gym, hot tub, massage, sauna; no a/c* ▤ *AE, MC, V* ☾ *Closed May* ⏍ *BP.*

★ **$$$** ▥ **Palace Bron.** In a lovely stand of pines above the town, this elegant and tranquil hotel is an ideal spot to relax. Guest rooms are bright and pretty, furnished with antiques and local designs. The sitting room has picture windows with magnificent views of Monte Bianco, and for chilly nights the high-quality restaurant offers a cozy fireplace. In winter there's a free shuttle between the hotel, the town center, and ski lifts. ✉ *Via Plan Gorret 41, 11013* ☎ *0165/846742* 🖷 *0165/844015* ⊕ *www. palacebron.it* ↱ *26 rooms, 1 suite* ⚬ *Restaurant, minibars, bar, piano bar, meeting room, some pets allowed (fee); no a/c* ▤ *AE, DC, MC, V* ☾ *Closed Apr.–mid-June and mid-Sept.–Nov.* ⏍ *BP.*

$$$ ▥ **Villa Novecento.** Run with the friendly charm and efficiency of Franco
Fodor's Choice Cavaliere and his son Stefano, the Novecento is a peaceful haven near
★ Courmayeur's busy center. In keeping with the style of a comfortable mountain lodge, colors throughout are warm and muted. The lounge, with deeply cushioned chairs, is lighted by a fire in winter, and the guest rooms are soothingly furnished with traditional fabrics, wooden fixtures, and early-19th-century prints. The hotel restaurant, with only a few extra tables for nonguests, serves creative adaptations of traditional cuisine; it's a good choice for a relaxed evening meal. ✉ *Viale Monte Bianco 64, 11013* ☎ *0165/843000* 🖷 *0165/844030* ⊕ *www.villanovecento. it* ↱ *24 rooms, 2 suites* ⚬ *Restaurant, gym, sauna, Turkish bath, bar,*

meeting rooms, some pets allowed; no a/c ⊟ *AE, DC, MC, V* ☽ *Closed May and Oct.* ⬦❘ *BP.*

$$ ▣ **Croux.** This bright, comfortable hotel is near the town center on the road leading to Monte Bianco. Friendly management makes it feel like a more intimate place than you'd expect for its size. Half the rooms have balconies, the other half great views of Monte Bianco. ⊠ *Via Croux 8, 11013* ☎ *0165/846735* 🖷 *0165/845180* ⊕ *www.hotelcroux.it* ⤹ *33 rooms* ⬦ *Bar, sauna, Turkish bath; no a/c* ⊟ *AE, DC, MC, V* ☽ *Closed mid-Apr.–mid-June and mid-Sept.–mid-Dec.* ⬦❘ *BP.*

Sports & the Outdoors

SKIING Courmayeur pales in comparison to its French neighbor, Chamonix, in both number (it has only 24) and quality of trails. Nevertheless, especially with good natural snow cover, the trails and Alpine vistas are spectacular. A huge gondola leads from the center of Courmayeur to Plan Checrouit, where gondolas and lifts lead to the actual ski slopes. The skiing around Monte Bianco is particularly good, and the off-piste options are among the best in Europe. The off-piste routes from Cresta d'Arp (the local peak) to Dolonne, and from the La Palud area into France, should be done with a guide. Contact the **Funivie Courmayeur/Mont Blanc** (☎ 0165/846658) for complete information about lift tickets, ski runs, and weather conditions. For Alpine guide services contact the **Società delle Guide Alpine** (⊠ Strada Villair 2 ☎ 0165/842064 ⊕ www. guidecourmayeur.com) in Courmayeur.

SPORTS CENTER The **Courmayeur Sports Center** presents you with numerous athletic alternatives to skiing. There are courts for squash, tennis, basketball, and volleyball, as well as a rock-climbing wall, a skating rink, a five-to-a-side soccer field, and an indoor golf course. ⊠ *Via dello Stadio 2* ☎ *0165/844096* ⊕ *www.sportcourmayeur.com* ☽ *Daily 10* AM–11 PM.

Cogne & the Parco Nazionale del Gran Paradiso

㉛ *52 km (32 mi) southeast of Courmayeur, 134 km (83 mi) northwest of Turin.*

Cogne is the gateway to the Parco Nazionale del Gran Paradiso. This huge park, once the domain of King Vittorio Emanuele II (1820–78) and bequeathed to the nation after World War I, is one of Europe's most rugged and unspoiled wilderness areas, with wildlife and many plant species protected by law. It's open free of charge throughout the year and is managed by a park board, the **Ente Parco Nazionale Gran Paradiso** (⊠ Via della Rocca 47, Turin, 10123 ☎ 011/8606211 ⊕ www.parks.it/parco. nazionale.gran.paradiso). Try to visit in May, when spring flowers are in bloom and most of the meadows are clear of snow. This is one of the few places in Europe where you can see the ibex (a mountain goat with horns up to 3 feet long) and the chamois (a small antelope).

Sports & the Outdoors

HIKING There's wonderful hiking to be done here, both on daylong excursions and longer journeys with overnight stops in the park's mountain refuges. The **Cogne tourist office** (⊠ Piazza E. Chanoux 36 ☎ 0165/

74040 ⊕ www.cogne.org) has a wealth of information and trail maps to help.

FORTIFIED CITIES OF THE PO PLAIN

Southeast of Turin, in the hilly wooded area around Asti known as the Monferrato and farther south in a similar area around Alba known as the Langhe, the rolling landscape is a patchwork of vineyards and dark woods dotted with hill towns and castles. This is wine country, producing some of Italy's most famous reds and sparkling whites. And hidden away in the woods are the secret places where hunters and their dogs unearth the precious, aromatic truffles worth their weight in gold at Alba's truffle fair. To the north of these hills, across the Po, are the cities of the plain. Beyond them lies Lago Maggiore, and eastward, across the Ticino River, is Milan.

Asti

32 *60 km (37 mi) southeast of Turin.*

Asti is best known outside of Italy for its wines—excellent reds as well as the famous sparkling white Spumante—but its strategic position on trade routes between Turin, Milan, and Genoa has given it a broad economic base. In the 12th century Asti began to develop as a republic, at a time when other Italian cities were also flexing their economic and military muscles. It flourished in the following century, when the inhabitants began erecting lofty **towers** (⊠ West end of Corso Vittorio Alfieri) for its defense, giving rise to the medieval nickname "city of 100 towers." In the center of Asti some of these remain, among them the 13th-century **Torre Comentina** and the well-preserved **Torre Troyana,** a tall, slender tower attached to the **Palazzo Troya.** The 18th-century church of **Santa Caterina** has incorporated one of Asti's medieval towers, the **Torre Romana** (itself built on an ancient Roman base), as its bell tower. Corso Vittorio Alfieri is Asti's main thoroughfare, running west–east across the city. This road, known in medieval times as Contrada Maestra, was built by the Romans.

The **Duomo** in Asti is an object lesson in the evolution of the Gothic architectural style. Built in the early 14th century, it's decorated so as to emphasize geometry and verticality: pointed arches and narrow vaults are counterbalanced by the earlier, Romanesque attention to balance and symmetry. The porch on the south side of the cathedral facing the square was built in 1470 and represents Gothic at its most florid and excessive. ⊠ *Piazza Cattedrale* ☏ *0141/592924* ⊘ *Daily 8:30–noon and 3:30–5:30.*

The Gothic church of **San Secondo** is dedicated to Asti's patron saint, reputedly decapitated on the spot where the church now stands. Secondo is also the patron of the city's favorite folklore and sporting event, the annual **Palio,** the colorful medieval-style horse race (similar to Siena's) held each year on the third Sunday of September in the vast Campo del Palio to the south of the church. ⊠ *Piazza San Secondo, south of*

Corso Vittorio Alfieri ☎ *0141/530066* ☺ *Mon.–Sat. 10:45–noon and 3:30–5:30, Sun. 3:30–5:30.*

Where to Stay & Eat

$$$
Fodor'sChoice
★

✕ **Gener Neuv.** The family-run Gener Neuv is one of Italy's best restaurants. The setting on the bank of the Tanaro River is splendid, and the menu of regional specialties is served with rustic elegance. Your choices may include agnolotti *ai tre stufati* (with a filling of ground rabbit, veal, and pork), and to finish, *composta di prugne e uva* (prune and grape compote). Fixed-price menus are available with or without the wine included. As you might expect, the wine list is first-rate. ✉ *Lungo Tanaro 4* ☎ *0141/557270* 🖷 *0141/436723* 🗐 *AE, DC, MC, V* ☺ *Closed Aug. and Mon., no dinner Sun.; Jan.–July, closed Sun.*

$$
✕ **L'Angolo del Beato.** Regional specialties such as bagna cauda and *tagliolini al ragu di anatra* (pasta with a duck sauce) are the main attraction at this central Asti restaurant, housed in a building that dates back to the 12th century. There's also a good wine list. ✉ *Via Guttuari 12* ☎ *0141/531668* 🗐 *AE, DC, MC, V* ☺ *Closed Sun., last wk of Dec., 1st wk of Jan., and 3 wks in Aug.*

$$
🏨 **Reale.** This hotel in a 19th-century building is conveniently located on Asti's main square. Rooms are spacious though somewhat eclectically decorated. ✉ *Piazza Alfieri 6, 14100* ☎ *0141/530240* 🖷 *0141/ 34357* ⊕ *www.hotel-reale.com* 🛏 *25 rooms, 2 suites* ♻ *Cable TV, parking (fee), some pets allowed; no a/c* 🗐 *AE, DC, MC, V* ⦿ *BP.*

$
🏨 **Rainero.** An older hotel near the train station, Rainero has been under the same family management for three generations. It's fitted with cheerful modern furnishings but has no restaurant. Ask for one of the "green rooms," done out in a green-and-white decor. ✉ *Via Cavour 85, 14100* ☎ *0141/353866* 🖷 *0141/594985* ⊕ *www.hotelrainero.com* 🛏 *53 rooms, 2 suites* ♻ *Bar, Internet, meeting rooms, parking (fee), some pets allowed* 🗐 *AE, DC, MC, V* ☺ *Closed Jan. 1–15* ⦿ *BP.*

Festivals

September is a month of fairs and celebrations in Asti, and the **Palio di Asti,** a horse race run through the streets of town, highlights the festivities. First mentioned in 1275, this annual event has been going strong ever since. After an elaborate procession in period costumes, nine horses and jockeys representing different sections of town vie for the honor of claiming the *palio,* a symbolic flag of victory. Call the **tourist office** (☎ 0141/530357 ⊕ www.atasti.it) for the schedule of events. For 10 days in early September Asti is host to the **Douja d'Or National Wine Festival**—an opportunity to see Asti and celebrate the product that made it famous. During the course of the festival a competition is held to award "Oscars" to the best wine producers, and stands for wine tastings allow visitors to judge the winners for themselves. Musical events and other activities accompany the festival. A complete program is available from the Asti tourist information office.

Shopping

The **Enoteca** on Piazza Alfieri, a square adjacent to Campo del Palio, is a wine center and shop, open Monday–Saturday 9–4:30, where you can try a range of Asti vintages, buy a bottle, and have a light snack. Be aware, though, that prices for Spumante in Asti are not necessarily lower than those elsewhere.

The **McArthur Glen designer outlet** (✉ Serravalle, 30 km [19 mi] south of Alessandria ☎ 0143/609000 ⊕ www.mcarthurglen.com) is a bit of a detour from Asti but may be worth it for fans of designer labels. Discounts are about 50% at more than 60 shops, including Armani, Burberry, Ralph Lauren, Versace, Levi's, and Marina Yachting. Directions can be found on the Web site.

Alba

❸❸ *30 km (18 mi) southwest of Asti.*

This small town has a gracious atmosphere and a compact core studded with medieval towers and Gothic buildings. In addition to being a wine center of the region, Alba is known as the "City of the White Truffle" for the dirty little tubers that command a higher price per ounce than diamonds. For picking out your truffle and having a few wisps shaved on top of your food, expect to shell out an extra €16—which is well worth it. Visit in October for the Fiera del Tartufo (National Truffle Fair), Cento Torri Joust (a medieval jousting festival), and the Palio degli Asini (donkey races), held the first Sunday of the month.

> off the beaten path

BAROLO – Some of Italy's finest wines are made within a radius of about 15 km (10 mi) of Alba. Barbaresco is produced to the east, and to the southwest the small town of Barolo lends its name to the "king of Italian wines." The zone is dotted with castles, and every town has an enoteca where you can sample the local vino. In the town of Barolo the **Castello di Barolo** houses a wine shop and a museum of wine making. ☎ *0173/56277* ☉ *Fri.–Wed. 10–12:30 and 3–6:30. Closed Jan.*

Where to Stay

$ ⌂ **La Meridiana.** If Alba strikes your fancy, consider a night at this reasonably priced belle-epoque–style bed-and-breakfast, on a hill overlooking the historic center and surrounded by Dolcetto and Nebbiolo grapevines. ✉ *Località Altavilla 9* ☎ *0173/440112* ✉ *cascinareine@libero.it* ⇆ *7 rooms, 2 apartments* ♨ *Pool, gym; no a/c, no room phones* ▭ *No credit cards* ⊙ *BP.*

> en route

From Alba, double back to Asti to pick up the A21 autostrada. The road east from Asti to Alessandria is straight, skirting the southern edge of the Po plain, but for the first half of the drive you see to the south green hillsides covered with vineyards. If you find yourself driving along this road during a thunderstorm (quite common on late summer afternoons), don't be surprised by the sound of explosions. Wine growers will often let off cannons loaded with blanks to persuade heavy clouds to rain rather than build up and develop destructive hailstones.

Casale Monferrato

㉞ *42 km (26 mi) northeast of Asti, 75 km (46 mi) southwest of Milan.*

Casale Monferrato, strategically situated on the southern bank of the Po, was held by the Gonzaga, rulers of Mantua, before falling into the hands of the Savoy. The 16th-century **Torre Civica**, marking the heart of town in Piazza Mazzini, commands extensive views up and down the Po. It's open the second Saturday and Sunday of every month for free guided visits. In the second half of March the **Festa di San Giuseppe** brings artisans, musicians, and vendors of traditional sweets to the central Piazza del Castello.

Casale's most enlightening sight is the **Museo Israelitico** (Jewish Museum) in the women's section of its synagogue. Inside is a collection of documents and sacred art of a community that was vital to the prosperity of this mercantile city. The synagogue dates from the late 16th century, and neighboring buildings on the same street formed the Jewish ghetto of that period. ⊠ *Vicolo Olper 44, south of Torre Civica* ☎ *0142/71807* ◷ *Mar.–Dec., Sun. 10–noon and 3:30–5:30; other times by appointment.*

Vercelli

㉟ *23 km (14 mi) north of Casale Monferrato, 80 km (50 mi) northeast of Turin.*

Vercelli is the rice capital of Italy and of Europe. Northern Italy's mainstay risotto owes its existence to the crop that was introduced to this fertile area in the late Middle Ages. **Piazza Cavour** is the heart of the medieval city and former market square. It was to this small square that merchants across northern Italy came in the 15th century to buy bags of rice, then a novelty grain from the East. Rising above the low rooftops around Piazza Cavour is the **Torre dell'Angelo** (not open to the public), whose forbidding military appearance reflects its origins as a watchtower.

The Vercelli **Duomo,** a mainly late-16th-century construction on the site of what was a 5th-century church, contains tombs of several Savoy rulers in an octagonal chapel along the south (right) wall. The cathedral's **Biblioteca** (chapter library; for entrance, see cathedral office) contains the *Gospel of St. Eusebius,* a 4th-century manuscript, and the *Codex Vercellensis,* an 11th-century collection of Anglo-Saxon poetry. ⊠ *Piazza Sant'Eusebio* ☎ *0161/255205* ◷ *Daily 8–12:30 and 3–6:30, except during mass on Sun.*

The **Basilica di Sant'Andrea,** a Cistercian abbey church built in the early 13th century with funds from another Abbey of St. Andrew (in England), witnessed the growing influence of northern Europe on Italy. Sant'Andrea is one of Italy's earliest examples of Gothic architecture, a style that came from the north but adapted to suit local Italian traditions and tastes. The church interior is a soaring flight of Gothic imagination, with slender columns rising up to the ribbed vaults of the high ceiling. The gardens on the north side of the basilica hold the remains of the abbey itself and some of its secondary buildings. It's only here that the Gothic style is interrupted. The buildings surround a cloister in which you can see pointed Gothic arches resting on severe and more solid 12th-century Romanesque bases. ⊠ *Piazza G. Bicheri* ☎ *0161/255513* ⊙ *Daily 8–noon and 3–6:30.*

The **Città Vecchia** is a collection of narrow streets and alleys that includes the Basilica di Sant'Andrea. Many of the houses are five centuries old, and you can see partly hidden gardens and courtyards beyond the wrought-iron gates.

On Tuesday and Friday mornings you can take an unusual guided tour of the **Borsa Merci** (⊠ Via Zumaglini 4 ☎ 0161/5981), the commodities market where rice has been traded for centuries. Vercelli's is the largest rice market in Europe. Contact the **Vercelli tourist office** (⊠ Viale Garibaldi 90, 13100 ☎ 0161/257888) for more information.

Novara

36 *23 km (14 mi) northeast of Vercelli, 95 km (59 mi) northeast of Turin.*

Novara is the easternmost city in Piedmont, only about 10 km (6 mi) west of the Ticino River, which forms the border with Lombardy, and 32 km (20 mi) from Milan. Much of the present city dates from the late 19th and early 20th centuries, but there are interesting buildings from earlier periods scattered about, most notably the tall, slender cupola of **San Gaudenzio**. The church itself, built between 1577 and 1690, is wholly baroque in design, with twisted columns and sumptuous statues. The main attraction, though, is its **cupola**, built from 1840 to 1888 and soaring to a height of just under 400 feet. This spire is visible everywhere in the city and in the surrounding countryside and has become as much a symbol of Novara as the Mole Antonelliana is of Turin—not a complete coincidence, since Alessandro Antonelli (1798–1888) designed this cupola and spire as well. ☎ *0321/629894* ⊙ *Daily 8–noon and 3–7.*

The **Duomo** in Novara is medieval in origin but was reconstructed in neoclassical style by Alessandro Antonelli between 1863 and 1869. The **Battistero** (Baptistery), outside the entrance to the cathedral, shows its age more clearly. The rotunda-shape building dates from the 5th century, although it was substantially enlarged in the 10th and 11th centuries. Restoration work has uncovered 10th-century frescoes on the interior walls; apocalyptic scenes are made all the more frightening by the use of vivid colors and a flat, two-dimensional Byzantine style. Also neighboring the cathedral is the **Broletto**, a cluster of well-preserved late-medieval buildings. ⊠ *Piazza Martiri della Libertà* ☎ *0321/35634* ⊙ *Daily 8–noon.*

Where to Stay

$$ ▦ **Italia.** Modern, functional rooms and the location, just a short walk from the Duomo and the central business and shopping areas of Novara, are the main attractions here. Some of the rooms have good views of the town, and the hotel's restaurant is one of Novara's best. ⊠ *Via Solaroli 8, 28100* ☎ *0321/399316* 🖷 *0321/399310* ⊕ *www.pancionihotels.it* ⤸ *59 rooms, 4 suites* ☖ *Restaurant, minibars, bar, meeting rooms* ▤ *AE, DC, MC, V* ⦿ *BP.*

PIEDMONT/VALLE D'AOSTA A TO Z

To research prices, get advice from other travelers, and book travel ar-rangements, visit www.fodors.com.

AIRPORTS

The region's only international airport, Aeroporto Torino Caselle, is 18 km (11 mi) north of Turin. It's notoriously foggy in winter, and many flights are diverted to Genoa, on the coast, with bus connections provided for the two-hour drive to Turin. From Aeroporto Caselle, local buses to Turin arrive at the bus station on Corso Inghilterra in the city center.

🛪 Airport Information **Aeroporto Torino Caselle** ☎ 011/5676361.

BUS TRAVEL

Turin's main bus station is on the corner of Corso Inghilterra and Corso Vittorio Emanuele. Urban buses and trams are operated by the agency ATM. The Turin-based SADEM line services the autostrada network to Milan and other destinations in Italy. Turin-based SAPAV services the same area—both specialize in bus transportation in Piedmont and Valle d'Aosta. SAVDA specializes in mountain service, providing frequent links between Aosta, Turin, and Courmayeur as well as Milan. SITA buses, part of the nationwide system, also connect Turin with the rest of Italy. There's also a major bus station at Aosta, across the street from the train station. General bus information is available at the numbers below.

🚌 Bus Information **ATM** ✉ Corso Turati 19/6, 10128 Turin ☎ 800/019152 ⊕ www.atm. to.it. **SADEM** ✉ Via della Repubblica 14, Grugliasco, Turin 10095 ☎ 800801600. **SAPAV** ✉ Corso Torino 396, Pinerolo, Turin 10064 ☎ 800/801901. **SAVDA** ✉ Strada Ponte Suaz 6, Aosta 11100 ☎ 0165/361244.

CAR RENTAL

🚗 Local Agencies **Avis** ✉ Porto Nuova, Turin ☎ 011/6699800 ✉ Corso Turati 37, Turin ☎ 011/500852 ✉ Aeroporto Torino Caselle, Turin ☎ 011/4701528. **Hertz** ✉ Via Mag-ellano 12, Turin ☎ 011/502080 ✉ Aeroporto Torino Caselle, Turin ☎ 011/5678166 ✉ Via Ascoli 39, Turin ☎ 011/4378175.

CAR TRAVEL

Italy's autostrada network links the region with the rest of Italy and neighboring France. Aosta, Turin, and Alessandria all have autostrada connections, with the A4 heading east to Milan and the A6 heading south to the Ligurian coast and Genoa. Turin is the hub of all the transportation systems in Piedmont, with autostrada connections to the north, south, and east.

For travel across the French, Swiss, and Italian borders in Piedmont–Valle d'Aosta, only a few routes are practicable year-round: the 12-km (7-mi) Mont Blanc tunnel connecting Chamonix with Courmayeur, the Colle del Gran San Bernardo/Col du Grand St. Bernard (connecting Martigny with Aosta on Swiss highway E27 and Italian highway SS27, with 6-km [4-mi] of tunnel), and the Traforo del Fréjus (between Modane and Susa, with 13 km [8 mi] of tunnel). There are other passes, but they become increasingly unreliable between November and April.

EMERGENCY SERVICES If you have a breakdown on the road, you can walk to one of the roadside stations marked SOS and push the button. You'll be connected to the Automobile Club of Italy (ACI), which will come and assist you, for free if you have a membership card for the automobile club in your home country. (Otherwise, you must pay a fee.) For emergency road assistance, ACI can also be reached at the phone number below.

🚹 **ACI** ☎ 803/116.

ROAD CONDITIONS Well-paved secondary roads (*superstrade*) run through the region, following the course of mountain valleys in many places. Sudden winter storms can close off some of the mountain stretches; contact local tourist offices for up-to-date road information before you set out. Bear in mind that this is very rough country, so no matter what time of year and what route you choose, you are always advised to check with the tourist office or, in a pinch, with the police, to make sure roads are passable and safe.

EMBASSIES & CONSULATES

🚹 United Kingdom **U.K. Consulate** ✉ Via Saluzzo 60, Turin ☎ 011/6509202, open Mon. and Thurs. 9–noon.

EMERGENCIES

Pharmacies throughout the region take turns staying open late and on Sunday. Dial 192 for the latest information (in Italian) on which are open. The Farmacia Boniscontro in Turin takes a lunch break between 12:30 and 3 but is open all night.

🚹 **Emergencies** ☎ 113. **Police** ☎ 112. **Ambulance service** ☎ 118. **Farmacia Boniscontro** ✉ Corso Vittorio Emanuele II, 66, Turin ☎ 011/538271.

MAIL & SHIPPING

🚹 Post Offices **Turin** ✉ Via Alfieri 10 ☎ 011/5060040.

OVERNIGHT SERVICES 🚹 Major Services **DHL** ✉ Via Bertolla all'Abbadia Stura, 176, Turin ☎ 800/345345.

PASSPORTS & VISAS

You should have your passport with you when day-tripping into France, even though it's unlikely you'll be asked to show it.

TOURS

Turin's group and personally guided tours are organized by the city's tourist office. Here you can also get information about the Touristibus, a two-hour guided bus trip that leaves from Piazza Castello, at the corner of Via Po, every day but Tuesday at 2:30. Touristibus goes through the historic center of Turin, including Via Roma and Porta Nuova, and then out to view such locations as the Palazzina di Caccia in Stupinigi and the Parco Valentino.

BOAT TOURS Two boats, the *Valentino* and the *Valentina*, ply the waters of the Po between the Murazzi, the Borgo Medioevale, and Moncalieri. With room for 100 passengers each, they provide a comfortable, slow, and rather pleasant way to see the sights of Turin that line this 8 km (5 mi) stretch of river.

🖅 Fees & Schedules **ATM** ✉ Corso Turati 19/6, Turin 10128 ☎ 800/019152 ⊕ www. atm.to.it

PRIVATE GUIDES Alpine guides are not only recommended but essential if you're planning to traverse some of the dramatic ranges outside St. Vincent, Courmayeur, or Breuil-Cervinia. Before embarking on an excursion (however short) into the mountains in these areas, contact the representative of the CAI (Club Alpino Italiano) for information about hikes and the risks. Guides from the Alpine Guides Association can accompany you on treks and also lead skiing, canyoning, and ice-climbing excursions.
🖅 **Alpine Guides Association** ✉ Strada Villair 2, Courmayeur ☎ 0165/842064. **CAI** ✉ Piazza E. Chanoux 8, Aosta ☎ 0165/40194.

TRAIN TRAVEL

Turin is on the main Paris–Rome TGV express line and is also connected with Milan, only 90 minutes away on the fast train. The fastest (Eurostar) trains cover the 667-km (400-mi) trip to Rome in about six hours, but most trains take about nine hours.

Services to the larger cities east of Turin are part of the extensive and reliable train network serving the Lombard Plain. West of the region's capital, however, the train services soon peter out in the steep mountain valleys. Continuing connections by bus serve these valleys, and information about train-bus mountain services can be obtained from train stations and tourist information offices, or by contacting the Ferrovie dello Stato (FS), the Italian national train service.
🖅 Train Information **FS–Trenitalia** ☎ 892021 ⊕ www.trenitalia.com.

VISITOR INFORMATION

🖅 Tourist Information **Alba** ✉ Piazza Medford 3, 12051 ☎ 0173/35833 ⊕ www. langheroero.it. **Aosta** ✉ Piazza E. Chanoux 8, 11100 ☎ 0165/236627 ⊕ www.regione. vda.it/turismo. **Asti** ✉ Piazza Alfieri 29, 14100 ☎ 0141/530357 ⊕ www.atasti.it. **Bardonecchia** ✉ Viale Vittoria 44, 10052 ☎ 0122/99032 ⊕ www.comune.bardonecchia. to.it. **Breuil-Cervinia** ✉ Via Carrel 29, 11021 ☎ 0166/949136 ⊕ www.cervinia.it. **Cogne** ✉ Piazza E. Chanoux 36, 11012 ☎ 0165/74040 ⊕ www.cogne.org. **Courmayeur** ✉ Piazzale Monte Bianco 13, 11013 ☎ 0165/842060 ⊕ www.courmayeur.net. **Novara** ✉ Baluardo Quintino Sella 40, 28100 ☎ 0321/394059. **Saluzzo** ✉ Via Griselda 6, 12037 ☎ 0175/46710 ⊕ www.comune.saluzzo.cn.it. **Sestriere** ✉ Via Pinerolo 14, 10058 ☎ 0122/755444 ⊕ www.comune.sestriere.to.it. **Turin** ✉ Piazza Castello 161, 10122 ☎ 011/535181 ✉ Stazione Porta Nuova, 10121 ☎ 011/531327 ⊕ www.turismotorino.org. **Vercelli** ✉ Viale Garibaldi 90, 13100 ☎ 0161/58002 ⊕ www.turismovalsesiavercelli.it.

THE ITALIAN RIVIERA

6

HIKE THE RUGGED COASTLINE
of the timeless Cinque Terre ⇨*p.248*

WATCH THE YACHTS DRIFT BY
from the harbor of luxurious Portfino ⇨*p.255*

IMAGINE GENOA'S PALATIAL PAST
on the palazzo-lined Via Garibaldi ⇨*p.266*

TASTE THE WORLD'S FINEST PESTO
in the region where it was born ⇨*p.271*

JOIN THE LOCALS FOR A *PASSEGGIATA*
on the promenade at Nervi ⇨*p.272*

TAKE YOUR CHANCES AT THE TABLES
of San Remo's Art Nouveau casino ⇨*p.278*

Updated by
Peter Blackman

LIKE THE FAMILY JEWELS that bedeck its habitual visitors, the Italian Riviera is glamorous, but in the old-fashioned way. The resort towns and coastal villages that stake intermittent claims on the rocky shores of the Ligurian Sea are the long-lost cousins of newer, overbuilt seaside paradises. Here the grandest palazzi share space with frescoed, angular, late-19th-century apartment buildings, and high-rise glitz seems as foreign as the Maine lobster that some of the region's tiniest restaurants incongruously fly in for dinner. The rustic and elegant, the provincial and chic, the cosmopolitan and the small-town are blended together here in a sun-drenched pastiche that makes up this, the "other" Riviera.

The serpentine arc of Liguria's coastline, sweeping serenely from La Spezia to Ventimiglia, is the defining mark of the region's identity. Although the province technically extends inland to the tops of the Ligurian Alps, Liguria is Italy's seaside region, and its greatest charms are those of the sea (the "Mare Ligure," never the "Mediterraneo"). For centuries the region has inspired poets and artists. This is where a captivated Percy Shelley praised the "soft blue Spezian bay" and the daredevil Lord Byron swam from Portovenere to Lerici. Today travelers escaping the conceits of civilization still head to the Italian Riviera for a cure. Mellowed by the balmy breezes blowing off the sea, they bask in the sun and explore the tiny coastal towns whose greatest treasures—peace, quiet, and dramatic natural beauty—remain for the most part undiscovered.

Liguria's narrow strip of mountain-protected coastline varies considerably between the two Rivieras. The western Riviera di Ponente (Riviera of the Setting Sun), which reaches from the French border to Genoa, has protected bays and wide sandy beaches and is generally more developed and commercialized than its counterpart to the east, the Riviera di Levante (Riviera of the Rising Sun). Beginning at the French border, the Ponente includes the fanciful seaside resorts of Bordighera and San Remo, similar to their glittery French cousins to the west in their unabashed dedication to the pursuit of pleasure. Much of the eastward sweep of the Ponente coastline has been developed for the packs of sun worshippers who descend upon it in the summer. The minuscule bays and inlets spanning the Levante coastline from Genoa to Portovenere become steeper, sculpted by nature into rocky cliffs.

If this coast is a necklace hung with jewels, the most dazzling pendant is the Portofino promontory. This must be the most photographed village in the world, and one look is enough to tell you why. Smooth-faced, brightly painted houses frame the port in a burst of color that becomes sheer enchantment at sunset, when the houses are reflected in the dancing waters of the harbor. And the people you encounter are attractions in themselves—it was, after all, Bogart and Bacall and Taylor and Burton who put the place on the map.

Farther east is a second peninsula where the road weaves inland, leaving you to hike or take a train or boat to explore the Cinque Terre, a collective community of five fishing villages perched on bluffs above the sea. Here are some of Liguria's least-crowded beaches, its sweetest white wine, its most colorful and quaintest village squares, and certainly its best views. From the hiking trails that link the Cinque Terre, the tiny

Numbers in the text correspond to numbers in the margin and on the Italian Riviera and Genoa maps.

If you have 3 days

With tour time limited, you should rent a car and concentrate on selected towns. On your first day begin on the eastern Riviera di Levante. Stop at the fishing villages of Vernazza in the **Cinque Terre** ④ ☞ and **Camogli** ⑩. Check into a hotel in ⊡ **Santa Margherita Ligure** ⑧, then take a short afternoon jaunt to **Portofino** ⑨. On the second day see ⊡ **Genoa** ⑪–㉟, exploring the old center and old harbor. The western Riviera should be the focus of the third day; head for ⊡ **San Remo** ㊻, allowing about a half day along the way to visit the medieval centers of **Albenga** ㊷ and **Cervo** ㊸.

If you have 5 days

Make Genoa your base and alternate excursions along the coast and into the interior with city sightseeing. On your first day explore ⊡ **Genoa** ⑪–㉟ ☞. If the day is a clear one, take the **Zecca-Righi funicular** ⑭ to the top for an aerial view of the city. On the second day head west, making a detour to Spotorno, and proceed to Noli, one of the best-preserved medieval towns on the entire Riviera. Then see the medieval delights of **Cervo** ㊸ before going on to sophisticated ⊡ **San Remo** ㊻ or palm-studded ⊡ **Bordighera** ㊼, where you can bask in the sun on Day 3. On the fourth and fifth days explore the eastern Riviera, starting with stately **Nervi** ㊱. Among the many allurements on the Portofino promontory, explore the fishing village of **Camogli** ⑩ and chichi **Portofino** ⑨; don't miss the hamlets of San Rocco, San Niccolò, and Punta Chiappa, accessible on foot from Camogli. Overnight in ⊡ **Santa Margherita Ligure** ⑧ or the similarly stylish ⊡ **Rapallo** ⑦. On the fifth day, take an excursion by train or boat to the five rock-perched coastal villages of the ⊡ **Cinque Terre** ④, with Vernazza the first priority.

If you have 7 days

Begin your visit in ⊡ **Genoa** ⑪–㉟ ☞, spending two days there. Budget time for an excursion to **Nervi** ㊱. On the third day head west, going directly to **Ventimiglia** ㊽ and working your way back toward Genoa. See the extraordinary cactus collection in the **Giardini Botanici Hanbury** ㊾, then turn inland to medieval Dolceacqua, only 10 km (6 mi) away. Stop in ⊡ Bordighera ㊼ or the much busier and more commercial resort of ⊡ **San Remo** ㊻ for an overnight stay. On the fourth day discover Noli (bus transport to Noli is via Spotorno). With the exception of **Albisola Marina** ㊳ and **Pegli** ㊲, you can skip the industrialized coast between **Savona** ㊵ and Genoa, where you can spend another night, or press on. On the fifth day, see the offhand charm of **Camogli** ⑩. Take the turnoff for ⊡ **Rapallo** ⑦ and ⊡ **Santa Margherita Ligure** ⑧. Spend a night in either of these towns, or if the traffic isn't heavy head for **Portofino** ⑨. (At the height of the season, opt for an excursion boat to Portofino from Camogli, Santa Margherita Ligure, or Rapallo.) On the sixth night stay in the ⊡ **Cinque Terre** ④ and experience its magical nocturnal calm. Hike the paths in Cinque Terre, and then, on your seventh day, head east to **La Spezia** ② and look for signs to **Portovenere** ③. Doubling back to La Spezia, take the coast road to charming **Lerici** ①. The La Spezia turnoff on the A12 and S1 highways is only about 15 km (9 mi) from the Tuscany border and it's 106 km (66 mi) back to Genoa.

villages seem like colorful blooms of flowers clinging to hulking black cliffs that plunge into the sea. Though this is still the Italian Riviera at its unbuttoned best, Vernazza's growing trinket-shop trade and Monterosso's ever-booked hotels are certain signs that even the Cinque Terre have been "discovered."

Set in the heart of the region is Genoa, Italy's largest commercial port, where magnificent Renaissance palaces wearing the dusty patina of time attest to the wealth of the city's seafaring past, intermixed with layers of loud urbanity. Every schoolchild knows Genoa as the birthplace of Christopher Columbus, and many would become wide-eyed upon learning it's also the home of Europe's largest aquarium. Despite the curiously seamy city's considerable charm, most visitors to Liguria are more interested in the waters found up or down the coast—not surprising, given the relaxed, easy lifestyle found along their shores.

Exploring the Italian Riviera

Though the pace of life in the region is leisurely, getting around the Riviera is an expedient affair. Public transportation is excellent: trains connect all sights along the coast, and buses snake inland. It takes two hours for a fast train to cover the entire coast (though local trains make innumerable stops and take upward of five hours). With the freedom of a car, you could drive from one end of the Riviera to the other on the autostrada in less than three hours. The A10 and A12 on either side of Genoa, engineering wonders with literally hundreds of long tunnels and towering viaducts, skirt the coast, avoiding local traffic on the beautiful Via Aurelia, which was laid out by the ancient Romans. The Via Aurelia, now known as national highway S1, connects practically all the towns along the coast.

If urban artistic and cultural treasures are your passion but you also want some seaside relief, stay in Genoa and make it your base for exploring the rest of the region on day trips. For a more relaxed approach, sea views, and recreation, settle into a resort and take a day trip into Genoa. Be forewarned: driving in Genoa is harrowing and should be avoided whenever possible—if you want to see the city on a day trip, go by train; if you're staying in the city, park in a garage or by valet and traverse the city on foot and by taxi throughout your stay.

About the Restaurants & Hotels

In Liguria there are certainly pizzerias, but look for bakeries and small eateries serving focaccia; the flatbread that is the region's answer to the pizza is ubiquitous. Also popular, especially in fast-paced Genoa, are the *enoteche* (wine bars) that have a large number of wines by the glass and serve simply prepared meals and snacks until the early hours of the morning. As in the rest of Italy, the types of eating establishments in Liguria include cafeterialike *tavole calde,* family-run *trattorie,* chic and formal *osterie,* and sophisticated *ristoranti.* Lunch is served between 12:30 and 2–2:30 and dinner between 7:30–8 and 10.

Most good hotels in Genoa are set in modern buildings, not in the grand old restored villas as you might hope. Genoa at its center is one

6

Boating

With so much coastline—350 km (217 mi)—and so many pretty little harbors, it's no wonder that boat travel is sometimes the most efficient way to get from place to place in Liguria. Use ferries to connect between the five villages of the Cinque Terre, or make a day's excursion from your coastal base to Portofino. The Riviera also attracts pleasure craft of all shapes and sizes, from rowboats to mega-yachts. San Remo, Rapallo, Santa Margherita Ligure, Chiavari, Finale Ligure, and Sestri Levante have large, well-equipped marinas, and nearly every town has a harbor and at least one marine shop. Every October, Genoa hosts the Salone Nautico Internazionale, a mammoth international boat show.

Hiking & Walking

Liguria's hilly terrain makes walking strenuous but rewarding, with stunning views of the sea and castles and little villages dotting the coast. Portofino invites walking, whether you opt for the popular and relatively easy walk from Portofino to the Abbazia di San Fruttuoso or the more challenging hike from Ruta to the top of Monte Portofino. Even the large town of Genoa has hiking options nearby: take the Zecca-Righi funicular up to Righi and walk along the ring of fortresses that used to defend the city, or ride the Genova–Casella railroad to one of the many rugged trailheads near the station stops. One of the best treks in the region is between the Cinque Terre fishing towns—rigorous walks rewarded with beautiful views. Everywhere in Liguria roads, mule paths, or footpaths lead into the hills, where you can discover the region at its unspoiled best.

---

of Italy's noisiest cities: when choosing a hotel make sure yours has windows that are *doppi vetri* (double-glazed). Lodging in Genoa and Liguria, as in much of the north, is somewhat expensive, especially in summer. If visiting in the fall, winter, or spring, ask for a *sconto bassa stagione* (low-season discount rate). The best bargains and the warmest welcomes can be found in the less-visited inland areas; there aren't a great number of hotels in this part of Liguria, but many of them are family-run and special because of it. Reserve ahead year-round for Genoa, and during the peak Easter and summer seasons (June to August) for resorts. Beware also of conferences and conventions for which lodging fills up far in advance. Note that many hotels and resorts in the area close for a number of weeks each year, usually late fall and early winter, and some in summer.

WHAT IT COSTS In euros					
	$$$$	$$$	$$	$	¢
RESTAURANTS	over €22	€16–€22	€11–€16	€7–€11	under €7
HOTELS	over €220	€160–€220	€110–€160	€70–€110	under €70

Restaurant prices are for a second course (secondo piatto). Hotel prices are for two people in a standard double room in high season, including tax and service.

Italian Riviera

Portofino Promontory

- **8** Santa Margherita Ligure
- **9** Paraggi
- **9** Portofino
- **10** Camogli
- Ruta
- Monte Portofino
- Pietre Strette
- Olmi
- Punta Chiappa
- ◆ Abbazia a di San Fruttuoso

KEY

- Beaches
- Ferry
- ▲ Start of itinerary

Genoa 11 - 35 see detail map

Nervi **36**

Pegli **37**

Arenzano
Varazze **38**
Albisola Marina **39**
Savona **40**
Spotorno
Noli
Finale Ligure **41**
Borghetto Santo Spirito
Albenga **42**
Garlenda
Bardineto
Alassio
Diano Marina
Cervo **43**
Imperia **44**
Dolcedo
Taggia **45**
Bussana Vecchia
San Remo **46**
Ospedaletti
Pigna
Dolceacqua
Bordighera **47**
Ventimiglia
Mortola Inferiore
Giardini Botanici Hanbury **49**
Balzi Rossi **48**

FRANCE

La Spezia
San Terenzo
Lerici **1**
Tellaro
Portovenere **2**
3
Riomaggiore
Manarola
Corniglia
Vernazza
Monterosso al Mare
Parco Nazionale delle Cinque Terre **4**
Levanto
Moneglia
Chiavari **5**
Lavagna
Sestri Levante
Zoagli
Rapallo **7**
6
Cavi di Lavagna

RIVIERA DI LEVANTE

RIVIERA DI PONENTE

Golfo di Genova

LIGURIA

Acqui Terme
Campo Ligure
Millesimo
Alba
Mondovì
Cuneo

TO CORSICA

TO ELBA, SARDINIA, SICILY, AND NAPLES

TO CORSICA

TO CORSICA

TO CORSICA

TO BARCELONA

ITALY

10 miles
15 km

SS45
SS35
SS334
SS29
SS28
SS582
SS1
A12
A15
A10
A26
A6
A7

N

Timing

Perhaps more than anywhere else in Italy, season is crucial on the Italian Riviera. Though shops, cafés, clubs, and restaurants stay open late in resorts during high season (at Easter and from June through August), during the rest of the year they close early, if they're open at all. Everything from the yacht-dotted playground of Portofino to the rows of seaside restaurants and bars that line the Riviera's quieter shores shuts down from October to February (with the occasional exception of the week around Christmas), leaving little more than starkly barren coasts, boarded-up cafés, and crashing waves. April, May, and September are the best times to visit, with flowers in bloom, pleasant weather, and moderate levels of activity. October and November often bring torrential rains, floods, and landslides to the region, making such excursions as the Cinque Terre walk temporarily impossible.

RIVIERA DI LEVANTE

Of the two Ligurian Rivieras, the Riviera di Levante, east of Genoa, is overall the wilder and more rugged, yet here you can also find towns like Portofino and Rapallo, world famous for their classic, elegant style. Around every turn of this area's twisting roads the hills plummet sharply to the sea, forming deep, hidden bays and inlets. Beaches on this coast are rocky, backed by spectacular sheer cliffs. The Portofino promontory has one sandy beach, on the east side, at Paraggi. From Chiavari to Cavi di Lavagna, the coast becomes a bit gentler, with a few sandy areas. Sailing conditions along the rugged coast from Sestri Levante down to Portovenere are good. Waterskiing, tennis, and golf are also popular. You may want to choose a base and take short day trips or explore the area by boat from the larger towns. You can anchor your boat in the relatively calm waters of small *ciazze* (coves) found all along the coast.

Lerici

① *106 km (66 mi) southeast of Genoa, 65 km (40 mi) west of Lucca.*

Near Liguria's border with Tuscany, this town is set on a magnificent coastline of gray cliffs and pine forests. Shelley was one of Lerici's best-known visitors and spent some of the happiest months of his life in the lovely white village of San Terenzo, 2 km (1 mi) away. After his death in 1822 the bay was renamed the Golfo dei Poeti, in his and Byron's honor.

Lerici once belonged to Tuscan Pisa, and the 13th-century Pisan **Castello di Lerici** has stood above the splendid bay for centuries. The castle now houses a museum of paleontology. ⊠ *Piazza S. Giorgio 1* ☎ *0187/969042* ⊕ *www.museocastello.lerici.sp.it* ☑ *€4.60* ⊙ *Mar. 16–June and Sept.–Oct. 19, Tues.–Sun. 10:30–1 and 2:30–6; July–Sept., daily 10:30–12:30 and 6:30 PM–midnight; Oct. 20–Dec. 9 and Dec. 27–Mar. 15, Tues.–Fri 10:30–12:30, Sat.–Sun. 10:30–12:30 and 2:30–5:30.*

Where to Stay & Eat

$$ ✕🏠 **Miranda.** Perched amid the clustered old houses in seaside Tellaro, 4 km (2½ mi) southeast of Lerici, this small family-run inn has become a gourmets' destination ($$$$) because of chef Angelo Cabani's imag-

ON THE MENU

LIGURIA'S COOKING might surprise you; it does employ all sorts of seafood—especially anchovies, sea bass, squid, and octopus—but it makes even wider use of vegetables and the aromatic herbs that grow wild on the hillsides, together with liberal amounts of olive oil and garlic. Basil- and garlic-rich pesto is Liguria's classic pasta sauce. You may also find pansoti (round pockets of pasta filled with a cheese mixture) and trofie (doughy, short pasta twists sometimes made with chestnut flour) with salsa di noci, an intense sauce of garlic, walnuts, and cream that, as with pesto, is ideally pounded with a mortar and pestle. Spaghetti allo scoglio is mixed with a tomato-based sauce containing an assortment of local frutti di mare (seafood). Fish is the best bet for a second course: the classic preparation is a whole grilled or baked whitefish—branzino (sea bass) and orata (dorado) are good choices—served with olives, potatoes, Ligurian spices, and

a drizzle of olive oil. A popular meat dish is cima alla Genovese, breast of veal stuffed with a mixture of eggs and vegetables and rolled, served as a cold cut. You should also try the succulent agnello (lamb), coniglio (rabbit), and fresh wild mushrooms foraged from the hills.

The Genovese and other Ligurians snack on torta pasqualina (vegetable pie) and focaccia, which comes simply salted and dribbled with olive oil, flavored with rosemary and olives, covered with cheese or anchovies, and even ripiena (filled), usually with cheese and/or vegetables and herbs. Local vineyards produce mostly light and refreshing whites such as Pigato, Vermentino, and Cinque Terre. Rossese di Dolceacqua, from near the French border, is the best red wine the region has to offer, but for a more robust accompaniment to meats opt for the more full-bodied reds of the neighboring Piedmont region.

---

inative way with Ligurian cooking. His unusual seafood menu changes daily, but might include *insalata di gamberoni e aragosta con finocchio* (shrimp and lobster salad with fennel) and risotto *mantecato con asparagi e gamberi* (with butter, asparagus, and shrimp). If you stay in one of the seven comfortable rooms with bath you have the option of half board at €194 for two people. ⊠ *Via Fiascherino 92, 19030 Tellaro* ☎ *0187/968130* 🖷 *0187/964032* 🖉 *locandamiranda@libero.it* 🛏 *5 rooms, 2 suites* 🗘 *Restaurant; no a/c* ☰ *AE, DC, MC, V* ☉ *Closed Jan.; restaurant closed Mon.* ⦿ *BP.*

$$ 🏨 **Florida.** This seafront, family-run establishment is not the most beautiful from the outside, but it has bright rooms with all the extras you would expect in a higher category, including soundproofing and a balcony with a sea view. For an even better view, loll in one of the deck chairs on the roof terrace. The Florida overlooks a small beach area and is close to tennis courts and a golf course; a solarium is also on the premises. ⊠ *Lungomare Biaggini 35, 19032* ☎ *0187/967332* 🖷 *0187/967344* 🌐 *www.hotelflorida.it* 🛏 *37 rooms* 🗘 *In-room safes, minibars, beach, bar, Internet* ☰ *AE, DC, MC, V* ☉ *Closed Dec. 20–Mar. 1* ⦿ *BP.*

La Spezia

❷ *11 km (7 mi) northwest of Lerici, 103 km (64 mi) southeast of Genoa.*

La Spezia is a large, industrialized naval port on routes to the Cinque Terre and to Portovenere. It lacks the quiet charm of the smaller towns. However, its decaying palm-lined Morin promenade, fertile citrus parks, and lively, balcony-lined streets make parts of La Spezia surprisingly beautiful. The remains of the massive 13th-century **Castel San Giorgio** now house a small museum dedicated to local archaeology. ✉ *Via XX Settembre* ☎ *0187/751142* 🎫 *€5* 🕒 *Wed.–Mon. 9:30–12:30 and 2–5.*

Portovenere

★ **❸** *12 km (7 mi) south of La Spezia, 114 km (70 mi) southeast of Genoa.*

Portovenere's small colorful houses, some dating from the 12th century, were once connected to the 12th- to 16th-century citadel, so that in times of attack the villagers could reach the safety of the battlements. The town commands a strategic position at the end of a peninsula that extends southeast from the Cinque Terre and forms the western border of the Gulf of La Spezia.

Lord Byron (1788–1824) is said to have written *Childe Harold's Pilgrimage* in Portovenere. Near the entrance to the huge, strange **Grotto Arpaia,** at the base of the sea-swept cliff, is a plaque recounting the poet's strength and courage as he swam across the gulf to the village of San Terenzo, near Lerici, to visit his friend Shelley (1792–1822); the feat is commemorated as well by the name of the stretch of water, Golfo dei Poeti (Poets' Gulf). **San Pietro,** a 13th-century Gothic church open daily 7–6, is built on the site of an ancient pagan shrine, on a formidable solid mass of rock above the Grotto Arpaia. With its black-and-white-stripe exterior, it is a landmark recognizable from far out at sea.

Where to Stay & Eat

$$–$$$ ✕ **Da Iseo.** Try to get one of the tables outside at this waterfront restaurant with bistro accents and paintings of Portovenere. Seafood is the only choice, but it's fresh and plentiful. Pasta courses are inventive; try spaghetti *alla Giuseppe* (with shellfish and fresh tomato) or *alla Iseo* (with a seafood curry sauce). ✉ *Waterfront* ☎ *0187/790610* ▭ *AE, DC, MC, V* 🕒 *Closed Wed. and Jan. 2–Feb. 15.*

¢–$ ✕ **Antica Osteria del Carrugio.** Near the castle built to defend the coast from Pisan incursions is this 100-year-old tavern with maritime decorations. The menu, which varies from day to day, emphasizes seafood. Specialties might include *mesc-ciùa* (soup of beans, chickpeas, and wheat), *polpo in insalata* (octopus salad), and *cozze ripiene* (mussels stuffed with garlic, anchovies, oregano, salami, and cheese). ✉ *Via Cappellini 66* ☎ *0187/790617* ⚲ *Reservations not accepted* ▭ *No credit cards* 🕒 *Closed Thurs. and Nov.*

★ **$$$** 🏨 **Royal Sporting.** Appearances are deceptive at this modern hotel on the beach about a 10-minute walk from the village. From the outside, the stone construction seems austere, but the courtyards and interior— with fresh flowers, potted plants, and cool, airy rooms—are colorful and vibrant. The sports facilities are among the best in the area. ⊠ *Via dell'Olivo 345, 19025* ☎ *0187/790326* 🖷 *0187/777707* ⊕ *www. royalsporting.com* ⇆ *56 rooms, 4 suites* △ *Restaurant, minibars, tennis court, saltwater pool, beach, bar, Internet, meeting rooms, some pets allowed (fee)* ⊟ *AE, DC, MC, V* ⊘ *Closed Nov.–mid-Mar.* ⑩ *BP.*

Parco Nazionale delle Cinque Terre

★ ▻ ❹ *Monterosso al Mare 93 km (58 mi) southeast of Genoa, Riomaggiore 14 km (9 mi) west of La Spezia.*

The aura of isolation that has surrounded five coastal villages known as the Cinque Terre, together with their dramatic coastal scenery, has made them one of the eastern Riviera's most stunning attractions. The towns and the pathways that link them are part of a national park that has become a standard, if not requisite, stop on Italy's tourist trail, in spite of the relative inaccessibility. Clinging haphazardly to steep cliffs, these five enchanting villages are linked by ocean-side footpaths, by train, and by narrow, unpaved, and rather tortuous roads.

For much of the villages' history the hiking paths were the only way to get from town to town on land; they still provide breathtaking ocean views as well as access to rugged, secluded beaches and grottoes. The most famous and easiest of the Cinque Terre trails is the **Via dell'Amore** (Lover's Lane), which links Riomaggiore with Manarola (2 km [1 mi], 30 minutes) by a flat path cut into the cliff side. The same trail continues to Corniglia (3 km [2 mi], 1 hour), then becomes more difficult between Corniglia and Vernazza (3 km [2 mi], 1½ hours) and even more difficult from Vernazza to Monterosso (2 km [1 mi], 1½ hours). Still, because of the relative elevations, walking east to west is easier than walking west to east. Additionally, trails lead from Monterosso up the mountainside and back down to Vernazza, and into the mountains from Corniglia, Manarola, and Riomaggiore, with old churches and great views along the way.

Be sure to wear sturdy shoes (hiking boots are best) and a hat, and bring a water bottle, as there is little shade. Also check weather reports before hiking; especially in late fall and winter, frequent thunderstorms flying in off the coast can send townspeople running for cover and make the shelterless trails slippery and dangerous. Rainfall in October and November can cause landslides and close the hiking paths for periods in fall and winter. Try to see the Cinque Terre in September or May, when the weather is good but the waves of tourists aren't so substantial and the towns can be seen in a somewhat more natural state. Advance hotel reservations are essential if you plan to spend the night here in July or August. The area's numerous *affittacamere* (rooms for rent in private homes) are often indicated only by a simple handwritten sign on a front door. Tourist offices in Riomaggiore and Monterosso—a booking service is provided by the latter—have a list of officially licensed affittacamere. These rooms vary considerably in comfort, amenities, and cost.

The local train on the Genoa–La Spezia line stops at each of the villages. The easiest to reach by car is Riomaggiore, the easternmost one and closest to La Spezia and the A12 autostrada. Entrance tickets for use of the trails, as well as tickets that combine use of the trails with unlimited use of the second-class trains or boats that connect the five towns of the Cinque Terre, are available at the Levanto, Monterosso, Vernazza, Corniglia, Manarola, Riomaggiore, and La Spezia train stations. Offsetting, to a small degree, the cost of your ticket are the maps, general information leaflets, and train and boat schedules included in the price. ⊕ *www.5terre. com* ✆ *1-day pass for footpaths €3.50, 1-day pass with train €6, 1-day pass with train and boat €15, 3-day pass with train €15, 7-day pass with train €20.*

need a break? For refreshments about halfway along the 20-minute walk on the Via dell'Amore trail, stop at the water's-edge **Bar Amore** (☎ 0187/921026 ⊠ Between Riomaggiore and Manarola).

Riomaggiore

11 km (7 mi) west of Portovenere.

The same sort of flowery little squares that bedeck the town's four siblings are found in Riomaggiore, interspersed with modern stucco houses and a sense that the population is less isolated here. This may be because Riomaggiore is comparatively convenient to La Spezia; you can get here by car by following signs from La Spezia's port.

WHERE TO STAY & EAT

$–$$

✕ **Ripa del Sole.** Try some of the great local wine with one of the house specialties: *calamari con gran farro* (steamed squid with lemon sauce and barley), tagliatelle *fresche con scampi e tartufo bianco* (fresh pasta with scampi and white truffles), or *filetto di branzino al piatto rovente* (sea bass cooked on the griddle with herbs and garlic). In summer you can eat on the terrace of this seafood restaurant. ⊠ *Via de' Gaspari 282* ☎ *0187/920143* ▭ *No credit cards* ☾ *Closed mid-Jan.–mid-Feb. and Mon. Nov.–Mar.*

$

▦ **Due Gemelli.** Set above the sea, this small hotel has fabulous views of the turquoise water. The rooms have simple, mismatched furnishings, but they all have balconies making them bright and airy. ⊠ *Via Litoranea 1, 19017* ☎ *0187/920111* 🖷 *0187/920678* ⊕ *www.duegemelli.it* ⇖ *14 rooms* ♿ *Restaurant, bar; no a/c* ▭ *AE, DC, MC, V* �‖ *BP.*

Manarola

1½ km (1 mi) west of Riomaggiore.

Multicolor houses spill down a dark hillside to town squares that hang over the port like balconies overlooking the tiny turquoise harbor. Manarola is the center of Cinque Terre wine-making, and you can taste the fruits of local labor in a number of wineries, as well as at the **Cooperativa Agricoltura di Riomaggiore, Manarola, Corniglia, Vernazza e Monterosso** (⊠ Via Groppo ☎ 0187/920435).

WHERE TO STAY

$

▦ **Ca' d'Andrean.** If you want to stay in one of the less crowded of the Cinque Terre, this tiny simple hotel is one of your best options. White-tile floors cool off the rooms, some of which have balconies. In summer, breakfast, an optional extra at €6 per person, is served in a flower garden. ⊠ *Via Discovolo 101, 19010* ☎ *0187/920040* 🖷 *0187/920452*

⊕ *www.cadandrean.it* ⇱ *10 rooms* ⚭ *Bar; no a/c* ▭ *No credit cards* ☺ *Closed mid-Nov.–mid-Dec.*

Corniglia

3 km (2 mi) west of Manarola.

Tiny, isolated Corniglia, strung back from a hilltop overlooking the sea, is unquestionably the most difficult of the Cinque Terre to visit. It has no port and no (usable) access road for automobiles, so you have to arrive by local train or on foot, along the difficult trail from Vernazza or the easy one from Manarola. On a pretty pastel square sits the 14th-century church of **San Pietro.** The rose window of marble imported from Carrara is impressive, particularly considering the work required to transport it here. ✉ *Main square* ☎ *0187/3235582* ☺ *Wed. 4–6, Sun. 10–noon.*

WHERE TO STAY & EAT ✗▦ **Cecio.** On the outskirts of Corniglia, many of the spotless rooms at the family-run Cecio have spectacular views of the town clinging to ¢ the cliffs above the bay. The same memorable vista can be enjoyed from the hotel's restaurant, which serves inexpensive and well-prepared local seafood dishes. ✉ *Via Serra 58, 19010, toward Vernazza* ☎ *0187/812043* 🖷 *0187/812138* ⇱ *12 rooms* ⚭ *Restaurant; no a/c, no room phones, no TV in some rooms* ▭ *DC, MC, V* ❮❯ *BP.*

Vernazza

3 km (2 mi) west of Corniglia.

Lovely Vernazza has the largest and best-equipped port of the Cinque Terre towns. Its pink, slate-roof houses and colorful squares contrast with the remains of a medieval fort and castle. The castle's tower was struck by lightning in 1896; it's been rebuilt and today has some of the best views in Cinque Terre. Summertime in Vernazza brings smart-set Italians to the town's cafés and restaurants. Stay in town and delve right in, escape on one of the many footpaths leading up through the hillsides' terraced vineyards, or head to one of the other towns on a relaxing boat ride from the port.

WHERE TO STAY & EAT ✗ **Gambero Rosso.** Relax on Vernazza's main square, looking out at a church. This fine trattoria serves such delectable dishes as shrimp salad, **$$–$$$** vegetable torte, and squid-ink risotto. The creamy pesto, served atop spaghetti, is some of the best in the area. End your meal with Cinque Terre's own *sciacchetrà*, a dessert wine served with semisweet biscotti. Don't drink it out of the glass—dip the biscotti in the wine instead. ✉ *Piazza Marconi 7* ☎ *0187/812265* ▭ *AE, DC, MC, V* ☺ *Closed Mon. Jan. and Feb.*

¢ ✗▦ **Trattoria Gianni Franzi.** Order your pesto with *fagiolini* (green beans), a Ligurian specialty that somehow tastes better when you're eating it outside in a beautiful *piazzetta* (small square) with a view of the port, as you can here. Above the restaurant, a number of simply furnished, economical rooms are available. Your choice here is between the smaller, older rooms without private bathrooms, but with tiny balconies and great views of the port, or those in the newer section, with bathrooms but no view. ✉ *Via G. Marconi 1, 19018* ☎ *0187/821003* 🖷 *0187/812228* ⇱ *20 rooms, 12 with bath* ⚭ *Restaurant, bar* ▭ *AE, DC, MC, V*

⊗ *Closed Jan. 8–Mar. 8; restaurant closed* Wed. early Mar.–mid-July *and mid-Sept.–early Jan.* |○| BP.

Monterosso al Mare
3 km (2 mi) west of Vernazza.

The narrow alleys and colorful houses of the old center are clustered on a hilltop above the port and its seaside promenade. Monterosso is also the largest, most developed, and least idyllic of the five fishing towns, with the Cinque Terre's biggest beach, its only sizable hotels, and most of its restaurants. Stone stairways link the two areas of town, affording lovely views of the mountains that tumble down onto the wide, sandy stretch below, which is mobbed in summer. On Thursday morning the whole town comes alive with the weekly market, where you can pick up local fruits, vegetables, and freshly caught seafood, among other delicacies.

In Monterosso's old town center, the 12th-century **church** (⊠ Piazza Garibaldi) is striped black and white in the Ligurian Gothic fashion. The **Pro Loco tourist office** (⊠ Via Fegina 38, below train station ☎ 0187/817506) can help with trail maps and boat schedules, and also provides a booking service for the many affittacamere in the area.

WHERE TO STAY & EAT

$$$ ✕ **Il Gigante.** A good introduction to Ligurian seafood is the *zuppa di pesce* (fish soup) served at this traditional trattoria. It's usually served as a first course but is filling enough to be an entrée. Daily specials might include risotto *ai frutti di mare* (with a seafood sauce) and spaghetti with an octopus sauce. ⊠ *Via IV Novembre 9* ☎ *0187/817401* ⌖ *Reservations essential* ⊟ *AE, DC, MC, V* ⊗ *Closed Mon.*

★ **$$$** ✕ **Miki.** Specialties here are anything involving seafood. The *insalata di mare* (seafood salad), with squid and fish, is more than tasty; so are the grilled fish and any pasta with seafood. If you're in the mood for a pizza, you can order that here as well. Miki has a beautiful little garden in the back, perfect for lunch on a sunny day. ⊠ *Via Fegina 104* ☎ *0187/817608* ⊟ *AE, DC, MC, V* ⊗ *Closed Nov. and Dec., and Tues. Sept.–July.*

★ **$$–$$$** ✕ **Il Pirata.** Bright and rustic, this trattoria near the port should be the first stop for lunch, especially if you make it in time to grab a seat at the long tables on the front porch outside. Specialties are those of the region, with a few surprising gourmet touches like the French wines lining the shelves and Maine lobster on the menu. Reservations are essential on weekends and in summer. ⊠ *Via Molinelli 6/8* ☎ *0187/817536* ⊟ *MC, V* ⊗ *Closed Wed. and mid-Jan.–mid.-Feb.*

¢ ✕ **Il Frantoio.** Some of the best focaccia on the coast is available here. It's a good place for a light lunch or a snack before heading out on the walk to Vernazza. ⊠ *Via Gioberti 1* ☎ *0187/818333* ⊟ *No credit cards.*

$$$–$$$$ ▦ **Porto Roca.** In a panoramic position above the sea, Porto Roca is set slightly apart, blessedly removed from the crowds. It has the look of a well-kept villa; its interiors have authentic antiques, and there are ample terraces. The rooms with views of the sea are bright and airy; avoid the back rooms, which are dark, dank, and without a view. ⊠ *Via Corone 1, 19016* ☎ *0187/817502* 🖷 *0187/817692* ⊕ *www.portoroca.it* ⇱ *43 rooms* ⌂ *Restaurant, bar, some pets allowed* ⊟ *AE, MC, V* ⊗ *Closed Nov. 4–Mar. 27* |○| BP.

| en route | From the Cinque Terre, small highways connect back out through the edge of La Spezia to state highway S1, which heads inland to the spectacular Passo del Bracco and then turns back out to the sea at Sestri Levante. After Sestri, S1 (which becomes Via Aurelia) hugs the coast, affording dazzling seaside scenery all the way to Genoa, the Riviera Ponente, and the French border. |

Moneglia

❺ *34 km (21 mi) northwest of Monterosso al Mare, 56 km (35 mi) southeast of Genoa.*

The town of Moneglia, sheltered by the wooded hills of a nature preserve, faces a little bay guarded by ruined castles. An out-of-the-way alternative to fussier resorts, it's a quiet base for walks and excursions by boat, car, or train to Portofino and the Cinque Terre towns. A classical guitar festival is held here in September.

Where to Stay

$$ 🏨 **Villa Edera.** Ingeniously merging an older building on a verdant hillside with a smart stone-and-glass wing, Villa Edera has a contemporary style. Terraces, a garden, luminous bedrooms, and lounges with stylish wicker armchairs are among the comforts. This hotel is owned by a family committed to personal attention; Mamma Ida's cooking is special, too. ⊠ *Via Venino 12, 16030* ☎ *0185/49291* 🖷 *0185/49470* ⊕ *www.villaedera.com* ⌁ *27 rooms* ⌂ *Restaurant, cable TV, pool, gym, sauna, bar, Internet, no-smoking rooms; no a/c in some rooms* ⊟ *AE, MC, V* ☉ *Closed Nov. 8–Feb.* ⊚⑴ *BP.*

Chiavari

❻ *19 km (12 mi) northwest of Moneglia, 38 km (23 mi) southeast of Genoa.*

Chiavari is a fishing town (rather than village) of considerable character, with narrow, twisting streets and a good harbor. Chiavari's citizens were intrepid explorers, and many emigrated to South America in the 19th century. The town boomed, thanks to the wealth of the returning voyagers, but Chiavari retains many medieval traces in its buildings.

In the town center, the **Museo Archeologico** displays objects from an 8th-century BC necropolis, or ancient cemetery, excavated nearby. The museum closes the first and third Sundays of the month. ⊠ *Palazzo Costaguta, Via Costaguta 4, Piazza Matteotti* ☎ *0185/320829* 🎟 *Free* ☉ *Tues.–Thurs. 9–1, Fri.–Sun. 2–7.*

Shopping

The traditional, light—they weigh only 3 pounds—*campanine*, wood chairs made of olive or walnut, are still produced by a few Chiavari craftsmen. Macramé lace can also be found here.

Rapallo

7 *9 km (5½ mi) northwest of Chiavari, 28 km (17 mi) east of Genoa.*

Rapallo was once one of Europe's most fashionable resorts, but it passed its heyday before World War II and has suffered from the building boom brought on by tourism. Ezra Pound and D. H. Lawrence lived here, and many other writers, poets, and artists have been drawn to it. Today, the town's harbor is filled with yachts. A single-span bridge on the eastern side of the bay is named after Hannibal, who is said to have passed through the area after crossing the Alps.

The highlight of the town center, the cathedral of **Santi Gervasio e Protasio**, at the western end of Via Mazzini, was founded in the 6th century. ⊠ *Via Mazzini* ☎ *0185/52375* ⊠ *Free* ☉ *Daily 6:30–noon and 3–6:30.*

The **Museo del Pizzo a Tombolo**, in a 19th-century mansion, has a collection of antique lace, a dying art for which Rapallo was once renowned. ⊠ *Villa Tigullio* ☎ *0185/63305* 🖼 *Free* ☉ *Oct.–Aug., Tues. and Wed. and Fri. and Sat. 3–6, Thurs. 10–11:30.*

Where to Stay & Eat

$$-$$$ ✕ **Roccabruna.** In a splendid villa outside Rapallo, seafood specialties adorn an abundant menu that changes regularly. Take the Casello–Savagna highway 2 km (1 mi) west from Rapallo. ⊠ *Via Sotto la Croce 6, Savagna* ☎ *0185/261400* ▭ *MC, V* ☉ *Closed Mon. and late Nov.–early Dec. No lunch Tues.–Sat. Oct.–June.*

$$-$$$
Fodor'sChoice ✕ **U' Giancu.** Owner Fausto Oneto is a man of many hats—don't be surprised if he wears six different ones during the course of a meal. Though
★ original cartoons cover the walls and a children's playground is the main feature of the outdoor seating area, Fausto is completely serious about his cooking. Lamb dishes are particularly delicious, and the vegetables from the restaurant's garden provide the freshest of ingredients. Those who want to learn the secrets of Ligurian cuisine can attend the lively morning cooking lessons. ⊠ *Via San Massimo 28, Località San Massimo, 3 km (2 mi) northwest of Rapallo* ☎ *0185/261212* ▭ *DC, MC, V* ☉ *Closed Wed. and mid.-Dec.–early Jan. No lunch.*

$-$$ ✕ **Da Mario.** Simply decorated and brightly lighted, this small and usually crowded trattoria serves some of the best seafood in Rapallo. Don't miss the spaghetti with seafood and tomatoes. A small terrace provides outdoor seating in summer. ⊠ *Piazza Garibaldi 23* ☎ *0185/51736* 🍽 *Reservations essential* ▭ *AE, DC, MC, V* ☉ *Closed Wed., and Oct. and Nov.*

$$$$ 🏨 **Grand Hotel Bristol.** This Victorian showcase is in an elevated position overlooking road and sea outside Rapallo and is set in lush gardens with a huge seawater pool. Spacious rooms, many with balcony and sea view, are decorated in soft blues and greens in a smart, contemporary style and have extra-large beds. You can choose between a Rapallo view and a Portofino view. In summer, dinner is served on the roof terrace. ⊠ *Via Aurelia Orientale 369, 16035* ☎ *0185/273313* 📠 *0185/55800* ⊕ *www.tigullio.net/bristol* 🛏 *85 rooms, 6 suites* �å *2 restaurants, minibars, cable TV, saltwater pool, hot tub, sauna, bil-*

liards, horseback riding, bar, meeting rooms, some pets allowed ⊟ AE, MC, V ⊘ Closed Dec.–Feb. ⏚ BP.

Shopping

Guido Porati's aromatic shop, **Bottega dei Sestieri** (✉ Via Mazzini 44 ☎ 0185/230530) sells Ligurian cheeses, wines, and other delicacies. For something truly regional, try the *trarcantu*, a cow's-milk cheese aged in grape skins. The store is on a narrow lane that runs parallel to Rapallo's waterfront.

The attractive coastal village of **Zoagli** (✉ On S1, 4 km [2½ mi] east of Rapallo) has been famous for silk, velvet, and damask since the Middle Ages.

Santa Margherita Ligure

❽ *3 km (2 mi) south of Rapallo, 31 km (19 mi) southeast of Genoa.*

A beautiful old resort town favored by well-to-do Italians, Santa Margherita Ligure has everything a Riviera playground should have—plenty of palm trees and attractive hotels, cafés, and a marina packed with yachts. Some of the older buildings here are still decorated on the outside with the trompe-l'oeil frescoes typical of this part of the Riviera. This is a pleasant, convenient base, which for many represents a perfect balance on the Italian Riviera: bigger and less Americanized than the Cinque Terre; less glitzy than San Remo; more relaxing than Genoa and environs; and ideally situated for day trips, such as an excursion to Portofino.

Where to Stay & Eat

$$$–$$$$ ✕ **La Paranza.** From the piles of tiny *bianchetti* (whitebait) in oil and lemon that are part of the antipasto *di mare* (of the sea) to the simple, perfectly grilled whole sole, fresh seafood in every shape and form is the specialty here. Mussels, clams, octopus, salmon, or whatever else is fresh that day is what's on the menu. Locals say this is the town's best restaurant, but if you're looking for a stylish evening out, look elsewhere— La Paranza is about food, not fashion. It's just off Santa Margherita's port. ✉ *Via Jacopo Ruffini 46* ☎ *0185/283686* ⚓ *Reservations essential* ⊟ *AE, DC, MC, V* ⊘ *Closed Mon. and Nov.*

$$$–$$$$ ✕ **La Stalla.** The breathtaking, hilltop views of Santa Margherita from this villa-turned-restaurant are worth the harrowing 3-km (2-mi) drive northwest to get here from Santa Margherita's port. Cesare Frati, your congenial host, is likely to tempt you with his homemade fettuccine ai frutti di mare followed by the *pescato del giorno alla moda ligure* (catch of the day baked Ligurian style, with potatoes, olives, and pine nuts) and a delightfully fresh lemon sorbet to complete the feast. ✉ *Via G. Pino 27, Nozarego* ☎ *0185/289447* ⊟ *AE, DC, MC, V* ⊘ *Closed Mon. and Nov.*

★ $$$–$$$$ ✕ **Oca Bianca.** Angelo, son of Cesare Frati at Santa Margherita's La Stalla, has broken away from the norm at this excellent small restaurant—there is no seafood on the menu. Meat dishes are the specialty, and choices may include mouthwatering preparations of lamb from France or New Zealand, steak from Ireland or Brazil, South African ostrich, and Italian pork. Delicious antipasti, an extensive wine list, and the attentive service add to the experience. The Oca Bianca serves dinner until 1 AM. ⊠ *Via XXV Aprile 21* ☎ *0185/288411* ⌲ *Reservations essential* ⊟ *AE, DC, MC, V* ⊘ *Closed Mon. and Jan.–mid-Feb. No lunch Tues.–Thurs. Sept.–Dec.*

\$\$–\$\$\$ ✕ **Trattoria Cesarina.** This typical trattoria serves classic local fare—and that means seafood. The white interior is refreshingly free of bric-a-brac, allowing you to focus on your meal. Don't expect a menu; instead, allow the friendly staff to tell you what to eat. Among other treats, you may encounter a delectable antipasto of local frutti di mare, a seafood-theme pasta dish, and the catch of the day delicately grilled or baked in that laissez-faire Ligurian style. ⊠ *Via Mameli 2/C* ☎ *0185/286059* ⊟ *MC, V* ⊘ *Closed Tues., and Dec. and Jan.*

★ **\$\$\$\$** ▦ **Grand Hotel Miramare.** Classic Riviera elegance prevails at this palatial hotel overlooking the bay south of the town center. Stroll through the lush garden, then take a dip in the curvaceous (heated) swimming pool or at the private swimming area on the sea. Antique furniture, such as crystal chandeliers and Louis XV chairs, fills the high-ceiling rooms, and there are marble bathrooms. ⊠ *Via Milite Ignoto 30, 16038* ☎ *0185/287013* ⊠ *0185/284651* ⊕ *www.grandhotelmiramare.it* ⤳ *75 rooms, 9 suites* ⌲ *2 restaurants, in-room safes, minibars, pool, beach, waterskiing, 2 bars, Internet, meeting rooms, some pets allowed* ⊟ *AE, DC, MC, V* ⦿*❙ BP.*

\$\$\$\$ ▦ **Imperiale Palace.** Via Pagana climbs north out of Santa Margherita Ligure on its way toward Rapallo; outside town it passes this traditional luxury hotel in an extensive park. The former villa was built in 1889. Reception rooms with tall windows, plush chairs, and potted plants create a warm welcome. The rooms are furnished with antiques; many overlook the shore drive to the sea. ⊠ *Via Pagana 19, 16038* ☎ *0185/288991* ⊠ *0185/284223* ⊕ *www.hotelimperiale.com* ⤳ *78 rooms, 14 suites* ⌲ *Restaurant, in-room safes, minibars, pool, beach, 2 bars, babysitting, meeting rooms* ⊟ *AE, DC, MC, V* ⊘ *Closed Nov.–Mar.* ⦿*❙ BP.*

\$\$\$ ▦ **Continental.** This stately seaside mansion with a columned portico was built in the early 1900s and stands in a lush garden shaded by tall palms and pine trees. The style is a blend of classic furnishings, mostly inspired by the 19th century, with some more functional pieces. There's also a modern wing. The hotel's own cabanas and swimming area are at the bottom of the garden. ⊠ *Via Pagana 8, 16038* ☎ *0185/286512* ⊠ *0185/ 284463* ⊕ *www.hotel-continental.it* ⤳ *68 rooms, 4 suites* ⌲ *Restaurant, in-room safes, minibars, bar, meeting rooms, some pets allowed* ⊟ *AE, DC, MC, V* ⊘ *Closed Jan. 8–Mar. 5* ⦿*❙ BP.*

Portofino

❾ *5 km (3 mi) south of Santa Margherita Ligure, 36 km (22 mi) east of Genoa.*

One of the most photographed villages along the coast, with a decidedly romantic and affluent aura, Portofino has long been a popular destination for foreigners. Once an ancient Roman colony and taken by the Republic of Genoa in 1229, it has also been ruled by the French, English, Spanish, and Austrians, as well as marauding bands of 16th-century pirates. Elite British tourists first flocked to the lush harbor in the mid-1800s. Some of Europe's wealthiest lay anchor in Portofino in summer, but they stay out of sight by day, appearing in the evening after buses and boats have carried off the day-trippers.

There's not actually much to *do* in Portofino, other than stroll around the wee harbor, see the castle, walk to Punta del Capo, look at the pricey boutiques, and sip a coffee while people-watching. However, weaving through picture-perfect cliff-side gardens and gazing at yachts framed by the turquoise Ligurian Sea and the cliffs of Santa Margherita can make for quite a relaxing afternoon. There are also several tame, photo-friendly hikes into the hills to nearby villages. Note the meticulous up-keep of streets and public flora in what is surely Italy's cleanest town.

Unless you're traveling on a deluxe budget, you may want to stay in Ra-pallo or Santa Margherita Ligure rather than at one of Portofino's few very expensive hotels. Restaurants and cafés are good but also pricey (don't expect to have a beer here for much under €8). Trying to reach Portofino by bus or car on the single narrow road can be a nightmare in summer and on holiday weekends. No trains go directly to Portofino: you must stop at Santa Margherita and take the public bus from there (€1). An alternative is to take a boat from Santa Margherita, though even this can be a harrowing experience, as cruise ships also anchor here to disgorge their passengers for outings.

From the harbor, follow the signs for the climb to the **Castello di San Giorgio,** the most worthwhile sight in Portofino, with its medieval relics, im-peccable gardens, and sweeping views. The castle was founded in the Middle Ages but restored in the 16th through 18th century. In true Portofino form, it was owned by Genoa's English consul from 1870 until its opening to the public in 1961. ✛ *Above harbor* ☎ *0185/269046* ☜ €3 ☾ *Apr.–Sept., Wed.–Mon. 10–6; Oct.–Mar., Wed.–Mon. 10–5.*

The small church **San Giorgio,** sitting on a ridge, was rebuilt four times during World War II. It is said to contain the relics of its namesake, brought back from the Holy Land by the Crusaders. Portofino enthusiastically celebrates St. George's Day every April 23. ✛ *Above harbor* ☎ *0185/ 269337* ☾ *Daily 7–6.*

Pristine views can be had from the deteriorating *faro* (lighthouse) at **Punta Portofino,** a 15-minute walk along the point that begins at the southern end of the port. Along the seaside path you can see numerous impres-sive, sprawling private residences behind high iron gates.

The only sand beach near Portofino is at **Paraggi,** a cove on the road between Santa Margherita and Portofino (the bus will stop there on request).

off the beaten path

ABBAZIA A DI SAN FRUTTUOSO – On the sea at the foot of Monte Portofino, the medieval Abbey of San Fruttuoso—built by the Benedictines of Monte Cassino—protects a minuscule fishing village that can be reached only on foot or by water (a 20-minute boat ride from Portofino and also reachable from Camogli, Santa Margherita Ligure, and Rapallo). The restored abbey is now the property of a national conservation fund (FAI) and occasionally hosts temporary exhibitions. The church contains the tombs of some illustrious members of the Doria family. The old abbey and its grounds are a delightful place to spend a few hours, perhaps lunching at one of the modest beach trattorias nearby (open only in summer). But boatloads of visitors can make it very crowded very fast; you might appreciate it most off-season. Last entrance is 30 minutes before closing time.

⊹ *15-min boat ride or a 2-hr walk northwest of Portofino* ☎ *0185/ 772703* ☞ *€4* ⊙ *Mar.–May and Oct., Tues.–Sun. 10–4; June–Sept., daily 10–6; Dec.–Feb., weekends 10–4.*

Where to Stay & Eat

$$$–$$$$ ✕ **Il Pitosforo.** A chic clientele, many with luxury yachts in the harbor, gives this waterfront restaurant a high glamour quotient, which is augmented by outlandish prices. Spaghetti ai frutti di mare is recommended; adventurous diners might try *lo stocco accomodou* (dried cod in a sauce of tomatoes, raisins, and pine nuts). ☒ *Molo Umberto I 9* ☎ *0185/269020 or 0335/5615833* ⌂ *Reservations essential* ▭ *AE, DC, MC, V* ⊙ *Closed Mon. and Tues., and Jan.–mid-Feb. No lunch.*

$$–$$$ ✕ **Ristorante Puny.** A table at this tiny restaurant is difficult to come by in summer, as the manager caters mostly to friends and regulars. If you are lucky enough to get in, however, the food will not disappoint you, nor will the cozy but elegant yellow interior. The unforgettable *pappardelle* (large, flat noodles) *al portofino* delicately blends two of Liguria's tastes: tomato and pesto in a sauce. Ligurian seafood specialties include baked fish with bay leaves, potatoes, and olives as well as the inventive *moscardini al forno* (baked octopus with lemon and rosemary in tomato sauce). ☒ *P. Martiri dell'Olivetta 4–5, on the harbor* ☎ *0185/269037* ⌂ *Reservations essential* ▭ *AE, DC, MC, V* ⊙ *Closed Thurs., and Jan. and Feb.*

¢ ✕ **Canale.** If the staggering prices of virtually all of Portofino's restaurants put you off, the long line outside this family-run bakery indicates that you're not alone and that something special is in store. Here all the focaccia is baked on the spot and served fresh from the oven, along with all kinds of sandwiches, pastries, and other refreshments. The only problem is there's nowhere to sit—time for a picnic! ☒ *Via Roma 30* ☎ *0185/269248* ▭ *No credit cards* ⊙ *Closed Nov. and Dec. No lunch Oct. and Jan.–Apr.*

$$$$ ▦ **San Giorgio.** If you decide to stay in Portofino, this is perhaps your best choice. Tucked away on a quiet backstreet with no views of the harbor, the San Giorgio offers rooms that are immaculate, comfortable, and soothingly designed with canopied beds, pastel walls and white linens, and ultramodern bathrooms. Two small 19th-century town houses were joined to form the hotel, and hallways seem like a labyrinth, but the level of service is high and the peaceful location—there's a secluded garden at the back—are a definite plus. ☒ *Via Del Fondaco 11, 16034* ☎ *0185/26991* ⊟ *0185/267139* ⊕ *www.portofinohsg.it* ⟿ *17 rooms, 1 suite* ⌂ *Bar, Internet, some pets allowed* ▭ *AE, DC, MC, V* ⊙ *Closed Dec.* ��◯�ӏ *BP.*

$$$$ ▦ **Splendido.** Arriving is so much like entering a Jazz Age film set that you'd almost expect to see a Bugatti or Daimler roll up the winding drive from the seaside and Portofino below. In this 1920s luxury hotel there's a particular attention to color, from the coordinated floral linens in corals and gold to the fresh flowers in the reception rooms and on the large terrace. Even grander than the hotel are its prices (more than €500), and the large numbers of American guests smoking Cuban cigars. ⊠ *Salita Baratta 16, 16034* ☎ *0185/267801* 🖨 *0185/267806* ⊕ *www. splendido.orient-express.com* ⇝ *34 rooms, 32 suites* ⚭ *Restaurant, tennis court, pool, gym, sauna, 2 bars, meeting rooms, some pets allowed* ▭ *AE, DC, MC, V* ⊗ *Closed mid-Nov.–late Mar.* ❑| *BP.*

Sports & the Outdoors

HIKING If you have the stamina, you can hike to the Abbazia di San Fruttuoso from Portofino. It's a steep climb at first, and the walk takes about 2½ hours one-way. If you're extremely ambitious and want to make a whole day of it, you can then hike another 2½ hours all the way to Camogli. Much more modest hikes from Portofino include a one-hour uphill walk to Cappella delle Gave, a bit inland in the hills, from where you can continue downhill to Santa Margherita Ligure (another 1½ hours) and a gently undulating paved trail leading to the beach at Paraggi (½ hour). Finally, there's a 2½-hour hike from Portofino that heads farther inland to Ruta, through Olmi and Pietre Strette.

Camogli

★ ❿ *15 km (9 mi) northwest of Portofino, 20 km (12 mi) east of Genoa.*

Camogli, at the edge of the large promontory and nature reserve known as the Portofino Peninsula, has always been a town of sailors. By the 19th century it was leasing its ships throughout the continent. Today, multi-color houses, remarkably deceptive trompe-l'oeil frescoes, and a massive 17th-century seawall mark this appealing harbor community, perhaps as beautiful as Portofino but without the glamour. When exploring on foot, don't miss the boat-filled second harbor, which is reached by ducking under a narrow archway at the northern end of the first one.

The **Castello Dragone,** built onto the sheer rock face near the harbor, is home to the **Acquario** (Aquarium), which has display tanks of local marine life actually built into the ramparts. ⊠ *Via Isola* ☎ *0185/773375* 💳 *€3* ⊗ *May–Sept., daily 10–noon and 3–7; Oct.–Apr., Fri.–Sun. 10–noon and 2:30–6, Tues.–Thurs. 10–noon.*

off the
beaten
path

SAN ROCCO, SAN NICCOLÒ, AND PUNTA CHIAPPA – You can reach these hamlets along the western coast of the peninsula on foot or by boat from Camogli. They are more natural and less fashionable than those facing south on the eastern coast. In the small Romanesque church at San Niccolò, sailors who survived dangerous voyages came to offer thanks.

RUTA – The footpaths that leave from Ruta, 4 km (2½ mi) east of Camogli, up to and around Monte Portofino and Camogli thread through rugged terrain, containing a multitude of plant species. Weary hikers are sustained by stunning views of the Riviera di Levante from the various vantage points along the way.

Where to Stay & Eat

$$–$$$ ✕ **Vento Ariel.** This small, friendly restaurant serves some of the best seafood in town. Dine on the shaded terrace in summer months and watch the bustling activity in the nearby port. Only the freshest of seafood is served; try the spaghetti *alle vongole* (with clams) or the mixed grilled fish. ✉ *Calata Porto* ☎ *0185/771080* ☰ *AE, DC, MC, V* ⊘ *Closed Wed. and Jan. 2–15.*

¢–$ ✕ **Pizzeria Il Lido.** As the name suggests, this popular spot is right across from Camogli's narrow beach, and the outside tables have great views of the sea. If you don't fancy one of the many varieties of pizza, you can choose one of the pasta dishes. ✉ *Via Garibaldi 133* ☎ *0185/770141* ☰ *MC, V* ⊘ *Closed Tues.*

★ **$$$** ⌂ **Cenobio dei Dogi.** Perched majestically a step above Camogli, overlooking harbor, peninsula, and sea, Cenobio dei Dogi is indisputably the best address in town. Genoa's doges once summered here. Ask for one of the rooms with expansive balconies; though unimaginative in design, they have commanding vistas of Camogli's cozy port. You can relax in the well-kept park or enjoy a game of tennis. Cenobio dei Dogi caters to business travelers and conventions. ✉ *Via Cuneo 34, 16032* ☎ *0185/7241* ☐ *0185/772796* ⊕ *www.cenobio.it* ⇄ *102 rooms, 4 suites* ♨ *Restaurant, tennis court, pool, gym, beach, bar, Internet, business services, meeting rooms* ☰ *AE, DC, MC, V* ⊠ *BP.*

$$ ⌂ **Hotel Augusta.** This friendly, family-run hotel is an economic and quiet choice in the center of Camogli. Though you won't have a view of the sea, it's just a short walk away. Guest rooms, all with parquet floors, are bright and modern. ✉ *Via Schiaffino 100, 16032* ☎ *0185/770592* ☐ *0185/770593* ⊕ *www.htlaugusta.com* ⇄ *15 rooms* ♨ *Restaurant, bar* ☰ *AE, DC, MC, V* ⊠ *BP.*

Nightlife & the Arts

Fodor'sChoice
★

The highlight of the festival of San Fortunato, held on the second Sunday of May each year, is the **Sagra del Pesce,** a crowded, festive, and free-to-the-public feast of freshly caught fish, cooked outside at the port in a frying pan 12 feet wide.

GENOA

Ligurian beach bums, beware: Genoa (Genova, in Italian) is a busy, sprawling, and cosmopolitan city, apt to break the spell of the coastal towns in a hurry. This isn't necessarily bad news, though; with more than two millennia of history under its belt, magnificent palaces and art, and an elaborate network of ancient hilltop fortresses, Genoa may be just the dose of curious culture you were looking for. The city's faded splendor can be seen through dark shadows and centuries of grime in the narrow alleyways of the old center—the largest in Europe.

Genoa's winding streets haven't always been so haunted and obscure. This is the birthplace of Columbus, but the city's proud history of trade and navigation predates him by several hundred years. Known as *La Superba* (The Proud), Genoa was from the 13th century a great maritime center rivaling Venice and Pisa in power and splendor. Loud and modern container ships now unload at docks that centuries before served galleons and vessels bound for the spice routes. By the 3rd century BC, when the Romans conquered Liguria, Genoa was already an important trading station. The Middle Ages and the Renaissance saw its rise into a jumping-off place for the Crusaders, a commercial center of tremendous wealth and prestige, and a strategic bone of international contention. A network of fortresses defending the city connected by a wall second only in length to the Great Wall of China was constructed in the hills above, and Genoa's bankers, merchants, and princes adorned the city with palaces, churches, and impressive art collections.

Genoa's downfall began more than 500 years ago as it became eclipsed by other Mediterranean ports and northern Italian powerhouses. By the 17th century Genoa was no longer a great sea power—but more modern enemies were yet to arrive. Since World War II the city has fought with—and often lost to—every evil associated with industrialization and urbanity. Crammed into a thin crescent of land between sea and mountains, Genoa has expanded up rather than out, taking on the form of a multilayer wedding cake, with streets, highways, churches, and entire residential neighborhoods built on others' rooftops. Public elevators and funiculars are as common as buses and trains. Traffic-, pollution-, and crime-ridden (by Italian standards), Genoa has lost precious tourist revenue due to its urban-planning follies.

And yet, Europe's biggest boat show, the annual Salone Nautico Internazionale, is held here. Fine restaurants are abundant, and classical dance and music are richly represented; the Teatro Carlo Felice is the local opera venue, and where the internationally renowned annual Niccolò Paganini Violin Contest takes place. Due to its location and its shipping industry, Genoa is also the most diverse city in Italy; it's one of the only places on the mostly homogeneous boot where you can find well-established North African, Asian, and South American communities. Just steps away from the port, walking down the darkly shadowed Via del Prè, with its street bazaars and spooky branching alleyways, seems like a momentary excursion to a third-world country.

Genoa has been struggling, mostly unsuccessfully, to change its seamy image. A port-side promenade, a spider-shape elevator with a harbor view, and Europe's largest aquarium were installed for the expensive, much-criticized Columbus quincentennial celebrations of 1992. Another hurried face-lift took place in preparation for Genoa's designation as one of Europe's "Capitals of Culture" for the year 2004, but it will take more than a flattering label to rescue this once-proud, still fascinating city. But should it be rescued? Perhaps the time to visit is now, before the old port is completely overbuilt, and before the city's gritty charm is gone.

Exploring Genoa

The ancient center of Genoa, threaded with tiny streets flanked by 11th-century portals, is roughly the area between the port and Piazza de Ferrari; this mazelike pedestrian zone—no car could fit—is officially called the Caruggi District, but the Genoese, in their matter-of-fact way, simply refer to the area as the place of the *vicoli* (narrow alleys). Between the 12th and 16th century the city expanded—with wider streets—to occupy the area now bounded by Stazione Principe to the west and Stazione Brignole to the east. Divided into *sestieri* (six neighborhoods), this is where the majority of Genoa's most important landmarks are found.

Medieval & Renaissance Genoa

a good walk

The best way to begin your exploration of Genoa is to see it from above. From Piazza Acquaverde, behind Stazione Principe, start your walk along Via Balbi, which runs southeast from Stazione Principe toward the medieval town. On Via Balbi you pass Palazzo Balbi Durazzo, also known as **Palazzo Reale** ⑪ ⌐, and **Palazzo dell'Università** ⑫. Continue straight past Piazza dellà Nunziata, stopping at **Santissima Annunziata** ⑬, to Largo di Zecca, where you can take the **Zecca-Righi funicular** ⑭ up to a marvelous lookout point on the edge of Genoa's network of fortresses. From Righi you can also walk along the ancient city walls in either direction. After descending, go southeast on Via Cairoli to reach the famed **Via Garibaldi** ⑮, a majestic street where you can pause to see the collections in the museums of **Palazzo Rosso** ⑯ and **Palazzo Bianco** ⑰. Stop in at **Palazzo Tursi** ⑱, Genoa's town hall, and ask the guard at the door if it happens to be open to visitors that day; if it is, you can see one of Paganini's violins. At the end of Via Garibaldi go left and left again to Piazza del Portello, where you can take the **Castelletto** ⑲ elevator for another panoramic view of the city and the port (a fine view is also to be had from the terrace of the **Museo d'Arte Orientale Chiossone** ⑳, just above Piazza del Portello). Returning to Piazza Fontane Marose at the end of Via Garibaldi, turn southwest, taking Via Luccoli into the medieval Caruggi District. Beyond Piazza Soziglia, detour to the left, taking Via Campetto to Piazza San Matteo, flanked by the well-preserved houses of the Dorias and the church of **San Matteo** ㉑. Follow Salita Arcivescovado and turn right on Via Reggio to the cathedral of **San Lorenzo** ㉒, medieval Genoa's religious heart. North of the cathedral is Vico degli Indoratori, onto which you turn northwest. Follow it to Via degli Orefici, on which you turn left to reach the **Loggia dei Mercanti** ㉓. Head north on Via San Luca, Genoa's best shopping street (hopping on weekend afternoons), to the **Galleria Nazionale** ㉔. At the northern end of Via San Luca is the spooky church of **San Siro** ㉕. From there, if it is daytime and if you're adventurous, you can continue on to Via del Campo back toward Principe until the street becomes Via del Prè, where you can find Genoa's seamy, multicultural underbelly, in some senses the true center of the ancient port. Prepare yourself for a tour through the human vices; women should not walk alone on Via del Prè.

TIMING   Allow a full day for this walk, with time to stop in churches and museums. Note that the Galleria Nazionale is closed on Monday. Do not walk on Via del Prè at night.

What to See

Caruggi District. The winding alleys—known as *caruggi*—that make up the popular side of medieval Genoa are the city's heart and soul. Wealthy Genovese built their homes in this quarter in the 16th century, and prosperous guilds, such as the goldsmiths for whom Vico degli Indoratori and Via degli Orefici were named, set up shop here. In this warren of

KEY

▶ Start of walk

narrow, cobbled streets extending north from Piazza Caricamento, the city's oldest churches punctuate blocks of 500-year-old apartment buildings, and tiny shops sell antique furniture, coffee, rifles, cheese, wine, gilt picture frames, camping gear, even live fish. The apartment buildings along the tiny streets lean in so precariously that penthouse balconies in some cases nearly touch those across the street, blocking what little sunlight would have shone down onto the cobblestones. When exploring these shady passageways, bear in mind that this quarter is one of the city's most disreputable. Don't come here at night or on holidays, when shops are closed and the alleys deserted, unless you're willing to part with your valuables.

⑲ Castelletto. One of Genoa's handy municipal elevators whisks you skyward from Piazza Portello, at the end of Via Garibaldi, for a good view of the old city. ⊠ *Piazza Portello, Castelletto* 🖭 *€1* ⊙ *6:40 AM–midnight.*

㉔ Galleria Nazionale. This gallery, housed in the richly adorned **Palazzo Spinola** north of Piazza Soziglia, contains masterpieces by Luca Giordano and Guido Reni. The *Ecce Homo,* by Antonello da Messina, is a hauntingly beautiful painting, of historical interest because it was the Sicilian da Messina who first brought Flemish oil paints and techniques to Italy from his sojourns in the Low Countries. ⊠ *Piazza Pellicceria 1, Maddalena* 🕾 *010/2705300* 🖭 *€4.50, €6.50 including Palazzo Reale* ⊙ *Tues.–Sat. 8:30–7:30, Sun. 1–8.*

Granarolo funicular. Take a cog railway up the steeply rising terrain to another part of the city's fortified walls. It takes 15 minutes to hoist you from Stazione Principe, on Piazza Acquaverde, to **Porta Granarolo,** 1,000 feet above, where the sweeping view gives you a sense of Genoa's size. The funicular departs about every half hour. ⊠ *Piazza del Principe, San Teodoro* 🕾 *010/5582414* ⊕ *www.amt.genova.it* 🖭 *1€, free with bus ticket* ⊙ *Daily 6 AM–10 PM, at 10:40 PM and 11:20 PM.*

㉓ Loggia dei Mercanti. This merchants' row dating from the 16th century is lined with shops selling local foods and gifts as well as raincoats, rubber boots, and fishing line. ⊠ *Piazza Banchi, Maddalena.*

⑳ Museo d'Arte Orientale Chiossone. In the Villetta di Negro park on the hillside above Piazza Portello, the Chiossone Oriental Art Museum has one of Europe's most noteworthy collections of Japanese, Chinese, and Thai objects. There's a fine view of the city from the museum's terrace. ⊠ *Piazzale Mazzini 1, Piazza Corvetto, Maddalena* 🕾 *010/542285* 🖭 *€3.10, free Sun.* ⊙ *Tues.–Fri. 9–1, weekends 10–7.*

⑰ Palazzo Bianco. It's difficult to miss the splendid white facade of this town palace as you walk down Via Garibaldi, once one of Genoa's most important streets. The building, completely restored in 2003–2004, houses a fine collection of 17th-century art, with the Spanish and Flemish schools well represented. ⊠ *Via Garibaldi 11, Maddalena* 🕾 *010/ 5572013* 🖭 *€3.10, €5.16 combined ticket with Palazzo Rosso, free Sun.* ⊙ *Tues.–Fri. 9–7, weekends 10–7.*

⑫ Palazzo dell'Università. Built in the 1630s as a Jesuit college, this has been Genoa's university since 1803. The exterior is unassuming, but climb the stairway flanked by lions to visit the handsome courtyard, with its portico of double Doric columns. ⊠ *Via Balbi 5, Pré.*

▶ ⑪ **Palazzo Reale.** Lavish rococo rooms provide sumptuous display space for paintings, sculptures, tapestries, and Asian ceramics. The 17th-century palace—also known as Palazzo Balbi Durazzo—was built by the Balbi family, enormously wealthy Genovese merchants. Its regal pretensions were not lost on the Savoy, who bought the palace and turned it into a royal residence in the early 19th century. The gallery of mirrors and the ballroom on the upper floor are particularly decadent. Look for works by Sir Anthony Van Dyck, who lived in Genoa for six years, beginning in 1621, and painted many portraits of the Genovese nobility. The formal gardens provide a welcome respite from the bustle of the city beyond the palace walls, as well as great views of the harbor. ⊠ *Via Balbi 10, Pré* ☎ *010/27101* ⊠ *€4, €1 gardens only, €6.50 including Galleria Nazionale* ⊗ *Tue. and Wed. 9–1:30, Thurs.–Sun. 9–7.*

⑯ **Palazzo Rosso.** This 17th-century baroque palace was named for the red stone used in its construction. It now contains, apart from a number of lavishly frescoed suites, works by Titian, Veronese, Reni, and Van Dyck. ⊠ *Via Garibaldi 18, Maddalena* ☎ *010/2476351* ⊠ *€3.10, €5.16 combined ticket with Palazzo Bianco, free Sun.* ⊗ *Tues.–Fri. 9–7, weekends 10–7.*

⑱ **Palazzo Tursi.** In the 16th century, wealthy resident Nicolò Grimaldi had a palace built of pink stone quarried in the region. It's been reincarnated as Genoa's Palazzo Municipale (Municipal Building), and so most of the goings-on inside are the stuff of local politics and quickie weddings. When Genovese civic proceedings are not taking place, however, you are welcome to view the richly decorated rooms and the famous Guarnerius violin that belonged to Niccolò Paganini (1782–1840), which is played once a year on Columbus Day (October 12). ⊠ *Via Garibaldi 9, Maddalena* ☎ *010/557111* ⊠ *Free* ⊗ *Weekdays 8–noon.*

㉒ **San Lorenzo.** Contrasting black slate and white marble, so common in Liguria, embellished the cathedral at the heart of medieval Genoa—inside and out. Consecrated in 1118, the church honors St. Lawrence, who passed through the city on his way to Rome in the 3rd century. For hundreds of years the building was used for state and religious purposes such as civic elections. Note the 13th-century Gothic portal, fascinating twisted barbershop columns, and the 15th- to 17th-century frescoes inside. The last campanile dates from the early 16th century. The **Museo del Tesoro di San Lorenzo** (San Lorenzo Treasury Museum) housed inside has some stunning pieces from medieval goldsmiths and silversmiths, for which medieval Genoa was renowned. ⊠ *Piazza San Lorenzo, Molo* ☎ *010/2471831* ⊠ *Cathedral free, museum €5.16* ⊗ *Cathedral daily 8–11:45 and 3–6:45, museum Mon.–Sat. 9–11:30 and 3–5:30.*

㉑ **San Matteo.** This typically Genovese black-and-white-stripe church dates from the 12th century; its crypt contains the tomb of Andrea Doria (1466–1560), the Genovese admiral who maintained the independence of his native city. The well-preserved Piazza San Matteo was, for 500 years, the seat of the Doria family, which ruled Genoa and much of Liguria from the 16th to the 18th century. The square is bounded by 13th-to 15th-century houses decorated with portals and loggias. ⊠ *Piazza San Matteo, Maddalena* ☎ *010/2474361* ⊘ *Mon.–Sat. 8–noon and 4–7, Sun. 9:30–10:30 and 4–5.*

㉕ San Siro. Genoa's oldest church was the city's cathedral from the 4th to the 9th century. Rebuilt in the 16th and 17th centuries, it now feels a bit like a haunted house—imposing frescoes line dank hallways, and chandeliers hold crooked candles flickering in the darkness. ⊠ *Via San Luca, Maddalena* ☎ *010/22461468* ⊘ *Daily 7:30–noon and 4–7.*

⓭ Santissima Annunziata. Exuberantly frescoed vaults decorate the 16th-to 17th-century church, which is an excellent example of Genovese baroque architecture. ⊠ *Piazza della Nunziata, Pré* ☎ *010/297662* ⊘ *Daily 9–noon and 3–7.*

★ ⓯ Via Garibaldi. Thirteen palaces were built along what was once known as the Via Aurea (Golden Street) in just 10 years. Genoa's leading patrician families constructed their residences here from 1554 onward to escape the cramped conditions of the medieval section. It is one of the most impressive streets in Italy, and the palace-museums today house some of the finest art collections in the country. Most of the palaces without museums on Via Garibaldi can be visited only by special application, but many have courtyards open to the public. ⊠ *West from Piazza Fontane Marose, Maddalena.*

⓮ Zecca-Righi funicular. This is a seven-stop commuter funicular beginning at Piazza della Nunziata and ending at a high lookout on the fortified gates in the 17th-century city walls. Ringed around the circumference of the city are a number of huge fortresses; this gate was part of the city's system of defenses. From Righi you can undertake scenic all-day hikes from one fortress to the next. ⊠ *Piazza della Nunziata, Pré* ☎ *010/5582414* ⊕ *www.amt.genova.it* ⊠ *€1, free with bus ticket* ⊘ *Daily 6 AM–11:45 PM.*

Southern Districts & the Aquarium

a good walk

Start downhill from **Porta Soprana ㉖** ⌐ and pay homage to the small, purported **childhood home of Christopher Columbus ㉗** on the square. Then follow Via Dante into Piazza de Ferrari to **Teatro Carlo Felice ㉘** and the **Accademia delle Belle Arti ㉙**. From Piazza de Ferrari, Genoa's unofficial center, you can make a detour and head down and back up Via XX Settembre, Genoa's wide main thoroughfare, with leading-name boutiques, cafés, and bookstores. Back in Piazza de Ferrari, on the west side of the piazza stands the **Palazzo Ducale ㉚**. Follow the palazzo around to its back side, which presents a neoclassical facade on Piazza Matteotti. Leading uphill from Piazza Matteotti, Salita Pollaiuoli takes you to **San Donato ㉛**. On the west side of the church is Stradone Sant'Agostino, which leads to Piazza Negri and **Sant'Agostino ㉜**. At the top of Stradone Sant'Agostino, from the west end of elongated Piazza Sarzano, take Via Santa Croce and turn right and then left onto Via Santa Maria di Castello, climbing up to the church of **Santa Maria di Castello ㉝**. From Piazza Embriaci turn west and follow the little streets downhill to Via Canneto il Curto, turning downhill on Via San Lorenzo to reach Piazza Caricamento and the old port, where you can take a ride in the panoramic **Il Bigo** ㉞ elevator, visit the **Acquario di Genova** ㉟, or take a boat tour of the port.

TIMING This walk takes from 2½ to 4 hours, with stops at churches and the museum at Sant'Agostino; add an hour or two if you are stopping at the Acquario di Genova.

What to See

㉙ **Accademia delle Belle Arti.** Founded in 1751, the Academy of Fine Arts, as well as being a school, houses a collection of paintings from the 16th to the 19th century. Genovese artists of the baroque period are particularly well represented. ⊠ *Largo Pertini 4, Portoria* ☎ *010/581957* 🎟 *Free* 🕙 *Mon.–Sat. 9–1.*

㉟ **Acquario di Genova.** Europe's biggest aquarium, second in the world only to Osaka's in Japan, is the third most-visited museum in Italy and a must for children. Fifty tanks of marine species, including sea turtles, dolphins, seals, eels, penguins, and sharks, share space with educational displays and re-creations of marine ecosystems, including a tank of coral from the Red Sea. If coming in by car just for the aquarium, take the Genova Ovest exit from the autostrada. Entrance is permitted every half hour and the ticket office closes 1½ hours before the aquarium. ⊠ *Ponte Spinola, Porto Vecchio* ☎ *0101/23451* ⊕ *www.acquario.ge.it* 🎟 *€12.50* 🕙 *July and Aug., daily 9 AM–11 PM; Sept.–June, Mon.–Wed. and Fri. 9:30–7:30, Thurs. 9:30 AM–10 PM, and weekends 9:30–8:30.*

㉗ **Childhood home of Christopher Columbus.** The ivy-covered remains of this fabled medieval house stand in the gardens below the Porta Soprana. A small and rather disappointing display of objects and reproductions relating to the life and travels of Columbus are on display inside. ⊠ *Piazza Dante, Molo* ☎ *No phone* 🎟 *€3* 🕙 *Tues.–Sun. 9–5.*

Harbor. A boat tour gives you a good perspective on the layout of the harbor, which dates back to Roman times. The Genoa inlet, the largest along the Italian Riviera, was also used by the Phoenicians and Greeks as a harbor and a staging area from which they could penetrate inland to form settlements and to trade. The port is guarded by the Diga Foranea, a striking wall 5 km (3 mi) long built into the ocean. The **Lanterna,** a lighthouse more than 360 feet high, was built in 1544 at the height of Andrea Doria's career; it's one of Italy's oldest lighthouses and a traditional emblem of Genoa. Boat tours of the harbor, provided by the Cooperativa Battellieri, launch from the aquarium pier (€6, 1 hour). ⊠ *Stazione Marittima, Ponte dei Mille* ☎ *010/265712* ⊕ *www. battellierigenova.it.*

㉞ **Il Bigo.** The bizarre white structure erected in 1992 to celebrate the Columbus quincentennial looks like either a radioactive spider or an overgrown potato spore, depending on your point of view. Its most redeeming feature is the **Ascensore Panoramico Bigo** (Bigo Panoramic Elevator), from which you can take in the harbor, city, and sea. Next to the elevator, in an area covered by sail-like awnings, there's an ice-skating rink in winter. ⊠ *Ponte Spinola, Porto Vecchio* ☎ *010/23451, 010/2461319 ice skating* 🎟 *Elevator €3.30, skating rink €7* 🕙 *Elevator Feb. and Nov., weekends 10–5; June–Aug., Tues. and Wed. and Sun. 10–8, Thurs.–Sat.*

10 AM–11 PM; Mar.–May and Sept., Tues.–Sun. 10–6; Oct., Tues.–Sun. 10–5; Dec. 26–Jan. 6, daily 10–5; skating rink Nov. or Dec.–Mar., weekdays 8 AM–9:30 PM, Sat. 10 AM–2 AM, Sun. 10 AM–midnight.

30 Palazzo Ducale. This palace was built in the 16th century over a medieval hall, and its facade was rebuilt in the late 18th century and later restored. It now houses temporary exhibitions and a restaurant-bar serving fusion cuisine. Reservations are necessary to visit the dungeons and tower. Guided tours of the palace and its exhibitions are sometimes available. ✉ *Piazza Matteotti 9 and Piazza de Ferrari, Portoria* ☎ *010/5574004* ⊕ *www.palazzoducale.genova.it* ☒ *Free* ☉ *Tues.–Sun. 9–9.*

▶ **26 Porta Soprana.** A striking 12th-century twin-tower structure, this medieval gateway stands on the spot where a road from ancient Rome entered the city. It is just steps uphill from Columbus's boyhood home, and legend has it that the explorer's father was employed here as a gatekeeper. It's also known as Porta di Sant'Andrea (note the flags, with a red cross on a white background, flying atop the towers). ✉ *Piazza Dante, Molo.*

31 San Donato. Although somewhat marred by 19th- and 20th-century restorations, the 12th-century San Donato—with its original portal and octagonal campanile—is a fine example of Genovese Romanesque architecture. Inside, an altarpiece by the Flemish artist Joos Van Cleve (circa 1485–1540) depicts the Adoration of the Magi. ✉ *Piazza San Donato, Portoria* ☎ *010/2468869* ☉ *Mon.–Sat. 8–noon and 3–7, Sun. 9–12:30 and 3–7.*

32 Sant'Agostino. This 13th-century Gothic church was damaged during World War II, but it still has a fine campanile and two well-preserved cloisters, which house an excellent museum displaying fragments of medieval architecture and fresco paintings. Highlighting the collection are the enigmatic fragments of a tomb sculpture by Giovanni Pisano (circa 1250–circa 1315). ✉ *Piazza Sarzano 35/r, Molo* ☎ *010/2511263* ☒ *€3.10, free Sun.* ☉ *Tues.–Fri. 9–7, weekends 10–7.*

33 Santa Maria di Castello. One of Genoa's most significant religious buildings, an early Christian church, was rebuilt in the 12th century and finally completed in 1513. You can visit the adjacent cloisters and see the fine artwork contained in the museum. Museum hours may occasionally vary during religious services. ✉ *Salita di Santa Maria di Castello 15, Molo* ☎ *010/2549511* ☒ *Free* ☉ *Daily 9–noon and 3:30–6.*

28 Teatro Carlo Felice. The World War II–ravaged opera house in Genoa's modern center, Piazza de Ferrari, was rebuilt and reopened in 1991 to host the fine Genovese opera company; its massive tower has been the subject of much criticism. ✉ *Passo Eugenio Montale 4, Piazza De Ferrari, Portoria* ☎ *010/53811* ⊕ *www.carlofelice.it.*

off the beaten path

CIMITERO MONUMENTALE DI STAGLIENO – One of the most famous of Genovese landmarks is this bizarrely beautiful cemetery; its fanciful marble and bronze sculptures sprawl haphazardly across a hillside on the outskirts of town. A **Pantheon** holds indoor tombs and some remarkable works like an 1878 *Eve* by Villa. Don't miss Rovelli's 1896 **Tomba Raggio,** which shoots Gothic spires out of the hillside forest. The cemetery began operation in 1851 and has been lauded by such visitors as Mark Twain and Evelyn Waugh. It covers a good deal of ground; allow at least half a day to explore. It's difficult to locate; the no. 12 and 14 buses from the Stazione Genova Brignole, or a taxi, take you there. ⊠ *Piazzale Resasco, Piazza Manin* ☎ *010/870184* ⊕ *www.cimiterodistaglieno.it* ☞ *Free* ⊙ *Daily 7:30–5.*

GENOVA–CASELLA RAILROAD – In continuous operation since 1929, the Genova–Casella railroad runs from Piazza Manin in Genoa (follow Via Montaldo from the center of town, or take Bus 33 or 34 to Piazza Manin) through the beautiful countryside above the city, finally arriving in the rural hill town of Casella. On the way, the tiny train traverses a series of precarious switchbacks that afford sweeping views of the forested Ligurian hills. In Casella Paese (the last stop) you can hike, eat lunch, or just check out the view and ride back. There are two restaurants and two pizzerias near the Casella station; try local cuisine at Trattoria Teresin in Località Avosso. **Canova** (two stops from the end of the line) is the start of two possible hikes through the hills: one a two-hour, one-way trek to a small sanctuary, **Santuario della Vittoria**, and the other a more grueling four-hour hike to the hill town of **Creto.** Another worthwhile stop along the rail line is **Sant'Olcese Tullo,** where you can take a half-hour (one-way) walk along a river and through the **Sentiero Botanico di Ciaé,** a botanical garden and forest refuge with labeled specimens of Ligurian flora and a tiny medieval castle. For Canova and Sant'Olcese, inform your conductor that you want him to stop. The Casella railroad is a good way to get a sense of the rugged landscape around Genoa, and you may have it to yourself. The train runs about every hour. ⊠ *Piazza Manin* ☎ *010/837321* ⊕ *www. ferroviagenovacasella.it* ☞ *€3.60 round-trip Mon.–Sat., €5 Sun.* ⊙ *Mon.–Sat. 7:30–7:30, Sun. 9–9.*

Where to Stay & Eat

$$$–$$$$ ✕ **Antica Osteria del Bai.** Look out from a large dark wood–paneled room over the Ligurian Sea from this romantic upscale restaurant perched on a cliff. A seaside theme pervades the wall art and menu, which might include black gnocchi with lobster sauce, and ravioli ai frutti di mare. The restaurant's traditional elegance is reflected in its white tablecloths, its dress code, and its prices. ⊠ *Via Quarto 16, Quarto* ☎ *010/387478* 🏛 *Jacket and tie* ⊟ *AE, DC, MC, V* ⊙ *Closed Mon., Jan. 10–20, and Aug. 1–20.*

$$$–$$$$ ✕ **Gran Gotto.** Innovative regional dishes are served in this posh, spacious restaurant festooned with contemporary paintings. Try *cappellacci di borragine con vellutata di pinoli* (borage pasta with a pine-nut sauce) followed by *calamaretti brasati con porri e zucchine* (braised baby squid with leeks and zucchini), one of the many excellent second courses. Service is quick and helpful. ⊠ *Viale Brigata Bisagno 69/r, Piazza della Vittoria, Foce* ☎ *010/564344* ⌕ *Reservations essential* ⊟ *AE, DC, MC, V* ⊙ *Closed Sun. and Aug. 12–31. No lunch Sat.*

$$$–$$$$ ╳ **Zeffirino.** The five Belloni brothers share chef duties at a well-known restaurant full of odd combinations, including decor that has both rustic wood and modern metallic pieces. Try the *passutelli* (ravioli stuffed with ricotta cheese, herbs, and fruit) or any of the homemade pasta dishes. With a Zeffirino restaurant in Las Vegas and another in Hong Kong, the enterprising Bellonis have gone international. ⊠ *Via XX Settembre 20, Portoria* ☎ *010/591990* ⌁ *Reservations essential* ⌂ *Jacket required* ⊟ *AE, DC, MC, V.*

$$–$$$ ╳ **Enoteca Sola.** Menus are chosen specifically to complement wines at Pino Sola's airy, casually elegant *enoteca* (wine bar) in the heart of the modern town. The short menu emphasizes seafood and varies daily but might include stuffed artichokes or baked stockfish. The real draw, though, is the wine list, which includes some of the winners of the *Tre Bicchieri* (Three Glasses) award denoting only the very best. ⊠ *Via C. Barabino 120/r, Foce* ☎ *010/594513* ⊟ *AE, DC, MC, V* ⊙ *Closed Sun. and Aug.*

$–$$ ╳ **Da Domenico.** Don't be dismayed by the labyrinth of rooms and wood passages that lead to your table at this restaurant in a quiet square near Piazza Dante—you've found one of those hidden corners that only the Genovese know. Traditional seafood and meat dishes are on the menu. ⊠ *Piazza Leonardo 3, Molo* ☎ *010/540289* ⌁ *Reservations essential* ⊟ *AE, DC, MC, V* ⊙ *Closed Mon.*

¢–$ ╳ **Bakari.** Hip styling and ambient lighting hint at the creative, even daring, takes on Ligurian classics here. Sure bets are the spinach-and-cheese gnocchi, any of several carpaccios, and the delicate beef dishes. Reserve ahead, requesting a table on the more imaginative ground floor. ⊠ *Vico del Fieno 16/r, northwest of Piazza San Matteo, Maddalena* ☎ *010/291936* ⊟ *AE, MC, V* ⊙ *Closed Sun. No dinner Wed. or Fri.*

$$$$ ▦ **City.** The location of this hotel can't be beat—it's off Via Roma, the grand shopping street, and one block from Piazza de Ferrari, which divides new Genoa from old Genoa in the heart of the city. A bland apartment-building exterior gives way to a polished lobby and light, modern rooms that are a bit small but very comfortable. Most have only mediocre views; try for a street-side room on a high floor. ⊠ *Via San Sebastiano 6, Portoria, 16123* ☎ *010/5545* 🖶 *010/586301* ⊕ *www.bestwestern. it/city_ge* ⏎ *63 rooms, 3 suites* ⌂ *Restaurant, in-room data ports, in-room safes, bar, parking (fee)* ⊟ *AE, DC, MC, V* ⏐⊙⏐ *BP.*

★ $$$ ▦ **Bristol Palace.** The 19th-century grand hotel in the heart of the shopping district carefully guards its reputation for courtesy and service. Spacious, individual guest rooms all have high ceilings and elegant wood wardrobes or headboards. Public rooms, all connected to the hotel's central oval staircase, are comfortable, small, and pleasantly discreet with paneled walls and soft lighting. ⊠ *Via XX Settembre 35, Portoria, 16121* ☎ *010/592541* 🖶 *010/561756* ⊕ *www.hotelbristolpalace.com* ⏎ *128 rooms, 5 suites* ⌂ *Restaurant, room TVs with movies, gym, bar, Internet, meeting rooms, parking (fee), some pets allowed* ⊟ *AE, DC, MC, V* ⏐⊙⏐ *BP.*

$ ▦ **Agnello d'Oro.** The friendly owner at Agnello d'Oro does double duty as a travel agent: he's happy to help you with plane reservations and travel plans. Only a few of the simple, modern rooms have balconies, but a surprisingly varied Continental breakfast awaits you in the morn-

THE ART OF THE PESTO PESTLE

YOU MAY HAVE KNOWN GENOA primarily for its salami or its brash explorer, but the city's most direct effect on your life away from Italy may be through its cultivation of one of the world's best pasta sauces. The sublime blend of basil, extra-virgin olive oil, garlic, pine nuts, and grated pecorino and Parmigiano Reggiano cheeses that forms pesto alla Genovese is one of Italy's crowning culinary achievements, a concoction that Italian food guru Marcella Hazan has called "the most seductive of all sauces for pasta." Unlike in the United States, where various versions of pesto bedeck everything from pizza to grilled-chicken sandwiches, Ligurian pesto is served only over spaghetti, gnocchi, lasagne, or—most authentically—trenette (a flat, spaghettilike pasta) or trofie (short, doughy pasta twists), and then typically mixed with boiled potatoes and green beans. Pesto is also occasionally used to

flavor minestrone. The small-leafed basil grown in the region's sunny seaside hills is considered by many to be the best in the world, and your visit to Liguria affords you the chance to savor pesto in its original form. Pesto sauce was invented primarily as a showcase for that singular flavor, and the best pesto brings out the fresh basil's alluring aroma and taste rather than masking it with the complementary ingredients. The simplicity and rawness of pesto is one of its virtues, as cooking (or even heating) basil ruins its delicate flavor. In fact, pesto aficionados refuse even to subject the basil leaves to an electric blender; Genovese (and other) foodies insist that true pesto can be made only with mortar and pestle. Although satisfactory versions can surely be prepared less laboriously, the pesto purists' culinary conservatism is supported by etymology: the word pesto is derived from the Italian verb pestare (to pound or grind).

ing. The hotel is about 100 yards from Stazione Principe, near the Palazzo Reale. ⊠ *Vico delle Monachette 6, Pré, 16126* ☎ *010/2462084* 🖷 *010/2462327* ⊕ *www.hotelagnellodoro.it* ↘ *25 rooms* ☖ *Restaurant, bar, parking (fee), some pets allowed, no-smoking rooms; no a/c in some rooms* ⊟ *AE, DC, MC, V* ⦿⃝ *BP.*

$ 🏨 **Cairoli.** This central family-run hotel is on a street near the aquarium that is closed to traffic, and rooms are soundproofed—an important plus in this noisy city. Three of the plainly decorated rooms open onto the hotel's pleasant terrace. A simple Continental breakfast costs €8 extra. ⊠ *Via Cairoli 14/4, Maddalena, 16124* ☎ *010/2461454* 🖷 *010/2467512* ⊕ *www.hotelcairoligenova.com* ↘ *12 rooms* ☖ *Bar* ⊟ *AE, DC, MC, V.*

Nightlife & the Arts

Especially in summer, the place for nightlife is on the waterfront to the *levante* (southeast) side of the city. From the center, take Corso Italia in the direction of Quarto, Quinto, and nearby Nervi to reach the outdoor nighttime hub. Several beachfront *bagni* (literally, baths) and their accompanying restaurants and bars in the area serve as nighttime summer hangouts.

Nightclubs

Makò. Big, well-known discotheques such as the famous Makò perch on a cliff about halfway to Nervi, attracting attention from Genovese twenty- and thirtysomethings. ⊠ *Corso Italia 28/r, Quarto* ☎ *010/367652.*

Opera

Teatro Carlo Felice. Genoa's well-respected opera company, Fondazione Teatro Carlo Felice, stages lavish productions and occasionally the debut of a work from October to May. ⊠ *Passo Eugenio Montale 4, Piazza De Ferrari, Portoria* ☎ *010/53811* ⊕ *www.carlofelice.it.*

Shopping

Liguria is famous for its fine laces, silver and gold filigree work, and ceramics. Look also for bargains in velvet, macramé, olive wood, and marble. Genoa is the best spot to find all these specialties. In the heart of the medieval quarter, Via Soziglia is lined with shops selling handicrafts and tempting foods. Via XX Settembre is famous for its exclusive shops. High-end shops line Via Luccoli. The best shopping area for trendy-but-inexpensive Italian clothing is near San Siro, on Via San Luca.

Clothing & Leather Goods

Bruno Magli. The Bologna-based designer makes an impeccable line of leather shoes, boots, handbags, and jackets. ⊠ *Via XX Settembre 135, Foce* ☎ *010/561890.*

Pescetto. Look for designer clothes, perfumes, and gifts at this fancy shop. ⊠ *Via Scurreria 8, Molo* ☎ *010/2473433.*

Stefanel. Come to the local venue of choice for modern Italian women's clothing. ⊠ *Via XX Settembre 36–39, Foce* ☎ *010/714755.*

Jewelry

Codevilla. The well-established Codevilla is one of the best jewelers on a street full of goldsmiths. ⊠ *Via Orefici 53, Maddalena* ☎ *010/2472567.*

Wines

Vinoteca Sola. Buy Italian and Ligurian wines and have them shipped overseas—or you can even buy futures for advance purchase. ⊠ *Piazza Colombo 13–15/r, near Stazione Brignole, Foce* ☎ *010/594513* ⊕ *www.vinotecasola.it.*

Side Trip from Genoa

Nervi

㊱ *11 km (7 mi) east of Genoa, 19 km (12 mi) west of Rapallo.*

The identity of this stately late-19th-century resort, famous for its seaside promenade, the **Passeggiata Anita Garibaldi** (1½ km [1 mi] long), its palm-lined roads, and 300 acres of parks rich in orange trees and exotics, is given away only by the sign on the sleepy train station in the center of town; the town is technically part of the city of Genoa. Its attractions are peace and quiet, lush gardens, and dramatic black cliffs that drop into the sea; it is as different from Genoa's hustle and bustle as its clear blue water is from Genoa's crowded port. From the Nervi train station, walk east along the seaside promenade to reach beach stations, a cliff-hanging restaurant, and the 2,000 varieties of roses in the public **Parco Villa Grimaldi,** all the while enjoying one of the most breathtaking views on the Riviera. Nervi—and the road along the way— also becomes a hotbed of nightlife in summer. Take one of the frequent trains for the 15-minute ride from Stazione Principe or Brignole (buy a ticket for Genova–Nervi), or take Bus 15 or 17 from Brignole or Piazza de Ferrari to Nervi. Alternatively, a taxi from town center runs about €20 one-way.

WHERE TO STAY &
EAT

$–$$

✕ **Marinella.** The impressive wrought-iron chandelier inside takes second billing to the great sea views from windows and terrace. The restaurant perches on seaside shoals. Try the *zuppa di pesce* (fish soup); main dishes change according to the day's catch. There's an inexpensive hotel annex, too. ⊠ *Passeggiata Anita Garibaldi 18/r* ☏ *010/3728343* ▤ *MC, V* ⊗ *Closed Mon. and Nov.*

★ $$$

▥ **Romantik Hotel Villa Pagoda.** Housed in a 19th-century merchant's mansion modeled after a Chinese pagoda, the top-quality hotel has a private park, private access to Nervi's famed cliff-top sea walk, and magnificent sea views. It's the best of both worlds—luxurious peace and quiet with the city's attractions just 15 minutes away. Request a tower room to look out over it all from the best vantage point. ⊠ *Via Capolungo 15, 16167* ☏ *010/3726161* 🖷 *010/321218* ⊕ *www.villapagoda. it* 🛏 *13 rooms, 4 suites* ♨ *Restaurant, in-room safes, minibars, tennis court, pool, piano bar, meeting room, some pets allowed* ▤ *AE, DC, MC, V* ▧ *BP.*

NIGHTLIFE & THE
ARTS

An **International Ballet Festival** (Tourist office ⊠ Stazione Principe, San Teodoro ☏ 010/2462633) is held every July in the Villa Gropallo park, drawing performers and audiences from all over the world.

Extraordinarily popular with locals, **Senhor do Bonfim** (⊠ Passeggiata Anita Garibaldi ☏ 010/3726312), a nightclub along the water on Nervi's beautiful seaside promenade, has live music late into the night on weekends, and mellower-than-disco dancing every night.

RIVIERA DI PONENTE

The Riviera di Ponente (Riviera of the Setting Sun) stretches from Genoa to Ventimiglia on the French border. For the most part it's an unbroken chain of popular beach resorts sheltered from the north by the Ligurian and Maritime Alps, mountain walls that guarantee mild winters and a long growing season—resulting in its other nickname, the Riviera dei Fiori (Riviera of Flowers). Actually, the name is more evocative than the sight of once-verdant hillsides now swathed in plastic to form massive greenhouses. Many towns on the western Riviera have suffered from an epidemic of overdevelopment, but most have preserved their old cores, usually their most interesting features. In major resorts, large, modern marinas cater to the pleasure-craft crowd. The Riviera di Ponente has both sandy and pebbly beaches with some quiet bays.

Pegli

🗗 *13 km (8 mi) west of Genoa.*

Once a popular summer home for many patrician Genovese families, Pegli has museums, parks, and some regal old villas with well-tended gardens. This residential suburb manages to maintain its dignity despite industrial development and the proximity of airport and port facilities. Two lovely villas make it worth an excursion. Pegli can be reached conveniently by commuter train from Stazione Porta Principe in Genoa.

Villa Doria, near the Pegli train station, has a large park. The villa itself, built in the 16th century by the Doria family, has been converted into a **naval museum.** ⊠ *Piazza Bonavino 7* ☎ *010/6969885* 🎟 *Villa €3.10, park free* ☉ *Villa Tues.–Fri. 9–1, Sat. 10–1, park daily 9–noon and 2–6.*

Villa Durazzo Pallavicini, set in 19th-century gardens with temples and artificial lakes, contains an **archaeological museum.** ⊠ *Via Pallavicini 11* ☎ *010/6981048* ⊕ *www.doit.it/pallavicini* 🎟 *€3.10* ☉ *Tues.–Fri. 9–7, weekends 10–7.*

Varazze

🗗 *23 km (14 mi) southwest of Pegli, 35 km (22 mi) west of Genoa.*

Well-preserved medieval ramparts surround the town, with the remains of a Romanesque church and facade built directly into one of the walls. Varazze is nicknamed *la città delle donne* (the city of women) after an annual festival once held in celebration of women. The name has remained but the festival, last given in 1999, has passed, at least for the moment, from fashion.

Albisola Marina

🗗 *11 km (7 mi) southwest of Varazze, 43 km (26 mi) west of Genoa.*

Albisola Marina has a centuries-old tradition of ceramic-making. Numerous shops here sell the distinctive wares, and even a whole sidewalk, **Lungomare degli Artisti,** has been transformed by the colorful ceramic works of well-known artists. It runs along the beachfront. The 18th-century **Villa Faraggiana** has interesting antique ceramics and exhibits on the history of the craft. ⊠ *Near the parish church on Via dell'Oratorio* ☎ *019/480622* 🎟 *Free* ☉ *Apr.–Sept., Wed.–Mon. 3–7.*

Shopping

Ceramiche San Giorgio (⊠ Corso Matteotti 5 ☎ 019/482747) has been producing ceramics since the 17th century, and is known for both classic and modern designs. **Mazzotti** (⊠ Corso Matteotti 25 ☎ 019/481626) has an exclusive ceramics selection and a small museum. **Ernan** (⊠ Corso Mazzini 77, Albisola Superiore ☎ 019/489916) sells blue-and-white Old Savona patterns typical of the 18th century.

Savona

40 *5 km (3 mi) southwest of Albisola Marina, 46 km (29 mi) southwest of Genoa.*

Savona is the fifth-largest seaport in Italy and handles vast oil and coal cargoes, as well as car and truck ferries. As it was considerably damaged during World War II, much of the town is modern and not very interesting, although a small austere older quarter near the harbor contains some fine homes of the town's merchant class. The large **Palazzo della Rovere** (⊠ *Via Pia 28*), which now houses magistrates' offices and is closed to the public, was designed for Pope Julius II by the Florentine Giuliano da Sangallo in 1495. The 12th-century **Torre del Brandale** (⊠ Piazza del Brandale 2 ☎ 019/821915), with its 14th-century annex, the **Palazzo degli Anziani,** and two other remaining medieval towers, is open by appointment.

Shopping

Watch for shops selling crystallized fruit, a local specialty. In Millesimo, a town 4 km (2½ mi) west and 36 km (18 mi) inland from Savona, little rum chocolates known as *millesimi* are produced. Look for bargains, too, in wrought-iron work, relief work on copperplate, and pieces in local sandstone.

Finale Ligure

41 *24 km (15 mi) southwest of Savona, 72 km (44 mi) southwest of Genoa.*

Palms, sand strips, *gelaterie* (gelato shops), and good rock-climbing terrain make Finale Ligure a nice break from gaudiness and pastel villages. Finale Ligure is actually made up of three small villages: Finalmarina, Finalpia, and Finalborgo. The former two have fine sandy beaches and modern resort amenities. The most attractive of the villages is Finalborgo, less than 1 km (½ mi) inland, a hauntingly preserved medieval settlement, planned to a rigid blueprint, with 15th-century walls. The surrounding countryside is pierced by deep, narrow valleys and caves; the limestone outcroppings provide the warm pinkish stone found in many buildings in Genoa. Here lurk rare reptiles and exotic flora.

Finalborgo is crowned by the impressive ruins of the huge **Castel Gavone.** ⊠ *Via Beretta.*

The baroque church of **San Biagio** houses many works of art. ⊠ *Piazza San Biagio* ☎ *019/695617* ⊙ *Daily 8–11:30 and 2:30–5.*

Enjoy the shade of the courtyard in the 14th- to 15th-century Dominican convent **Santa Caterina,** or step in to see the museum of local paleontology and natural history. ⊠ *Museo Civico* ☎ *019/690020* ⊒ *€2.60* ⊙ *July–Oct., Tues.–Sat. 9–noon and 3–6, Sun. 9–noon; Nov.–June, Tues.–Sat. 9–noon and 2:30–4:30, Sun. 9–noon.*

Where to Stay & Eat

$$$–$$$$ ✕ **Ai Torchi.** You could easily become a homemade-pesto snob here. The high prices are justified by excellent inventive seafood and meat dishes and by the setting—a restored 5th-century olive-oil refinery. ⊠ *Via del-*

l'Annunziata 12 ☎ *019/690531* ⊟ *AE, DC, MC, V* ⊘ *Closed Jan. 7–Feb. 10, and Tues. Sept.–July.*

¢ 🏨 **Hotel Riviera.** Your agreeable host, Marzio Alberto, welcomes you to this smartly run hotel. Rooms are cheerfully furnished and brightly lighted, and some have views of the sea. There's an additional charge for breakfast if you stay for less than three nights during August. ⊠ *Via Ruffini 11, 17024* ☎ *019/692814* 🖷 *019/680013* ⊕ *www.hotelrivierafinale.it* ⤶ *20 rooms* ⚲ *Bar; no a/c in some rooms* ⊟ *AE, DC, MC, V* ⊘ *Closed mid-Oct–mid-Dec.* ⦿ *BP.*

> **off the beaten path**
>
> **NOLI –** Just 9 km (5½ mi) northeast of Finale Ligure, the ruins of a castle loom benevolently over the tiny medieval gem of Noli. It's hard to imagine that this charming village was—like Genoa, Venice, Pisa, and Amalfi—a prosperous maritime republic in the Middle Ages. If you don't have a car, get a bus for Noli at Spotorno, where local trains stop.

Albenga

42 *20 km (12 mi) southwest of Finale Ligure, 90 km (55 mi) southwest of Genoa.*

Albenga has a medieval core, with narrow streets laid out by the ancient Romans. A network of alleys is punctuated by centuries-old towers surrounding the 18th-century Romanesque cathedral, with a late-14th-century campanile and a baptistery dating back to the 5th century.

> **off the beaten path**
>
> **BARDINETO –** For a look at some of the Riviera's mountain scenery, make an excursion by car to this attractive village in the middle of an area rich in mushrooms, chestnuts, and raspberries, as well as local cheese. A ruined castle stands above the village. From Borghetto Santo Spirito (between Albenga and Finale Ligure), drive inland 25 km (15 mi).

Where to Stay

$$$$ 🏨 **La Meridiana.** An oasis of Italian hospitality and refinement occupies a handsome farmhouse compound surrounded by a garden. The interiors are those of a comfortably luxe home, with tasteful, bright prints and colors; fresh flowers; and a mix of traditional and period-style furniture in the common and guest rooms. Il Rosmarino restaurant serves fine wine and seafood dishes. You can enjoy privileges at the golf, tennis, and equestrian clubs nearby. ⊠ *Via ai Castelli, off A10, 17033 Garlenda, 8 km (5 mi) north of Albenga* ☎ *0182/580271* 🖷 *0182/580150* ⊕ *www.relaischateaux.com/meridiana* ⤶ *13 rooms, 15 suites* ⚲ *Restaurant, golf privileges, pool, sauna, bicycles, Ping-Pong, bar, Internet, some pets allowed (fee)* ⊟ *AE, DC, MC, V* ⊘ *Closed Nov.–Mar.* ⦿ *BP.*

Cervo

43 *23 km (14 mi) southwest of Albenga, 106 km (65 mi) southwest of Genoa.*

Cervo is the quintessential sleepy Ligurian coastal village, nicely polished for the tourists who come to explore its narrow byways and street staircases. It's a remarkably well-preserved medieval town, crowned with a big baroque church. In July and August the square in front of the church is the site of chamber music concerts.

Imperia

44 *12 km (7 mi) west of Cervo, 116 km (71 mi) southwest of Genoa.*

Imperia actually consists of two towns: Porto Maurizio, a medieval town built on a promontory, and Oneglia, now an industrial center for oil refining and pharmaceuticals. Porto Maurizio has a virtually intact medieval center, the Parasio quarter, an intricate spiral of narrow streets and stone portals, and some imposing 17th- and 18th-century palaces. There's little of interest in more modern Oneglia, but the 1½-km (1-mi) trip northeast along the seafront from Porto Maurizio into the new town is worth taking for a visit to the olive-oil museum.

Imperia is king when it comes to olive oil, and the story of the olive—its cultivation and pressing into oil—is the theme of the small **Museo dell' Olivo** set up by the Fratelli Carli olive-oil company. Displays of the history of the olive tree, farm implements, presses, and utensils show how olive oil has been made in many countries throughout history. ⊠ *Via Garessio 11* ☎ *0183/720000* ⊕ *www.museodellolivo.com* ⊠ *Free* ⊗ *Wed.–Mon. 9–noon and 3–6:30.*

Where to Eat

★ ¢–$ ✗ **Candidollo.** In this rustic country inn, with checkered tablecloths and worn terra-cotta floors, host Bruno Ardissone uses fresh, local ingredients to make traditional, seasonal recipes. The menu usually includes *coniglio al timo* (rabbit with thyme and other herbs) and *lumache all'agliata* (grilled snails in piquant sauce). It's well worth the detour to get to this village on the valley road a mile or so north of Diano Marina. ⊠ *Corso Europa 23, Diano Borello, 6 km (4 mi) east of Imperia* ☎ *0183/43025* ☰ *No credit cards* ⊗ *Closed Tues. and Nov.–Mar. No lunch Mon.*

Taggia

45 *20 km (12 mi) west of Imperia, 135 km (84 mi) southwest of Genoa.*

The town of Taggia has a medieval core and one of the most imposing medieval bridges in the area. The church of **San Domenico,** with a small museum, was once part of a monastery founded in the 15th century that remained a beacon of faith and learning in western Liguria for 300 years. An antiques market is held here, just south of Taggia, on the fourth weekend of the month. ⊠ *Piazzale San Domenico, Arma di Taggia* ☎ *No phone* ⊠ *Free* ⊗ *Fri.–Wed. 9–5.*

San Remo

★ **46** *10 km (6 mi) west of Taggia, 146 km (90 mi) southwest of Genoa.*

The self-styled capital of the Riviera di Ponente, San Remo is also the area's largest resort, lined with polished, world-class hotels, exotic gardens, and seaside promenades. Renowned for its royal visitors, famous casino, and romantic setting, San Remo still maintains some of the glamour of its heyday from the late 19th century to World War II. Waterside palm fronds conceal a sizable old center that, unlike in other Ponente towns, is lively even in the off-season. Restaurants, wine bars, and boutiques are second in Liguria only to Genoa's, and San Remo's cafés bustle with afternoon activity.

The newer parts of San Remo suffer from the same epidemic of overbuilding that changed so many towns on the western Riviera for the worse. The Mercato dei Fiori, Italy's most important wholesale flower market, is held here in a market hall between Piazza Colombo and Corso Garibaldi and open to dealers only. More than 20,000 tons of carnations, roses, mimosa flowers, and innumerable other cut flowers are dispatched from here each year. As the center of northern Italy's flower-growing industry, the town is surrounded by hills where verdant terraces are now blanketed with plastic to form immense greenhouses.

Consult the San Remo **tourist office** for information on the flowers and about events in town. ⊠ *Palazzo Riviera, Largo Nuvoloni 1* ☎ *0184/ 571571* ⊕ *www.sanremonet.com.*

Explore the warren of alleyways in the old part of San Remo, **La Pigna** ("the pinecone"), which climbs upward to Piazza Castello and a splendid view of the town.

The onion-domed Russian Orthodox church of **San Basilio** is a legacy of Russian empress Maria Alexandrovna, wife of Czar Alexander II, who built a summerhouse here. ⊠ *Corso dell'Imperatrice.*

In addition to gaming, the Art Nouveau **San Remo Casinò** has a restaurant, a nightclub, and a theater that hosts concerts and the annual San Remo Music Festival. ⊠ *Corso Inglese* ☎ *0184/5951* 🎰 *Slot machines no cover charge; tables no cover charge Mon.–Thurs., €7.50 Fri.–Sun.* ☉ *Slot machines Sun.–Fri. 10 AM–2:30 AM, Sat. 10 AM–3:30 AM, tables Sun.–Fri. 2:30 PM–2:30 AM, Sat. 2:30 PM–3:30 AM.*

off the beaten path

BUSSANA VECCHIA – In the hills where flowers are cultivated for export sits Bussana Vecchia, a self-consciously picturesque former ghost town largely destroyed by an earthquake in 1877. The inhabitants packed up and left en masse after the quake, and for almost a century the houses, church, and crumbling bell tower were empty shells, overgrown by weeds and wildflowers. Since the 1960s an artists colony has evolved among the ruins. Painters, sculptors, artisans, and bric-a-brac dealers have restored dwellings for themselves and sell their wares to you. ⊹ *8 km (5 mi) east of San Remo.*

Where to Stay & Eat

★ ¢–$ ✕ **Nuovo Piccolo Mondo.** Old wooden chairs dating from the 1920s, when the place opened, evoke the homey charm of this small, family-run trattoria. The place has a faithful clientele, so get there early to grab a table and order Ligurian specialties such as *sciancui* (a roughly cut flat pasta with a mixture of beans, tomatoes, zucchini, and pesto) and *polpo* *e patate* (stewed octopus with potatoes). ⊠ *Via Piave 7* ☎ *0184/509012* ⊟ *No credit cards* ۞ *Closed Sun. and Mon., and July.*

$$$$ 🏨 **Royal.** It's a toss-up whether this deluxe hotel or the Splendido in Portofino is the most luxurious in Liguria. Rooms here have a mixture of modern amenities and antique furnishings. The heated seawater swimming pool, open April–September, is in a subtropical garden. On the terrace, candlelight dining and music are offered each night in warm weather. Keep your eyes open for spectacular off-season discounts. Only a few paces from the casino and the train station, the Royal is definitely part of San Remo (unlike the Splendido, which is set above the town). ⊠ *Corso Imperatrice 80, 18038* ☎ *0184/5391* 🖨 *0184/661445* ⊕ *www. royalhotelsanremo.com* ⋖ *121 rooms, 17 suites* ۍ *2 restaurants, room service, in-room dataports, in-room safes, cable TV, golf privileges, miniature golf, tennis court, saltwater pool, hair salon, gym, 2 bars, baby-sitting, playground, dry cleaning, laundry service, convention center* ⊟ *AE, DC, MC, V* ۞ *Closed Oct. 8–Dec. 20* ۞| *MAP.*

$$ 🏨 **Paradiso.** A quiet palm-fringed garden gives the Paradiso an air of seclusion in this sometimes hectic resort city. Rooms are modern and bright; many have little terraces. The hotel restaurant has a good fixed-price menu. This small central hotel is adjacent to a lush public park. ⊠ *Via Roccasterone 12, 18038* ☎ *0184/571211* 🖨 *0184/578176* ⊕ *www.paradisohotel.it* ⋖ *41 rooms* ۍ *Restaurant, pool, bar, Internet, no-smoking rooms* ⊟ *AE, DC, MC, V* ۞| *BP.*

Bordighera

47 *12 km (7 mi) west of San Remo, 155 km (96 mi) southwest of Genoa.*

This garden spot was the first town in Europe to grow date palms, and its citizens still have the exclusive right to provide the Vatican with palm fronds for Easter celebrations. Bordighera, on a large, lush promontory, wears its genteel past as a famous winter resort with unstudied ease. A large English colony, attracted by the mild climate, settled here in the second half of the 19th century and is still very much in evidence today; you regularly find people taking afternoon tea in the cafés, and streets named after Queen Victoria and Shakespeare. Thanks partly to its many year-round English residents, Bordighera does not close down entirely in the off-season like some Riviera resorts but rather serves as a quiet winter haven for elderly people. With plenty of hotels and restaurants, Bordighera makes a good base for beach-going and excursions and is quieter and less commercial than San Remo.

Running parallel to the railway tracks that skirt the seafront, **Lungomare Argentina** is a pleasant promenade, 1½ km (1 mi) long, which begins at the western end of the town and provides good views westward to the French Côte d'Azur.

Where to Stay & Eat

$$$$ ✕ **Le Chaudron.** A charming rustic interior, with ancient Roman arches, has the look of restaurants across the French border in Provence. Ligurian specialties are highlights on the predominantly seafood menu: try the cheese *pansoti con salsa di noci* (ravioli with walnut sauce) and the branzino with artichokes or mushrooms. ⊠ *Via Vittorio Emanuele 9*

☎ *0184/263592* ⌖ *Reservations essential* ☰ *DC, MC, V* ⊘ *Closed Mon.,* *1st 2 wks in Feb., and 1st 2 wks in July.*

$$–$$$ ✕ **La Reserve Restaurant.** This informal trattoria has access to the beach and excellent views of the sea from the dining room; there are even changing rooms for anyone who wants to take a post-lunch dip. Concentrate on the seafood here: specialties are seafood ravioli *al finocchio selvatico* (with wild fennel) and assorted grilled fish. La Reserve is part of the Hotel Parigi, 1½ km (1 mi) east of the center on the road to San Remo. ⊠ *Via Arziglia 20* ☎ *0184/261322* ☰ *AE, DC, MC, V* ⊘ *Closed Mon. and mid-Nov.–mid-Dec. No dinner Wed.*

$–$$ ✕ **Il Tempo Ritrovato.** A small wine bar and restaurant combine forces here on Bordighera's main street. Simple pasta dishes and a spectacular wine list make this a great spot to stop. ⊠ *Via Vittorio Emanuele 144* ☎ *0184/261207* ☰ *AE, DC, MC, V* ⊘ *Closed Sun. and Mon.*

$–$$ ✕ **Piemontese.** Both the Ligurian seafood and the hearty cuisine of the neighboring Piedmont region served here are very popular with locals. Risotto *al Barolo* is cooked with Barolo wine, sausage, and porcini mushrooms, and the winter specialty is *bagna cauda* (raw vegetables with a garlic, oil, and anchovy sauce). ⊠ *Via Roseto 8, off Via Vittorio Emanuele* ☎ *0184/261651* ☰ *AE, MC, V* ⊘ *Closed Tues. and mid-Nov.–mid-Dec.*

$$ ▣ **Grand Hotel Capo Ampelio.** This converted villa overlooks the town and the coastline. Traditional architectural details in the reception rooms and staircases are paired with modern guest rooms, all of which have balconies. The hotel is somewhat outside the town center, so the rooms are quiet. ⊠ *Via Virgilio 5, 18012* ☎ *0184/264333* 🖷 *0184/264244* ⇨ *104 rooms* ⌂ *Restaurant, pool, gym, massage, bar, recreation room* ☰ *DC, MC, V* ⊘ *Closed Nov.–Dec. 22* ⦿ *BP.*

$ ▣ **Pensione Villa Miki.** Tucked away on a quiet residential street, this small family-run pension has simple rooms, only four of which have balconies and private bathrooms. Full- and half-pension plans are available, which, because the food is good and the price is right, are worth considering. ⊠ *Via Lagazzi 14 18012* ☎ *0184/261844* 🖷 *0184/265808* ⇨ *10 rooms, 4 with bath* ⌂ *Restaurant, bar; no a/c* ☰ *No credit cards* ⦿ *BP.*

Ventimiglia

48 *5 km (3 mi) west of Bordighera, 159 km (98 mi) southwest of Genoa.*

From its past life as a pre-Roman settlement known as Albintimilium, Ventimiglia retains some important archaeological remains, including a 2nd-century AD amphitheater. A vital trade center for hundreds of years, it declined in prestige as Genoa grew and is now little more than a frontier town that lives on tourism and the cultivation of flowers. (On Friday the large flower market, open to the trade only, creates traffic gridlock; it's best to avoid the town on that day.) Ventimiglia is divided in two by the Roia River. The **Città Vecchia** is a well-preserved medieval old town on the western bank. The 11th-century **Duomo** has a Gothic portal dating from 1222. Walk up Via del Capo to reach the **ancient walls,** which have fine views of the coast.

> **en route**

From Ventimiglia, a provincial road swings 10 km (6 mi) up the Nervi River valley to a lovely-sounding medieval town, Dolceacqua (its name translates as Sweetwater), with a ruined castle. Liguria's best-known red wine is the local Rossese di Dolceacqua. A farther 6 km (4 mi) along the road lies Pigna, a fascinating medieval village built in concentric circles on its hilltop.

Where to Stay

$$ ⊡ **La Riserva.** More than 1,100 feet above sea level are the village of
Fodor'sChoice Castel d'Appio and this innlike establishment. Rooms are bright, airy,
★ and simply decorated with contemporary furnishings and coral fabrics. The staff is very helpful, providing, for example, regular lifts into town if you have no car. In addition to its excellent restaurant, La Riserva has numerous activities and a lovely panoramic terrace for drinks, sunbathing, or candlelight dinners. Full-board rates are a good deal. ⊠ *Via Peidago 79, 18039 Castel d'Appio, 5 km (3 mi) west of Ventimiglia* ☎ *0184/229533* 🖶 *0184/229712* ⊕ *www.lariserva.it* 🛏 *16 rooms* ⚘ *Restaurant, pool, bicycles, Ping-Pong, bar, Internet* 🖃 *AE, DC, MC, V* ⊘ *Closed mid-Oct.–Mar.* ❑| *BP.*

Giardini Botanici Hanbury

★ ㊾ *6 km (4 mi) west of Ventimiglia, 165 km (102 mi) southwest of Genoa.*

Mortola Inferiore, only 2 km (1 mi) from the French border, is the site of the world-famous Giardini Hanbury (Hanbury Gardens), one of the largest botanical gardens in Italy. Planned and planted in 1867 by a wealthy English merchant, Sir Thomas Hanbury, and his botanist brother Daniel, the terraced gardens contain species from five continents, including many palms and succulents. There are panoramic views of the sea from the gardens, which descend to the beach. The ticket office closes one hour before the garden. ⊠ *Giardini Hanbury, Località Mortola* ☎ *0184/229507* 🖾 *€6* ⊘ *Mar.–June 15, daily 9:30–6; June 16–Sept. 15, daily 9:30–7; Sept. 16–last Sat. in Oct., daily 9:30–6; last Sun. in Oct.–Feb., Tues.–Sun. 10–5.*

> **off the beaten path**

BALZI ROSSI – Prehistoric humans left traces of their lives and magic rites in the Balzi Rossi (Red Rocks), caves carved in the sheer rock. You can visit the caves and a small museum displaying some of the objects found there. ⊠ *Via Balzi Rosso 9, 2 km (1 mi) west of Giardini Botanici Hanbury* ☎ *0184/38113* 🖾 *€2* ⊘ *Tues.–Sun. 8:30–5:30.*

THE ITALIAN RIVIERA A TO Z

To research prices, get advice from other travelers, and book travel arrangements, visit www.fodors.com.

AIR TRAVEL
There is daily air service between Genoa and Zürich (on Swiss International Air Lines), London (on British Airways), Paris (on Air France), Munich (on Air Dolomiti), and Milan and Rome (on Alitalia).

🛫 Carriers **Air Dolomiti** ☎ 800/013366 ⊕ www.airdolomiti.it. **Air France** ☎ 848/884466 ⊕ www.airfrance.com. **Alitalia** ☎ 848/865641 ⊕ www.alitalia.com. **British Airways** ☎ 848/812266 ⊕ www.britishairways.com. **Swiss International Air Lines,** ☎ 848/852000 ⊕ www.swiss.com.

AIRPORTS

Aeroporto Internazionale Cristoforo Colombo is only 6 km (4 mi) from the center of Genoa. The nearest airports for direct U.S. flights are Nice, in France, about 2½ hours west of Genoa (an easy bus connection), and Milan's Linate and Malpensa, about two hours northeast.

🛫 Airport Information **Aeroporto Internazionale Cristoforo Colombo** ⊠ Sestri Ponente, Genoa ☎ 010/60151.

TRANSFERS Volabus services from Cristoforo Colombo Airport connect with Genoa's Stazione Brignole, stopping also at Piazza Acquaverde (Stazione Principe). Tickets cost €2.10 and may be purchased on the bus.
🛫 **Volabus** ☎ 010/5582414.

BOAT & FERRY TRAVEL

Genoa is Italy's largest port and can be reached from the United States as well as other parts of Liguria and Italy (Sardinia, La Spezia, and Savona). Ships berth in the heart of Genoa, including cruise ships of the Genoa-based Costa Cruise Line. Ferries to various ports around the Mediterranean are operated by Tirrenia Navigazione, whose most popular destination is Sardinia (a 13-hour trip). Grimaldi Lines sends cruise ship–like overnight ferries to Barcelona (an 18-hour trip) and Palermo, Sicily (a 20-hour trip). Corsica Ferries runs car ferries from Savona to Bastia and Ile-Rousse in Corsica.

Boat or ferry travel is the most pleasant—and sometimes only—way to get from place to place within Liguria. A busy network of local ferry lines, such as Servizio Marittimo del Tigullio and Alimar, connects many of the resorts. Golfo Paradiso lines run between Camogli, San Fruttuoso (on the Portofino promontory), and Recco, and in summer from the port of Genoa and Nervi to Portofino, Cinque Terre, and Portovenere, stopping in Recco and Camogli. Navigazione Golfo dei Poeti runs frequent ferry-shuttle services between Portofino, Portovenere, and Cinque Terre.

🚢 Boat & Ferry Information **Alimar** ⊠ Calata Zingari, Molo, Genoa ☎ 010/256775. **Corsica Ferries** ⊠ Calata Nord, Porto Vado, Savona ☎ 019/2155300 ⊕ www.corsicaferries. com. **Costa Cruise Line** ⊠ Via Gabriele D'Annunzio 2 ☎ 010/54831. **Golfo Paradiso** ⊠ Via Scalo 3, Camogli ☎ 0185/772091 ⊕ www.golfoparadiso.it. **Grimaldi Lines** ⊠ Stazione Marittima, Ponte dei Mille, Genoa ☎ 010/589331. **Navigazione Golfo dei Poeti** ⊠ Viale Mazzini 21, La Spezia ☎ 0187/732987 ⊕ www.navigazionegolfodeipoeti. it. **Servizio Marittimo del Tigullio** ⊠ Via Palestro 8/1b, Santa Margherita Ligure ☎ 0185/284670 ⊕ www.traghettiportofino.it. **Tirrenia Navigazione** ⊠ Stazione Marittima, Ponte dei Mille, Genoa ☎ 010/2758041 ⊕ www.tirrenia.it.

BUS TRAVEL

The main bus station in Genoa is at Piazza Principe. Local buses, operated by the municipal transport company AMT, serve the steep valleys that run to some of the towns along the western coast. Tickets may be bought at local bus stations or at newsstands for local buses. Buy your ticket before you board the bus. AMT also operates the funicular railways and the elevators that service the steeper sections of the city. Tigullio Trasporti provides connections along the Levante coast. Diana Tours operates a bus service between Genoa and the Nice airport in France, but no regular bus service connects Genoa with the towns along the Ponente coast itself.

🚌 Bus Information **AMT** ⊠ Piazza Acquaverde, Genoa ☎ 010/5582414 ⊕ www.amt. genova.it. **Diana Tours** ⊠ Via G. Ardoino 151, Diano Marina ☎ 800/651931. **Tigullio Trasporti** ⊠ Piazza Nostro Signore dell'Orto, Chiavari ☎ 0185/373233 ⊠ Piazza Vittorio Veneto 1, Santa Margherita Ligure ☎ 0185/288834.

CAR RENTAL

🚗 Agencies **Avis** ⊠ Via delle Casacce 3, Piazza Acquaverde, Genoa ☎ 010/540906 ⊠ Aeroporto Internazionale Cristoforo Colombo, Sestri Ponente Genoa ☎ 010/6507280 ⊠ Via Fratelli Rosselli 74/76, La Spezia ☎ 0187/770270 ⊠ Corso Imperatrice 96, San Remo ☎ 0184/532462, 199/100133 for national inquiries. **Budget** ⊠ Aeroporto Internazionale Cristoforo Colombo, Genoa ☎ 010/6512467. **Hertz** ⊠ Via Casaregis 76/78, Genoa ☎ 010/5702625 ⊠ Aeroporto Internazionale Cristoforo Colombo, Sestri Ponente, Genoa ☎ 010/6512422 ⊠ Via San Bartolomeo 392, La Spezia ☎ 0187/512140 ⊠ Via XX Settembre 17, San Remo ☎ 0184/500470.

CAR TRAVEL

Autostrada A12 southeast from Genoa links up with the autostrada network for all northern and southern destinations; Rome is a six-hour drive from Genoa. The 150-km (93-mi) trip north to Milan on A7 takes two hours. Nice is 2½ hours of tunnels west on A10.

Two good roads run parallel to each other along the coast of Liguria. Closer to shore and passing through all the towns and villages is the Via Aurelia, S1, which has excellent views at almost every turn but gets crowded in July and August. More direct and higher up than S1 is the autostrada, A10 west of Genoa and A12 to the south. These routes save time on weekends, in summer, and on days when festivals slow traffic in some resorts to a standstill. Any time of year, do your best to avoid driving in the center of Genoa.

EMBASSIES & CONSULATES

🏴 United Kingdom **British Consulate** ⊠ Piazza della Vittoria 15/16, 16121 Genoa ☎ 010/416828 🖷 010/416958.
🏴 United States **U.S. Consular Agency** ⊠ Via Dante 2, 16121 Genoa ☎ 010/584492 🖷 010/5533033.

EMERGENCIES

Europa and Ghersi are two late-night pharmacies in Genoa.

If you break down on the highway, walk along the side of the road until you come to an emergency telephone. Call and the emergency highway road service comes to tow you to the nearest service station—for a hefty fee. On a smaller road, unless you have a cell phone you'd be better off walking to the nearest town or gas station (usually not too far) and calling ACI Emergency Service (a free call) from any pay phone. In order to describe where you are, be prepared to seek out the help of locals. (*Dove siamo?*—Where are we?)

ACI ☎ 803/116. **Ambulance** ☎ 118. **Europa** ✉ Corso Europa 676, Genoa ☎ 010/380239. **Police** ☎ 112. **Ghersi** ✉ Corso Buenos Aires 18/r, Genoa ☎ 010/541661. **Ospedale Generale Regionale San Martino** ✉ Largo Rosanna Benzi 10, Genoa ☎ 010/5551. **General emergencies** ☎ 113.

MAIL & SHIPPING

Post Offices Genoa ✉ Via Dante 4A/B ☎ 010/5705913. **La Spezia** ✉ Piazza Verdi, 19121 ☎ 0187/735191. **San Remo** ✉ Via Roma 156, 18038 ☎ 0184/523277.

TOURS

Informal harbor cruises or excursion cruises between coastal towns are scheduled and operated by the main ferry lines, but you can have as much fun—if not more—negotiating a price with a boat owner at one of the smaller ports. You're likely to get a boat operator with a rudimentary command of English at best. You can also take a boat tour of Genoa harbor with Cooperativa Battellieri del Porto di Genova. The tour, which starts from the aquarium pier, costs €6, lasts about an hour, and includes a visit to the breakwater outside the harbor, the Bacino delle Grazie, and the Molo Vecchio (Old Port).

A bus tour of Genoa with an English-speaking guide is a good way to see the city and its panoramic upper reaches. A coach leaves every afternoon at 3 from Piazza Caricamento, by the port, and does the Giro Giro Tour, a two-hour narrated loop of the city (€15). It's operated by Genoa's municipal transport company in conjunction with the agency Macrame Viaggi.

Boat Tours Cooperativa Battellieri ✉ Stazione Marittima, Ponte dei Mille, Genoa ☎ 010/265712 ⊕ www.battellierigenova.it.

Bus Tours Macrame Viaggi ✉ Piazza Colombo 3, Maddalena, Genoa ☎ 010/5959779.

TRAIN TRAVEL

Frequent and fast train service by the Ferrovie dello Stato (Italian State Railways), or Trenitalia, connects Liguria with the rest of Italy. Genoa is 1½ hours from Milan and 5½–6 hours from Rome (4½ with the Eurostar). Many services from France (in particular, the French Riviera) pass along the Ligurian Coast on the way to all parts of Italy. Regular service connecting all parts of Liguria operates from Genoa's two stations: depart from Stazione Principe to points west and Stazione Brignole to points east and south. All the coastal resorts are on this line, and many international trains stop along the coast west of Genoa on their way between Paris and Milan or Rome.

Train stations Stazione Brignole ✉ Piazza Giuseppe Verdi, Foce, Genoa ☎ 892021. **Stazione Principe** ✉ Piazza del Principe, San Teodoro, Genoa ☎ 892021.

Train lines Ferrovie dello Stato ☎ 892021 ⊕ www.trenitalia.com.

VISITOR INFORMATION

Most towns have a local tourist office, called Agenzia di Promozione Turistica (APT), that can provide general information, and for a small fee, can help you book accommodations Monday–Saturday, 9–5. Note that the Terminale Crociere branch in Genoa is open only May–September, for the arrival of major ferries and cruise ships.⚐ Tourist Information **Genoa** ✉ Palazzina Santa Maria, Molo ☎ 010/248711 ⊕ www.apt.genova.it ✉ Stazione Principe, San Teodoro ☎ 010/2462633 ✉ Aeroporto Internazionale Cristoforo Colombo, Sestri Ponente ☎ 010/6015247 ✉ Via Roma 11 ☎ 010/576791 ✉ Terminale Crociere, Ponte dei Mille ☎ 010/6015247. **Alassio** ✉ Viale Mazzini 62, 17021 ☎ 0182/647027 ⊕ www.inforiviera.it. **Albenga** ✉ Viale Martiri della Libertà 1, 17031 ☎ 0182/558444 ⊕ www.inforiviera.it. **Bordighera** ✉ Via Roberto 1, 18012 ☎ 0184/262322 ⊕ www.rivieradeifiori.org. **Camogli** ✉ Via XX Settembre 33, 16032 ☎ 0185/771066. **Imperia** ✉ Viale Matteotti 37, 18100 ☎ 0183/660140 ⊕ www.rivieradeifiori.org. **La Spezia** ✉ Via Mazzini 45, 19100 ☎ 0187/770900 ⊕ www.aptcinqueterre.sp.it. **Lerici** ✉ Via Biaggini 6, 19032 ☎ 0187/967346 ⊕ www.aptcinqueterre.sp.it. **Levanto** ✉ Piazza Cavour 12, 19015 ☎ 0187/808125 ⊕ www.aptcinqueterre.sp.it. **Monterosso** ✉ Via Fegina 38, 19016 ☎ 0187/817506 ⊕ www.aptcinqueterre.sp.it. **Portofino** ✉ Via Roma 35, 16034 ☎ 0185/269024 ⊕ www.apttigullio.liguria.it. **Rapallo** ✉ Lungomare V. Veneto 7, 16035 ☎ 0185/230346 ⊕ www.apttigullio.liguria.it. **Riomaggiore** ✉ Stazione Ferroviaria, 19017 ☎ 0187/920633 ⊕ www.aptcinqueterre.sp.it. **San Remo** ✉ Palazzo Riviera, Largo Nuvoloni 1, 18038 ☎ 0184/571571 ⊕ www.rivieradeifiori.org. **Santa Margherita Ligure** ✉ Via XXV Aprile 28, 16038 ☎ 0185/2929 ⊕ www.apttigullio.liguria.it. **Varazze** ✉ Viale Nazioni Unite, 17019 ☎ 019/935043 ⊕ www.inforiviera.it. **Ventimiglia** ✉ Via Cavour 61, 18039 ☎ 0184/351183 ⊕ www.rivieradeifiori.org.

EMILIA-ROMAGNA

7

Updated by
Robin S.
Goldstein

GOURMETS THE WORLD OVER claim that Emilia-Romagna's greatest contribution to humankind has been gastronomic. Birthplace of fettuccine, tortellini, lasagna, prosciutto, and Parmesan cheese, the region has a spectacular culinary tradition. But there are also many cultural riches in the flat, fertile Po plain and its surroundings: Parma's Correggio paintings, Giuseppe Verdi's villa at Sant'Agata, the medieval splendor of Bologna's palazzi and Ferrara's alleyways, and the Byzantine beauty of mosaic-rich Ravenna—glittering as brightly today as it did 1,500 years ago.

Emilia-Romagna owes its beginnings to a road. In 187 BC the Romans laid out the Via Aemilia, a long highway running straight northwest from the Adriatic port of Rimini to the central garrison town of Piacenza, and it was along this central spine that the primary towns of the region developed. Two millennia later the old Roman road (SS9) is still called Via Emilia, and the autostrada (A1 and A14) runs parallel to it.

Despite the unifying factor of the Via Emilia, the region has had a fragmented history. Its eastern portion, roughly the area from Faenza to the coast, known as Romagna, has looked first to the Byzantine east and then to Rome for art, political power, and, some say, national character. The western portion, Emilia, from Bologna to Piacenza, had a more northern, rather dour sense of self-government and dissent.

The principal city of the region is Bologna, a busy cultural and culinary capital less trodden but just as exciting to visit as Italy's more famous tourist destinations. It was founded by the Etruscans but eventually came under the influence of the Roman Empire. The Romans established a garrison there, renaming the old Etruscan settlement Bononia, the Bologna of today. It was after the fall of Rome that the region began its fragmentation. Romagna, centered in Ravenna, was ruled from Constantinople. Ravenna eventually became the capital of the empire in the west in the 5th century, passing to papal rule in the 8th century. Even today, however, the city is still filled with reminders of two centuries of Byzantine rule.

The other cities of the region, from the Middle Ages on, became the fiefs of important noble families—the Este in Ferrara and Modena, the Pallavicini in Piacenza, the Bentivoglio in Bologna, and the Malatesta in Rimini. Today all these cities bear the marks of their noble patrons. When in the 16th century the papacy managed to exert its power over the entire region, some of these cities were divided among the families of the reigning popes— hence the stamp of the Farnese family on Parma, Piacenza, and Ferrara.

In the years since, Bologna and Emilia-Romagna have established a robust tradition of rebellion and dissent. The Italian socialist movement was born in the region, as was Benito Mussolini (in keeping with the political climate of his home state, he was a firebrand socialist during the early part of his career). Emilia-Romagna did not take to fascism, however: it was in this region that the antifascist resistance was born, and during World War II the region suffered terribly at the hands of the Fascists and the Nazis.

Despite a long history of bloodletting, turmoil, and rebellion, the arts— both decorative and culinary—have always flourished in Emilia-Romagna.

The great families financed painters, sculptors, and writers (Dante found a haven in Ravenna after being expelled from his native Florence). In modern times Emilia-Romagna has given to the arts such famous sons as painter Giorgio Morandi, writer Giorgio Bassani (author of *The Garden of the Finzi-Continis*), filmmakers Michelangelo Antonioni and Federico Fellini, and tenor Luciano Pavarotti.

Nowadays the sprawling plants of the industrial food giants of Italy, such as Barilla and Fini, stand side by side with the fading villas and deteriorating farmhouses that have long punctuated the flat, fertile land of the Po plain. Each fall the region's trademark low-lying fog rolls in off of the Adriatic and hangs over those Romagnan flatlands for the winter, coloring cities and countryside alike with a spooky, gray glow. As Antonioni once mused: "On the plain in late September, evening comes quickly. The day ends when headlights are turned on unexpectedly. The sunset is not soft, it is mysterious. It is so hard to see what is before my eyes."

Bologna is acknowledged as the leading city of Italian cuisine, and the rest of the region follows—eating is a seminal part of any Emilia-Romagnan experience. The area's history is replete with culinary legends, such as how the original *tortellino* (singular of tortellini) was modeled on the shape of Venus's navel and the original *tagliolini* (long, thin egg pasta) were served at the wedding banquet of Annibale Bentivoglio and Lucrezia d'Este. It's almost impossible to eat badly in Emilia-Romagna, and everything is worth trying—Parma's famed prosciutto and Parmigiano Reggiano cheese, Modena's balsamic vinegar, and the best pasta in the world.

Exploring Emilia-Romagna

The predominantly flat landscape of Emilia-Romagna has a geographical logic—the Via Emilia (SS9) and its parallel big brother, the Autostrada del Sole (highway A1), bisect the Po Valley and Romagna plain, making it easy to cover most of the major destinations in the region in order by driving straight through. From Bologna there are three choices of itineraries: head north on A13 to Ferrara and then southeast on S16 to Ravenna, or continue east or west along the Via Emilia (SS9), stopping for short visits at some of the smaller towns en route northwest to Piacenza or southeast to Rimini and the sea.

About the Restaurants & Hotels

Eating light in Emilia-Romagna might mean leaving half of your tortellini *con noci e panna* (with walnuts and cream) on your plate. Ravioli stuffed with spinach and ricotta cheese, *tortelli* (triangular pasta dumplings) stuffed with squash, and tortellini stuffed with minced pork and beef all have in common one key word—stuffed—and you may feel that way, too. Although the highest-end restaurants boast world-class creativity, you don't need to spend a lot for a memorable culinary experience. Some of the very best versions of local staples, like tortellini *in brodo* (in broth) and tagliatelle *al ragù* (in a tomato sauce with minced pork and beef, elsewhere known as Bolognese), can be found in the simplest, most inexpensive, of kitchens, where a caring grandmother has likely been doting on the simmering sauce since early morning.

Numbers in the text correspond to numbers in the margin and on the Emilia-Romagna and Bologna maps.

If you have 3 days

Given three days, you should set aside two nights to see ⊠ **Bologna** ❻–❿ ► and its environs. Make a point of seeing the sights in and around Piazza Maggiore and to sample the city's legendary cuisine. Where you spend your third day depends on your route out of Emilia-Romagna. If you're going to Milan or Turin, make a stop about 100 km (62 mi) northwest of Bologna at ⊠ **Parma** ❸, where you could cover the major sights in two or three hours. If you're heading toward the Adriatic coast, the calm unspoiled Renaissance city of ⊠ **Ferrara** ❺ should be your priority.

If you have 6 days

Coming from Milan or the west, stop for lunch in **Piacenza** ❶, an elegant and harmonious town. If opera's your thing, make a detour to see the cluster of places associated with the composer Verdi centered in **Busseto** ❷. Spend the first night in ⊠ **Parma** ❸ or ⊠ **Modena** ❹, where you can sample the region's fine food and wine. On the second day ⊠ **Bologna** ❻–❿ is your destination, where you should stay for at least two days and nights to take in the sights. On Day 4 turn north to ⊠ **Ferrara** ❺, enjoying an amble around medieval streets and spending your fifth night. Day 6 you could drop into the ceramic center of **Faenza** ⓰, famed for its faience pottery, or stop a night in a spa town, such as Castrocaro Terme near **Forlì** ⓱ or ⊠ **Bagno di Romagna** ⓲, before heading to ⊠ **Ravenna** ⓳–㉔ to see the excellent Byzantine mosaics.

Emilia-Romagna has a reputation for an efficiency uncommon in most of the rest of Italy. Even the smallest hotels are well run, with high standards of quality and service. Bologna is very much a businessperson's city, and most hotels there cater to the business traveler, but there are smaller, more intimate hotels as well. Though prices are high, you can expect an experience delightfully free of the condescending attitude and manipulative pricing schemes that sometimes mar Italy's tourist meccas. The one exception to the rule is Rimini, whose business is tourism. Its numerous hotels, unlike those in the rest of Emilia-Romagna, have tourist-oriented full- and half-board packages. They overflow during July and August but are closed for much of the off-season.

WHAT IT COSTS In euros					
	$$$$	**$$$**	**$$**	**$**	**¢**
RESTAURANTS	over €22	€16–€22	€12–€16	€7–€11	under €7
HOTELS	over €220	€160–€220	€110–€160	€70–€110	under €70

Restaurant prices are for a second course *(secondo piatto)*. Hotel prices are for two people in a standard double room in high season, including tax and service.

Timing

You would never visit Emilia-Romagna for the weather. Winters are gray and cold, and summers are airless and hot, though sea breezes on the coast offer some respite. Fall (September–October) and spring (April–May) have the best weather and are considered high season at hotels. If you are here in summer, get up early and do as much as you can in the morning. In winter make sure you are equipped for the frequent rain and damp, penetrating cold. Dense, low-lying fog is common throughout the plains in fall and winter and can be starkly beautiful, but it can also be very hazardous on the road.

EMILIA

The Via Emilia runs through Emilia's heart in a straight shot from medieval Piacenza to thoroughly modern Modena. On the way from the past to the present you encounter many of Italy's cultural riches—from the culinary and artistic treasures of Parma to the birthplace and home of Giuseppe Verdi and the mist-shrouded tangle of streets that make up Ferrara's old Jewish ghetto. It may be tempting to imitate Modena's Ferraris and zoom over the short (113-km [70-mi]) stretch of highway spanning the region, but take time to detour into the countryside, with its decaying farmhouses and 800-year-old abbeys, and to stop for a taste of prosciutto.

Piacenza

❶ *66 km (41 mi) southeast of Milan, 150 km (94 mi) northwest of Bologna.*

The city of Piacenza has always been associated with industry and commerce. Its position on the Po River has made it an important inland port since the earliest times; the Etruscans, and then the Romans, had thriving settlements on this site. As you approach the city today you could be forgiven for thinking that it holds little of interest. Piacenza is surrounded by ugly industrial suburbs (with particularly unlovely concrete factories and a power station), but forge ahead to discover that they surround a delightfully preserved medieval downtown and an unusually clean city. The prosperity is evidenced by the great shopping along Corso Vittorio Emanuele II.

The heart of the city is the **Piazza dei Cavalli** (Square of the Horses). The flamboyant equestrian statues from which the piazza takes its name are depictions of Ranuccio Farnese (1569–1622) and, on the left, his father, Alessandro (1545–92). Alessandro was a beloved ruler, enlightened and fair; Ranuccio, his successor, was less admired. Both statues are the work of Francesco Mochi, a master sculptor of the baroque period. Dominating the square is the massive 13th-century **Palazzo del Comune,** also known as the Palazzo Gotico. This two-tone, marble-and-brick, turreted and crenellated building was the seat of town government before Piacenza fell under the iron fists of the ruling Pallavicini and Farnese families.

Attached like a sinister balcony to the bell tower of Piacenza's 12th-century **Duomo** is a *gabbia* (iron cage), where miscreants were incarcerated

Byzantine Splendor Nowhere is Byzantine mosaic art more spectacular than in Ravenna. The city, which was conquered by the Byzantines in the 6th century AD, is filled with beautifully preserved mosaics that put more of an emphasis on nature—green pastures, sheep, and starry skies, for instance—than you might be used to during your tour of Italy's ancient artistic treasures. Tiny glittering tiles cover walls of churches and tombs that have the most unassuming exteriors. Outside Ravenna, the town of Classe hides even more mosaic gems. Every few years seems to bring yet another accidental mosaic discovery in the area—and another few pieces fit into the puzzle of Romagna's fascinating Byzantine past.

7

Political Talk Emilia-Romagna might seem staid: city after city has immaculate streets filled with smartly dressed businessmen in impeccable shoes, murmuring to each other through the winter fog over cups of coffee. But after dark, from Parma to Bologna, Piacenza to Ferrara, the middle managers are replaced on the streets by young, energetic would-be intellectuals, and the murmurs turn into impassioned political discussion—usually with a leftist slant—over jugs of table wine. If you enjoy this type of conversation, take time to stop for a drink after dinner in one of Parma's back-alley wine bars or Bologna's up-and-coming nightspots. Don't be afraid to join in—all ages are welcome, and divergent opinions, thoughtfully argued, are treated with respect. (Locals are usually happy to practice their English, which can often be quite good.) You'll experience another side of the region—a side that's important to understanding the culture and history.

---

naked and subjected to the scorn (and projectiles) of the crowd in the marketplace below. Inside the cathedral a less-evocative but equally impressive medieval stonework decorates the pillars and the crypt, and there are extravagant frescoes by Il Guercino (a.k.a. Giovanni Barbieri, 1591–1666) in the dome of the cupola. The Duomo can be reached by following Via XX Settembre from Piazza dei Cavalli. ⊠ *Piazza Duomo* ☎ *0523/335154* ☉ *Mon.–Sat. 7–noon and 4–7, Sun. 7–1 and 4–7.*

The **Museo Civico,** the city-owned museum of Piacenzan art and antiquities, is housed in the vast **Palazzo Farnese.** The ruling family had commissioned a monumental palace, but construction, begun in 1558, was never completed. The highlight of the museum's rather eclectic exhibit is the 2nd-century BC Etruscan *Fegato di Piacenza,* a bronze tablet in the shape of a *fegato* (liver), with the symbols of the gods of good and ill fortune marked on it. By comparing this master "liver" with one taken from the body of a freshly slaughtered sacrifice, priests could predict the future. The collection also contains Botticelli's *Madonna with St. John the Baptist.* Reserve ahead for free one-hour guided tours. ⊠ *Piazza Cittadella* ☎ *0523/326981* ⊕ *www.musei.piacenza.it* 🎫 *€5.25* ☉ *Tues.–Thurs. 8:45–1, Fri. and Sat. 8:45–1 and 3–6, Sun. 9:30–1 and 3–6; tours Tues.–Thurs. 9:30, Fri. 9:30 and 3:30, weekends 9:30, 11, 3, and 4:30 by appointment.*

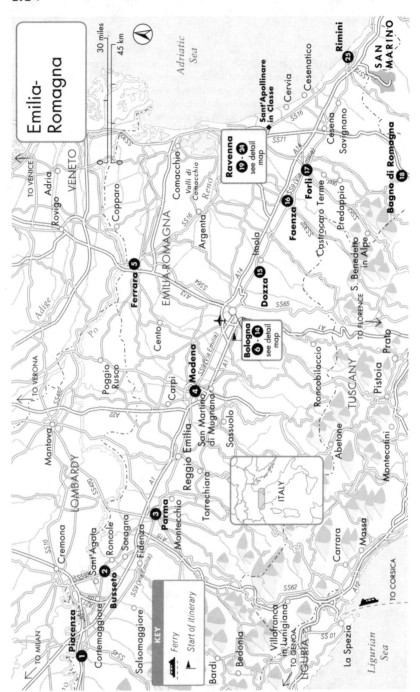

The **Galleria d'Arte Moderna Ricci Oddi** has been getting increasing attention for its unusually good collection of paintings from the 1800s and 1900s by luminaries from all over northern and central Italy—with a focus on Tuscany and Emilia. ⊠ *Via San Siro 13* ☏ *0523/320742* 🖂 *€4* ☉ *Tues.–Sun. 10–noon and 3–6.*

Where to Eat

★ **$$$$** ✕ **Antica Osteria del Teatro.** On a lovely little square in the center of town, this restaurant is one of the best in all Emilia-Romagna. The 15th-century building, with coffered ceilings and sober furniture, effuses elegance. The pricey, French-influenced menu might be best described as haute Italian; some of the more nouveau flights of fancy might include, for example, a terrine of duck liver with marzipan-stuffed dates. The two tasting menus are an excellent way to sample the kitchen at its best. Service is excellent and the wine list impeccable. ⊠ *Via Verdi 16* ☏ *0523/ 323777* ⊕ *www.anticaosteriadelteatro.it* ⌖ *Reservations essential* ⊟ *AE, DC, MC, V* ☉ *Closed Sun. and Mon., Aug. 1–25, and Jan. 1–10.*

$ ✕ **Agnello da Renato.** Simple, small, and cheap, Agnello is an excellent place to plop down for lunch. Try the *tortelli alla Piacentina* (small pasta pillows stuffed with ricotta and spinach and bathed in butter and Parmesan) or the *coniglio alla cacciatore* (rabbit in a tomato and white-wine sauce). It's very central (steps from the Palazzo Gotico). ⊠ *Via Calzolai 9* ☏ *0523/320874* ⊟ *No credit cards* ☉ *Closed Mon.*

Busseto

❷ *30 km (19 mi) southeast of Piacenza, 124 km (79 mi) northwest of Cremona.*

Busseto's main claim to fame is the 15th-century **Villa Pallavicino,** where master composer Giuseppe Verdi (1813–1901) worked and lived with his mistress (and later wife) Giuseppina Strepponi. On display are the maestro's piano, scores, composition books, and walking sticks. At this writing the villa was closed for renovation with a reopening date uncertain. ⊠ *Via Provesi 36* ⊕ *www.bussetolive.com* ☏ *0524/92239.*

In the center of Busseto is the lovely **Teatro Verdi,** dedicated, as one might expect, to the works of the hamlet's famous son. Once inside the well-preserved, ornate 19th century–style theater, use your imagination to get a feel for where he worked. Check with the Busseto tourist office for the performance schedule. Nonperformance visits are by appointment only. ⊠ *Piazza G. Verdi 10* ☏ *0524/931732 reservations* 🖂 *€4* ☉ *Mar.–Oct., Tues.–Sun. 9:30–noon and 3:30–6:30; Nov.–Feb., Tues.–Sun. 9:30–noon and 3–5.*

off the beaten path

VILLA SANT'AGATA – For Verdi lovers Sant'Agata (also known as Villa Verdi) is a veritable shrine. It's the grand country home Verdi built for himself in 1849, the place where some of his greatest works were composed. Tours are required, and you have to reserve a few days in advance by phone or on the Web. ⊠ *Via Verdi 22, Sant'Agata Villanova sull'Arda, 4 km (2½ mi) north of Busseto on S588, toward Cremona* ☏ *0523/830000* ⊕ *www.villaverdi.org*

ON THE MENU

E**MILIA-ROMAGNA'S REPUTATION** as Italy's gourmet haven is well deserved; a visit wouldn't be complete without sampling what the region does best. The specialties are nothing new in name, they're just better here, where they were born—for example, Parma's world-famous prosciuttos and crumbly Parmigiano Reggiano cheese (not just grated, but also often served by itself as an appetizer or dessert, perhaps drizzled with balsamic vinegar). Bologna's pasta (especially tagliatelle) al ragù is in a heavenly, slow-cooked sauce of onions, carrots, minced pork and beef, and fresh tomatoes that in no way resembles the "Bolognese" sauce served worldwide. The rich, soft, garlicky mortadella has been reincarnated elsewhere to its detriment as "baloney."

Among the many Emilian variations on stuffed pasta, tortelli and cappellacci are larger pasta pillows, about the size of a Brussels sprout, but with the same basic form as tortellini; they're often stuffed with pumpkinlike squash or spinach and cheese. Tortelloni are, in theory, even bigger, although their size varies. Stuffed pastas are generally served simply, with melted butter, sage, and (what else) Parmigiano Reggiano cheese, or in brodo (in beef or chicken broth), which brings out the subtle richness of the fillings.

Look also for the local specialties: although most are served throughout the region, traditionalists have zampone (pig's feet stuffed with minced meat) and aceto balsamico (balsamic vinegar) in Modena; their risotto in padella (with fresh herbs and tomatoes) in Piacenza; their brodetto (tangy seafood stew) in Rimini; their ancient Roman piadine (chewy, flat griddle breads) in Romagna; their cappellacci di zucca (pasta filled with pumpkinlike squash) and salama da sugo (salty, oily sausage aged and then cooked) in Ferrara; and

everything else in Bologna. Also along the Adriatic coast, don't miss the simply grilled seafood: the scampi from the Adriatic, for instance, are a thin, shrimplike crustacean whose tender meat is so sweet that you may swear there's something added. (It's also great in tomato-based pasta sauce.) Razor clams, mussels, and little noci (tiny clamlike mussels) are among the sweet, warm-water shellfish available.

From Piacenza to the Adriatic, ham is the king of meats in Emilia-Romagna, but nowhere is this truer than in Parma, where it's served as an appetizer, a great panino (grilled sandwich) filling, and even as a pizza topping. Note, however, that in Parma, as elsewhere in Italy, prosciutto (also called prosciutto cotto, or cotto) means "cooked ham," which is closer to (but much better than) what Americans would put in a ham sandwich. The product that Americans call prosciutto—raw, cured ham—is prosciutto crudo (crudo for short). For the best crudo di Parma look for slices, always cut to order, that are razor thin and bright red (not grayish red). Parma ham's even more prized, and pricey, cousin, is the sweet and flavorful culatello di Zibello, which is produced along the banks of the Po River, and is cured and aged for more than 11 months.

Emilia-Romagna's wines accompany the region's fine food rather than vying with it for accolades. The best known is Lambrusco, a sparkling red produced on the Po plain that has some admirers and many detractors. It's praised for its tartness and condemned for the same quality. The region's best wines include Sangiovese di Romagna, which can be similar to Chianti, from the Romagnolan hills, and Barbera, from the Colli Piacetini and Apennine foothills. Castelluccio, Bonzara, Zerbina, Leone Conti, and Tre Monti are among the region's top producers—keep your eyes out for their bottles.

€6 ⊙ Apr.–Sept., Tues.–Sun. 9–11:45 and 3–6:45; Jan. 16–Mar. and Oct.–Dec. 15, Tues.–Sun. 9–11:45 and 2:30–5:30; Dec. 16–Jan. 15, Tues.–Sun. by appointment.

Parma

❸ *40 km (25 mi) southeast of Busseto, 97 km (61 mi) northwest of Bologna.*

Dignified, delightful Parma stands on the banks of a tributary of the Po River. Much of the lively historic center has been untouched by modern times, despite heavy damage during World War II. Almost every major European power has had a hand in ruling Parma at one time or another. The Romans founded the city—then little more than a garrison on the Via Aemilia—after which a succession of feudal lords held sway. In the 16th century came the ever-avaricious Farnese family (who are still the dukes of Parma) and then, in fast succession, the Spanish, French, and Austrians (after the fall of Napoléon). The French influence is strong. The novelist Stendhal (1783–1842) lived in the city for several years and set his classic *The Charterhouse of Parma* here.

Bursting with gustatory delights, Parma now draws crowds for its sublime cured ham, prosciutto crudo di Parma (known locally simply as prosciutto *crudo*); and for the delicate, pale yellow Parmigiano Reggiano cheese, the original—and best—of a class now known around the world as Parmesan. The city's prosperity has long been tied to the Parmalat dairy empire, but at the end of 2003 the once-proud company was brought down by a huge corporate scandal. As the public learned of fictional $4 billion bank accounts and shell holding companies offshore, Parmalat went bankrupt (and even sold off the star players of Parma, the company-owned soccer team). It remains to be seen how the city will recover from the economic shock of Parmalat's spectacular collapse.

Fodor'sChoice
★

The **Piazza del Duomo**, site of the cathedral, the baptistery, the church of San Giovanni, and the palaces of the bishop and other notables, is the heart of the city. This square and its buildings make up one of the most harmonious, tranquil city centers in Italy. The magnificent 12th-century **Duomo** has two vigilant stone lions standing guard beside the main door. The arch of the entrance is decorated with a delicate frieze of figures representing the months of the year, a motif repeated inside the baptistery on the right-hand side of the piazza. Some of the church's original artwork still survives, notably the simple yet evocative *Descent from the Cross,* a carving in the right transept by Benedetto Antelami (1150–1230), a sculptor and architect whose masterwork is this cathedral's baptistery.

It is odd to turn from this austere work of the 12th century to the exuberant fresco in the dome, the *Assumption of the Virgin* by Antonio Correggio (1494–1534). The fresco was not well received when it was unveiled in 1530. "A mess of frogs' legs," the bishop of Parma is said to have called it. Today Correggio is acclaimed as one of the leading masters of Mannerist painting. ⊠ *Piazza del Duomo* ☎ *0521/235886* ⊙ *Daily 9–12:30 and 3–7.*

The **Battistero** is a solemn, simple baptistery—Romanesque on the exterior and an uplifting Gothic inside. The doors are richly decorated with figures, animals, and flowers, and the interior is adorned with figures carved by Antelami showing the months and seasons. ⊠ *Piazza del Duomo* ☎ *0521/235886* ⬚ *€3* ☉ *Daily 9–12:30 and 3–6:30.*

Once beyond the elaborate baroque facade of **San Giovanni Evangelista,** the Renaissance interior reveals several works by Correggio; his *St. John the Evangelist* (left transept) is considered the finest. Also in this church (in the second and fourth chapels on the left) are works by Girolamo Parmigianino (1503–40)—a contemporary of Correggio's and the spearhead of the Mannerist art movement. Once seen, Parmigianino's swan-necked Madonnas are never forgotten: they pose with all the precious élan of today's fashion models. ⊠ *Piazzale San Giovanni* ☎ *0521/ 235311* ☉ *Daily 8–noon and 3:30–6.*

In the monastery adjoining the church of San Giovanni Evangelista is the **Spezieria di San Giovanni**—once a pharmacy where Benedictine monks mixed medicines and herbals. Although production stopped in 1881, the 16th-century decorations survive. ⊠ *Borgo Pipa 1, off Piazzale San Giovanni* ☎ *0521/233309* ⬚ *€2* ☉ *Tues.–Sun. 8:30–1:45.*

★ Works by Parma's own Correggio and Parmigianino as well as Leonardo da Vinci (1452–1519), El Greco (1541–1614), and Bronzino (1503–72) hang at the **Galleria Nazionale.** The museum is housed on the bank of the river in the rather grim-looking **Palazzo della Pilotta,** which was built in about 1600. It's so big that from the air the building is Parma's most recognizable sight—hence the destruction it suffered from Allied bombs in 1944. Much of the building has been restored. The palazzo takes its name from the game *pilotta*, a sort of handball played within the palace precincts in the 17th century.

To enter the Galleria Nazionale, on the ground floor of the palace, you pass through the magnificent baroque **Teatro Farnese,** built in 1628 and based on Palladio's theater in Vicenza. Built entirely of wood, it was burned badly during Allied bombing but has been flawlessly restored. ⊠ *Piazza Pilotta* ☎ *0521/233309* ⊕ *www.artipr.arti.beniculturali.it* ⬚ *€6, Galleria only €4* ☉ *Tues.–Sun. 8:30–1:45.*

The **Camera di San Paolo** is the former dining room of the abbess of the Convent of St. Paul. It was extensively frescoed by Correggio, and despite the building's religious character the decorations aren't Christian but rather ravishingly beautiful depictions of mythological scenes—the *Triumphs of the Goddess Diana*, the *Three Graces*, and the *Three Fates*. It's near the Palazzo della Pilotta, off Strada Garibaldi. ⊠ *Via Melloni* ☎ *0521/233309* ⬚ *€2* ☉ *Tues.–Sun. 8:30–1:45.*

Near Parma's central Piazza Garibaldi is **Santa Maria della Steccata,** a delightful 16th-century domed church with a wonderful fresco cycle by Parmigianino. The painter took so long to complete it that his patrons imprisoned him briefly for breach of contract. ⊠ *Piazza Steccata 9, off Via Dante* ☎ *0521/234937* ⊕ *www.santuari.it/steccata* ☉ *Daily 9–noon and 3–6.*

Where to Stay & Eat

$$$-$$$$ ✕ **La Greppia.** The most elegant, most talked-about restaurant in the city is also one of the best. Taste well-known chef Paola Cavazzini's innovative treats like the *anelli con cavolo nero e mostarda della Paola* (small ring-shape pasta with black cauliflower and caramelized fruits) and the *faraona al tartufo nero di Fragno* (guinea hen with black truffle and chestnut puree). Service is personal and friendly, thanks to the place's tiny size, and the unpretentious surroundings keeps the focus on the food. There's often a bargain set-price lunch for less than €30. ☒ *Via Garibaldi 39/a,* ☎ *0521/233686* ⌕ *Reservations essential* ⊟ *AE, DC, MC, V* ⊘ *Closed Mon. and Tues., July, and 1 wk in Dec.–Jan.*

$$-$$$ ✕ **Croce di Malta.** The appealing, old-fashion restaurant occupies what was once a convent and then an inn. Traditional local fare includes delicate homemade pasta—try the tortelli (with squash filling) or tagliatelle in any fashion. Second courses include well-prepared, hearty versions of classic veal and cheese dishes. The place is also quite serious about wine. ☒ *Borgo Palmia 8,* ☎ *0521/200272* ⌕ *Reservations essential* ⊟ *AE, DC, MC, V* ⊘ *Closed Sun.*

$$-$$$ ✕ **Parizzi.** Named for its exciting young chef, Marco Parizzi, this restaurant rivals La Greppia for the title of Parma's finest. A stylish art nouveau interior with Persian rugs complements antipasti such as *culatello di Zibello* (the most highly touted of Parma prosciuttos, aged more than 11 months). Try traditional Parma classics like stuffed tortelli and sublime risotto di Parmigiano Reggiano with shaved white truffle (in season). The wine list is top-notch. ☒ *Strada Repubblica 71* ☎ *0521/ 285952* ⊕ *www.parmacucina.com* ⌕ *Reservations essential* ⊟ *AE, DC, MC, V* ⊘ *Closed Mon., Aug., and 3 wks in Dec.–Jan.*

$$ ✕ **Osteria dei Mascalzoni.** This hip, romantic spot just off Via Farini is thoroughly modern in both conception and execution. Mood lighting is carefully placed, and the walls and tables exude expensive design and refinement, yet the place remains somehow young and casual. Meat dishes, such as the fillet of beef with a delicate cream of leeks, are good. The wine list is carefully chosen, though pricey, with a particularly good selection from Sicily. Leave satisfied and charmed, if a bit poorer for your wine tab. It stays open until 1 AM. ☒ *Vicolo delle Cinque Piaghe 1* ☎*0521/ 281809* ⊟ *AE, DC, MC, V* ⌕ *Reservations essential* ⊘ *Closed Sun. and 3 wks in Aug.*

★ $-$$ ✕ **Parma Rotta.** In an old inn about 2 km (1 mi) from downtown, the Parma Rotta is an informal neighborhood trattoria serving hearty dishes like spit-roasted lamb and meats cooked on a wood-fired grill, topped off with homemade desserts. Dine outdoors under a pleasant trellis in summer. ☒ *Via Langhirano 158* ☎ *0521/966738* ⊕ *www.parmarotta. com* ⊟ *AE, DC, MC, V* ⊘ *Closed Sun. and Mon. June–Aug. and Mon. Oct.–May.*

★ ¢ ✕ **Enoteca Antica Osteria Fontana.** At lunch and before dinner, gregarious locals flock to this bright blue, old-school *enoteca* (wine bar) serving a star-studded selection of wines at shockingly good prices. You have to queue up in anarchic fashion for a table—or eat at the bar—and service is brusque. But that's all part of the experience. The delicious grilled *panini* (sandwiches), filled with Emilia's best *salumi* (deli meats) and other delights, make it worthwhile. The panini come quartered, so you can share with the table. The enoteca is also the best take-out wine store in town. Closing time is early (9 PM, sometimes earlier). ⊠ *Strada Farini 24/a, near the Piazza del Duomo* ☎ *0521/286037* 🖃 *MC, V* ☺ *Closed Sun.*

$$$–$$$$ 🏨 **Hotel Stendhal.** The Stendhal is one of Parma's finest hotels. Rooms are thickly carpeted and spacious, some with chandeliers and antique furniture. A few rooms have views of the Palazzo della Pilotta on the edge of the old center of town. The hotel is newly affiliated with the Jolly chain, but it's best to reserve through the property directly. ⊠ *Via Bodoni 3, 43100* ☎*0521/208057* 🖷*0521/285655* ⊕*www.hotelstendhal. it* ⇱ *62 rooms* ⚿ *Restaurant, minibars, bar, Internet, meeting room, some pets allowed* 🖃 *AE, DC, MC, V* ⵏⵣ *BP.*

$$$ 🏨 **Palace Hotel Maria Luigia.** Top-quality, convenient to Old Parma and the train station: the Maria Luigia is popular with business travelers. Some of the traditional rooms, with heavy draperies and wood furniture, have lovely vistas of Parma. It's part of the Italian Sina Hotel chain. ⊠ *Viale Mentana 140, 43100* ☎ *0521/281032* 🖷 *0521/231126* ⊕*www. sinahotels.com* ⇱ *89 rooms, 12 suites* ⚿ *Restaurant, minibars, bar, meeting room* 🖃 *AE, DC, MC, V* ⵏⵣ *BP.*

$$ 🏨 **Hotel Torino.** A warm reception and pleasant, relaxed surroundings welcome you to this former convent tucked away in a quiet pedestrian zone in the heart of town. It has modern, smallish rooms with Correggio reproductions on the walls. If traveling by car, fax ahead for a detailed map with driving directions—it's difficult to find. ⊠ *Via Mazza 7, 43100* ☎ *0521/281046* 🖷 *0521/230725* ⊕ *www.hotel-torino.it* ⇱ *33 rooms* ⚿ *Bar, some pets allowed* 🖃 *AE, DC, MC, V* ⵏⵣ *BP.*

Nightlife & the Arts
Opera in Parma is taken just as seriously as in Milan, although tickets are a little easier to come by. Performances are staged at the landmark **Teatro Regio** (⊠ Via Garibaldi 16 ☎ 0521/218678 ⊕ www. teatroregioparma.org). The main opera season is January–March, and the Verdi festival is May–mid-June.

Playwright Dario Fo, the 1997 Nobel Prize winner for literature, helped found the **Teatro Due** (⊠ Viale Basetti 12 ☎ 0521/230242), where productions mix comedy and politics—understanding is limited without a knowledge of Italian.

Modena

❹ *56 km (35 mi) southeast of Parma, 38 km (23 mi) northwest of Bologna.*

Modena has gained recognition for three very contemporary names: the high-performance cars Maserati and Ferrari come from here, and so does the opera star Luciano Pavarotti. But, with apologies to the Tenor and the Testarossa, Modena's syrupy balsamic vinegar, aged for up to 40 years, is still perhaps its greatest achievement. The town has become another Emilian food mecca, with delicious home cooking at every turn. Extensive modern industrial sprawl encircles the center; although the

BALSAMIC NECTAR

BEWARE: the balsamic vinegar you've probably tried—even the pricier versions sold at specialty stores—may be good on salads, but it bears only a fleeting resemblance to the real thing, Aceto Balsamico Tradizionale di Modena. The vinegar that passes the strict governmental standards (a winelike D.O.C.—Denominazione di Origine Controllata—regulation) is officially a condiment rather than a vinegar, and it is made with Trebbiano grape must, which is cooked over an open fire, reduced and fermented from 12 to 25 or more years in a series of specially made wooden casks. As the vinegar becomes more concentrated, so much liquid evaporates through the years that it takes more than 6 gallons of must to produce one quart of vinegar 12 years later. The result is an intense and syrupy concoction best enjoyed sparingly on grilled meats, strawberries, or Parmigiano

Reggiano cheese. The vinegar has such a complexity of flavor that some even drink the stuff as an after-dinner liqueur.

Written documentation of serious vinegar production in Modena goes back as far as 1508, when Alfonso I d'Este, then the duke of Modena, had a facility, although the term "balsamic" did not appear until the 18th century. The Consorzio Produttori Aceto Balsamico Tradizionale di Modena, which can be visited, monitors the quality of the authentic balsamic vinegar, made only by a few licensed restaurants and small producers. The consortium also limits production, keeping prices sky high (expect to pay €50 for a 100-ml bottle of tradizionale which is generally aged 12 to 15 years, or €80 and up for the older tradizionale extra vecchio variety), which is aged 25 years. In the United States, though, expect to pay up to double those prices—if you can even find the product.

old quarter is small, it is filled with narrow medieval streets, pleasant piazzas, and typical Emilian architecture.

The 12th-century **Duomo,** also known as the Basilica Metropolitana, is one of the finest examples of Romanesque architecture in the country. The exterior is decorated with medieval sculptures depicting scenes from the life of San Geminiano, the city's patron saint, and fantastic beasts, as well as a realistic-looking scene of the sacking of a city by barbarian hordes—a reminder to the faithful to be ever vigilant in defense of the church. The bell tower is made of white marble and is known as **La Ghirlandina** (The Little Garland) because of its distinctive weather vane. The somber church interior is divided by an elaborate gallery carved with scenes of the Passion of Christ. The carvings took 50 years to complete and are by an anonymous Modenese master of the 12th century. The tomb of San Geminiano is in the crypt. ⊠ *Piazza Grande* ☎ *059/ 216078* ⊕ *www.duomodimodena.it* ⊙ *Daily 7–12:30 and 3:30–7.*

Modena's principal museum is housed in the **Palazzo dei Musei,** a short walk from the Duomo. The collection was assembled in the mid-17th century by Francesco d'Este (1610–58), Duke of Modena, and the **Galleria Estense** is named in his honor. The gallery also houses the duke's

Biblioteca Estense, a huge collection of illuminated books, of which the best known is the beautifully illustrated 15th-century *Bible of Borso d'Este.* A map dated 1501 was one of the first in the world to show Columbus's discovery of America. To get here, follow Via Emilia, the old Roman road that runs through the heart of the town, to Via di Sant'Agostino. ✉ *Piazza Sant'Agostino 337* ☎ *059/4395711* ⊕ *www. galleriaestense.it* ✆ *€4* ☉ *Tues.–Sun. 8:30–7:30.*

At the **Consorzio Produttori Aceto Balsamico Tradizionale di Modena** you can do a tasting, have a tour of the small facility with the friendly staff, and, of course, buy their famous balsamic vinegar. ✉ *Corso Cavour 60* ☎ *059/236981* ⊕ *www.balsamico.it* ✆ *Free* ☉ *By appointment.*

Where to Stay & Eat

★ **$$$–$$$$** ✕ **Borso d'Este.** Highly regarded by the *crema* of the region's monied set, Borso d'Este serves some delicious variations on old themes, like ravioli stuffed with game and Parmesan. The space is ultratrendy and modern, despite antiques throughout. In season don't miss the *tartufo* (truffle) specialties: ricotta- and spinach-stuffed *tortelloni* (large tortellini) in a truffle-mushroom sauce, and the mushroom tart with truffles. ✉ *Piazza Roma 5* ☎ *059/214114* ⚐ *Reservations essential* ▤ *AE, DC, MC, V* ☉ *Closed Sun. and Aug. 1–20. No lunch Sat.*

$$$–$$$$ ✕ **Hosteria Giusti.** The ancient stone walls here are shared with what is reputedly the world's oldest deli, the Salumeria Giusti, founded in 1605. There are only four tables and a host of antique furnishings in the tiny room, where the kitchen turns out dishes like your Italian grandmother might have cooked—handmade tagliolini, *gnocco fritto* (fried dough) with salumi from next door, and items using Modena's famous balsamic vinegar. Reserve well ahead; it's an unforgettable Modena experience. ✉ *Vicolo Squallore 46* ☎ *059/222533* ⊕ *www.giusti1605.com* ⚐ *Reservations essential* ▤ *AE, DC, MC, V* ☉ *Closed Sun. and Mon., Dec., and Aug. No dinner.*

$–$$ ✕ **Da Enzo.** This big, cheerful, well-patronized trattoria is in the old town's pedestrian zone, a few steps from Piazza Mazzini. All the classic Modenese specialties are represented, including *zampone* (bladder) and *cotechino* (creamy pork sausage). For starters, try the tortelloni *di ricotta e spinaci* (stuffed with ricotta and spinach). ✉ *Via Coltellini 17* ☎ *059/225177* ▤ *AE, DC, MC, V* ⚐ *Reservations essential weekends* ☉ *Closed Mon. and Aug. No dinner Sun.*

$$$ ▦ **Canal Grande.** Once a ducal palace, the Canal Grande has large, airy rooms appointed with ornate dark-wood upholstered pieces. The garden has a fountain in back and breakfast is served on a pretty terrace there in summer. The hotel's restaurant, La Secchia Rapita (closed August), gets rave reviews. ✉ *Corso Canalgrande 6, 41100* ☎ *059/217160* ⎙ *059/221674* ⊕ *www.canalgrandehotel.it* ⇆ *75 rooms, 3 suites* ⚒ *Restaurant, in-room safes, minibars, bar* ▤ *AE, DC, MC, V* ◉⧦ *BP.*

$–$$ ▦ **Hotel Centrale.** The name says it all: this old-school hotel couldn't be better located, right around the corner from Piazza Grande. Rooms are basic and functional, with the classic feel of an Italian building whose layers of renovation don't quite cover up its aging design. The beige lobby is spiced up with cheery checkered floors. ✉ *Via Rismondo 55, 41100*

☏ *059/218808* 🖨 *059/238201* ⊕ *www.hotelcentrale.it* ➹ *40 rooms, 36 with bath* ⟁ *In-room safes, bar* ▭ *AE, DC, MC, V* ⊘ *Closed 3 wks in Aug.*

Ferrara

★ ❺ *47 km (29 mi) northeast of Bologna, 74 km (46 mi) northwest of Ravenna.*

When the legendary Ferrarese filmmaker Michelangelo Antonioni called his beloved hometown "a city that you can see only partly, while the rest disappears to be imagined," perhaps he was referring to the low-lying fog that rolls in off the Adriatic each winter and shrouds Ferrara's winding knot of medieval alleyways, turreted pleasure palaces, and ancient wine bars—once inhabited by the likes of Copernicus—in a ghostly mist. But perhaps Antonioni was also suggesting that Ferrara's striking beauty often conceals a dark and tortured past. The picturesque maze of twisting cobblestone streets that forms the old ghetto witnessed the persecution of its Jews once fascist Italy came under the spell of Nazi Germany.

And although the site was first settled before the time of Christ and was once ruled by Ravenna, Ferrara's history really begins with an ominous event—the arrival of the Este in 1259. For more than three centuries the infamous dynasty ruled with an iron fist; brother killed brother, son fought father, husband murdered wife. The majestic castle with moat, which now guards the heart of Ferrara's old town in innocuous splendor, was originally built as a fortress to protect the ruthless Este dukes from their own citizens; deep within the castle's bowels the Este kept generations of political dissidents in dank cells barely larger than a human body. The greatest of the dukes, Ercole I (1433–1505), attempted to poison a nephew who challenged his power, and when that didn't work he beheaded him. Yet it is to this pitiless man that Ferrara owes its great beauty. In one of his more empathetic moments, Ercole invited Sephardic Jews exiled from Spain to settle in Ferrara, spawning half a millennium of Jewish history that came to a spectacular end as Italy succumbed to Axis ideology, a tragedy documented in Giorgio Bassani's book and Vittorio De Sica's canonical neo-realist film, *The Garden of the Finzi-Continis*.

Today you are likely to be charmed by Ferrara's prosperous air and meticulous cleanliness, its excellent local restaurants and fin-de-siècle coffeehouses, and its hospitable, youthful spirit, marked by the boisterous mass of winedrinkers that gathers outside the Duomo on even the foggiest of weekend evenings. Though Ferrara is now a UNESCO world heritage site, the city still draws amazingly few tourists—which only adds to its mysterious appeal.

A museum card sold at the Palazzo dei Diamanti and at several art museums around town grants admission to every museum, palace, and castle in Ferrara for €12.40. A combined ticket for the Palazzo Schifanoia and its museum, the Palazzina Marfisa d'Este, and the Museo della Cattedrale costs €6.70.

Naturally enough, the building that was the seat of Este power dominates the town: it is the massive **Castello Estense,** a perfectly preserved and placed square in the center of the city in Piazza Castello. It is a suitable symbol for the ruling family: cold and menacing on the outside, lavishly decorated within. The public rooms are grand, but deep in the bowels of the fortress are chilling dungeons where enemies of the state were held in wretched conditions—a function these quarters served as recently as 1943, when antifascist prisoners were detained there. In particular, the **Prisons of Don Giulio, Ugo, and Parisina** have some fascinating features, like 15th-century smoke graffiti protesting the imprisonment of the young lovers Ugo and Parisina, who were beheaded in 1425.

The castle was established as a fortress in 1385, but work on its luxurious ducal quarters continued into the 16th century. Representative of Este grandeur are the **Sala dei Giochi** (Game Room), extravagantly painted with pagan athletic scenes, and the **Sala dell'Aurora,** decorated to show the times of the day. From the terraces of the castle and from the hanging garden, reserved for the private use of the duchesses, are fine views of the town and the surrounding countryside. You can cross the castle's moat, traverse its drawbridge, and wander through many of its arcaded passages at any time; in the still of a misty night, the experience is haunting. ⊠ *Piazza Castello* ☎ *0532/299233* ⌨ *Castle €6, tower €1 extra* ⏱ *Castle Tues.–Sun. 9:30–5:30, tower Tues.–Sun. 10–4:45.*

The magnificent Gothic **Duomo,** a few steps away from the Castello Estense, has a three-tiered facade of bony arches and beautiful carvings over the central door. It was begun in 1135 and took more than 100 years to complete. The interior was completely remodeled in the 17th century. Some of the original decorations of the town's main church, the Ex-chiesa e chiostro di San Romano, reside in the on-site **Museo del Duomo.** ⊠ *Piazza Cattedrale* ☎ *0532/207449* ⊕ *www.comune.fe.it/ musei-aa/schifanoia/catte.html* ⏱ *Duomo Mon.–Sat. 7:30–noon and 3–6:30, Sun. 7:30–12:30 and 3:30–7:30; Museo Tues.–Sun. 9–1 and 3–6* ⊠ *Duomo free, Museo €4.20.*

The oldest and most characteristic area of Ferrara is to the south of the Duomo, stretching between the Corso Giovecca and the city's ramparts. Here various members of the Este family built pleasure palaces, the most famous of which is the **Palazzo Schifanoia** (*schifanoia* means "carefree" or, literally, "fleeing boredom"). Begun in the 14th century, the palace was remodeled in 1466 and was the city's first Renaissance palazzo. The interior is lavishly decorated, particularly the **Salone dei Mesi,** with an extravagant series of frescoes showing the months of the year and their mythological attributes. The adjacent **Museo Civico Lapidario** has a collection of coins, statuary, and paintings. ⊠ *Via Scandiana 23* ☎ *0532/ 209998* ⊕ *www.comune.fe.it/musei-aa/schifanoia/skifa.html* ⌨ *Palace and museum €4.20, 1st Mon. of month free* ⏱ *Tues.–Sun. 9–6.*

The grand but unfinished courtyard is the most interesting part of the luxurious **Palazzo di Ludovico il Moro,** a magnificent 15th-century palace built for Ludovico Sforza, husband of Beatrice d'Este. The palazzo contains the region's **Museo Archeologico,** a repository of relics of early man, Etruscans, and Romans found in the country surrounding the city. ✉ *Via XX Settembre 124, near the Palazzo Schifanoia* ☎ *0532/66299* 🎟 *€4* ⊙ *Tues.–Sun. 9–2.*

The courtyard of the peaceful **Palazzo del Paradiso** contains the tomb of the great writer Ariosto (1474–1533), author of the most popular work of literature of the Renaissance, the poem *Orlando Furioso.* The building now houses the city library, the **Biblioteca Ariostea.** ✉ *Via delle Scienze 17* ☎ *0532/418200* 🎟 *Free* ⊙ *Weekdays 9–7:30, Sat. 9–1:30.*

One of the best-preserved of the Renaissance palaces along Ferrara's old streets is the charming **Casa Romei.** Downstairs are rooms with 15th-century frescoes and several sculptures collected from destroyed churches. The house stands not far from the Palazzo del Paradiso, in the area behind Ferrara's castle. The schedule varies with exhibits. ✉ *Via Savonarola 30* ☎ *0532/240341* 🎟 *€2* ⊙ *Tues.–Sun. 8:30–7:30.*

On the busy Corso Giovecca is the **Palazzina di Marfisa d'Este,** a grandiose 16th-century home that belonged to a great patron of the arts. The house has painted ceilings, fine 16th-century furniture, and a garden containing a grotto and an outdoor theater. At this writing, it was closed indefinitely for restoration. ✉ *Corso Giovecca 170* ☎ *0532/209988* ⊕ *www.comune.fe.it/musei-aa/schifanoia/marfi.html.*

The collection of ornate religious objects in the **Museo Ebraico** (Jewish Museum) bears witness to the long history of the city's Jewish community. This history had its high points—1492, for example, when Ercole I invited the Jews to come over from Spain—and its lows, notably 1624, when the papal government closed the **ghetto,** which was reopened only with the advent of a united Italy in 1859. The triangular warren of narrow, cobbled streets that made up the ghetto originally extended as far as Corso Giovecca (originally Corso Giudecca, or Ghetto Street); when it was enclosed, the neighborhood was restricted to the area between Via Scienze, Via Contrari, and Via di San Romano. The museum, in the center of the ghetto, is also the site of Ferrara's **synagogue.** ✉ *Via Mazzini 95* ☎ *0532/210228* 🎟 *€4* ⊙ *1-hr guided tours Sun. and Thurs. at 10, 11, and noon.*

The **Palazzo dei Diamanti** (Palace of Diamonds) is so called for the 12,600 faceted stone blocks that famously stud the facade. The palace was built in the 15th and 16th centuries and today contains the **Pinacoteca Nazionale,** an extensive art gallery devoted primarily to the painters of Ferrara. ✉ *Corso Ercole I d'Este 19–21* ☎ *0532/205844* 🎟 *€4* ⊙ *Tues. and Wed. and Fri. and Sat. 9–2, Thurs. 9–7, Sun. 9–1.*

Where to Stay & Eat

$$–$$$ ✕ **Trattoria La Romantica.** The former stables of a 17th-century merchant's house have been transformed into this casually elegant, welcoming restaurant, which is a great favorite among well-fed locals. Although the decor (warm light and wood-beam ceilings, incongruous prints, and a piano) seems to be in perpetual transition, the haute-rustic food is fully realized: Ferrarese specialties like cappellacci di zucca (pasta stuffed with a pumpkinlike squash) dumplings in a cream sauce with tomato, walnuts, and Parmesan) are served side by side with French oysters. ⊠ *Via Ripagrande 36* ☎ *0532/765975* ☰ *AE, DC, MC, V* ⊘ *Closed Wed., Jan. 7–17, and July 1–17.*

\$\$ ✕ **Osteria del Ghetto.** Though the Osteria is buried deep in the old Jewish ghetto, its seasonal menu is anything but old-fashioned. This casually elegant eatery represents the cutting edge of Ferrarese cooking. Creative dishes like basmati rice torte with Colonnata lard and boletus mushrooms, eggplant flan with cold Grana cream, and a lukewarm pheasant salad with balsamic vinegar span the new culinary spectrum of northern Italy. The interior is modern and relaxing, with wood-beamed ceilings, a no-smoking section, and tables on the street in summer. The wine list is excellent. ⊠ *Via Vittorio 26/28* ☎ *0532/764936* ☰ *AE, DC, MC, V* ⊘ *Closed Tues.*

\$–\$\$ ✕ **Antica Trattoria Volano.** Local businessmen often fill this white-walled, traditional-to-the-core neighborhood trattoria. The decor is rustic and the food includes such local treats as cappellacci di zucca and a good version of *salama da sugo*, a salty and oily boiled sausage served over mashed potatoes. Try the *tris* (a sampler of three different pastas). ⊠ *Via Volano 20* ☎ *0532/761421* ☰ *AE, DC, MC, V* ⊘ *Closed Fri.*

\$–\$\$ ✕ **Guido Ristorante.** The menu here is made up of Ferrarese specialties, plus some inventive dishes you won't find anywhere else, such as gnocchi in curry sauce with black olives and zucchini. The fish is fresh, and pastas are delicate and perfectly cooked. The cozy dining room has exposed brick and old wooden beams. Locals in the know frequent this restaurant on a cobbled street in the Jewish ghetto. ⊠ *Via Vignatagliata 61* ☎ *0532/761052* ☰ *AE, DC, MC, V* ⊘ *Closed Thurs. and July.*

\$–\$\$ ✕ **Hostaria Savonarola.** Into the wee hours, an avant-garde buzz emanates from this bright, bustling wine bar and informal restaurant. Despite the hip scene, the menu—scrawled on a chalkboard—is simple and traditional, focusing on a few daily preparations of good local ingredients. Risotto *in crema di zucca* makes creamy use of Ferrara's trademark small, pumpkinlike squash, and *papardelle al sugo d'anatra* pairs wide, flat noodles with a duck sauce. Service is warm, and outdoor tables couldn't be better for castle views. You can also buy good local salumi to go, just inches away from the castle in the very heart of town. ⊠ *Piazza Savonarola 12/16* ☎ *0532/200214* ☰ *AE, DC, MC, V.*

★ ¢–\$ ✕ **Osteria Al Brindisi.** Ferrara is a city of wine bars, beginning with this, Europe's oldest, which began pouring in 1435. Wine bottles from all over the world line the ancient walls of Al Brindisi. There's romantic ambient lighting and a memorable spread of salumi and local cheeses, as well as tasty hot dishes such as tortellini in brodo. This might just be the most perfect place to drink wine in Italy—Copernicus, who once lived upstairs, seemed to think so. Prices are low, and even the music (Otis Redding and the like) somehow feels just right. ⊠ *Via degli Adelardi 11* ☎ *0532/209142* ☰ *AE, DC, MC, V* ⊘ *Closed Mon.*

The **Prenotel hotel reservation hot line** (☎ 0532/462046), run by the city, allows you to make reservations at any of the accommodations listed below, among many others.

$$$ ⊞ **Hotel Ripagrande.** The courtyards, vaulted brick lobby, and breakfast
FodorsChoice room of this 15th-century noble's palazzo retain much of their lordly
★ Renaissance flair, but rooms are decidedly more down-to-earth. Every-
thing here from the room service to the showers is impeccable. Stan-
dard doubles and many enormous bi- and tri-level suites have faux-Persian
rugs, tapestries, and cozy antique furniture; top-floor rooms and suites
with terraces are like a Colorado ski lodge. The suites are a good deal,
the location is quiet but prime, and the friendly restaurant is worth a
try. ⊠ *Via Ripagrande 21, 44100* ☎ *0532/765250* 🖷 *0532/764377*
⊕ *www.ripagrandehotel.it* 🛏 *20 rooms, 20 suites* ⌂ *Restaurant, in-room
safes, minibars, bar, meeting room* ☰ *AE, DC, MC, V* ⦿ *BP.*

$ ⊞ **Locanda Borgonuovo.** This lovely bed-and-breakfast is in a 17th-cen-
tury monastery on a quiet but central pedestrians-only street. It books
up months in advance, partly because musicians and actors from the
local theater make this their home away from home. Rooms are fur-
nished with antiques, and one has its own kitchen for longer stays. Sum-
mer breakfasts are served in the leafy courtyard. ⊠ *Via Cairoli 29, 44100*
☎ *0532/211100* 🖷 *0532/246328* ⊕ *www.borgonuovo.com* 🛏 *4 rooms*
⌂ *Dining room, in-room safes, minibars, bicycles, library* ☰ *AE, MC,
V* ⦿ *BP.*

¢–$ ⊞ **Hotel San Paolo.** On the edge of the old city, San Paolo is the best
inexpensive choice in town. The 10-minute walk from the heart of Fer-
rara's medieval quarter is pleasant, and there are good restaurants in
the vicinity. Singles are a particularly good value. ⊠ *Via Baluardi 9,
44100* ☎ *0532/762040* 🖷 *0532/762040* ⊕ *www.hotelsanpaolo.it*
🛏 *31 rooms.* ⌂ *Bicycles, pets allowed; no a/c in some rooms* ☰ *AE,
DC, MC, V.*

Nightlife

The dim, stylish **Enobar Estense** (⊠ Piazza Cattedrale 7 ☎ 339/4831510),
right next to the cathedral, accompanies wines from all over Italy with
endless plates of delightful free Italian tapas and soothing jazz. **Enoteca
I Contrari** (⊠ Via Contrari 52 at Via Mazzini ☎ 0532/) has huge wooden
beams, high ceilings, good music, and good feelings. They serve panini,
plates of local salumi and cheeses, specialty rums and Scotches, and great
wines by the glass.

For live jazz, check out the **Jazz Club Ferrara** (⊠ Torrione San Giovanni
☎ 0532/211573 ⊕ www.jazzclubferrara.com), which has a star-stud-
ded lineup. The low-key **Leon d'Oro** (⊠ Piazza Cattedrale 2–10 ☎ 0532/
209318) is a grand old café serving expensive drinks, coffee, and sig-
nature Ferrarese fruitcakes (as well as a few basic pasta dishes at
lunchtime) in a truly regal environment. It's closed Wednesday. **Orsatti
1860** (⊠ Via Cortevecchia 33 ☎ 0532/207572) is one of the oldest and
best places in town for local pastries and great espresso (standing at the
bar, of course).

Sports & the Outdoors

BICYCLES Cycling is extremely popular in Ferrara. For guided bike trips, call **Ci-
cloclub Estense** (☎0532/900931). For bike rental, try **Pirana e Bagni** (⊠ Pi-
azzale Stazione 2 ☎ 0532/772190).

BOLOGNA

The centuries of wars, sackings, rebellions, and bombings that left such dramatic evidence in other cities of Emilia-Romagna have not taken their toll on Bologna's old city center. Narrow, cobblestone streets remain intact, as do the ancient churches, massive palaces, and medieval towers. Arcades line many of the main thoroughfares, shading the walkways to such an extent that you can stroll around town in a rainstorm for hours without feeling a drop.

Through its long history, first as an Etruscan city then a Roman one, then as an independent city-state in the Middle Ages, Bologna has always played a significant role in the north of Italy. Over the centuries the city has acquired a number of nicknames: Bologna the Learned, in honor of its venerable university, the oldest in the world; Bologna the Red, for its rosy rooftops and communist leanings; Bologna the Turreted, recalling the forest of medieval towers that once rose from the city center (two remarkable examples survive); and Bologna the Fat, a tribute to its preeminent position in the world of cuisine, the birthplace of mortadella, tortellini, and ragù.

Today one might also be tempted to dub it Bologna the Hip, for its position at the cutting edge of Italian culture. Recent years have brought an explosion of trendy *newyorkese* bars and lounges with postmodern music and Germanic track lighting, American brunches and California construction cuisine, and pricey boutiques in primary colors. The result is a jarring juxtaposition of leaning medieval towers and towering modernist fashion billboards. Unfortunately, the influx of people and industry that has accompanied these changes has also brought air and noise pollution, a further distraction from the city's architectural and culinary gems.

Although foreign tourists have lately begun to discover Bologna's special charm and arrive (along with Italians) in increasing numbers, the city's urban vitality still comes in large part from its student population. The university was founded in about the year 1088, and by the 13th century already had more than 10,000 students. It was a center for the teaching of law and theology, and it was ahead of its time in that many of the professors were women. Guglielmo Marconi, the inventor of the wireless telegraph, first formulated his groundbreaking theories in the physics labs of the university. Today the university has prominent business and medical faculties.

Exploring Bologna

Piazza Maggiore and the adjacent Piazza del Nettuno make up the core of the city. Arranged around these two squares are the imposing Basilica di San Petronio, the massive Palazzo Comunale, the Palazzo del Podestà, the Palazzo di Re Enzo, and the Fontana del Nettuno—one of the most visually harmonious groupings of public buildings in the entire country. From here, sights that aren't on one of the piazzas are but a short walk away, along delightful narrow cobbled streets or under the ubiquitous arcades that double as municipal umbrellas.

a good walk

Start at the southern end of sprawling Piazza Maggiore at the 14th-century **Basilica di San Petronio** ⑥ ▶, peeking into its museum to see the church's original designs, some never realized. On the west side of Piazza Maggiore is the **Palazzo Comunale** ⑦, especially worthwhile if you like the work of modern artist Giorgio Morandi. Next it's on to the **Palazzo del Podestà** ⑧ and its Torre dell'Arengo, at the north end of Piazza Maggiore in the adjoining Piazza Nettuno, where stands the Fontana del Nettuno, a.k.a. *Il Gigante*. To the left (west) is **Palazzo Re Enzo** ⑨, with its dark medieval associations. Toward the busy, chic Via Rizzoli, which runs east from Piazza Nettuno, is the gleaming, glass, modern tourist office complex that has drawn mixed reviews from locals. Follow Via Rizzoli directly into the medieval section of the city to Piazza di Porta Ravegnana, where you can climb the slightly off-kilter Torre degli Asinelli, the taller of **Le Due Torri** ⑩, Bologna's two landmark towers. From Piazza di Porta Ravegnana you have two choices: you might walk five minutes southeast down Via Santo Stefano to the remarkable church of **Santo Stefano** ⑪, and from there, head west on Via Farini and take a left on Via Garibaldi and another left a few blocks down to reach Piazza San Domenico and **San Domenico** ⑫. You could then continue northeast along Via Zamboni for the last three important sights. Or from the Piazza di Porta Ravegnana you might walk northeast on Via Zamboni to Via delle Belle Arte and the **Pinacoteca Nazionale** ⑬, with works by Raphael, Giotto, Parmigianino, and Bolognese masters, and finally stroll north to the **Università di Bologna** ⑭ district for a *caffè* and snack.

TIMING   Take at least a full day to explore Bologna; it's compact and lends itself to easy exploration, but there is plenty to see. The full walk should take at least five hours, plus a lunch break to sample Bologna's culinary bounty.

What to See

▶ ⑥ **Basilica di San Petronio.** Construction on this cathedral began in the 14th century, and work was still in progress on this vast building some 300 years later. It's not finished yet, as you can see: the wings of the transept are missing and the facade is only partially decorated, lacking most of the marble face the architects had intended. The main doorway was carved by the great Sienese master of the Renaissance, Jacopo della Quercia. Above the center of the door is a Madonna and Child flanked by Saints. Ambrose and Petronius, the city's patrons.

The interior of the basilica is huge: the Bolognans had planned an even bigger church—you can still see the columns erected to support the larger church outside the east end—but had to tone down construction when the university seat was established next door in 1561. The **Museo di San Petronio** contains models showing how the church was originally intended to look. The most important artworks in the church are in the left aisle, frescoes by Giovanni di Modena dating from the first years of the 1400s. ✉ *Piazza Maggiore* ☎ *051/225442* 🎟 *Free* ⊙ *Basilica Apr.–Sept., daily 7:30–1:15 and 2:30–6; Oct.–Mar., daily 7:30–1 and 2:30–6. Museo di San Petronio Mon.–Sat. 9:30–12:30 and 2:30–5:30, Sun. 2:30–5:30.*

Fontana del Nettuno. Sculptor Giambologna's elaborate 1566 baroque monument to Neptune occupying Piazza Nettuno has been aptly nicknamed *Il Gigante* (The Giant). Its exuberantly sensual mermaids and undraped God of the Sea drew fire when it was constructed, but not enough, apparently, to dissuade the populace from using the fountain as a public washing stall for centuries. It's also known for another reason: walk behind Neptune and to his right for an infamously lewd angle on the statue. ⊠ *Piazza Nettuno, next to the Palazzo Re Enzo, Piazza Maggiore.*

★ ❿ **Le Due Torri.** Two landmark towers, the **Torre degli Asinelli** and the **Torre Garisenda,** stand side by side in the compact Piazza di Porta Ravegnana. Torre degli Asinelli (circa 1109) is at 320 feet the taller of the two. It leans an alarming 7½ feet off perpendicular. The Torre Garisenda (from the late 11th century), tilting 10 feet, was shortened to 165 feet for safety in the 1500s, and is now closed to visitors. The towers were mentioned by Dante in *The Inferno.* They are two of the 60 that remain out of more than 200 that once presided over the city: every family of importance had a tower as a symbol of prestige and power, and as a potential fortress. For a fine view of Bologna's rooftops, climb up the 500 steep stairs of Torre degli Asinelli. ⊠ *Piazza di Porta Ravegnana, east of Piazza Maggiore* 🎫 €3 🕙 *Apr.–Sept., daily 9–6; Oct.–Mar., daily 9–5.*

❼ Palazzo Comunale. A mélange of building styles and constant modifications characterize this huge palace dating from the 13th to 15th centuries. When Bologna was an independent city-state, this was the seat of government, a function it still serves today. Over the door is a statue of Bologna-born Pope Gregory XIII, most famous for reorganizing the calendar. There are good views from the upper stories of the palace. The first-floor Red Room (City Council Hall) is open on advance request and during some exhibitions.

Within the palazzo there are also two museums. The **Collezioni Comunali d'Arte** exhibits paintings from the Middle Ages as well as some Renaissance works by Luca Signorelli (circa 1445–1523) and Tintoretto. The **Museo Morandi** is dedicated to the 20th-century still-life artist Giorgio Morandi; in addition to his paintings, there's a re-creation of his studio and living space. ⊠ *Piazza Maggiore 6* ☎ *051/203111 Palazzo, 051/ 203526 Collezioni, 051/203332 Museo* ⊕ *www.museomorandi.it* 🖭 *Palazzo free, each museum €4, combined ticket €6* ۞ *Palazzo Mon. 2:30–9:30, Tues.–Sat. 9 AM–9:30 PM, Sat. 9–7; Collezioni Tues.–Sat. 9–6:30, Sun. 10–6:30; Museo Tues.–Sun. 10–6.*

The **Biblioteca Sala Borsa,** connected to the Palazzo Comunale (toward Via Indipendenza), has an impressive interior courtyard surrounded by the library. Underground caves and the foundations of the old cathedral can be visited by appointment made through the tourist office. ⊠ *Piazza Nettuno, Piazza Maggiore* ☎ *051/204400* ⊕ *www.bibliotecasalaborsa. it* 🖭 *Free* ۞ *Mon. 2:30–9, Tues.–Fri. 9 AM–9:30 PM, Sat. 9–7.*

❽ Palazzo del Podestà. This classic Renaissance palace facing the Basilica di San Petronio was erected in 1484, and attached to it is the soaring **Torre dell'Arengo.** The bells in the tower have rung whenever the city has celebrated, mourned, or called its citizens to arms since 1453. ⊠ *Piazza Nettuno, Piazza Maggiore* ☎ *051/224500* ۞ *During exhibitions only.*

❾ Palazzo Re Enzo. King Enzo of Sardinia was imprisoned in this 13th-century medieval palace for 23 years, until his death in 1272. He had waged war on Bologna and was captured after the fierce battle of Fossalta in 1249. The palace has other macabre associations: common criminals received the last rites of the Church in the tiny chapel in the courtyard before being executed in Piazza Maggiore. The courtyard is worth peeking into, but the palace merely houses government offices. ⊠ *Piazza Re Enzo, Piazza Maggiore* ☎ *051/224500* ۞ *During exhibitions only.*

❿ Pinacoteca Nazionale. Bologna's principal art gallery contains many works by the immortals of Italian painting, including Raphael's famous *Ecstasy of St. Cecilia.* There's also a beautiful multipanel painting by Giotto, as well as a Parmigianino *Madonna and Saints.* The centerpieces of the collection, however, are the many rooms devoted to the two most important late-16th-century Bolognese masters, Guido Reni and Annibale Carracci. Other canvases convey the boisterous, earthy life of Old Bologna. ⊠ *Via delle Belle Arti 56, University* ☎ *051/4209411* ⊕ *www. pinacotecabologna.it* 🖭 *€4* ۞ *Tues.–Sun. 9–7.*

⑫ San Domenico. The tomb of St. Dominic, who died here in 1221, is called the **Arca di San Domenico** and is found in this church in the sixth chapel on the right. Many artists participated in its decoration, notably Niccolò di Bari, who was so proud of his contribution that he changed his name to Niccolò dell'Arca to recall this famous work. The young Michelangelo carved the angel on the right. In the right transept of the church is a tablet marking the last resting place of the hapless King Enzo, the Sardinian ruler imprisoned in the Palazzo Re Enzo. The attached museum displays religious relics and art. ✉ *Piazza San Domenico 13, off Via Garibaldi, south of Piazza Maggiore* ☎ *051/6400411* ⊙ *Weekdays 7:30–1 and 3:30–8, Sat. 7:30–1 and 3:30–7:30, Sun. 8–1 and 3:30–7:30; museum weekdays 10–noon and 3:30–6, Sat. 9:30–noon and 3:30–5:30, Sun. 3:30–5:30.*

⑪ Santo Stefano. This splendid and unusual basilica actually contains between four and seven connected churches (authorities differ). The oldest is **Santi Vitale e Agricola,** which dates from the 8th century and contains a 14th-century nativity scene much loved by Bologna's children, who come at Christmastime to pay their respects to the baby Jesus. The church of **San Sepolcro** (12th century) contains the **Cortile di Pilato** (Courtyard of Pontius Pilate), so named for the basin in its center said to be where Pilate washed his hands after condemning Christ. Also in the building is a **museum** displaying various medieval religious works and with a shop where you can buy sundry items such as honey, shampoo, and jam made by the monks. ✉ *Via Santo Stefano 24, Piazza Santo Stefano, University* ⊕ *www.settechiese.it* ☎ *051/223256* ✉ *Free* ⊙ *Mon.–Sat. 9–12:15 and 3:30–6, Sun. 9–noon and 3:30–7.*

FodorśChoice
★

Tourist Office. Guided walking tours of Bologna—in English—are run by the tourist office in Piazza Maggiore. Tours cost €13 and begin at 10:30 AM Wednesday, Saturday, and Sunday. ✉ *Piazza Maggiore 1* ☎ *051/246541* ⊕ *www.comune.bologna.it/bolognaturismo.*

⑭ Università di Bologna. Take a stroll through the streets of the university area, a jumble of buildings, some dating as far back as the 15th century and most to the 17th and 18th. The neighborhood, as befits a college town, is full of bookshops, coffee bars, and cheap restaurants. None of them are particularly distinguished, but they're all characteristic of student life in the city. Try eating at the *mensa universitaria* (cafeteria) if you want to strike up a conversation with local students (most speak English). Political slogans and sentiments are scrawled on walls all around the university and tend to be ferociously leftist. The **university museums,** in Palazzo Poggi, display scientific instruments and paleontological, botanical, and university-related artifacts. ✉ *Via Zamboni 33, University* ☎ *051/2099360* ⊕ *www.unibo.it/musei-universitari* ✉ *Free* ⊙ *Mon.–Sat. 9–4, Sun. 10:30–3:30.*

> off the
> beaten
> path

BASILICA DI SAN LUCA – It's a spectacular one-hour walk (or 10-minute drive) uphill from Porta Saragozza to the Basilica di San Luca at the edge of Bologna's center (follow Via Saragozza). It's an impressive hilltop church that has perched dramatically atop Monte della Guardia since 1160. The entire road is remarkably arcaded the entire way; you walk beneath 666 arches before arriving at the round basilica, which has a famous Madonna icon. But it's the sweeping views of the Emilian countryside and city from the 990-foot altitude that make the trip worthwhile—most of all in autumn, when the leaves of the hills on one side play off the blazing red rooftops of Bologna on the other. If you go by car (or, better yet, scooter), it's possible to ask for directions at the church and take an unmarked route back through the hills, winding past wonderful, rustic Emilian restaurants before reentering the city center through Porta San Mammolo. ⊠ *Via Saragozza, 3½ km (2 mi) southwest of Bologna.*

Where to Stay & Eat

$$–$$$$ ╳ **Rosteria Luciano.** A changing list of daily specials at this classic art deco restaurant augments what is already one of Bologna's most varied menus. Some of the best choices are tortelli *di zucca* (with pumpkinlike squash filling) and a pork chop with ham and cheese. Among the desserts, the *ricottina al forno* (oven-baked ricotta with a charcoal flavor) is worth the splurge. ⊠ *Via Nazario Sauro 19, Piazza Maggiore* ☎ *051/231249* ⌕ *Reservations essential* ═ *AE, DC, MC, V* ⊘ *Closed Wed., Aug., and Sun. in July.*

★ **$$–$$$** ╳ **Da Cesari.** Bologna classics such as tortellini in brodo and veal cutlet Bolognese (with ham and melted cheese) are well executed. But it's the delectable appetizers—such as *coppa di testa con cipolla e aceto balsamico* (cold, sliced head meat and red onion with balsamic vinegar) and white truffle with celery and shaved Parmesan—that make Da Cesari truly memorable. The romantic lighting in the dining room is warm and welcoming. Accompany the meal with wine made by the owner's family: Cesari's Liano is excellent. ⊠ *Via de' Carbonesi 8, south of Piazza Maggiore* ☎ *051/ 226769* ⊕ *www.da-cesari.com* ⌕ *Reservations essential* ═ *AE, DC, MC, V* ⊘ *Closed Sun., Sat. in July, Aug. 1–24, and Jan. 1–6.*

★ **$$–$$$** ╳ **Godot Wine Bar.** The buzzing, modern, expansive bilevel restaurant-wine bar is equally popular with students and foodies. This is the new face of Bologna. The extraordinary wine list is so diverse that you might find, say, a world-class Pugliese bottle so scarce that it's impossible to find in Puglia. Although the food may be the side attraction here, the basics are solid: they make a mean tagliatelle al ragù, for instance. ⊠ *Via Cartoleria 12, University* ☎ *051/226315* ⊕ *www.godotwine.it* ═ *AE, MC, V* ⊘ *Closed Sun. and 3 wks. in Aug.*

$$–$$$ ╳ **Le Stanze.** Sip an *aperitivo* (aperitif) or a late-night drink at a modern bar under the 17th-century frescoes that line the ceiling of what was the private chapel of the 1576 Palazzo Bentivoglio. If you choose to eat at the adjoining avant-garde restaurant, expect modern Italian fusion cooking—traditional ingredients used in new ways. Try the tasting of three soups, including an excellent chickpea ragù and a curried spinach concoction. The bar's open until 1:30 AM (2:30 on Saturday). ⊠ *Via del Borgo di S. Pietro 1, University* ☎ *051/228767* ⊘ *Closed July and Aug.* ═ *DC, MC, V.*

$$ ╳ **Nuovi Notai.** On the right side of the basilica, this spot is practically in Piazza Maggiore itself. The building is 14th century, the decor a bit overdone in a 19th-century way, and the food a rich, complex blend of classic regional and Tuscan specialties. Try the lamb cutlets with *aceto balsamico tradizionale* (Modena's prized balsamic vinegar) and Tropea onions. Formal service makes the place feel a bit touristy, but it's a classic Bologna experience. ⊠ *Via de' Pignattari 1, Piazza Maggiore* ☎ *051/ 228694* ⌲ *Reservations essential* ▭ *AE, DC, MC, V* ⊘ *Closed Sun.*

¢–$ ✕ **Cantina Bentivoglio.** This two-floor wine-jazz extravaganza is a classic place to relax by night. The ground floor is a dim, bottle-clad wine cellar; in the cavernlike basement downstairs live jazz is staged every night (for a €4 cover). The wine list includes labels from many of Italy's lesser-known regions, and the menu lists pastas, meats, and interesting salads and lighter plates, such as *crostini* (toasted bread) with mozzarella, eggplant, tomato, and roasted peppers. Vegetarian options are plentiful. Doors stay open until 2 AM, and wine is also available to go. ⊠ *Via Mascarella 4, University* ☎ *051/265416* ⊕ *www.affari.com/bentivoglio* ⊘ *Closed Sun. and Mon. Oct.–May* ▭ *AE, DC, MC, V.*

¢–$ ✕ **Da Bertino.** Happy diners don't seem to mind the close quarters in the large, bustling space here. Maybe it's because of the incredibly low prices, or maybe it's because popularity hasn't spoiled this traditional neighborhood trattoria and its simple home-style dishes. Highlights are the homemade *paglia e fieno* (yellow and green, plain and spinach, pasta) with sausage and the choices on the steaming tray of *bollito misto* (boiled meats). Ask to be seated in the back, rather than the less attractive room up front. ⊠ *Via delle Lame 55, Porta San Felice* ☎ *051/522230* ▭ *AE, DC, MC, V* ⊘ *Closed Sun. and Mon. Oct.–May, and Aug. 4–31. No dinner Sat. in June and July.*

¢–$ ✕ **La Scuderia.** A bit of New York chic comes to Bologna via the cutting-edge café/wine bar/performance space in a stunning vaulted ballroom of an old palazzo. Next door to the university, La Scuderia serves as an informal meeting place for hip students and intellectuals. Salads, desserts, lunches, wines by the glass, and American-style Sunday brunches are options. You can just as easily drink coffee over a newspaper at breakfast as flirt over a piña colada in the evening. Many nights there's live jazz. ⊠ *Piazza G. Verdi 2, off Via Zamboni, University* ☎ *051/6569619* ▭ *AE, DC, MC, V* ⊘ *Closed Mon.*

★ ¢–$ ✕ **Victoria.** It's not unusual for this unpretentious and charming trattoria-pizzeria off Via dell'Indipendenza to have lines, so reserve ahead. Although locals come for the cheap pizzas, the rest of the menu is not to be overlooked, particularly the tortellini *con noci e speck,* a ridiculously rich treatment of Bologna's classic pasta in a sauce of cream, ground walnuts, and cured ham. The back room has a lovely 17th-century painted wooden ceiling. ⊠ *Via Augusto Righi 9/c, north of Piazza Maggiore* ☎ *051/233548* ⌲ *Reservations essential* ▭ *AE, DC, MC, V* ⊘ *Closed Thurs.*

★ ¢ ✕ **Tamburini.** Smells of all that is good about Bolognese food waft through the room and out into the streets. Breads, numerous cheeses, salumi such as Parma and Bologna hams and prosciuttos, roasted peppers, inventive salads, balsamic vinegars, local olive oils, smoked salmon, and fresh pasta are among the delights. This upscale deli–cum–self-service buffet is *the* lunch spot. Tamburini also vacuum-packs foods for shipping or air travel. ✉ *Via Drapperie 1, Piazza Maggiore* ☎ *051/234726* ➡ *AE, MC, V* ⊗ *No dinner.*

★ **\$\$\$\$** 🏨 **Corona d'Oro 1890.** A medieval printing house in a former life, this hotel is delightful, lyrically art nouveau in its public space and atrium, with enough flowers for a wedding. Guest rooms make opulent use of original 15th- and 16th-century decorations such as painted wood ceilings and Gothic-vault windows. The morning English breakfast buffet is worth getting up for. ✉ *Via Oberdan 12, north of Piazza Maggiore, 40126* ☎ *051/236456* 🖷 *051/262679* ⊕ *http://corona.hotel-bologna. net* ➪ *35 rooms* ⧉ *In-room safes, minibars, bicycles, bar, meeting room* ➡ *AE, DC, MC, V* ⊗ *Closed 1st 3 wks in Aug.* ⦿ *BP.*

★ **\$\$\$\$** 🏨 **Grand Hotel Baglioni.** Sixteenth-century paintings and frescoes by the Bolognese Carracci brothers are rarely seen outside a museum or church, but in this 15th-century palazzo they provide the stunning backdrop for the public rooms and restaurant of one of Italy's most glamorous hotels. Lady Di slept here, and you may feel no less royal in a handsome room with antique furniture and brocaded walls. The highly regarded I Carracci restaurant serves top-notch food in regal, formal surroundings. ✉ *Via dell'Indipendenza 8, north of Piazza Maggiore, 40121* ☎ *051/225445* 🖷 *051/234840* ⊕ *www.baglionihotels.com* ➪ *113 rooms, 11 suites* ⧉ *Restaurant, in-room safes, minibars, bar, babysitting, meeting room, parking (fee), no-smoking rooms* ➡ *AE, DC, MC, V* ⦿ *BP.*

\$\$\$–\$\$\$\$ 🏨 **Dei Commercianti.** Rooms here were designed to retain the structural integrity of the 11th-century palace and tower the hotel occupies, and are therefore cozy and unique, with original wood beams built into the walls. Tower rooms and suites have balconies with magnificent views of San Domenico church; all are stylishly furnished with, among other things, Carrara marble desks custom-built following a 15th-century design. ✉ *Via De' Pignattari 11, south of Piazza Maggiore, 40124* ☎ *051/233052* 🖷 *051/224733* ⊕ *http://commercianti.hotel-bologna.net* ➪ *32 rooms, 2 suites* ⧉ *Dining room, in-room safes, minibars, bicycles, bar* ➡ *AE, DC, MC, V* ⦿ *BP.*

★ **\$\$\$–\$\$\$\$** 🏨 **Novecento.** A design-oriented hotel inspired by 1930s Europe, Novecento is at its core modern, modern, modern. Clean lines and elegant restraint are the hallmarks of the rooms, the lobby, and even the elevators. Breakfast is great, there's free wine and snacks for happy hour, and it's in the middle of everything in downtown Bologna. Call ahead if you need a parking space, and be advised that the garage closes mid-evening for the night. ✉ *Piazza Gallilei, Piazza Maggiore, 40126* ☎ *051/7457311* 🖷 *051/7457322* ⊕ *http://novecento.hotel-bologna.net* ➪ *25 rooms* ⧉ *Dining room, in-room safes, minibars, bar, parking (fee), no-smoking rooms* ➡ *AE, DC, MC, V* ⦿ *BP.*

\$\$\$–\$\$\$\$ 🏨 **Orologio.** Although occupying an old palazzo, which was originally a public building, the Orologio achieves a contemporary effect. A mid-level lounge and Internet room is a pleasant place to relax, and top-floor rooms have good views of Bologna's skyline. Under the same management as the Corona d'Oro and the Dei Commercianti, this hotel is in a quiet pedestrian zone off Piazza Grande—an ideal sightseeing location. Fax ahead or check the Web site for driving directions. ✉ *Via IV*

Novembre 10, Piazza Maggiore, 40123 ☏ *051/231253* 🖶 *051/260552* ⊕ *http://orologio.hotel-bologna.net* ⟿ *29 rooms* ⚒ *Dining room, minibars, bicycles, Internet* ▭ *AE, DC, MC, V* ⌾ *BP.*

$–$$ 🏨 **Accademia.** Looking for a midrange, comfortable base for exploring the area? This small hotel is right in the center of the university quarter. The rooms are adequate, the staff friendly. Look for discounted prices on the Web site. A few more inexpensive rooms are without bath. ⊠ *Via delle Belle Arti 6, at Via delle Moline, University, 40126* ☏ *051/232318* 🖶 *051/263590* ⊕ *www.hotelaccademia.it* ⟿ *28 rooms, 24 with bath* ⚒ *Bar, parking (fee)* ▭ *No credit cards* ⌾ *BP.*

$ 🏨 **San Vitale.** Modern furnishings and a garden distinguish this modest hostelry, about 1 km (½ mi) from the center of town. The service is courteous, and rooms are clean and bright. There are private bathrooms, but facilities are very basic. ⊠ *Via San Vitale 94, University, 40125* ☏ *051/225966* 🖶 *051/239396* ⟿ *17 rooms* ⚒ *Internet, parking (fee)* ▭ *No credit cards.*

Nightlife & the Arts

The Arts

BALLET **Arena del Sole.** You can see ballet performances at this theater opened in 1810. ⊠ *Via Indipendenza 44, north of Piazza Maggiore* ☏ *051/2910910* ⊕ *www.arenadelsole.it.*

FESTIVALS **Festa di San Petronio.** The first weekend in October crowds celebrate with bands, fireworks, and free *mortadella di Bologna* sandwiches in Piazza Maggiore.

Made in BO. Named after city's two-letter license-plate abbreviation, Made in BO runs for a month and a half from June to August. It's a series of nightly outdoor concerts, popular with locals, in the Parco Nord (near the Fiera). ☏ *051/533880* ⊕ *www.madeinbo.it.*

Open-air Cinema. Free movies are shown in Piazza Unità from June through August. The tourist office has the schedule.

MUSIC & OPERA **Cantina Bentivoglio.** For jazz this cantina is one of Bologna's most appealing nightspots. ⊠ *Via Mascarella 4/b, University* ☏ *051/265416.*

Sala Bossi. Come to Sala Bossi for all types of classical music—and opera. ⊠ *Piazza Rossini 2, University* ☏ *051/233975.*

Sala Mozart. Accademia Filarmonica, the city's principal music school, calls the Sala Mozart home. ⊠ *Via Guerrazzi 13, University* ☏ *051/222997.*

Teatro Comunale. The 18th-century theater presents concerts by Italian and international orchestras throughout the year, but is dominated by the highly acclaimed opera performances in the winter season. Reserve seats well in advance. ⊠ *Largo Respighi 1, University* ☏ *051/529999* ⊕ *www.comunalebologna.it.*

Nightlife

As a university town, Bologna has long been known for its hopping nightlife. As early as 1300 it was said to have had 150 taverns. Most of the city's current 200-plus pubs and lounges are frequented by Italian students, young adults, and the international study-abroad crowd, with the university district forming the epicenter. In addition to the university area, the pedestrian-only zone on Via del Pratello, lined with a host of pubs, is also a hopping night scene, as is Via delle Moline, with cutting-edge cafés and bars. A more upmarket, low-key evening experience can be had at one of Bologna's many new wine bars that are also restaurants, such as Cantina Bentivoglio and Godot Wine Bar. And then there are the hypertrendy bar-lounges that represent the newest, and most *newyorkese,* of Bologna's many faces; some of these joints make even Milan look old-school.

Bar Calice. The elegant and trendy bar runs an indoor-outdoor operation year-round with heat lamps; it's a cocktail and wine bar that's extremely popular with the see-and-be-seen thirtysomethings. ⊠ *Via Clavature 13/a, at Via Marchesana, Piazza Maggiore* ☎ *051/264508.*

Bar de' Marchi. Across from the picturesque San Francesco church and its pleasant piazza is the real thing—a local hangout with a raucous mix of old men and students playing cards and drinking cheap wine by the glass. ⊠ *Piazza San Francesco 4, University* ☎ *051/238945.*

Cantavalli. A wine bar with romantic ambient lighting and a good draft beer selection, Cantavalli is relaxing choice. (⊠ Via Belle Arti 2, University ☎ 051/268395).

The Cluricaune. For a young, tipsy, boisterous international crowd, head for this Irish pub. ⊠ *Via Zamboni 18/b, University* ☎ *051/263419.*

Divinis. The casually hip Divinis wine bar has a remarkable, if pricey, selection by the glass (as well as high-end food) served in chichi surroundings until 1:30 AM. ⊠ *Via Battibecco 4/c University* ☎ *051/2961502.*

Lord Lister. If your taste runs toward the English pub, try Lord Lister, which draws loads of students, study-abroaders, and expats. ⊠ *Via Zamboni 56, University* ☎ *051/240886.*

Nu Bar Lounge. On the Buco San Petronio, a tunnel-like street tucked near the cathedral, a loud, modern, haywire lounge hosts a self-confident crowd. Join the crowd sipping *prosecco,* a dry, sparkling white wine, or cocktails here and sometimes munching on light food. ⊠ *Via de' Musei 6, Piazza Maggiore* ☎ *051/222532* ⊕ *www.nu-lounge.com.*

Room. This postmodern fantasy lounge with exposed pipes, industrial furnishings, and low-to-the-ground pillow-seats has a staff composed entirely of beautiful people. The place serves midrange food and Sunday brunch. ⊠ *Via Fossalta 3, Piazza Maggiore* ☎ *051/2961274* ⊕ *www.roomrestaurant.it.*

Shopping

Books

Feltrinelli. Next to the Due Torri is the best bookstore in the region, which capitalizes on the university clientele. ⊠ *Piazza Ravegnana 1, east of Piazza Maggiore* ☎ *051/266891* ⊕ *www.lafeltrinelli.it.*

Feltrinelli International. Look here for innumerable travel guides and maps, and Italy's best selection of English and other foreign-language books. ⊠ *Via Zamboni 7/b, east of Piazza Maggiore* ☎ *051/268070.*

Clothing

A host of small clothing and jewelry shops lines Via d'Azeglio in the center of town. For cheaper goods, Via dell'Indipendenza between the station and downtown is often lined with street vendors hawking bargain-basement clothing.

Galleria Cavour. One of the most upscale malls in Italy, the Galleria Cavour houses many of the fashion giants, including Gucci, Versace, and the jeweler and watchmaker Bulgari. ⊠ *Piazza Cavour, south of Piazza Maggiore.*

Wine & Food

Bologna is a good place to buy wine. Several shops have a bewilderingly large selection—to go straight to the top, ask the managers which wines were awarded the prestigious *Tre Bicchieri* (Three Glasses) award from Gambero Rosso's wine bible, *Vini d'Italia.*

City Market. The gargantuan market is open daily except Sunday during daylight hours, housing vendors of every imaginable sort hawking wares of variable quality, including food, clothing, shoes, books, and every imaginable household necessity. ⊠ *Piazza VIII Agosto, off Via dell'Indipendenza north toward the train station.*

Enoteca Italiana. Repeatedly recognized as one of the best wine stores in Italy, Enoteca Italiana lives up to its reputation with shelves lined with excellent selections from all over Italy at reasonable prices. Their delicious sandwiches with wine by the glass also make a great stand-up light lunch. ⊠ *Via Marsala 2/b, north of Piazza Maggiore* ☎ *051/227132.*

Scaramagli. Friendly owners run this midsize, down-to-earth wine store. The shop is closed in the afternoon from 1 until 5, but reopens from 5 to 8 every evening except Thursday. ⊠ *Strada Maggiore 31/d, University* ☎ *051/227132.*

Via Oberdan. For fresh produce, meats, and other foods sold in traditional Italian markets, head to Via Oberdan, the street just off Indipendenza downtown. ⊠ *Piazza Maggiore.*

ROMAGNA

Anywhere in Emilia-Romagna, the story goes, a weary, lost traveler will be invited into a family's home and offered a drink. But the Romagnese claim that he'll be served water in Emilia and wine in Romagna. The hilly, mostly rural, and largely undiscovered Romagna region has crumbling farmhouses dotting rolling hills, smoking chimneys, ancient Christian temples, and rowdy local bars dishing out rounds and rounds of *piadine* (flat griddle breads). Ravenna, the site of shimmering Byzantine mosaics, dominates the region, and Rimini is one of Italy's most popular seaside resorts.

Heading southeast out of Bologna, Via Emilia (SS9) and the parallel A14 Autostrada lead to the towns of Dozza and Faenza. From there, cut north to the Adriatic coast on the S71 to reach Ravenna, or continue on southeast on the A14 to reach Rimini. Alternatively, the slower S16 cuts a northwest–southeast swath through Romagna, directly connecting Ravenna and Rimini.

Dozza

⑮ *85 km (53 mi) southeast of Ferrara, 31 km (19 mi) southeast of Bologna.*

Dozza is a small village just off the Via Emilia (SS9) where artists from all over flock in September of odd years to take part in a mural competition. As a result, virtually every square foot of the town is covered with colorful scenes, executed with varying degrees of skill.

Dozza is crowned with a splendidly restored medieval castle museum, the **Rocca Sforzesca di Dozza.** ☎ *0542/678240* ⊠ *€4* ⊗ *Apr.–Sept., Tues.–Sat. 10–1 and 3–7, Sun. 10–1 and 3–7:30; Oct.–Mar., Tues.–Sat. 10–12:30 and 3–5, Sun. 10–1 and 2:30–6.*

Enoteca Regionale, in Dozza's castle, is the wine "library" for the region. While wine shopping in this cozy stone building, you can sample the different vintages from the surrounding countryside, particularly Dozza's own Albana, a white wine that comes dry or sweet. For larger consumption, the on-site wine bar is open afternoon until evening. ⊠ *Rocca di Dozza* ☎ *0542/678089* ⊕ *www.enotecaemiliaromagna.it* ⊗ *Tues.–Fri. 9:30–1 and 2:30–6:30, weekends 10–1 and 3–7.*

Where to Eat

$$$$ ✕ **San Domenico.** Some superstar restaurants come and go, but San

FodorśChoice Domenico is anything but a flash in the pan, having defended its posi-

★ tion as one of Italy's most refined dining destinations year after year. The majestic appointments complement celebrity chef Valentino Marcattilii's wondrous creations, such as hand-stuffed pasta with rabbit and eggplant in lemon-thyme sauce, and risotto with scampi, black truffle, and artichoke. Service is like a silent, perfectly choreographed ballet, and the staggering wine list has more than 3,000 choices. Reserve well in advance. ⊠ *Via G. Sacchi 1, Imola, 15 km (9 mi) east of Dozza* ☎ *0542/ 29000* ⊕ *www.sandomenico.it* ⚎ *Reservations essential* ▭ *AE, DC, MC, V* ⊗ *Closed Mon., Aug., and Jan. No dinner Sun.*

Faenza

⑯ *23 km (14 mi) southeast of Dozza, 49 km (30 mi) southeast of Bologna.*

The renowned style of pottery called faience has been produced in Faenza, on the Via Emilia, since the 12th century. In the central **Piazza del Popolo** are dozens of shops selling the native wares. Faenza, not surprisingly, is home to the **Museo delle Ceramiche,** one of the largest ceramics museums in the world. ⊠ *Viale Baccarini 19* ☎ *0546/ 697311* ⊕ *www.racine.ra.it/micfaenza* ⊠ *€6* ⊗ *Apr.–Oct., Tues.–Sat. 9–7, Sun. 9:30–1 and 3–7; Nov.–Mar., Tues.–Fri. 9–1:30, weekends 9:30–5:30.*

Forlì

⑰ *16 km (10 mi) southeast of Faenza, 74 km (46 mi) southeast of Bologna.*

The biggest city on the Via Emilia between Bologna and Rimini is Forlì. It's a pretty, prosperous, provincial Romagnan city with a huge but harmonious piazza and duomo. Some of the true riches of Romagna lie along the smaller roads branching off to the north and south of Forlì. Castrocaro Terme is one of the spa towns in the hills to the south.

★ **$$$$** ✕ **La Frasca.** Chef Gianfranco Bolognesi is an artist with fresh Adriatic seafood, delectable fowl, and Romagnan produce. Expect far-fetched, haute-cuisine delights such as a pastry-crust quail stuffed with foie gras and black truffle. A beautiful drive brings you to this elegant country restaurant in the secluded spa town of Castrocaro Terme, 11 km (7 mi) southeast of Forlì. Sit in the garden for alfresco summer dining. ⊠ *Viale Mateotti 34, Castrocaro Terme, 11 km (7 mi) southeast of Forlì* ☎ *0543/ 767471* ⊕ *www.lafrasca.it* ⌖ *Reservations essential* ⊟ *AE, DC, MC, V* ☾ *Closed Tues., Jan. 1–21, and Aug. 15–Sept. 1.*

Bagno di Romagna

⑱ *66 km (41 mi) southeast of Forlì, 74 km (46 mi) southeast of Bologna.*

Bagno di Romagna is one of the spa hill towns that dot the bucolic Romagnan countryside. There's not a lot to see, but the public hot springs in the center can be enjoyed year-round.

Where to Stay & Eat

★ **$$$$** ✕ **Paolo Teverini.** The chef-owner—and restaurant's namesake—is one of the star culinary personalities of the region. His relentlessly modern preparations are punctuated by essences, foams, gelatins, and reductions that display an almost conniving flair for drama, matched only by the outlandishly pink and posh decor. Most impressive of all is the voluminous wine list, a showcase of older vintages from Italy's best producers at lower-than-wine-store prices. ⊠ *Piazza Dante 2* ☎ *0543/911260* ⊕ *www.paoloteverini.it* ⌖ *Reservations essential* ⊟ *AE, DC, MC, V* ☾ *Closed Mon. and Tues. Sept.–June.*

$$ ▦ **Tosco Romagnolo.** Right near Bagno di Romagna's thermal baths, the Tosco Romagnolo is in the same spa complex (and under the same ownership) as the inimitable Paolo Teverini restaurant. Rooms are reasonably priced (rates drop dramatically in winter) and suites, though more expensive, are top-notch and sparkling. The hot tub and pool (heated) on the hotel's roof command calming views of the surrounding Romagnan hills. The attached spa, Gaia Teverini, has all manner of health treatments, massage, and so on. ⊠ *Piazza Dante 2, 47021* ☎ *0543/911260* ▦ *0543/911014* ⊕ *www.paoloteverini.it* ⬚ *45 rooms, 4 suites* ⌂ *2 restaurants, some in-room safes, minibars, pool, health club, outdoor hot tub, spa, bicycles, bar, meeting rooms, car rental* ⊟ *AE, DC, MC, V.*

en route   On Via Emilia, beyond the turnoff for Bagno di Romagna on the way to Rimini, you pass Savignano. A reminder that no matter how new the towns might look, you are still traveling in a place of great history: Just outside the town is a small stream, the Rubicone. Cross it and you, too, have crossed the Rubicon, the river made famous by Julius Caesar when in 49 BC he defied the Roman Senate by bringing his army across the river and plunging the country into civil war.

Ravenna

▶ *52 km (84 mi) north of Bagno di Romagna, 76 km (47½ mi) east of Bologna.*

Ravenna is a small, quiet city of brick palaces and cobbled streets whose magnificent monuments remind you of its storied past. The high point in Ravenna's history was 1,500 long years ago, when the city became the capital of the Roman Empire. The honor was short-lived—the city was taken by the barbarian Ostrogoths in the 5th century; in the 6th century it was conquered by the Byzantines, who ruled it from Constantinople.

Because Ravenna spent much of its history looking to the East, its greatest art treasures show much Byzantine influence: above all, Ravenna is a city of mosaics, the finest in Western art. A combination ticket, costing €8.50 from April to September, €6.50 October to March (available at ticket offices of all included sights), admits you to six of Ravenna's most important monuments: the Tomba di Galla Placidia, the Basilica di San Vitale, the Battistero Neoniano, Sant'Apollinare Nuovo, the church of Spirito Santo, and the Museo Arcivescovile e Cappella Sant'Andrea. The Battistero Neoniano is the only attraction that sells a single-site ticket, and that's only from March to May.

a good walk

Start your day at the spectacular **Mausoleo di Galla Placidia** ⑲, an unassuming brick building that conceals some of the most impressive mosaics in Italy. From the Mausoleo, turn right onto Via Galla Placidia and move on to the octagonal **Basilica di San Vitale** ⑳ and its brilliant Byzantine mosaics. In the same area, down Via San Vitale to the right of the Basilica, stands the **Museo Nazionale** ㉑, with a well-presented display of early religious art. Then backtrack along Via San Vitale toward the center. Take a right at Via Salara, then a quick left onto Cavour and up to Piazza Costa. Take a right on Mateotti just before the piazza. You're now in the heart of the *centro storico* (historic center). Depending on your timing, you could have lunch at a restaurant in the area before a visit to the **Battistero Neoniano** ㉒. To get to the Battistero, follow Matteotti, which becomes Mentana after Piazza XX Settembre; take a right on Via Gessi and follow it to its end at the baptistery. Then continue on to the **Tombe di Dante** ㉓ and **Sant'Apollinare Nuovo** ㉔.

TIMING Start out early in the morning to avoid lines (reservations are required for the Mausoleo and Basilica in May and June). Allow an hour each for the Mausoleo, the Basilica, and the Museo Nazionale. A half day should suffice for the walk alone.

What to See

⑳ **Basilica di San Vitale.** The octagonal church of San Vitale was built in AD 547, after the Byzantines conquered the city, and its interior shows a strong Byzantine influence. In the area behind the altar are the most famous works

Ravenna

KEY

▶ *Start of walk*

🛈 *Tourist information*

in the church, accurate portraits of the Emperor of the East, Justinian, attended by his court and the bishop of Ravenna, Maximian. Notice how the mosaics seamlessly wrap around the columns and curved arches on the upper sides of the altar area. Reservations are required from March through mid-June. ✉ *Via San Vitale, off Via Salara* ☎ *0544/217522 for reservations, 0544/215193, 800/303999* ⊕ *www.ravennavisitcard.com* 🎫 *Combination ticket €8.50 Apr.–Sept., €6.50 Oct.–Mar.* ☉ *Jan. and Feb., daily 9–4:30; Mar. and Oct., daily 9–5; Apr.–Sept., daily 9–7.*

②② Battistero Neoniano. The Battistero, next door to Ravenna's 18th-century cathedral, is one of the town's most important mosaic sights. In keeping with the building's baptismal role, the great mosaic in the dome shows the baptism of Christ, and beneath that scene are the Apostles. The lowest band of mosaics contains Christian symbols, the Throne of God and the Cross. Note the naked figure kneeling next to Christ—he is the personification of the River Jordan. The Battistero building is said to have been a Roman bath dating from the 5th century AD. ✉ *Via Battistero* ☎ *0544/219938* ⊕ *www.ravennavisitcard.com* 🎫 *Single-site ticket €2 Mar.–May; combination ticket €8.50 Apr.–Sept., €6.50 Oct.–Mar.* ☉ *Jan. and Feb., daily 9–4:30; Mar. and Oct., daily 9–5:30; Apr.–Sept., daily 9–7.*

Domus dei Tappeti di Pietra. This underground archeological site (Ancient Home of the Stone Carpets) was uncovered during the course of routine maintenance work by the city in 1993 and opened to the public in 2002. Below ground level (10 feet down) lie the remains of a 6th-century AD Byzantine palace, whose beautiful and well-preserved network of mosaics on the floor display themes that are fascinatingly un-Christian. The ticket office closes a half hour before the museum. ⊠ *Via Barbiani, enter through Sant'Eufemia* ☎ *0544/32512* ⌨ *Combination ticket €8 Apr.–Sept., €6 Oct.–Mar.* ⊕ *www.ravennantica.it* ⊗ *Tues.–Sat. 8:30–6:30, Sun. 8:30–7:30.*

⑲ Mausoleo di Galla Placidia. The little tomb and the great church stand
FodorsChoice side by side, but the tomb predates the Basilica di San Vitale by at least
★ a hundred years. These two adjacent sights are decorated with the best-known, and most elaborate, mosaics in Ravenna. Galla Placidia was the sister of Rome's emperor, Honorius, the man who moved the imperial capital to Ravenna in AD 402. She is said to have been beautiful and strong-willed, and to have taken an active part in the governing of the crumbling empire. This tomb, constructed in the mid-5th century, is her memorial.

Outside, the tomb is a small, unassuming redbrick building; the exterior's seeming poverty of charm only serves to enhance the richness of the interior mosaics, in deep midnight blue and glittering gold. The tiny, low central dome is decorated with symbols of Christ and the evangelists and striking gold stars. Over the door is a depiction of the Good Shepherd. Eight of the Apostles are represented in groups of two on the four inner walls of the dome; the other four appear singly on the walls of the two transepts. Notice the small doves at their feet, drinking from the water of faith. Also in the tiny transepts are some delightful pairs of deer (representing souls), drinking from the fountain of resurrection. There are three sarcophagi in the tomb, none of which are believed to contain the remains of Galla Placidia. She died in Rome in AD 450, and there is no record of her body having been transported back to the place where she wished to lie. Reservations are required for the Mausoleo from March through mid-June. ⊠ *Via San Vitale, off Via Salara* ☎ *0544/ 215193, 0544/217522 reservations, 800/303999 toll-free information* ⊕ *www.ravennavisitcard.com* ⌨ *Combination ticket €8.50 Apr.–Sept., €6.50 Oct.–Mar.* ⊗ *Jan. and Feb., daily 9–4:30; Mar. and Oct., daily 9–5; Apr.–Sept., daily 9–7.*

㉑ Museo Nazionale. The National Museum of Ravenna, next to the Church of San Vitale, contains artifacts from ancient Rome, Byzantine fabrics and carvings, and pieces of early Christian art. The collection is housed in a former monastery, but is well displayed and artfully lighted. ⊠ *Via Fiandrini* ☎ *0544/34424* ⌨ *€3* ⊗ *Tues.–Sun. 10–4:30.*

㉔ Sant'Apollinare Nuovo. The mosaics displayed in this church date from the early 6th century, making them slightly older than the works in San Vitale. Since the left side of the church was reserved for women, it's only fitting that the mosaic decoration there is a scene of 22 virgins offering crowns to the Virgin Mary. On the right wall are 26 men carrying the crowns of martyrdom. They are approaching Christ, surrounded by angels. ⊠ *Via Roma and Via Guaccimanni* ☎ *0544/219518 or 800/303999* ⊕ *www.ravennavisitcard.com* ✉ *Combination ticket € 8.50 Apr.–Sept., €6.50 Oct.–Mar.* ⊙ *Daily 9:30–4:30.*

㉓ Tomba di Dante. The tomb of Dante is in a small neoclassical building next door to the large church of St. Francis. Exiled from his native Florence, the author of *The Divine Comedy* died here in 1321. The Florentines have been trying to reclaim their famous son for hundreds of years, but the Ravennans refuse to give him up, arguing that since Florence did not welcome Dante in life it does not deserve him in death. The small **Museo Dantesco** has displays on the writer's life and the history of the tomb. ⊠ *Via Dante Alighieri 4 and 9* ☎ *0544/30252* ✉ *Free* ⊙ *Tomb Apr.–Sept., daily 9–7; Oct.–Mar., daily 9–noon and 2–5. Museum Apr.–Sept., Tues.–Sun. 9–noon and 3:30–6; Oct.–Mar., Tues.–Sun. 9–noon.*

> **off the beaten path**

SANT'APOLLINARE IN CLASSE – This church, about 5 km (3 mi) southeast of Ravenna, is landlocked now, but when it was built it stood in the center of the busy shipping port of Classis. The arch above and the area around the high altar are rich with mosaics. Those on the arch, older than the ones behind it, are considered superior. They show Christ in Judgment and the 12 lambs of Christianity leaving the cities of Jerusalem and Bethlehem. In the apse is the figure of Sant'Apollinare himself, a bishop of Ravenna, and above him is a magnificent Transfiguration against blazingly green grass, animals in skewed perspective, and flowers. ⊠ *Via Romea Sud, Classe* ☎ *0544/473661* ✉ *€2, free Sun.* ⊙ *Mon.–Sat. 8:30–7:30, Sun. 1–7:30.*

Where to Stay & Eat

$–$$ ✕ **Bella Venezia.** Graceful low archways lead into this attractive restaurant's two small dining rooms. Lighting is bright and styling is pink and white. Try the beans with olive oil and *bottarga* (cured roe), the owner's special risotto with butter, Parmesan, cured ham, mushrooms, and peas and, for the second course, the *fegato alla Veneziana* (grilled liver with onions). ⊠ *Via IV Novembre 16* ☎ *0544/212746* ⊕ *www.bellavenezia. it* ▭ *AE, DC, MC, V* ⊙ *Closed Sun. and 3 wks in Jan.*

★ $–$$ ✕ **Ca' de Ven.** A vaulted wine cellar in the heart of the old city, the Ca' de Ven is great for a hearty meal. You sit at long tables with other diners and feast on platters of delicious cold cuts, flat breads, and cold, heady white wine. The tortelli *di radicchio e pecorino* (with radicchio and goat cheese) are the best first course. ⊠ *Via C. Ricci 24* ☎ *0544/30163* ▭ *AE, DC, MC, V* ⊙ *Closed Mon., 3 wks in Jan.–Feb., and 1st wk of June.*

$ ✕ **La Gardèla.** The kitchen seems to operate with an otherworldly efficiency, making this bright, bustling downtown restaurant extremely popular with the local business crowd—especially at lunch (always a good sign). The place is best for classics like tagliatelle al ragù and simple Adriatic fish, such as *sardoncini* (breaded, fried sardines). ⊠ *Via Ponte Marino 3* ☎ *0544/217147* ▭ *AE, DC, MC, V* ⊙ *Closed Thurs., 10 days in Aug., and 10 days in Jan.*

$$–$$$ 🖼 **Hotel Bisanzio.** Just steps from San Vitale and the Tomb of Galla Placidia, this Best Western hotel is the most convenient lodging for mosaic enthusiasts. The outside is drab, but rooms are comfortable and modern, and the lobby's Florentine lamps add a touch of style. Ask for a room on the top floor and you may get a view of the basilica. ⊠ *Via Salara 30, 48100* ☎ *0544/217111* 🖷 *0544/32539* ⊕ *www.bisanziohotel.com* ⤴ *38 rooms* ⚭ *Dining room, in-room safes, minibars, 2 bars, meeting room, parking (fee)* ⊟ *AE, DC, MC, V* 🍽 *BP.*

$ 🖼 **Hotel Centrale Byron.** Tranquillity is assured here in the center of Ravenna's old town, because it's in a pedestrian zone. The old-fashioned, well-managed hotel has spotless if uninspiring rooms. You can drop off your luggage at the door, but you have to park your car in one of the nearby garages or lots. ⊠ *Via IV Novembre 14, 48100* ☎ *0544/33479* 🖷 *0544/34114* ⊕ *www.hotelbyron.com* ⤴ *54 rooms* ⚭ *Cable TV, in-room safes, minibars, bar* ⊟ *AE, DC, MC, V* 🍽 *BP.*

¢   🖼 **Hotel Ravenna.** A functional stopover near the train station, the Ravenna is still only a few minutes' walk from the center. This modern hotel has smallish rooms; two rooms are equipped for people with disabilities. ⊠ *Via Maroncelli 12, 48100* ☎ *0544/212204* 🖷 *0544/212077* ⤴ *26 rooms* ⚭ *Bar, parking (fee); no a/c* ⊟ *MC, V* 🍽 *BP.*

Nightlife & the Arts

Mosaics by Night. Friday evenings in July and August the Byzantine mosaic masterpieces in town are lighted. Guided tours are available from the tourist office.

Ravenna Festival. A musical extravaganza, held every year throughout June and July, brings in orchestras from all over the world to perform in Ravenna's mosaic-clad churches and theaters.

en route   There are two routes from Ravenna to Rimini. The coastal road, S16, hugs the shoreline much of the way, passing through Cervia. Although its length of 52 km (32 mi) is not great, this scenic route is naturally slower (beware of fog in winter). The coast north of Rimini is lined with dozens of small resort towns, only one having any charm—the seaport of Cesenatico; the others are mini-Riminis, and in summer the narrow road is hopelessly clogged with traffic. A faster route is to start on the inland S71 straight out of Ravenna, then take the A14 back out to the coast, which leads directly into Rimini; the distance is 64 km (39 mi).

Rimini

㉕   *52 km (32 mi) southeast of Ravenna, 121 km (76 mi) southeast of Bologna.*

Rimini is the principal summer resort on the Adriatic Coast and one of the most popular holiday destinations in Italy, flooded with Italians and other Europeans from June to August (if you must go then, reserve ahead). There are hundreds of hotels, and you are as likely to find a Bierkeller or an English tearoom as an Italian restaurant. Beach clubs that rent deck chairs and umbrellas line the waterfront. Hotels have staked out

CloseUp

SAN MARINO, A COUNTRY ON A CLIFF

THE WORLD'S SMALLEST and oldest republic," as San Marino dubs itself, is landlocked entirely by Italy. It consists of three ancient castles perched high on cliffs of sheer rock rising implausibly out of the flatlands of Romagna, and a tangled knot of cobblestoned streets below, which are, unfortunately, lined with tourist boutiques, cheesy hotels and restaurants, and gun shops. The 45-minute drive from Rimini is easily justified, however, by the castle-top view of the stunning green countryside far below the tiny country. The 1,000-meter-plus precipices of sheer rock will make jaws drop and acrophobes quiver.

San Marino was founded in the 4th century AD by a stonecutter named Marino who settled with a small community of Christians, escaping persecution by pagan emperor Diocletian. Over the millennia, largely because of the logistical and strategic nightmares associated with attacking a fortified rock, San Marino was more or less left alone by Italy's various conquerors, and continues to this day to operate as a politically independent country (population 26,000) and a member of the United Nations, economically supported almost entirely by its 3-million-visitor-per-year tourist industry.

San Marino's headline attractions are its **tre castelli** (three castles)—medieval architectural wonders that appear on every coat of arms in the city. Starting in the center of town, you can walk quickly past the trinket shops along a paved cliff-top ridge from the 10th-century Rocca della Guaita to the 13th-century Rocca della Cesta (which contains a museum of ancient weapons that's worthwhile mostly for the views from its terraces and turrets), and finally to the 14th-century Rocca Montale (closed to the public), the most remote of the castles. Every step of the way affords spectacular views of Romagna and the Adriatic Sea; it is said that from the castle-

top perches, on a clear day, you can see across the sea to Croatia. The walks make for a good day's exercise but are by no means arduous. The longest—and windiest—hike is the one between the second and third castle. Even if you arrive after castle visiting hours, the ridge walk from castle to castle is supremely worthwhile. 🏰 Rocca della Guaita and Rocca della Cesta: €3 ⊙ Oct.–Mar., daily 8:50–5; Apr.–Sept., daily 8–8.

A must-see while in San Marino is the **Piazza della Libertà**, whose battlemented and clock-topped Palazzo Pubblico is guarded by San Marino's real-life soldiers in their green uniforms. As you'll notice by peering into the shops along the old town's winding streets, the republic is famous for its crossbows—and more: shopping for fireworks, firearms, and other items illegal for sale elsewhere is another popular tourist activity.

Most of San Marino's 26,000 residents live not in the medieval town above but rather along the more modern and accessible streets below the rock. Visiting San Marino in winter—off-season—increases the appeal of the experience, as tourist establishments shut down and you more or less have the castles to yourself. In August, on the other hand, every inch of walkway on the rock is mobbed with sightseers. To get to San Marino by car, take highway SS72 west from Rimini. From Borgo Maggiore, at the base of the rock, a harrowing but scenic cable car will whisk you up to the castles and town. Alternatively, drive all the way up the winding road; public parking is available in the town itself. Don't worry about changing money, showing passports, learning telephone codes, and the like (although the tourist office will stamp your passport for €1); San Marino is, for all practical purposes, Italy—except, that is, for its majestic perch, its gun laws, and its reported 99% national voter turnout rate.

their own private beach turf; at the public beaches, expect to be packed in like sardines. Prepare also for murky seawater; tourists come to Rimini mostly for the company and nightlife. In the off-season (October–March) Rimini is a cold, windy ghost town with few places open. The town stands at the junction of two great Roman consular roads, the Via Emilia and the Via Flaminia. In addition, in Roman times it was an important port, making it a strategic and commercial center.

From the 13th century onward, Rimini was controlled by the Malatesta family, an unpredictable group capable of grand gestures and savage deeds. The famous lovers immortalized in Dante's *Inferno,* Paolo (died 1304) and Francesca (died 1283 or 1284), were Malatestas. Sigismondo Malatesta (1417–68), lord of the city in the middle of the 15th century, banished his first wife, strangled his second, and poisoned his third. He lived with his beautiful mistress Isotta until her death, upon which he was so grief-stricken that he raised a magnificent monument ★ in her honor, the **Tempio Malatestiano,** which is the principal sight in the town. The Renaissance facade by Leon Battista Alberti (1404–72) is considered a masterpiece.

The interior is light and spacious and contains the tombs of both the lovers. The dollar-sign-like intertwined *I,* for Isotta, and *S,* for Sigismondo, are everywhere. To the right of the entrance, in what is now the Tempio's book and gift shop, is a wonderful fresco by Piero della Francesca (1420–92); when the shop is closed, one of the cathedral's staff can unlock the room. ⊠ *Via IV Novembre 35* ☎ *0541/51130* ⊕ *www.diocesi. rimini.it* 🎟 *Free* ⊙ *Mon.–Sat. 8–12:30 and 3:30–7, Sun. 9–1 and 3:30–7.*

Rimini's oldest monument is the **Arco d'Augusto,** now stranded in the middle of a square just inside the city ramparts. It was erected in 27 BC, making it the oldest surviving Roman arch. ⊠ *Largo Giulio Cesare.*

Where to Stay & Eat

★ **$$** ✕ **Dallo Zio.** Nothing but seafood is served here, and all of it is good—and a good value. Two small rooms are unpretentious; one has antiques. Recommended are the delicious, tangy *brodetto dell'Adriatica* (shellfish broth) and *passatelli al pesce* (pasta twists with fish). ⊠ *Vicolo Santa Chiara 16* ☎ *0541/786747* 🍴 *Reservations essential* ▭ *DC, MC, V* ⊙ *Closed Mon. No lunch Tues.–Fri.*

★ **$$** ✕ **La Locanda di San Martino.** Patrons have been known to drive all the way from the Ligurian coast just for the seafood delights here. Dishes like *spaghettoni ai frutti di mare* (thick spaghetti with seafood sauce) and *grigliata di pesce mista* (mixed seafood grill) are uniformly fresh and superbly prepared, and the mixed antipasto served with lunch is exquisite. An outdoor patio in the back is more romantic than the nondescript main dining room. It's off the road out of Rimini heading toward Bologna. ⊠ *Via Emilia 226* ☎ *0541/680127* ▭ *AE, MC, V* ⊙ *Closed Mon. Oct.–May.*

¢ ✕ **Piada e Cassoni da Jonny.** Come here for the grilled flatbread, one of the traditional specialties of Romagnan cooking. A brisk staff member fills a *piada* (grilled flatbread) with cheese, tomato, and meat or vegetables, or *cassoni* (a bigger filled pocket of bread, more like a calzone, but also grilled) to order while you wait, for only a couple of euros—just don't expect to sit down at this bustling take-out place. Jonny also delivers. ⊠ *Via Giovanni XXIII 101* ☎ *0541/29675* ▤ *No credit cards.*

★ **$$$$** ⌂ **Grand Hotel.** This fin-de-siècle extravaganza, made famous by Fellini in his *Amarcord*, is grander than ever. The hyperluxe stage is set by enormous crystal chandeliers in the lobby, bright pink hallways, and inlaid wood in the rooms that seems playful rather than formal. A spotless private beach completes the scene. Entourages and steamer trunks would not be out of place here; neither would it be a surprise to see a greyhound loping through the restaurant on her way to the pool with her owner. ⊠ *Via Ramusio 1, Parco Federico Fellini, 47900* ☎ *0541/56000* 🖷 *0541/56866* ⊕ *www.grandhotelrimini.com* ⊅ *98 rooms, 19 suites* ⌂ *2 restaurants, minibars, tennis court, 2 outdoor pools, health club, hair salon, massage, sauna, beach, 2 bars, nightclub, meeting room* ▤ *AE, DC, MC, V* ⍾⍾ *BP.*

¢–$ ⌂ **Annarita.** The main benefits here are proximity to the beach promenade and a friendly price. It's on a residential road leading off the main Viale Vespucci, and off-season rates are so low that they border on ridiculous. Facilities at the small, modern block hotel are rudimentary, and rooms are basic, but a loyal clientele means availability may be limited. ⊠ *Viale Misurata 24, 47900* ☎ *0541/391044* ⊕ *www.hotelannarita. it* ⊅ *14 rooms* ⌂ *Restaurant, bar* ▤ *No credit cards* ⍾⍾ *BP.*

EMILIA-ROMAGNA A TO Z

To research prices, get advice from other travelers, and book travel arrangements, visit www.fodors.com.

AIR TRAVEL

Bologna is an important business and convention center and is therefore well served by European airlines linking it with Italian cities and European capitals, including Rome and Milan (on Alitalia), Paris (on Air France), London on British Airways (and from London Stansted on easyJet), Barcelona (on Iberia), Amsterdam (on KLM), and Frankfurt (on Lufthansa). There are no direct flights from the United States, however. Those wishing to fly direct often choose instead to fly into and rent a car at Milan Malpensa airport, a 45-minute drive on the A1 Autostrada from Piacenza and an easy two hours from Bologna. Parma, Rimini, and Forlì are the smaller hubs in the region. Alitalia operates a daily Rome–Parma flight; the low-cost operator Ryanair runs daily service between London (Stansted) and Forlì; easyJet, another low-cost operator, serves Bologna from London's Stansted, and Air Minerva, which code-shares with Alitalia, connects Rimini with Rome and Milan.

✈ Carriers **Air France** ☎ 848/884466 ⊕ www.airfrance.com. **Alitalia** ☎ 848/865641 ⊕ www.alitalia.com. **British Airways** ☎ 848/81266 ⊕ www.british-airways.com. **easyJet** ☎ 848/887766 ⊕ www.easyjet.com. **Iberia** ☎ 848/870000 ⊕ www.iberia.com. **KLM** ☎ 02/218981 ⊕ www.northwest.com. **Lufthansa** ☎ 0516477730 ⊕ www.lufthansa. com. **Ryanair** ☎ 199/114114 ⊕ www.ryanair.com.

AIRPORTS

The main airport of the region, Guglielmo Marconi, is 10 km (6 mi) north-west of Bologna. Aerobus service (Bus 54, €4.15) connects Guglielmo Marconi with Bologna's central train station as well as a downtown stop. It runs every half hour from 6 AM to 11:30 PM. Parma's small airport is Aero-porto G. Verdi, and Rimini's is called Aeradria; both are connected by bus to their respective cities at arrival and departure times. The airport at Forlì, 6 km (4 mi) from the A14 autostrada, is convenient to Ravenna, Rimini, and Bologna (a Bologna-bound bus waits for all Ryanair arrivals).

✈ Airport Information Aeradria Rimini Airport ⊠ Rimini ☎ 0541/715711 ⊕ www.riminiairport.com. **Aeroporto di Forlì** ⊠ Forlì ☎ 0543/474990 ⊕ www.forli-airport.it. **Aeroporto G. Verdi** ⊠ Parma ☎ 0521/982626 ⊕ www.aeroportoparma.it. **Guglielmo Marconi** ⊠ Via Triumvirato 84, Bologna ☎ 051/6479615 ⊕ www.bologna-airport.it.

CAR RENTAL

✈ Local Agencies Avis ⊠ Guglielmo Marconi airport, Via Triumvirato 84, Bologna ☎ 051/6472032 ⊠ Via Pietrammellara 27/D, Bologna ☎ 051/255024 ⊠ Via Marco Polo 91, Bologna ☎ 051/6341632 ⊠ Aeroporto G. Verdi, Via Dell'Aeroporto 44/A, Parma ☎ 0521/291238 ⊠ Viale Trieste 16D, Rimini ☎ 0541/51256. **Europcar** ⊠ Via Amendola 12/f, Bologna ☎ 051/247101 ⊠ Guglielmo Marconi airport, Bologna ☎ 051/6472111 ⊠ Hotel Baglioni, Viale Piacenza 51/c, Parma ☎ 0521/293035 ⊠ Aeroporto Verdi, Parma ☎ 0521/293035 ⊠ Via Giovanni XXIII 126, Rimini ☎ 0541/54746. **SIXT Autonoleggio** ⊠ Piazza XX Settembre 6, Bologna ☎ 051/4210079 ⊠ Guglielmo Marconi airport, Sala Arrivi, Bologna ☎ 051/6472027.

CAR TRAVEL

Bologna is on the autostrada network, so driving between cities is a breeze. The Via Emilia (SS9), one of the oldest roads in the world, runs through the heart of the region. It's a straight, low-lying modern road, the length of which can be traveled in a few hours. Ferrara and Ravenna are joined to it by good modern highways. Although less scenic, the A1 ("Autostrada del Sole") and A14 highways, which run parallel to the Via Emilia, can get you where you're going about twice as fast. Note that much of the historic center of Bologna is closed off to cars daily 7 AM–8 PM.

Beware of low-lying fog in fall and winter, especially in Romagna nearer to the Adriatic coast. On some nights the fog can render driving an impossibility.

EMERGENCIES

For first aid, call the police and ask for *pronto soccorso,* and be prepared to give your address. Pharmacies take turns staying open late and on Sunday; for the latest information, consult the current list posted on the front door of each pharmacy or ask at the local tourist office. ACI emergency service provides 24-hour roadside assistance.

✈ ACI ☎ 803/116. **Carabinieri** ☎ 112. **Police, ambulance** ☎ 113. **Doctors and dentists** ☎ 113.

MAIL & SHIPPING

✈ Post Offices Bologna ⊠ Piazza Minghetti 1, 40124. **Ferrara** ⊠ Viale Cavour 27, 44100. **Modena** ⊠ Via Emilia Centro 86, 41100. **Parma** ⊠ Via Pisacane 1, 43100. **Ravenna** ⊠ Piazza Garibaldi 1, 48100. **Rimini** ⊠ Largo G. Cesare 1, 47900.

TRAIN TRAVEL

Bologna is an important rail hub for the entire northern part of Italy and has frequent, fast train service to Rome, Milan, Florence, and Venice. The railway follows the Via Emilia (SS9), and all the cities covered can be easily reached by train. Contact Ferrovie dello Stato, the national train operator, for more information.

🚩 Train Information **Ferrovie dello Stato (FS)** ☎ 892021 ⊕ www.trenitalia.com.

VISITOR INFORMATION

🚩 Tourist Information **Bologna** ✉ Guglielmo Marconi airport ☎ 051/246541 ✉ Stazione Centrale, 40121 ☎ 051/246541 ✉ Piazza Maggiore 1, 40124 ☎ 051/246541 ⊕ www.comune. bologna.it/bolognaturismo. **Busseto** ✉ Comune, Piazza G. Verdi 10, 43011 ☎ 0524/92487. **Dozza** ✉ Via XX Settembre, 40050 ☎ 0542/678052. **Faenza** ✉ Piazza del Popolo 1, 48018 ☎ 0546/691602. **Ferrara** ✉ Castello Estense, 44022 ☎ 0532/209370 ⊕ www. ferraraterraeacqua.it. **Modena** ✉ Via Scudari 12, 41100 ☎ 059/206660 ✉ Palazzo dei Musei, Via Vittorio Veneto 5 ☎ 059/200125 ⊕ www.comune.modena.it. **Parma** ✉ Via Melloni 1/a, 43100 ☎ 0521/218889 ⊕ turismo.comune.parma.it. **Piacenza** ✉ Piazza Cavalli 7 29100 ☎ 0523/329324 ⊕ www.provincia.pc.it. **Ravenna** ✉ Via Salara 8, 48100 ☎ 0544/35404 ⊕ www.turismo.ravenna.it. **Rimini** ✉ Piazzale Cesare Battisti, 47037 ☎ 0541/51331 ✉ Piazzale Fellini 3, Marina Centro, 47037 ☎ 0541/56902 ⊕ www. riminiturismo.it. **San Marino** ✉ Contra Omagnano 20, 47890 ☎ 0549/882400.

FLORENCE

8

Updated by
Patricia Rucidlo

FLORENCE, THE CITY OF THE LILY, gave birth to the Renaissance and changed the way we see the world. For centuries it has captured the imagination of travelers, who come here to walk in the footsteps of Dante, Donatello, Botticelli, and Michelangelo. You will find sublime art at almost every turn, but Florence isn't simply one large museum. Even if *David* and the Duomo didn't exist, you could still fall in love with the city for its views at sunset over the Arno, its earthy yet sophisticated food and wine, or the way the natives manage to lead thoroughly modern lives in a place that hasn't changed all that much since the 16th century.

Though Florence (Firenze in Italian) can lay claim to a modest importance in the ancient world, it did not fully emerge into its own until the 11th century. In the early 1200s, the city, like most of the rest of Italy, was rent by civic unrest. Two factions, the Guelphs and the Ghibellines, competed for power. The Guelphs supported the papacy, and the Ghibellines supported the Holy Roman Empire. Bloody battles—most notably one at Montaperti in 1260—tore Florence and other Italian cities apart. Sometimes the Guelphs were in power and exiled the Ghibellines; at other times, the reverse was true. By the end of the 13th century the Guelphs ruled securely and Ghibellines had been vanquished. This didn't end civic strife, however: the Guelphs split into the Whites and the Blacks for reasons still debated by historians. Dante, author of the *Divine Comedy* (arguably Italy's greatest work of literature) was banished from Florence in 1301 because he was a White.

Local merchants had organized themselves into guilds by 1250. In that year they proclaimed themselves the *"primo popolo"* (literally, "first people"), making a landmark attempt at elective, republican rule. Though the episode lasted only 10 years, it constituted a breakthrough in Western history. Such a daring stance by the merchant class can be attributed to its new-found power, as Florence was emerging as one of the economic powerhouses in 13th-century Europe. Florentines were papal bankers; they instituted the system of international letters of credit; and the gold florin became the international standard of currency. With this economic strength came a building boom. Public and private palaces, churches, and basilicas were built, enlarged, or restructured. Sculptors such as Donatello and Ghiberti were commissioned to decorate them; painters such as Giotto and Botticelli were commissioned to fresco their walls.

Though ostensibly a republic, Florence was blessed (or cursed, depending on your point of view) with one very powerful family, the Medici, who came to prominence in the 1430s and were the de facto rulers of Florence for several hundred years. The Medici originally came from north of Florence, and it was not until the time of Cosimo il Vecchio (1389–1464) that the family's foothold in Florence was securely established. Florence's golden age occurred during the reign of his grandson Lorenzo de' Medici (1449–92). Lorenzo was not only an astute politician but also a highly educated man and a great patron of the arts. Called "Il Magnifico" (the Magnificent), he gathered around him poets, artists, philosophers, architects, and musicians and organized all manner of cultural events, festivals, and tournaments.

You can see nearly all of Florence's most renowned sights in three days. Plan your day around the opening hours of museums and churches; to gain an edge on the tour groups in high season, go to the most heavily trafficked sights very early in the morning or around closing time. If you can, allow a day to explore each neighborhood.

8

If you have 3 days Spend Day 1 exploring Florence's centro storico, which will give you an eyeful of such masterpieces as Ghiberti's bronze doors at the Battistero (these are copies; the originals are in the nearby Museo dell'Opera del Duomo), Giotto's Campanile (bell tower), Brunelleschi's cupola majestically poised atop the Duomo, and Botticelli's mystical *Primavera* and *Birth of Venus* at the Galleria degli Uffizi. On Day 2, wander north of the Duomo and take in the superb treasury of works ranging from Michelangelo's *David* at the Galleria dell'Accademia to the lavish frescoes at the Cappella dei Magi and the Museo di San Marco (don't miss San Lorenzo, Michelangelo's Biblioteca Medicea Laurenziana, and the Cappelle Medicee). On this afternoon (or on the afternoon of Day 3) head southeast to Santa Croce or west to Santa Maria Novella. On the third day, cross the Ponte Vecchio to the Arno's southern bank and explore the Oltrarno, being sure not to miss the gargantuan Palazzo Pitti, testament to the power of the Medici, and the Giardino di Boboli, once their own private garden.

If you have 5 days Break down the tours in the above itinerary into shorter ones, adding a few sights such as Piazzale Michelangelo, halfway up a hill on the Arno's southern bank, and San Miniato—both with expansive views of the city. Climb Giotto's Campanile, which rewards you with sweeping views of the city and hills beyond, or if you're feeling even more adventurous, climb the narrow, twisting stairs to the top of the Duomo. Take Bus 7 from the station or Piazza del Duomo to enchanting Fiesole. Spend more time in the Galleria degli Uffizi and Bargello or at one of the smaller museums such as the Museo dell'Opificio delle Pietre Dure, around the corner from the Galleria dell'Accademia. The little-visited but nevertheless wonderful Museo di Storia della Scienza is worth a trip, as is the Museo di Santa Maria Novella.

If you have 8 days Add an all-day excursion south to the Tuscan city of Siena or a couple of half-day trips to the Medici villas around Florence. Visit more of Florence's interesting smaller churches; there's a dazzling fresco by Perugino at Santa Maria Maddalena dei Pazzi and a brilliant Pontormo in the Oltrarno's Santa Felicita. On the trail of additional, lesser-known artistic gems, check out Andrea del Castagno's fresco of the *Last Supper* in the former refectory at Sant'Apollonia, northwest of the Museo di San Marco. It's worth the trip to see Andrea del Sarto's stunning grisaille frescoes in the Chiostro dello Scalzo, north of the Museo di San Marco. The church of Santo Spirito, west of Piazza Pitti, is a fine example of 15th-century architectural rationalism.

Lorenzo's son, Piero (1471–1503), proved inept at handling the city's affairs. He was run out of town in 1494, and Florence briefly enjoyed its status as a republic while dominated by the Dominican friar Girolamo Savonarola (1452–98). Savonarola preached against perceived pagan abuses and persuaded his followers to destroy their books, art, women's wigs, and jewelry in public "bonfires of the vanities." Eventually, he so annoyed the pope that he was declared a heretic and hanged.

After a decade of internal unrest, the republic fell and the Medici were recalled to power. But even with the return of the Medici Florence never regained its former prestige. By the 1530s most of the major artistic talent had left the city—Michelangelo, for one, had settled in Rome. The now-ineffectual Medici, eventually attaining the title of grand dukes, remained nominally in power until the line died out in 1737, after which time Florence passed from the Austrians to the French and back again until the unification of Italy (1865–70), when it briefly became the capital under King Vittorio Emanuele II (1820–78).

Florence was "discovered" in the 18th century by upper-class northerners making the grand tour. It became a mecca for travelers, particularly the Romantics, who were inspired by the elegance of its palazzos and its artistic wealth. Today millions of modern visitors follow in their footsteps. As the sun sets over the Arno and, as Mark Twain described it, "overwhelms Florence with tides of color that make all the sharp lines dim and faint and turn the solid city to a city of dreams," it's hard not to fall under the city's spell.

EXPLORING FLORENCE

Sightseeing in Florence is easy: everything that you'll want to see is concentrated in the relatively small historic center of the city. But there is so much packed into the area that you may find yourself slogging from one mind-boggling sight to another and feeling overwhelmed. If you are not an inveterate museum enthusiast, take it easy. Don't try to absorb every painting or fresco that comes into view. There's second-rate art even in the Galleria degli Uffizi and the Palazzo Pitti (*especially* the Pitti), so find some favorites and enjoy them at your leisure.

Walking through the streets and alleyways in Florence is a discovery in itself, but to save time and energy (especially after a few days in the city), make use of the efficient bus system. Buses also provide the least-fatiguing way to reach Piazzale Michelangelo, San Miniato, and the Forte di Belvedere. It's easy to make excursions to, say, Fiesole or the Medici villas by city bus. Most churches are open from 8 or 9 until noon or 12:30 and from 3 or 4 until about 6. The Duomo has continuous hours.

In between tracking the Renaissance and beyond, stop to breathe in the city, the marvelous synergy between history and modern Florentine life. Firenze is a living, bustling metropolis that has managed to preserve its predominantly medieval street plan and mostly Renaissance infrastructure while successfully adapting to the insistent demands of 21st-century life.

8

Looking at Art The abundance of Renaissance art in Florence is staggering—so much so that you may find yourself literally staggering as you try to take it all in. To avoid an art hangover, accept the fact that, no matter how determined you may be, you will not see everything. You're likely to have a more satisfying experience if you pick and choose sights that strike your interest, give yourself the freedom to follow your whims, and ignore any pangs of guilt if you'd rather nap at your hotel than stand in line at the Uffizi. Florence isn't a city that can be "done"; instead, it's a place you can return to again and again, confident that there will always be more treasures to discover.

Shopping Since the days of the medieval guilds, Florence has been synonymous with fine craftsmanship and good business. Such time-honored Florentine specialties as antiques (and reproductions), bookbinding, jewelry, lace, leather goods, silk, and straw attest to this. Lovely paper products are made here and sold all over town. The leather produced here is of especially good quality. The various shopping areas are a throwback to the Middle Ages, when each district supplied a different product. During the Renaissance, the Oltrarno was the neighborhood where the artisans lived, and if you wander around there now you'll find that little has changed: there are still goldsmiths, leatherworkers, and furniture restorers, among others, plying their trade.

During the 12th and 13th centuries, Florence, like most other Italian towns, was a forest of towers—more than 200 of them, if the smaller three- and four-story towers are included. Today only a handful survive, but if you look closely you'll find them as you explore the *centro storico* (historic city center).

Numbers in the text correspond to numbers in the margin and on the Florence map.

Centro Storico: The Duomo to the Ponte Vecchio

Florence's centro storico, a relatively small area stretching from the Piazza del Duomo south to the Arno, is as dense with artistic treasures as anyplace in the world. The churches, medieval towers, Renaissance palaces, and world-class museums and galleries contain some of the most outstanding aesthetic achievements of Western history.

a good walk

Start at the **Duomo** ❶ ▶ and **Battistero** ❷, climb the **Campanile** ❸ if you wish, and then visit the **Museo dell'Opera del Duomo** ❹, behind the Duomo. Go directly south from the Duomo on Via dei Calzaiuoli, turning right on Via degli Speziali for a detour to **Piazza della Repubblica** ❺ and **Orsanmichele** ❻. Alternatively, go directly south from the Museo dell'Opera del Duomo along Via del Proconsolo to the **Bargello** ❼ museum, opposite the ancient church **Badia Fiorentina** ❽. Head west on Via della Condotta to Via Calzaiuoli, then south to the **Piazza della Signoria** ❾,

with its Loggia dei Lanzi and **Palazzo Vecchio** ⑩. The **Galleria degli Uffizi** ⑪, perhaps Italy's most important art gallery, is at the south side of the piazza. Exit from the piazza's southwest corner along Via Vacchereccia. At the corner of Via Por Santa Maria is the **Mercato Nuovo** ⑫, lined with stores. Follow Via Por Santa Maria to the river; walk east along the north side of the Arno to Piazza dei Giudici to see the **Museo di Storia della Scienza** ⑬. Backtrack west along the Arno to wind up your walk on the **Ponte Vecchio** ⑭.

TIMING Though much of Florence's centro storico is closed to automobile traffic, you still must dodge mopeds, cyclists, and masses of fellow tourists as you walk the narrow streets, especially in the area bounded by the Duomo, Piazza della Signoria, Galleria degli Uffizi, and Ponte Vecchio. It takes about 40 minutes to walk the route, with 45 minutes to 1 hour each for the Museo dell'Opera del Duomo and the Palazzo Vecchio; 1 to 1½ hours for the Bargello; and a minimum of 2 hours for the Uffizi (reserve tickets in advance to avoid long lines).

What to See

❽ Badia Fiorentina. This ancient church was rebuilt in 1285; its graceful bell tower, best seen from the interior courtyard, is beautiful for its unusual construction—a hexagonal tower built on a quadrangular base. The interior of the church was halfheartedly remodeled in the baroque style during the 17th century; its best-known work of art is the delicate *Vision of St. Bernard* by Filippino Lippi (circa 1457–1504), on the left as you enter. The painting—one of Lippi's finest—is in superb condition; note the Virgin Mary's beautifully rendered hands. ⊠ *Via Dante Alighieri 1, near Bargello* ☎ *055/264402* 🎫 *Free* ☉ *Mon. 3–6.*

★ **❼ Bargello.** During the Renaissance, this building was headquarters for the *podestà,* or chief magistrate. It was also used as a prison, and the exterior served as a "most wanted" billboard: effigies of notorious criminals and Medici enemies were painted on its walls. Today it houses the **Museo Nazionale,** containing what is probably the finest collection of Renaissance sculpture in Italy. The concentration of masterworks by Michelangelo (1475–1564), Donatello (circa 1386–1466), and Benvenuto Cellini (1500–71) is remarkable; they're distributed among an eclectic array of arms, ceramics, and enamels. For Renaissance art lovers, the Bargello is to sculpture what the Uffizi is to painting.

In 1401 Filippo Brunelleschi (1377–1446) and Lorenzo Ghiberti (circa 1378–1455) vied for the most prestigious commission of the day: the decoration of the north doors of the baptistery in Piazza del Duomo. For the competition, each designed a bronze bas-relief panel depicting the Sacrifice of Isaac; both panels are displayed, together, in the room devoted to the sculpture of Donatello on the upper floor. The judges chose Ghiberti for the commission; see if you agree with their choice. ⊠ *Via del Proconsolo 4, Bargello* ☎ *055/2388606* ⊕ *www.arca.net/db/musei/ bargello.htm* 🎫 *€4* ☉ *Daily 8:15–1:50. Closed 2nd and 4th Mon. of month and 1st, 3rd, and 5th Sun. of month.*

★ **❷ Battistero** (Baptistery). The octagonal Baptistery is one of the supreme monuments of the Italian Romanesque style and one of Florence's oldest structures. Local legend has it that it was once a Roman temple of Mars; modern excavations, however, suggest that its foundations date from the 4th to 5th and the 8th to 9th century AD, well after the collapse of the Roman Empire. The round-arched Romanesque decoration on the exterior probably dates from the 11th century. The interior dome mosaics from the early 14th century are justly renowned, but—glittering beauties though they are—they could never outshine the building's famed bronze Renaissance doors decorated with panels crafted by Lorenzo Ghiberti. The doors—or at least copies of them—on which Ghiberti spent most of his adult life (1403–52) are on the north and east sides of the Baptistery, and the Gothic panels on the south door were designed by Andrea Pisano (active circa 1290–1348) in 1330. The original Ghiberti doors were removed to protect them from the effects of pollution and have been beautifully restored; some of the panels are now on display in the Museo dell'Opera del Duomo.

Ghiberti's north doors depict scenes from the life of Christ; his later east doors (dating 1425–52), facing the Duomo facade, render scenes from the Old Testament. Very different in style, they illustrate the artistic changes that marked the beginning of the Renaissance. Look at the far right panel of the middle row on the earlier (1403–24) north doors (*Jesus Calming the Waters*). Ghiberti captured the chaos of a storm at sea with great skill and economy, but the artistic conventions he used are basically pre-Renaissance: Jesus is the most important figure, so he is the largest; the disciples are next in size, being next in importance; the ship on which they founder looks like a mere toy.

The exquisitely rendered panels on the east doors are larger, more expansive, more sweeping—and more convincing. Look at the middle panel on the left-hand door. It tells the story of Jacob and Esau, and the various episodes—the selling of the birthright, Isaac ordering Esau to go hunting, the blessing of Jacob, and so forth—have been merged into a single beautifully realized street scene. Ghiberti's use of perspective suggests depth: the background architecture looks far more credible than on the north door panels, the figures in the foreground are grouped realistically, and the naturalism and grace of the poses (look at Esau's left leg and the dog next to him) have nothing to do with the sacred message being conveyed. Although the religious content remains, the figures and their place in the natural world are given new prominence and are portrayed with a realism not seen in art since the fall of the Roman Empire more than a thousand years before.

As a footnote to Ghiberti's panels, one small detail of the east doors is worth a special look. To the lower left of the Jacob and Esau panel, Ghiberti placed a tiny self-portrait bust. From either side, the portrait is extremely appealing—Ghiberti looks like everyone's favorite uncle—but the bust is carefully placed so that there is a single spot from which you can make direct eye contact with the tiny head. When that contact is made, the impression of intelligent life is astonishing. It is no wonder that these doors received one of the most famous compliments in the history of art from an artist known to be notoriously stingy with praise: Michelangelo himself declared them so beautiful that they could serve as the Gates of Paradise. ⊠ *Piazza del Duomo* ☎ *055/2302885* ⊕ *www. operaduomo.firenze.it* 🎫 *€3* 🕓 *Mon.–Sat. noon–7, Sun. 8:30–2.*

❸ **Campanile.** The Gothic bell tower designed by Giotto (1266–1337) is a soaring structure of multicolored marble originally decorated with reliefs that are now in the Museo dell'Opera del Duomo. A climb of 414 steps rewards you with a close-up of Brunelleschi's cupola on the Duomo next door and a sweeping view of the city. ⊠ *Piazza del Duomo* ☎ *055/ 2302885* ⊕ *www.operaduomo.firenze.it* 🎫 *€6* 🕓 *Daily 8:30–7:30.*

★ ▶ ❶ **Duomo** (Cattedrale di Santa Maria del Fiore). In 1296 Arnolfo di Cambio (circa 1245–circa 1310) was commissioned to build "the loftiest, most sumptuous edifice human invention could devise" in the Romanesque style on the site of the old church of Santa Reparata. The immense Duomo was not completed until 1436, the year when it was consecrated. The imposing facade dates only from the 19th century; it was added in the neo-Gothic style to complement Giotto's genuine Gothic 14th-century campanile. The real glory of the Duomo, however, is Filippo Brunelleschi's dome, presiding over the cathedral with a dignity and grace that few domes to this day can match.

Brunelleschi's **cupola** was an ingenious engineering feat. The space to be enclosed by the dome was so large and so high above the ground that traditional methods of dome construction—wooden centering and scaffolding—were of no use whatsoever. So Brunelleschi developed entirely new building methods, which he implemented with equipment of his own design (including a novel scaffolding method). Beginning work in 1420, he built not one dome but two, one inside the other, and connected them with common ribbing that stretched across the intervening empty space, thereby considerably lessening the crushing weight of the structure. He also employed a new method of bricklaying, based on an ancient Roman herringbone pattern, interlocking each new course of bricks with the course below in a way that made the growing structure self-supporting. The result was one of the great engineering breakthroughs of all time: most of Europe's later domes, including that of St. Peter's in Rome, were built employing Brunelleschi's methods, and today the Duomo has come to symbolize Florence in the same way that the Eiffel Tower symbolizes Paris. The Florentines are justly proud, and to this day the Florentine phrase for "homesick" is *nostalgia del cupolone* (homesick for the dome).

The interior is a fine example of Florentine Gothic. Much of the cathedral's best-known art has been moved to the nearby Museo dell'Opera del Duomo. Notable among the works that remain, however, are two towering equestrian frescoes honoring famous soldiers: *Niccolò da Tolentino,* painted in 1456 by Andrea del Castagno (circa 1419–57), and *Sir John Hawkwood,* painted 20 years earlier by Paolo Uccello (1397–1475); both are on the left-hand wall of the nave. A 10-year restoration, completed in 1995, repaired the dome and cleaned the vast and crowded fresco of the *Last Judgment,* executed by Vasari and Zuccaro, on its interior. Originally Brunelleschi wanted mosaics to cover the interior of the great ribbed cupola, but by the time the Florentines got around to commissioning the decoration, 150 years later, tastes had changed.

Too bad: it's a fairly dreadful *Last Judgment* and hardly worth the effort of craning your neck to see it.

You can explore the upper and lower reaches of the cathedral. The remains of a Roman wall and an 11th-century cemetery have been excavated beneath the nave; the way down is near the first pier on the right. The climb to the top of the dome (463 steps) is not for the faint of heart, but the view is superb. ⊠ *Piazza del Duomo* ☎ *055/2302885* ⊕ *www. operaduomo.firenze.it* ⊠ *Free, crypt €3, cupola €6* ☉ *Crypt: weekdays 10–5, Sat. 10–5:45, 1st Sat. of month 10–4. Cupola: weekdays 8:30–7, Sat. 8:30–5:40, 1st Sat. of month 8:30–4. Duomo: Mon.–Wed. and Fri. 10–5, Thurs. 10–3:30, Sat. 10–4:45, Sun. 1:30–4:45, 1st Sat. of month 10–3:30.*

⓫ **Galleria degli Uffizi.** The venerable Uffizi Gallery occupies the top floor
FodorśChoice of the U-shape **Palazzo degli Uffizi** (Uffizi Palace) fronting on the Arno,
  ★   designed by Giorgio Vasari (1511–74) in 1560 to hold the *uffizi* (administrative offices) of the Medici grand duke Cosimo I (1519–74). Later, the Medici installed their art collections here, creating what was Europe's first modern museum, open to the public (at first only by request) since 1591. Hard-core museum aficionados can pick up a complete guide to the collections at bookshops and newsstands.

Among the highlights are Paolo Uccello's *Battle of San Romano,* its brutal chaos of lances one of the finest visual metaphors for warfare ever captured in paint; the *Madonna and Child with Two Angels,* by Fra Filippo Lippi (1406–69), in which the impudent eye contact established by the angel would have been unthinkable prior to the Renaissance; the *Birth of Venus* and *Primavera* by Sandro Botticelli (1445–1510), the goddess of the former seeming to float on air and the fairy-tale charm of the latter exhibiting the painter's idiosyncratic genius at its zenith; the portraits of the Renaissance duke Federico da Montefeltro and his wife, Battista Sforza, by Piero della Francesca (circa 1420–92); the *Madonna of the Goldfinch,* by Raphael (1483–1520), which, though darkened by time, captures an aching tenderness between mother and child; Michelangelo's *Doni Tondo* (the only panel painting that can be securely attributed to him); a *Self-Portrait as an Old Man* by Rembrandt (1606–69); the *Venus of Urbino* by Titian (circa 1488/90–1576); and the splendid *Bacchus* by Caravaggio (circa 1571/72–1610). In the last two works, the approaches to myth and sexuality are diametrically opposed, to put it mildly. If panic sets in at the prospect of absorbing all this art at one go, visit later in the afternoon when it's less crowded. Advance tickets can be reserved by phone (all the operators speak English) or, once in Florence, at the Uffizi reservation booth at least one day in advance of your visit. If you book by phone, remember to keep the confirmation number and take it with you to the door at the museum marked "Reservations." Usually you will be ushered in almost immediately. Come with cash, because credit cards are not accepted. ⊠ *Piazzale degli Uffizi 6, near Piazza della Signoria* ☎ *055/23885* ⊠ *Advance tickets* ⊠ *Consorzio ITA, Piazza Pitti 1, 50121* ☎ *055/294883* ⊕ *www.uffizi.firenze. it* ⊠ *€5.50, reservation fee €3* ☉ *Tues.–Sun. 8:15–6:50.*

need a break? GustaVino (✉ Via della Condotta 37/r, near Piazza della Signoria ☎ 055/2399806) calls itself an *"enoteca con cucina,"* which means that you can drink and eat. Its handy location (a minute or two from Piazza Signoria) makes it a perfect spot to recover after a trip to the Uffizi.

⑫ Mercato Nuovo (New Market). This open-air loggia was new in 1551. Beyond its slew of souvenir stands, its main attraction is a copy of Pietro Tacca's bronze *Porcellino* (which translates as "little pig," despite the fact that the animal is, in fact, a wild boar) on the south side, dating from around 1612 and copied from an earlier Roman work now in the Uffizi. The Porcellino is Florence's equivalent of the Trevi Fountain: put a coin in his mouth, and if it falls through the grate below (according to one interpretation), it means that one day you'll return to Florence. ✉ *Corner of Via Por Santa Maria and Via Porta Rossa, near Piazza della Repubblica* ☉ *Market Tues.–Sat. 8–7, Mon. 1–7.*

❹ Museo dell'Opera del Duomo (Cathedral Museum). Ghiberti's original Baptistery door panels and the *cantorie* (choir loft) reliefs by Donatello and Luca della Robbia (1400–82) keep company with Donatello's *Mary Magdalen* and Michelangelo's *Pietà* (not to be confused with his more famous *Pietà* in St. Peter's in Rome). Renaissance sculpture is in part defined by its revolutionary realism, but in its palpable suffering Donatello's *Magdalen* goes beyond realism. Michelangelo's heart-wrenching *Pietà* was unfinished at his death; the female figure on the left was added by one Tiberio Calcagni (1532–65), and never has the difference between competence and genius been manifested so clearly. ✉ *Piazza del Duomo 9* ☎ *055/2302885* ⊕ *www.operaduomo.firenze.it* 🎫 *€6* ☉ *Mon.–Sat. 9–7:30, Sun. 9–1:40.*

⑬ Museo di Storia della Scienza (Museum of the History of Science). Though it tends to be obscured by the glamour of the neighboring Uffizi, this science museum has much to recommend it: Galileo's own instruments, antique armillary spheres—some of them real works of art—and other reminders that the Renaissance made not only artistic but also scientific history. ✉ *Piazza dei Giudici 1, near Piazza della Signoria* ☎ *055/ 265311* ⊕ *www.imss.fi.it* 🎫 *€6.50* ☉ *Mon. and Wed.–Sat. 9:30–5, Tues. 9:30–1; Oct.–May, also open 2nd Sun. of month 10–1.*

❻ Orsanmichele. This multipurpose structure began as an 8th-century oratory, then in 1290 was turned into an open-air loggia for selling grain. Destroyed by fire in 1304, it was rebuilt as a loggia-market. Between 1367 and 1380 the arcades were closed and two stories added above; finally, at century's end it was turned into a church. Inside is a beautifully detailed 14th-century Gothic tabernacle by Andrea Orcagna (1320–68); you'll have to come back another time to see it, because the interior is closed indefinitely for restoration. The exterior niches contain copies of sculptures dating from the early 1400s to the early 1600s by Donatello and Verrocchio (1435–88), among others, that were paid for by the guilds. Though it is a copy, Verrocchio's *Doubting Thomas* (circa 1470) is particularly deserving of attention. Here you see Christ, like the building's other figures, entirely framed within the niche, and

MEET THE MEDICI

The Medici were the dominant family of Renaissance Florence, wielding political power and financing some of the world's greatest art. You'll see their names at every turn around the city. These are some of the clan's more notable members:

Cosimo il Vecchio (1389–1464), incredibly wealthy banker to the popes, was the first in the family line to act as de facto ruler of Florence. He was a great patron of the arts and architecture; he was the moving force behind the family palace and the Dominican complex of San Marco.

Lorenzo il Magnifico (1449–92), grandson of Cosimo il Vecchio, presided over a Florence largely at peace with her neighbors. A collector of cameos, a writer of sonnets, and lover of ancient texts, he was the preeminent Renaissance man.

Leo X (1475–1521), also known as Giovanni de' Medici, became the first Medici pope, helping extend the family power base to include Rome and the Papal States. His reign was characterized by a host of problems, the biggest one being a former friar named Martin Luther.

Catherine de' Medici (1519–89) was married by her cousin Pope Clement VII to Henry of Valois, who later became Henry II of France. Wife of one king and mother of three, she was the first Medici to marry into European royalty. Lorenzo il Magnifico, her great-grandfather, would have been thrilled.

Cosimo I (1537–74), the first grand duke of Tuscany, should not be confused with his ancestor Cosimo il Vecchio. A country boy, he grew up north of Florence and returned as a 17-year-old who quickly caught on to the foibles and intrigues of Florentine government.

St. Thomas standing on its bottom ledge, with his right foot outside the niche frame. This one detail, the positioning of a single foot, brings the whole composition to life. It's possible to see the original sculptures at the **Museo di Orsanmichele** within. ⊠ *Via dei Calzaiuoli, near Piazza della Repubblica* ☎ *055/284944* ⊘ *Closed indefinitely.*

❿ **Palazzo Vecchio** (Old Palace). Florence's forbidding, fortresslike city hall, presumed to have been designed by Arnolfo di Cambio, was begun in 1299, and its massive bulk and towering campanile dominate the Piazza della Signoria. It was built as a meeting place for the elected guildsmen who governed the city at the time; over the centuries it has served lesser purposes, but today it is once again City Hall. The interior courtyard is a good deal less severe, having been remodeled by Michelozzo (1396–1472) in 1453; the copy of Verrocchio's bronze *puttino* (little child), topping the central fountain, softens the space.

Two adjoining rooms on the second floor supply one of the starkest contrasts in Florence. The vast **Sala dei Cinquecento** (Room of the Five Hundred) is named for the 500-member Great Council, the people's assembly established by Savonarola, which met here. The Sala was later decorated by Giorgio Vasari, around 1563–65, with huge—almost grotesquely huge—frescoes celebrating Florentine history; depictions of battles with nearby cities predominate. Continuing the martial theme, the Sala also contains Michelangelo's *Victory* group, intended for the never-completed tomb of Pope Julius II (1443–1513), plus other sculptures of lesser quality.

The little **Studiolo** is to the right of the Sala's entrance. The study of Cosimo I's son, the melancholy Francesco I (1541–87), it was designed by Vasari and decorated by Vasari and Bronzino (1503–72). It is intimate, civilized, and filled with complex allegorical art. ⊠ *Piazza della Signoria* ☏ *055/2768465* ⚏ *€5.70* ☉ *Mon.–Wed., and Fri. and Sat. 9–7, Thurs. 9–2, Sun. 9–7.*

⑤ Piazza della Repubblica. This was the site of the ancient forum at the core of the original Roman settlement that was to become Florence. The street plan in the area around the piazza still reflects the carefully plotted grid of the Roman military encampment. The Mercato Vecchio (Old Market), dating from the Middle Ages, was demolished and the current piazza was constructed between 1885 and 1895 as a neoclassical showpiece. The piazza is lined with outdoor cafés affording excellent spots to people-watch.

★ ⑨ Piazza della Signoria. This is by far the most striking square in Florence. It was here, in 1497, that the famous "bonfire of the vanities" took place, when the fanatical friar Savonarola induced his followers to hurl their worldly goods into the flames; it was also here, a year later, that he was hanged as a heretic and, ironically, burned. A bronze plaque in the pavement marks the exact spot of his execution.

The statues in the square and in the 14th-century **Loggia dei Lanzi** on the south side vary in quality. Cellini's famous bronze *Perseus* holding the severed head of Medusa is certainly the most important sculpture in the loggia. Other works include *The Rape of the Sabines* and *Hercules and the Centaur,* both late-16th-century works by Giambologna (1529–1608), and, in the back, a row of sober matrons dating from Roman times. (*The Rape of the Sabines* is scheduled to be removed for safekeeping and to be replaced with a copy.)

In the square, the Neptune Fountain, dating from between 1550 and 1575, wins the booby prize. It was created by Bartolomeo Ammannati, who considered it a failure himself. The Florentines call it *Il Biancone,* which may be translated as "the big white one" or "the big white thing." Giambologna's equestrian statue to the left of the fountain pays tribute to Grand Duke Cosimo I. Occupying the steps of the Palazzo Vecchio are a copy of Donatello's heraldic lion of Florence, known as the *Marzocco* (the original is in the Bargello); a copy of Donatello's *Judith and Holofernes* (the original is inside the Palazzo Vecchio); a copy of Michelangelo's *David* (the original is now in the Galleria dell'Accademia); and Baccio Bandinelli's insipid *Hercules* (1534).

⑭ Ponte Vecchio (Old Bridge). This charming bridge was built in 1345 to replace an earlier bridge that was swept away by flood, and its shops housed first butchers, then grocers, blacksmiths, and other merchants. But in 1593 the Medici grand duke Ferdinand I (1549–1609), whose private corridor linking the Medici palace (Palazzo Pitti) with the Medici offices (the Uffizi) crossed the bridge atop the shops, decided that all this plebeian commerce under his feet was unseemly. So he threw out the butchers and blacksmiths and installed 41 goldsmiths and eight jewelers. The bridge has been devoted solely to these two trades ever since.

Take a moment to study the **Ponte Santa Trinita,** the next bridge downriver. It was designed by Bartolomeo Ammannati in 1567 (possibly from sketches by Michelangelo), blown up by the retreating Germans during World War II, and painstakingly reconstructed after the war. The view from Ponte Santa Trinita is beautiful, which might explain why so many young lovers hang out there.

In Michelangelo's Footsteps: San Lorenzo to the Accademia

A sculptor, painter, architect, and even a poet, Florentine native son Michelangelo was a consummate genius, and some of his finest creations remain in his hometown. The Biblioteca Medicea Laurenziana is perhaps his most fanciful work of architecture. A key to understanding Michelangelo's genius can be found in the magnificent Cappelle Medicee, where both his sculptural and architectural prowess can be clearly seen. Planned frescoes were never completed, sadly, for they would have shown in one space the artistic triple threat that he certainly was. The towering yet graceful *David,* his most famous work, resides in the Galleria dell'Accademia.

a good walk

Start at the church of **San Lorenzo** ⑮ ➤, visiting the **Biblioteca Medicea Laurenziana** ⑯ and its famous anteroom before circling the church to the northwest and making your way through the San Lorenzo outdoor market on Via del Canto de' Nelli to the entrance of the **Cappelle Medicee** ⑰. Retrace your steps through the market and take Via dei Gori east to Via Cavour and the **Palazzo Medici-Riccardi** ⑱, the home of Florence's most important family throughout the Renaissance. Follow Via Cavour two blocks north to Piazza San Marco and the church of the same name, attached to which is the **Museo di San Marco** ⑲, containing marvelous works by the pious and exceptionally talented painter-friar Fra Angelico. If you have time, go northwest from Piazza San Marco to see Castagno's *Last Supper* at Sant'Apollonia and then north to the Chiostro dello Scalzo. From Piazza San Marco, walk a half block south down Via Ricasoli to the **Galleria dell'Accademia** ⑳. Return to the east side of Piazza San Marco and take Via Cesare Battisti east into Piazza della Santissima Annunziata, one of Florence's prettiest squares, site of the **Spedale degli Innocenti** ㉑ and, at the north end of the square, the church of **Santissima Annunziata** ㉒. One block southeast of the entrance to Santissima Annunziata, through the arch and on the left side of Via della Colonna, is the **Museo Archeologico** ㉓. Continue down Via della Colonna to **Santa Maria Maddalena dei Pazzi** ㉔, harboring a superb fresco by Perugino. Return to Via della Colonna and continue heading southeast; take a right on Via Luigi Carlo Farini, where you'll find the **Sinagoga** ㉕ and its Museo Ebraico.

TIMING The walk alone takes about one hour, plus 45 minutes for the Cappelle Medicee, 20 minutes for the Palazzo Medici-Riccardi, 40 minutes for the Museo di San Marco, 30 minutes for the Galleria dell'Accademia (*David*), and 40 minutes for the Museo Archeologico. Note that the Museo di San Marco closes at 1:50 on weekdays. After visiting San Lorenzo, resist the temptation to explore the market that surrounds the church before going to the Palazzo Medici-Riccardi; you can always come back later, when the churches and museums have closed; the market is open until 7 PM.

What to See

⑯ Biblioteca Medicea Laurenziana (Laurentian Library). Michelangelo the architect was every bit as original as Michelangelo the sculptor. Unlike Brunelleschi (the architect of San Lorenzo), however, he was not obsessed with proportion and perfect geometry. He was interested in experimentation, invention, and expressing a personal vision at times highly idiosyncratic.

It was never more idiosyncratic than in the Laurentian Library, begun in 1524 and finished in 1568, and its famous **vestibolo.** This strangely shaped anteroom has had scholars scratching their heads for centuries. In a space more than two stories high, why did Michelangelo limit his use of columns and pilasters to the upper two-thirds of the wall? Why didn't he rest them on strong pedestals instead of on huge, decorative curlicue scrolls, which rob them of all visual support? Why did he recess them into the wall, which makes them look weaker still? The architectural elements here do not stand firm and strong and tall, like those inside the church next door; instead, they seem to be pressed into the wall as if into putty, giving the room a soft, rubbery look that is one of the strangest effects ever achieved by aping classical architecture. It is almost as if Michelangelo purposely set out to defy his predecessors, intentionally flouting the conventions of the High Renaissance to see what kind of bizarre, mannered effect might result. His innovations were tremendously influential and produced a period of architectural experimentation, known as Mannerism, that eventually evolved into the baroque. As his contemporary Giorgio Vasari put it, "Artisans have been infinitely and perpetually indebted to him because he broke the bonds and chains of a way of working that had become habitual by common usage."

Nobody has ever complained about the anteroom's staircase (best viewed head-on), which emerges from the library with the visual force of an unstoppable lava flow. In its highly sculptural conception and execution, it's quite simply one of the most original and fluid staircases in the world. ⊠ *Piazza San Lorenzo 9, entrance to the left of San Lorenzo* ☎ *055/210760* ⊕ *www.bml.firenze.sbn.it* 🎟 *Special exhibitions €5* ☉ *Daily 8:30–1:30.*

★ **⑰ Cappelle Medicee** (Medici Chapels). This magnificent complex includes the **Cappella dei Principi,** the Medici chapel and mausoleum that was begun in 1605 and kept marble workers busy for several hundred years, and the **Sagrestia Nuova** (New Sacristy), designed by Michelangelo and so called to distinguish it from Brunelleschi's Sagrestia Vecchia (Old Sacristy).

Michelangelo received the commission for the New Sacristy in 1520 from Cardinal Giulio de' Medici (1478–1534), who later became Pope Clement VII and who wanted a new burial chapel for his cousins Giuliano (1478–1534) and Lorenzo (1492–1519). The result was a tour de force of architecture and sculpture. Architecturally, Michelangelo was as original and inventive here as ever, but it is, quite properly, the powerful sculpture that dominates the room. The scheme is allegorical: on the tomb to the right are figures representing Day and Night, and on the tomb to the left are figures representing Dawn and Dusk; above them are idealized sculptures of the two men, usually interpreted to represent the active life and the contemplative life. But the allegorical meanings are secondary; what is most important is the intense presence of the sculptural figures. Michelangelo's contemporaries were so awed by this force (in his sculpture here and elsewhere) that they invented an entirely new word to describe the phenomenon: *terribilità* (dreadfulness). To this day it's used only when describing his work, and it's in evidence here at the peak of its power. During his stormy relations with the Medici, Michelangelo once hid out in a tiny room that is accessed from the left of the altar. The room contains charcoal sketches once thought to be Michelangelo's; art historians now think otherwise, but they're a nice example of centuries-old grafitti. Admission is on the hour (at 9, 10, 11, and noon) and is limited to 12 people; tell the ticket seller that you want to see them. Your chances of getting in are better for one of the earlier hours. ⊠ *Piazza di Madonna degli Aldobrandini, near San Lorenzo* ☎ *055/ 294883 reservations* 🖃 *€6* ⊘ *Daily 8:15–5. Closed 1st, 3rd, and 5th Mon. and 2nd and 4th Sun. of month.*

★ ❷⓿ **Galleria dell'Accademia** (Accademia Gallery). The collection of Florentine paintings here, dating from the 13th to the 18th century, is largely unremarkable, but the sculptures by Michelangelo are worth the price of admission. The unfinished *Slaves,* fighting their way out of their marble prisons, were meant for the tomb of Michelangelo's overly demanding patron, Pope Julius II (1443–1513). But the focal point is the original *David,* moved here from Piazza della Signoria in 1873. The *David* was commissioned in 1501 by the Opera del Duomo (Cathedral Works Committee), which gave the 26-year-old sculptor a leftover block of marble that had been ruined by another artist. Michelangelo's success with the block was so dramatic that the city showered him with honors, and the Opera del Duomo voted to build him a house and a studio in which to live and work.

Today *David* is beset not by Goliath but by tourists, and seeing the statue at all—much less really studying it—can be a trial, as it is surrounded by a Plexiglas barrier. The statue is not quite what it seems. It is so poised and graceful and alert—so miraculously alive—that it is often considered the definitive embodiment of the ideals of the High Renaissance in sculpture. But its true place in the history of art is a bit more complicated.

As Michelangelo well knew, the Renaissance painting and sculpture that preceded his work were deeply concerned with ideal form. Perfection of proportion was the ever-sought Holy Grail; during the Renaissance, ideal proportion was equated with ideal beauty, and ideal beauty was equated with spiritual perfection. But *David,* despite its supremely calm and dignified pose, departs from these ideals. Michelangelo did not give the statue perfect proportions. The head is slightly too large for the body, the arms are too large for the torso, and the hands are dramatically large for the arms. The work was originally commissioned to adorn the facade of the Duomo and was intended to be seen from below at a distance. Michelangelo knew exactly what he was doing, calculating that the perspective of the viewer would be such that, in order for the statue to appear properly proportioned, the upper body, head, and arms would have to be bigger, as they are farther away from the viewer's line of vision. But he also did it to express and embody, as powerfully as possible in a single figure, an entire biblical story. David's hands *are* big, but so was Goliath, and these are the hands that slew him. Save yourself a long and tiresome wait at the museum entrance by reserving your tickets in advance. ⊠ *Via Ricasoli 60, near San Marco* ☎ *055/294883 reservations, 055/2388609 gallery* ◻ *€6.50, reservation fee €3* ⊙ *Tues.–Sun. 8:15–6:50.*

off the beaten path

MUSEO DELL'OPIFICIO DELLE PIETRE DURE – Ferdinand I established a workshop in 1588 to train craftsmen in the art of working with precious and semiprecious stones and marble. Four hundred–plus years later, the workshop is renowned as a center for the restoration of mosaics and inlays in semiprecious stones. The little museum is highly informative and includes some magnificent antique examples of this highly specialized and beautiful craft. ⊠ *Via degli Alfani 78, near San Marco* ☎ *055/26511* ◻ *€2* ⊙ *Mon., Wed., and Fri. and Sat. 8:15–2, Thurs. 8:15–7.*

㉓ **Museo Archeologico.** Of the Etruscan, Egyptian, and Greco-Roman antiquities in this museum, the Etruscan collection is particularly notable—one of the largest in Italy. The famous bronze *Chimera* was discovered (without the tail, a reconstruction) in the 16th century. ⊠ *Via della Colonna 38, near Santissima Annunziata* ☎ *055/23575* ⊕ *www.comune.fi.it/sogetti/sat* ◻ *€4* ⊙ *Mon. 2–7, Tues. and Thurs. 8:30–7, Wed. and Fri.–Sun. 8:30–2.*

⑲ **Museo di San Marco.** A former Dominican convent adjacent to the church of San Marco now houses this museum, which contains many stunning works by Fra Angelico (circa 1400–55), the Dominican friar famous for his piety as well as for his painting. When the friars' cells were restructured between 1439 and 1444, he decorated many of them with frescoes meant to spur religious contemplation. His paintings are simple and direct and furnish a compelling contrast to those in the Palazzo Medici-Riccardi chapel. Whereas Gozzoli's frescoes celebrate the splendors of the Medici, Fra Angelico's exalt the simple beauties of the contemplative life and quiet reflection. Fra Angelico's works are everywhere in this complex, from the friars' cells to the superb panel paintings on view in the museum. Don't miss the famous *Annunciation* on the upper floor and the works in the gallery off the cloister as you enter. Here you can see his beautiful *Last Judgment*; as usual, the tortures of the damned

FLORENCE'S TRIAL BY FIRE

One of the most striking figures of Renaissance Florence was Girolamo Savonarola, a Dominican friar who, for a moment, captured the conscience of the city. In 1491 he became prior of the convent of San Marco, where he adopted a life of austerity and delivered sermons condemning Florence's excesses and the immorality of his fellow clergy. Following the death of Lorenzo de' Medici, Savonarola was instrumental in the formation of the republic of Florence, ruled by a representative council with Christ enthroned as monarch. In one of his most memorable acts, he urged Florentines to toss worldly possessions—from frilly dresses to Botticelli paintings—onto a "bonfire of the vanities" in Piazza della Signoria. Savonarola's antagonism toward church hierarchy led to his undoing: he was excommunicated in 1497, and the following year was hanged and burned on charges of heresy. Today, at the Museo di San Marco, you can visit Savonarola's cell and see his arresting portrait.

are far more inventive and interesting than the pleasures of the redeemed. ⊠ *Piazza San Marco 1* ☎ *055/2388608* 🎟 *€4* ☉ *Weekdays 8:15–1:50, weekends 8:15–6:50. Closed 1st, 3rd, and 5th Sun., and 2nd and 4th Mon. of month.*

off the
beaten
path

CENACOLO DI SANT'APOLLONIA – The frescoes of the refectory of a former Benedictine nunnery were painted in sinewy style by Andrea del Castagno, a follower of Masaccio (1401–28). The *Last Supper* is a powerful version of this typical refectory theme. From the entrance, walk around the corner to Via San Gallo 25 and take a peek at the lovely 15th-century cloister that belonged to the same monastery but is now part of the University of Florence. ⊠ *Via XXVII Aprile 1, near San Marco* ☎ *055/2388607* ☉ *Tues.–Sun. 8:15–1:50. Closed 2nd and 4th Mon. of month.*

CHIOSTRO DELLO SCALZO – Often overlooked, this small, peaceful 16th-century cloister was frescoed in grisaille by Andrea del Sarto (1486–1530), with scenes from the life of St. John the Baptist, Florence's patron saint. ⊠ *Via Cavour 69, near San Marco* ☎ *055/ 2388604* ☉ *Mon., Thurs., and Sat. 9–1.*

★ ⑱ **Palazzo Medici-Riccardi.** The main attraction of this palace, begun in 1444 by Michelozzo for Cosimo de' Medici, is the interior chapel, the so-called **Cappella dei Magi** on the upper floor. Painted on its walls is Benozzo Gozzoli's famous *Procession of the Magi,* finished in 1460, which celebrates both the birth of Christ and the greatness of the Medici family. Like Ghirlandaio, Gozzoli was not a revolutionary painter and is today considered less interesting than other 15th-century stars such as Masaccio, Botticelli, and Leonardo. Gozzoli's gift, however, was for entrancing the eye, not challenging the mind, and on those terms his success here is beyond question. The paintings are full of activity yet somehow frozen in time in a way that fails utterly as realism but succeeds triumphantly when the demand for realism is set aside. Entering the chapel is like walking into the middle of a magnificently illustrated children's storybook, and this beauty makes it one of the most enjoyable rooms in the entire city. ⊠ *Via Cavour 1, near San Lorenzo* ☎ *055/2760340* ⌷ *€4* ⊗ *Thurs.–Tues. 9–7.*

▶ **⓯ San Lorenzo.** The interior of this church, like that of Santo Spirito on the other side of the Arno, was designed by Filippo Brunelleschi in the early 15th century. Both proclaim with ringing clarity the beginning of the Renaissance in architecture (neither was completed by Brunelleschi, and which he worked on first is unknown). San Lorenzo's most dramatic element is its floor grid of dark, inlaid marble lines. The grid makes the rigorous geometry of the interior immediately visible and is an illuminating lesson on the laws of perspective. If you stand in the middle of the nave at the church entrance, on the line that stretches to the high altar, every element in the church—the grid, the nave columns, the side aisles, the coffered nave ceiling—seems to march inexorably toward a hypothetical vanishing point beyond the high altar, exactly as in a single-point-perspective painting. Brunelleschi's **Sagrestia Vecchia** (Old Sacristy) has stucco decorations by Donatello; it's at the end of the left transept. The facade of the church was never finished. ⊠ *Piazza San Lorenzo* ☎ *055/290184* ⌷ *€2.50* ⊗ *Mon.–Sat. 10–5.*

㉔ Santa Maria Maddalena dei Pazzi. One of Florence's hidden treasures, Perugino's (circa 1445/50–1523) cool and composed *Crucifixion* is in the chapter house of the monastery below this church. Here you can see the Virgin Mary and St. John the Evangelist with Mary Magdalen and Sts. Benedict and Bernard of Clairvaux posed against a simple but haunting landscape. The figure of Christ crucified occupies the center of this brilliantly hued fresco. Perugino's colors radiate—note the juxtaposition of the yellow-green cuff against the orange tones of the Magdalen's robe. ⊠ *Borgo Pinti 58, near Santa Croce* ☎ *055/2478420* ⌷ *Donation requested* ⊗ *Mon.–Sat. 10–noon and 5–7, Sun. 9–10:45 and 3–6:50.*

㉒ Santissima Annunziata. Dating from the mid-13th century, this church was restructured in 1447 by Michelozzo, who gave it an uncommon (and lovely) entrance cloister with frescoes by Andrea del Sarto (1486–1530), Pontormo (1494–1556), and Rosso Fiorentino (1494–1540). The interior is a rarity for Florence: a sumptuous example of the baroque. But it's not really a fair example, since it is merely 17th-century baroque decoration applied willy-nilly to an earlier structure—exactly the sort of violent remodeling exercise that has given the baroque a bad name. The **Cappella dell'Annuziata,** immediately inside the entrance to the left, illustrates the point. The lower half, with its stately Corinthian columns and carved frieze bearing the Medici arms, was commissioned by Piero de' Medici in 1447; the upper half, with its erupting curves and impish sculpted cherubs, was added 200 years later. Each is effective in its own way, but together they serve only to prove that dignity is rarely comfortable wearing a party hat. ⊠ *Piazza di Santissima Annunziata* ☎ *055/ 266186* ⊗ *Daily 7–12:30 and 4:30–6:30.*

㉕ Sinagoga (Synagogue). Jews were well settled in Florence by 1396, when the first money-lending operations became officially sanctioned. Medici patronage helped Jewish banking houses to flourish, but by 1570 Jews were required to live within the large "ghetto," near today's Piazza della Repubblica, by decree of Pope Pius V (1504–72). Construction of the modern Moorish-style synagogue, with its lovely garden, began in 1874 as a bequest of David Levi, who wished to endow a synagogue "worthy of the city." Falcini, Micheli, and Treves designed the building on a domed Greek-cross plan with galleries in the transept and a roofline bearing three distinctive copper cupolas. The exterior has alternating bands of tan travertine and pink granite, reflecting an Islamic style repeated in Giovanni Panti's ornate interior. Of particular interest are the cast-iron gates by Pasquale Franci, the eternal light by Francesco Morini, and the Murano glass mosaics by Giacomo dal Medico. The gilded doors of the Moorish ark, which fronts the pulpit and is flanked by extravagant candelabra, are decorated with symbols of the ancient Temple of Jerusalem and bear bayonet marks from vandals. The synagogue was used as a garage by the Nazis, who failed to inflict much damage in spite of an attempt to blow up the place with dynamite. Only the columns on the left side were destroyed, and, even then the women's balcony above did not collapse. Note the Star of David in black and yellow marble inlaid in the floor. The original capitals can be seen in the garden.

Some of the oldest and most beautiful Jewish ritual artifacts in all of Europe are displayed in the small **Museo Ebraico** upstairs, accessible by stairs or elevator. Exhibits document the Florentine Jewish community and the building of the synagogue. The donated objects all belonged to local families and date from as early as the late 16th century. Take special note of the exquisite needlework and silver objects. A small but well-stocked gift shop is downstairs. *Synagogue and museum ⊠ Via Farini 4, near Santa Croce ☎ 055/2346654 ⊡ Synagogue and museum €4 ⊙ Apr. and May, and Sept. and Oct., Sun.–Thurs. 10–5, Fri. 10–2; June–Aug., Sun.–Thurs. 10–6, Fri. 10–2; Nov.–Mar., Sun.–Thurs. 10–3, Fri. 10–2. English-guided tours 10:10, 11, noon, 1, 2 (no tour at 2 on Fri.).*

> **need a break?**
>
> Adjacent to Florence's synagogue is **Ruth's** (⊠ Via Farini 2/a, near Santa Croce ☎ 055/2480888), the only kosher-vegetarian restaurant in Tuscany. Inexpensive vegetarian and Mediterranean dishes and a large selection of kosher wines highlight the menu. It's closed for Friday dinner and Saturday lunch.

㉑ Spedale degli Innocenti. Built by Brunelleschi in 1419 to serve as a foundling hospital, this takes the prize as the very first Renaissance building. Brunelleschi designed its portico with his usual rigor, employing the two shapes he considered mathematically (and therefore philosophically and aesthetically) perfect: the square and the circle. Below the level of the arches the portico encloses a row of perfect cubes; above the arch level the portico encloses a row of intersecting hemispheres. The whole geometric scheme is articulated with Corinthian columns, capitals, and arches borrowed directly from antiquity. At the time he designed the portico, Brunelleschi was also designing the interior of San Lorenzo, using the same basic ideas. But since the portico was finished before San Lorenzo, the Spedale degli Innocenti can claim the honor of ushering in Renaissance architecture. The 10 ceramic medallions depicting swaddled infants that decorate the portico are by Andrea della Robbia (1435–1525/28), done in about 1487. Inside is a small museum devoted to lesser-known Renaissance works. ✉ *Piazza di Santissima Annunziata 12* ☎ *055/20371* 💴 *€2.60* 🕙 *Thurs.–Tues. 8:30–2.*

Santa Maria Novella to the Arno

Piazza Santa Maria Novella is near the train station and is marked by a degree of squalor, especially at night. Nevertheless, the streets in and around the piazza have their share of architectural treasures, including some of Florence's most tasteful palazzos.

a good walk

Start in Piazza Santa Maria Novella, its north side dominated by the church of **Santa Maria Novella** ㉖ ☞; then take Via delle Belle Donne, which leads from the east side of the piazza to a minuscule square, at the center of which stands a curious shrine known as the Croce al Trebbio. Take Via del Trebbio east and turn right onto Via Tornabuoni, Florence's finest shopping street. At the intersection of Via Tornabuoni and Via Strozzi is the overwhelming **Palazzo Strozzi** ㉗. If you want a dose of contemporary sculpture, follow Via della Spada to the **Museo Marino Marini** ㉘. One block west from Palazzo Strozzi, down Via della Vigna Nuova, is Leon Battista Alberti's groundbreaking **Palazzo Rucellai** ㉙. Follow the narrow street opposite the palazzo (Via del Purgatorio) east almost to its end; then zigzag right and left, turning east on Via Parione to reach Piazza di Santa Trinita, where, in the middle, stands the Colonna della Giustizia (the Column of Justice), a column from Rome's Terme di Caracalla, given to the Medici grand duke Cosimo I by Pope Pius IV in 1560. Cosimo placed it here in 1565 to mark the spot where he heard news that Florentine ducal forces had prevailed over a ragtag army of Florentine republican exiles and their French allies at the 1554 battle of Marciano; the victory made his power in Florence all but absolute. Halfway down the block to the south (toward the Arno) is the church of **Santa Trinita** ㉚, home to Ghirlandaio's glowing frescoes. From there go east on Borgo Santi Apostoli, a typical medieval street flanked by tower houses, and take a right on Via Por Santa Maria to get to the Ponte Vecchio. Alternatively, walk from Piazza Santa Trinita to Ponte Santa Trinita, which leads into the Oltrarno.

TIMING The walk takes about 30 minutes, plus 30 minutes for Santa Maria Novella and 15 minutes for Santa Trinita. A visit to the Museo di Santa Maria Novella and the cloister takes about 30 minutes.

What to See
Croce al Trebbio. A little granite column near Piazza Santa Maria Novella was erected in 1338 by Dominican friars (the Dominican basilica Santa Maria Novella is down the street) to commemorate a famous local victory: it was here in 1244 that they defeated their avowed enemies, the Patarene heretics, in a bloody street brawl. ✉ *Via del Trebbio, near Santa Maria Novella.*

28 Museo Marino Marini. One of the few museums in Florence that shows significant art from the last century is this one dedicated to sculptor and painter Marini (1901–80). His 21-foot-tall bronze of a horse and rider dominates the main gallery. The museum itself is an eruption of contemporary space in a deconsecrated 9th-century church, designed with a series of open stairways, walkways, and balconies that allow you to peer at Marini's work from all angles. In addition to his Etruscanesque sculpture, the museum houses Marini's paintings, drawings, and engravings. ⊠ *Piazza San Pancrazio, near Santa Maria Novella* ☎ *055/ 219432* 🖃 *€4* ⊘ *Mon. and Wed.–Sat. 10–5.*

29 Palazzo Rucellai. Architect Leon Battista Alberti (1404–72) designed perhaps the very first private residence inspired by antique models—going a step further than the Palazzo Strozzi. A comparison between the two is illuminating. Evident on the facade of the Palazzo Rucellai, dating between 1455 and 1470, is the ordered arrangement of windows and rusticated stonework seen on the Palazzo Strozzi, but Alberti's facade is far less forbidding. Alberti devoted a larger proportion of his wall space to windows, which lighten the facade's appearance, and filled in the remainder with rigorously ordered classical elements borrowed from antiquity. The result, though still severe, is less fortresslike, and Alberti strove for this effect purposely (he is on record as saying that only tyrants need fortresses). Ironically, the Palazzo Rucellai was built some 30 years *before* the Palazzo Strozzi. Alberti's civilizing ideas here, it turned out, had little influence on the Florentine palazzos that followed. To Renaissance Florentines, power—in architecture, as in life—was as impressive as beauty. The palace now serves as apartments for wealthy Florentines. ⊠ *Via della Vigna Nuova, near Santa Maria Novella.*

27 Palazzo Strozzi. The Strozzi family built this imposing palazzo in an attempt to outshine the nearby Palazzo Medici. The design is based on a model by Giuliano da Sangallo (circa 1452–1516) dating from around 1489 that was in fact inspired by the Palazzo Medici; construction took place between 1489 and 1504 under Il Cronaca (1457–1508) and Benedetto da Maiaino (1442–97). The exterior is simple, severe, and massive: it's a testament to the wealth of a patrician, 15th-century Florentine family. The interior courtyard is another matter altogether. It is here that the classical vocabulary—columns, capitals, pilasters, arches, and cornices—is given uninhibited and powerful expression. Blockbuster art shows frequently occur here. ⊠ *Via Tornabuoni, near Piazza della Repubblica* ☎ *055/2776461* ⊕ *www.firenzemostre.com* 🖃 *Free except during exhibitions* ⊘ *Daily 10–7.*

▶ **26 Santa Maria Novella.** The facade of this church looks distinctly clumsy by later Renaissance standards, and with good reason: it is an architectural hybrid. The lower half was completed mostly in the 14th century; its pointed-arch niches and decorative marble patterns reflect the Gothic style of the day. About a hundred years later (around 1456), architect Leon Battista Alberti was called in to complete the job. The marble decoration of his upper story clearly defers to the already existing work below, but the architectural motifs he added evince an entirely different style. The central doorway, the four ground-floor half columns with Corinthian capitals, the triangular pediment atop the second story, the inscribed frieze immediately below the pediment—these are borrowings from antiquity, and they reflect the new Renaissance era in architecture, born some 37 years earlier at Florence's Spedale degli Innocenti. Alberti's most important addition, however, the S-curve scrolls that surmount the decorative circles on either side of the upper story, had no precedent in antiquity. The problem was to soften the abrupt transition between wide ground floor and narrow upper story. Alberti's solution turned out to be definitive. Once you start to look for them, you will find scrolls such as these (or sculptural variations of them) on churches all over Italy, and every one of them derives from Alberti's example here.

The architecture of the interior is, like the Duomo, a dignified but somber example of Florentine Gothic. Exploration is essential, however, because the church's store of art treasures is remarkable. Highlights include the 14th-century stained-glass rose window depicting the *Coronation of the Virgin* (above the central entrance); the Cappella Filippo Strozzi (to the right of the altar), containing late-15th-century frescoes and stained glass by Filippino Lippi; the *cappella maggiore* (the area around the high altar), displaying frescoes by Domenico Ghirlandaio (1449–94); and the Cappella Gondi (to the left of the altar), containing Filippo Brunelleschi's famous wood crucifix, carved around 1410 and said to have so stunned the great Donatello when he first saw it that he dropped a basket of eggs.

Of special interest for its great historical importance and beauty is Masaccio's *Trinity,* on the left-hand wall, almost halfway down the nave. Painted around 1426–27 (at the same time he was working on his frescoes in Santa Maria del Carmine), it unequivocally announced the arrival of the Renaissance. The realism of the figure of Christ was revolutionary in itself, but what was probably even more startling to contemporary Florentines was the barrel vault in the background. The mathematical rules for employing perspective in painting had just been discovered (probably by Brunelleschi), and this was one of the first works of art to employ them with utterly convincing success. ✉ *Piazza Santa Maria Novella* ☎ *055/ 210113* 💶 *€2.50* ☉ *Mon.–Thurs. and Sat. 9–3, Sun. 9–2.*

In the cloisters of the **Museo di Santa Maria Novella,** to the left of Santa Maria Novella, is a faded fresco cycle by Paolo Uccello depicting tales from Genesis, with a dramatic vision of the Flood. Earlier and better-preserved frescoes painted between 1348 and 1355 by Andrea da Firenze are in the chapter house, or the Cappellone degli Spagnoli (Spanish Chapel), off the cloister. ✉ *Piazza Santa Maria Novella 19* ☎ *055/282187* 💶 *€2.60* ☉ *Wed.–Mon. 9–2.*

➌⓪ Santa Trinita. Started in the 11th century by Vallombrosian monks and originally Romanesque in style, this church underwent a Gothic remodeling during the 14th century. (Remains of the Romanesque construction are visible on the interior front wall.) Its major work is the cycle of frescoes and the altarpiece in the Cappella Sassetti, the second to the high altar's right, painted by Domenico Ghirlandaio between 1480 and 1485. Ghirlandaio was a wildly popular but conservative painter for his day, and generally his paintings show little interest in the laws of perspective that other Florentine painters had been experimenting with for more than 50 years. But his work here has such graceful decorative appeal it hardly seems to matter. The frescoes illustrate the life of St. Francis, and the altarpiece, depicting the Adoration of the Shepherds, veritably glows. ⊠ *Piazza Santa Trinita, near Santa Maria Novella* ☎ *055/216912* ☺ *Mon.–Sat. 8–noon and 4–6, Sun. 4–6.*

The Oltrarno

A walk through the Oltrarno (literally "the other side of the Arno") takes in two very different aspects of Florence: the splendor of the Medici, manifest in the riches of the mammoth Palazzo Pitti and the gracious Giardino di Boboli; and the charm of the Oltrarno, a slightly gentrified but still fiercely proud working-class neighborhood with artisans' and antiques shops.

a good walk

Starting from Santa Trinita, cross the Arno over Ponte Santa Trinita and continue south down Via Maggio until you reach the crossroads of Sdrucciolo dei Pitti (on the left) and the short Via Michelozzi (on the right). Turn left onto the Sdrucciolo dei Pitti. **Palazzo Pitti** ㉛ ▶, Florence's largest palace, lies before you as you emerge onto Piazza Pitti. Behind the palace is the **Giardino di Boboli** ㉜. Find time to walk through the splendidly landscaped gardens. If you have the energy, walk up the hill to the nearby **Forte di Belvedere** ㉝, which commands a wonderful view and sometimes has art exhibits. If you want to take a Mannerist detour to see the Pontormo *Deposition* at **Santa Felicita** ㉞, head northeast from Palazzo Pitti on Via Guicciardini back toward the Ponte Vecchio. Walk down Borgo Sant'Jacopo, cross Via Maggio, and take a left at Via del Presto di San Martino. Notice the unassuming facade of the church of **Santo Spirito** ㉟. Diagonally across the square from the church entrance, turn right on Via Sant'Agostino to Via dei Serragli. Cross and follow Via Santa Monaca west through the heart of the Oltrarno to Piazza del Carmine and the church of **Santa Maria del Carmine** ㊱, where the famous fresco cycle by Masaccio, Masolino, and Filippino Lippi fills the Cappella Brancacci. Go to the far end of Piazza del Carmine and turn right onto Borgo San Frediano; then follow Via di Santo Spirito and Borgo Sant'Jacopo east to reach the Ponte Vecchio.

TIMING   The walk alone takes about 45 minutes; allow one hour to visit the Galleria Palatina in Palazzo Pitti and more if you visit the other galleries. Spend at least 30 minutes to an hour savoring the graceful elegance of the Giardino di Boboli. When you reach the crossroads of the Sdrucciolo dei Pitti and Via Michelozzi, you have a choice. If it's around noon, you may want to postpone the first stop temporarily to see the churches of Santo Spirito, Santa Felicita, and Santa Maria del Carmine before they close for the afternoon. Otherwise, proceed to Palazzo Pitti. The churches can each be visited in 15 minutes.

What to See

㉝ **Forte di Belvedere.** This impressive structure was built in 1590 to help defend the city against siege. But time has brought about a transformation, and what was once a first-rate fortification is now a first-rate exhibition venue. Farther up the hill is Piazzale Michelangelo, but, as the natives know, the best views of Florence are right here. To the north, all the city's monuments are spread out in a breathtaking panorama. To the south, the nearby hills furnish a complementary rural view, in its way equally memorable. The fortress, occasionally a host of art exhibitions (contact the tourist office for schedule), is adjacent to the top of the Giardino di Boboli. ⊠ *Porta San Giorgio, near San Niccolò* 🖼 *Varies with exhibit.*

㉜ Giardino di Boboli (Boboli Garden). The main entrance to this landscaped garden is from the courtyard of Palazzo Pitti. The garden began to take shape in 1549, when the Pitti family sold the palazzo to Eleanora of Toledo, wife of the Medici grand duke Cosimo I. The initial landscaping plans were laid out by Niccolò Tribolo (1500–50). After his death work was continued by Vasari, Ammannati, Giambologna, Bernardo Buontalenti (circa 1536–1608), and Giulio (1571–1635) and Alfonso Parigi (1606–56), among others, resulting in the most spectacular backyard in Florence. The Italian gift for landscaping—less formal than the French but still full of sweeping drama—is displayed here at its best. A copy of the famous *Morgante*, Cosimo I's favorite dwarf astride a particularly unhappy tortoise, is near the exit. Sculpted by Valerio Cioli (circa 1529–99), the work shows a perfectly executed potbelly. ⊠ *Enter through Palazzo Pitti* 🕾 *055/294883* 🖼 *€4, combined ticket with Museo delle Porcellane and Museo degli Argenti* ☉ *Apr.–Oct., daily 8:15–5:30; Nov.–Mar., daily 8:15–4:30. Closed 1st and last Mon. of month.*

▶ ㉛ Palazzo Pitti. This palace is one of Florence's largest—if not one of its best—architectural set pieces. The original palazzo, built for the Pitti family around 1460, comprised only the main entrance and the three windows on either side. In 1549 the property was sold to the Medici, and Bartolomeo Ammannati was called in to make substantial additions. Although he apparently operated on the principle that more is better, he succeeded only in proving that more is just that: more.

Today it houses several museums: The **Museo degli Argenti** (🖼 €4, combined ticket with Giardino di Boboli ☉ Daily 8:15–1:50) displays a vast collection of Medici household treasures. The **Galleria del Costume** (🖼 €5, combined ticket with Galleria d'Arte Moderna ☉ Daily 8:15–1:50) showcases fashions from the past 300 years. The **Galleria d'Arte Moderna** (🖼 €5, combined ticket with Galleria del Costume ☉ Daily 8:15–1:50) holds a collection of 19th- and 20th-century paintings, mostly Tuscan. And, most famous of all, the **Galleria Palatina** (🖼 €6.50 ☉ Tues.–Sun. 8:15–6:50) contains a broad collection of paintings from the 15th to 17th century. High points include a number of portraits by Titian and an unparalleled collection of paintings by Raphael, notably the double portraits of Angelo Doni and his wife, the sullen Maddalena Strozzi. The rooms of the Galleria Palatina remain much as the Medici left them. Their floor-to-ceiling paintings are considered by some to be Italy's most egregious exercise in conspicuous consumption, aesthetic overkill, and trumpery. The price of admission also allows you to explore the former **Appartamenti Reali,** containing furnishings from a remodeling done in the 19th century. ⊠ *Piazza Pitti* ☎ *055/210323* ☉ *All but Galleria Palatina closed 2nd and 4th Sun. and 1st, 3rd, and 5th Mon. of month.*

❸❹ Santa Felicita. This late baroque church (its facade was remodeled 1736–39) contains the Mannerist Jacopo Pontormo's (1494–1556) tour de force, the *Deposition,* the centerpiece of the Cappella Capponi (executed 1525–28), a masterpiece of 16th-century Florentine art. The remote figures, which transcend the realm of Renaissance classical form, are portrayed in tangled shapes and intense pastel colors (well preserved because of the low lights in the church), in a space and depth that defy reality. Note, too, the exquisitely frescoed *Annunciation,* also by Pontormo, at a right angle to the *Deposition.* The granite column in the piazza was erected in 1381 and marks a Christian cemetery. ⊠ *Piazza Santa Felicita, Via Guicciardini, near Palazzo Pitti* ☉ *Mon.–Sat. 9–noon and 3–6, Sun. 9–1.*

❸❻ Santa Maria del Carmine. The **Cappella Brancacci,** at the end of the right transept of this church, houses a masterpiece of Renaissance painting: a fresco cycle that changed the course of Western art forever. Fire nearly destroyed the church in the 18th century; miraculously, the Brancacci Chapel survived almost intact. The cycle is the work of three artists: Masaccio and Masolino (1383–circa 1440/47), who began it around 1424, and Filippino Lippi, who finished it some 50 years later, after a long interruption during which the sponsoring Brancacci family was exiled. It was Masaccio's work that opened a new frontier for painting, as he was among the first to employ single-point perspective; tragically, he did not live to experience the revolution his innovations caused—he died in 1428 at the age of 27.

Masaccio collaborated with Masolino on several of the frescoes, but by himself he painted the *Tribute Money* on the upper-left wall; *St. Peter Baptizing* on the upper altar wall; the *Distribution of Goods* on the lower altar wall; and, most famous, the *Expulsion of Adam and Eve* on the chapel's upper-left entrance pier. If you look closely at the last painting and compare it with some of the chapel's other works, you will see a pronounced difference. The figures of Adam and Eve have a startling presence, primarily due to the dramatic way in which their bodies seem to reflect light. Masaccio here shaded his figures consistently, so as to suggest a single, strong source of light within the world of the painting but outside its frame. In so doing, he succeeded in imitating with paint the real-world effect of light on mass, and he thereby imparted to his figures a sculptural reality unprecedented in his day.

These matters have to do with technique, but with the *Expulsion of Adam and Eve* his skill went beyond mere technical innovation. In the faces of Adam and Eve you see more than finely modeled figures. You see terrible shame and suffering depicted with a humanity rarely achieved in art. Reservations to see the church are mandatory, but can be booked on the same day. Your time inside is limited to 15 minutes—a frustration that's only partly mitigated by the 40-minute DVD about the history of the chapel you can watch either before or after your visit.

⊠ *Piazza del Carmine, near Santo Spirito* ☎ *055/2382195, reservations 055/2768224* 🖭 *€4* ⊙ *Mon. and Wed.–Sat. 10–5, Sun. 1–5.*

㉟ Santo Spirito. The plain, unfinished facade gives nothing away, but the interior, although it appears chilly (cold, even) compared with later churches, is one of the most important examples of Renaissance architecture in Italy. The interior is one of a pair designed in Florence by Filippo Brunelleschi in the early 15th century (the other is San Lorenzo). It was here that Brunelleschi supplied definitive solutions to the two main problems of interior Renaissance church design: how to build a cross-shaped interior using architectural elements borrowed from antiquity and how to reflect in that interior the order and regularity that Renaissance scientists (among them Brunelleschi himself) were at the time discovering in the natural world around them.

Brunelleschi's solution to the first problem was brilliantly simple: turn a Greek temple inside out. To see this clearly, look at one of the stately arch-topped arcades that separate the side aisles from the central nave. Whereas ancient Greek temples were walled buildings surrounded by classical colonnades, Brunelleschi's churches were classical arcades within walled buildings. This brilliant architectural idea overthrew the previous era's religious taboo against pagan architecture once and for all, triumphantly reclaiming that architecture for Christian use.

Brunelleschi's solution to the second problem—making the entire interior orderly and regular—was mathematically precise: he designed the church so that all its parts were proportionally related. The transepts and nave have exactly the same width; the side aisles are precisely half as wide as the nave; the little chapels off the side aisles are exactly half as deep as the side aisles; the chancel and transepts are exactly one-eighth the depth of the nave; and so on, with dizzying exactitude. For Brunelleschi, such a design technique would have been a matter of passionate conviction. Like most theoreticians of his day, he believed that mathematical regularity and aesthetic beauty were flip sides of the same coin, that one was not possible without the other. In the **refectory of Santo Spirito** (⊠ Piazza Santo Spirito 29 ☎ 055/287043), adjacent to the church, you can see the remains of Andrea Orcagna's fresco of the *Crucifixion*. ⊠ *Piazza Santo Spirito* ☎ *055/210030* 🖭 *Church free, refectory €2.20* ⊙ *Church: Thurs.–Tues. 10–noon and 4–5:30; Wed. 9–noon. Refectory: Tues.–Sat. 9–1:50.*

need a break?

Cabiria (⊠ Piazza Santo Spirito 4/r ☎ 055/215732), across the piazza from the church of Santo Spirito, draws a funky crowd in search of a cappuccino or quenching ade. When it's warm, sit outside on the terrace. Snacks and light lunches are also available.

From Santa Croce to San Miniato al Monte

The Santa Croce quarter, on the southeast fringe of the historic center, was built up in the Middle Ages outside the second set of medieval city walls. The centerpiece of the neighborhood was the basilica of Santa Croce, which could hold great numbers of worshippers; the vast piazza could accommodate any overflow and also served as a fairground and playing field for traditional, no-holds-barred soccer games. A center of leather working since the Middle Ages, the neighborhood is still packed with leather craftsmen and leather shops.

a good walk

Begin your walk at the church of **Santa Croce** ③⑦ ▶; from here you can take a quick jaunt up Via delle Pinzochere to **Casa Buonarroti** ③⑧ to see works by Michelangelo. Return to Santa Croce, and at the southwest end of the piazza go south on Via de' Benci and cross the Arno over Ponte alle Grazie. Turn left onto Lungarno Serristori and continue to Piazza Giuseppe Poggi; a series of ramps and stairs climbs to **Piazzale Michelangelo** ③⑨, where the city lies before you in all its glory. From Piazzale Michelangelo, climb the stairs behind La Loggia restaurant to the church of San Salvatore al Monte, and go south on the lane leading to the stairs that climb to **San Miniato al Monte** ④⓪, cutting through the fortifications hurriedly built by Michelangelo in 1529 when Florence was threatened by troops of the Holy Roman Emperor Charles V (1500–58). You can avoid the long walk by taking Bus 12 or 13 at the west end of Ponte alle Grazie and getting off at Piazzale Michelangelo or at the stop after for San Miniato al Monte; you still have to climb the monumental stairs to and from San Miniato, but you can then take the bus from Piazzale Michelangelo back to the center of town.

TIMING The walk alone takes about 1½ hours one-way, plus 30 minutes in Santa Croce, 30 minutes in the Museo di Santa Croce, and 30 minutes in San Miniato. Depending on the amount of time you have, you can limit your sightseeing to Santa Croce and Casa Buonarroti or continue on to Piazzale Michelangelo. The walk to Piazzale Michelangelo is a long uphill hike, with the prospect of another climb to San Miniato from there. If you decide to take a bus, remember to buy your ticket before you board. Finally, since you go to Piazzale Michelangelo for the view, skip it if it's a hazy day.

What to See

③⑧ **Casa Buonarroti.** Michelangelo Buonarroti the Younger, the grand-nephew of the famed Michelangelo, turned his family house into a shrine honoring the life of his great-uncle. It's full of works executed by Michelangelo, including a marble bas-relief, the *Madonna of the Steps*, carved when Michelangelo was a teenager, and his wooden model for the facade of San Lorenzo. ✉ *Via Ghibellina 70, near Santa Croce* ☎ *055/241752* ⊕ *www.casabuonarroti.it* 🎟 *€6.50* ⊗ *Wed.–Mon. 9:30–4.*

③⑨ **Piazzale Michelangelo.** From this lookout you have a marvelous view of Florence and the hills around it, rivaling the vista from the Forte di Belvedere. It has a copy of Michelangelo's *David* and outdoor cafés packed with tourists during the day and with Florentines in the evening. The **Giardino dell'Iris** (Iris Garden) off the piazza is in full flower in May. The **Giardino delle Rose** (Rose Garden) on the terraces below the piazza is in full bloom in May and June, and open only then.

④⓪ **San Miniato al Monte.** This church, like the Baptistery, is a fine example of Romanesque architecture and one of the oldest churches in Florence, dating from the 11th century. The lively green-and-white marble facade has a 12th-century mosaic topped by a gilt bronze eagle, emblem of San Miniato's sponsors, the Calimala (cloth merchants' guild). Inside are a 13th-century marble floor and apse mosaic. Spinello Aretino (1350–1410) covered the walls of the **Sagrestia** with frescoes on the life of St. Benedict. The adjacent **Cappella del Cardinale del Portogallo** is one of the richest Renaissance works in Florence. Built to hold the tomb of a Portuguese cardinal, Prince James of Lusitania, who died young in Florence in 1459, it has a glorious ceiling by Luca della Robbia, a sculptured tomb by Antonio Rossellino (1427–79), and inlaid pavement in multicolor marble. ⊠ *Viale Galileo Galilei, Piazzale Michelangelo, Lungarno South* ☎ *055/2342731* ⊘ *Apr.–Oct., daily 8–noon and 3–7; Nov.–Mar., daily 8–noon and 3–4:30.*

▶ ㉗ **Santa Croce.** Like the Duomo, this church is Gothic, but, also like the
Fodor'sChoice Duomo, its facade dates from the 19th century. The interior is most fa-
★ mous for its art and its tombs. As a burial place, the church is a Florentine pantheon, probably containing more skeletons of Renaissance celebrities than any other church in Italy. Among others, the tomb of Michelangelo is immediately to the right as you enter; he is said to have chosen this spot so that the first thing he would see on Judgment Day, when the graves of the dead fly open, would be Brunelleschi's dome through Santa Croce's open doors. The tomb of Galileo Galilei (1564–1642), who produced evidence that Earth is not the center of the universe, and was not granted a Christian burial until 100 years after his death because of it, is on the left wall, nearly opposite Michelangelo's. The tomb of Niccolò Machiavelli (1469–1527), the political theoretician whose brutally pragmatic philosophy so influenced the Medici, is halfway down the nave on the right. The grave of Lorenzo Ghiberti, creator of the Baptistery doors, is halfway down the nave on the left. Composer Gioacchino Rossini (1792–1868) is entombed at the end of the nave on the right. The monument to Dante Alighieri (1265–1321), the greatest Italian poet, is a memorial rather than a tomb (he is buried in Ravenna); it's on the right wall near the tomb of Michelangelo.

The collection of art within the church complex is by far the most important of any church in Florence. Historically, the most significant works are probably the Giotto frescoes in the two chapels immediately to the right of the high altar. They illustrate scenes from the lives of St. John the Evangelist and St. John the Baptist (in the right-hand chapel) and scenes from the life of St. Francis (in the left-hand chapel). Time has not been kind to these frescoes; over the centuries, wall tombs were placed in the middle of them, they were whitewashed and plastered over, and in the 19th century they suffered a clumsy restoration. But the reality that Giotto introduced into painting can still be seen. He did not paint beautifully stylized religious icons, as the Byzantine style that preceded him prescribed; he instead painted drama—St. Francis surrounded by grieving friars at the very moment of his death. This was a radical shift in emphasis, and it changed the course of Western art. Before Giotto, painting's role was to symbolize the attributes of God; after him, it was to imitate life. His work is indeed primitive, compared with later painting, but in the early 14th century it caused a sensation that was not equaled for another 100 years. He was, for his time, the equal of both Masaccio and Michelangelo.

Among the church's other highlights are Donatello's *Annunciation,* a moving expression of surprise (on the right wall two-thirds of the way down the nave); 14th-century frescoes by Taddeo Gaddi (circa 1300–66) illustrating scenes from the life of the Virgin Mary, clearly showing the influence of Giotto (in the chapel at the end of the right transept); and Donatello's *Crucifix,* criticized by Brunelleschi for making Christ look like a peasant (in the chapel at the end of the left transept). Outside the church proper, in the **Museo dell'Opera di Santa Croce** off the cloister, is the 13th-century *Triumphal Cross* by Cimabue (circa 1240–1302), badly damaged by the flood of 1966. A model of architectural geometry, the **Cappella Pazzi,** at the end of the cloister, is the work of Brunelleschi. ⊠ *Piazza Santa Croce 16* ☎ *055/2466105* 🖃 *Basilica and museum (combined ticket):* €4 ⊙ *Daily 9:30–5.*

WHERE TO EAT

Dining hours are earlier here than in Rome, starting at 1 for the midday meal and at 8 for dinner. Many of Florence's restaurants are small, so reservations are a must. You can sample such specialties as creamy *fegatini* (a chicken-liver spread) and *ribollita* (minestrone thickened with bread and beans and swirled with extra-virgin olive oil) in a bustling, convivial *trattoria,* where you share long wooden tables set with paper place mats, or in an upscale *ristorante* with linen tablecloths and napkins. Follow the Florentines' lead and take a break at an *enoteca* (wineshop or wine bar) during the day and discover some excellent Chiantis and Super Tuscans from small producers who rarely export.

WHAT IT COSTS In euros					
	$$$$	**$$$**	**$$**	**$**	**¢**
AT DINNER	over €22	€16–€22	€11–€16	€7–€11	under €7

Prices are for a second course (secondo piatto).

Centro Storico

$$$–$$$$ ✕**Osteria n. 1.** The name "Osteria" is the only pretentious aspect of this romantic restaurant in an old palazzo in the historic center. The place is suffused with a rosy glow from the tablecloths and cream-color walls, lined with painted landscapes and the occasional coat of arms. The food is expertly prepared—try *tagliatelle verdi ai broccoli e salsiccia* (flat noodles with sausage and broccoli) before moving on to any of the grilled meats. ⊠ *Via del Moro 18–20/r, near Santa Maria Novella* ☎ *055/284897* 🖃 *AE, DC, MC, V* ⊙ *Closed Sun. and 20 days in Aug. No lunch Mon.*

$ ✕**Osteria delle Belle Donne.** Down the street from the church of Santa Maria Novella, this gaily decorated spot, festooned with ropes of garlic and other vegetables, has an ever-changing menu and stellar service led by the irrepressible Giacinto. Even the checkered cloth napkins are cheery. The kitchen offers Tuscan standards, but shakes up the menu with alternatives such as *sedani con bacon, verza, e uova* (thick noodles sauced with bacon, cabbage, and egg). If you want to eat al fresco, request a table outside when booking. ⊠ *Via delle Belle Donne 16/r, near Santa Maria Novella* ☎ *055/2382609* ▤ *AE, DC, MC, V.*

Oltrarno

★ **$$–$$$** ✕ **Beccofino.** Forget that the noise level here often reaches the pitch of the Tower of Babel, and ignore the generic urban decor. Concentrate, instead, on the food, which might be the most creative and best in town. A pale-wood serpentine bar separates the ochre-walled wine bar from the green-walled restaurant. Chef Francesco Berardinelli has paid some dues in the United States, and it shows in the inventiveness of his food (such as his pairing of scallops with bitter greens), which ends up tasting wholly and wonderfully Italian. ⊠ *Piazza degli Scarlatti 1/r, Lungarno Guicciardini, Lungarno South* ☎ *055/290076* ⚄ *Reservations essential* ▤ *MC, V* ☯ *No lunch Mon.–Sat.*

$–$$ ✕ **Quattro Leoni.** The eclectic staff at this trattoria in a small piazza is an appropriate match for the diverse menu. In winter, you can sample the offerings in one of two rooms with high ceilings, and in summer you can sit outside and admire the scenery. Traditional Tuscan favorites, such as *taglierini con porcini* (long, thin, flat pasta with porcini mushrooms), are on the menu, but so, too, are less typical dishes such as the earthy cabbage salad with avocado, pine nuts, and drops of *olio di tartufo* (truffle oil). Reservations are a good idea. ⊠ *Piazza della Passera, Via dei Vellutini 1/r, near Palazzo Pitti* ☎ *055/218562* ▤ *AE, DC, MC, V* ☯ *No lunch Wed.*

¢–$ ✕ **La Casalinga.** *Casalinga* means "housewife," and this place has the nostalgic charm of a 1950s kitchen with Tuscan comfort food to match. If you eat ribollita anywhere in Florence, eat it here—it couldn't be more authentic. Mediocre paintings clutter the semi-paneled walls, tables are set close together, and the place is usually jammed. The menu is long, portions are plentiful, and service is prompt and friendly. Save room for dessert: the *sorbetto al limoncello* perfectly caps off the meal. ⊠ *Via Michelozzi 9/r, near Santo Spirito* ☎ *055/218624* ▤ *AE, DC, MC, V* ☯ *Closed Sun., 1 wk at Christmas, and 3 wks in Aug.*

¢ ✕ **Osteria Antica Mescita San Niccolò.** It's always crowded, always good, and always cheap. The osteria is next to the church of San Niccolò, and if you sit in the lower part you'll find yourself in what was once a chapel dating from the 11th century. Such subtle but dramatic background plays off nicely with the food, which is simple Tuscan at its best. The *pollo con limone* is tasty pieces of chicken in a lemon-scented broth. In winter, try the *spezzatino di cinghiale con aromi* (wild boar stew with herbs). Reservations are advised. ⊠ *Via San Niccolò 60/r, near San Niccolò* ☎ *055/2342836* ▤ *AE, MC, V* ☯ *Closed Sun. and Aug.*

San Lorenzo & Beyond

★ **$$$$** ✕ **Taverna del Bronzino.** Want to have a sophisticated meal in a 16th-century Renaissance artist's studio? There's nothing outstanding about the decor in the former studio of Santi di Tito, a student of Bronzino's,

ON THE MENU

A TYPICAL FLORENTINE MEAL starts with an antipasto of crostini (grilled bread spread with various savory toppings) or cured meats such as prosciutto crudo (ham thinly sliced) and finocchiona (salami seasoned with fennel). Primi piatti (first courses) can consist of local versions of pasta dishes available throughout Italy. Peculiar to Florence, however, are the vegetable-and-bread soups such as pappa al pomodoro (bread and tomato soup) and ribollita (minestrone with bread and beans), and, in summer, a salad called panzanella (tomatoes, onions, vinegar, oil, basil, and bread). Before they are eaten, these are often christened with un "C" d'olio, a generous C-shape drizzle of the sumptuous local olive oil.

Unparalleled among the secondi piatti (main courses) is bistecca alla fiorentina—a thick slab of local Chianina beef, often grilled over charcoal, seasoned with olive oil, salt, and pepper, and served rare. Arista (roast loin of pork seasoned with rosemary) is also a local specialty, as are many other roasted meats that pair especially well with Chianti. A secondo is usually served with a contorno (side dish) of white beans, sautéed greens, or artichokes in season, all of which can be drizzled with more of that fruity olive oil.

Desserts in Florence are more or less an afterthought. The meal often ends with a glass of vin santo (literally, "holy wine") an ochre-colored sweet dessert wine that pairs beautifully with biscotti ("twice cooked" cookies).

Those with a sense of culinary adventure should not miss the tripe sandwich. This Florentine favorite, served from stands throughout town, comes with a fragrant salsa verde (green sauce) or a piquant red hot sauce—or both.

---

save for its simple formality, with white tablecloths and place settings. Lots of classic, superb Tuscan food, however, graces the artful menu, and the presentation is often dramatic. A wine list of solid, affordable choices rounds out the menu. The service is outstanding. Reservations are advised, especially for eating at the wine cellar's only table. ⊠ *Via delle Ruote 25/r, near San Marco* ☎ *055/495220* ▤ *AE, DC, MC, V* ☉ *Closed Sun. and 3 wks in Aug.*

★ **$–$$** ✕ **Le Fonticine.** Owner Silvano Bruci is from Tuscany and his wife, Gianna, is from Emilia-Romagna, and their fine-dining oasis near the train station combines the best of two Italian cuisines. Start with the mixed-vegetable antipasto plate and then move on to any of their house-made pastas. The feathery light tortelloni *nostro modo* are stuffed with fresh ricotta and served with a tomato and cream sauce, and should not be missed. The restaurant's interior, filled with the Brucis' painting collection, provides a cheery space for this soul-satisfying food. ⊠ *Via Nazionale 79/r, near San Lorenzo* ☎ *055/282106* ▤ *AE, DC, MC, V* ☉ *Closed Sun. and Mon., Nov. 24–Jan. 5, and July 25–Aug. 25.*

★ **¢–$** ✕ **Mario.** Florentines flock to this narrow family-run trattoria near San Lorenzo to feast on Tuscan favorites served at simple tables under a wooden ceiling dating from 1536. A distinct cafeteria feel and genuine

Map labels (streets and piazzas):

V. Guelfa · V. S. Gallo · V. Cavour · V. Ricasoli · V. Pucci · V. Gino Capponi · Piazza SS. Annunziata · V. Laura · V. Colonna · V. degli Alfani · V. dei Servi · V. del Castellaccio · V. Bufalini · V. della Pergola · V. Nuova dei Caccini · Piazza del Duomo · V. delle Oche · V. d. Studio · V. dell'Oriuolo · V. S. Egidio · Borgo Pinti · V. di Fiesolana · V. dei Pepi · Mezzo · Proconsolo · Piazza San Pier Maggiore · Piazza V. Salvemini Pietrapiana · Borgo degli Albizi · V. dei · V. Matteo Palmieri · V. San Pier Maggiore · V. dell'Ulivo · V. D. Alighieri · V. dei Pandolfini · V. Ghibellina · V. della Vigna Vecchia · V. dell'Agnolo · V. dei Cimatori · della Condotta · Piazza S. Firenze · V. d. Gondi · V. d. Burella · Via Torta · V. Verrazzano · V. Ghibellina · Borgo Allegri · V. San Cristofano · za della gnoria · Borgo dei Greci · Piazza Santa Croce · V. di S. Giuseppe · V. Leoni · Via d. Corno · Via d'Acqua · Via Vinegia · Via Parlascio · Via d. Magalotti · V. dei · Neri · Via d. Rustici · V. de Benci · V. Antonio Magliabecchi · Borgo S. Croce · V. d. Vagelli · V. V. Malenchini · Lung. Diaz · Corso Tintori · V. Tripoli · Lung. d. Grazie · Ponte alle Grazie · Lung. Torrigiani · V. dei Bardi · Piazza del Mozzi · V. dei Renai · Lung. Serristori · Via V. di S. Niccolò · V. S. Miniato · Via di Belvedere · V. Giorgio · martelli · azo · peziali · reccia · hibustieri

0 — 440 yards
0 — 400 meters

Restaurants ▼

Hotels ▼

Florentine hospitality prevail: you'll be seated wherever there's room, which often means with strangers. Yes, there's a bit of extra oil in most dishes, which imparts calories as well as taste, but aren't you on vacation in Italy? Worth the splurge is *riso al ragù* (rice with ground beef and tomatoes). ⊠ *Via Rosina 2/r, corner of Piazza del Mercato Centrale, near San Lorenzo* ☎ *055/218550* ⌲ *Reservations not accepted* ▭ *No credit cards* ⊘ *Closed Sun. and Aug. No dinner.*

Santa Maria Novella to the Arno

$$–$$$ ✕ **Cantinetta Antinori.** After a rough morning of shopping on Via Tornabuoni, stop for lunch in this 15th-century palazzo in the company of Florentine ladies (and men) who lunch and come to see and be seen. The panache of the food matches its clientele: expect treats such as *tramezzino con pane di campagna al tartufo* (country pâté with truffles served on bread) and the *insalata di gamberoni e gamberetti con carciofi freschi* (crayfish and prawn salad with shaved raw artichokes). ⊠ *Piazza Antinori 3, near Santa Maria Novella* ☎ *055/292234* ▭ *AE, DC, MC, V* ⊘ *Closed weekends, 20 days in Aug., and Dec. 25–Jan. 6.*

Santa Croce

$$$$ ✕ **Alle Murate.** Creative versions of classic Tuscan dishes are served in this sleek and sophisticated spot. The *involtini di vitella ripieni di melanzane coi fagiolini al dente* (veal rolls stuffed with eggplant garnished with green beans) is remarkably light and flavorful. The main dining room has a rich, uncluttered look, with warm wood floors and paneling and soft lights. In a smaller adjacent room called the *vineria* you get the same splendid service but substantially reduced prices. There's no middle ground with the wine list—there's only a smattering of inexpensive bottles before it soars to exalted heights. ⊠ *Via Ghibellina 52/r, near Santa Croce* ☎ *055/240618* ▭ *AE, DC, MC, V* ⊘ *Closed Mon. No lunch.*

$$$$ ✕ **Cibrèo.** The food at this upscale trattoria is fantastic, from the creamy
Fodor'sChoice crostini *di fegatini* (a savory chicken-liver spread) to the melt-in-your-
★ mouth desserts. If you thought you'd never try tripe—let alone like it—this is the place to lay any doubts to rest: the *trippa in insalata* (cold tripe salad) with parsley and garlic is an epiphany. Construe chef Fabio Picchi's unsolicited advice as a sign of his enthusiasm for cooking; it's warranted, as the food is among the best and most creative in town. Around the corner is Cibreino, Cibrèo's budget version, with a shorter menu and a no-reservations policy. ⊠ *Via A. del Verrocchio 8/r, near Santa Croce* ☎ *055/2341100* ⌲ *Reservations essential* ▭ *AE, DC, MC, V* ⊘ *Closed Sun. and Mon., July 25–Sept. 5, and Dec. 31–Jan. 7.*

$$$$ ✕ **Enoteca Pinchiorri.** A sumptuous Renaissance palace with high, frescoed ceilings and bouquets in silver vases provides the backdrop for this restaurant, one of the most expensive in Italy. Some consider it one of the best, and others consider it a non-Italian rip-off, as the kitchen is presided over by a Frenchwoman with sophisticated, yet internationalist, leanings. Prices are high and portions are small; the vast holdings of the wine cellar, as well as stellar service, dull the pain, however, when the bill is presented. Interesting pasta combinations such as the *ignudi*—

ricotta-and-spinach dumplings with a lobster-and-coxcomb fricassee—
are always on the menu. ✉ *Via Ghibellina 87, near Santa Croce* ☎ *055/
242777* ⌚ *Reservations essential* ▭ *AE, MC, V* ⊘ *Closed Sun. and Mon.,
and Aug. No lunch Tues. or Wed.*

$$$ ✕ **Cantina Barbagianni.** *"Diverso dal solito"* (different from the usual)
is the leitmotif here, and this attitude is reflected in the funky furnish-
ings (lots of strategically placed drapery) and avant-garde paintings on
the walls. Cristina, the proprietor, presides over it all with great ease.
The regularly changing menu strays far from the typical Tuscan path:
l'anatra con mirtillo (duck with blueberries) is a rare thing in these parts,
and the chef is to be commended for his inventiveness. The *risotto al
carciofi con scamorza* (artichoke risotto with smoked cheese) is fragrant
and tasty. ✉ *Via Sant'Egidio 13, near Santa Croce* ☎ *055/248–0508*
▭ *AE, DC, MC, V* ⊘ *Closed Sun.*

★ **$$$** ✕ **La Giostra.** The clubby La Giostra, which means "carousel" in Ital-
ian, is owned and run by Prince Dimitri Kunz d'Asburgo Lorena, and
his way with mushrooms is as remarkable as his charm. The unusually
good pastas may require explanation from Soldano, one of the prince's
good-looking twin sons. In perfect English he'll describe a favorite dish,
taglierini con tartufo bianco, a decadently rich pasta with white truffles. Leave room for dessert: this might be the only show in town with
a sublime tiramisu *and* a wonderfully gooey Sacher torte. ✉ *Borgo Pinti
12/r, near Santa Croce* ☎ *055/241341* ▭ *AE, DC, MC, V.*

$–$$ ✕ **Acquacotta.** With its closely spaced, red-checked tablecloths, you could-
n't get any more "Italian" than this. You almost expect the chef to come
out of the kitchen with an accordion and serenade you while you eat.
Not to worry: service is offhand (sometimes dismissive), and the chef has
better things to do than break into song. The highlight of the menu, with
the usual list of grilled meats and pasta starters, is the *acquacotta*, literally "cooked water"—a favorite from southern Tuscany that rarely appears on Florentine menus. It's a vegetable-based soup with mushrooms
and onions that's topped with a poached egg. ✉ *Via dei Pilastri 51/r, near
Santa Croce* ☎ *055/242907* ▭ *MC, V* ⊘ *Closed Sun. and Aug.*

★ **$–$$** ✕ **Osteria de'Benci.** A few minutes from Santa Croce, this charming os-
teria serves some of the most eclectic food in Florence. Try the spaghetti
degli eretici (in tomato sauce with fresh herbs). The grilled meats are
justifiably famous; the *carbonata* is a succulent piece of grilled beef served
rare. When it's warm, you can dine outside with a view of the 13th-cen-
tury tower belonging to the prestigious Alberti family. Right next door
is Osteria de'Benci Caffè (¢–$), serving selections from the menu from
8 AM to midnight. ✉ *Via de'Benci 11-13/r, near Santa Croce* ☎ *055/
2344923* ▭ *AE, DC, MC, V* ⊘ *Closed Sun.*

$–$$ ✕ **Pallottino.** With its tiled floor, photograph-filled walls, and wooden
tables, Pallottino is the quintessential Tuscan trattoria, with hearty,
heartwarming classics such as pappa al pomodoro and *peposa alla
toscana* (a beef stew laced with black pepper). The menu changes frequently to reflect what's seasonal; the staff is friendly, as are the diners,
who often share a table and, eventually, conversation. ✉ *Via Isola delle
Stinche 1/r, near Santa Croce* ☎ *055/289573* ▭ *AE, DC, MC, V*
⊘ *Closed Mon. and 2–3 wks in Aug.*

¢ ✕ **da Rocco.** These are some of the hottest tables (booths, actually) in one of Florence's biggest markets. You can get lunch to go, or cram yourself into one of the booths, swill from the straw-cloaked flask (wine here is *da consumo*—which means they charge you for how much you drink). Food is abundant, Tuscan, and fast. Locals pack it in at lunchtime; the menu changes daily, and the prices are just right. ⊠ *In the Mercato Sant'Ambrogio, Piazza Ghiberti, near Santa Croce* ☎ *No phone* ⊟ *No credit cards* ⊘ *Closed Sun. No dinner.*

Pizzerias

The *pizziauoli* (pizza-makers) successfully merge the Roman (thin) crust with the Neapolitan (thick) crust at **Le Campane** (⊠ Borgo La Croce 85-87/r, near Santa Croce ☎ 055/2341101). **Baldovino** (⊠ Via San Giuseppe 22/r, near Santa Croce ☎ 055/241773) makes pizzas to delight the kids and more sophisticated stuff to satisfy the parents. In the Oltrarno, try **Borgo Antico** (⊠ Piazza S. Spirito 6/r, near San Spirito/San Frediano ☎ 055/210437), which serves pizza and other trattoria fare.

Enoteche

Most wine bars also serve light fare, making them yet another option for lunch or dinner. Tranquil **Coquinarius** (⊠ Via delle Oche 15/r, near Duomo ☎ 055/2302153) provides a great place to rest one's soul one block away from the Duomo (except on Sunday, when it's closed). **Fuori Porta** (⊠ Via Monte alle Croci 10/r, near San Niccolò ☎ 055/2342483), one of the oldest and best wine bars in Florence, has cured meats and cheeses, as well as daily specials such as a sublime spaghetti al curry. It's closed Sunday. **Frescobaldi Wine Bar** (⊠ Via de'Magazzini 2-4/r, near Piazza della Signoria ☎ 055/284724) sells wine by the glass at its small wine bar and terrific plates of pasta in its romantic restaurant. **Le Volpi e l'Uva** (⊠ Piazza de'Rossi 1, near Palazzo Pitti ☎ 055/2398132), just off Piazza Santa Trinita, is an oenophile's dream: the well-informed barmen pour significant wines by the glass and serve equally impressive cheeses and other savory delights.

Cafés

Cafés in Italy serve not only coffee concoctions and pastries but also drinks and panini; some offer light lunches as well. They open early in the morning and usually close around 8 PM. The always-crowded **Caffè Giacosa/Roberto Cavalli** (⊠ Via della Spada 10 near Santa Maria Novella ☎ 055/2776328), joined at the hip with a Florentine fashion designer's shop, is open for breakfast, lunch, tea, and cocktails. All bars in Italy ought to be like **Caffètteria Piansa** (⊠ Borgo Pinti 18/r, near Santa Croce ☎ 055/2342362). It's rare that one can pull off a great breakfast and lunch, plus fine drinks at night. **Gran Caffè** (⊠ Piazza San Marco 11/r ☎ 055/215833) is down the street from the Accademia, so it's a perfect stop for a marvelous *panino* (sandwich) or sweet while raving about the majesty of Michelangelo's *David*. Classy **Procacci** (⊠ Via Tornabuoni 64/r, near Santa Maria Novella ☎ 055/211656) is a Florentine institution dating back to 1885; try one of the panini tartufati and swish it down with a glass of

Prosecco. It's closed Sunday and Monday. Perhaps the best spot for people-watching is **Rivoire** (✉ Via Vacchereccia 4/r, Piazza della Signoria ☎ 055/214412). Stellar service, light snacks, and terrific aperitivi are the norm. Think twice, however, before ordering more substantial fare.

Gelaterie & Pasticcerie

The *pasticceria* (bakery) **Dolci e Dolcezze** (✉ Piazza C. Beccaria 8/r, near Sant'Ambrogio ☎ 055/2345458), on colorful Borgo La Croce, probably has the prettiest and tastiest cakes, sweets, and tarts in town. It's closed Monday. Most people consider **Vivoli** (✉ Via Isola delle Stinche 7/r, near Santa Croce ☎ 055/292334) the best gelateria in town. **Vestri** (✉ Borgo Albizi 11/r, near Santa Croce ☎ 055/2340374) is devoted to chocolate in all its guises. The small but sublime selection of chocolate-based gelati includes one with hot peppers.

Salumerie

Salumerie are food shops specializing in fresh meats and cheeses; they're great for picking up a picnic lunch or assembling dinner. Most are closed Monday morning. **Antico Salumificio Anzuini-Massi** (✉ Via de' Neri 84/r, near Santa Croce ☎ 055/294 901) shrink-wraps their own pork products, making it a snap to take home some *salame di cinghiale* (wild boar salami). If you find yourself in the Oltrarno and hungry for lunch or a snack, drop into **Azzarri Delicatesse** (✉ Borgo S. Jacopo 27b/cr, near Santo Spirito ☎ 055/2381714) for a sandwich, meat for the grill, wine, or French cheeses. **Conti** (✉ Mercato Centrale, enter at Via Signa, near San Lorenzo ☎ 055/2398501), closed Sunday, sells top-quality wines, olive oils, and dried fruits; they'll shrink-wrap the highest-quality dried porcini for traveling. Looking for some cheddar cheese to pile in your panino? **Pegna** (✉ Via dello Studio 8, near Duomo ☎ 055/282701)— closed Saturday afternoon in July and August, Wednesday afternoon the rest of the year, and Sunday year-round—has been selling both Italian and non-Italian food since 1860. **Perini** (✉ Mercato Centrale, enter at Via dell'Aretino, near San Lorenzo ☎ 055/2398306), closed Sunday, sells everything from prosciutto and mixed meats to sauces for pasta and a wide assortment of antipasti. They're generous with their free samples. At **Salumeria Verdi** (✉ Via Verdi 36/r, near Santa Croce ☎ 055/244517), options include well-prepared sandwiches and everything to assemble a dinner. You can eat in or take out. It's closed Sunday.

WHERE TO STAY

No stranger to visitors, Florence has hotels for all budgets throughout the city; for instance, you can find both budget and luxury hotels in the centro storico and along the Arno. Whether you are in a five-star hotel or a more modest establishment, you may have one of the greatest pleasures of all: a room with a view. Florence has so many famous landmarks that it's not hard to find lodgings with a panoramic vista. And the equivalent of the genteel pensioni of yesteryear still exists, with the benefit of modern plumbing.

Florence's importance not only as a tourist city but as a convention center and site of the Pitti fashion collections throughout the year means a high demand for rooms. Except in winter, reservations are a must. If you find yourself in Florence with no reservations, go to **Consorzio ITA** (⊠ Stazione Centrale, near Santa Maria Novella ☎ 055/282893). You must go there in person to make a booking.

WHAT IT COSTS In euros				
$$$$	**$$$**	**$$**	**$**	**¢**
FOR 2 PEOPLE over €290	€210–€290	€140–€210	€80–€140	under €80

Prices are for two people in a standard double room in high season.

Centro Storico

$$$$ 🏨 **Hotel Savoy.** From the outside, it looks very much like the turn-of-the-19th-century building that it is. Inside, sleek minimalism and up-to-the-minute amenities prevail. Sitting rooms have a funky edge, their cream-color walls dotted with contemporary prints. Rooms are decorated in muted colors, with streamlined furniture and soaring ceilings; many have views of the Duomo's cupola or the Piazza della Repubblica. The deep marble tubs might be reason enough to stay here—but you'll also appreciate the efficient and courteous staff. ⊠ *Piazza della Repubblica 7, 50123* ☎ *055/27351* 🖷 *055/2735888* ⊕ *www.roccofortehotels.com* ⌨ *98 rooms, 9 suites* 🛆 *Restaurant, room service, in-room data ports, in-room fax, in-room safes, minibars, cable TV with movies and video games, in-room VCRs, exercise equipment, bar, children's programs (ages 0–12), dry cleaning, laundry service, concierge, Internet, business services, meeting rooms, parking (fee), no-smoking rooms* ⊟ *AE, DC, MC, V* ❙❙❙ *EP.*

$$$ 🏨 **Hermitage.** A stone's throw from the Ponte Vecchio, this is a fine little hotel with an enviable location. All rooms are decorated differently with lively wallpaper; some have views of Palazzo Vecchio and others of the Arno. The rooftop terrace, where you can have breakfast or an aperitivo, is decked with flowers. The lobby suggests a friend's living room—its warm yellow walls are welcoming. Double glazing and air-conditioning help keep street noise at bay. (The hotel has an elevator at the top of a short flight of stairs from the street.) ⊠ *Vicolo Marzio 1, Piazza del Pesce, Ponte Vecchio, near Piazza della Signoria 50122* ☎ *055/287216* 🖷 *055/212208* ⊕ *www.hermitagehotel.com* ⌨ *27 rooms, 1 suite* 🛆 *In-room safes, cable TV, babysitting, laundry service, parking (fee), some pets allowed* ⊟ *MC, V* ❙❙❙ *BP.*

$$$ 🏨 **Hotel Benivieni.** This quiet, tranquil former 15th-century palace is one block away from the Duomo. Rooms are spacious, with high ceilings, hardwood floors, and sweeping draperies. A winter garden provides a wonderful place to while away some time. The affable Caldana family, wholly fluent in English, ably staffs the front desk. ⊠ *Via delle Oche 5, near Duomo, 50122* ☎ *055/2382133* 🖷 *055/2398248* ⊕ *www.hotelbenivieni.it* ⌨ *15 rooms* 🛆 *In-room safes, cable TV, babysitting, dry cleaning, laundry service, Internet, parking (fee), some pets allowed, no-smoking rooms* ⊟ *AE, DC, MC, V* ❙❙❙ *BP.*

$$ 🏨 **Torre Guelfa.** Enter this hidden hotel through an immense wooden door on a narrow street, and continue through an iron gate and up a few steps to an elevator that will take you to the third floor. A few more steps and you're in a 13th-century Florentine *torre* (tower). The Torre Guelfa once protected the fabulously wealthy Acciaiuoli family; now it's one of the best-located small hotels in Florence. Each guest room is different, some with canopied beds, some with balconies. Those on a budget might want to consider one of the six less-expensive rooms on the second floor, which are comparable to the rest of the rooms except that they have no TVs. ✉ *Borgo Santi Apostoli 8, near Santa Maria Novella, 50123* 🕾 *055/2396338* 🖷 *055/2398577* 🛏 *24 rooms, 2 suites* ⚲ *Some in-room safes, babysitting, dry cleaning, laundry service, Internet, parking (fee), some pets allowed, no-smoking rooms; no TV in some rooms* 🚪 *AE, MC, V* ⦿❘ *BP.*

$–$$ 🏨 **Alessandra.** The location a block from the Ponte Vecchio, and the clean, ample rooms make this a good choice. The building, known as the Palazzo Roselli del Turco, was designed in 1507 by Baccio d'Agnolo, a contemporary of Michelangelo's. Though little remains of the original design save for the high wood ceilings, there's still an aura of grandeur. Several of the rooms have views of the Arno, and the sole suite is spacious and a steal for this category. Friendly hosts Anna and Andrea Gennarini speak fluent English. ✉ *Borgo Santi Apostoli 17, near Santa Maria Novella 50123* 🕾 *055/283438* 🖷 *055/210619* ⊕ *www.hotelalessandra. com* 🛏 *26 rooms, 19 with bath, 1 suite, 1 apartment* ⚲ *In-room safes, some minibars, cable TV, dry cleaning, laundry service, Internet (fee), parking (fee), no-smoking rooms* 🚪 *AE, MC, V* ⦿ *Closed Dec. 10–26* ⦿❘ *BP.*

$ 🏨 **Albergo Firenze.** A block from the Duomo, this hotel is in one of the oldest piazzas in Florence. Though the reception area and hallways have all the charm of a college dormitory, the similarity ends upon entering the spotlessly clean rooms. For the location, the place is a great bargain; its rooms (including a good number of triples and quadruples) make this an inviting place for families and travelers on a budget. ✉ *Piazza Donati 4, near Duomo, 50122* 🕾 *055/214203* 🖷 *055/ 212370* ⊕ *www.hotelfirenze-fi.it* 🛏 *58 rooms* ⚲ *Parking (fee)* 🚪 *No credit cards* ⦿❘ *BP.*

The Oltrarno

$$$$ 🏨 **Lungarno.** Many rooms and suites here have private terraces that jut out right over the Arno, granting views of the Palazzo Vecchio and Duomo opposite. Four suites in a 13th-century tower preserve details like exposed stone walls and old archways and look out onto a little square with a medieval tower covered in jasmine. The very chic decor approximates a breezily elegant home, with lots of crisp white fabrics with blue trim. A wall of windows and a sea of white couches make the lobby bar one of the nicest places in the city to stop for a drink. Inquire about the Lungarno Suites, across the river; they include kitchens, making them attractive if you're planning a longer stay. ✉ *Borgo San Jacopo 14, Lungarno South, 50125* 🕾 *055/27261* 🖷 *055/268437* ⊕ *www. lungarnohotels.com* 🛏 *60 rooms, 13 suites* ⚲ *Restaurant, in-room*

*data ports, in-room fax, cable TV with movies, bar, babysitting, dry clean-
ing, laundry service, concierge, Internet, meeting rooms, parking (fee),
no-smoking rooms* ☰ *AE, DC, MC, V* ❍❘ *BP.*

$$$$ ⌷ **Palazzo Magnani Feroni.** The perfect place to play the part of a Florentine aristocrat is this 16th-century palazzo, which despite its massive halls and sweeping staircase could almost feel like home. Suites include
large sitting rooms and bedrooms, all decorated with luxurious fabrics,
chandeliers, and Renaissance-inspired furniture. The rooftop terrace, complete with bar, has citywide views that startle. Though it's only a five-
minute walk from the Ponte Vecchio, the street is surprisingly quiet.
✉ *Borgo San Frediano 5, near Santo Spirito, 50124* ☎ *055/2399544*
📠 *055/2608908* ⊕ *www.florencepalace.com* ⟋ *11 suites* ♢ *Room
service, in-room data ports, in-room safes, minibar, cable TV, exercise
equipment, billiards, bar, dry cleaning, laundry service, parking (fee),
no-smoking rooms* ☰ *AE, DC, MC, V* ❍❘ *BP.*

$ ⌷ **Albergo La Scaletta.** For a tremendous view of the Boboli Garden, look
no farther than this exquisite pensione run by a mother-and-son team.
Near the Ponte Vecchio and Palazzo Pitti, it has simply furnished yet
rather large rooms and a sunny breakfast room. In warm weather two
flower-bedecked terraces are open, one with a stunning 360-degree
view of Florence. ✉ *Via Guicciardini 13, near Palazzo Pitti, 50125* ☎ *055/
283028* 📠 *055/289562* ⊕ *www.lascaletta.com* ⟋ *11 rooms, 10 with
bath* ♢ *Parking (fee), some pets allowed; no TV in some rooms* ☰ *MC,
V* ❍❘ *BP.*

Piazza San Marco & Beyond

$$ ⌷ **Loggiato dei Serviti.** Though this hotel was not designed by Brunelleschi,
Florence's architectural genius, it might as well have been. A mirror image
of the architect's famous Spedale degli Innocenti across the way, the Log-
giato is tucked away on one of the city's loveliest squares. Occupying
a 16th-century former convent, the building was once an inn for trav-
eling priests. Vaulted ceilings, tasteful furnishings (some antique), canopy
beds, and rich fabrics make this spare Renaissance building with mod-
ern comforts a find. ✉ *Piazza Santissima Annunziata 3, 50122* ☎ *055/
289592* 📠 *055/289595* ⊕ *www.loggiatodeiservitihotel.it* ⟋ *29 rooms*
♢ *In-room data ports, in-room safes, minibars, cable TV, bar, babysit-
ting, dry cleaning, laundry service, parking (fee), some pets allowed* ☰ *AE,
DC, MC, V* ❍❘ *BP.*

$$ ⌷ **Morandi alla Crocetta.** Near Piazza Santissima Annunziata, this is a
Fodor's Choice charming and distinguished residence in which you're made to feel like
★ privileged friends of the family. The former convent is close to the sights
but very quiet, and is furnished comfortably in the classic style of a gracious Florentine home. One room retains original 17th-century fresco
fragments, and two others have small private terraces. The Morandi is
not only an exceptional hotel but also a good value. It's very small, so
try to book well in advance. ✉ *Via Laura 50, near Santissima Annunziata, 50121* ☎ *055/2344747* 📠 *055/2480954* ⊕ *www.hotelmorandi.
it* ⟋ *10 rooms* ♢ *In-room data ports, in-room safes, minibars, cable
TV, dry cleaning, laundry service, concierge, Internet, parking (fee), some
pets allowed* ☰ *AE, DC, MC, V* ❍❘ *EP.*

¢ 🔲 **Residenza Johanna I.** Savvy travelers and those on a budget should look no farther, as this *residenza* (residence) is a tremendous value for quality and location. Though it's very much in the centro storico, the place is rather homey: indeed, you'll be given a large set of keys to let you into the building, as the staff goes home at 7 PM. Rooms have high ceilings and are simply decorated in pale pastel floral prints; morning tea and coffee (but no breakfast) are taken in one's room. ⊠ *Via Bonifacio Lupi 14, near San Marco, 50129* 🕾 *055/481896* 🖷 *055/482721* ⊕ *www.johanna.it* 🛏 *11 rooms* ⚲ *Fans, parking (fee); no a/c, no room phones, no room TVs* 🖃 *No credit cards* ⃝ *EP.*

FodorśChoice
★

Santa Croce

$$$–$$$$ 🔲 **J&J.** On a quiet street within walking distance of the sights, this unusual hotel is a converted 16th-century convent. Its large, suitelike rooms are ideal for honeymooners, families, and small groups of friends. Some rooms are on two levels, and many are imaginatively arranged around a central courtyard. Some bathrooms have been refitted with pale travertine tiles, providing a pleasing ultramodern juxtaposition to the rest of the place. The smaller rooms are more intimate, some opening onto a little shared courtyard. The gracious owners enjoy chatting in the light and airy lounge; breakfast is served in a glassed-in Renaissance loggia or in the central courtyard. ⊠ *Via di Mezzo 20, near Santa Croce, 50121* 🕾 *055/26312* 🖷 *055/240282* ⊕ *www.jandjhotel.com* 🛏 *19 rooms, 7 suites* ⚲ *In-room data ports, cable TV, bar, babysitting, dry cleaning, laundry service, parking (fee), no-smoking rooms* 🖃 *AE, DC, MC, V* ⃝ *BP.*

★ **$$$–$$$$** 🔲 **Monna Lisa.** Housed in a 15th-century palazzo, with parts of the building dating from the 13th century, this hotel retains some of its original wood-coffered ceilings from the 1500s, as well as its original marble staircase. Though some rooms are small, they are tastefully decorated, each with different floral wallpaper. The public rooms retain a 19th-century aura, and the intimate bar, with its red velveteen wallpaper, is a good place to unwind. ⊠ *Borgo Pinti 27, near Santa Croce, 50121* 🕾 *055/2479751* 🖷 *055/2479755* ⊕ *www.monnalisa.it* 🛏 *45 rooms* ⚲ *In-room safes, minibars, cable TV, bar, babysitting, dry cleaning, laundry service, concierge, parking (fee), some pets allowed, no-smoking rooms* 🖃 *AE, DC, MC, V* ⃝ *BP.*

¢ 🔲 **Albergo Losanna.** Most major sights are within walking distance of this tiny pensione just within the Viale, the edge of the city center. Though dated and a little worn around the edges, the property is impeccably clean and the rooms have high ceilings; the mother and son who run the place are enthusiastic and cordial. Try to get a room facing away from the street; you won't have a view but you will get a quiet night's sleep. ⊠ *Via V. Alfieri 9, near Santa Croce, 50121* 🕾🖷 *055/245840* ⊕ *www.albergolosanna.com* 🛏 *8 rooms, 3 with bath* ⚲ *Parking (fee); no a/c in some rooms, no room TVs* 🖃 *MC, V* ⃝ *BP.*

¢ 🔲 **Istituto Oblate dell'Assunzione.** Twelve nuns run this perfectly situated convent just minutes from the Duomo. Rooms are spotlessly clean and simple; some of them offer views of the cupola, and others look out onto a carefully tended garden where guests are encouraged to relax.

Several rooms have three and four beds, making them well suited for families. Curfew is at 11:30 PM, and those of you who want to attend Mass can do so every morning at 7:30. The nuns will provide half or full pension for groups of 10 or more. ⊠ *Borgo Pinti 15* ☏ *055/ 2480582* 🖷 *055/2346291* 📟 *50 rooms, 25 with bath* ⚓ *Parking (fee), no-smoking rooms; no a/c in some rooms, no room phones, no room TVs* ▭ *No credit cards* ⊚ *EP.*

Santa Maria Novella to the Arno

$$$$ ⊞ **Grand.** Long the mainstay of sophisticated, moneyed travelers, this Florentine classic provides all the luxurious amenities. Rooms are decorated in either Renaissance or Empire style; the former have rich, deeply hued damask brocades crisp prints and patterned fabric offsetting white walls. The overall effect is sumptuous, and the views—either of the Arno or overlooking a small rectangular courtyard lined with potted orange trees—are equally impressive. A summer 2003 refurbishment has brought a lift to public rooms, which dazzle with their dark-wood fittings and shiny white marble. Il Fiorino, the sleek restaurant, has a cutting-edge menu. ⊠ *Piazza Ognissanti 1, Lungarno North, 50123* ☏ *055/288781* 🖷 *055/217400* ⊕ *www.starwood.com* 📟 *107 rooms* ⚓ *Restaurant, room service, in-room data ports, in-room safes, minibars, cable TV with movies, gym, bar, piano bar, babysitting, dry cleaning, laundry service, concierge, Internet, business services, meeting rooms, parking (fee), some pets allowed, no-smoking rooms* ▭ *AE, DC, MC, V* ⊚ *EP.*

★ **$$$** ⊞ **Beacci Tornabuoni.** Florentine pensioni do not come any more classic than this. In a 14th-century palazzo, it has old-fashioned style and enough modern comfort to keep you happy. The sitting room has a large fireplace, the terrace has a tremendous view of some major Florentine monuments, and the wallpapered rooms are inviting. On Monday, Wednesday, and Friday nights from May through October, the dining room opens, serving Tuscan specialties. ⊠ *Via Tornabuoni 3, near Santa Maria Novella 50123* ☏ *055/212645* 🖷 *055/283594* ⊕ *www. bthotel.it* 📟 *28 rooms* ⚓ *Restaurant, minibars, cable TV, bar, babysitting, dry cleaning, laundry service, Internet, parking (fee), some pets allowed* ▭ *AE, DC, MC, V* ⊚ *BP.*

$$ ⊞ **Villa Azalee.** Five minutes on foot from the train station and steps from the Fortezza da Basso (site of the Pitti fashion shows), this 19th-century villa deftly recalls its previous incarnation as a private residence. Furniture has quilted, floral-print slipcovers, and the floors are scattered with throw rugs. Many of the rooms have views of the hotel's garden, and some have private terraces. ⊠ *Viale Fratelli Rosselli 44, near Santa Maria Novella 50123* ☏ *055/214242* 🖷 *055/268264* ⊕ *www.villa-azalee.it* 📟 *25 rooms* ⚓ *Minibars, cable TV, bicycles, bar, dry cleaning, laundry service, parking (fee), some pets allowed* ▭ *AE, DC, MC, V* ⊚ *BP.*

★ **$** ⊞ **Bellettini.** You're in good hands at this small hotel on three floors run by sisters Marzia and Gina Naldini along with their husbands. Public rooms are simple but comfortable; the good-size guest rooms have Venetian or Tuscan provincial decor; bathrooms are bright and modern. The top floor has two rooms with a view, and a handful of triples and quadruples make this the perfect place for families or friends traveling together. There's an ample buffet breakfast, including tasty home-made cakes. ☒ *Via dei Conti 7, near Santa Maria Novella, 50123* ☏ *055/213561* 🖷 *055/283551* ⊕ *www.hotelbellettini.com* ⟿ *28 rooms* ⚙ *In-room safes, minibars, cable TV, bar, Internet, parking (fee), some pets allowed* ⊟ *AE, DC, MC, V* ❾⊙❾ *BP.*

$ 🏨 **Nuova Italia.** Near the train station and within walking distance of the sights, this hotel is run by a genial English-speaking family. Its homey rooms are clean and simply furnished. Air-conditioning and triple-glazed windows ensure restful nights. Some rooms can accommodate extra beds. ☒ *Via Faenza 26, near Santa Maria Novella, 50123* ☏ *055/268430* 🖷 *055/210941* ⊕ *www.hotelnuovaitalia.com* ⟿ *20 rooms* ⚙ *Cable TV, parking (fee), some pets allowed* ⊟ *AE, MC, V* ❾⊙❾ *BP.*

¢–$ 🏨 **Pensione Ferretti.** Minutes away from Piazza Santa Maria Novella, this pensione has views onto the tiny piazza containing the Croce al Trebbio, as well as easy access to the historic center. English-speaking owner Luciano Michel and his South African–born wife, Sue, do just about anything to make you feel at home (including providing 24-hour free Internet access). Ceiling fans make warmer months more bearable. Though it's housed in a 16th-century palazzo, accommodations are simple and no-frills. ☒ *Via delle Belle Donne 17, near Santa Maria Novella, 50123* ☏ *055/2381328* 🖷 *055/219288* ⊕ *www.emmeti.it/Hferretti* ⟿ *16 rooms, 6 with bath; 1 apartment* ⚙ *Fans, Internet, parking (fee), some pets allowed; no a/c, no room TVs* ⊟ *AE, DC, MC, V* ❾⊙❾ *BP.*

Outside the City

$$–$$$ 🏨 **Relais Villa l'Olmo.** Alberto and Claudia Giannotti have turned a former 16th-century country villa into an elegantly comfortable agriturismo just 20 minutes south from the center of Florence. If you're looking for a country experience but crave easy access to the city, this place just outside the small town of Impruneta does the trick. Many of the apartments look out over a gently terraced field of olive trees. (The estate produces top-notch olive oil, as well as some respectable wine.) The cheerfully decorated apartments are suitable for couples; some adjoin together, making them good options for families or groups. Unlike at many agriturismi, there's no minimum stay during high season here. ☒ *Via Impruneta 19, 50023 Impruneta* ☏ *055/2311311* 🖷 *055/2311313* ⊕ *www.relaisfarmholiday.it* ⟿ *8 apartments, 1 farmhouse, 2 cottages* ⚙ *Picnic area, BBQs, a/c (fee), fans, in-room safes, kitchens, refrigerators, cable TV with movies, golf privileges, 3 pools, massage, mountain bikes, babysitting, dry cleaning, laundry facilities, laundry service, Internet, free parking, some pets allowed, no-smoking rooms* ⊟ *AE, DC, MC, V* ❾⊙❾ *EP.*

NIGHTLIFE & THE ARTS

The Arts

Florence is justifiably famous for its musical offerings. Its annual Maggio Musicale attracts the best international talent; theaters also host visiting American rock stars and cabaret performers. Major traveling art exhibitions are mounted at Palazzo Strozzi and Forte Belvedere throughout the year.

Film

You can find movie listings in *La Nazione,* the daily Florentine newspaper. Note that most American films are dubbed into Italian rather than subtitled. The **Odeon** (✉ Piazza Strozzi, near Piazza della Repubblica ☎ 055/214068) shows first-run English-language films on Monday, Tuesday, and Thursday at its magnificent art deco theater. The **Fulgor** (✉ Via Maso Finiguerra 22/r, Lungarno North ☎ 055/238 1881) screens films in English on Thursday.

Music

The **Maggio Musicale Fiorentina,** a series of internationally acclaimed concerts and recitals, is held in the **Teatro Comunale** (✉ Corso Italia 16, Lungarno North ☎ 055/211158 ⊕ www.maggiofiorentina.com). Tickets can be obtained directly at the **box office** (✉ Via Alamanni 39 ☎ 055/210804) or by **phone** (☎ 800/112211) within Italy from late April through June. Other events—opera, ballet, and additional concerts—occur regularly throughout the year at different venues in town. November to June is the concert season of the **Orchestra della Toscana** (✉ Via Ghibellina 101, near Santa Croce ☎ 055/210804). **Amici della Musica** (⊕ www.amicimusica.fi.it) organizes concerts at the **Teatro della Pergola** (✉ Via della Pergola 18/32, box office Via Alamanni 39, near Santissima Annunziata ☎ 055/210804 ⊕ www.pergola.firenze.it).

Opera

Operas are performed in the **Teatro Comunale** (✉ Corso Italia 12, Lungarno North ☎ 055/211158) from September through December.

Nightlife

Florentines are rather proud of their nightlife options. Most bars have some sort of happy hour, which usually lasts for many hours, often accompanied by substantial snacks. Dance clubs typically don't open until very late in the evening and don't get crowded until 1 or 2 in the morning. Cover charges are steep, but it's fairly easy to find free passes in trendier bars around town.

Bars

For a swanky experience lubricated with trademark Bellinis and fine martinis, head to **Harry's Bar** (✉ Lungarno Vespucci 22/r, Lungarno North ☎ 055/2396700). **Rex** (✉ Via Fiesolana 23–25/r, near Santa Croce ☎ 055/2480331) attracts a trendy, artsy clientele. From June to September, **Via di Fuga** (✉ Via Ghibellina, near Santa Croce ☎ No phone) is one of the coolest spots to be; once the courtyard of Le Murate, a former Renaissance convent and 19th-century prison, it hosts big bands, performance art, movies, and more. **Zoe** (✉ Via dei Renai 13/r, near San Niccolò ☎ 055/243111) calls itself a *caffetteria,* and although coffee may indeed be served, twentysomething Florentines flock here for the fine (and expensive) cocktails. **Negroni** (✉ Via dei Renai 17/r, near San Niccolò ☎ 055/243647) teems with well-dressed young Florentines at happy hour. **Capocaccia** (✉ Lungarno Corsini 12-14/r, Lungarno North

☎ 055/210751) is relatively calm at lunch and aperitivo time, but at night the crowds flow out of the bar and onto the street. **Sant'Ambrogio Caffè** (✉ Piazza Sant'Ambrogio 7–8/r, near Santa Croce ☎ 055/241035) has outdoor summer seating with a view of an 11th-century church (Sant'Ambrogio) directly across the street.

Zona 15 (✉ Via del Castellaccia 53-55/r [Piazza Brunelleschi], Duomo ☎ 055/211678) is coolly chic with its pale interior, blond woodwork, and metallic surfaces. Lunch, dinner, cocktails, and live music are on offer for Florentine cognoscenti and others. The oh-so-cool—bordering on pretentious—vibe at **La Dolce Vita** (✉ Piazza del Carmine 6/r, near Santo Spirito ☎ 055/284595) attracts Florentines and the occasional visiting American movie star. If you want to have a light lunch, a sparkling aperitivo, or simply check your e-mail, stop in at the **Astor** (✉ Piazza del Duomo 20/r, near Duomo ☎ 055/2399000). It's open from early in the morning until late at night.

Nightclubs
Most clubs are closed either Sunday or Monday. **Yab** (✉ Via Sassetti 5/r, near Piazza della Repubblica ☎ 055/215160) is one of the largest clubs; it attracts a young clientele. Young, up-to-the-minute Florentines drink and dance till the wee hours at **Maramao** (✉ Via dei Macci 79/r, near Santa Croce ☎ 055/244341); it opens at 11 PM and doesn't really get going until around 2 AM. **Maracaná** (✉ Via Faenza 4, near Santa Maria Novella ☎ 055/210298) is a restaurant and pizzeria featuring Brazilian specialties; at 11 PM it transforms itself into a cabaret floor show and then opens the floor to dancing. Book a table if you want to eat. If you had a transvestite grandmother, her home would look like **Montecarla** (✉ Via de' Bardi 2, near San Niccolò ☎ 055/2340259). On its two crowded floors people sip cocktails against a backdrop of exotic flowers, leopard-print chairs and chintz, and red walls and floors. **BeBop** (✉ Via dei Servi 76/r, near Santissima Annunziata) has loud, live music and Beatles nights. **Jazz Club** (✉ Via Nuova de' Caccini 3, corner of Borgo Pinti, near Santa Croce ☎ 055/2479700) puts on live music in a smoky basement.

When last call's come and gone, go where the bartenders unwind after their shift: **Loch Ness** (✉ Via de' Benci 19/r, near Santa Croce). They pour drinks there until 5 AM.

SPORTS

Health Clubs
Palestra Ricciardi (✉ Borgo Pinti 75, near Santa Croce ☎ 055/2478444 or 055/2478462), with daily admission of €10.40 and weekly of €33, has stretching, aerobics, step aerobics, and bodybuilding classes; it also has free weights, stationary bikes, treadmills, and rowing machines.

Running
Don't even think of running on the narrow city streets, as tour buses and triple-parked Alfa Romeos leave precious little space for pedestrians. Instead, head for **Le Cascine,** the park along the Arno at the western end of the city. You can run to Le Cascine along the Lungarno (stay

on the sidewalk), or take Bus 17 from the Duomo. A cinder track lies on the hillside below **Piazzale Michelangelo,** across the Arno from the city center. A scenic, but not serene, run can be had along the Lungarno, the streets that line both sides of the Arno.

Soccer

Italians are passionate about *calcio* (soccer), and the Florentines are no exception; indeed, *tifosi* (fans) of Fiorentina, the local team, are fervent supporters. It plays home matches at the **Stadio Comunale** (Municipal Stadium; ⊠ Top of Viale Manfredo Fanti, northeast of the center) in Campo di Marte, usually on Sunday from late August to May. Tickets are sold at the ticket booth **Chiosco degli Sportivi** (⊠ Via Anselmi, southwest side of Piazza della Repubblica ☎ 055/292363). A medieval version of soccer, **Calcio Storico,** is played around the Festa di San Giovanni on June 24 each year by teams dressed in costumes representing the six Florence neighborhoods. Games take place in Piazza Santa Croce, where they have allegedly been played since the middle of the 16th century.

SHOPPING

Window-shopping in Florence is like visiting an enormous contemporary art gallery, for many of today's greatest Italian artists are fashion designers, and most keep shops in Florence. Shops are generally open 9–1 and 3:30–7:30 and are closed Sunday and Monday morning most of the year. Summer (June–September) hours are usually 9–1 and 4–8, and some shops close Saturday afternoon instead of Monday morning. When looking for addresses of shops, you will see two color-coded numbering systems on each street. The red numbers are commercial addresses and are indicated, for example, as 31/r. The blue or black numbers are residential addresses. Most shops take major credit cards and will ship purchases, but because of possible delays it's wise to take your purchases with you.

Markets

Roam through the stalls under the loggia of the **Mercato Nuovo** (⊠ Corner of Via Por Santa Maria and Via Porta Rossa, near Piazza della Repubblica) for cheery, inexpensive trinkets. In the streets next to the church of San Lorenzo, the clothing and leather-goods stalls of the **Mercato di San Lorenzo** have bargains. It's also a great place to take children who are weary of looking at Renaissance monuments. The flea market on **Piazza dei Ciompi** (⊠ Sant'Ambrogio, near Santa Croce) takes place on the last Sunday of the month. An open-air market is held in **Le Cascine park** every Tuesday morning.

In the huge, two-story **Mercato Centrale** (⊠ Near San Lorenzo ◷ Mon.–Sat. 7–2), food is everywhere, some of it remarkably exotic. The ground floor contains meat and cheese stalls, as well as some very good bars selling *panini* (sandwiches), and the second floor teems with vegetable stands. If you're looking for dill or mangoes in Florence, this is most likely where you'll find them.

Shopping Districts

Florence's most fashionable shops are concentrated in the center of town. The fanciest designer shops are mainly on **Via Tornabuoni** and **Via della Vigna Nuova**. The city's largest concentrations of antiques shops are on **Borgo Ognissanti** and the Oltrarno's **Via Maggio**. The **Ponte Vecchio** houses reputable but very expensive jewelry shops, as it has since the 16th century. The area around **Santa Croce** is the heart of the leather merchants' district.

Specialty Stores

Antiques

Galleria Luigi Bellini (⊠ Lungarno Soderini 5, Lungarno South ☎ 055/214031) claims to be Italy's oldest antiques dealer, which may be true, since father Mario Bellini was responsible for instituting Florence's international antiques biennial. **Giovanni Pratesi** (⊠ Via Maggio 13, near Santo Spirito ☎ 055/2396568) specializes in furniture, with some fine paintings, sculpture, and decorative objects turning up from time to time. Vying with Luigi Bellini as one of Florence's oldest antiques dealers, **Guido Bartolozzi** (⊠ Via Maggio 18/r, near Santo Spirito ☎ 055/215602) sells predominately period Florentine pieces. **Roberto Innocenti e C. S.N.C** (⊠ Borgo Pinti 11–13/r and Via Matteo Palmieri 29/r, near Santa Croce ☎ 055/2478668) specializes in things more recently antique such as art nouveau and art deco.

Books & Paper

Long one of Florence's best art-book shops, **Libreria Salimbeni** (⊠ Via Matteo Palmieri 14–16/r, near Santa Croce ☎055/2340905) has an outstanding selection. **Libreria d'Arte Galleria degli Uffizi** (⊠ Piazzale degli Uffizi 6, near Piazza della Signoria ☎ 055/284508) carries monographs on famous artists, some of whose work can be found in the Uffizi; it also carries scholarly works from both the Italian and Anglophone worlds.

Pineider (⊠ Piazza della Signoria 13/r ☎ 055/284655) has shops throughout the world, but the business began in Florence and still does all its printing here. Personalized stationery and business cards are a mainstay, but so are fine leather desk accessories, as well as a less stuffy, more light-hearted line of products.

One of Florence's oldest paper-goods stores, **Giulio Giannini e Figlio** (⊠ Piazza Pitti 37/r ☎ 055/212621) is *the* place to buy the marbleized stock, which comes in many shapes and sizes, from flat sheets to boxes and even pencils.

Alberto Cozzi (⊠ Via del Parione 35/r, near Santa Maria Novella ☎ 055/294968) keeps an extensive line of Florentine papers and paper products, and the artisans in the shop rebind and restore books and works on paper.

Clothing

The usual fashion gurus—such as Prada and Armani—all have shops in Florence, and nearly all of them populate Via Tornabuoni, which more and more resembles a giant *passarella* (catwalk). If you want to buy Florentine haute fashion while in Florence, stick to Pucci, Gucci, Ferragamo, and Roberto Cavalli, all of which call Florence home.

Prada (✉ Via Tornabuoni 51/r-53/r, near Santa Maria Novella ☎ 055/267471 ✉ Outlet ✉ Levanella Spacceo, Estrada Statale 69, Montevarchi ☎ 055/91911), known to mix schoolmarmish sensibility with sexy cuts and funky fabrics, appeals to an exclusive clientele. Cognoscenti will drive or taxi about 45 minutes out of town to the Prada Outlet.

The sleek, classic **Giorgio Armani** (✉ Via Tornabuoni 48/r, near Santa Maria Novella ☎ 055/219041) is a centerpiece of the dazzling high-end shops clustered in this part of town. The aristocratic Marchese di Barsento, **Emilio Pucci** (✉ Via Tornabuoni 20-22/r, near Santa Maria Novella ☎ 055/2658082), became an international name in the late 1950s when the stretch ski clothes he designed for himself caught on with the dolce vita crowd—his pseudopsychedelic prints and "palazzo pajamas" became all the rage.

Native son **Roberto Cavalli** (✉ Via Tornabuoni 83/r, near Santa Maria Novella ☎ 055/2396226), whose outlandish designs appeal to Hollywood celebrities and those who want to look like more expensive versions of Britney Spears, has a corner shop with a trendy café attached.

Some Florentine boutiques require you to stray off the beaten fashion path. **Paola Pardini** (✉ Borgo Albizzi 70/r, near Santa Croce ☎ 055/2001340) has a fine line of knitwear in cashmere and other fine wool for women who don't aspire to dress like 20-year-olds (though many 20-year-olds would find the line quite appealing as well).

Florentine **Patrizia Pepe** (✉ Piazza San Giovanni 12/r, near Duomo ☎ 055/2645056) has body-conscious clothes perfect for all ages, especially for women with a tiny streak of rebelliousness. At **L'essentiel** (✉ Via del Corso 10/r, near Piazza della Signoria ☎ 055/294713) Lara Caldieron has spun her club-going years into fashion that works well on the street as well as in the office.

You can take home a custom-made suit or dress from **Giorgio Vannini** (✉ Via Borgo Santi Apostoli 43/r, near Santa Maria Novella ☎ 055/293037), who has a showroom for his prêt:à-porter designs. **Bernardo** (✉ Via Porta Rossa 87/r, near Piazza della Repubblica ☎ 055/283333) specializes in men's trousers, cashmere sweaters, and shirts with details like mother-of-pearl buttons.

Though it may seem American, **Diesel** (✉ Via dei Lamberti 13/r, near Piazza della Signoria ☎ 055/2399963) started in Vicenza; its gear is on the "must-have" list of many self-respecting Italian teens. **Piccolo Slam** (✉ Via de'Neri 9/11r, near Santa Croce ☎ 055/214504) has classic styles for members of the junior set.

Embroidery & Linens

Loretta Caponi (✉ Piazza Antinori 4/r, near Santa Maria Novella ☎ 055/213668) is synonymous with Florentine embroidery, and her luxury lace, linens, and lingerie have earned her worldwide renown. **Valmar** (✉ Via Porta Rossa 53/r, near Piazza della Repubblica ☎ 055/284493) is filled with tangled spools of cords, ribbons, and fringes, plus buttons, tassels, sachets, and hand-embroidered cushions. You can also bring in your own fabric, choose the adornments, and they will custom-make your cushion or table runner.

Sant'Jacopo Show (✉ Borgo Sant'Jacopo 66/r, near Santo Spirito ☎ 055/2396912) is an offbeat shop specializing in mannequins, decorations, and shop fittings. Sumptuous silks, beaded fabrics, lace, wool, and tweeds can be purchased at **Valli** (✉ Via Strozzi 4/r, near Piazza della Repubblica ☎ 055/282485). It carries fabrics created by Armani, Valentino, and other high-end designers.

Gifts & Housewares

The essence of a Florentine holiday is captured in the sachets of the **Officina Profumo Farmaceutica di Santa Maria Novella** (✉ Via della Scala 16, near Santa Maria Novella ☎ 055/216276), a turn-of-the-19th-century emporium of herbal cosmetics and soaps that are made following centuries-old recipes created by friars. **Antica Officina del Farmacista Dr. Vranjes** (✉ Borgo La Croce 44/r near Santa Croce ☎ 055/241748 ✉ Via San Gallo 63/r ☎ 055/494537) makes aromatic oils and perfumes for people and for spaces. For housewares, nothing beats **Bartolini** (✉ Via dei Servi 30/r, near Santissima Annunziata ☎ 055/211895) for well-designed, practical items. **Sbigoli Terrecotte** (✉ Via Sant'Egidio 4/r, near Santa Croce ☎ 055/2479713) carries traditional Tuscan terracotta and ceramic vases, pots, and cups and saucers, made by the mother-daughter team of Antonella Chini and Lorenza Adami, who turn out Florentine-inspired designs based on Antonella's extensive ceramics training in Faenza. **Rampini Ceramiche** (✉ Borgo Ognissanti 32/34, Lungarno North ☎ 055/219720 ⊕ www.rampiniceramics.com) sells exquisitely crafted ceramics in various patterns, shapes, and sizes.

Jewelry

Cassetti (✉ Ponte Vecchio 54/r, near Piazza della Signoria, ☎ 055/2396028) combines precious and semiprecious stones and metals in contemporary settings. **Gherardi** (✉ Ponte Vecchio 5/r, near Piazza della Signoria ☎ 055/211809), Florence's king of coral, has the city's largest selection of finely crafted pieces, as well as cultured pearls, jade, and turquoise. **Carlo Piccini** (✉ Ponte Vecchio 31/r, near Piazza della Signoria, ☎ 055/292030) has sold antique jewelry as well as made pieces to order for several generations; you can also get old jewelry reset. One of Florence's oldest jewelers, **Tiffany** (✉ Via Tornabuoni 25/r, near Santa Maria Novella ☎ 055/215506), has supplied Italian (and other) royalty with finely crafted gems for centuries. Its selection of antique-looking classics has been updated with a choice of contemporary silver.

Gatto Bianco (✉ Borgo Santi Apostoli 12/r, near Santa Maria Novella ☎ 055/282989) has breathtakingly beautiful jewelry worked in semiprecious and precious stones; the look is completely contemporary. Affordable necklaces and rings, mostly in silver, can be purchased at **La Gazza Ladra** (✉ Piazza Salvemini 6, near Santa Croce ☎ 055/2466008). **Oreria** (✉ Borgo Pinti, 87/a, near Santa Croce ☎ 055/244708), run by two women who create divine designs using silver and semiprecious stones, is the place to direct someone to buy you something significant.

Shoes & Leather Accessories

At peak tourist times, status-conscious shoppers often stand in line outside **Gucci** (✉ Via Tornabuoni 73/r, near Santa Maria Novella ☎ 055/264011), ready to buy anything with the famous logo. Beware, however, of shop assistants with severe attitude problems. Born near Naples, the late Salvatore **Ferragamo** (✉ Via Tornabuoni 2/r, near Santa Maria Novella ☎ 055/292123) earned his fortune custom-making shoes for famous feet, especially Hollywood stars. The elegant store, in a 13th-century Renaissance palazzo, displays designer clothing and accessories, but elegant footwear still underlies the Ferragamo success. **Cellerini** (✉ Via del Sole 37/r, near Santa Maria Novella ☎ 055/282533) is a Florentine institution in a city where it seems that nearly everybody is wearing an expensive leather jacket.

For sheer creativity in both color and design, check out the shoes at **Sergio Rossi** (✉ Via Roma 15/r, near Duomo ☎ 055/294873) and fantasize about having a life to go with them. **Pollini** (✉ Via Calimala 12/r, near Piazza della Repubblica ☎ 055/214738) has beautifully crafted shoes and leather accessories for those willing to pay that little bit extra. **Giotti** (✉ Piazza Ognissanti 3–4/r, Lungarno North ☎ 055/294265) has a full line of leather goods and leather clothing.

The **Scuola del Cuoio** (✉ Piazza Santa Croce 16 ☎ 055/355644 ⊕ www.leatherschool.com), in the former dormitory of Santa Croce, is a consortium for leatherworkers who ply their trade and sell their wares on the premises.

Paolo Carandini (✉ Via de' Macci 73/r, near Santa Croce ☎ 055/245397) works exclusively in leather, producing exquisite objects such as picture frames, jewelry boxes, and desk accessories.

Il Bisonte (✉ Via del Parione 31/r, off Via della Vigna Nuova, near Santa Maria Novella ☎ 055/215722) is known for its natural-looking leather goods, all stamped with the store's bison symbol. **Madova** (✉ Via Guicciardini 1/r, near Palazzo Pitti ☎ 055/2396526) has a rainbow of high-quality leather gloves. **Furla** (✉ Via Calzaiuoli 47/r, near Piazza della Repubblica ☎ 055/2382883) makes beautiful leather bags and wallets in up-to-the-minute designs.

SIDE TRIPS FROM FLORENCE
FIESOLE & GRACIOUS GARDENS

Fiesole

A half-day excursion to Fiesole, in the hills 8 km (5 mi) above Florence, gives you a pleasant respite from museums and a wonderful view of the city. Fiesole began life as an ancient Etruscan and later Roman village that held some power until it succumbed to barbarian invasions. Eventually it gave up its independence in exchange for Florence's protection. The medieval cathedral, ancient Roman amphitheater, and lovely old villas behind garden walls are clustered on a series of hilltops. The trip from Florence by car or bus takes 20–30 minutes. Take Bus 7 from the Stazione Centrale di Santa Maria Novella, Piazza San Marco, or the Duomo. (You can also get on and off the bus at San Domenico.) There are several possible routes for the two-hour walk from central Florence to Fiesole. One route begins in residential Salviatino (Via Barbacane, near Piazza Edison, on the Bus 7 route), and after a short time offers peeks over garden walls of beautiful villas, as well as a panorama of Florence in the valley. A walk around Fiesole can take a couple of hours, depending on how far you stroll from the main piazza.

The **Duomo** reveals a stark medieval interior. In the raised presbytery, the **Cappella Salutati** was frescoed by 15th-century artist Cosimo Rosselli, but it was his contemporary the sculptor Mino da Fiesole (1430–84) who put the town on the artistic map. The Madonna on the altarpiece and the tomb of Bishop Salutati are fine examples of his work. ⊠ *Piazza Mino da Fiesole* ☎ *055/59400* ⊗ *Nov.–Mar., daily 7:30–noon and 2–5; Apr.–Oct., daily 7:30–noon and 3–6.*

Fiesole's beautifully preserved 2,000-seat **Anfiteatro Romano** (Roman Amphitheater) dates from the 1st century BC and is used for the summer concerts of the **Estate Fiesolana** (⊠ Teatro Romano ☎ 055/5978403), a festival of theater, music, dance, and film that also utilizes the churches of Fiesole. To the right of the amphitheater are the remains of the **Terme Romani** (Roman Baths), where you can see the gymnasium, hot and cold baths, and rectangular chamber where the water was heated. A beautifully designed **Museo Archeologico**, an intricate series of levels connected by elevators, is built amid the ruins and contains objects dating from as early as 2000 BC. The nearby **Museo Bandini** is a small collection with a lot of interesting paintings. It's filled with the private collection of Canon Angelo Maria Bandini (1726–1803); he fancied 13th- to 15th-century Florentine paintings, terra-cotta pieces, and wood sculpture, which he later bequeathed to the Diocese of Fiesole. ⊠ *Via Portigiani 1* ☎ *055/59477* ⊠ *€6.50, includes access to the archaeological park and museums* ⊗ *Apr.–Sept., daily 9:30–7; Oct.–Mar., Wed.–Mon. 9:30–5.*

The hilltop church of **San Francesco** has a good view of Florence and the plain below from its terrace and benches. Halfway up the hill you'll see sloping steps to the right; they lead to a lovely wooded **park** with trails that loop out and back to the church.

If you really want to stretch your legs, walk 4 km (2½ mi) back toward Florence center along Via Vecchia Fiesolana, a narrow lane in use since Etruscan times, to the church of **San Domenico.** Sheltered in the church is the *Madonna and Child with Saints* by Fra Angelico, who was a Dominican friar here. ⊠ *Piazza San Domenico, off Via Giuseppe Mantellini* ☎ *055/59230* ⊗ *Daily 9–noon.*

It's only a five-minute walk northwest from the church of San Domenico to the **Badia Fiesolana,** which was the original cathedral of Fiesole. Parts of it date from the 11th century, but it was substantially enlarged after 1456. ⊠ *Via della Badia dei Roccettini 11* ☎ *055/59155* ⊗ *Weekdays 9–6, Sat. 9:30–12:30.*

Where to Stay

$$$$ ⊞ **Villa San Michele.** The cypress-lined driveway provides an elegant preamble to this incredibly gorgeous (and incredibly expensive) hotel nestled in the hills of Fiesole. The 16th-century building was originally a Franciscan convent designed by Santi di Tito. Not a single false note is struck in the reception area (formerly the chapel), the dining rooms (a covered cloister and former refectory), or the tasteful antiques and art that decorate the rooms. The open-air loggia, where lunch and dinner are served, provides one of the most stunning views of Florence—a good thing, too, as the food is overpriced and bland. ⊠ *Via Doccia 4, 50014* ☎ *055/59451* 🖷 *055/5678250* ⊕ *www.villasanmichele.com* ⇆ *19 rooms, 26 suites* ⟡ *Restaurant, room service, in-room fax, in-room data ports, in-room safes, minibars, cable TV with movies, in-room VCRs, pool, gym, mountain bikes (fee), piano bar, babysitting, dry cleaning, laundry service, concierge, Internet, free parking, some pets allowed, no-smoking rooms* ⊟ *AE, DC, MC, V* ⊗ *Closed Dec.–Easter* ⦿⦶ *BP.*

¢–$ ⊞ **Fattoria di Maiano.** In the foothills between Florence and Fiesole, these lovely apartments sleep from 4 to 11 people and are rented by the week. You'll have wood floors, simple and sturdy furniture, and very modern kitchens. Most apartments have splendid views onto olive tree groves (olive oil is produced by the Fattoria owners). Here you'll have all the pleasures of the country, with one significant city (Florence) 5 km (3 mi) away. ⊠ *Via Benedetto da Maiano 11, 50016* ☎ *055/599600* 🖷 *055/599640* ⊕ *www.fattoriadimaiano.com* ⇆ *8 apartments* ⟡ *Kitchenettes, some pets allowed; no a/c in some rooms* ⊟ *DC, MC, V* ⦿⦶ *EP.*

Gracious Gardens Around Florence

Like any well-heeled Florentine, you too can get away from Florence's hustle and bustle by heading for the hills. Take a break from city sightseeing to enjoy the gardens and villas set like jewels in the hills around the city. Villa di Castello and Villa La Petraia, both northwest of the center of town in Castello, can be explored in one trip. The garden at Villa Gamberaia is a quick 8-km (5-mi) jaunt east of the center near Settignano. Plan for a full-day excursion, picnic lunch included, if visiting all three. Spring and summer are the ideal time to visit, when flowers are in glorious bloom. For a taste of Medici living, venture farther afield to the family's Villa Medicea in Poggio a Caiano, south of Prato.

Villa di Castello

A fortified residence in the Middle Ages, Villa di Castello was rebuilt by the Medici in the 15th century. The Accademia della Crusca, the 400-year-old institution that is the official arbiter of the Italian language, now occupies the palace, which is not open to the public. The gardens are the main attraction. From the villa entrance, walk uphill through the 19th-century park set above part of the formal garden. You'll reach the terrace, which affords a good view of the geometric layout of the Italian garden below; stairs on either side descend to the parterre.

Though the original garden design has been altered somewhat over the centuries, the allegorical theme of animals devised by Tribolo to the delight of the Medici in 1537 is still evident. The artificial cave, Grotta degli Animali (Animal Grotto), displays an imaginative menagerie of sculpted animals by Giambologna and his assistants. An Ammannati sculpture, a figure of an old man representing *Gennaio* (January) is at the center of a pond on the terrace overlooking the garden. Two bronze sculptures by Ammannati, centerpieces of fountains studding the Italian garden, can now be seen indoors in Villa La Petraia. Allow about 45 minutes to visit the garden; you can easily visit Villa La Petraia from here, making for a four-hour trip in total.

To get to Villa di Castello by car, head northwest from Florence on Via Reginaldo Giuliani (also known as Via Sestese) to Castello, about 6 km (4 mi) northwest of the city center in the direction of Sesto Fiorentino; follow signs to Villa di Castello. Or take Bus 28 from the city center and tell the driver you want to get off at Villa di Castello; from the stop, walk north about ½ km (¼ mi) up the tree-lined allée from the main road. ⊠ *Via di Castello 47, Castello* ☎ *055/454791* 🖙 *€2, includes entrance to Villa La Petraia* ⊗ *Garden Nov.–Feb., daily 8:15–4:30; Mar.–Oct., daily 9–7. Closed 2nd and 3rd Mon. of month* ☞ *Palace closed to public.*

Villa La Petraia

The splendidly planted gardens of Villa La Petraia lie high above the Arno plain with a sweeping view of Florence. The villa was built around a medieval tower and reconstructed after it was purchased by the Medici sometime after 1530. Virtually the only trace of the Medici having lived here is the 17th-century courtyard frescoes depicting glorious episodes from the clan's history. In the 1800s the villa served as a hunting lodge for King Vittorio Emanuele II (1820–78), who kept his mistress here while Florence was the temporary capital of the newly united country of Italy.

An Italian-speaking guide will take you through the 19th-century–style salons. The garden—also altered in the 1800s—and the vast park behind the palace suggest a splendid contrast between formal and natural landscapes. Allow 60 to 90 minutes to explore the park and gardens, plus 30 minutes for the guided tour of the villa interior. This property is best visited after the Villa di Castello.

To reach Villa La Petraia by car, travel as though you're going to Villa di Castello (head northwest from Florence on Via Reginaldo Giuliani), but take the right off Via Reginaldo Giuliani, following the sign for Villa La Petraia. You can walk from Villa di Castello to Villa La Petraia in about 15 minutes; turn left beyond the gate of Villa di Castello and continue straight along Via di Castello and the imposing Villa Corsini; take Via della Petraia uphill to the entrance. ⊠ *Via della Petraia 40, Località Castello* ☎ *055/451208* 🖙 *€2, includes entrance to Villa di Castello* ⊗ *Oct.–Mar., garden daily 8:15–4:30, villa tours daily at 9:15, 10, 10:45, 11:30, 12:10, 1:30, 2:20, 3, and 3:40; Apr., May, and Sept., garden daily 9–5, villa tours daily at 9:15, 10, 10:45, 11:30, 12:10, 1:30, 2:20, 3, 3:40, and 4:45; June–Aug., garden daily 9–7, villa tours daily at 9:15, 10, 10:45, 11:30, 12:10, 1:30, 2:20, 3, 3:40, 4:45, 5:35, and 6:35. Closed 2nd and 3rd Mon. of month.*

Villa Gamberaia

Villa Gamberaia, near the village of Settignano on the eastern outskirts of Florence, was the rather modest 15th-century country home of Matteo di Domenico Gamberelli, the father of noted Renaissance sculptors Bernardo, Antonio, and Matteo Rossellino. In the early 1600s the villa passed into the hands of the wealthy Capponi family. They spared no expense in rebuilding it and, more important, creating its garden, one of the finest near Florence. Studded with statues and fountains, the garden suffered damage during World War II but has been restored according to the original 17th-century design. This excursion takes about 1½ hours, allowing 45 minutes to visit the garden.

To get here by car, go to Piazza Beccaria and turn onto Via Gioberti. This eventually becomes Via Aretina; follow the sign to the turnoff to the north to Villa Gamberaia, about 8 km (5 mi) from the center. To arrive by bus, take Bus 10 to Settignano. From Settignano's main Piazza Tommaseo, walk east on Via di San Romano; the second lane on the right is Via del Rossellino, which leads southeast to the entrance of Villa Gamberaia. The walk from the piazza takes about 10 minutes. ⊠ *Via del Rossellino 72, near Settignano* ☎ *055/697205* ✉ *€10* ☉ *Garden Mon.–Sat. 9–6, Sun. 9–6.*

FLORENCE A TO Z

To research prices, get advice from other travelers, and book travel arrangements, visit www.fodors.com.

AIRPORTS & TRANSFERS

Florence's Aeroporto A. Vespucci, called Peretola, receives flights from Milan, Rome, London, and Paris. To get into Florence by car, take the A11. Tickets for the local bus service into Florence are sold at the airport's second-floor bar. Take Bus 62, which goes directly to the train station at Santa Maria Novella; the airport's bus shelter is beyond the parking lot.

Pisa's Aeroporto Galileo Galilei is the closest landing point with significant international service. It's relatively easy to get to Florence, as the SS67 leads directly there. For flight information, call the airport or Florence Air Terminal (an office at Santa Maria Novella, Florence's main train station). A train service connects Pisa's airport station with Santa Maria Novella, roughly a one-and-a-half-hour trip. Trains start running about 7 AM from the airport, 6 AM from Florence, and continue service every hour until about 7 PM from the airport, 4 PM from Florence. You can check in for departing flights at the Florence Air Terminal, which is around the corner from train tracks 1 and 2.

🛈 Airport Information **Aeroporto Galileo Galilei** ⊠ 12 km [7 mi] south of Pisa and 80 km [50 mi] west of Florence ☎ 050/500707 ⊕ www.pisa-airport.com. **Florence Air Terminal** ⊠ Stazione Centrale di Santa Maria Novella ☎ 055/216073. **Peretola** ⊠ 10 km [6 mi] northwest of Florence ☎ 055/373498 ⊕ www.airport.florence.it.

BIKE & MOPED TRAVEL

Brave souls (cycling in Florence is difficult at best) may rent bicycles at easy-to-spot locations at Fortezza da Basso, the Stazione Centrale di Santa Maria Novella, and Piazza Pitti. Otherwise try Alinari. You'll be up against hordes of tourists and those pesky *motorini* (mopeds). Le Cascine, a former Medici hunting ground turned into a large public park with paved pathways, admits no cars. The historic center can be circumnavigated via bike paths lining the Viali, a road that runs along the center's circumference. If you want to go native and rent a noisy Vespa (Italian for "wasp") or other make of motorcycle or *motorino* (moped), you may do so at Maxirent. Massimo also rents mopeds. However unfashionable, helmets must be rented at either place, and by law are mandatory, much to the chagrin of many Italians.

🚲 Rentals **Alinari** ✉ Via Guelfa 85/r, San Marco ☎ 055/280500. **Massimo** ✉ Via Campo d'Arrigo 16/r ☎ 055/573689. **Maxirent** ✉ Borgo Ognissanti 155/r, Santa Maria Novella ☎ 055/265420.

BUS TRAVEL TO & FROM FLORENCE

Long-distance buses provide inexpensive if somewhat claustrophobic service between Florence and other cities in Italy and Europe.

🚌 Bus Information **Lazzi Eurolines** ✉ Via Mercadante 2, Santa Maria Novella ☎ 055/363041 ⊕ www.lazzi.it. **SITA** ✉ Via Santa Caterina da Siena 17/r, Santa Maria Novella ☎ 055/214721 ⊕ www.sita-on-line.it.

BUS TRAVEL WITHIN FLORENCE

Maps and timetables are available for a small fee at the ATAF (Trasporti Area Fiorentina) booth, or for free at visitor information offices. Tickets must be bought in advance at tobacco stores, newsstands, from automatic ticket machines near main stops, or at ATAF booths. The ticket must be canceled in the small validation machine immediately upon boarding. Small electric buses make the rounds of the centro storico and provide an easy alternative to footing it around town. Use the same ticket as for the regular bus.

FARES & SCHEDULES Two types of tickets are available, both valid for one or more rides on all lines. One costs €1 and is valid for one hour from the time it is first canceled. A multiple ticket–four tickets, each valid for 60 minutes–costs €3.90. A 24-hour tourist ticket costs €4.50. Two-, three-, and seven-day passes are also available.

🚌 Bus Information **ATAF** ✉ Next to train station; Piazza del Duomo 57/r, Santa Maria Novella ☎ 800/019794 toll free.

CAR RENTAL

🚗 Local Agencies **Avis** ✉ Via Borgo Ognissanti, 128/r, Santa Maria Novella ☎ 055/2398826. **Hertz Italiana** ✉ Via Finiguerra 33/r, Santa Maria Novella ☎ 055/317543. **Maggiore-Budget Autonoleggio** ✉ Via Termine 1, Santa Maria Novella ☎ 055/311256.

CAR TRAVEL

Florence is connected to the north and south of Italy by the Autostrada del Sole (A1). It takes about one hour of driving on scenic roads to get to Bologna (although heavy truck traffic over the Apennines often makes for slower going), about 3 hours to Rome, and 3 to 3½ hours to

Milan. The Tyrrhenian Coast is an hour west on the A11. In the city, abandon all hope of using a car, since most of the downtown area is accessible only to locals with properly marked vehicles. For assistance or information, call the ACI (Automobile Club Firenze).

🚹 **ACI** ⊠ Viale Amendola 36, outside &town ☎ 055/2486246.

EMBASSIES & CONSULATES

🚹 United Kingdom **U.K. Consulate** ⊠ Lungarno Corsini 2, Lungarno North ☎ 055/284133 ⊕ www.britain.it.

🚹 United States **U.S. Consulate** ⊠ Lungarno Vespucci 38, Lungarno North ☎ 055/266951 ⊕ www.usembassy.it.

EMERGENCIES

You can get a list of English-speaking doctors and dentists at the U.S. Consulate, or contact the Tourist Medical Service. If you need hospital treatment and an interpreter, you can call AVO, a group of volunteer interpreters; it's open Monday, Wednesday, and Friday 4–6 PM and Tuesday and Thursday 10–noon. Comunale No. 13, a local pharmacy, is open 24 hours a day, seven days a week. For a complete listing of other pharmacies that have late-night hours on a rotating basis, dial 192.

🚹 **AVO** ☎ 055/2344567. **Tourist Medical Service** ⊠ Via Lorenzo il Magnifico, 59 ☎ 055/475411.

🚹 Emergency Services **Ambulance** ☎ 118. **Emergencies** ☎ 113. **Misericordia** (Red Cross) ⊠ Piazza del Duomo 20 ☎ 055/212222. **Police** ⊠ Via Zara 2, near Piazza della Libertà ☎ 055/49771.

🚹 24-Hour Pharmacies **Comunale No. 13** ⊠ Stazione Centrale di Santa Maria Novella ☎ 055/289435.

ENGLISH-LANGUAGE MEDIA

BOOKS 🚹 **BM Bookshop** ⊠ Borgo Ognissanti 4/r, Santa Maria Novella ☎ 055/294575. **Edison** ⊠ Piazza della Repubblica 27/r ☎ 055/213110. **Feltrinelli International** ⊠ Via Cavour 12-20/r, near Duomo ☎ 055/219524. **Paperback Exchange** ⊠ Via Fiesolana 31/r, Santa Croce ☎ 055/2478154.

WHERE TO STAY

VILLA RENTALS 🚹 Local Agents **The Best in Italy** ⊠ Via Ugo Foscolo 72 50124 ☎ 055/223064 🖷 055/2298912 ⊕ www.thebestinitaly.com. **Florence and Abroad** ⊠ Via San Zanobi 58, 50129 San Marco Florence ☎ 055/487004 ⊕ www.florenceandabroad.com. **Custom Travel and Special Events** ⊠ Via dell'Ardiglione 19 near Santo Spirito, 50124 ☎ 055/2645526 ⊕ www.customitaly.com.

MAIL & SHIPPING

🚹 Post Offices **Florence** ⊠ Via Pellicceria 3, Piazza della Repubblica ☎ 055/27361. **Florence** ⊠ Via Pietrapiana 53/55, Santa Croce ☎ 055/211415.

OVERNIGHT 🚹 Major Services **DHL** ⊠ Via della Cupola 234/5 ☎ 800/123800 toll free. **Federal Ex-**
SERVICES **press** ⊠ Via Gioberti 3 ☎ 055/8974001, 800/123800 toll free.

SAFETY

LOCAL SCAMS Florence is subject to the same types of petty thievery practiced in Italy's other large, heavily touristed cities. Pickpockets are known to frequent crowded places, particularly buses. Purse-snatchers sometimes operate on mopeds, making them quick and potentially dangerous. Groups of gypsy children have a number of ruses to part you from your property. Although the odds are against you falling prey to such crimes, it's always wise to keep your valuables well guarded, to be alert to your surroundings, and to err on the side of caution if you find yourself in suspicious circumstances.

TAXIS
Taxis usually wait at stands throughout the city (in front of the train station and in Piazza della Repubblica, for example), or you can call for one. The meter starts at €2.30, with a €3.60 minimum and extra charges at night, on Sunday, or for radio dispatch. A tip of about 10% will be much appreciated.

Taxi Companies **Taxis** ☎ 055/4390 or 055/4798.

TOURS
BIKE TOURS Florence by Bike sets off several times a day for one- to three-hour tours of major monuments or for tours with specific themes such as Renaissance Florence or 13th-century Florence. I Bike Italy has one-day tours around Fiesole and Chianti, as well as a two-day tour around Siena.

Companies **Florence by Bike** ✉ Via San Zanobi 120-122/r, San Lorenzo ☎ 055/488992 ⊕ www.florencebybike.it. **I Bike Italy** ✉ Borgo degli Albizi 11, Santa Croce ☎☎ 055/2342371 ⊕ www.ibikeitaly.com.

BUS TOURS The major bus operators have half-day itineraries, all of which use comfortable buses staffed with English-speaking guides. Morning tours begin at 9, when buses pick visitors up at the main hotels. Stops include the cathedral complex, the Galleria dell'Accademia, Piazzale Michelangelo, and the Palazzo Pitti (or, on Monday, the Museo dell'Opera del Duomo). Afternoon tours stop at the large hotels at 2 PM and take in Piazza della Signoria, the Galleria degli Uffizi (or the Palazzo Vecchio on Monday, when the Uffizi is closed), nearby Fiesole, and, on the return, the church of Santa Croce. A half-day tour costs about €24.75, including museum admissions.

Fees & Schedules **Lazzi Eurolines** ✉ Via Mercadante 2, Santa Maria Novella ☎ 055/363041 ⊕ www.lazzi.it. **SITA** ✉ Via Santa Caterina da Siena 17/r, Santa Maria Novella ☎ 055/214721.

WALKING TOURS Companies **Custom Travel and Special Events** ✉ Via dell'Ardiglione 19, near Santo Spirito, 50124 ☎ 055/2645526 ⊕ www.customitaly.com. **Salon in Florence: Florence Art Lectures** ☎ 416/322-3334 in U.S. ⊕ www.florenceart.org.

TRAIN TRAVEL
Florence is on the principal Italian train route between most European capitals and Rome, and within Italy it is served frequently from Milan, Venice, and Rome by Intercity (IC) and nonstop Eurostar trains. Stazione Centrale di Santa Maria Novella is the main station and is in the center of town. Be sure to avoid trains that stop only at the Campo di Marte or Rifredi stations, which are not convenient to the center.

Train Information **Stazione Centrale di Santa Maria Novella** ☎ 892021 ⊕ www.trenitalia.com.

TRAVEL AGENCIES

🎁 Local Agent Referrals **American Express** ✉ Via Dante Alighieri 22/r, near Duomo 🕿 055/50981. **Brunelleschi Travel** ✉ Via dell'Oriuolo 50–52/r, near Santa Croce 🕿 055/2340228. **CIT Italia** ✉ Piazza Stazione 51/r, near Santa Maria Novella 🕿 055/ 284145 or 055/212606. **Travelex** ✉ Lungarno Acciaiuoli 6/r, Lungarno North 🕿 055/ 289781.

VISITOR INFORMATION

The main Florence tourist office, APT, has offices next to the Palazzo Medici-Riccardi, in the main train station, and around the corner from the Basilica di Santa Croce. Its Web site is in Italian only. Fiesole's office is on the main piazza.

🎁 Tourist Information **Fiesole** ✉ Via Portigiani 3, 50014 🕿 055/598720 ⊕ www.comune. fiesole.fi.it. **Florence** Agenzia Promozione Turistica (APT) ✉ Via Cavour 1/r, next to Palazzo Medici-Riccardi, near San Lorenzo 50100 🕿 055/290832 ✉ Stazione Centrale di Santa Maria Novella, 50100 🕿 055/212245 ✉ Borgo Santa Croce 29/r 🕿 055/2340444 ⊕ www.comune.firenze.it.

TUSCANY

9

Updated by
Patricia Rucidlo

HILLSIDES BLANKETED WITH VINEYARDS, silver-green olive groves, and enchanting towns are the essence of Tuscany, one of the most beautiful places in the world. Much seems unchanged since the Renaissance; Siena's piazza continues to captivate, while Chianti's narrow roads wind their way through cypress-filled countryside. A visit here is magic and food for the soul.

Midway down the Italian peninsula, Tuscany, with its hills, snowcapped mountains, dramatic cypress trees, and miles of coastline on the Tyrrhenian Sea, provides breathtaking views everywhere you look. The Arno, its most famous river, stretches clear across the region from Florence before making its way to the sea just beyond Pisa. The beauty of its landscape proves a perfect foil for the abundance of superlative art and architecture typical of the region. It also produces some of Italy's finest wines and olive oils. The combination of unforgettable art, sumptuous views, and eminently drinkable wines that pair beautifully with its simple food makes a trip to Tuscany something beyond special.

Tuscany (Toscana in Italian) was populated, at least by the 7th century BC, by the Etruscans, a mysterious lot who chose to live on hills—the better to see the approaching enemy—in such places as present-day Arezzo, Chiusi, Cortona, Fiesole, and Volterra. Some 500 years later, the Romans came, saw, and conquered; by 241 BC they had built the Aurelia, a road from Rome to Pisa that is still in use today. The crumbling of the Roman Empire and subsequent invasions by marauding Lombards, Byzantines, and Holy Roman Emperors meant centuries of turmoil. By the 12th century city-states were being formed throughout Tuscany in part, perhaps, because it was unclear exactly who was in charge.

The two groups vying for power were the Guelphs and the Ghibellines, champions of the pope and the Holy Roman Emperor, respectively. They jostled for control of individual cities and of the region as a whole. Florence was more or less Guelph, and Siena more often than not Ghibelline. This led to bloody battles, most notably the 1260 battle of Montaperti, in which the Ghibellines roundly defeated the Guelphs.

Eventually—by the 14th century—the Guelphs became the dominant force. But this did not mean that the warring Tuscan cities settled down to a period of relative peace and tranquillity. The age in which Dante wrote his *Divine Comedy* and Giotto and Piero della Francesca created their incomparable frescoes was one of internecine strife. Florence was the power to be reckoned with; it coveted Siena, which it conquered, lost, and reconquered during the 15th and 16th centuries. Finally, in 1555, following in the footsteps of Volterra, Pisa, Prato, and Arezzo, Siena fell for good. They were all united under Florence to form the grand duchy of Tuscany. The only city to escape Florence's dominion was Lucca, which remained fiercely independent until the arrival of Napoléon. Eventually, however, even Florence's influence waned, and the 17th and 18th centuries saw the decline of the entire region as various armies swept across it.

Some contend that the purest form of the Italian language is spoken in Tuscany. Tuscans—and Florentines in particular—proudly claim Dante as a native son, and his *Divine Comedy* certainly did much to put the

Numbers in the text correspond to numbers in the margin and on the Tuscany, Lucca, Pisa, and Siena maps.

If you have
3 days

Florence is a practical starting point. See **Lucca** ④–⑩ ▶ and the **Leaning Tower** ⑪ in **Pisa** ⑪–⑯, then head for ▦ **San Gimignano** ⑲ to overnight. The next day, explore the medieval alleyways of **Siena** ㉕–㉜ for a few hours; then move on to ▦ **Montepulciano** ㊱ for the night. The following day, detour south to the thermal waters of **Saturnia** ㊸ and stroll through the medieval town of **Pitigliano** ㊹; then go north to **Arezzo** ㉝ and head back to Florence via the A1 or, if you have time, along the twisting roads of Chianti (SS69, SS408, SS429, and SS222).

If you have
5 days

From Florence, head for industrial **Prato** ① ▶ to see its striking *centro storico* (historic center); **Pistoia** ②, site of bitter Guelph-Ghibelline feuding; and, if you enjoy resorts, **Montecatini Terme** ③, once one of Europe's most famous spas. Stay over in ▦ **Lucca** ④–⑩ and spend part of the next day exploring. Head for **Pisa** ⑪–⑯, then move on to the enchanting hilltop town of **San Miniato** ⑰ and either ▦ **Volterra** ⑱ or ▦ **San Gimignano** ⑲, the quintessential Tuscan town and a good place to spend your second night. On the third day visit Chianti en route to ▦ **Siena** ㉕–㉜, perhaps Italy's loveliest medieval city. After a night there, visit the **Abbazia di Monte Oliveto Maggiore** ㉟, **Montalcino** ㊳, and the **Abbazia di Sant'Antimo** ㊴, overnighting in or around ▦ **Montepulciano** ㊱. On the morning of your fifth day drive to **Saturnia** ㊸ and enjoy a thermal bath, then make quick visits to **Pitigliano** ㊹ and **Pienza** ㊲. Move on to handsome and heavily trafficked **Cortona** ㉞, where you can see work by Fra Angelico in the Museo Diocesano; in **Arezzo** ㉝ stop at the church of San Francesco to marvel at Piero della Francesca's glorious frescoes.

If you have
7 days

As you approach **Prato** ① ▶, you'll have time to visit the modern collection at the Centro per l'Arte Contemporanea L. Pecci. If you opt to see the resort town of **Montecatini Terme** ③, take the waters at one of the local *terme* (spas) or ride the funicular up to older Montecatini Alto. Extend your ▦ **Pisa** ⑪–⑯ exploration beyond the Piazza del Duomo to include the **Museo Nazionale di San Matteo** ⑯, and stay the night. From Pisa head toward Chianti. Take the SS67 east toward Florence, and before entering the city turn south to pick up the meandering SS222, also known as the Strada Chiantigiana. It runs through the heart of Chianti by way of **Panzano** ㉒, where you can sample local wine at one of the many *enoteche* (wine bars). Carry on to ▦ **Castellina in Chianti** ㉔ and plan to stay two nights there or in nearby ▦ **Radda in Chianti** ㉓, dedicating a day to vineyard-hopping. Next settle into a ▦ **Siena** ㉕–㉜ hotel and take a day to see the city. From Siena head south to discover **Montepulciano** ㊱, **Pienza** ㊲, and ▦ **Montalcino** ㊳ for a night. For a moving sight, detour to the **Abbazia di San Galgano** ㊵. East of Siena, well worth the trip and last overnight, are ▦ **Cortona** ㉞ and ▦ **Arezzo** ㉝.

9

For a taste of a more rugged landscape on the way back to Florence, detour through the Casentino, a mountainous region blanketed with a vast forest that is a far cry from the pastoral images associated with Tuscany. You'll take the winding SS70, called the Consuma, a splendidly scenic road with hairpin turns and blind curves.

Tuscan vernacular on the map. Boccaccio followed suit with his bawdy *Decameron,* written in the 1350s. However, it was the Aretine Petrarch (1304–74), one of the earliest humanists of the Italian Renaissance, whose use of the vernacular in his poetry was most widely imitated.

To many, Tuscan art is synonymous with the art of Florence, and that bias can be attributed in part to another Aretine named Giorgio Vasari (1511–74), who in his *Lives of the Artists* created an inescapably Florentine canon. Florentine art is indeed dazzling, but the rest of Tuscany should not be overlooked. Nicola Pisano (circa 1215/20–1278/84) carved a groundbreaking pulpit in Pisa, then worked with his son Giovanni on another in Siena. Giovanni carried the tradition to Pistoia. Ambrogio Lorenzetti (documented 1319–48) produced wonderful frescoes representing *Good and Bad Government* in the Palazzo Pubblico in Siena. The frescoes of the *Legend of the True Cross* by Piero della Francesca (circa 1420–92) in Arezzo are among the 15th century's most stunning fresco cycles. Siena-born Aeneas Silvius Piccolomini (1405–64), later Pope Pius II, carried out his vision of an ideal Renaissance city in Pienza.

Many of Tuscany's cities and towns have retained the same fundamental character over the past 500 years. Civic rivalries that led to bloody battles so many centuries ago have given way to soccer rivalries. Renaissance pomp lives on in the celebration of local feast days and centuries-old traditions such as the Palio in Siena and the Giostra del Saraceno (Joust of the Saracen) in Arezzo. Often present-day Tuscans look as though they might have served as models for paintings produced hundreds of years ago. In many ways, the Renaissance still survives in Tuscany.

Exploring Tuscany

Although Tuscany is relatively small—no important destination is more than a few hours' drive from Florence—the desire to linger is strong: can you really get enough of sitting on a *terrazza* (terrace) with a good *caffè* (espresso) or a full-bodied Chianti, watching the evening settle over a landscape of soft-edged hills, proud medieval towns, quiet villages, and cypress-ringed villas?

It's best to have a car when traveling in Tuscany to fully enjoy the region's riches—it's the only way to get to many small towns and vineyards. The cities west of Florence are easily reached by the A11, which heads from Florence to Lucca and then to the sea; the A1 heads south from Florence toward Arezzo. Florence and Siena are connected by a *superstrada* and also the panoramic SS222, which threads through Chianti wine country. The hill towns north and west of Siena lie along superstrade and winding local roads—all are well marked, but you should still arm yourself with a good map.

About the Restaurants & Hotels

Long gone are the days of the four-course Italian midday meal. Italians now eat lighter at both lunchtime and dinnertime—it's fairly typical to have a plate of pasta for lunch with a half carafe of wine, followed by a sweet or fresh fruit. It's also fine to mix up the menu; if you'd like to start lunch or dinner with an antipasto and then segue directly to a *secondo* (second course), have no fear that you're acting like a tourist—Italians eat this way, too. Savvy travelers and those on a budget might want to consider keeping dining costs down by eating a big lunch instead of a big dinner: many restaurants offer lunch specials. Consider drinking the house wine instead of ordering a bottle: you are, after all, in Tuscany; even house wines are generally more than simply drinkable. And if a sandwich is all you're hankering for, drop in to any *alimentari* (delicatessen) and ask the man or woman behind the counter to make you a *panino*: select from any of the ingredients before you in the glass case, and they'll do so.

Staying in Tuscany is not inexpensive, especially in highly visited cities such as Siena, Lucca, San Gimignano, and Arezzo. But the area is full of options, from five-star luxe complete with swimming pools and helipads to delightful one-star hotels. Some midrange hotels provide the best value, as rooms are often spacious and prices fair. To keep costs down, overnight in less-frequented towns. You might want to consider staying at an *agriturismo,* a farm that has opened its rooms or apartments to guests; choices range from rustic to stately (note that some require a minimum stay of several days). Villa rental can also be an economical and enjoyable option for groups and families.

WHAT IT COSTS In euros				
$$$$	**$$$**	**$$**	**$**	**¢**
RESTAURANTS over €22	€16–€22	€11–€16	€7–€11	under €7
HOTELS over €220	€160–€220	€110–€160	€70–€110	under €70

Restaurant prices are for a second course (un secondo). Hotel prices are for two people in a standard double room in high season, including tax and service.

Timing

Spring and fall are the best times to come to Tuscany, when the weather is warm but the volume of tourists is relatively low. In summer, try to arrive in towns early in the morning to avoid crowds and the often oppressive heat. Rising early is not hard, as Tuscany is not about late nights (unless you are in Forte dei Marmi or Elba during high season). Most bars and restaurants close their shutters well before midnight. If you plan to visit the frescoes in the Palazzo Pubblico in Siena at midday, be prepared to wait in line and, once inside, to be shuffled along by iron-willed attendants eager to see you in and out as quickly as possible. If you want to photograph the towers of San Gimignano from a distance, do it in early morning, when the light is good and lines of neon-color tour buses snaking up the hill will not ruin a perfect picture.

WESTERN TUSCANY

In the shadows of the rugged coastal Alpi Apuane, where Michelangelo quarried his marble, this area isn't as lush as southern Tuscany—the hills flatten out, and there are hints of industry. It's well worth the effort to visit these spots, however—there's wonderful art, and there are some very fine restaurants with prices slightly lower than what you'll find in Florence.

Prato

▶ ❶ *17 km (11 mi) northwest of Florence, 60 km (37 mi) east of Lucca.*

The wool industry in this city, one of the world's largest manufacturers of cloth, was known throughout Europe as early as the 13th century. It was further stimulated in the 14th century by a local cloth merchant, Francesco di Marco Datini, who built his business, according to one of his ledgers, "in the name of God and of profit." A cumulative €5 ticket provides admission to the Museo dell'Opera del Duomo (Cathedral Museum), Museo di Pittura Murale, and il Castello.

Prato's **Centro per l'Arte Contemporanea L. Pecci** (L. Pecci Center of Contemporary Art) has acquired a burgeoning collection of works by Italian and other artists. ⊠ *Viale della Repubblica 277* ☎ *0574/5317* ⊕ *www.centropecci.it* 🎟 *€7* ☉ *Wed.–Mon. 10–7.*

Prato's Romanesque **Duomo** is famous for its **Pergamo del Sacro Cingolo** (Chapel of the Holy Girdle), to the left of the entrance, which enshrines the girdle of the Virgin Mary. It is said that the Virgin presented it to the apostle Thomas in a miraculous appearance after her Assumption. The Duomo also contains 15th-century frescoes by Prato's most famous son, Fra Filippo Lippi (1406–69), who executed scenes from the life of St. Stephen on the left wall and scenes from the life of John the Baptist on the right in the **Cappella Maggiore** (Main Chapel). As of this writing, the frescoes were undergoing restoration; to find out about possible guided visits on the scaffolding, call 0574/24112. ⊠ *Piazza del Duomo* ☎ *0574/26234* ☉ *Mon.–Sat. 7–12 and 3–7, Sun. 7–12:30 and 3–8.*

Sculptures by Donatello (circa 1386–1466) that originally adorned the Duomo's exterior pulpit are now on display in the **Museo dell'Opera del Duomo** (Cathedral Museum). ⊠ *Piazza del Duomo 49* ☎ *0574/29339* 🎟 *€5, includes Museo di Pittura Murale and il Castello* ☉ *Mon. and Wed.–Sat. 9:30–12:30 and 3–6:30, Sun. 9:30–12:30.*

Installed in the **Museo di Pittura Murale** (Museum of Mural Painting) is a collection of paintings by Fra Filippo Lippi and other works from the 13th to 15th century in a special exhibit called Treasures of the City, on view through 2005. The permanent collection contains frescoes removed from sites in Prato and environs. ⊠ *Piazza San Domenico 8* ☎ *0574/440501* 🎟 *€5, includes Museo dell'Opera del Duomo and il Castello* ☉ *Mon. and Wed.–Sat. 10–6, Sun. 10–1.*

The church of **Santa Maria delle Carceri** was built by Giuliano Sangallo in the 1490s and is a landmark of Renaissance architecture. ⊠ *Piazza*

9

Hiking & Biking
Serious hikers and trekkers come to Tuscany for its network of trails and incredible views. The Apennines' Parco dell'Orecchiella in the Garfagnana has extensive forests with trails for hiking and biking, as well as horseback riding and cross-country skiing in winter.

In spring, summer, and fall, bicyclists are as much a part of the landscape as the cypress trees. A drive on any steep Chianti road takes you past groups of bikers peddling up and down endless hills. Many are on weeklong organized tours, but it's also possible to rent bikes for jaunts in the countryside or to join afternoon or day minitours. Most Tuscan roads are in excellent condition, though often narrow, winding, and steep. That said, be cautious—especially as some of the drivers on these narrow, twisting roads may have just stopped at a vineyard for a tasting.

Thermal Baths
Southern Tuscany is shadowed with smoky clouds of steam billowing from natural geysers. There are also several outdoor naturally heated pools that smell of sulfur but are reputed to be therapeutic. Saturnia is the most famous; others are Venturina, near Piombino; Galleraie, near Montieri; Bagno Vignoni, near San Quirico d'Orcia; and Chianciano Terme, near Chiusi and not far from Lago Trasimeno in neighboring Umbria. But be aware that the baths can be crowded in summer.

Vineyards
Those picturesque vineyards on the Chianti hillsides are not cinematic backdrops; they are working farms, and when fall comes and their grapes are harvested and processed, they produce that world-famous *vino rosso* (red wine) that has been complementing Tuscan food for ages. Chianti's heritage dates back thousands of years, but the borders that define Chianti Classico weren't officially drawn until 1932. The Chianti region is actually surprisingly large, stretching from Pistoia, north of Florence, to Montalcino, south of Siena. (It includes all the areas where various types of Chianti grapes are grown.)

Chianti Classico is at the heart of the Chianti region. Its *gallo nero* (black rooster) logo dates from the 12th century, when the rooster was the symbol of the Chianti League, a military alliance that defended the Florentine border against Siena. Now that rooster signifies some of the highest-quality wines in the entire Chianti region.

Wine tasting lures travelers who want to give their eyes a rest after looking at all those halos in the churches and museums of Florence and Siena. Most of the vineyards have figured this out and offer direct sales and samplings of their products. Some have roadside stands, and others have elaborate sampling rooms in which snacks are served. Tourist information offices in most Chianti towns have maps to guide you through an itinerary of vineyard hopping.

CloseUp

ON THE MENU

JUST AS THE ANCIENT ETRUSCANS introduced cypress trees to the Tuscan landscape, their influence on regional food—in the use of fresh herbs—still lingers after more than three millennia. Simple and earthy, Tuscan food celebrates the seasons with a host of fresh vegetable dishes, wonderful bread-based soups, and savory meats and game perfumed with sage, rosemary, and thyme. Saltless Tuscan bread is grilled and drizzled with olive oil (crostino), or spread with chicken liver (crostino di fegatini), or rubbed with garlic and topped with tomatoes (bruschetta) or fettunta. For their love of beans—particularly cannellini simmered in olive oil and herbs until creamy—Tuscans have been disparagingly nicknamed mangiafagioli (bean eaters) by Italians from other regions. Pecorino, a cheese made from sheep's milk, is particularly good in these parts—try it when it's young and in a soft, practically spreadable state,

as well as when it's stagionato, or aged. When it's good, it's the equal of the finest Parmesan. Relatively new to Tuscan cuisine is the reintroduction of dishes featuring cinta senese, a once nearly extinct pig.

Grapes have been cultivated here since Etruscan times, and Chianti still dominates. The robust red wine is a staple on most tables; however, the discerning can select from a multitude of other varieties, including such reds as Brunello di Montalcino and Vino Nobile di Montepulciano and such whites as Vermentino and Vernaccia. Super Tuscans, a fanciful name given to a group of wines by American journalists, now command attention as some of the best wines produced in Italy; they have great depth and complexity. The dessert wine vin santo is produced throughout the region and is often sipped with biscotti (twice-baked cookies), perfect for dunking.

Santa Maria delle Carceri, off Via Cairoli and southeast of the cathedral ☎ *0574/27933* ☉ *Daily 7–noon and 4–7:30.*

Though in ruins, the formidable **Castello** (Castle) built for Frederick II Hohenstaufen, adjacent to Santa Maria delle Carceri, is an impressive sight, the only castle of its type outside southern Italy. ⊠ *Piazza Santa Maria delle Carceri* ☎ *0574/38207* 🎫 *€5, includes Museo dell'Opera del Duomo and Museo di Pittura Murale* ☉ *Nov.–Mar., Mon. and Wed.–Fri. 10–1, weekends 9–1 and 3–5; Apr.–Oct., Wed.–Mon. 10–7.*

off the beaten path

POGGIO A CAIANO - For a look at gracious country living Renaissance style, detour south of Prato to the Villa Medicea in Poggio a Caiano. Lorenzo "il Magnifico" (1449–92) commissioned Giuliano da Sangallo (circa 1445–1516) to redo the villa, which was lavished with frescoes by important Renaissance painters such as Andrea del Sarto (1486–1530) and Pontormo (1494–1557). You can take a walk around the austerely ornamented grounds while waiting for entry. ⊠ *Poggio a Caiano, 7 km (4½ mi) south of Prato, follow signs* ☎ *055/877012* 🎫 *€2* ☉ *Garden: Mar. and Apr., Sept. and Oct., Mon.–Sat. 9–5:30; Nov.–Feb., Mon.–Sat. 9–4:30; May–Aug., Mon.–Sat. 9–6:30, Sun. 9–12:30. Villa: Mon.–Sat. 9–1:30, Sun.*

9–noon. Guided visits only, hourly on the ½ hr, 9:30–1 hr before closing. Closed 2nd and 3rd Mon. of month.

Where to Eat

★ **$$–$$$** ✕ **Da Delfina.** Delfina Cioni began cooking many years ago for hungry hunters, and now her son Carlo effectively oversees four comfortably rustic rooms. Nestled amid vineyards and olive trees, the place has a glorious view of the Tuscan countryside, including a Medici villa (Ferdinando I de'Medici also enjoyed hunting in the area). Dishes celebrate Tuscan food, with an emphasis on fresh local ingredients. The seasonal menu is complemented by a fine wine list, and service is gracious. *Secondi* (second courses) such as *coniglio con olive e pignoli* (rabbit sautéed with olives and pine nuts) are a real treat. ⊠ *Via della Chiesa 1, Artimino* ☎ *055/8718074* ⌕ *Reservations essential* ▭ *No credit cards* ⊘ *Closed Mon. and 2 wks in Aug. No lunch Tues. No dinner Sun.*

¢ ✕ **La Vecchia Cucina di Soldano.** Local Pratesi specialties, including the odd but tasty *sedani ripieni* (stuffed celery), are served here in a completely unpretentious place. You could be sitting in your Italian grandmother's kitchen; tablecloths are red-and-white checked, and the service is friendly and casual. The place teems with locals enjoying the superb *tagliolini sui fagioli* (thin noodles with beans). Clearly they, too, like the rock-bottom prices. ⊠ *Via Pomeria 23* ☎ *0574/34665* ▭ *No credit cards* ⊘ *Closed Sun.*

Shopping

Prato's biscotti (twice-cooked cookies) have an extra-dense texture, lending themselves to submersion in caffè or vin santo. The best in town are at **Antonio Mattei** (⊠ Via Ricasoli 20/22 ☎ 0574/25756).

The centuries-old tradition of selling fine textiles crafted into fine clothing continues in Prato. **Enrico Pecci di A. Pecci & C** (⊠ Via del Pantano 16/e ☎ 055/89890) sells fabric by the meter.

Pistoia

❷ *18 km (11 mi) northwest of Prato, 36 km (22 mi) northwest of Florence.*

Pistoia can claim a Roman past, as well as a bloody history during the Middle Ages, when the town was rent by civil strife. Its historic center is a jewel and little visited, which makes coming here all the more worthwhile. The **Cattedrale di San Zeno** in the main piazza houses the Dossale di San Jacopo, a magnificent silver altar. The two half figures on the left were executed by Filippo Brunelleschi (1377–1446). ⊠ *Piazza del Duomo* ☎ *0573/25095* ▨ *Illumination of altarpiece €2* ⊘ *Church daily 9–noon and 4–7; altar daily 10–noon and 4–5:45.*

The **Palazzo del Comune,** begun around 1295, houses the **Museo Civico,** with works by local artists from the 14th to 20th century. ⊠ *Piazza del Duomo 1* ☎ *0573/371296* ▨ *€3.50, free Sat. 3–7* ⊘ *Tues.–Sat. 10–7, Sun. 9–12:30.*

Founded in the 13th century and still a working hospital today, the **Spedale del Ceppo** (literally, Hospital of the Tree Stump) has a glorious early-

16th-century exterior terra-cotta frieze begun by Giovanni della Robbia (1469–1529) and completed by the workshop of Santi and Benedetto Buglioni in 1526–28. ⊠ *Piazza Ospedale, a short way down Via Pacini from Piazza del Duomo.*

An architectural gem in green-and-white marble, the medieval church of **San Giovanni Fuorcivitas** contains a *Visitation* by Luca della Robbia (1400–82), a painting attributed to Taddeo Gaddi, and a holy-water font that may have been executed by Fra Guglielmo around 1270. ⊠ *Via Cavour* ☎ *0573/24784* ⊙ *Daily 8–noon and 4–6:30.*

Although it's not as grand as the silver altar in Pistoia's cathedral, Giovanni Pisano's powerfully sculpted pulpit, executed between 1298 and 1301 in the church of **Sant'Andrea,** is considered by many the town's greatest art treasure. ⊠ *Via Sant'Andrea* ☎ *0573/21912* ⊙ *Nov.–Mar., daily 8–1 and 4–6:30; Apr.–Oct., daily 8–12:30 and 3:30–7.*

☺ The **Giardino Zoologico,** a small zoo especially laid out to accommodate the wiles of both animals and children, is a 20-minute drive out of town. Take Bus 29 from the train station. ⊠ *Via Pieve a Celle 160/a* ☎ *0573/ 911219* ▨ *€9* ⊙ *Apr.–Sept., daily 9–7; Oct.–Mar., daily 9–5.*

Where to Eat

¢–$ ✕ **La BotteGaia.** Just off Piazza del Duomo, this popular wine bar has rustic tables in a couple of rooms with exposed brick-and-stone walls. Jazz plays softly in the background. Typical wine-bar fare such as plates of *salami e formaggi* (cured ham and cheeses) shares the menu with a surprisingly sophisticated list of daily specials that can include *insalatina con foie gras condita con vinaigrette* (foie gras with dressed greens). Dine al fresco with a view of the splendid Piazza del Duomo in summer. ⊠ *Via del Lastrone 4* ☎ *0573/365602* ⌂ *Reservations essential* ▭ *AE, DC, MC, V* ⊙ *Closed Mon. and 15 days in Aug. No lunch Sun.*

Montecatini Terme

❸ *16 km (10 mi) west of Pistoia, 49 km (30 mi) northwest of Florence.*

Immortalized in Fellini's 8½, Montecatini Terme has Italy's premier thermal waters, known for their curative powers and, at least once upon a time, for their great popularity among the wealthy. The town's abundance of art nouveau buildings went up during its heyday at the beginning of the 20th century. Like most other well-heeled resort towns, Montecatini attracts the leisured traveler; aside from taking the waters and people-watching in Piazza del Popolo, there's not a whole lot to do here. The mineral springs flow from five sources and are used to treat liver and skin disorders. Those "taking the cure" report each morning to one of the town's *stabilimenti termali* (thermal establishments; ⊠ Via Verdi 73 ☎ 0572/778509 information) to drink their prescribed cupful of water, whose curative effects became known in the 1800s.

Of Montecatini Terme's art nouveau structures, the most attractive is the **Terme Tettuccio** (⊠ Viale Verdi 41 ☎ 0572/778501), a neoclassical edifice with colonnades. Here Montecatini's healthful tonic spouts from fountains set up on marble counters, the walls are decorated with bucolic scenes on painted ceramic tiles, and in the morning an orchestra plays under a frescoed dome.

LUCCA

In this fortress town, Caesar, Pompey, and Crassus agreed to rule Rome as a triumvirate in 56 BC; it was later the first town in Tuscany to accept Christianity. Lucca still has a mind of its own, and when most of Tuscany was voting Communist as a matter of course, its citizens rarely followed suit. Within the city's ramparts, built between 1544 and 1645, the composer Giacomo Puccini (1858–1924) was born. He is celebrated, along with his peers, during the summer Opera Theater of Lucca Festival.

Exploring Lucca

The historic center of Lucca is walled, and motorized traffic is restricted. Walking or biking is the most efficient and most enjoyable way to get around. You can rent bicycles, and the center is quite flat, so biking is easy without the threat of traffic.

a good walk

Start at the **Museo Nazionale di Palazzo Mansi** ❹ ▶ on Via Galli Tassi, just within the walls. Walk down Via del Toro to Piazza del Palazzo Dipinto, and follow Via di Poggio to **San Michele in Foro** ❺. From Piazza San Michele, walk around to the back of the church and follow Via Beccheria south through Piazza Napoleone. Make a left through the smaller Piazza San Giovanni, which leads directly to the **Duomo** ❻. Check out the charming facade before going into the church and looking at the *Volto Santo* crucifix and the tomb of Ilaria del Carretto. Walk down Via dell'Arcivescovado, which is behind the Duomo; the street name changes to Via Guinigi just after crossing Via Santa Croce. Climb the tower of the **Palazzo Guinigi** ❼ and admire the view. Make a right heading out of Palazzo Guinigi and proceed down Via Sant'Andrea; make a right onto Via Fillungo. At Via Fontana take a left and follow it to Via Cesare Battisti. Make a right and head toward the church of **San Frediano** ❽, with its strangely mummified St. Zita, the patron saint of domestic workers. From the church, walk along Via San Frediano back toward the Fillungo; make a right and then a left, and head into the **Piazza del Anfiteatro Romano** ❾, where the Roman amphitheater once stood. Relax and have an aperitivo at one of the many cafés lining the piazza. Exit the piazza through the doorway to the left where you entered. Veer toward the right, following the curve of the buildings. Make a quick left onto Via del Portico and bear right. You will pass the church and piazza of San Pietro Somaldi on your left; just after the piazza make a left onto Via della Fratta. Continue straight; just after passing the church of San Francesco, you will find yourself at the **Museo Nazionale di Villa Guinigi** ❿.

TIMING The walk will take about three hours; add a half hour for lingering in each of the museums.

What to See

★ ❻ **Duomo.** The round-arched facade of the cathedral is an example of the rigorously ordered Pisan Romanesque style, in this case happily enlivened by a varied collection of small carved columns. Take a closer look at the decoration of the facade and of the portico below, which make for one of the most entertaining church exteriors in Tuscany. The Gothic interior contains a moving wood crucifix (called the *Volto Santo*, or Holy Face) brought here, as legend has it, in the 8th century (though it probably dates from between the 11th and early 13th century). The marble tomb of Ilaria del Carretto (1408) is the masterpiece of the Sienese sculptor Jacopo della Quercia (1371/74–1438). ⊠ *Piazza del Duomo* 🕾 *0583/ 490530* 💳 *€2* ☉ *Duomo: weekdays 7–5:30, Sat. 9:30–6:45, Sun. 11:30–11:50 and 1–5:30. Tomb: Nov.–Mar., weekdays 9:30–4:45, Sat. 9:30–6:45, Sun. 11:30–11:50 and 1–5; Apr.–Oct., weekdays 9:30–5:45, Sat. 9–6:45, Sun. 9–10 and 1–5:45.*

▶ ❹ **Museo Nazionale di Palazzo Mansi.** Highlights here are the brightly colored *Portrait of a Youth* by Pontormo and portraits of the Medici painted by Bronzino (1503–72) and others. ⊠ *Palazzo Mansi, Via Galli Tassi 43, San Donato* 🕾 *0583/55570* 💳 *€4, combination ticket with Museo Nazionale di Villa Guinigi €6.50* ☉ *Tues.–Sat. 9–7, Sun. 9–2.*

❿ **Museo Nazionale di Villa Guinigi.** On the east end of the historic center, the museum houses an extensive collection of local Romanesque and Renaissance art. ⊠ *Villa Guinigi, Via della Quarquonia, Lucca East* 🕾 *0583/496033* 💳 *€4, combination ticket with Museo Nazionale di Palazzo Mansi €6.50* ☉ *Tues.–Sat. 9–7, Sun. 9–2.*

❼ **Palazzo Guinigi.** The tower of the medieval palace contains one of the city's most curious sights: six ilex trees have established themselves at the top, and their roots have grown into the room below. From the tower there's a magnificent view of the city and the surrounding countryside. ⊠ *Palazzo Guinigi, Via Sant'Andrea 42, Amfiteatro* 🕾 *0583/919931 for tourist information* 💳 *€3.50* ☉ *Sept. 16–Feb. 28, Tues.–Sat. 9:30–6, Sun. 9–2; Mar., Tues.–Sat. 9:30–7, Sun. 9–2; Apr. 1–Sept. 15, Tues.–Sun. 9–midnight.*

★ **Passeggiata delle Mura** (walk on the walls). Any time of day when the weather is agreeable, you can find the citizens of Lucca cycling, jogging, strolling, or playing ball in this large, unusual park atop the ring of ramparts that surrounds the *centro storico* (historic center). Sunlight streams through two rows of tall plane trees to dapple the walkway, a loop almost 5 km (3 mi) in total length. Ten bulwarks are topped with lawns, many with picnic tables, some with play equipment for children. One caution: there are no railings along the ramparts' edge, and the drop to the ground is a precipitous 40 feet.

❾ **Piazza del Anfiteatro Romano.** A Roman amphitheater once stood on this spot; the medieval buildings built over the amphitheater retain its original oval shape and brick arches. It's a popular gathering place, with numerous cafés and some eclectic shops. ⊠ *Off Via Fillungo.*

❽ **San Frediano.** The church contains works by Jacopo della Quercia and, bizarrely, the lace-clad mummy of the patron saint of domestic servants, St. Zita. ⊠ *Piazza San Frediano, Amfiteatro* ☉ *Mon.–Sat. 8:30–noon and 3–5, Sun. 10:30–5.*

Lucca

KEY

▲ Start of walk

0 | 200 yards

0 | 200 meters

⑤ San Michele in Foro. The facade of this church, slightly west of the centro storico, is even more fanciful than the Duomo's. Check out the superb panel painting of Sts. Girolamo, Sebastian, Rocco, and Helen by Filippino Lippi (1457/58–1504) in the right transept. ⊠ *Piazza San Michele, San Michele* ⊙ *Daily 7:40–noon and 3–6.*

off the beaten path

FORTE DEI MARMI – One of Tuscany's most exclusive summer beach resorts, Forte dei Marmi is a favorite of moneyed Tuscans and Milanese, whose villas are neatly laid out in a vast pine woods. In summer a beachcomber's bonanza takes place on Wednesday morning, when everything from faux designer sunglasses to plastic sandals and terry towels goes on sale. It's 35 km (22 mi) northwest of Lucca and 65 km (40 mi) northwest of Florence—also near the marble-producing towns of Carrara (where Michelangelo quarried his stone), Seravezza, and Pietrasanta.

VILLA REALE – Eight kilometers (5 mi) north of Lucca in Marlia, this villa was once the home of Napoléon's sister, Princess Elisa. Restored by the Counts Pecci-Blunt, the estate is celebrated for its spectacular gardens, originally laid out in the 16th century and redone in the middle of the 17th century. Gardening buffs adore the legendary *teatro di verdura,* a theater carved out of hedges and topiaries; concerts are occasionally held here. Contact the **Lucca tourist office** (⊠ Piazza Santa Maria 125 ☎ 0583/919931) for details. ⊠ *Villa Reale* ☎ *0583/30108* ⌦ *€6* ⊙ *Mar.–Nov., guided visits Tues.–Sun. at 10, 11, noon, 3, 4, 5, and 6; Dec.–Feb., by appointment.*

Where to Stay & Eat

$$–$$$ ✕ **La Mora.** Just 9 km (5½ mi) outside Lucca, this former stagecoach station now serves classic Lucchese food. Start with the *minestra di farro* (soup made with emmer, a grain that resembles barley) with beans, or the exquisite homemade *tacconi* (a thin, short, wide pasta) with rabbit sauce. Though Lucca is not near the sea, La Mora's rendition of *cacciucco* (a Livornese fish stew) is succulent and not to be missed. The wine list offers some great wines from the area, as well as from just about everywhere else in Italy. ⊠ *Via Sesto di Ponte a Moriano 1748* ☎ *0583/406402* ▤ *AE, DC, MC, V* ⊙ *Closed Wed., Jan. 1–15, and June 15–30.*

$$ ✕ **Bucadisantantonio.** It's been around since 1782, and you can understand why. The staying power of the place is the result of its superlative Tuscan food, brought to the table by waitstaff that doesn't miss a beat. A white-walled interior hung with copper pots and brass musical instruments provides a classy, comfortable setting for enjoying the menu, which ranges from the simple but blissful *tortelli lucchesi al sugo* (meat-stuffed pasta with a tomato-and-meat-sauce) to such daring dishes as roast *capretto* (kid) with herbs. ⊠ *Via della Cervia 3, San Michele* ☎ *0583/55881* ⌲ *Reservations essential* ▤ *AE, DC, MC, V* ⊙ *Closed Mon., 2 wks in Jan., and 2 wks in July. No dinner Sun.*

FodorśChoice ★

$$ ✕ **Il Giglio.** Just off Piazza Napoleone, this restaurant is a place for all seasons, with a big fireplace in the dining room and an outdoor terrace in summer. A 2003 refurbishment spruced up the carpets and the walls while maintaining the 19th-century charm. The menu comprises Tuscan favorites such as *farro garfagnino* (a thick soup made with grain and beans) and *coniglio con olive* (rabbit stew with olives). Amiable white-jacketed waiters speak knowledgeably about the wine list. ⊠ *Piazza del Giglio 2, Duomo* ☎ *0583/494058* ▤ *AE, DC, MC, V* ⊘ *Closed Wed. and 15 days in Feb. No dinner Tues.*

$–$$ ✕ **Osteria del Neni.** Tucked away on a side street a block from San Michele, this delightful little place offers up tasty treats in a cozy space with paper place mats, wooden tables, and walls sponged in two different hues of warm orange. All the pasta is made in house, and if you're lucky enough to find ravioli *spinaci ed anatra in salsa di noci* (stuffed with duck and spinach, with a creamy but light walnut sauce), by all means order it. The menu changes regularly; in summer this splendid food can be enjoyed alfresco. ⊠ *Via Pescheria 3, San Michele* ☎ *0583/ 492681* ⌕ *Reservations essential* ▤ *MC, V* ⊘ *Closed Sun. and Jan.*

$$$$ ✕▨ **Locanda l'Elisa.** A stay here could evoke home—that is, if home is a neoclassical villa with a lush garden a short ride from the city. Most rooms are suites, with fresh flowers, antiques, and fine fabrics, and you're served by a caring staff. The restaurant Il Gazebo, a former Victorian conservatory, merits a visit even if you're not staying here. Sicilian chef Corrado Spinola offers two menus (one typically Tuscan, the other less rigidly so) and two divine tasting menus (one meat, one fish) in either "piccolo" or "grande" portions. ⊠ *Via Nuova per Pisa 1952, 55050, outside of town* ☎ *0583/379737* ▤ *0583/379019* ⊕ *www.locandaelisa. com* ↸ *3 rooms, 7 suites* ⌕ *Restaurant, in-room data ports, in-room safes, minibars, cable TV, pool, massage, bar, babysitting, dry cleaning, laundry service, concierge, Internet, free parking, some pets allowed* ▤*AE, DC, MC, V* ⊘ *Closed Jan. 7–Feb. 11* ⦿❘ *EP.*

$$$ ▨ **Hotel Ilaria.** The former stables of the Villa Bottini have been transformed into this modern hotel within the historic center. Rooms are done in warm wood veneer, and the second-floor terrace overlooking the villa makes a comfortable place to relax. The availability of free bikes is a great bonus in this bike-friendly city. ⊠ *Via del Fosso 26, Lucca East, 55100* ☎ *0583/469200* ▤ *0583/991961* ⊕ *www.hotelilaria.com* ↸ *30 rooms* ⌕ *In-room safes, minibars, cable TV, bicycles, bar, babysitting, dry cleaning, laundry service, concierge, meeting room, free parking, some pets allowed (fee), no-smoking rooms* ▤ *AE, DC, MC, V* ⦿❘ *BP.*

★ $$$ ▨ **Palazzo Alexander.** This small, elegantly appointed boutique hotel tucked into a quiet side street is a stone's throw from San Michele in Foro. The building, dating from the 12th century, has been restructured to create the ease common to Lucchesi nobility: timbered ceilings, warm yellow walls, and brocaded chairs adorn the public rooms, and the motif is carried into the guest rooms, all of which have high ceilings and that same glorious damask. Top-floor suites have sweeping views of the town. ⊠ *Via S. Giustina 48, San Michele, 55100* ☎ *0583/583571* ▤ *0583/583610* ⊕ *www.palazzo-alexander.com* ↸ *9 rooms, 3 suites, 1 apartment* ⌕ *In-room data ports, in-room safes, minibars, cable TV, bicycles, wine bar, babysitting, dry cleaning, laundry service, concierge, Internet, parking (fee), no-smoking rooms* ▤ *AE, DC, MC, V* ⦿❘ *BP.*

$ ⊞ **Piccolo Hotel Puccini.** Steps away from the busy square and church of San Michele, this little hotel is quiet, calm, and handsomely decorated. It also has parking (which must be reserved in advance) at a reasonable fee, a great advantage. ⊠ *Via di Poggio 9, San Michele, 55100* ☎ *0583/ 55421* 🖷 *0583/53487* ⊕ *www.hotelpuccini.com* ↳ *14 rooms* ♨ *Fans, in-room safes, cable TV, bar, babysitting, dry cleaning, laundry service, Internet, parking (fee), some pets allowed, no-smoking rooms; no a/c* ▭ *AE, DC, MC, V* ¶◎¶ *EP.*

Nightlife & the Arts

The **Estate Musicale Lucchese,** one of many Tuscan music festivals, runs throughout the summer in Lucca. Contact the **Lucca tourist office** (⊠ Piazza Santa Maria 125, Lucca East ☎ 0583/919931) for details. The **Opera Theater of Lucca Festival,** sponsored by the Opera Theater of Lucca and the school of music of the University of Cincinnati, runs from mid-June to mid-July; performances are staged in open-air venues. Call the Lucca tourist office for information.

Lucca Comics and Games (⊠ Via della Cavallerizza 11, outside of town ☎ 0583/48522 🖷 0583/91203 ⊕ www.luccacomicsandgames.com) plays host to a three-week festival running from mid-October to early November. Comics aficionados flock to Lucca for exhibitions, a comics market, and, of course, to meet one another. Check the Web site for exact dates and locations.

Sports & the Outdoors

The centro storico is flat and easily navigated because automobile traffic is severely limited. A splendid bike ride may be had by circling the entire historic center along the top of the bastions—affording something of a bird's-eye view. You can rent bikes at **Barbetti Cicli** (⊠ Via Amfiteatro 23, Amfiteatro ☎ 0583/517073). Bikes are also available for rental at **Poli Antonio Biciclette** (⊠ Piazza Santa Maria 42, Lucca East ☎ 0583/493787).

Shopping

Lucca's justly famed olive oil, available throughout the city, is exported around the world. Look for those made by Fattoria di Fubbiano and Fattoria Fabbri—two of the best.

A particularly delicious version of *buccellato,* a sweet, anise-flavored bread with raisins that is a specialty of Lucca, is baked at **Pasticceria Taddeucci** (⊠ Piazza San Michele 34, San Michele ☎ 0583/494933).

★ Chocoholics can get their fix at **Caniparoli** (⊠ Via S. Paolino 96, San Donato ☎ 0583/53456); they are so serious about their sweets that they do not make them from June through August because of the heat. On the second Sunday of the month there's a **flea market** in Piazza San Martino.

Bargain-hunters won't want to miss **Benetton Stock Outlet** (⊠ Via Mordini 17/19, Amfiteatro ☎ 0583/464533), with its brightly colored garments at reduced prices.

PISA

Pisa may have been inhabited as early as the Bronze Age. It was certainly populated by the Etruscans and, in turn, became part of the Roman Empire. In the early Middle Ages it flourished as an economic powerhouse—along with Amalfi, Genoa, and Venice, it was one of the maritime republics. The city's economic and political power ebbed in the early 15th century as it fell under the domination of Florence, though it enjoyed a brief resurgence under Cosimo I in the mid-16th century. Pisa endured heavy Allied bombing—miraculously, the Duomo and Leaning Tower were spared, along with some other grand Romanesque structures. Beyond the kitsch that the Leaning Tower has spawned, Pisa has much to offer. Its treasures are more subtle than Florence's, to which it is inevitably compared, though the city's cathedral-baptistery-campanile complex on Piazza del Duomo is among the most dramatic ensembles in Italy.

Exploring Pisa

Pisa, like many other Italian cities, is best seen on foot, and most of what's worth seeing is within walking distance. The views along the Arno are particularly grand and shouldn't be missed—there's a sense of spaciousness that is missing along the Arno in Florence. You should weigh the different options for combination tickets to sights on the Piazza del Duomo when you begin your visit. (The combination tickets are sold at the sights.)

a good walk   Start in the Campo dei Miracoli, exploring the complex containing the **Leaning Tower** ⓫, **Duomo** ⓬, **Battistero** ⓭, **Camposanto** ⓮, and **Museo dell'Opera del Duomo** ⓯. After a coffee or gelato, walk down Via Santa Maria—the Campanile will be behind you. At Piazza Felice Cavallotti, go left onto Via dei Mille and continue through Piazza dei Cavalieri to Via Dini, and make a right onto Borgo Stretto, a major thoroughfare lined with cafés. On the left, before the river, is the church of San Michele in Borgo. With its ornate 14th-century Pisan Romanesque facade and columns, it's vaguely reminiscent of a wedding cake. Walk up to Piazza Garibaldi and turn left along the Lungarno Mediceo. Practically at the Ponte alla Fortezza, on the left, is the **Museo Nazionale di San Matteo** ⓰.

TIMING   The walk takes about an hour and a half without stops—but there's lots to see along the way; stops could take a few hours, depending upon how long you stay in the Museo Nazionale di San Matteo.

What to See

⓭ **Battistero.** The Gothic Baptistery, which stands across from the Duomo's facade, is best known for the pulpit carved by Nicola Pisano in 1260. Ask one of the ticket takers if he'll sing for you inside the baptistery. The acoustics are remarkable; a tip of €3 is appropriate. ⊠ *Piazza del Duomo, Campo dei Miracoli* ☎ *050/561820* ⊕ *www.duomo.pisa.it* 🎫 *€5* ⊙ *June 22–Sept. 21, daily 8–7:40; Mar. 22–June 21 and Sept. 22–Dec. 21, daily 9–5:40; Dec. 22–Mar. 21, daily 9–4:40.*

KEY

🛈 Tourist information

▶ Start of walk

⓮ **Camposanto.** According to legend, the cemetery, a walled structure on the western side of the Campo dei Miracoli, is filled with earth from the Holy Land brought back by returning Crusaders. Contained within are numerous frescoes, notably the *Drunkenness of Noah* by Renaissance artist Benozzo Gozzoli and the disturbing *Triumph of Death* (14th century), whose authorship is disputed but whose subject matter shows what was on people's minds in a century that saw the ravages of the Black Death. ✉ *Camposanto, Campo dei Miracoli* ☎ *050/561820* ⊕ *www.duomo. pisa.it* 💶 *€5* ⊘ *June 22–Sept. 21, daily 8–7:40; Mar. 22–June 21 and Sept. 22–Dec. 21, daily 9–5:40, Dec. 22–Mar. 21, daily 9–4:40.*

⓬ **Duomo.** Pisa's cathedral was the first building to use the horizontal marble stripe motif (borrowed from Moorish architecture in the 11th century) common to Tuscan cathedrals. It's famous for the Romanesque panels depicting the life of Christ on the transept door facing the tower and for its expertly carved 14th-century pulpit by Giovanni Pisano. ✉ *Piazza del Duomo, Campo dei Miracoli* ☎ *050/561820* ⊕ *www.duomo. pisa.it* 💶 *€2, free Oct.–Mar.* ⊘ *Mar. 22–Dec. 21, Mon.–Sat. 10–7:40, Sun. 1–7:40; Dec. 22–Mar. 21, Mon.–Sat. 10–12:45, Sun. 3–4:45.*

★ ☝ ⓫ **Leaning Tower.** The Leaning Tower (Torre Pendente) provided the final grace note for the complex comprising the Duomo, Baptistery, and the

Camposanto. Construction started in 1174, and the lopsided settling was evident by the time work began on the third story. The tower's architects attempted to compensate by making the remaining floors slightly taller on the tilting side, but the extra weight only made the problem worse. The settling continued, to a point that by the end of the 20th century many feared it would simply topple over, despite all efforts to prop the structure up. Now it has been firmly anchored to the earth. In early 2000 the final step of restoring the tower to its original tilt of 300 years ago was executed, and it appears to have been successful. After years of being closed, it is once again open to the public for climbing. Legend holds that Galileo conducted an experiment on the nature of gravity by dropping metal balls from the top of the 187-foot-high tower; historians say this legend has no basis in fact (which is not quite to say that it is false). ⊠ *Campo dei Miracoli* ☎ *050/560547, reservations online at www.opapisa.it only* ⊕ *torre.duomo.pisa.it* ☎ *€15* ☉ *Nov.–Mar., daily 9–5:50; Apr.–Oct., daily 8–8.*

⑮ **Museo dell'Opera del Duomo.** At the southeast corner of the sprawling Campo dei Miracoli, the museum holds a wealth of medieval sculptures and the ancient Roman sarcophagi that inspired the figures of Nicola Pisano (circa 1220–84). ⊠ *Via Arcivescovado, Campo dei Miracoli* ☎ *050/560547* ⊕ *www.duomo.pisa.it* ☎ *€5* ☉ *June 22–Sept. 21, daily 8–7:20; Mar. 22–June 21 and Sept. 22–Dec. 21, daily 9–5:20; Dec. 22–Mar. 21, daily 9–4:20.*

⑯ **Museo Nazionale di San Matteo.** On the north bank of the Arno, this museum contains wonderful early Renaissance sculpture and a stunning reliquary by Donatello (circa 1386–1466). ⊠ *Lungarno Mediceo, Lungarni* ☎ *050/541865* ☎ *€4* ☉ *Tues.–Sat. 8:30–7:30, Sun. 8:30–1.*

Where to Stay & Eat

★ **$$$** ✕ **La Mescita.** High, vaulted ceilings and stencilled walls lined with wine bottles provide the simple decor at this trattoria. There's nothing simple, however, about the menu, as chef-owner Stefano Saviozzi and his wife, Elisabetta Bauti, turn out highly inventive, Tuscan-spirited dishes. The constantly changing menu draws produce and inspiration from the market just outside the door. Unusual *primi* (first courses) include *garganelli all'uovo con il guanciale croccante e passata di fagioli bianchi* (egg pasta with fried bacon and puréed beans), which gives new meaning to the idea of pork and beans. Desserts are not to be missed: save room for the *ricotta montata col cioccolato fuso* (fresh sheep's milk cheese topped with chocolate sauce). ⊠ *Via Cavalca 2, Santa Maria* ☎ *050/ 544294* ▤ *AE, DC, MC, V* ☉ *Closed Mon. and 3 wks in Jan., last 3 wks in Aug. No lunch Tues.*

$–$$ ✕ **Osteria dei Cavalieri.** This charming white-walled osteria a few steps from Piazza dei Cavalieri is reason enough to come to Pisa. The chef does it all—serves up grilled fish, pleases vegetarians, and prepares *tagliata* (thin slivers of rare beef) for meat lovers. There are three set menus—from the sea, garden, and earth—or you can order à la carte; at lunchtime, *piatti unici* (single plates) offer a quick alternative. Service can be a bit rushed, but try to linger over your wine anyway. Finish your meal with a lemon sorbet bathed in Prosecco (dry sparkling wine), and walk away feeling you've eaten like a king at plebeian prices. ⊠ *Via San Frediano 16, Santa Maria* ☎ *050/580858* ⊟ *AE, DC, MC, V* ⊘ *Closed Sun., July 25–Aug. 25, Dec. 29–Jan. 7. No lunch Sat.*

¢ ✕ **Vineria alla Piazza.** Translated, the name means, "wine store on the square," and the food here is as straightforward as the name: a simple blackboard lists two or three primi as well as secondi. When the kitchen runs out, the offering is erased from the board and a new one added— a guarantee the food is made-that-moment fresh. The primi are particularly good, especially the light-as-a-feather *polenta gratinata al gorgonzola* (cornmeal mixed with Gorgonzola and run briefly under the broiler). ⊠ *Piazza delle Vettovaglie 13, Santa Maria* ☎ *No phone* ⌂ *Reservations not accepted* ⊟ *No credit cards* ⊘ *Closed Sun.*

$$$$ ▦ **Hotel Relais dell'Orologio.** What used to be a private family palace is now an intimate hotel just around the corner from Campo dei Miracoli. As it opened in spring 2003, everything is sparkling new. Eighteenth-century decor fills the rooms and public spaces; some rooms have stencilled walls and wood-beamed ceilings. On the third floor, sloped ceilings add a decided air of romance. A large sitting room complete with fireplace provides a relaxing spot to read or sip a glass of wine. ⊠ *Via della Faggiola 12/14, Santa Maria, 56126* ☎ *050/830361* ▦ *050/ 551869* ⊕ *www.hotelrelaisorologio.com* ⏎ *16 rooms, 5 suites* ♨ *Dining room, room service, in-room data ports, in-room safes, minibars, refrigerators, cable TV, bar, babysitting, dry cleaning, laundry service, concierge, business services, meeting rooms, parking (fee), some pets allowed, no-smoking rooms* ⊟ *AE, DC, MC, V* |⊘| *EP.*

$$ ▦ **Royal Victoria.** In a pleasant palazzo facing the Arno a 10-minute walk from the Campo dei Miracoli, this hotel has been in the Piega family since 1837—such continuity probably explains why Charles Dickens and Charles Lindbergh, among others, have stayed here. Rooms, though dated, are simply furnished; many have splendid views of the river. The fourth-floor terrace is a perfect spot for an apertivo or postcard writing. An added plus is the hotel's rental-car service, which rents by the day, allowing easy access to beaches and points of interest outside town. ⊠ *Lungarno Pacinotti 12, Lungarni, 56126* ☎ *050/940111* ▦ *050/940180* ⊕ *www.royalvictoria.it* ⏎ *48 rooms, 40 with bath* ♨ *Room service, in-room data ports, cable TV, bicycles, bar, babysitting, dry cleaning, laundry service, concierge, parking (fee), some pets allowed; no a/c in some rooms, no fans in some rooms* ⊟ *AE, DC, MC, V* |⊘| *BP.*

Nightlife & the Arts

The **Luminaria** feast day on June 16 honors San Ranieri, the city's patron saint. Palaces along the Arno are lit with white lights, and there are plenty of fireworks; this is the city at its most beautiful. Pisa has a lively arts scene, most of which happens at the 19th-century Teatro Verdi. Music and dance performances are presented from September through May. Contact **Fondazione Teatro di Pisa** for schedules and information (⊠ *Via Palestro 40, Lungarni* ☎ *050/941111* ⊕ *www.teatrodipisa.pi.it.*).

HILL TOWNS SOUTHWEST OF FLORENCE

Submit to the draw of Tuscany's enchanting fortified cities, many dating to the Etruscan period, which crown the hills west of Siena. San Gimignano, known as the "medieval Manhattan" because of its forest of towers built by rival families, is perhaps the most heavily visited; but visitors are old hat to this Roman outpost, and with its tilted cobble streets and stout medieval buildings the days of Guelph-Ghibelline conflicts can seem palpable. Rising from a series of bleak gullied hills and valleys, Volterra has always been popular for its minerals and stones, particularly alabaster, which was used by the Etruscans for many implements, some now displayed in the exceptional and unwieldy Museo Etrusco Guarnacci. Blissfully off the tour-bus circuit, San Miniato is a peaceful hill town with a pleasant local museum and a convent where you can spend the night.

San Miniato

⑰ *42 km (26 mi) southeast of Pisa, 43 km (27 mi) southwest of Florence.*

Dating from Etruscan and Roman times, San Miniato was so named when the Lombards erected a church here in the 8th century and consecrated it to the saint. The Holy Roman Empire had very strong ties to San Miniato. Today the pristine, tiny hill town's narrow, cobbled streets are lined with austere facades dating from the 13th to 17th century. Its artistic treasures are on a par with those of other similar-size towns in the area, but the real reason for a trip is simply that the place is so pretty. St. Francis founded the 1211 **Convento e Chiesa di San Francesco** (Convent and Church of St. Francis), containing two cloisters and an ornate wooden choir. For a dose of monastic living, you can stay overnight. ✉ *Piazza San Francesco* ☎ *0571/43051* ⊙ *Daily 9–noon and 3–7; or ring bell.*

Although the **Museo Diocesano** is small, the collection has a number of subtle and pleasant works of art. Note the rather odd Fra Filippo Lippi *Crucifixion, Il Redentore* by Verrocchio (1435–88), and the small but sublime *Education of the Virgin,* by Tiepolo (1696–1770). ✉ *Piazza del Castello* ☎ *0571/418071* 🎟 *€2.58* ⊙ *Nov.–Mar., Tues.–Sun. 10–12:30 and 3–6; Apr.–Oct., Tues.–Sun. 9–noon and 3–6.*

Where to Stay & Eat

$–$$ ✕ **Il Convio.** A short drive down a steeply serpentine road from San Miniato brings you to this rustic country ristorante. Though the decor is simple (sponged walls with stenciled decoration), the menu is anything but. Four tasting menus (including a vegetarian option) give appropriately named chef Angelo Madonna a chance to show his stuff. And what stuff it is: he mixes up seemingly odd concoctions such as *crocette di alici fredde* (cold anchovy croquettes) topped with an emulsion of Worcestershire sauce and shrimp. Surprisingly, it works. ✉ *Via San Maiano 2* ☎ *0571/408114* ⊟ *AE, DC, MC, V* ⊙ *Closed Wed.*

¢ ⊡ **Convento di San Francesco.** For a complete change of pace, stay in this 13th-century convent in the company of five Franciscan friars. Rooms are simple, bordering on spartan, but clean and quiet. You can participate in religious devotions or or skip them altogether. All rooms have baths, and there are five rooms that groups can rent. It's a 10-minute walk from the town center. Plan to arrive before 8 PM and they'll give you a set of keys—thus sparing the usually obligatory convent curfew. ⊠ *Piazza San Francesco, 56020* ☎ *0571/43051* ᕔ *0571/43398* ⊳ *30 rooms* ⚒ *No a/c, no room phones, no room TVs, no kids under 12* ⊟ *No credit cards* ⍥ *EP.*

Volterra

🔞 *50 km (31 mi) west of Siena, 27 km (17 mi) southwest of San Gimignano.*

Unlike other Tuscan hill towns that rise above sprawling vineyards and rolling fields of green, Volterra—described by D. H. Lawrence in his *Etruscan Places* as standing "somber and chilly alone on her rock"—is surrounded by desolate terrain marred with industry and mining equipment. The fortress, walls, and gates still stand mightily over Le Balze, a stunning series of gullied hills and valleys to the west that were formed by irregular erosion. The town has long been known for its alabaster, which has been mined since Etruscan times; today the Volterrans use it to make ornaments and souvenirs sold all over town. A €7 combined ticket allows entry to the Museo Etrusco Guarnacci, the Pinacoteca e Museo Civico, and the Museo di Arte Sacra.

Volterra has some of Italy's best small museums. The extraordinarily large and unique collection of the **Museo Etrusco Guarnacci** is an enigma in a region from which many of the Etruscan artifacts have landed in state museums and at the Vatican. If only a curator had thought to cull the best of the 700 funerary urns rather than to display every last one of them. ⊠ *Via Don Minzoni 15* ☎ *0588/86347* ᕳ *Combined ticket* €7 ⊗ *Mar. 16–Nov. 3, daily 9–7; Nov. 4–Mar. 15, daily 9–2.*

The **Pinacoteca e Museo Civico** houses a highly acclaimed collection of religious art, including a *Madonna and Child with Saints* by Luca Signorelli (1445/50–1523) and a *Deposition* by Rosso Fiorentino (1494–1541) that is reason enough to visit Volterra. ⊠ *Via dei Sarti 1* ☎ *0588/87580* ⊕ *www.comune.volterra.pi.it* ᕳ *Combined ticket* €7 ⊗ *Mar. 16–Nov. 3, daily 9–7; Nov. 4–Mar. 15, daily 9–2.*

Next to the altar in the town's unfinished **Duomo** is a magnificent 13th-century carved-wood *Deposition*. Note the fresco by Benozzo Gozzoli (1420–97) in the Cappella della Addolorata. Along the left wall of the nave you can see the arrival of the Magi. ⊠ *Piazza San Giovanni* ☎ *0588/86192* ⊗ *Daily 7–7.*

Among Volterra's best-preserved ancient remains is the Etruscan **Porta all'Arco,** an arch dating from the 4th century BC now incorporated into the city walls. The ruins of the 1st-century BC **Teatro Romano,** a beautifully preserved Roman theater, are worth a visit. Adjacent to the theater are the remains of the **Roman terme** (baths). The theater complex is just outside the walls past Porta Fiorentina. ⊠ *Viale Francesco Ferrucci* ☎ *0586/260837* ᕳ €2 ⊗ *Mar.–May and Sept.–Nov., daily 10–1 and 2–4; June–Aug., daily 10–6:45; Dec.–Feb., weekends 10–1 and 2–4.*

Where to Stay & Eat

$ ✕ **Il Sacco Fiorentino.** The understated tone of this small two-room restaurant gives nothing away—its white walls, tile floors, and pink tablecloths are unremarkable. You'll forgive the lack of ambience, however, once the food starts arriving. The *antipasti del Sacco Fiorentino* are a medley of sautéed chicken liver, porcini, and polenta drizzled with balsamic vinegar. It just gets better: the *tagliatelle del Sacco Fiorentino* are a riot of curried spaghetti with chicken and roasted red peppers. ⊠ *Piazza XX Settembre 18* ☎ *0588/88537* ⊟ *AE, DC, MC, V* ⊘ *Closed Wed.*

$ ▦ **San Lino.** This hotel, once a convent, has wood beams and terra-cotta floors paired with modern-day comforts. It's within the town walls and a 10-minute walk from the main piazza. The restaurant, open only for guests and groups of 20 or more, serves regional specialties, including *zuppa alla volteranna*, a thick vegetable soup. ⊠ *Via San Lino 26, 56048* ☎ *0588/85250* ⊟ *0588/80620* ⊕ *www.hotelsanlino.com* ⇦ *43 rooms* ⚱ *Restaurant, minibars, cable TV, pool, dry cleaning, laundry service, concierge, Internet, parking (fee); no a/c in some rooms* ⊟ *AE, DC, MC, V* ⊘ *Closed Nov.–Jan.* ⦿ *BP.*

Shopping

A number of shops in Volterra sell boxes, jewelry, and other objects made of alabaster. The **Cooperativa Artieri Alabastro** (⊠ Piazza dei Priori 5 ☎ 0588/87590) has two large showrooms of alabaster pieces. In what was once a medieval monastery, the **Galleria Agostiniane** (⊠ Piazza XX Settembre 3 ☎ 0588/86868) crafts alabaster objects of all kinds. You can also see a free video on how the mineral is quarried and carved. At **Camillo Rossi** (⊠ Via Lungo le Mura del Mandorlo 7 ☎ 0588/86133) you can actually see craftspeople at work, creating alabaster objects for all tastes and budgets.

San Gimignano

⑲ *27 km (17 mi) east of Volterra, 57 km (35 mi) southwest of Florence.*

When you're high on a hill surrounded by centuries-old towers silhouetted against the blue sky, it's difficult not to fall under the medieval spell of San Gimignano. Its high walls and narrow streets are typical of Tuscan hill towns, but it is the surviving medieval "skyscrapers" that set the town apart from its neighbors and create its uniquely photogenic silhouette. Today 15 towers remain, but at the height of the Guelph-Ghibelline conflict there was a forest of more than 70, and it was possible to cross the town by rooftop rather than street. The towers were built partly to defend the town—they provided a safe refuge and were useful for pouring boiling oil on attacking enemies—and partly to bolster the egos of their owners, who competed with deadly seriousness to build the highest tower in town. When the Black Death devastated the population in 1348, power and independence faded fast and civic autonomy was ultimately surrendered to Florence.

Today San Gimignano isn't much more than a gentrified walled city, amply prepared for its booming tourist trade but still very much worth exploring. Despite the remarkable profusion of chintzy souvenir shops lining its main drag, there's some serious Renaissance art to be seen here and an equally important local wine (Vernaccia) to be savored. Escape at midday to the uninhabited areas outside the city walls for a hike and a picnic, and return to explore the town in the afternoon and evening, when things quiet down and the long shadows cast by the imposing towers take on fascinating shapes. You can buy two types of combination tickets for the sights; one costs €7.50 and covers just about everything, while the other costs €5.50 and is slightly more limited.

San Gimignano's most important medieval buildings are clustered around the central **Piazza del Duomo.** The imposing **Torre Grossa** is the biggest tower in town, with views that are well worth the climb. ⊠ *Piazza del Duomo 1* ☎ *0577/940008* ☜ *€5* ☉ *Mar.–Oct., daily 9:30–7:30; Nov.–Feb., daily 10–5:30.*

The **Palazzo del Popolo** houses the **Museo Civico,** featuring Taddeo di Bartolo's celebratory scenes from the life of San Gimignano. The town's namesake was a bishop of Modena who achieved sainthood by driving hordes of barbarians out of the city in the 10th century. Dante visited San Gimignano as an ambassador from Florence for only a single day in 1300, but it was long enough to get a room named after him, which now holds a *Maestà* by 14th-century artist Lippo Memmi. A small room contains frescoes by Memmo di Filippuccio (active 1288–1324) depicting a young couple's courtship, shared bath, and wedding. The highly charged eroticism of the frescoes may be explained, in part, by the fact that they were in what were probably the private rooms of the commune's chief magistrate. ⊠ *Piazza del Duomo* ☎ *0577/940008* ☜ *Museo Civico €5* ☉ *Mar.–Oct., daily 9:30–7:30; Nov.–Feb., daily 10–5:30.*

★　The Romanesque **Collegiata** is a treasure trove of frescoes, including Bartolo di Fredi's cycle of scenes from the Old Testament on the left nave wall dating from 1367. Taddeo di Bartolo's otherworldly *Last Judgment,* on the arch just inside the facade, depicts distorted and suffering nudes—avant-garde stuff for the 1390s. The New Testament scenes on the right wall, which may have been executed by Barna da Siena in the 1330s, suggest a more reserved, balanced Renaissance manner. The **Cappella di Santa Fina** contains glorious frescoes by Domenico Ghirlandaio (1449–94) depicting the story of this local saint. ⊠ *Piazza del Duomo* ☎ *0577/940316* ☜ *€3.50* ☉ *Mar.–Oct., weekdays 9:30–7:30, Sat. 9:30–5, Sun. 1–3; Nov.–Jan. 20, Mon.–Sat. 9:30–5, Sun. 1–5.*

The **Museo di Criminologia Medievale** (Museum of Medieval Criminology) displays cutting-edge medieval torture technology, along with operating instructions and a clear description of the intended effect. Though some scholars dispute the historical accuracy of many of the instruments displayed, the final, very contemporary object—an electric chair imported from the United States—does give pause. ⊠ *Via del Castello 1–3* ☎ *0577/ 942243* ☜ *€8* ☉ *Mar. 16–July 18, daily 10–7; July 19–Sept. 17, daily 10–midnight; Sept. 18–Nov. 1, weekdays 10–7, weekends 10–8; Nov. 2–Mar. 15, Mon.–Sat. 10–6, Sun. 10–7.*

Before leaving San Gimignano, be sure to see its most revered work of art, at the northern end of town, in the church of **Sant'Agostino:** Benozzo

Gozzoli's utterly stunning 15th-century fresco cycle depicting scenes from the life of St. Augustine. ✉ *Piazza Sant'Agostino* ☎ *0577/907012* ⊘ *Nov.–Mar., daily 7–noon and 3–6; Apr.–Oct., daily 7–noon and 3–7.*

Where to Stay & Eat

\$\$ ✕ **La Mangiatoia.** Gaily colored gingham tablecloths provide an interesting juxtaposition with rib-vaulted ceilings dating from the 13th century in this cozy spot. The lighthearted feminine touch might be explained by chef Susi Cuomo, who has been presiding over her kitchen for more than 20 years. The menu is seasonal—in the autumn, don't miss her *sacottino di pecorino al tartufo* (little packages of pasta stuffed with cheese and seasoned with truffles), and in summer enjoy lighter fare on the intimate, flower-bedecked terrace in the back. ✉ *Via Mainardi 5, off Via San Matteo* ☎ *0577/941528* ☰ *MC, V* ⊘ *Closed Tues., 3 wks in Nov., and 1 wk in Jan.*

¢ ✕ **Enoteca Gustavo.** The ebullient Maristella Becucci reigns supreme in this tiny wine bar (three small tables in the back, two in the bar, two bar stools) serving divine, and ample, crostini. The *crostino con carciofini e pecorino* (toasted bread with artichokes topped with semi-aged pecorino) packs a punch. So, too, does the selection of wines by the glass: the changing list has about 16 reds and whites, mostly local, all good. The cheese plate is a bit more expensive than the other offerings, but it's worth it. ✉ *Via San Matteo 29* ☎ *0577/940057* ⌁ *Reservations not accepted* ☰ *AE, DC, MC, V* ⊘ *Closed Tues.*

\$–\$\$ ✕▦ **Bel Soggiorno.** One wall of the spacious restaurant here (\$\$–\$\$\$) is glass, and beyond it is a sweeping view of a Tuscan hillside. The dining room is simple and rustic; the food, however, is not: the *petto di faraona con mele condite, salsa al miele e pecorino di fossa* (breast of guinea fowl with apples, honey, and aged pecorino) is a real treat. The restaurant and the hotel attached to it, with simple, airy rooms, have been in the same family since 1886. If you're looking for a place right within the town walls, look no farther. ✉ *Via San Giovanni 91, 53037* ☎ *0577/ 940375* ▤ *0577/940375* ⊕ *www.hotelbelsoggiorno.it* ⇨ *17 rooms, 4 suites* △ *Restaurant, minibars, cable TV, babysitting, dry cleaning, parking (fee)* ☰ *AE, DC, MC, V* ⊘ *Closed Jan. 6–Feb.; restaurant closed Wed.* ⊠ *BP.*

\$\$ ▦ **Pescille.** A rambling farmhouse 4 km (2½ mi) outside San Gimignano has been transformed into a handsome hotel with understated contemporary and country-classic motifs. From this charming spot you get a splendid view of San Gimignano and its towers. ✉ *Località Pescille, Strada Castel San Gimignano, 53037* ☎ *0577/940186* ▤ *0577/943165* ⊕ *www. pescille.it* ⇨ *38 rooms, 12 suites* △ *Cable TV, tennis court, pool, gym, bar, Internet, free parking; no a/c in some rooms* ☰ *AE, DC, MC, V* ⊘ *Closed Nov.–Mar.* ⊠ *BP.*

Colle Val d'Elsa

❷⓿ *50 km (31 mi) southwest of Florence, 24 km (15 mi) northwest of Siena.*

On the road from Florence to Siena, Colle Val d'Elsa rises dramatically along a winding road, its narrow streets lined with palazzos dating from the 15th and 16th centuries. For art enthusiasts, it's perhaps best known as the birthplace of Arnolfo di Cambio (circa 1245–1310), architect of Florence's Duomo. Once a formidable producer of wool, the town now produces glass and crystal sold in local shops. Colle has two distinct parts: the relatively modern and less interesting Colle Bassa and the older Colle Alta.

Where to Stay & Eat

★ $$$$ ✕ **Ristorante Arnolfo.** Food lovers should not miss Arnolfo, one of Tuscany's most highly regarded restaurants. Chef Gaetano Trovato sets high standards of creativity; his dishes daringly ride the line between innovation and tradition, almost always with spectacular results. The menu changes frequently and has two fixed-price options, but you are always sure to find fish in the summer and lots of fresh vegetables and herbs. The location is a tranquil spot in the center of town. ✉ *Piazza XX Settembre 52* 🕿🕿 *0577/920549* ▤ *AE, DC, MC, V* ⊘ *Closed Tues., mid-Jan.–mid-Feb., and 2 wks in Aug.*

★ $$$$ 🏨 **La Suvera.** Pope Julius II once owned this luxurious estate in the valley of the River Elsa, 28 km (17 mi) west of Siena and 56 km (33 mi) south of Florence. The papal villa and adjacent building have magnificently furnished guest rooms and suites appointed with antiques and modern comforts. La Suvera's first-rate facilities, including drawing rooms, a library, an Italian garden, a park, and the Oliviera restaurant (serving organic estate wines), make it hard to tear yourself away. ✉ *Pievescola (Casola d'Elsa), off SS541, 53030* 🕿 *0577/960300* 🖷 *0577/960220* ⊕ *www.lasuvera.it* ➾ *16 rooms, 16 suites* ⚒ *Restaurant, room service, in-room safes, minibars, cable TV, tennis court, pool, exercise equipment, massage, Turkish bath, mountain bikes, bar, library, dry cleaning, laundry service, concierge, Internet, meeting room; no kids under 12* ▤ *AE, DC, MC, V* ⊘ *Closed Nov.–Easter* ¶⊙¶ *BP.*

Greve in Chianti

❷❶   *27 km (17 mi) south of Florence, 40 km (25 mi) north of Siena.*

If there is a capital of Chianti, it is Greve, a friendly market town with no shortage of cafés, enoteche, and craft shops lining its main piazza. The sloping, asymmetrical **Piazza Matteotti** is attractively arcaded and has a statue of Giovanni da Verrazano (circa 1480–1528), the explorer who discovered New York harbor, in the center. At one end of the piazza is the **Chiesa di Santa Croce**, with works from the school of Fra Angelico (circa 1400–55). ✉ *Piazza Matteotti* ⊙ *Daily 9–1 and 3–7.*

Where to Stay & Eat

★ $$$ ✕ **Osteria di Passignano.** Sophisticated country dining may not get better than this seemingly simple restaurant next to the Vallombrosan abbey. A tiny sampling (in one case, a *sformatino di pecorino di fosso,* or flan made with aged pecorino) deliciously whets the appetite for what's to come. The kitchen team, a group of chefs all under 30, can do traditional as well as whimsical Tuscan—and then divine things such as the *maccheroni del Martelli al ragù bianco di agnelli e carciofi morellini* (pasta with a lamb and artichoke sauce), which really isn't Tuscan at all. The wine list is unbeatable, as is the service. ✉ *Via Passignano 33,*

Località Badia a Passignano ☎ *055/8011278* ▭ *AE, DC, MC, V* ⊗ *Closed Sun., Jan. 7–Feb. 1, and 15 days in Aug.*

★ **$–$$** ✕ **Ristoro di Lamole.** Although off the beaten path (in this case, the SS222), on a narrow, winding road lined with olive trees and vineyards, this place is worth the effort to find: the view from the outdoor terrace is divine, as is the simple, exquisitely prepared Tuscan cuisine. Start with the bruschetta drizzled with olive oil or the sublime *verdure sott'olio* (vegetables marinated in oil) before moving on to any of the fine secondi. The kitchen has a way with *coniglio* (rabbit); don't pass it up if it's on the menu. ⊠ *Lamole in Chianti* ☎ *055/8547050* ▭ *AE, DC, MC, V* ⊗ *Closed Jan. 6–Feb. 28.*

$$$ ▥ **Fonte de' Medici.** The Antinori family has been making wine since 1180, and in 2001 they extended their efforts into an agriturismo—appropriately, each of the individually decorated rooms and apartments bears the name of a grape. All are decorated with sponged walls, some with canopy beds, most with fireplaces and deep bathtubs, and nearly all with views of the tranquil countryside. Rooms are scattered between three structures, the busiest being Santa Maria a Macerata, and the most remote Podere Vivaio. If you're after bliss in the middle of Chianti, look no farther. ⊠ *Via Santa Maria a Macerata 31, 50020 Montefiridolfi* ☎*055/8244700* 🖶*055/8244701* ⊕*www.fontedemedici.com* ⇘*25 apts., 2 cottages* ♿ *Restaurant, picnic area, BBQs, fans, in-room data ports, in-room safes, kitchens, microwaves, refrigerators, cable TV, tennis court, pool, wading pool, exercise equipment, massage, sauna, steam room, mountain bikes, soccer, wine bar, wine shop, babysitting, laundry facilities, laundry service, Internet, meeting rooms, free parking, some pets allowed (fee); no a/c in some rooms, no fans in some rooms* ▭ *AE, DC, MC, V* ⊗ *Restaurant closed Nov.–Feb.*

Fodor'sChoice
★

$$ ▥ **Villa Vignamaggio.** This historic estate has guest rooms and apartments in a villa, as well as two small houses and a cottage on the grounds. The villa, surrounded by manicured classical Italian gardens, dates from the 14th century but was restored in the 16th. It's reputedly the birthplace of Mona Lisa, the woman later made famous by Leonardo da Vinci. The place also does tastings of its very fine wine; inquire at reception to organize a tasting. ⊠ *Via Petriolo 5, 50022* ☎ *055/854661* 🖶 *055/ 8544468* ⊕*www.vignamaggio.com* ⇘*3 rooms, 4 suites, 13 apartments, 2 cottages* ♿ *Minibars, cable TV, tennis court, 2 pools, playground, babysitting, laundry service, some pets allowed, no-smoking rooms* ▭ *AE, DC, MC, V* ⊗ *Closed mid-Nov.–mid-Mar.* ⍓ *BP.*

Panzano

㉒ *7 km (4½ mi) south of Greve, 29 km (18 mi) south of Florence.*

With its magnificent views, Panzano is one of the prettiest stops in Chianti. The town centerpiece is the church of **Santa Maria Assunta,** where you can see an *Annunciation* attributed to Michele di Ridolfo del Ghirlandaio (1503–77). ⊠ *Panzano Alto* ⊗ *Daily 7–noon and 4–6.*

Ancient even by Chianti standards, the hilltop church of **San Leolino** probably dates from the 10th century, but was completely rebuilt in the Romanesque style sometime in the 13th century. The 3-km (2-mi) trip south

CloseUp

BACCHUS IN TUSCANY

TUSCANY IS ITALY'S CLASSIC wine country. In addition to the world-famous Chianti, Tuscan winemakers produce other renowned wines, many of them labeled DOCG (Denominazione di Origine Controllata e Garantita) or DOC (Denominazione di Origine Controllata), indicating rigorous standards of production. Don't be afraid to sample something that doesn't bear this label, however; Tuscans have been making wine for 25 centuries, and DOC or not, they know what they're doing.

Vino Nobile di Montepulciano, the "Noble Wine," lays claim to its title by virtue of royal patronage and ancient history: the Etruscans were making wine here before Rome was founded. Much later, in 1669, England's William III sent a delegation to Montepulciano to procure this splendid wine. Less noble but no less popular is **Rosso di Montepulciano,** a light, fruity DOC red.

With its velvety black berries and structured tannins, **Brunello di Montalcino** is just as sophisticated as Vino Nobile. The strain of the Sangiovese grape variety used to make it was developed in 1870 by a local winemaker in need of vines that would better cope with windy weather. The resulting wine quicky became popular. Brunello has a younger sibling, the DOC **Rosso di Montalcino.**

Not all of Tuscany's great wines are reds; in fact, many give the region's highest honors to a white wine, **Vernaccia di San Gimignano.** This golden wine is made from grapes native to Liguria, and it's thought that its name is a corruption of Vernazza, a village that's part of the Ligurian coast's Cinque Terre.

To the foreigner, **Chianti** evokes Tuscany as readily as gondolas evoke Venice. This firm, full-bodied, and powerful wine pressed from mostly Sangiovese grapes is the region's most popular, and it's easy to taste why. More difficult to understand is the difference between the many kinds of Chianti: this DOCG region has seven subregions, including Chianti Classico, the oldest, whose wines have a gallo nero (black rooster) on the label. Each subregion has its own particularities, but the most noticeable—and costly—difference is between regular Chianti and the riserva (reserve) stock, aged for at least four years.

Some Italian winemakers, chafing at the strict regulations for making Chianti, sought to break free of the chains by mixing wines the way they wanted. Thus was born the so-called **Super Tuscan,** a largely fanciful title dreamed up by American journalists. But there's nothing fanciful (or inexpensive) about these French oak–aged wines, which are the toast of Tuscany.

Since most vineyards are in the country, the best way to visit is by car. The SS222 (aka the Strada Chiantigiana) will lead you through the heart of Chianti and to many local producers. More specifically, Le Strade del Vino (the Wine Roads) are routes marked out in various regions of Tuscany. You can hit the road with a map and stop at any number of wineries for tours and tastings. Many—especially smaller producers—offer free tastings without an appointment. Larger producers usually charge a small fee for a three-glass tasting, and sometimes require a reservation for a tour. Preliminary research can be conducted at www.terreditoscana.it (click on "Strade del Vino"), or visit any tourist information center in wine country (Greve, Montalcino, and Montepulciano are the best places to start) for guidance. Remember: always have a designated driver. These vineyards are usually off narrow, curving roads. Sobriety is a must.

of Panzano is worth it for the simplicity of the church's exterior and its 14th-century cloister. The 16th-century terra-cotta tabernacles are attributed to Giovanni della Robbia, and there's also a remarkable triptych attributed to the Master of Panzano that was executed sometime in the mid-14th century. Check with the **tourist office in Greve** (⊠ Viale Giovanni da Verrazano 33 ☎ 055/8546287) for open days and hours. ⊠ *Località San Leolino* ☎ *No phone* 🎫 *Free.*

Where to Stay & Eat

$$ ✕ **Oltre il Giardino.** An ancient stone farmhouse has been converted into a cozy dining area with a large terrace and spectacular views of the valley. Terra-cotta–colored, stenciled walls and simple wood tables provide the background for very tasty Tuscan food—the *peposo* (a beef stew laced with black pepper) is particularly piquant; the *tagliatelle sul piccione* (flat noodles with a delicate squab sauce) delightfully fragrant. If it's warm, enjoy your meal in the carefully planted garden. The wine list is particularly strong on the local variety, which in this case is Chianti Classico. ⊠ *Piazza G. Bucciarelli 42* ☎ *055/852828* 🖃 *AE, DC, MC, V* ⊘ *Closed Mon. and mid-Nov.–mid-Dec.*

$–$$ ▥ **Villa La Barone.** Formerly the home of the Viviani della Robbia family, this 16th-century villa retains many aspects of a private home. The honor bar allows you to enjoy an aperitivo in the tile barroom or on the terrace while admiring the view. And there are views here in abundance, from the pool to the rose garden to the back of the villa. Guest rooms have tile floors, white walls, and timber ceilings. The once-mandatory meal plan has been abolished, making this place a delight for budgeters. ⊠ *Via San Leolino 19, 50020 Panzano in Chianti* ☎*055/852621* 🖶*055/852277* ☎*30 rooms* ⚭ *Dining room, tennis court, pool, babysitting, laundry service, concierge, Internet; no a/c in some rooms, no room TVs* 🖃 *AE, MC, V* ⊘ *Closed Nov.–Easter* ⦿ *BP.*

Radda in Chianti

★ ㉓ *33 km (20 mi) south of Greve, 52 km (32 mi) south of Florence.*

Radda in Chianti sits on a hill separating Val di Pesa from Val d'Arbia. It's one of many tiny Chianti villages that invite you to stroll their steep streets; follow the signs pointing you toward the *camminamento,* a covered medieval passageway circling part of the city inside the walls. In Piazza Ferrucci, you'll find the **Palazzo del Podestà,** or Palazzo Comunale, the city hall that has served the people of Radda for more than four centuries. It has 51 coats of arms embedded in its facade. ⊠ *Piazza Ferrucci.*

| off the beaten path | **VOLPAIA –** Perched atop a hill 10 km (6 mi) north of Radda is this fairy-tale hamlet, a military outpost from the 10th to the 16th century and once a shelter for religious pilgrims. Every August, for the Festa di San Lorenzo, people come to Volpaia to watch for falling stars and a traditional fireworks display put on by the family that owns the adjacent wine estate and agriturismo lodging, **Castello di Volpaia** (⊠ Piazza della Cisterna 1, 53017 ☎ 0577/738066). |

Where to Stay & Eat

¢ ✕ **Osteria Le Panzanelle.** Nada Michelassi and Silvia Bonechi combined their accumulated wisdom in the hotel and restaurant worlds to create this hospitable place a few minutes outside Radda. Its small but carefully crafted menu has typical tastes of Tuscany, such as the exquisite *trippa alla fiorentina* (Florentine-style tripe) as well as unexpected treats like *crostone con salsiccia fresca* (toasted bread with fresh sausage). Two small, simple rooms and tables outdoors provide the setting to the tasty fare. The wine list, equally well thought out, is particularly strong on the local products—in this case, Chianti Classico and Super Tuscans. ⊠ *Località Lucarellia 29* ☎ *0577/733511* ☰ *MC, V* ☉ *Closed Mon.*

★ $$$–$$$$ ✕▥ **Relais Fattoria Vignale.** On the outside it's an unadorned manor house with an annex across the street. Inside it's refined country-house comfortable, with terra-cotta floors, sitting rooms, and nice stone- and woodwork. White rooms with exposed brick and wood beams contain simple wooden bed frames and furniture, charming rugs and prints, and modern white-tile bathrooms. The grounds, flanked by vineyards and olive trees, are equally inviting, with lawns, terraces, and a pool. The sophisticated Ristorante Vignale ($$$$) serves excellent wines and Tuscan specialties; the in-house enoteca ($$$), simpler Tuscan fare. ⊠ *Via Pianigiani 9, 53017* ☎ *0577/738300 hotel, 0577/738701 restaurant, 0577/738012 enoteca* ☎ *0577/738592* ⊕ *www.vignale.it* ⤴ *35 rooms, 5 suites* ⏢ *2 restaurants, in-room safes, minibars, cable TV, pool, bar, wine shop, library, laundry service, concierge, Internet, meeting room, free parking, no-smoking rooms* ☰ *AE, DC, MC, V* ☉ *Closed Jan.–Mar. 15, restaurant closed Thurs., enoteca closed Wed.* ¶ *BP.*

$$$ ▥ **Palazzo Leopoldo.** A former 15th-century palazzo has been turned into an invitingly intimate small hotel on Radda's main street. Rooms have high ceilings, and a contemporary interpretation of neoclassicism predominates. Chandeliers, in some of the suites and in public rooms, are 19th-century handcrafted reproductions of Venetian Renaissance originals. The staff speaks English, the tasty breads at breakfast are made locally, and when it's warm there's an inviting terrace. A spa has beauty treatments, and the restaurant serves mostly Tuscan food. ⊠ *Via Roma 33, 53017* ☎ *0577/735605* ☎ *0577/738031* ⊕ *www.palazzoleopoldo. it* ⤴ *8 rooms, 9 suites* ⏢ *Restaurant, room service, in-room data ports, in-room safes, some kitchenettes, minibars, refrigerators, cable TV, hot tub, massage, sauna, spa, bar, babysitting, dry cleaning, laundry service, concierge, Internet, meeting room, free parking, some pets allowed, no-smoking rooms* ☰ *AE, DC, MC, V* ☉ *Closed Jan. and Feb.* ¶ *BP, FAP, MAP.*

¢ ▥ **La Bottega di Giovannino.** The name is actually that of the wine bar run by Giovannino Bernardoni and his daughter Monica, who also rent rooms in the house just next door. This is a fantastic place for the budget-conscious traveler, as rooms are immaculate and beds comfortable. Most rooms have a stunning view of the surrounding hills. All have their own bath, though most of them necessitate taking a short trip outside one's room. ⊠ *Via Roma 6–8, 53017* ☎ *0577/738056* ⊕ *www. labottegadigiovannino.it* ⤴ *10 rooms* ⏢ *Bar; no a/c, no room phones* ☰ *MC, V* ¶ *EP.*

Castellina in Chianti

㉔ *14 km (8 mi) west of Radda, 21 km (13 mi) northwest of Siena.*

Castellina in Chianti, or simply Castellina, is on a ridge above the Val di Pesa, Val d'Arbia, and Val d'Elsa, and the panorama is bucolic in almost every direction you look. The imposing 15th-century tower hints at the history of this village, which was an outpost during the continuing wars between Florence and Siena.

Where to Stay

$$ ⊞ **Palazzo Squarcialupi.** This refurbished 15th-century palace on the main street in town offers a pleasant, restful place to stay. Rooms have high ceilings, white walls, and tile floors; bathrooms are tiled in local stone. Many of the rooms have a view of the valley below. Common areas are elegant but comfortable, and the breakfast buffet is ample. The multilingual staff goes out of its way to be helpful. Though there's no restaurant, the hotel will arrange for a light lunch in the warmer months. ⊠ *Via Ferruccio 22, 53011* ☎ *0577/741186* 🖷 *0577/740386* ⊕ *www. chiantiandrelax.com* 🛏 *9 rooms, 8 suites* ⚿ *Minibars, cable TV, bar, babysitting, dry cleaning, laundry service, Internet, free parking, some pets allowed* ⊟ *AE, DC, MC, V* ⊘ *Closed Nov.–Mar.* ⦿| *BP.*

$–$$ ⊞ **Collelungo.** One of the loveliest agriturismi in the area, Collelungo consists of a series of abandoned farmhouses that have been carefully remodeled. Set amid a notable vineyard (it produces internationally recognized Chianti Classico), the apartments—all with cooking facilities and dining areas—have exposed stone walls and that typical Tuscan tile floor. The *salone* (lounge), which possibly dates from the 14th century, has satellite TV; adjacent to it is an honor bar. In high season a minimum one-week stay is required. ⊠ *Podere Collungo 53011* ☎ *0577/740489* 🖷 *0577/741330* ⊕ *www.collelungo.it* 🛏 *12 apartments* ⚿ *BBQ, pool, bar, laundry service, free parking; no a/c, no room phones, no room TVs, no kids under 8* ⊟ *MC, V* ⊘ *Closed Nov.–Mar.* ⦿| *EP.*

SIENA

One of Italy's most enchanting medieval cities, Siena is the one city you should visit in Tuscany if you visit no other. Florence's great historical rival was in all likelihood founded by the Etruscans. During the late Middle Ages it was both wealthy and powerful, for it saw the birth of the world's oldest bank, the Monte dei Paschi, still very much in business. It was bitterly envied by Florence, which in 1254 sent forces that besieged the city for more than a year, reducing its population by half and laying waste to the countryside. The city was finally absorbed by the grand duchy of Tuscany, ruled by Florence, in 1559.

Sienese identity is still defined by its 17 medieval *contrade* (neighborhoods), each with its own church, museum, and emblem. Look for streetlights painted in the contrada's colors, plaques displaying its symbol, and statues embodying the spirit of the neighborhood. The various contrade uphold ancient rivalries during the centuries-old Palio, a twice-yearly horse race (held in July and August) around the main piazza.

Exploring Siena

Practically unchanged since medieval times, Siena stretches over the slopes of three steep hills, but you will find the most interesting sights in a fairly compact area. Be sure to leave some time to wander off the main streets. Most sights are concentrated in the pedestrian-only centro storico, so you will end up walking up and down a lot of steep streets. If you have only one day in Siena, see the Piazza del Campo, the Duomo and its Museo dell'Opera Metropolitana, and the Palazzo Pubblico. If you are seeing more sights, it will probably be worthwhile to buy a cumulative ticket (valid for three days, €7.50), good for entrance to the Duomo's Biblioteca Piccolomini, the Battistero, and the Museo dell'Opera Metropolitana. If you can overnight here, by all means do so: the city is filled with day-trippers and tour buses, and in the late afternoon and evening it empties out. Siena's medieval charm and narrow streets are thrown into high relief, and Piazza del Campo positively glows.

From Florence there are two basic routes to Siena. The speedy modern SS2 is good if you're making a day trip from Florence, as it's a four-lane divided highway. For a jaunt through Chianti, take the narrower and more meandering SS222, known as the Strada Chiantigiana. It's a gorgeous ride on only two lanes—patience is a necessity.

a good walk

Begin at the **Piazza del Campo** ㉕ ▶, one of Italy's finest squares, where you can visit the **Palazzo Pubblico** ㉖ and climb its adjacent tower, the Torre del Mangia. Cross the piazza and exit on the stairs to the left to Via di Città, one of Siena's main shopping streets. Up on the left is the enchanting Palazzo Chigi-Saracini, where concerts are often held. Step in to admire the especially well-preserved courtyard and cistern. Continue up the hill and take the second right, Via del Capitano, which leads to Piazza del Duomo. The **Duomo** ㉗ is a must-see, along with its **Battistero** ㉘ and **Museo dell'Opera Metropolitana** ㉙. Opposite the front of the Duomo is the **Spedale di Santa Maria della Scala** ㉚. Chief among Siena's other gems is the **Pinacoteca Nazionale** ㉛, a short walk straight back down Via del Capitano (which becomes Via San Pietro). The church of **San Domenico** ㉜ lies in the other direction; you could take Via della Galluzza to Via della Sapienza.

TIMING This walk should last a full day, taken at a leisurely pace and allowing some time to relax in the Piazza del Campo. Allow two days to really explore Siena. The *passeggiata* (evening stroll) along the main shopping streets should not be missed. Keep in mind that most shops are closed on Sunday and museums have variable hours.

What to See

㉘ **Battistero.** The Duomo's 14th-century Gothic Baptistery was built to prop up one side of the Duomo. There are frescoes throughout, but the highlight is a large bronze 15th-century baptismal font designed by Jacopo della Quercia and adorned with bas-reliefs by various artists, including two by Renaissance masters: the *Baptism of Christ* by Lorenzo Ghiberti (1378–1455) and the *Feast of Herod* by Donatello. ✉ *Piazza San Giovanni, Duomo* ⊕ *www.operaduomo.it* 🎟 *€2.50, combined ticket*

€ 7.50 ⊗ Nov.–Mar. 14, Mon.–Sat. 10–1 and 2–5, Sun. 2–5; Mar. 15–Oct., Mon.–Sat. 9–7:30, Sun. 2–7:30.

㉗ Duomo. A few minutes' walk west of Piazza del Campo, Siena's Duomo is beyond question one of the finest Gothic cathedrals in Italy. The facade, with its multicolor marbles and painted decoration, is typical of the Italian approach to Gothic architecture, lighter and much less austere than the French. The cathedral as it now stands was completed in the 14th century, but at the time the Sienese had even bigger plans. They had decided to enlarge the building by using the existing church as a transept for a new one, with a new nave running toward the southeast. But in 1348 the Black Death decimated Siena's population, the city fell into decline, funds dried up, and the plans were never carried out. The beginnings of the new nave can be seen from the steps outside the Duomo's right transept.

The Duomo's interior, with its coffered and gilded dome, is striking. It's most famous for its magnificent inlaid marble floors, which took almost 200 years to complete (beginning around 1370); more than 40 artists contributed to the work, made up of 56 separate compositions depicting biblical scenes, allegories, religious symbols, and civic emblems. They are covered for most of the year for conservation purposes but are usually unveiled every September for the entire month. The Duomo's pulpit, also much appreciated, was carved by Nicola Pisano between 1266 and 1268; the life of Christ is depicted on the rostrum frieze. In the **Biblioteca Piccolomini,** a room painted by Pinturicchio (circa 1454–1513) between 1502 and 1509, frescoes show scenes from the life of native son Aeneas Sylvius Piccolomini (1405–64), who became Pope Pius II in 1458. They are in excellent condition and reveal a freshness rarely seen in Renaissance frescoes. ⊠ *Piazza del Duomo, Città* ☎ *0577/ 283048* ⊕ *www.operaduomo.it* ⊡ *Biblioteca Piccolomini €1.50, combined ticket €7.50* ⊙ *Duomo Nov.–mid-Mar., Mon.–Sat. 7:30–5, Sun. 2–5; mid-Mar.–Oct., Mon.–Sat. 7:30–7:30, Sun. 2–7:30. Biblioteca Piccolomini Nov.–mid-Mar., Mon.–Sat. 10–1 and 2–5, Sun. 2–5; mid-Mar.–Oct., Mon.–Sat. 9–7:30, Sun. 2–7:30.*

> **need a break?**
>
> Not far from the Duomo and the Pinacoteca, Siena's **Orto Botanico** (Botanical Garden; ⊠ Via Pier Andrea Mattioli 4, Città ☎ 0577/ 232874) is a great place to relax and enjoy views of the countryside. It's open weekdays 8–12:30 and 2:30–5:30, Sat. 8–noon, with an entrance fee of €8. Guided tours in English are available with a reservation.

㉙ **Museo dell'Opera Metropolitana.** Built into part of the unfinished new cathedral's nave, the museum contains a small but important collection of Sienese art and the cathedral treasury. Its masterpiece is unquestionably the *Maestà* by Duccio (circa 1255–1318), painted around 1310 and magnificently displayed in a room devoted entirely to the artist's work. The tower inside the museum offers a splendid view. ⊠ *Piazza del Duomo, next to the Duomo, Città* ☎ *0577/283048* ⊕ *www.operaduomo.it* ⊡ *€5.50, combined ticket €7.50* ⊙ *Nov.–mid-Mar., daily 9–1:30; mid-Mar.–Sept., daily 9–7:30; Oct., daily 9–6.*

㉖ **Palazzo Pubblico.** The focal point of the Piazza del Campo, the Gothic Palazzo Pubblico has served as Siena's town hall since the 1300s. It now also contains the **Museo Civico,** its walls covered with early Renaissance frescoes. The nine governors of Siena once met in the Sala della Pace, famous for Ambrogio Lorenzetti's frescoes called *Allegories of Good and Bad Government,* painted in the late 1330s to demonstrate the dangers of tyranny. The good government side depicts a utopia, showing first the virtuous ruling council surrounded by angels and then scenes of a perfectly running city and countryside. Conversely, the bad government fresco tells a tale straight out of Dante. The evil ruler and his advisers have horns and fondle strange animals, while the town scene depicts the seven mortal sins in action. Interestingly, the bad government fresco is severely damaged, and the good government fresco is in terrific condition. The **Torre del Mangia,** the palazzo's famous bell tower, is named after one of its first bell ringers, Giovanni di Duccio (called Mangiaguadagni, or earnings eater). The climb up to the top is long and steep, but the view makes it worth every step. ⊠ *Piazza del Campo 1, Città* ☎ *0577/292226* ⊡ *Torre del Mangia €5.50, Museo Civico €6.50, combined ticket for Torre and Museo €9.50* ⊙ *Torre del Mangia Nov.–Mar. 15, daily 10–4; Mar. 16–Oct., daily 10–7. Museo Civico Nov.–Mar. 15, daily 10–6:30; Mar. 16–Oct., daily 10–7.*

㉕ Piazza del Campo. Known simply as Il Campo (The Field), this fan-shaped
FodorsChoice   piazza is one of the finest in Italy. Constructed toward the end of the
★   12th century on a market area unclaimed by any contrada, it's still the
heart of town. The bricks of the Campo are patterned in nine different
sections—representing each member of the medieval Government of Nine.
At the top of the Campo is a copy of the **Fonte Gaia,** decorated in the
early 15th century by Siena's greatest sculptor, Jacopo della Quercia,
with 13 sculpted reliefs of biblical events and virtues. Those lining the
rectangular fountain are 19th-century copies; the originals are in the
Spedale di Santa Maria della Scala. On Palio days (July 2 and August
16), the Campo and all its surrounding buildings are packed with cheer-
ing, frenzied locals and tourists craning their necks to take it all in.

㉛ Pinacoteca Nazionale. The national picture gallery contains an excellent
collection of Sienese art, including works by native sons Ambrogio
Lorenzetti (active 1319–48), Duccio, and Domenico Beccafumi
(1486–1551). ⊠ *Via San Pietro 29, Città* ☎ *0577/281161* 🎫 *€4*
🕙 *Mon. 8:30–1:15, Tues.–Sat. 8:30–7:15, Sun. 8:30–1:15.*

㉜ San Domenico. In the church of San Domenico is the **Cappella di Santa
Caterina,** with frescoes by Sodoma portraying scenes from the life of St.
Catherine of Siena. Catherine was a much-respected diplomat, noted for
ending the Great Schism by persuading the pope to return to Rome from
Avignon. The saint's preserved head and finger are on display in the chapel.
⊠ *Costa di Sant'Antonio, Camollìa* ☎ *0577/280893* 🕙 *Nov.–mid-Mar.,
daily 9–1 and 3–6; mid-Mar.–Oct., daily 7–1 and 2:30–6:30.*

★ **㉚ Spedale di Santa Maria della Scala.** A former hospital and hostel for weary
pilgrims, built beginning in the late 9th century, continues to evolve into
a grand exhibition space, hosting major contemporary art shows and
housing, among other gems, some of the Fonte Gaia sculpted reliefs by
Jacopo della Quercia (1371/74–1438). Even if you are not particularly
taken with Etruscan objects, the subterranean archaeological museum
contained within the ospedale is not to be missed. Its interior design is
sheer brilliance—it's beautifully lighted, eerily quiet, and an oasis of cool
on hot summer days. ⊠ *Piazza del Duomo, opposite the front of the
Duomo, Città* ☎ *0577/224811* 🎫 *€5.20* 🕙 *Mar. 17–Oct., daily 10–6;
Nov. and Dec. 23, daily 10:30–4:30; Dec. 24–Jan. 6, daily 10–6; Jan.
7–Mar. 16, daily 10:30–4:30.*

Where to Stay & Eat

$$$–$$$$ ✕ **Antica Trattoria Botteganova.** Just outside the city walls, along the
road that leads north to Chianti, the Botteganova is arguably the best
restaurant in Siena. Chef Michele Sorrentino's cooking is all about
clean flavors, balanced combinations, and inviting presentation. Look
for inspiring dishes such as spaghetti *alla chitarra in salsa di astice pic-
cante* (with a spicy lobster sauce). The interior, with high vaulting, is
relaxed yet classy, and the service is first rate. There's a small room for
nonsmokers. ⊠ *Strada per Montevarchi (SS408) 29, 2 km (1 mi) north
of Siena* ☎ *0577/284230* 🖃 *AE, DC, MC, V* 🕙 *Closed Sun.*

$$–$$$ ✕ **Le Logge.** Bright flowers provide dashes of color in this classic Tuscan
dining room with stenciled ceilings. The wooden cupboards (now filled

with wine bottles) lining the walls recall the turn-of-the-19th-century food store it once was. The menu, with four or five primi and secondi, changes regularly, but almost always includes their classic *malfatti all'osteria* (ricotta and spinach dumplings in a cream sauce). Inventive desserts such as *coni con mousse al cioccolato e gelato allo zafferano* (two diminutive ice cream cones with chocolate mousse and saffron ice cream) provide a perfect ending to the meal. ⊠ *Via del Porrione 33, San Martino* ☎ *0577/48013c* ⊟ *AE, DC, MC, V* ☉ *Closed Sun. and 3 wks in Jan.*

\$\$ ✕ **Hosteria il Carroccio.** For an intimate meal, angle for one of the few seats here to try dishes both creative and deliciously simple. The *palline di pecorino con lardo e salsa di pere* (pecorino cheese balls wrapped with pork fat and briefly grilled), for instance, are sublime. So, too, are the amply proportioned *primi*—the *pici* (a local specialty resembling spaghetti) is especially good. In summer you can sit outdoors. ⊠ *Via Casato di Sotto 32* ☎ *0577/41165* ⊟ *MC, V* ☉ *Closed Wed.*

\$–\$\$ ✕ **La Taverna di San Giuseppe.** Though it's not too far from il Campo, you would have to know about this place to find it, as it's on a residential street with very few tourist attractions. It's one long, cavernous room filled mostly with people speaking Italian. The menu teems with Tuscan favorites with Sienese twists, including prosciutto *di cinta senese* (prosciutto made from local, once nearly extinct, porcines). Here they make their version of *fegatini* (chicken livers) with spleen; it's aromatic and flavorful. ⊠ *Via G. Duprè 132, San Martino* ☎ *0577/42286* ⊟ *AE, DC, MC, V* ☉ *Closed Sun.*

\$ ✕ **Osteria Castelvecchio.** In a stall in the oldest part of town, this little restaurant with high, ribbed vaults mixes past and present on its daily-changing menu. You're likely to find such Sienese standards as spaghetti *saporiti con gli aromi* (with tomatoes and herbs) as well as offbeat selections such as *sformatino del pastore con soia e cardi al vino* (a ricotta and greens concoction with cardoons and tofu). Husband-and-wife proprietors Simone Romi and Sabrina Fabi are committed to *piatti di verdura* (vegetarian dishes), and they've got a great wine list. ⊠ *Via Castelvecchio 65, Città* ☎ *0577/49586* ⊟ *AE, DC, MC, V* ☉ *Closed Tues.*

\$\$\$\$ ⊞ **Certosa di Maggiano.** A former 14th-century monastery converted into an exquisite country hotel, this haven of gracious living is about 1½ km (1 mi) from the center of Siena. Rooms have the style and comfort of an aristocratic villa, with classic prints and bold colors such as a happy daffodil yellow. Common rooms are luxurious, with fine woods and leather. In warm weather, breakfast is served on the patio next to the garden ablaze with flowers. Half board is required in high season. ⊠ *Via Certosa 82, take the Siena Sud exit off superstrada, 53100* ☎ *0577/288180* 🖷 *0577/288189* ⊕ *www.certosadimaggiano.it* ⇥ *6 rooms, 11 suites* ⚹ *Restaurant, minibars, cable TV, tennis court, pool, exercise equipment, dry cleaning, laundry service, concierge, helipad, no-smoking rooms; no kids under 12* ⊟ *AE, MC, V* ⍥ *MAP.*

\$\$\$\$ ⊞ **Park.** What began life in the 16th century as a home for the prosperous Gori family is now an elegant hotel a short ride from the centro storico. Many of the rooms, with plush carpeting, large bathrooms, and flowered drapery, face a courtyard complete with well and stunning view of olive trees and Siena beyond. Public rooms have sweeping ceilings, highly polished terra-cotta floors, and comfortable couches. The Olivo restaurant serves regional cuisine, and the breakfast buffet includes splendid scrambled eggs. The staff is extraordinarily helpful and polite. ⊠ *Via Marciano 18, 53100* ☎ *0577/290290* 🖷 *0577/49020* ⊕ *www. royaldemeure.com* 📾 *65 rooms, 1 suite* ♨ *Restaurant, room service, minibars, cable TV, 6-hole golf course, tennis court, pool, bar, babysitting, dry cleaning, laundry service, concierge, Internet, business services, meeting rooms, some pets allowed, no-smoking rooms* ⊟ *AE, DC, MC, V* ⊘ *Closed Nov.–Mar.* ⦿| *BP.*

★ **$$$** 🏨 **Palazzo Ravizza.** There might not be a more romantic and prettier place in the center of Siena than this quietly charming pensione just outside Porta San Marco and a 10-minute walk to the Duomo. Rooms have high ceilings, antique furniture, big windows, and bathrooms decorated with hand-painted tiles. The attached restaurant serves tasty Tuscan classics, which can be eaten outdoors when it's warm. ⊠ *Pian dei Mantellini 34, Città, 53100* ☎ *0577/280462* 🖷 *0577/221597* ⊕ *www. palazzoravizza.it* 📾 *40 rooms, 4 suites* ♨ *Restaurant, some in-room safes, some minibars, cable TV, bar, laundry service, concierge, free parking, some pets allowed* ⊟ *AE, DC, MC, V* ⦿| *BP.*

$$ 🏨 **Antica Torre.** A restored 16th-century tower within the town walls in the southeast corner of Siena, Antica Torre is a 10-minute walk from Piazza del Campo. It's the work of a cordial couple who have carefully evoked a private home, with only eight simply but tastefully furnished guest rooms. The old stone staircase, wooden beams, and original brick vaults here and there are reminders of the building's great age. ⊠ *Via Fieravecchia 7, San Martino, 53100* ☎ *0577/222255* ⊕ *www. anticatorresiena.it* 📾 *8 rooms* ♨ *Minibars, cable TV, Internet* ⊟ *AE, DC, MC, V* ⦿| *BP.*

¢ 🏨 **Alma Domus.** If you're after a contemplative, utilitarian experience, this might be the place for you. Run by the committed parishioners of the Santurario Santa Caterina (Sanctuary of St. Catherine), it's just around the corner from the church of San Domenico. Rooms are spartan and very clean. Many have a view of the Duomo and the rest of Siena, which might make the 11:30 curfew liveable. ⊠ *Via Camporeggio 37, Camollia, 53100* ☎ *0577/44177* 🖷 *0577/47601* 📾 *31 rooms* ♨ *No-smoking floors; no room phones, no room TVs* ⊟ *No credit cards* ⦿| *EP.*

Nightlife & the Arts

Music

In the last week of July, Siena hosts the **Settimane Musicali Senesi,** a series of concerts held in churches and courtyards with performances of local and other music. Contact **Accademia Musicale Chigiana** (⊠ Via di Città 89, Duomo ☎ 0577/22091 ⊕ www.chigiana.it) for information. Other musical events occur throughout the year; inquire at the tourist information office for details.

Sports

Siena's **Palio** horse race takes place every year on July 2 and August 16, but its spirit lives all year long. Three laps around a makeshift track in

Piazza del Campo by horses and riders representing the city's contrade earn participants the respect or scorn of the city. The event is so important to the Sienese that bribery, kidnapping of the jockeys, and other brutalities are commonplace—sabotaging a horse's reins is the only thing that remains taboo. A horse doesn't even need its rider to be considered a valid winner. Festivities kick off three days prior to the main event, with trial races, banquets lining the streets, and late-night celebrations. As the Palio approaches, residents don scarves with their contrada's colors and march through city streets in medieval costumes. Tickets are usually sold out months in advance; call the **tourist office** (✉ Piazza del Campo 56 ☎ 0577/280551) for information. It's possible you might luck out and get an unclaimed seat or two; if not, the center of the piazza is free to all on a first-come, first-served basis, until just moments before the start.

Shopping

Siena is known for its cakes and cookies, their recipes of medieval origin—look for *cavallucci* (sweet spice biscuits), *panforte* (a densely packed concoction of honey, hazelnuts, almonds, and spices), and *ricciarelli* (almond-paste cookies). The best place in town to find Sienese baked goods, as well as to grab a cappuccino, is **Nannini** (✉ Banchi di Sopra 24, Camollìa ☎ 0577/236009).

Siena has excellent specialty food and wine shops. **La Bottega dei Sapori Antichi** (✉ Via delle Terme 41, Camollìa ☎ 0577/285501) is a good option for local products. Italy's only state-sponsored enoteca, **Enoteca Italiana** (✉ Fortezza Medicea, Camollìa ☎ 0577/288497) sells wines from all over Italy.

Siena Ricama (✉ Via di Città 61, Duomo ☎ 0577/288339) has embroidered linens and other housewares. Chiara Perinetti Casoni at **Bottega dell'Arte** (✉ Via Stalloreggi 47, Città ☎ 0577/40755) creates high-quality copies of 14th- and 15th-century Sienese paintings using tempera and gold leaf on panels.

AREZZO & CORTONA

The hill towns of Arezzo and Cortona carry on age-old local traditions—in June and September, for example, Arezzo's Romanesque and Gothic churches are enlivened by the Giostra del Saracino, a costumed medieval joust. Arezzo has been home to important artists since ancient times, when Etruscan potters produced their fiery-red vessels here. Fine examples of the work of Luca Signorelli are preserved in Cortona, his hometown.

Arezzo

 81 km (50 mi) southeast of Florence, 74 km (46 mi) northwest of Perugia

Arezzo was the birthplace of both the poet Petrarch and the Renaissance artist and art historian Giorgio Vasari. Guido d'Arezzo, the inventor of musical notation, was also born here. Today Arezzo is best known for the magnificent frescoes by Piero della Francesca (circa 1420–92) in the

Fodor'sChoice **Basilica di San Francesco.** Painted between 1452 and 1466, they depict
★ scenes from the *Legend of the True Cross* on three walls of the *cappella
maggiore,* or altar choir. What Sir Kenneth Clark called "the most perfect morning light in all Renaissance painting" may be seen in the lowest section of the right wall, where the troops of the emperor Maxentius
flee before the sign of the cross. Unveiled in 2000 after a painstaking
15-year restoration, they may now be seen in all their brilliance. ⊠ *Piazza San Francesco* ☎ *0575/900404* ⊕ *www.pierodellafrancesca.it*
⊠ *€5.03* ☉ *Nov.–Mar., weekdays 9–5:30, Sat. 9–5, Sun. 1–5; Apr.–Oct.,
weekdays 9–6:30, Sat. 9–5:30, Sun. 1–5:30. Admission limited to 25
people every ½ hr. Reservations required.*

Some historians maintain that Arezzo's oddly shaped, sloping **Piazza
Grande** was once the site of an ancient Roman forum. Now it plays host
to a first-Sunday-of-the-month antiques fair as well as the **Giostra del
Saracino** (Joust of the Saracen), featuring medieval costumes and competition, held here in the middle of June and on the first Sunday of September. Check out the 16th-century loggia designed by native son Giorgio
Vasari on the northeast side of the piazza.

The curving, tiered apse on Piazza Grande belongs to **Santa Maria della
Pieve,** one of Tuscany's finest Romanesque churches, built in the 12th
century. Don't miss the Portale Maggiore (great door) with its poly-
chromed figures representing the months; restored in 2002, they are remarkably vibrant. ⊠ *Corso Italia* ☎ *0575/377678 for tourist information*
☉ *Daily 8–noon and 3–6.*

Arezzo's medieval **Duomo** (at the top of the hill) contains a fresco of a
somber *Magdalen* by Piero della Francesca; look for it next to the large
marble tomb near the organ. ⊠ *Piazza del Duomo 1* ☎ *0575/23991*
☉ *Daily 7–12:30 and 3–6:30.*

The **Casa di Giorgio Vasari** (Giorgio Vasari House) was designed and decorated as his private home by the region's leading art historian and architect around 1540. ⊠ *Via XX Settembre 55* ☎ *0575/409040* ⊠ *€2*
☉ *Mon. and Wed.–Sat. 8:30–6:30, Sun. 8:30–1:30.*

Where to Stay & Eat

★ ¢ ✕ **La Torre di Gnicche.** If you're looking for a small, intimate place with
Italian home cooking, grab a light lunch or dinner here. This one-room
eatery seating about 30 is part of a Renaissance palazzo. The short menu
includes assorted crostini, sensational *delicatezze sott'olio* (vegetables
marinated in oil), cheese plates, and an earthy *polpettone* (meat loaf).
The formidable and eminently affordable wine list makes eating *ribollita* (a hearty, traditional Tuscan soup) a heightened experience. ⊠ *Piaggia San Martino 8* ☎ *0575/352035* ▤ *MC, V* ☉ *Closed Wed.*

$–$$ ▦ **Castello di Gargonza.** Enchantment reigns at this tiny 13th-century
hamlet in the countryside near Monte San Savino, part of the fiefdom
of the aristocratic Florentine Guicciardini and restored by the modern
Count Roberto Guicciardini as a way to rescue a dying village. A castle, church, and cobbled streets set the stage. A minimum two-night stay
in any of the rooms is appreciated; cottages and apartments rent Saturday to Saturday throughout the year. These have one to six rooms each,

sleep 2 to 10 people, and have as many as four baths. La Torre restaurant (closed Tuesday) serves local fare. ⊠ *52048 Monte San Savino* ☏ *0575/847021* 🖷 *0575/847054* ⊕ *www.gargonza.it* ⤢ *18 rooms, 11 apartments, 1 suite* 🍴 *Restaurant, pool, meeting room; no a/c, no room TVs* 🖃 *AE, DC, MC, V* ⊘ *Closed 3 wks in Jan. and 3 wks in Nov.* ⦿⦙ *BP.*

★ $ 🎥 **Calcione Country and Castle.** The elegant Marchesa Olivella Lotteringhi della Stufa has turned her six-centuries-old family homestead into a top-notch agriturismo. Think sophisticated rustic; many of the apartments have open fireplaces, the houses have a private pool (the rest share the estate pool), and there are private lakes for fishing and windsurfing. Calcione is convenient to Arezzo, Siena, San Gimignano, and the delights of Umbria. From June to mid-September, a minimum one-week stay is mandatory. ⊠ *Lucignano, 52046* ☏ *0575/837100* 🖷 *0575/837153* ⊕ *www.calcione.com* ⤢ *2 houses, 1 cottage, 6 apartments* 🍴 *BBQ, 3 pools, 3 lakes, babysitting, some pets allowed; no a/c, no phones in some rooms, no room TVs* 🖃 *No credit cards* ⊘ *Closed Nov.–Mar.* ⦿⦙ *EP.*

Shopping

FLEA MARKET On the first Sunday of each month a colorful flea market with antiques and other less precious objects for sale takes place in the **Piazza Grande.**

GOLD Gold production here is on an industrial scale. Uno-A-Erre is the largest of several factories supplying local shops. Big-time baubles can be purchased in the town center. For gold jewelry set with precious or semi-precious stones, try **Il Diamante** (⊠ Via Guido Monaco 69 ☏ 0575/353450). **Borghini** (⊠ Corso Italia 130 ☏ 0575/24678) has an impressive collection of fine jewelry. **Prosperi** (⊠ Corso Italia 76 ☏ 0575/20746) works wonders in gold, silver, and platinum.

OUTLET MALLS Savvy shoppers head to **I Pelletieri d'Italia** (⊠ Località Levanella, SS69, Montevarchi ☏ 055/91901) for discounted Prada products. Go during the week, or if a weekend is your only option remember that patience is a virtue. If you're on an outlet roll, continue north to **The Mall** (⊠ Via Europa 8, Leccio Reggello ☏ 055/8657775), where discounted lines such as Gucci, Yves Saint Laurent, Armani, Sergio Rossi—to name but a few—abound.

TEXTILES At **Busatti** (⊠ Corso Italia 48 ☏ 0575/355295 ⊕ www.busatti.com), the Busatti-Sassolini family has been making sumptuous handwoven linen, wool, hemp, and cotton for more than a century, most adorned with hand-stitched hems, embroideries, and lace.

Cortona

㉞ *29 km (18 mi) south of Arezzo, 117 km (73 mi) southeast of Florence.*

Magnificently situated, with olive trees and vineyards creeping up to its walls, pretty Cortona commands sweeping views over Lake Trasimeno and the plain of the Valdichiana. Its two galleries and churches are rarely visited; its delightful medieval streets are a pleasure to wander for their own sake.

Cortona is considered one of Italy's oldest towns—popularly known as the "Mother of Troy and Grandmother of Rome." Tradition claims that it was founded by Dardanus, also the founder of Troy (after whom the Dardanelles were named). He was fighting a local tribe, so the story goes, when he lost his helmet (*corythos* in Greek) on Cortona's hill. In time a town grew up that took its name (Corito) from the missing headgear. By the 5th century BC the Etruscans had built the first set of town walls, whose cyclopean traces can still be seen in the 3-km (2-mi) sweep of the present fortifications. As a member of the Etruscans' 12-city league, it became one of the leading northern cities. An important consular road, the Via Cassia, which passed by the foot of its hill, assured the town's importance under the Romans. Its fortunes waned in the Middle Ages, however, as the plain below reverted to marsh. After holding out against neighbors like Perugia, Arezzo, and Siena, the *comune* was captured by King Ladislas of Naples in 1409 and sold to the Florentines two years later.

The heart of Cortona is formed by **Piazza della Repubblica** and the adjacent **Piazza Signorelli,** where you'll find pleasant shops to browse through. The **Museo Diocesano** (Diocesan Museum) houses an impressive number of large and splendid paintings by native son Luca Signorelli, as well as a stunning *Annunciation* by Fra Angelico, a delightful surprise in this small town. ⊠ *Piazza del Duomo 1* ☎ *0575/62830* ⚊ *€5* ⊙ *Nov.–Mar., Tues.–Sun. 10–5; Apr.–Oct., Tues.–Sun. 10–7.*

Where to Stay & Eat

$–$$ ✕ **Osteria del Teatro.** Just off Cortona's large Piazza del Teatro, this small osteria is lined with photographs from theatrical productions spanning many years. The food is deliciously simple—try the *filetto in crema di tartufo* (beef in a creamy truffle sauce); service is warm and friendly. ⊠ *Via Maffei 2* ☎ *0575/630556* ⊟ *AE, DC, MC, V* ⊙ *Closed Wed. and 2 wks in Nov.*

★ **$$$$** ✕▦ **Il Falconiere.** Run by the husband-and-wife team of Riccardo and Silvia Baracchi, this heavenly hotel just minutes outside Cortona consists of rooms in an 18th-century villa and suites in the *chiesetta* (little church) once belonging to an obscure 19th-century Italian poet and hunter. If you desire a little bit more privacy, you can stay at Le Vigne del Falco, at the opposite end of the property, where most rooms are suites with their own entrances and all have grand views of the plain below. The restaurant's inventive menu is complemented by the wine list, the product of Silvia's extensive sommelier training. By all means sample their own estate-produced olive oil. Gourmands should inquire into the week-long cooking classes offered on-site. ⊠ *Località San Martino 370, 52044* ☎ *0575/612679* ⊟ *0575/612927* ⊕ *www.ilfalconiere.com* ⟲ *13 rooms, 6 suites* ⚇ *Restaurant, room service, in-room safes, minibars, cable TV, 2 pools, bar, babysitting, dry cleaning, laundry service, concierge, Internet, free parking, some pets allowed (fee), no-smoking rooms* ⊟ *AE, MC, V* ⊙ *Restaurant closed Mon. Nov.–Mar.* ⦿ *BP.*

SOUTHERN TUSCANY

Along the roads leading south from Siena, soft green olive groves give way to a blanket of oak, cypress, and reddish-brown earth. Towns are the size of the roads—small—and as old as the hills. The scruffy mountain landscapes of Monte Amiata make up some of the wildest parts of Tuscany, and once you're across the mountains the landscape is still full of cliffs, like the one Pitigliano perches on. Southern Tuscany offers good wine (try Brunello di Montalcino or the exceptional, lesser-known Morellino di Scansano for a true treat), thermal baths at Saturnia, Etruscan ruins, and the strands and fishing villages of Elba.

Abbazia di Monte Oliveto Maggiore

35 *37 km (23 mi) southeast of Siena, 104 km (65 mi) southeast of Florence.*

This Benedictine abbey, Tuscany's most visited religious houses, is an oasis of olive and cypress trees amid the harsh landscape of a zone known as the Crete, where erosion has sculpted the hills starkly, laying open barren rock in lush farmland. Surrounded by thick woodlands in the deep-cut hills south of Siena, it is accessible by car but not easily by bus.

Olivetans, or "White Benedictines," founded the abbey in 1313; this breakaway group sought to return to the simple ideals of the early Benedictine order. The monastery's mellow brick buildings in one of Tuscany's most striking landscapes protect a treasure or two. Only the **main cloister** and portions of the **park** are open to the public. The wooden choir in the church, with its intarsia designs, is an understated work of art that dates from 1503 to 1505. In the main cloister, frescoes by Luca Signorelli and Sodoma depict scenes from the life of St. Benedict with earthy realism, a quality that came easily to Sodoma, described by Vasari as "a merry and licentious man of scant chastity." ⊠ *SS451 south of Asciano* ☎ *0577/707611* ☉ *Daily 9:15–noon and 3:15–5:45.*

Montepulciano

36 *13 km (8 mi) west of the A1, 119 km (74 mi) southeast of Florence.*

Perched high on a hilltop, Montepulciano is made up of a pyramid of clustered Renaissance buildings set within a circle of cypress trees. At an altitude of almost 2,000 feet, it's cool in summer and chilled in winter by biting winds that sweep its spiraling streets. Montepulciano has an unusually harmonious look, the result of the work of three architects, Michelozzo (1396–1472), Antonio da Sangallo il Vecchio (circa 1455–1534), and Giacomo da Vignola (1507–73), who graced it with palaces and churches in an attempt to impose Renaissance architectural
★ ideals on an ancient Tuscan hill town. The pièce de résistance is the **Piazza Grande,** a wide expanse of urban space lined with 15th-century family palazzos and the equally grand, but facadeless, Duomo. On the hillside below the town walls is the church of **San Biagio,** designed by Sangallo, a paragon of Renaissance architectural perfection considered to be his masterpiece. ⊠ *Via di San Biagio* ☎ *0578/7577761* ☉ *Daily 9–12:30 and 3:30–7:30.*

Where to Stay & Eat

★ **$$$** ✕ **La Grotta.** Just across the street from the Tempio di San Biagio (Church of San Biagio), this place has an innocuous entrance that might lead you to pass right by. Don't, for the food is fantastic. The *tagliolini con car-*

ciofi e rigatino (thin noodles with artichokes and bacon) is heavenly, as is the *tagliatelle di grano saraceno con asparagi e zucchine* (flat noodles with asparagus and zucchini). Follow with any of the wonderful *secondi*, and wash it down with the local wine, which just happens to be one of Italy's finest—Vino Nobile di Montepulciano. ⊠ *Località San Biagio* ☎ *0578/757479* ⊟ *AE, MC, V* ☙ *Closed Wed. and Jan. 8–Feb. 28.*

$$$$ ✕▥ **Locanda dell'Amorosa.** A majestic cypress-lined drive leads to the main gate of this country inn outside Sinalunga. A self-sufficient hamlet in the 14th century with its own chapel, it's now a romantically refined place to rest your head. Owners Carlo and Alessandra Citterio live on site and tend to every detail. Some rooms offer stunning views, others a private garden or terrace. All have sumptuous fabrics, and many have large bathrooms. The lusciously landscaped grounds teem with color in spring and summer. The restaurant, which once stabled horses, has candle-lit tables, stone walls, and a menu grounded in Tuscan classics with flights of fantasy. ⊠ *Località Amorosa, Sinalunga 53048, 10 km (6 mi) from the Valdichiana exit off the A1* ☎ *0577/679497* ▤ *0577/ 632001* ⊕ *www.amorosa.it* ⬎ *17 rooms, 8 suites* ☖ *Restaurant, room service, in-room data ports, in-room safes, minibars, cable TV, pool, mountain bikes, wine bar, wine shop, baby-sitting, dry cleaning, laundry service, concierge, Internet, meeting rooms, no-smoking rooms* ⊟ *AE, DC, MC, V* ☙ *Closed Jan. and Feb.* ⦶ *EP.*

$ ▦ **Il Marzocco.** A 16th-century building within the town walls, this hotel evokes the 19th century, complete with old-fashioned parlors and a billiard room. Furnished in heavy late-19th-century style or in spindly white wood, many bedrooms have large terraces overlooking the countryside and are big enough to accommodate extra beds. ⊠ *Piazza Savonarola 18, 53045* ☎ *0578/757262* ▤ *0578/757530* ⬎ *16 rooms* ☖ *Restaurant, fans, billiards; no a/c* ⊟ *AE, DC, MC, V* ☙ *Closed Jan. 20–Feb. 10* ⦶ *BP.*

Nightlife & the Arts

The **Cantiere Internazionale d'Arte** (⊠ Piazza Grande 7 ☎ 0578/757341 for tourist information office), held in July and August, is a festival of art, music, and theater ending with a major theatrical production in Piazza Grande. For information on scheduling and events, contact the local tourist information office.

Pienza

 120 km (75 mi) southeast of Florence.

Pienza owes its urban design to Pope Pius II, who had grand plans to transform his home village of Corsignano—the town's former name—into a model Renaissance town. The man entrusted with the project was Bernardo Rossellino (1409–64), a protégé of the great Renaissance architectural theorist Leon Battista Alberti (1404–74). His mandate was to create a cathedral, a papal palace, and a town hall (plus miscellaneous other buildings) that adhered to the humanist pope's principles. The result was a project that expressed Renaissance ideals of art, architecture, and civilized good living in a single scheme: it stands as a fine example of the architectural canons that Alberti formulated in the early Renaissance and that were utilized by later architects, including Michelangelo (1475–1564), in designing many of Italy's finest buildings and piazzas. Today the cool nobility of Pienza's center seems almost surreal in this otherwise unpretentious village, known locally for its pecorino. Although the cheese is made all over Italy, here it is a superior gastronomic experience.

The **Palazzo Piccolomini,** the seat of Pius II's papal court, was designed by Rossellino in 1459, using Florence's Palazzo Rucellai by Alberti as a model. You can visit the papal apartments, including a library, as well as the **Sala delle Armi,** with an impressive weapons collection, and the music room, with its extravagant wooden ceiling. ⊠ *Piazza Pio II* ☎ *0578/748503* 🔳 *€3* ۞ *Guided tours Tues.–Sun. 10–noon and 3–5:30. Closed 2nd half of Feb., 1st wk in Mar., Nov. 16–Dec. 7.*

The interior of the **Duomo** is simple but richly decorated with paintings from the Sienese school. Begun in 1459 and finished in a record three years' time, the facade is divided into three parts. Renaissance pilasters on the facade draw attention to the pope's coat of arms encircled by a wreath of fruit, the papal tiara, and keys above it. ⊠ *Piazza Pio II* ۞ *Daily 8:30–1 and 2:30–7.*

Where to Stay & Eat

¢–$$ ✕ **La Porta.** Montichiello is a hamlet minutes away from Pienza, and this osteria–wine bar is basically the only show in town. But what a show it is—from start to finish, the food is delicious. The menu changes regularly, but you can always count on top-quality cheeses (pecorino di Pienza, among others) and lively pasta dishes such as *tagliolini alla chianina* (thin noodles with a hearty minced beef sauce). Second courses are just as strong; if rabbit's on the menu, don't miss it. Reservations are a good idea, especially in summer. ⊠ *Montichiello* ☎ *0578/755163* ▭ *MC, V* ۞ *Closed Thurs. and 3 wks in Jan.*

¢–$ ✕ **La Chiocciola.** A no-frills trattoria a few minutes' walk from the historic center, this place offers typical Pienza fare, including homemade *pici* (thick, short spaghetti) with hare or wild boar sauce. Their take on *formaggio in forno* (baked cheese) with assorted accompaniments such as fresh porcini mushrooms is reason enough to come here. ⊠ *Via Mencattelli 4* ☎ *0578/748683* ▭ *MC, V* ۞ *Closed Wed. and 10 days in Feb.*

★ $ ▦ **La Foce.** The various farmhouses and apartments scattered about the former estate of noted Anglo-American historian Iris Origo and her husband, Antonio, have been converted into this agriturismo, furnished in simple, rustic style, with wooden furniture, sponged walls, and extraordinary views. Kitchens are fully equipped, and some of the rooms have working fireplaces. If you're looking for peace and quiet, look no farther. From May through October, a minimum one-week stay is obligatory. ⊠ *Strada della Vittoria 61, Chianciano Terme, 53042* ☎🖶 *0578/69101* ⊕ *www.lafoce.com* ⤳ *9 apartments, 6 farmhouses* ⚒ *Fans, kitchens, refrigerators, some cable TV, tennis court, 8 pools, playground, laundry facilities, laundry service, free parking; no a/c* ▭ *MC, V* ⓞ *EP.*

Montalcino

38 *24 km (15 mi) west of Pienza, 41 km (25 mi) south of Siena*

Another medieval hill town with a special claim to fame, Montalcino is the source for Brunello di Montalcino, one of Italy's most esteemed red wines. You can sample it in wine cellars in town or visit a nearby winery for a free guided tour and tasting; you must call ahead for reservations. One Montalcino winery worth visiting is **Fattoria dei Barbi e del Casato** (✉ Località Podernuovi ☎ 0577/841200). The 14th-century **La Fortezza** (✉ Via Panfilo dell'Oca ☎ 0577/849211 ☎€3 ✆ Nov.–Mar., daily Tues.–Sun. 9–6; Apr.–Oct., daily 9–8) has an enoteca for tasting wines. In the very heart of the centro storico is **Alle Logge** (✉ Piazza del Popolo ☎ 0577/846186 ✆ Thurs.–Tues. 7 AM–1 AM), a sophisticated wine bar where selections by the glass always include a significant Brunello.

Where to Stay & Eat

$$$$ ✕ **Poggio Antico.** One of Italy's renowned chefs, Roberto Minnetti, abandoned his highly successful restaurant in Rome and moved to the country just outside Montalcino. Now he and his wife, Patrizia, serve Tuscan cuisine masterfully interpreted by Roberto in a relaxed but regal dining room with arches and beamed ceilings. The seasonal menu offers *pappardelle al ragù di agnello* (flat, wide noodles in a lamb sauce) and venison in a sweet-and-sour sauce. ✉ *Località I Poggi, 4 km (2½ mi) outside Montalcino on road to Grosseto* ☎ 0577/849200 ▤ MC, V ✆ *Closed Mon. and 20 days in Jan. No dinner Sun.*

¢ ✕▦ **Fattoria dei Barbi e del Casato.** The rustic taverna ($$) of this family-owned wine estate, which produces excellent Brunello as well as its younger cousin, Rosso di Montalcino, is set among vineyards and has a large stone fireplace. The estate farm produces many of the ingredients used in such traditional specialties as *stracotto nel brunello* (braised beef cooked with beans in Brunello wine). Six comfortable, traditionally furnished apartments are next to the cantina; a two-night minimum stay is required throughout the year. ✉ *Località Podernuovi, 53024* ☎ *0577/841200 taverna, 0577/841111 fattoria* ▤ *0577/841112* ⟨ *Reservations essential* ↝ *6 apartments* ⟨ *Fans, kitchenettes, cable TV, some pets allowed; no a/c* ▤ AE, DC, MC, V ✆ *Taverna closed Wed. and mid-Jan.–mid Feb. No dinner Tues. Nov.–Mar.* ⦿ EP.

Abbazia di Sant'Antimo

★ **39** *10 km (6 mi) south of Montalcino, 51 km (32 mi) south of Siena.*

It's well worth your while to visit this abbey, a 12th-century Romanesque gem of pale stone in the silvery green of an olive grove. The exterior and interior sculpture is outstanding, particularly the nave capitals, a combination of French, Lombard, and Spanish influences. According to legend, the **sacristy** (rarely open) formed part of the primitive Carolingian church (founded in AD 781), its entrance flanked by 9th-century pilasters. The small **vaulted crypt** dates from the same period. An unusual element is the ambulatory, whose three radiating chapels (rare in Italian churches) were probably copied from the French model. Throughout the day the monks fill this magnificent space with Gregorian chant. ⊠ *Castelnuovo dell'Abate* ☎ *0577/835659* ⊕ *www.antimo. it* ☉ *Daily 10–12:30 and 6–8.*

Monte Amiata

④⓪ *86 km (52 mi) southeast of Siena, 156 km (94 mi) southeast of Florence.*

At 5,702 feet high, the dormant volcano Monte Amiata is one of Tuscany's few ski resorts, but it's no match for the Alps or the Dolomites. Its main attraction is a wide-open view of Tuscany. From here you can meander along panoramic mountaintop roads in your car and visit Castel del Piano, Arcidosso, Santa Flora, and Piancastagnaio—towns dating from the Middle Ages.

Abbazia di San Galgano

★ **④①** *33 km (20 mi) southwest of Siena, 70 km (43 mi) northwest of Montalcino.*

This Gothic cathedral missing its roof is a hauntingly beautiful sight. The church was built in the late 12th century by Cistercian monks, who designed it after churches built by their order in France. Starting in the 15th century it fell into ruin, declining gradually over the centuries. Grass has grown through the floor, and the roof and windows are gone. What's left of its facade and walls makes a grandiose and desolate picture. Behind it, a short climb up a hill brings you to the charming little church of San Galgano, with frescoes by Ambrogio Lorenzetti (active 1319–48), as well as a famous sword of local legend. As the story goes, Galgano, a medieval knight, had an epiphany on this spot and gave up fighting. He thrust his sword into a stone, where it remains to this day.

Elba

④② *Portoferraio: 1 hr by ferry from Piombino.*

The largest island in the Tuscan archipelago, ringed with pristine beaches and pocked with rugged vegetation, Elba is an hour by ferry or a halfhour by hydrofoil from Piombino, or a short hop by air from Pisa. Its main port is Portoferraio, fortified in the 16th century by the Medici grand duke Cosimo I. Be sure to sample the local wines, including Moscato and Aleatico. Lively **Portoferraio** is the best base for exploring the island. Good beaches are Biodola, Procchio, and Marina di Campo.

Victor Hugo spent his boyhood on Elba, and Napoléon was here during his famous exile in 1814–15, which resulted in the building of the **Palazzina dei Mulini.** More interesting is the **Villa San Martino** (⊠ Località San Martino ☎ 0565/914688) a couple of miles outside town, whose grandiose neoclassical facade was built by the emperor's nephew. ⊠ *Piazzale Napoleone 1, Portoferraio* ☎ *0565/915846* ⊠ *€3 for one site, €5 for both* ☉ *Palazzina: Apr.–Sept., Mon. and Wed.–Sat. 9–7, Sun. 9–1; Oct.–Mar., Mon. and Wed. 9–4, Sun. 9–1. Villa: Apr.–Sept., Tues.–Sat. 9–7, Sun. 9–1; Oct.–Mar., Tues.–Sat. 9–4, Sun. 9–1.*

The **Museo Archeologico** reconstructs the island's ancient history through a display of Etruscan and Roman artifacts recovered from shipwrecks. ⊠ *Calata Buccari, Portoferraio* ☎ *0565/944024* ⊡ *€2* ⊙ *June 15–Sept. 15, Fri.–Wed. 9–2:30 and 6–midnight; Sept. 16–June 14, Tues.–Sun. 9–noon and 3–6.*

Where to Stay & Eat

$–$$$ ✕ **La Canocchia.** In the center of Rio Marina on the eastern shore of Elba is this airy, 40-seat place across from a public garden. Seafood takes center stage here. Specialties include ravioli *scampi e asparagi o calamari* (stuffed with shrimp or squid, in light asparagus sauce) and various saffron-perfumed catches of the day. The *frittura di paranza* (mixed fried fish) are crisp and light, and the *involtini di pescespada* (swordfish rolls) also shouldn't be missed. Book ahead in summer, as it can get very crowded. ⊠ *Via Palestro 3, Rio Marina* ☎ *0565/962432* ▤ *MC, V* ⊙ *Closed Mon. and Nov.–mid-Feb.*

$–$$ ✕ **Trattoria da Lido.** In the historic center of Portoferraio, at the beginning of the road to the old Medici walls, this bustling, casual restaurant serves commendable *gnocchetti di pesce* (bite-size potato-and-fish dumplings) with a white cream sauce and fresh *pesce all'elbana* (whitefish baked with vegetables and potatoes). ⊠ *Salita del Falcone 2, Portoferraio* ☎ *0565/914650* ▤ *AE, DC, MC, V* ⊙ *Closed mid-Dec.–mid-Feb.*

$$$$ ▥ **Hermitage.** This fine hotel on the most exclusive bay on Elba, 8 km (5 mi) from Portoferraio, consists of a central building with guest rooms as well as little cottages, each with six to eight rooms and its own separate entrance. You have private access to a white sandy beach, where you'll find the hotel's own bar and restaurant. During high season half board is mandatory. ⊠ *Biodola, 57037* ☎ *0565/936911* ▤ *0565/ 969984* ⊕ *www.elba4star.it* ⮡ *110 rooms* ⚫ *2 restaurants, cable TV, 6-hole golf course, 9 tennis courts, 3 pools, soccer, volleyball, 3 bars, Internet, meeting room, some pets allowed* ▤ *AE, DC, MC, V* ⊙ *Closed Nov.–Apr.* ⊙ *FAP, MAP.*

Saturnia

㊸ *47 km (30 mi) southwest of Monte Amiata, 129 km (77 mi) south of Siena.*

Etruscan and pre-Etruscan tombs cut into the local rock can be seen in this town, a lively center in pre-Etruscan times. Today it is known for its hot sulfur **thermal baths.** There's a modern spa with a luxury hotel attached to it called **Terme di Saturnia,** or you can soak for free at the tiered natural pools of Cascate del Gorello, next to the road to Montemerano.

Where to Stay & Eat

$$$$ ✕ **Da Caino.** At this excellent restaurant in the nearby town of Montemerano (on the road to Scansano), specialties include tomatoes and peppers on crisp phyllo dough, lasagna with pumpkin, and such hearty dishes as *cinghiale lardolato con olive* (wild boar larded with olives). Prices are among the highest in the region; locals consider it a serious splurge. ⊠ *Via della Chiesa 4, Montemerano, 7 km (4½ mi) south of Saturnia* ☎ *0564/602817* ⚛ *Reservations essential* ▤ *AE, DC, MC, V* ⊙ *Closed Wed., and Jan. and Feb. No dinner Thurs.*

$–$$$ ✕ **I Due Cippi–Da Michele.** Owner Michele Aniello has a terrific restaurant with a lengthy and creative menu; emphasis is placed on Maremman cuisine such as wild boar and duck—though there are other treats as well; try the *tortelli di castagne al seme di finocchio* (chestnut-stuffed tortelli with butter sauce and fennel seeds). In good weather you can enjoy your meal on a terrace overlooking the town's main square. ✉ *Piazza Veneto 26/a* ☎ *0564/601074* ⏣ *Reservations essential* ▭ *AE, DC, MC, V* ⊘ *Closed Tues. Oct.–June, Dec. 20–26, and Jan. 10–25.*

★ **$$$$** ▥ **Terme di Saturnia.** Spa living might not get any more lush than at this top-notch spa, where every possible health and beauty treatment is available. Guests roam the public rooms in plush white bathrobes (available in every room) in between treatments and dip into the 37.5°C sulfurous thermal pools (which can be accessed directly from inside the hotel). A complete overhaul in 2003 has made the place—both public and private rooms—sleekly elegant. Half and full board are options, and should be considered, as the on-site restaurant is worth a trip in itself. The multilingual staff is incredibly helpful. ✉ *Saturnia, 58050* ☎ *0564/601061* ⊟ *0564/601266* ⊕ *www.termedisaturnia.it* ⟿ *140 rooms, 10 suites* ⏣ *3 restaurants, snack bar, room service, in-room safes, minibars, cable TV with movies, in-room VCRs, driving range, 2 tennis courts, 2 pools, 2 wading pools, health club, hair salon, sauna, spa, steam room, bar, piano bar, shops, dry cleaning, laundry facilities, concierge, Internet, helipad, some pets allowed* ▭ *AE, DC, MC, V* ⏐⊙⏐ *BP.*

$ ▥ **Villa Garden.** All the rooms at this small place, charmingly furnished with comfortable beds, floral curtains and bedspreads, and tiled bathrooms, are named for flowers. Just a few minutes from the center of town, it's a perfect place to stay if you want to take the waters without breaking the bank. The buffet breakfast is good and filling, the staff courteous and efficient. ✉ *Via Sterpeti 56, 58014* ☎ *0564/601182* ⊟ *0564/ 601207* ⊕ *www.laltramaremma.it/villa_garden* ⟿ *10 rooms* ⏣ *Minibars, cable TV, bar, Internet, free parking, some pets allowed; no a/c in some rooms* ▭ *AE, DC, MC, V* ⏐⊙⏐ *BP.*

Pitigliano

④ *33 km (21 mi) southeast of Saturnia, 147 km (92 mi) southeast of Siena.*

From a distance, the medieval stone houses of Pitigliano look as if they melt into the cliffs of the soft tufa rock on which they are set. Etruscan tombs, which locals use for storing wine, are connected by a network of caves and tunnels. In 1293 the Orsini family moved its base from Sovana to the more easily defended Pitigliano. They built up the town's defenses and fortified their home, Palazzo Orsini. Later, in the early 1500s, Antonio da Sangallo the Younger added more to the town's fortresslike aspect, building bastions and towers throughout the town and adding a noteworthy aqueduct below the fortress as well.

Savory local specialties include the famous Pitigliano white wine, olive oil, cured meats, and cheeses; local restaurants serve good food at modest prices. Wander down the narrow streets of the old **Jewish Ghetto.** Though Jews had settled in Pitigliano as early as the 15th century, they arrived in much greater numbers after a 1569 papal bull of Pope Pius V evicted the Jews from Rome.

TUSCANY A TO Z

To research prices, get advice from other travelers, and book travel arrangements, visit www.fodors.com.

AIRPORTS

The largest airports in the region are Pisa's Aeroporto Galileo Galilei and Florence's Aeroporto A. Vespucci, known as Peretola, which connects to Amsterdam, Brussels, Frankfurt, London, Munich, and Paris.

🎦 Airport Information **Aeroporto Galileo Galilei** ☎ 050/500707 ⊕ www.pisa-airport.com. **Peretola** ⊠ 10 km [6 mi] northwest of Florence ☎ 055/315874 ⊕ www.airport.florence.it.

BIKE TRAVEL

Italy by Design will provide you with bikes and hand-tailored itineraries, and pick you up and drop you off; it also organizes hiking and other tours in Tuscany and elsewhere. The Massachusetts-based Ciclismo Classico offers guided bike tours throughout Italy.

🎦 Bike Rentals **Italy by Design** ⊠ Via degli Artigiani 20, Panzano in Chianti ☎ 055/852418 🖶 055/852418 ⊕ www.italybydesign.com. **Ciclismo Classico** ⊠ 30 Marathon St., Arlington, MA 02474 ☎ 800/866-7314 ⊕ www.ciclismoclassico.com.

BOAT & FERRY TRAVEL

Boat services link the Tuscan islands with the mainland. Passenger and car ferries leave from Piombino and Livorno for Elba. From Piombino, Moby Lines travels to Porto Azzurro and Portoferraio on Elba. Toremar runs ferries between Capraia and Livorno, Pianosa and Elba's Porto Azzurro, and Giglio and Giannutri and Porto Santo Stefano. Prices can differ drastically, so comparison shop before buying your tickets; check both counters, or call both offices, before booking.

🎦 Boat & Ferry Information **Moby Lines** ⊠ Piazzale Premuda, Piombino ☎ 0565/221212 ⊕ www.mobylines.it. **Toremar** ⊠ Nuova Stazione 57025, Piombino ☎ 0565/31100 ⊠ Porto Mediceo, Livorno ☎ 0586/896113 ⊠ Piazzale A. Candi, Porto Santo Stefano ☎ 0564/810803 ⊕ www.toremar.it.

BUS TRAVEL

Tuscany is crisscrossed by bus lines connecting smaller towns and cities on the autostradas and superhighways. Buses can be a good mode of transport for touring, though getting information and making arrangements, particularly for a non-Italian speaker, can be a test of patience. To see the hill towns around Siena, such as San Gimignano, you can take a Siena-to-Arezzo Tra-In or Lazzi bus; at either Siena or Arezzo you can connect with the main train line. From Colle Val d'Elsa you can catch a CPT bus to get to Volterra. SENA connects Rome with Siena on several scheduled daily trips.

🎦 Bus Information **CPT (Compagnia Pisana Trasporti)** ⊠ Piazza Sant'Antonio 1, Pisa ☎🖶 050/505511 ⊕ www.cpt.pisa.it. **Lazzi Eurolines** ⊠ Via Mercante 2, Florence ☎ 055/363041 ⊕ www.lazzi.it. **SENA** ⊠ Piazza Gramsci, Siena ☎ 0577/283203 🖶 0577/40731. **Tra-In** ⊠ Statale 73, Levante 23, Due Ponti, Siena ☎ 0577/204111.

CAR RENTAL

Hertz and Avis are the tried and true options. It is usually less expensive to arrange for car rental from the United States; explore options before traveling. If you want an automatic transmission, make that clear when placing your reservation. Also double-check to make sure that the drop-off point is open on weekends, which is often not the case except at airports.

🚘 Local Agencies **Avis** ✉ Piazza della Repubblica 1/a, Arezzo ☎ 0575/354232 ✉ Via Città Gemelli, Lucca ☎ 0583/513614 ✉ Via Simone Martini 36, Siena ☎ 0577/270305. **Hertz** ✉ Aeroporto Galileo Galilei, Pisa ☎ 050/49187 ✉ Via Montegrappa 208, Prato ☎ 0574/527774 ✉ Viale Sardegna 37, Siena ☎ 0577/45085.

CAR TRAVEL

The best way to see Tuscany is by car, making it possible to explore the tiny towns and country restaurants that are so much a part of the region's charm. Drivers should be prepared to navigate through bewildering suburban sprawl around Tuscan cities; to reach the historic centers where most of the sights are, look for the CENTRO STORICO signs. In many small towns you must park outside the city walls.

The Autostrada del Sole (A1) connects Florence with Bologna, 105 km (65 mi) to the north, and with Rome, 277 km (172 mi) to the south, passing by Arezzo and Chiusi (where you turn off for Montepulciano). The A11 leads west from Florence and meets the coastal A12 between Viareggio and Livorno. A toll-free superstrada links Florence with Siena. For Chianti wine-country scenery, take the SS222 south of Florence through the undulating hills between Strada in Chianti and Greve in Chianti.

EMERGENCY SERVICES — If you have a breakdown on the autostrada, or any toll road, you will find along the side of the road "SOS" boxes placed every couple of kilometers. You push a button on the box, a green light pops on, and help is sent—you don't actually talk to a person. If you are on other roads, call ACI, the Italian Auto Club.

🚘 **ACI** ☎ 803/116.

EMERGENCIES

Pharmacies stay open at off hours on a rotating basis. To find out who's open, check the schedule posted in all pharmacy windows.

🚘 **Ambulance, medical emergency** ☎ 118. **Police, fire** ☎ 113.

MAIL & SHIPPING

🚘 Post Offices **Lucca** ✉ Via Vallisneri 2 ☎ 0583/43351. **Pisa** ✉ Piazza Vittoria Emanuele ☎ 050/43352. **Siena** ✉ Via Petrilli Savina ✉ Via Rispini 3 ☎ 0577/50286. 🚘 Internet Points **Pisa** ✉ Internet Planet, Piazza Cavallotti 3/4 ☎ 050/830702 ✉ Odissea, via F. Turati 20 ☎ 050/2200738. **Radda in Chianti** ✉ Bar Sampoli & Lapis, via XI febbraio 2 ☎ No phone. **San Gimignano** ✉ La Tuscia di Panichi Sandra ☎ 0577/942087.

TOURS

From Florence, American Express operates one-day excursions to Siena and San Gimignano and can arrange for cars, drivers, and guides for special-interest tours in Tuscany. Another option is the Florence-based, American-owned and -operated Custom Travel and Special Events, which runs day trips into Chianti wine country and other selected spots in Tuscany.

🗊 Fees & Schedules **American Express** ⊠ Via Dante Alighieri 22/r, Florence ☎ 055/50981. **Custom Travel and Special Events** ⊠ Via dell'Ardiglione 19, Florence ☎ 055/2645526.

BOAT TOURS Charters in Tuscany are available through the Centro Nautico Italiano. Depart from either Marciana Marina in Elba or Talamone (on the mainland, south of Follonica) for journeys through the Tuscan archipelago, including the islands of Giglio, Capraia, Gorgona, Pianosa, Montecristo, and Giannutri. You can either skipper your own vessel or hire a crew; fleets can accommodate as few as 2 people or as many as 12. Exploring the Ligurian coast, or Corsica or Sardinia, is also a possibility.
🗊Fees & Schedules **Centro Nautico Italiano** ⊠Piazza della Signoria 8, Florence ☎055/287419 🖨 055/284690 ⊕ www.centronautico.it.

BUS TOURS Bus tours can be arranged through any travel agency. Brunelleschi Travel, for instance, will tailor bus itineraries to suit your tastes and budget.
🗊 Fees & Schedules **Brunelleschi Travel** ⊠ Via dell'Oriuolo 50-52/r, Florence ☎ 055/2340228.

HOT-AIR Ballooning in Tuscany will arrange for a one-hour balloon ride over the
BALLOON TOURS Crete Senese. Flights depart from just outside Pienza and sail over the hills of Montepulciano, Montalcino, and Pienza. The location of touchdown depends on local weather conditions; two cars follow the balloon and are ready for prompt pickup as well as a champagne breakfast on the flight's completion.
🗊 **Ballooning in Tuscany** ⊠ Podere La Fratta, Montisi ☎ 0577/665310 🖨 0577/632973 ⊕ www.ballooningintuscany.com.

WALKING TOURS A terrific way to discover Tuscany is by walking it. Two companies offer guided tours that cater to anyone from the novice hiker to the expert. Country Walkers offers weeklong (and longer) walking tours throughout Tuscany in spring and fall. Italian Connection, Walking & Culinary Tours offers walking and culinary itineraries through Tuscan hill towns at various times between April and November.
🗊 Fees & Schedules **Country Walkers** ⬦ Box 180, Waterbury, VT 05676 ☎ 802/244-5661 or 888/742-0770. **Italian Connection, Walking & Culinary Tours** ⊠ 11 Fairway Dr., Suite 210, Edmonton, Alberta, Canada ☎ 800/462-7911.

TRAIN TRAVEL

The coastal line from Rome to Genoa passes through Pisa and all the beach resorts. The main line from Rome to Bologna passes through Arezzo, Florence, and Prato. Italy's main rail line, which runs from Milan to Calabria, links Florence and Arezzo in Tuscany and runs past Chiusi and Cortona on its way south. Another main line connects Florence with Pisa. There's also regular, nearly hourly service from Florence to Lucca via Prato, Pistoia, and Montecatini. Call FS, the Italian State Railway, toll-free for information.
🗊 Train Information **FS** ☎ 892021 ⊕ www.trenitalia.com.

TRAVEL AGENCIES

🗊 Local Agent Referrals **American Express** ⊠ Via Dante Alighieri 22, Florence ☎ 055/50981. **Artemisia** ⊠ Via Ricasoli 29, Montalcino ☎ 0577/846021 🖨 0577/846020 ⊕ www.artemisiaviaggi.it. **ATUV** ⊠ Piazza Martiri della Libertà 4/6, Volterra

☎ 0588/86333 📠 0588/86333. **CIT Italia** ✉ Piazza Stazione 51/r, Florence ☎ 055/284145. **Brunelleschi Travel** ✉ Via dell'Oriuolo 50–52/r, Florence ☎ 055/2340228. **Solimano Viaggi** ✉ Via Don Minzoni 29, Volterra ☎ 0588/81364 📠 0588/81356.

VISITOR INFORMATION

🚹 Agritourist Information **Terranostra** ✉ Via dei Magazzini 2, Florence, 50122 ☎ 055/280539 ⊕ www.terranostra.it. **Turismo Verde** ✉ Via Verdi 5, Florence ☎ 055/2344925. 🚹 Tourist Information **Arezzo** ✉ Piazza della Repubblica 28 ☎ 0575/377678 ⊕ www.apt.arezzo.it. **Colle Val d'Elsa** ✉ Via F. Campana 43 ☎ 0577/922791. **Cortona** ✉ Via Nazionale 42 ☎ 0575/630352 ⊕ www.cortonaweb.com. **Greve in Chianti** ✉ Viale Giovanni da Verrazzano 33 ☎ 055/8546287. **Lucca** ✉ Piazza Santa Maria 125 ☎ 0583/919931 ⊕ www.lucca.tourist.it. **Montalcino** ✉ Costa del Municipio 1 ☎ 0577/442944 ⊕ www.prolocomontalcino.it. **Montecatini Terme** ✉ Viale Verdi 66 ☎ 0572/772244 ⊕ www.montecatini.it. **Montepulciano** ✉ via di Gracciano nel Corso 59/r ☎ 0578/757341 ⊕ www.prolocomontepulciano.it. **Pienza** ✉ Palazzo Pubblico, Piazza Pio II ☎ 0578/749071 ⊕ www.infinito.it/utenti/ufficio.turistico. **Pisa** ✉ Piazza del Duomo ☎ 050/560464 ⊕ www.pisa.turismo.toscana.it. **Pistoia** ✉ Palazzo dei Vescovi, Via Roma 1 ☎ 0573/21622 ⊕ www.comune.pistoia.it. **Pitigliano** ✉ via Roma 6 ☎ 0564/614433. **Portoferraio** ✉ Calata Italia 26 ☎ 0565/914671 ⊕ www.aptelba.it. **Prato** ✉ Piazza delle Carceri 15 ☎ 0574/24112 ⊕ www.prato.turismo.toscana.it. **Radda in Chianti** ✉ Piazza Castello 1 ☎ 0577/738494. **San Gimignano** ✉ Piazza del Duomo 1 ☎ 0577/940008 ⊕ www.sangimignano.com. **San Miniato** ✉ Piazza del Popolo 3 ☎ 0571/42745 ⊕ www.cittadisanminiato.it. **Siena** ✉ Piazza del Campo 56 ☎ 0577/280551. **Volterra** ✉ Piazza dei Priori 20 ☎ 0588/87257 ⊕ www.comune.volterra.pi.it.

UMBRIA &
THE MARCHES

10

Updated by
Peter Blackman **BIRTHPLACE OF SAINTS** and home of some of the country's greatest artistic treasures, central Italy is a collection of misty green valleys and picture-perfect hill towns laden with centuries of history. Umbria and the Marches are the Italian countryside as you've imagined it: verdant farmland, steep hillsides topped with fairy-tale fortresses, winding country roads traveled by horses and Fiat 500s carrying crates of fresh olives. No single town here has the extravagant wealth of art and architecture of Florence, Rome, or Venice, but this works in your favor: small jewels of towns feel knowable, not overwhelming. This is not to suggest that the cultural cupboard is bare—far from it. Orvieto's cathedral and Assisi's basilica are two of the most important sights in Italy, and Perugia, Todi, Spoleto, and Urbino are rich in art and architecture. Virtually every small town in the region has a castle, church, or museum worth a visit—but without them you'd still be compelled to stop for the interesting streets, panoramic views, and natural beauty.

The earliest inhabitants of Umbria, the Umbri, were thought by the Romans to be the most ancient inhabitants of Italy. Little is known about them; with the coming of Etruscan culture the tribe fled into the mountains in the eastern portion of the region. The Etruscans, who founded some of the great cities of Umbria, were in turn supplanted by the Romans. Unlike Tuscany and other regions of central Italy, Umbria had few powerful medieval families to exert control over the cities in the Middle Ages—its proximity to Rome ensured that it would always be more or less under papal domination.

In the center of the country, Umbria has for much of its history been a battlefield where armies from north and south clashed. Hannibal destroyed a Roman army on the shores of Lake Trasimeno, and the bloody course of the interminable Guelph-Ghibelline conflict of the Middle Ages was played out here. Dante considered Umbria the most violent place in Italy. Trophies of war still decorate the Palazzo dei Priori in Perugia, and the little town of Gubbio continues a warlike rivalry begun in the Middle Ages—every year it challenges the Tuscan town of Sansepolcro to a crossbow tournament. Today the bowmen shoot at targets, but neither side has forgotten that 500 years ago its ancestors shot at each other. In spite of—or perhaps because of—this bloodshed, Umbria has produced more than its share of Christian saints. The most famous is St. Francis, the decidedly pacifist saint whose life shaped the Church of his time. His great shrine at Assisi is visited by hundreds of thousands of pilgrims each year. St. Clare, his devoted follower, was Umbria-born, as were St. Benedict, St. Rita of Cascia, and the patron saint of lovers, St. Valentine.

East of Umbria, the Marches (Le Marche to Italians) stretch between the hills of the southern Apennines and the Adriatic Sea. It's a region of great turreted castles standing on high peaks defending passes and roads—silent testament to the region's bellicose past. The Marches have passed through numerous hands. First the Romans supplanted the native cultures; then Charlemagne supplanted the Romans (and gave the region its name—it was divided into "marks," or provinces, under the rule of the Holy Roman Emperor); then began the seemingly never-end-

Numbers in the text correspond to numbers in the margin and on the Umbria and the Marches, Perugia, Spoleto, and Assisi maps.

10

If you have 3 days

In 🔲 **Perugia** ❶–❺ ↸, your main stops should be the Galleria Nazionale dell'Umbria and the Collegio del Cambio, both housed in the atmospheric **Palazzo dei Priori** ❷. Spend the rest of your day ambling along Corso Vannucci and toiling up and down the steep lanes on either side. Devote your second day to the medieval hill town of 🔲 **Assisi** ❻–❾ and its magnificently restored basilica. On your third day, get an early start and head south to **Spoleto** ⓭–⓳, where narrow streets abound with evocative views and delightful surprises.

If you have 5 days

Given five days, you have time to spend a couple of them exploring the unspoiled neighboring region of the Marches. The area is somewhat remote, and your means of transportation will dictate what you can see. In any case, start your tour in 🔲 **Perugia** ❶–❺ ↸, and follow the itinerary above for your first two days. If you are traveling by public transportation, spend your third night in 🔲 **Spoleto** ⓭–⓳, where you can jump on a train bound for **Ancona** ㉕; from here you can board a bus or a train for Pésaro and 🔲 **Urbino** ㉔. This hilltop gem retains its proud, self-contained character, almost untouched by modern construction. Plan for at least half a day for reaching Urbino from Spoleto, and it's not much shorter by car, crossing the Marches border from 🔲 **Gubbio** ❿, where you might spend your last day appreciating the views, shops, and choice hotels and restaurants.

If you have 7 days

Reserve four days for Umbria and three for the Marches. With greater flexibility you can choose how many nights you want to spend in Umbria's capital, 🔲 **Perugia** ❶–❺ ↸, and how many in the region's smaller centers. Two nights in Perugia allows you to explore the city thoroughly, including the archaeological museum, and you could take the easy excursion to the wine village of **Torgiano** ⓫ or the ceramics town of **Deruta** ⓬. Or spend a night in 🔲 **Gubbio** ❿. 🔲 **Spoleto** ⓭–⓳ and 🔲 **Assisi** ❻–❾ are essential stops; you might stay for a night in each. From Spoleto you can explore the classic hill town of **Todi** ㉓, unspoiled **Narni** ㉑, and the wine mecca **Orvieto** ㉒ (they can also be seen on your way to or from Rome, only about 90 minutes away). From Spoleto drive north to the Marches region for your last three days. 🔲 **Urbino** ㉔ is a must-see in the Marches. Head south for the inland town of 🔲 **Ascoli Piceno** ㉗—there is little in the way of hotels, galleries, or sophisticated shops here, but it's marvelously quaint. On the way—or on the way back—drop in at the sanctuary of **Loreto** ㉖, nestled in the mountains 24 km (15 mi) south of Ancona.

ing struggle between popes and local lords. Despite all this martial tussling, it was in the lonely mountain town of Urbino that the Renaissance came to its fullest flower; the small town became a haven of culture and learning that rivaled the larger, richer, and more powerful city of Florence, and even Rome itself.

Exploring Umbria & the Marches

The region of Umbria is compact enough that you can have a satisfying tour in a relatively limited amount of time. If you have a car, Perugia makes a convenient base for exploring the region; you can see all the major sights in the regional capital in one day, then make easy excursions to the hill towns on your other days without feeling overwhelmed by constant travel. Without a car, plan overnights in towns farther afield. East of Perugia, the Marches invite leisurely exploring, but expect some lengthy rides between the main points of interest.

The steep hills and deep valleys that make Umbria and the Marches so idyllic also make for challenging driving. Choose routes carefully to avoid tortuous mountain roads; major towns are not necessarily linked to each other by train, bus, or highway. A detailed local road map is always helpful.

About the Restaurants & Hotels

With a preponderance of rustic, hearty regional food on the menu, it's no surprise that Umbria and the Marches abound with simple eateries, such as trattorias, in both town and country. Bakeries and storefronts sell *torta al testo* in Umbria, and *crescie* in the Marches. Both are traditional forms of flat, pitalike bread that can be filled to order with various combinations of meat, cheese, and vegetables. Less common than in the more wine-conscious regions of Italy is the *enoteca* (wine bar), which serves simple meals as well as wine by the glass. Sophisticated restaurants are few and far between, and generally do not reflect the culinary traditions of these regions. Lunch is served between 12:30 and 2–2:30 and dinner between 7:30–8 and 10.

Virtually every old town in Umbria and the Marches has some kind of hotel, no matter how small the place may be. A popular trend in Umbria, particularly around Gubbio, Orvieto, and Todi, is the conversion of old villas, farms, and monasteries into first-class hotels. These tend to be out in the countryside, and the natural splendor often outweighs the problem of getting into town—although you definitely need a car. Interestingly, hotels in town tend to be simpler than their country cousins, with notable exceptions in Spoleto, Gubbio, and Perugia. No-smoking rooms are rare. Chains are few, and most hotels are small, so it's always worth your while to call ahead, and absolutely necessary when traveling in July and August or during one of the numerous festivals—especially in Assisi, Spoleto, Orvieto, Gubbio, and Urbino.

WHAT IT COSTS In euros				
$$$$	**$$$**	**$$**	**$**	**¢**
RESTAURANTS over €22	€16–€22	€11–€16	€7–€11	under €7
HOTELS over €220	€160–€220	€110–€160	€70–€110	under €70

Restaurant prices are for a second course *(secondo piatto)*. Hotel prices are for two people in a standard double room in high season, including tax and service.

Timing

The forested hills of Umbria and the Marches ensure beguiling colors in the fall and an explosion of greenery in spring. Bear in mind that winter is longer and colder here than in nearby Rome, so bring warm clothes to enjoy the outdoors from October to April. The consolation is that winter is the best season for the region's cuisine: January to April is truffle time in Norcia and Spoleto, and October to December brings a bounty of fresh local mushrooms. Book accommodations well in advance if you are planning to visit in June and July, when the Spoleto Festival dei Due Mondi and the Jazz Festival of Perugia take place. Sightseers and pilgrims throng the streets of Assisi year-round, but the religious festivals of Christmas, Easter, the feast of St. Francis (October 4), and the Calendimaggio Festival (May 1) draw even bigger crowds.

PERUGIA

The painter Perugino (the Perugian) filled his work with images of his home: soft hills with sparse trees, wide plains dotted with lakes. Despite the development of undistinguished modern suburbs, this peaceful landscape still survives, and venerable Perugia's medieval hilltop city remains almost completely intact. Perugia is the best-preserved hill town of its size; there are few better examples of the self-contained city-state that so shaped the course of Italian history. Little remains of Perugia's earliest ancestors, although the Arco di Augusto (Arch of Augustus) in Piazza Fortebraccio, the northern entrance to the city, is of Etruscan origin.

Exploring Perugia

The best approach to the city is by train—the station is in the unlovely suburbs, but there are frequent buses running directly to Piazza d'Italia, the heart of the old town. If you are driving, leave your car in one of the parking lots near the station and then take the bus or the escalator, which passes through subterranean excavations of the city's Roman foundations, from Piazza Partigiani to the Rocca Paolina.

a good walk

Starting in Piazza d'Italia, stroll down Corso Vannucci and head to the **Duomo** ① ▶ in Piazza IV Novembre. Visit the **Palazzo dei Priori** ②, being sure to explore the **Galleria Nazionale dell'Umbria** ③ and the **Collegio del Cambio** ④, with its fine Perugino frescoes. A 10-minute walk south of the center along Via Oberdan and Corso Cavour leads to the **Museo Archeologico Nazionale** ⑤. After perusing the Etruscan relics in the museum, return to Piazza IV Novembre, breaking for lunch or an espresso at a café.

TIMING A walk through Perugia takes about an hour, and if stopping at all sights along this itinerary you should plan on at least a half day.

What to See

★ ④ **Collegio del Cambio.** The series of elaborate rooms at Bankers' Guild Hall housed the meeting hall and chapel of the guild of bankers and money changers. The walls were frescoed from 1496 to 1500 by the most important Perugian painter of the Renaissance, Pietro Vannucci, better known as Perugino (circa 1450–1523). The iconography prevalent in the works includes common religious themes, like the Nativity and the Transfiguration (on the end walls), but also figures intended to inspire the businessmen who congregated here. On the left wall are female figures representing the Virtues, beneath them the heroes and sages of antiquity. On the right wall are the prophets and sibyls. Perugino's most famous pupil, Raffaello Sanzio, or Raphael (1483–1520), is said to have painted here, his hand, experts say, most apparent in the figure of Fortitude. On one of the pilasters is a remarkably honest self-portrait of Perugino, surmounted by a Latin inscription. The Collegio is on the ground floor of the Palazzo dei Priori, and is entered from Corso Vannucci. ⊠ *Corso Vannucci 25* ☎ *075/5728599* ⊡ *€2.60* ☉ *Mar.–Oct., Mon.–Sat. 9–12:30 and 2:30–5:30, Sun. 9–12:30; Nov.–Dec. 19 and Jan. 7–Feb., Tues.–Sat. 8–2, Sun. 9–12:30; Dec. 20–Jan. 6, Tues.–Sat. 9–12:30 and 2:30–5:30, Sun. 9–12:30.*

Corso Vannucci. The heart of the city is the broad stately pedestrian street that runs from Piazza d'Italia to Piazza IV Novembre. As evening falls, Corso Vannucci is filled with Perugians out for their evening *passeggiata,* a pleasant predinner stroll that may include a pause for an *aperitivo* (aperitif) at one of the many cafés that line the street.

▶ ❶ **Duomo.** This church's prize relic is the Virgin Mary's wedding ring, stolen in 1488 from the nearby town of Chiusi. The ring, kept in a chapel on the left aisle, is the size of a large bangle and is kept under lock—15 locks actually—and key year-round except July 30 and the second-to-last Sunday in January. The first date commemorates the day the ring was brought to Perugia, the second Mary's wedding anniversary. The cathedral itself is large and rather plain, dating from the Middle Ages but with many additions from the 15th and 16th centuries. There are some elaborately carved choir stalls, executed by Giovanni Battista Bastone in 1520. Precious objects associated with the cathedral are on display at the associated **Museo Capitolare,** including vestments, vessels, manuscripts, and gold work. An early masterpiece by Luca Signorelli (circa 1450–1523) is the altarpiece showing the Madonna with St. John the Baptist, St. Onophrio, and St. Lawrence (1484). ⊠ *Piazza IV Novembre* ☎ *075/5723832* ⊡ *Duomo free, museum €2.60* ☉ *Duomo Mon.–Sat. 7–12:30 and 4–6:45, Sun. 8–12:30 and 4–6:45; museum weekdays 10–1, Sun. 10–1 and 4–6.*

❸ **Galleria Nazionale dell'Umbria.** On the third floor of the **Palazzo dei Priori** is the region's most comprehensive art gallery. Well-placed information panels (in Italian and English) describe work by native artists—most notably Pinturicchio (1454–1513) and Perugino—along with others of the Umbrian and Tuscan schools. The gallery also exhibits frescoes, sculptures, and several superb painted crucifixes from the 13th and 14th centuries; other rooms are dedicated to Perugia itself, illustrating the evolution of the medieval city. The last admission is a half hour before closing, and the gallery is closed the first Monday of each month. ⊠ *Corso Vannucci 19, Piazza IV Novembre* ☎ *075/5721009* ⊕ *www. gallerianazionaledellumbria.it* ⊡ *€6.50* ☉ *Sept. 16–June 15, daily 8:30–7:30; June 16–Sept. 15, Sun.–Fri. 8:30–7:30, Sat. 8:30 AM–11 PM.*

☾ **La Città della Domenica.** Umbria's only attraction aimed directly at the younger set is the theme park–like La Città della Domenica. Five hun-

10

Cathedrals

Churches all over Italy are architectural masterpieces and repositories of splendid art, but Umbria has two of the country's most notable gems. In Orvieto the Duomo's facade alone is reason enough to visit the region; inside, Luca Signorelli's frescoes have an incandescent glow that's thrilling to behold. In Assisi the Basilica di San Francesco—actually two large churches, one Gothic and one Romanesque—is a major pilgrimage site. Throngs of the faithful have been drawing inspiration from the works of Giotto and Cimabue for more than 700 years.

Hiking

Magnificent scenery makes the heart of Italy excellent hiking and mountaineering country. In Umbria, the rocky area around Spoleto is particularly good, and the tourist office supplies itineraries of walks and climbs to suit all ages and levels of ability. From Cannara you can walk for a half hour to get to the fields of Pian d'Arca, the site of St. Francis's sermon to the birds. Follow in the footsteps of the saint on innumerable trails leading from Assisi toward nearby Monte Subasio. For more challenging hiking, the northern reaches of the Valnerina are exceptional; the mountains around Norcia should not to be missed.

Shopping

Wine and pottery are the two most celebrated Umbrian exports. Torgiano, south of Perugia, is one of the best-known centers of wine production, where you can watch the process and buy the product. Orvieto is a white winemaking center in its own right. Ceramic designs with the most flair are for sale in Deruta, south of Torgiano on S3bis. And the red glazes of Gubbio pottery have been renowned since medieval times. The secret of the original glaze died with its inventor some 500 years ago, but some contemporary potters produce a fair facsimile.

---

dred acres contain buildings based on fairy tales—Snow White's House, the Witches' Wood—as well as a reptile house, aquarium, medieval museum, exhibit of shells from all over the world, game rooms, and a choice of restaurants. Entrance is free for children under four years of age. West from Perugia, take the secondary road that leads to Corciano. ⊠ *Via Col di Tenda 140, Località Montepulito, 8 km (5 mi) west of Perugia* ☎ *075/5054941* ✆ *€10* ☉ *Easter–mid-Sept., daily 10–7; mid-Sept.–Oct., weekends 10–7; Nov.–Easter, aquarium and reptile house only, Sat. 2–7, Sun. 10–7.*

❺ **Museo Archeologico Nazionale.** Perugia was a flourishing Etruscan site long before it fell under Roman domination in 310 BC. This museum next to the imposing church of San Domenico contains an excellent collection of Etruscan artifacts from throughout the region. ⊠ *Piazza G. Bruno 10* ☎ *075/5727141* ⊕ *www.archeopg.arti.beniculturali.it* ✆ *€2* ☉ *Mon. 2:30–7:30, Tues.–Sun. 8:30–7:30.*

★ ❷ **Palazzo dei Priori.** The imposing palace, begun in the 13th century, has an unusual staircase that fans out into Piazza IV Novembre. The facade

is decorated with symbols of Perugia's former power: the griffin is the city's symbol; the lion denotes Perugia's allegiance to the medieval Guelph (or papal) cause. Both figures support the heavy chains of the gates of Siena, which fell to Perugian forces in 1358. Most of the building now houses the town's municipal offices, which are not open to tourists, with access permitted only to the third-floor **Galleria Nazionale dell'Umbria**. ✉ *Corso Vannucci 19* ☎ *075/5771*.

Where to Stay & Eat

$$ ✕ **La Taverna.** Medieval steps lead to a rustic two-story restaurant where wine bottles and artful clutter decorate the walls. Good choices from the regional menu include *ravioli fatti in casa al tartufo nero e pinoli* (homemade ravioli with black truffles and pine nuts) and grilled meat dishes. ✉ *Via delle Streghe 8, off Corso Vannucci* ☎ *075/5724128* ⚑ *Reservations essential* ☰ *AE, DC, MC, V* ☉ *Closed Mon.*

$-$$ ✕ **Il Falchetto.** Exceptional food at reasonable prices makes this Perugia's best bargain. Service is smart but relaxed in the two medieval dining rooms that put the kitchen and chef on view. The house specialty is *falchetti* (homemade gnocchi with spinach and ricotta cheese). ✉ *Via Bartolo 20* ☎ *075/5731775* ☰ *AE, DC, MC, V* ☉ *Closed Mon. and last 2 wks in Jan.*

★ ¢ ✕ **Dal Mi' Cocco.** A great favorite with Perugia's university students, this is a fun, crowded, and truly inexpensive place to enjoy a multicourse, fixed-price meal (€13). You may find yourself seated at a long table with other diners, but some language help from your neighbors could come in handy—the menu is in pure Perugian dialect. Meals change with the seasons, and each day of the week brings some new creation *dal cocco* (from the "coconut," or head) of the chef. ✉ *Corso Garibaldi 12* ☎ *075/5732511* ⚑ *Reservations essential* ☰ *No credit cards* ☉ *Closed Mon. and July 25–Aug. 15.*

$$$$ ▦ **Brufani Palace.** A 19th-century palazzo has been turned into an elegant lodging choice. The Brufani's public rooms and first-floor guest rooms have high ceilings and are done in grand belle epoque style. Second-floor rooms are more modern; many on both floors have a marvelous view of the Umbrian countryside or the city. ✉ *Piazza d'Italia 12, 06121* ☎ *075/5732541* 🖷 *075/5720210* ⊕ *www.brufanipalace. com* 🖙 *63 rooms, 31 suites* ⚐ *Restaurant, pool, gym, bar, meeting room* ☰ *AE, DC, MC, V* ⊙l *BP.*

$$$ ▦ **Locanda della Posta.** Reside at the center of Perugia's old district in an 18th-century palazzo. Renovation has left the reception and other public areas rather bland, but the rooms, all of which are carpeted, are tastefully and soothingly decorated in muted colors. Though soundproofed, rooms at the front of the hotel face the busy Corso Vannucci and should be avoided in favor of those on the upper floors at the back of the building, which also have great views. ✉ *Corso Vannucci 97, 06121* ☎ *075/5728925* 🖷 *075/5732562* 🖙 *38 rooms, 1 suite* ⚐ *Minibars, bar, parking (fee)* ☰ *AE, DC, MC, V* ⊙l *BP.*

¢ ▦ **Paola.** You can be certain of a warm and friendly welcome from the owner, Signora Paola, at this small family-run pensione. The beds may be on the soft side, but if you stay for more than three nights you're offered access to the kitchen in the evening. Paola is easily reached by bus from the train station and is moments from the center via a nearby public escalator. ⊠ *Via della Canapina 5, 06121* ☎ *075/5723816* 🖂 *8 rooms without bath* ♻ *No a/c, no room phones, no room TVs* ▭ *No credit cards.*

¢ 🖭 **Rosalba.** Here's a bright and friendly choice with scrupulously clean, basic rooms; the ones at the back enjoy a view. On the top floor, Room 9 has a private terrace and sleeps up to five people, making it perfect for a family or group of friends. Although somewhat out of the way, the hotel is only a matter of minutes from Corso Vannucci by virtue of a nearby public escalator stop. ⊠ *Via del Circo 7, 06100* ☎ *075/ 5728285* 🖷 *075/5720626* 🖂 *11 rooms* ♻ *Free parking; no room TVs* ▭ *No credit cards.*

Nightlife & the Arts

The monthly *Viva Perugia* (sold at newsstands), with a section in English, is a good source of information about what's going on in town. Summer sees two international music festivals in Perugia.

Festival delle Nazioni di Musica da Camera. Music lovers should make the trek to the International Chamber Music Festival, a two-week event held

ON THE MENU

Central Italy is mountainous, and its food is hearty and straightforward, with a stick-to-the-ribs quality that sees hardworking farmers and artisans through a long day's work and helps them make the steep climb home at night. The region has made several important contributions to Italian cuisine. Particularly prized are winter's tartufi neri (black truffles) from the area around Spoleto and from the hills around the tiny town of Norcia. The delicacy shows up on menus stuffed in ravioli, layered in lasagna, and mixed with

risotto. Local pasta specialties, such as thick, handmade ciriole (roughly shaped, fat spaghetti) or strangozzi (long, thin pasta)—also spelled stringozzi or strengozzi—are even better prepared al tartufo, enriched with excellent local olive oil and truffles. Norcia's pork products—especially sausages, salami, and arista (roast loin perfumed with rosemary)—are so famous that pork butchers throughout Italy are called norcini, and pork butcher shops are called norcinerie.

in late August and early September. ✉ On S3bis, 80 km (50 mi) north of Perugia, Città di Castello ☎ 075/8521142 📠 075/8552461.

Sagra Musicale Umbra. Celebrate the traditional music of the region at performances during 10 days in September. ☎ 075/5732800 ⊕ www.umbria.org/eng/eventi.

Umbria Jazz Festival. The world-famous concert series lasts for 10 days in July. ☎ 075/5732432 📠 075/572256 ⊕ www.umbriajazz.com.

Shopping

Judging by the expensive shops around the Corso Vannucci, the Perugians are not afraid to part with their euros. Clothing shops selling Italian designers such as Gucci, Ferragamo, Armani, and Fendi line the streets. The town is also known for its famous Perugina chocolate, although the brand (a Nestlé company since the early 1990s) is easily found all over Italy. Cioccolato al latte (milk chocolate) and fondente (dark chocolate)—in tiny jewel-like boxes or in giant gift boxes the size of serving trays—are sold all over town. Round hazelnut-filled chocolate candies, baci (literally, kisses), come wrapped in silver foil and, like fortune cookies, contain romantic sayings in several languages, English included.

Eurochocolate Festival. The third week in October is especially sweet, when Perugia hosts the Eurochocolate Festival, and the streets are filled with stands, sculptures, and—best of all—tastings. ☎ 075/5732670 ⊕ www.eurochocolate.perugia.it.

ASSISI

The legacy of St. Francis, founder of the Franciscan monastic order, pervades the rosy hills of Assisi, 47 km (30 mi) north of Spoleto and 25 km (16 mi) east of Perugia. Each year the city hosts several million pilgrims, but not even the massive flow of visitors to this town of only 3,000 residents can spoil the singular beauty of one of Italy's most significant religious centers. The hill on which Assisi sits rises dramatically from the flat plain, and the town is dominated at the top of the mount by a medieval castle; on the lower slope of the hill is the massive Basilica di San Francesco, sitting majestically on graceful arched supports.

Like most other towns in the region, Assisi began as an Umbri settlement in the 7th century BC and was conquered by the Romans 400 years later. The town was Christianized by St. Rufino, its patron saint, in AD 238, but it is the spirit of St. Francis, patron saint of Italy and founder of the Franciscan Order, that is felt throughout its narrow medieval streets. The famous 13th-century basilica built in his honor was decorated by the greatest artists of the period. Assisi is pristinely medieval in architecture and appearance, due in large part to relative neglect from the 16th century until 1926, when the celebration of the 700th anniversary of St. Francis's death brought more than 2 million visitors. Since then, Assisi has become one of the most important pilgrimage destinations in the Christian world.

Exploring Assisi

The train station is 4 km (2½ mi) from town, with bus service about every half hour. The walled town is closed to outside traffic, so cars must be left in the parking lots at Porta San Pietro, near Porta Nuova, or beneath Piazza Matteotti. Frequent city minibuses run between the parking lots and the center of town.

a good walk

Much of your time in Assisi will likely be spent visiting churches and walking through the quiet streets. At the top of your list should be the **Basilica di San Francesco** ⑥ ▶, with its spectacularly restored frescos. Via San Francesco leads back to Piazza del Comune and its Pinacoteca, Museo Civico, and the **Tempio di Minerva** ⑦. From the piazza, Via di San Rufino leads to **San Rufino** ⑧, Assisi's town cathedral. Double back to the piazza and take Corso Mazzini to **Santa Chiara** ⑨. Also of interest outside the city walls are the Eremo delle Carceri, east of the center along Via Santuario delle Carceri, and the church of Santa Maria degli Angeli, near the train station.

TIMING Devote a half day or more to this walk. After seeing the basilica, stroll the length of town, stopping at churches and shops.

What to See

▶ ⑥ **Basilica di San Francesco.** The basilica is not one church but two, the Gothic upper part built a scant half century after the Romanesque lower one. Work on this two-tiered monolith was begun a few years after the death of St. Francis. His coffin, unearthed from its secret hiding place after a 52-day search in 1818, is on display in the crypt below the Lower Basilica. Both churches are magnificently decorated artistic treasure-houses, covered floor to ceiling with some of Europe's finest frescoes: the Lower Basilica is dim and full of candlelight shadows, while the Upper Basilica is bright and airy.

FodorsChoice
★

Assisi

TO EREMO DELLE CARCERI

S-444

Anfiteatro Romano

V. Santuario d. Carceri

Perlici

Via Porta Perlici

Via Bovi

Pza. San Rufino

V. di San Rufino

V. Dono Doni

Via S. Gabriele

Pza. Matteotti

Viale Umberto I

Via Galeazzo Alessi

Via Borgo Aretino

Porto Nuova

Viale Umberto I

Emanuele II

Vittorio

Viale

KEY

▲ *Start of walk*

TO SAN DAMIANO

Rocca Maggiore

V. della Rocca

Via del Colle

Via Santa Croce

Via S. Maria delle Rose

Via S. Paolo

Via Giotto

Via del Seminario

Via Metastasio

Via S. Francesco

Via Fontebella

Pza. d. Comune

Via Portica

Via Rocchi

V. B. da Quintavalle

Via Brizi

Via A. Cristofani

V.-di-San-Rufino

Corso Mazzini

Via S. Antonio

Via S. Agnese

Vittorio

Emanuele II

Via S. Giacomo

Via Merry del Val

Pza. San Francesco

Via del

Pza. San Pietro

Fosso Cupo

V. degli Ancajani

Via Borgo S. Pietro

San Pietro

Pza. Unità d'Italia

Viale Vittorio

Viale G. Marconi

Sizi

TO STAZIONE CENTRALE

TO SANTA MARIA DEGLI ANGELI

0   200 yards

0   200 meters

Basilica di
San Francesco **6**
San Rufino **8**
Santa Chiara **9**
Tempio di Minerva **7**

The first chapel to the left of the nave in the **Lower Basilica** was decorated by the Sienese master Simone Martini (1284–1344). Dating from 1322–26, the frescoes show the life of St. Martin—the sharing of his cloak with the poor man, the saint's knighthood, and his death. There is some dispute about the paintings in the third chapel on the right, which depict the life of Mary Magdalen. Experts have argued for years, with many attributing them to Giotto (1266–1337). There is a similar dispute about the works above the high altar, depicting the marriage of St. Francis to Poverty, Chastity, and Obedience—some say they are by Giotto; others claim them for an anonymous pupil. In the right transept are frescoes by Cimabue (circa 1240–1302), including a Madonna and saints, one of them St. Francis himself. In the left transept are some of the best-known works of the Sienese painter Pietro Lorenzetti (circa 1280–1348). They depict the *Madonna with Sts. John and Francis,* the *Crucifixion,* and the *Descent from the Cross.*

It's quite a contrast to climb the steps next to the altar and emerge into the bright sunlight and airy grace of the double-arched Renaissance **Chiostro dei Morti** (Cloister of the Dead). A door to the right leads to the **Tesoro** (Treasury) of the church and contains relics of St. Francis and other holy objects associated with the order.

In the **Upper Basilica** the frescoes show that Giotto, only in his twenties when he painted them, was a pivotal artist in the development of Western painting, breaking away from the stiff, unnatural styles of earlier generations and moving toward realism and three-dimensionality. The paintings are meant to be viewed from left to right, starting in the transept. The most beloved of the scenes is probably *St. Francis Preaching to the Birds,* a touching painting that seems to sum up the saint's gentle spirit. In the scene of the dream of Innocent III (circa 1160–1216), the pope dreams of a humble monk who will steady the church; in the panel next to the sleeping pope, you see a strong Francis supporting a church that seems to be on the verge of tumbling down—a scene that resonates with irony today. ⊠ *Piazza di San Francesco* ☏ *075/819001* ☉ *Lower Basilica Easter–Oct., daily 6 AM–6:50 PM; Nov.–Easter, daily 6–5:50. Upper Basilica Easter–Oct., daily 8:30–6:50; Nov.–Easter, daily 8:30–5:50.*

Eremo delle Carceri. In the caves on the slope of Monte Subasio, Francis and his followers established their first home, to which he returned often during his life. The church and monastery—in dense woodlands—retain the tranquil, contemplative air St. Francis so prized. True to their Franciscan heritage, the friars here are entirely dependent on alms from visitors. ⊠ *Via Santuario delle Carceri, 4 km (2½ mi) east of Assisi* ☏ *075/ 812301* 🖃 *Donations accepted* ☉ *Nov.–Mar., daily 6:30–5; Apr.–Oct., daily 6:30 AM–7 PM.*

❽ **San Rufino.** St. Francis and St. Clare were among those baptized in Assisi's Duomo, the principal church in town until the 12th century. The baptismal font has since been redecorated, but it is possible to see the **crypt** of San Rufino, the martyred 3rd-century bishop who brought Christianity to Assisi. Admission to the crypt includes a look at the small **Museo Capitolare** and its detached frescoes and artifacts. ⊠ *Piazza San Rufino* ☏ *075/812283* 🖃 *Duomo free, crypt and museum €2.07* ☉ *Duomo*

CloseUp
FRANCIS, ITALY'S PATRON SAINT

St. Francis was born in Assisi in 1181, the son of a noblewoman and a well-to-do merchant. His troubled youth included a year in prison; he planned a military career, but after a long illness he heard the voice of God, renounced his father's wealth, and began a life of austerity. His mystical embrace of poverty, asceticism, and the beauty of man and nature struck a responsive chord in the medieval mind; he quickly attracted a vast number of followers. He was the first saint to receive

the stigmata (wounds in his hands, feet, and side corresponding to the torments of Christ on the cross). He died on October 4, 1226, in the Porziuncola, the secluded chapel in the woods where he had first preached the virtue of poverty to his disciples. St. Francis was declared patron saint of Italy in 1939, and today the Franciscans make up the largest of the Catholic orders.

daily 7–noon and 2–sunset; crypt and museum Mar. 16–Oct. 15, daily 10–1 and 2–5; Oct. 16–Mar. 15, daily 10:30–1 and 3–6.

❾ Santa Chiara. This striking red-striped 13th-century church is dedicated to St. Clare, one of the earliest and most fervent of St. Francis's followers and the founder of the Order of Poor Clares, in imitation of the Franciscans. The church contains the body of the saint, and in the **Cappella del Crocifisso** is the crucifix that spoke to St. Francis and led him to a life of piety. A heavily veiled member of St. Clare's order is stationed before the cross in perpetual adoration of the image. ⊠ *Piazza Santa Chiara* ☎ *075/812282* ⊘ *Daily 7–noon and 2–sunset.*

Santa Maria degli Angeli. The shrine here is much venerated because it was in the **Cappella del Transito,** then a humble cell, that St. Francis died in 1226. This baroque church is built over the **Porziuncola,** a chapel restored by St. Francis. It's on the outskirts of town, near the train station. ⊠ *Località Santa Maria degli Angeli* ⊘ *Daily 7 AM–sunset.*

❼ Tempio di Minerva. Pieces of a Roman temple dating from the time of Augustus (63 BC–AD 14) make up this sanctuary dedicated to the goddess of wisdom. The expectations raised by the perfect classical facade are not met by the interior, subjected to a thorough baroque assault in the 17th century, but both are worth a look. ⊠ *Piazza del Comune* ⊘ *Daily 7–noon and 2:30–sunset.*

off the beaten path

CANNARA – A pleasant excursion 16 km (10 mi) southwest of Assisi leads to this tiny town; a half hour's walk then brings you to the fields of Pian d'Arca, the legendary site of St. Francis's sermon to the birds. The first week of September the town's Sagra della Cipolla (Onion Festival) is in full swing, with everything from soup to ice cream flavored with the town's favorite vegetable. *Pro Loco tourist office* ⊠ *Piazza Umberto I* ☎ *0742/72177.*

Where to Stay & Eat

Advance room reservations are absolutely essential if you are visiting Assisi between Easter and October or during Christmastime; latecomers are often left to choose from lodging in modern Santa Maria degli Angeli, 8 km (5 mi) out of town. Ask at the Assisi **tourist office** for a list of pilgrim hostels, an interesting and economical alternative to conventional lodgings. Private convents, churches, or other Catholic organizations run these *ostelli* (hostels) or *conventi* (convents). Rooms are on the spartan side, but you are virtually assured of a peaceful night's stay (€20–€32). ⊠ *Piazza del Comune 12, 06081* ☎ *075/812534* ⊕ *www.comune.assisi.pg.it.*

$–$$ ✕ **Buca di San Francesco.** In summer dine in a cool green garden; in winter under the low brick arches of the restaurant's cozy cellars: no wonder this central restaurant is Assisi's busiest. The food is first-rate, too. Try spaghetti *alla buca,* homemade pasta served with a roasted mushroom sauce. ⊠ *Via Brizi 1* ☎ *075/812204* ⊟ *AE, DC, MC, V* ☉ *Closed Mon. and July.*

$ ✕ **La Fortezza.** Romans built parts of the walls that make up this family-run restaurant. The service is personable and the kitchen reliable. A particular standout is *anatra al finocchio selvatico* (duck with wild fennel). La Fortezza also has seven simple but clean guest rooms available. ⊠ *Vicolo della Fortezza 2/b* ☎ *075/812418* ⌂ *Reservations essential* ⊟ *AE, DC, MC, V* ☉ *Closed Thurs. and Feb.*

★ ¢–$ ✕ **Osteria Piazzetta dell'Erba.** Avoid stodgy tourist eateries and come here for an informal meal or a light snack. There are two different *primi piatti* (first courses) every day, along with various salads and a good selection of fillings to go in the ever-present *torta al testo.* The goat cheese is from Sardinia and is a delicious surprise. ⊠ *Via San Gabriele dell'Addolorata 15b* ☎ *075/815352* ⊟ *AE, DC, MC, V* ☉ *Closed Mon. and 3 wks in Jan.*

¢ ✕ **La Stalla.** A simple and rustic restaurant occupies a onetime stable. The kitchen turns out hearty country fare; for something light, try the torta al testo with your choice of local cheeses, salami, grilled meats, and vegetables. In summer enjoy your meal outside under a trellis shaded with vines and flowers. This is a good place to stop on your way to or from the Eremo delle Carceri. ⊠ *Via Santuario delle Carceri 8, 1 km (½ mi) east of center* ☎ *075/812317* ⊟ *No credit cards* ☉ *Closed Mon. Oct.–June.*

¢ ✕▦ **La Pallotta.** One of the best hotels in its category and a great family-run restaurant are found here under one roof. Upstairs, the beds are firm, and some of the upper-floor rooms look out across the rooftops of town. Downstairs, with a separate entrance on the alley around the corner, Vicolo della Volta Pinta ($) is a cozy trattoria with a fireplace and stone walls. The *menu di degustazione* (tasting menu) is a good way to sample the tasty local dishes, such as *strangozzi* (a long, thin pasta also spelled *stringozzi* and *strengozzi*) with *salsa di funghi* (mushroom sauce). ⊠ *Via San Ruffino 6, 06081* ☎ *075/812649* 📠 *075/812307* ⊕ *www.pallottaassisi.it* ⇝ *8 rooms* ⌂ *Restaurant, bar; no a/c* ⊟ *AE, DC, MC, V* ❙❘❙ *BP.*

FodoršChoice ★

$$$ ⌖ **Castello di Petrata.** Built as a fortress in the 14th century, the Petrata
Fodor'sChoice rightfully dominates its position—with Monte Subasio, Assisi, and the
★ distant hills and valleys of Perugia all in view. Every room is different
from the last: wood beams and sections of exposed medieval stonework
set the stage, and firm beds, comfortable couches, and upholstered
chairs turn each room into a delightful retreat. The bathrooms with tubs
are considerably more spacious than those with showers. ⊠ *Località
Petrata 22, Pieve San Nicolò, 06081, 6 km (4 mi) east of Assisi* ☏ *075/
815451* 🖷 *075/8043026* ⊕ *www.castellopetrata.com* ⤻ *21 rooms, 2
suites* ⌂ *Restaurant, minibars, pool, bar, Internet, meeting rooms, some
pets allowed; no a/c* ▭ *AE, DC, MC, V* ⊙ *Closed Jan. and Feb.* ¶⊙¶ *BP.*

$$$ ⌖ **Hotel Subasio.** The Subasio, housed in a converted monastery, has
counted Marlene Dietrich and Charlie Chaplin among its guests. Some
of the rooms remain a little monastic, but the splendid views, comfortable old-fashioned sitting rooms, flower-decked terraces, and a lovely
garden more than balance out a certain austerity in the furnishings. Ask
for a room overlooking the valley. The hotel is close to the Basilica di
San Francesco. ⊠ *Via Frate Elia 2, 06082* ☏ *075/812206* 🖷 *075/
816691* ⊕ *www.umbria.org/hotel/subasio* ⤻ *54 rooms, 8 suites*
⌂ *Restaurant, bar, parking (fee)* ▭ *AE, DC, MC, V* ¶⊙¶ *BP.*

$$ ⌖ **San Francesco.** You can't beat the location—the roof terrace and
some of the rooms look out onto the Basilica di San Francesco, which
is opposite the hotel. Rooms and facilities range from simple to homely,
but you may be reminded that looks aren't everything by the nice
touches like slippers, a good-night piece of chocolate, and soundproof-
ing. Fruit, homemade tarts, and fresh ricotta make for a first-rate break-
fast. ⊠ *Via San Francesco 4, 06082* ☏ *075/812281* 🖷 *075/816237*
⊕ *www.hotelsanfrancescoassisi.it* ⤻ *44 rooms* ⌂ *Restaurant, mini-
bars, bar, Internet, some pets allowed* ▭ *AE, DC, MC, V* ¶⊙¶ *BP.*

$ ⌖ **Hotel Umbra.** A 16th-century town house is the setting for this charm-
ing hotel in a tranquil part of the city, an area closed to traffic and near
Piazza del Comune. The rooms are arranged as small suites, each with
tiny living room and balcony. Ask for an upper room with a view over
the Assisi rooftops to the valley below. The restaurant, closed for lunch
on Tuesday and Wednesday, has a charming vine-covered terrace lead-
ing to a secluded garden. ⊠ *Via degli Archi 6, 06081* ☏ *075/812240*
🖷 *075/813653* ⊕ *www.hotelumbra.it* ⤻ *25 suites* ⌂ *Restaurant, mini-
bars, bar* ▭ *AE, DC, MC, V* ⊙ *Closed mid-Jan.–mid-Mar.* ¶⊙¶ *BP.*

NORTHERN UMBRIA

To the north of Perugia, placid, walled Gubbio watches over green
countryside, true to its nickname, City of Silence—except for its fast and
furious festivals in May, as lively today as when they began more than
800 years ago. To the south, along the Tiber River valley, are the towns
of Deruta and Torgiano, best known for their hand-painted ceramics
and wine—as locals say, go to Deruta to buy a pitcher and to Torgiano
to fill it.

Gubbio

⑩ *48 km (30 mi) north of Assisi, 40 km (25 mi) northeast of Perugia.*

There is something otherworldly about this small jewel of a medieval town tucked away in a rugged, mountainous corner of Umbria. Even at the height of summer the cool serenity of the City of Silence's streets remains intact. Since medieval times Gubbio has been known for its red pottery. The town teeters on the slopes of Monte Ingino, and the streets are dramatically steep. Parking in the central Piazza dei Quaranta Martiri (40 Martyrs Square), named for 40 hostages murdered by the Nazis in 1944, is easy and secure, and it is wise to leave your car there and explore the narrow lanes on foot.

★ The striking Piazza Grande is dominated by the **Palazzo dei Consoli,** the 14th-century meeting place of Gubbio's parliament. The palace is the home of a small museum, famous chiefly for the **Tavole Eugubine** (Gubbio Tablets), seven bronze tablets written in the ancient Umbrian language, employing Etruscan and Latin characters and providing the best key to understanding this obscure tongue. Also in the museum are a captivating miscellany of coins, medieval arms, paintings, and majolica and earthenware pots, not to mention the exhilarating views over Gubbio's roofscape and beyond from the lofty loggia. For a few days at the beginning of May the palace also displays the famous *ceri* (ceremonial pillars) that are the focus of Gubbio's annual festivities. ⊠ *Piazza Grande* ☎ *075/9274298* ⊕ *www. comune.gubbio.pg.it* ☎ €5 ⊙ *Apr.–Oct., daily 10–1 and 3–6; Nov.–Mar., daily 10–1 and 2–5.*

The **Duomo,** on a narrow street on the highest tier of the town, dates from the 12th century, with some baroque additions—in particular, a lavishly decorated bishop's chapel. ⊠ *Via Ducale* ⊙ *Daily 8–12:45 and 3–7:30.*

The **Palazzo Ducale** is a scaled-down copy of the Palazzo Ducale in Urbino (Gubbio was once the possession of that city's ruling family, the Montefeltro). Gubbio's version contains a small museum and a courtyard. ⊠ *Via Ducale* ☎ *075/9275872* ☎ €2 ⊙ *Tues.–Sun. 8:30–7:30.*

Outside Gubbio's walls at the eastern end of town (follow Corso ⓒ Garibaldi or Via XX Settembre to the end), a **gondola** provides a bracing panoramic ride to the top of Monte Ingino. ⊠ *Via S. Girolamo* ☎ *075/ 9273881* ☎ €5 *round-trip* ⊙ *Nov.–Feb., Thurs.–Tues. 10–1:15 and 2:30–5; Mar., Mon.–Sat. 10–1:15 and 2:30–5:30; Apr. and May, Mon.–Sat. 10–1:15 and 2:30–6:30, Sun. 9:30–1:15 and 2:30–7; June, Mon.–Sat. 9:30–1:15 and 2:30–7, Sun. 9–7:30; July and Aug., Mon.–Sat. 8:30–7:30, Sun. 8:30–8; Sept., Mon.–Sat. 9:30–1:15 and 2:30–7, Sun. 9–1:15 and 2:30–7:30; Oct., daily 10–1:15 and 2:30–6.*

Monte Ingino, along with its spectacular views, has the basilica of **Sant'-Ubaldo,** repository of Gubbio's famous ceri, three 16-foot poles crowned with statues of Sts. Ubaldo, George, and Anthony. The pillars are transported to the Palazzo dei Consoli on the first Sunday of May in preparation for the race that takes place during the Festival of the Ceri. You can reach the church by car from the SP298, by hiking, or by taking a gondola. ✠ *Top of Monte Ingino* ☉ *Daily 9–noon and 4–7.*

Where to Stay & Eat

$$–$$$ ✕ **Taverna del Lupo.** One of the city's most famous taverns, this popular restaurant seats 150 people and gets hectic on weekends and during the high season. Lasagna made in the Gubbian fashion, with ham and truffles, is an unusual indulgence, and the *coniglio di "Buon Ricordo"* (rabbit stew with herbs and spices) is a specialty. Peruse the extensive wine list and save room for the excellent desserts. ⊠ *Via Ansidei 21* ☎ *075/9274368* ≣ *AE, DC, MC, V* ☉ *Closed Mon. Oct.–Apr.*

$–$$$ ✕ **Bosone Garden.** Succulent treats here include a two-mushroom salad with truffles, risotto *alla porcina* (with porcini mushrooms, sausage, and truffles), and leg of pork. This was once the stables of the palace that now houses the Hotel Bosone. A pleasant garden provides outdoor seating in summer. ⊠ *Via Mastro Giorgio 2* ☎ *075/9221246* ≣ *AE, DC, MC, V* ☉ *Closed Wed. Oct.–May, and 2 wks in Jan.*

¢ ✕▥ **Grotta dell'Angelo.** Angel's Grotto is a simple, rustic hotel and trattoria in the lower part of the old town, near the main square and tourist information office. Rooms are basic, with wood furnishings. Breakfast is optional at €3 per person. The restaurant ($), with a few tables under a pergola in the hotel's garden, serves simple local specialties, including salami, stringozzi, and lasagna *tartufata* (with truffles). ⊠ *Via Gioia 47, 06024* ☎▱ *075/9273438* ⊕ *www.grottadellangelo.it* ⤴ *18 rooms* ♿ *No a/c* ≣ *AE, DC, MC, V* ☉ *Closed 3 wks in Jan.*

$$ ▥ **Relais Ducale.** Three 15th-century town palaces unite to form this hotel with small, antiques-filled guest rooms. Ask for one on the upper floors to enjoy views of the town and valley. Especially impressive is the panorama from the hotel's hanging garden, where tables are set for breakfast during the summer months. The hotel is off Gubbio's Piazza Grande. ⊠ *Via Galeotti 19, 06024* ☎ *075/9220157* ▱ *075/9220159* ⊕ *www.mencarelligroup.com* ⤴ *20 rooms, 5 suites* ♿ *Bar, meeting rooms* ≣ *AE, DC, MC, V* �📶 *BP.*

$ ▥ **Hotel Bosone Palace.** A former palace, Palazzo Raffaelli, serves as home to Hotel Bosone. Elaborate frescoes grace the ceilings of the two enormous suites, furnished with painted antiques, and top the hotel's small and delightful breakfast room. Standard rooms are comfortably though soberly decorated with heavy wooden furniture. Ask for a room facing the valley and away from the sometimes noisy street. ⊠ *Via XX Settembre 22, 06024* ☎ *075/9220688* ▱ *075/9220552* ⊕ *www.mencarelligroup.com* ⤴ *28 rooms, 2 suites* ♿ *Dining room, minibars, bar; no a/c* ≣ *AE, DC, MC, V* ☉ *Closed 3 wks in Jan.* �📶 *BP.*

Nightlife & the Arts

☾ Gubbio explodes with exuberance every May 15 during the **Corsa dei Ceri** (Race of the Poles), held annually since 1151 in honor of St. Ubaldo, the town's patron saint. Three 16-foot poles, elaborately decorated and crowned with statues of Sts. Ubaldo, George, and Anthony (representing three medieval guilds), are carried by teams who race up Mount Ingino. Don't place any bets, though; Ubaldo always wins.

At Christmastime, kitsch is king in Gubbio. From December 7 to January 10, colored lights are strung down the mountainside in a tree pattern as the town stakes its claim as the home of the **world's largest Christmas tree.**

Sports & the Outdoors

A costumed medieval pageant with its roots in Gubbio's warring past, the **Palio della Balestra** (Crossbow Tournament) takes place on the last Sunday in May. *Gubbio tourist office* ⊠ *Piazza Oderisi 6, 06024* ☎ *075/9220693.*

Torgiano

❶ *48 km (30 mi) southeast of Gubbio, 15 km (9 mi) southeast of Perugia.*

Torgiano's **Cantine Lungarotti** winery is best known for Rubesco Lungarotti, San Giorgio, and chardonnay. ⊠ *Via Mario Angeloni 12* ☎ *075/ 9880348* 🔄 *Free* ☉ *Tours weekdays 8–1 and 3–6 by appointment.*

The **Museo del Vino** has a large collection of ancient wine vessels, presses, documents, and tools that tell the story of viticulture in Umbria and beyond. ⊠ *Corso Vittorio Emanuele 31* ☎ *075/9880200* 🔄 *€4* ☉ *Apr.–Oct., daily 9–1 and 3–7; Nov.–Mar., daily 9–1 and 3–6.*

The **Osteria del Museo,** next door to the Museo del Vino, is devoted exclusively to the Lungarotti winery. You can buy the highly regarded wines there and, for €4 to €10, take part in a tasting. ⊠ *Corso Vittorio Emanuele 33* ☎☎ *075/9880069.*

Deruta

❷ *7 km (4 mi) south of Torgiano, 20 km (12 mi) southeast of Perugia.*

Deruta has been known for its ceramics since the 16th century. Notable in this medieval hill town are the 14th-century church of San Francesco and the Palazzo Comunale, but Deruta's main attraction is the magnificent ceramics collection in the **Museo Regionale della Ceramica.** ⊠ *Largo San Francesco* ☎ *075/9711000* 🔄 *€3* ☉ *Apr.–June, daily 10:30–1 and 3–6; July–Sept., daily 10–1 and 3:30–7; Oct.–Mar., Wed.–Mon. 10:30–1 and 2:30–5.*

Shopping

Deruta has more than 70 ceramics workshops and boutiques. Start your browsing in the central Piazza dei Consoli.

Maioliche Cynthia (⊠ Via Umberto I 1 ☎ 075/9711255) specializes in reproductions of antique ceramic designs. **Ceramiche El Frate** (⊠ Piazza dei Consoli 29 ☎ 075/9711435) sells unusual ceramic tiles and jugs. The workshop at **Fabbrica Maioliche Tradizionali** (⊠ Via Tiberina Nord 37 ☎ 075/9711220) is open for visits weekdays 8:30–1 and 2:30–4:30 and also operates one of the largest shops in the area.

SPOLETO

For most of the year Spoleto is one in a pleasant succession of sleepy hill towns. But for three weeks every summer it shifts into high gear for its turn in the spotlight: the Festival dei Due Mondi, a world-class extravaganza of theater, opera, music, painting, and sculpture, where the world's top artists vie for honors and throngs of art aficionados vie for hotel rooms.

But there is good reason to visit Spoleto any time of the year. Roman and medieval attractions and superb natural surroundings make it one of Umbria's most inviting towns. From the churches set among silvery olive groves on the outskirts of town to the soaring Ponte delle Torri behind it, Spoleto has sublime views in every direction.

Exploring Spoleto

Spoleto is small, and its sights are clustered in the upper part of town, meaning it's best explored on foot. Several walkways cut down the hill, crossing the Corso Mazzini, which turns up the hill. Parking in Spoleto is always difficult; park outside the walls in Piazza della Vittoria.

a good walk

Begin at Piazza del Duomo, and visit the **Duomo** ⑬ ▶, which stands against a backdrop of hill and sky with La Rocca towering overhead. Cross the piazza and go up the stairs to Via Saffi and the church of **Sant'Eufemia** ⑭ and its museum. If you are short on time, skip Sant'Eufemia and head straight up to **La Rocca** ⑮ and **Ponte delle Torri** ⑯. Retrace your steps back to Via Fontesecca (Sant'Eufemia), with its shops selling local pottery and other handicrafts. Past the church of Sant'Eufemia, turn left onto Via Visiale, which brings you to the **Casa Romana** ⑰. Stop in or continue on Via Brigone west to Piazza del Mercato, built on the site of the Roman forum and home to Spoleto's open-air produce market, open Monday–Saturday 8–1:30. At the narrow end of Piazza del Mercato is the **Arco di Druso** ⑱. Turn right on Via Brignone and cross Piazza della Libertà to Via Sant'Agata, which leads to the **Teatro Romano** ⑲ and Museo Archeologico.

TIMING Sightseeing in Spoleto is relaxed; one day allows you to see the highlights and still have time for a leisurely lunch and a walk across the Ponte delle Torri.

What to See

⑱ **Arco di Druso.** This arch was built in the 1st century AD by the Senate of Spoleto to honor the Roman general Drusus (circa 13 BC–AD 23), son of the emperor Tiberius. It once marked the entrance to the Foro Romano (Roman Forum). ⊠ *Piazza del Mercato.*

⑰ **Casa Romana.** The house excavated at the end of the 19th century is thought to have belonged to Vespasia Polla, the mother of the Roman Emperor Vespasian. The design is typical for houses of the 1st century AD, and some of the original decoration is still intact, including geometrically patterned marble mosaics and plaster moldings. ⊠ *Palazzo del Municipio, Via Visiale 9* ☎ *0743/224656* 🎟 *€2.50* ⊙ *Oct. 16–Mar., daily 10–6; Apr.–Oct. 15, daily 10–8.*

🅭 Duomo. A Renaissance loggia, eight rose windows, and an early-13th-century gold mosaic of the Benedictory Christ lightens the church's rather dour 12th-century Romanesque facade. The contrast makes this one of the finest church exteriors in the region. Inside, the Duomo holds the most notable art in town, including the immaculately restored frescoes in the apse by Fra Filippo Lippi (1406–69), showing the *Annunciation,* the *Nativity,* and the *Dormition of Mary,* with a marvelous *Coronation of the Virgin* adorning the dome; be ready with a €.50 coin to illuminate the masterpiece. The Florentine artist died shortly after completing the work, and his tomb—designed by his son, Filippino Lippi (1457–1504)—lies in the right transept. Another fresco cycle, including work by Pinturicchio, is in the **Cappella Eroli** off the right aisle. ⊠ *Piazza Duomo* ☎ *0743/44307* ◷ *Mar.–Oct., daily 8–1 and 3–6:30; Nov.–Feb., daily 8–1 and 3–5:30.*

🅭 La Rocca. The fortress built in 1359–63 by the Gubbio-born architect Gattapon dominates Spoleto. The structure served as a prison between 1860 and 1982 and now houses a small museum dedicated to medieval Spoleto. Plans for future development include an open-air theater and an international school for book restoration. You can admire the formidable exterior from the road that circles the extensive park beneath the castle. Tickets include a shuttle up to the entrance. Guided visits start on the hour; the last tour starts an hour before closing. ✉ *Via del Ponte* ☎ *0743/223055* ✉ *€4.65* 🕙 *Mid-Mar.–June 10 and Sept. 16–Oct., weekdays 10–noon and 3–7, weekends 10–7; June 11–Sept. 15, weekdays 10–7, weekends 10–9; Nov.–mid-Mar., weekdays 10–noon and 3–5, weekends 10–5.*

★ ⑯ **Ponte delle Torri.** Striding massively and gracefully across the gorge that separates Spoleto from Monteluco, this 14th-century bridge is one of Umbria's most-photographed sights, and justifiably so. Built by Gattapone over the foundations of a Roman-era aqueduct, it's 750 feet long and soars up to 262 feet above the forested gorge. Postcard valley views make a walk across the bridge a must, particularly on a starry night. Beyond are the slopes of Monteluco, where well-marked trails invite further exploration on foot. ✉ *Via del Ponte.*

⑭ **Sant'Eufemia.** Ancient and austere, this 11th-century church sits in the courtyard of the archbishop's palace. Its most interesting feature is the gallery, where female worshippers were required to sit—a holdover from the Eastern Church and one of the few such galleries in this part of Italy. Enter through the attached **Museo Diocesano,** which contains paintings including a Madonna by Fra Filippo Lippi. ✉ *Via Saffi, between Piazza del Duomo and Piazza del Mercato* ☎ *0743/23101* ✉ *€3* 🕙 *Oct.–Mar., Wed.–Sat. and Mon. 10–12:30 and 3–6, Sun. 11–5; Apr.–Sept., Wed.–Sat. and Mon. 10–1 and 4–7, Sun. 10:30–1 and 3–6.*

⑲ **Teatro Romano.** The small but well-preserved Roman theater was the site of a gruesome episode in Spoleto's history. During the medieval struggle between Guelph (papal) and Ghibelline (imperial) factions for control of central and northern Italy, Spoleto took the side of the Holy Roman Emperor. And woe to those who disagreed: 400 Guelph supporters were massacred in the theater, their bodies burned in an enormous pyre. In the end, however, the Guelphs were triumphant, and Spoleto was incorporated into the states of the Church in 1354. Through a door in the west portico, the **Museo Archeologico** displays assorted artifacts and the *Lex Spoletina* (Spoleto Law) tablets dating from 315 BC. This ancient legal document prohibited the destruction of the *Bosco Sacro* (Sacred Forest), south of town on Monteluco, a pagan prayer site later frequented by St. Francis. The theater is used in summer for Spoleto's arts festival. ✉ *Piazza della Libertà* ☎ *0743/223277* ✉ *€2* 🕙 *Daily 8:30–7:30.*

off the beaten path

SAN SALVATORE – The church and cemetery of San Salvatore seem very much forgotten, ensconced in solitude and cypress trees on a peaceful hillside, with the motorway rumbling below. One of the oldest churches in the world, it was built by eastern monks in the 4th century, largely of Roman-era materials. The highlight is the facade, with three exquisite marble doorways and windows, one of the earliest and best preserved in Umbria. It dates from a restoration in the 9th century and has hardly been touched since. ✉ *Via della Basilica di San Salvatore, outside town, off Via Flaminia* 🕙 *Nov.–Feb., daily 7–5; Mar. and Apr., and Sept. and Oct., daily 7–6; May–Aug., daily 7–7.*

TRUFFLE TROUBLE

Umbria is rich with truffles—more are found here than anywhere else in Italy—and those not consumed fresh are processed into pastes or flavored oils. The primary truffle areas are around the tiny town of Norcia, which holds a truffle festival every February, and near Spoleto, where signs warn against unlicensed truffle hunting at the base of the Ponte delle Torri. Although grown locally, the rare delicacy can cost a small fortune, up to $200 for a quarter pound—fortunately,

a little goes a long way. At such a price there's great competition among the nearly 10,000 registered truffle hunters in the province, who use specially trained dogs to sniff them out among the roots of several types of trees, including oak and ilex. Despite one or two incidences of poisoning truffle-hunting dogs and importing inferior tubers from China, you can be reasonably assured that the truffle shaved onto your pasta has been unearthed locally.

Where to Stay & Eat

$$–$$$ ✕ **Il Tartufo.** As the name indicates, dishes prepared with truffles are the specialty here—don't miss the risotto *al tartufo,*—but there are also choices not perfumed with this expensive delicacy on the menu. Incorporating the ruins of a Roman villa, the restaurant's decor is rustic on the ground floor with more modern furnishings upstairs. In summer, outdoor seating opens and traditional fare is spiced up to appeal to the cosmopolitan crowd attending (or performing in) the Festival dei Due Mondi. ⊠ *Piazza Garibaldi 24* ☎ *0743/40236* ⌂ *Reservations essential* ▤ *AE, DC, MC, V* ☾ *Closed Mon. and last 2 wks in July. No dinner Sun.*

$$–$$$ ✕ **Ristorante Panciolle.** In the heart of Spoleto's medieval quarter, this restaurant has one of the most appealing settings you could wish for: a small piazza filled with lemon trees. Dishes change throughout the year, and may include pastas served with asparagus or mushrooms, as well as grilled meats. When in season, more expensive dishes prepared with fresh truffles are also available. ⊠ *Vicolo degli Eroli 1* ☎ *0743/45598* ⊕ *www. ristoranteilpanciollespoleto.com* ⌂ *Reservations essential* ▤ *AE, DC, MC, V* ☾ *Closed Wed. and last 2 wks in Nov.*

$–$$$ ✕ **Apollinare.** Low wooden ceilings and candlelight make Apollinare the romantic "in" spot in town. The kitchen serves good-sized portions of sophisticated, innovative variations on local cooking: cherry tomatoes, mint, and a touch of red pepper top the usual long, thin pasta, or strangozzi. The *caramella* (light puff pastry roll filled with local cheese, served with a creamy Parmesan sauce) is a must-have. In late spring and summer you can dine under a pergola on the piazza. ⊠ *Via Sant'Agata 14* ☎ *0743/223256* ▤ *AE, D, MC, V* ☾ *Closed Tues. Nov.–Mar.*

$–$$ ✕ **Il Pentagramma.** A former stable-turned-restaurant serves fresh local dishes such as *tortelli ai carciofi e noci* (artichoke-filled pasta with a hazelnut sauce) and lamb in a truffle sauce. It's quite central, off the Piazza della Libertà. ⊠ *Via Martani 4* ☎ *0743/223141* ▤ *DC, MC, V* ⊘ *Closed Mon. No dinner Sun.*

★ **$$$** ⬚ **Cavaliere Palace Hotel.** Turn into an arched passage off one of Spoleto's busy shopping streets and enter an elegant world through a quiet courtyard. Built in the 17th century for an influential cardinal, the rooms, particularly on the second floor, retain their sumptuously frescoed ceilings; care has been taken to retain a sense of old-world comfort throughout. In warm weather enjoy breakfast on a terrace and in a peaceful garden at the back of the hotel. ⊠ *Corso Garibaldi 49, 06049* ☎ *0743/220350* 🖷 *0743/224505* ⊕ *www.cavalierehotels.com* ⮐ *29 rooms, 2 suites* ⚷ *Restaurant, bar, meeting rooms* ▤ *AE, DC, MC, V* ⦿❘ *BP.*

$$ ⬚ **Hotel San Luca.** The elegant San Luca is Spoleto's finest hotel, thanks
Fodor'sChoice to its commendable attention to detail: hand-painted friezes decorate
★ guest-room walls, linen sheets cover firm beds, and some of the spacious rooms are wheelchair accessible. Enjoy an ample breakfast buffet, including homemade cakes, which is served in a pleasant room facing the central courtyard. You can sip afternoon tea in oversize armchairs by the fireplace, and the hotel's rose garden provides a sweet-smelling backdrop for a walk or a nap. Service is cordial and prices are surprisingly modest. ⊠ *Via Interna delle Mura 21, 06049* ☎ *0743/223399* 🖷 *0743/223800* ⊕ *www.hotelsanluca.com* ⮐ *33 rooms, 2 suites* ⚷ *Bar, Internet, parking (fee)* ▤ *AE, DC, MC, V* ⦿❘ *BP.*

$$ ⬚ **Palazzo Dragoni.** Housed in the 15th-century palazzo of a Spoletan noble and decorated with antiques and frescoes, all the rooms of this hotel differ in size and aspect. Room 8 with a canopied bed and Room 10 with elegant picture windows are particularly beautiful. The plain tile bathrooms, while simple and functional, lack the charm of the rest of the building. Look out at the cathedral and the sloping rooftops of the town from the guest rooms that face the valley and from the loggia, where the buffet breakfast is served. ⊠ *Via del Duomo 13, 06049* ☎ *0743/222220* 🖷 *0743/222225* ⊕ *www.palazzodragoni.it* ⮐ *15 rooms* ⚷ *Bar, meetings rooms, parking (fee), some pets allowed; no a/c* ▤ *MC, V* ⦿❘ *BP.*

$ ⬚ **Hotel Clitunno.** A renovated 18th-century building houses this pleasant hotel in the center of town. Cozy bedrooms and intimate public rooms, some with timbered ceilings, have the sense of a traditional Umbrian home—albeit one with a good restaurant. The hotel staff is glad to light the fireplace in Room 212 in advance of winter arrivals. Upper-floor rooms look over Spoleto's rooftops. ⊠ *Piazza Sordini 6, 06049* ☎ *0743/223340* 🖷 *0743/222663* ⊕ *www.hotelclitunno.com* ⮐ *47 rooms* ⚷ *Restaurant, bar, library, meeting rooms; no a/c in some rooms* ▤ *AE, DC, MC, V* ⦿❘ *BP.*

Nightlife & the Arts

Festival dei Due Mondi. Thousands of spectators flock to the Festival of Two Worlds, held mid-June–mid-July, to watch music, opera, and theater artists perform. Order tickets as far in advance as possible; full program information is available starting in February. *Box office* ⊠ *Piazza Duomo 8* ☎ *800/565600* ⊕ *www.spoletofestival.it.*

Valnerina

㉕ *Terni 27 km (17 mi) south of Spoleto.*

The Valnerina (the valley of the River Nera, to the east of Spoleto), is the most beautiful of Central Italy's many well-kept secrets. The twisting roads that serve the rugged landscape are poor, but the drive is well worth the effort for its forgotten medieval villages and dramatic mountain scenery. You can head into the area from Terni on the S209, or on the SP395bis north of Spoleto, which links the Via Flaminia (S3) with the middle reaches of the Nera valley through a tunnel.

The **Cascata delle Marmore** are waterfalls engineered by the Romans in the 3rd century BC. To find them, drive east from Terni on the road to Lake Piediluco and Rieti. The waters are diverted on weekdays to provide hydroelectric power. On summer evenings, when the falls are in full spate, the cascading water is floodlighted. *Falls information office* ⊠ *SP79, 3 km (2 mi) east of Terni* ☎ *0744/62982* 🎫 *Free* 🕙 *Light displays May, weekends 8 PM–10 PM; June–Aug., daily 8 PM–10 PM; mid-Mar.–Apr. and Sept., weekends 8 PM–9 PM.*

The Terni **tourist office** can provide information on the operating schedule of the Cascata delle Marmore, and on the region in general. ⊠ *Viale Cesare Battisti 7/a, 05100* ☎ *0744/423047.*

Close to the town of Ferentillo is the outstanding 8th-century abbey of **San Pietro in Valle,** with fine frescoes in the church nave and a peaceful cloister. One of the abbey outbuildings houses an excellent restaurant with moderate prices. ⊠ *S209, 22 km (14 mi) northeast of Terni* ☎ *0743/54395.*

Norcia, the birthplace of St. Benedict, is better known for its Umbrian pork and truffles. Norcia exports truffles to France and hosts a truffle festival, the Mostra Internazionale del Tartufo Nero di Norcia, every November. The surrounding mountains provide spectacular hiking. ⊹ *67 km (42 mi) northeast of Terni.* **Piano Grande,** a mountain plain 25 km (15 mi) to the northeast of the valley, is a hang-glider's paradise.

SOUTHERN UMBRIA

Orvieto, built on a tufa mount, produces one of Italy's favorite white wines and has one of the country's greatest cathedrals and most compelling fresco cycles. Nearby Narni and Todi are pleasant medieval hill towns. The former stands over a steep gorge, its Roman pedigree evident in dark alleyways and winding streets; the latter is a fairy-tale village with incomparable views and one of Italy's most perfect piazzas.

Narni

㉑ *13 km (8 mi) southwest of Terni in Valnernia, 45 km (28 mi) southwest of Spoleto.*

At the edge of a steep gorge, Narni—like so many other towns in Umbria—is a medieval city of Roman origins. Below its finely paved streets and pretty Romanesque churches, excavations provide glimpses of an intriguing past. The **Lacus,** under Piazza Garibaldi, is an ancient Roman cistern with remnants of a Roman floor that was in use until the late Middle Ages. Two cisterns and assorted Roman fragments are visible in the crypt of the 8th-century church of **Santa Maria Impensole.** ⊠ *Via Mazzini* ☎ *0744/242226* ⊙ *Daily 9:30–noon and 4:30–6:30.*

A macabre note is struck by the symbols and dates on the walls of the rooms under the former church of **San Domenico,** inscribed by prisoners held there during the Inquisition. The best day to visit is Sunday, when the excavated sites are open and tours are given in English. ⊠ *Via Mazzini* ☎ *0744/722292* 🎫 *€4* ⊙ *Apr.–Oct., Sun. 10–1 and 3–6; Nov.–Mar., Sun. 11–1 and 3–5.*

You can take a unique tour of Narni's underground **Roman aqueduct**— the only one open to the public in all of Italy, but it's not for the claustrophobic. Contact the Associazione Culturale Subterranea at least one week ahead to book a visit. *Associazione Culturale Subterranea* ⊠ *Via San Bernardino 12* ☎ *0744/722292* ⊕ *www.narnisotterranea.it* ⊙ *Sun. 10–1 and 3–6, and by appointment.*

The town **tourist office** can also help you book a tour of the Roman aqueduct. ⊠ *Piazza dei Priori 3* ☎ *0744/423047.*

Where to Eat

$–$$ ✕ **Il Cavallino.** Run by the third generation of the Bussetti family, Il Cavallino is a first-rate trattoria outside Narni. There are always several pastas to choose from, but it's the meat that makes this a worthy detour. Rabbit roasted with rosemary and sage and juicy grilled T-bone steaks are house favorites. The wine list has the best of what's local. ⊠ *Via Flaminia Romana 220, 3 km (2 mi) south of center* ☎ *0744/761020* ▭ *AE, DC, MC, V* ⊙ *Closed Tues., July 13–30, and Dec. 20–26.*

Orvieto

㉒ *66 km (41 mi) northwest of Narni, 53 km (32 mi) west of Spoleto.*

Carved out of an enormous plateau of volcanic rock high above a green valley, Orvieto has natural defenses that made the high walls seen in many Umbrian towns unnecessary. The Etruscans were the first to settle here, digging a honeycombed network of more than 1,200 wells and storage caves out of the soft stone. The Romans attacked, sacked, and destroyed the city in 283 BC; since then, it has grown up out of the rock into an enchanting maze of alleys and squares. Orvieto was solidly Guelph in the Middle Ages, and for several hundred years popes sought refuge in the city, at times needing protection from their enemies, at times from the summer heat of Rome.

When painting his frescoes inside the Duomo, Luca Signorelli asked that part of his contract be paid in Orvietan wine, and he was neither the first nor the last to appreciate the region's popular white. In past times the caves carved underneath the town were used to ferment the Trebbiano grapes used in making Orvieto Classico; now local wine production has moved out to more traditional vineyards, but you can still while away the afternoon in tastings at any number of shops in town.

★ Orvieto's **Duomo** is a dazzling triumph of Romanesque-Gothic architecture. It was built to commemorate a local miracle: a priest in the nearby town of Bolsena suddenly found himself assailed by doubts about the transubstantiation—he could not bring himself to believe that the body of Christ was contained in the consecrated communion host. His doubts were put to rest, however, when a wafer he had just blessed suddenly started to drip blood onto the linen covering the altar. The pope certified the miracle and declared a new religious holiday—the Feast of Corpus Christi.

The stunning carved-stone church facade is the work of some of Italy's finest artists and took 300 years to complete. The bas-reliefs on the lower parts of the pillars by Lorenzo Maitani (circa 1275–1330), one of the Duomo's architects, show scenes from the Old Testament and some scary renderings of the *Last Judgment and Hell,* as well as a more tranquil *Paradise.*

Inside the cathedral a vast expanse of space leads to the major works, at the far end of the church in the transepts. To the left is the **Cappella del Corporale,** where the famous stained altar cloth is kept in a golden reliquary modeled after the cathedral and inlaid with enamel images of the miracle. The cloth is removed for public viewing on Easter and on Corpus Christi (the ninth Sunday after Easter). A trio of local artists executed frescoes depicting the miracle on the chapel walls. Signorelli's *Stories of the Antichrist,* the artistic jewel of the Duomo, deck the walls of the **Cappella Nuova** (Cappella di San Brizio), in the right transept (buy tickets in the tourist office across the square). In these delightfully gruesome works, the damned fall to hell, and lascivious demons bite off ears, step on heads, and spirit away young girls. Dante would surely have approved; in the chapel, his portrait accompanies *Scenes from Purgatorio.* Signorelli and Fra Angelico, who also worked on the chapel, witness the gory scene. ⊠ *Piazza del Duomo* ☎ *0763/342477* 🖃 *Church free, Cappella Nuova €3* ⊗ *Nov.–Feb., daily 7:30–12:45 and 2:30–5:15; Mar. and Oct., daily 7:30–12:45 and 2:30–6:15; Apr.–Sept., daily 7:30–12:45 and 2:30–7:15.*

The **Museo Claudio Faina,** across the piazza from the Duomo, holds Etruscan and Roman artifacts. Its Roman coins, bronze pieces, and sarcophagi are accessible and interesting. ⊠ *Palazzo Faina* ☎ *0763/341511* 🖃 *€4.50* ⊗ *Oct.–Mar., Tues.–Sun. 10–5; Apr.–Sept., daily 9:30–6.*

On Piazza Cahen, the **Fortezza,** built in the mid-14th century, encloses a public park with benches, shade, and an incredible view. The **Pozzo di San Patrizio** (Well of St. Patrick) was commissioned by Pope Clement VII (1478–1534) in 1527 to ensure a plentiful water supply in case of siege. Descend into the well on a pair of winding mule paths designed to avoid traffic jams. ⊠ *Viale Sangallo, off Piazza Cahen* ☎ *0763/ 343768* 🖃 *€3.50* ⊗ *Oct.–Mar., daily 10–5:45; Apr.–Sept., daily 9:30–6:45.*

Where to Stay & Eat

$$$ ✕ **Osteria dell'Angelo.** Come here for a decidedly nouvelle alternative to heavy Umbrian cuisine; tempting ingredients are delicately spiced and thoughtfully prepared. From the changing menu you might try the *sformato di sogliola e scampi in fondente di verza e fonduta* (sole and prawn flan with a cabbage and cheese sauce) as a starter, and continue with the *carrè d'agnello in crosta di nocciole tostate* (lamb ribs baked in a crust of toasted hazelnuts). Desserts are spectacular, and the wine list is a book with an intoxicating array of wines and vintages. ⊠ *Piazza XXIX Marzo 8/a* ☎ *0763/341805* ⚐ *Reservations essential* ▭ *MC, V* ⊘ *Closed Tues. and July 28–Aug. 16.*

$–$$ ✕ **Le Grotte del Funaro.** This restaurant has an extraordinary location, deep in a series of caves within the volcanic rock beneath Orvieto. Once you have negotiated the steep steps, typical Umbrian specialties like tagliatelle *al vino rosso* (with red wine sauce) and grilled beef with truffles await. Sample the fine Orvieto wines, either the whites or the lesser-known reds. ⊠ *Via Ripa Serancia 41* ☎ *0763/343276* ⊕ *www.ristorantiorvieto.it* ⚐ *Reservations essential* ▭ *AE, DC, MC, V* ⊘ *Closed Mon. and 1 wk in July.*

¢–$ ✕ **Cantina Foresi.** For a light lunch of cheese, salami, bread, and salad accompanied by a glass of cool white wine, this small enoteca is hard to beat. Opposite the cathedral, the cantina's umbrella-shaded tables have one of the best views of the church facade in town. ⊠ *Piazza del Duomo 2* ☎ *0763/341611* ▭ *AE, DC, MC, V* ⊘ *Closed Tues. Nov.–Mar.*

$ ✕▥ **Villa Bellago.** Three farmhouses overlooking Lake Corbara have been completely renovated, resulting in a lodging with bright, spacious guest rooms and ample facilities. The hotel's fine restaurant specializes in imaginatively prepared Umbrian and Tuscan dishes; fresh fish is always on the menu. ⊠ *On S448, 05023 Baschi, 7 km (4½ mi) south of Orvieto* ☎ *0744/950521* ⚐ *0744/950524* ⊕ *www.argoweb.it/hotel_villabellago* ⊅ *12 rooms, 2 suites* ⚐ *Restaurant, minibars, tennis court, pool, gym, sauna, bar; no a/c* ▭ *AE, DC, MC, V* ⊘ *Closed 4 wks in Jan.–Feb. Restaurant closed Tues.* ⦿| *BP.*

★ **$$$$** ▥ **Hotel La Badia.** One of the best-known country hotels in Umbria occupies a 12th-century building—a former monastery. Vaulted ceilings and exposed stone walls establish the rustic elegance in the guest rooms. The rolling park around the hotel provides wonderful views of the valley and the town of Orvieto in the distance. ⊠ *Località La Badia, 05018 Orvieto Scalo, 4 km (2½ mi) south of Orvieto* ☎ *0763/301959* ⚐ *0763/305396* ⊕ *www.labadiahotel.it* ⊅ *21 rooms, 7 suites* ⚐ *Restaurant, 2 tennis courts, pool, bar, meeting room* ▭ *AE, MC, V* ⊘ *Closed Jan. and Feb.* ⦿| *BP.*

$$ ▥ **Palazzo Piccolomini.** Once a 16th-century palace, this is perhaps your best bet for a pleasant stay in central Orvieto. Though the entrance hall and bar are austere, the guest rooms, which vary in size, are modern and comfortable. Try for one of the larger rooms on an upper floor. Service is friendly and efficient. ⊠ *Piazza Ranieri 36, 05018* ☎ *0763/341743* ⚐ *0763/391046* ⊅ *34 rooms* ⚐ *Bar, Internet* ▭ *AE, DC, MC, V* ⊘ *Closed Jan. 15–31* ⦿| *BP.*

Shopping

CHEESE Like most places in Italy, Orvieto produces several local cheeses. With several small tables, a cheese counter that is second to none, a short menu, and a carefully chosen wine list, the specialty store **Carraro** (⊠ Corso Cavour 101 ☎ 0763/342870) is an excellent place for either a *degustazione* (tasting) of Orvietan cheese, or a light lunch ($).

EMBROIDERY & LACE Embroidery and lace making flourish in Orvieto. One of the best shops for *merletto* (lace) is **Duranti** (⊠ Corso Cavour 105 ☎ 0763/342222).

WINE Excellent Orvieto wines are justly prized throughout Italy and the world. The whites pressed from the region's Trebbiano grapes are fruity, with a tart finish. Orvieto also produces its own version of the Tuscan dessert wine *vin santo*. It's darker than its Tuscan cousin and is aged five years before bottling. You can stop for a glass of vino at the **Wine Bar Nazzaretto** (⊠ Corso Cavour 40 ☎ 0763/340868), where there's also a good selection of sandwiches and snacks, and vin santo is for sale.

WOODWORKING Orvieto is a well-known center for woodworking, particularly fine inlay and veneer work. The Corso Cavour has a number of artisan shops specializing in woodwork, the best known being the **Michelangeli family studio** (⊠ Via Michelangeli 3, at Corso Cavour ☎ 0763/342377), chock-full of imaginatively designed creations ranging in size from a giant *armadio* (wardrobe) to a simple wooden spoon.

Todi

㉓ *30 km (19 mi) east of Orvieto, 41 km (27 mi) northwest of Spoleto.*

As you stand on **Piazza del Popolo**, it's easy to see why Todi is often described as Umbria's prettiest hill town. The square is a model of spatial harmony, with stunning views over the surrounding countryside. Narrow cobblestone streets go winding around the hill, every so often finishing in a tiny quiet piazza. Todi's 12th-century Romanesque-Gothic **Duomo** is famed for its choir stalls by Antonio Bencivenni da Mercatello and his son Sebastiano, dating from 1530. Its simple square facade is echoed by the solid Palazzo dei Priori across the way. The Renaissance church of **Santa Maria della Consolazione,** with an elegant pale-green dome, is a pleasant surprise on the outskirts of town.

Where to Stay & Eat

$–$$ ✕ **Ristorante Umbria.** Todi's most popular restaurant for more than four decades, the Umbria is reliable for sturdy country food, plus a wonderful view from the terrace. There's always a hearty soup simmering, as well as homemade pastas with truffles, game, and the specialty of the house, *palombaccio alla ghiotta* (roasted squab). ⊠ *Via San Bonaventura 13* ☎ *075/8942737 or 075/8942390* ▤ *AE, DC, MC, V* ✆ *Closed Tues. and July.*

★ $$ ▥ **Tenuta di Canonica.** The affable hosts here, Daniele and Maria Fano, have retained the architectural integrity of this brick farmhouse and medieval tower in the Tiber Valley. You're bound to marvel at the exposed stone walls, high beamed ceilings, brick floors, and terra-cotta tiles, all in soothing colors. Guest rooms are filled with family furniture and antique pieces. You can hike or ride on horseback through olive groves, orchards, and the forest on the grounds. ⊠ *Località La Canonica 75–76, 06059, 5 km (3 mi) northwest of center* ☎ *075/8947545* 🖶 *075/ 8947581* ⊕ *www.tenutadicanonica.com* ⤴ *10 rooms, 3 apartments* ⚘ *Dining room, pool, bar, library; no a/c, no room TVs* ▭ *MC, V* ⼌❙ *BP.*

$ 🏠 **San Lorenzo Tre.** More in tune with the 19th than the 21st century, the hotel doesn't pamper you with modern comforts; surrounded by antique furniture, paintings, and period knickknacks, you get the sense of a time long past. Only three of the six rooms have private bathrooms, but all share a magnificent view over the valleys and hills to the north of town. A narrow alley off Todi's main square and a long flight of stairs lead up to this tiny guesthouse. ⊠ *Via San Lorenzo 3, 06059* ☎☎ *075/ 8944555* ⊕ *www.todi.net/lorenzo* ⤴ *6 rooms, 3 with bath* ⚘ *No a/c, no room phones, no room TVs* ▭ *No credit cards* ⊘ *Closed Jan. and Feb.* ⼌❙ *BP.*

THE MARCHES
HIDDEN ITALY

Less touristed than Tuscany or Umbria, the Marches (Le Marche in Italian) have comparably diverse and attractive landscapes. Like those of its neighbors, the region's patchwork of hills is stitched with grapevines and olive trees producing delicious wine and oil. You're off the beaten path here and services tend to be less luxurious than in the regions to the west, but with a little luck you may have the place to yourself.

A car is recommended for traveling the region. Beyond the narrow coastal plain and away from major towns the roads are steep and twisting. There is efficient bus service between the coastal town of Pésaro and Urbino, the principal tourist destinations of the region. Train travel is slow and stops are limited, although you can reach Ascoli Piceno by rail.

Urbino

㉔ *101 km (63 mi) northeast of Perugia, 107 km (66 mi) northeast of Arezzo.*

Majestic Urbino, atop a steep hill with a skyline of towers and domes, is something of a surprise—it's oddly remote—and it's humbling to reflect that it was once a center of learning and culture almost without rival in western Europe. The town looks much as it did in the glory days of the 15th century, a cluster of warm brick and pale stone buildings, all topped with russet-color tiled roofs. The focal point is the immense and beautiful Palazzo Ducale.

Urbino's tradition of learning continues today, and the city takes great pride in its intellectual and humanistic heritage. It is home to the small but distinguished Università di Urbino—one of the oldest in the world— and during school term the streets are filled with students. It is very much a college town, with the usual bookshops, record stores, bars, and coffeehouses. In summer the Italian student population is replaced by foreigners who come to study Italian language and arts at several prestigious private fine-arts academies.

Urbino's fame rests on the reputations of three of its native sons: Duke Federico da Montefeltro (1422–82), the enlightened warrior-patron who built the Palazzo Ducale; Raffaello Sanzio (1483–1520), or Raphael, one of the most influential painters in history and an embodiment of the spirit of the Renaissance; and the architect Donato Bramante (1444–1514), who translated the philosophy of the Renaissance into buildings of grace and beauty. Unfortunately, there's little work by either Bramante or Raphael in the city, but the duke's influence can still be felt strongly, even now, some 500 years after his death.

Fodor'sChoice
★ The **Palazzo Ducale** holds the place of honor in the city, and in no other palace of its era are the principles of the Renaissance stated quite so clearly. If the Renaissance was, in ideal form, a celebration of the nobility of man and his works, of the light and purity of the soul, then there is no place in Italy, the birthplace of the Renaissance, where these tenets are better illustrated.

Today the palace houses the **Galleria Nazionale delle Marche,** with a superb collection of paintings, sculpture, and objets d'art, well arranged and properly lighted. Masterworks in the collection include Paolo Uccello's *Profanation of the Host,* Titian's *Resurrection* and *Last Supper,* and Piero della Francesca's *Madonna of Senigallia.* But the gallery's highlight is Piero's enigmatic masterpiece, long known as *The Flagellation of Christ.* Much has been written about this painting, and few experts agree on its meaning. It's one of the few works Piero signed (on the lowest step supporting the throne). The last tickets are sold 90 minutes before closing. ⊠ *Piazza Duca Federico* ☎ *0722/2760* ⊕ *www.comune. urbino.ps.it* ⊡ *€4* ⊗ *Apr.–Oct., Mon. 8:30–2, Tues.–Sun. 8:30 AM–10 PM; Nov.–Mar., Mon. 8:30–2, Tues.–Sun. 8:30–7:15.*

The **Casa Natale di Raffaello** is where the painter Raphael was born and, under the direction of his artist father, took his first steps in painting. There is debate about the fresco of the Madonna here; some say it is by Raphael, whereas others attribute it to the father—with Raphael's mother and the young painter himself standing in as models for the Madonna and Child. ⊠ *Via Raffaello 57* ☎ *0722/320105* ⊡ *€3* ⊗ *Mon.–Sat. 9–2, Sun. 10–1.*

Where to Stay & Eat

$–$$ ✕ **La Vecchia Fornarina.** Locals often fill the small, two-room trattoria near the Piazza della Repubblica to capacity. The specialty is meaty country fare, such as *coniglio* (rabbit) and *vitello alle noci* (veal cooked with walnuts) or *ai porcini* (with mushrooms). There's also a good selection of pasta dishes. ⊠ *Via Mazzini 14,* ☎ *0722/320007* ⟡ *Reservations essential* ☐ *AE, DC, MC, V.*

¢ ▥ **Hotel San Giovanni.** This hotel in the old town is housed in a renovated medieval building. The rooms are basic, clean, and comfortable—with a wonderful view from Rooms 24 to 30. There's a handy restaurant-pizzeria below. ⊠ *Via Barocci 13, 61029* ☎ *0722/2827* ⎙ *0722/329055* ⇦ *31 rooms, 17 with bath* ⚒ *Restaurant; no a/c* ☐ *No credit cards* ⊗ *Closed July and Christmas wk* ⎊ *BP.*

Shopping

Historically, Urbino has been a center for the production of fine majolica ceramic designs, and you can find pretty reproductions as well as contemporary designs at shops throughout. A unique, though hard-to-carry, gift would be the Stella Ducale (Ducal Star), a complex three-dimensional decorative wooden star designed out of pyramid shapes by Renaissance mathematician Luca Pacioli.

Ancona

㉕ *87 km (54 mi) southeast of Urbino, 139 km (87 mi) northeast of Perugia.*

Set on an elbow-shaped bluff (hence its name; *ankon* is Greek for "elbow") jutting out into the Adriatic, Ancona is one of Italy's most important ports. It's well served by trains, which makes it a good base for an excursion to Loreto or to Ascoli Piceno, farther south along the Adriatic coast. The city was the target of serious aerial bombing during World War II, and much was reduced to rubble, only to be rebuilt in a nondescript sprawl of boxy concrete. A few blocks from the main ferry terminal, what's left of the city's old center proves that Ancona was, and still is in parts, a lovely city. Narrow, cobbled streets wind steeply up from the waterfront, opening onto wide piazzas edged with handsome 19th-century brick-and-stucco buildings painted deep orange, pink, and ochre. The alleys leading downhill from central Piazza del Plebiscito are lined with chic shops selling everything from handmade linens to herbal cosmetics, and there are cafés and *pasticcerie* (pastry shops) aplenty to stave off hunger before your ferry leaves. There are enough sights to fill the longest layover, too.

The 12th-century Romanesque church of **Santa Maria della Piazza** is built over a church from the 5th century; parts of the foundation and original hand-cut mosaic pavement are visible through handy glass cutouts in the floor. The 2nd-century **Arco di Traiano** (Trajan's Arch) out on the point is worth a look. The **Duomo di San Ciriaco**, built over a Greek temple, was redesigned in the 13th century to make it more visible to ships coming in to Ancona's port. The **Loggia dei Mercanti**, dating from the 15th century, was Ancona's bazaar, where merchants and traders dealt in all manner of goods from the Far East.

Where to Stay & Eat

$-$$ ✕ **La Moretta.** This family-run trattoria is on the central Piazza del Plebiscito, and in summer there's dining outside in the square. Among the specialties here are *stoccafisso all'Anconetana* (cod baked with capers, anchovies, potatoes, and tomatoes) and the famous *brodetto* (fish stew). ⊠ *Piazza del Plebiscito 52* ☎ *071/202317* ▭ *AE, DC, MC, V* ⊙ *Closed Sun., Jan. 1–10, and Aug. 13–18.*

$-$$ ✕ **Osteria del Pozzo.** The *antipasto di mare* (seafood appetizer), delicately flavored with a few drops of light olive oil and mixed with tiny pieces of seasonal fruit, is one reason the predominantly seafood restaurant is popular with locals. Pastas and main courses are equally delicious, and you should definitely finish with the restaurant's *sorbetto di limone* (lemon sorbet), served in a glass as a cool refreshing drink. This small, plain place is on a narrow cobblestone street between the port and Piazza del Plebiscito. ⊠ *Via Bonda 2* ☎ *071/2073996* ☰ *AE, DC, MC, V* ⊘ *Closed Sun., Jan. 6–15, and Aug. 7–31.*

$$$ 🏨 **Grand Hotel Palace.** Widely held to be the best hotel in town, it's the extras here—slippers, bath salts, and shaving kits—that earn the ranking. Rooms are on the small side but beautifully furnished with French beds dressed in yellow damask, and half have a view directly over the port. Public rooms are grand and elegant, and the breakfast room is on the top floor with a panoramic view. ⊠ *Lungomare Vanvitelli 24, 60100* ☎ *071/201813* 🖨 *071/2074832* ✐ *palace.ancona@libero.it* ⇗ *39 rooms, 1 suite* ⚭ *Dining room, gym, bar, Internet, meeting rooms* ☰ *AE, DC, MC, V* ⊘ *Closed Dec. 23–Jan. 1* ⏅ *BP.*

Loreto

㉖ *31 km (19 mi) south of Ancona, 118 km (73 mi) southeast of Urbino.*

★ Thousands of pilgrims come to Loreto every year to visit one of the world's best-loved shrines, the **Santuario della Santa Casa** (House of the Virgin Mary), within the **basilica.** According to legend, angels moved the house from Nazareth to this hilltop in 1295, when Nazareth fell into the hands of Muslim invaders. Excavations made at the behest of the Church have shown that the house did once stand elsewhere and was brought to the hilltop—by either crusaders or a family named Angeli—around the time the angels (*angeli*) are said to have done the job.

Easter week and the Feast of the Holy House on December 10 are marked by processions, prayers, and a deluge of pilgrims; the rest of the year the shrine is relatively quiet. The house itself consists of three rough stone walls contained within an elaborate marble tabernacle; built around this centerpiece is the giant basilica of the Holy House, which dominates the town. The basilica was begun in Gothic style in 1468 and continued in Renaissance style through the late Renaissance with the help of some of the period's greatest architects: Bramante, Antonio da Sangallo (the Younger, 1483–1546), Giuliano da Sangallo (circa 1445–1516), and Sansovino (1467–1529).

The Holy Virgin of Loreto is the patroness of air travelers; you can pick up Pope John Paul II's prayer for a safe flight in the church, where it's available in a dozen languages. ⊠ *Piazza della Madonna* ☎ *071/970104* ⊕ *www.santuarioloreto.it* ⊘ *June–Sept., daily 6:45–12:30 and 2:30–8; Oct.–May, daily 6:45–12:30 and 2:30–7.*

Ascoli Piceno

㉗ *74 km (38 mi) south of Loreto, 175 km (109 mi) southeast of Perugia.*

Ascoli Piceno is not a hill town; rather, it sits in a valley ringed by steep hills and cut by the fast-racing Tronto River. The town is almost unique in Italy in that it seems to have its traffic problems pretty much under control—in the old center, at any rate; you can drive *around* the quaint part of the city, but driving *through* it is most difficult. This feature makes Ascoli Piceno one of the most pleasant large towns in the country for exploring on foot. There is traffic, but without the jams, noise, and exhaust fumes of other Italian cities.

★ The heart of Ascoli Piceno is the majestic **Piazza del Popolo,** dominated by the Gothic church of **San Francesco** and the **Palazzo dei Capitani del Popolo,** a 13th-century town hall that contains a graceful Renaissance courtyard. The square functions as the city's living room: at dusk each evening the piazza fills with people strolling and exchanging news and gossip. Ascoli Piceno's **Giostra della Quintana** (Joust of the Quintana) is held on the first Sunday in August. Children love this medieval-style joust and the processions of richly caparisoned horses that wind through the streets of the old town. *Ascoli tourist office* ⊠ *Piazza del Popolo 1* ☎ *0736/253045.*

Where to Stay & Eat

★ **$–$$** ✕ **Ristorante Tornasacco.** At one of Ascoli Piceno's oldest restaurants you won't find nouvelle cuisine: the owners pride themselves on meaty local specialties such as *olive ascolane* (olives stuffed with minced meat, breaded and deep-fried), *maccheroncini alla contadina* (homemade short pasta in a lamb, pork, and veal sauce), and *bistecca di toro* (bull steak). ⊠ *Piazza del Popolo 36* ☎ *0736/254151* ☰ *AE, DC, MC, V* ⊙ *Closed Fri., July 15–31, and Dec. 23–28.*

$ 🏨 **Il Pennile.** Look for this modern, family-run hotel in a quiet residential area outside the old city center, amid a grove of olive trees. Rooms are functional; some have views of the city. ⊠ *Via G. Spalvieri, 63100* ☎ *0736/41645* 🖷 *0736/342755* ⊕ *www.hotelpennile.com* ⇨ *33 rooms* ⚏ *Minibars, gym, bar, Internet* ☰ *DC, MC, V* ⦿ *BP.*

UMBRIA & THE MARCHES A TO Z

To research prices, get advice from other travelers, and book travel arrangements, visit www.fodors.com.

AIR TRAVEL

Central Italy's closest major airports are in Florence, Rome, and Pisa—a 2-, 2½-, and 3-hour drive respectively. Perugia's tiny Aeroporto Sant'Egidio has flights to and from Milan, Rome Ciampino, and Palermo.
🛈 **Aeroporto Sant'Egidio** ☎ 075/592141 ⊕ www.airport.umbria.it. **Alitalia** ☎ 848/865642 ⊕ www.alitalia.it.

BUS TRAVEL

Perugia is served by the Sulga Line, with daily departures from Rome's Stazione Tiburtina and from Piazza Adua in Florence. Connections between Rome, Spoleto, and the Marches are provided by the associated bus companies Bucci and Soget.

There is good local bus service between all the major and minor towns of Umbria. Some of the routes in rural areas, especially in the Marches, are designed to serve as many destinations as possible and are, therefore, quite roundabout and slow, and schedules often change.
🛈 Bus Information **Bucci–Soget** ⊠ Strada delle Marche 56, Pesaro ☎ 0721/32401 ⊕ www.mediaworks.it/bucci.htm. **Sulga Line** ⊠ Stazione Tiburtina, Rome ☎ 075/5009641 ⊕ www.sulga.it.

CAR RENTAL

⊞ Agencies **Avis** ✉ Sant'Egidio airport, Perugia ☎ 075/6929796 ✉ Stazione Ferroviaria Fontivegge, Perugia ☎ 075/5000395 ✉ Località S. Chiodo 164, Spoleto
☎ 0743/46272 ✉ Via XX Settembre 80/d, Terni ☎ 0744/287170. **Europcar** ✉ Via
Ruggero d'Andreotto 7, Perugia ☎ 075/5731704 ✉ Via degli Artigiani 10, Terni ☎ 0744/
817337 ✉ Raffaello Sanzio airport, Ancona ☎ 071/9162240. **Hertz** ✉ Via 7 Martiri 32/
f, Orvieto ☎ 0763/301303 ✉ Piazza Vittorio Veneto 4, Perugia ☎ 075/5002439 ✉ San-
t'Egidio airport, Perugia ☎ 075/5002439 ✉ Via Cerquiglia 144, Spoleto ☎ 0743/46703.

CAR TRAVEL

On the western edge of the region is the Umbrian section of the Autostrada
del Sole (A1), Italy's principal north–south highway. It links Florence
and Rome with Orvieto and passes near Todi and Terni. The S3 inter-
sects with A1 and leads on to Assisi and Urbino. The Adriatica super-
highway (A14) runs north–south along the coast, linking the Marches
to Bologna and Venice.

Umbria has an excellent, modern road network. Central Umbria is
served by a major highway, S75bis, which passes along the shore of Lake
Trasimeno and ends in Perugia. Assisi is served by the modern highway
S75; S75 connects to S3 and S3bis, which cover the heart of the region.
Major inland routes connect coastal A14 to large towns in the Marches,
including Urbino, Jesi, Macerata, and Ascoli Piceno, but inland secondary
roads in mountain areas can be tortuous and narrow. Always carry a
good road map, a flashlight, and, if possible, a cellular phone in case of
a breakdown.

EMERGENCIES

Emergency numbers are accessible from every phone, including cellular phones, all over Italy. If you have ongoing medical concerns, it's a
good idea to make sure someone is on duty all night where you're staying—not a given in Umbria, less so in the Marches. As elsewhere in Italy,
every pharmacy in Umbria and the Marches bears a sign at the door
listing area pharmacies open in off-hours. Perugia, Spoleto, Assisi, Gubbio, and Urbino all have at least one so-called "night" pharmacy, but
out in the countryside you may need a car to get to one. Try to bring
extras with you of all medications you take regularly.

In car emergencies, call ACI for towing and repairs—you can ask to be
transferred to an English-speaking operator; be prepared to tell the operator which road you're on, the direction you're going (e.g., *verso* [in
the direction of] Perugia") and the *targa* (license plate number) of your
car. The great majority of Italians carry cellular phones, so if you don't
have one, flag down someone who does for help.

⊞ **ACI** ☎ 803/116. **Ambulance** ☎ 118. **Carabinieri** (Military Police) ☎ 112. **Emergencies** ☎ 113. **Fire** ☎ 115.

MAIL & SHIPPING

⊞ Post Offices **Assisi** ✉ Piazza del Comune 23 ☎ 075/812355. **Perugia** ✉ Piazza Matteotti 1 ☎ 075/5720395. **Spoleto** ✉ Piazza della Libertà 12 ☎ 0743/223198.

TRAIN TRAVEL

Intercity trains of the Ferrovie dello Stato (Italian State Railways), or Trenitalia, connect Florence and Rome with Perugia and Assisi several times a day in 2–2½ hours. Local service, requiring a change of trains in either Terontola (to and from Florence), or Foligno (to and from Rome), is also available. The main Rome–Ancona line passes through Narni, Terni, Spoleto, and Foligno, and intercity trains on the Rome–Florence line make stops at Orvieto. Branch lines link Ancona with the inland towns of Fabriano and Ascoli Piceno. In Umbria, a small, privately owned railway operated by Ferrovia Centrale Umbra (FCU) runs from Città di Castello in the north to Terni in the south via Perugia.

🚆 Train Lines **Ferrovia Centrale Umbra (FCU)** ☎ 075/5729121 ⊕ www.fcu.it. **Ferrovie dello Stato** ☎ 892021 ⊕ www.trenitalia.com.

VISITOR INFORMATION

Turismo Verde, as well as local tourist offices, can provide you with information about *agriturismi* (farm stays) in the countryside. Though officially working farms, these range in style from rustic, with little more than a bed and breakfast, to luxury resorts with swimming pools and restaurants.

🚆 Tourist Information **Ancona** ✉ Via Thaon de Revel 4, 60100 ☎ 071/358991 ⊕ www.comune.ancona.it. **Ascoli Piceno** ✉ Piazza del Popolo 1, 63100 ☎ 0736/253045 ⊕ www.ascolipiceno.com. **Assisi** ✉ Piazza del Comune 12, 06081 ☎ 075/812534 ⊕ www.comune.assisi.pg.it. **Gubbio** ✉ Via Ansidei 32, 06024 ☎ 075/9220790 ⊕ www.comune.gubbio.pg.it. **Loreto** ✉ Via Solari 3, 60025 ☎ 071/970276 ⊕ www.turismo.marche.it. **Narni** ✉ Piazza dei Priori 3, 05035 ☎ 0744/715362 ⊕ www.comune.narni.tr.it. **Orvieto** ✉ Piazza Duomo 24, 05018 ☎ 0763/341772 ⊕ www.comune.orvieto.tr.it. **Perugia** ✉ Piazza IV Novembre 3, 06123 ☎ 075/5723327 ⊕ www.umbria2000.it. **Spoleto** ✉ Piazza della Libertà 7, 06049 ☎ 0743/49890 ⊕ www.comune.spoleto.pg.it. **Terni** ✉ Viale Cesare Battisti 7/a, 05100 ☎ 0744/423047. **Todi** ✉ Piazza Umberto I 6, 06059 ☎ 075/8943395. **Turismo Verde** ✉ Via Maria Angeloni 1, 06124 Perugia ☎ 075/5002953 🖷 075/5002956 ⊕ www.turismoverde.it. **Urbino** ✉ Piazza Duca Federico 35, 61029 ☎ 0722/2613.

ROME

11

Updated by
Clare Pedrick
& Dana
Klitzberg

ROME IS A HEADY BLEND of artistic and architectural masterpieces, classical ruins, and extravagant baroque churches and piazzas. The city's 2,700 years of history are on display everywhere you look. The ancient rubs shoulders with the medieval, the modern runs into the Renaissance, and the result is like nothing so much as an open-air museum. Julius Caesar and Nero, the Vandals and the Borgias, Raphael and Caravaggio, Napoléon and Mussolini—they and countless other political, cultural, and spiritual luminaries have left their mark on the city. More than Florence, more than Venice, Rome is Italy's treasure trove, packed with masterpieces from more than two millennia of artistic achievement. This is where a metropolis once bustled around the carved marble monuments of the Roman Forum, where centuries later Michelangelo Buonarotti painted Christian history in the Sistine Chapel, where Gian Lorenzo Bernini's nymphs and naiads dance in their fountains, and where an empire of gold was worked into the crowns of centuries of rulers.

Today Rome's formidable legacy is upheld by its people, their history knit into the fabric of their everyday lives. Students walk dogs in the park that was once the mausoleum of the family of the emperor Augustus; Raphaelesque madonnas line up for buses on busy corners; priests in flowing robes walk through medieval piazzas talking on cell phones. Modern Rome has one foot in the past, one in the present—a delightful stance that allows you to have an espresso in a square designed by Bernini, then take the metro back to your hotel room in a renovated Renaissance palace. "When you first come here you assume that you must burrow about in ruins and prowl in museums to get back to the days of Numa Pompilius or Mark Antony," Maud Howe observes in her book *Roma Beata*. "It is not necessary; you only have to live, and the common happenings of daily life—yes, even the trolley car and your bicycle—carry you back in turn to the Dark Ages, to the early Christians, even to prehistoric Rome."

EXPLORING ROME

Updated by
Clare Pedrick

Visitors to Rome often face a conundrum: the more you see of the city, the more you'll realize how little you have seen. Take heart; Rome wasn't built in a day. The Italian author Silvio Negro said it best: "*Roma, non basta una vita*" (Rome, a lifetime is not enough). It's wise to start out knowing this and to have a focused but flexible itinerary. A ramble through a picturesque quarter of Old Rome can be just as enchanting as the quiet contemplation of a chapel or a trek through marbled museum corridors.

Though spread out, Rome invites walking, and taxis are rarely far off for the weary. Plan your day taking into account the varying opening hours of the sights you want to visit, which usually means mixing the ancient, classical, and baroque, museums and parks, the center and the environs. Most churches are usually open from 8 or 9 until noon or 12:30 and from 3 or 4 until about 6:30 or 7.

The Rome Archeologia Card, a combination ticket for the Colosseum, Palatine, and the various branches of the Museo Nazionale Romano

If you have 3 days

Begin your first day by surveying Rome from atop the Campidoglio, then explore the Roman Forum and see the Palatine Hill and the Colosseum (⇨ see Ancient Rome, *below*). In the afternoon, combine sightseeing with shopping and make your way through the neighborhood around the Spanish Steps and the Trevi Fountain (⇨ Piazza Venezia to the Spanish Steps). The following day, visit the Vatican Museums and Sistine Chapel (⇨ The Vatican Museums), then St. Peter's (⇨ The Vatican), breaking between the two for lunch. Take it easy on your third morning: explore a museum or sight of interest and then relax at a café and watch the passing parade. Spend your final afternoon and evening exploring the Ghetto and Trastevere neighborhoods (⇨ Across the Tiber).

11

If you have 5 days

On the morning of the fourth day wander through Villa Borghese and see the Canova and Bernini sculptures in the Galleria Borghese (which requires a reservation; ⇨ Villa Borghese to the Ara Pacis). Bring a picnic to eat beneath a shady tree in the magnificent gardens, then, in the afternoon, wander down Via Veneto for some shopping and a gelato. On the fifth day take an early-morning excursion along Via Appia Antica (⇨ The Catacombs & Via Appia Antica). After lunch back in town, see some of Rome's most historic churches, with San Clemente a highlight (⇨ Historic Churches).

If you have 7 days

Devote your remaining time to further exploration of the historic center city, with caffè stops along the way. Make sure you pass by the Pantheon, an architectural jewel of ancient Rome, and linger in Piazza Navona to see Bernini's fabulous fountains (⇨ Old Rome). Finally, return to the neighborhood you've liked best in your week here and don't be shy about poking into its courtyards and churches.

(Palazzo Altemps, Crypta Balbi, Terme di Diocleziano, Terme di Caracalla, Villa dei Quintili, the Mausoleo di Cecilia Metella, and Palazzo Massimo alle Terme), valid for seven consecutive days, is available at each participant's ticket office for €20—a good deal for ancient-history buffs.

Numbers in the text correspond to numbers in the margin and on the Rome and Old Rome maps.

Ancient Rome: Glories of the Caesars

A walk through the very core of Roman antiquity, through what was once the capital of the Western world, the Roman Forum, is an impressive introduction to the glories of the ancient city. Although the millennia have reduced this grand complex to fields of picturesque ruins, it is nonetheless awe-inspiring to consider that this square was the birthplace of Western civilization. Roman law and powerful armies were created here, banishing the barbarian world for a millennium. Here all Rome shouted as one, "Caesar has been murdered," and crowded to hear Mark Antony's eulogy for the fallen leader. Legend has it that St. Paul traversed the Forum en route to his audience with Nero. Up on the Campidoglio the harmony of Michelangelo's Renaissance piazza is an appropriate homage to the seat of the ancient governments based here 2,000 years before. In the heyday of the Empire, the Forum below occasionally became an enormous banquet hall, where all imperial Rome could be entertained in one place (as our times have observed thanks to such Hollywood epics as *Quo Vadis, Ben-Hur,* and *Cleopatra*). It's fitting that in the aftermath of centuries of such pageantry Percy Bysshe Shelley and Edward Gibbon reflected here on the meaning of *sic transit gloria mundi* (so passes away the glory of the world).

a good walk

Begin your walk on the **Campidoglio** ❶ ▷—the site of Michelangelo's spectacular piazza and Rome's city hall, Palazzo Senatorio, which was built over the Tabularium, the ancient hall of records. Flanking the palazzo are both halves of Rome's most noteworthy museum complex, the **Musei Capitolini** ❷, made up of the Museo Capitolino, the Palazzo dei Conservatori, the Pinacoteca Capitolina, the Tabularium, and Palazzo Caffarelli. They contain works of art gathered by Pope Sixtus IV, one of the Renaissance papal patrons of the arts. Off to the side of the Campidoglio, at the head of its formidable flight of steps, stands the ancient redbrick church of **Santa Maria d'Aracoeli** ❸. Walk down the road to the left of Palazzo Senatorio, behind the piazza, and look out over the remains of the Roman Forum. From here steps descend to the gloomy **Carcere Mamertino** ❹, the Mamertine Prison. The road leads out past the Forum of Caesar to Via dei Fori Imperiali. Across the street are the Forum of Trajan and the **Colonna di Traiano** ❺. Continue along the Via dei Fori Imperiali, passing the fora built by Augustus and Nerva, and cross back over the road to the entrance of the **Foro Romano** ❻. At the side of the ancient Via Sacra inside the Forum is the entrance to the **Colle Palatino** ❼, site of Rome's earliest settlement, which dates back to the late Bronze Age. Take the ramp that leads from the Forum–Palatine Hill area to the **Arco di Costantino** ❽ and, beyond it, the **Colosseo** ❾, one of antiquity's most famous monuments. Don't forget to check out the view from the park laid out over the ruins of Nero's **Domus Aurea** ❿, his sumptuous palace, behind the Colosseum.

TIMING It takes about an hour to walk the route, plus two hours to visit the Musei Capitolini, and two to three hours to explore the Roman Forum and Palatine Hill. The Colosseum takes about a half hour to visit, plus 20 minutes waiting in line.

What to See

❽ **Arco di Costantino.** This imposing arch was erected in AD 315 to celebrate the victory of the emperor Constantine (280–337) over Maxentius (died 312). The largest (69 feet high, 85 feet long, 23 feet wide) and best preserved of Rome's triumphal arches, it's one of the finest remaining monuments of ancient Rome.

★ ▷ ❶ **Campidoglio.** Though most of the buildings on Michelangelo's piazza date from the Renaissance, this hill was once the nerve center of the Roman Empire, the place where the city's first and holiest temples stood, including its most sacred, the Tempio di Giove (Temple of Jupiter). The city's archives were kept in the Tabularium (hall of records), the tall tufa structure that forms the foundation of today's city hall, the **Palazzo Sen-**

Opera Alfresco

Roman nightlife moves outdoors in summertime, and that goes not only for pubs and discos but for higher culture as well. Open-air opera is one venerable Italian tradition that has staged a comeback. Competing opera companies commandeer church courtyards, ancient villas, and soccer stadiums for performances that range from student-run mom-and-pop-eras to full-scale extravaganzas. The quality of performances is generally quite high, even if small productions often resort to school-play scenery and folding chairs to cut costs. Tickets run from about €15 to €40. Look for old-fashion posters plastered all over the city, advertising classics like *Tosca* and *La Traviata,* or contact the companies directly to find out what's on.

11

Shopping

The city's most famous shopping district is conveniently compact, fanning out at the foot of the Spanish Steps in a galaxy of boutiques offering gorgeous wares with glamorous labels. Here you can ricochet from Gucci to Prada to Valentino to Versace with less effort than it takes to pull out your platinum credit card. If your budget is designed for lower altitudes, you also can find great clothes and accessories at less extravagant prices. But buying is not necessarily the point. Taking in window displays that are works of art or imagining you or yours in a little red dress by Valentino or a lean Armani suit can be satisfactions in themselves.

Sidewalk Cafés

Café-sitting is the most popular leisure-time activity in Rome, practiced by all and involving nothing more strenuous than gesturing to catch the waiter's eye. Cafés are meant for relaxing, chatting with a companion, and watching the passing parade, possibly within view of one of the city's spectacular fountains or churches. Part of the pleasure is resting your tired feet; you will never be rushed, even when the cafés are most crowded, just before lunch and dinner. (Be aware, though, that you pay for your seat—prices are higher at tables than at the counter.)

---

atorio. By the Middle Ages, Monte Caprino (Goat Hill), as the hill was already called, had fallen into ruin. In 1536 Pope Paul III (1468–1549) decided to restore its grandeur for the triumphal entry into the city of Charles V (1500–58), the Holy Roman Emperor, and called upon Michelangelo to create the staircase ramp; the buildings and facades on three sides of Capitol Hill; the slightly convex pavement and its decoration; and the pedestal for the bronze equestrian statue of Marcus Aurelius. A work from the 2nd century AD, the statue stood here from the 16th century until 1981. The only celebrated equestrian bronze statue to survive from classical antiquity, it was mistakenly believed to represent the Christian emperor Constantine rather than the pagan Marcus Aurelius, hence its endurance through the centuries. A legend foretells that some day the statue's original gold patina will return, heralding the end of the world. The city's authorities had it restored and placed in the courtyard of the Museo Capitolino, saving not only what was left of

Rome

See Old Rome Map

CITTÀ DEL VATICANO

Villa Borghese

Zoological Gardens

Botanical Gardens

Parco Gianicolense

Forum of Trajan

Forum of Caesar

Arco di Settimio Severo

CAPITOLINE HILL

PALATINO HILL

AVENTINE HILL

Circo Massimo

TO CIMITERO ACATTOLICO

Parco di Porta Capena

KEY

▶ Start of walk

0 ——— 880 yds

0 ——— 800 m

the gold but also the statue's bronze, which had been seriously damaged by air pollution. A copy was placed on the original pedestal in 1997. As Michelangelo's preeminent urban set piece, the piazza sums up all the majesty of High Renaissance Rome.

❹ Carcere Mamertino (Mamertine Prison). This series of gloomy cells under a 17th-century church is where Rome's vanquished enemies were finished off. Some historians believe that St. Peter was held prisoner here, and legend has it that he miraculously brought forth a spring of water with which to baptize his jailers. ⊠ *Via del Tulliano, near Piazza Venezia* ☎ *06/6792902* ☞ *Donation requested* ☉ *Daily 9–12:30 and 2–5.*

Circo Massimo (Circus Maximus). In the giant arena laid out between Palatine and Aventine hills, more than 300,000 spectators watched chariot races while the emperor surveyed the scene from his palace on the Palatine Hill.

❼ Colle Palatino (Palatine Hill). A lane known as the Clivus Palatinus, whose worn paving stones were once trod by emperors and their slaves, climbs from the Forum area to a site that historians identify with Rome's earliest settlement. From 1878 to 1889, illustrious archaeologist Rodolfo Lanciani excavated a site on the Palatine Hill and found evidence of Romulus's presence, thereby contradicting early critics who deemed Romulus a mythical figure. The story goes that the twins Romulus and Remus were abandoned as infants but were nursed by a she-wolf on the banks of the Tiber and adopted by a shepherd. Encouraged by the gods to build a city, the twins chose a site in 735 BC, fortifying it with a wall that Lanciani identified by digging on the Palatine Hill. During the building of the city, the brothers quarreled, and in a fit of anger Romulus killed Remus.

Fodor'sChoice
★

In ancient times, despite the location overlooking the Forum with its traffic, congestion, and attendant noise, the Palatine Hill was Rome's most coveted address. More than a few of the 12 Caesars called the Palatine Hill home—including Caligula, who met his premature end in the Cryptoporticus tunnel, which today still stands (and remains unnerving). The palace of Tiberius was the first to be built here; others followed, most notably the gigantic extravaganza constructed for Emperor Domitian. Views from the ruins of the imperial palaces extend over the Circus Maximus. Today the Palatine is one of the most tranquil places in town, its Renaissance gardens a welcome respite, especially on a hot day. The Palatine Antiquarium holds relics found during excavations on the hill, as well as models of late Bronze Age villages. ⊠ *Entrances at the Arch of Titus in the Roman Forum and Via S. Gregorio 30, near Colosseo* ☎ *06/39967700* ⊕ *www.pierreci.it* ☞ *€8, includes Colosseo admission; €20, multisight ticket; reservation fee €1.50* ☉ *Tues.–Sun. 9–1 hr before sunset.*

❺ Colonna di Traiano. The ashes of Trajan (AD 53–117) were buried inside the base of this column, built to commemorate the emperor and his military campaigns in Dacia (Romania). It stands in what was once the **Foro di Traiano,** near the huge semicircular **Mercati di Traiano** (Trajan's Market) and the ruins of the **Foro di Augusto.** *Entrance* ⊠ *Via dei Fori Imperiali and Via IV Novembre 6, near Colosseo* ☎ *06/69780532* ☞ *€6.20* ☉ *Tues.–Sun. 9–4:30.*

★ ❾ **Colosseo.** The massive and majestic Colosseum, ancient Rome's most famous monument, was begun by the Flavian emperor Vespasian (AD 7–79)
in AD 72 and inaugurated eight years later with a program of games and
shows lasting 100 days. More than 70,000 spectators could sit within
the arena's 573-yard circumference, which had marble facing, hundreds of statues for decoration, and a velarium—an ingenious system
of sail-like awnings rigged on ropes manned by imperial sailors—to protect the audience from the sun and rain. Before the imperial box, gladiators would salute the emperor and cry, "*Ave, imperator, morituri te
salutant*" ("Hail, emperor, men soon to die salute you"); it is said that
when one day they heard the emperor Claudius respond, "Or maybe
not," they were so offended that they called a strike.

Originally known as the Flavian Amphitheater, it took the name Colos-
seum after a truly colossal gilt bronze statue of Nero that stood nearby.
Gladiator combat and staged animal hunts ended by the 6th century. The
arena later served as a quarry from which materials were looted to build
Renaissance churches and palaces. Finally, it was declared sacred by the
Vatican in memory of the many Christians believed martyred here.
(Scholars now maintain that Christians met their death elsewhere.) Dur-
ing the 19th century, romantic poets lauded the glories of the ruins when
viewed by moonlight. Now its arches glow at night with mellow golden
spotlights—less romantic, perhaps, but still impressive. ⊠ *Piazza del
Colosseo* ☎ *06/7005469, 06/39967700 reservations* ✆ *€8, includes
Palatine Hill admission; €20, multisight ticket; reservation fee €1.50*
⊙ *Tues.–Sun. 9–1 hr before sunset.*

❿ **Domus Aurea.** Nero's "Golden House" gives a good sense of the excesses
of Imperial Rome. After fire destroyed much of the city in AD 64, Nero
took advantage of the resulting open space to construct a lavish palace
so large that it spread over four of Rome's seven hills. A circular opening in the roof of the banquet hall created the illusion that the room itself was revolving. Today the palace remains impressive in scale, although
it requires a bit of imagination to envision its former grandeur (a
mediocre audio guide is some help). One wing caved in in early 2000
and remains closed at least through 2005. The underground site is cold
even in summer, so take something warm to wear. Reservations are highly
recommended. ⊠ *Via della Domus Aurea, near Colosseo* ☎ *06/39967700
reservations* ⊕ *www.pierreci.it* ✆ *€5 plus €1.50 reservation fee; €10
with tour; audio guide €2* ⊙ *Wed.–Mon. 9–7:45.*

**need a
break?**

The gardens of the **Oppian Hill,** directly above Nero's Golden
House, are a favorite place for modern-day Roman children to play.
Take a seat at the small outdoor bar among the palms and
bougainvillea and enjoy an *aperitivo* against the dramatic backdrop
of the Colosseum.

Foro di Cesare. Caesar built this forum, including a temple dedicated to
himself and the goddess Minerva, to expand the then-crowded original
Roman Forum, which had been built up over the preceding 500 years.
In doing so, Caesar set a trend that several emperors followed, building what are now called the Imperial Fora.

★ ❻ **Foro Romano.** Built in what was once a marshy valley between the Capitoline and Palatine hills, the Forum was the civic heart of Republican Rome, the austere enclave that preceded the hedonistic society that grew up under the emperors in the 1st to 4th century AD. The area was once filled with stately and magnificent buildings—temples, palaces, shops—and crowded with people from all corners of the world. Today this series of ruins and marble fragments interspersed with crumbling columns is impressive, but it's not easy to envision the grandeur that once was. It may help to bear in mind that what you see today are the ruins not of one period but of almost 900 years, from about 500 BC to AD 400.

Rome's timeless landscape is suggestive enough that you will probably be content to wander, letting your imagination dwell on Cicero (106 BC–43 BC), Julius Caesar (100 BC–44 BC), and Mark Antony (circa 81 BC–30 BC), who delivered the funeral address in Caesar's honor from the rostrum just left of the **Arco di Settimio Severo.** This arch, one of the grandest of all antiquity, was built in AD 203 to celebrate the victory of the emperor Severus (AD 146–211) over the Parthians, and was topped by a bronze equestrian statuary group with six horses. Most visitors also explore the reconstruction of the large brick senate hall, the **Curia;** the three Corinthian columns (a favorite of 19th-century poets), all that remains of the **Tempio di Vespasiano** (Temple of Vespasian); the circular **Tempio di Vesta,** where the highly privileged vestal virgins kept the sacred flame alive; and the **Arco di Tito,** which stands in a slightly elevated position on a spur of the Palatine Hill. The view of the Colosseum from the arch is superb, and reminds us that it was the Emperor Titus (AD 39–81) who helped finish the vast amphitheater begun by his father, Vespasian. Now cleaned and restored, the arch was erected in AD 81 to celebrate the sack of Jerusalem 10 years earlier, after the great Jewish revolt. A famous relief shows the captured contents of Herod's Temple—including its huge seven-branched menorah—being carried in triumph down Rome's Via Sacra. Audio guides are available at the bookshop–ticket office at the Via dei Fori Imperiali entrance. ✉ *Entrances at Via dei Fori Imperiali and Piazza del Colosseo* ☎ *06/39967700* ⊕ *www.pierreci.it* ✇ *Free, guided tour €3.50, audio guide €4* ◷ *Daily 9–1 hr before sunset.*

★ ❷ **Musei Capitolini.** The collections in the twin Museo Capitolino and Palazzo dei Conservatori were assembled by Pope Sixtus IV (1414–84), one of the earliest of the Renaissance popes. Although parts of the collection may excite only archaeologists and art historians, others contain some of the most famous pieces of classical sculpture, such as the poignant *Dying Gaul,* the regal *Capitoline Venus,* and the *Exquiline Venus* (identified as another Mediterranean beauty, Cleopatra herself). The delicate *Marble Faun* inspired Nathaniel Hawthorne's novel of the same name. Many of the works here and in Rome's other museums were copied from Greek originals. For hundreds of years, craftsmen of ancient Rome prospered by producing exact replicas of Greek statues using a process called "pointing."

Portraiture, however, was one area in which the Romans outdid the Greeks. The hundreds of Roman busts of emperors in the Sala degli Im-

AN EMPEROR CHEAT SHEET

OCTAVIAN, later known as Caesar Augustus, was Rome's first emperor (27 BC–AD 14). His rule began a 200-year period of peace known as the Pax Romana.

The name of **NERO** (AD 54–68) lives in infamy as a violent persecutor of Christians and as the murderer of his wife, his mother, and countless others. Although it's not certain whether he actually fiddled as Rome burned in AD 64, he was well known as a singer and a composer of music.

DOMITIAN (AD 81–96) was the first emperor to declare himself "Dominus et Deus," Lord and God. He stripped away power from the Senate, and as a result after his death he suffered "Damnatio Memoriae"—the Senate had his name and image erased from all public records.

TRAJAN (AD 98–117), the first Roman emperor to be born outside Italy (in southern Spain), enlarged the empire's boundaries to include modern-day Romania, Armenia, and Upper Mesopotamia.

HADRIAN (AD 117–138) expanded the empire in Asia and the Middle East. He's best known for designing and rebuilding the Pantheon, constructing a majestic villa at Tivoli, and initiating myriad other constructions across the empire, including the famed wall across Britain.

MARCUS AURELIUS (AD 161–180) is remembered as a humanitarian emperor, a Stoic philosopher whose Meditations are still read today. Nonetheless, he was an aggressive leader devoted to expanding the empire.

CONSTANTINE I (AD 306–337) made his mark by legalizing Christianity, an act that changed the course of history, legitimizing the once-banned religion and paving the way for the papacy in Rome.

peratori and of philosophers in the Sala dei Filosofi of the **Museo Capitolino** constitute a Who's Who of the ancient world. Within these serried ranks are 48 Roman emperors, ranging from Augustus to Theodosius (AD 346–395). On one console you'll see the handsomely austere Augustus, who "found Rome a city of brick and left it one of marble." On another rests Claudius "the stutterer," an indefatigable builder brought vividly to life in the novel *I, Claudius* by Robert Graves (1895–1985). Also in this company is Nero, one of the most notorious emperors—though by no means the worst—who built for himself the fabled Domus Aurea. And, of course, there are the baddies: cruel Caligula (AD 12–41) and Caracalla (AD 186–217), and the dissolute, eerily modern boy-emperor, Heliogabalus (AD 203–222).

Unlike the Greeks, whose portraits are idealized, the Romans preferred the "warts and all" school of representation. Many of the busts that have come down to us, notably that of Commodus (AD 161–192), the emperor-gladiator (found in a gallery on the upper level of the museum), are almost brutally realistic. As you leave the museum, be sure to stop in the courtyard. To the right is the original equestrian statue of Marcus Aurelius that once stood in the piazza outside, restored and safely kept behind glass. At the center of the courtyard is the gigantic, reclining figure of Oceanus, found in the Roman Forum and later dubbed *Marforio,* one of Rome's "talking statues" to which citizens from the 1500s to the 1900s affixed anonymous satirical verses and notes of political protest. (Another talking statue still in use today sits at Piazza Pasquino, near Piazza Navona.)

The **Palazzo dei Conservatori** is a trove of ancient and baroque treasures. Lining the courtyard are the colossal fragments of a head, leg, foot, and hand—all that remains of the famous statue of the emperor Constantine the Great, who believed that Rome's future lay with Christianity. These immense effigies were much in vogue in the later days of the Roman Empire. The resplendent Salone dei Orazi e Curiazi on the first floor is a ceremonial hall with a magnificent gilt ceiling, carved wooden doors, and 16th-century frescoes. At either end of the hall reign statues of the baroque era's most charismatic popes, a marble Urban VIII (1568–1644) by Bernini (1598–1680) and a bronze Innocent X (1574–1655) by Bernini's rival Algardi (1595–1654). The renowned symbol of Rome, the *Capitoline Wolf,* a 6th-century BC Etruscan bronze, holds a place of honor in the museum; the suckling twins were added during the Renaissance to adapt the statue to the legend of Romulus and Remus. The museum's Pinacoteca, or painting gallery, holds some of baroque painting's great masterpieces, including Caravaggio's *La Buona Ventura* (1595) and *San Giovanni Battista* (1602), Peter Paul Rubens's (1577–1640) *Romulus and Remus* (1614), and Pietro da Cortona's (1596–1669) sumptuous portrait of Pope Urban VIII (1627). The museum complex includes the adjacent **Palazzo Caffarelli,** where temporary exhibitions take place and where you can enjoy the view and refreshments on a large open terrace. Admission to the Pinacoteca is included in your ticket. ✉ *Piazza del Campidoglio, near Piazza Venezia* ☎ *06/39967800 or 06/67102475* ⊕ *www.pierreci.it* ✆ €6.20, *free last Sun. of month* ⊙ *Tues.–Sun. 9–8.*

❸ **Santa Maria d'Aracoeli.** This stark redbrick church was one of the first Christian churches in Rome. According to legend, on this spot the Sibyl predicted to Augustus the coming of a redeemer. The emperor is believed to have responded by erecting the Ara Coeli, the Altar of Heaven. The church is best known for its seemingly endless, steep stairs from Piazza Venezia and for the 15th-century frescoes by Pinturicchio (1454–1513) in the first chapel on the right. ✉ *Piazza d'Aracoeli, near Piazza Venezia* ⊙ *Oct.–May, daily 7–noon and 4–6; June–Sept., daily 7–noon and 4–6:30.*

The Vatican: Rome of the Popes

This tiny walled city-state, capital of the Catholic Church, draws millions of visitors every year to its wealth of treasures and spiritual monuments. You might go to the Vatican for its exceptional art holdings—Michelangelo's frescoes, rare archaeological marbles, and Bernini's statues—or to immerse yourself in the unique and grandiose architecture of St. Peter's Square. Or you may go in pilgrimage, spiritual or otherwise, to the most overwhelming architectural achievement of the Renaissance and the seat of world Catholicism, St. Peter's Basilica. In between the sacred and the profane lie sights for every taste and inclination: magnificent rooms decorated by Raphael, sculptures such as the *Apollo Belvedere* and the *Laocoön,* frescoes by Fra Angelico, paintings by Giotto and Leonardo, and the celebrated ceiling of the Sistine Chapel. The power that emerged as the Rome of the emperors declined—the Church—gave impetus to a profusion of artistic expression and shaped the destiny of the city for a thousand years. Note: ushers at the entrance of St. Peter's Basilica and the Vatican Museums will not allow entry to people with inappropriate clothing—which means no bare knees or shoulders.

a good walk

Start your walk at the **Castel Sant'Angelo** ⑪ ⌐, the fortress that once served as the pope's refuge, and take in the stage-set beauty of the Ponte Sant'-Angelo before turning right onto Via della Conciliazione (or following the more intimate route west along Borgo Pio) to the Vatican. Once inside **Piazza San Pietro** ⑫, rich architectural detail awaits at **Basilica di San Pietro** ⑬, the magnificent seat of the Catholic Church. Below the basilica, visit the Vatican Grottoes, the last resting place of many of the popes, and, if you have time, arrange a tour of the Vatican Gardens and the excavations below the church.

TIMING Allow an hour for a visit to Castel Sant'Angelo. You'll also need an hour to see St. Peter's, plus 30 minutes for the Museo Storico, 15 minutes for the Vatican Grottoes, and an hour to climb to the top of the dome. Note that free one-hour English-language tours of the basilica are offered Monday–Saturday at 10 and 3, Sunday at 2:30 (sign up at the little desk under the portico).

Sights to See

★ ⑬ **Basilica di San Pietro.** The physical proportions of the sublime St. Peter's Basilica are staggering: it covers about 18,100 square yards, extends 212 yards in length, and carries a dome that rises 435 feet and measures 138 feet across its base. Its history is equally impressive: no fewer than five of Italy's greatest artists—Donato Bramante (1444–1514), Raphael (1483–1520), Baldassare Peruzzi (1481–1536), Antonio Sangallo the Younger (1483–1546), and Michelangelo (1475–1564)—died while working on the construction of this version of St. Peter's.

The history of the original St. Peter's goes back to the year AD 319, when the emperor Constantine built a basilica over the site of the tomb of St. Peter (died AD 64). This early church stood for more than 1,000 years, undergoing a number of restorations, until it was on the verge of collapse. Reconstruction began in 1452 but was abandoned for lack of funds. In 1506 Pope Julius II (1443–1513) instructed the architect Bramante to raze the existing structure and build a new and greater basilica. In 1546 Pope Paul III persuaded the aging Michelangelo to take on the job of completing the building. Revising Bramante's plan, Michelangelo designed the dome to cover the crossing, but his plans, too, were modified after his death. The cupola, one of the most beautiful in the world, was completed by Giacomo della Porta (circa 1537–1602) and Domenico Fontana (1543–1607). The new church wasn't completed and dedicated until 1626; by that time the ground plan had shifted from a Greek cross to a Latin one, creating a longer nave but obscuring the view of the dome from the piazza. Under the portico, 15th-century bronze doors by Filarete (circa 1400–1469), salvaged from the old basilica, fill the central portal. Off the entry portico, Bernini's famous *Scala Regia,* the ceremonial entryway to the Vatican Palace and one of the most magnificent staircases in the world, is graced with Bernini's dramatic statue of Constantine the Great.

The cherubs over the holy-water fonts will give you a sense of the grand scale of St. Peter's: the sole of each cherub's foot is as long as the distance from your fingertips to your elbow. It is because the proportions of this giant building are in such perfect harmony that its vastness may escape you at first. But in its megascale—inspired by the size of the ancient Roman ruins—it reflects Roman *grandiosità* in all its majesty.

Over an altar in a side chapel near the entrance is Michelangelo's **Pietà.** Legend has it that the artist, only 22 at the time the work was completed, overheard passersby expressing skepticism that such a young man could have executed such a sophisticated and moving piece. Offended at the implication, he crept back that night and signed the piece—in big letters, on a ribbon falling from the Virgin's left shoulder across her breast, where no one could possibly miss it. His name is there today.

Four massive piers support the dome at the crossing, where the mighty Bernini **baldacchino** (canopy) rises high above the papal altar. "What the barbarians didn't do, the Barberini did," 17th-century wags quipped when Barberini Pope Urban VIII had the bronze stripped from the Pantheon's portico and melted down to make the baldacchino (using what was left over for cannonballs). The pope celebrates mass here, over the grottoes holding the tombs of many of his predecessors. Deep in the excavations under the foundations of the original basilica is what is believed to be the tomb of St. Peter. The bronze throne behind the main altar in the apse, the Cathedra Petri (Chair of St. Peter), is Bernini's work (1656), and it covers a wooden-and-ivory chair that St. Peter himself is said to have used. However, scholars contend that this throne probably dates only from the Middle Ages. See how the adoration of a million lips has completely worn down the bronze on the right foot of the statue of St. Peter in front of the near right pillar in the transept. ⊕ *www. vatican.va* ☉ *Apr.–Sept., daily 7–7; Oct.–Mar., daily 7–6. Closed during ceremonies in the piazza.*

The entrance to the **Grotte Vaticane** (Vatican Grottoes), which hold the tombs of many popes, is at the crossing. The only exit from the grottoes leads outside St. Peter's, to the courtyard that holds the entrance to the dome. ☉ *Apr.–Sept., daily 7–6; Oct.–Mar., daily 7–5.*

A small but rich collection of Vatican treasures is housed in the **Museo Storico** in the Sacristy, among them precious antique chalices and the massive 15th-century sculptured bronze tomb of Pope Sixtus V (1520–90) by Antonio del Pollaiuolo (1431–98). ▱ €9 ☉ *Daily 8–5.*

The **roof** of the church, reached by elevator or stairs, is a landscape of domes and towers. A short interior staircase leads to the base of the dome for a dove's-eye view of the interior of St. Peter's. Then, only if you are stout of heart and sound of lung should you attempt the taxing and claustrophobic climb up the narrow stairs—there's no turning back!—to the balcony of the lantern, where the view embraces the Vatican Gardens and all of Rome. ☎ *06/69883462* 🛗 *Elevator €5, stairs €4* ☉ *Daily 8–5. Closed during ceremonies in the piazza.*

off the
beaten
path

VATICAN NECROPOLIS – Visit the pre-Constantine necropolis under St. Peter's for a fascinating glimpse of the underpinnings of the great basilica, which was built over the cemetery where archaeologists believe they have found St. Peter's tomb. Apply in advance by sending a fax or e-mail (scavi@fsp.va) with the name of each visitor, language spoken, possible days for the visit, and a local phone number. Reservations will be confirmed a few days in advance. No children under 15 are admitted. Tickets are sometimes available for same-day tours; apply in person at the Ufficio Scavi (Excavations Office), on the right beyond the Arco delle Campane (Arch of the Bells) entrance to the Vatican, which is left of the basilica. Tell the Swiss Guard you want the Ufficio Scavi, and he will let you by. ☎ *06/69885318* 🖨 *06/ 69885518* ⊕ *www.vatican.va* 🎫 *€9* ☉ *Ufficio Scavi Mon.–Sat. 8–5.*

☙ ⚑ **⑪ Castel Sant'Angelo.** For hundreds of years this fortress guarded the Vatican, to which it is linked by the Passetto, an arcaded passageway. According to legend, Castel Sant'Angelo got its name during the plague of 590, when Pope Gregory the Great (circa 540–604), passing by in a religious procession, had a vision of an angel sheathing its sword atop the stone ramparts. Though it may look like a stronghold, Castel Sant'Angelo was in fact built as a tomb for the emperor Hadrian (76–138) in AD 135. By the 6th century it had been transformed into a fortress, and it remained a refuge for the popes for almost 1,000 years. It has dungeons, battlements, cannon and cannonballs, and a collection of antique weaponry and armor. The lower levels formed the base of Hadrian's mausoleum; ancient ramps and narrow staircases climb through the castle's core to courtyards and frescoed halls, where temporary exhibits are held. Off the loggia is a café.

The upper terrace, with the massive angel statue commemorating Gregory's vision, evokes memories of Tosca, Puccini's poignant heroine in the opera of the same name, who threw herself off these ramparts with the cry, *"Scarpia, avanti a Dio!"* ("Scarpia, we meet before God"). On summer evenings a book fair with musical events and food stalls surrounds the castle. One of Rome's most beautiful pedestrian bridges, **Ponte Sant'Angelo** spans the Tiber in front of the fortress and is studded with graceful angels designed by Bernini. ⊠ *Lungotevere Castello 50, San Pietro* ☎ *06/39967700* ⊕ *www.pierreci.it* 🎫 *€5* ☉ *Tues.–Sun. 9–8.*

Giardini Vaticani. Generations of popes and cardinals have mulled over affairs of church and state in these beautifully manicured gardens, originally laid out in the 16th century. A two-hour guided tour, half by bus and half on foot, with a guide, takes you through a haven of shady walkways, elaborate fountains, and exotic plants. A second option is a combined gardens tour and guided visit to the Sistine Chapel. Tickets are

CloseUp

A MORNING WITH THE POPE

The pope holds audiences in a large, modern hall (or in St. Peter's Square in summer) on Wednesday morning at 10. To attend, you must get tickets; apply in writing at least 10 days in advance to the **Papal Prefecture** (Prefettura della Casa Pontificia; ⌖ 00120 Vatican City ☎ 06/69883273 🖷 06/69885863), indicating the date you prefer, your language, and your hotel. Or go to the prefecture, through the Porta di Bronzo, the bronze door at the end of the colonnade on the right side of the piazza; the office is open Monday–Saturday 9–1, and last-minute tickets may be available. You can also arrange to pick up free tickets on Tuesday from 5 to 6:45 at the **Santa Susanna American Church** (⌖ Via XX Settembre 15, near Termini ☎ 06/42014554); call first. For a fee, travel agencies make arrangements that include transportation. Arrive early, as security is tight and the best places fill up fast.

available at the **Guided Visit to Vatican Museums Office** (⌖ Piazza San Pietro ☎ 06/69884466), open Monday–Saturday 8:30–7. Make reservations two or three days in advance. ⊕ *www.vatican.va* 🖾 €9 for gardens tour, €19 for gardens and Sistine Chapel ☉ Mon.–Sat.

⑫ Piazza San Pietro. As you enter St. Peter's Square you are officially entering Vatican territory. The piazza is one of Bernini's most spectacular masterpieces. Completed in 1667 after 11 years' work—a relatively short time in those days, considering the vastness of the task—the piazza can hold 400,000 people. It's surrounded by a curving pair of quadruple colonnades, which are topped by a balustrade and statues of 140 saints. Look for the two disks set into the pavement on either side of the obelisk at the center of the piazza. When you stand on either disk, a trick of perspective makes the colonnades seem to consist of a single row of columns. Bernini had an even grander visual effect in mind when he designed the square. By opening up this immense, bright, airy space in a neighborhood of narrow, shadowy streets, he created a contrast that would surprise and impress anyone who emerged from the darkness into the light, in a characteristically baroque metaphor. But in the 1930s Mussolini spoiled the effect. To celebrate the "conciliation" between the Vatican and the Italian government under the Lateran Pact of 1929, he conceived of the Via della Conciliazione, the broad, rather soulless avenue that now forms the main approach to St. Peter's and gives the eye time to adjust to the enormous dimensions of the square and church. Remember to take a look at the Swiss Guards in their 16th century–style uniforms; they stand at the Vatican City entrances to the right and left of St. Peter's.

Vatican Museums: The Sistine Chapel & Beyond

The Vatican Palace has been the papal residence since 1377. Actually, it represents a collection of buildings that covers more than 13 acres, containing an estimated (no one has bothered to count them) 1,400 rooms, chapels, and galleries. Other than the pope and his court, the occupants are some of art's greatest masterpieces. The main entrance to the museums, on Viale Vaticano, is a long walk from Piazza San Pietro. Some city buses stop near the main entrance: Bus 49 from Piazza Cavour stops right in front; Buses 81 and 492 and Tram 19 stop at Piazza Risorgimento, halfway between St. Peter's and the museums. The Ottaviano–S. Pietro and the Cipro–Musei Vaticani on Metro A also are in the vicinity.

a good tour

There are many sections of the **Musei Vaticani** ⑩ besides the Sistine Chapel that are not to be overlooked: the Museo Egizio; the Chiaramonti and Museo Pio Clementino, which are given over to classical sculptures (among them some of the best-known statues in the world—the *Laocoön*, the *Belvedere Torso,* and the *Apollo Belvedere*—which with their vibrant humanism had a tremendous impact on Renaissance art); and the Museo Etrusco. Finally, you should make sure to visit the Stanze di Raffaello and see Raphael's paintings in the Pinacoteca.

TIMING   Plan on about two hours if you just want to see highlights; an in-depth visit will take at least a full morning. To minimize time spent in line, it's usually a good idea to get here just before opening time.

Sights to See

⑭ **Musei Vaticani** (Vatican Museums). The immense collections housed

Fodor'sChoice   here are so rich that unless you are an art history buff you will proba-
★   bly just want to skim the surface, concentrating on pieces that strike your fancy. The Sistine Chapel is a must, of course, and that's why you may have to wait in line to see it; after all, every tourist in Rome has the same idea. Pick up a leaflet at the main entrance to the museums to see the overall layout. The Sistine Chapel is at the far end of the complex, and the leaflet charts two abbreviated itineraries through other collections to reach it. You can rent a taped commentary (€4, about 90 minutes) in English for the Sistine Chapel, the Stanze di Raffaello, and the other main attractions. Or you can book a guided tour with the **Guided Visit to Vatican Museums Office** (☎ 06/69884676). Phone at least a day in advance. Cost, including entrance fee, is €16.50.

The exhibition halls of the **Biblioteca Vaticana** (Vatican Library) are bright with frescoes and contain a sampling of the library's rich collections of precious manuscripts. Room X, the Room of the Aldobrandini Marriage, holds a beautiful Roman fresco of a nuptial rite. More classical statues are on view in the new wing. At the Quattro Cancelli you'll find the cafeteria. The **Pinacoteca** (Picture Gallery) displays works by such artists as Giotto (circa 1266–1337), Fra Angelico, and Filippo Lippi (circa 1406–69), and Raphael's exceptional *Transfiguration, Coronation* and *Foligno Madonna.*

The **Stanze di Raffaello** (Raphael Rooms) are second only to the Sistine Chapel in artistic interest—and draw crowds comparable to the Sistine's as well. In 1508 Pope Julius II employed Raphael, on the recommendation of Bramante, to decorate the rooms with biblical scenes. The result was a Renaissance tour de force. Of the four rooms, the second and third were decorated mainly by Raphael. The others were decorated by

Giulio Romano (circa 1499–1546) and other assistants of Raphael; the first room is known as the Stanza dell'Incendio, with frescoes of the fire (*incendio*) in the Borgo neighborhood by Romano.

The frescoed **Stanza della Segnatura** (Room of the Signature), where papal bulls were signed, is one of Raphael's finest works; indeed, they are thought by many to be some of the finest paintings in the history of Western art. This was Julius's private library, and the room's use is reflected in the frescoes' themes, philosophy and enlightenment. A paradigm of High Renaissance painting, the works here demonstrate the revolutionary ideals of the time: naturalism (Raphael's figures lack the awkwardness of those painted only a few years earlier); humanism (the idea that human beings are the noblest and most admirable of God's creations); and a profound interest in the ancient world, the result of the 15th-century rediscovery of classical antiquity. Theology triumphs in the fresco known as the *Disputa,* or *Debate on the Holy Sacrament.* The *School of Athens* glorifies some of philosophy's greats, including Plato and Aristotle at the fresco's center. The pensive figure on the stairs is thought to be modeled after Michelangelo, who was painting the Sistine ceiling at the same time Raphael was working here. Michelangelo does not appear in preparatory drawings, so Raphael may have added his fellow artist's portrait after admiring his work.

The tiny **Cappella di Nicholas V** (Chapel of Nicholas V) is aglow with frescoes by Fra Angelico (1387–1455), the Florentine monk whose sensitive paintings were guiding lights for the Renaissance. The **Appartamento Borgia** (Borgia Apartment) is worth seeing for the elaborately painted ceilings, designed and partially executed by Pinturicchio. Among the frescoes, look for the Borgia's family emblem, the bull, and for the blond Lucrezia, the Borgia pope's daughter, posing piously as St. Catherine.

In 1508, while Raphael was put to work on his series of rooms, the redoubtable Pope Julius II commissioned Michelangelo to paint single-handedly the more than 10,000-square-foot ceiling of the **Cappella Sistina** (Sistine Chapel). The task cost the artist four years of mental and physical anguish. It's said that for years afterward Michelangelo couldn't read anything without holding it up over his head. The result, however, was the masterpiece that you now see, its colors cool and brilliant after restoration. Bring a pair of binoculars to get a better look at this incredible work (unfortunately, you're not allowed to lie down on the floor to study the frescoes above, the viewing position of choice in decades past; by the time you leave the chapel your neck may feel like Michelangelo's, so you may also want to study it—to take a cue from 19th-century visitors—with the aid of a pocket mirror).

The ceiling is in essence a painted Bible: Michelangelo's subject was the story of humanity before the coming of Christ. Although some of the frescoed panels are veritable stews of figures, others—especially the depiction of God's outstretched hand giving Adam the spark of life in the *Creation of Adam*—are forcefully simple, revealing how much Michelangelo brought to painting from the discipline of sculpture. In 1541, some 30 years after completing the ceiling, Michelangelo was commissioned to paint the *Last Judgment* on the chapel's altar wall. If the artist's ceiling may be taken as an expression of the optimism of the High Renaissance, the *Last Judgment,* by contrast, is a virtual guided tour through hell. The aged and embittered Michelangelo painted his own face on the wrinkled human skin in the hand of St. Bartholomew, below and to the right of the figure of Christ, which he clearly modeled on the *Apollo Belvedere* (on exhibit in the Vatican galleries). This is not surprising, since in the intervening years Rome had been sacked and pillaged by mercenary troops of Charles V in 1527, who used the Sistine Chapel as a stable.

In only a few years the grim Counter-Reformation began, and suddenly the nudity in Michelangelo's *Last Judgment* was so repugnant to the papal court that the artist Daniele da Volterra (1509–66)—forever after known as *il braghettone* (the breeches-maker)—was ordered to paint loincloths over the offending parts. Like the ceiling, the *Last Judgment* has been cleaned; the restoration was unveiled in April 1994, surprising viewers with its clarity and color. Was Michelangelo truly a master of vibrant color? Or is the "new" Sistine a travesty of the artist's intentions? Opinions remain divided, but most art historians believe the restoration is true to Michelangelo's original vision.

In all, the Vatican Museums offer a staggering foray into the realms of art and history—so much that it's foolhardy to try to see all the collections in one day. ⊠ *Viale Vaticano, San Pietro* ☎ *06/69883332* ⊕ *www. vatican.va* ✉ *€12; free last Sun. of month* ☉ *Mid-Mar.–Oct., weekdays 8:45–4:45, no admission after 3:45, Sat. and last Sun. of month 8:45–1:45, no admission after 12:20; Nov.–mid-Mar., Mon.–Sat. and last Sun. of month 8:45–1:45, no admission after 12:20* ☞ *Note: ushers at the entrance of St. Peter's and the Vatican Museums will not allow entry to people with bare knees or bare shoulders.*

need a break? There are neighborhood trattorias far better and far less popular with tourists than those opposite the Vatican Museums entrance. Among them is the **Hostaria Dino e Toni** (⊠ Via Leone IV 60, near San Pietro), where you can dine on typical Roman fare at moderate, even inexpensive prices. **La Caravella** (⊠ Via degli Scipioni 32, at Via Vespasiano, off Piazza Risorgimento, near San Pietro) serves Roman specialties, including pizza at lunch, every day but Thursday, when it's closed.

Old Rome: Gold & Grandeur

The neighborhood between the Corso and the Tiber bend is one of Rome's most beautiful districts, filled with narrow streets bearing curious names, airy baroque piazzas, and picturesque courtyards. It has been an integral part of the city since ancient times, and its position between the Vatican and the Lateran palaces, both seats of papal rule, put it in the mainstream of Rome's development from the Middle Ages onward. It includes such world-famous sights as the Pantheon, but it is mainly an excursion into the 16th and 17th centuries, when baroque art triumphed. Some of Rome's most coveted residential addresses are here.

The most important clue to the Romans is their baroque art—not its artistic technicalities but its spirit. When you understand this, you will no longer be a stranger in Rome. Flagrantly emotional, heavily expressive, and sensuously visual, the 17th-century artistic movement known as the baroque was born in Rome, the creation of three geniuses, the sculptor and architect Gianlorenzo Bernini, the painter and architect Pietro da Cortona (1596–1669), and the architect and sculptor Francesco Borromini (1599–1667). From the drama found in the artists' paintings to the jewel-laden, gold-on-gold detail of 17th-century Roman palaces, baroque style was intended both to shock and delight by upsetting the placid, "correct" rules of the Renaissance. The style's appeal to the emotions made it a powerful weapon in the hands of the Counter-Reformation.

a good walk

Start on Via del Plebiscito, near Piazza Venezia, at the huge church of **Il Gesù** ⑮ ▶, the grandmother of all baroque churches. Walk west along Via Celso to Via della Botteghe Oscure and **Crypta Balbi** ⑯, then head north past **Largo di Torre Argentina** ⑰, the site where Caesar was slain by Brutus, to Piazza della Minerva and the church of **Santa Maria sopra Minerva** ⑱. Turn down Via della Minerva to reach the **Pantheon** ⑲. From Piazza della Rotonda, in front of the Pantheon, take Via Giustiniani onto Via della Dogana Vecchia to the church of **San Luigi dei Francesi** ⑳, a pilgrimage spot for art lovers everywhere. Just north is the church of **Sant'Agostino in Campo Marzio** ㉑, in the piazza of the same name. Visit historic **Palazzo Altemps** ㉒, off Piazza Sant'Apollinare, before arriving at **Piazza Navona** ㉓, one of Rome's showpiece piazzas, home to Bernini's Fontana dei Quattro Fiumi and the church of Sant'Agnese in Agone, the quintessence of baroque architecture. Leave the piazza at the south end and cross one of Rome's great thoroughfares, Corso Vittorio Emanuele II, to the **Campo de' Fiori** ㉔. Flowing naturally out of the campo is a short promenade that will take you to **Palazzo Farnese** ㉕, perhaps the most beautiful Renaissance palace in Rome. Then proceed south to inspect **Palazzo Spada** ㉖ and its picture gallery. Take Via Baullari to one of the outstanding architectural monuments of Renaissance Rome, the **Palazzo Massimo alle Colonne** ㉗, and, two blocks east along the bustling street, the huge, 17th-century church of **Sant'Andrea della Valle** ㉘. Finally, head down Corso del Rinascimento to No. 40, the church of **Sant'Ivo alla Sapienza** ㉙, with a golden lantern atop the dome in the shape of a spiral.

TIMING This walk can take from four to six hours, including time to linger at Crypta Balbi, Palazzo Altemps, and Palazzo Spada.

What to See

★ ㉔ **Campo de' Fiori.** This bustling square is home to a famed morning market, a must-see dose of local culture for any Roman holiday. Each morning, vendors fill temporary stalls with all manner of local produce, nuts, cheese, spices, flowers, and seafood; by early afternoon it's all gone, to resurface in the city's homes and restaurants at dinnertime. If you don't want to join the fray, step back and take a break at one of the many pleasant cafés that border the market. The view has certainly improved since the Middle Ages, when the square was the scene of public executions, including that of philosopher-monk Giordano Bruno (1548–1600). His statue still broods in the center of the square.

Old Rome

KEY

▲ Start of walk

220 yards

200 meters

River Tiber

Santa Maria
della Pace

need a break?
Some of Rome's best pizza comes out of the ovens of **Il Forno di Campo de' Fiori** (☎ 06/68806662) on Campo de' Fiori. Choose pizza *bianca* (topped with olive oil) or *rossa* (with tomato sauce), and move to the annex next door to have your warm pizza filled with prosciutto and figs, or other mouthwatering combinations.

⑯ Crypta Balbi (Crypt of Balbus). After 20 years of excavation and restoration, these fascinating remains of a porticoed courtyard and theater built in 13 BC, now part of the Museo Nazionale Romano, afford a unique look at Roman history. Rather than focus on one era, the museum peels back the layers of the site, following the latest techniques in conservation. The well-explained exhibits (with text in English and Italian) give you a tangible sense of the sweeping changes that this spot—and Rome—underwent from antiquity to the 20th century. A partially restored wall provides an example of what marble and tufa constructions looked like before weather took its toll and medieval builders stripped the marble off for reuse. Copies of documents and reconstructed coins and other everyday objects found in drains, rubbish dumps, and tombs are a window into the world of the people who lived and worked here over the ages. ⊠ *Via Delle Botteghe Oscure 31, near Piazza Venezia* ☎ *06/39967700* 🖅 *€4* ☉ *Tues.–Sun. 9–7:45.*

▶ ⑮ Il Gesù. Grandmother of all baroque churches, this huge structure was designed by the architect Vignola (1507–73) to be the tangible symbol of Jesuits, a major force in the Counter-Reformation in Europe. It remained unadorned for about 100 years, but when it finally was decorated, no expense was spared. Its interior drips with gold and lapis lazuli, gold and precious marbles, gold and more gold—all covered by a fantastically painted ceiling by Baciccia (1639–1709) that seems to merge with the painted stucco figures at its base. St. Ignatius's apartments, reached from the side entrance of the church, are also worth a visit (afternoons only) for the trompe-l'oeil frescoes and relics of the saint. ⊠ *Piazza del Gesù, near Piazza Venezia* ☎ *06/3613717* ☉ *Daily 6:30–12:30 and 4–7.*

⑰ Largo di Torre Argentina. In the middle of this busy piazza lies Rome's largest fully excavated Republican-era ruins. The site was discovered in 1885 and further dug up from 1926 to 1929. What came to light was the Area Sacra (sacred area), with columns, altars, and foundations from four temples dating as far back as the 1st century BC. On the west side of the square lies the Curia Pompeia, the site where Caesar was slain in 44 BC. The frescoes on the taller brickwork are from the 12th century church of San Nicola de' Cesarini, which was built into one of the temples. While here it's hard to miss the many cats lounging around the site: the ruins serve as a cat sanctuary for hundreds of the city's strays. In the southwest corner take the staircase down to visit the cats and the *gattare* (cat ladies) who look after them. Volunteer cat tenders are welcome, even for a few hours.

㉒ Palazzo Altemps. If you're interested in ancient sculpture, you should not miss one of Rome's greatest collections of classical antiquities, housed in this 16th-century building. It displays the collections of ancient

Roman and Egyptian sculpture of the **Museo Nazionale Romano.** Look for two works in the famed Ludovisi collection: the large, intricately carved Ludovisi Sarcophagus and *Galata,* a poignant work portraying a barbarian warrior who chooses death for himself and his wife rather than humiliation by the enemy. The palace's stunning courtyard and gorgeously frescoed ceilings and loggia make an impressive setting for the sculptures. ⊠ *Piazza Sant'Apollinare 46, near Piazza Navona* ☎ *06/39967700* ⊑ *€5* ⊘ *Tues.–Sun. 9–7:45.*

㉕ **Palazzo Farnese.** The Farnese family rose to great power during the Renaissance, in part due to the favor Pope Alexander VI showed to the beautiful Giullia Farnese. The large palace was begun when, with Alexander's aid, Giullia's brother became cardinal; it was further enlarged on his election as Pope Paul III in 1534. The uppermost frieze decorations and main window overlooking the piazza are the work of Michelangelo, who also designed part of the courtyard, as well as the graceful arch over Via Giullia at the back. The facade on Piazza Farnese has been recently cleaned, further revealing geometrical brick configurations that have long been thought to hold occult meaning. When looking at the palace from outside you can catch a glimpse of the splendid frescoed ceilings, including the **Galleria Carracci** vault painted by Annibale Carracci between 1597 and 1604—the second-greatest ceiling in Rome. For permission to view it from the inside, write to the French Embassy, which now occupies the palace. Specify the number in your party, when you wish to visit, and a local phone number for confirmation a few days before the visit. ⊠ *Servizio Culturale, French Embassy, Piazza Farnese 67, 00186 Rome* ☎ *06/686011* ⊑ *Free* ⊘ *By appointment only.*

㉗ **Palazzo Massimo alle Colonne.** A graceful columned portico marks this inconspicuous but seminal architectural monument of Renaissance Rome, built by Baldassare Peruzzi in 1527. Via del Paradiso, across Corso Vittorio Emanuele II, affords a better view. ⊠ *Corso Vittorio Emanuele II 141, near Piazza Navona.*

㉖ **Palazzo Spada.** A dazzling stuccoed facade tucked away in Piazza Capo di Ferro, west of Piazza Farnese, fronts an equally magnificent inner courtyard. On the southeast side of the inner courtyard, the gallery designed by Borromini creates an elaborate optical illusion, appearing to be much longer than it really is. On the first floor there are paintings and sculptures that belonged to Cardinale Bernardino Spada, an art connoisseur who collected works by Italian and Flemish masters. ⊠ *Piazza Capo di Ferro 13, Campo de' Fiori* ☎ *06/6832409* ⊕ *www.galleriaborghese.it* ⊑ *€5* ⊘ *Tues.–Sun. 8:30–7:30.*

⑲ **Pantheon.** One of Rome's most impressive and best-preserved ancient monuments, the Pantheon is particularly close to the hearts of Romans. The emperor Hadrian designed it around AD 120 and had it built on the site of an earlier temple that had been damaged by fire. The most striking thing about the Pantheon is not its size, immense though it is (until 1960 the dome was the largest ever built); rather, it is the remarkable harmony of the building. Notice that the height of the dome is equal to

FodorśChoice
★

the diameter of the circular interior. The oculus, or opening in the ceiling, is meant to symbolize the all-seeing eye of heaven; in practice, it illuminates the building and lightens the heavy stone ceiling. The original bronze doors have survived more than 1,800 years, centuries longer than the interior's rich gold ornamentation, which was plundered by popes and emperors. Art lovers can pay homage to the tomb of Raphael, who is buried in an ancient sarcophagus under the alter of Madonna del Sasso. ⊠ *Piazza della Rotonda, Pantheon* ☎ *06/68300230* ⊗ *Mon.–Sat. 9–7:30, Sun. 9–5:30.*

★ ⟳ ㉓ **Piazza Navona.** This famed 17th-century piazza, built over the site and following the form of the 1st-century Stadium of Domitian, is one of Rome's showpiece attractions. It still has the carefree air of the days when it was the scene of Roman circus games, medieval jousts, and 17th-century carnivals. Today it often attracts fashion photographers and Romans out for their evening *passeggiata* (promenade). The Christmas fair held from early December through January 6 fills the piazza with games, nativity scenes (some well crafted, many not so), and multiple versions of the Befana, the ugly but good witch who brings candy and toys to Italian children on Epiphany. (Her name is a corruption of the Italian word *Epifania.*) Bernini's splashing **Fontana dei Quattro Fiumi** (Fountain of the Four Rivers), with an enormous rock squared off by statues representing the four corners of the world, makes a fitting centerpiece. Behind the fountain is the church of **Sant'Agnese in Agone,** an outstanding example of baroque architecture built by the Pamphili Pope Innocent X and still owned by his descendants, the Doria Pamphili. The facade—a wonderfully rich mélange of bell towers, concave spaces, and dovetailed stone and marble—is by Carlo Rainaldi (1611–91) and Francesco Borromini (1599–1667), a contemporary and sometime rival of Bernini. One story has it that the Bernini statue nearest the church, which represents the River Plate, has its hand up before its eye because it can't bear the sight of the Borromini facade. Though often repeated, the story is a fiction: the facade was built after the fountain.

㉔ **San Luigi dei Francesi.** The clergy of San Luigi considered Caravaggio's roistering and unruly lifestyle scandalous enough, but his realistic treatment of sacred subjects—seen in three paintings in the last chapel—was too much for them. They rejected outright his first version of the altarpiece, and they weren't especially happy with the other two works. Thanks to the intercession of Caravaggio's patron, the influential Cardinal Francesco del Monte, they were persuaded to keep them—a lucky thing, since they are now thought to be among the artist's finest paintings. Have a few one-euro coins handy for the light machine. ⊠ *Piazza San Luigi dei Francesi, near Piazza Navona* ☎ *06/688271* ⊗ *Fri.–Wed. 8–12:30 and 3:30–7:30.*

㉑ **Sant'Agostino in Campo Marzio.** Caravaggio's celebrated *Madonna of the Pilgrims*—which scandalized all Rome because it pictured pilgrims with dirt on the soles of their feet—can be found in this small church over the first altar on the left. Also of interest are Raphael's *Prophet,* on the first pilaster on the left, and the dozens of heart-shape ex-votos to Madonna del Parto (Mary of Childbirth) at the entrance. ⊠ *Piazza di*

Sant'Agostino, near Piazza Navona ☎ *06/68801962* ⊗ *Mon.–Sat. 7–1 and 4:30–7:30, Sun. 7–1 and 3:30–7:30.*

㉘ Sant'Andrea della Valle. This huge 17th-century church looms mightily over a busy intersection. Aficionados of Puccini, who set the first act of his *Tosca* here, have been known to hire a horse-drawn carriage at night for an evocative journey that traces the course of the opera (from Sant'Andrea up Via Giulia to Palazzo Farnese—Scarpia's headquarters—to the locale of the opera's climax, Castel Sant'Angelo). Inside, above the apse are striking frescoes depicting scenes from St. Andrew's life by the Bolognese painter Domenichino (1581–1641). ⊠ *Corso Vittorio Emanuele II, near Campo de' Fiori* ☎ *06/6861339* ⊗ *Daily 7–noon and 4:30–7:30.*

㉙ Sant'Ivo alla Sapienza. Borromini's eccentric church has what must surely be Rome's most unusual dome—topped by a golden spiral said to have been inspired by a bee's stinger. ⊠ *Corso Rinascimento 40, near Piazza Navona* ⊗ *Sun. 10–noon.*

⑱ Santa Maria sopra Minerva. In practically the only Gothic-style church in Rome, the attractions are Michelangelo's *Risen Christ* and the tomb of the gentle 15th-century artist Fra Angelico. Have some coins handy to light up the **Carafa Chapel** in the right transept, where exquisite 15th-century frescoes by Filippino Lippi (circa 1457–1504) are well worth the small investment. (Lippi's most famous student was Botticelli.) In front of the church, Bernini's charming elephant bearing an Egyptian obelisk has an inscription on the base stating that it takes a strong mind to sustain solid wisdom. ⊠ *Piazza della Minerva, Pantheon* ☎ *06/6793926* ⊗ *Daily 7–noon and 4–7.*

Via Giulia. Named after Pope Julius II and serving for more than four centuries as the "salon of Rome," this street is still the address of choice for Roman aristocrats. Built with funds garnered by taxing prostitutes, the street is lined with elegant palaces, including the Palazzo Falconieri, and old churches (one, San Eligio, reputedly designed by Raphael himself). The area around Via Giulia is a wonderful place to wander in to get the feeling of daily life as carried on in a centuries-old setting—an experience enhanced by the dozens of antiques shops in the neighborhood.

Piazza Venezia to the Spanish Steps: Vistas & Views

Though it has a bustling commercial air, this part of the city also holds great visual allure, from the gaudy marble confection that is the monument to Vittorio Emanuele II to the theatrical Piazza di Sant'Ignazio. Among the things to look for are stately palaces, baroque ballrooms, and the greatest example of portraiture in Rome, Velázquez's incomparable *Innocent X* at the Galleria Doria Pamphilj. Those with a taste for the sumptuous theatricality of Roman ecclesiastical architecture—illusionistic ceiling painting in particular—will find this a rewarding stop. Highlights are the Trevi Fountain and the Spanish Steps, 18th-century Rome's most famous example of city planning.

a good
walk

Start at the flamboyant **Monumento a Vittorio Emanuele II** ㉚ ▶ in Piazza Venezia, a mass of marble studded with statuary that has the city's best view from its top. As you look up Via del Corso, to your left is **Palazzo Venezia** ㉛, an art-filled Renaissance palace from whose balcony Mussolini once addressed the crowds. On Saturday you can visit the picture gallery, known as the Galleria Colonna, in the **Palazzo Colonna** ㉜, east of Piazza Venezia. From Piazza Venezia head north on Via del Corso, one of the city's busiest shopping streets, to the **Palazzo Doria Pamphilj** ㉝, home to an important painting gallery. A quick detour west will bring you to the sumptuous 17th-century church of **Sant'Ignazio** ㉞. As you continue north on Via del Corso you will reach Piazza Colonna and the ancient **Colonna di Marco Aurelio** ㉟. Continue north on Via del Corso and take a right onto chic Via Condotti, which gives you a head-on view of the **Spanish Steps** ㊱ and Piazza di Spagna; to the right of the steps, at No. 26, is the **Keats-Shelley Memorial House** ㊲, where the English Romantic poet John Keats died. A great view across Rome's skyline awaits at the top of the Spanish Steps. From the narrow (southern) end of Piazza di Spagna, take Via Propaganda to Sant'Andrea delle Fratte, turn left onto Via del Nazareno, and then cross busy Via del Tritone to Via della Stamperia. This street leads to the **Fontana di Trevi** ㊳, one of Rome's most famous landmarks.

TIMING   The walk takes approximately three hours.

What to See

㉟ **Colonna di Marco Aurelio.** This ancient column—like the one Trajan erected—is an extraordinary stone history book. Its detailed reliefs spiraling up to the top illustrate the victorious campaigns of emperor Marcus Aurelius (AD 121–80) against the barbarians. ⊠ *Piazza Colonna, near Piazza di Spagna.*

★ ㊳ **Fontana di Trevi** (Trevi Fountain). Tucked away on a small piazza off Via del Tritone, this huge fountain designed by Nicola Salvi (1697–1751) is a spectacular fantasy of mythical sea creatures amid cascades of splashing water. It was featured in the 1954 film *Three Coins in the Fountain* and, of course, was the scene of Anita Ekberg's aquatic frolic in Fellini's *La Dolce Vita*. The fountain is the world's most spectacular wishing well: legend has it that you can ensure your return to Rome by tossing a coin into the fountain. By day it's one of the busiest sites in town; at night the spotlighted piazza takes on the festive air of a crowded outdoor party. ⊠ *Piazza di Trevi.*

off the
beaten
path

TIME ELEVATOR ROMA – If you're in need of a basic primer on Roman history, or you're traveling with kids and want to rouse their enthusiasm for the monuments and galleries they'll be traipsing though, try this fun, educational 45-minute joyride back in time. After participating in a group quiz show on Roman history, you sit in a small theater with moving chairs (equipped with seat belts) and watch a movie on the history of Rome. The chairs jostle and slide to create the effect that you are within the film. It's not cheap, but for the Disney generation it may succeed in arousing enthusiasm about the past. Groups are let in every half hour. ⊠ *Via dei S.S. Apostoli*

20, near Piazza di Trevi ☎ *06/6990053* ⊕ *www.time-elevator.it*
🎟 *€11* ⊙ *Daily 10–10.*

㊲ Keats-Shelley Memorial House. English Romantic poet John Keats (1795–1821) once lived in what is now a museum dedicated to him and his great contemporary and friend Percy Bysshe Shelley (1792–1822). You can visit his tiny rooms, preserved as they were when he died here. ✉ *Piazza di Spagna 26, next to the Spanish Steps* ☎ *06/6784235* ⊕ *www.keats-shelley-house.org* 🎟 *€2.60* ⊙ *Weekdays 9–1 and 3–6, Sat. 11–2 and 3–6.*

> **off the beaten path**
>
> **CIMITERO ACATTOLICO AND PIRAMIDE DI CAIO CESTIO** – Behind the Piramide, a stone pyramid built in 12 BC at the order of the Roman *praetor* (senior magistrate) who was buried here, is a cemetery reminiscent of a country churchyard. It was intended for non-Catholics, and here you'll find Keats's tomb and the place where Shelley's heart was buried, as well as the tombs of Italian communist Antonio Gramsci and beat poet Gregory Corso. It's about a 20-minute walk south from the Arch of Constantine along Via San Gregorio and Viale Aventino. On the site of the pyramid is a cat colony run by the famous Roman *gattare* (cat ladies). They look after and try to find homes for some 300 of Rome's thousands of stray cats. On Saturday afternoon they give free tours of the graveyard, the pyramid, and their cat shelter. ✉ *Via Caio Cestio 6, Piramide* ☎ *06/5741900* ⊕ *www. protestantcemetery.it* 🎟 *Donation of €1 appreciated* ⊙ *Tues.–Sat. 9–4:30. Sun. 9–2; ring bell for cemetery custodian.*

▶ **㉚ Monumento a Vittorio Emanuele II.** The huge bronze sculpture group atop this vast marble monument is visible from many parts of the city, making this modern Rome's most flamboyant landmark. It was erected in the late 19th century to honor Italy's first king, Vittorio Emanuele II (1820–78), and the unification of Italy. Sometimes said to resemble a wedding cake or a typewriter in the Victorian style, it also houses the **Tomb of the Unknown Soldier** with its eternal flame. A side entrance to the monument will take you to the **Museo del Risorgimento**, which charts Italy's struggle for nationhood. The red shirt and boots of revolutionary hero Giuseppe Garibaldi (1807–82) are among the mementos. The views from the top of the "Vittoriano" are unforgettable. Opposite the monument, note the enclosed wooden veranda fronting the palace on the corner of Via del Plebiscito and Via Corso. For the many years that she lived in Rome, Napoléon's mother had a fine view from here of the local goings-on. ✉ *Entrance at Piazza Ara Coeli, next to Piazza Venezia* ☎ *06/6991718* ⊕ *www.ambienterm.arti.beniculturali. it/vittoriano/index.html* 🎟 *Museum €5* ⊙ *Daily 9:30–5:30.*

㉜ Palazzo Colonna. This fabulous private palace is open to the public once a week. The entrance to the picture gallery, the **Galleria Colonna,** is a secondary one, behind a plain, inconspicuous door. The old masters are lackluster, but the gallery should be on your must-see list because the **Sala Grande** is truly the grandest 17th-century room in Rome. More than 300 feet long, with bedazzling chandeliers, colored marble, and enormous paintings, it's best known today as the site where Audrey Hepburn met the press in *Roman Holiday.* ⊠ *Via della Pilotta 17, near Piazza di Trevi* ☎ *06/6784350* ⊕ *www.galleriacolonna.it* ⊠ *€7* ☾ *Sept.–July, Sat. 9–1; free guided tour in English with reservation.*

③③ Palazzo Doria Pamphilj. The 18th-century facade of this palazzo on Via del Corso is only a small part of a bona fide patrician palace, still home to a princely family that rents out many of its 1,000 rooms. Visit the remarkably well preserved **Galleria Doria Pamphilj,** a picture gallery that gives you a sense of the sumptuous surroundings of a Roman noble family and how art was once put on display: numbered paintings (the museum catalog, available from the bookshop, comes in handy) are packed onto every available wall space. Pride of place is given to the famous (and pitiless) portrait of the 17th-century Pamphilj pope Innocent X by Diego Velázquez (1599–1660), but don't overlook Caravaggio's poignant *Rest on the Flight into Egypt.* The audio guide is by the current Doria Pamphilj prince himself and gives a fascinating personal history of the palace. ⊠ *Piazza del Collegio Romano 2, near Piazza Venezia* ☎ *06/ 6797323* ⊕ *www.doriapamphilj.it* ⊠ *Galleria Doria Pamphilj €7.30, includes audio guide* ☾ *Fri.–Wed. 10–5.*

③① Palazzo Venezia. A blend of medieval solidity and genuine Renaissance grace, this building houses temporary exhibits and a haphazard collection of mostly early Renaissance weapons, ivories, and paintings in its grand salons, some of which Mussolini used as his offices. Notice the balcony over the main portal, from which Il Duce addressed huge crowds in Piazza Venezia below. The palace hosts major touring art exhibits, so check to see what's currently showing. ⊠ *Piazza San Marco 49, near Piazza Venezia* ☎ *06/69994318* ⊠ *€4* ☾ *Tues.–Sun. 9–7.*

③④ Sant'Ignazio. The false interior dome in this sumptuous 17th-century church is a trompe-l'oeil oddity among the lavishly frescoed domes of the Eternal City. To get the full effect of the illusionistic ceiling painted by Andrea del Pozzo (1642–1709), stand on the small disk set into the floor of the nave to view his *Glory of St. Ignatius Loyola.* The church contains some of Rome's most splendorous, jewel-encrusted altars. If you're lucky, you might be able to catch an evening concert performed here. The church is the focus of Filippo Raguzzini's 18th-century rococo piazza, where the buildings are arranged almost as in a stage set, a reminder that theatricality was a key element of almost all the best baroque and rococo art. ⊠ *Piazza Sant'Ignazio, Pantheon* ☎ *06/ 6794406* ☾ *Daily 7:30–12:30 and 4–7:30.*

★ **③⑥ Spanish Steps.** Both the steps and the Piazza di Spagna get their names from the Spanish Embassy to the Vatican on the piazza, opposite the American Express office, though the staircase was built with French funds in 1723. In an allusion to the church of Trinità dei Monti at the top of the hill, the staircase is divided by three landings (beautifully banked with azaleas from mid-April to mid-May). This area has always welcomed tourists: 18th-century dukes and duchesses on their Grand Tour, 19th-century artists and writers in search of inspiration—among them Stendhal, Balzac, Thackeray, and Byron—and today's enthusiastic hordes. The **Fontana della Barcaccia** (Fountain of the Old Boat) at the base of the steps is by Pietro Bernini, father of the famous Gian Lorenzo. ⊠ *Piazza di Spagna.*

Historic Churches: Heavenly Monuments of Faith

Rome's history can be told through its churches. In both their historical import and artistic mastery, the ubiquitous and incredibly varied buildings bear witness to the centuries they have withstood; they have something for every visitor, regardless of faith. The churches that highlight this walk date to the early centuries of Christianity.

a good walk

Begin at **Santa Maria Maggiore** ㊴ �застdeep off Via Cavour. From here go south on Via Merulana, which leads straight to **San Giovanni in Laterano** ㊵. The adjoining Palazzo Laterano houses the Museo Storico Lateranense; across the street, a small building contains the **Scala Santa** ㊶, or Sacred Stairs, supposedly from Pilate's Jerusalem palace. Circle Palazzo Laterano to see the 4th-century octagonal Battistero di San Giovanni, forerunner of many such buildings throughout Italy. Follow Via San Giovanni in Laterano to **San Clemente** ㊷, and explore the ancient church buried underground.

TIMING The walk alone takes approximately 90 minutes, plus 15–20 minutes in each of the churches. Allow at least an hour to explore San Clemente. A visit to the Museo Storico Lateranense will take you about 30 minutes.

What to See

★ ㊷ **San Clemente.** This church is one of the most extraordinary archaeological sites in Rome. San Clemente is a 12th-century church built on top of a 4th-century church, which in turn was built over a 2nd-century pagan temple to the god Mithras. Little of the temple remains, but the 4th-century church is largely intact, perhaps because it wasn't unearthed until the 19th century. (It was discovered by Irish Dominican monks; members of the order still live in the adjacent monastery.) The upper church, which you enter from street level, holds a beautiful early-12th-century mosaic showing a cross on a gold background, surrounded by swirling green acanthus leaves teeming with little scenes of everyday life. The marble choir screens, salvaged from the 4th-century church, are decorated with early Christian symbols: doves, vines, and fish. In the left aisle is the Castiglioni chapel, holding frescos painted around 1400 by the Florentine artist Masolino da Panicale (1383–1440), a key figure in the introduction of realism and one-point perspective into Renaissance painting. Note the large Crucifixion and scenes from the lives of Sts. Catherine, Ambrose, and Christopher, plus an Annunciation (over the entrance). Before you leave the upper church, take a look at the pretty cloister— evening concerts are held here in summer.

From the right aisle, stairs lead down to the remains of the 4th-century church, which was active until 1084, when it was damaged beyond repair during a siege of the neighborhood by the Norman prince Robert Guiscard. The vestibule is decorated with marble fragments found during the excavations (which are still under way), and in the nave are colorful 11th-century frescoes depicting stories from the life of St. Clement.

Another level down is the Mythraeum, a shrine dedicated to the god Mithras, whose cult spread from Persia and gained a hold in Rome during the 2nd and 3rd centuries. ⊠ *Via San Giovanni in Laterano 108, near Colosseo* ☎ *06/70451018* ✉ *€3* ⊘ *Mon.–Sat. 9–noon and 3–6, Sun. 10–12:30 and 3–6.*

40 **San Giovanni in Laterano.** You may be surprised to discover that the cathedral of Rome is not St. Peter's but this church. (St. Peter's is in Vatican City, technically not a part of Rome.) Dominating the piazza whose name it shares, this immense building is where the pope officiates in his capacity as bishop of Rome. The towering facade and Borromini's cool baroque interior emphasize the majesty of its proportions. The **cloister** is one of the city's finest, with beautifully carved columns surrounding a peaceful garden.

The adjoining **Palazzo Laterano** (Lateran Palace) was the official papal residence until the 13th century, and is still technically part of the Vatican. It houses the offices of the Rome Diocese and the rather bland **Museo Storico Laterano** (Lateran Historical Museum). Behind the palace are the 4th-century octagonal **Battistero di San Giovanni** (St. John's Baptistery), forerunner of many similar buildings throughout Italy, and Rome's oldest and tallest obelisk, brought from Thebes and dating from the 15th century BC. ⊠ *Piazza San Giovanni in Laterano, near Colosseo* ☎ *06/69886464* ✉ *Cloister €2.50, museum €3.50* ⊘ *Church Apr.–Sept., daily 7–7; Oct.–Mar., daily 7–6. Cloister 9–½ hr before church closing. Museum Sat. guided tours at 9:15, 10:30, and noon. 1st Sun. of each month 8:45–1. Baptistery daily 9–1 and 5–1 hr before sunset.*

off the beaten path

SAN PIETRO IN VINCOLI – The church takes its name from the *vincoli* (chains) that once held St. Peter (they're on display in the case under the altar), but throngs of tourists come to see Michelangelo's *Moses,* a powerful statue almost as famed as his frescoes in the Sistine Chapel. The *Moses* was destined for the tomb of Julius II, designed to be the largest in St. Peter's Basilica. But Julius's successors had Michelangelo work on other projects, and the tomb was never finished. ⊠ *Piazza San Pietro in Vincoli, near Colosseo* ☎ *06/4882865* ⊘ *Daily 7–12:30 and 3:30–6.*

SANTI QUATTRO CORONATI – The 12th-century church of the Four Crowned Martyrs, part of a fortified abbey that provided refuge to early popes and emperors, is in an unusual corner of Rome, a quiet island that has resisted the tide of time and traffic flowing beneath its ramparts. Few places in Rome are so reminiscent of the Middle Ages. Don't miss the cloister with its well-tended gardens and 12th-century fountain. The entrance is the door in the left aisle; ring the bell if it's not open. You can also ring at the adjacent convent for the key to the Oratorio di San Silvestro (Oratory of St. Sylvester), with 13th-century frescoes. ⊠ *Largo Santi Quattro Coronati, near Colosseo* ☎ *06/70475427* ⊘ *Easter–Christmas, daily 9:30–12:30 and 3:30–6; Christmas–Easter, daily 9:30–12:30.*

▶ ❸❾ **Santa Maria Maggiore.** One of Rome's four great pilgrimage churches was built on the spot where a 3rd-century pope witnessed a miraculous midsummer snowfall (which is reenacted every August 15). The gleaming mosaics on the arch in front of the main altar date from the 5th century. The apse mosaic dates from the 13th century, and the opulently carved wood ceiling is believed to have been gilded with the first gold brought from the New World. To view the elaborate 14th-century facade mosaics, inquire at the souvenir shop. ✉ *Piazza Santa Maria Maggiore, off Via Cavour, near Termini* ☎ *06/4465836* ☉ *Daily 7 AM–8 PM.*

❹❶ **Scala Santa** (Sacred Stairs). A small building opposite the Lateran Palace houses what is claimed to be the staircase from Pilate's palace in Jerusalem. The faithful climb it on their knees. ✉ *Piazza San Giovanni in Laterano, near Colosseo* ☉ *Daily 6:15–noon and 3:30–6:30.*

Il Quirinale to Piazza della Repubblica: Palaces & Fountains

On this walk you'll see ancient Roman sculptures and early Christian churches, but the highlights are from the 16th and 17th centuries, when Rome was conquered by the baroque—and by Bernini.

a good
walk

Begin on **Il Quirinale** ❹❸ ▶, the highest of Rome's seven hills. Here you'll find the Palazzo Quirinale, official residence of the president of Italy and once home of the popes. See what's on at Le Scuderie Papale al Quirinale (the Quirinale Stables), which houses topflight touring art exhibits. Along Via del Quirinale (which becomes Via XX Settembre) is the church of **Sant'Andrea Sant'Andrea al Quirinale** ❹❹, considered by many to be Bernini's finest work, and, at the Quattro Fontane (Four Fountains) crossroads, the church of **San Carlino alle Quattro Fontane** ❹❺, designed by Bernini's rival Borromini. Take a left on Via delle Quattro Fontane to reach the imposing **Palazzo Barberini** ❹❻, where the Galleria Nazionale d'Arte Antica houses masterpieces by Raphael and Caravaggio. Down the hill are the Piazza Barberini and the **Fontana del Tritone** ❹❼ by Bernini. Cross the piazza and begin your gradual climb up Via Vittorio Veneto, which bends past **Santa Maria della Concezione** ❹❽ and the U.S. Embassy, and turn off onto Via Bissolati. On the corner of Piazza San Bernardo is the church of **Santa Maria della Vittoria** ❹❾, known for Bernini's baroque decoration. It's not far down Via Orlando to **Piazza della Repubblica** ❺⓿. On one side of the square is an ancient Roman brick facade that marks the church of Santa Maria degli Angeli. Beyond, on the near corner of Piazza del Cinquecento, the vast square in front of Stazione Termini, is the last stop. **Palazzo Massimo alle Terme** ❺❶ houses part of the Museo Nazionale Romano's collections, highlighting examples of the fine mosaics and masterful paintings that decorated ancient Rome's villas and palaces.

TIMING You could devote a full afternoon or a leisurely day to this tour. The walk itself takes approximately 90 minutes, plus 10 to 15 minutes for each church visited, and 1½ hours each for visits to the Galleria Nazionale in Palazzo Barberini and Palazzo Massimo alle Terme.

What to See

❹❼ **Fontana del Tritone** (Triton Fountain). The centerpiece of Piazza Barberini is Bernini's graceful fountain designed in 1637 for the sculptor's patron,

Pope Urban VIII, whose Barberini coat of arms, featuring bees, is at the base of the large shell. Close by is the **Fontana delle Api** (Fountain of the Bees), the last fountain designed by Bernini. ⊠ *Piazza Barberini, near Via Veneto.*

▶ ❹ **Il Quirinale.** The highest of ancient Rome's seven hills, this is where ancient Romans, and later popes, built their residences in order to escape the deadly miasmas and malaria of the low-lying area around the Forum. The fountain in the square has ancient statues of Castor and Pollux reining in their unruly steeds and a basin salvaged from the Roman Forum. The **Palazzo del Quirinale** (⊠ €5 ☉ Sept.–July, Sun. 8:30–12:30) passed from the popes to Italy's kings in the 19th century; it's now the official residence of the nation's president. Every day at 4 PM the ceremony of the changing of the guard at the portal includes a miniparade complete with band.

Directly opposite the main entrance of the Palazzo del Quirinale sits **Le Scuderie Papale al Quirinale** (the Quirinal Stables), which once housed more than 120 horses for the exclusive use of the pope and his guests. The low-lying building was designed by Alessandro Specchi (1668–1729) in 1722 and was among the major achievements of baroque Rome. The stables were remodeled in the late 1990s by eminent architect Gae Aulenti and now serve as a venue for major touring art exhibits. ⊠ *Piazza del Quirinale, near Piazza di Trevi* ☎ *06/39967500 or 06/696271* ⊕ *www.scuderiequirinale.it* ⊠ *Admission varies depending on exhibit* ☉ *Sun.–Thurs. 10–8, Fri. and Sat. 10 AM–11 PM.*

❹ **Palazzo Barberini.** Along with architect Carlo Maderno (1556–1629), Borromini helped make the splendid 17th-century Palazzo Barberini a residence worthy of Rome's leading art patron, Pope Urban VIII, who began the palace for his family in 1625. Inside, the **Galleria Nazionale d'Arte Antica** offers some fine works by Raphael and Caravaggio. Rome's biggest ballroom is here; its ceiling, painted by Pietro da Cortona, depicts Immortality bestowing a crown upon Divine Providence escorted by a "bomber squadron"—to quote Sir Michael Levey—of mutant bees. (Bees featured prominently in the heraldic device of the Barberini.) ⊠ *Via Barberini 18, near Via Veneto* ☎ *06/328101* ⊕ *www. galleriaborghese.it* ⊠ *€6* ☉ *Tues.–Sun. 9–7.*

❺ **Palazzo Massimo alle Terme.** This 19th-century palace in neo-baroque style holds part of the collections of antiquities belonging to the Museo Nazionale Romano (also exhibited in the Palazzo Altemps). Here you can see extraordinary examples of the fine mosaics and masterful paintings that decorated ancient Rome's palaces and villas. Don't miss the fresco—depicting a lush garden in bloom—that came from the villa that Livia, wife of Emperor Augustus, owned outside Rome. ⊠ *Largo Villa Peretti 2, near Termini* ☎ *06/48903501* ⊠ *€6* ☉ *Tues.–Sun. 9–7.*

❺ **Piazza della Repubblica.** This piazza has a typical 19th-century layout, but the curving porticoes echo the immense **Terme di Diocleziano** (Baths of Diocletian; ☎ *06/39967700* ⊠ *€5* ☉ *Tues.–Sun. 9–7:45*). Built in the 4th century AD, they were the largest and most impressive of the baths of ancient Rome, with vast halls, pools, and gardens that could accommodate 3,000 people at a time. Also part of the great baths was an **Aula Ottagonale** (Octagonal Hall; ☎ 06/4870890 ☑ Free ☉ Tues.–Sat. 9–2, Sun. 9–1), which now holds a sampling of the ancient sculptures found there, including two beautiful bronzes. ☒ *Via Romita 8, near Termini.*

The racy **Fontana delle Naiadi** (Fountain of the Naiads), an 1870 addition to the piazza, depicts voluptuous bronze ladies wrestling happily with marine monsters. The curving ancient Roman brick facade on one side of the piazza marks the church of **Santa Maria degli Angeli,** adapted by Michelangelo from the vast central chamber of the colossal baths. Look for the sundial carved on the floor. ☒ *Via Romita 8, near Termini* ☎ *06/4870690* ☑ *Free* ☉ *Tues.–Sat. 9–2, Sun. 9–1.*

45 **San Carlino alle Quattro Fontane.** Borromini's church at the Four Fountains crossroads is an architectural gem. In a space no larger than the base of one of the piers of St. Peter's, Borromini attained geometric perfection. Characteristically, he chose a subdued white stucco for the interior decoration, so as not to distract from the form. Don't miss the cloister, which you reach through the door to the right of the altar. The exterior of the church is Borromini at his bizarre best, all curves and rippling movement. Outside, four charming fountains frame views in four directions. ☒ *Via del Quirinale 23, near Piazza di Trevi* ☎ *06/4883261* ☉ *Daily 9–1 and 4–6.*

48 **Santa Maria della Concezione.** In the crypt under the main Capuchin church, the bones of some 4,000 dead Capuchin monks are arranged in odd decorative designs around the shriveled and decayed skeletons of their kinsmen, a macabre reminder of the impermanence of earthly life. Signs declare WHAT YOU ARE, WE ONCE WERE. WHAT WE ARE, YOU SOMEDAY WILL BE. Although not for the easily spooked, the crypt is touching and oddly beautiful. ☒ *Via Veneto 27* ☎ *06/4871185* ☑ *Donation expected* ☉ *Fri.–Wed. 9–noon and 3–6.*

49 **Santa Maria della Vittoria.** The most famous feature here is Bernini's baroque decoration of the **Cappella Cornaro,** an exceptional fusion of architecture, painting, and sculpture in which the *Ecstasy of St. Teresa* is the focal point. Bernini's audacious conceit was to model the chapel after a theater: members of the Cornaro family—sculpted in white marble—watch from theater boxes as, center stage, St. Teresa, in the throes of mystical rapture, is pierced by a gilded arrow held by an angel. To quote one 18th-century observer, President de Brosses: "If this is divine love, I know it well." ☒ *Via XX Settembre 17, Termini* ☎ *06/42740571* ☉ *Daily 8:30–noon and 4:30–6.*

44 **Sant'Andrea al Quirinale.** This small but imposing baroque church was designed and decorated by Bernini, who considered it one of his finest works. ☒ *Via del Quirinale, Piazza di Trevi* ☎ *06/48903187* ☉ *Mon. and Wed.–Sat. 8–noon and 4–6, Sun. 4–7.*

off the
beaten
path

GALLERIA COMUNALE DI ARTE MODERNA E CONTEMPORANEA –
Located in the former Peroni beer factory, the City Gallery of
Modern and Contemporary Art is an example of some of the most
interesting industrial design of the early 20th century. The factory,

devised by Gustavo Giovannoni and located in a former warehouse district of Rome, now houses touring avant-garde art exhibits that provide a refreshing change from Rome's baroque. ⊠ *Via Reggio Emilia 54, near Porta Pia* ☎ *06/4742848* ⊕ *www.comune.roma.it/ galleriacomunale* ☑ *€ 3* ⊙ *Tues.–Sat. 9–7, Sun. 9–1:30.*

Villa Borghese to the Ara Pacis: Amid Sylvan Glades

Touring Rome's artistic masterpieces while staying clear of its hustle and bustle can be, quite literally, a walk in the park. Some of the city's finest sights are tucked away in or next to green lawns and pedestrian piazzas, offering a breath of fresh air for weary sightseers. Villa Borghese, one of Rome's largest parks, can alleviate gallery gout by offering an oasis in which to cool off under the ilex trees. If you feel like a picnic, have an *alimentare* (food shop) make you some *panini* (sandwiches) before you go, as you'll find only overpriced food carts within the park.

a good walk

Start at **Porta Pinciana** ㊿ ▶, one of the entrances to Villa Borghese. Follow Viale del Museo Borghese to the **Museo e Galleria Borghese** ㊾ and its fabulous art collection in an extraordinary setting. (Make sure to reserve a ticket for your visit in advance.) Head west inside the park past the zoo and exit the park gates at Viale delle Belle Arti. A five-minute walk downhill will take you to the **Museo Nazionale Etrusco di Villa Giulia** ㊿, perhaps the best collection in the world of Etruscan artifacts. From Villa Giulia take the wide flight of steps at Piazzale M. Cervantes back into Villa Borghese. Head to the southwest corner of the park to enjoy the view of Rome from the **Pincio** ㊿ belvedere before descending the ramps to pedestrian-only **Piazza del Popolo** ㊿. At the north end of the piazza, next to the 400-year-old city gate, the Porta del Popolo, is the church of **Santa Maria del Popolo** ㊿, with one of the richest art collections of any church in the city. If you're not out of steam, stroll south along Via di Ripetta to glance at Mausoleo di Augusto, built by Caesar Augustus; next to it is the **Ara Pacis Augustae** ㊿, built in 13 BC and currently closed for restoration.

TIMING The walk takes approximately two hours; allow an additional 1½ hours for the Galleria Borghese, 1½ hours for Villa Giulia, and 45 minutes for the stroll past the Mausoleo di Augusto and the Ara Pacis.

Sights to See

㊿ **Ara Pacis Augustae** (Altar of Augustan Peace). This altar on the northwest corner of Piazza Augusto Imperatore was erected in 13 BC to celebrate the era of peace ushered in by Augustus's military victories. Next to it is the imposing bulk of the marble-clad **Mausoleo di Augusto** (Mausoleum of Augustus), built by the emperor for himself and his family. The Ara Pacis is closed while a museum to house it is being built. ⊠ *Via Ripetta, near Piazza di Spagna* ⊙ *Closed for restoration.*

☾ **Explora: Il Museo dei Bambini di Roma** (Explore: the Museum for the Children of Rome). One of the very few sites in the city geared specifically to kids, Explora provides two floors of open space filled with hands-on activities and games; kids ranging from toddlers to 12-year-olds are let in for two-hour shifts. (There's also a child-friendly restaurant.) Just steps from the car-free Piazza del Popolo and a short hike downhill from the playground in Villa Borghese, the museum is well suited to a child-oriented day in the neighborhood. ⊠ *Via Flaminia 82, near Villa Borghese* ☎ *06/3613776* ⊕ *www.mdbr.it* ⊠ *€7 for children 3 and up, €6 for adults* ☉ *Tues.-Fri admission at 9:30, 11:30, 3, and 5; weekends admission at 10, noon, 3, and 5; reservations essential on weekends.*

㊾ Museo e Galleria Borghese (Borghese Museum and Gallery). The palace, completed in 1613 for Cardinal Scipione Borghese (1576–1633) as a place to flaunt his fabulous antiquities collection and hold elegant fetes, is today a monument to 18th-century Roman interior decoration at its most luxurious, dripping with porphyry and alabaster. Throughout the grand salons are ancient Roman mosaic pavements and statues of various deities, including one officially known as *Venus Victrix*. There has never been any doubt, however, as to the statue's real subject: Pauline Bonaparte, Napoléon's sister, who married Prince Camillo Borghese in one of the storied matches of the 19th century. Sculpted by Canova (1757–1822), the princess reclines on a chaise longue, bare-bosomed, her hips swathed in classical drapery, the very model of haughty detachment and sly come-hither. Pauline is known to have been shocked that her husband took pleasure in showing off the work to his guests. This coyness seems curious given the reply she is supposed to have made to a lady who asked her how she could have posed for the work: "Oh, but the studio was heated." Other rooms hold important sculptures by Bernini, including *David* and *Apollo and Daphne*. The renowned picture collection has splendid works by Titian, Caravaggio, and Raphael, among others. Be sure to reserve admission at least a day ahead of time. ⊠ *Piazza Scipione Borghese 5, off Via Pinciana, Villa Borghese* ☎ *06/8548577 information, 06/32810 reservations* ⊕ *www.galleriaborghese.it* ⊠ *€8.50, plus €2 reservation fee; audio guide or English guided tour €5* ☉ *Tues.–Sun. 9–7; reservations required, entrance every 2 hrs.*

★ ㊿ Museo Nazionale Etrusco di Villa Giulia (National Etruscan Museum at Villa Giulia). This Renaissance papal palace built by Julius III between 1550 and 1555 sits in the Villa Borghese Gardens and holds a well-laid-out collection of art and artifacts of the Etruscans, who predated the Romans. Known for their sophisticated art and design, the Etruscans left a legacy of sarcophagi, bronze sculptures, terra-cotta vases, and stunning jewelry. (Unlike the Greeks, Etruscan women sat at the banquet tables with men and enjoyed displaying their wealth on their bodies.) Acclaimed pieces of statuary in the gallery include *Dea con Bambino* (*Goddess with Infant*) and *Sarcophagus degli Sposi* (*Sarcophagus of the Married Couple*). In the villa's courtyard visit the atmospheric underground Ninfeo, the remains of the Virgin's Aqueduct from the Augustan period. ⊠ *Piazzale Villa Giulia 9, near Villa Borghese* ☎ *06/3201951* ⊠ *€4* ☉ *Tues.–Sun. 9–7:30.*

need a break? **Caffè delle Arti** (⊠ Viale delle Belle Arti 131, near Villa Borghese ☎ 06/32651236), an exquisite, light-filled space with towering ceilings and bronze statues, is located inside the Galleria Nazionale d'Arte Moderna, across the street from Villa Giulia. The menu includes tea with a variety of homemade pastries as well as Roman and Neapolitan dishes. In warm weather sit out on the huge terrace and take in the splendor of the surrounding Villa Borghese.

56 **Piazza del Popolo.** Designed by neoclassical architect Giuseppe Valadier (1762–1839) in the early 1800s, this piazza is one of the largest in Rome, and it has a 3,000-year-old obelisk in the middle. Always a favorite spot for café-sitting and people-watching, the piazza is closed to motorized traffic, creating a pedestrian oasis. The bookend baroque churches **Santa Maria dei Miracoli** and **Santa Maria in Montesanto** are not, first appearances to the contrary, twins. On the plaza's eastern side, stairs lead uphill to the Pincio. To the north, at the end of the square is the 400-year-old **Porta del Popolo,** Rome's northern city gate. It was designed by Bernini to welcome the Catholic convert Queen Christina of Sweden to Rome in 1605.

55 **Pincio.** At the southwestern corner of Villa Borghese, the Pincio belvedere and gardens were laid out by architect Giuseppe Valadier as part of his overall plan for Piazza del Popolo. Nineteenth-century counts and countesses liked to take their evening passeggiata here in the hope of meeting Pius IX (1792–1878), the last pope to go about Rome on foot. Nowadays you're more likely to see runners and in-line skaters, as well as throngs of Romans out for a stroll. It's a good place to take in the summer concerts and New Year's fireworks staged in Piazza del Popolo below.

52 **Porta Pinciana.** One of the historic city gates in the Aurelian Walls surrounding Rome, Porta Pinciana was built in the 6th century AD, about three centuries after the walls were built to keep out the barbarians. These days it's one of the entrances to Villa Borghese.

57 **Santa Maria del Popolo.** This church next to the Porta del Popolo goes almost unnoticed, but it has one of the richest art collections of any church in Rome. Here you'll find Raphael's High Renaissance masterpiece the **Cappella Chigi,** as well as two stunning Caravaggios in the **Cappella Cerasi.** Each December an exhibit of Christmas nativity scenes is held in the adjacent building. ⊠ *Piazza del Popolo, near Villa Borghese* ☎ *06/3610836* ☉ *Mon.–Sat. 7–noon and 4–7, Sun. 7:30–1:30 and 4:30–7:30.*

Across the Tiber: The Ghetto, Tiberina Island & Trastevere

This walk takes you through separate communities, each staunchly resisting the tides of change, including the old Jewish Ghetto. In Trastevere you will find a resident colony of foreigners coexisting with "the Romans of Rome." Despite rampant gentrification, Trastevere remains about the most tightly knit community in the city, its natives proudly proclaiming their descent from the ancient Romans.

Beginning at Largo Argentina, take Via Paganica to Piazza Mattei, where one of Rome's loveliest fountains, the 16th-century **Fontana delle Tartarughe** **59** ☞, is tucked away. Take Via della Reginella into Via Portico d'Ottavia, heart of the Jewish Ghetto. On the Tiber is the **Sinagoga** **60**. The **Teatro di Marcello** **61**, behind the Portico d'Ottavia, was originally a theater designed to hold 20,000 people. Follow Via di Teatro di Marcello south, passing the ruins of two small temples: the **Tempio della Fortuna Virilis** ⓺ and the circular **Tempio di Vesta** ⓺. Across **Piazza Bocca della Verità** ⓺ is the 12th-century church of Santa Maria in Cosmedin, with the marble Bocca della Verità. Retracing your steps, walk upstream along the Tiber, cross Ponte Fabricio over **Isola Tiberina** ⓺, and then head into Trastevere.

Begin your exploration of Trastevere at Piazza in Piscinula (you will need a good map to make your way around this intricate maze of winding side streets), take Via dell'Arco dei Tolomei, cross Via dei Salumi, and turn left onto Via dei Genovesi and then right to the piazza in front of **Santa Cecilia in Trastevere** ⓺. Baroque enthusiasts will want to walk several blocks southwest down Via Anicia to **San Francesco a Ripa** ⓺ to see a famous Bernini sculpture. Follow Via San Francesco a Ripa to the very heart of Trastevere, to **Piazza di Santa Maria in Trastevere** ⓺, site of the lovely 12th-century church of the same name. With a detailed map, find your way through the narrow byways to Piazza Sant'Egidio and Via della Scala, continuing on to Via della Lungara and **Villa Farnesina** ⓺, where you can see frescoes by Raphael. From Trastevere, climb Via Garibaldi to the Janiculum Hill, which offers views spanning the whole city, and where you'll find the church of **San Pietro in Montorio** ⓺, built in 1481.

TIMING   The walk takes approximately four hours, plus 10 to 15 minutes for each church visited, and about an hour for a visit to Villa Farnesina. It a full afternoon, made even better if you tack on the evening and have dinner in Trastevere.

What to See

▶ ⓹⓽ **Fontana delle Tartarughe.** The 16th-century Fountain of the Turtles in Piazza Mattei is one of Rome's loveliest. Designed by Giacomo della Porta (1539–1602) in 1581 and sculpted by Taddeo Landini (1550–96), the piece revolves around four bronze boys, each clutching a dolphin that jets water into marble shells. Several bronze tortoises, thought to have been added by Bernini, are held in each of the boys' hands and drink from the fountain's upper basin. The piazza is named for the Mattei family, which built **Palazzo Mattei** on Via Caetani (worth a peek for its sculpture-rich courtyard and staircase), and sits at the border of the old Jewish Ghetto. ⊠ *Piazza Mattei, Ghetto.*

⓺ **Isola Tiberina.** Ancient Ponte Fabricio and Ponte Cestio link the old Jewish Ghetto and the neighborhood of Trastevere to this island, where a city hospital stands on a site that has been dedicated to healing ever since a temple to Aesculapius was erected here in 291 BC. If you have time, and if the river's not too high, walk down the stairs for a different perspective on the island and the Tiber.

Jewish Ghetto. Rome has had a Jewish community since the 1st century BC, and from that time until the present its living conditions have varied widely according to its relations with the city's rulers. In 1555 Pope Paul II established Rome's Jewish ghetto in the neighborhood marked off by the Portico d'Ottavia, the Tiber, and Via Arenula. The area quickly became Rome's most squalid and densely populated. At one point,

Jews—who had engaged in many businesses and professions in Trastevere—were limited to the sale of used iron and clothing as a trade. The laws were rescinded around the time of the Italian unifications in the 1870s, and not much remains of the ghetto as it was, but some of Rome's 15,000 Jews still live in the area, and a few families still run clothing shops on the Via di Portico d'Ottavia. German troops occupied Rome during World War II, and on October 16, 1943, many of Rome's Jews were rounded up and deported to Nazi concentration camps. In 1982 the synagogue here was attacked with grenades and machine guns by Palestinian terrorists, and in 1986, as a gesture of reconciliation, Pope John Paul II paid a visit to Rabbi Elio Toaff, becoming the first pope ever to pray in a Jewish synagogue. Today the ghetto is home to Rome's few Judaica shops and kosher groceries, bakeries, and restaurants, as well as linen and shoe stores and the trendy cafés and bars that have moved in with gentrification. Quiet, winding alleys are a shady respite from the center's hustle and are well worth a half hour's stroll.

Palazzo Corsini. This elegant palace holds the 16th- and 17th-century painting collection of the **Galleria Nazionale d'Arte Antica;** even if you're not interested in the paintings, stop in to climb the extraordinary 17th-century stone staircase, itself a drama of architectural shadows and sculptural voids. The adjacent Corsini gardens, now Rome's **Giardino Botanico,** offer a welcome break with native and exotic plants and a stunning view at the top. ⊠ *Via della Lungara 10, Trastevere* ☎ *06/68802323* ⊕ *www.galleriaborghese.it* 🎫 *€4* ⊘ *Tues.–Sun. 8:30–1.*

⑥④ Piazza Bocca della Verità. On the site of the Forum Boarium, ancient Rome's cattle market, this square was later used for public executions. Its name is derived from the marble **Bocca della Verità** (Mouth of Truth) set into the entry portico of the 12th-century church of **Santa Maria in Cosmedin.** In the Middle Ages, legend had it that any person who told a lie with his hand in the mouth of the ancient drain-hole cover would have it chomped off. Today tour groups line up in this noisy, traffic-jammed piazza to give this ancient lie detector a try.

off the
beaten
path

COLLE AVENTINO – One of the seven hills of ancient Rome, the Aventine is now a quiet residential neighborhood that most tourists don't see. It's home to some of the city's oldest and least-visited churches and some unusual views. Peek through the keyhole in the gate to the **garden of the Knights of Malta** (⊠ Piazza Cavalieri di Malta, Aventino) for a surprise view of the dome of St. Peter's. The city panorama from the walled park next to the church of Santa Sabina, off Via Santa Sabina, is wider, if more conventional.

TERME DI CARACALLA – The scale of the towering ruins of ancient Rome's most beautiful and luxurious public baths, the Baths of Caracalla, hints at their past splendor. Inaugurated by the emperor Caracalla in 217, the baths were used until the 6th century. An ancient version of a swank athletic club, the baths were open to all, though men and women used them separately; citizens could bathe, socialize, and exercise in huge pools and richly decorated halls. ⊠ *Via delle*

Terme di Caracalla 52 Aventino ☎ *06/39967700* ⊕ *www.pierreci.it* ▨ *€5* ⊙ *Tues.–Sun. 9–1 hr hour before sunset, Mon. 9–2.*

★ ⑱ **Piazza di Santa Maria in Trastevere.** This piazza is a popular spot for afternoon coffees and evening cocktails at its outdoor cafés, but the showpiece of the square is the 12th-century church of **Santa Maria in Trastevere.** The 13th-century mosaics on the church's facade—which add light and color to the piazza, especially at night when they are in spotlight—are believed to represent the Wise and Foolish Virgins. Inside, the enormous golden mosaic in the apse is the city's finest, a shining burst of Byzantine color and light set off by giant columns. In August, processions honoring the Virgin Mary gather at the church as part of Trastevere's traditional feast, called *Festa de Noantri* (Our Own Feast). ⊠ *Trastevere* ☎ *06/5814802* ⊙ *Church daily 7:30–1 and 4–7.*

⑰ **San Francesco a Ripa.** This church in Piazza San Francesco d'Assisi holds one of Bernini's most dramatic sculptures, the figure of the Blessed Ludovica Albertoni ecstatic at the prospect of entering heaven. Ask the sacristan to show you the cell where St. Francis slept when he came to seek the pope's approval for his new order. ⊠ *Piazza San Francesco d'Assisi, Trastevere* ☎ *06/5819020* ⊙ *Daily 7–noon and 4–7.*

⑳ **San Pietro in Montorio.** One of Rome's key Renaissance buildings, the **Tempietto,** stands in the cloister of this church built by order of Ferdinand and Isabella of Spain in 1481. Bramante built the Tempietto over the spot where St. Peter was thought to have been crucified. It's an architectural gem and was one of his earliest and most successful attempts to design a building in an entirely classical style. ⊠ *Via Garibaldi, Gianicolo, Trastevere* ☎ *06/5813940* ⊙ *Daily 9–noon and 4–6; Tempietto, Oct.–Mar., daily 9:30–12:30 and 2–4; Apr.–Sept., daily 4–6.*

⑯ **Santa Cecilia in Trastevere.** Mothers and children love to dally in the delightful little garden in front of this church in Piazza Santa Cecilia. Duck inside for a look at the 9th-century mosaics and the languid statue of St. Cecilia under the altar. Fragments of a *Last Judgment* fresco cycle by Cavallini, dating from the late 13th century, remain one of his most important works. Though the Byzantine-influenced fragments are obscured by the structure, what's left reveals a rich luminosity in the seated apostles' drapery and a remarkable depth in their expressions. A pretty cloister and remains of Roman houses are visible under the church. Ask to see them at the booth to the left of the main nave. ⊠ *Piazza Santa Cecilia, Trastevere* ☎ *06/5899289* ▨ *Frescoes €2* ⊙ *Daily 10–noon and 4–6; frescoes Tues. and Thurs. 10–11:30, Sun. 11:30–noon.*

⑳ **Sinagoga.** The large, bronze-roof synagogue on the Tiber is a Roman landmark. The **Museo Ebraico** documents the history of the Jewish community in Rome. Most of the decorative crowns, prayer books, holy chairs, and tapestries dating from the 17th century were donated by prominent Jewish families whose ancestors once lived in the Ghetto. The collection offers a change of pace from the predominantly Christian art found elsewhere in Rome. ⊠ *Lungotevere Cenci 15, Ghetto* ☎ *06/68400661* ▨ *€6* ⊙ *Mon.–Thurs. 9–7:30, Fri. 9–2, Sun. 9–12:30.*

61 **Teatro di Marcello.** The Teatro, hardly recognizable as a theater today, was originally designed to hold 20,000 spectators. It was begun by Julius Caesar; today, the 16th-century apartment building that sprouted out of its remains has become one of Rome's most prestigious residential addresses. The area south of the theater makes a grand stage for chamber music concerts in summer. ⊠ *Via del Teatro di Marcello, Ghetto* ⊙ *Open during concerts only.*

62 **Tempio della Fortuna Virilis.** This rectangular temple devoted to "manly fortune" dates from the 2nd century BC and is built in the Greek style, as was the norm in the early years of Rome. For its age, it is remarkably well preserved, in part due to its subsequent consecration as a Christian church. ⊠ *Piazza Bocca della Verità, near Piazza Venezia.*

63 **Tempio di Vesta.** All but one of the 20 original Corinthian columns in Rome's most evocative small ruin remain intact. It was built in the 2nd century BC. Researchers now believe the temple was devoted to Hercules by a successful olive merchant. ⊠ *Piazza Bocca dell Verità, near Piazza Venezia.*

Trastevere. This area consists of a maze of narrow streets that is still, despite evident gentrification, one of the city's most authentically Roman neighborhoods. Literally translated, its name means "across the Tiber," and indeed Trastevere and the Trasteverini—the neighborhood's natives— are a breed apart. The area is hardly undiscovered, but among its self-consciously picturesque trattorias and trendy tearooms you'll also find old shops and dusty artisans' workshops in alleys festooned with laundry hung out to dry. One of the least affected parts of Trastevere centers on Piazza in Piscinula, where San Benedetto, the smallest medieval church in the city, stands opposite the restored medieval Casa dei Mattei. Stroll along Via dell'Arco dei Tolomei and Via dei Salumi, shadowy streets showing the patina of the ages.

Via del Portico d'Ottavia. Along this street in the heart of the Jewish Ghetto are buildings where medieval inscriptions, ancient friezes, and half-buried classical monuments attest to the venerable history of the neighborhood. The old **Chiesa di Sant'Angelo in Pescheria** was built right into the ruins of the Portico d'Ottavia, which was a monumental area enclosing a temple, library, and other buildings within colonnaded porticoes.

★ **69** **Villa Farnesina.** Money was no object to extravagant host Agostino Chigi, a Sienese banker who financed many a papal project. His munificence is evident in his elegant villa, built about 1511. When Raphael could steal some precious time from his work on the Vatican Stanze and from his wooing of the Fornarina, he executed some of the frescoes, notably a luminous *Galatea*. Chigi delighted in impressing guests by having his servants cast precious dinnerware into the Tiber when it was time to clear the table. The guests didn't know of the nets he had stretched under the waterline to catch everything. ⊠ *Via della Lungara 230, Trastevere* ☎ *06/68027268* ⊕ *www.lincei.it* ✉ *€5* ⊙ *Mon.–Sat. 9–1 and first Sun. of month.*

The Catacombs & Via Appia Antica

The Early Christian sites on the ancient Appian Way are some of the religion's oldest. Catacombs, where early Christians (whose religion prohibited cremation) buried their dead and gathered to worship in secret, lie below the very road where tradition says Christ appeared to St. Peter. The Via Appia Antica, built 400 years before, offers a quiet, green place to walk and ponder the ancient world. The Rome APT office provides an informative free pamphlet for this itinerary.

a good tour

Resist any temptation to undertake the 1½-km (1-mi) walk between Porta San Sebastiano and the catacombs; it's a dull and tiring hike on a heavily trafficked cobblestone road, with stone walls the only scenery. Instead, hop on Bus 660 from the Colli Albani metro stop on Line A to the **Via Appia Antica** ⓐ ▶. (Bus 218 from San Giovanni in Laterano also passes near the catacombs, but you have to walk about ½ km [¼ mi] east from Via Ardeatina to Via Appia Antica.) A slightly more expensive but hassle-free option is to take Bus 110 from Piazza Venezia; it's air-conditioned and allows you to hop on and off as you please.

TIMING   Allow one hour for this tour, plus one hour for the catacombs.

Sights to See

★ ▶ ⓐ **Via Appia Antica.** This Queen of Roads, "Regina Viarium," was the most important of the extensive network of roads that traversed the Roman Empire, a masterful feat of engineering that made possible Roman control of a vast area by allowing for the efficient transport of armies and commercial goods. Completed in 312 BC by Appius Claudius, the road was ancient Europe's first highway, connecting Rome with Brindisi, 584 km (365 mi) away on the Adriatic coast. Today part of the route still exists (as Via Appia, SS7), but most of it is a paved, modern highway. The stretch indicated here is the opposite: closed to traffic, the ancient roadway passes through grassy fields and shady groves and by the villas of movie stars (Marcello Mastroianni and Gina Lollobrigida had homes here) and other VIPs. This part is still paved with the ancient *basoli* (basalt stones) over which the Romans drove their carriages. Taverns, houses, temples, and tombs flanked the ancient road, and the occasional lone statue, crumbling wall, or column is still visible, draped in ivy or alone in a patch of wildflowers. Pick a sunny day for your visit, wear comfortable shoes, and bring a bottle of water. **San Callisto** is one of the best preserved of the underground catacombs. A friar will guide you through its crypts and galleries. ⊠ *Via Appia Antica 110* ☎ *06/51301580* ⊠ *€5* ⊙ *Mar.–Jan., Thurs.–Tues. 8:30–noon and 2:30–5:30.*

The 4th-century **San Sebastiano** catacomb, named for the saint who was buried here, burrows underground on four levels. The only one of the catacombs to remain accessible during the Middle Ages, it's the origin of the term "catacomb," for it was in a spot where the road dips into a hollow, a place the Romans called *catacumbas* ("near the hollow"). Eventually the Christian cemetery that had existed here since the 2nd century came to be known by the same name, which was applied to all underground cemeteries discovered in Rome in later centuries. ⊠ *Via*

Appia Antica 136 ☎ *06/7850350* 🖃 *€5* ⊘ *Mid-Nov.–mid-Oct., Mon.–Sat. 8:30–noon and 2:30–5:30.*

On the east side of Via Appia Antica are the ruins of the **Circo di Massenzio,** where the obelisk now in Piazza Navona once stood. ⊠ *Via Appia Antica 153* ☎ *06/7801324* 🖃 *€3* ⊘ *Oct.–Mar., Tues.–Sun. 9–5; Apr.–Sept., Tues.–Sun. 9–7.*

The circular **Tomba di Cecilia Metella,** the mausoleum of a Roman noblewoman who lived at the time of Julius Caesar, was transformed into a fortress in the 14th century. The tomb houses a small museum with sculptures from the Via Appia Antica and an interesting reconstruction of the area's geological and historical past. ⊠ *Via Appia Antica 161* ☎ *06/78021465 or 06/39967700* ⊕ *www.pierreci.it* 🖃 *€2* ⊘ *Mon.–Sat. 9–1:30 and 2:30–7.*

WHERE TO EAT

Updated by
Dana Klitzberg

Rome has been known since ancient times for its great feasts and banquets, and though the days of the triclinium and the Saturnalia are long past, dining out is still the Romans' favorite pastime. The city is distinguished more by its good attitude toward eating out than by a multitude of world-class restaurants; simple, traditional cuisine reigns supreme, although things are slowly changing as talented young chefs explore new culinary frontiers. Many of the city's restaurants cater to a clientele of regulars, and atmosphere and attitude are usually friendly and informal. The flip side is that in Rome the customer is not always right—the chef and waiters are in charge, and no one will beg forgiveness if you wanted *skim* milk in that cappuccino. Be flexible and you're sure to *mangiar bene* (eat well). Lunch is served from 12:30 to 2:30 and dinner from 8 until about 11, though some restaurants stay open later, especially in summer, when patrons linger at sidewalk tables to enjoy the parade of people and the *ponentino* (evening breeze).

WHAT IT COSTS In euros				
	$$$$	**$$$**	**$$**	**$**	**¢**
AT DINNER	over €22	€16–€22	€11–€16	€7–€11	under €7

Prices are for a second course (*secondo piatto*).

Campo de' Fiori

$$$–$$$$ ✕ **Osteria del Pesce.** The entrance to this restaurant looks like an upscale *pescheria* (fish market), which is a good indicator of what awaits you inside: seafood from the coast south of Rome that's beautiful enough to display like aquatic jewels. From starters such as tuna or sea bass carpaccio to seafood-laced pasta dishes, to secondi of grilled or sauteed fish and crustaceans, all dishes are simply prepared and of the highest quality. The space—all hardwood floors, subtle lighting, and walls in royal blue and chili-pepper red—brims with energy. The wine list is a comprehensive selection of whites, and there's also a wide range of after-dinner liqueurs. ⊠ *Via di Monserrato 32 near Campo de' Fiori* ☎ *06/6865617* ☐ *AE, DC, MC, V* ☺ *Closed Sun and 2 wks in Aug. No lunch.*

$$ ✕ **Roscioli.** Marco Roscioli, longtime proprietor of an upscale food counter and bakery, opened this restaurant (with a gourmet deli counter and wine shop up front) in December 2002 around the corner from his famous *forno* (bakery). The menu offers a mix of tasty and often uncommon Italian meats and cheeses, as well as pasta, meat, and fish dishes, all of which are meant to be paired with one of the 800 wines on offer. Try the homemade pasta with duck prosciutto or the potato gnocchi with sea-urchin sauce, or splurge on the foie gras. If you book ahead you can get a table in the cozy, appealing wine cellar. ⊠ *Via dei Giubbonari 21/22 near Campo de' Fiori* ☎ *06/6875287* ☐ *AE, DC, MC, V* ☺ *Closed Sun.*

$–$$ ✕ **Grappolo d'Oro Zampanò.** This Campo area favorite expanded in late
Fodor'sChoice 2003 to include a pizzeria in addition to its restaurant serving eclectic
★ regional Italian cuisine. The kitchen and service are as good as ever: expertly prepared pizzas come steaming to the table, and in the restaurant, specials such as an eggplant flan with Gorgonzola sauce are light and flavorful. Second plates, from beef stewed in Sangiovese wine to a delicate grouper fillet oven-baked in foil with potatoes, tomatoes, and oregano, satisfy every palate. There's a well-selected (though not bargain-priced) wine list. ⊠ *Piazza della Cancelleria 80 near Campo de' Fiori* ☎ *06/6897080* ☐ *AE, MC, V* ☺ *Closed Mon. and Aug.*

Piazza di Spagna

$$$–$$$$ ✕ **Reef.** This seafood restaurant is all about ultramodern design, with sand beneath a Plexiglas floor, rusted-iron accents, huge fish-photo blowups, and a full wall of windows that look onto Ara Pacis. An outpost in famed chef Antonello Colonna's consulting empire, Reef produces Roman fare with a modern twist: try the spigola in *crosta di arachidi* (with a peanut crust). There's a sushi bar at the entrance, where you can sit and view the full workings of the kitchen through a glass wall. ⊠ *Piazza Augusto Imperatore 47, near Piazza di Spagna* ☎ *06/68301430* ☐ *AE, DC, MC, V* ☺ *Closed Mon. No lunch Tues.*

$$–$$$ ✕ **Dal Bolognese.** This classic restaurant on Piazza del Popolo is a convenient shopping-spree lunch spot, and an "in-crowd" dinner destination. The expansive pedestrian piazza offers prime people-watching real estate, and tables inside are perfectly spaced for table-hopping and lots of two-cheek kisses. As the name promises, the cooking here adheres to the hearty tradition of Bologna, with delicious homemade tortellini *in brodo* (in broth), fresh pastas in creamy sauces, and steaming trays of boiled meats. Among the desserts, try the *dolce della mamma* (a concoction of gelato, zabaglione, and chocolate sauce) and the fruit-shape gelato. ⊠ *Piazza del Popolo 1, near Piazza di Spagna* ☎ *06/3611426* ☐ *AE, DC, MC, V* ☺ *Closed Mon. and Aug.*

$ ✕ **GINA.** "Homey minimalism" isn't a contradiction at this white-washed café with a modern edge (block seats, single flowers in mason jars, white chandeliers, and mirrors). With a menu ranging from salads, sandwiches, and pastas to American-style desserts, this is the perfect spot for a late lunch, an aperitivo, or a light dinner that won't break the bank

Where to Eat in Rome

in this high-end neighborhood. Also available are fully stocked gourmet picnic baskets to pick up on the way to nearby Villa Borghese. For a relaxed Saturday evening, join the friendly owners for live jazz from 9:30 to midnight. ⊠ *Via San Sebastianello 7A, near Piazza di Spagna* ☎ *06/ 6780251* ▤ *AE, MC, V* ☉ *Closed Sun. and Aug.*

★ ¢–$ ✕ **Osteria della Frezza.** You can get regular osteria fare and service at this member of the 'Gusto restaurant empire (which dominates the surrounding block), or you can sample *cicheti* (Venetian dialect for bar snacks). These are miniature portions of what's on the regular menu: cured meats and a head-spinning selection of cheeses; pastas, including thick spaghetti with octopus, tomato, and pecorino cheese; and such secondi as grilled lamb chops and meatballs in tomato sauce. Homemade desserts are also available in tiny portions. The wine list is full of interesting choices; trust the knowledgable staff to point you in the right direction. ⊠ *Via della Frezza 16, near Piazza di Spagna* ☎ *06/3226273* ▤ *AE, DC, MC, V.*

Piazza Navona

$$$$ ✕ **Il Convivio.** The Troiani brothers came to Rome in the late 1980s and
Fodor'sChoice ever since have been leaders of a small circle of top Italian gourmands.
★ Their inventive fare can be characterized as Italian cuisine revisited—classic dishes made from the best ingredients, given a unique, elegant tweak. The raw "lacquered" tuna and the foie gras are luscious starters, and Roman broccoli soup is a classic that's disappeared from other menus. For secondi, the pigeon is exquisitely cooked, and the fish are all first-rate. Desserts are delicious, if a bit restrained, service is excellent, and the wine selection, although pricey, would impress any connoisseur. ⊠ *Vicolo dei Soldati 31, near Piazza Navona* ☎ *06/6869432* 🪑 *Reservations essential* ▤ *AE, DC, MC, V* ☉ *Closed Sun., 1 wk in Jan., and 2 wks in Aug. No lunch.*

$$$–$$$$ ✕ **L'Altro Mastai.** Executive chef Fabio Baldassare (former sous-chef to La Pergola's renowned Heinz Beck) turns out beautiful Mediterranean dishes at this recent entry on the fine-dining scene. Pastas are homemade and flavored with a delicate hand (think Roman broccoli ravioli in a truffle-scented sauce), and secondi such as sea bass with tomatoes and olives taste of the sea and sun. Portions are small, especially for the prices, so partake heartily in the breads and *assaggini* (nibbles) throughout the meal. Desserts are luscious and beautifully executed, and the wine list ample. The restaurant has a casual wine-bar sibling across the street. ⊠ *Via G. Giraud 53 (Via dei Banchi Nuovi), near Piazza Navona* ☎ *06/68301296* ▤ *AE, DC, MC, V* ☉ *Closed Sun. and Mon., and Aug.*

$$$–$$$$ ✕ **Sangallo.** Small and intimate, this quiet fish restaurant snuggled between Piazza Navona and the Pantheon is an outpost of high-quality seafood in the tradition of Anzio, the coastal town south of Rome the owner hails from. The menu has some sophisticated touches, such as oysters tartare, snapper with foie gras, and pasta dishes made with toothsome Gragnano pasta. There are precious few tables in the tiny dining room, so make sure to book ahead. ⊠ *Vicolo della Vaccarella 11/a, near Piazza Navona* ☎ *06/6865549* 🪑 *Reservations essential* ▤ *AE, DC, MC, V* ☉ *Closed Sun., 1 wk in Jan., and 2 wks in Aug. No lunch Mon.*

ON THE MENU

ROMAN COOKING IS SIMPLE. *Dishes rarely have more than a few ingredients, and meat and fish are most often roasted, baked, or grilled. The best meat is often* abbacchio *(milk-fed lamb)—legs are usually roasted with rosemary and potatoes, and chops served* alla scottadito *(literally "burn your finger"—hot off the grill). Most Mediterranean fish are light, yet flavorful, among them* spigola *(sea bass),* orata *(bream), and* rombo *(turbot). Romans swoon for batter-fried* baccalà *(cod).*

The quintessential Roman pasta dishes are made with guanciale *(cured pork cheek) or* pancetta *(bacon) and pecorino Romano cheese. All'*amatriciana *adds onion and tomato to the mix and is classically served with* bucatini *(a thick, hollow spaghetti); alla* carbonara *tosses the pork and cheese with egg yolk and black pepper; and alla* gricia *is amatriciana without tomatoes. Potato gnocchi with a tomato sauce and Parmesan or pecorino is a favorite for Thursday dinner.*

Seasonal vegetables may not appear on the menu but are usually available. Cicoria *and* spinaci ripassati *(sautéed chicory and spinach) are perennial favorites, and many restaurants specialize in vegetable* fritto misto *(literally "mixe fried"). Rome is famous for* carciofi *(artichokes)—available from November to April—prepared* alla rom *(stuffed with garlic and mint and braised) or* alla giudia *(fried whole, making each petal crisp). A springtime treat is* vignarola, *a mixture of tender peas, fava beans, artichokes, and guanciale.*

Typical wines of Rome are from the Castelli Romani, the towns in the hills to the southeast: Frascati, Colli Albani, Marino, and Velletri. Though tap water in Rome is drinkable, restaurants usually offer bottled water, either gassata *(sparkling) or* liscia *(still).*

$$ ✕ **Osteria dell'Ingegno.** This casual but trendy spot is great for a glass of wine or a meal in the city center. The simple but innovative menu focuses on regional and seasonal produce and changes weekly. The walls are hung with colorful paintings by local artists, and service is friendly. ✉ *Piazza di Pietra 45, near Piazza Navona* ☏ *06/6780662* ▭ *AE, DC, MC, V* ☻ *Closed Sun. and 2 wks in Aug.*

San Pietro

$$$$ ✕ **La Pergola.** High atop Monte Mario, the Cavalieri Hilton's rooftop La Pergola restaurant offers a commanding view of the city below. Trompe-l'oeil ceilings and handsome wood paneling combine with low lighting to create an intimate atmosphere. Celebrated Wunder-chef Heinz Beck brings Rome its most polished example of Mediterranean *alta cucina* (haute cuisine); dishes are balanced and light, and presentation is striking. For a window table reserve a month in advance; otherwise, two weeks. ✉ *Cavalieri Hilton, Via Cadlolo 101, Monte Mario* ☏ *06/3509221* ⌖ *Reservations essential* 🏛 *Jacket and tie* ▭ *AE, DC, MC, V* ☻ *Closed Sun. and Mon., and 2 wks in Dec. No lunch.*

$$$–$$$$ ✕ **Il Simposio di Costantini.** At the classiest wine bar in town, done out in wrought-iron vines, wood paneling, and velvet, you can choose from about 30 wines. Food is appropriately fancy: marinated and smoked fish, composed salads, top-quality salami and other cured meats, terrines and pâtés, vegetable dishes, and several inventive secondi, mostly meat/game selections. Finish off with a plate from an assortment of 80 cheeses grouped according to origin or type, and a well-balanced dessert menu. ⊠ *Piazza Cavour 16, near San Pietro* ☎ *06/3211502* ⊟ *AE, DC, MC, V* ⊘ *Closed Sun. and last 2 wks of Aug. No lunch Sat.*

★ $$–$$$ ✕ **Siciliainbocca.** Finally, Rome has a straight-up, no-nonsense Sicilian restaurant. The owners, both Sicily natives, decided to open up Siciliainbocca after years of frustration at not finding a decent pasta *alla norma* (with eggplant, tomato sauce, and aged ricotta cheese) in the capital. Try specialties such as caponata, risotto *ai profumi di Sicilia* (with lemon, orange, mozzarella, and zucchini), and delicious grilled swordfish, shrimp, and squid. Even in the dead of winter, Siciliainbocca's yellow walls and brightly colored ceramic plates warm you up. There's outdoor seating in summer. ⊠ *Via E. Faà di Bruno 26, near San Pietro* ☎ *06/37358400* ⊟ *AE, DC, MC, V* ⊘ *Closed Sun.*

$$ ✕ **Taverna Angelica.** The area surrounding St. Peter's Basilica isn't known for culinary excellence, but Taverna Angelica is an exception. Its tiny size (just 20 seats) allows the chef to concentrate on each individual dish, and the results are impressive. The menu is creative without being pretentious; such dishes as chickpeas with a fondue of pecorino cheese, lentil soup with pigeon breast, and breast of duck in balsamic vinegar are exquisitely executed. The candlelit dining room, tasteful decor, and excellent service are icing on the cake. ⊠ *Piazza A. Capponi 6, near San Pietro* ☎ *06/6874514* ⌂ *Reservations essential* ⊟ *AE, V.*

$ ✕ **Alfredo e Ada.** There's no place like home, and you'll feel like you're back there from the moment you squeeze into a table at this hole in the wall just across the river from Castel Sant'Angelo. There's no menu, just plate after plate of whatever Ada thinks you should try, from hearty, classic pastas to *involtini di vitello* (savory veal rolls with tomato) and homemade sausage. Sit back, relax, and enjoy—it's all good. By the time you leave you may have made some new friends, too. ⊠ *Via dei Banchi Nuovi 14, near San Pietro* ☎ *06/6878842* ⊟ *No credit cards* ⊘ *Closed weekends.*

¢–$ ✕ **Tre Pupazzi.** The "three puppets," after which the trattoria is named, are the worn stone figures on a fragment of an ancient sarcophagus that embellishes a building on this byway near the Vatican. Little has changed here since the place was built in 1625, and the restaurant upholds a tradition of good food, courteous service, and reasonable prices. The menu offers classic Roman and Abruzzese trattoria fare, including fettuccine and abbacchio, plus pizzas at lunchtime, a rarity in Rome. The restaurant opens early, at noon for lunch and 7 for dinner. ⊠ *Borgo Pio 183 at Via dei Tre Pupazzi, near San Pietro* ☎ *06/68803220* ⊟ *AE, DC, MC, V* ⊘ *Closed Sun. and Aug.*

Termini & San Lorenzo

★ $$$–$$$$ ✕ **Agata e Romeo.** The husband-and-wife team of Agata Parisella and Romeo Caraccio runs one of Rome's top restaurants. Agata puts an inspired twist on Roman cuisine with dishes such as crepes with chestnut flour and ewe's-milk ricotta, and breaded lamp chops. Romeo acts as maître d' and expert sommelier. A tasting menu, complete with wine, changes monthly to reflect seasonal dishes and allows you to try a range of specialties. Desserts are scrumptious and the wine list is excellent. ⊠ *Via Carlo Alberto 45, near Termini* ☎ *06/4466115* ⊟ *AE, DC, MC, V* ⊗ *Closed weekends, 2 wks in July, and 2 wks in Aug.*

$$-$$$$ ✕ **F.I.S.H.** The name stands for Fine International Seafood House, which sums up the kitchen's approach to its cuisine. The menu is divided into three sections: sushi (both traditional and "new generation"), Asian, and Mediterranean. All dishes are well executed, and range from Italian fish-based pastas to a Thai mollusk soup with lemongrass and coconut milk that is a party for the senses. This is fresh, fresh fish in capable and creative hands. Seating is limited, so book ahead, especially on weekends. ⊠ *Via dei Serpenti16, Monti* ☎ *06/47824962* ⚐ *Reservations essential* ⊟ *AE, D, MC, V* ⊗ *Closed Mon. and 2 wks in Aug.*

★ $$ ✕ **Uno e Bino.** Giampaolo Gravina's restaurant in an artsy corner of the San Lorenzo neighborhood is popular with Romans from all over town. He works the dining room, offering suggestions from an impressive wine list, and his sister Gloria is in the kitchen turning out inventive cuisine inspired by the family's Umbrian and Sicilian roots. Octopus salad with asparagus and carrots, and spaghetti with swordfish, tomatoes, and capers are specialties. ⊠ *Via degli Equi 58, San Lorenzo* ☎ *06/4460702* ⊟ *AE, D, MC, V* ⊗ *Closed Mon. and Aug. No lunch.*

$ ✕ **Arancia Blu.** Owner and chef Fabio Passan has a mission—to prove that "vegetarian cuisine" isn't an oxymoron. He succeeds, with flavorful, creative dishes that have won him a devoted clientele of vegetarians and omnivores alike. Start with a leek-and-almond quiche or lemon-ricotta ravioli with squash and sage, and move on to *polpettine vegetali* (meatless meatballs) with a tomato–coriander seed sauce. Gourmet palates will be tickled by the selections of coffee and olive oil, and by the chocolate tasting, 14 chocolate wafers of every flavor and origin. Vegan and wheat-free dishes are available on request. ⊠ *Via dei Latini 65, San Lorenzo* ☎ *06/4454105* ⊟ *No credit cards* ⊗ *No lunch.*

¢–$ ✕ **Pommidoro.** Mamma's in the kitchen and the rest of the family greets, serves, and keeps you happy and well fed at this trattoria popular with artists, filmmakers, and actors. It's near Rome's main university in the counterculture San Lorenzo neighborhood, a short cab ride east of Stazione Termini. The menu offers especially good grilled meats and game birds as well as classic home-style cucina. You can dine outside in warm weather. ⊠ *Piazza dei Sanniti 44, San Lorenzo* ☎ *06/4452692* ⊟ *AE, DC, MC, V* ⊗ *Closed Sun. and Aug.*

Trastevere & Testaccio

$$$ ✕ **Antico Arco.** Founded by three friends with a passion for wine and fine food, Antico Arco has won the hearts of foodies from Rome and beyond with its culinary inventiveness and high style. The menu changes with the season, but you may find such delights as *flan di taleggio con salsa di funghi* (taleggio cheese flan with mushrooms), or a *carré d'agnello* (rack of lamb) with foie-gras sauce and pears in port wine. Don't miss dessert, especially the chocolate soufflé with melted chocolate center: it's justly famous among chocoholics all over the city. ⊠ *Piazzale Aurelio 7, Trastevere* ☎ *06/5815274* ♣ *Reservations essential* ▭ *AE, DC, MC, V* ☺ *Closed Sun. and 2 wks in Aug. No lunch.*

$$$ ✕ **Ferrara.** What used to be a well-stocked *enoteca* (wine bar) with a few nibbles has become what locals now know as the "Ferrara block": the enoteca has expanded to become a full-fledged restaurant, a wine bar, and a gastronomic boutique, taking over a good section of one of the area's famous streets. The renovations have resulted in an airy, modernist destination with an interesting, frequently changing menu; antipasti and primi are particularly strong. There's an exhaustive wine list, as well as several choices of coffees, teas, and digestives for sipping after a decadent dessert. ⊠ *Via del Moro 1A, Trastevere* ☎ *06/58333920* ▭ *DC, MC, V* ☺ *Closed Tues. and 2 wks in Aug.*

$$–$$$ ✕ **Spirito di Vino.** At this restaurant on the less-traveled side of Viale Trastevere, the food ranges from inventive (mini meatballs seasoned with coriander) to traditional (spaghetti with cacio cheese and pepper) to historical (braised pork shoulder with apple and leeks, following a recipe dating back to the time of Apicius, ancient Rome's first cookbook author). The dining room is welcoming and refined, with walls in tomato-red and dark wood. The proud owner is happy to explain every dish on the menu and give you the history of his wine cellar, where several ancient sculptures, now in the Vatican and Capitoline museums, were unearthed. ⊠ *Via dei Genovesi 31 A/B, Trastevere* ☎ *06/5896689* ▭ *AE, MC, V* ☺ *Closed Sun. and 2 wks in Aug.*

★ $ ✕ **Alle Fratte.** Here you'll find staple Roman trattoria fare as well as dishes with a Neapolitan slant, so spaghetti alla carbonara shares the menu with penne *alla Sorrentina* (with tomato, basil, and fresh mozzarella). Again looking south, try the pressed octopus carpaccio with arugula to start, followed by a mixed seafood pasta or a grilled sea bass with oven-roasted potatoes. Service is always with a smile, with boisterous owner Francesco, his American wife, and their trusted waiter Peppe making you feel at home. ⊠ *Via delle Fratte di Trastevere 49/50* ☎ *06/ 5835775* ▭ *AE, DC, MC, V* ☺ *Closed Wed. and 2 wks in Aug.*

$ ✕ **Perilli.** A bastion of authentic Roman cooking since 1911 (the decor has changed very little), this trattoria is the place to go to try rigatoni *con pajata* (with calves' intestines)—if you're into this sort of thing. Pasta all'amatriciana and carbonara are also classics. The house wine is a golden nectar from the Castelli Romani. ⊠ *Via Marmorata 39, Testaccio* ☎ *06/ 5742415* ▭ *AE, DC, MC, V* ☺ *Closed Wed.*

Via Veneto

$$$$ ✕ **La Terrazza dell'Eden.** The Hotel Eden's La Terrazza restaurant has an unparalleled view of Rome's seven hills and food as spectacular as the view. Chef Enrico Derfligher, formerly of Buckingham Palace, refreshes the menu every six months with superb culinary creations that are high on flavor and low on butter. If you're a wine enthusiast, ask the maître d' to let you view the restaurant's showcase cellar. ⊠ *Hotel Eden, Via Ludovisi 49, near Via Veneto* ☎ *06/47812752* ♣ *Reservations essential* 🏛 *Jacket and tie* ▭ *AE, DC, MC, V.*

★ **$$$–$$$$** ✕ **Papá Baccus.** Italo Cipriani takes his meat as seriously as any Tuscan. He uses real Chianina beef, the prized breed traditionally used for the house-specialty *bistecca alla fiorentina*, a thick grilled steak left rare in the middle. Cipriani brings many ingredients from his hometown on the border of Emilia-Romagna and Tuscany. Try the sweet and delicate prosciutto from Pratomagno or the *ribollita,* a traditional bread-based minestrone soup. The welcome is warm, the service excellent. ⊠ *Via Toscana 36, near Via Veneto* ☎ *06/42742808* ⊟ *AE, DC, MC, V* ⊘ *Closed Sun. and 2 wks in Aug. No lunch Sat.*

Pizzerias

Pizza may have been invented somewhere else, but in Rome it's hard to walk a block without encountering it in one form or another. Pizza from a bakery is usually made without cheese—pizza *bianca* (with olive oil and salt) or pizza *rossa* (with tomato sauce). Many small shops specialize in pizza *al taglio* (by the slice), priced by the *etto* (100 grams, about ¼ pound), according to the kind of topping. Both types make a great snack any time of day. Some good places to find the real thing on the go:

Il Forno di Campo de' Fiori (⊠ Campo de' Fiori), closed Sunday, makes hot pizza bianca and rossa and is crowded all day. Try pizza *farcita,* "stuffed" pizza bianca filled with meats, cheeses, vegetables, and even prosciutto and warm figs in season at their sandwich bar next door. **La Renella** (⊠ Via del Moro 16, Trastevere ☎ 06/5817265) is a truly excellent bakery and pizzeria, and it stays open late. **Zí Fenizia** (⊠ Via Santa Maria del Pianto 64, Ghetto) makes kosher pizza in the old Jewish Ghetto; it closes Friday at sundown and remains closed Saturday.

But don't leave Rome without sitting down to a classic, wafer-thin, crispy Roman pizza in a lively, no-frills pizzeria. Most are open only for dinner, usually from 8 PM to midnight. Look for a place with a *forno a legna* (wood-burning oven), a must for a good thin crust on your plate-size Roman pizza. Standard models are the *margherita* (tomato, mozzarella, and basil) and the *capricciosa* (a little bit of everything, depending upon the "caprices" of the pizza chef: tomato, mozzarella, sausage, olives, artichoke hearts, prosciutto, even egg), and most pizzerias have a long list of additional options, including tasty mozzarella *di bufala* (made from buffalo milk).

$ ✕ **Acchiapafantasmi.** The name translates as "ghostbusters," after the restaurant's award-winning pizza shaped like a ghost with mozzarella, cherry tomatoes, and oregano. But the menu extends beyond pizza to spicy treats of the Commisso brothers' native Calabria, such as the spreadable *'nduja* sausage (half pork, half hot peppers) and an innovative version of eggplant parmigiana. The gelato, brought up from the southern town of Pizzo Calabria, is considered by some the best in Italy. ⊠ *Via dei Cappellari 66, near Campo de' Fiori* ☎ *06/6873462* ⊟ *AE, DC, MC, V* ⊘ *Closed Tues. and 1 wk in Aug.*

★ **¢–$** ✕ **Dar Poeta.** It's always crowded and lively at this Trastevere innovator. Pizza is offered in traditional Roman style (paper-thin) or the thicker Neapolitan *pizza alta*. The menu offers toppings beyond the average (try the house pizza, with sauteed zucchini, sausage, and hot pepper), and there are several types of *bruschette* (grilled bread with various toppings) and salads. A must-try: the dessert calzone, filled with ricotta cheese and chocolate-hazelnut Nutella. ⊠ *Vicolo del Bologna, Trastevere* ☎ 06/5880516 ⊟ *AE, MC, V.*

¢–$ ✕ **La Soffitta.** You pay more, but hey, it's imported. This is Rome's hottest spot for classic Neapolitan pizza (thick, though crunchy on the bottom, rather than paper-thin and crispy like the Roman kind), and one of the few pizzerias in town certified by the True Neapolitan Pizza Association. Desserts are brought in daily from Naples. ⊠ *Via dei Villini 1/e, Termini* ☎ 06/4404642 ⚠ *Reservations not accepted* ⊟ *AE, DC, MC, V* ⊙ *Closed Aug. 10–31. No lunch.*

¢–$ ✕ **Remo.** Expect a wait at this perennial favorite in Testaccio frequented by students and neighborhood locals. You won't find tablecloths or other nonessentials, just classic Roman pizza and boisterous conversation. ⊠ *Piazza Santa Maria Liberatrice 44, Testaccio* ☎ 06/5746270 ⚠ *Reservations not accepted* ⊟ *No credit cards* ⊙ *Closed Sun., Aug., and Christmas wk. No lunch.*

Enoteche

It was not so long ago that wine in Rome (and other towns) was strictly local; you didn't have to walk far to find an *osteria,* a tavernlike establishment where you could buy wine straight from the barrel or sit down to drink and nibble a bit, chat, or play cards. The tradition continues today, as many Roman wineshops are also open as *enoteche* (wine bars). Most have done away with the folding chairs and rickety tables in favor of designer interiors and chic ambience. Shelves are lined with hundreds of bottles from all over the country, representing the best in Italian wine making, and many selections are available by the glass. Behind the bar you'll usually find a serious wine enthusiast, maybe even a sommelier.

$$$ ✕ **Bistro.** The atmosphere here is both airy and intimate; high, pale yellow arched ceilings, immense guilt mirrors, rich oak paneling, and an original wrought-iron bar counter are all true to the art nouveau style. Chef Emanuele Vizzini serves up fusion dishes such as fettuccine *al Cabernet con scampi* (red-wine fettuccine with scampi and vegetables) and Nasdaq *taglionini* with lobster (the dollar-green pasta is made with curaçao liqueur). The sommelier has selected 300 labels (12 available by the glass) of lesser-known, high-quality wines. ⊠ *Via Palestro 40, Termini* ☎ 06/44702868 ⊟ *AE, DC, MC, V* ⊙ *No lunch Sun.*

★ $ ✕ **Cul de Sac.** This is a classic Roman enoteca, frequented by everyone from local soccer fans to the Fendi sisters. Quarters are cramped, both inside and at the tables outside on the small piazza, but once you've snagged a seat and begin sipping the wine and sampling the food, you realize it's worth it. The selection of Italian regional cheeses and cured meats is vast, and the soups, pastas, and salads have homemade appeal. Especially refreshing are the international dishes: hummus, Greek salad, and various pâtés that can be difficult to find in these parts. The wine list is tremendous and constantly changing. ⊠ *Piazza Pasquino 73, near Piazza Navona* ☎ 06/68801094 ⊟ *AE, MC, V* ⊙ *Closed 2 wks in Aug.*

★ ¢–$ ✕ **Cavour 313.** Wine bars are popping up all over the city, but Cavour 313 has been around much longer than most. Open for lunch and dinner, it serves an excellent variety of cured meats, cheeses, and salads. Choose from about 25 wines by the glass or uncork a bottle (there are more than 1,200) and stay a while. ✉ *Via Cavour 313, Colosseo* ☎ *06/ 6785496* ☐ *AE, DC, MC, V* ☉ *Closed Aug. No lunch weekends. No dinner Sun. June 15–Sept.*

Cafés

As elsewhere in Italy, there's a *bar* (coffee bar) on nearly every corner in Rome where you can get coffee drinks, fruit juices, pastries, sandwiches, liquor, and beer. Locals usually stop in for a quick caffeine hit at the counter. If you want to sit at a table, beware: prices can be up to four times higher. Don't be shy about asking what the extra cost is before sitting. Pricey **Antico Caffè Greco** (✉ Via Condotti 86, near Piazza di Spagna ☎ 06/6791700) is a national landmark popular with tourists; its red-velvet chairs and marble tables have hosted the likes of Byron, Shelley, Keats, Goethe, and Casanova. **Caffè Sant'Eustachio** (✉ Piazza Sant'-Eustachio 82, near Pantheon ☎ 06/6861309) makes one of the smoothest cappuccinos anywhere. Its secret? *Crema di caffè* (coffee cream)—a rich, homemade addition slipped into each cup. If you want your *caffè* (espresso) without sugar Sant'Eustachio, ask for it *amaro*. **Tazza d'Oro** (✉ Via degli Orfani 84, near Pantheon ☎ 06/6789792) serves some of the best coffee in the city, as well as decadent *granita di caffè* (iced coffee) with a thick wallop of whipped cream mixed in. **Rosati** (✉ Piazza del Popolo 5, near Piazza di Spagna ☎ 06/3225859) is Piazza del Popolo's premier people-watching spot. Tables on the car-free piazza fill up quickly on weekends, when it seems the whole city is here. **Antico Caffè della Pace** (✉ Via della Pace 3, near Piazza Navona ☎ 06/ 6861216) has an ornate, old-fashioned atmosphere. **Ciampini** (✉ Piazza San Lorenzo in Lucina 29, near Piazza di Spagna ☎ 06/6876606), off the Corso in a jewel of a piazza, is a prime spot for a predinner aperitivo. Be sure to ask for the free assaggini.

Gelaterie & Pasticcerie

For Italians, gelato is more a snack than a serious dessert. **Il Gelato di San Crispino** (✉ Via della Panetteria 42, near Piazza di Trevi ☎ 06/ 6793924), closed Tuesday, is perhaps the most celebrated gelato in all of Italy, made without artificial colors or flavors. It's worth crossing town for. **Fiocco di Neve** (✉ Via del Pantheon 51 ☎ 06/6786025) is renowned for its zabaglione and *riso bianco* (rice) ice cream. **Fonte della Salute** (✉ Via Cardinal Marmaggi 2, Trastevere ☎ 06/5897471), literally "fountain of health," serves frozen yogurt as well as traditional gelato. It's closed Tuesday in winter. For decades, **Muse** (✉ Via Eleanora Duse 1E, Parioli ☎ 06/8079300), popularly known as da Giovanni (after the owner), has been a mecca for Romans in the know. Winter flavors include chestnut and almond. It's closed Sunday. **Giolitti** (✉ Via Uffici del Vicario 40, near Pantheon ☎ 06/6991243), just off Via Campo Marzio, has a quaint tearoom and delicious fruit-flavored gelato.

Romans are not known for their sweet tooths, and there are few *pasticcerie* (pastry shops) in town that distinguish themselves with particularly good examples of the few regional desserts. One exception is the **Forno del Ghetto** (✉ Via del Portico d'Ottavia 1, Ghetto ☎ 06/6878637), closed Friday at sundown, Saturday, and Jewish holidays. This hole in the wall—no sign, no tables, just a take-away counter—is an institution, preserving a tradition of Italian-Jewish sweets that cannot be found anywhere else. The ricotta cake (with sour-cherry jam or chocolate) is unforgettable. For a change of pace, try the Austrian cakes and American pies at **Dolceroma** (✉ Via del Portico d'Ottavia 20/b, Ghetto ☎ 06/6892196); the apple strudel and Sacher torte may not be Italian, but Romans come here in droves just the same. It's closed Sunday afternoon and Monday and four weeks July–August. **Dagnino** (✉ Galleria Esedra, Via VE Orlando 75, near Termini ☎ 06/4818660) is an outpost of all foods Sicilian. The pastries, such as ricotta-filled cannoli and the *cassata* cake, as well as colorful marzipan candies, are exquisite.

Salumerie

There are several hundred *salumerie* (gourmet food shops) in town, but a few stand out for a particularly ample selection and items of rare, superior quality. Foodies should head straight for **Franchi** (✉ Via Cola di Rienzo 200, near San Pietro ☎ 06/6864576), closed Sunday, with the city's best take-out treats, including salmon mousse, roast beef, vegetable fritters, and an endless selection of sliced meats and cheeses that you can have vacuum-packed for safe transport home. **Castroni** (✉ Via Cola di Rienzo 196, near San Pietro ☎ 06/6864383), closed Sunday, is a fine general food shop with lots of imported items. It's right next door to the Franchi shop. **Volpetti** (✉ Via Marmorata 47, Testaccio ☎ 06/5742352), closed Tuesday afternoon and Sunday, has the highest-quality meats and specializes in aged cheeses from small producers.

WHERE TO STAY

Updated by
Dana Klitzberg

Rome has the range of accommodations you would expect of any great city, from the squalid little hotels around the railway station to the grand monuments to luxury and elegance around major piazzas and Via Veneto. Appearances can be misleading: crumbling stucco facades may promise little from the outside, but they often hide interiors of considerable elegance. By the same token, elaborate reception areas may lead to surprisingly plain rooms. Generally, rooms tend to be small by U.S. standards. Many of the lower-price hotels are actually old-fashioned *pensioni* set on one or several floors of a large building. One disadvantage of staying in central hotels in lower categories is noise; you can ask for an inside room if you are a light sleeper, but you may end up looking out on a dark courtyard.

Rome is a year-round tourist destination, so you should always try to make reservations, even if only a few days in advance. Always inquire about special low rates, often available in both winter and summer if occupancy is low. If you arrive in Rome without reservations, try **Hotel**

Reservation Service (☎ 06/6991000), with an English-speaking operator available daily 7 AM–10 PM, and with desks at Aeroporto Fiumicino and Stazione Termini. A list of all the hotels in Rome, with prices and facilities, is available from the main **APT information office** (⊠ Via Parigi 5, Termini ☎ 06/48899255).

WHAT IT COSTS In euros				
$$$$	**$$$**	**$$**	**$**	**¢**
FOR 2 PEOPLE over €290	€210–€290	€140–€210	€80–€140	under €80

Prices are for two people in a standard double room in high season.

Campo de' Fiori

$$$–$$$$ 🏨 **Hotel Ponte Sisto.** The location just off the Ponte Sisto, the pedestrian bridge that connects the Campo de' Fiori neighborhood to Trastevere, gives you the convenience of the city center and access to the trattorias and bars of Trastevere, an area popular with both Romans and expats. Once the palazzo of the noble Venetian Palottini family, the hotel now features clean and bright, if basic rooms. Wall-to-wall carpeting and green-marble bathrooms add refinement, but the real draw is the large internal courtyard, where guests can get sun, read beneath the shade of the enormous palms, and sip cocktails under the stars. ⊠ *Via dei Pettinari 64, Campo de' Fiori 00186* ☎ *06/686310* 🖷 *06/68301712* ⊕ *www. hotelpontesisto.it* ⤳ *102 rooms, 1 suite* ⚘ *Dining room, in-room safes, minibars, cable TV, bar, meeting rooms, parking (fee)* ⊟ *AE, DC, MC, V* ¶⊙¶ *BP.*

★ **$$** 🏨 **Residenza Farnese.** The Renaissance charm of this former priests' convent has been preserved—its landmark status prevents the owners from making too many changes. In one of the rooms, believed to be a former chapel, they stripped the paint to find a colorfully frescoed ceiling, which they had professionally restored. The rooms run from understated antiques and deep blue fabrics to more ornate hand-painted floral dressers and original artwork. All have hardwood floors and clean, modern bathrooms with showers. There is a billiards room with a bar for socializing, and a large breakfast room that serves homemade breads and organic marmalades. ⊠ *Via del Mascherone 59, Campo de' Fiori 00186* ☎ *06/68891388* 🖷 *06/68210980* ✉ *residenzafarnese@libero. it* ⤳ *31 rooms* ⚘ *Cable TV, in-room safes, minibars, Internet, conference room* ⊟ *AE, MC, V* ¶⊙¶ *BP.*

$ 🏨 **Campo de' Fiori.** Frescoes, exposed brickwork, and picturesque effects throughout this little hotel could well be the work of a set designer. There's an aura of romanticism in the decoration, with the layout making the most of limited space. Though a few rooms are so compact they're almost claustrophobic, the decor reminds you that you're in the heart of Rome. There's no elevator, but the climb to the roof terrace rewards you with a marvelous view. ⊠ *Via del Biscione 6, Campo de' Fiori 00186* ☎ *06/68806865* 🖷 *06/6876003* ⊕ *www.hotelcampodefiori.com* ⤳ *27 rooms, 14 with bath* ⚘ *No a/c, no room TVs* ⊟ *MC, V* ¶⊙¶ *BP.*

Where to Stay in Rome

$ ⊞ **Smeraldo.** The location, a stone's throw from Campo de' Fiori on a quiet side street, makes this an excellent choice in its price category. All the guest rooms have been recently refurbished; they're decorated with white marble floors, salmon-color bedding and curtains, and wooden bed frames and furniture. Shiny new bathrooms in green marble have showers or a combination bath/shower. ⊠ *Vicolo dei Chiodaroli 9, Campo de' Fiori 00186* ☎ *06/6875929 or 06/6892121* 🖷 *06/68805495* ⤶ *25 rooms* ⚲ *In-room safes, cable TV, bar* ☰ *AE, DC, MC, V* ⦿ *BP.*

Colosseo

$$$$ ⊞ **Hotel Capo d'Africa.** Opened in September 2002, this hotel is part of the Celio area's resurgence. It's designed on the boutique hotel model, with '60s-style furnishings in bright purple and orange, commissioned artwork on the walls, and quirky light fixtures. The 1903 building was originally a school, and as a result rooms are different sizes, all done in earth tones and saffron, with marble-and-tile bathrooms. Two rooftop terraces, connected by the breakfast room, are a delightful bonus in warmer weather. ⊠ *Via Capo d'Africa 54, near Colosseo 00184* ☎ *06/ 772801* 🖷 *06/77280801* ⊕ *www.hotelcapodafrica.com* ⤶ *64 rooms, 1 suite* ⚲ *In-room safes, minibars, cable TV, gym, bar, Internet, meeting rooms, parking (fee), no-smoking rooms.* ☰ *AE, DC, MC, V* ⦿ *BP.*

$$ ⊞ **Duca d'Alba.** This elegant hotel has made a stylish contribution to the ongoing gentrification of the Suburra neighborhood, near the Colosseum and the Roman Forum. The tasteful neoclassical decor includes custom-designed furnishings and marble bathrooms. All rooms are entirely soundproof and offer satellite TV and modem ports. Breakfast consists of an ample buffet. With its attentive staff and reasonable rates, Duca d'Alba is an exceptional value. ⊠ *Via Leonina 14, near Colosseo 00184* ☎ *06/484471* 🖷 *06/4884840* ⊕ *www.hotelducadalba.com* ⤶ *27 rooms, 1 suite* ⚲ *In-room safes, some kitchenettes, minibars, cable TV, bar* ☰ *AE, DC, MC, V* ⦿ *BP.*

Piazza di Spagna

$$$$ ⊞ **D'Inghilterra.** Legendary names like Liszt, Mendelssohn, Hans Christian Andersen, Mark Twain, and Hemingway litter the guest book here. With a residential feel and a staff that is as warm as the surroundings are velvety, this hotel near the Spanish Steps was once the guesthouse of the fabulously rich Prince Torlonia. Rooms are so full of carpets, gilt-framed mirrors, and cozy bergères, you'll hardly notice the snug dimensions. Its chic ochre restaurant with vaulted ceilings, Café Romano, has tables on via Borgogna and serves eclectic cuisine nonstop from noon to midnight. ⊠ *Via Bocca di Leone 14, near Piazza di Spagna 00187* ☎ *06/ 699811* 🖷 *06/69922243* ⊕ *www.hoteldinghilterraroma.it* ⤶ *90 rooms, 8 suites* ⚲ *Restaurant, in-room safes, minibars, cable TV, bar, laundry service, parking (fee), no-smoking rooms* ☰ *AE, DC, MC, V* ⦿ *EP.*

★ $$$$ ⊞ **Hassler.** At the top of the Spanish Steps, the Hassler has sweeping views of Rome from its front rooms and rooftop restaurant; other rooms overlook the gardens of the Villa Medici. The public rooms have an extravagant 1950s elegance—especially the clubby winter bar, the summer garden bar, and the glass-roof lounge, with gold marble walls and a hand-painted tile floor. Comfortable guest rooms are decorated in a variety of classic styles, some with frescoed walls. The penthouse suite, resplendent with antiques, has a huge terrace. ⊠ *Piazza Trinità dei Monti 6, near Piazza di Spagna 00187* ☎ *06/699340* ᕤ *06/6789991* ⊕ *www.lhw.com* ᕥ *85 rooms, 15 suites* ⌂ *Restaurant, in-room safes, minibars, cable TV, gym, hair salon, bar, laundry service, concierge, parking (fee), no-smoking rooms* ▭ *AE, DC, MC, V* ⌾ *EP.*

$$$$ ▦ **Hotel Art.** Via Margutta has historically been an artists' haunt, so it's fitting that the Hotel Art, opened in 2002, is a favorite of creative types. In the futuristic lobby the concierge and check-in staff are stationed within glowing white pods, and the café/bar retains the arched ceiling from its days as a chapel. The four floors of rooms are identified by corridor color (yellow, green, orange, and blue). The color scheme is reflected in the rooms' bathroom tiles, but otherwise, the interiors are all the same: parquet floors, high-quality linens, clean lines, all in a neutral palette. A central courtyard is a good lounging spot in warmer months. ⊠ *Via Margutta 56, near Piazza di Spagna 00187* ☎ *06/328711* ᕤ *06/36003995* ⊕ *www.hotelart.it* ᕥ *46 rooms and suites* ⌂ *In-room safes, minibars, cable TV, gym, bar* ▭ *AE, DC, MC, V* ⌾ *EP.*

$$$$ ▦ **Hotel de Russie.** In the 19th century this historic hotel counted Russian princes among its guests. Later Picasso and Cocteau leaned out the windows to pick oranges from the trees in the terraced garden, a lush oasis just a few steps from Piazza del Popolo. Famed hotelier Sir Rocco Forte has restored the de Russie to a superlative standard of accommodations and service. Rooms are in chic Italian contemporary style, with Roman mosaic motifs in bathrooms. Many have garden views, and several suites have panoramic terraces. The spa is luxurious. ⊠ *Via del Babuino 9, near Piazza di Spagna 00187* ☎ *06/328881* ᕤ *06/32888888* ⊕ *www.rfhotels.com* ᕥ *130 rooms, 27 suites* ⌂ *Restaurant, in-room safes, minibars, cable TV, health club, hair salon, spa, bar* ▭ *AE, DC, MC, V* ⌾ *EP.*

$$$$ ▦ **The Inn at the Spanish Steps.** The name of this small, exclusive hotel tells it all. Staying here is like having your own little place on fabled Via Condotti, the elegant shopping street crowned by the Spanish Steps. The hotel occupies the upper floors of a centuries-old palazzo it shares with historic Caffè Greco. Rooms, all junior suites, are handsomely decorated with damask fabrics and antiques. ⊠ *Via Condotti 85, near Piazza di Spagna 00187* ☎ *06/69925657* ᕤ *06/6786470* ⊕ *www.atspanishsteps. com* ᕥ *22 rooms* ⌂ *In-room safes, minibars, cable TV, airport shuttle, no-smoking rooms* ▭ *AE, DC, MC, V* ⌾ *BP.*

★ **$$–$$$$** ▦ **Locarno.** Art aficionados and people in the cinema have long appreciated this hotel's preserved fin de siècle charm, intimate feel, and central location off Piazza del Popolo. Wallpaper and fabric prints are coordinated in the rooms, and some rooms have antiques. Everything is lovingly supervised by the owners, a mother-daughter duo. The buffet breakfast is ample, there's bar service on the panoramic roof garden, and complimentary bicycles are available if you feel like braving the traffic. ⊠ *Via della Penna 22, near Piazza di Spagna 00186* ☎ *06/3610841* ᕤ *06/3215249* ᕥ *64 rooms, 2 suites* ⌂ *Restaurant, in-room* *data ports, in-room safes, minibars, cable TV, bar, laundry service, no-smoking rooms* ▭ *AE, DC, MC, V* ⊕ *www.hotellocarno.com* ⓘⓞⓘ *BP.*

$$$ ⓘⓘ **Carriage.** The Carriage's location is its main appeal: it's two blocks from the Spanish Steps, in the heart of Rome. The decor of subdued baroque accents, richly colored wallpaper, and antique reproductions lends a touch of elegance. Some furniture has seen better days, and rooms can be pint-size, but several have small terraces. A roof garden adds to the appeal. ⊠ *Via delle Carrozze 36, near Piazza di Spagna 00187* ☎ *06/6990124* 🖷 *06/6788279* ⊕ *www.hotelcarriage.net* ⤳ *24 rooms, 3 suites* ▭ *AE, DC, MC, V* ⓘⓞⓘ *BP.*

$ ⓘⓘ **Margutta.** For location, good value, and friendly owner-managers, the Margutta is outstanding. The lobby and halls in this small hotel are unassuming, but rooms are a pleasant surprise, with a clean and airy look, attractive wrought-iron bedsteads, and modern baths. Three rooms have private terraces. Though it's in an old building, there's an elevator. The location is on a quiet side street between the Spanish Steps and Piazza del Popolo. ⊠ *Via Laurina 34, near Piazza di Spagna 00187* ☎ *06/ 3223674* 🖷 *06/3200395* ⤳ *24 rooms* ⚴ *Cable TV, Internet* ▭ *AE, DC, MC, V* ⓘⓞⓘ *BP.*

$ ⓘⓘ **Panda.** This is one of the best deals in the neighborhood, particularly remarkable given that the neighborhood is Via della Croce, one of Piazza di Spagna's chic shopping streets. Guest rooms are outfitted in terracotta and wrought iron; they're smallish, but quiet, thanks to double-glazed windows, and spotlessly clean. Pay even less by sharing a bath—in low season, you may have it to yourself anyway. ⊠ *Via della Croce 35, Piazza di Spagna 00187* ☎ *06/6780179* 🖷 *69942151* ⤳ *20 rooms, 14 with bath* ⚴ *No a/c in some rooms, no room TVs* ▭ *MC, V* ⓘⓞⓘ *BP.*

Trastevere

$–$$ ⓘⓘ **Hotel Santa Maria.** The rooms at this lovely former convent off of a small street behind Piazza Santa Maria in Trastevere are all ground-floor, surrounding a pebbled interior courtyard shaded by orange trees. Large double beds are covered in cream-color comforters, the floors are terra-cotta tiles, and the bathrooms are clean and bright, each with a shower/tub. In fair weather, breakfast or a drink in the courtyard is a real treat, with a backdrop of old Trastevere that seems more opera set than reality. ⊠ *Vicolo del Piede 2, Trastevere 00153* ☎ *06/5894626* 🖷 *06/5894815* ⊕ *www.htlsantamaria.com* ⤳ *18 rooms, 2 suites* ⚴ *In-room safes, minibars, cable TV, bar* ▭ *AE, DC, MC, V* ⓘⓞⓘ *BP.*

$ ⓘⓘ **Hotel Trastevere House.** Close to the pizzerias and bars of Viale Trastevere, yet off the beaten path in an 18th-century house tucked away on a tiny street, this bed-and-breakfast is a find. The cozy rooms are done in traditional dark wood and deep blue fabric, with wood-beam ceilings and terra-cotta floors. The owners have another hotel, Domus Tiberina, around the corner, complete with a suite with balcony. ⊠ *Vicolo del Buco 7, Trastevere 00153* ☎☎ *06/5883774* ⊕ *www. trasteverehouse.it* ⤳ *10 rooms, 7 with bath* ⚴ *Cable TV; no a/c* ▭ *MC, V* ⓘⓞⓘ *BP.*

Piazza Navona

$$$$ ⊞ **Raphaël.** This may be Rome's most fascinating hotel. The location is perfect—tucked away behind Piazza Navona—and the vine-covered facade creates a feeling of cozy mystery. The extensive lobby features an array of sculpture, genuine antiques, and original Picasso ceramics. Each room is uniquely decorated with its own treasures, and bathrooms are finished with travertine marble or hand-painted tiles. The two-level Bramante Terrace, where guests can arrange to have meals, has great city views. Some suites have private terraces. ⊠ *Largo Febo 2, near Piazza Navona 00186* ☎ *06/682831* 🖷 *06/6878993* ⊕ *www.raphaelhotel. com* ⟿ *51 rooms, 7 suites, 10 apartments* ♧ *Restaurant, cable TV, gym, sauna, bar, Internet, laundry services, parking (fee)* ⊟ *AE, DC, MC, V* ⦿ *EP.*

$$ ⊞ **Abruzzi.** Rarely do magnificent views of world-famous ancient monuments come so cheap. From the windows of this old-fashioned little establishment the Pantheon is literally in your face. Unfortunately, the facilities also recall a Rome of yesteryear: sink in the room, bathroom down the hall (some higher-price rooms have a private bath). But the rooms are clean, many have recently been redone, and the beds are comfortable. To make your reservation, you have to send a signed traveler's check with the name of the hotel also on it. ⊠ *Piazza della Rotonda 69, near Pantheon 00186* ☎ *06/6792021* 🖷 *06/69788076* ⊕ *www. hotelabruzzi.it* ⟿ *26 rooms, 15 with bath* ♧ *In-room safes, minibars, cable TV* ⊟ *AE, MC, V* ⦿ *BP.*

★ **$$** ⊞ **Cesàri.** The exterior of this intimate hotel on a traffic-free street is as it was when Stendhal stayed here in the 1800s. Inside, the cream-color walls are embellished with old prints of Rome and soft-green drapes and bedspreads, creating an air of comfort and serenity. Bathrooms are done in smart two-tone blue marble. ⊠ *Via di Pietra 89a, near Pantheon 00186* ☎ *06/6749701* 🖷 *06/67497030* ⟿ *47 rooms* ♧ *Cable TV, parking (fee)* ⊟ *AE, DC, MC, V* ⦿ *BP.*

★ **$$** ⊞ **Santa Chiara.** Three historic buildings form this gracious hotel behind the Pantheon. It has been in the same family for 200 years, and the personal attention shows in meticulously decorated and maintained lounges and rooms. Each room has built-in oak headboards, a marble-top desk, and an elegant travertine bath. Double-glazed windows look out over the Piazza della Minerva. There are three apartments, for two to five people, with full kitchens. ⊠ *Via Santa Chiara 21, near Pantheon 00186* ☎ *06/6872979* 🖷 *06/6873144* ⊕ *www.albergosantachiara.com* ⟿ *100 rooms, 4 suites, 3 apartments* ♧ *Cable TV, some kitchenettes, bar* ⊟ *AE, DC, MC, V* ⦿ *BP.*

$–$$ ⊞ **Coronet.** This small hotel occupies part of a floor in one wing of the vast Palazzo Doria Pamphilj; seven interior rooms overlook the family's lovely private garden court. Don't expect palatial ambience, but antique-style molding in the carpeted halls and beam ceilings in several rooms do lend a historic air. The good-size rooms have oldish baths, some very small. Several rooms can accommodate three or four beds. ⊠ *Piazza Grazioli 5, near Piazza Venezia 00186* ☎ *06/6792341* 🖷 *06/69922705* ⊕ *www. hotelcoronet.com* ⟿ *13 rooms, 10 with bath* ⊟ *AE, MC, V* ⦿ *BP.*

¢ 🔲 **Fraterna Domus.** Situated on a byway near Piazza Navona, this guest-house is run by nuns who do not wear religious habits. Rooms are spar-tan but have the essentials, including small private bathrooms. Meals are hearty and inexpensive, and the curfew is 11 PM. ⊠ *Vicolo del Leonetto 16, Piazza Navona 00186* ☎ *06/68802727* 🖷 *06/6832691* ⤶ *20 rooms* ⚌ *No a/c in some rooms, no room TVs* ☰ *DC, MC, V.* �‖ *BP.*

San Pietro

$$$–$$$$ 🔲 **Atlante Star.** The lush rooftop-terrace garden café and the restaurant of this comfortable hotel near St. Peter's have a knockout view of the basilica and the rest of Rome. In a distinguished 19th-century building, the rooms are attractively decorated with striped silks and prints for an old-world atmosphere; many bathrooms have hot tubs. The friendly fam-ily management is attentive to guests' needs and takes pride in offering extra-virgin olive oil from its own trees in the country. A sister hotel, the Atlante Garden, just around the corner, has larger rooms at slightly lower rates. ⊠ *Via Vitelleschi 34, near San Pietro 00193* ☎ *06/6873233* 🖷 *06/6872300* ⊕ *www.atlantehotels.com* ⤶ *65 rooms, 10 suites* ⚌ *Restaurant, in-room safes, minibars, cable TV, bar, laundry service, concierge, parking (fee), no-smoking rooms* ☰ *AE, DC, MC, V* �‖ *BP.*

$$$–$$$$ 🔲 **Giulio Cesare.** An aristocratic town house with a garden in the resi-dential but central Prati district, the Giulio Cesare is a 10-minute walk across the Tiber from Piazza del Popolo. It's beautifully run, with a friendly staff and a quietly luxurious air. The rooms are elegantly furnished, with chandeliers, thick rugs, floor-length drapes, and rich damasks in soft col-ors. Public rooms have Oriental carpets, old prints and paintings, mar-ble fireplaces, and a grand piano. The buffet breakfast is a veritable banquet. ⊠ *Via degli Scipioni 287, near San Pietro 00192* ☎ *06/3210751* 🖷 *06/3211736* ⤶ *90 rooms* ⚌ *Dining room, in-room safes, minibars, cable TV, Internet* ☰ *AE, DC, MC, V* �‖ *BP.*

★ $$$ 🔲 **Farnese.** A late-19th-century mansion, the Farnese is near the metro and within walking distance of St. Peter's. Furnished with great atten-tion to detail in belle-epoque style, it has an intimate atmosphere, daz-zling modern baths, lively fresco decorations, and a roof garden. ⊠ *Via Alessandro Farnese 30, near San Pietro 00192* ☎ *06/3212553* 🖷 *06/3215129* ⤶ *23 rooms* ⚌ *Minibars, cable TV, bar, laundry service, con-cierge, free parking* ☰ *AE, DC, MC, V* �‖ *EP.*

$$–$$$ 🔲 **Residenza Paolo VI.** Inside the Vatican walls, the Paolo VI (pro-nounced Paolo Sesto, Italian for Pope Paul VI) is a convenient base for seeing St. Peter's and the Vatican sights. Rooms in this former monastery are a little sterile, with simple furniture and marble floors, but they're balanced out by a wonderful roof terrace with a view of the basilica. Breakfast is an American-style buffet. ⊠ *Via Paolo VI 29, near San Pietro 00193* ☎ *06/68134108* 🖷 *06/6867428* ⊕ *www.residenzapaolovi.com* ⤶ *29 rooms* ⚌ *In-room safes, minibars, cable TV, bar, laundry service, parking (fee), no-smoking rooms* ☰ *AE, D, MC, V* �‖ *BP.*

$$ 🔲 **Sant'Anna.** An example of the gentrification of the picturesque old Borgo neighborhood in the shadow of St. Peter's, this fashionable small hotel

has ample bedrooms done in art deco style. The frescoes in the breakfast room and fountain in the courtyard are typical Roman touches. The spacious attic rooms have tiny terraces. ⊠ *Borgo Pio 134, near San Pietro 00193* ☎ *06/68801602* ⊟ *06/68308717* ⊕ *www.hotelsantanna.com* ⇌ *20 rooms* ⬧ *Minibars, cable TV, parking (fee)* ⊟ *AE, DC, MC, V* ¶⊙¶ *BP.*

¢ ⊞ **San Giuseppe della Montagna.** This convent is just outside the Vatican walls, near the entrance to the Vatican Museums. Some of the guest rooms have three beds and all have private bathrooms. There's no curfew; guests are given keys. ⊠ *Viale Vaticano 87, near San Pietro 00165* ☎ *06/39723807* ⊟ *06/39721048* ⇌ *15 rooms* ⬧ *No a/c, no room TVs* ⊟ *No credit cards* ¶⊙¶ *BP.*

Termini & Via Nazionale

★ **$$$$** ⊞ **Exedra.** If asked to define "luxury hotel," you might simply answer "the Exedra." When it opened in December 2002 it transformed a dilapidated piazza into a vibrant center. A red carpet leads to the entrance, where an attentive staff tends to your every need. Rooms are spacious, with high ceilings and chandeliers, king-size beds, soft carpets, and richly colored marble in the bathrooms. There's a rooftop terrace with a pool and bar, and a world-class spa. Construction of the hotel unearthed additional baths of Diocletian, on view under glass. ⊠ *Piazza della Repubblica 47, near VIa Nazionale 00185* ☎ *06/489381* ⊟ *06/48938000* ⊕ *www.boscolohotels.com* ⇌ *240 rooms* ⬧ *3 restaurants, in-room safes, minibars, cable TV, 2 bars, babysitting, dry cleaning, laundry service, concierge, Internet, meeting rooms, parking (fee), no-smoking rooms* ⊟ *AE, DC, MC, V* ¶⊙¶ *EP.*

$$$–$$$$ ⊞ **Mascagni.** Outside is one of Rome's busiest, most central streets, but not a sound filters into the interior of this elegant establishment. It has a cheerful staff and the particular charm of a small hotel. Decorated in early 1920s style, it has handsome mahogany furnishings and coordinated fabrics. The intimate lounges and pleasant bar follow the same decorating scheme, as does the breakfast room, where a lavish buffet is laid in the morning. Discounted rates can be a good deal, so be sure to ask. ⊠ *Via Vittorio Emanuele Orlando 90, near Via Nazionale 00185* ☎ *06/48904040* ⊟ *06/4817487* ⊕ *www.hotelmascagni.com* ⇌ *40 rooms* ⬧ *In-room safes, minibars, cable TV, bar, laundry service, concierge, business services, parking (fee), no-smoking rooms* ⊟ *AE, DC, MC, V* ¶⊙¶ *BP.*

$$$ ⊞ **Britannia.** You'll find here a very special small hotel. The attention
Fodor'sChoice to detail of owner Pier Paolo Biorgi is evident in every corner, from the
★ frescoed halls to the breakfast room. Each guest room has a unique layout and is furnished with cozy fabrics and original artwork, as well as a marble bathroom with a heat lamp. The caring management provides such amenities as English-language dailies and local weather reports delivered to your room each morning. The light-filled rooftop suite opens onto a private terrace. ⊠ *Via Napoli 64, near Via Nazionale 00184* ☎ *06/ 4883153* ⊟ *06/4882343* ⊕ *www.hotelbritannia.it* ⇌ *32 rooms, 1 suite* ⬧ *In-room safes, minibars, cable TV, bar, laundry service, free parking* ⊟ *AE, DC, MC, V* ¶⊙¶ *BP.*

$$ ⌨ **Montreal.** On a central avenue across the square from Santa Maria Maggiore, only three blocks from Stazione Termini, the compact Montreal occupies three floors of an older building. It's been totally renovated and offers fresh-looking, though small, rooms. The owner-managers are pleasant and helpful, and the neighborhood has plenty of reasonably priced restaurants. ⊠ *Via Carlo Alberto 4, near Termini 00185* ☎ *06/4457797* 🖷 *06/4465522* ⊕ *www.hotelmontrealroma.com* 🛏 *27 rooms* ⚘ *In-room safes, minibars, cable TV, parking (fee)* ▤ *AE, DC, MC, V* ⦿ *BP.*

$-$$ ⌨ **Des Artistes.** The three personable Riccioni brothers have transformed their hotel into one of the best in the Termini Station neighborhood in its price range, lavishing it with paintings, handsome furnishings in mahogany, attractive fabrics, and marble baths. There's a floor with 10 simpler rooms for travelers on a budget. ⊠ *Via Villafranca 20, near Termini 00185* ☎ *06/4454365* 🖷 *06/4462368* ⊕ *www.hoteldesartistes.com* 🛏 *40 rooms, 27 with bath* ⚘ *In-room data ports, in-room safes, minibars, cable TV, bar, concierge, parking (fee); no a/c in some rooms, no smoking* ▤ *AE, DC, MC, V* ⦿ *BP.*

$-$$ ⌨ **Hotel Venezia.** It's unusual to find a low-price hotel in Rome that's this *pretty*—16th-century wood tables and sideboards set off by cozy matching armchairs and tapestries give the public areas the feel of an elegant country house (in miniature). Guest rooms are somewhat simpler but still a cut above those of other hotels in this price range. They even offer a "pillow menu"—you can select the type of pillow you want to sleep on. The location is a few blocks from Termini. ⊠ *Via Varese 18, near Termini 00185* ☎ *06/4457101* 🖷 *06/4957687* ⊕ *www. hotelvenezia.com* 🛏 *60 rooms* ⚘ *In-room safes, minibars, cable TV; no a/c in some rooms* ▤ *AE, D, MC, V* ⦿ *BP.*

$-$$ ⌨ **Morgana.** Step into the richly marbled lobby and comfortable lounges (smoking and no-smoking) with antique accents, and experience elegance at its most cordial. Rooms are decorated with fine fabrics and plush carpeting. The location is convenient to the Stazione Termini. ⊠ *Via Filippo Turati 33, near Termini 00185* ☎ *06/4467230* 🖷 *06/4469142* ⊕ *www.hotelmorgana.com* 🛏 *103 rooms, 2 suites* ⚘ *In-room safes, minibars, cable TV, bar, laundry service, concierge, no-smoking rooms* ▤ *AE, DC, MC, V* ⦿ *BP.*

$ ⌨ **Adler.** This tiny pensione run by the same family for more than three decades provides a comfortable stay on a quiet street near the station for a very good price. Ideal for families, the Adler has six spacious rooms that sleep three, four, or five, as well as a single and a double. Rooms are basic but impeccably clean (owner Serena Biancalana sees to that). Worn but cozy chairs line the lobby, and in summer, breakfast can be taken on the leafy courtyard balcony. ⊠ *Via Modena 5, near Termini 00184* ☎ *06/484466* 🖷 *06/4880940* 🛏 *8 rooms* ⚘ *Cable TV, bar* ▤ *AE, DC, MC, V* ⦿ *BP.*

$ ⌨ **Tempio di Pallade.** This small hotel near Porta Maggiore is one of the best deals in its class. Rooms are simple but elegant, done in blue and gold with all basic amenities and private baths. The Ranieri siblings will be happy to make arrangements for you, from airport taxis to tours of the city to opera tickets. Triples and quads are available on request. ⊠ *Via Giolitti 425-427 near Termini 00185* ☎ *06/70451521* 🖷 *06/70452758*

⊕ *www.hoteltempiodipallade.com* ⤴ *50 rooms* ♻ *In-room safes, minibars, cable TV, concierge* ▭ *AE, DC, MC, V* ⦿ *BP.*

★ ¢ 🖭 **The Beehive.** Linda Martinez-Bremmer and Steve Bremmer are the friendly American couple who run this funky B&B, as well as apartment rentals, a few blocks from Termini Station. Rooms are bright, clean, and include ultramodern furniture and colorful artwork. One hostel-style room with eight bunk beds costs a mere 20 euros per person. In the communal kitchen, guests can socialize, make drinks, and surf the Web. There's free concierge service—while they book you a table for dinner you can sit in the lobby and wonder how something so good can cost so little. ⊠ *Via Marghera 8, near Termini 00185* ☎ *06/44704553* ⊕ *www.the-beehive.com* ⤴ *9 rooms, 10 rooms in apartments* ♻ *Internet, concierge; no a/c, no room TVs* ▭ *No credit cards* ⦿ *EP.*

Via Veneto

★ $$$$ 🖭 **Aleph.** The newest addition to Rome's high-end boutique hotels, the Aleph plays with themes of heaven and hell through Adam Tihany's playful design. The rooms are done in whimsical, modern Venetian style, in cream and deep blue with touches of black and white (full-wall photo blow-ups, furniture) and Murano-glass light fixtures. But it's the common areas that define the place: lusty red interiors in the library, the Angel lobby bar, the sushi bar, and the seafood restaurant, Maremoto. ⊠ *Via San Basilio 15, near Via Veneto 00187* ☎ *06/422901* 🖷 *06/42290000* ⊕ *www.boscolohotels.com* ⤴ *94 rooms, 2 suites* ♻ *Restaurant, in-room safes, minibars, cable TV, gym, spa, bar, laundry service, concierge, Internet, no-smoking rooms* ▭ *AE, DC, MC, V* ⦿ *EP.*

★ $$$$ 🖭 **Eden.** A superlative hotel that combines dashing elegance and stunning vistas of Rome with the warmth of Italian hospitality, the Eden was once a preferred haunt of Hemingway, Ingrid Bergman, and Federico Fellini. Antiques, sumptuous Italian fabrics, linen sheets, and marble baths are the essence of good taste. Views from the rooftop bar and terrace will take your breath away, and the hotel's top-floor restaurant, La Terrazza dell'Eden, merits raves, too. ⊠ *Via Ludovisi 49, near Via Veneto 00187* ☎ *06/478121* 🖷 *06/4821584* ⊕ *www.hotel-eden.it* ⤴ *112 rooms, 14 suites* ♻ *Restaurant, in-room safes, minibars, cable TV, gym, bar, laundry service, concierge, parking (fee), no-smoking rooms* ▭ *AE, DC, MC, V* ⦿ *EP.*

$$$$ 🖭 **Rose Garden Palace.** Tucked away behind the American Embassy, this elegant hotel is a marriage of the classic (marble floors, velvet sofas, patterned curtains) and the contemporary (clean lines, modern furniture). Guest rooms are done in calming tones of beige, slate blue, and terracotta. A state-of-the-art fitness room, pool, and sauna/steam room located below ground are small but perfect. Friday nights, jazz musicians play in the bar, and in warm weather the bar opens onto the namesake rose garden. ⊠ *Via Boncompagni 19, 00187* ☎ *06/421741* 🖷 *06/4815608* ⊕ *www.rosegardenpalace.com* ⤴ *59 rooms, 6 suites* ♻ *Restaurant, in-room safes, minibars, cable TV, indoor pool, gym, spa, bar, meeting rooms, parking (fee), no-smoking rooms* ▭ *AE, DC, MC, V* ⦿ *BP.*

$$$$ 🏨 **Westin Excelsior.** Next door to the American Embassy, the Excelsior is the hotel of choice for visiting diplomats, celebrities—and American business conferences. It's of the breed of old-fashion hotels that put the *luxe* in deluxe: every corner is lavished with mirrors, moldings, Oriental rugs, crystal chandeliers, and huge, baroque floral arrangements. Guest rooms have elegant drapery, marble baths, top-quality linens, and big, firm beds. ⊠ *Via Veneto 125 00187* ☎ *06/47081* 🖷 *06/4826205* ⊕ *www.westin.com/excelsiorrome* ⤵ *286 rooms, 35 suites* ⚴ *Restaurant, in-room safes, minibars, cable TV, indoor pool, gym, bar, laundry service, concierge, no-smoking rooms* ⊟ *AE, DC, MC, V* ⥮ *EP.*

★ **$$** 🏨 **La Residenza.** Mainly Americans frequent this cozy hotel in a converted town house near Via Veneto. Rooms are basic and comfortable (although single rooms are windowless), but the real charm of the hotel is found in its bar, terrace, and lounges (smoking and no-smoking) adorned with warm wallpaper and love seats. Rates include a generous American-style buffet breakfast and an in-house movie every night. ⊠ *Via Emilia 22, near Via Veneto 00187* ☎ *06/4880789* 🖷 *06/485721* ⊕ *www.thegiannettihotelsgroup.com* ⤵ *28 rooms* ⚴ *In-room safes, minibars, cable TV, bar, laundry service* ⊟ *AE, MC, V* ⥮ *BP.*

Beyond the City Center

$$$$ 🏨 **Cavalieri Hilton.** Though the Cavalieri is outside the city center, distance has its advantages, one of them being the magnificent view from the hotel's hilltop position (ask for a room facing the city). This hotel is an oasis of quiet good taste with a distinctive Italian flair. If you can tear yourself away from the gardens and pools, a courtesy shuttle bus to downtown Rome leaves every hour. Don't miss the acclaimed rooftop restaurant, La Pergola. ⊠ *Via Cadlolo 101, Monte Mario 00136* ☎ *06/35091* 🖷 *06/35092241* ⊕ *www.cavalieri-hilton.com* ⤵ *357 rooms, 17 suites* ⚴ *2 restaurants, cable TV, tennis court, 2 pools (1 indoor), health club, hair salon, spa, bar* ⊟ *AE, DC, MC, V* ⥮ *EP.*

★ **$$$–$$$$** 🏨 **Castello della Castelluccia.** Just 10 miles from the hustle and bustle of Rome's city center, this beautifully renovated 12th-century castle is an oasis of calm set in a small wooded park. The original structure has been preserved intact, complete with crumbling watchtower (now a three-level suite); all that's missing is a medieval knight clinking down the echoing stone halls. Guest rooms are luxuriously appointed, with inlaid-wood antiques and four-poster beds; a few have marble fireplaces, and two have giant, tiled hot-tub alcoves. There's shuttle-bus service to central Rome. ⊠ *Via Carlo Cavino, Località La Castelluccia 00123* ☎ *06/30207041* 🖷 *06/30207110* ⊕ *www.lacastelluccia.com* ⤵ *18 rooms, 6 suites* ⚴ *Restaurant, room service, in-room data ports, minibars, cable TV, pool, spa, horseback riding, bar, laundry service, meeting room, free parking, some pets allowed* ⊟ *AE, D, MC, V* ⥮ *BP.*

$$ 🏨 **Crowne Plaza.** Although outside the city center, this Crowne Plaza hotel (refurbished from the original 1972 Holiday Inn structure) is a sprawling, fine-tuned, American-style hotel. It has all the amenities needed for business conferences, but it's also great for families and vacationers who want to be surrounded by greenery. The luxurious Saturnia Spa has all the services you might require to unwind, with a modern gym, exercise classes, and indoor and outdoor pools. The rooms are comfortable and spacious, with two double beds qualifying as a double room: a breath of fresh air in often-cramped European quarters. ⊠ *Via Aurelia Antica 415, outside San Pietro 00165* ☎ *06/66420* 🖷 *06/6637190* ⊕ *www. crowneplaza.com/rome-stpeters* 🛏 *321 rooms* ⚬ *2 restaurants, in-room safes, minibars, cable TV, 4 tennis courts, 2 pools (1 indoor) health club, spa, piano bar, shop, Internet, convention center, airport shuttle, free parking, no-smoking rooms* ⊟ *AE, DC, MC, V* ⏐◯⏐ *BP.*

NIGHTLIFE & THE ARTS

The Arts

Updated by
Dana Klitzberg

Rome lacks the culture of some of Italy's other cities, but it is the capital, and so various offerings from the worlds of music, dance, theater, and film are to be found. Trends and performance offerings change constantly, so the best way to take stock of the leisure activities at hand is to consult one of the local publications devoted to the subject. You'll find comprehensive listings in English, along with handy bus and metro information, in the back of the weekly *roma c'è* booklet. A new issue is on sale at newsstands every Wednesday. The monthly *Time Out Roma* gives comprehensive event schedules as well as editors' picks; listings are mainly in Italian (with a small summary in English) but are easy to decipher. Schedules of events are also published in daily newspapers; pick up *Trovaroma,* the weekly entertainment guide published in Italian every Thursday as a supplement to the daily newspaper *La Repubblica.* The monthly *Where* magazine is distributed free at hotels and restaurants. An English-language biweekly, *Wanted in Rome,* is sold at central newsstands and has good listings of events.

Dance

The **Rome Opera Ballet** performs at the **Teatro dell'Opera** (⊠ Piazza Beniamino Gigli 8, near Termini ☎ 06/481601, 06/48160255 tickets), often with international guest stars. Rome is sporadically visited by classical ballet and modern dance companies from Russia, the United States, and Europe; performances are at the Teatro dell'Opera, **Teatro Olimpico** (⊠ Piazza Gentile da Fabriano 17, Stadio Olimpico ☎ 06/3265991), or one of the open-air venues in summer. Small dance companies from Italy and abroad perform in various places; check concert listings for details.

Film

A few theaters in the center reserve one night a week for original-language movies: check listings in *roma c'è*. Tickets range in price from €4.50 for matinees and some weeknights up to €8 for weekend evenings. The three-screen **Pasquino** (⊠ Piazza Sant'Egidio 10, near Trastevere ☎ 06/5815208) shows exclusively original-language films, mainly in English. The **Metropolitan** (⊠ Via del Corso 7, near Piazza di Spagna ☎ 06/32600500) has four screens, with one dedicated to English-language films from September to June; its location just off Piazza del Popolo makes it convenient for a post-shopping rest. The five-screen **Warner Village Mod-**

erno (⊠ Piazza della Repubblica 45–46, near Termini ☎ 06/47779202) is convenient to the train station.

Music

CLASSICAL There's a wide variety of classical music concerts held at numerous venues large and small throughout Rome, including churches. Christmastime, in particular, is a busy concert season in Rome. Depending on the venue, tickets run from about €8 to €30. Rome's brand new state-of-the-art **Auditorium-Parco della Musica** (⊠ Via de Coubertin 15, Flaminio ☎ 06/80241350 ⊕ www.musicaperroma.it), a 10-minute tram ride from Piazza del Popolo, has three halls with excellent acoustics and a large courtyard used for concerts and other events. Of the larger classical music companies, one principal concert series is organized year-round by the **Accademia di Santa Cecilia** (Concert hall and box office ⊠ Via della Conciliazione 4, near San Pietro ☎ 06/684391). In summer the Accademia moves into one of the most spectacular and enchanting outdoor stages in the world, the ancient **Terme di Caracalla** (⊠ Via delle Terme di Caracalla 52). The **Accademia Filarmonica Romana** (⊠ Via Flaminia 118, near Stadio Olimpico ☎ 06/3201752, 06/3265991 tickets) has concerts at the Teatro Olimpico. **Istituzione Universitaria dei Concerti** (⊠ Aula Magna, Piazzale Aldo Moro 5, near San Lorenzo ☎ 06/3610051) offers small concerts with music ranging from swing to Bach. The internationally respected **Oratorio del Gonfalone series** (⊠ Via del Gonfalone 32/a, Campo de' Fiori ☎ 06/6875952) focuses on baroque music. **Il Tempietto** (☎ 06/87131590 ⊕ www.tempietto.it) organizes classical music concerts indoors in winter and in the atmospheric settings of Teatro Marcello and Villa Torlonia in summer.

Many small concert groups perform in cultural centers and churches, and many such concerts are free, including all performed in Catholic churches, where a special ruling permits only religious music. Look for posters outside churches announcing concerts, particularly at the church of **Sant'Ignazio** (⊠ Piazza Sant'Ignazio, near Pantheon ☎ 06/6794560), which often hosts concerts in a spectacularly frescoed setting.

ROCK, POP & Pop, jazz, and world music concerts are frequent, especially in sum-
JAZZ mer, although even performances by big-name stars may not be well advertised. Many of the bigger-name acts perform outside the center, so it's worth asking about transportation *before* you buy your tickets. Tickets for major events are usually handled by **Orbis** (⊠ Piazza Esquilino 37, near Santa Maria Maggiore ☎ 06/4744776). **Box Office** (⊠ Viale Giulio Cesare 88, near San Pietro ☎ 06/37500375) sells concert tickets from Monday to Saturday. **Hello Ticket** (⊠ Termini station ☎ 06/47825710) sells tickets to concerts as well as theater and other cultural events.

Opera

Rome's opera season runs from November or December to May, and performances are staged in the **Teatro dell'Opera** (⊠ Piazza Beniamino Gigli 8, Termini ☎ 06/481601, 06/48160255 tickets). Prices range from about €16 to €120 for regular performances; they can go much higher for an opening night or an appearance by an internationally acclaimed guest singer. Standards may not always measure up to those set by Milan's fabled La Scala, but, despite strikes and shortages of funds, most performances are respectable. In summer the Teatro dell'Opera stages performances in various outdoor venues, such as Piazza del Popolo. Small, private companies hold sporadic performances of the classics in venues ranging from school auditoriums to church courtyards. **New Mendelflor Music** (☎ 06/21707618) usually has something in production.

Theater

Rome offers various theater performances throughout the year in Italian, English, and several other languages, depending upon who is sponsoring the performance. The beautiful and recently refurbished **Teatro Argentina** (✉ Largo Argentina 52, Campo de' Fiori ☎ 06/68804601) is a well-regarded center for important productions and festivals. The nearby **Teatro Valle** (✉ Via del Teatro Valle 23A ☎ 06/68803794) hosts performances of the same caliber as its neighbor, Teatro Argentina, but often with a more experimental bent, particularly during its fall season. For comic theater in English, check out **The Miracle Players,** a group of English-speaking actors who write and produce free public performances every summer in the Roman Forum, presenting a perfectly balanced mix of the historical and the hilarious.

Nightlife

La Dolce Vita notwithstanding, Rome's nightlife is not the world's most exciting, though discos, live-music spots, and late-night bars do exist. In keeping with the changing times, the "flavor of the month" factor is at work here, too, and many places fade into oblivion after their 15 minutes of fame. The best sources for an up-to-date list of late-night spots are *roma c'è* and *Where,* but if you'd prefer to see where the night takes you, head to Trastevere or the area around Piazza Navona, both filled with bars, restaurants, and people after dark. In summer, all discos and many bars and music clubs close to beat the heat (although some simply relocate to the beach, where many Romans spend their summer nights). The city-sponsored Estate Romana (Rome Summer) festival takes over, lighting up hot city nights with concerts, bars, and discos, all in the open air. Pick up the Roma Estate event guide at newsstands.

Bars

English- and Irish-style pubs have long been a prominent part of the bar scene in Rome, among Italians and foreigners alike. **Trinity College** (✉ Via del Collegio Romano 6, near Piazza Venezia ☎ 06/6786472) is one such drinking hall. **Sloppy Sam's** (✉ Campo de' Fiori 10 ☎ 06/68802637) is an American-run outpost on one of the city's busiest piazzas. Look for happy-hour specials and student discounts.

So where do you go for a cocktail? **Bar della Pace** (✉ Via della Pace 5, near Piazza Navona ☎ 06/6861216) has been the chic people-watching cocktail bar of choice since time immemorial. **Bar del Fico** (⊠ Piazza del Fico 26, near Piazza Navona ☎ 06/6865205) is a bustling, authentically Roman alternative to Bar della Pace around the corner, but expect huge crowds on weekend and summer nights. For a trendy, sophisticated scene, try **BarBar** (⊠ Via Crescenzio 18, near San Pietro), a lounge with ambient music and a cigar room. Quarters are cramped, but **Taverna del Campo** (⊠ Campo de' Fiori 16 ☎ 06/6874402) has music and tasty hors d'oeuvres. **La Vineria** (⊠ Campo de' Fiori 15 ☎ 06/68803268) is the original bar on a square that's now full of them. It remains the truest example of an old-school Roman enoteca, always in style and great for watching the "scenery."

For that essential predinner aperitivo, head for the buzzing **Friends** (⊠ Piazza Trilussa 34, Trastevere ☎ 06/5816111) across the Tiber from the historic center. **Crudo** (⊠ Via Degli Specchi 6, Campo de' Fiori ☎ 06/6838989 ⊕ www.crudoroma.it) is a spacious, modern, New York–style lounge serving cocktails and *crudo* (raw) nibbles such as sushi and carpaccio. For later in the evening, head to **Stardust** (⊠ Vicolo de' Renzi 4, Trastevere ☎ 06/58320875) for cocktails mixed up by an international bar staff and an ambience provided by eclectic music and local characters.

Music Clubs

Jazz, folk, pop, and Latin-music clubs are flourishing in Rome, particularly in Trastevere and Testaccio. Jazz clubs are especially popular, and talented local groups may be joined by visiting musicians from other countries. As admission, many clubs require that you buy a membership card, often valid for a month, at a cost of €6 and up. On weekend nights it's a good idea to reserve a table in advance no matter where you're going.

Just behind the Vatican Museums, **Alexanderplatz** (⊠ Via Ostia 9, near San Pietro ☎ 06/39742171), Rome's most famous jazz club, has a bar and a restaurant and features live jazz and blues played nightly by both local and internationally known musicians. **La Palma** (⊠ Via Giuseppe Mirri 35, Tiburtina ☎ 06/43599029) is the venue favored by experimental jazz musicians. It's near the Tiburtina metro stop. **Big Mama** (⊠ Vicolo San Francesco a Ripa 18, Trastevere ☎ 06/5812551) presents live blues, R&B, African, jazz, and rock. Latin rhythms are the specialty at **No Stress Brasil** (⊠ Via degli Stradivari 35, Trastevere ☎ 06/5813249), where there's a Brazilian orchestra from Tuesday to Saturday. Monday is karaoke night.

In trendy Testaccio, **Caffè Latino** (⊠ Via Monte Testaccio 96 ☎ 06/57288556) is a vibrant Roman locale that has live music (mainly Latin) almost every night, followed by recorded soul, funk, and '70s and '80s revival; it's closed Monday. **Il Locale** (⊠ Vicolo del Fico 3, near Piazza Navona ☎ 06/6879075), closed Monday, pulls in a lively crowd for Italian rock. **The Place** (⊠ Via Alberico II 27–29, near San Pietro ☎ 06/68307137) offers a mixture of live funk, Latin, and jazz sounds, accompanied by excellent fusion cuisine.

Nightclubs

Most clubs open about 10:30 PM and charge an entrance fee of about €20, which may include the first drink; subsequent drinks cost about €10. Most clubs are closed Monday, and all those listed here close in summer, some opening instead at the beaches of Ostia or Fregene. The liveliest areas for clubs with a younger clientele are the grittier working-class districts of Testaccio and Ostiense. **Gilda** (✉ Via Mario de' Fiori 97, near Piazza di Spagna ☎ 06/6784838) is a longtime favorite with the slightly older rich and the very young for dinner and disco dancing.

★ Jackets are required for men. **Art Café** (✉ Via del Galoppatoio 33, near Piazza di Spagna ☎ 06/36006578) is Rome's disco of the moment; it's large, with multiple levels, and there are theme nights (Tuesday fashion night, Thursday live jazz and dinner, Friday hip-hop), and *privé* (VIP) areas with a wading pool.

One of Rome's first discos, **Piper** (✉ Via Tagliamento 9, near Piazza Fiume ☎ 06/8414459) is still a magnet for young movers and shakers who favor disco and house beats and spectacular light effects. It's open Saturday and Sunday nights only. **Bloom** (✉ Via del Teatro Pace 29, near Piazza Navona ☎ 06/68802029) is a lounge/club in the city center, where Romans and visiting celebrities go to swill cocktails and dance in tight quarters. A young crowd frequents the row of discos on Via di Monte Testaccio. Among them, **Alibi** (✉ Via di Monte Testaccio 39 ☎ 06/5743448) is a multilevel complex that caters to a mixed gay and straight crowd. **Goa** (✉ Via Libetta 13, Testaccio ☎ 06/5748277) is among Rome's trendiest clubs. You can listen to hip-hop, tribal, and house played by some of Europe's most touted DJs. Decor takes its inspiration from Southeast Asia, with incense, exotic artifacts, and slide projections. **Suite** (✉ Via degli Orti di Trastevere 1 ☎ 06/5861888) is an inspired reproduction of a luxurious, futuristic hotel suite. The **Ex Magazzini** (✉ Via dei Magazzini Generali 8 bis, Ostiense ☎ 06/5758040) is a happening disco bar that offers a mix of live and DJ sets and hosts a vintage market on Sunday. The under-25 crowd lets loose to indie rock and weekend live shows at postindustrial **Black Out** (✉ Via Saturnia 18, near San

★ Giovanni ☎ 06/70496791). **La Maison** (✉ Vicolo dei Granari 4, near Piazza Navona ☎ 06/6833312), bedecked in purple velvet and chandeliers, offers two distinct spaces and one main dance floor, with DJs dishing up the latest dance tunes.

SPORTS & THE OUTDOORS

Biking

Updated by
Dana Klitzberg

You can rent a bike at **Collalti** (✉ Via del Pellegrino 82, Campo de' Fiori ☎ 06/68801084), which is also a reliable bike-repair shop; it's closed Monday. **St. Peter Moto** (✉ Via di Porta Castello 43, near San Pietro ☎ 06/6875714) is a good place to rent scooters as well as bikes.

Health Clubs

Day passes at the facilities listed here cost between €26 and €55. The **Roman Sport Center** (✉ Via del Galoppatoio 33, near Via Veneto ☎ 06/

3201667) is a vast full-fledged health club next to the underground parking lot in Villa Borghese; it has two swimming pools, a gym, aerobic workout areas, squash courts, and saunas. **Roman Sport Center 2** (⊠ Largo Somalia 60, Parioli ☎ 06/86212411) is an offshoot with fewer facilities. The **Cavalieri Hilton** (⊠ Via Cadlolo 101, Monte Mario ☎ 06/35091) has a running path on its grounds as well as outdoor and indoor pools, two clay tennis courts, and a luxurious spa, fitness center, and hair salon, all open to nonguests. The **Sheraton Roma** (⊠ Viale del Pattinaggio 100, EUR ☎ 06/54531) has a heated outdoor pool, a tennis court, two squash courts, a sauna, and a fitness center. The **Sheraton Golf** (⊠ Viale Parco de' Medici 167, Magliana ☎ 06/65288) has a fitness center and 27 holes of golf. Four tennis courts, an outdoor swimming pool, sauna, steam room, and a gym are available at the **Crowne Plaza** (⊠ Via Aurelia Antica 415 ☎ 06/66420).

Horseback Riding

There are numerous riding clubs in Rome. The most central is the **Centro Ippico Villa Borghese** (⊠ Via del Galoppatoio 23, near Via Veneto ☎ 06/3200487). **Società Ippica Romana** (⊠ Via Monti della Farnesina 18, near Stadio Olimpico ☎ 06/3240592) was the first riding club to open in Rome, and has large outdoor facilities and excellent instructors. The **International Riding Show,** held in May, draws a stylish crowd to the amphitheater of Piazza di Siena in Villa Borghese. The competition is stiff, and the program features a cavalry charge staged by the dashing mounted corps of the *carabinieri* (military police). Check with the **tourist office** (⊠ Via Parigi 5, Termini ☎ 06/36004399) for details.

Running

The best bet for running in central Rome is the **Villa Borghese,** with an approximately ⅔-km (½-mi) circuit of the Pincio, among the marble statuary. A longer run in the park itself might include a loop around Piazza di Siena, a grass riding arena. Although most traffic is barred from Villa Borghese, government and police cars sometimes speed through. Be careful to stick to the sides of the roads. For a long run away from all traffic, try the hilly and majestic **Villa Ada** in northern Rome, in the upscale Parioli neighborhood. **Villa Doria Pamphilj** on the Janiculum is a beautiful spot for a run south of the city. History-loving runners should do as the chariot horses did and run at the old **Circus Maximus.** A standard oval track open to runners is in the park flanked by the **Via delle Terme di Caracalla.**

Soccer

Italy's favorite spectator sport stirs passionate enthusiasm among partisans. Games are usually held on Sunday afternoons throughout the fall-to-spring season. The two home teams—Roma and Lazio—which are both in Serie A (the top division), play their home games in the **Stadio Olimpico** (⊠ Viale dello Stadio Olimpico ☎ 06/3237333), part of the Foro Italico complex built by Mussolini on the banks of the Tiber. There's a chance of soccer tickets being on sale at the box office at game time, but it's a better idea to buy them in advance from **Lazio Point** (⊠ Via Farini 34, near Termini ☎ 06/4826688) to see the Lazio team play. Go to **Orbis** (⊠ Piazza Esquilino 37, near Termini ☎ 06/4744776) for tickets to see the Roma soccer team.

Swimming

The outdoor pool of the **Cavalieri Hilton** (⊠ Via Cadlolo 101, Monte Mario ☎ 06/35091) is a summertime oasis open to nonguests for a fee of €40 on weekdays, €55 on weekends. A reasonably priced swimming option (€10 per day, €8 after 2 PM) is the **Piscina delle Rose** (⊠ Viale America 20, EUR ☎ 06/5926717), a pleasant outdoor pool in the leafy EUR suburb and only a five-minute walk from the EUR-Laurentina metro stop. The **Roman Sport Center** (⊠ Via del Galoppatoio 33, near Via Veneto ☎ 06/3201667) has two swimming pools. The entrance fee for nonmembers is €26 per day.

Tennis

Rome hosts the Italian Open each May, one of the more important European tournaments on clay courts. It's held at the **Foro Italico** (⊠ Viale dei Gladiatori 31, north Rome ☎ 06/36858218).

SHOPPING

Updated by
Clare Pedrick

They say when in Rome to do as the Romans do—and the Romans love to shop. Shops are generally open from 9 or 9:30 to 1 and from 3:30 or 4 to 7 or 7:30. There's a tendency for shops in central districts to stay open all day, and hours are becoming more flexible throughout the city. Remember that many stores are closed Sunday, though this is changing, too, especially in the city center. With the exception of food stores, most stores also close on Monday morning from September to mid-June and Saturday afternoon from mid-June through August. You can save some money taking advantage of the Tax-Free for Tourists VAT tax refunds, available at most large stores for purchases over €155. Or hit Rome in January and early February or in late July, when stores clean house with the justly famous biannual sales.

Bargains

On **Via Cola di Rienzo** (⊠ Near San Pietro) there are stands selling everything from CDs to handicrafts. The market at **Via Sannio** (⊠ Near San Giovanni in Laterano) features job lots of designer shoes and stalls selling new and used clothing at bargain prices; hours are weekdays 8–2, Saturday 8–5. The market **Borghetto Flaminio** (⊠ Piazza della Marina) sells good-quality vintage clothing on Sunday 9–2. The morning market in **Piazza Testaccio,** in the heart of the neighborhood of the same name, is known for stands selling last season's designer shoes at a third of the original price or less.

Romans and visitors alike flock to the **McArthurGlen Designer Outlet** (⊠ Via Ponte di Piscina Cupa, Castel Romano ☎ 06/5050050 ⊕ www. mcarthurglen.it), 10 km (6 mi) outside the city. Housed in a mock ancient Roman setting, the complex offers more than 90 stores selling major labels at prices 30–70% lower than normal. To get there, get on the Grande Raccordo Anulare ring road, take Exit 26 onto the Via Pontina SS148 toward Pomezia, exit at Castel Romano, and follow the signs. The mall is open daily 10–10.

Rome
Shopping

Department Stores & Malls

Italian department stores have little in common with their American and English cousins; most of them are much smaller and do not carry the same variety of merchandise. Still, they're worth a stop if you're looking for something in a hurry. **Rinascente** (⊠ Via del Corso 189, near Piazza di Trevi ☎ 06/6797691 ⊠ Piazza Fiume, Salario ☎ 06/8841231) sells only clothing and accessories in its main store. Its Piazza Fiume branch has the same stock, plus furniture and housewares. Both stores are open Monday–Saturday 9–9, Sunday 10:30–8. **Coin** (⊠ Piazzale Appio 7, near San Giovanni in Laterano ☎ 06/7080020 ⊠ Via Mantova 1/b Salario ☎ 06/8416279) carries a large and attractive collection of housewares as well as fashions for men and women, and is generally trendier than the other department stores. **Oviesse** (⊠ Via Candia 74, near San Pietro ☎ 06/39743518) offers moderately priced goods ranging from bathing suits to children's clothes. The midrange chain store **UPIM** (⊠ Piazza Santa Maria Maggiore, near Termini ☎ 06/4465579) is an institution in Italy; it sells stylish clothes, bed linen, and kitchenware at reasonable prices. **Cinecittà Due** (⊠ Viale Palmiro Togliatti 2 ☎ 06/7220910) was the first of Rome's several mega-malls, with 100 stores; take Metro A to the Subaugusta or Cinecittà stops.

Markets

All outdoor food markets are open Monday–Saturday from early morning to about 1 PM (a bit later on Saturday), but get there in the early part of the day for the best selection. Beware of pickpockets, and don't go if you can't stand crowds. Downtown Rome's most colorful outdoor food market is at **Campo de' Fiori**, south of Piazza Navona. The **Trionfale market** (⊠ Via Andrea Doria, near San Pietro) is big and bustling; it's about a five-minute walk north of the entrance to the Vatican Museums. There's room for bargaining at the Sunday-morning flea market at **Porta Portese** (⊠ Via Ippolito Nievo, Trastevere); it offers seemingly endless rows of dealers in new and secondhand clothing, bootleg CDs, old furniture, car stereos of suspicious origin, and all manner of old junk. Keep an eye on your wallet—the crowds and the money changing hands draw Rome's most skillful pickpockets.

Shopping Districts

If your shopping list starts with Gucci, Prada, Fendi, and the other big names, start your shopping day at **Piazza di Spagna,** in the vicinity of which are most of fashion's more exclusive shops. **Via Condotti** is the neighborhood's central axis, but you'll find elegant designer clothing and accessories on every block of this area, bordered by Piazza di Spagna on the east, Via del Corso on the west, from Piazza San Silvestro to Via della Croce.

There are so many hole-in-the-wall boutiques selling top-quality merchandise in Rome's center that even just wandering you're sure to find something that catches your eye. Shops along **Via Campo Marzio** and adjoining **Piazza San Lorenzo in Lucina** stock eclectic and high-quality

Via Condotti
Shopping

clothes and accessories, although without the big names and at slightly lower prices. Running from Piazza Venezia to Piazza del Popolo lies **Via del Corso**, the center's main shopping avenue, more than a mile of clothing, shoes, leather goods, and home furnishings from classic to cutting-edge. **Via Cola di Rienzo**, across the Tiber from Piazza del Popolo, has block after block of boutiques, shoe stores, and department stores, as well as street stalls and gourmet food shops. For top-quality antiques, look in shops along **Via del Babuino**, near Piazza di Spagna. **Via dei Coronari**, across the Tiber from Castel Sant'Angelo, has quirky antiques and home furnishings. Via Giulia and surrounding streets are good bets for decorative arts. Should your gift list include religious souvenirs, look for everything from rosaries to Vatican golf balls at the shops between Piazza San Pietro and **Borgo Pio.** Liturgical vestments and statues of saints make for good window-shopping on **Via dei Cestari,** near the Pantheon. **Via Nazionale** is a good bet for affordable fashions, including shoes, bags, and gloves. Since its refurbishment for the Jubilee in the year 2000, **Termini** station has become a good one-stop place for most shopping needs. Its 60-plus underground shops are open until 10 PM and include clothing, cosmetics, eyewear, and food stores as well as an UPIM department store on ground level.

Specialty Stores

Antiques & Prints

For old prints and antiques, **Tanca** (⊠ Salita dei Crescenzi 12, near Pantheon ☎ 06/6875272) is a good hunting ground. Early photographs of Rome and views of Italy from the archives at **Alinari** (⊠ Via Alibert 16/a, near Piazza di Spagna ☎ 06/69941998) make memorable souvenirs. **Nardecchia** (⊠ Piazza Navona 25 ☎ 06/6869318) is reliable for prints. Stands in **Piazza della Fontanella Borghese** (⊠ Near Via del Corso) sell prints and old books.

Crafts & Gifts

For fine pottery, handwoven textiles, and other handicrafts, **Myricae** (⊠ Piazza del Parlamento 38, near Pantheon ☎ 06/6873742) has a good selection. A bottle of liqueur, jar of marmalade, or bar of chocolate handmade by Cistercian monks in several monasteries in Italy makes an unusual, tasty gift to take home; pick from goodies at **Ai Monasteri** (⊠ Corso Rinascimento 72, near Piazza Navona ☎ 06/68802783). Stylish stationery, organized by color, as well as leather albums and pens of every description can be found at **Fabriano** (⊠ Via del Babuino 173, near Piazza di Spagna ☎ 06/6864268). Drop into **Panella** (⊠ Via Merulana 54, near Santa Maria Maggiore ☎ 06/4872344), one of Rome's most spectacular bakeries, for exquisite bread sculptures and a fine selection of pastas, oils, and preserves to take home. Pricey **C.u.c.i.n.a** (⊠ Via Mario de' Fiori 65, near Piazza di Spagna ☎ 06/6791275) is one of the best kitchen-supply stores in town. At **Spazio Sette** (⊠ Via dei Barbieri 7, near Campo de' Fiori ☎ 06/6869747) you'll find gadgets and furniture for the kitchen, living room, and bathroom from the biggest names in Italian and international design, for sale in a striking frescoed 17th-century palazzo.

Designer Clothing

All of Italy's top fashion houses and many international designers have stores near Piazza di Spagna. Rome's leading local couturier, recognized the world over by the "V" logo, is **Valentino** (⊠ Valentino **Donna** ⊠ Via Condotti 13, near Piazza di Spagna ☎ 06/6795862 ⊠ **Valentino Uomo** ⊠ Via Bocca di Leone 15, near Piazza di Spagna ☎ 06/6783656). If the king of Roman high fashion is Valentino, then its queen is **Laura Biagiotti** (⊠ Via Borgognona 43–44, near Piazza di Spagna ☎ 06/6795040), who is justly famous for luxurious knitwear, silk separates, and loose-fitting dresses. **Dolce & Gabbana** (⊠ Piazza di Spagna 82 ☎ 06/69924999), a spin-off of the top-of-the-line D&G store on Via Borgognona, shows the trendiest designer fashions in casual wear and accessories for men and women. **Fendi** (⊠ Via Borgognona 40, near Piazza di Spagna ☎ 06/69666001) has several stores in Rome; all stock a wide assortment of the Fendi sisters' signature furs and print fashions. Sleek, vaguely futuristic **Prada** (⊠ Via Condotti 92, near Piazza di Spagna ☎ 06/6790897) has two entrances: the one for the men's boutique is to the left of the women's. The shop is as understated and elegant as the designs at **Giorgio Armani** (⊠ Via Condotti 77, near Piazza di Spagna ☎ 06/6991460). **Gucci** (⊠ Via Condotti

8, near Piazza di Spagna ☎ 06/6783762) often has lines out the door of its two-story shop, testament to the continuing popularity of its rich leathers and edgy clothes designs. The two stores of **Gianni Versace** (✉ **Versace Uomo** ✉ Via Borgognona 24–25, near Piazza di Spagna ☎ 06/6795037 ✉ **Versace Donna** ✉ Via Bocca di Leone 26–27, near Piazza di Spagna ☎ 06/6780521) offer the rock-star styles that made the house's name.

MEN'S CLOTHING **Ermenegildo Zegna** (✉ Via Borgognona 7/e, near Piazza di Spagna ☎ 06/6789143) has the finest in men's elegant styles and accessories. **Il Portone** (✉ Via delle Carrozze 71, near Piazza di Spagna ☎ 06/69925170) embodies a tradition in custom shirtmaking. For decades a man was a fashion flop without Portone's classic cuts and signature stripes in his closet. **Brioni** (✉ Via Barberini 79, near Piazza di Trevi ☎ 06/6783635 ✉ Via Condotti 21, near Piazza di Spagna ☎ 06/6783428) has a well-deserved reputation as one of Italy's top tailors. There are ready-to-wear garments in addition to impeccable custom-made apparel.

WOMEN'S CLOTHING **Galassia** (✉ Via Frattina 21, near Piazza di Spagna ☎ 06/6797896) has expensive, extreme, and extravagant women's styles by Gaultier, Westwood, and Yamamoto—this is the place for feather boas and hats with ostrich plumes. **Mariselaine** (✉ Via Condotti 70, near Piazza di Spagna ☎ 06/6795817) is a top-quality women's fashion boutique. The garments at **Luisa Spagnoli** (✉ Via del Tritone 30, near Piazza di Trevi ☎ 06/69202220) are elegant but contemporary, and they go to large sizes. **Mariella Burani** (✉ Via Bocca di Leone 28, near Piazza di Spagna ☎ 06/6790630) mixes classy chic with judicious high-fashion overtones. **Arsenale** (✉ Via del Governo Vecchio 64, near Piazza Navona ☎ 06/6861380) is the boutique of designer Patrizia Pieroni, who creates funky—sometimes outrageous—clothes using from luxurious fabrics. If you're in the market for luxurious lingerie, **La Perla** (✉ Via Condotti 79, near Piazza di Spagna ☎ 06/69941934) has what you're looking for.

Embroidery & Linens

Frette (✉ Piazza di Spagna 11 ☎ 06/6790673) is a Roman institution for luxurious linens. **Venier Colombo** (✉ Via Frattina 79, Piazza di Spagna ☎ 06/6787705) has a selection of exquisite lace goods, including lingerie and linens. **Lavori Artigianali Femminili** (✉ Via Capo le Case 6, Piazza di Spagna ☎ 06/6781100) offers delicately embroidered household linens, infants' and children's clothing, and blouses.

Jewelry & Silver Objects

What Cartier is to Paris, **Bulgari** (✉ Via Condotti 10, near Piazza di Spagna ☎ 06/6793876) is to Rome; the shop's elegant display windows hint at what's beyond the guard at the door. **Buccellati** (✉ Via Condotti 31, near Piazza di Spagna ☎ 06/6790329) is a tradition-rich Florentine jewelry house renowned for its silverwork; it ranks with Bulgari for quality and reliability. At **Liliana Michilli** (✉ Via Dei Banchi Vecchi 37, near Campo de' Fiori ☎ 06/68392154) you can buy convincing copies of Bulgari and Gucci rings for a fraction of the price. **Bozart** (✉ Via Bocca di

Leone 4, near Piazza di Spagna ☎ 06/6781026) features dazzling costume jewelry in keeping with the latest fashions.

Shoes & Leather Accessories

For the latest styles in handbags and a selection of scarves and costume jewelry (all Italian made) at reasonable prices, go to **Furla** (✉ Piazza di Spagna 22 ☎ 06/69200363), which has a number of downtown stores. **Ferragamo Donna** (✉ Via Condotti 73, near Piazza di Spagna ☎ 06/6791565) has the ultimate in women's high-fashion shoes, handbags, and scarves. **Ferragamo Uomo** (✉ Via Condotti 65 near Piazza di Spagna ☎ 06/6781130) sells classic shoes for men. For a vast selection of affordable, high-quality Italian-made bags and accessories sold in a stylish setting, head for **Regal** (✉ Via Nazionale 254, near Termini ☎ 06/4884893). **Federico Polidori** (✉ Via Pie di Marmo 7, near Pantheon ☎ 06/6797191) crafts custom-made leather bags and briefcases complete with monograms. **Volterra Vague** (✉ Via Barberini 102, near Piazza di Trevi ☎ 06/4819315) is well stocked and offers a wide selection of handbags at moderate prices. For gloves as pretty as Holly Golightly's, head to **Sermoneta** (✉ Piazza di Spagna 61 ☎ 06/6791960). **Di Cori** (✉ Piazza di Spagna 53 ☎ 06/6784439) has gloves in every color of the spectrum. **Calzature Fausto Santini** (✉ Via Santa Maria Maggiore 165, near Santa Maria Maggiore ☎ 06/6784114) is the place for colorful, offbeat, and ever-fashionable Santini shoes at half price. (The flagship store is on upmarket Via Frattina.) **Bruno Magli** (✉ Via del Gambero 1, near Piazza di Spagna ☎ 06/6793802 ✉ Via Veneto 70 ☎ 06/42011671) is known for well-made shoes and matching handbags at both moderate and high prices. **Campanile** (✉ Via Condotti 58, near Piazza di Spagna ☎ 06/6790731) has two floors of shoes in the latest, as well as classic, styles; they also sell other leather goods. **Tod's** (✉ Via Borgognona 45, near Piazza di Spagna ☎ 06/6786828) might sound British, but the signature button-soled moccasins are strictly Italian made. This exclusive Tod's location carries every model and style as well as its line of handmade bags.

Silks & Fabrics

Fratelli Bassetti (✉ Corso Vittorio Emanuele II 73, near Campo de' Fiori ☎ 06/6892326) has a vast selection of world-famous Italian silks and fashion fabrics in a rambling palazzo. **Aston** (✉ Via Boncompagni 27, near Via Veneto ☎ 06/42871227) stocks couture-level fabrics for men and women. You can find some real bargains when *scampoli* (remnants) are on sale.

ROME A TO Z

To research prices, get advice from other travelers, and book travel arrangements, visit www.fodors.com.

AIRPORTS & TRANSFERS

Most international flights and all domestic flights arrive at Aeroporto Leonardo da Vinci, also known as Fiumicino, 30 km (19 mi) southwest of Rome. Some international and charter flights land at Ciampino, a civil and military airport 15 km (9 mi) southeast of Rome. To get to the city from Fiumicino by car, follow the signs for Rome on the expressway from the airport, which links with the GRA, the beltway around Rome. The direction you take on the GRA depends on where your hotel is, so get directions from the car-rental people at the airport. A taxi from Fiumicino to the center of town costs about €50, including *supplementi* (extra charges) for airport service and luggage, and the ride takes 30–40 minutes, depending on traffic. Private limousines can be hired at booths in the arrivals hall; they charge a little more than taxis but can take more passengers. Ignore gypsy drivers who approach you inside the terminal; stick to the licensed cabs, yellow or white, that wait by the curb. A booth inside the arrivals hall provides taxi information.

You have a choice of two trains to get to downtown Rome from Fiumicino Airport. Ask at the airport (at APT or train information counters) which train takes you closer to your hotel. The nonstop Airport–Termini express takes you directly to Track 22 at Stazione Termini, Rome's main train station, which is well served by taxis and is the hub of metro and bus lines. The ride to Termini takes 30 minutes; departures are every half hour beginning at 6:37 AM from the airport, with a final departure at 11:37 PM. From Termini to the airport, trains leave at 21 and 51 minutes past the hour. Tickets cost €8.80. FM1, the other airport train, runs from the airport to Rome and beyond, terminating in Monterotondo, a suburban town to the east. The main stops in Rome are at Trastevere, Ostiense, and Tiburtina stations; at each you can find taxis and bus and/or metro connections to other parts of Rome. This train runs from Fiumicino from 6:35 AM to 12:15 AM, with departures every 20 minutes, a little less frequently in off-hours. The ride to Tiburtina takes 40 minutes. Tickets cost €2.27. For either train buy your ticket at automatic vending machines. There are ticket counters at some stations (at Termini/Track 22, Trastevere, Tiburtina). Date-stamp the ticket at the gate before you board.

🔢 Airport Information **Aeroporto Leonardo da Vinci** ☎ 06/65951, 06/65953640 English-language flight information ⊕ www.adr.it. **Ciampino** ✉ Via Appia Nuova ☎ 06/794941.

BUS TRAVEL TO & FROM ROME

There's no central bus terminal in Rome. COTRAL is the suburban bus company that connects Rome with outlying areas and other cities in the Lazio region. Long-distance and suburban buses terminate either near Tiburtina Station or near outlying metro stops such as Rebbibia and Anagnina. For COTRAL bus information, call weekdays 8 AM–6 PM.

🔢 Bus Information **COTRAL** ☎ 800/150008 toll-free.

BUS TRAVEL WITHIN ROME

ATAC city buses and tram lines run from about 6 AM to midnight, with night buses (indicated N) on some lines. A 75-minute ticket costs €1 and a day pass €4. The compact electric buses of Lines 117 and 119 take routes through the center of Rome that can save lots of walking.

🔢 Bus Information **ATAC** ☎ 800/431784 toll free.

CAR RENTAL
🔝 Local Agencies **Avis** ✉ Via Sardenia 38 ☎ 06/42824728, 06/650011531 Fiumicino Airport. **Europcar** ✉ Via Lombardia 7 ☎ 06/4871274, 06/65010879 Fiumicino Airport. **Hertz** ✉ Via del Gallopatoio/Villa Borghese Parking Lot 33 ☎ 06/3216831, 06/65011553 Fiumicino Airport. **Maggiore** ✉ Termini Station ☎ 06/4880049, 06/65010678 Fiumicino Airport. **Thrifty** ✉ Termini Station ☎ 06/4747825, 06/65010347 Fiumicino Airport.

CAR TRAVEL
The main access routes from the north are A1 (Autostrada del Sole) from Milan and Florence and the A12–E80 highway from Genoa. The principal route to or from points south, including Naples, is the A2. All highways connect with the Grande Raccordo Anulare (GRA), which channels traffic into the city center. Markings on the GRA are confusing: take time to study the route you need.

EMBASSIES & CONSULATES
🔝 Australia **Australian Consulate** ✉ Via Alessandria 215, Piazza Fiume ☎ 06/852721.
🔝 Canada **Canadian Consulate** ✉ Via Zara 30, Piazza Fiume ☎ 06/445981.
🔝 New Zealand **New Zealand Consulate** ✉ Via Zara 28, Piazza Fiume ☎ 06/4417171.
🔝 United Kingdom **U.K. Consulate** ✉ Via Venti Settembre 80/a, Via Veneto ☎ 06/42200001.
🔝 United States **U.S. Consulate** ✉ Via Veneto 121, Via Veneto ☎ 06/46741.

EMERGENCIES
Farmacia Internazionale Capranica, Farmacia Internazionale Barberini, and Farmacia Cola di Rienzo are pharmacies that have some English-speaking staff. Most pharmacies are open 8:30–1 and 4–8; some are open all night. A schedule posted outside each pharmacy indicates the nearest pharmacy open during off-hours (afternoons, through the night, and Sunday). Dial ☎ 1100 for an automated list of three open pharmacies closest to the telephone from which you call. The hospitals listed below have English-speaking doctors. Rome American Hospital is about 30 minutes by cab from the center of town.
🔝 Emergency Services **Ambulance** ☎ 118. **Police** ☎ 113. **Red Cross** ☎ 06/5510.
🔝 Hospitals **Rome American Hospital** ✉ Via Emilio Longoni 69, Via Prenestina ☎ 06/22551 ⊕ www.rah.it. **Salvator Mundi International Hospital** ✉ Viale delle Mura Gianicolensi 67, Trastevere ☎ 06/588961 ⊕ www.smih.pcn.net.
🔝 Pharmacies **Farmacia Cola di Rienzo** ✉ Via Cola di Rienzo 213, San Pietro ☎ 06/3243130. **Farmacia Internazionale Barberini** ✉ Piazza Barberini 49, Via Veneto ☎ 06/4825456. **Farmacia Internazionale Capranica** ✉ Piazza Capranica 96, Pantheon ☎ 06/6794680.

ENGLISH-LANGUAGE MEDIA
BOOKS English-language books are expensive in Rome; most are imported from England, so prices in Rome reflect the strong pound and shipping costs. The Anglo-American Bookstore and the Economy Book and Video Center have the widest selection of genres. The English Bookshop has a smaller selection but better prices. Trastevere's Almost Corner Bookstore carries lots of offbeat new fiction and has a vast history section. For used books at lower prices, try the Open Door. At Fel-

trinelli International you can pick up novels and guidebooks in English as well.

Almost Corner Bookstore ⊠ Via del Moro 45, Trastevere ☎06/5836942. **Anglo-American Bookstore** ⊠ Via della Vite 102, near Piazza di Spagna ☎06/6795222 ⊕ www.aab. it. **Economy Book and Video Center** ⊠Via Torino 136, near Termini ☎06/4746877 ⊕www. booksitaly.com. **The English Bookshop** ⊠Via di Ripetta 24B, near Piazza di Spagna ☎06/3203301. **Feltrinelli International** ⊠ Via Vittorio Emanuele Orlando 78/81, near Termini ☎06/4870171. **Lion Bookshop** ⊠Via dei Greci 33/36, near Piazza di Spagna ☎06/32654007. **Open Door** ⊠ Via della Lungaretta 23, Trastevere ☎ 06/5896478.

NEWSPAPERS & MAGAZINES The ubiquitous *International Herald Tribune* is published in Italy with a four-page *Italy Weekly* insert, an English-language summary of main Italian news stories and local cultural events. Major English and American newsmagazines and a few daily papers are available at some newsstands, including those on Via Veneto, Via del Corso (at Via del Tritone), and Campo de' Fiori.

WHERE TO STAY

APARTMENT & VILLA RENTALS For families or groups of friends, an apartment or villa rental may be more convenient than a hotel. Always insist on photos, a map with indication of location, and a detailed description of the property. The English-language biweekly *Wanted in Rome* lists private-party rentals.

Local Agents Homes International ⊠ Via Bissolati 20, Via Veneto 00187 ☎ 06/4881800 🖷 06/4881808. **Property International** ⊠ Viale Aventino 79, Aventino 00153 ☎ 06/5743170 🖷 06/5743182.

Rental Listings Wanted in Rome ⊕ www.wantedinrome.com.

MAIL & SHIPPING

Post Offices Main post office ⊠ Piazza San Silvestro 19, Piazza di Spagna ☎ 06/6798495.

OVERNIGHT SERVICES Although DHL and UPS offices are far out of the city center, FedEx has walk-in service on Via Barberini; all three companies will pick up packages from anywhere in Rome.

Major Services DHL (800/345345). **Federal Express** ⊠ Via Barberini 115, Via Veneto ☎ 800/123800. **UPS** ☎ 800/877877.

MOPED TRAVEL

Zipping and careening through traffic on a *motorino* (moped) in downtown Rome is an attractive way to visit the city for some, but if you're risk averse, pass on it. If your impulses—and reflexes—are fast, you can join the craziness of Roman traffic by renting a moped and the mandatory helmet at numerous rental spots throughout the city. Be extremely careful of pedestrians when riding: Romans are casual jaywalkers and pop out frequently from between parked cars.

Moped Rentals Enjoy Rome ⊠Via Marghera 8A, 00185 Termini Rome ☎06/4451843 ⊕ www.enjoyrome.com. **Happy Rent** ⊠ Via Farini 3, Termini ☎ 06/4818185 ⊕ www. happyrent.it. **Scoot-a-Long** ⊠ Via Cavour 302, Termini ☎ 06/6780206. **St. Peter Moto** ⊠ Via di Porta Castello 43, San Pietro ☎ 06/6875714.

Rome Metro &
Suburban Railway

TO
ORTE
FM1

TO
REBIBBIA

S. Maria del
Soccorso

B LINE

Monti Tiburtini

Quintilliani

Pza.
Bologna

Policlinico

Staz. Tiburtina

TO
VITERBO

FM3

TO
GROSSETO

Villa
Borghese

Flaminio

Battistini
Cornelia

Ottaviano
Cipro

Lepanto

Spagna

Barberini

Castro
Pretorio

A LINE

Valle
Aurelia

San Pietro

Repubblica

Termini

Vittorio
Emanuele

TO
SULMONA

FM5

St. Peter's /
Vatican City

Cavour

FM2

Colosseo

Manzoni

S. Giovanni

Circo
Massimo

Re di Roma
Ponte Lungo

Trastevere

Tuscolana
Piramide
(Ostiense)

Furio Camillo
Colli Albani

Arco di Travertino

Porta Furba

Numidio Quadrato

Garbatella

Lucio Sestio
Giulio Agricola

Tiber

TO
FIUMICINO

FM1

S. Paolo

Subaugusta

Cinecittà

A LINE

TO
E. U. R.

B LINE

TO
NETTUNO/
LATINA

FM7

Anagnina
TO VELLETRI, ALBANO
LAZIALE, FRASCATI

Magliana

SAFETY

LOCAL SCAMS A word of caution: "gypsy" children, who hang around sights popular with tourists throughout Europe, are rife in Rome and are adept pick-pockets. Keep a close eye on your belongings when boarding the bus and subway, particularly at Termini Station. One modus operandi is to approach a tourist and proffer a piece of cardboard with writing on it. While the unsuspecting victim attempts to read the message *on* it, the children's hands are busy *under* it, trying to make off with purses or valuables. If you see such a group (recognizable by their unkempt appearance), do not even allow them near you—they are quick and know more tricks than you do. Also be aware of people, usually young men, who ride by on motorbikes, grab the shoulder strap of your bag or camera, and step on the gas. Wear or carry your bag on the side away from the street edge of the sidewalk, or, best of all, wear a concealed money belt. Don't carry more money than you need, and don't carry your passport unless you need it to exchange money. A useful expression to ward off pesky panhandlers or vendors is "*Vai via!*" (Go away!).

WOMEN IN ROME Foreign women can expect to attract extra attention from Italian men, but this is usually harmless flirtation, and rarely will become a safety issue. Do be careful of gropers on subways and buses, particularly on the metro and on Buses 64 (Termini–Vatican) and 218 and 660 (Catacombs). They're known to take advantage of the cramped space to press up against women. React like the locals: forcefully and loudly.

SUBWAY TRAVEL

The metro (subway) is an efficient, traffic-free way to get around and there are stops near many of the main tourist attractions. Service begins at 5:30 AM, and the last trains leave the most distant station at 11:30 PM (on Saturday night, trains run until 12:30 AM). There are two lines— A and B—which intersect at Stazione Termini. The fare is €1.

TAXIS

Taxis in Rome do not cruise, but if empty (look for an illuminated TAXI sign on the roof) they will stop if you flag them down. Taxis wait at stands and can also be called by phone, in which case you're charged a bit more. The meter starts at €2.33 from 7 AM to 10 PM, at €3.36 on Sunday and holidays, and at €4.91 after 10 PM. Each piece of baggage will add an extra €2.03 to your fare. Use only licensed, metered yellow or white cabs, identified by a numbered shield on the side, an illuminated taxi sign on the roof, and a plaque next to the license plate reading SERVIZIO PUBBLICO. Avoid unmarked, unauthorized, unmetered gypsy cabs (numerous at airports and train stations), whose renegade drivers actively solicit your trade and may demand astronomical fares. Some taxis accept some credit cards, but you must specify when calling that you will pay that way.

🚖 Taxi Companies **Taxi** ☎ 06/5551, 06/3570, 06/4994, or 06/88177.

TOURS

BIKE TOURS Enjoy Rome organizes all-day bike tours of Rome for small groups covering major sights and some hidden ones. Remember, Rome is famous for its seven hills; be prepared for a workout.

🚲 Fees & Schedules **Enjoy Rome** ✉ Via Marghera 8A, near Termini ☎ 06/4451843 ⊕ www.enjoyrome.com.

BUS TOURS American Express and CIT offer general orientation tours of the city, as well as specialized tours of particular areas such as the Vatican or Ancient Rome. Stop-'n'-go City Tours has English-speaking guides and the option of getting off and on at 14 key sites in the city. A day pass costs €12.

🚌 Fees & Schedules **American Express** ☎ 06/67641. **Appian Line** ☎ 06/487861. **ATAC** ☎ 800/431784. **CIT** ✉ Piazza della Repubblica 64, near Termini ☎ 06/4620311 ⊕ www. citonline.it. **Stop-'n'-go City Tours** ☎ 06/48905729

WALKING TOURS All About Rome, American Express, Enjoy Rome, Scala Reale, Through Eternity, and Walks of Rome offer walking tours of the city and its sites.

🚶 Fees & Schedules **All About Rome** ☎ 06/7100823 ⊕ www.allaboutromewalks. netfirms.com. **American Express** ☎ 06/67641. **Enjoy Rome** ✉ Via Marghera 8A, near Termini ☎ 06/4451843 ⊕ www.enjoyrome.com. **Scala Reale** ✉ Via dell'Olmata 30, near Termini ☎ 06/4745673 or 800/732–2863 Ext. 4052 ⊕ www.scalareale.org. **Through Eternity** ☎ 06/7009336 ⊕ www.througheternity.com. **Walks of Rome** ✉ Via Urbana 38 Quirinale ☎ 06/484853.

TRAIN TRAVEL

Stazione Termini is Rome's main train terminal; the Tiburtina and Ostiense stations serve some long-distance trains, many commuter trains, and the FM1 line to Fiumicino Airport. Some trains for Pisa and Genoa leave Rome from, or pass through, the Trastevere Station. You can find English-speaking staff at the information office at Stazione Termini, or ask for information at travel agencies. You can purchase tickets up to two months in advance at the main stations or at most travel agencies. Lines at station ticket windows may be very long: you can save time by using the electronic ticket machines, which have instructions in English, or by buying your ticket at a travel agency. You can reserve a seat up to one day in advance at a travel agency or up to an hour in advance at a train station. Tickets for train rides within a radius of 100 km (62 mi) of Rome can be purchased at tobacco shops and at some newsstands, as well as at ticket machines on the main concourse. All train tickets must be date-stamped before you board, at the machine near the track, or you will be fined.

🚆 Train Information **Trenitalia** ☎ 166/105050, 892021 from outside Rome (a small service charge applies) ⊕ www.trenitalia.it.

TRANSPORTATION AROUND ROME

Although most of Rome's sights are in a relatively circumscribed area, the city is too large to be seen solely on foot. Take the metro (subway), a bus, or a taxi to the area you plan to visit, and expect to do a lot of walking once you're there. Wear a pair of comfortable, sturdy shoes to cushion the impact of the *sanpietrini* (cobblestones). Get away from the noise and polluted air of heavily trafficked streets by taking parallel streets whenever possible. You can get free city and transportation-route maps at municipal information booths; the transportation maps are probably more up-to-date than those you can buy at newsstands.

Rome's integrated public transportation system includes buses and trams (ATAC), metro and suburban trains and buses (COTRAL), and some other suburban trains (Trenitalia) run by the state railways. Try to avoid the rush hours (8–9, 1–2:30, 7–8), and beware of pickpockets and gropers. When purchasing tickets for excursions outside Rome on COTRAL buses or trains, buy a return ticket, too, to save time at the other end.

FARES & SCHEDULES A ticket valid for 75 minutes on any combination of buses and trams and one entrance to the metro costs €1. You are expected to date-stamp your ticket when you board the first vehicle, stamping it again when boarding for the last time within 75 minutes (the important thing is to stamp it the first time). Tickets for the public transit system are sold at tobacconists, newsstands, some coffee bars, ATMs positioned in metro stations and some bus stops, and at ATAC and COTRAL ticket booths (in some metro stations, on the lower concourse at Stazione Termini, and at a few main bus terminals). A BIG tourist ticket, valid for one day on all public transport, costs €4. A weekly ticket (Settimanale, also known as CIS) costs €15 and can be purchased only at ATAC booths.

TRAVEL AGENCIES

🛈 Local Agent Referrals **American Express** ☎ 06/67641. **Appian Line** ☎ 06/487861. **Carrani Tours** ✉ Via Vittorio Emanuele Orlando 95, near Termini ☎ 06/4880510. **CIT** ✉ Piazza della Repubblica 64, near Termini ☎ 06/4620311 ⊕ www.citonline.it.

VISITOR INFORMATION

🛈 Tourist Information **Tourist office** (Azienda di Promozione Turistica di Roma/APT) ✉ Via Parigi 5, near Termini ☎ 06/48899255 ⊘ Monday–Saturday 9–7 ✉ Aeroporto Leonardo da Vinci ☎ 06/65951 ⊘ Daily 8:15–7.

LAZIO, ABRUZZO & MOLISE

12

Updated by
Mark Walters

PLAYGROUND OF THE ETRUSCANS, united under the Romans, and embellished by Renaissance popes, Lazio towers culturally over its Apennine neighbors to the east. But all three regions in this imposing swath across central Italy contain sites of undiluted charm. The dreamlike landscapes of Abruzzo and Molise are dotted with medieval castles and quaint villages, with many more remote areas begging for discovery. Fine cuisine and hospitality at highly affordable prices add to the appeal of these three lesser-known regions of central Italy.

For the better part of 2,000 years, the grandeur and glory of Rome have obscured the constellation of attractions in the region around it. Yet exploring Lazio (Latium to the ancient Romans) can immeasurably broaden one's understanding of the Roman empire and its legacy. You can explore selected sights of Lazio on day trips from Rome; the result is a more superficial experience of the region's pleasures, but nonetheless it can be worthwhile. One of the easiest excursions from the capital takes you southwest 25 km (15 mi) to the sea, where tall pines stand among the well-preserved ruins of Ostia Antica, the main port of ancient Rome and an archaeological site that rivals Pompeii. A visit to Ostia Antica tells you more about the way the ancient Romans lived than the Roman Forum does.

The rolling landscape of Lazio along the coast northwest of Rome was once Etruscan territory, and at Cerveteri and Tarquinia it holds some intriguing reminders of a people who taught the ancient Romans a thing or two about religion, art, and a pleasurable way of life. The Etruscan sites here give you a very concrete impression of the people whose skilled artwork and artifacts are displayed at local museums. Deep in the countryside farther north, larger Viterbo has an intact medieval core and historic traces of its days as a papal stronghold interspersed with modern industry.

East of Rome lie some of the region's star sites, along a route that loops through the hills where ancient Romans built their summer resorts. At Tivoli, Hadrian's Villa shows you the scale of individual imperial Roman egos, while Villa d'Este demonstrates that Renaissance egos were no smaller. Eastward at Palestrina lies a vast pagan sanctuary from ancient times. At Subiaco, St. Benedict founded the hermitage that gave rise to Western monasticism. Southeast of Rome are three romantic sites little known outside Italy: a castle at Sermoneta that once belonged to Cesare Borgia, a fairy-tale garden at Ninfa, and the seaside citadel of Sperlonga.

Still lands of shepherds and wolves, the mountainous regions of Abruzzo and Molise preserve much of their local traditions and culture. Craggy peaks, ruined castles, hill towns, and peasant life unchanged since the Middle Ages abound in both regions. Abruzzo's real treasure is its natural beauty, preserved pristinely in the Parco Nazionale d'Abruzzo. With its hiking trails, immense beech forests, and wildlife, it's a must-see for nature lovers. Neighboring Molise, one of the smallest of the Italian regions and blissfully unravaged by tourist development, has astounding archaeological sites set against an impressive Apennine backdrop.

Exploring Lazio, Abruzzo & Molise

Most of Lazio's attractions are within striking distance of Rome and can be covered in day trips from the capital, but there's much to be said for staying overnight and appreciating the area after the day-trippers have moved on. If you intend to combine more than two sights in one day, a car will be a necessity. For outlying Abruzzo and Molise the best months are May and June, when there's a profusion of spring flowers, though September and October also offer optimal traveling, hiking, and sightseeing conditions. L'Aquila lies in a frost pocket close to the Gran Sasso, the Apennines' highest peak, making traveling conditions sometimes treacherous in winter months. Whether bound for ski slopes or just driving through, you should always check road conditions and weather reports before setting out.

About the Restaurants & Hotels

Meal prices are generally a little lower in the rest of Lazio than in Rome, and good restaurants tend to attract large numbers from the capital on weekends. In Abruzzo and Molise, simplicity is the rule: the most satisfying meals are to be had at modest restaurants where often as not you won't find a menu, just daily specials prepared according to age-old traditions.

With relatively few exceptions (hotels at spas and beaches and hill resorts such as Viterbo), accommodations in the region cater more to commercial travelers than to tourists. Public rooms and guest rooms tend to be functional and short on character, though adequate for an overnight. Peak periods, especially in mountain resorts, are the New Year, Easter, and the first three weeks of August, when almost all accommodations have been booked up months in advance.

WHAT IT COSTS In euros					
	$$$$	$$$	$$	$	¢
RESTAURANTS	over €22	€16–€22	€11–€16	€7–€11	under €7
HOTELS	over €220	€160–€220	€110–€160	€70–€110	under €70

Restaurant prices are for a second course (un secondo). Hotel prices are for two people in a standard double room in high season, including tax and service.

OSTIA ANTICA

Founded around the 4th century BC, Ostia served as Rome's port city for several centuries until the Tiber changed course, leaving the town high and dry. What has been excavated here is a remarkably intact Roman town in a pretty, parklike setting. Fair weather and good walking shoes are essential. On hot days, be here when the gates open or go late in the afternoon. A visit to the excavations takes two to three hours, including 20 minutes for the museum.

Numbers in the text correspond to numbers in the margin and on the Lazio, Abruzzo & Molise and the Ostia Antica maps.

12

If you have 2 days

Only 20 minutes from Rome, **Ostia Antica** ❶–❽ ► is an obvious destination for the first day. Traveling by car, stop for a look at the ancient Etruscan center of **Tarquinia** ❷⓪ before continuing to the hill town of ▣ **Tuscania** ㉑ for your first night. On the second day take in the gardens of the Villa Lante in **Bagnaia** ㉓ and round the day off with a trip to ▣ **Tivoli** ㉖ and the Villa D'Este. Spend the night in Tivoli or head back to Rome. If dependent on public transport, choose two of these areas and cover them more thoroughly.

If you have 4 days

With four days you can focus on Lazio or head into the hills of Abruzzo. If you want to stick to Lazio, after seeing **Ostia Antica** ❶–❽ ► on the first day stop at the necropolis of **Cerveteri** ⑲ and continue on to medieval ▣ **Tarquinia** ⓴, where you'll spend the night. In the morning, drive inland, stopping at ▣ **Tuscania** ㉑ on your way to ▣ **Viterbo** ㉒, with its papal palaces and medieval quarter. Make either Tuscania or Viterbo home for your second night. The next morning, stop in **Bagnaia** ㉓ and ▣ **Tivoli** ㉖, seeing the Villa Adriana and Villa d'Este, then continue on to the ancient Roman religious site of ▣ **Palestrina** ㉗, a good place to overnight. On Day 4, check out the monasteries of **Subiaco** ㉘. If it's summer, head to the coast and spend an afternoon at the beach in ▣ **Sperlonga** ㉛ and stay the night there; otherwise, stretch Tivoli, Palestrina, and Subiaco out over two days. Alternatively: if you'd rather see some of Abruzzo, follow the above itinerary until Tivoli, then head through the mountains on the A24 autostrada, forking off toward Pescara and winding up in the valley town of ▣ **Sulmona** ㉟, an excellent choice for your third night. Come morning, head into the ▣ **Parco Nazionale d'Abruzzo** ㊱ and spend the last day in the heart of the Apennines.

If you have 7 days

Follow the Lazio itinerary above up through Subiaco on the third day; on Day 4, take the A25 highway through the mountains to ▣ **Sulmona** ㉟, where you'll spend your fourth night. From there, head into the ▣ **Parco Nazionale d'Abruzzo** ㊱, explore all day, and spend the night in Civitella Alfedena. Next comes a choice: if you're a city type and prefer more of Abruzzo, travel northwest, stopping at mysterious **Castel del Monte** ㉝ and **Santo Stefano di Sessanio** ㉞ before heading to the regional capital of ▣ **L'Aquila** ㉜, whose fine castle and churches make a good backdrop for your sixth night and seventh day. Alternatively, if the weather holds and you like antiquities, go east after the Parco Nazionale to see the Hellenistic theater in the hills of **Pietrabbondante** ㊳ and the medieval town of ▣ **Agnone** ㊴, spending the sixth night either there or in the Molise regional capital of **Isernia** ㊲. An ambitious seventh day would include the ancient Roman town of **Sepino** ㊵ to the east before heading back west . . . or continuing southeast into Puglia.

► **Ostia Antica** was inhabited by a cosmopolitan population of rich busi-
Fodor'sChoice nessmen, wily merchants, sailors, slaves, and their respective families.
★ The great *horrea* (warehouses) were built in the 2nd century AD to handle huge shipments of grain from Africa; the *insulae* (forerunners of the
modern apartment building) provided housing for the growing population. Under the combined assaults of the barbarians and the *Anophe-
les* mosquito, and after the Tiber changed course, the port was eventually
abandoned. Tidal mud and windblown sand covered the city, which lay
buried until the beginning of the 20th century. The **Scavi di Ostia Antica** (Ostia Antica excavations) have since been extensively excavated
and are well maintained. ⊠ *Via dei Romagnoli* ☎ *06/56358099* ⊕ *www.
itnw.roma.it/ostia/scavi* 🖃 *€4, includes admission to Museo Ostiense*
☉ *Tues.–Sun. 8:30–1 hr before sunset.*

Before exploring Ostia Antica's ruins, it's worthwhile to take a tour
❶ through the **Castello della Rovere,** in the medieval *borgo* (town). This
is the distinctive castle, easily spotted as you come off the footbridge
from the train station, built by Pope Julius II when he was the Cardinal Bishop of Ostia in 1483. Its triangular form is unusual for military
architecture. Inside are (badly faded) frescoes by Michelangelo's pupil
Baldassare Peruzzi.

❷ The **Porta Romana,** one of the city's three gates, is where you'll enter
the Ostia Antica excavations. It opens onto the Decumanus Maximus,
the main thoroughfare crossing the city from end to end. To your right,
a staircase leads up to a platform—the remains of the upper floor of the
❸ **Terme di Nettuno** (Baths of Neptune)—from which you get a good view
of the black-and-white mosaic pavements representing a marine scene
with Neptune and the sea goddess Amphitrite. Directly behind the baths
is the barracks of the fire department, which played an important role
in a town with warehouses full of valuable goods and foodstuffs.

❹ On the north side of the Decumanus Maximus is the beautiful **Teatro**
(Theater), built by Agrippa, remodeled by Septimius Severus in the 2nd
century AD, and finally restored by the Rome City Council in the 20th
century. In the vast Piazzale delle Corporazioni, where trade organi-
❺ zations similar to guilds had their offices, is the **Tempio di Cerere**
(Temple of Ceres), which is only appropriate for a town dealing in grain
imports—Ceres, who gave her name to cereal, was the goddess of agri-
❻ culture. You can visit the **Domus di Apuleio** (House of Apuleius), built
in Pompeian style, lower to the ground and with fewer windows than
❼ was characteristic of Ostia. Next door, the **Mithraeum** has balconies
and a hall decorated with symbols of the cult of Mithras. This male-
only religion, imported from Persia, was especially popular with le-
gionnaires.

❽ On Via Semita dei Cippi, just off Via dei Molini, the **Domus della Fortuna Annonaria** (House of Fortuna Annonaria) is the richly decorated
residence of a wealthy Ostian, which displays the skill of the mosaic artists
of the period. One of the rooms opens onto a secluded garden.

The Etruscan Past

The countryside in northern Lazio is generously dotted with Etruscan ruins and tombs. For centuries these remnants offered the only insight into the mysterious civilization that dominated the area before the rise of Rome and set the precedent for many of Rome's accomplishments. In his 1920s travelogue *Etruscan Places,* D. H. Lawrence wrote, "We know nothing about the Etruscans except what we find in their tombs." Fortunately, modern scientific techniques have since delved much further, and museums in Cerveteri, Tarquinia, and Tuscania, along with the main Etruscan museum in Rome, the Villa Giulia, regularly offer new exhibits. Still, basic questions remain unanswered, such as where exactly the Etruscans came from, what family of languages Etruscan belongs to, and why they left no proper literature to posterity. But wherever you go in northern Lazio, the Etruscans are never far away: signs point to *Riva degli Etruschi* (Shore of the Etruscans), shops and businesses use imitation Etruscan lettering, and right in the middle of Tuscania, Etruscan sarcophagi are laid out by the main square.

12

Mountain Hikes

Many of the upland areas in the three regions are crisscrossed by scenic trails. The Parco Nazionale d'Abruzzo is open year-round, although it's best appreciated at off-peak times. Avoid public holidays, especially Easter Monday, and the first three weeks of August: the crowds scare the animals away, and popular hiking routes are accessible by reservation only in an attempt to limit congestion. Higher trails may be snowbound from November to April. As in all mountain environments, the weather is prone to sudden changes even in midsummer, so you should take all the standard equipment, particularly sunscreen and rain gear.

Parks & Gardens

Dating back to antiquity, Lazio has been a preferred locale for the retreats of wealthy Romans, places where they could escape the city to relax in expansive surroundings and indulge their grand and sometimes eccentric gardening tastes. Today one of the primary pleasures of the region is visiting these estates: Hadrian's Villa and Villa d'Este are must-see destinations, but you can also be richly rewarded by visits to lesser-known spots, such as Villa Lante and Palazzo Farnese, where Renaissance cardinals took a break from the papal court; Bomarzo, where a 16th-century prince created a bizarre theme park; and Ninfa, where a modern oasis has developed among medieval ruins.

---

9 On Via dei Molini you can see a **molino** (mill), where grain for the warehouses next door was ground with stones that are still here. Along Via **10** di Diana you come upon a **thermopolium** (bar) with a marble counter and a fresco depicting the fruit and foodstuffs that were sold here. At **11** the end of Via dei Dipinti is the **Museo Ostiense** (Ostia Museum), open the same hours as the Scavi (but leave at least a half hour before closing to enter the museum), which displays sarcophagi, massive marble

columns, and statuary too large to be shown anywhere else, including a beautiful statue of Mithras slaying the bull that was taken from the underground Mithraeum.

⑫ The **Forum,** on the south side of Decumanus Maximus, holds the monumental remains of the city's most important temple, dedicated to Jupiter, Juno, and Minerva; other ruins of baths; a basilica (which in Roman times was a secular hall of justice); and smaller temples.

⑬ Via Epagathiana leads toward the Tiber, where there are large **horrea,** erected during the 2nd century AD to receive the enormous amounts of grain imported into Rome during that period, the height of the Empire.

⑭ West of Via Epagathiana, the **Domus di Amore e Psiche** (House of Cupid and Psyche), a residence, was named for a statue found there (now on display in the museum); you can see what remains of a large pool in an enclosed garden decorated with marble and mosaic motifs. Even in ancient times a premium was placed on water views: the house faces the shore, which would have been only about ⅓ km (⅕ mi) away. The

⑮ **Casa di Serapide** (House of Serapis) on Via della Foce is a 2nd-century multilevel dwelling; another apartment building stands one street

⑯ over on Via degli Aurighi. Nearby, the **Termi dei Sette Sapienti** (Baths of the Seven Wise Men) are named for a group of bawdy frescoes found there.

⑰ The **Porta Marina** leads to what used to be the seashore. About 1,000

⑱ feet to the southeast are the ruins of the **sinagoga** (synagogue), one of the oldest in the Western world.

Where to Eat

$–$$$ ✕ **Cipriani.** Handily located in the little medieval borgo near the excavations, this elegant trattoria serves Roman specialties and seafood and has an exquisite wine list. The more businesslike mood at lunchtime contrasts with an upgrade in menu, style, and price in the evening. ⊠ *Via del Forno 11* ☎ *06/56359560* ▭ *AE, DC, MC, V* ⊙ *Closed Wed.*

THE ETRUSCAN SEABOARD

Northwest of Rome lie Etruscan sites on coastal hills that dominate approaches from all directions. The Etruscans held sway over a vast territory mainly north of Rome from the 8th to the 4th century BC, before the Roman Republic's gradual expansion northward. According to the literary sources—mainly written by their Greek and Roman adversaries—Etruscans lived a fairly decadent life and had an unsurpassed reputation in fields as diverse as bronze-working and soothsaying. Though there are few remains of their settlements, they reserved some of their finest construction skills for assuring comfort and style in the afterlife: the Etruscan necropolis, or "city of the dead," was an agglomeration of tombs that most likely aimed to reproduce the homes and lifestyles of the living.

As you make the trip north beyond Rome's city limits, you traverse green countryside with pastures and endless fields of artichokes, a premium

Ostia Antica

KEY

▲ *Start of walk*

Fireman's
Barracks

Train
Station

TO ROME

220 yards
200 meters

crop in these parts. You catch glimpses of the sea to the west, where the coast is dotted with suburban developments. Because the beaches in this area are popular with today's Romans, highways (especially the coastal Via Aurelia) and public transportation can be crowded on weekends from spring to fall. Exploring the Etruscan sites requires some agility in climbing up and down uneven stairs, and you need shoes suitable for walking on rough dirt paths.

Cerveteri is the principal Etruscan site closest to Rome and features the Necropoli della Banditaccia, a sylvan setting among mossy stones and variously shaped monuments that are memorials to revered ancestors. Tarquinia is farther north and has impressive painted tombs, as well as an excellent museum full of objects recovered from tombs throughout the region. On the way, you'll pass Civitavecchia, Rome's principal port. From the highway or train you can see the port installations, which include a fort designed by Michelangelo. Northeast of Tarquinia is Tuscania, a finely preserved town brimming with cultural heritage and medieval atmosphere.

Cerveteri

⑲ *42 km (26 mi) northwest of Rome.*

The nucleus of Cerveteri, in the shadow of a medieval castle, stands on a spur of tufa rock that was the site of the Etruscan city of Caere, a thriving commercial center in the 6th century BC. The necropolis is about 2 km (1 mi) from Cerveteri's main piazza, a trip you can make on foot or by taxi.

In the **Necropoli della Banditaccia** (Banditaccia Necropolis), the Etruscan residents of Caere left a heritage of great historical significance. In this monumental complex of tombs—whose construction spans over 500 years, from the 7th to the 1st century BC—they laid their relatives to rest, some in simple graves, others in burial chambers that are replicas of Etruscan dwellings. The round tumulus tombs are prototypes of Rome's tombs of Augustus and Hadrian (in the Mausoleo di Augusto and Castel Sant'Angelo) and the Tomb of Cecilia Metella on the Via Appia. Look especially for the **Tomba dei Capitelli,** with carved capitals; the **Tomba dei Rilievi,** its walls decorated with stucco reliefs of household objects; and the similar **Tombe degli Scudi e delle Sedie.** The **Tomba Moretti** has a little vestibule with columns. Some tombs have several chambers. ⊠ *Necropoli della Banditaccia* ☎ *06/9940001* 🎟 *€4* ☉ *Tues.–Sun. 9–1 hr before sunset.*

Where to Eat

$$ ✕ **Tuchulcha.** About ½ km (⅓ mi) from the entrance to the Banditaccia Necropolis, on the road leading to the site, this country trattoria offers simple and satisfying home-style food; two specialties are handmade fettuccine and locally grown artichokes served in various ways. You can dine outside in good weather. ⊠ *Via della Necropoli Etrusca* ☎ *06/9914075* 🍴 *No credit cards* ☉ *Closed Mon.*

CloseUp

ON THE MENU

With a tradition of sumptuous banquets that stretches back millennia, there's no lack of good places to eat in the Lazio region. Each town has its own culinary specialties, including local cheese and wine. The bread that predominates—a dark, crusty country loaf—makes the ultimate bruschetta (toasted bread doused with extra virgin olive oil and topped with vine-ripe tomatoes). Restaurants on the coast, naturally, specialize in seafood.

The diets in Abruzzo and Molise—except along the coastal Adriatic strip—tend toward heartier, meat-based dishes. Homemade maccheroni alla chitarra (spaghetti with a square profile, usually eaten with tomato or mushrooms) is found in most areas, though specialties may vary from one town to the next. You'll also come across Alpine favorites such as polenta in Molise, as well as sheep's- and cow's-milk cheeses.

Tarquinia

 About 90 km (55 mi) northwest of Rome, 50 km (30 mi) northwest of Cerveteri, 20 km (12 mi) north of Civitavecchia.

Fortified Tarquinia sprawls on a hill overlooking the sea. Once a powerful Etruscan city, it was also a major center in the Middle Ages. Though it lacks the harmony of better-preserved medieval towns, Tarquinia offers unexpected pleasures, among them views of narrow medieval streets opening onto quaint squares dominated by palaces and churches, and the sight of the majestic 12th-century church of Santa Maria di Castello encircled by medieval walls and towers. Be sure to walk to the medieval wall at the inland edge of town for towering views over the Etruscan countryside. To focus on Tarquinia's Etruscan heritage, visit the museum in Palazzo Vitelleschi, then see the frescoed underground tombs in the necropolis just east of the city.

The **Museo Nazionale Tarquiniense** (National Museum of Tarquinia) is housed in Palazzo Vitelleschi, a splendid 15th-century building that contains a wealth of Etruscan treasures. Even if pottery and endless ranks of stone sarcophagi leave you cold, a visit here is memorable for the horses. A relief plaque of two marvelous terra-cotta winged horses gleams against the gray-stone wall on which it has been mounted in the main hall. The horses once decorated an Etruscan temple, and are vibrant proof of the degree of artistry attained by the Etruscans in the 4th century BC. The museum and its stately courtyard are crammed with sarcophagi from the tombs found beneath the meadows surrounding the town. The figures of the deceased recline on their stone couches, mouths curved in enigmatic smiles. Upstairs are vases and other Etruscan artifacts, together with some of the more precious frescoes from the tombs, removed to keep them from deteriorating. ⊠ *Piazza Cavour 1* ☎ *0766/856036* ⌨ *€4, €6.50 including necropolis* ☾ *Tues.–Sun. 8:30–7:30.*

The entrance to the **Necropolis,** the Etruscan city of the dead, is about 1 km (½ mi) outside the town walls—about a 20-minute walk from Piazza Matteotti, the main square. Alternatively, there is infrequent bus service from Piazza Cavour to the necropolis, with only a couple of morning and afternoon departures. (For directions and/or bus information, ask at the Museo Nazionale Tarquiniense ticket counter or nearby tourist office.) The tombs date from the 6th to the 2nd century BC, and they were painted with lively scenes of Etruscan life. The colors are amazingly fresh in some tombs, and the scenes show the vitality and highly civilized lifestyle of this ancient people. Of the thousands of tombs that exist throughout the territory of Etruria (there are 40,000 in the vicinity of Tarquinia alone), only a small percentage have been excavated scientifically. Many more have been plundered by "experts" called *tombaroli,* who dig illegally, usually at night. The tombs in the Tarquinia necropolis are bare; the only evidence of their original function is the stone platforms on which the sarcophagi rested. But the wall paintings are intriguing and in many cases quite beautiful. The visit takes about 90 minutes, and good explanations in English are posted outside each tomb. ⊠ *Monterozzi, on the Strada Provinciale 1/b, Tarquinia–Viterbo* ☎ *0766/856308, 06/ 9941098 English-language tours* 🖃 *€4, €6.50 including Museo Nazionale Tarquiniense* ⊙ *Tues.–Sun. 8:30–1 hr before sunset.*

off the beaten path

NORCHIA - About 20 km (13 mi) northeast of Tarquinia on the road to Vetralla (S1bis) is the junction for the Etruscan necropolis of Norchia, which lies about 5 km (3 mi) farther to the north. From the far corner of the parking lot, a five-minute walk along a path between fields will take you to the edge of a thickly wooded gorge. This is the perfect place to act out your Indiana Jones fantasies: you seemingly stumble upon Etruscan tombs sculpted out of the cliff face, you're unlikely to see other visitors, everything is covered in thick vegetation, *and* the site is unguarded. As you walk down to the bottom of the gorge—though it is not steep, good walking shoes and water bottles are recommended—look at the way parts of the rock face have been modeled to imitate architectural styles. To top it off, there are medieval ruins and a photogenic vantage point up the other side of the gorge (about 10 minutes away). As there is no site map on display and little by way of site information, stick to well-trodden paths.

Where to Stay & Eat

★ ¢–$ ✕ **Il Grappolo.** This central wine bar might just be your much-needed antidote to another pasta meal—a great place for a snack, a drink, or a light meal built around wine and good company. It's cold food only, but the menu includes such fresh creations as *insalata di pera, speck, e grana* (salad with pear, speck, and flakes of grana cheese), perhaps accompanied by Paterno wine, a local Sangiovese thoroughbred, considered Lazio's rival to fine Tuscan reds. The atmosphere is modern, youthful, and welcoming. ⊠ *Via Alberata Dante Alighieri 3* ☎ *0766/ 857321* 🖃 *AE, DC, MC, V* ⊙ *Closed Mon. and Jan. 7–31. No lunch Nov.–Mar.*

¢ ✕▦ **San Marco.** It would be impossible to find a better location for exploring the old center of Tarquinia than this ancient monastery, a huge, complex structure on the town's main square that's been operating as an inn since 1876. Rooms are simple, clean, and inviting, and the bar hops with locals on weekend nights. Lodging is merely the latest chapter in the San Marco's storied history; in the 1500s these hallowed halls housed the mysterious order of the Frati Neri (Black Monks)—an Augustinian sect whose cloisters remain intact in the hotel's courtyard. The menu at the excellent restaurant (**¢–$$**) even offers recipes reconstructed from the brothers' 16th-century cookbooks—or pizza, for the less daring. ✉ *Piazza Cavour 18, 01016* ☎ *0766/842234* 🖷 *0766/842306* ⊕ *www.san-marco.com* 🛏 *26 rooms* ⚐ *Restaurant, bar, dance club; no a/c.* ⊟ *AE, DC, MC, V* ⦵ *BP.*

Tuscania

★ ㉑ *24 km (15 mi) northeast of Tarquinia, 25 km (16 mi) west of Viterbo.*

Given its small size—a population of only 7,000—Tuscania seems to overflow with sites from a number of historical periods, much more so than neighboring Tarquinia and Viterbo. The medieval city walls were tastefully restored after a devastating earthquake in 1971, and the interior abutting the walls has been pleasingly landscaped with lawns and gardens. The long-abandoned ancient nucleus of the town, which includes the two outstanding Romanesque churches of Santa Maria Maggiore and San Pietro, lies a 20-minute walk outside the city walls to the southeast. Exploration back in the walled town also pays dividends: narrow cobblestone streets dotted with medieval towers make for great walks. Piazza Basile in front of the Palazzo Comunale presents a parapet with the sculpted lids of nine Etruscan sarcophagi, while below is the Fontana di Sette Cannelle, the restored city fountain dating from Etrusco-Roman times. North of the city walls is the archaeological museum, housed in the convent of the adjacent 15th-century church, Santa Maria del Riposo.

The **Museo Archeologico Tuscanese** displays the necropolis material from two main Etruscan families, the Curunas and Vipinanas, dating from the 4th to 2nd century BC. The family members are depicted on the sarcophagi in typical banqueting position, looking far from undernourished. Also displayed are the grave goods, which would have been buried with them, as well as some helpful photographs showing what the tombs looked like when first excavated. The rooms above have some more recent finds stretching back to the 8th century BC, along with some information panels in English. ✉ *Via del Riposo 36* ☎ *0761/436209* 🖂 *Free* ☉ *Tues.–Sun. 8:30–7:30.*

Where to Stay & Eat

★ $ ✕ **La Torre di Lavello.** Opposite the town's medieval tower, this trattoria-cum-pizzeria combines efficient service with stylish presentation at very reasonable prices. The menu is varied and imaginative. Highly recommended is the fettuccine *al ragù bianco* (a pasta dish with beans), as well as the ricotta cheese *con miele* (with honey) for dessert. To be assured of a seat, arrive early or make a reservation. ⊠ *Via Torre di Lavello 27* ☎ *0761/434258* ▭ *DC, MC, V* ⊗ *Closed Wed.*

¢ ▦ **Locanda di Mirandolina.** This courteously run guesthouse in Tuscania's

FodorsChoice old town makes a perfect base for visiting ancient Etruria. Rooms are

★ distinguished by door color rather than number, and are cozily furnished and immaculately kept. The intimate restaurant ($–$$) is an excellent place to sample local recipes. Book well in advance as this is a popular choice, especially with northern Europeans. ⊠ *Via del Pozzo Bianco 40/ 42* ☎▦ *0761/436595* ⊕ *www.mirandolina.it* ⇗ *10 rooms* ▭ *MC, V* ⦿ *BP* ⊗ *Closed Jan. 6–Feb. 12. Restaurant closed Tues.*

TUSCIA

The Viterbo region, north of the capital, is rich in history, embodied in cameo scenes of dark medieval stone, dappled light on wooded paths, a prelate's palace worthy of Rome itself, and another prelate's pleasure garden, where splashing fountains were aquatic jokes played on unsuspecting guests. From Viterbo and Bagnaia to Caprarola and Villa Lante, this region has a concentration of first-rate attractions—with the surprising Renaissance theme park at Bomarzo thrown in for good measure. The city of Viterbo, which overshadowed Rome as a center of papal power for a time during the Middle Ages, lies in the heart of Tuscia, the modern name for the Etruscan domain of Etruria, a landscape of dramatic beauty punctuated by thickly forested hills and deep, rocky gorges. The farmland east of Viterbo conceals small quarries of the dark, volcanic *peperino* stone that shows up in the walls of so many buildings here, as well as in portals and monumental fireplaces. Lake Bolsena is an extinct volcano, and the sulfur springs still bubbling up in Viterbo's spas were used by the ancient Romans.

Bagnaia is the site of Villa Lante, where there are Italian gardens and a vast park; at Caprarola are the huge Renaissance palace and gardens designed for the Farnese family. Both sites were the work of the virtuoso architect Giacomo Barozzi (circa 1535–1584), known as Vignola, who later worked with Michelangelo on St. Peter's. He rearranged the little town of Caprarola, too, to enhance the palazzo's setting.

The ideal way to explore this region is by car, making Bomarzo your first stop. By train, you can start at Viterbo and get to Bagnaia by local bus. If you're traveling by train or bus you will have to check schedules carefully, and you may have to allow for an overnight if you want to see all four attractions.

Viterbo

②② *104 km (64 mi) northwest of Rome.*

Viterbo's moment of glory was in the 13th century, when it became the seat of the papal court. The medieval core of the city still sits within 12th-century walls. Its old buildings, with windows bright with geraniums, are made of dark peperino, the local stone that colors the medieval part of Viterbo a dark gray, contrasted here and there with the golden tufa rock of walls and towers. Peperino is also used in the characteristic and typically medieval exterior staircases that you see throughout the old town. More recently, Viterbo has blossomed into a regional commercial center, and much of the modern city is loud and industrial. However, Viterbo's San Pellegrino district is a place to get the feel of the Middle Ages, seeing how daily life is carried on in a setting that has remained practically unchanged over the centuries. The Palazzo Papale and the cathedral enhance the effect. The city has also remained a renowned spa center for its natural hot springs just outside of town, frequented by popes—and the laity—since medieval times.

The Gothic **Palazzo Papale** (Papal Palace) was built in the 13th century as a residence for popes looking to get away from the city. At that time Rome was a notoriously unhealthy place, ridden with malaria and plague and rampaging factions of rival barons. In 1271 the palace was the scene of a novel type of rebellion. A conclave held here to elect a new pope had dragged on for months, apparently making no progress. The people of Viterbo were exasperated by the delay, especially as custom decreed that they had to provide for the cardinals' board and lodging for the duration of the conclave. So they tore the roof off the great hall where the cardinals were meeting, and put them on bread and water. Sure enough, a new pope—Gregory X—was elected in short order. The interior of the Palazzo, which houses a museum of sacred art, is currently closed for restoration, but you can climb the stairs to what was once the loggia. ⊠ *Piazza San Lorenzo* 🕾 *0761/341124.*

The facade and interior of Viterbo's duomo, **Chiesa di San Lorenzo,** date from the Middle Ages. On the ancient columns inside the cathedral you can see the chips that an exploding bomb took out of the stone during World War II. There's a small adjoining museum. ⊠ *Piazza San Lorenzo* 🕾 *0761/309623* ⊘ *8–12:30 and 3:30–7.*

The medieval district of **San Pellegrino** is one of the best-preserved such precincts in Italy. It has charming vistas of arches, vaults, towers, exterior staircases, worn wooden doors on great iron hinges, and tiny hanging gardens. You pass many antiques shops as you explore the little squares and byways. The **Fontana Grande** in the piazza of the same name is the largest and most extravagant of Viterbo's authentic Gothic fountains. ⊠ *Via San Pellegrino.*

☺ Viterbo has been a spa town for centuries, and the **Terme dei Papi** continues the tradition. This excellent spa offers the usual rundown of health and beauty treatments with an Etruscan twist: try a facial with local volcanic mud, or a steam bath in an ancient cave, where scalding hot mineral water direct from the Bullicam spring splashes down a waterfall to a pool under your feet. The Terme dei Papi's main draw, however, is the *terme* (baths) themselves: a 100,000-square-foot outdoor limestone pool of Viterbo's famous hot water, which pours into the shallow end at 59°C (138°F)—though the pool feels much hotter than that—and intoxicates with its sulfurous odor. Floats and deck chairs are for rent, but bring your own bathrobe and towel unless you're staying at the hotel. ⊠ *Strada Bagni 12, Viterbo* 🕾 *0761/3501* ⊕ *www.*

termedeipapi.it ✉ *Weekdays €12; weekends €15* ⊙ *Pool, daily 9–5:30; spa, daily 9–6.*

Where to Stay & Eat

★ **$$** ✕ **Enoteca La Torre.** One of the best wine cellars in Italy takes center stage at the elegant Enoteca La Torre. It's also a temple to good eating: in addition to an ever-changing menu there are lists for cheeses, mineral waters, oils, and vinegars. Chestnut fritters and rabbit stew are unusual delicacies, but whatever you choose will be local, traditional, and of the highest quality. ✉ *Via della Torre 5* ☎ *0761/226467* ▭ *AE, DC, MC, V* ⊙ *Closed Sun.*

★ **¢–$$** ✕ **Tre Re.** Viterbo's oldest restaurant—and one of the most ancient in Italy—has been operating in (predictably) the city's historic center since 1622, and it still focuses on nothing but traditional local cooking and open, friendly service. A gregarious buzz of Viterbese businessmen and families fills the small, wood-paneled and white-walled room to overflowing at lunchtime, as diners enjoy the truest versions of such Lazio specialties as *acquacotta viterbese* (literally "cooked water," a hearty vegetable and hot-pepper soup that was the ancient sustenance of shepherds and stockmen. ✉ *Via Macel Gattesco 3* ☎ *0761/304619* ▭ *AE, MC, V* ⊙ *Closed Thurs.*

¢–$ ✕ **Cantina Palazzo dei Mercanti.** The casual Cantina, which shares a
Fodor'sChoice kitchen and wine list with the elegant Enoteca La Torre, offers the best
★ lunch value in town, with impeccably executed classics served up for pocket change. Try whatever is offered as the daily rotating special, such as *pappardelle* (wide, flat fresh pasta noodles) with a tomato-and-meat sauce, or just select a glass or bottle from the Enoteca's epic wine list, which includes a complex matrix of ratings from Italy's foremost wine reviewers. ✉ *Via della Torre 1* ☎ *0761/226467* ▭ *AE, DC, MC, V* ⊙ *Closed Sun.*

$$$ ▦ **Hotel Niccolò V.** This upscale, airy hotel is connected to Viterbo's mineral baths and spa at Terme dei Papi. While the Niccolò, 5 km (3 mi) from the center of town, is certainly the most convenient lodging to the baths, the complex is also a surreal mix of doctors in scrubs, half-naked bathers, and lost hotel guests wandering through an enormous maze-like lobby. In the guest rooms, though, marble baths and wooden floors give an air of country-house elegance. Breakfast, a sumptuous buffet, is taken in a wood-beamed gallery overlooking a small garden. Hotel guests are also offered the option of dinner for a mere €7 extra per person, as well as free use of the outdoor and indoor pools. ✉ *Strada Bagni 12, 01100* ☎ *0761/350555* ▤ *0761/350273* ⊕ *www.termedeipapi.it* ⊃ *20 rooms, 3 suites* ⚏ *Restaurant, in-room safes, minibars, pool, bar, meeting rooms* ▭ *AE, DC, MC, V* ⦿ *BP.*

Bagnaia

㉓ *5 km (3 mi) east of Viterbo.*

The village of Bagnaia is the site of 16th-century cardinal Alessandro Montalto's summer retreat. Small twin residences are but an excuse for the hillside garden and park that surround them, designed by Vignola for a member of the papal court.

Villa Lante is a terraced extravaganza. On the lowest terrace a delightful Italian garden has a centerpiece fountain fed by water channeled down the hillside. On another, higher terrace a stream of water runs through a groove carved in a long stone table where the cardinal entertained his friends alfresco, chilling wine in the running water. That's only one of the most evident and innocent of the whimsical water games that were devised for the cardinal. The symmetry of the formal gardens contrasts with the wild, untamed park adjacent to it, reflecting the paradoxes of nature and artifice that are the theme of this pleasure garden. ⊠ *Via G. Baroni 71* ☎ *0761/288008* ✉ *Park free, gardens and residences €2* ⊘ *Tues.–Sun. 8:30–1 hr before sunset.*

Caprarola

㉔ *19 km (12 mi) southeast of Viterbo.*

The wealthy and powerful Farnese family took over this sleepy village in the 1500s and endowed it with a palace that rivals the great residences of Rome.

The massive, magnificent, 400-year-old **Palazzo Farnese,** built on an unusual pentagonal plan, has an ingenious system of ramps and terraces designed by Vignola that leads right up to the main portal. This nicety allowed carriages and mounts to arrive directly in front of the door. Though the salons are unfurnished, the palace's grandeur is still evident. An artificial grotto decorates one wall, the ceilings are covered with frescoes glorifying the splendors of the Farnese family, and an entire room is frescoed with maps of the world as it was known to 16th-century cartographers. From the windows you can glimpse the garden, which can be visited only by appointment. ⊠ *Via Nicolai* ☎ *0761/646052* ✉ *€2* ⊘ *Tues.–Sun. 8:30–1 hr before sunset.*

Bomarzo

㉕ *15 km (9 mi) northeast of Viterbo.*

☾ The eerie 16th-century **Parco dei Mostri** (Monster Park) is populated by weird and fantastic sculptures of mythical creatures and eccentric architecture. It was created by Prince Vicino Orsini for his wife, Giulia Farnese, who is said to have taken one look at the park and died of heart failure. No one really knows why the prince had the sculptures carved in outcroppings of stone in a dusky wood on his estate, but it probably has something to do with the artifices that were an artistic conceit of his time. Children love it, and there are photo ops galore. However, be advised that the park's staff can be brusque. ⊠ *1½ km (1 mi) west of town* ☎ *0761/924029* ✉ *€8* ⊘ *Daily 8:30–1 hr before sunset.*

TIVOLI, PALESTRINA & SUBIACO

East of Rome are two of Lazio's star attractions—the Villa Adriana and the Villa d'Este in Tivoli—and, off the beaten path in the mountains beyond them, the lesser-known and wonderfully peaceful Palestrina and

Subiaco. The road from Rome to Tivoli passes through uninspiring industrial areas and burgeoning suburbs that used to be lush countryside. You'll know you're close to Tivoli when you see vast quarries of travertine marble and smell the sulfurous vapors of the little spa, Bagni di Tivoli. Both sites in Tivoli are outdoors and entail walking.

With a car you can continue your loop through the mountains east of Rome, taking in two very different sights that are both focused on religion. The ancient pagan sanctuary at Palestrina is set on the slopes of Mt. Ginestro, from which it commands a sweeping view of the green plain and distant mountains. Subiaco, the cradle of Western monasticism, is tucked away in the mountains above Tivoli and Palestrina. Unless you start out very early and have lots of energy, plan an overnight stop along the way if you want to take in all three.

Tivoli

🔢 *36 km (22 mi) northeast of Rome.*

★ **Villa Adriana** (Hadrian's Villa), 6 km (4 mi) south of Tivoli, was an emperor's theme park, an exclusive retreat where the marvels of the classical world were reproduced for a ruler's pleasure. Hadrian, who succeeded Trajan as emperor in AD 117, was a man of genius and intellectual curiosity. Fascinated by the accomplishments of the Hellenistic world, he decided to re-create it for his own enjoyment by building this villa over a vast tract of land below the ancient settlement of Tibur. From AD 118 to 130, architects, laborers, and artists worked on the villa, periodically spurred on by the emperor himself when he returned from another voyage full of ideas for even more daring constructions. After his death in AD 138 the fortunes of his villa declined. It was sacked by barbarians and Romans alike; many of his statues and decorations ended up in the Musei Vaticani, but the expansive ruins are nonetheless compelling.

It's not the single elements but the peaceful and harmonious effect of the whole that makes Hadrian's Villa such a treat. Oleanders, pines, and cypresses growing among the ruins heighten the visual impact. To help you get your bearings, maps are issued free with the audio guides (€4) at the ticket office. A visit here should take about two hours, more if you like to savor antiquity slowly. After sunset on Fridays, a special one-hour tour under spotlights is available for €4.65. In summer there's a sound-and-light show at night; check with your hotel concierge or call the ticket office for the schedule. Otherwise, in summer the park should be visited early to take advantage of cool mornings. ⊠ *Bivio di Villa Adriana, off Via Tiburtina, 6 km (4 mi) southwest of Tivoli* ☎ *0774/ 530203* 🎫 *€6.50* 🕙 *Daily 9–1 hr before sunset.*

★ **Villa d'Este,** a late-Renaissance estate, is a playground of artistic whimsy, manifested in the 80-some fountains of all shapes and sizes that tumble down the vast, steep hillside garden. Cardinal Ippolito d'Este (1509–72), an active figure in the political intrigues of mid-16th-century Italy, set about proving his dominance over man and nature by commissioning this monument to architectural excess. His builders tore down part of a Franciscan monastery to clear the site, then diverted the Aniene River to water the garden and feed the fountains. History shows it was worth the effort, and the Villa d'Este is still considered one of Italy's most beautiful spots. A major showpiece fountain—Fontana dell'Organo—was restored in 2003 and now pipes out music at regular intervals (check at the ticket office for precise times). On the other side of the garden the more timeworn Fontana di Roma is a scale model representing Rome's river network and mythology as well as some of its ancient buildings. Allow an hour for this visit, and bear in mind that you'll be climbing a lot of stairs. ⊠ *Piazza Trento 1* ☎ *0774/312070* ⊕ *www.villadestetivoli.info* ⊠ *€6.50* ☉ *Tues.–Sun. 9–1 hr before sunset.*

Where to Stay & Eat

$ ✕ **Del Falcone.** A central location—on Tivoli's main street leading off Largo Garibaldi—means that this restaurant is popular and often crowded. In the ample and rustic dining rooms you can try homemade *crespella* (a rolled pancake), flavored with nuts or ricotta cheese and spinach. Country-style grilled meats are excellent. ⊠ *Via Del Trevio 34* ☎ *0774/312358* ▤ *AE, DC, MC, V.*

$$ ✕▥ **Adriano.** At the entrance to Hadrian's Villa, this restaurant-inn is a handy place to have lunch before heading up the hill to Villa d'Este. It's also a good base for the night before or after exploring. The restaurant ($$–$$$) is Italian with a sophisticated touch, as in risotto *ai fiori di zucchine* (with zucchini flowers). The atmosphere is relaxing, especially at outdoor tables in summer. The green surroundings also provide a restful backdrop for the Adriano's 10 rooms, which are casually elegant and immaculately kept. ⊠ *Via di Villa Adriana 194* ☎ *0774/ 382235* ▤ *0774/535122* ⊕ *www.hoteladriano.it* ⇩ *10 rooms* ⬧ *Tennis court, bar; no smoking* ▤ *AE, DC, MC, V* ☉ *No dinner Sun.* ❏ *BP.*

Palestrina

㉗ *27 km (17 mi) southeast of Tivoli on S636, 37 km (23 mi) east of Rome along Via Prenestina.*

Palestrina is surprisingly little known outside Italy, except to students of ancient history and music lovers. Its most famous native son, Giovanni Pierluigi da Palestrina, born here in 1525, was the renowned composer of 105 masses, as well as madrigals, magnificats, and motets. But the town was celebrated long before the composer's lifetime.

Ancient Praeneste (modern Palestrina) flourished much earlier than Rome. It was the site of the Temple of Fortuna Primigenia, which dates from the 2nd century BC. This was one of the largest, richest, most frequented temple complexes in all antiquity—people came from far and wide to consult its famous oracle. In modern times no one had any idea of the extent of the complex until World War II bombings exposed ancient foundations occupying huge artificial terraces stretching from the upper part of the town as far downhill as its central Duomo.

Large arches and terraces scale the hillside up to the imposing **Palazzo Barberini,** built in the 17th century along the semicircular lines of the original temple. It's now a museum containing material found on the site, dating from throughout the classical period. This well-labeled collection of Etruscan bronzes, pottery, and terra-cotta statuary as well as Roman artifacts takes second place to the chief attraction, a 1st-century BC mosaic representing the Nile in flood. This delightful work—a large-scale composition in which form, color, and innumerable details captivate the eye—is alone worth the trip to Palestrina. But there's more: a model of the temple as it was in ancient times will help you appreciate the immensity of the original construction. ⊠ *Museo Nazionale Archeologico, Palazzo Barberini* ☎ *06/9538100* ⌦ *€3* ⊗ *Daily 9–7:30; archaeological zone of the temple: daily 9–1 hr before sunset.*

Where to Stay & Eat

¢ ✕🏠 **Hotel Stella.** In the restaurant ($–$$) of this small central hotel in Palestrina's public garden you'll receive a cordial welcome, and find on the menu local dishes such as light and freshly made fettuccine served with a choice of sauces, as well as unusual combinations such as *pasta e fagioli con frutti di mare* (pasta and bean soup with shellfish). Decor tends toward the bright and fanciful. The guest rooms are frilly and a bit worn, but clean and comfortable. ⊠ *Piazzale Liberazione 3 00036* ☎ *06/9538172* 🖷 *06/9573360* ⊕ *www.hotelstella.it* ⤺ *30 rooms* ⚶ *Restaurant, bar; no a/c in some rooms* ▤ *AE, DC, MC, V* �ⓘ○ⓘ *BP.*

Subiaco

28 *54 km (33 mi) northeast of Rome.*

Tucked in among wooded mountains in the deep and narrow valley of the Aniene River, which empties into the Tiber in Rome, Subiaco is a modern town built over World War II rubble. It is chiefly known (aside from being the birthplace of Gina Lollobrigida, whose family name is common in these parts) as the site of the monastery where St. Benedict devised his rule of communal religious life in the 6th century, founding the order that was so important in transmitting learning through the ages. Even earlier, the place was a refuge of Nero, who built a villa here said to have rivaled that of Hadrian at Tivoli, damming the river to create three lakes and a series of waterfalls. The road to the monastery passes the ruins of the emperor's villa.

The 6th-century **Monastero di San Benedetto** is a landmark of Western monasticism. It was built over the grotto where the saint lived and meditated. Clinging to the cliff on nine great arches, it has resisted assaults for almost 900 years. Over the little wooden veranda at the entrance, a Latin inscription wishes PEACE TO THOSE WHO ENTER. The upper church is covered with frescoes by Umbrian and Sienese artists of the 14th century. In front of the main altar a stairway leads to the lower church, carved out of the rock, with another stairway leading down to the grotto where Benedict lived as a hermit for three years. The frescoes here are even earlier than those above; look for the portrait of St. Francis of Assisi, painted from life in the early 13th century, in the **Cappella di San Gregorio** (Chapel of St. Gregory), and for the monastery's oldest fresco, painted in the Byzantine style in the 8th century, in the **Grotta dei Pastori** (Shepherds' Grotto). ⊠ *Subiaco* 🕾 *0774/85039* ⊕ *www.benedettini-subiaco.it* 🖃 *Free* ⊘ *Daily 9–12:30 and 3–6.*

Where to Stay & Eat

¢–$ ✕ **Frà Diavolo.** About 5 km (3 mi) outside Subiaco on the road up to Cervara—right at the junction to Monte Livata—is this cheerful restaurant-cum-pizzeria. Choose between the sunny eating area inside or the fairly makeshift outdoor terrace. Brisk but courteous service ensures that you are plied at regular intervals with local specialties such as *strozzapreti alla Frà Diavolo* (homemade pasta with tomatoes, eggplant, mozzarella, and basil). ⊠ *Contrada Colle Perino* 🕾 *0774/83850* 🖃 *AE, DC, MC, V* ⊘ *Closed Mon.*

¢ 🏨 **Foresteria del Monastero.** If you're looking for a quiet retreat in pristine natural surroundings and the added bonus of spiritual refreshment, this is the place. Part of the Santa Scolastica monastery complex—the rooms are not nearly as spartan as the original monks' cells—has been tastefully renewed to create an efficiently run hotel, with the added option of half board for only €6 per person per day. Well-marked trails lead from the Foresteria up to the monastery of St. Benedict and beyond into the wilderness area of the Parco dei Monti Simbruini. There's just one caveat: the monastery's bells start ringing at 8 AM, so late sleepers might think twice. ⊠ *Monastero Santa Scolastica, 00028* 🕾 *0774/85569* 🖶 *0774/822862* 🖄 *foresteria@benedittini-subiaco.it* 🛏 *45 rooms* ♿ *Restaurant, bar, 2 meeting rooms* 🖃 *AE, DC, MC, V* ⦿❘ *BP.*

SERMONETA, NINFA & SPERLONGA

This trio of romantic places south of Rome, set in a landscape defined by low mountains and a broad coastal plain, lures you into a past that seems centuries away from the city's bustle. Sermoneta is a castle town. Ninfa, nearby, is a noble family's fairy-tale garden that is open to the public only at limited times. Both are on the eastern fringe of the Pontine Plain, once a malaria-infested marshland that was ultimately reclaimed for agriculture by one of the most successful projects of Mussolini's regime. Several new towns were built here in the 1930s, among them Latina and Pontinia. Sperlonga is a medieval fishing village perched above the sea near one of emperor Tiberius's most fabulous villas. You need a car to see them all in a day or so, and to get to Ninfa. But Sermoneta and Sperlonga are accessible by public transit.

Sermoneta

㉙ *80 km (50 mi) southeast of Rome.*

In Sermoneta the town and castle are one. In medieval times concentric rings of walls protected the townspeople and provided shelter from marauders for nearby farmers. The lords—in this case the Caetani family—

held a last line of defense in the tall tower, where if necessary they could cut themselves off by pulling up the drawbridge.

The **Castello Caetani** dates from the 1200s. In the 15th century, having won the castle by ruse from the Caetanis, Borgia Pope Alexander VI transformed it into a formidable fortress and handed it over to his son Cesare. The chiaroscuro of dark and light stone, the quiet of the narrow streets, and the bastions that hint at siege and battle take you back in time. ⊠ *Via della Fortezza* ☎ *0773/695404* ✉ *€5* ↻ *Guided tours only* ⊙ *Apr.–Oct., Fri.–Wed. 10–11, 3–4, and 5–6; Nov.–Mar., Fri.–Wed. 10–11:30, 2–3, and 4–5.*

Ninfa

30 *75 km (47 mi) southeast of Rome, 5 km (3 mi) north of Sermoneta.*

In the Middle Ages **Ninfa** was a thriving village, part of the Caetani family's vast landholdings around Sermoneta. It was abandoned when malaria-carrying mosquitoes infested the plain, and it fell into ruin. Now it's a place of rare beauty, a dream garden of romantic ruins and rushing waters, of exotic flora and fragrant blooms. Ninfa is an oasis of the Worldwide Fund for Nature (WWF), managed in collaboration with the Caetani heirs. Generations of the Caetani family, including English and American spouses and gardening buffs, created the garden over the course of the 20th century. ⊠ *Via Ninfina, Doganella di Ninfa* ☎ *0773/ 632231, 0773/695404 APT Latina-Provincial Tourist Office* ✉ *€8* ↻ *Guided tours only* ⊙ *Apr.–Oct: usually weekends 9:30–noon and 2:30–6, but call for designated days and reservations.*

Sperlonga

31 *127 km (79 mi) southeast of Rome.*

Sperlonga is a labyrinth of whitewashed alleys, arches, and little houses, like a casbah wrapped around a hilltop overlooking the sea, with broad, sandy beaches on either side. Long a favorite haunt of artists and artisans in flight from Rome's quick pace, the town has ancient origins. The medieval town gates, twisting alleys, and watchtower were vital to its defense when pirate ships came in sight. Now they simply make this former fishing town even more picturesque.

Under a cliff on the shore only 1 km (½ mi) south of Sperlonga are the ruins of a grandiose villa built for Roman emperor Tiberius and known as the **Grotta di Tiberio.** The villa incorporated several natural grottoes, in one of which Tiberius dined with guests on an artificial island. The various courses were served on little boats that floated across the shallow seawater pool to the emperor's table. Showpieces of the villa were the colossal sculpture groups embellishing the grotto. The **Museo Nazionale** (National Museum) was built on the site especially to hold the fragments of these sculptures, discovered by chance by an amateur archaeologist. The huge statues had been smashed to pieces centuries earlier by Byzantine monks unsympathetic to pagan images. For decades the subject and appearance of the originals remained a mystery, and the museum was a work in progress as scholars there tried to put together the 7,000 pieces of this giant puzzle. Their achievement, the immense Scylla group, largest of the sculptures, is on view here. ⊠ *Via Flacca (SS 213, km 16.5)* ☎ *0771/548028* 🖭 *€2* 🕙 *Daily 9–7.*

Where to Stay & Eat

$$–$$$ ✕ **Gli Archi.** Tucked into a landing of Sperlonga's myriad stairways, this attractive restaurant has brick-arch interiors and tables on a cute *piazzetta* for fair-weather dining. A touch of refinement puts it a cut above the establishments closer to the beach, and its owners take pride in serving high-quality ingredients with culinary simplicity. Seafood, including the house favorite *pennette alla seppiolina* (pasta with cuttlefish ink), predominates, but there are a few meat platters, too. ⊠ *Via Ottaviano 17* ☎ *0771/548300* 🖃 *AE, DC, MC, V* 🕙 *Closed Wed. and Jan.*

$–$$ 🏨 **La Sirenella.** This family-run hotel occupies a prime position on Sperlonga's sandy beach and is a short walk from the old town. Rooms are bright and airy—ask for a room on one of the upper floors in the *ala mare* (sea wing) to enjoy views over the Circeo promontory and the audiotherapy of lapping waves. ⊠ *Via Cristoforo Colombo 25, 01100* ☎ *0771/549186* 🖶 *0771/549189* ⊕ *www.lasirenella.com* 🛏 *40 rooms* 🍴 *Restaurant, bar, free parking* 🖃 *AE, MC, V* 🍽 *MAP, FAP.*

ABRUZZO

Central Italy isn't all tranquil hills dotted with picturesque hill towns and vineyards. East of Lazio the terrain of the often-overlooked Abruzzo region turns rugged, with isolated mountain villages and some of the country's best-preserved wildlife sanctuaries. In Abruzzo, you can enjoy nature in the rough, and there's no better place than the Parco Nazionale d'Abruzzo for hiking and horseback riding. L'Aquila, a walkable town well worth an afternoon stroll, is a good base for exploring the central part of the region. Abruzzese cooking is mountain-style—hearty, simple, local foods. You are likely to find plenty of lamb, mutton, and pork, pecorino cheese and ricotta, and wild mushrooms and lentils on restaurant menus, along with dishes spiced with saffron, which is grown near L'Aquila. The local wines tend toward the robust and the spicy; white Trebbiano and red Montepulciano d'Abruzzo are the best-known types.

L'Aquila

㉜ *125 km (78 mi) northeast of Rome.*

The regional capital of L'Aquila was founded when Emperor Frederick II (1482–1556) united the 99 surrounding kingdoms under one flag (which bore an eagle, or *l'aquila*). The town's most famous fountain, **Fontana Delle 99 Canelle,** commemorates the event with 99 spouts, and the church bells in the Duomo ring 99 times each night. A good place to begin a walk is Piazza Battaglione Alpini, which serves as a bus terminal. ★ L'Aquila's austere **Castello** (fortress) looms over the city, offering sweeping vistas of the nearby Gran Sasso mountain range. Built by the Spanish rulers in the 16th century to discourage popular revolt, the Castello also served as a prison. The formidable defense works—which were never put to the test—include a warren of underground passages around the bastions, which are now open to the public.

The castle is the site of temporary art exhibitions and the **Museo Nazionale dell'Abruzzo,** which has a good collection drawn from the region's earthquake-ravaged churches and a gallery of modern art on the top floor. The highlight of the visit is the reconstructed skeleton of a million-year-old mammoth discovered nearby in 1954. ⊠ *Viale delle Medaglie d'Oro* ☎ *0862/633200* ☑ *€4* ⊙ *Tues.–Sun. 9–8. Free guided tours around castle: weekends 10:30, noon, 3, 4, and 5:30.*

The main road from Piazza Battaglione Alpini leads to the center of town. Up on the right is the small Piazza Santa Maria Paganica; a little farther ahead is Via di San Bernardino, which climbs to the left to the Renaissance church of **San Bernardino.** It was built in honor of St. Bernardine of Siena and has a lovely facade featuring the classical orders of columns. The mausoleum that holds the saint's remains was built by a pupil of Donatello (circa 1386–1466), and the altarpiece is by Andrea della Robbia (1435–1525). The rest of the interior was given a baroque makeover in the early 18th century. ⊠ *Via di San Bernardino* ⊙ *Daily 8–noon and 4–6.*

A 15-minute walk from the church of San Bernardino along Via Fortebraccio brings you outside the city walls to **Santa Maria di Collemaggio,** probably the most famous church in Abruzzo. It was built at the end of the 13th century by the hermit Peter of Morrone, who was later elected Pope Celestine V, and its fame stems from Peter's. He was so attached to the church that he insisted on being crowned and buried here rather than in Rome; his remains rest in the mausoleum to the right of the altar. The church's simple Romanesque facade is strikingly laced with a geometric pattern of white and pink marble. Gothic elements include the rose windows and decorative portals. The interior is rather bare—it was stripped of its baroque embellishments in the 1970s—although the floor has decorative patterns, and several fine 15th-century frescoes adorn the nave walls. ⊠ *Piazzale Collemaggio 1* ☎ *0862/26744* ⊙ *Daily 9–6:30.*

Where to Stay & Eat

★ **$$** ✕ **Elodia.** A curious but successful blend of elegance and simplicity, Elodia specializes in hard-to-find traditional Abruzzese dishes such as *crespelle di ricotta alla montanara* (thin ricotta pancakes), rustic flavors such as chickpea-and-chestnut soup (in winter), and foodie touches such as an olive oil list and wine-tasting menus. Delicious homemade desserts such as apple-chocolate cake and pears baked in Montepulciano d'Abruzzo wine should not be missed. After dinner, ask for a tour of the wine cellar. ⊠ *Frazione Camarda, S17bis del Gran Sasso* ☎ *0862/ 606219* 🖃 *AE, DC, MC, V* ⊙ *Closed Mon. and 1st 2 wks in July. No dinner Sun.*

¢–$ ✕ **Le Fiaccole.** Occupying tastefully restored vaulted cellars a short walk from the Duomo, Le Fiaccole is an atmospheric venue for both quick snacks—such as a €4 pizzalike *crostino* from the wood-burning oven—

and more challenging pasta dishes, like homemade *pizzicuni ai cinque sapori* (five-flavored pasta served with mushrooms, bacon, saffron, arugula, and Parmesan flakes). The modest markup on good wines also goes down well with the youngish clientele. ⊠ *Via degli Ortolani 10* ☎ *0862/414221* ⊟ *AE, DC, MC, V* ☺ *Closed Wed.*

$ ⊞ **Duomo.** The quiet Duomo, housed in 18th-century quarters, is as central as it can be. Many rooms have a view of the lovely square below, and the decor is a nice blend of traditional touches and modern comforts: expect terra-cotta floors and wrought-iron beds matched with practical wooden furniture. The buffet breakfast includes local honey, cakes, and cookies. ⊠ *Via Dragonetti 10, 67100* ☎ *0862/410893* ⊜ *0862/413058* ⊕ *www.hotel-duomo.it* ☟ *28 rooms* ☖ *Bar; no a/c* ⊟ *AE, DC, MC, V* ⦿❘ *BP.*

Shopping

There's a good **antiques market** in Piazza Santa Maria della Paganica the second weekend of each month. Piazza del Duomo is the location for the town's **produce market** Monday–Saturday 8–1.

Medieval Abruzzo

The landscape surrounding L'Aquila is studded with old castles, guard towers, and tiny hamlets, some perfectly preserved and still inhabited, others in ruins and haunted by the ghosts of past battles. Castel del Monte and Santo Stefano di Sessanio are two medieval *borghi* (hamlets) east of L'Aquila on the S17bis that make a pleasant half-day excursion.

㉝ Castel del Monte, 14 km (9 mi) east of Santo Stefano di Sessanio on the S17bis, is an unusual example of a *ricetto,* a type of fortified village without external walls. A single steep access road rises to the center of the town, which is crossed by narrow alleys and dark tunnels leading to the more distant houses. In case of attack, the inhabitants could barricade themselves in their houses, block the narrow streets, and pour hot oil down the main street.

㉞ Santo Stefano di Sessanio was first the property of the powerful Roman Piccolomini family, then passed to the Medici. It has the most sophisticated guard tower in the area, built with rounded instead of squared sides to make an attack more difficult. Climb to the top to enjoy a panoramic view of the Campo Imperatore valley and its striking rock formations.

Skiing

The area around L'Aquila is dominated by the **Apennines,** central Italy's greatest mountains. The Alps they're not, but in winter you can find ample choice for a day's skiing at **Campo Imperatore** (☎ 0862/22146), **Campo Felice** (☎ 0862/917803), and **Ovindoli** (☎ 0863/705087), which have a total of 60 km (40 mi) of runs and 100 km (60 mi) of cross-country trails. Note that winter weekends see a heavy influx of Romans and Neapolitans on the slopes, so to avoid long waits at the ski lifts opt for midweek skiing if conditions are right.

Sulmona

35 *63 km (39 mi) southeast of L'Aquila.*

Sulmona may be best known for producing some of Italy's best *confezioni* (candies), but the little town is also one of the visual gems of Abruzzo, buried in a river valley in the region's mountainous heartland. Its winding pedestrian shopping streets and alleyways reveal the fanciful fonts of centuries-old storefronts, fading shades of orange palazzi, and a jumble of grand mirrored candy shops. While Sulmona has little in the way of well-known sights, its jovial evening *passeggiata* (stroll), down-home cooking, and kinship with Abruzzese tradition are unlike anything you might see in the big city. It's also an excellent base for exploring the national parkland nearby.

Corso Ovidio is Sulmona's main strip, worthy of a long stroll, especially in the before-dinner hours. The 18th-century candy stores along the street are all similar, so take your pick if souvenir-shopping; look for exquisite silver candied almonds or Sulmona's trademark, the tiny, white, spherical *confetti*. The Romanesque **Cattedrale di San Panfilo**, at the end of Corso Ovidio, is piled atop the age-old ruins of a Roman temple. In the wide-open Piazza Garibaldi in the shadow of the mountains at the edge of the old town, the central **Fontana del Vecchio** is the terminus of a 13th-century aqueduct that divides the new and old towns.

Where to Stay & Eat

$ ✕ **Da Gino.** A local crowd flocks to this casual basement trattoria in the *centro storico* (historic center), especially at lunchtime, to sample from a careful selection of well-priced Abruzzo classics. A cool yellow room with cathedral-like arches occupies the underground space next to the 15th-century Santa Maria della Tomba. Daily specials (don't even think about asking for a menu) might include tasty *involtini* (veal or chicken rolled with ham, mushrooms, peppers, rosemary, and white wine sauce). Don't miss the assortment of *contorni* (vegetables) such as stuffed pepper and zucchini with egg batter. Wash it down with the local red, Montepulciano d'Abruzzo. ⊠ *Piazza Plebiscito 12* 🕾 *0864/52289* ➡ *No credit cards* ⊗ *Closed Sun. No lunch Mon.*

¢ 🏨 **Hotel Italia.** Frozen in time, this no-frills hotel in the very heart of the old town will transport you to Italy's past. Beautiful old furniture, fading mirrors, and winding staircases lead to a maze of skeleton-keyed rooms with little in the way of modern facilities, but an abundance of belle-epoque character. If you want to go even more rustic, rooms without bath are half the price. A rickety ladder on the top floor leads to a roof with views over the nearby dome of Sant'Annunziata and a panorama of Abruzzo's surrounding mountain terrain—especially spectacular at sunrise. ⊠ *Piazza Salvatore Tommasi* 🕾🕾 *0864/52308* ➡ *27 rooms, 18 with bath* 🕭 *No a/c* ➡ *No credit cards* ⊙ *EP.*

Parco Nazionale d'Abruzzo

★ ㊱ *Civitella Alfedena 109 km (68 mi) southeast of L'Aquila, 18 km (11 mi) east of Pescasseroli.*

Italy's national park system is for the most part underdeveloped, but the 440-square-km (170-square-mi) Abruzzo National Park is a notable exception. Full of lakes, streams, ruined castles, wildlife, and rugged terrain crossed by hiking trails, the park is home to Apennine wolves, Marsican brown bears, Abruzzan chamois, and an interesting mix of Mediterranean and Alpine birds. The Carta Turistica, on sale at local tobacconists or newsagents, is a comprehensive topographical map with nearly 150 trails marked and identified with symbols indicating their relative difficulty and the animals that you're most likely to meet along the way. One of the most popular short walks (2½ hours) begins near Opi (path F2) and crosses the lovely Valle Fondillo, with chamois to be spotted on the higher ground of Monte Amaro in the early morning. (Should you miss them, the Opi entrance has a semi-enclosed chamois preserve.) For a full-day loop in the green, try path I1 to the Val di Rosa forest, and then head up to Passo Cavuto and return to town via Valle Ianna'nghera (path K6).

Helpful information offices at the edges of the park in the towns of **Pescasseroli** (✉ Via Piave 2 ☎ 0863/910097) and **Civitella Alfedena** (✉ Museo del Lupo, Via Santa Lucia ☎ 0864/890141) have all the information you will need for a hike through the scenery and can also arrange guided tours in English. The visitor centers, open daily 10–1 and 3–7, each themed toward a different kind of wildlife found inside the park, provide great opportunities for children to learn about animals. There's a wolf reserve and wolf museum with exhibits and films in the quasi-Alpine village of Civitella Alfedena, which is the starting point for several major trails. The more bustling town of Pescasseroli at the valley bottom has a nature reserve for injured animals and a nature museum and ecolab with interactive displays for kids.

Where to Stay

¢ 🏨 **Albergo Antico Borgo La Torre.** Close to Civitella's medieval tower, this hotel is a hospitality landmark for hikers and family groups, with owner-manager Antonio dispensing both bonhomie and local knowledge in abundance. If available, ask for one of the refurbished wood-paneled rooms in the newer wing. A small adjoining garden has lounge chairs for warm-weather basking. Most guests prefer to stay on half-board terms, and enjoy hearty *cucina abruzzese* in a cozy dining room at the end of the day. ✉ *Via Castello 3, 67030 Civitella Alfedena* ☎ *0864/890121* 🖷 *0864/890210* ⊕ *www.albergolatorre.com* ⤳ *19 rooms* ⚐ *Restaurant, bar; no a/c* ▭ *No credit cards* ⊙| *BP.*

MOLISE

Established in 1965 after splitting from Abruzzo to the north, the region of Molise has long lived in the shadow of its more glamorous neighboring regions. This has spared it many of the ravages of development:

its mountains have much of their original woodland and grassland, the hill villages are generally well preserved, the archaeological sites are delightfully undervisited, and the cucina has retained its distinct *molisano* flavor with the best of local ingredients. With the exception of Valle d'Aosta, Molise is Italy's smallest region and lends itself to a few days' exploration from a single base. Of the two provincial centers, Isernia has more history and character than its rather brash counterpart to the east, Campobasso.

Isernia

③⑦ *111 km (70 mi) north of Naples, 176 km (110 mi) southeast of Rome.*

Isernia perches at just under 1,500 feet above sea level on what in the distant past must have been an easily defensible ridge overlooking river valleys and busy viaducts. The town suffered severe collateral damage during Allied bombing raids in World War II—they were aiming for the bridge down in the valley. The northern part of the town is laid out in the standard grid pattern of Italian postwar development. Previous damage had been wrought by an earthquake in 1837, a notable victim being the **Cattedrale,** rebuilt in rather incongruous neoclassical style shortly afterward. Beneath the campanile to the east of the cathedral are four marble statues (in desperate need of restoration) from the Roman era positioned at the corners of the gateway.

In the heart of the old town is the **Museo Nazionale,** which houses finds from Roman necropoli outside ancient Aesernia. You can view an impressive array of funerary sculptures and the remarkably preserved remains of local fauna (including elephant and rhino species) hunted by *Homo aeserniensis* on a grassy river plain more than 700,000 years ago. Ask to see the helpful video (in good English) contextualizing the finds. ⊠ *Ex-convento Santa Maria delle Monache, Corso Marcelli 48* ☎ *0865/ 415179* ⊡ *€2* ⊙ *Daily 8:30–7:30* ⊙ *Closed 1st and 3rd Mon. of every month.*

---

off the beaten path

PESCHE – Travel 4 km (2 mi) northeast of Isernia to Pesche, a village clinging both to its past and the steep limestone slope beneath it. From here two paths head up and around the Riserva Naturale di Pesche above the village, mainly through holm-oak and deciduous oak forests. In springtime look for orchids among the bare limestone rocks, and enjoy the woodland concert of blackcaps and finches.

Where to Stay & Eat

$ ✕ **Taverna Maresca.** Don't be misled by the rustic, unassuming air of this family restaurant in the heart of Isernia's old town—it's long been an excellent place for sampling local cucina. Warming dishes in winter include such peasant fare as *ceci e fagioli* (beans and chickpeas; Isernia claims to have Molise's best), and *involtini di melanzane* (eggplant rolls stuffed with meat and cheese) are thankfully served year-round. Dinner reservations are essential on Saturday. ⊠ *Corso Marcelli 186* ☎ *0865/ 3976* ⊕ *web.tiscali.it/tavernamaresca* ⊟ *AE, DC, MC, V* ⊙ *Closed Sun., Dec. 24–Jan. 2, and Aug.*

¢ ⊞ **Hotel S. Maria del Bagno.** Though definitely not a traditional stone-built *molisano* building, this quiet, well-run hotel is functional and fairly spacious, and its location—just outside the picturesque medieval hill village of Pesche—makes it a perfect base for local country walks exploring nearby Isernia (3 km [2 mi]) and excursions into the rest of Molise. ⊠ *Viale S. Maria del Bagno 1, 86090 Pesche* ☎ *0865/460129* 🖷 *0865/460136* ⇨ *45 rooms* ♨ *Restaurant, bar, playground, meeting room; no a/c* ⊟ *AE, DC, MC, V* ⦿ *BP.*

Pietrabbondante

➌➑ *26 km (17 mi) northeast of Isernia, 25 km (16 mi) south of Agnone.*

Identified by some scholars as Bovianum Vetus, the capital of Samnium in antiquity, the site of Pietrabbondante consists of a theater and temple complex built between the 4th and 1st century BC, 3,000 feet up in the wilds of Molise. Though attempts to restore two of the monuments are in questionable taste—concrete sits uncomfortably with the local limestone—seeing a **Hellenistic theater** this high up verges on a supernatural experience. ⊠ *Via Macere* ☎ *0865/76129* 🖾 *€2* ⊙ *8:30–1 hr before sunset.*

Agnone

➌➒ *43 km (27 mi) northeast of Isernia.*

Known since medieval times for its thriving production of bells, Agnone has a rambling old town that's worth exploring. Make a stop at the **Museo Storico della Campana,** which chronicles the history of campanology (bell-making) in the area. ⊠ *C/o Fonderia Marinelli, Via F. D'Onofrio 14* ☎ *0865/78235* 🖾 *€4.50* ⊙ *Tours daily at noon and 4; in August at 10, noon, 4, and 6; all tours in Italian only.*

Where to Stay

¢ ⊞ **Albergo Sammartino.** Strategically located at the entrance to the old town and with views from most rooms sweeping over the Verrino valley, this hotel has been owned by the Sammartino family for almost 90 years. Rooms are simple, light, and usually quiet—except for Sunday mornings, when church bells start up their concerto around dawn. ⊠ *Largo Pietro Micca 44, 86081* ☎ *0865/77577* 🖷 *0865/78239* ⇨ *22 rooms* ♨ *Restaurant, bar, meeting room; no a/c* ⊟ *AE, DC, MC, V* ⦿ *BP.*

Sepino

➍⓪ *41 km (26 mi) southeast of Isernia, 25 km (16 mi) south of Campobasso.*

The hill town of Sepino takes its name from the ancient Roman town of **Saepinum,** situated off the main S17 near the village of Altìlia. The site, whose monuments were mainly laid out in the Augustan age (27 BC–AD 14), is like a miniature Pompeii, but refreshingly without the hordes of visitors. Saepinum is best tackled by entering through the Porta Tammaro 300 feet from the main road and working your way around counterclockwise via the theater, the baths (note the original stucco on the walls), the *decumanus* (main street) to the basilica (identified by its peristyle of columns), and then out onto the forum, with its standard complement of civic buildings. Southwest of the forum, just off the *cardo* (main cross street) leading to the southwestern gate of Porta Terravecchia are the administrative offices and visitor center, where site maps and descriptions (in Italian) can be obtained. ⊠ *Contrada Altilia* ☎ *0874/ 790207* ☜ *Free* ⊘ *Daily 8–8.*

LAZIO, ABRUZZO & MOLISE A TO Z

To research prices, get advice from other travelers, and book travel arrangements, visit www.fodors.com.

AIRPORTS

Central Italy's closest major airports are in Rome, Pescara, and Naples. Pescara is served by Ryanair from London and Frankfurt, and by Air One from Milan.

🔢 Airport Information **Naples** ☎ 081/7896259 Capodichino ⊕ www.gesac.it. **Pescara** ☎ 085/4324200 Abruzzo ⊕ www.abruzzo-airport.it. **Rome** ☎ 06/65953640 Fiumicino.

BUS TRAVEL

COTRAL buses leave Rome for Cerveteri from the Lepanto stop of Metro A, with service every 40 minutes or so during the day. The ride takes about 70 minutes. Tuscania has a regular bus connection with Viterbo.

Buses leave Rome for Tivoli every 15 minutes from the terminal at the Ponte Mammolo stop on Metro B, but not all take the route that passes near Hadrian's Villa. Inquire which bus passes closest to the villa and tell the driver to let you off there. The ride takes about one hour. From Rome to Palestrina, take the COTRAL bus from the Anagnina stop on Metro A. From Rome to Subiaco, take the COTRAL bus from the Rebibbia stop on Metro B; buses leave every 40 minutes; the circuitous trip takes one hour and 45 minutes.

COTRAL buses for Viterbo depart from the Saxa Rubra stop of the Ferrovie COTRAL train. The *diretta* (direct) bus takes about 75 minutes. Bagnaia can be reached from Viterbo by local city bus. For Caprarola, COTRAL buses leave from the Saxa Rubra station on the Roma Nord line.

COTRAL buses for Sermoneta leave Rome from the EUR Fermi stop of Metro B. The ride takes about one hour.

For Abruzzo, L'Aquila is served by hourly ARPA buses leaving Stazione Tiburtina in Rome, while for the National Park it's best to take the train to Avezzano and then travel the rest of the way on the ARPA bus. Buses for Molise (Molise Trasporti) leave Rome (Stazione Tiburtina) roughly every two hours and take about 2½ hours to reach Isernia.

🔢 Bus Information **ARPA** ☎ 0863/26561. **COTRAL** ☎ 800/431784 toll-free ⊕ www. cotralspa.it. **Molise Trasporti** ☎ 0874/493080.

CAR TRAVEL

To get from Rome to Ostia (a 30- to 40-minute trip), follow Via del Mare southwest, which leads directly there. If approaching from Rome's ring road, the Gran Raccordo Anulare, look for the Ostiense or Ostia Antica exit.

For Cerveteri, take either the A12 Rome–Civitavecchia toll highway to the Cerveteri-Ladispoli exit, or take the more scenic coastal route with stoplights, the Via Aurelia. The trip takes about 40 minutes on the autostrada, twice that on the slow road. To get to Tarquinia, take the A12 Rome–Civitavecchia highway all the way to the end, where you continue on the Via Aurelia to Tarquinia. The trip takes about one hour. From that point, Tuscania is reached by cutting inland for another half hour.

For Tivoli, take the Rome–L'Aquila autostrada (A24). To get to Palestrina directly from Rome, take the Autostrada del Sole (A2) to the San Cesareo exit and follow signs for Palestrina; this trip takes about one hour. From Rome to Subiaco, take S155 east for about 40 km (25 mi) and the S411 for 25 km (15½ mi); the trip takes about 70 minutes.

For Viterbo, Bagnaia, and Bomarzo, head out of Rome on the A1 autostrada, exiting at Attigliano. Bomarzo is only 3 km (2 mi) from the autostrada. The trip takes one hour.

The fastest route to sites south of Rome is the Via Pontina, an expressway. For Sermoneta, turn northeast at Latina. The trip takes about 50 minutes. For out-of-the-way Ninfa, proceed as for Sermoneta, but before reaching Sermoneta follow the signs for Doganella/Ninfa. The trip takes about one hour. For Sperlonga, take the Via Pontina to Latina, then the Via Appia to Terracina and Sperlonga. The trip takes about 1½ hours.

For Abruzzo and Molise, head east from Rome on the scenic A24 autostrada toward L'Aquila, about an hour's drive from Rome. Before L'Aquila, the A25 splits off toward Pescara. For the Parco Nazionale d'Abruzzo, take the A25 past Avezzano, exit at Pescina, and follow signs to Pescasseroli. Sulmona is farther along the A25, just off the autostrada about two hours from Rome. For Molise, take autostrada A2 to the Cassino exit, and then follow the main road (SS 6) eastward via Venafro to Isernia, about 2½ hours from Rome.

EMERGENCY   When you're on the road, always carry a good road map, a flashlight,
SERVICES   and, if possible, a cellular phone so that in case of a breakdown you can call ACI for towing and repairs—ask and you will be transferred to an English-speaking operator. Be prepared to tell the operator which road you're on, the direction you're going (e.g., "*verso* [in the direction of] Perugia") and the *targa* (license plate number) of your car. The great majority of Italians carry cellular phones, so if you don't have one, flag down someone who does for help.
🚩 **ACI** ☎ 803/116.

EMERGENCIES

Emergency numbers (listed below) are accessible from every phone, including cellular phones, all over Italy. If you have ongoing medical concerns, it's a good idea to make sure someone is on duty all night where you're staying—not a given in Lazio, less so in Abruzzo and Molise. As elsewhere in Italy, every pharmacy in Lazio, Abruzzo, and Molise bears a sign at the door listing area pharmacies open in off-hours, though in the countryside you may need a car to get to one. Try to bring extras with you of all medications you take regularly.

🛈 **Emergencies** ☎ 113. **Ambulance** ☎ 118. **Carabinieri** (Military Police) ☎ 112. **Fire** ☎ 115.

TOURS

CIT has half-day excursions to Villa d'Este in Tivoli. American Express has tours to Hadrian's Villa. Appian Line has excursions to Hadrian's Villa. Carrani Tours has tours that include Hadrian's Villa. For Viterbo, authorized guides are available through the APT office.

🛈 Fees & Schedules **American Express** ☎ 06/67641. **Appian Line** ☎ 06/487861. **Carrani Tours** ☎ 06/4742501. **CIT** ☎ 06/478641. **Viterbo APT** ✉ Piazza San Carluccio ☎ 0761/304795.

TRAIN TRAVEL

Regular train service links the Ostia Antica station with Rome's Piramide Metro B Line station, near Porta San Paolo. Exit the Metro and go to the station called Ostia Lido adjacent to the Metro station. The ride takes about 35 minutes. Trains depart every half hour throughout the day.

For many destinations in the three regions, you may need to take a combination of train and bus. From stations in Rome, FS and Metropolitana suburban trains take you to the Cerveteri-Ladispoli station, where you can get a bus for Cerveteri. The train takes 30 minutes; the bus ride then takes 15 minutes. To get to Tarquinia, take an FS train (Rome–Genoa line) from Rome or from Cerveteri to the Tarquinia station (this service is sometimes operated by bus between Civitavecchia and Tarquinia), then a local bus from the station up to the hilltop town. The trip takes about 75–90 minutes. There's a fast mainline train service from Rome to Viterbo, which takes an hour and 40 minutes. Tuscania is accessible by bus from Viterbo. Trains also stop at Bagnaia, 10 minutes beyond Viterbo.

FS trains connect Rome's Termini and Tiburtina stations with Tivoli in about 30 minutes; Villa d'Este is about a 20-minute uphill walk from the station at Tivoli. The FS train from Stazione Termini to Palestrina takes about 40 minutes; you can then board a bus from the train station to the center of town.

FS trains on the Rome–Formia–Naples line stop at Latina Scalo, where you can get a local bus to Sermoneta, though service is erratic. Traveling time is about one hour. For Sperlonga, on the same line, get off at the Itri station, from which buses leave for Sperlonga. The trip takes about 1½ hours.

Abruzzo is served by trains to Avezzano (10 trains daily from Roma Termini), from where you can get an ARPA bus direct to Pescasseroli and Civitella Alfedena. Sulmona is directly on the Rome-Tivoli-Pescara train line, 2½ hours from Rome. In Molise, as an alternative to direct bus links from Rome, Isernia and Campobasso are reached by local train from Vairano-Caianello, a junction on the Rome–Caserta railway.

🚆 Train Information **FS–Trenitalia** ☎ 892021 ⊕ www.trenitalia.com.

VISITOR INFORMATION

🚩 Tourist Information **Cerveteri** ✉ Piazza Risorgimento 19 ☎ 06/99551971. **Isernia** ✉ Via Farinacci 9 ☎ 0865/3992. **L'Aquila** ✉ Piazza Santa Maria di Paganica 5 ☎ 0862/410808 ⊕ www.abruzzoturismo.it. **Latina** ✉ Piazza del Popolo ☎ 0773/480672. **Palestrina** ✉ Piazza Santa Maria degli Angeli ☎ 06/9573176. **Parco Nazionale d'Abruzzo** ✉ Via Piave 2, Pescasseroli ☎ 0863/910097 ⊕ www.regione.abruzzo.it/turismo/parchi/nazionale/index.html. **Subiaco** ✉ Via Cadorna 59 ☎ 0774/822013. **Sulmona** ✉ Corso Ovidio 208 ☎ 0864/53276. **Tarquinia** ✉ Piazza Cavour 1 ☎ 0766/856384 ⊕ www.tarquinia.net. **Tivoli** ✉ Largo Garibaldi ☎ 0774/334522. **Tuscania** ✉ Via del Comune 1 ☎ 0761/436371. **Viterbo** ✉ Piazza Verdi 4/a ☎ 0761/226666.

NAPLES & CAMPANIA

13

FEEL THE PULSE OF NAPLES
on the streets of Spaccanapoli ⇨*p.615*

GET SERENADED AT TABLESIDE
by guitar-strumming folk singers ⇨*p.620*

CLIMB MOUNT VESUVIUS
for views of the towns it's buried ⇨*p.632*

UNLOCK THE VILLA OF THE MYSTERIES
at the ancient city of Pompeii ⇨*p.637*

VISIT SOUTHERN ITALY'S VERSAILLES
at the Reggio in Caserta ⇨*p.639*

WATCH THE STYLISH PEOPLE-WATCHERS
on the Piazzetta in Capri Town ⇨*p.644*

GAZE INTO AN INFINITE EMERALD SEA
from Ravello's Villa Cimbrone ⇨*p.662*

Updated by
Francesca
Marretta &
Chris Rose

CAMPANIA IS A REGION OF EVOCATIVE NAMES—Capri, Sorrento, Pompeii, Herculaneum—that conjure up visions of cliff-shaded coves, sun-dappled waters, and mighty ruins. The gateway to these treasures is the regional capital of Naples (Napoli in Italian), the most operatic of cities, lording over its fabled bay. Campania stretches south in flat coastal plains and low mountains from Baia Domizia, Capua, and Caserta to Naples and Pompeii on the magnificent bay; past the isles of Capri and Ischia; along the rocky coast to Sorrento, Amalfi, and Salerno; and farther still past the Cilento National Park to Sapri and the Basilicata border. Inland lies the rugged Apennine chain and the rolling countryside around Benevento.

On each side of Naples the earth fumes and grumbles, a reminder that all this beauty was born of cataclysm. Toward Sorrento, Vesuvius smolders sleepily over the ruins of Herculaneum and Pompeii, while west of Naples, beyond Posillipo, the craters of the Solfatara spew steaming gases. And nearby are the dark, deep waters of Lago d'Averno, legendary entrance to Hades. With these reminiscences of death and destruction so close at hand, it's no wonder that the southerner in general, and the Neapolitan in particular, plunges so enthusiastically into the task of living each moment to the fullest.

Lying on Mediterranean trade routes plied by several pre-Hellenic civilizations, Campania was systematically settled by the ancient Greeks from approximately 800 BC onward. Here myth and legend blend confusingly with historical fact: the town of Herculaneum is said—rather improbably—to have been established by Hercules himself, and Naples in ancient times was called Parthenope, the name attributed to one of the Sirens who preyed on hapless sailors in antiquity. Nearby Cumae, thought to be the first Greek settlement on the Italian mainland, was home to the famous Sibyl who pronounced her oracles from the recesses of a dark vaulted chamber. Thanks to archaeological research, some of the layers of myth have been stripped away to reveal an extensive pattern of occupation and settlement well before Rome became established. Greek civilization flourished for hundreds of years all along this coastline, but there was nothing in the way of centralized government until centuries later when the Roman Republic, uniting all Italy for the first time, surged southward and absorbed the Greek colonies with little opposition. Generally, the peace of Campania was undisturbed during these centuries of Roman rule.

Naples and Campania, with the rest of Italy, decayed with the Roman Empire and collapsed into the abyss of the Middle Ages. Naples itself regained some importance under the rule of the Angevins in the latter part of the 13th century and continued its progress in the 1440s under Aragonese rule. The nobles who served under the Spanish viceroys in the 16th and 17th centuries, when their harsh rule made all Italy quail, enjoyed their pleasures, and taverns and gaming houses thrived, even as Spain milked the area with its taxes. After a short-lived Austrian occupation, Naples became the capital of the Kingdom of the Two Sicilies, which the Bourbon kings established in 1738. Their rule was generally benevolent as far as Campania was concerned, and their support of papal

Numbers in the text correspond to numbers in the margin and on the Campania, Naples, and Pompeii maps.

If you have 3 days

In 🗺 **Naples** ①–⑭ 🏴, a visit to the **Museo Archeologico Nazionale** ⑬ is an essential preparation (or follow-up) for an expedition to **Herculaneum** ⑲ and **Pompeii** ㉒–㊴, indispensable sights for anyone visiting Campania. The islands of **Ischia** ㊸ and **Capri** ㊹–㊾ can also be reached from Naples and make an ideal retreat from the city's noise. It's worth spending at least one night out of Naples, and a good alternative to the islands is 🗺 **Sorrento** ㊿, an easy hydrofoil ride away and a good base from which to tour the nearby Amalfi Coast, where you could visit the towns of **Positano** ㊿, **Amalfi** ㊿, or **Ravello** ㊿ on a third day's excursion.

13

If you have 5 days

In 🗺 **Naples** ①–⑭ 🏴 more time will enable you to take in one of the region's greatest palace-museums, the **Museo di Capodimonte** ⑭, housed in one of the Bourbon royal palaces. Outside of town you can also see more than just one of the classical sights, including a visit to the Greek temples of **Paestum** ㊿, highly recommended for a glimpse at some of Magna Graecia's most stunning relics. You might also venture north to **Caserta** ㊿ to wander around the royal palace and its vast grounds. Back in the Bay of Naples, spend your fourth and fifth days exploring 🗺 **Ischia** ㊸ and 🗺 **Sorrento** ㊿, both undemanding holiday resorts with plenty of natural beauty.

If you have 7 days

A week in Campania will allow you to discover some of the more esoteric pleasures that Naples has to offer. Apart from the sheer vibrancy of its shopping streets and alleys and the glorious views over the waterfront, 🗺 **Naples** ①–⑭ 🏴 has plenty of diversions within its tight mesh of streets, and you should make time for visiting some of its many famous churches—the **Duomo** ⑪, of course, but also **Santa Chiara** ⑧, the art gallery of the **Girolamini** ⑫, and the **Cappella Sansevero** ⑨, with its 18th-century sculptures. Outside town, head west to the volcanic region of the **Phlegrean Fields** ⑮–⑱, where Roman remains lie within a smoking, smoldering area rich with classical history. Spend three nights on the Amalfi Coast, making sure to visit inland 🗺 **Ravello** ㊿ and pass some time in pretty 🗺 **Positano** ㊿, which requires at least a day. 🗺 **Capri** ㊹–㊾, too, deserves a couple of nights to appreciate fully its beauty. You might pass a last day, perhaps en route out of Campania, in **Benevento** ㊶, which holds a well-preserved Roman theater and the renowned Arco di Traiano.

---

authority in Rome was an important factor in the development of the rest of Italy. Their rule was important artistically, too, for not only did it contribute greatly to the architectural beauty of the region, but it attracted great musicians, artists, and writers only too willing to enjoy the easy life at court in such magnificent natural surroundings. Finally, Giuseppe Garibaldi launched his famous expedition, and in 1860 Naples was united with the rest of Italy.

Times were relatively tranquil through the years that followed—with visitors of one nation or another thronging to Capri, to Sorrento, to Amalfi, and, of course, Naples—until World War II. Allied bombings did considerable damage in Naples and the bay area. At the fall of the fascist government the sorely tried Neapolitans rose up against Nazi occupation troops and in four days of street fighting drove them out of the city. A monument was raised to the *scugnizzo* (the typical Neapolitan street urchin), celebrating the youngsters who participated in the battle. The war ended. Artists, tourists, writers, and other lovers of beauty began to flow again into the Campania region that one ancient writer called "most blest by the Gods, most beloved by man." As the years have gone by, some parts gained increased attention from knowing visitors, while others lost the cachet they once had. Though years of misgovernment have left an indelible mark, the tide appears to be turning: the region's immense cultural and natural heritage is finally being revalued as local authorities and inhabitants alike appreciate the importance of nurturing the area's largest industry—tourism.

Exploring Campania

Many of Campania's attractions are on the Golfo di Napoli (Bay of Naples)—including the city itself and its satellite islands Capri and Ischia, and the archaeological sites of Pompeii, Herculaneum, and the Campi Flegrei (Phlegrean Fields) at the northern end of the bay. At the southern end Sorrento also lies in this charmed circle, within easy distance of Positano and the pleasures of the and Coast. Farther afield, Paestum offers more classical sights, while inland Caserta has a Bourbon palace and Benevento more majestic Roman remains.

If art and antiquities are high on your list, consider spending a few days in Naples before retreating to the beauty of Capri, Ischia, or the Amalfi Coast. Few fall in love with Naples at first sight, and many complain about its obvious flaws: urban decay and delinquency. But practically everyone who takes the time and trouble to discover its artistic riches and appreciate its vivacious nature considers it worth the effort. Naples is close to Italy's most fabled classical ruins, and you should dedicate at least a morning or afternoon to Pompeii or Herculaneum.

About the Restaurants & Hotels

Campania restaurants are known for their flexible mealtimes; in the evening many will continue serving until the wee hours. Following the strong oral tradition of southern Italians, many restaurants in Campania don't have menus, or, if there is a menu the best dishes may not be on it. Instead you're likely to be told what's on offer by your waiter—creating great opportunities for you to expand your Italian culinary vocabulary.

Most areas have fine accommodations in all price categories, but they get very busy (especially the small establishments), so reserve well in advance. High-season rates apply at all coastal resorts from April or May through September, and Christmas and Easter also draw crowds and command top rates. Whereas coastal resorts elsewhere close up tight from

13

Archaeology The regions to the west and east of Naples are two of of the great treasure troves of Greek and Roman antiquity. The classical world becomes strikingly tangible when you visit sites such as Pompeii, preserved by Vesuvius's dust; Herculaneum, said to be founded by that hard-laboring Greek Hercules; Baia, pleasure pot of Roman emperors; Lago d'Averno, legendary entrance to Hades; Oplontis, once home to Mr. and Mrs. Nero; Pozzuoli, with its great amphitheater; and Cumae, where a noted Sibyl made prophecies. The Romans dubbed the lovely terrain of the region *Campania Felix* (Happy Land) and filled it with palatial country residences, resort towns, and artwork that reflected their famously cosmopolitan tastes. Much of the best art has been carted off to the Museo Archeologico in Naples, but there are notable exceptions, including the eye-opening murals at Pompeii's Villa of the Mysteries, the finest surviving paintings from classical antiquity.

Vistas *Dolce far niente*—literally "the sweetness of doing nothing"—is a major leisure activity of coastal Campania. Sorrento and the Amalfi Coast are studded with belvederes ("beautiful viewing spots") and roadside rest stops built on the roadside—especially prized if you're the driver and miss what your passengers are oohing and aahing about. Sorrento's views are wider and more serene than the Amalfi Coast's mountain-meets-sea drama. Positano and Ravello have the most dramatic in-town vistas, although great ones peek out and pop up just about everywhere. The Lattari Mountains behind the coast are exceptional for wider panoramas. When booking hotels, ask to be on the water side, throw open the shutters, and, at least once, worship the sun: rising on the Amalfi Coast, setting in Sorrento, or doing both on the peninsula.

fall to spring, some hotels and restaurants are open in Sorrento and on the Amalfi Coast year-round (many lodgings reopen just for the Christmas and New Year period). It's always a good idea to book far in advance, and it's imperative in high season (July through September). In summer, hotels on the coast that serve meals almost always require that you take half board. Recent years have seen a boom in *agriturismo* or farmhouse lodgings, especially in the Cilento south of Salerno and the province of Benevento. This is an increasingly attractive option for families, budget travelers, and those wanting to practice their Italian.

WHAT IT COSTS In euros					
	$$$$	**$$$**	**$$**	**$**	**¢**
RESTAURANTS	over €22	€16–€22	€11–€16	€7–€11	under €7
HOTELS	over €220	€160–€220	€110–€160	€70–€110	under €70

Restaurant prices are for a second course (*secondo piatto*). Hotel prices are for two people in a standard double room in high season, including tax and service.

Timing

Campania is not at its best in high summer: Naples can be stifling, though thankfully devoid of crowds and traffic especially in August, while coastal resorts such as Sorrento, the islands, and the Amalfi Coast are overrun with tour buses and bad tempers. Any other time of year would be preferable, including winter, when the temperature rarely falls below the comfort threshold. Swimming is feasible year-round, though you will see only the hardiest bathers out between October and May.

Summer is also the worst time for ascents to Vesuvius; the best visibility occurs in spring and fall. Watch the clock, however, as the days get shorter; excursions to Vesuvius, Pompeii, Herculaneum, and the islands all require some traveling, and it's easy to get caught with little daylight left. At most archaeological sites you are rounded up one hour before sunset, so the earlier you arrive the better.

NAPLES

Before its decline after Italy's unification in 1860, Naples was a city that rivaled Paris as a brilliant and refined cultural capital, the ultimate destination for northern European travelers on their Grand Tour. A decade of farsighted city administration and a massive injection of European Union funds have kick-started the city back on course, though it is still a difficult place for the casual visitor to take a quick liking to: noise and air pollution levels are uncomfortably high, and unemployment protest marches and industrial disputes frequently disrupt public transportation and may even result in the temporary closure of major tourist attractions. Armed with the right attitude—"be prepared for the worst but hope for the best"—you will find that Napoli does not disappoint. Among other things, it's one of Italy's top *città d'arte,* with world-class museums and a staggering number of fine churches. The most important finds from Pompeii and Herculaneum are on display at the Museo Archeologico Nazionale—a cornucopia of sculpture, frescoes, and mosaics—and seeing them will add to the pleasure of trips to the ancient ruins. And Naples has a wonderful location: thanks to the backdrop of Vesuvius and the islands in the bay, it's one of those few cities in the world that are instantly recognizable.

Exploring Naples

In Naples you need a good sense of humor and a firm grip on your pocketbook and camera. You'll probably be doing a lot of walking (take care crossing the chaotic streets), for buses are crowded and taxis get stalled in traffic. If you come to Naples by car, park it in a garage, agree on the cost in advance, and then keep it there for the duration of your stay. (If you park it on the street, smashed windows and theft are constant risks.) Use the funiculars or the new metro (Line 1) to get up and down the hills, and take the quick—but erratic—metro Line 2 (the city's older subway system) when crossing the city between Piazza Garibaldi and Pozzuoli. For Pompeii, Herculaneum, and Sorrento, take the private Circumvesuviana Line, and the Cumana line from Piazza Monte-

ON THE MENU

CAMPANIA'S SIMPLE CUISINE *relies heavily on the bounty of the region's fertile farmland. Locally grown tomatoes are exported all over the world, but to try them here is another experience completely. Even in winter you can find tomato sauce made with small sun-dried tomatoes plucked from bright red strands that you can see hanging outdoors on kitchen balconies. Pasta is a staple here, and spaghetti al pomodoro (with tomato sauce) and alle vongole (with clam sauce, either white or red) appear on most menus.*

Naples is the homeland of pizza, and you'll encounter it here in two classic forms: alla margherita (with tomato, mozzarella, and basil) and marinara (with tomato, garlic, and oregano). Mozzarella—produced by Campania's thriving buffalo population—is used in many dishes; one of the most gratifying on a hot day is insalata caprese (salad with mozzarella, tomatoes,

and basil). Melanzane (eggplant) and even zucchini are served parmigiana (fried and layered with tomato sauce and mozzarella). Meat may be served alla pizzaiola (cooked in a tomato-and-garlic sauce). Fish and seafood in general can be expensive, though fried calamari and totani (cuttlefish) are usually reasonably priced. Lemons, grown locally, are widely used in cooking and for the sweet and heady liqueur limoncello, especially popular around Sorrento and on the Amalfi Coast. Among the region's grape varieties, Fiano, Greco di Tufo, and Falanghina make fine whites, and the Aglianico grape produces Campania's prestigious red, Taurasi. Wine production here has an impressive pedigree: Falerno wines (red and white) are mentioned by the Latin poet Horace, and Lacryma Christi (a blend of grape varieties) is produced from grapes grown around the slopes of Vesuvius.

santo takes in Pozzuoli and leads toward Baia and Cumae. The *artecard* allows you to combine public transport and entry to major museums: a three-day card (€25) includes free entry to two museums or archaeological sites, a 50% discount on other attractions, and free transport throughout the museum area—including return trips on fast craft across the bay from Pozzuoli as far afield as Salerno; a seven-day card (€28) gives free entry to all sights covered by the program but doesn't include a travel pass. You can purchase the artecard and find out more information on the sights covered at the airport stand (outside customs), at the train station at Piazza Garibaldi, and at the Web site ⊕ www.campaniartecard.it.

For standard public transportation, a Giranapoli pass costs €0.77 and is valid for 90 minutes on all public transit within the city boundaries; €2.32 buys a *biglietto giornaliero* (ticket for the whole day). A Fascia 1 ticket (€1.29 for 100 minutes) covers trips between Naples and a radius of about 10 km (6 mi), which includes Pozzuoli and Portici; Fascia 2 (€1.55 for 120 minutes) takes in Ercolano (Herculaneum), Baia, and Cumae; Fascia 3 (€2.01 for 140 minutes) includes Pompeii, Boscoreale, and Castellammare; Fascia 4 (€2.48 for 160 minutes) will take you as far as Vico Equense; and Fascia 5 (€2.84 for 180 minutes) covers trips to Sorrento and beyond.

Royal Naples

Naples hasn't been a capital for more than 150 years, but it still prides itself on its royal heritage. Most of the modern center of the town owes its look and feel to various members of the Bourbon family, who built their palaces and castles in this area.

a good walk

Start at the **Castel Nuovo** ❶ ⏵, facing the harbor on Piazza Municipio and housing a museum of mainly religious art. Pass the **Teatro San Carlo** ❷ on your way to the imposing **Palazzo Reale** ❸, a royal palace rich with the indulgences of Naples's past rulers. Next turn back to the seafront where about 15 minutes' walk south another royal fortress, the **Castel dell'Ovo** ❹, overlooks the Santa Lucia waterfront. From there head back onto Via Caracciolo and walk as far as the long, elegant Villa Comunale park. Go to the bandstand, then turn right and take the quiet Via Bausan to Via Colonna, turn left, and go to the funicular stop at Piazza Amedeo; take a ride up to the Vomero to visit the **Castel Sant'Elmo** ❺ and the adjacent **Certosa di San Martino** ❻, both commanding magnificent vistas over city and sea to Vesuvius.

TIMING   Seeing these sights takes a full day. Allow about two hours for the museum visits, with the majority of time devoted to the Palazzo Reale and the Certosa di San Martino. The views from the latter over the bay are good at any time, but are especially fine at sunset.

What to See

❹ **Castel dell'Ovo.** Dangling over the Porto Santa Lucia on a thin promontory, this 12th-century fortress built over the ruins of an ancient Roman villa commands a view of the whole harbor—proof, if you need it, that the Romans knew a premium location when they saw one. For the same reason, some of the city's top hotels share the site. It's a peaceful spot for strolling and enjoying the views. ⊠ *Santa Lucia waterfront, Via Partenope, Santa Lucia* ☎ *081/2400055* ☞ *Free* ☉ *Mon.–Sat. 9–5, Sun. 9–1:30.*

⏵ ❶ **Castel Nuovo.** Also known as the Maschio Angioino, this massive fortress was built by the Angevins (related to the French monarchy) in the 13th century and completely rebuilt by the Aragonese rulers (descendants of an illegitimate branch of Spain's ruling line) who succeeded them. The decorative marble triumphal arch that forms the entrance was erected during the Renaissance in honor of King Alfonso V of Aragon (1396–1458), and its rich bas-reliefs are credited to Francesco Laurana (circa 1430–1502). Set incongruously into the castle's heavy stone walls, the arch is one of the finest works of its kind. Within the castle you can see sculptures and frescoes from the 14th and 15th centuries, as well as the city's **Museo Civico,** comprising mainly local artwork from the 15th to 19th centuries. It's hard to avoid the impression that these last were rejects from the much finer collection at the Museo di Capodimonte, though there are also regular exhibitions worth visiting, and the windows offer views over the piazza and the port below. You can also visit the Palatine Chapel and the octagonal **Sala dei Baroni,** where Ferrante I disposed of a group of rebellious barons in 1485 by inviting them to a mock wedding party and then pouring boiling oil on their heads from the ceiling. The room is still regularly used for city council meetings. In the left corner of the courtyard is the **Sala dell'Armeria,** the Armory, where part of the flooring has been conveniently glassed over to reveal the remains of a Roman villa and a medieval necropolis. ⊠ *Piazza Municipio* ☎ *081/7952003* ✉ *€5, free Sun.* ☉ *Mon.–Sat. 9–7, ticket office closes at 6; Sun. courtyard only 9–1.*

❺ Castel Sant'Elmo. Perched on the Vomero, this castle was built by the Angevins in the 14th century to dominate the port and the old city and remodeled by the Spanish in 1537. The stout fortifications are still in use today by the military, and occasionally there are performances, exhibitions, and fairs. ⊠ *Largo San Martino, Vomero* ☎ *081/5784020* ✉ *€1* ☉ *Tues.–Sun. 9–7.*

★ ❻ Certosa di San Martino. A Carthusian monastery restored in the 17th century in exuberant Neapolitan baroque style, this structure has now been transformed into a diverse museum complex. The **Museo dell'-Opera,** with its impressive galleries around the Chiostro Grande (great cloister), gives a sound introduction to monastic life and a well-signposted history of the Carthusians and San Martino. Room 24 has a helpful 18th-century scale model of the monastic complex, and Room 26 has 19th-century paintings of monastic life. Dalbono's 13 gouaches of Vesuvius in various angry poses are attractively displayed in Room 28; moving back in time, Room 32 contains part of the anonymous Tavola Strozzi, depicting the Naples waterfront in the 15th century and the return of the Aragonese fleet from the Battle of Ischia. The *presepi* (Christmas crèches) are a popular exhibit, and the splendidly decorated church and annexes and the panoramic garden terraces are two other good reasons for coming up here. Take the funicular from Piazza Montesanto to Vomero. ⊠ *Museo Nazionale di San Martino, Vomero* ☎ *081/5781769* ✉ *€6, includes admission to Castel Sant'Elmo* ☉ *Tues.–Sun. 8:30–7.*

❸ Palazzo Reale. Dominating Piazza del Plebiscito, the huge palace—best described as overblown imperial—dates from the early 1600s. It was renovated and redecorated by successive rulers, including Napoléon's sister Caroline and her ill-fated husband, Joachim Murat (1767–1815), who reigned briefly in Naples after the French emperor had sent the Bourbons packing and before they returned to reclaim their kingdom. Don't miss seeing the **royal apartments,** sumptuously furnished and full of precious paintings, tapestries, porcelains, and other objets d'art. The monumental marble staircase gives you an idea of the scale on which Neapolitan rulers lived. ⊠ *Piazza del Plebiscito* ☎ *081/5808111* ✉ *€4* ☉ *Thurs.–Tues. 9–7:30.*

need a break?

The most famous coffeehouse in town is the **Caffè Gambrinus** (⊠ Piazza Trieste e Trento, near Piazza Plebiscito ☎ 081/417582), catercorner to the Palazzo Reale across the Piazza Trieste e Trento. Founded in 1850, this 19th-century jewel functioned as a brilliant intellectual salon in its heyday but has fallen into a Sunset Boulevard–type existence, relying on past glamour, at the mercy of

KEY

⊢ Funicular
Ⓜ Metro stop
▲ Start of walk

0 — 300 yards
0 — 300 meters

Golfo di Napoli

Cappella Sansevero **9**
Castel dell'Ovo **4**
Castel Nuovo **1**
Castel Sant'Elmo **5**
Certosa di
San Martino **6**
Duomo **11**
Gesù Nuovo **7**
Museo Archeologico
Nazionale **13**

Museo di
Capodimonte **14**
Palazzo Reale **3**
Quadreria dei
Girolamini **12**
San Lorenzo
Maggiore **10**
Santa Chiara **8**
Teatro San Carlo **2**

tourists and their pitiless cameras, and with often indifferent service. But the opening of some of its long-closed inside rooms with amazing mirrored walls and gilded ceilings makes this an essential stop for any visitor to the city.

Piazza del Plebiscito. The vast square next to the Palazzo Reale was laid out by order of Murat, whose architect was clearly inspired by the colonnades of St. Peter's in Rome. The large church of **San Francesco di Paola** in the middle of the colonnades was added as an offering of thanks for the Bourbon restoration by Ferdinand I, whose titles reflect the somewhat garbled history of the Kingdom of the Two Sicilies, made up of Naples (which included most of the southern Italian mainland) and Sicily. They were united in the Middle Ages, then separated, then unofficially reunited under Spanish domination during the 16th and 17th centuries. In 1816, with Napoléon out of the way on St. Helena, Ferdinand IV (1751–1825) of Naples, who also happened to be Ferdinand III of Sicily, officially merged the two kingdoms, proclaiming himself Ferdinand I of the Kingdom of Two Sicilies. His reactionary and repressive rule earned him a few more colorful titles among his rebellious subjects.

Quartieri Spagnoli. The Spanish garrison was quartered in the now-decaying tenements aligned in a tight-knit grid along incredibly narrow alleys in this neighborhood roughly between Via Toledo (downhill border) and Via Pasquale Scura (western leg of Spaccanapoli). It's a hectic, sometimes dangerous area, chock-full of local color, brooding in the shadow of Vomero. Though still largely impoverished, the neighborhood is showing signs of improvement. It's a five-minute walk west of Piazza Municipio, accessible from Via Toledo.

② Teatro San Carlo. This large theater was built in 1737, 40 years earlier than Milan's La Scala—though it was destroyed by fire and had to be rebuilt in 1816. You can visit the impressive interior, decorated in the white-and-gilt stucco of the neoclassical era, as part of a prearranged tour, and visitors are sometimes allowed in during morning rehearsals. ⊠ *Via San Carlo between Piazza Municipio and Piazza Plebiscito, Piazza Plebiscito* ☎ *081/7972331 or 081/7972412* ⊕ *www.teatrosancarlo. it* €5 ☺ Tours by appointment.

need a break?   Across from the Teatro San Carlo towers the imposing entrance to the glass-roof neoclassical **Galleria Umberto** (⊠ Via San Carlo, near Piazza Plebiscito), a shopping arcade where you can sit at one of several cafés and watch the vivacious Neapolitans as they go about their business.

Via Toledo. Sooner or later you'll wind up at one of the busiest commercial arteries, also known as Via Roma, which has thankfully been closed to through traffic—at least along the stretch leading from the Palazzo Reale. Don't avoid dipping into this parade of shops and coffee bars where plump pastries are temptingly arranged.

Vomero. Heart-stopping views of the Bay of Naples are framed by this gentrified neighborhood on a hill served by the Montesanto, Centrale, and Chiaia funiculars. Stops for all three are an easy walk from Piazza Vanvitelli, a good starting point for exploring this thriving district with no shortage of smart bars and trattorias.

Spaccanapoli & Capodimonte

This is the old Greek center of the city, around the two *decumani* (Via Tribunali and Via San Biagio dei Librai) that later formed the Roman town center. Capodimonte was open countryside until the Bourbon kings built a hunting lodge there, after which it rapidly became part of the city itself.

a good walk

Start your walk in Piazza Gesù, built over the old Greco-Roman city, and stroll east along Spaccanapoli (the unofficial name for the long street that cuts a straight line through the heart of Old Naples), taking in the churches of **Gesù Nuovo 7** ⌐ and **Santa Chiara 8** en route. Farther up Spaccanapoli you need only detour a few steps to see some other art-rich religious monuments: **Cappella Sansevero 9**, **San Lorenzo Maggiore 10**, the **Duomo 11**, and **Quadreria dei Girolamini 12**. Continuing north on Via Duomo, take a left onto Via Foria, and you will end up at one of Italy's most important museums, the **Museo Archeologico Nazionale 13**, packed with archaeological relics of the classical era and a must before venturing out of town to see Pompeii and Herculaneum. From here, footsore and weary, you deserve a taxi or bus to reach **Museo di Capodimonte 14**, the greatest of the Bourbon palaces, where, after ogling at the artistic masterpieces on display you can siesta in the Bosco di Capodimonte (park) and admire the wonderful views over the Bay of Naples.

TIMING Allow the better part of a day for this tour. You should aim to arrive at the Museo Archeologico shortly after lunchtime when the crowds have thinned out. Two hours will be just enough to get your bearings and cover the more important collections. The museum in Capodimonte—unlike many of the churches and the archaeological museum—is well lighted and can be viewed in fading daylight, so it's best left till last.

What to See

9 Cappella Sansevero. Off Spaccanapoli, the Cappella di Santa Maria della Pietà dei Sangro, better known as the Cappella Sansevero, holds the tombs of the noble Sangro di San Severo family. Much of it was designed in the 18th century by Giuseppe Sammartino, including the centerpiece, a striking *Veiled Christ* carved from a single block of alabaster. If you can stomach it, take a peek in the crypt, where some of the anatomical experiments conducted by Prince Raimondo, a scion of the family and noted 18th-century alchemist, are gruesomely displayed. ⊠ *Via de Sanctis 19, Spaccanapoli* ☎ *081/5518470* ⊠ *€5* ⊙ *Oct.–Apr., Mon. and Wed.–Sat. 10–4:40, Sun. 10–1; May–Sept., Mon. and Wed.–Sat. 10–6:40, Sun. 10–1.*

11 Duomo. Though the Duomo was established in the 1200s, the building you see was erected a century later and has since undergone radical changes, especially during the baroque age. Inside the cathedral 110 ancient columns salvaged from pagan buildings are set into the piers that support the 350-year-old wooden ceiling. Off the left aisle you step down into the 4th-century church of **Santa Restituta,** which was incorporated into the cathedral; though Santa Restituta was redecorated in the late 1600s in the prevalent baroque style, a few very old mosaics remain in the **Battistero** (Baptistery). The chapel also gives access to an archaeological zone, a series of paleochristian rooms dating from the Roman era.

On the right aisle of the cathedral, in the **Cappella di San Gennaro,** are multicolor marbles and frescoes honoring St. Januarius, miracle-working patron saint of Naples, whose altar and relics are encased in silver. Three times a year—on September 19 (his feast day); on the Saturday preceding the first Sunday in May, which commemorates the transference of his relics to Naples; and on December 16—his dried blood, contained in two sealed vials, is believed to liquefy during rites in his honor. On these days large numbers of devout Neapolitans offer up prayers in his memory. The **Museo del tesoro di San Gennaro** houses a rich collection of treasures associated with the saint. Paintings by Solimena and Luca Giordano hang alongside statues, busts, candelabras, and tabernacles in gold, silver, and marble by Cosimo Fanzago and other 18th-century baroque masters. A guided visit is included in the ticket price. ⊠ *Via Duomo 147, Spaccanapoli* ☎ *081/449097* ⌑ *Duomo and Cappella di San Gennaro free, Battistero and archaeological zone €3, museum €5* ۩ *Duomo and Cappella di San Gennaro daily 8–12:30 and 4:30–7; Battistero and archaeological zone Mon.–Sat. 9–noon and 4:30–6:30, Sun. 9–noon; museum daily 9–5.*

▶ **❼ Gesù Nuovo.** The oddly faceted stone facade of the church was designed as part of a palace dating from between 1584 and 1601, but plans were changed as construction progressed, and it became the front of an elaborately decorated baroque church. Be sure not to miss the votive chapel dedicated to San Ciro (Saint Cyrus) in the far left corner of the church. Here hundreds of tiny silver ex-voto images have been hung on the walls to give thanks to the saint for his assistance in medical matters. You can buy ex-votos at any of the jewelers that line the street outside. ⊠ *Piazza Gesù Nuovo, Spaccanapoli* ☎ *081/5518613* ۩ *Mon.–Sat. 7–12:30 and 4:15–7:30, Sun. 7–2.*

★ **⓭ Museo Archeologico Nazionale.** The National Archaeological Museum's huge red building, a cavalry barracks in the 16th century, is undergoing a massive restoration program that will fit it out with new galleries, a cafeteria, and a direct entrance from the Museo metro station. At any given time you may find several rooms closed to the public as the restoration progresses. The museum holds one of the world's great collections of Greek and Roman antiquities, including such extraordinary sculptures as the *Hercules Farnese,* an exquisite Aphrodite attributed to the 4th-century BC Greek sculptor Praxiteles, and an equestrian statue of Roman emperor Nerva. Vividly colored mosaics and countless artistic and household objects from Pompeii and Herculaneum provide insight into the life and art of ancient Rome. For a free guided tour of the limited-access Gabinetto Segreto and its collection of erotic art, ask for information at the ticket office. Invest in an up-to-date printed museum guide or audio guide, because exhibits tend to be poorly labeled. ⊠ *Piazza Museo 19 Spaccanapoli* ☎ *081/5648941* ⊕ *www.archeona.arti. beniculturali.it* 🎫 *€6.50* 🕙 *Wed.–Mon. 9–7.*

need a break? **Timpani e Tempura** (⊠ Vico della Quercia 17, Spaccanapoli ☎ 081/5512280) is a tiny shrine to local culinary culture. There are no tables; instead you perch yourself at the counter, but it's worth squeezing in for the *timballi di maccheroni* (baked pasta cakes) and the unique *mangiamaccheroni* (spaghetti in broth with *caciocavallo* cheese, butter, basil, and pepper). High-quality wines by the glass make this a place for a quick, delicious lunch. You can also buy cheese and salami to take home with you.

★ ⑭ **Museo di Capodimonte.** The grandiose 18th-century neoclassical Bourbon royal palace houses an impressive collection of fine and decorative art. Capodimonte's greatest treasure is the excellent collection of paintings well displayed in the **Galleria Nazionale,** on the palace's 1st and 2nd floors. Besides the art collection, part of the **royal apartments** still has a complement of beautiful antique furniture, most of it on the splashy scale so dear to the Bourbons, and a staggering collection of porcelain and majolica from the various royal residences. The walls of the apartments are hung with numerous portraits, providing a close-up of the unmistakable Bourbon features, a challenge to any court painter. Most rooms have fairly comprehensive, portable information cards in English, whereas the audio guide is overly selective and somewhat quirky. The main galleries on the 1st floor are devoted to work from the 13th to 18th century, including many pieces by Dutch and Spanish masters, as well as by the great Italians. On the 2nd floor look out for stunning paintings by Simone Martini (circa 1284–1344), Titian (1488/90–1576), and Caravaggio (1573–1610). The palace is situated in the vast Bosco di Capodimonte (Capodimonte Park), which served as the royal hunting preserve and later as the site of the Capodimonte porcelain works. ⊠ *Via Miano 2, Porta Piccola, Via Capodimonte* ☎ *848/800288 information and bookings for special exhibitions* 🎫 *€7.50, €6.50 after 2 PM* 🕙 *Tues.–Sun. 8:30–7:30, ticket office closes 6:30 PM.*

Piazza Dante. This square, which has a metro station linking up with the Vomero and beyond, is a bibliophile's paradise. The Via Port'Alba on the eastern side is lined with bargain book stalls. ⊠ *Spaccanapoli.*

⑫ **Quadreria dei Girolamini.** Off an improbably quiet cloister enclosing a prolific forest of lemon and loquat trees, the Girolamini art museum is attached to the restored Girolamini church. Its intimate, high-quality collection of 16th- and 17th-century paintings is one of the city's best-kept secrets, well worth a half-hour visit. ⊠ *Via Duomo 142, Spaccanapoli* 🎫 *Free* 🕙 *Daily 9:30–12:50.*

⑩ **San Lorenzo Maggiore.** It's unusual to find French Gothic style in Naples, but it has survived to great effect in this church, which was built in the

Middle Ages and decorated with 14th-century frescoes. Outside the 17th-century cloister is the entrance to **excavations** revealing what was once part of the Roman forum, and before that the Greek agora. You can walk among the streets, shops, and workshops of the ancient city and see a model of how the Greek Neapolis might have looked. ⊠ *Via Tribunali, 316 Spaccanapoli* ☎ *081/2110860* ⊕ *www. sanlorenzomaggiorenapoli.it* ☎ *Excavations €4* ☉ *Daily 8–noon and 5–7; excavations Mon.–Wed. 9–1 and 3–5:30, Sat. 9–5:30, Sun. 9:30–1:30.*

❽ Santa Chiara. This monastery church is a Neapolitan landmark and the subject of a famous old song. It was built in the 1300s in Provençal Gothic style, and it's best known for the quiet charm of its cloister garden, with columns and benches sheathed in 18th-century ceramic tiles painted with delicate floral motifs and vivid landscapes. An adjoining museum traces the history of the convent; the entrance is off the courtyard at the left of the church. ⊠ *Piazza Gesù Nuovo, Spaccanapoli* ☎ *081/5526209* ☎ *Museum and cloister €4* ☉ *Church Apr.–Sept., daily 8:30–noon and 4–7; Oct.–Mar., daily 8:30–noon and 4–6. Museum and cloister Mon.–Sat. 9:30–1 and 2:30–5:30, Sun. 9:30–1.*

need a break? Walk up Via Santa Maria di Costantinopoli, which is lined with shops selling antiques and musical instruments. You'll come upon Piazza Bellini, a leafy square that holds **Intra Moenia** (☎ 081/290720), a bookstore and café open every day from 10 AM to 3 AM, serving snacks, salads, and drinks—and selling books, prints, and postcards of Naples. It also stages art exhibitions and neighbors the city's main Internet café.

Spaccanapoli. Nowhere embodies the spirit of backstreet Naples better than this arrow-straight street divided into tracts bearing several names. It runs through the heart of the old city (*spacca* means "split") from west to east, retracing one of the main arteries of the Greek, and later Roman, settlement. **Via Benedetto Croce** was named in honor of the illustrious philosopher born here in 1866, in the building at No. 12. You'll walk past peeling palaces, dark workshops where artisans ply their trades, and many churches and street shrines. Where the street changes to **Via San Biagio dei Librai** and **Via San Gregorio Armeno,** the shops stage special exhibitions of *presepi* (nativity scenes) in the weeks before Christmas. ✛ *Beginning with Via Pasquale Scura, just west of Via Toledo, and ending with Via Vicaria Vecchia east of Via Duomo.*

need a break? While you're exploring the old part of town, take a break at what the Neapolitans call "the best pastry shop in Italy"—**Scaturchio** (⊠ Piazza S. Domenico Maggiore 19, Spaccanapoli ☎ 081/5516944). The café was founded in 1918 by two brothers, one of whom, Francesco, invented the cakes called *ministeriali* to attract Anna Fouché, a famous actress of the time. You can still buy these cakes today, along with other Neapolitan specialties such as *babà*, *rafioli*, and *pastiera*, which you can eat there with a coffee or have gift-wrapped in the room at the back.

Where to Stay & Eat

$$$ ✕ **La Sacrestia.** Neapolitans flock to this upscale patrician villa for the restaurant's location—on the slopes of the Posillipo hill—and high culinary standards. The specialties include tasty antipasti, linguine in *salsa di scorfano* (scorpion-fish sauce), and fettuccine with small squid, black olives, and potatoes. ⊠ *Via Orazio 116, Posillipo* ☎ *081/664186* ▭ *AE, DC, MC, V* ⊘ *Closed 2 wks mid-Aug. No lunch Mon., no dinner Sun.*

★ **$$–$$$** ✕ **Da Dora.** Despite its location up an unpromising-looking *vicolo* (alley) off the Riviera di Chiaia, this small restaurant has achieved cult status for its seafood platters. It's remarkable what Giovanni, the owner-chef, can produce in his tiny kitchen. Start with the pasta dish *mezzanello,* which is laden with local seafood, and perhaps follow up with *pezzogna* (blue-spotted bream). Like many restaurants on the seafront, Da Dora has its own guitarist, who is often robustly accompanied by the kitchen staff. ⊠ *Via Fernando Palasciano 30, Mergellina* ☎ *081/680519* ⌣ *Reservations essential* ▭ *AE, DC, MC, V* ⊘ *Closed Sun. and two wks in mid-Aug.*

$$ ✕ **La Bersagliera.** You'll inevitably be drawn to eating at the Santa Lucia waterfront, in the shadow of the looming medieval Castel dell'Ovo. This spot is big and touristy but fun, with an irresistible combination of spaghetti and mandolins. The menu suggests uncomplicated, timeworn classics, such as spaghetti *alla pescatora* (with seafood sauce) and *tagliatelle alla bersagliera* with handmade pasta, cherry tomatoes, tiny octopi, and clams. ⊠ *Borgo Marinaro 10, Santa Lucia* ☎ *081/7646016* ▭ *AE, DC, MC, V* ⊘ *Closed Tues. and 2 wks in Jan.*

★ **$$** ✕ **La Stanza del Gusto.** The name means "The Room of Taste," and this restaurant lives up to the billing. A minute's walk from some of the city's busiest streets, up a flight of stairs opposite the Teatro Sannazzaro on Via Chiaia, it feels removed from the hectic world outside. The kitchen aims to make the most of local products, including buffalo—both its milk (in the form of mozzarella) and its meat are on the menu. Serious gastronomes will want to try the *menu degustazione,* eight courses for €60. ⊠ *Vicoletto Sant'Arpino 21, Piazza Plebiscito* ☎ *081/401578* ▭ *AE, DC, MC, V* ⌣ *Reservations essential* ⊘ *Closed Sun. and Mon., and Aug. Lunch by appointment only.*

$$ ✕ **Mimì alla Ferrovia.** Near the central station, this bustling fish restaurant is as close as you get in Naples to a Parisian brasserie. It's a local institution popular with lawyers from the nearby law courts and local businessmen. The service is polite but not obsequious, the atmosphere relaxed, sometimes noisy. Try the *paccheri ai frutti di mare* (flat pasta with seafood), the *rigatoni fiori di zucca e gamberetti* (pasta tubes with zucchini flowers and shrimp), or the filling *pasta e patate con provola* (pasta, potatoes, and smoky provola cheese). ⊠ *Via Alfonso D'Aragona 21, Piazza Garibaldi* ☎ *081/5538525* ▭ *AE, DC, MC, V* ⊘ *Closed Sun. and last 2 wks in Aug.*

$–$$ ✕ **Osteria Castello.** The walls are covered with shelves full of wine bottles, and there are red-check tablecloths with candles on them—it looks like the quintessential Italian restaurant, and it is, with simple

FOLK SONGS À LA CARTE

I F YOU WANT TO HEAR canzoni napoletane—the fabled Neapolitan folk songs—performed live, you can try to catch the city's top troupes, such as the Cantori di Posillipo and I Virtuosi di San Martino, in performances at venues like the Teatro Trianon. But an easier alternative is to head for one of the city's more traditional restaurants, such as La Bersagliera or Mimì alla Ferrovia, where most every night you can expect your meal to be interrupted by a posteggiatore. These singers aren't employed by the restaurants, but they're encouraged to come in, swan around the tables with a battered old guitar, and belt out classics such as "Santa Lucia," "O' Surdat' Innamurate," "Torna a Surriento" (Come Back to Sorrento), and, inevitably, "Funiculì Funiculà."

These songs are the most famous of a vast repertoire that found international fame with the mass exodus of southern Italians to the United States in the early 20th century. "Funiculì Funiculà" was written by Peppino Turco and Luigi Danza in 1880 to herald Naples's new funicular railways. "O Sole Mio," by Giovanni Capurro and Eduardo di Capua, has often been mistakenly taken for the Italian national anthem. "Torna a Surriento" was composed by Ernesto di Curtis in 1903 to help remind the current Italian prime minister how wonderful he thought Sorrento was (and how many government subsidies he had promised the township).

The singers are more than happy to do requests, even inserting the name of your innamorato or innamorata into the song. When they've finished they'll stand discreetly by your table. Give them a few euros and you'll have friends for life (or at least for the night).

dishes at excellent prices and friendly service. Start at the excellent antipasto buffet, followed by the essential *pasta e patate con la provola* (pasta and potatoes with smoked mozzarella—it sounds like carbohydrate overload, but it's actually divine) and then the grilled, flat *pleos* mushrooms. You can sip wine (preferably the local *aglianico* red) or a liqueur and sit for hours talking with friends. ⊠ *Via S. Teresa a Chiaia 38, Chiaia* ☎ *081/400486* ⌂ *Reservations essential* ▤ *AE, DC, MC, V* ☉ *Closed Sun.*

$–$$ ✕ **Umberto.** Run by the Di Porzio family since 1916, Umberto has become one of the city's classic restaurants. It's divided into a simple pizzeria and a more elegant restaurant, both of which offer the class of the Chiaia area and the friendliness of other parts of the city. Try the *tubettini 'do tre dita* ("three finger maccheroni" with a mixture of seafood), which bears the nickname of the original Umberto. Owner Massimo and sister Lorella (Umberto's grandchildren) are both wine experts and oversee a fantastically well-curated cellar. Umberto is also the only restaurant in the city that caters to those who have a gluten allergy. ⊠ *Via Alabardieri 30-31, Chiaia* ☎ *081/418555* ▤ *AE, DC, MC, V* ☉ *Closed Mon.*

★ **$–$$** ✕ **Vadinchenia.** Though it identifies itself as a cultural and gastronomic association, Vadinchenia has all the trimmings of a high-class restaurant at surprisingly modest prices. Husband-and-wife team Saverio and Silvana steer their guests through an innovative menu against a backdrop of refreshingly minimalist decor. Adventurous palates will enjoy such bold combinations as *paccheri alle alici e pecorino* (pasta with sardines and sheep's cheese), and meat eaters will delight in the *filletto al vino e sale grosso* (steak cooked in wine and rock salt). In winter round off the meal with the *purée di castagna* made from local chestnuts. ✉ *Via Pontano 21, Chiaia* ☎ *081/660265* ▭ *AE, DC, MC, V* ⌦ *Reservations essential* ⊙ *Closed Sun. and Aug. No lunch.*

¢–$ ✕ **L'Ebbrezza di Noè.** A small bar leads into a larger dining area decorated in the style of a very elegant farmhouse. Owner Luca has an enthusiasm for what he does that is quite moving—as you sip a recommended wine you can sense that he hopes you like it as much as he does. The attention paid to the quality of the wine carries over to the food—here you can taste delicate *carpaccio di chianina* (thinly sliced Tuscan steak), rare cheeses such as the Sicilian *ragusano di razza modicani,* the local *caciocavallo podolico,* and a cholesterol-boosting three-cheese plate of Gorgonzola, Roquefort, and Stilton. ✉ *Vico Vetriera a Chiaia 8b/9, Chiaia* ☎ *081/400104* ▭ *AE, DC, MC, V* ⊙ *Closed Mon. No lunch.*

¢ ✕ **Cantina della Tofa.** Located on one of the narrow alleys that lead off Via Toledo up into the Spanish Quarter, this small, welcoming restaurant serves traditional Neapolitan fare that goes beyond standard pasta with seafood or tomatoes. Try the *vellutata di cicerchie,* a creamy soup made from the beans that are a cross between chickpeas and fava beans. The orange-walled dining room has large wooden tables that are more Tuscan than Campanian in style. The service is friendly and unhurried. ✉ *Vico Tofa 71, Piazza Municipio* ☎ *081/406840* ▭ *No credit cards* ⊙ *Closed Sun.*

¢ ✕ **Da Michele.** You have to love a place that has, for more than 130 years, offered only two types of pizza—marinara and margherita—and a small selection of drinks, and still manages to attract long lines. The prices have something to do with it, but the pizza itself suffers no rivals, and even those waiting in line are good-humored; the boisterous, joyous atmosphere wafts out with the smell of yeast and wood smoke onto the street. ✉ *Via C. Sersale 1/3* ☎ *081/5539204* ▭ *No credit cards* ⊙ *Closed Sun. and last 2 wks in Aug.*

¢ ✕ **Lombardi.** Lombardi is one of the city's most highly regarded old-style pizzerias. Simple decor and slightly cramped tables are more than compensated for by the excellent pizzas, including the Bassolino (named after Naples's popular former mayor), with buffalo-milk mozzarella and fresh tomatoes. The location is handy for a quick pizza before or after a visit to the Archaeological Museum. ✉ *Via Foria 12, near Museo* ☎ *081/456220* ▭ *No credit cards* ⊙ *Closed Sun.*

¢ ✕ **Sorbillo.** Don't be put off by the lines—the locals know the wait is worth it. Take their advice and order a basic Neapolitan pizza (try the unique pizza al pesto or the stunningly simple marinara—just tomato and oregano). They're cooked to perfection by the third generation of pizza makers who run the place. Don't expect tablecloths: here you have the joy of eating on traditional white-marble tabletops. ☒ *Via dei Tribunali 32, Spaccanapoli* ☎ *081/446643* ▤ *MC, V* ⊘ *Closed Sun.*

¢ ✕ **Vecchia Cantina.** The location is on a rather dark side street in the tattier section of the Spaccanapoli, but this place is well worth seeking out for its combination of old-style Neapolitan hospitality, high-quality food and wine, and excellent prices. It's a family affair, with Gianni out front and his mother, Nunzia, and wife, Maria, busy in the kitchen—much like in a typical Neapolitan household. The decorations are an accumulation of kitsch, and everyone who comes here seems to know everyone else. The pasta *e ceci* (with chickpeas) shouldn't be missed, and *baccalà fritto* (fried salt cod) is a specialty. The wine list includes selections from all over Italy. ☒ *Via S. Nicola alla Carità 13-14, Spaccanapoli* ☎ *081/5520226* ⬥ *Reservations essential* ▤ *AE, DC, MC, V* ⊘ *Closed Tues.*

$$$$ ☷ **Grand Hotel Vesuvio.** You'd never guess from the somewhat dull exterior that this is the oldest of Naples's great seafront hotels—the place where Enrico Caruso died, Oscar Wilde escaped with lover Lord Alfred Douglas, and Bill Clinton charmed the waitresses. Fortunately the spacious, soothing interior compensates for what's lacking on the outside. Guest rooms are done in luxurious, traditional style with antique accents, vibrantly colored walls, and gleaming bathrooms; many have grand views of the bay. You can pamper yourself at the spa, and there are myriad special services on request. The famous Caruso restaurant sits atop the hotel, affording wonderful views. ☒ *Via Partenope 45, Santa Lucia, 80121* ☎ *081/7640044* ☐ *081/7644483* ⊕ *www.vesuvio.it* ⇆ *163 rooms, 17 suites* ⚭ *Restaurant, in-room safes, minibars, cable TV, health club, bar, babysitting, meeting room, some pets allowed* ▤ *AE, DC, MC, V* ⦿⫟ *BP.*

★ $$$$ ☷ **Parker's.** This landmark hotel has been serving up doses of elegant, old-style atmosphere to visiting VIPs since 1870. The gilt-trimmed Empire bureaus, 19th-century paintings, shimmering chandeliers, fluted pilasters, and ornate ceilings all create a splendidly glittering environment. From the hotel's perch midway up the Vomero Hill (and convenient to funicular lines) you get fine views of the bay and Capri; if your room doesn't have one of these vistas, drink it all in from the excellent rooftop restaurant. There's also a day spa providing a full complement of health and beauty treatments. ☒ *Corso Vittorio Emanuele 135, Chiaia, 80121* ☎ *081/7612474* ☐ *081/663527* ⊕ *www.grandhotelparkers.it* ⇆ *73 rooms, 10 suites* ⚭ *Restaurant, in-room safes, minibars, cable TV, gym, massage, sauna, spa, bar, meeting rooms, parking (fee)* ▤ *AE, DC, MC, V* ⦿⫟ *BP.*

$$$–$$$$ ☷ **San Francesco al Monte.** This high-end hotel retains hints of its former life as a Franciscan monastery: the small lobby leads to narrow corridors lined with doors that look dauntingly cell-like, until you enter and find surprisingly spacious, simply decorated rooms, many with their own Jacuzzis, antique furnishings, majolica-tile floors, and stunning views of the city below and the bay beyond. The hotel's restaurant is equally upscale, its French chef adding a Gallic twist to Italian fare. ☒ *Corso Vittorio Emanuele 328, 80135* ☎ *081/4239111* ☐ *081/*

2512485 ⊕ *www.hotelsanfrancesco.it* ⤳ *50 rooms* ⚴ *Restaurant, in-room safes, minibars, swimming pool, bar, meeting rooms* ⊟ *AE, DC, MC, V* ⦿ *BP.*

$$$ ▦ **Caravaggio Hotel.** The old town's first top-level hotel, opened in December 2002 in a 17th-century palazzo on a tiny square behind the Duomo, takes its name from the painter of the amazing *Sette Opere della Misericordia,* which can be seen in the chapel opposite. The entrance hall is atmospherically furnished with blocks of volcanic stone, and the remains of the city's original Greek walls are visible. The guest rooms are all modern—each even has a power shower. Breakfast includes a selection of meats and cheeses from local Campanian farms. ⊠ *Via Rioario Sforza 157, Spaccanapoli, 80139* ☎ *081/2110066* 🖷 *081/4421578* ⊕ *www.caravaggiohotel.it* ⤳ *16 rooms* ⚴ *Cable TV, bar, Internet, some pets allowed* ⊟ *AE, DC, MC, V* ⦿ *BP.*

$$$ ▦ **Paradiso.** You can take a taxi or funicular from downtown to this modern air-conditioned hotel perched on a hill above the port of Mergellina. Huge window walls in the lobby and front rooms provide gorgeous views. Blue and beige tones make for a restful, attractive setting. Smallish rooms are smart, with built-in furnishings of rosy wood with marble surfaces. A roof terrace invites sitting, dining, and contemplating the entire bay and Vesuvius. ⊠ *Via Catullo 11, Posillipo, 80122* ☎ *081/7614161* 🖷 *081/7613449* ⊕ *www.hotelparadisonapoli. it* ⤳ *74 rooms* ⚴ *Restaurant, minibars, bar, parking (fee)* ⊟ *AE, DC, MC, V* ⦿ *BP.*

$$ ▦ **Chiaja.** A two-minute walk from Piazza Plebiscito and the Royal Palace takes you to this hotel in a spruced up 18th-century palazzo, part of which was once a brothel. Above the fireplace in the homely entrance hall is a portrait of the marchese Nicola Le Caldano Sasso III, original owner of the building; her granddaughter Mimi now runs the place. Rooms are small but comfortable; any sense of claustrophobia (a hazard with buildings in this old part of town) is offset by the opulent period furnishings. Vouchers for breakfast at nearby Gambrinus café are available on request. Helpful and friendly service is always available. ⊠ *Via Chiaia 216, 80121, Chiaia* ☎ *081/415555* 🖷 *081/ 422344* ⊕ *www.hotelchiaia.it* ⤳ *27 rooms* ⚴ *Minibars, bar* ⊟ *AE, DC, MC, V* ⦿ *EP.*

$$ ▦ **Hotel Toledo.** A centuries-old palazzo has been tastefully transformed into this boutique hotel a two-minute walk up from Via Toledo, near Spaccanapoli and the Royal Palace. Rooms are furnished in a pleasing rustic style, and the leafy rooftop terrace provides a quintessentially Neapolitan backdrop for your breakfast. ⊠ *Via Montecalvario 15, Quartieri Spagnoli, 80134* ☎🖷 *081/406800* ⊕ *www.hoteltoledo.com* ⤳ *18 rooms* ⚴ *Minibars, bar* ⊟ *AE, DC, MC, V* ⦿ *BP.*

$$ ▦ **Pinto Storey.** This fascinating old pensione overflows with warmth and charm. The simple and airy guest rooms are on the 4th floor of an elegant late-19th-century building off the chic Piazza Amedeo. Rooms here are always in high demand, so book early. ⊠ *Via G. Martucci 72, 80121, Chiaia* ☎ *081/681260* 🖷 *081/667536* ⊕ *www.pintostorey.it* ⤳ *18 rooms* ⚴ *Minibars, bar* ⊟ *AE, MC, V* ⦿ *EP.*

$–$$ 🖼 **Il Convento.** The Convento occupies a 17th-century palazzo that's tucked away in the Spanish Quarter but is conveniently close to Via Toledo. Rooms are small but elegantly decorated in simple, modern Mediterranean style, maintaining original architectural features such as arched or beamed ceilings. Two junior suites have private roof gardens. ✉ *Via Speranzella 137/A, 80132, Piazza Municipio* 🕾 *081/403977* 🖬 *081/ 400332* ⊕ *www.hotelilconvento.it* 🛏 *12 rooms, 2 suites* ⚭ *Minibars, cable TV, bar, Internet* ▤ *AE, DC, MC, V* ⦿ *BP.*

$ 🖼 **Donna Regina.** This bed-and-breakfast is in part of the 14th-century monastery of Donna Regina, and has been lovingly restored by a family of Neapolitan artists. In the old part of town, it has views of the cloisters and the two churches of Santa Maria Donna Regina. Inside it's filled with antique Neapolitan furniture and family works of art. Donna Gabriella will cook delightful traditional evening meals on request. There are only four rooms, so you need to book well in advance throughout the year. ✉ *Via Settembrini 80, Spaccanapoli, 80139* 🕾🖬 *081/446799* 🛏 *4 rooms* ⚭ *Lounge* ▤ *MC, V* ⦿.

$ 🖼 **Neapolis.** Situated on a narrow alley just off the humming Via Tribunali close to Piazza Bellini, this small hotel looks out over the 13th-century Pietrasanta bell tower. The mix of modern and traditional furnishings, the lovely terra-cotta floors, and data ports in every room make this a good base for exploring Naples's medieval center. ✉ *Via Francesco Del Giudice 13, Spaccanapoli* 🕾 *081/4420815* 🖬 *081/ 4420819* ⊕ *www.hotelneapolis.com* 🛏 *18 rooms* ⚭ *In-room data ports, minibars, bar* ▤ *AE, DC, MC, V* ⦿ *BP.*

$ 🖼 **Soggiorno Sansevero.** Within the very heart of Spaccanapoli, this pensione occupies a floor in the former palace of the princes di Sangro di San Severo. Although the palazzo overlooks the opera-set Piazza San Domenico, the tiny Soggiorno is on the palazzo's quiet inner courtyard. Rooms are simply furnished—linoleum floors, modern beds, great-grandmama's boudoir bureau—and may even come with ghosts: Carlo Gesualdo, inventor of the madrigal song, murdered his wife and her lover on the palace's staircase. The staff is very friendly and helpful. ✉ *Piazza San Domenico 9 (Palazzo Sansevero), 80131 Spaccanapoli* 🕾 *081/ 4201336* 🖬 *081/211698* ⊕ *www.albergosansevero.it* 🛏 *6 rooms, 4 with bath* ▤ *AE, DC, MC, V.*

Nightlife & the Arts

The Arts

CLASSICAL MUSIC   A classical music festival known as **International Music Weeks** takes place throughout May in Naples. Concerts are held at the Teatro San Carlo, the Teatro Mercadante, and in the neoclassical Villa Pignatelli. For information, contact the **Teatro San Carlo box office** (🕾 081/7972331 or 081/7972412).

OPERA   Opera is a serious business in Naples—not in terms of the music so much as the costumes, the stage design, the players, and the politics. What's happening on stage can be secondary to the news of who's there, who they're with, and what they're wearing. Given the circumstances, it's hardly surprising that the city's famous San Carlo company doesn't offer a particularly innovative repertoire. Nonetheless, the company is usually of very high quality—and if they're not in form the audience lets them know it. Performances take place in the historic **Teatro San Carlo** (⊠ Via San Carlo, Piazza Plebiscito ☎ 081/7972331 or 081/7972412 ⊕ www. teatrosancarlo.it), the luxury liner of southern Italian opera houses. The hall still gleams with its mid-19th-century gilded furnishings and thick red-velvet drapes. For the opera and ballet seasons (generally December through June), many seats are presold by subscription, but there are often some available at the box office a few days before the performance. You can also book ahead by calling **Concerteria** (⊠ Via Schipa 23 Chaia ☎ 081/7611221). For an additional fee you can order tickets on the theater Web site.

Nightlife

Nightclubs and bars are found in many areas around Naples. The sophisticated crowd heads to Posillipo and the Vomero, Via Partenope along the seafront, and the Chiaia area (between Piazza dei Martiri and Via Dei Mille). A more bohemian and literary crowd makes for the *centro storico* (city center) and the area around Piazza Bellini. Bear in mind that clubs, and their clientele, may change rapidly, so do some investigating before you hit the town. Following are specific venues to check out.

In Piazza Bellini there's a relatively relaxed night scene—you might even be able to sit down at a proper table. **Caffè Intramoenia** (⊠ Piazza Bellini 70, Spaccanapoli ☎ 081/290720) is the granddaddy of all the bars here; it was set up as a bookshop in the late 1980s and still has its own small publishing house and a variety of the attractive titles on sale. Seats in the heated veranda are at a premium over the winter, though many sit outside all year round. **Bere Vino** (⊠ 62 Via San Sebastiano, Spaccanapoli ☎ 081/29313) looks like a shop from the outside, but inside you'll find long wooden tables and shelves of wine from all over Italy that are consumed on the premises. Peppery *taralli* biscuits, olives, and selections of cheeses and smoked meats can be used to *apoggiare* ("prop up") whatever you're drinking. Look for recommended wines by the glass on the chalkboard or spend ages perusing the encyclopedic list. **Aret' 'a Palm** (⊠ Piazza S. Maria la Nova, Spaccanapoli) is Neapolitan for "behind the palm tree," and that's exactly where you'll find this agreeably dark bar on Piazza Santa Maria La Nova. Its long marble bar and mirrored walls suggest Paris more than Naples.

The **Enoteca Belledonne** (⊠ Vico Belledonne a Chiaia 18, Chiaia ☎ 081/403162) is something of an institution among inhabitants of the more upscale Chiaia area. Between 8 and 9 in the evening it seems like the whole neighborhood has descended into the tiny space for an *aperitivo* (cocktail). The small tables and low stools are notably uncomfortable, but the cozy atmosphere and the pleasure of being surrounded by glass-fronted cabinets full of wine bottles with beautiful labels more than makes up for it. Excellent local wines are available by the glass at great prices. **Marshal Lounge** (⊠ 12 Vicoletto Belledonne a Chiaia, Chiaia ☎ 081/405216) has a sleek, minimalist design that makes the space seem larger than it is. There are monthly art exhibits. **Siddharta**

(⊠ Via Vito Fornari 15 ☎ 081/422334) has a slightly exotic touch, as it's one of the city's first sushi bars, though the stylish restaurant also offers excellent local fare. On the other side of the large underground space are a bar and disco that fill up with the area's bright young things on Friday and Saturday.

Sports & the Outdoors

Bicycling

To rent a bike in town and for information on group excursions, contact **Napoli Bike** (⊠ Riviera di Chiaia 201 ☎ 081/411934 ⊕ www. napolibike.com), conveniently close to the Villa Comunale.

Boat Tours

Summer evening boat tours take in the Naples waterfront from the port at Mergellina to Cape Posillipo, with a view of Castel dell'Ovo on the way back. For bookings contact **Seafront Tours** (⊠ Galleria Umberto I 17, Piazza Plebiscito ☎ 081/5519188).

Shopping

Leather goods, jewelry, and cameos are some of the best items to buy in Campania. In Naples you'll generally find good deals on handbags, shoes, and clothing. If you want the real thing, make your purchases in shops, but if you don't mind imitation goods rummage around at the various street-vendor *bancherelle* (stalls). Most boutiques and department stores follow roughly these hours: Monday 4:30–8, Tuesday–Saturday 9:15–1 and 4:30–8. Food shops are open Monday morning, but most close about 2 PM on Thursday afternoon.

Shopping Districts

The immediate area around **Piazza dei Martiri** has the densest concentration of luxury shopping, with perfume shops, fashion outlets, and antiques on display. Browse there on **Via dei Mille** and **Via Filangieri.** The small, pedestrian-only **Via Calabritto** is where you'll find high-end retailers such as Prada, Gucci, Versace, Vuitton, Cacharel, Damiani, and Cartier. The **Vomero** district yields more commercial shops—especially in the **Galleria Scarlatti,** on Via Scarlatti, and the **Galleria Vanvitelli,** off Piazza Vanvitelli. **Via Chaia** and **Via Toledo** are the two busiest shopping streets for most Neapolitans; there you'll find reasonably priced clothes and shoes, with a sprinkling of cafés and food shops. **Via Santa Maria di Costantinopoli** is the street for antiques shops, and you'll find an antiques market on the third weekend of each month in the gardens of Villa Comunale and a flower market early every morning in the Castel Nuovo moat.

Specialty Stores

Colonnese (⊠ Via San Pietro a Maiella 32/33, Spaccanapoli ☎ 081/459858) is an old-fashion bookstore with antique wooden cabinets and tables laden with volumes on art, local history, and esoterica. **Melinoi** (⊠ Via Benedetto Croce, 34, Spaccanapoli ☎ 081/5521204) stands out from the many small boutiques in Naples for its originality; they stock clothes and accessories by Romeo Gigli as well as a number of French designers. **Lo Stock** (✉ Via Fiorelli 7, Piazza dei Martiri ☎ 081/2405253) is a large basement in which designer-label remainders can be found at hugely reduced prices. Be prepared to rummage and hope they have your size.

Gay Odin (✉ Via Toledo 214, Piazza Plebiscito ☎ 081/400063) produces handmade chocolates that you can find only in its Naples shops. Buy a delicious chocolate Mount Vesuvius, or try the famous *foresta* (flaked chocolate). You can also visit the **Gay Odin factory** (✉ Via Vetriera 12, Chiaia ☎ 081/417843). **Mario Raffone** (✉ Via Santa Maria di Costantinopoli 102, Spaccanapoli ☎ 081/459667) is a family printing business where they still use old presses. They sell prints of nativity figures and Vesuvius and have a catalog of old prints from the 20th century. The **Ospedale delle Bambole** (✉ Via San Biagio dei Librai 81, Spaccanapoli ☎ 081/203067), a tiny storefront operation, is a world-famous "hospital" for dolls; it's a wonderful photo-op and a great place to take kids. **Nel Regno di Pulcinella** (✉ Vico San Domenico Maggiore 9, Spaccanapoli ☎ 081/5514171) is the workshop of famous Pulcinella maker Lello Esposito. The shop, a converted 16th-century stable, also has wonderful model volcanoes and the traditional good-luck symbol of the city, a red horn. **Marinella** (✉ Via Riviera di Chiaia 287/a, Chiaia ☎ 081/2451182) sells old-fashion made-to-measure ties that are favorites of the British royal family.

THE PHLEGREAN FIELDS

The name Campi Flegrei—the fields of fire—was once given to the entire region west of Naples, including the island of Ischia. The whole area floats freely on a mass of molten lava very close to the surface. The fires are still smoldering. Greek and Roman notions of the Underworld were not the blind imaginings of a primitive people; they were the creations of poets and writers who stood on this very ground and wrote down what they saw. Today it should take about half a day to assess it yourself.

Solfatara

⑮ *8 km (5 mi) west of Naples.*

Here at the sunken volcanic crater Solfatara you can experience firsthand the volcanic nature of this otherworldly terrain. In fact, the only eruption of this semiextinct volcano was in 1198, though according to one legend, every crater in the Phlegrean Fields is one of the mouths of a hundred-headed dragon named Typhon that Zeus hurled down the crater of Epomeo on the island of Ischia. According to another, the sulfurous springs of the Solfatara are poisonous discharges from the wounds the Titans received in their war with Zeus. The stark, scorched area, slightly marred by the modern apartment blocks peering over the rim, exerts a strange fascination. The area has good visitor facilities, is well signposted, and is safe for walking if you stick to the path. ☎ *081/5262341* ⊕ *www. solfatara.it* 🎫 *€5* ☉ *Daily 8:30–1 hr before sunset.*

Pozzuoli

16 *2 km (1 mi) west of Solfatara, 8 km (5 mi) west of Naples.*

The small fishing town of Pozzuoli once boasted of its difference from nearby Naples, and though in recent years it has become a suburb of its neighbor, it still retains enough character and sights of interest to make it worth at least a half-day trip—or longer if you want to visit one of the town's famous fish restaurants. The **Anfiteatro Flavio** is the third-largest amphitheater in Italy, after the Colosseum and Santa Maria Capua Vetere, and once held 40,000 spectators. Judging from the complex underground network of *carceres* (cells), which definitely merit a visit, entertainment consisted mainly of *venationes* (fights), often involving exotic animals such as lions and tigers brought from far-flung corners of the Roman Empire. The *fossa,* the large ditch in the middle of the arena, may well have contained the stage, which could be raised when necessary. If visiting between June and September, ask at the ticket office for information about outdoor evening concerts. ☎ *081/5266007* ✇ *€4 includes Cumae and the museum and site of Baia* ☉ *Daily 9–1 hr before sunset.*

You may want to make a short trip to Pozzuoli's **harbor** and imagine St. Paul landing here en route to Rome in AD 61, only 18 years before the eruption of Vesuvius. His own ship had been wrecked off Malta, and he was brought here on the *Castor and Pollux,* a grain ship from Alexandria.

Where to Eat

Pozzuoli is justly famed for its fish restaurants. On weekends in summer the town's narrow streets are packed with Neapolitans who take the trip out to Pozzuoli to eat.

$–$$ ✕ **La Taverna di Angelo.** There are only a few tables at this wonderful restaurant hidden on one of the backstreets off the main square, so try to book ahead. The menu consists of what's fresh that day, but the tagliatelle with *ricci di mare* (sea urchins) is a specialty. Angelo himself works in the kitchen, and the helpful waiters will recommend the right wine to go with your meal. ⊠ *Via Maria Puteolana 12* ☎ *081/3131002, 081/5262612* ⌂ *Reservations essential* ▤ *MC, V* ☉ *Closed Mon.*

$ ✕ **Ristorante Don Antonio.** Neapolitans flock to this restaurant up a *vicolo* (alley) one block from the Pozzuoli waterfront for fresh seafood and unbeatable prices. Unlike other hostelries, which will happily serve well into the afternoon siesta or late at night, Don Antonio rolls down the shutters as soon as the day's catch has been consumed. ⊠ *Via Magazzini 20, off Piazza San Paolo* ☎ *081/5267941* ⌂ *Reservations not accepted* ▤ *No credit cards* ☉ *Closed Mon.*

Baia

17 *7 km (4½ mi) south of Pozzuoli, 12 km (7 mi) west of Naples.*

Now largely under the sea, this was once the most opulent and fashionable resort area of the Roman Empire, a place where Sulla, Pompey, Cicero, Julius Caesar, Tiberius, and Nero all built holiday villas. Petronius's *Satyricon* is a satire on the corruption, intrigue, and wonderful licentiousness of Roman life at Baia. (Petronius was hired to arrange parties and entertainments for Nero, so he was in a position to know.) It was here at Baia that Emperor Claudius built a great villa for his wife, Messalina (who spent her nights indulging herself at public brothels); here that Agrippina poisoned her husband and was, in turn, murdered by her son Nero; and here that Cleopatra was staying when Julius Caesar was murdered on the Ides of March in 44 BC. You can visit the excavations of the famous *terme* (baths). ⊠ *Via Fusaro 35* ☎ *081/8687592* 💰 *€4 includes Cumae, the museum of Baia and the Pozzuoli amphitheater* ☉ *Tues.–Sun. 9–2 hrs before sunset.*

en route   Follow the southern loop around Lago Miseno (a volcanic crater believed by the ancients to be the Styx, across which Charon ferried the souls of the dead) and Lago del Fusaro. You'll take in some fine views of the Golfo di Pozzuoli (Bay of Pozzuoli).

Cumae

18   *5 km (3 mi) north of Pozzuoli, 16 km (10 mi) west of Naples.*

Perhaps the oldest Greek colony in Italy, Cumae (Cuma in Italian) overshadowed the Phlegrean Fields, including Naples, in the 7th and 6th centuries BC. The **Antro della Sibilla** (Sibyl's Cave)—one of the most venerated sites in antiquity—is in Cumae. In the 6th or 5th century BC the Greeks hollowed the cave from the rock beneath the present ruins of Cumae's acropolis. You walk through a dark, massive stone tunnel that opens into a vaulted chamber where the Sibyl uttered her oracles. Standing here, the sense of mystery is overwhelming. "This is the most romantic classical site in Italy," wrote the English travel writer H. V. Morton (1892–1979). "I would rather come here than to Pompeii."

Virgil (70–19 BC) wrote in his epic *Aeneid* of the Trojan prince Aeneas's descent to the Underworld to speak to his father. To find his way in he needed the guidance of the Cumaean Sibyl. Virgil did not dream up the Sibyl's cave or the entrance to Hades—he must have stood both in her chamber and on the rim of Lago d'Averno, where you can stand yourself. When he wrote *"Facilis descensus Averno"*—"The way to hell is easy"—it was because he knew the way. In Book VI of the *Aeneid* Virgil described how Aeneas, arriving at Cumae, sought Apollo's throne (remains of the **Tempio di Apollo** can still be seen) and "the deep hidden abode of the dread Sibyl / An enormous cave. . . ."

Sibyls were not necessarily charlatans; they were mediums, prophets, old women whom the ancients believed could communicate with the other world. The three most famous Sibyls were at Erythrae, Delphi, and Cumae. Governments consulted the Sibyls before mounting campaigns. Wealthy aristocrats came to commune with their dead relatives. Businessmen came to get their dreams interpreted or to seek favorable omens before entering into financial agreements or setting off on journeys. Farmers came to remove curses on their cows. Love potions were a good source of revenue—women from Baia lined up for potions to slip into the wine of handsome charioteers.

Little of ancient Cumae now stands aboveground—the Temple of Apollo has suffered woefully over the millennia—but the underground passages are virtually intact, though not entirely visitable. There are detailed information panels to guide you through the site, with extra information on flora and fauna supplied by the local Worldwide Fund for Nature. As you walk through, you'll soon appreciate what a good choice it was to colonize at this location: it was surrounded by fertile land, had relatively easy access to the sea (though no natural harbor), and an acropolis at the top providing an excellent vantage in all directions. Allow at least two hours for this visit to soak up the ambience, study the ruins, and reach the top level overlooking the Acherusia Palus—now Lago Fusaro—to the south and part of the Silva Gallinaria, the thick holm-oak ground cover to the north, once an immense forest stretching almost all the way to Rome. ⊠ *Via Acropoli 39* ☎ *081/8543060* 🎫 *€4 includes the Pozzuoli amphitheater and the museum and site of Baia* ⊙ *Daily 9–2 hrs before sunset.*

Lago d'Averno

4 km (2½ mi) south of Cumae, 11 km (7 mi) west of Naples.

Regarded by the ancients as the gateway to Hades, the fabled Lago d'Averno (Lake Avernus) was well known by the time Virgil settled here to write *The Aeneid*. Today the scene has changed a fair amount: in summer the area pulsates to the sound of disco music, and you would be more likely to come across members of the 21st-century underworld than meet the shades of the dead that Virgil so evocatively describes. As with Lago Lucrino (the Lucrine Lake) less than 1 km (½ mi) to the south, a tarmac road skirts much of the lake. However, some of the spell is restored by the backdrop: forested hills rise on three sides and the menacing cone of Monte Nuovo looms on the fourth. The smell of sulfur sometimes hangs over the landscape, and blocked-off passages lead into long-abandoned caves into which Virgil might well have ventured. ✢ *Drive west from Pozzuoli on S7 toward Cumae; then turn left (south) on the road to Baia. About 1 km (½ mi) along, turn right; follow signs to Lago d'Averno.*

HERCULANEUM, VESUVIUS & POMPEII

Volcanic ash and mud preserved the Roman towns of Herculaneum and Pompeii almost exactly as they were on the day Mt. Vesuvius erupted in AD 79, leaving them not just archaeological ruins but museums of daily life in the ancient world. The two buried cities and the volcano responsible can be visited from either Naples or Sorrento, thanks to the Circumvesuviana, the suburban railway that provides fast, frequent, and economical service.

Herculaneum

★ *10 km (6 mi) southeast of Naples.*

Lying more than 60 feet below the town of Ercolano, the ruins of Herculaneum are set among the acres of greenhouses that make this area one of Europe's principal flower-growing centers. It had about 5,000 inhabitants when it was destroyed; many of them were fishermen, craftsmen, and artists. In AD 79 the gigantic eruption of Vesuvius (which also destroyed Pompeii) buried the town under a tide of volcanic mud. The semiliquid mass seeped into the crevices and niches of every building, covering household objects and enveloping textiles and wood—sealing all in a compact, airtight tomb.

Casual excavation—and haphazard looting—began in the 18th century, but systematic digs were not initiated until the 1920s. Today less than half of Herculaneum has been excavated; with present-day Ercolano and the unlovely Resina Quarter (famous among bargain hunters as the area's largest secondhand-clothing market) sitting on top of the site, progress is limited. From the ramp leading down to Herculaneum's neatly laid-out streets and well-preserved edifices, you get a good overall view of the site, as well as an idea of the amount of volcanic debris that had to be removed to bring it to light.

Though Herculaneum had only one-fourth the population of Pompeii and has been only partially excavated, what has been found is generally better preserved. In some cases you can even see the original wooden beams, staircases, and furniture. Much excitement is presently focused on one excavation in a corner of the site, the Villa dei Papiri, built by Julius Caesar's father-in-law. The building is named for the 1,800 carbonized papyrus scrolls dug up here in the 18th century, leading scholars to believe that this may have been a study center or library. Given the right funds and political support, it is hoped that the villa can be properly excavated and ultimately opened to the public. Little of the site can be seen aboveground, though visitors to the Getty Villa (formerly the J. Paul Getty Museum) in Malibu, California, can see a modern version, built following 18th-century drawings made by the Swiss archaeologist Carl Weber.

At the entrance to the archaeological park you should pick up a map showing the gridlike layout of the dig. Splurge on an audio guide (€6 for one, €9 for two; you'll need to leave an ID card) and head down the tunnel to start the tour at the old shoreline. Though many of the houses are closed and some are in dire need of restoration, a fair cross section of domestic, commercial, and civic buildings is still accessible. Decorations are especially delicate in the **Casa del Nettuno ed Anfitrite** (House of Neptune and Amphitrite), named for the subjects of a still-bright mosaic on the wall of the nymphaeum (a recessed grotto with a fountain), and in the **Terme Femminili** (Women's Baths), where several delicate black-and-white mosaic pavements embellished the various rooms. Annexed to the former house is a remarkably preserved wineshop, where amphorae still rest on carbonized wooden shelves. On the other side of the house is the **Casa del Bel Cortile** (House of the Beautiful Courtyard). In one of its inner rooms is the temporary display of a cast taken of some skeletons found in the storerooms down at the old seafront, where almost 300 inhabitants sought refuge from the eruption and were ultimately encapsulated for posterity. The palaestra, the sumptuously decorated **Terme Suburbane** (Suburban Baths)—open only mornings—and the **Casa dei Cervi** (House of the Stags), with an elegant garden open to the sea breezes, are all evocative relics of a lively and luxurious way of life. ⊠ *Corso Ercolano, a 5-min walk downhill from the Ercolano Circumvesuviana station* ☎ *081/8575347* ⊕ *www.pompeiisites.org* ✑ *€10; €18 including Oplontis, Pompeii, and 2 other sites over 3 days* ☉ *Apr.–Oct., daily 8:30–7:30, ticket office closes at 6; Nov.–Mar., daily 8:30–5, ticket office closes at 3:30.*

Vesuvius

❷⓿ *8 km (5 mi) northeast of Herculaneum, 16 km (10 mi) east of Naples.*

The profile of Vesuvius is so inseparable from the Bay of Naples area, and the ferocious power it can unleash so vivid as you tour the sights of the cities that it destroyed, you may be overwhelmed by the urge to explore the crater itself. In summer especially, the prospect of rising above the sticky heat of the city and sights below is a heady one. The view when clear is magnificent, with the curve of the coast and the tiny white houses among the orange and lemon blossoms. If the summit is lost in mist you'll be lucky to see your hand in front of your face. When you see the summit clearing—it tends to be clearer in the afternoon—head for it. If possible, see Vesuvius after you've toured the ruins of buried Herculaneum to appreciate the magnitude of the volcano's power.

Reaching the crater takes some effort. From the Ercolano stop of the Circumvesuviana, take scheduled buses (trip takes one hour; there are four or five departures a day—check for the latest schedule at the bar just outside the train station) or your own car to Quota 1000 (the parking lot and cafeteria area near the top). From here you must climb the soft, slippery cinder track on foot, a 30-minute ascent, and pay €6 for access, which includes compulsory guide service, usually young geologists with a smattering of English. At the bottom you'll be offered a stout walking stick (a small tip is appreciated on return). The climb can be tiring if you're not used to steep hikes. Wear nonskid shoes (not sandals). ☎ *081/7775720* ✑ *€6* ☉ *Daily 9 AM–2 hrs before sunset.*

You can visit **Osservatorio Vesuviano** (the old observatory)—2,000 feet up—and view instruments used to study the volcano, some dating back to the mid-19th century. ☎ *081/7777149 or 081/7777150* ⊕ *www.ov. ingv.it* ✑ *Free* ☉ *Weekends 10–2.*

Oplontis

 20 km (12 mi) southeast of Naples, 5 km (3 mi) west of Pompeii.

The spectacular archaeological site of Oplontis (surrounded by the fairly drab urban landscape of Torre Annunziata) is a villa complex that's been imaginatively ascribed—based on a mere inscription on an amphora—to Nero's second wife, Poppaea Sabina, whose family was well known among the landed gentry of neighboring Pompeii. As Roman villas go, Poppaea's Villa is truly exceptional. Excavation so far has uncovered an area of more than 100 by 75 meters (325 by 250 ft), and because the site is bound by a road to the west and a canal to the south, it may never be possible to gauge its full extent. What's been found includes porticoes, a large peristyle, a *piscina* (pool), baths, and extensive gardens, as well as the standard atria, triclinia, and a warren of *cubicula* (bedrooms). The villa is thought by some to have been a training school for young philosophers and orators.

Access is easiest from the Circumvesuviana station of Torre Annunziata, about 650 feet away. Outside the station turn left and then right downhill; the site is just after the crossroads down on the left. If coming by car, take the Torre Annunziata turnoff from the Naples–Salerno autostrada, turn right, and then look for signs on the left for Oplontis at the first major crossroads. The main entrance to the site is from the north—you basically go into the villa through the gardens, with the atrium on the southern side lying under about 10 feet of pumice and pyroclastic material from Vesuvius.

Oplontis offers the full gamut of Roman wall paintings, with a particular penchant for the illusionist motifs of the so-called Second Pompeian Style. There are some good examples in the west wing of the villa, especially in the triclinium (Room 14—look for the room numbers above the doors) giving onto the small portico (Room 13), which abuts the west end of the site and the road above. Although the stuccowork in the thermae, or baths, is less impressive than in Pompeii and Herculaneum, the calidarium (Room 8) has a delightful miniature landscape scene surmounted by a peacock in a niche at its eastern end (binoculars are useful). Nearby, in the tepidarium (Room 18), there's an interesting glimpse into the structural design of Roman baths; here the floor is raised by *suspensurae,* small brick supporting pilasters, enabling warm air to pass beneath. ⊠ *Via Sepolcri 1, Torre Annunziata* ☎ *081/8575347* ⊕ *www.pompeiisites.org* ✉ *€5 including Boscoreale and Stabiae in 1 day; €18 including Herculaneum, Pompeii, and the 2 other sites over 3 days* ☉ *Apr.–Oct., daily 8:30–7:30, ticket office closes at 6; Nov.–Mar., daily 8:30–5, ticket office closes at 3:30.*

Pompeii

Fodor'sChoice
★
11 km (7 mi) southeast of Herculaneum, 24 km (15 mi) southeast of Naples.

Ancient Pompeii was much larger than Herculaneum; a busy commercial center with a population of 10,000–20,000, it covered about 160 acres on the seaward end of the fertile Sarno Plain. In 80 BC the Roman general Sulla turned Pompeii into a Roman settlement, colonized by the standard complement of army veterans. The town was laid out in a grid pattern, with two main intersecting streets. The wealthiest took a whole block for themselves; those less fortunate built a house and rented out the front rooms, facing the street, as shops. The facades of these houses were relatively plain and seldom hinted at the care and attention lavished on the private rooms within. When visitors arrived they passed the shops and entered an open atrium. In the back was a receiving room. Behind was another open area, called the peristyle, with rows of columns and perhaps a garden with a fountain. Only good friends ever saw this private part of the house, which was surrounded by bedrooms and the dining area.

Pompeian houses were designed around an inner garden, so that families could turn their backs on the world outside. Not that public life was so intolerable. There were good numbers of *tabernae* (taverns), *thermopolia* (hot-food shops) on almost every corner, and frequent shows at the amphitheater. The public fountains and toilets were fed by huge cisterns connected by lead pipes beneath the sidewalks. Since garbage and rainwater collected in the streets of Pompeii, the sidewalks were raised, and huge stepping-stones were placed at crossings so pedestrians could keep their feet dry. Herculaneum had better drainage, with an underground sewer that led to the sea.

All households would have had slaves, though in varying numbers depending on financial resources. A small, prosperous family had as many as eight engaged in tasks ranging from estate management to education to cooking. Judging from archaeological finds and depictions on wall frescoes, the Pompeians enjoyed a balanced diet, including meat, seafood, walnuts, eggs, bread (made from wheat and barley), grapes, pears, and figs—all washed down with wine made of grapes grown on the slopes of Vesuvius.

Thanks to those deep layers of pyroclastic deposits from Vesuvius that protected the site from natural wear and tear over the centuries, Pompeii provides unique insights into the sort of things that the locals found important 2,000 years ago. Some 15,000 graffiti have been found in Pompeii and Herculaneum. Many were political announcements—one person recommending another for office, for example, and spelling out his qualifications. Some were announcements of upcoming events—a play at the theater, a gladiatorial show at the amphitheater. Others were public notices—that wine was on sale, that an apartment would be vacant on the Ides of March. A good many were personal and lend a human dimension to the disaster that not even the sights can equal. Here are a couple:

At the baths: "What is the use of having a Venus if she's made of marble?"

At the entrance to the front lavatory at a private house: "May I always and everywhere be as potent with women as I was here."

Pompeii

To get the most out of Pompeii rent an audio guide (€6 for one, €9 for two; you'll need to leave an ID card) and allow at least three or four hours. Come armed with bottled water and a snack—there are some shady, underused picnic tables outside the Porta di Nola to the northeast of the site. Two buildings within the site—Terme Suburbane (daily 10–2) and Casa del Menandro (weekends 2–4)—are open for restricted viewing on a first-come, first-served basis. Pompeii has its own stop (Pompei–Villa dei Misteri) on the Naples–Sorrento Circumvesuviana line, close to the main entrance at the Porta Marina (there's another entrance to the excavations at the far end of the site, near the amphitheater).

▶ ㉒ The first buildings to the left after you've gone through the ticket turnstiles are the **Terme Suburbane** (Suburban Baths), built—by all accounts without planning permission—right up against the city walls. The baths have eyebrow-raising frescoes in the *apodyterium* (changing room) that strongly suggest that more than just bathing and massaging went on here.

㉓ Enter the remains of the old city walls through **Porta Marina**, so called because it faces the sea. You'll note the two entrances here, the smaller one on the left being used only by pedestrians in antiquity. Past the Tem-
㉔ ple of Venus is the **Basilica**, the city's law court and the economic center. These oblong buildings ending in a semicircular projection (apse) were the model for early Christian churches, which had a nave (central aisle) and two side aisles separated by rows of columns. Standing in the Basilica, you can recognize the continuity between Roman and Christian architecture.

㉕ The Basilica opens onto the **Foro** (forum), the public meeting place surrounded by temples and public buildings. It was here that elections were held and speeches and official announcements made. At the far (north-
㉖ ern) end of the forum is the **Tempio di Giove** (Temple of Jupiter). The
㉗ renowned **Casa del Fauno** (House of the Faun) displayed wonderful mosaics, which can now be viewed in the Museo Archeologico Nazionale in Naples.

㉘ The **Terme di Foro** (Forum Baths) on Via delle Terme is smaller than
㉙ the Terme Stabiane, but with more delicate decoration. The **Casa del Poeta Tragico** (House of the Tragic Poet) is a typical middle-class house from the last days of Pompeii. On the floor is a mosaic of a chained dog and the inscription CAVE CANEM ("Beware of the dog").

㉚ The beautiful **Porta Ercolano** (Herculaneum Gate) was a main gate that led to Herculaneum and Naples, one of seven gates in the ancient city
㉛ walls. The **Villa dei Misteri** (Villa of the Mysteries), outside Pompeii's walls, contains what some consider the greatest surviving group of paintings from the ancient world, telling the story of a young bride (Ariadne) being initiated into the mysteries of the cult of Dionysus. Bacchus (Dionysus), the god of wine, was popular in a town so devoted to the pleasures of the flesh. But he also represented the triumph of the irrational—of all those mysterious forces that no official state religion could fully suppress. The cult of Dionysus, like the cult of the Cumaean Sibyl, gave people a sense of control over fate and, in its focus on the other world, helped pave the way for Christianity.

UNLOCKING THE VILLA OF THE MYSTERIES

N ITS DAY, *Pompeii was celebrated as the Côte d'Azur, the seaside Brighton, the Fire Island of the ancient Roman empire. Evidence of a Sybaritic bent is everywhere. In the town's grandest villas and rowdiest lupanaria (brothels), murals reveal a worship of hedonism engaged in by satyrs, bacchantes, hermaphrodites, and acrobatic couples.*

Pompeii's most magnificently memorable frescoes are found at the Villa dei Misteri, or Villa of the Mysteries, and the finest of these are in the triclinium (banquet room). Painted in the most glowing Pompeian reds and oranges, the panels relate the saga of Ariadne, a young bride, and her initiation into the sacred mysteries of the cult of Dionysus, a god imported to Italy from Greece and then given the Latin name Bacchus.

The Villa of the Mysteries frescoes were painted circa 50 BC, most art historians believe, and represent the peak of the Second Style of Pompeian wall painting. The triclinium frescoes are thought to be the work of a local artist, although the theme may have been copied from an earlier cycle of paintings of the Hellenistic period.

In all there are 10 scenes, depicting children and matrons, musicians and satyrs, phalluses and gods. There are no inscriptions with the names of the main characters (such as are found on Greek vases), and after 2,000 years historians remain puzzled by many aspects of the triclinium cycle. Though some of the frescoes' mysteries may never be solved, it's pleasure enough to come here, marvel at their vibrant beauty, and contemplate love among the ruins.

32 The **Casa degli Amorini Dorati** (House of the Gilded Cupids) is an elegant, well-preserved home with original marble decorations in the garden. **33** On the walls of **Lupanare** (brothel) are scenes of erotic games in which **34** clients could engage. The **Terme Stabiane** (Stabian Baths) had underground furnaces, the heat from which circulated beneath the floor, rose through flues in the walls, and escaped through chimneys. The water temperature could be set for cold, lukewarm, or hot. Bathers took a lukewarm bath to prepare themselves for the hot room. A tepid bath came next, and then a plunge into cold water to tone up the skin. A vigorous massage with oil was followed by rest, reading, horseplay, and conversation.

35 Togas were washed at **Fullonica Stephani.** The cloth was dunked in a tub full of water and chalk and stomped on like so many grapes. Once clean, the material was stretched across a wicker cage and exposed to sulfur fumes. The fuller (cleaner) carded it with a long brush, then placed it under a press. The harder the pressing, the whiter and brighter **36** it became. Many paintings and mosaics were executed at **Casa del Menandro,** a patrician's villa named for a fresco of the Greek playwright Menander. The **Orto dei Fuggiaschi** (Garden of the Fugitives) contains **37** poignant plaster casts of those overwhelmed by the eruption in AD 79.

38 The **Anfiteatro** (Amphitheater) was the ultimate in entertainment for local Pompeians and offered a gamut of experiences, but essentially this was for gladiators rather than wild animals. Unlike the amphitheater at Pozzuoli, here there are no underground *cellae* for the penning of animals (and *venationes,* or combat with wild animals really became popular only late in the 1st century AD). With the large palaestra close by and the gladiatorial barracks near the theater area, there were extensive facilities to train gladiators in many types of combat. Teams worked for impresarios, who hired them out to wealthy citizens, many of whom were running for office and hoping that the gory entertainment would buy them some votes. Most gladiators were slaves or prisoners, but a few were men from the far-flung reaches of the empire who enjoyed fighting.

By Roman standards, Pompeii's amphitheater was quite small (seating 20,000). Built in about 80 BC, it was oval and divided into three seating areas like a theater. There were two main entrances—at the north and south ends—and a narrow passage on the west called the *Porta Libitinensis,* through which the dead were most probably dragged out. A wall painting found in a house near the theater (now in the Naples Museum) depicts the riot in the amphitheater in AD 59 when several citizens from the nearby town of Nucera were killed. After Nucerian appeals to Nero, shows in the amphitheater were suspended for 10 years. ✉ *Pompei Scavi* 🕾 *081/8575347* ⊕ *www.pompeiisites.org* 🖼 *€10; €18 including Oplontis, Herculaneum, and 2 other sites over 3 days* ☺ *Apr.–Oct., daily 8:30–7:30, ticket office closes at 6; Nov.–Mar., daily 8:30–5, ticket office closes at 3:30.*

Many visitors to ancient Pompeii are unaware of the modern pilgrimage that many Italians make to visit the **Santuario,** consecrated in 1891, which dominates the central square in modern Pompei. Its main altar contains a painting, *The Virgin of the Rosary with Child,* which has been worshipped all over the world since it was claimed to have healing powers in 1876. The bell tower stands more than 250 feet high and has great views over the Lattari Mountains, Mount Vesuvius, the Sorrento coast, the ruins of Pompeii, and modern Pompei. ✉ *Piazza Bartolo Longo* 🕾 *081/8577111* 🖼 *Bell tower elevator €0.50* ☺ *Church daily 6:30–2 and 3–7:30; bell tower May–Sept., Sat.–Thurs. 9–1 and 3–6; Oct.–Apr., Sat.–Thurs. 9–1 and 3–5.*

Where to Eat

$$$–$$$$ ✕ **President.** Brother-and-sister team Ornella and Paolo Gramaglia preside over what's commonly recognized as the finest restaurant in the area. Fish is a specialty, with dishes giving modern twists to classic recipes— try the *paccheri con straccetti di triglia, vongole e zucchine* (large pasta with red mullet, clams, and zucchini). The main room is elegantly decorated with 19th-century Neapolitan furniture, and there's an extensive wine cellar. ✉ *Piazza Schettini 12, 80045* 🕾 *081/8507245* 🖶 *AE, DC, MC, V* ☺ *Closed Mon. and mid-Aug. No lunch Sun.*

¢–$ ✕ **Ristorante Pizzeria Carlo Alberto.** This small, efficiently run restaurant with an impressive range of choices is comfortably out of the reach of large tour groups. If you're a vegetarian, try pizza *regina* (pizza with buffalo mozzarella and cherry tomatoes). The *focaccetta* (flatbread) is a pleasant change from regular bread. Reservations are essential on weekends. ⊠ *Via Carlo Alberto 15* ☎ *081/8633231* ▤ *DC, MC, V.*

CASERTA & BENEVENTO

From Caserta, the Italian answer to Versailles, if you proceed to Benevento you'll view an almost perfectly preserved Roman arch. Benevento was badly damaged by World War II bombings, but among the modern structures there are some medieval and even older relics still standing in the old town. If you go by car, make a brief detour to the medieval hamlet of Caserta Vecchia on the hillside, where there are one or two good restaurants and a very old cathedral.

Caserta

★ ❸❾ *11 km (7 mi) northeast of Herculaneum, 25 km (16 mi) northeast of Naples.*

The palace known as the **Reggia** shows how Bourbon royals lived in the mid-18th century. Architect Luigi Vanvitelli devoted 20 years to its construction under Bourbon ruler Charles III, whose son, Ferdinand IV (1751–1825), moved in when it was completed in 1774. Both king and architect were inspired by Versailles, and the rectangular palace was conceived on a massive scale, with four interconnecting courtyards, 1,200 rooms, and a vast park. Though the palace is not as well maintained as its French counterpart, the main staircase puts the one at Versailles to shame, and the **royal apartments** are sumptuous. It was here, in what Eisenhower called "a castle near Naples," that the Allied High Command had its headquarters in World War II, and here German forces in Italy surrendered in April 1945. There's also a museum showing items relating to the palace and the Caserta area. Most enjoyable are the gardens and parks, particularly the Cascades, adorned with sculptures of the classical goddess Diana and her maidens. ⊠ *Piazza Carlo III* ☎ *0823/448084* ▦ *Royal apartments, Museo dell'Opera, park, and English garden €6; park only €2; minibus €1* ☉ *Royal apartments Tues.–Sun. 8:30–7:30. Park Mar., Tues.–Sun. 8:30–5; Apr., Tues.–Sun. 8:30–6; May and Aug., Tues.–Sun. 8:30–6:30; June and July, Tues.–Sun. 8:30–7; Sept. and Oct., Tues.–Sun. 8:30–5:30; Nov.–Feb., Tues.–Sun. 8:30–3:30; ticket office closes 1 hr before closing.*

Santa Maria Capua Vetere

❹⓿ *8 km (5 mi) west of Caserta, 30 km (18 mi) north of Naples.*

A short hop from Caserta—through somewhat unlovely development—is a cluster of fascinating sites dating back to the Roman period and beyond. The **Anfiteatro Campano** was modeled on the Colosseum and built under the emperor Hadrian (AD 117–138). It's been stripped of much of its superstructure, but some of the surviving sculptural decorations are on display at the small adjoining Museo dei Gladiatori. The museum's highlight is the helpful reconstruction of one of the amphitheater's original 76 *vomitoria* (entrances), together with then-and-now scale models of the amphitheater. All information panels are in Italian only. ⊠ *Piazza I Ottobre* ☎ *0823/844206* 🖃 *€2.50* ☉ *Tues.–Sun. 9–6:30.*

Benevento

④① *35 km (22 mi) east of Caserta, 60 km (37 mi) northeast of Naples.*

Benevento owes its importance to its establishment as the capital of the Lombards, a northern tribe that invaded and settled what is now Lombardy when they were forced to move south by Charlemagne's conquests in the 8th century. The tough and resourceful Lombards moved farther south and set up a new duchy in Benevento, later moving its seat to Salerno, where they saw the potential of the natural harbor. Under papal rule in the 13th century, Benevento built a fine cathedral and outfitted it with bronze doors that were a pinnacle of Romanesque art. The cathedral, doors, and a large part of the town were blasted by World War II bombs. The **Duomo** has been rebuilt, and the remaining panels of the original bronze doors are in the chapter library. Fortunately, the

★ majestic 2nd-century AD **Arco di Traiano** (Trajan's Arch) was unscathed by the World War II bombing that hit Benevento. Roman emperor Trajan, who sorted out Rome's finances, brought parts of the Middle East into the empire, and extended the Appian Way through Benevento to the Adriatic. The ruins of the **Teatro Romano,** which had a seating capacity of 20,000, have been extensively restored and host a summer music and theater season. ⊠ *Take Via Carlo from the Duomo* 🖃 *€2* ☉ *Daily 9–1 hr before sunset.*

PROCIDA, ISCHIA & CAPRI

History's hedonists have long luxuriated on Campania's famous islands. The Roman emperor Tiberius built a dozen villas on Capri in which to indulge his sexual whims. Later residents have included dancer Rudolf Nureyev and droves of artists and writers. These days, day-trippers make up the majority of visitors, diminishing the islands' social cachet. Ischia, less pretty and less chic than Capri, is still a popular destination on account of its spas, beaches, and hot springs. Procida, long the poor relation of the three, and the closest to Naples, is starting to capitalize on its chief natural asset, the unspoiled isle of Vivara. The pastel colors of Procida's main harbor will be familiar to anyone who has seen the widely acclaimed film *Il Postino,* scenes of which were shot there.

Procida

④② *35 mins by hydrofoil, 1 hr by car ferry from Naples.*

Lying barely 3 km (2 mi) from the mainland and 10 km (6 mi) from the nearest port of Pozzuoli, Procida is an island of enormous contrasts. It is the most densely populated island in Europe—almost 11,000 people crammed into less than 3½ square km (2 square mi)—and yet there are oases such as Marina Corricella and Vivara that seem to have been bypassed by modern civilization. It's no surprise that picturesque Procida has strong artistic traditions and is widely considered a painters' island par excellence.

The sleepy fishermen's village of **Corricella,** used as the setting for the waterfront scenes in the Oscar-winning film *Il Postino,* has been relatively immune to life in the limelight, and apart from the opening of an extra restaurant and bar there have been few changes. This is the type of place where even those with failing grades in art class feel like reaching for a paintbrush to record the delicate pinks and yellows of the waterfront buildings. The **Graziella** bar at the far end of the seafront offers the island's famous lemons squeezed over crushed ice to make an excellent granita.

Where to Stay & Eat

$–$$ ✕ **La Gorgonia.** This atmospheric restaurant sits right on the waterfront at Corricella. The specialties here are combinations of seafood and locally grown vegetables, such as pasta *con fagioli e cozze* (with beans and mussels). ⊠ *Marina Corricella 50* ☎ *081/8101060* ▱ *AE, DC, MC, V* ✸ *Closed Mon. and Nov.–Jan.*

$ ▦ **Casa Gentile.** Spacious rooms overlook Corricella at this quiet hotel designed to blend in tastefully with the local Mediterranean architecture. If you're interested in fishing, ask the owner, Vincenzo, if you can join him on his nighttime travels around the Bay of Naples. The hotel offers a water-taxi service to and from port. ⊠ *Marina Corricella 88 80079* ☎ *081/8967799* ▱ *081/8969011* ➲ *10 rooms* ⚭ *Minibars; no a/c* ▱ *MC, V* ✸ *Closed Nov.–mid-Mar.* ▯ *BP.*

Ischia

⑬ *45 mins by hydrofoil, 90 mins by car ferry from Naples, 60 mins by ferry from Pozzuoli.*

Whereas Capri wows you with its charm and beauty, Ischia takes time to cast its spell. In fact, an overnight stay is probably not long enough for the island to get into your blood. It does have its share of vine-growing villages beneath the lush volcanic slopes of Monte Epomeo, and unlike Capri it enjoys a life of its own that survives when the tourists head home. But there are few signs of antiquity here, the architecture is unremarkable, the traffic can be overwhelming, and hoteliers have yet to achieve a balanced mix of clientele—most are either German (off-season) or Italian (in-season). But should you want to plunk down in the sun for a few days and tune out the world, this is an ideal place to go; just don't expect Ischia to be an unspoiled, undiscovered Capri. When Augustus gave the Neapolitans Ischia for Capri, he knew what he was doing.

Ischia is volcanic in origin. From its hidden reservoir of seething molten matter come the thermal springs said to cure whatever ails you. As early as 1580 a doctor named Lasolino published a book about the mineral wells at Ischia. "If your eyebrows fall off," he wrote, "go and try the baths at Piaggia Romano. If you know anyone who is getting bald, anyone who suffers from elephantiasis, or another whose wife yearns for a child, take the three of them immediately to the Bagno di Vitara; they will bless you." Today the island is covered with thermal baths, often surrounded by tropical gardens.

A good 35-km (22-mi) road makes a circuit of the island; the ride takes most of a day at a leisurely pace if you're stopping along the way to enjoy the views and perhaps have lunch. You can book a boat tour around the island at the booths in various ports along the coast; there's a one-hour stop at Sant'Angelo. The information office is at the harbor. You may drive on Ischia year-round. There's also fairly good bus service, and you'll find plenty of taxis.

Ischia Porto is the largest town on the island and the usual point of debarkation. It's no workaday port, however, but a lively resort with plenty of hotels, Ischia's best shopping area, and low flat-roof houses on terraced hillsides above the water. Its narrow streets often become flights of steps that scale the hill, and its villas and gardens are framed by pines.

Most of the hotels are along the beach in the part of town called **Ischia Ponte,** which gets its name from the *ponte* (bridge) built by Alfonso of Aragon in 1438 to link the picturesque castle on a small islet offshore with the town and port. For a while the castle was the home of Vittoria Colonna, poetess, granddaughter of Renaissance Duke Federico da Montefeltro (1422–82), and platonic soul mate of Michelangelo, with whom she carried on a lengthy correspondence. You'll find a typical resort atmosphere: countless cafés, shops, and restaurants, and a 1-km (½-mi) stretch of fine-sand beach. **Casamicciola,** a popular beach resort, is 5 km (3 mi) west of Ischia Porto. Chic and upscale **Lacco Ameno,** next to Casamicciola, is distinguished by a mushroom-shape rock offshore and some of the island's best hotels. Here, too, you can enjoy the benefits of Ischia's therapeutic waters.

The far western and southern coasts of Ischia are more rugged and attractive. **Forio,** at the extreme west, has a waterfront church and is a good spot for lunch or dinner. The sybaritic hot pools of the **Giardini Poseidon Terme** (Poseidon Gardens) spa establishment are on the Citara beach, south of Forio. You can sit like a Roman senator on a stone chair recessed in the rock and let the hot water cascade over you—all very campy, and fun. **Sant'Angelo,** on the southern coast, is a charming village; the road doesn't reach all the way into town, so it's free of traffic, and it's a five-minute boat ride from the beach of Maronti, at the foot of cliffs. The inland town of Fontana is the base for excursions to the top of **Monte Epomeo,** the long-dormant volcano that dominates the island landscape. You can reach its 2,585-foot peak in less than 1½ hours of relatively easy walking.

Where to Stay & Eat

★ **$$$** ╳ **Il Melograno.** A 10-minute walk south from the center of Forio takes you to the tranquil setting of one of Campania's finest restaurants. With antipasti such as *calamaretti crudi con pera* (raw squid with pears) and many tempting pasta dishes, you could be forgiven for skipping the main course. Try the very reasonably priced local wines (both white and red) from the Pietratorcia winery up the road. Dessert, appropriately called *dulcis in fundo* (the best for last), also merits attention. ⊠ *Via G. Mazzella 110, Forio* ☎ *081/998450* ⚞ *Reservations essential* ▤ *AE, DC, MC, V* ⊘ *Closed Mon. and Tues. in Nov. and Dec., and Jan. 7–Mar. 15.*

$$ ✕ **Gennaro.** This small family restaurant on the seafront in Ischia Porto serves excellent fish in a convivial atmosphere. Specialties include spaghetti alle vongole and linguine *all'aragosta* (with lobster). ⊠ *Via Porto 66, Ischia Porto* ☎ *081/992917* ▤ *AE, DC, MC, V* ⊘ *Closed Nov.–mid-Mar.*

$$$$ ▦ **Grand Hotel Punta Molino.** Set in its own pinewood grounds on Ischia's northeastern coastline yet within walking distance of the island's shopping boulevards, this pleasingly modern hotel provides privacy, relaxation, and low-key evening entertainment. Rooms are decorated in gentle Mediterranean hues—some of the best are in the villa annex. A crescent-shape swimming pool wraps around part of the main building, and the gardens have walkways and shady pergolas. Rates include a buffet lunch or candlelight dinner. ⊠ *Lungomare C. Colombo 23, 80077* ☎ *081/991544* 🖷 *081/9991562* ⊕ *www.puntamolino.it* ⤴ *90 rooms* ⚭ *2 restaurants, 3 pools, health club, spa, beach, piano bar, meeting rooms* ▤ *AE, DC, MC, V* ⊘ *Closed Oct.–Mar.* ⵌ⊘ *MAP.*

$$$$ ▦ **Hotel San Montano.** Modern San Montano is perched commandingly 300 feet up on Monte Vico. Nautical motifs and materials are used in much of the hotel, with portholes in the lobby, brass finishings to the room furniture, and tiller-shape headboards. With the full gamut of spa treatments available you could be forgiven for not venturing down to sea level. Note that half board is required in high season. ⊠ *Via Montevico 20, 80076, Lacco Ameno* ☎ *081/994033* 🖷 *081/980242* ⊕ *www.sanmontano.com* ⤴ *65 rooms, 12 suites* ⚭ *Restaurant, minibars, tennis court, 2 pools, spa* ▤ *AE, DC, MC, V* ⊘ *Closed Nov.–Mar.* ⵌ⊘ *MAP.*

$$$ ▦ **Villarosa.** A highlight at this gracious family-run hotel—a villa with bright and airy rooms—is the thermally heated pool in the villa garden. In high season, half board is required, and you must reserve well in advance. It's in the heart of Ischia Porto and only a short walk from the beach. ⊠ *Via Giacinto Gigante 5, Ischia Porto 80077* ☎ *081/991316* 🖷 *081/992425* ⊕ *www.lavillarosa.it* ⤴ *37 rooms* ⚭ *Restaurant, pool* ▤ *AE, DC, MC, V* ⊘ *Closed Nov.–Mar.* ⵌ⊘ *MAP.*

$ ▦ **La Pergola.** Here you'll find one of the few opportunities to stay on a working farm on Ischia. La Pergola is a whitewashed villa perched attractively on the slopes of Monte Epomeo and surrounded by vineyards and olive and fruit trees, with sweeping views westward over Citara Beach. Its dynamic young owners also operate a thriving restaurant serving local specialties including the fabled rabbit dish *coniglio all'ischitana.* ⊠ *Via San Giuseppe 8, Forio 80075* ☎☎ *081/909483* ⚭ *giosocol@tin.it* ⤴ *7 rooms* ⚭ *Restaurant; no a/c, no room phones, no room TVs* ▤ *No credit cards* ⵌ⊘ *MAP.*

Capri

75 mins by boat, 40 mins by hydrofoil from Naples.

Erstwhile pleasure dome to Roman emperors and now Italy's most glamorous seaside getaway, Capri (pronounced with an accent on the first syllable) is a craggy island at the southern approach to the Bay of Naples. The summer scene on Capri calls to mind the stampeding of bulls through the narrow streets of Pamplona: if you can visit in spring or fall, do so. Yet even the crowds are not enough to destroy Capri's very special charm. The town is a Moorish opera set of shiny white houses, tiny squares, and narrow medieval alleyways hung with flowers. You can take a bus or the funicular to reach the town, which rests on top of rugged limestone cliffs hundreds of feet above the sea, and on which herds of *capre* (goats) once used to roam (giving the name to the island). Unlike the other islands in the Bay of Naples, Capri is not of volcanic origin; it may be a continuation of the limestone Sorrentine peninsula.

Limestone caves on Capri have yielded rich prehistoric and neolithic finds. The island is thought to have been settled by Greeks from Cumae in the 6th century BC and later by other Greeks from Neapolis, but it was the Romans in the early imperial period who really left their mark. Emperor Augustus vacationed here; Tiberius built 12 villas scattered over the island, and, in later years, he refused to return to Rome, even when he was near death. Capri was one of the strongholds of the 16th-century pirate Barbarossa, who first sacked it and then made it a fortress. In 1806 the British wanted to turn the island into another Gibraltar and were beginning to build fortifications when the French took it away from them in 1808. Over the next century, from the opening of its first hotel in 1826, Capri saw an influx of visitors that reads like a Who's Who of literature and politics, especially in the early decades of the 20th century.

Like much else about Capri, the island's rare and delicious white wine is sensuous and intoxicating. Note that most of the wine passed off as "local" on Capri comes from the much more extensive vineyards of Ischia.

On arrival at the port, pick up the excellent map of the island at the tourist office (€1). You may have to wait in line for the cog railway (€2.60 round-trip) to **Capri Town,** perched some 450 feet above the harbor. If it's not operating, there's a bus and taxi service, as well as a network of steps leading all the way up. From the upper station, walk out into Piazza Umberto I, much better known as the Piazzetta, the island's social hub. You can window-shop in expensive boutiques and browse in souvenir shops along Via Vittorio Emanuele, which leads south toward the many-domed **Certosa di San Giacomo.** You can visit the church and cloister of this much-restored monastery and also pause long enough to enjoy the breathtaking view of Punta Tragara and the Faraglioni, three towering crags, from the viewpoint at the edge of the cliff. ⊠ *Via Certosa* ☎ *081/8376218* ☾ *Tues.–Sun. 9–2.*

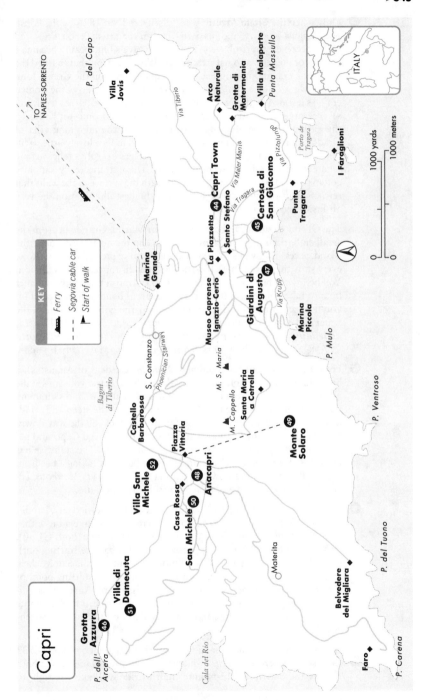

Capri

KEY

◆ Ferry

– – – Segovia cable car

▶ Start of walk

Grotta Azzurra **46**

Villa di Damecuta **51**

Villa Jovis

Arco Naturale

Grotta di Matermania

Villa Malaparte
Punta Massullo

Capri Town **44**

La Piazzetta

Santo Stefano

Certosa di San Giacomo **45**

Punta Tragara

I Faraglioni

Marina Grande

Museo Caprense Ignazio Cerio

Giardini di Augusto **47**

Marina Piccola

P. Mulo

Castello Barbarossa

S. Constanzo

Phoenician Stairway

Bagni di Tiberio

Piazza Vittoria

M. S. Maria

M. Cappello

Santa Maria a Cetrella

Monte Solaro **49**

Villa San Michele **52**

Casa Rossa **50**

Anacapri **48**

San Michele

Materita

Belvedere del Migliara

Faro

P. del Capo

TO NAPLES-SORRENTO

Via Tiberio

Via Mater Mania

Via Tragara

Via Pizzolungo

Porto di Tragara

Via Krupp

P. Ventroso

P. del Tuono

Cala del Rio

P. dell' Arcera

P. Carena

ITALY

1000 yards

1000 meters

46 Only when the **Grotta Azzurra** was "discovered" in 1826 by the Polish poet August Kopisch and his Swiss friend, the artist Ernest Fries, did Capri become a tourist haven. The watery cave's blue beauty became a symbol of the return to nature and revolt from reason that marked the Romantic era, and it soon became a required stop on the Grand Tour. In fact, the grotto had long been an island landmark. During the Roman era—as testified by the extensive remains, primarily below sea level, and several large statues now at the Certosa di San Giacomo—it had been the elegant, mosaic-decorated nymphaeum of the adjoining villa of Gradola. Historians can't quite agree if it was simply a lovely little pavilion where rich patricians would cool themselves or truly a religious site where sacred mysteries were practiced. The extraordinary sapphire color is caused by a hidden opening beneath the surface of the walls that refracts light through the blue water. At highest illumination the very air inside seems tinted blue.

The Grotta Azzurra can be reached from Marina Grande or from the small embarkation point below Anacapri on the northwest side of the island, accessible by bus from Anacapri. If you're pressed for time, however, skip this sometimes frustrating and disappointing excursion. You board one boat to get to the grotto, then transfer to another smaller boat to take you inside. If there's a backup of boats waiting to get in, you'll be given precious little time to enjoy the gorgeous color of the water and its silvery reflections. ⊠ *Marina Grande* ⛴ *About €11–€13, depending on boat company, including €4 admission to grotto* ☉ *Apr.–Sept., daily 9:30–2 hrs before sunset; Oct.–Mar., daily 10–noon.*

47 From the terraces of the **Giardini di Augusto** (Gardens of Augustus), a beautifully planted public garden with excellent views, you can see the village of Marina Piccola below—restaurants, cabanas, and swimming platforms huddle among the shoals—and admire the steep and winding Via Krupp, actually a staircase cut into the rock, all the way down. Friedrich Krupp, the German arms manufacturer, loved Capri and became one of the island's most generous benefactors. The staircase has been closed for years, but you can reach the beach by taking a bus from the Via Roma terminus down to Marina Piccola. ⊠ *Via Matteotti, beyond the monastery of San Giacomo* ☉ *Daily dawn–dusk.*

48 A tortuous road leads up to **Anacapri**, the island's "second city," about 3 km (2 mi) from Capri Town. To get there you can take a bus either from Via Roma in Capri Town or from Marina Grande (both €1.30), or a taxi (about €15 one-way; agree on the fare before starting out). Crowds are thick down Via Capodimonte leading to Villa San Michele and around the square, Piazza Vittoria, which is the starting point of the chairlift to the top of Monte Solaro. Elsewhere, Anacapri is quietly appealing. It's a good starting point for walks, such as the 80-minute round-trip journey to the **Migliara Belvedere**, on the island's southern coast.

49 An impressive limestone formation and the highest point on Capri (1,932 feet), **Monte Solaro** affords gasp-inducing views toward the bays of both Naples and Salerno. A 12-minute chairlift ride will take you right to the top (refreshments available at bar), which is a starting point for a number of scenic trails on the western side of the island. Picnickers should note that even in the summer it can get windy at this height, and there are few trees to provide shade or refuge. ✉ *Piazza Vittoria, Anacapri* ☎ *081/8371428* 🎟 *€4 one-way, €5.50 round-trip* ⊙ *Daily 9–5:30.*

50 In the heart of Anacapri, the octagonal baroque church of **San Michele,** finished in 1719, is best known for its exquisite majolica pavement designed by Solimena and executed by the *mastro-riggiolaro* (master tiler) Chiaiese from Abruzzo. A walkway skirts the rich ceramic carpet depicting Adam and a duly contrite Eve being expelled from the Garden of Eden, but you can get a fine overview from the organ loft, reached by a winding staircase near the ticket booth (a privileged perch you have to pay for). Outside the church is the Via Finestrale, which leads to Anacapri's noted **Le Boffe quarter.** This section of town, slightly lower on the hillside, is centered on the Piazza Ficacciate and the Church of Santa Sofia, and owes its name to the distinctive domestic architecture prevalent here, which uses vaults and sculpted groins instead of cross beams. ✉ *Piazza Nicola, Anacapri* ☎ *081/8372396* 🎟 *€2* ⊙ *Nov.–Mar., daily 9:30–5; Apr.–Oct., daily 9–7.*

One of the best excursions from Anacapri is to the ruins of the Roman **51 Villa di Damecuta.** Sited strategically on a ridge with views sweeping across the Bay of Naples toward Procida and Ischia, the villa would have had its main access point at the landing stage right by the Blue Grotto at Gradola. This was probably one of the villas mentioned by Tacitus in his *Annals* as having been built by Tiberius: "Here on Capreae, in twelve spacious, separately named villas, Tiberius settled." Like Villa Jovis to the east, Villa di Damecuta was extensively plundered over the centuries prior to its proper excavation in 1937. Below the medieval tower (Torre Damecuta) there are two rooms (*domus* and *cubiculum*) that are thought to have been Tiberius's secret summer refuge. Affinities with Villa Jovis may be seen in the *ambulatio* (walkway) complete with seats and a stunning backdrop. To reach Villa Damecuta, get the bus from Anacapri to Grotta Azzurra and ask the driver to let you off at the proper stop. Alternatively, you can walk from the center of Anacapri down the bus route (about 30 minutes, but no sidewalks) or try your luck in the network of virtually traffic-free little alleyways running parallel to the main road. ✉ *Via A. Maiuri* 🎟 *Free* ⊙ *Daily 9–1 hr before sunset.*

From Anacapri's Piazza della Vittoria, picturesque Via Capodimonte leads ★ **52** to **Villa San Michele,** the charming former home of Swedish doctor and philanthropist Axel Munthe (1857–1949) that Henry James called "the most fantastic beauty, poetry, and inutility that one had ever seen clustered together." At the ancient entranceway to Anacapri just at the top of the Scala Fenicia and occupying the site of an ancient Roman villa, Villa San Michele was built (beginning in 1896) in accordance with Munthe's instructions. Physician to the Swedish royal family, Munthe practiced in Paris and in Rome, thereby building up a substantial fortune, much of which he plowed into real estate in Anacapri. He was also a philanthropist with a lifelong dedication to the sick and destitute.

Munthe's *The Story of San Michele* is an evocative—if not entirely re-liable—autobiography.

The villa is set around Roman-style courtyards, marble walkways, and atriums. Rooms display the doctor's varied collections, which range from bric-a-brac to antiquities. Medieval choir stalls, Renaissance lecterns, and gilded statues of saints are all part of the setting, with some rooms preserving the doctor's personal memorabilia. A spectacular pergola path overlooking the entire Bay of Naples leads from the villa to the famous Sphinx Parapet, where an ancient Egyptian sphinx looks out toward Sorrento; you cannot see its face—on purpose. It is said that if you touch the sphinx's hindquarters with your left hand while making a wish, it will come true. The parapet is connected to the little Chapel of San Michele, which once stood on the grounds of one of Tiberius's villas.

Besides hosting summer concerts, the Axel Munthe Foundation has an ecomuseum that fittingly reflects Munthe's fondness for animals. There you can learn about various bird species—accompanied by their songs—found on Capri. Munthe bought up the hillside and made it a sanctuary for birds. ⊠ *Via Axel Munthe* ☎ *081/837401* ⊕ *www.sanmichele. org* ⌨ *€5* ⊗ *May–Sept., daily 9–6; Mar., daily 9:30–4:30; Apr. and Oct., daily 9:30–5; Nov.–Feb., daily 10:30–3:30.*

> **off the beaten path**

BELVEDERE AND ARCO NATURALE – A short walk along Via Tragara leads to a belvedere overlooking the Faraglioni; another takes you out of town on Via Matermania to the so-called Natural Arch, an unusual rock formation near a natural grotto that the Romans transformed into a shrine. The 20-minute walk from the Piazzetta up picturesque Via Madre Serafina and Via Castello to the belvedere at Punta Cannone gives you a panoramic view of the island.

VILLA JOVIS – From Capri Town, the 45-minute hike east to Villa Jovis, the grandest of those built by Tiberius, is strenuous but rewarding. Follow the signs for Villa Jovis, taking Via Le Botteghe from the Piazzetta, then continuing along Via Croce and Via Tiberio. At the end of a lane that climbs the steep hill, with pretty views all the way, you come to the precipice over which the emperor reputedly disposed of the victims of his perverse attentions. From a natural terrace above, near a chapel, are spectacular views of the entire Bay of Naples and, on clear days, part of the Gulf of Salerno. Below are the ruins of Tiberius's palace. Allow 45 minutes each way for the walk alone. ⊠ *Via Tiberio* ☎ *081/8370381* ⌨ *€2* ⊗ *Daily 9–1 hr before sunset.*

Where to Stay & Eat

$$$ ✕ **La Capannina.** One of Capri's finest restaurants, La Capannina is only a few steps from the busy social hub of the Piazzetta. It has a discreet covered veranda—open in summer—for dining by candlelight; most of the regulars avoid the stuffy indoor rooms. The specialties are home-made ravioli and linguine *con lo scorfano* (flat spaghetti with scorpion fish). Look for the authentic Capri wine with the house label. ⊠ *Via*

Le Botteghe 12 bis and 14, Capri Town ☎ *081/8370732* ⌦ *Reservations essential* ⊟ *AE, DC, MC, V* ⊘ *Closed mid-Jan.–mid-Mar. and Wed. Mar. and Nov.*

\$\$–\$\$\$ ✕ **La Canzone del Mare.** This is the legendary bathing lido of the Marina Piccola, erstwhile haunt of Grace Fields, Emilio Pucci, Noël Coward, and any number of 1950s and '60s glitterati. The VIPs may have departed for the Bagni di Tiberio beach, but the setting is as magical as ever: enjoy luncheon (no dinner served) in the thatch-roof pavilion looking out over the sea and I Faraglioni in the distance—this is Capri as picture-perfect as it comes. ⊠ *Via Marina Piccola 93, Capri Town* ☎ *081/8370104* ⊟ *AE, DC, MC, V* ⊘ *Closed Nov.–Mar. No dinner.*

\$\$–\$\$\$ ✕ **Ristorante Pizzeria Aurora.** Though often frequented by celebrities—their photographs adorn the walls—this restaurant offers courtesy and *simpatia* regardless of your fame. Sit outside for maximum visibility or go for extra privacy within. The cognoscenti start off by sharing a pizza *all'acqua,* a thin pizza with mozzarella and a sprinkling of *peperoncino* (dried chili peppers). If tiring of pasta, try the *sformatino alla Franco* (rice pie in a prawn sauce). Reservations are essential for dinner. ⊠ *Via Fuorlovado 18–20, Capri Town* ☎ *081/8370181* ⊟ *AE, DC, MC, V* ⊘ *Closed Jan. and Feb.*

★ \$\$ ✕ **Da Tonino.** It is well worth making the short detour off the beaten track to the Arco Naturale to be pampered by creative chef Tonino. The emphasis here is on land-based dishes; try the *terrina di coniglio* (rabbit terrine) or ask for the pigeon dish with pesto, rosemary, and pine nuts, accompanied by wine from a well-stocked cellar. ⊠ *Via Dentecala 34, Capri Town* ☎ *081/8376718* ⊟ *AE, DC, MC, V* ⊘ *Closed Jan. 10–Mar. 15.*

\$\$ ✕ **I Faraglioni.** With natural shade provided by a 100-year-old wisteria plant, this is a popular, fairly stylish restaurant centrally located and immersed in Mediterranean greenery. Meals here usually kick off with *uovo alla Monachina,* an egg-shape dish stuffed with mystery ingredients. For the first course, try the *straccetti con gamberi e pomodorini* (fresh green pasta with shrimp and cherry tomatoes). ⊠ *Via Camerelle 75, Capri Town* ☎ *081/8370320* ⌦ *Reservations essential* ⊟ *AE, DC, MC, V* ⊘ *Closed Nov.–Mar.*

\$–\$\$ ✕ **Al Grottino.** At this small and friendly family-run restaurant near the Piazzetta you'll find arched ceilings and autographed photos of celebrity customers on the walls. House specialties are gnocchi with tomato sauce and mozzarella, and linguine with scampi. ⊠ *Via Longano 27, Capri Town* ☎ *081/8370584* ⌦ *Reservations essential* ⊟ *AE, DC, MC, V* ⊘ *Closed Tues. and Nov. 3–Mar. 20.*

\$ ✕ **La Giara.** About a two-minute walk from the bustling Piazza Vittoria in Anacapri, this pizzeria-ristorante has a variety of palatable dishes served briskly and courteously. For a change from seafood, try the *pennette aum aum,* pasta pleasingly garnished with eggplant, mozzarella, cherry tomatoes, and basil. ⊠ *Via Orlandi 67, Anacapri* ☎ *081/8373860* ⊟ *AE, DC, MC, V* ⊘ *Closed Wed., and Dec. and Jan.*

\$\$\$\$ ✕▥ **Villa Brunella.** This opulent family-run gem is nestled in a garden just below the lane leading to the Faraglioni. Comfortable and tastefully furnished, the hotel has spectacular views and a swimming pool overlooking the sea. The terrace restaurant ($$) also benefits from the superb panorama and is renowned for its seafood and other local dishes. ⊠ *Via Tragara 24, Capri Town 80073* ☎ *081/8370122* 🖷 *081/8370430* ⊕ *www.villabrunella.it* ⇨ *20 rooms* ♻ *Restaurant, cable TV, pool, bar* ⊟ *AE, DC, MC, V* ⊘ *Closed Nov.–Mar.* ¶⊘l *BP.*

$$$$
FodorsChoice
★
🖭 **Punta Tragara.** Clinging to the Punta Tragara, this gorgeous hotel has a hold-your-breath perch directly over the rocks of I Faraglioni. Originally a villa visited by Churchill and Eisenhower, its exterior was renovated by Le Corbusier in traditional Capri style, then opened as a hotel in the 1970s. Baronial fireplaces, gilded antiques, and travertine marble set the style in the main salons, while guest rooms—no two are alike—are sumptuously cozy-casual. The garden area has two drop-dead beautiful saltwater pools and an arbor-covered restaurant, La Bussola, which might be the prettiest spot on the island. To top it off, the staff seems to have been sent to the finest finishing schools. ⊠ *Via Tragara 57, Capri Town 80073* ☎ *081/8370844* 🖷 *081/8377790* ⊕ *www. hoteltragara.com* ⇨ *48 rooms* ♻ *Restaurant, 2 pools, bar* ⊟ *AE, DC, MC, V* ¶⊘l *BP.*

$$$$
🖭 **Quisisana.** This is the most luxurious and traditional hotel in the center of Capri Town. Spacious rooms have some antique accents. Many have arcaded balconies with views of the sea or the charming enclosed garden surrounding a swimming pool. The Quisisana is particularly popular with Americans. ⊠ *Via Camerelle 2, Capri Town 80073* ☎ *081/ 8370788* 🖷 *081/8376080* ⊕ *www.quisi.com* ⇨ *149 rooms* ♻ *2 restaurants, cable TV, tennis court, pool, gym, sauna, bar, Internet, convention center* ⊟ *AE, DC, MC, V* ⊘ *Closed Nov.–mid-Mar.* ¶⊘l *MAP.*

★ **$$$$**
🖭 **Scalinatella.** The name means "little stairway," and that's how this charming but modern small hotel is built, on terraces following the slope of the hill, overlooking the gardens, pool, and sea. The bedrooms are intimate, with alcoves and fresh, bright colors; the bathrooms have whirlpool baths. ⊠ *Via Tragara 8, Capri Town 80073* ☎ *081/8370633* 🖷 *081/8378291* ⊕ *www.scalinatella.com* ⇨ *30 rooms* ♻ *Restaurant, tennis court, pool, bar* ⊟ *AE, DC, MC, V* ⊘ *Closed Nov.–mid-Mar.* ¶⊘l *BP.*

$$–$$$
🖭 **Villa Sarah.** The whitewashed Mediterranean building here has a homey look and bright, simply furnished rooms. It's close enough to the Piazzetta (a 10-minute walk) to give easy access to the goings-on there, yet far enough away to ensure restful nights. There's a garden and a small bar. ⊠ *Via Tiberio 3/a, Capri Town 80073* ☎ *081/8377817* 🖷 *081/8377215* ⊕ *www.villasarah.it* ⇨ *20 rooms* ♻ *Cable TV, bar, Internet* ⊟ *AE, DC, MC, V* ⊘ *Closed Nov.–Mar.* ¶⊘l *BP.*

$$
🖭 **Villa Krupp.** Occupying a quiet location overlooking the Gardens of Augustus, this historic hostelry was the onetime home of Maxim Gorky, whose guests included Vladimir Lenin. Rooms are plain but spacious; a renovation of the ground floor in summer 2003 has given the place a more modern look. ⊠ *Viale Matteotti 12, Capri Town 80073* ☎ *081/ 8370362* 🖷 *081/8376489* ⇨ *12 rooms* ♻ *No a/c in 1 room, no room TVs* ⊟ *MC, V* ⊘ *Closed Nov.–Mar.* ¶⊘l *BP.*

$
🖭 **Aida.** A 10-minute walk from the town center on a tiny lane that borders the Gardens of Augustus, the Aida offers a tranquil haven from

Capri's bustle and hard sell. The staff is sociable, and the rooms, which look onto a small garden, are spacious, comfortably furnished, and immaculately clean. ⊠ *Via Birago, Capri Town 80073* ☎ *081/ 8370366* ➳ *4 rooms* ⚫ *No a/c* ▭ *No credit cards* ⊘ *Closed Oct.–May.* |◎| *BP.*

$ 🏠 **Villa Eva.** Villa Eva is a glimpse of how Capri once was, or might have been. Before it became home to vacationing film stars and the super-rich, the island was famous for its bohemian artistic community. Salvatore (you'll recognize him by the beard) and Eva have managed to capture the atmosphere of this "other" Capri; accommodations are in modest cottages, where beds may sag a bit and you may have to fend off mosquitoes, but the lush gardens and laid-back atmosphere are just the ticket if you want a uniquely Caprese experience at budget prices. ⊠ *Via La Fabbrica 8, Anacapri 80071* ☎ *081/8371549* 🖷 *081/8372040* ⊕ *www.villaeva.com* ➳ *24 rooms* ⚫ *Pool, bar; no a/c, no room TVs* ▭ *AE, DC, MC, V* ⊘ *Closed mid-Nov.–mid-Mar.* |◎| *BP.*

THE AMALFI COAST

As travelers journey down the fabled Amalfi Coast, their route takes them past rocky cliffs plunging into the sea and small boats lying in sandy coves like brightly colored fish. Erosion has contorted the rocks into shapes resembling figures from mythology and hollowed out fairy grottoes where the air is turquoise and the water an icy blue. In winter nativity scenes of moss and stone are created in the rocks. White villages dripping with flowers nestle in coves or climb like vines up the steep, terraced hills. Lemon trees abound, loaded with blossom or fruit—and netting in winter to protect the fruit. The inhabitants jest that they look after their lemons better than their children. The road must have a thousand turns, each with a different view, on its dizzying 69-km (43-mi) journey from Sorrento to Salerno.

Sorrento

🔢 *50 km (31 mi) south of Naples, 50 km (31 mi) west of Salerno.*

Sorrento is across the Bay of Naples from Naples itself, on autostrada A3 and SS145. The Circumvesuviana railway, which stops at Herculaneum and Pompeii, provides another connection. The coast between Naples and Castellammare, where road and railway turn off onto the Sorrento peninsula, seems at times depressingly overbuilt and industrialized. Yet Vesuvius looms to the left, you can make out the 3,000-foot-high mass of Monte Faito ahead, and on a clear day you can see Capri off the tip of the peninsula. The scenery improves considerably as you near Sorrento, where the coastal plain is carved into russet cliffs rising perpendicularly from the sea. This is the Sorrento (north) side of the peninsula; on the other side is the more dramatically scenic Amalfi Coast. But Sorrento has at least two advantages over Amalfi: the Circumvesuviana railway terminal and a fairly flat terrain. A stroll around town is a pleasure—you'll encounter narrow alleyways and interesting churches, and the views of the Bay of Naples from the Villa Comunale and the Museo Correale are priceless.

Until the mid-20th century Sorrento was a small, genteel resort favored by central European princes, English aristocrats, and American literati. During World War I American soldiers came to recuperate at the Hotel Vittoria. Now the town has grown and spread out along the crest of its famous cliffs, and apartments stand where citrus groves once bloomed. Like most resorts, Sorrento is best off-season, in spring, autumn, or even winter, when Campania's mild climate can make a stay pleasant anywhere along the coast.

A highlight of Sorrento is **Museo Correale di Terranova,** an 18th-century villa with a lovely garden on land given to the patrician Correale family by Queen Joan of Aragon in 1428. It has an excellent private collection amassed by the count of Terranova and his brother. The building itself is fairly charmless, with few period rooms, but the garden offers an allée of palm trees, citrus groves, floral nurseries, and an esplanade with a panoramic view of the Sorrento coast. The collection itself is one of the finest devoted to Neapolitan paintings, decorative arts, and porcelains, so for connoisseurs of the *seicento* (Italian 17th century), this museum is a must. Magnificent 18th-century inlaid tables by Giuseppe Gargiulo, Capodimonte porcelains, and rococo portrait miniatures are reminders of the age when pleasure and delight were all. Also on view are regional Greek and Roman archaeological finds, medieval marble work, glasswork, old master paintings, 17th-century majolicas—even Tasso's death mask. ⊠ *Via Correale* ☎ *081/8781846* 🖃 *Museum and gardens €6* ⊙ *Wed.–Mon. 9–2.*

Worth checking out is the **Museo Bottega della Tarsialignea,** set up by local architects to ensure the continuity of the intarsia (wood inlay) tradition. It houses historical collections as well as exhibitions of modern work. There's a shop where you can pick up an unusual souvenir. ⊠ *Via San Nicola 28* ☎ *081/8771942* ⊕ *www.alessandrofiorentinocollection.it* 🖃 *€8* ⊙ *Museum guided visits (required) every ½ hr Apr.–Oct., Tues.–Sun. 9:30–noon and 5–7; Nov.–Mar., Tues.–Sun. 9:30–noon and 3–5. Shop Tues.–Sun. 9:30–1 and 5–8 (Nov.–Mar. 3–6).*

Via Marina Grande turns into a pedestrian lane, then a stairway leading to Sorrento's only real beach at **Marina Grande,** where fishermen pull up their boats and there are some good seafood restaurants. A frequent bus also plies this route; tickets are sold at the *tabacchi* (tobacconist).

off the beaten path

CAPO DI SORRENTO AND THE BAGNO DELLA REGINA GIOVANNA – Just 2 km (1 mi) west of Sorrento, turn right off Statale 145 toward the sea, and then park and walk a few minutes through citrus and olive groves to get to Capo di Sorrento, the craggy tip of the cape, with the most interesting ancient ruins in the area. They were identified by the Latin poet Publius Papinius Statius as the ancient Roman villa of historian Pollio Felix, patron of the great authors Virgil and Horace. Next to the ruins is Bagno della Regina Giovanna

(Queen Joan's Bath). A cleft in the rocks allows the sea to channel through an archway into a clear, natural pool, with the water turning iridescent blue, green, and violet as the sunlight changes angles. The easiest way to see all this is to rent a boat at Sorrento; afterward, sailing westward will bring you to the fishermen's haven of Marina di Puolo, where you can lunch on fresh catch at a modest restaurant.

Where to Stay & Eat

★ **$$$$** ✕ **Don Alfonso 1890.** The most heralded restaurant in Campania is the domain of Alfonso Iaccarino; *haute*-hungry pilgrims come here to feast on culinary rarities, often centuries-old recipes given a unique spin. The braciola of lamb with pine nuts and raisins is a recipe that dates back to the Renaissance, and the cannoli stuffed with foie gras pays homage to the Neapolitan Bourbon court. Nearly everything is homegrown, and the wine cellar is one of the finest in Europe. Those who want to make a night of it can stay in one of five apartments above the restaurant. ⊠ *Corso Sant'Agata 13, Sant'Agata sui due Golfi, 7 km south of Sorrento* ☎ *081/8780026* ☐ *AE, DC, MC, V* ☉ *Closed Mon. and Jan. 10–Mar.; closed Tues. Oct.–May.*

$$$–$$$$ ✕ **Antica Trattoria.** An old-fashion dining room inside and garden tables in fair weather make this a pleasant place to enjoy the local cooking. The atmosphere is homey and the menu is voluminous; specialties include spaghetti alle vongole and *pappardelle all'antica trattoria* (fresh pasta with porcini mushrooms, prosciutto, tomatoes, and basil). You can also opt for one of four prix-fixe menus. ⊠ *Via Giuliani 33* ☎ *081/ 8071082* ☐ *AE, DC, MC, V* ☉ *Closed Mon. and 4 wks in Jan.–Feb.*

$$–$$$ ✕ **Antico Francischiello da Peppino.** Overlooking olive groves seeming to run into the sea, this fourth-generation establishment is situated away from the throng, halfway between Sorrento and Massa Lubrense. Two huge, beamed rooms with sprays of fern, antique mirrored sideboards, hundreds of mounted plates, brick archways, old chandeliers, fresh flowers, and tangerine-hued tablecloths make for quite a sight. Specialties include ravioli filled with sea bass, baked bream in a potato crust with lemon, and limoncello ice cream. ⊠ *Via Partenope 27, Massa Lubrense,* ☎ *081/533–9780* ☐ *AE, DC, MC, V* ☉ *Closed Wed. in winter.*

★ **$–$$** ✕ **"La Favorita"—O' Parrucchiano.** This restaurant is set in a sprawling, multilevel, high-ceilinged greenhouse and orchard, with tables and chairs amid enough tropical greenery to fill a Victorian conservatory; the effect is enchantingly 19th century. Opened in 1890 by an ex-priest (O' Parrucchiano means "the priest's place" in the local dialect), La Favorita continues to serve classic Sorrentine cuisine. Though the white-bean soup, cheese baked in lemon leaves, ravioli caprese, lemon tart, and profiteroles are all excellent, they can't compete with the unique decor. ⊠ *Corso Italia 71* ☎ *081/8781321* ☐ *MC, V* ☉ *Closed Wed. Nov.–Mar.*

$ ✕ **Trattoria da Emilia.** You can sit outside here, right on the Marina Grande, and watch the life of the port go by. This simple, rustic restaurant with wooden tables has been run by Donna Emilia and her offspring since 1947 and provides typical Sorrento home cooking and a family atmosphere. Fried seafood is the specialty. Sofia Loren came to eat here

while filming *Pane, amore, ...* ✉ *Via Marina Grande 62* ☎ *081/
8072720* ▭ *No credit cards* ☉ *Closed Tues. Oct.–Mar. No dinner
Oct.–Mar.*

$$$$ ⊞ **Bellevue Syrene.** This exclusive hotel is set in a cliff-top garden close
to the center of Sorrento. It retains its solid, old-fashion comforts and
sumptuous charm, with Victorian nooks and alcoves, antique paintings,
and exuberant frescoes. You can find interior-facing rooms at lower prices
if you're willing to forgo the splendid views over the sea. ✉ *Piazza della
Vittoria 5, 80067* ☎ *081/8781024* 🖷 *081/8783963* ⊕ *www.
bellevuesyrene.it* ↘ *73 rooms* ♦ *2 restaurants, minibars, gym, beach,
dock, bar, meeting room, some pets allowed* ▭ *AE, DC, MC, V* ⦿*BP.*

★ **$$$$** ⊞ **Cocumella.** A grand hotel in every sense, the Cocumella seems little
changed since the days when Goethe and the Duke of Wellington stayed
here. Set in a cliff-top garden overlooking the Bay of Naples, the hotel
occupies a 17th-century monastery complete with frescoed ceilings and
antique reliquaries. The amenities are hardly monastic: they include a
spectacular pool area, a workout room, summer concerts in the hotel's
baroque church, and Empire-style suites, some with fireplaces. For
around €140 per person you can spend a day cruising in the hotel's 90-
foot-long 19th-century yacht. Given the hotel's high standards, the
restaurant is a disappointment. ✉ *Via Cocumella 7, Sant'Agnello,
80065* ☎ *081/8782933* 🖷 *081/8783712* ⊕ *www.cocumella.com* ↘ *50
rooms, 18 suites* ♦ *Restaurant, cable TV, pool, gym, spa, bar, Internet,
some pets allowed* ▭ *AE, DC, MC, V* ☉ *Closed Nov.–Mar.* ⦿*BP.*

★ **$$$$** ⊞ **Excelsior Vittoria.** Magnificently situated overlooking the Bay of
Naples, this is a belle-epoque dream come true. Gilded salons, stunning gardens, and an impossibly romantic terrace where orchestras lull
you twice a week with Neapolitan and modern music: in all, it's a truly
intoxicating experience. Caruso stayed here and, more recently, Luciano Pavarotti. A new outdoor swimming pool and gym were added
in spring 2004. ✉ *Piazza Tasso 34, 80067* ☎ *081/8071044* 🖷 *081/
8771206* ⊕ *www.exvitt.it* ↘ *98 rooms, 20 suites* ♦ *Restaurant,
cable TV, pool, bar, Internet, meeting room, some pets allowed* ▭ *AE,
DC, MC, V* ⦿*BP.*

$$ ⊞ **Settimo Cielo.** Here's an excellent choice if you want to stay on the
water but your budget doesn't extend to one of the luxury hotels. There
are gardens and a swimming pool on the grounds, and the beach is a
few steps away. The rooms, which all face the sea, are simple and mod-
ern. ✉ *Via Capo 27, 80067* ☎ *081/8781012* 🖷 *081/8073290* ⊕*www.
hotelsettimocielo.com* ↘ *20 rooms* ♦ *Restaurant, pool, bar* ▭ *AE, DC,
MC, V* ☉ *Closed Nov.–mid-Dec., Jan.–Mar.* ⦿*BP.*

$ ⊞ **Lorelei et Londres.** Once favored by Room-with-a-View ladies from
FodorsChoice England, this amazing relic still looks like E. M. Forster's Lucy Hon-
★ eychurch might pull up at any moment. Out front is a beautiful terrace
café, aflutter with red awnings and tablecloths. The welcoming lobby
always seems to be filled with laughter, so apparently few guests mind
that the rooms upstairs are tatterdemalion, furnished with simple beds,
linoleum flooring, and creaking cupboards. Ask for sea-view rooms away
from the noisy road. For luxe and modernity, go elsewhere; come here
to take a trip back to the *bella*19th century. ✉ *Via Califano 2, 80067*

☎ 081/8073187 🖷 081/5329001 ⬠ 27 rooms ▤ AE, DC, MC, V ☾ Closed mid-Nov.–mid-Mar. ⦿| BP.

$ 🖭 **Mignon Meublé.** Spacious and simple yet stylish accommodations, a central location, friendly service, and bargain rates: with this combination of characteristics you'll understand why it's advisable to book well in advance here. Breakfast is served in your room, but there's a small sitting area where you can also relax. ⬠ Via Sersale 9, 80067 ☎ 081/ 8073824 🖷 081/5329001 ⬠ 23 rooms ⬩ No room phones ▤ AE, DC, MC, V ⦿| BP.

Shopping

Around **Piazza Tasso** are a number of shops selling embroidered goods and intarsia woodwork, a centuries-old tradition here. **Fattoria Terranova** (⬠ Piazza Tasso 161 ☎ 081/8781263) sells all kinds of produce ranging from cheeses to preserves to liqueurs, all made on a family-run farm in nearby Massa.

Along narrow **Via San Cesareo,** where the air is pungent with the perfumes of fruit and vegetable stands, there are shops selling local and Italian crafts—everything from jewelry boxes to trays and coffee tables with intarsia decoration. **Ferdinando Corcione,** in his shop on Via San Francesco, gives demonstrations of intarsia work, producing decorative plaques with classic or contemporary motifs. You may want to stop in one of the many shops selling **limoncello,** the famous lemon liqueur. Piemme and Villa Massa are recommended brands; the latter is exported to the United States.

Positano

★ ➎➍ 14 km (9 mi) east of Sorrento, 57 km (34 mi) south of Naples.

When John Steinbeck lived here in 1953, he wrote that it was difficult to consider tourism an industry because "there are not enough *tourists.*" Alas, Positano, a village of white Moorish-style houses clinging to slopes around a small sheltered bay, has since been discovered. The artists came first, and, as so often happens, the wealthy followed and the artists fled. Another Steinbeck observation still applies, however: "Positano bites deep. It is a dream place that isn't quite real when you are there and becomes beckoningly real after you have gone. Its houses climb a hill so steep it would be a cliff except that stairs are cut in it. I believe that whereas most house foundations are vertical, in Positano they are horizontal. The small curving bay of unbelievably blue and green water laps gently on a beach of small pebbles. There is only one narrow street and it does not come down to the water. Everything else is stairs, some of them as steep as ladders. You do not walk to visit a friend, you either climb or slide."

In the 10th century Positano was part of Amalfi's maritime republic, which rivaled Venice as an important mercantile power. Its heyday was in the 16th and 17th centuries, when its ships traded in the Near and Middle East carrying spices, silks, and precious woods. The coming of the steamship in the mid-19th century led to the town's decline; some three-fourths of its 8,000 citizens emigrated to America, most to New York.

What had been reduced to a forgotten fishing village is now the number one attraction on the coast. From here you can take hydrofoils to Capri during the summer, escorted bus rides to Ravello, and tours of the Grotta dello Smeraldo. If you're staying in Positano, check whether your hotel has a parking area. If not, you will have to pay for space in a parking lot, which is almost impossible to find during the high season, from Easter to September. The best bet for day-trippers is to arrive by bus—there is a good, regular service—or else get to Positano early enough to find a parking space.

No matter how much time you spend in Positano, make sure you have some comfortable walking shoes (no heels) and that your back and legs are strong enough to negotiate those daunting *scalinatelle* (little stairways). Alternatively, you can ride the municipal bus, which frequently plies along the one-and-only-one-way Via Pasitea, hairpinning from Positano's central Piazza dei Mulini to the mountains and back, making a loop through the town every half hour. Heading down from the Sponda bus stop toward the beach, you pass Le Sirenuse, the hotel where John Steinbeck stayed in 1953. Its stepped terraces offer vistas over the town, so you might splurge on lunch or a drink here on the pool terrace, a favorite gathering place for Modigliani-sleek jet-setters. Continue to Piazza dei Mulini, and make a left turn onto Via dei Mulini.

need a break? If you want to catch your breath after a bus ride to Positano, take a quick time-out for an espresso, a slice of Positanese (a delectable chocolate cake), or a fresh-fruit iced granita in the lemon-tree garden at **Bar-Pasticceria La Zagara** (⊠ Via Mulini 8 ☎ 089/875964).

Past a bevy of resort boutiques, head to Via dei Mulini 23 to view the prettiest garden in Positano—the 18th-century courtyard of the **Palazzo Murat,** named for Joachim Murat, who sensibly chose the palazzo as his summer residence. This was where Murat, designated by his brother-in-law Napoléon as King of Naples in 1808, came to forget the demands of power and lead the simple life. Since Murat was one of Europe's leading style setters, it couldn't be *too* simple, and he wound up building a grand abode (now a hotel) just steps from the main beach.

Beyond the Palazzo Murat is the Chiesa Madre, or parish church of **Santa Maria Assunta,** its green-and-yellow majolica dome topped by a perky cupola visible from just about anywhere in town. Built on the site of the former Benedictine abbey of St. Vito, the 13th-century Romanesque structure was almost completely rebuilt in 1700. The last piece of the ancient mosaic floor can be seen under glass near the apse. Note the carved wooden Christ, a masterpiece of devotional religious art, with its bathetic face and bloodied knees, on view before the altar. At the altar is a Byzantine 13th-century painting on wood of Madonna with Child, known as the Black Virgin, carried to the main beach every August 15 to celebrate the Feast of the Assumption. Legend claims that the painting was once stolen by Saracen pirates, who, fleeing in a raging storm, heard from a voice on high saying, "*Posa, posa*"—"Put it down, put it down." When they placed the image on the beach near the church, the storm calmed, as did the Saracens. Positano was saved, and the town's name was established (yet again). Embedded over the doorway of the church's bell tower, set across the tiny piazza, is a medieval bas-relief of fishes, a fox, and a pistrice, the mythical half-dragon, half-dog sea monster. This is one of the sole relics of the medieval abbey of St. Vito. ⊠ *Piazza Flavio Gioia above the main beach* ☎ *089/875067* ☉ *Daily 8:30–noon and 4:30–7.*

The walkway from the Piazza Flavio Gioia leads down to the **Spaggia Grande,** or main beach, bordered by an esplanade and some of Positano's best restaurants. Head over to the stone pier to the far right of the beach as you face the water. A staircase leads to the **Via Positanesi d'America,** a lovely seaside walkway. Halfway up the path you'll find the Torre Trasita, the most distinctive of Positano's three coastline defense towers, which, in various states of repair, define the edges of Positano. The Trasita—now a residence occasionally available for summer rental—was one of the defense towers used to warn of pirate raids. Continuing along the Via Positanesi d'America you pass tiny inlets and emerald coves until the large beach, Spaggia di Fornillo, comes into view.

If the Spaggia Grande is too orderly for you, take the small boat to the **Spaggia di Laurito.** (Look for the boat on the right side of the harbor as you approach the beach—it has a sign with a big red smiling fish on it.) You can spend an entire day in this little cove, taking the two steps up to the restaurant **Da Adolfo** when the exertion of swimming has worked up your appetite.

Where to Stay & Eat

$$-$$$ ✕ **Buca di Bacco.** After an aperitif at the town's most famous and fashionable café downstairs, you dine on a veranda overlooking the beach. The specialties include *zuppa di cozze* (mussel soup), fresh *spigola* (sea bass), and figs and oranges in caramel. ⊠ *Via Rampa Teglia 8* ☎ *089/ 875699* ▤ *AE, DC, MC, V* ☉ *Closed Nov.–Mar.*

$$-$$$ ✕ **Donna Rosa.** This minimalist little hideaway in one-street Montepertuso, the hamlet high over Positano, is truly original. Everybody gets into the act: Mamma does the creative cooking to order; Pappa "makes noise"; and the daughters rule out front. Homemade pasta is the house specialty, along with delectable desserts, which may include walnut or strawberry mousse and *crostata all'arancio* (orange tart). A wide selection of fine wines is on hand, and live music can be anything from jazz to Australian gospel, with a daughter singing sweetly. Reservations are essential at dinner. ⊠ *Via Montepertuso* ☎ *089/811806* ▤ *AE, DC, MC, V* ☉ *Closed Mon.*

$$-$$$ ✕ **'O Capurale.** Even though *o' capurale* ("the corporal") himself no longer runs the place, his eponymous restaurant is still a great find in the crowded center of Positano. There's one large dining room with simple wooden tables, a marble floor, and a high coved ceiling with Fauvist-style frescoes. The space remains cool even in the height of summer when filled with diners digging into fresh pasta with mussels and pumpkin, or rockfish *all'acqua pazza,* with a few tomatoes and garlic. ⊠ *Via Regina Giovanna 12* ☎ *089/875374* ▤ *AE, DC, MC, V* ☉ *Closed Nov.–mid-Feb.*

$–$$$ ✕ **Il Ritrovo.** Stretching alongside the tiny town square of the mountain
FodorsChoice hamlet of Montepertuso is Il Ritrovo, one of the finest restaurants in
★ the area. Tables outside (heated in winter) provide a dizzying view of
the coast, and inside, the wood-paneled dining room has the feel of a
ship's cabin. The menu is a mix of sea and mountain food; try the
scialatielli ai frutti di mare (thick spaghetti with all manner of things
from the sea), accompanied by grilled vegetables or followed by *scamorza*
(a mozzarella-like cheese) baked in lemon leaves. Save room for hazel-
nut *semifreddo* (soft ice cream) and a homemade liqueur. The wine list
is excellent. ⊠ *Via Montepertuso, 77* ☎ *089/812005* ⌚ *Reservations
essential* ▤ *AE, DC, MC, V.*

$$ ✕ **Da Adolfo.** At this completely informal spot on Spaggia di Laurito,
most diners sit for hours in their swimsuits, whiling away the time read-
ing or chatting over a jug of the light local wine (with peaches in the
summer) or a hefty plate of *totani con patate* (squid and potatoes with
garlic and oil). The brusque but amusing waiters are part of the scene.
⊠ *Spaggia di Laurito* ☎ *089/875022* ⌚ *Reservations not accepted*
▤ *No credit cards* ⊘ *Closed Oct.–Apr.*

$$$$ ▥ **Casa Albertina.** Clinging to the cliff, this little house is well loved for
its Italian charm, its homey restaurant, and its owners, the Cinque family. Rooms have high ceilings, bright fabrics, tile flooring, and sunny terraces or balconies overlooking the sea and coastline. Cars can't drive
to the doorway, but porters will ferry your luggage. Note: it's 300 steps
down to the main beach. Half or full board is required in summer (and
is reflected in the price category here). ⊠ *Via della Tavolozza 3, 84017*
☎ *089/875143* ⎙ *089/811540* ⊕ *www.casalbertina.it* ⮎ *21 rooms*
⌂ *Restaurant, minibars, cable TV, parking (fee), some pets allowed* ▤ *AE,
DC, MC, V* ⊓⊙⊩ *MAP.*

$$$$ ▥ **Il San Pietro.** A luxurious oasis for the affluent international set, the
San Pietro lies a few bends outside the town and is set high above the
sea with garden terraces. The hotel has sumptuous Neapolitan baroque
decor and masses of flowers in the lounges, elegantly understated rooms
(most with terraces), and marvelous views. There's a pool on an upper
level, and an elevator whisks you down to the private beach and beach
bar. The proprietors organize boating excursions and provide car and
minibus service into town. ⊠ *Via Laurito 2, 84017* ☎ *089/875455* ⎙ *089/
811449* ⊕ *www.ilsanpietro.it* ⮎ *60 rooms* ⌂ *Restaurant, cable TV, tennis court, pool, beach, gym, dock, 2 bars* ▤ *AE, DC, MC, V* ⊘ *Closed
mid-Nov.–mid-Mar.* ⊓⊙⊩ *BP.*

★ **$$$$** ▥ **Le Sirenuse.** A handsome 18th-century palazzo in the center of town
has been transformed into this luxury hotel with bright tile floors, precious antiques, and tasteful furnishings. The bedrooms are spacious and
comfortable; most have splendid views from balconies and terraces. The
top-floor suites have huge bathrooms and whirlpool baths. One side of
a large terrace has an inviting swimming pool; on the other is an excellent restaurant. ⊠ *Via Cristoforo Colombo 30, 84017* ☎ *089/875066*
⎙ *089/811798* ⊕ *www.sirenuse.it* ⮎ *60 rooms* ⌂ *Restaurant, cable
TV, pool, gym, sauna, bar* ▤ *AE, DC, MC, V* ⊓⊙⊩ *BP.*

$$$$ ▥ **Palazzo Murat.** The location is perfect—in the heart of town, near the
beachside promenade, but set in a quiet, walled garden. The old wing

is a historic palazzo with tall windows and wrought-iron balconies; the modern wing is a whitewashed Mediterranean building with arches and terraces. You can relax in antiques-accented lounges or in the charming vine-draped patio and enjoy gorgeous views from the comfortable bedrooms. ☒ *Via dei Mulini 23, 84017* ☎ *089/875177* 🖷 *089/811419* ⊕ *www.palazzomurat.it* ⇦⌐ *31 rooms* ᗰ *Restaurant, minibars, bar* ▤ *AE, DC, MC, V* ⊗ *Closed Nov.–Mar.* ⦿| *BP.*

$$ 🏨 **La Fenice.** This tiny, friendly, unpretentious hotel on the peaceful outskirts of town beckons with bougainvillea-laden vistas, castaway cottages, and a turquoise pool (open only in summer), all perched over a private beach. Guest rooms—accented with coved ceilings, whitewashed walls, and native folk art—are simple havens of tranquillity; book the best, those closest to the sea, only if you can handle *very* steep walkways. ☒ *Via G. Marconi 4, 84017* ☎ *089/875513* 🖷 *089/811309* ⇦⌐ *9 rooms, 6 cottages* ᗰ *Pool; no a/c, no room phones, no room TVs* ▤ *No credit cards* ⦿| *BP.*

$$ 🏨 **Villa Rosa.** Sharing almost the same views as hotels with twice the price tag, this family-run lodging has long been a favorite with independent travelers. It's extremely central but slightly set back from the road up the inevitable steps. Ask for one of the rooms on the 1st floor, which are quieter and have better views. ☒ *Via C. Colombo 127, 84017* ☎ *089/811955* 🖷 *089/812112* ⊕ *www.villarosapositano.it* ⇦⌐ *18 rooms* ▤ *AE, DC, MC, V* ⊗ *Closed Nov.–Feb.*

$ 🏨 **La Ginestra.** Set in hikers' paradise at about 2,000 feet over Positano, the farming cooperative La Ginestra dominates the coastline with its converted 18th-century manor house. The peasants' quarters have been transformed into a thriving restaurant, and the guest rooms above are decorated in simple country style. Positano is reached via a network of footpaths—be aware that it's a good hour's slog up from the bottom. If arriving by train, get off the Circumvesuviana train at Vico Equense and take the local orange bus uphill to the village of Santa Maria del Castello, which is about 300 meters from the cooperative. Access by car is also easiest from Vico Equense. ☒ *Via Tessa 2, Santa Maria Del Castello, Vico Equense 80069* ☎🖷 *081/8023211* ⊕ *www.laginestra.org* ⇦⌐ *7 rooms* ᗰ *Restaurant; no a/c, no room phones* ▤ *MC, V* ⦿| *MAP.*

Nightlife

L'Africana (☒ Vettica Maggiore, Praiano, 10 km [6 mi] east of Positano on the coast road ☎ 089/874042) is the premier nightclub on the Amalfi Coast, built into a fantastic grotto above the sea.

Grotta dello Smeraldo

13 km (8 mi) east of Positano, 27 km (17 mi) east of Sorrento.

A peculiar green light that casts an eerie emerald glow over impressive formations of stalagmites and stalactites, many of them underwater, inspired the name of the Grotta dello Smeraldo (Emerald Grotto). You can park at the signposts for the grotto along the coast road and take an elevator down, or you can drive on to Amalfi and return to the grotto by more romantic means—via boat. Boat tours leave from the Amalfi seafront regularly, according to demand; the charge is €6 per person. Call ahead, as hours are subject to change. ☎ *Tourist information, 089/871107 ☒ Grotto €5.50 ☉ Apr.–Sept., daily 9–5; Oct.–Mar., daily 10–4.*

Amalfi

 17 km (11 mi) east of Positano, 35 km (22 mi) east of Sorrento.

"The sun—the moon—the stars, and—Amalfi," Amalfitans used to say. During the Middle Ages Amalfi was an independent maritime state with a population of 50,000. The ship's compass, trivia fans will be interested to know, was invented here in 1302. The republic also brought the art of papermaking to Europe from Arabia. Before World War II there were 13 mills making paper by hand in the Valle Molini, but now only two small ones remain. The town is romantically situated at the mouth of a deep gorge and has some good-quality hotels and restaurants. It's also a convenient base for excursions to Capri and the Grotta dello Smeraldo. The parking problem here is as bad as that in Positano. The small lot in the center of town fills quickly; if you're willing to pay the steep prices, make a lunch reservation at one of the hotel restaurants and have your car parked for you.

Amalfi's main historical sight is its **Duomo** (also known as Cattedrale di Sant'Andrea), which shows an interesting mix of Moorish and early Gothic influences. You're channeled first into the adjoining **Chiostro del Paradiso** (Paradise Cloister), built around 1266 as a burial ground for Amalfi's elite and one of the architectural treasures of southern Italy. Its flower-and-palm-filled quadrangle has a series of exceptionally delicate intertwining arches on slender double columns in a combination of Byzantine and Arabian styles. Next stop is the 9th-century basilica, a **museum** housing sarcophagi, sculpture, Neapolitan goldsmithing, and other treasures from the cathedral complex.

Steps from the basilica lead down into the **Cripta di Sant'Andrea** (Crypt of St. Andrew). The cathedral above was built in the 13th century to house the saint's bones, which came from Constantinople and supposedly exuded a miraculous liquid believers call the "manna of St. Andrew." Following the one-way traffic up to the cathedral itself, you finally get to admire the elaborate polychrome marbles and painted, coffered ceilings from its 18th-century restoration; art historians shake their heads over this renovation, as the original decoration of the apse must have been one of the wonders of the Middle Ages. ☒ *Piazza del Duomo* ☎ *089/ 871059 ☒ €2.50 ☉ Daily: Mar.–June and Oct., 9–7; July–Sept., 9–9; Nov.–Feb., 10–1 and 2:30–5:30.*

The **Valle dei Mulini** (Valley of the Mills), uphill from town, was for centuries Amalfi's center for papermaking, an ancient trade learned from the Arabs (who learned it from the Chinese). Beginning in the 12th century former flour mills in the town were converted to produce paper made from cotton and linen, being among the first in Europe to do so. In 1211 Frederick II of Sicily prohibited this lighter, more readable paper for use in the preparation of official documents, favoring traditional sheepskin parchment, but by 1811 more than a dozen mills here, with more along the coast, were humming. Natural waterpower ensured that the handmade paper was cost-effective, but catastrophic flooding in 1954 closed most of the mills for good, and many of them have now been converted into private housing. The **Museo della Carta** (Museum of Paper) opened in 1971 in a 15th-century mill; paper samples, tools of the trade, old machinery, and the audiovisual presentation are all enlightening. ⊠ *Via delle Cartiere 23* ☎ *089/8304561* ⊕ *www. museodellacarta.it* ☜ €3.40 ☉ *Nov.–Mar., Tues.–Sun. 10–3; Apr.–June and Oct., daily 10–6; July–Sept., daily 10–8.*

Where to Stay & Eat

★ **$$$–$$$$** ✕ **Da Gemma.** Cognoscenti have sung the praises of this understated landmark since 1872. Tile floors, green tablecloths, and a terrace set above the main street are soothing elements. The kitchen glistens, the menu is printed on local handmade paper, and Amalfi foodies appreciate such favorites as oven-baked fish with lemon peel and the *tubettoni alla masaniello* (tiny pieces of pasta with capers, mussels, and prawns). Traces of Amalfi's Arabic roots can be found in the sweets made with almonds and citrus fruits. ⊠ *Via Fratello Gerardo Sasso 9* ☎ *089/ 871345* ☰ *AE, DC, MC, V* ☉ *Closed mid-Jan.–mid-Feb. and Wed. Sept.–June.*

$$$ ✕ **Trattoria di Maria.** At this friendly locals' haunt presided over by the convivial Enzo (son of Maria) you can dine on delicious pizza cooked in a wood oven, local fish dishes, and lemon profiteroles. Ask for a glass of the limoncello or one of the other homemade liqueurs made from bay leaves, fennel, or bilberries (similar to blueberries). ⊠ *Piazza ad Amalfi* ☎ *089/871880* ☰ *AE, DC, MC, V* ☉ *Closed Mon. and Nov.*

$$–$$$ ✕ **A Paranza.** Located in the hamlet of Atrani, a 15-minute walk from the center of Amalfi along the coast road toward Salerno, A Paranza is worth the walk. The two dining rooms, with coved ceilings and immaculate linen tablecloths, are at once homey and quite formal. Entirely seafood based, each day's menu depends on the catch; the tasting menu (antipasti ranging from marinated tuna to fried rice balls, pasta, and risotto, and a choice of dessert) is a good option. If that sounds like too much, go for the scialatielli ai frutti di mare. Finish your meal with one of the divine cakes. ⊠ *Via Dragone 1/2* ☎ *089/871840* ☰ *AE, DC, MC, V* ☉ *Closed Dec. 8–26 and Tues. Oct.–May.*

★ **$$$$** ⌂ **Santa Caterina.** A large mansion perched above a terraced and flowered hillside on the coast road just outside Amalfi proper, the Santa Caterina is one of the top hotels on the entire coast. The rooms are tastefully decorated; most have small terraces or balconies with great views. There are lovely lounges, gardens, and terraces for relaxing, and an elevator delivers you to the seaside saltwater pool, bar, and swimming area. On grounds lush with lemon and orange groves, there are two romantic villa annexes. ⊠ *Strada Amalfitana 9, 84011* ☎ *089/871012* 🖷 *089/871351* ⊕ *www.hotelsantacaterina.it* ⇗ *66 rooms* ☜ *2 restaurants, cable TV, saltwater pool, gym, beach, 2 bars, Internet, meeting room, free parking* ☰ *AE, DC, MC, V* ⧖ *BP.*

$$ ⌂ **Piccolo Paradiso.** The location in the Amalfi harbor area across from the Arsenale makes this upscale B&B a special choice. A small elevator deposits you in the cozy house, sunny yellow with green shutters, and with a casually furnished, sun-bright terrace. A common area has tile flooring; rooms are smallish but comfortable, with wicker seating and wrought-iron headboards. Some rooms have private terraces. ☒ *Via M. Camera 5, 84011* ☏ *089/873001* ⬅ *6 rooms* ☰ *AE, MC, V.*

$–$$ ▦ **Hotel dei Cavalieri.** This terraced white Mediterranean-style hotel on the main road outside Amalfi has three villa annexes on grounds just across the road that extend all the way to a beach below. Bright rooms are functionally furnished, with splashy majolica-tile floors. An ample buffet breakfast is served. ☒ *Via M. Comite 32, 84011* ☏ *089/831333* 🖷 *089/831354* ⊕ *www.hoteldeicavalieri.it* ⬅ *54 rooms* ♨ *Restaurant, cable TV, bar* ☰ *AE, DC, MC, V* |◎| *BP.*

Shopping

A must for lovers of art, vintage prints, and fine books is down by the waterfront: **Andrea de Luca** (☒ Largo Cesareo Console 8 ☏ 089/871954), a publisher of fine books and postcards, whose shop sells desk accessories, objets d'art, and art tomes. You'll find paper creations, maps, and other souvenirs near the Duomo at **Amalfi nelle Stampe Antiche** (☒ Piazza Duomo 10 ☏ 089/872368).

Ravello

⑥ *5 km (3 mi) northeast of Amalfi, 40 km (25 mi) east of Sorrento.*

Fodor'sChoice
★

Perched on a ridge high above Amalfi and the neighboring town of Atrani, the enchanting village of Ravello has stupendous views, quiet lanes, two important Romanesque churches, and several irresistibly romantic gardens. Set "closer to the sky than the sea," according to André Gide, the town has been the ultimate aerie ever since it was founded as a smart suburb for the richest families of Amalfi's 12th-century maritime republic. Rediscovered by English aristocrats a century ago, the town now hosts one of Italy's most famous music festivals.

In Ravello pride of place is taken by the **Duomo,** dedicated to patron saint Pantaleone and founded in 1086 by Orso Papiro, the town's first bishop. Rebuilt in the 12th and 17th centuries, it retains traces of medieval frescoes in the transept, an original mullioned window, a marble portal, and a three-story 13th-century bell tower playfully interwoven with mullioned windows and arches. The 12th-century bronze door has 54 embossed panels depicting Christ's life, and saints, prophets, plants, and animals, all narrating biblical lore. It was crafted by Barisano da Trani, who also fashioned the doors of the cathedrals of Trani and Monreale. The nave's three aisles are divided by ancient columns, and treasures include sarcophagi from Roman times and paintings by southern Renaissance artist Andrea da Salerno. Most impressive are the two medieval pulpits: the earlier one (on your left as you face the altar), used for reading the Epistles, is inset with a mosaic scene of Jonah and the whale, symbolizing death and redemption. The more famous one opposite, used for reading the Gospels, was commissioned by Nicola Rufolo in 1272 and created by Niccolò di Bartolomeo da Foggia. It seems almost Tuscan in style, with exquisite Cosmatesque mosaic work and bas-reliefs and six

twisting columns sitting on lion pedestals. An eagle grandly tops the inlaid marble lectern.

A chapel to the left of the apse is dedicated to St. Pantaleone, a physician who was beheaded in the 3rd century in Nicomedia. Every July 27
devout believers gather in hope of witnessing a miracle (similar to that
of San Gennaro in Naples), in which the saint's blood, collected in a
vial and set out on an inlaid marble altar, appears to liquefy and come
to a boil; it hasn't happened in recent years. In the crypt is the **Museo
del Duomo,** which displays treasures from about the 13th century, during the reign of Frederick II of Sicily. ⊠ *Piazza del Duomo* *€1.50*
☉ *Church: daily 9–1 and 3–7; museum: Apr.–Oct., daily 9:30–1 and
3–7; Nov.–Mar., weekends 9:30–1 and 3–7.*

Directly off Ravello's main piazza is the **Villa Rufolo,** which—if the master storyteller Boccaccio is to be believed—was built in the 13th century by Landolfo Rufolo, whose immense fortune stemmed from trade
with Moors and Saracens. Within is a scene from the earliest days of
the Crusades. Norman and Arab architecture mingle in profusion in a
welter of color-filled gardens so lush that composer Richard Wagner used
them as his inspiration for the home of the Flower Maidens in his opera
Parsifal. Beyond the Arab-Sicilian cloister and the Norman tower are
two flower-bedded terraces that offer a splendid vista of the Bay of Salerno;
the lower "Wagner Terrace" is the site for the yearlong **Festival Musicale di Ravello** (☎ 089/858149 Ravello Concert Society 089/858249
⊕ www.ravelloarts.org). ⊠ *Piazza Duomo, 84010* *€4* ☉ *Daily
9–sunset.*

From Ravello's main piazza, head west along Via San Francesco and
Via Santa Chiara to the **Villa Cimbrone,** a medieval-style fantasy that sits
1,500 feet above the sea. Created in 1905 by England's Lord Grimthorpe
and made world famous when Greta Garbo stayed here in 1937, the
Gothic castle-palazzo is set in fragrant rose gardens that lead to the
Belvedere dell'Infinità (Belvedere of Infinity), a grand stone parapet
that overlooks the impossibly blue Gulf of Salerno and frames a panorama
that former Ravello resident Gore Vidal has called "the most beautiful
in the world." The villa itself is now a hotel. ⊠ *Via Santa Chiara 26*
☎ *089/857459* *€4.50* ☉ *Daily 9–sunset.*

Where to Stay & Eat

★ **$–$$$** ✕ **Cumpà Cosimo.** This family-run restaurant a few steps from the cathe-
dral square offers a cordial welcome in two simple but attractive din-
ing rooms. There's no view, but the food is excellent, most of it coming
from owner Donna Netta's garden or her butcher shop next door.
Among the specialties are cheese crepes, roast lamb, and a dish includ-
ing seven types of homemade pasta. ⊠ *Via Roma 44* ☎ *089/857156*
 AE, DC, MC, V ☉ *Closed Mon. and Jan. 10–Feb.*

$–$$ ✕ **Vittoria.** Down the bustling arcade of pottery shops adjacent to the
grounds of the Villa Rufolo, this is a good place for a return to reality
and an informal bite. Vittoria's thin-crust pizza with loads of fresh toppings is the star attraction, but also consider the pasta, maybe fusilli with
tomatoes, zucchini, and mozzarella. Decor is extremely simple, with white

walls and a few etchings of Ravello. ⊠ *Via dei Rufolo 3* ☎ *089/857947* ⊟ *AE, DC, MC, V* ☺ *Closed Tues. Nov.–Mar.*

$$$$ ▦ **Hotel Palumbo.** Occupying a 12th-century patrician palace outfitted with antiques and modern comforts, this elegant hotel has the feel of a lovely private home. It has beautiful garden terraces, breathtaking views, and a sumptuous upstairs dining room. In summer you can descend to a villa at sea level and be pampered in the hotel's coastal retreat. Note that half board is compulsory except in winter, when the restaurant is closed. ⊠ *Palazzo Confalone, Via San Giovanni del Toro 16, 84010* ☎ *089/857244* ⊞ *089/858133* ⊕ *www.hotel-palumbo.it* ⇌ *20 rooms* ⌂ *Restaurant, cable TV, bar* ⊟ *AE, DC, MC, V* ⦿❘ *MAP.*

★ **$$$$** ▦ **Palazzo Sasso.** The whole experience at this 12th-century palace, from the marble atrium and lofty coastal views to courteous attentive service and finer details of hotel decor, makes it one of the finest hotels in southern Italy. The Rossellini restaurant, open to the public only in the evenings, is also highly recommended. ⊠ *Via San Giovanni del Toro 28, 84010* ☎ *089/818181* ⊞ *089/858900* ⊕ *www.palazzosasso. com* ⇌ *36 rooms, 8 suites* ⌂ *Restaurant, cable TV, pool, outdoor hot tub, bar, library, Internet, some pets allowed* ⊟ *AE, DC, MC, V* ☺ *Closed Nov.–Mar* ⦿❘ *BP.*

$$$$ ▦ **Villa Cimbrone.** Suspended over the azure sea and set amid rose-laden gardens, this magical place was once the home of Lord Grimthorpe and the holiday hideaway of Greta Garbo. Now the Gothic-style *castello* (castle) has guest rooms ranging from palatial to cozy (opt for the Peony Room, which has its own terrace). Tapestried armchairs, framed prints, vintage art books, and other antiques that belonged to Viscountess Frost, the lord's daughter, still grace the enchantingly elegant sitting room. Best of all, guests have the villa's famous gardens all to themselves once their gates are closed at sunset. The villa is a strenuous hike from the town center, but porters will carry your luggage and the distance helps keep this the most peaceful place on the Amalfi Coast. ⊠ *Via Santa Chiara 26, 84010* ☎ *089/857459* ⊞ *089/857777* ⊕ *www.villacimbrone.it* ⇌ *13 rooms* ⌂ *Minibars, library* ⊟ *AE, DC, MC, V* ☺ *Closed Nov.–Easter* ⦿❘ *BP.*

$$ ▦ **Parsifal.** In 1288 this diminutive property was a convent housing an order of Augustinian friars. Today the ancient, ivy-covered stone arches and a tile walkway looking out over the coastline lead to a cozy interior that still feels a bit like a retreat. Sun lounges, a garden, a fountain with reflecting pool, and an alfresco dining area all overlook the sea. Rooms are small (monks' cells, after all), so ask for one with a balcony; Nos. 20, 22, 23, 24, and 26 are best. ⊠ *Viale Gioacchino d'Anna 5, Ravello 84010* ☎ *089/857144* ⊞ *089/857972* ⊕ *www.hotelparsifal.com* ⇌ *19 rooms* ⌂ *Restaurant, bar* ⊟ *AE, DC, MC, V* ⦿❘ *MAP.*

$ ▦ **Villa Amore.** A 10-minute walk from the Piazza Duomo, this family-run hotel has a garden and an exhilarating view of the sea from most of its bedrooms. If you're looking for tranquillity, you've found it, especially at dusk, when the valley is tinged with a glorious purple light. Rooms are small, with modest modern furnishings; one of the treats is delicious homemade jam at breakfast. Full board is available, and at least half board is required from July through September. Reserve ahead, and specify time of arrival if you need help with luggage from the parking lot or bus stop; you pay €4 per bag. ⊠ *Via del Fusco 5, 84010* ☎☎ *089/ 857135* 🛏 *12 rooms* ⚭ *Restaurant, bar, some pets allowed; no a/c, no room TVs* ▭ *DC, MC, V* ⦿ *MAP.*

Salerno

❺❼ *6 km (4 mi) east of Vietri sul Mare, 56 km (35 mi) southeast of Naples.*

Spread out along its bay, Salerno was long a sad testimony to years of neglect and overdevelopment, but the antique port is now reevaluating its artistic heritage. It's a well-connected base for exploring the Cilento area to the south, which has such lovely sea resorts as San Marco di Castellabate and Palinuro, and inland some fine mountain walks and spectacular gorges and caves, such as Castelcivita and Pertosa.

Salerno has an imposing Romanesque **Duomo** founded in the mid-9th century and substantially rebuilt by Robert Guiscard from 1076 to 1085. The scene is set by the doorway—see the marble lions at the base— which gives way to a spacious atrium. The Cosmatesque pulpits rival Ravello's for elegance, and ornately carved marbled sarcophagi reinforce the cathedral's stately pedigree. ⊠ *Piazza Duomo* ☎ *089/231387* ⊗ *Daily 10–1:30 and 3–6.*

The **Museo Archeologico Provincale**, in Salerno's medieval Benedictine abbey, has interesting displays of ancient artifacts from the region, with many of the higher-quality finds coming from the Greco-Etruscan necropolis in what is now the suburb of Fratte. Some fine Attic and Corinthian vases are on the upper floor, but the show-stealer is the 1st-century BC bronze head of Apollo fished out of the Gulf of Salerno in 1930. ⊠ *Via San Benedetto 28* ☎ *089/231135* ⊡ *Free* ⊗ *Mon.–Sat. 9–7, Sun 9–1.*

Where to Stay

$ ⊞ **Plaza.** You can easily walk to the harbor, shops, and transportation from these clean, no-frills lodgings, right across from the train station and tourist office. The interior is decorated in warm, mellow tones, and guest rooms are spacious, some with air-conditioning and all with TVs. When booking, ask for a room on one of the upper floors, which tend to be quieter, or in the back over the courtyard. ⊠ *Piazza Vittorio Veneto 42, 84123* ☎ *089/224477* ⊟ *089/237311* ⊕ *www.plazasalerno. it* 🛏 *42 rooms* ⚭ *Minibars, cable TV, lobby lounge; no a/c in some rooms,* ▭ *AE, DC, MC, V* ⦿ *BP.*

Paestum

★ ❺❽ *42 km (26 mi) southeast of Salerno, 99 km (62 mi) southeast of Naples.*

One of Italy's most majestic sights lies on the edge of a flat coastal plain: the remarkably well-preserved **Greek temples** of Paestum. SS18 from the north passes the train station (Stazione di Paestum), which is about 800 yards from the ruins through the perfectly preserved **Porta Sirena** archway. This is the site of the ancient city of Poseidonia, founded by Greek colonists probably in the 6th century BC. When the Romans took over the colony in 273 BC and the name was latinized to Paestum, they changed the layout of the settlement, adding an amphitheater and a forum. Much of the archaeological material found on the site is displayed in the well-labeled **Museo Nazionale,** and several rooms are devoted to the unique tomb paintings discovered in the area, rare examples of Greek and pre-Roman pictorial art.

At the northern end of the site opposite the ticket barrier is the **Tempio di Cerere** (Temple of Ceres). Built in about 500 BC, it's now thought to have been originally dedicated to the goddess Athena. Follow the Roman road southward through the site, past the **Foro Romano** (Roman forum), to the **Tempio di Nettuno** (Temple of Poseidon), a magnificent Doric edifice with 36 fluted columns and an extraordinarily well-preserved entablature (area above the capitals), which rivals those of the finest temples in Greece. Beyond is the so-called **Basilica,** the earliest of Paestum's standing edifices; it dates from early in the 6th century BC. The name is an 18th-century misnomer, for the structure was in fact a temple sacred to Hera, the wife of Zeus. Try to see the temples in the late afternoon, when the light enhances the deep gold of the limestone and the temples are almost deserted. ☎ 0828/722654 🖾 *Excavations €4, museum €4, excavations and museum €6.50* ☉ *Excavations July–Sept., daily 9 AM–10 PM; Oct.–June, daily 9–1 hr before sunset. Museum July–Sept., daily 9 AM–10 PM; Oct.–June, daily 9–6:30; closed 1st and 3rd Mon. of each month.*

Where to Stay & Eat

¢–$ ✕🖼 **Helios.** Directly across the road from the Porta della Giustizia and a few steps from the temples, the Helios has cottage-type rooms in a garden setting. Seven rooms have whirlpool baths. A pleasant restaurant serves local specialties and seafood. The home-produced ricotta and mozzarella are especially recommended. The hotel also organizes visits to a local mozzarella producer and excursions around the area on horseback. ✉ *Via Nettuno 7, Zona Archeologica, 84063* ☎ *0828/811451* 🖶 *0828/811600* 🛏 *27 rooms* ♨ *Restaurant, pool; no a/c in some rooms, no TV in some rooms* ☰ *AE, DC, MC, V* ‖◎‖ *MAP.*

NAPLES & CAMPANIA A TO Z

To research prices, get advice from other travelers, and book travel arrangements, visit www.fodors.com.

AIRPORTS

Aeroporto Capodichino, 8 km (5 mi) north of Naples, serves the Campania region. It handles domestic and international flights, including several daily between Naples and Rome (flight time 45 minutes). Throughout the year there is direct helicopter service with Cab Air between Aeroporto Capodichino and Capri, Ischia, or Positano. The cost is €1,200, regardless of the destination.

Taxis are available at the airport for the ride to downtown Naples (€15–€20). The transportation company ANM runs the Alibus service, which leaves the airport every 30 minutes with stops at Piazza Garibaldi and Piazza Muncipio (€2). The more frequent but slightly slower Bus

3S also goes to Piazza Garibaldi and to the port (Molo Beverello) beyond. Tickets, bought from the newsstands inside the airport, run €0.77. 🗷 Airport Information **Aeroporto Capodichino** ☎ 081/7896259. **ANM (Azienda Napoletana Mobilità)** ☎ 081/7631111. **Cab Air** ☎ 081/2587110.

BOAT & FERRY TRAVEL

A variety of fast craft and passenger and car ferries connect the islands of Capri and Ischia with Naples and Pozzuoli year-round. In summer Capri and Ischia are serviced by boats from the Amalfi Coast. Boats and hydrofoils for these islands and for Sorrento leave from Naples's Molo Beverello. Hydrofoils also leave from Mergellina.

Information on departures is published every day in the local paper, *Il Mattino*, and in local editions of national dailies (*Corriere della Sera* or *La Repubblica*). Alternatively, ask at the tourist office or at the port, or contact the companies—Caremar, Navigazione Libera del Golfo, SNAV, and Alilauro—directly. Always double-check schedules in stormy weather. The Coop Sant'Andrea, a boat company based in Amalfi, organizes trips to many places along the coast, as well as special disco and fireworks cruises.

FARES & SCHEDULES · 🗷 Boat & Ferry Information **Alilauro** ☎ 081/7614909 ⊕ www.alilauro.it. **Caremar** ☎ 081/5513882 ⊕ www.caremar.it. **Coop Sant'Andrea** ☎ 089/873190 ⊕ www.coopsantandrea.it. **Mergellina** ⊠ About 1½ km [1 mi] to the west of Piazza Municipio. **Molo Beverello** ⊠ Southeast of Piazza Municipio. **Navigazione Libera del Golfo** (NLG) ☎ 081/5527209 ⊕ www.navlib.it. **SNAV** ☎ 081/7612348 ⊕ www.snavali.com.

BUS TRAVEL

Marozzi, a Rome-based line, runs direct air-conditioned buses from Rome to Pompeii, Salerno, Sorrento, and Amalfi. Buses leave Rome's Stazione Tiburtina weekdays at 3 PM, weekends at 7 AM.

There's an extensive network of local buses in Naples and throughout Campania. ACTP buses connect Naples with Caserta in one hour, leaving every 20 minutes from Piazza Garibaldi (every 40 minutes on Sunday). Buses to Santa Maria Capua Vetere leave Piazza Garibaldi approximately every 30–40 minutes Monday to Saturday (travel time 45 minutes). There are six buses a day Monday to Saturday from Piazza Garibaldi to Benevento. The trip takes 90 minutes. SITA buses for Salerno leave every 30 minutes Monday to Saturday and every two hours on Sunday from the SITA terminal on Via Pisanelli. SITA buses also serve the Amalfi Coast, connecting Sorrento with Salerno. Curreri operates a service (six runs daily) between Sorrento and Aeroporto Capodichino. 🗷 Bus Information **ACTP** ☎ 081/7001111. **Curreri** ☎ 081/8015420. **Marozzi** ☎ 06/4076140. **SITA** ⊠ Via Pisanelli, near Piazza Municipio ☎ 081/5522176 ⊕ www.sita-on-line.it.

CAR RENTAL

🗷 Local Agencies **Avis** ⊠ Aeroporto di Capodichino, Naples ☎ 081/7805790 ⊕ www.avis.com ⊠ Stazione Centrale, Naples ☎ 081/284041 ⊠ Via Piedigrotta 44, Naples ☎ 081/7618354 ⊠ Viale Nizza 53, Sorrento ☎ 081/8782459. **Hertz** ⊠ Via G. Bosco, Caserta ☎ 0823/356383 ⊕ www.hertz.it ⊠ Aeroporto Capodichino, Naples ☎ 081/7802971, 199112211 toll-free in Italy ⊠ Piazza Garibaldi 91/b, Naples ☎ 081/206228 ⊠ Garage Di Leva, Via degli Aranci 9, Sorrento ☎ 081/8071646.

CAR TRAVEL

Italy's main north–south route, the A2 (also known as the Autostrada del Sole), connects Rome with Naples and Campania. In good traffic the drive to Naples takes less than three hours. Autostrada A3, a continuation of the A2, runs south from Naples through Campania and into Calabria. It also connects with the autostrada A16 to Bari, which passes Avellino and is linked with Benevento by expressway. For Herculaneum (Ercolano), Pompeii (Pompei), and Oplontis, take the A3 southeast and turn off at the appropriate exit (for Vesuvius, Ercolano is quickest); for the Sorrento peninsula and the Amalfi Coast, exit at Castellammare di Stabia. To get to Paestum, take A3 to the Battipaglia exit and take the road to Capaccio Scalo–Paestum.

GARAGES   In Naples, Garage dei Fiori is near Villa Pignatelli, Grilli is near Stazione Centrale, and Turistico is near the port.

🚗 **Garage dei Fiori** ⊠ Via Colonna 21 ☎ 081/414190. **Grilli** ⊠ Via Ferraris 40 ☎ 081/264344. **Turistico** ⊠ Via de Gasperi 14 ☎ 081/5525442.

ROAD   All roads on the Sorrento peninsula and Amalfi Coast are narrow and
CONDITIONS   twisting, but they have outstanding views. In high season, from about April through October, only residents' cars are allowed on Ischia and Capri.

EMBASSIES & CONSULATES

🚗 United Kingdom **British Consulate** ⊠Via Dei Mille 40, Naples ☎081/4238911 ⊕www.ukinitalia.it.

🚗 United States **U.S. Consulate** ⊠ Piazza della Repubblica 2, Naples ☎ 081/5838111 ⊕ www.usembassy.it.

EMERGENCIES

🚗 **Police** ☎ 112. **Ambulance** ☎ 118.

🚗 Pharmacies **Farmacia Helvethia** ⊠ Piazza Garibaldi 11, opposite Stazione Centrale ☎ 081/5548894.

ENGLISH-LANGUAGE MEDIA

The monthly *Qui Napoli,* free from tourist offices, has useful information in English on museums, exhibitions, and transportation. For a more comprehensive monthly listing of entertainment and events, buy *Le Pagine dell'Ozio,* available at most newsstands. (Two pages are in English.)

MAIL & SHIPPING

UPS has a location in Casoria, near Naples, but shipping services should be arranged using the toll-free number. Federal Express doesn't have a Naples office but works in conjunction with the service SDA. The main Naples post office is open Monday–Saturday 9 to 7.

🚗 Post Offices **Naples Main Post Office** ⊠ Piazza Matteotti, off Via Toledo ☎ 081/5511456.

🚗 Major Overnight Services **Federal Express** ☎ 02/25088001, 800/123800 toll-free. **SDA** ⊠ Via Botteghelle di Portici 203/a, Naples ☎ 081/2583411. **UPS** ⊠ Via Pascoli 8, Casoria ☎ 02/25088001, 800/877877 toll-free.

SAFETY

LOCAL SCAMS The main risks in Naples are car break-ins, bag-snatching, pickpocketing, and fraud. As a general rule, give twosomes on scooters a wide berth—it's the one riding pillion that does the snatching—and never make major purchases such as digital cameras from unlicensed dealers. Goods can be artfully switched with worthless packages right under your nose. Be particularly vigilant around the central station area of Piazza Garibaldi in Naples; make sure your valuables are carefully stowed away in an inside pocket.

SUBWAY TRAVEL

Naples's rather old Metropolitana (subway system), also called Linea 2, provides frequent service and can be the fastest way to get across the traffic-clogged city. Tickets cost €0.77, and trains run from 5 AM until 10:30 PM. The other urban subway system, Metropolitana Collinare (or Linea 1), links the hill area of the Vomero and beyond with the National Archaeological Museum and Piazza Dante. Construction is under way to extend the route to Piazza Garibaldi, though the discovery of an ancient Roman port during work on the proposed Piazza Municipio station in December 2003 may delay work.

🚇 Subway Information **FS** ☎ 892021.

TOURS

Fine Arts organizes made-to-measure guided tours and stays. The Associazione di Donnaregina, run by two Neapolitan artists, organizes small group tours (six to eight people) of Naples and surroundings, offering insights into the culture, traditions, and lesser-known places of the region. Other operators include Milleviaggi, Tourcar, and STS. A welcome center for visitors to Naples's old town, the Centro di Accoglienza Turistica Museo Aperto Napoli, offers a museum-style audio guide (€6) you can to listen to as you wander the area.

🚇 **Associazione di Donnaregina** ✉ Via Luigi Settembrini 80, Naples ☎ 081/446799 or 338/6401301. **Centro di Accoglienza Turistica Museo Aperto Napoli** ✉ Via Pietro Colletta 89 ☎ 081/5636062 ⊕ www.museoapertonapoli.com. **Fine Arts** ✉ Via San Paolo 13, Naples ⊕ www.artifexgallery.it ☎ 081/291634. **Milleviaggi** ✉ Riviera di Chiaia 252, Naples ☎ 081/7642064. **Tourcar** ✉ Piazza Matteotti 1, Naples ☎ 081/5521938 ⊕ www.tourcar.it. **STS** ✉ Via Bernini 90, Naples ☎ 081/5565164.

TRAIN TRAVEL

There are trains every hour between Rome and Naples. Eurostar and Intercity trains make the trip in less than two hours. Trains take either the inland route (through Cassino) or go along the coast (via Formia). Almost all trains to Naples stop at Stazione Centrale.

A network of suburban trains connects Naples with several points of interest. The line used most by visitors is the Circumvesuviana, which runs from Corso Garibaldi Station and stops at Stazione Centrale before continuing to Ercolano (Herculaneum), Pompeii, and Sorrento. Frequent local trains connect Naples with Caserta and Salerno. Travel time between Naples and Sorrento on the Circumvesuviana line is about 75 minutes. Benevento is on the main line between Naples and Foggia. The Circumflegrea runs from Piazza Montesanto Station in Naples toward the archaeological zone of Cumae, with three departures in the morning. The Ferrovia Cumana runs from Piazza Montesanto Station to Pozzuoli and Lucrino. For the archaeological zone of Baia, get the shuttle bus outside Lucrino station.

🚆 Train Information **Circumflegrea and Cumana** ☎ 081/5513328 ⊕ www.sepsa.it. **Circumvesuviana** ☎ 081/7722444 ⊕ www.vesuviana.it. **Stazione Centrale** ✉ Piazza Garibaldi ☎ 892021 ⊕ www.trenitalia.it.

VISITOR INFORMATION

The EPT (Ente Provinciale per il Turismo) handles information for the province—which in this case could be the province of Naples or that of Salerno—whereas information offices run by the local tourist organizations are more ubiquitous, though they cover much the same ground.

🚆 Tourist Information **EPT** ✉ Piazza dei Martiri 58, 80121 Naples ☎ 081/4107211 ✉ Stazione Centrale, 80142 Naples ☎ 081/268779 ✉ Stazione Mergellina, Naples 80122 ☎ 081/7612102 ⊕ www.ept.napoli.it.

Amalfi ✉ Corso delle Repubbliche 27, 84011 ☎ 089/871107. **Benevento** ✉ Piazza Roma 11, 82100 ☎ 0824/319938 ⊕ www.eptbenevento.it. **Capri** ✉ Marina Grande pier, 80073 ☎ 081/8370634 ✉ Piazza Umberto I, Capri Town, 80073 ☎ 081/8370686 ⊕ www.capritourism.com. **Caserta** ✉ Piazza Dante 35, 81100 ☎ 0823/321137. **Ercolano** ✉ Via 4 Novembre 82, 80056 ☎ 081/7881243. **Naples** ✉ Piazza del Gesù, 80135 ☎ 081/5523328. **Pompeii** ✉ Via Sacra 1, 80045 ☎ 081/8507255. **Porto d'Ischia** ✉ Via Iasolino, Porto Salvo, 80077 ☎ 081/5074231. **Ravello** ✉ Piazza Duomo 1, 84010 ☎ 089/857096. **Salerno** ✉ Piazza Vittorio Veneto, 84100 ☎ 089/231432, 800/213289 toll-free ⊕ www.crmpa.it/ept. **Sorrento** ✉ Via de Maio 35, 80067 ☎ 081/8074033 ⊕ www.sorrentotourism.com.

PUGLIA

14

Updated by
Nick Bruno

THE HEEL AND SPUR OF ITALY'S BOOT, the ancient land of Puglia has some of the country's most unspoiled scenery, most fascinating artistic and historical sites, and finest beaches. Once merely associated with train or car journeys for Greece-bound travelers, Puglia (known to some English speakers as Apulia, from its Latin name) is slowly gaining recognition as a destination in its own right. In recent years there has been an influx of Northern Europeans, including many Brits, jetting in on budget flights to buy a piece of the region's rustic bliss as a relatively cheap holiday home.

Beyond the seaside resorts and the few major sights lies sunbaked countryside where expanses of silvery olive trees, vineyards of *primitivo* grapes, and giant prickly-pear cacti fight their way through the rocky soil in defiance of the relentless summer heat. Country trattorias, oil refineries, buildings eternally under construction, and fairy-tale-like *trulli*—curious conical structures dating from the Middle Ages—complete the rural landscape. Meanwhile, the cities and fishing villages do their best to dispel the effects of the sun: whitewashed ports stand coolly over the turquoise Mediterranean, their castles guarding mazes of medieval alleyways dotted with wide-open doorways and grandmothers drying their handmade *orecchiette,* the most Puglian of pastas, in the midday heat.

Puglia has long been inhabited, conquered, and visited. On sea voyages to their colonies and trading posts in the west, the ancient Greeks invariably headed for Puglia first—it was the shortest crossing—before filtering southward into Sicily and westward to the Tyrrhenian coast. In turn, the Romans—often bound in the opposite direction—were quick to recognize the strategic importance of the peninsula. Later centuries were to see a procession of other empires raiding or colonizing Puglia: Byzantines, Saracens, Normans, Swabians, Turks, and Spaniards all swept through, each group leaving its mark. Romanesque churches and the powerful castles built by 13th-century Holy Roman Emperor Frederick II (who also served as king of Sicily and Jerusalem), are among the most impressive of the buildings in the region. Frederick II, dubbed *Stupor Mundi* (Wonder of the World) for his wide-ranging interests in literature, science, mathematics, and nature, was one of the foremost personalities of the Middle Ages.

The last 50 years have brought a huge economic revival after the centuries of neglect following Puglia's golden age under the Normans and Swabians. Having benefited from EU funding, state incentive programs, and subsidies for irrigation, Puglia is now Italy's second-biggest producer of wine, with most of the rest of the land devoted to olives, citrus fruits, and vegetables. The rugged Gargano peninsula has done well as a summer retreat, and the baroque city of Lecce continues to sparkle with vitality. The main ports of Bari, Brindisi, and Taranto are thriving centers, though there remain serious problems of unemployment and poverty. However, the much-publicized arrival of thousands of asylum seekers from Eastern Europe and beyond has not significantly destabilized these cities, as had been feared, and the economic and political refugees have dispersed throughout Italy. Compared with neighboring Albania a mere 70 km (44 mi) away across the Straits of Otranto, Puglia oozes with

Puglia and the bordering state of Basilicata, particularly Matera, are well suited to be combined into a single trip, and Calabria can also be easily added to form a pan-*mezzogiorno* (southern Italy) itinerary.

Numbers in the text correspond to numbers in the margin and on the Puglia and Bari maps.

14

If you have 3 days

With three days in Puglia, make the southeastern part of the region your priority. If your first landfall is **Bari** ❶–❺ ▶, leave on the Brindisi road and head into the trulli district toward ▦ **Martina Franca** ㉔ or ▦ **Alberobello** ⑳, good bases for the first night. Make your second stop ▦ **Lecce** ㉗, spending the day in this glorious baroque town. On the third day, keep Lecce as your base, but explore the Salentine peninsula, visiting the well-preserved historic towns of **Gallipoli** ㉙ and **Otranto** ㉘.

If you have 5 days

Start out by spending a day or two exploring the forested **Gargano Promontory** ⑪–⑲ ▶ and the coastline northwest of **Bari** ❶–❺. Take the coast road (SS16) from Bari toward **Trani** ❼, a historic port with a famed waterside cathedral. After **Barletta** ❽, the coast road (SS159) heads northwest through abandoned salt pans and marshes, now nature preserves of international importance. The seaside fishing villages–cum–resorts of the Gargano Promontory—▦ **Vieste** ⑭, ▦ **Peschici** ⑮, and ▦ **Rodi Garganico** ⑯—offer the best choice of accommodations, although ▦ **Foggia** ⑪ and nearby ▦ **Lucera** ⑫ make good bases, too. Aim to spend your third night in ▦ **Alberobello** ⑳, the capital of trulli country—touristy, but engaging—or in whitewashed ▦ **Ostuni** ㉓. From Alberobello, it's a short run to **Taranto** ㉕ for a look around the archaeological museum. Break for an hour or two in **Brindisi** ㉖, stopping at the famous column marking the end of the Via Appia, but save your last two nights for the Salentine peninsula and ▦ **Lecce** ㉗, a treat that will provide some of your most abiding memories of Puglia.

If you have 7 days

Choose ▦ **Bari** ❶–❺ ▶, with its bustling port and winding medieval old town, as your first base. Stay there two nights, devoting a good part of one day to exploring **Polignano a Mare** ❾, an atmospheric seaside town with good road and rail links to the regional capital. From Bari, venture up to the Gargano Promontory. A car is indispensable since transport connections are tortuous and slow, but be prepared to abandon it for a half-day ramble through the **Foresta Umbra** ⑰, **Monte Sant'Angelo** ⑱, and **San Giovanni Rotondo** ⑲. Proceed down the Adriatic Coast back toward Bari, staying a night in ▦ **Trani** ❼, perhaps taking in the fine cathedrals of **Barletta** ❽ and **Molfetta** ❻, and making an inland detour to the fascinatingly geometrical **Castel del Monte** ⑩. Head southeast toward trulli country, spending a night in ▦ **Alberobello** ⑳ or ▦ **Martina Franca** ㉔. At some point take a trip underground at the **Grotte di Castellana** ㉑, a soothing respite from summer heat. The bustling cities of **Taranto** ㉕ and **Brindisi** ㉖ are worth a stop for their archaeological relics. Spend your last three nights in the heel of Italy, with ▦ **Lecce** ㉗ as a base, venturing out to the seaside towns of ▦ **Otranto** ㉘ or ▦ **Gallipoli** ㉙.

prosperity—though it can be difficult to find an abundance of lodging facilities outside the business circuit.

Exploring Puglia

Driving is the best—and some say only—way to get around the region. The autostrada and superstrada networks connect Bari and Brindisi with the smaller towns. Note that entering the historic centers of many towns requires a small car, folding side-view mirrors, and a bit of nerve; tentative drivers should park outside the center and venture in by foot.

If your main interest is spending time at the beach, head to the Gargano Promontory, which has some of Puglia's best coastline but lacks the small-town country character of much of the region. Otherwise, convenient travel bases include Alberobello and Martina Franca in the trulli country; Lecce and Otranto near the tip of the heel; and the small coastal towns of Trani and Polignano, within easy reach of Bari.

Bari and Brindisi are notorious for purse-snatchings, car thefts, and break-ins. If you are driving in these cities, do not leave valuables in the car or trunk, and find a guarded parking space if possible.

About the Restaurants & Hotels

The best—and cheapest—way to eat in Puglia might be to ask around for a rustic family-run trattoria, sometimes referred to as a *casareccia* or *casalinga*, often found in the countryside or outskirts of a city. These bare-bones locales usually don't offer menus—just tastes that rival those of any highbrow restaurant in the region. Assent to the waiter's suggestions with a simple *va bene* (that's fine) and leave yourself in the chef's hands. You'll rarely be disappointed. Note that in many of the region's restaurants, especially the more rural or local ones, you pay one set price for your food, regardless of what you end up ordering.

Outside of the larger cities, hotel accommodations are limited and modest—both in amenities and price—but offer friendly service. Along the miles of sandy beaches on the Gargano spur and elsewhere on the coast, big, white, Mediterranean-style beach hotels have sprung up in profusion. Most are similar in design, price, and quality. In summer many require guests to stay multiple days and take full or half board. During Easter, rooms in the Alberobello area may be at a premium. Reserve in advance throughout the region. Many establishments, particularly the beach resorts, close during the winter months. Remember that in a region like this—blazing hot in summer and bitter cold in winter—air-conditioning and central heating are important.

Agriturismi (farm stays) in Puglia are an increasingly popular lodging option. Most *fattorie* and *masserie* (small farms and grander farm estates) offering accommodation are listed at local tourist offices, and they vary widely in cost, facilities, and English-language competence. This may be the closest you will get to experiencing the Puglian rural lifestyle. If you don't mind forgoing some modern convenience you'll experience Puglia at its best this way.

14

Beaches Italians and foreign visitors alike return summer after summer to Puglia, drawn by the sea. Though no longer undiscovered, the shores of the Gargano Promontory offer safe swimming and sandy beaches. The whole coastline between Bari and Brindisi is well served with beach facilities. In even the smallest villages you'll find beaches with changing rooms and—essential in the blazing sun—beach umbrellas. If you don't mind venturing farther afield, Gallipoli, on the south coast of the heel, has wonderful sand dunes and nearby pine forests. From Brindisi south to Leuca on the Adriatic coast, however, the coastline consists of rock, not sand.

Festivals In keeping with the provincial nature of Puglia, the arts take on a folk flavor, with processions on religious occasions more prevalent than performing arts in theaters or opera houses. Seeking out festivals and pageants will enrich your experience of life in Italy's deep south. To give just one example: in early March Bari commemorates the arrival of St. Nicholas's bones with two days of flamboyant costumed processions near the basilica and along the shoreline, followed by open-air parties and fireworks. The best newspaper for festival listings is the daily *Gazzetta del Mezzogiorno* (⊕ www.gdmland.it), which covers the entire region.

Shopping Puglia is rich in folk art, reflecting the influences of the many nations that have passed through the region or ruled it. Look for handmade goods such as pottery, baskets, textiles, carved-wood figures, and painted clay whistles. You won't find many boutiques here, but rather modest shops and open-air markets, where some bargaining can enter into the purchase.

	WHAT IT COSTS In euros				
	$$$$	**$$$**	**$$**	**$**	**¢**
RESTAURANTS	over €22	€16–€22	€11–€16	€7–€11	under €7
HOTELS	over €220	€160–€220	€110–€160	€70–€110	under €70

Restaurant prices are for a second course *(secondo piatto)*. Hotel prices are for two people in a standard double room in high season, including tax and service.

Timing

Summers are torrid this far south, and even the otherwise perfect villages of the interior are too dazzlingly white for easy comfort from July to early September. So unless you are planning to be thoroughly idle—always an alluring prospect in Puglia—avoid the hot season. Of course, if you're on the Gargano Promontory, which has Puglia's only significant elevation, you'll be able to appreciate the forested interior during these months. And the Gargano and Bari-to-Brindisi coastal regions are strictly summer-holiday zones. Italians vacation in August, and sometimes July, but never June or September.

Wintertime in Puglia can see heavy rain and wind, often lasting several days at a time. The temperatures rarely fall to freezing, however. In spring, days are usually warm and the skies clear; you can generally find water warm enough for swimming through October. Note that many lodgings can be closed off-season, especially along the coast.

BARI & THE ADRIATIC COAST

The coast has a strong flavor of the Norman presence in the south, embodied in the distinctive Puglian-Romanesque churches, the most atmospheric being in Trani. The busy commercial port of Bari offers architectural nuggets in its compact, labyrinthine Old Quarter abutting the sea, while Polignano a Mare combines accessibility to the major centers with the charm of a medieval town. For a unique excursion, drive inland to the imposing Castel del Monte, an enigmatic 13th-century octagonal fortification.

Bari

260 km (162 mi) southeast of Naples, 450 km (281 mi) southeast of Rome.

Bari is a big rough-and-tumble port and a transit point for travelers catching ferries across the Adriatic to Greece, but also a cosmopolitan city with one of the most interesting historic centers in the region. Most of Bari is set out in a logical 19th-century grid, following the designs of Joachim Murat (1767–1815), Napoléon's brother-in-law and King of the Two Sicilies. The heart of the modern town is **Piazza della Libertà** , but just beyond it, across Corso Vittorio Emanuele, is the *città vecchia* (old town), a maze of narrow streets on the promontory that juts out between Bari's old and new ports, circumscribed by Via Venezia, offering elevated views of the Adriatic in every direction. Stop for an outdoor drink at **Greta** (⊠ Via Venezia 22) for a commanding view of the port and sea. By day, explore the old town's winding alleyways, where Bari's open-door policy offers a glimpse into the daily routine of southern Italy—matrons hand-rolling pasta with their grandchildren home from school for the midday meal, and handymen perched on rickety ladders, patching up centuries-old arches and doorways. Back in the new town, join the evening *passeggiata* (stroll) on pedestrian-only **Via Sparano**, then saunter among the outdoor bars in Piazza Ferrarese, at the end of Corso Vittorio Emanuele, when night falls.

In the città vecchia, overlooking the sea and just off Via Venezia, is the **Basilica di San Nicola**, built in the 11th century to house the bones of St. Nicholas, also known as St. Nick, or Santa Claus. His remains, buried in the crypt, are said to have been stolen by Bari sailors from Myra, where St. Nicholas was bishop, in what is now Turkey. The basilica, of solid and powerful construction, was the only building to survive the otherwise wholesale destruction of Bari by the Normans in 1152. ⊠ *Piazza San Nicola* ☎ *080/5237247* ⊘ *Daily 7–noon and 4–7:45.*

Bari's 12th-century **Cattedrale** is the seat of the local bishop and was the scene of many significant political marriages between important fam-

ON THE MENU

ANYONE WHO LIKES TO EAT *will find pleasure in Puglia, where the cuisine has evolved from more than 2,000 years of foreign influence. Southern cuisine is hearty and healthful, based around homemade pastas and cheeses, fresh vegetables, seafood, and local olive oil. Here you will find dishes unavailable elsewhere in Italy, such as 'ncapriata, also called favi e fogghi (a first-course fava-bean puree topped with bitter chicory or other cooked vegetables and drizzled with extra virgin olive oil; mix it all together before eating). Focaccia barese (stuffed with fried onions, black olives, anchovies, and ricotta) makes a great snack or lunch.*

Puglia's pasta specialties include orecchiette (ear-shape pasta) and strascenate (rectangles of pasta with one rough side and one smooth side), all served with tomato-based sauces or cime di rape (bitter greens). Look for handmade

fusilli (spiral pasta) or any pasta fatto in casa or pasta fatto a mano—rolled out only hours before being served. Don't miss the dairy products, such as ricotta and burrata cheese, which is actually stuffed with butter.

Puglia produces almost a fifth of Italy's wine. In the last few years, the region has begun to compete on a national scale. The ancient primitivo grape, thought by many to have been brought to California and renamed Zinfandel, yields strong, heady wines. Look for the powerful Primitivo di Manduria, best with food; the robust Salice Salentino, made from Negroamaro grapes; and the sweet red Aleatico di Puglia. Blends like Amativo (a creation from Ca'ntele blending Negroamaro and Primitivo) have recently livened up the Pugliese wine scene. Top winemakers to look for include Conti Zecca, Leone di Castris, Rubino, and Tormaresca.

ilies in the Middle Ages. The cathedral's solid architecture reflects the Romanesque style favored by the Normans of that period. ⊠ *Piazza dell'Odegitria* ☎ *080/5288215* ☒ *Free* ☉ *Daily 7–1:30 and 4–7.*

❺ Looming over Bari's cathedral is the huge **Castello Svevo.** The current building dates from the time of Holy Roman Emperor Frederick II (1194–1250), who rebuilt an existing Norman-Byzantine castle to his own exacting specifications. Designed more for power than beauty, it looks out beyond the cathedral to the small Porto Vecchio (Old Port). Inside is a haphazard collection of medieval Puglian art and archaeological artifacts, and rotating exhibits of works by local artists. ⊠ *Piazza Federico II di Svevia* ☎ *080/5286218, 0339/1146908 for tour reservations* ☒ *€2* ☉ *Tues.–Sun. 9–7:30, ticket office closes at 7 PM. Guided tours Sat. 5:30, Sun. 11 and 5:30.*

Where to Stay & Eat

$$–$$$ ✕ **Trattoria al Pescatore.** This is one of Bari's best fish restaurants, in the old town opposite the castle and just around the corner from the cathedral. Summer cooking is done outside, where you can sit amid a cheerful clamor of quaffing and dining. Try the grilled *céfalo* (mullet) if it is available, accompanied by crisp salad and a carafe of invigorating local

KEY

► *Start of walk*

wine. Reservations are essential in July and August. ⊠ *Piazza Federico
II di Svevia 6* ☎ *080/5237039* ▤ *AE, DC, MC, V* ⊙ *Closed Mon.*

★ **$$$** 🏨 **Hotel Palace.** This downtown landmark is stationed steps away from
Corso Vittorio Emanuele in the new city, but is also extremely conve-
nient to the medieval center. The large, comfortable rooms are furnished
lightly and tastefully. For an extra €20, some rooms (ask in advance)
whimsically cater to a variety of special tastes, including pet rooms, chil-
dren's rooms, and a room for music lovers, complete with stereo and clas-
sical CD collection. Other amenities include Smart Car rental service (€36
per day) and a buffet breakfast. ⊠ *Via Lombardi 13, 70122* ☎ *080/
5216551* 🖷 *080/5211499* ⊕ *www.palacehotelbari.it* 🛏 *189 rooms*
🍴 *Restaurant, bicycles, bar, convention center, meeting room, parking
(fee), some pets allowed (fee)* ▤ *AE, DC, MC, V* ⏐⊙⏐ *MAP.*

 ¢ 🏨 **Adria.** This lodging's virtues are its convenience to the train station
and relative low cost in a city short on inexpensive lodgings. Facilities
are undistinguished, but this is primarily a one-night stopover, with guest
rooms that are basic but fine. The American Bar has coved ceilings and
some intriguing artwork. ⊠ *Via L. Zuppetta 10, 70121, turn right out
of the station to find it.* ☎ *080/5246699* 🖷 *080/5213207* ⊕ *http://space.
tin.it/viaggi/mlippol* 🛏 *35 rooms, 28 with bath* 🍴 *Restaurant, bar,
parking (fee); no a/c* ▤ *AE, DC, MC, V* ⏐⊙⏐ *BP.*

Nightlife & the Arts

While Bari's famous Teatro Petruzzelli awaits restoration after a fire in 1991, most drama and ballet have been diverted to the **Teatro Piccinni.** Italian rock/pop concerts can also be seen here. (⊠ Corso Vittorio Emanuele 84 ☎ 080/5210878 ⊗ Tickets on sale 10:30–12:30 and 5–8). Ticket prices range from €15 to €35.

Leopard spots, zebra stripes, and African artwork give **Matiti Brown** (⊠ Piazza Ferrarese ☎ 080/5227693) in Bari Vecchia a dash of the exotic. Cocktails are quaffed and Kenyan dishes sampled by a friendly crowd who chat on the terrace before dancing to the DJ's upbeat mix inside.

Sports & the Outdoors

BIKING **G. S. De Benedictis** (⊠ Via Nitti 23 ☎ 080/5744345) rents bikes, which are a great way to explore the flat roads of the trulli region.

Molfetta

❻ *25 km (16 mi) northwest of Bari, 108 km (67 mi) east of Foggia.*

The unusual 13th-century **Duomo di San Corrado** of Molfetta, crowning Molfetta's circular old town surrounded on three sides by water, reveals distinct Byzantine features, such as the pyramid-shape covers of the three main domes. If you're in the area around Easter, don't miss Molfetta's colorful Holy Week processions, a hit for young and old alike. ⊠ *Banchina Seminario* ⊗ *Daily 7–noon and 4–7.*

Trani

❼ *18 km (11 mi) northwest of Molfetta, 43 km (27 mi) northwest of Bari.*

Smaller than the other ports along this coast, Trani has a quaint old town with polished stone streets and buildings, medieval churches, and a harbor filled with fishing boats. Trani is also justly famous for its sweet dessert wine, Moscato di Trani. The stunning, pinkish-white hued 11th-century **Duomo** (⊠ Piazza Duomo ⊗ Daily 8–noon and 3:30–7), considered one of the finest in Puglia, is built on a spit of land jutting into the sea. The boxy well-preserved **Castle** (☎ 0883/506603 ⊗ Daily 8:30–7:30) was built by Frederick II in 1233. The Jewish community flourished here in medieval times, and on **Via Sinagoga** (Synagogue Street) two of the four synagogues still exist: the 13th-century **Santa Maria Scolanova** and **Santa Anna,** which still bears a Hebrew inscription.

Where to Stay & Eat

★ **$$** ✕🏠 **La Regia.** This small hotel-restaurant occupies a 17th-century palazzo superbly positioned in front of the Duomo, on a swath of land jutting out into the sea. Don't expect grand or spacious rooms, though they are perfectly adequate. The restaurant ($$–$$$) has attractive stonework, vaulted ceilings, and a terra-cotta tiled floor. Regional specialties are presented imaginatively: try the baked crepes (similar to cannelloni) or grilled fish. Reservations are essential for Sunday lunch and dinner on summer weekends. ⊠ *Piazza Mons. Addazi 2, 70059* ☎ *0883/ 584444* 🖶 *0883/506595* 🛏 *10 rooms* ⚱ *Restaurant, bar* ▭ *AE, DC,*

MC, V ⊘ *Restaurant closed Mon. Hotel and restaurant closed 15 days in Jan.* ⦾ *BP.*

$ ⊞ **Royal.** This is an unpretentious, 1950s-built, modern hotel near the train station. Rooms are trim and tidy, suited to stopovers rather than extended stays. ⊠ *Via De Robertis 29, 70059* ☎ *0883/588777* ⊟ *0883/582224* ⊕ *www.hotelroyaldam.com* ⤳ *40 rooms* ⚿ *Restaurant, meeting room* ⊟ *AE, DC, MC, V* ⦾ *BP.*

Barletta

❽ *13 km (8 mi) northwest of Trani, 56 km (35 mi) northwest of Bari.*

The **Colossus,** a bronze statue more than 15 feet tall, is thought to be of the Byzantine emperor Valentinian and to date from the 5th century AD. Part of Venice's booty after the sack of Byzantium's capital, Constantinople, in the 1200s, the Colossus was abandoned on the beach near Barletta when the ship carrying it to Venice foundered in a storm. ⊠ *Next to the church of San Sepolcro, Corso Vittorio Emanuele.*

Where to Eat

$ ⤬ **La Casaccia.** Near a picturesque castle, this restaurant prides itself on its *zuppa di pesce* (fish soup), made fresh every day, as well as local dishes like *orecchiette* (small ear-shaped pasta). There's nothing fancy here; the tone is calm and down-home, most tables occupied by discriminating regulars who appreciate the good Puglian cooking and the moderate prices. ⊠ *Corso Cavour 40* ☎ *0883/533719* ⊟ *No credit cards.*

Polignano a Mare

❾ *40 km (24 mi) southeast of Bari, 14 km (9 mi) north of Castellana.*

With a well-preserved whitewashed old town perched on limestone cliffs overlooking the Adriatic, Polignano a Mare makes an atmospheric base for exploring the surrounding area. Bari is only a half hour's train ride up the coast. The town is virtually lifeless all winter, but becomes something of a weekend hot spot for city-dwellers in summer.

Where to Stay & Eat

$-$$$ ⤬ **Le Antiche Mura.** Built dramatically into the 16th-century stone walls of the old town, this family-run restaurant is popular with locals and visitors alike. Specialties here are mainly—but not exclusively—seafood platters like *cozze a gratin* (mussels filled with bread crumbs) and *seppie al forno* (baked cuttlefish). Reservations are essential on weekends. ⊠ *Via Roma 11* ☎ *080/4242476* ⊕ *www.polignano.com/antichemura* ⊟ *AE, DC, MC, V* ⊘ *Closed Mon.*

$$ ⤬⊞ **Grotta Palazzese.** Carved out of a cliff opening onto the Adriatic,
Fodor'sChoice the Grotta Palazzese inhabits a stunning group of rocks and grottoes
★ that have wowed onlookers from time immemorial. Though all rooms but one have sea views, ask for one of the cave-apartments across the road rather than the more boxlike rooms in the main 1960s block. (Suites 18, 25, and 139 are the most impressive.) The Grotta Palazzese's true tour de force is its summer restaurant ($$$–$$$$), serving impeccably prepared fish (try the assortment of raw Adriatic shellfish called *frutti*

di mare crudi). The dramatic setting incorporates rock formations, with tables actually standing on an implausible bridge inside a jagged cave, while waves cast blue-green shadows on the grotto walls. It's one of the most romantic settings in all Italy. ✉ *Via Narciso 59, 70059* ☎ *080/ 4240677* 🖷 *080/4240767* ⊕ *www.grottapalazzese.it* ⇋ *14 rooms, 14 small apartments* ⌖ *2 restaurants, beach, bar, meeting room, parking (fee)* ⊟ *AE, DC, MC, V* ⊘ *Outdoor restaurant closed Oct.–Apr.* ⑩ *BP.*

Castel del Monte

★ ❿   *30 km (19 mi) south of Barletta, 56 km (35 mi) southwest of Bari.*

Built by Frederick II in the first half of the 13th century on an isolated hill, Castel del Monte is an imposing octagonal castle with eight austere towers. Very little is known about the structure, since virtually no records exist: the gift shop has many books that explore its mysterious past and posit fascinating theories based on its dimensions and Federico II's love of mathematics. It has none of the usual defense features associated with medieval castles, so it probably had little military significance. Some theories suggest it might have been built as a hunting lodge or may have served as an astronomical observatory, or even a stop for pilgrims on their quest for the Holy Grail. ✛ *On signposted minor road 18 km (11 mi) south of Andria* ◪ *€3* ☎ *0883/569997, 0339/1146908 tour reservations* ⊕ *www.castelli-puglia.org/it/index.html* ⊘ *Daily 10–1:30 and 2:30–7:30; June–Sept. also Sat. 9 PM–midnight. Optional guided tours in English and Italian available every 1–2 hrs.*

GARGANO PROMONTORY

Forming the spur of Italy's boot, the Gargano Promontory (Promontorio del Gargano) is a striking contrast to the Adriatic's generally flat, unenthralling coastline. This is a land of whitewashed coastal towns, wide sandy beaches interspersed with secluded coves, and craggy limestone cliffs topped by deep-green pine and lush Mediterranean maquis. Not surprisingly, it pulls in the crowds in July and August, including many Germans and northern Italians. Prices are higher than elsewhere in Puglia as a result of its popularity. Camping is almost always an option, as plentiful and pretty campgrounds dot the Gargano's curvy, cliff-hugging roads. (Driving some of them at night can be harrowing.) For the kids, the beaches and the Foresta Umbra national park are great places to let off steam, and many towns stage puppet shows in public gardens.

Foggia

▶ ⓫   *95 km (60 mi) west of Bari.*

Foggia, the chief city in Puglia's northernmost province, is not the most inspiring destination, though it makes a useful overnight stop for visitors to the Gargano. The old town is pleasant but fairly modern, having sustained significant war damage. On the main line from Rome and Naples, and easily accessible from the autostrada, Foggia has all the amenities you would expect from a major commercial center, hosting numerous fairs and conventions throughout the year. This means that, although it enjoys a decent selection of lodgings and restaurants, you'll need to reserve to ensure accommodations. This is the place to get or exchange cash or rent a car for excursions to the Gargano.

Where to Stay & Eat

★ **$$** ✕ **La Nuova Mangiatoia.** Set in an old farmhouse, this seafood restaurant looks like a medieval tavern, with arches and wood-beamed ceilings. You can also dine in a large garden, where tables made from wagon wheels surround an old well. The chef will supply recipes for Adriatic dishes, such as spaghetti *ai datteri di mare al cartoccio* (with razor clams). The location is on the main road to Bari, near the Foggia Agricultural Fairgrounds. ⊠ *Via Virgilio 2* ☏ *0881/634457* ⟪ *Reservations essential on weekends.* ⊟ *AE, DC, MC, V* ⊗ *Closed Mon.*

$ ✕ **Ambasciata Orsarese.** This hidden pizzeria and restaurant near Foggia's market, also referred to as "Trilussa," is very local, very good, and very small. In the tiny dining room the few tables are surrounded by rows of bottles of the region's best wines, which accompany pizza prepared in a 16th-century oven. Local antipasti and *primi* (first courses) are also available. Try their famed *pane divino,* a tasty and healthful bread that apparently aids digestion. ⊠ *Via Tenente Iorio 50, at the corner of Rosati* ☏ *0881/709253* ⊟ *No credit cards* ⊗ *Closed Mon.*

★ **$$$** ✕▥ **Cicolella.** This 1920s hotel near the station, on a tree-lined *viale* (road), has tasteful rooms with floor-length curtains, regal wallpaper, and restful, discreet lighting. Some have balconies. The excellent restaurant ($$) specializes in international cuisine, plus well-prepared local dishes. Service is impeccable, and a good regional wine list complements such country classics as puree of fava beans with chicory, drizzled with Puglian olive oil infused with hot peppers. Homemade *cavatelli neri* (dark pasta twists) are paired with a delectable tomato sauce made with pungent *ricotta dura* (hard ricotta) and have salty *grano bruccinto* (grated Parmesan-like cheese) sprinkled on top. ⊠ *Viale Ventiquattro Maggio 60, 71100* ☏ *0881/566111* ≞ *0881/778984* ⊕ *www.hotelcicolella. isnet.it* ⇔ *91 rooms, 13 suites* ⚭ *Restaurant, meeting room* ⊟ *AE, DC, MC, V* ⊗ *Restaurant closed weekends and Aug. 1–20* ¶ *BP.*

Wine Bars

Foggia has a surprisingly active nightlife, with several decent wine bars. The **Wine Bar Cairoli** (⊠ Via Martire 60 ☏ 0881/722472), a multiroom, cavernlike restaurant and bar, is a great place to sample local wines as well as antipasti and pizza. **Coniglio Mannaro** (⊠ Via Bruno 16 ☏ 0881/740752) is an *osteria* beloved by arty types who spill out onto the nearby square.

Lucera

⑫ *18 km (12 mi) northwest of Foggia.*

Occupying a commanding position over the Tavoliere, Puglia's flat coastal plains, Lucera flourished during the Roman era, long before Frederick II—in what was considered an enlightened gesture for the 13th century—relocated more than 10,000 Sicilian Arabs here in 1224.

Though subsequent decades of religious intolerance removed the Arab mosques, Lucera has retained an impressive complement of historical sites and an attentively preserved old town.

After you've explored Lucera's cobblestone streets, head for the 14th-century **Cattedrale,** a curious blend of Romanesque and Gothic architecture, commissioned by Charles II of Anjou to replace an earlier mosque. ⊠ *Piazza Duomo* ☎ *0881/520880* ⊙ *Daily 8–noon and 4–7.*

Lying rather incongruously beyond one of the poorer parts of the modern town is Lucera's partially reconstructed **Anfiteatro Augusteo,** built at the end of the 1st century BC. Although much of the superstructure has been lost, the grandiose entrance gates have been rebuilt, complete with dedication inscriptions. ⊠ *Viale Augusteo* ☎ *0881/522762* ⊙ *Oct.–Apr., Tues.–Sun. 9–2 and 4–8; May–Sept., Tues.–Sun. 9–8.*

The so-called **Fortezza Svevo Angioina,** a 10-minute walk northwest of the old town, is an impressive sight. It was plundered for building material up to modern times, and little but the base remains of Frederick's *palatium* (royal palace), built in 1233. The castle owes its present form to the Angevins, who transformed it over the next century into a military stronghold, complete with drawbridge, moat, 24 towers, and a wall more than 1 km (½ mi) long. ⊠ *Via Castello* ☎ *0881/522762* ⊙ *Oct.–Apr., Tues.–Sun. 9–2 and 4–8; May–Sept., Tues.–Sun. 9–8.*

In the spirit of cultural enlightenment that pervades Lucera, **guided tours** (☎ 0881/548626 for bookings) are available in Italian and occasionally English, free of charge, at the museum, amphitheater, and castle.

Where to Stay

¢ ⊡ **La Balconata 2.** This family-run hotel occupies part of a modern condominium and is two minutes' walk from the south gate of Porta Troia leading to the old town. When booking, ask for the quieter rooms away from the main road. The restaurant's regional cuisine is also well worth a try, but you'll need to be immune to cigarette smoke. ⊠ *Viale Ferrovia 15, 71036* ☎ *0881/520998 or 0881/546725* ⊕ *www.labalconata. it* ⊅ *49 rooms* ᗝ *Restaurant, bar* ⊟ *AE, DC, MC, V* ⊚ *BP.*

Mattinata

⑬ *53 km (32 mi) northeast of Foggia, 138 km (86 mi) northwest of Bari.*

Just inland from a fine sandy beach, where you'll find most of the campsites and hotels, this is a generally quiet village that comes into its own in the summer season.

Where to Stay & Eat

$$–$$$ ✕ **Trattoria della Nonna.** The waves lapping at the shore just inches outside the picture windows of this elegant but unpretentious coastal restaurant, a few kilometers outside of Mattinata, are an indication of how fresh the fish will be. The memorable assorted raw seafood antipasto includes some shellfish you might not find anywhere else. *Cozze peruse* (an indigenous Puglian clam), hiding inside spiked-hair shells, are briny and buttery; tiny *noci* shellfish have a wonderful sweetness; and big, rich

local oysters are all about texture. Try sweet grilled scampi with oil and lemon, and wash it all down with one of the great white wines on the extensive list. ⊠ *Mattinata Mare* ☎ *0884/559205* ▤ *AE, DC, MC, V* ☺ *Closed Mon. Oct.–May.*

$$$–$$$$ 🏨 **Baia delle Zagare.** This secluded, modern group of cottages overlooks an inlet and lies on the shore road around the Gargano Promontory, well north of Mattinata. An elevator built into the cliffs takes you down to a long private beach complete with limestone caves. The hotel restaurant is good enough to warrant staying on the premises all day. (You're expected to take half board in August.) Be careful when approaching on the road, as the gated entrance is easy to miss. ⊠ *Località Valle dei Mergoli, 17 km (10 mi) northeast of Mattinata, 71030* ☎ *0884/550155* 📠 *0884/550884* ⊕ *www.hotelbaiadellezagare.it* ➷ *150 rooms* ⚭ *Restaurant, minibars, tennis court, pool, health club, beach, dance club, theater* ▤ *MC, V* ☺ *Closed Sept. 15–May* ⦿| *MAP.*

$–$$ 🏨 **Alba del Gargano.** Although it's in the town center, this whitewashed modern hotel provides a restful atmosphere. Large balconies overlook a quiet courtyard garden, and a frequent (and free) bus service connects with a private, rocky beach 2 km (1 mi) away, where you can use the hotel's beach chairs and umbrellas. Rooms are comfortably furnished, and there's a good restaurant. Half or full board is mandatory in August. ⊠ *Corso Matino 102, 71030* ☎ *0884/550771* 📠 *0884/550772* ⊕ *www.albadelgargano.it* ➷ *40 rooms, 3 suites* ⚭ *Restaurant, beach, bar* ▤ *MC, V* ⦿| *MAP.*

Vieste

⑭ *93 km (58 mi) northeast of Foggia, 179 km (111 mi) northwest of Bari.*

This large whitewashed town jutting off the tip of the spur of Italy's boot is the Gargano's main commercial center and an attractive place to wander around. Though curvy mountain roads render it slightly less accessible from the autostrada and mainline rail stations than, say, Peschici and Mattinata, the range of accommodations (including camping) makes it a useful base for exploring Gargano. The resort attracts legions of tourists in summer, some bound for the Isole Tremiti, a tiny archipelago connected to Vieste by regular ferries. While in Vieste, make for the **castle,** its interior not open to the public but offering good views from its high position overlooking the beaches and town.

Where to Stay & Eat

★ $$–$$$ ✕ **San Michele.** Dine on exquisite Gargano fare at this charmingly intimate eatery on the town's main street. Their legendary antipasti include grilled eggplant and marinated anchovies. The porcini mushrooms picked from the region's Foresta Umbra are worth the visit alone. ⊠ *Viale XXIV Maggio 72* ☎ *0884/708143* ▤ *AE, DC, MC, V* ☺ *Closed Mon. and Jan.–mid-Mar.*

★ $$$$ 🏨 **Pizzomunno.** Probably the most luxurious resort on the Gargano, Pizzomunno is right on the beach and surrounded by an extensive park. It is large, white, modern, air-conditioned, and well equipped. The rooms are ample and plush, all with terraces. Here you can unwind, or try your hand at tennis or archery. ⊠ *Spiaggia di Pizzomunno, 71019* ☎ *0884/*

708741 ☎ 0884/707325 ⬦ 183 rooms ⚬ 3 restaurants, 3 tennis courts, 2 pools, health club, sauna, archery, cinema, dance club, children's programs ☰ AE, DC, MC, V ☉ Closed mid-Oct.–early Apr. ⎰○⎱ BP.

$ ⌂ **Punta San Francesco.** After starting its life as an olive-oil factory, this hotel was tastefully refurbished in the mid-1990s. Thanks to its location near the waterfront in the heart of old Vieste, it is both quiet and close to the action. The owner is a warm, welcoming friend (and ardent promoter of local culture) to all who arrive, and the view from the rooftop is beautiful, especially at dawn. ⊠ Via San Francesco 2, 71019 ☎ 0884/701422 ☎ 0884/701424 ⬦ 14 rooms ☰ MC, V ⎰○⎱ EP.

Peschici

⑮ 22 km (14 mi) northwest of Vieste, 199 km (124 mi) northwest of Bari.

Peschici is a pleasant resort on Gargano's north shore, a cascade of white-washed houses and streets with a beautiful view over a sweeping cove. Some surrounding areas are particularly popular with campers from northern Europe. Development has not wreaked too much havoc on the town: the mazelike center retains its characteristic low houses topped with little Byzantine cupolas.

Rodi Garganico

⑯ 20 km (12 mi) west of Peschici, 40 km (25 mi) west of Vieste.

This fishing village squeezed between the hills and the sea takes its name from the island of Rhodes, recalling its former Greek population. Ringed by pine woods and citrus groves, Rodi is linked by hydrofoils with the Isole Tremiti. Warning: the place gets hectic in July and August.

off the beaten path

ISOLE TREMITI – A ferry service from Termoli, west of the Gargano (1¾ hours), and hydrofoil service from Vieste, Peschici, and Rodi Garganico (40 minutes to one hour) connect the mainland with these three small islands north of the Gargano. Although somewhat crowded with Italian tourists in summer, they are famed for their sea caves, pine forests, and craggy limestone formations. Interesting medieval churches and fortifications dot the islands.

Where to Eat

$–$$ ✕ **Il Gabbiano.** Admire the view facing the sea in Rodi Garganico at this cheerful restaurant (which also serves as a private beach in summer) while savoring freshly caught seafood. Order the sublime *fritto misto* and squeeze lemon juice onto the various sea creatures lightly fried in flour. ⊠ Via Trieste 16 ☎ 0884/965283 ☰ AE, V ☉ Closed Thurs. in Nov.–Mar.

Foresta Umbra

★ **⑰** 25 km (16 mi) south of Rodi Garganico, 30 km (19 mi) southwest of Vieste.

In the middle of the Gargano Promontory is the majestic Foresta Umbra (Shady Forest), a dense growth of beech, maple, sycamore, and oak generally found in more northerly climates, thriving here because of the altitude, 3,200 feet above sea level. Between the trees in this national park are occasional dramatic vistas opening out over the Golfo di Manfredonia. From the north coast, take harrowingly curvy S528 (midway between Peschici and Rodi Garganico) south to head through the interior of the Gargano (do it during the day), or try the gentler ascent between Mattinata and Vieste on S89.

Monte Sant'Angelo

★ ⑱ *16 km (10 mi) north of Manfredonia, 60 km (19 mi) southwest of Vieste.*

Perched amid olive groves on the limestone cliffs overlooking the gulf is the town of Monte Sant'Angelo. Pilgrims have flocked here for nearly 1,500 years—among them, St. Francis of Assisi and crusaders setting off for the Holy Land from the then-flourishing port of Manfredonia. Monte Sant'Angelo is centered on the **Santuario di San Michele** (Sanctuary of San Michele), built over the grotto where the archangel Michael is believed to have appeared before shepherds in the year 490. Walk down a long series of steps to get to the grotto itself; on its walls you can see the hand tracings left by pilgrims.

The **Tomba di Rotari** (Tomb of Rotari), believed to have been a medieval baptistery, has some remarkable 12th-century reliefs. It's reached by steps down and to the left from the Santuario di San Michele. Steep steps lead up to the large, ruined **Castello Normano** (Norman Castle) that dominates the town, with a view of the intricate pattern of the streets and steps winding their way up the side of the valley. Monte Sant'Angelo's medieval quarter, the **Rione Junno,** is a maze of little white houses squeezed into a corner of the narrow valley.

Where to Stay

¢–$ 🏨 **Rotary Hotel.** This simple but welcoming modern hotel is set amid olive and almond groves just outside town. Most rooms have basic decor and terraces with views of the Golfo di Manfredonia. ⊠ *Via Pulsano, Km. 1, 71037* ☎ *0884/562146* 🖷 *0884/562147* ⊕ *www.hotelsantangelo. com/rotary_hotel.htm* 🛏 *24 rooms* ⚘ *Restaurant; no a/c* ⊟ *AE, MC, V* ⏐⚇⏐ *BP.*

Shopping

Most food shops in the Junno sell a local specialty called *ostia piena,* a pastry made with candied almonds and wafers of a type similar to communion hosts. The best place to get them—and munch on them—is at the southern end of the Junno, by the Villa Comunale.

San Giovanni Rotondo

⑲ *25 km (16 mi) west of Monte Sant'Angelo, 85 km (52 mi) southwest of Vieste.*

The ancient village of San Giovanni Rotondo, on the winding S272, is a relatively recent center of religious pilgrimage. Devotees flock here to pay their respects to the shrine and **Tomba di Padre Pio** (⊠ Chiesa Santa Maria delle Grazie, Piazzale Santa Maria delle Grazie). Pio (1887–1968) was a monk revered for his pious life, his miraculous intercessions, and his having received the stigmata (the signs of Christ's wounds).

> **en route** A short ride south on S273, and then east (left) at L'Annunziata, will take you back to Manfredonia, where you can link up with the coastal road to return to Bari.

Where to Stay

$$ 🏨 **Grand Hotel degli Angeli.** Indeed grand, this hotel lies amid verdant gardens, fountains, and a mixture of pious and flamboyant statues. Relax on the expansive terrace before dining in one of the very decent restaurants. The functional guest rooms are decorated in light, soothing colors. ⊠ *Viale Padre Pio, 71013* ☎ *0882/454646* 🖷 *0882/454645* ⊕ *www.grandhoteldegliangeli.it* ⤵ *98 rooms* ⚲ *2 restaurants, minibars, playground* ☰ *AE, DC, MC, V* ⏐⭘⏐ *BP.*

THE TRULLI DISTRICT

The inland area to the southeast of Bari is one of Italy's oddest enclaves, mostly flat terrain given over to olive cultivation and interspersed with the idiosyncratic habitations that have lent their names to the district. The origins of the beehive-shape trulli go back to the 13th century and maybe further. The trulli, found nowhere else in the world, are built of local limestone, without mortar, and with a hole in the top for escaping smoke. Some are painted with mystical or religious symbols; some are isolated, and others are joined together with roofs on various levels. Legends of varying credibility surround the trulli (for example, that they were originally built so that residents could quickly take apart their homes when the tax collectors came by). The center of trulli country is Alberobello in the enchanting Valle d'Itria: it has the greatest concentration of the buildings. You will spot them all over this region, some in disrepair but always adding a quirky charm to the landscape.

Alberobello

⓴   *59 km (37 mi) southeast of Bari, 45 km (28 mi) north of Taranto.*

Although Alberobello is something of a tourist trap, the amalgamation of more than 1,000 trulli huddled together along steep, narrow streets is nonetheless an unusual sight (as well as a national monument and a UNESCO World Heritage Site). As one of the most popular tourist destinations in Puglia, Alberobello has spawned some excellent restaurants (and some not-so-excellent trinket shops). Alberobello's largest trullo, the **Trullo Sovrano,** is up the hill through the trulli zone (head up Corso Vittorio Emanuele past the obelisk and the Basilica). Though you can go inside, where you'll find a fairly conventional domestic dwelling, the real interest is the structure itself.

Where to Stay & Eat

$$$–$$$$ ✕ **Il Poeta Contadino.** Proprietor Marco Leonardo serves "creative regional **Fodor's**Choice cooking" in this upscale country restaurant in the heart of the attractive ★ trulli zone. The room features ancient stone walls, candlelight tables, and a refined, understated ambience. Dishes might include *triglie vinaigrette alla menta* (red mullet with a mint vinaigrette) or *coda di rospo con pomodoro candito salsa al basilico* (monkfish in a tomato and basil sauce). In season, try anything with white truffle. The well-respected *L'espresso* magazine rates the extensive wine list and dining experience very highly. ⊠ *Via Indipendenza 21* ☎ *080/4321917* ⌖ *Reservations essential* ☰ *AE, DC, MC, V* ☯ *Closed Mon. and Jan. 7–31. No dinner Sun.*

★ **$–$$$** ✕ **Trullo d'Oro.** This welcoming rustic restaurant set in five trulli houses has dark-wood beams, whitewashed walls, and an open hearth. Local country cooking includes dishes using lamb and veal, vegetable and cheese antipasti, pasta dishes with crisp raw vegetables on the side, and almond pastries. Among the specialties are roast lamb with *lampasciuni* (a type of wild onion) and spaghetti *al trullo,* made with tomatoes, *rughetta* (arugula), and four cheeses. ⊠ *Via F. Cavallotti 27* ☎ *080/4323909* ⌖ *Reservations essential* ☰ *AE, DC, MC, V* ☯ *Closed Mon. (except in June–Aug.) and Jan. 10–31. No dinner Sun.*

$$–$$$ ▤ **Dei Trulli.** Trulli-style cottages in a pine wood near the trulli zone make this a magical place to stay. It's decorated with rustic furnishings and folk-art rugs. The modestly priced restaurant serves local specialties. You're expected to take half or full board in high season. ⊠ *Via Cadore 28–32, 70011* ☎ *080/4323555* ⤶ *080/4323560* ⊕ *http://www.hoteldeitrulli. it* ⇆ *28 rooms* ⌂ *Restaurant, minibars, pool* ☰ *AE, MC, V* ▯⊙▯ *MAP.*

Grotte di Castellana

㉑ *20 km (12 mi) northwest of Alberobello, 63 km (52 mi) southeast of Bari.*

The Grotte di Castellana is a huge network of caves discovered in 1938. You can take one of the hourly guided tours through the grottoes filled with fantastically shaped stalagmites and stalactites, part of the largest network of caves on the Italian mainland. The two-hour tour takes you on an extra 2-km (1½-mi) hike to another cave (Grotta Bianca). ⊠ *Piazzale Anelli* ☎ *080/4998211* ⊕ *www.grottedicastellana.it* ▱ *€9 1-hr tour, €14 2-hr tour* ☯ *Apr.–Oct., daily 8:30–7, until 9 in Aug.; Nov.–Mar., daily 9:30–4. Last 2-hr tour leaves 1 hr before closing. English 1-hr tours at 1 and 6:30; English 2-hr tours at 11 and 4.*

Locorotondo

㉒ *9 km (5½ mi) southeast of Alberobello, 40 km (25 mi) north of Taranto.*

Locorotondo is an attractive hilltop town within the trulli district in the Itria Valley (take S172 from Alberobello). The *rotondo* in the town's name refers to the circular pattern of the houses, swirling down from the top. From the top of the town, on the road to Martina Franca, a verdant public garden gives way to lookout points over the entire Valle d'Itria, a landscape dotted with olive groves and trulli. Wander around the evocative alleyways of the *centro storico* (historic center) and look for the blazing yellow cathedral in Piazza Fra Giuseppe Andria Rolleo.

Where to Eat

$ ✕ **Centro Storico.** The refined ambience and cuisine of this restaurant, set apart from the tourist haunts, make it pricier than its neighbors. But the food and service are worth it. Try such regional dishes as *sformato di verdura* (vegetable stew) and *agnello alla castellanese* (local lamb). ⊠ *Via Eroi di Dogali 6* ☎ *080/4315473* ⌲ *Reservations essential* ⊟ *AE, MC, V* ☺ *Closed Wed. and 2 wks in Mar.*

Ostuni

㉓ *50 km (30 mi) west of Brindisi, 40 km (25 mi) northeast of Locorotondo.*

This sun-bleached, medieval town lies on three hills a short distance from the coast. From a distance, Ostuni is a jumble of blazingly white houses and churches spilling over a hilltop and overlooking the sea—thus earning it the nickname *la città bianca* (the White City). The **old town**, on the highest of the hills, has steep cobbled lanes, wrought-iron lanterns, some good local restaurants, and stupendous views out over the coast and the surrounding plain. **Piazza Libertà**, the city's main square, divides the new town to the west and the old town to the east.

Where to Stay & Eat

$$ ✕ **Osteria del Tempo Perso.** Buried in the side streets of the old town, this laid-back restaurant has rough-hewn stone interiors, with intriguing objects adorning the walls. It is open July–September nightly and October–June for Saturday dinner and Sunday lunch. Service is friendly and preparations focus on local cuisine such as delectable stuffed hot peppers and orecchiette with bitter greens and olive oil. ⊠ *Via G. Tanzarella Vitale 47* ☎ *0831/303320* ⊟ *AE, MC, V* ☺ *Closed Mon. and Dec. 27–Jan. 15; no lunch July–Sept.; Oct.–June, Sat. dinner and Sun. lunch only.*

$ ✕ **Vecchia Ostuni.** In the heart of the old town, enjoy Puglian grills and seafood, loved of the locals and served up here. Savor the restaurant's famed antipasti before settling down to *scallopine al vino bianco e funghi* (veal scallops with white wine and mushrooms) or *costata di maiale alla brace* (pork chop char-grilled). The homemade desserts are worthwhile, and there's a good selection of local wines. ⊠ *Largo Lanza 9* ☎ *0831/303308* ⊟ *AE, DC, MC, V* ☺ *Closed Tues. and Jan.*

$ ▦ **Incanto.** From the guest rooms of this large, modern hotel about a mile outside the old town, you can admire the expansive countryside, sea, and whitewashed hilltop city in the distance. It makes a convenient overnight base for visiting the area. ⊠ *Via dei Colli, 72017* ☎ *0831/301781* ▤ *0831/338302* ⊕ *www.hotelincanto.it* ⇱ *75 rooms, 5 suites* ⌂ *2 restaurants, minibars, 2 bars* ⊟ *AE, DC, MC, V* ¶☺◉ *BP.*

Nightlife

Especially in summer, Ostuni is livelier by night than you might expect. **Riccardo Cafè** (⊠ Via G. Tanzarello Vitale ☎ 0831/306046) is the hippest spot in town for a drink or a coffee before or after dinner. Grottoes, neon lighting, and contemporary sofas transport you to another Ostuni entirely.

Martina Franca

㉔ *6 km (4 mi) south of Locorotondo, 36 km (22 mi) north of Taranto.*

Martina Franca is a beguiling town with a dazzling mixture of medieval and baroque architecture in the light-color local stone. Ornate balconies hang above the twisting, narrow streets, with little alleys leading off into the hills. Martina Franca was developed as a military stronghold in the 14th century, when a surrounding wall with 24 towers was built, but now all that remains of the wall are the four gates that had once been the only entrances to the town. Each July and August, the town holds a music festival.

Where to Stay & Eat

$ ✕ **Da Gianni.** Sample the best *pizze* in town at this welcoming wood-filled eatery replete with curious collages on the walls. Try their fabulous antipasti, including *scamorzine calde e speck* (small melting soft cheese balls and bacon) and bountiful plates of mozzarella served with roast potatoes. ✉ *Via Vittorio Emmanuelle 7* ☎ *080/4306323* ▤ *MC, V* ⊘ *Closed Mon.*

$–$$ ▦ **Park Hotel San Michele.** This garden hotel makes a pleasant base in the warm months, thanks to its pool. The two categories of single rooms have a small price difference; if alone, opt for the higher-price ones. All rooms are spacious, some embellished with handsome furniture and including complimentary bowls of fruit. ✉ *Viale Carella 9, 74015* ☎ *080/4807053* ▤*080/4808895* ⊕*www.parkhotelsm.it* ⬎*85 rooms* ⑃*Restaurant, pool, bar* ▤ *AE, DC, MC, V* ⑲| *BP.*

ACROSS THE HEEL & SOUTH TO LECCE

This far south, the mountains run out of steam and the land is uniformly flat. The monotonous landscape, besides being agriculturally important, is redeemed by some of the region's best sandy coastline and a handful of small, alluring fishing towns, such as Otranto and Gallipoli. Taranto and Brindisi don't quite fit this description: both are big ports where historical importance is obscured by unsightly heavy industry. Nonetheless, Taranto has its archaeological museum, and Brindisi marks the end of the Via Appia (the Imperial Roman road). Farther south, in Salento (the Salentine Peninsula), Lecce is an unexpected oasis of grace and sophistication, and its swirling architecture will melt even the most uncompromising critic of the baroque.

Taranto

㉕ *100 km (62 mi) southeast of Bari, 40 km (25 mi) south of Martina Franca.*

Taranto (the stress is on the first syllable) was an important port even in Roman times. It lies toward the back of the instep of the boot on the broad Mare Grande bay, which is connected to a small internal Mare Piccolo basin by two narrow channels, one artificial and one natural. The old town is a series of old *palazzi* in varying states of decay and narrow cobblestone streets on an island between the larger and smaller bodies of water, linked by causeways; the modern city stretches inward along the mainland. Circumnavigate the old town and take in a dramatic panorama to the north, revealing Italy's shipping industry at its busiest: steel works, dockyards, a bay dotted with fishing boats, and a fish market teeming with pungent activity along the old town's western edge. Little remains of Taranto's past except the 14th-century church of **San Domenico** (⊠ Via Duomo 33) jutting into the sea at one end of the island, and its famous naval academy.

★ A compendium on the millennia of local history, Taranto's **Museo Nazionale** has a large collection of prehistoric, Greek, and Roman artifacts discovered mainly in the immediate vicinity, including Puglian tombs dating from before 1000 BC. The museum is just over the bridge from the old town, on the promontory. The collection is a testament to the importance of this ancient port, which has always taken full advantage of its unique trading position at the end of the Italian peninsula. Telephone ahead before visiting the museum, as hours can be irregular. ⊠ *Corso Umberto 41* ☎ *099/4532112* ☞ *€3* ☉ *Daily 8:30–7:30.*

Where to Stay

$$ ☐ **Grand Hotel Delfino.** This well-equipped hotel on the waterfront caters mainly to business clients, but it's a good, central place to unwind after exploring the city. There are sea views from the large modern lounge, the attractive terrace, and the airy rooms with balconies. The restaurant features regional seafood. ⊠ *Viale Virgilio 66, 74100* ☎ *099/ 7323232* ☒ *099/7304654* ⊕ *www.grandhoteldelfino.it* ☞ *204 rooms* ☆ *Restaurant, minibars, pool, meeting room* ▭ *AE, DC, MC, V* ☉ *BP.*

Brindisi

❷⁶ *114 km (71 mi) southeast of Bari, 72 km (45 mi) east of Taranto.*

Occupying the head of a deep inlet on the eastern Adriatic coast, Brindisi (the stress is on the first syllable) has long been one of Italy's most important ports. Today most travelers think of it only as a terminus for the ferry crossing that links Italy with Greece, and the seedy area around the port seems to confirm this. However, the impression fails to give credit to the broader importance of the city (which has a population of nearly 100,000) and to the assortment of interesting 13th- and 14th-century churches in the atmospheric old town. Brindisi has always played an important role as gateway to the eastern Mediterranean and beyond and in the Middle Ages it was the departure point for several crusades to the Holy Land. That said, if you're looking for a place to spend the night in conjunction with a ferry departure or arrival, you'd be better served in nearby Lecce or Ostuni.

The core of Brindisi is at the head of a deep channel, which branches into two harbors, with the city between them. Look for the steeple of the cathedral to get your bearings, but go beyond it and down the steps to the water's edge. To the left is a tall **Roman column** and the base of another one next to it. These columns were built in the 2nd century AD and marked the end of the Via Appia (Appian Way), the Imperial Roman road that led from the capital to this important southeastern seaport. ⊠ *Viale Regina Margherita.*

The **Duomo,** a short walk from Brindisi's Roman column, has a mosaic floor in its apse that is worth the stop; the floor dates from the 12th century, although much of the rest of the cathedral was rebuilt in the 18th. ⊠ *Piazza Duomo* ☉ *Daily 7–1 and 4–8.*

The **Castello Svevo,** one of the defense fortifications built by the illustrious Frederick II in the 13th century, guards the larger of Brindisi's two inner harbors. It isn't accessible to the public. ☒ *Piazza Castello.*

Where to Stay

$ 🏨 **Mediterraneo.** Comfort and a central location are the advantages of this modern business-oriented Best Western hotel. Rooms have double-glazed windows and most have balconies. ☒ *Viale Aldo Moro 70, 72100* ☎ *0831/582811* 🖷 *0831/587858* ⊕ *www.hotelmediterraneo.it* 🛏 *65 rooms* 🗠 *Restaurant* ▤ *AE, DC, MC, V* ⏐○⏐ *BP.*

★ $$ ✕ **Lanterna.** An elegant dining experience awaits at this handsome, high-celinged 16th-century palazzo near the Duomo. Cool off in the equally enchanting courtyard under pergolas while sampling superb fish creations like *tubettini con frutti di mare* (small tubular pasta with seafood). ☒ *Via Tarantini 14-16* ☎ *081/564026* ▤ *AE, DC, MC, V* ⊘ *Closed Sun. and Aug.*

Lecce

❷❼ *40 km (25 mi) southeast of Brindisi, 87 km (54 mi) east of Taranto.*

Fodor'sChoice
★
Lecce is the crown jewel of the mezzogiorno. While the city may be affectionately referred to as "the Florence of the South," that sobriquet does an injustice to Lecce's uniqueness in the Italian landscape. Though the city's great shopping, modern bars, and the impossibly intricate baroque architecture conjure up images of the Renaissance masterpieces of the North, Lecce's lively streets, laid-back student cafés, magical evening passeggiata (stroll), and openness to visitors are distinctively southern. The city is a cosmopolitan oasis two steps from the idyllic Otranto-Brindisi coastline and a hop from the olive-grove countryside of Puglia. Undiscovered by tourists, Lecce exudes an optimism and youthful joie de vivre unparalleled in any other baroque showcase. There is no Lecce of the North.

Although Lecce was founded before the time of the ancient Greeks, it's often associated with the term *Lecce baroque,* the result of a citywide impulse in the 17th century to redo the town in the baroque fashion. But this was baroque with a difference. Although such architecture is often heavy and monumental, here it took on a lighter, more fanciful air. Just look at the church of **Santa Croce,** with the **Palazzo della Prefettura** abutting it. Although every column, window, pediment, and balcony is given a curling baroque touch—and then an extra one for good measure—the overall effect is lighthearted. The buildings' scales are unintimidating and the local stone is a glowing honey color: it couldn't look menacing if it tried. ☒ *Via Umberto I* ☎ *0832/241927* ⊘ *Daily 8–1 and 5–8.*

Lecce's ornate **Duomo,** first built in 1114 but reconstructed in baroque style from 1659 to 1670, is uncharacteristically set in a solitary lateral square off a main street, rather than at a crossroads of pedestrian traffic. To the left of the Duomo, the more austere **bell tower,** reconstructed by master baroque architect Giuseppe Zimbalo in the 17th century, takes on a surreal golden hue each dusk. The facades of the adjoining 18th-century **Palazzo Vescovile,** farther past the right side of the Duomo, and the **Seminario** on the Piazza's right edge, complement the rich ornamentation of the Duomo to create an effect almost as splendid as that of Santa Croce. The Seminario's tranquil **cloister** is also worth a visit. ✉ *Piazza Duomo, off Corso V. Emanuele* ☎ *0832/308884* ☉ *Daily 8–1 and 5–8.*

In the middle of **Piazza Sant'Oronzo,** the city's putative center, surrounded by cafés, pastry shops, and newsstands, is a **Roman column** of the same era and style as the one in Brindisi, but imaginatively surmounted by an 18th-century statue of the city's patron saint, Orontius. Next to the column, the shallow rows of seats in the **Anfiteatro Romano** suggest Verona's arena or a small-scale Roman Colosseum.

Where to Stay & Eat

$–$$ ✕ **Villa G. C. della Monica.** Set in a gracious 17th-century villa complete with palm trees, courtyard, and fountain, this restaurant comes into its own with summer alfresco dining in the garden. The menu focuses almost entirely on seafood, with the traditional Puglian *antipasto misto,* a generous spread of appetizers, followed by seasonal seafood dishes such as *maccheroni con vongole veraci, cozze tarantine, e fagioli bianchi* (macaroni with small Adriatic clams, mussels, and white beans) and fresh grilled fish. It's particularly suitable for families with young children, as there's lots of space to run around. ✉ *Via SS. Giacomo e Filippo 40* ☎ *0832/458432* ▤ *AE, MC, V* ☉ *Closed Tues.*

$ ✕ **La Torre di Merlino.** This lively eatery with handsome old-stone interiors and dark wooden furniture serves generous, innovative salads. Customers are predominantly students and arty types, tended to by an amiable staff. ✉ *Vico G.B. del Tufo 10* ☎ *0832/241874* ⟡ *Reservations essential* ▤ *AE, MC, V* ☉ *No dinner Mon.*

★ **¢–$** ✕ **Trattoria Casareccia.** This is an excellent place to try traditional *pugliese* cooking in a warm and casual setting—white walls and loud chatter. Don't expect a menu; choose from the daily specials, which might include homemade whole wheat pasta served with a delicate sauce of tomato and ricotta forte. The rustic *purè di fave e cicoria* (puree of fava bean with chicory) is topped with local olive oil; mix it together before eating. Service is informal and welcoming. ✉ *Via Costadura 19* ☎ *0832/ 245178* ▤ *AE, MC, V* ☉ *Closed Mon., Aug. 27–Sept. 11, 1 wk for Easter, and Dec. 23–Jan. 2. No dinner Sun.*

$–$$ 🏨 **President.** Rub elbows with visiting dignitaries at this new business hotel near Piazza Mazzini. The reception is expansive and furnishings are 1980s tasteful, with an emphasis on primary colors and modernist lamps. ✉ *Via Salandra 6, 73100* ☎ *0832/311881* 🖶 *0832/372283* ⇨ *154 rooms* ₰ *Restaurant, minibars, bar, lounge, meeting room, parking (fee)* ▤ *AE, DC, MC, V* ℔ *BP.*

$–$$ 🏨 **Risorgimento.** An old-fashioned Liberty-style hotel in an 18th-century palace, this hotel combines historic charm with modern comfort. For undisturbed sleep and summertime siestas during longer stays, ask for rooms overlooking the backstreets or the courtyard. The roof garden has great views. ✉ *Via Augusto Imperatore 19, Piazza S. Oronzo, 73100* ☎ *0832/242125* 🖶 *0832/245571* ⊕ *www.webshop.it/*

hotelrisorgimento ⤳ *57 rooms* ⟂ *Restaurant, minibars, lounge, meeting room, parking (fee)* ⊟ *AE, DC, MC, V* ⊠ *BP.*

¢ ⌘ **Cappello.** You'll find the grand art nouveau facade of this decent hotel in easy distance from the train station, outside the old city walls (a mere 10-minute walk from the town center). Space is dear in the guest rooms, but they are fine enough for a short stay. Rooms at the back get a little noisy because of the nearby railroad. ⊠ *Via Montegrappa 4, 73100* ☎ *0832/308881* 🖷 *0832/301535* ⊕ *www.webshop.it/hotelcappello* ⤳ *32 rooms* ⟂ *Bar, parking (fee)* ⊟ *AE, DC, MC, V* ⊠ *BP.*

Shopping

The best place in town to buy gastronomical delights from the Salento region, including olive oil, ricotta forte, hot pepper sauce, and an assortment of local baked goods, is **Golosità del Salento da Valentina** (⊠ Via A. Petronelli 3 ☎ 0832/300549), a few steps from the Piazza del Duomo. The friendly and helpful owner presses his own olive oil and has infinite patience with—and interest in—visitors from abroad.

Nightlife & the Arts

The most popular hangout for the university crowd is **I Merli** (⊠ Via Federico D'Aragona ☎ 0832/241874), a classy café where scores of locals gather each afternoon and evening for coffee, spirits, and gossip. Hours are 5:30 PM–2 AM (weekends open earlier); closed Monday.

In July, the public gardens are the setting for **drama productions** and, sometimes, opera. A **baroque music festival** is held in churches throughout the city in September. For details on forthcoming events call the **Tourist Information Office** (☎ 0832/248092).

Otranto

28 *36 km (22 mi) southeast of Lecce, 188 km (117 mi) southeast of Bari.*

In one of the first great Gothic novels, Horace Walpole's 1764 *The Castle of Otranto,* the English writer immortalized the city and its mysterious medieval fortress. Otranto (the stress is on the first syllable) has likewise had more than its share of dark thrills. As the easternmost point in Italy—and therefore closest to the Balkan peninsula—it's often borne the brunt of foreign invasions during its checkered history. A flourishing port from ancient Greek times, Otranto (*Hydruntum* to the Romans) has a history like most of southern Italy: after the fall of the western Roman Empire, centuries of Byzantine rule interspersed with Saracen incursions, followed by the arrival of the Normans and other dynasties from northern Europe. The town was sacked by Turkish forces in 1480 and occupied for a year, never recovering its former glory. Modern Otranto's dank cobblestone alleyways alternatively reveal dusty, forgotten doorways and modern Italian fashion chains, and the spooky castle still looms above, between city and sea. On a clear day you can see across to Albania.

The historic city center nestles within impressive city walls and bastions, dominated by the famous **Castello,** which is attributed to the Spanish of the 16th century. ⊠ *Piazza Castello* ☎ *0832/930722* ⊙ *Tues.–Sun. 9–1* ⊠ *Free.*

The real jewel in Otranto is the **Cattedrale,** originally begun by the Normans and conserving an extraordinary 12th-century mosaic pavement in the nave and aisles. ⊠ *Piazza Basilica* ☎ *0836/802720* ✆ *Free* ⊙ *Daily 8:30–noon and 5–7:30.*

off the beaten path

COASTLINE SOUTH TO LEUCA – The coastal road between Otranto and Leuca is one of the most beautiful in southern Italy. Sandy beaches are replaced by rocky outcrops and sheer cliffs watched over by scattered castles and seaside pleasure palaces. Along the way, **Santa Cesarea Terme,** with a pleasant shoreline and famous fanciful Moorish resort, and **Castro,** with another attractive marina, are worthwhile stops; this is land that few foreign tourists traverse. At the end of the journey, **Capo Santa Maria di Leuca** has a lighthouse at the southeasternmost point in Italy, the end of the Puglian Aqueduct, and the quiet, sparse basilica of **Santa Maria Finibus Terrae** (land's end). The **Marina di Leuca,** below, is a little fishing village with excursion boats and a few summertime hotels and bars. If, after the drive, you're heading back to Lecce or points east, the inland highway is a faster route.

Where to Stay

¢ 🏨 **La Fattoria.** This working farm (dairy cows and olives) lies 3 km (2 mi) southwest of Otranto, off the road to Uggiano. It makes an excellent base for visiting Lecce, Gallipoli, and other sights in the Salentine Peninsula. The restaurant specializes in organic food but operates only weekends (and evenings in summer), which means you have to fend for yourself the rest of the time. Bring bath towels and soap! ⊠ *SS Otranto–Uggiano Bivio Casamassetta, 73028* ☎☎ *0836/804651* ⇱ *5 apartments, 5 bungalows* ⚙ *Restaurant, playground* ⊟ *AE, DC, MC, V* ⍑⊙⍑ *BP.*

Shopping

Otranto's old town has been tastefully gentrified and has an array of shops displaying local products and chain boutiques. **Texum** (⊠ Corso Garibaldi 43) specializes in objects d'art sculpted from *pietra leccese,* the soft local limestone used for much of the baroque architecture in the Salentine Peninsula. If you want to stock up on regional wines and olive oil, stop off at **Il Giardino del Re** (⊠ Corso Garibaldi 64), where wine-tasting sessions are frequently arranged.

Gallipoli

㉙ *37 km (23 mi) south of Lecce, 190 km (118 mi) southeast of Bari.*

The fishing port of Gallipoli, on the Golfo di Taranto, is divided between a new town, on the mainland, and a pleasant fortified town, across a 17th-century bridge, crowded onto its own small island in the gulf. The Greeks called it Kallipolis, the Romans Anxa. Like the infamous Turkish town of the same name on the Dardanelles, the Italian Gallipoli occupies a strategic location and thus was repeatedly attacked through the centuries—by the Normans in 1071, the Venetians in 1484, the British in 1809. Today, life in Gallipoli revolves around its fishing trade. Bright fishing boats in primary colors breeze in and out of the bay during the day, and Gallipoli's fish market, below the bridge, throbs with activity all morning.

Gallipoli's historic quarter, a mix of narrow alleys and squares, is guarded by **Castello Aragonese,** a massive fortification that grew out of an earlier Byzantine fortress that you can still see at the southeast corner. After being an operative base for the busy *Guardia di Finanza* (revenue police), it's now being renovated and adapted for future use as a public monument. Gallipoli's **Duomo** (⊠ Via Antonietta De Pace ☎ 0833/261987) open daily 9–12:30 and 5–8, is a notable baroque church. The church of **La Purissima** (⊠ Riviera Nazario Sauro ☎ 0833/261699) has a stuccoed interior as elaborate as a wedding cake, with an especially noteworthy tiled floor. You can visit daily 9–12:30 and 5–7:30.

Where to Stay & Eat

$–$$ ✕ **Marechiaro.** Unless you arrive by boat—as many do—you have to cross a little bridge to reach this simple port-side restaurant, not far from the town's historic center. It's built out onto the sea, replete with wood paneling, flowers, and terraces with panoramic coastal views. Try the renowned *zuppa di pesce alla gallipolina* (fish stew), succulent shellfish, and linguine with seafood. ⊠ *Lungomare Marconi* ☎ *0833/266143* ▤ *AE, DC, MC, V* ☺ *Closed Tues. Oct.–May.*

★ $$$ ▥ **Costa Brada.** The rooms all have terraces with sea views at this modern white beach hotel of classic Mediterranean design. The interiors are uncluttered and tasteful; rooms 110 through 114 are particularly spacious and overlook the beach. The hotel accepts only half- or full-board guests in high season. ⊠ *Baia Verde, Litoranea Santa Maria di Leuca, 73014* ☎ *0833/202551* ▤ *0833/202555* ⊕ *www.grandhotelcostabrada. it* ⇖*78 rooms* ⚹ *2 restaurants, snack bar, 2 pools (1 indoor), gym, sauna, shop* ▤ *AE, DC, MC, V* ▮◉▮ *MAP.*

Sports & the Outdoors

BEACHES Ample swimming, water sports, and clean, fine sand make Gallipoli's **beaches** a good choice for families. The 5-km (3-mi) expanse of sand sweeping south from town has both public and private beaches, the latter equipped with changing rooms, sun beds, and umbrellas. Water sports equipment can be bought or rented at the waterfront shops in town.

PUGLIA A TO Z

To research prices, get advice from other travelers, and book travel arrangements, visit www.fodors.com.

AIR TRAVEL

CARRIERS Several airlines serve the cities of Bari and Brindisi: Alitalia flies regularly between Bari and Brindisi and Rome and Milan; Volare-Air Europe connects Bari with Rome and Milan; Air One serves Bari with flights from Turin, Milan, and Rome, and operates one daily Brindisi-Milan flight; and Air Dolomiti connects Bari with Verona and Turin. Pescara, farther up the Adriatic in Abruzzo, but convenient to Puglia, is served by Ryanair from London and Air One from Milan.

🛪 Airlines & Contacts **Air Dolomiti** ☎ 800/013366 ⊕ www.airdolomiti.it. **Air Europe** ☎ 848/848130, 080/5370495 in Bari ⊕ www.aireurope.it. **Air One** ☎ 848/848130, 080/5316153 in Bari ⊕ www.air-one.it. **Alitalia** ☎ 848/865641 ⊕ www.alitalia.com. **Ryanair** ☎ 199/114114 ⊕ www.ryanair.com.

AIRPORTS

A regular bus service connects the two airports, Bari-Palese (about 10 km [7 mi] northwest of the city center) and Brindisi-Papola (8 km [5 mi] to the north), with their respective cities. Alitalia buses provide service from the cities to arrivals and departures at both airports. Many hotels and taxis within other outlying cities provide service directly to and from the airports, which can be much simpler than public transport—call your hotel for details.

🛪 Airport Information **Bari-Palese** ⊠ Strada Provinciale Aeroporto ☎ 080/5835204 ⊕ www.seap-puglia.it. **Brindisi-Papola** ⊠ Via de Simone Ruggero 1 ☎ 0831/4117208 ⊕ www.seap-puglia.it

BOAT & FERRY TRAVEL

Ferries ply the waters from Bari and Brindisi to Greece (Corfu, Igoumenitsa, Patras, and Kephalonia), Turkey, Albania, and even Egypt and Croatia. Brindisi's connection to Patras is covered by some rail passes, thus immensely popular with backpackers.

🛳 Boat & Ferry Information **Adriatica di Navigazione** to Albania and the Tremiti islands; agents at A. Galli e Figlio ⊠ Corso Manfredi 4, 71043 Manfredonia ☎ 0884/582520 ⊠ Gargano Viaggi Piazza Roma 7, 71019 Vieste ☎ 0884/708501 ⊕ www.adriatica.it. **Blue Star Ferries** only Brindisi to Corfu and Igoumenitsa; agents at Il Globo ⊠ Corso Garibaldi 65, 72100 Brindisi ☎ 0831/527684 ⊕ www.bluestarferries.com.

BUS TRAVEL

Compared with rail, travel times by bus into Puglia from Naples on the far side of the Apennines are substantially shorter. From Rome, contact Autolinee Marozzi, at their Rome office or in Bari. If traveling between Naples and Foggia, contact CLP. Miccolis runs a daily Naples-Lecce service, which takes five hours, about half as long as by train.

Direct, if not always frequent, connections operate between most destinations in Puglia. SITA is the main bus company operating in the region. In many cases bus service is the backup when problems with train service arise. to the train service.

🚌 Bus Information **Autolinee Marozzi** ☎ 06/44249519 in Rome, 080/5562446 in Bari. **CLP** ☎ 081/5311706. **Miccolis** ☎ 081/200380. **SITA** ⊠ Piazza Aldo Moro 15/a ☎ 080/5213714.

CAR RENTAL

🚗 Local Agencies **Avis** ⊠ Via L. Zuppetta 5/a, Bari ☎ 080/5247154 ⊠ Aeroporto Palese, Bari ☎ 080/5316168 ⊠ Piazza Cairoli 25, Brindisi ☎ 0831/526407 ⊠ Aeroporto Papola, Brindisi ☎ 0831/418826 ⊠ Train station, Foggia ☎ 0881/678912 ⊠ Viale Grassi 158, Lecce ☎ 0832/228585 ⊠ Corso Umberto 61, Taranto ☎ 099/4532278 ⊕ www.avis.com. **Hertz** ⊠ Aeroporto Palese, Bari ☎ 080/5316171 ⊠ Aeroporto Papola, Brindisi

☎ 0831/413060 ⊕ www.hertz.com. **Maggiore-Budget** ⊠ Viale Ventiquattro Maggio 76, Foggia ☎ 0881/773173.

CAR TRAVEL

Driving is the best way to get around Puglia and the only way to see remote sights. Puglia is linked with the Italian autostrada system, making it just a four- or five-hour drive from Rome to the Gargano Promontory or Bari. Roads are good, and major cities are linked by fast autostrade. Secondary roads connect the whole region; more direct—but sometimes less scenic—routes provide a convenient link between Bari, Brindisi, and Lecce. Highways along the coast are usually accompanied by parallel, slower coastal roads with fewer lanes but beautiful vistas. If you're squeamish about getting lost, don't plan on any night driving in the countryside—the roads can become confusing without the aid of landmarks or large towns.

EMERGENCY   ACI Emergency Service offers 24-hour roadside assistance.
SERVICES   🖪 **ACI dispatchers** ☎ 803/116.

EMERGENCIES

For general emergencies, dial 113. Pharmacies take turns staying open late and on Sunday. A list of hours is posted on each *farmacia* (pharmacy). 🖪 **General Emergencies** ☎ 113.

MAIL & SHIPPING

🖪 Post Offices **Bari** ⊠ Via Amendola 116 ☎ 080/5507236. **Brindisi** ⊠ Piazza Vittoria 8 ☎ 0831/525058.

SAFETY

WOMEN IN   The usual precautions apply here as throughout the south of Italy.
PUGLIA   Women should pay particular attention in Bari and Brindisi, more so by the port in Brindisi and in Bari's old town at night, where seedy characters still abound and evening outings are best done in groups.

TOURS

The Azienda di Promozione Turistica in Bari is the best connection for guided tours in Puglia, otherwise poorly served by tour operators. The office can put you in touch with one of a number of local operators that offer everything from chauffeur-driven cars to a quick regional primer as part of a longer excursion.
🖪 Fees & Schedules **Azienda di Promozione Turistica della Provincia di Bari** ⊠ Piazza Moro 32/a, 70122 ☎ 080/5242244or 080/5242361 ⊕ www.pugliaturismo.it.

TRAIN TRAVEL

Bari is a transit hub for train connections with northern Italy. Good train service, operated by FS (Italian State Railways), links Bari to Brindisi, Lecce, and Taranto, but smaller destinations can often be reached only by completing the trip on a connecting bus operated by the railroad. The private Ferrovie Sud-Est (FSE) line connects the trulli area and Martina Franca with Bari and Taranto, and the fishing port of Gallipoli with Lecce.
🖪 Train Information **FS** ☎ 848/888088. **Ferrovie Sud-Est (FSE)** ☎ 080/5462111 or 0832/668111.

TRAVEL AGENCIES
🔝 Local Agent Referrals **Carlson Wagonlit Travel** ✉ Via Cardassi 56, Bari ☎ 080/5540588 ⊕ www.ewt.it. **Crusi Viaggi e Turismo** ✉ Piazza S. Oronzo 21, Lecce 73100 ☎ 0832/305522 🖷 0832/306208. **Utac Viaggi** ✉ Via Santa Lucia 11, Brindisi 72100 ☎ 0831/524921 🖷 0831/529040 ⊕ www.utacviaggi.it.

VISITOR INFORMATION
🔝 Tourist Information **Alberobello** ✉ Piazza Ferdinando IV, 70011 ☎ 080/4325171. **Bari** ✉ Piazza Moro 32/a, 70122 ☎ 080/5242361 ⊕ www.pugliaturismo.it. **Brindisi** ✉ Lungomare R. Margherita, 72100 ☎ 0831/523072. **Foggia** ✉ Via Perrone 17, 71100 ☎ 0881/723141. **Lecce** ✉ Via Vittorio Emanuele 24, 73100 ☎ 0832/248092. **Ostuni** ✉ Corso Mazzini 6, 72017 ☎ 0831/301268. **San Giovanni Rotondo** ✉ Piazza Europa 104, 71013 ☎ 0882/456240. **Taranto** ✉ Corso Umberto 113, 74100 ☎ 099/4532392. **Trani** ✉ Piazza Trieste 10, 70059 ☎ 0883/585530. **Vieste** ✉ Piazza Kennedy, 71019 ☎ 0884/708806 ✉ Kiosk in Piazza della Repubblica, summer only ☎ 0883/43295.

BASILICATA & CALABRIA

15

Updated by
Mark Walters

THE *MEZZOGIORNO,* the informal name for Italy's south, reaches its full apotheosis in the regions of Basilicata and Calabria, often referred to as the instep and toe of Italy's boot. Here, in an area of Italy not on most tourist itineraries, the southern sun burns on a quiet, sparsely populated landscape where government neglect and archaic social patterns have prevented the kind of industrialization and rush to modernity experienced in other parts of the country. Half-built structures dot the countryside, road signs are few and far between, and cities become ghost towns for up to five hours at midday. Despite the undeveloped state of large tracts of these two regions, however, Basilicata and Calabria have become increasingly popular among Italians, and hotels and leisure facilities along the coasts are more than adequate, if lacking character. Among the untrammeled scenery here, hardly altered since the city-states of Magna Graecia (Greek colonies) ruled the coasts, you'll find the bizarre cave dwellings of Matera, a shining example of Byzantine church-building at Stilo, country *trattorie* buried in the hills, the tranquil and sun-drenched beaches of Tropea and Scilla—and some of Italy's friendliest people.

Exploring Basilicata & Calabria

The regions of Basilicata and Calabria can be toured as either brief side trips from Campania, Puglia, or Sicily or as a series of select stops en route to these other regions. Basilicata, particularly Matera, makes a natural and convenient accompaniment to any visit to Puglia. The best and fastest way to explore these regions is to stick to the coasts, making inland jaunts from there. West of Taranto, follow the Ionian coast for the classical remains at Metaponto, Crotone, and other Greek sights strung along the S106, making brief detours to visit such curiosities as the troglodyte city of Matera and, if time allows, the Norman stronghold of Gerace. South of Salerno the route along the Tyrrhenian coast takes in a brief stretch of Basilicata—among whose cliffs nestles the smart resort of Maratea—before swooping down into Calabria, where you can divide your time between first-class beaches on the Tropea promontory and the high inland ranges of Sila and Aspromonte.

Basilicata and Calabria are well served by transport connections, and drivers and bus and train passengers alike should find no difficulty circulating within these regions. The toll-free A3 autostrada gives a clear run from Salerno all the way down to Reggio di Calabria (although you get what you pay for—it's under eternal construction, so allow extra time), while the much more scenic S18 runs parallel, hugging the Tyrrhenian coast; the S106 traces the Ionian coast from Taranto to Reggio and is often empty of traffic. Trains also follow these coastal routes, with frequent connections on the Naples–Villa San Giovanni line and fewer trains on the Ionian side. Things get much busier in midsummer, when beaches and resorts burst into activity and hotel rooms can be hard to find.

About the Restaurants & Hotels

Following the oral tradition in southern Italy, many restaurants in the region will either not have a menu or will not update it on a daily basis. Always ask the serving staff what they recommend, as it may not be listed.

15

Your itinerary while exploring Basilicata and Calabria will depend on the direction you're traveling. An ideal route is to come from the north either along the Tyrrhenian coast—from Campania on the S18 or the faster A3 highway—or from Puglia on the S106. If you're traveling in Basilicata, you can cross over to the Tyrrhenian coast without any difficulty on the panoramic S653, passing through the Pollino range and enabling you to make a stop at Maratea. Farther south you can change coasts at Sibari, Catanzaro, Stilo, and Locri. From the Tyrrhenian coast, head inland at Paola to go through the Sila range to Crotone on the Ionian Sea.

Numbers in the text correspond to numbers in the margin and on the Basilicata and Calabria map.

If you have
3 days

If it's summer and you're heading south from Campania, spend a night in the resort of ⊞ **Maratea** ❺ ⌐, a perfect marriage of cliffs and beaches. On your second day, stop for lunch at **Diamante** ❻, then catch a glimpse of **Pizzo** ❿ and stop for the night at ⊞ **Tropea** ⓫, close to some of Calabria's best beaches. From here it's a short trip to the Sicily ferries at Villa San Giovanni. Alternatively, coming from Puglia, make a stop at the archaeological site at **Metaponto** ❶ before crossing over to Basilicata's west coast for a night at ⊞ **Maratea** ❺, then continue south as above. With an extra day at your disposal you might return to the Ionian coast to see the lovely Byzantine La Cattólica church at ⊞ **Stilo** ⓱. Spend the night here, and then drive the brief distance down the coast to see the classical ruins of **Locri** ⓯ before heading west to the archaeological museum at **Reggio di Calabria** ⓭, then continue on to Sicily or head back up to Stilo for the final night. If traveling in fall or winter, substitute a night in either ⊞ **Cosenza** ❼, Calabria's layered hillside metropolis, or the wondrous cave town of ⊞ **Matera** ❷, for Maratea and other beach towns.

If you have
5 days

From Puglia, allow two or three hours to explore the classical remains at **Metaponto** ❶ before heading inland on the fast S407 to ⊞ **Matera** ❷ ⌐, a must for its fascinating *sassi,* prehistoric rock dwellings, and an ideal first overnight stop. Cross over to the Tyrrhenian and spend your second night at ⊞ **Maratea** ❺, then head south via **Diamante** ❻. At Paola, veer east across the coastal chain to get a taste of inland Calabria, spending your third night in ⊞ **Cosenza** ❼, the frozen-in-time provincial capital. Explore Cosenza's old town, or take a day trip to hike or ski in neighboring **Camigliatello** ❽. Before you head south, deviate to the ancient Greek site of **Crotone** ❾, cut back westward at Catanzaro to the attractive seaside town of ⊞ **Pizzo** ❿, and later head to beautiful ⊞ **Tropea** ⓫, either of which makes a good fourth-night stop. If you can pull yourself away, continue down the coast the following day; you might have lunch by the harbor at **Bagnara Calabra** ⓬, siesta on the beach, and if archaeology strikes your fancy, pass through **Reggio di Calabria** ⓭, where the archaeological museum is one of southern Italy's best. If you have time left over, either make an excursion on to the brooding massif of **Aspromonte** ⓮ or skirt south around this range to the Greek site at **Locri** ⓯ and the nearby Norman town of **Gerace** ⓰. Otherwise, it's just a short hop over the Straits to Messina and Sicily.

Hotels are generously distributed throughout this region. They range from grand, if slightly faded, high-class complexes with pools, tennis courts, and copious grounds to family-run places where the famous southern hospitality compensates for a lack of amenities. Note that many seaside hotels open up just for the summer season and are closed almost eight months a year. Children are welcome everywhere and are usually a prominent presence in the region's hotels. Many families vacation in the numerous campsites along both coasts, most fully equipped and often with bungalows or apartments for rent by the week or less; these can get congested in August. Most campsites are closed in winter.

WHAT IT COSTS In euros					
	$$$$	**$$$**	**$$**	**$**	**¢**
RESTAURANTS	over €22	€16–€22	€11–€16	€7–€11	under €7
HOTELS	over €220	€160–€220	€110–€160	€70–€110	under €70

Restaurant prices are for a second course *(secondo piatto)*. Hotel prices are for two people in a standard double room in high season, including tax and service.

Timing

The regions of Basilicata and Calabria suffer from intense heat in summer and, away from the coasts, bitter cold in winter. Unless coming for the beach party scene, avoid August, since accommodations can be limited and facilities generally strained; any time on either side of August, though, would be ideal for touring these regions. Beaches are comparatively empty and the water temperature is comfortable in June, July, and September. Avoid the coastal resorts in winter if you want to find hotels open and anything more than a lonely dog on the streets. The months of January and February see snow inland, which can make driving conditions difficult. Spring and fall see the forests of Basilicata and Calabria at their best.

BASILICATA

Occupying the instep of Italy's boot, Basilicata has long been one of Italy's poorest regions, memorably described by Carlo Levi in his *Christ Stopped at Eboli*, a book that brought home to the majority of the Italians the depths of deprivation to which this forgotten region was subject. (The tale of Levi's internment was poignantly filmed by Francesco Rosi in 1981.) Basilicata was not always so desolate, however. For the ancient Greeks, the area formed part of Magna Graecia, the loose collection of colonies founded along the coasts of southern Italy whose wealth and military prowess rivaled those of the city-states of Greece itself. Metaponto (formerly Metapontion or Metapontum) was one of the most important of these colonies; its remains are easily reached along the coastal S106. Farther inland, the city of Matera, the region's true highlight, is built on the side of an impressive ravine that is honeycombed with *sassi* (prehistoric dwellings), some of them still occupied, forming a separate enclave that contrasts vividly with the attractive baroque town above.

15

Beaches The lack of industry in Basilicata and Calabria has one positive result for beach fans—acres of sand and a largely unpolluted sea running almost continuously down both coasts of the peninsula. This is not the place for you if you like your beaches impeccably tended but crowded with regimented lines of sunbathers and ranks of uniform beach umbrellas. Here you can pick and choose strands at whim and spread out. What's more, there's a pronounced difference between the two coasts: the more developed Tyrrhenian littoral, on the western side, has more villages and facilities and is more scenic, with the mountains a constant backdrop; the eastern Ionian shore, on the other hand, is flatter and wilder, has fewer towns and villages, and holds less visual interest. The best Tyrrhenian spots are around Maratea, Praia a Mare, Amantea, Tropea, and Scilla. On the Ionian, head for Lido di Metaponto, Sibari, Capo Rizzuto, and Soverato. Remember that if you don't have your own beach umbrella, the summer sun can be oppressive and even dangerous: borrow or buy one if you can, and arm yourself with plenty of sunscreen. Alternatively, stick to your hotel beach or seek out those few spots where there are lidos and amenities to rent, such as at Metaponto, Soverato, and around Tropea.

Hiking Most vacationers in Basilicata and Calabria think of only swimming and sunbathing as the main pastimes, unaware of the hiking that can be done in the forested or craggily bare peaks and valleys of the predominantly mountainous landscape. Three zones have been made into nature reserves: Farthest north, the Parco Nazionale del Monte Pollino, riddled with lush canyons and marked paths, straddles the boundary between Basilicata and Calabria and is a good place to spot eagles and wild boars. The village of Terranova di Pollino, off the S653 to the north, is a good starting point for these mountains, which reach up to 7,500 feet. Occupying the widest part of the Calabrian peninsula, the Sila Massif (which rises to 6,300 feet) attracts the most visitors, though the thick pine, beech, and chestnut forests are vast enough for you to find your own space. Farthest south, the Aspromonte Massif, with peaks as high as 6,500 feet soaring above Reggio di Calabria, is a welcome retreat from summer temperatures. Access is easiest from the S183 between Melito di Porto Salvo and Gambarie. For further information, including walking and hiking itineraries, contact local tourist offices.

Metaponto

❶ *48 km (30 mi) southwest of Taranto, 182 km (114 mi) south of Bari.*

Greek Metapontion was founded around 700 BC, most probably by Achaeans from the Greek mainland. The great mathematician and philosopher Pythagoras, banished from Kroton, established a school here in about 510 BC and eventually died in the city. Punished for its support of the Carthaginian general Hannibal (247–183 BC) after his victory over Rome at Cannae (216 BC), Metapontum, as it was known by the Romans, endured long years of decline—sacked by the slave-rebel

Spartacus (died 71 BC) and subsequently ravaged both by malaria and Saracen raids. Most of what remained was used for building elsewhere in the region, but the *zona archeologica* (archaeological zone), which covers a vast area, retains enough interest to merit a visit. You'll need a car: allow about an hour for the museum, which is best seen before the site, to view the plans and maps and put it all into context, and then an hour or two for the excavations. When you've finished here, you might take a dip at Lido di Metaponto, where there are sandy, well-equipped beaches.

The modern **Museo Archeologico Nazionale** displays 4th- and 5th-century AD statuary, ceramics, jewelry, and coins—sadly, representing only a small fraction of the total number of finds until work on the new exhibition rooms is completed. Perhaps most interesting are examples of coins stamped with ears of barley, symbolizing the cereal production to which Metapontion owed its prosperity. Also noteworthy is the section showing how the study of fingerprints on shards found in the artisans' quarter has revealed information on the social makeup of the ancient city. Maps and aerial photographs of the site with accounts of the excavations are useful for your visit. The museum lies about 2 km (1 mi) outside Lido di Metaponto (look out for the scanty signs). ⊠ *Borgo Metaponto, Via Laveran 21* ☎ *0835/ 745327* 🎟 *€2.50* ☉ *Tues.–Sun. 9 AM–8 PM, Mon. 2 PM–8 PM.*

Highlights of Metaponto's sprawling **zona archeologica,** accessible to the east of the Museo Archeologico Nazionale, include the **Santuario di Apollo Licio** (Sanctuary of Apollo Lykaios), a 6th-century BC Doric temple that, archaeologists have deduced, once had 32 columns. Only the foundations and a few capitals and shafts are to be seen today. Nearby, encircled by an expanse of grass, lie the remains of a 4th-century BC **Teatro,** much restored. More compelling is the better-preserved Tempio di Hera (Temple of Hera), commonly known as **Tavole Palatine,** found 2–3 km (1–2 mi) north, where the main S106 crosses the Bradano River. With 15 of its fluted Doric columns surviving, it's the most evocative remnant of this once mighty state. ⊠ *Metaponto Borgo* ☎ *0835/745327* 🎟 *Free* ☉ *Daily 9–1 hr before sunset.*

Matera

▶ **2** *45 km (28 mi) north of Metaponto, 62 km (39 mi) south of Bari.*

Matera is one of southern Italy's most unusual towns. On their own, the elegant baroque churches, palazzi, and broad piazzas—filled to bursting during the evening *passeggiata*, when the locals turn out to stroll the streets—would make Matera stand out in Basilicata's impoverished landscape. But what really sets this town apart is its sassi.

Fodor'sChoice Matera's **sassi** are rock-hewn dwellings piled chaotically atop one an-
★ other, strewn across the sides of a steep ravine. They date from Paleolithic times, when they were truly cave homes. In the years since, the grottoes were slowly adapted as houses only slightly more modern, with their exterior walls closed off and canals regulating rainwater and sewage. Until relatively recently, these troglodytic abodes presented a Dante-esque vision of squalor and poverty, graphically described in Carlo Levi's *Christ Stopped at Eboli*, but in the 1960s most of them were

ON THE MENU

WHILE CALABRIA is renowned for its seafood—calamari, bream, sea bass, and swordfish to name a few—Basilicata is better known for its land produce. In both regions look for various types of funghi (mushrooms), particularly in the fall; intense ricotta forte; antipasti of roasted vegetables soaked in local olive oil; lamb stew; and handmade fusilli (pasta twists). Pork is one of the region's meat staples, and it takes many forms, including roast suckling pig; salame piccante (Calabrian spicy salami infused with peppercorns); and savory salsiccia piccante, hot Italian sausage (often sold by street vendors in a roll with peppers, onions, french fries, and mayonnaise).

Methods of preparing and even naming mezzogiorno dishes vary widely, providing many opportunities for adventurous eating. One taste experience universally available, however, is peperoncini (small dried hot chile peppers), the sweat-inducing seeds of which are often added to pasta dishes, especially pasta prepared simply with garlic, oil, and fresh pomodorini (cherry tomatoes), boiled down.

Drinking wine in southern Italy used to be a hit-or-miss affair, but now if you are prepared to spend upward of €8–10 you're likely to be in for something good. Red wines have undergone a major revolution: several producers are using the Aglianico grape variety in Basilicata to outstanding effect—try Paternoster's range of wines—while in Calabria producers like Librandi have worked wonders with the local Gaglioppo variety. White wines have traditionally posed fewer problems: good wine is produced under the Cirò DOC denomination on Calabria's eastern seaboard from the Greco Bianco variety.

emptied of their inhabitants, who were then largely consigned to the ugly blocks seen on the way into town. Today, however, having been designated a World Heritage Site, the area has been cleaned up and is gradually being populated once again—and even gentrified, as evidenced by the bars and restaurants that have moved in. The wide Strada Panoramica leads you safely through this desolate region, which still retains its eerie atmosphere and panoramic views.

There are two areas of sassi, the **Sasso Caveoso** and the **Sasso Barisano**, and both can be seen from vantage points in the upper town. Then follow the Strada Panoramica down into the sassi and feel free to ramble among the strange structures, which, in the words of H. V. Morton in his *A Traveller in Southern Italy*, "resemble the work of termites rather than of man." Among them you will find several *chiese rupestri*, or rock-hewn churches, some of which have medieval frescoes, notably **Santa Maria de Idris**, right on the edge of the Sasso Caveoso, near the ravine. A few minutes east of Santa Maria, in the so-called Albanian quarter (settled by refugees in the 15th century), the 10th-century **Santa Lucia alle Malve** has Byzantine-style frescoes dating from 1250. ⊠ *Sasso Caveoso* 🎫 *€5.20 for all 8 churches in the sassi* ☉ *Oct.–Mar., daily 9:30–1:30 and 2:30–5:30; Apr.–Sept., daily 9:30–1:30 and 2:30–8.*

The **Duomo** in Matera was built in the late 13th century and occupies a prominent position between the two areas of sassi. It has a pungent Apulian-Romanesque flavor; inside, some of the columns came from Metaponto, and there's a recovered fresco, probably painted in the 14th century, showing scenes from the *Last Judgment.* On the Duomo's facade the figures of Sts. Peter and Paul stand on either side of a sculpture of Matera's patron, Madonna della Bruna. ⊠ *Via Duomo* ☎ *0835/ 335201* ☉ *Daily 8–noon and 3:30–7.*

In town you'll find the 13th-century Romanesque church of **San Giovanni Battista,** restored to its pre-Baroque simplicity in 1926. As you go in through a side door—the original end door and facade were incorporated into later buildings—note the interesting sculpted decorations in the porch. The interior still conserves its original cross vaulting, ogival arches, and curious capitals. ⊠ *Via San Biagio* ☉ *Daily 8–noon and 3:30–7.*

Matera's excellent **Museo Ridola** is housed in the ex-monastery of Santa Chiara. Illustrating the human and geological history of the area, the museum includes an extensive selection of prehistoric and classical finds, notably Bronze Age weaponry and beautifully decorated Greek pottery. One room displays stolen art treasures recovered by a special department of the *carabinieri* (national police). ⊠ *Via Ridola 24* ☎ *0835/ 310058* 🎫 *€2.50* ☉ *Tues.–Sun. 9–8, Mon. 2–8.*

Where to Stay & Eat

$–$$ ✕ **Le Botteghe.** This stylish restaurant is right in the heart of the sassi, occupying pleasingly restored vaulted premises. Try *gli ortaggi de Le Botteghe* (a sample of seasonal vegetables) served as an antipasto. Carnivores will delight in the charcoal-grilled *bistecca di Podolico,* a steak made from a local cattle breed, best washed down with local Aglianico del Vulture red wine. ⊠ *Piazza San Pietro Barisano 22* ☎ *0835/344072* ⌘ *Reservations essential* ▤ *AE, DC, MC, V* ☉ *Closed Wed. No dinner Sun.*

¢–$$ ✕ **Oi Marì.** Along the main road below the Hotel Sassi, this lively restaurant is an excellent choice within the sassi themselves. Friendly servers cater to a mix of tourists and locals in a network of ancient, cavelike rooms that are painted brightly enough not to be spooky. The sassi ambience accompanies great pizza, salumi, and a good selection of typical local dishes at very reasonable prices. The wine list includes many of Puglia and Basilicata's most up-and-coming reds. ⊠ *Vico Fiorentini 66, Rione Sassi* ☎ *0835/346121* ▤ *AE, DC, MC, V* ☉ *Closed Tues. and first 2 wks in Oct.*

$ 🏨 **Hotel Sassi.** Hotel Sassi lies right in the heart of the Sasso Barisano, directly across from the Duomo. It has a raw, cavelike design, with rough-hewn walls and stairs (and so is not advised for anyone with mobility difficulties). Facilities are minimal; rooms are small and plain but clean, comfortable, and air-conditioned. Two rooms are set aside for hostel-type bunk accommodation at budget rates. Parking is a bit of a hike from the hotel, something to consider if you have heavy baggage. ⊠ *Via San Giovanni Vecchio 89, 75100* ☎ *0835/331009* 🖷 *0835/333733* ⊕ *www.hotelsassi.it* ⤳ *17 rooms, 1 suite* ♨ *Minibars, bar* ▤ *AE, DC, MC, V* ⦿I *BP.*

$ **⊡ Locanda di San Martino.** Combining the right aura, good taste, and value,
Fodor'sChoice   the Locanda is a welcome new entry among Matera's sassi. The historic
★   rooms—formerly cave dwellings—have been impeccably restored under
the sensitive ownership of Antonio Panetto and American anthropologist
Dorothy Zinn, and stepping out onto your terrace overlooking the old
town is like being on a film set. ⊠ *Via San Martino 22, 75100* 📠📠 *0835/
256600* ⊕ *www.locandadisanmartino.it* ↪ *15 rooms, 6 suites* ⚑ *Restaurant, minibars, bar, library, some free parking* ⊟ *AE, DC, MC, V* ⦿⫶ *BP.*

The Outdoors

WALKING TOURS   The agency **SIC** (⊠ Via Casalnuovo 15, 75100 ☎ 0835/314244 ⊕ www.
stoneincoming.it) arranges tours of the sassi area on request, charging
around €8 per person for a group of four or more. Call ahead to request an English-speaking guide. Independent guides also offer their services on the spot, pricing by length of tour and the number in your party.

Aliano

❸ *127 km (79 mi) southwest of Matera, 102 km (63 mi) southeast of
Potenza.*

This remote village off S598 in the center of Basilicata's empty interior
was the site of Carlo Levi's internment during 1936 and 1937. After the
war, Levi (1902–75) published his account of that time in his classic *Christ
Stopped at Eboli*, later filmed by Francesco Rosi. Not significantly different from any of the countless villages scattered over the featureless clay
gullies and outcrops stretching out on all sides, Aliano (called Gagliano
by Levi) has not altered much, and readers can identify the church, the
piazza where the Fascist mayor addressed the impassive peasants, and
the timeless views. The house in Aliano where Carlo Levi stayed has been
preserved as the **Museo Storico Carlo Levi,** displaying some personal artifacts as well as other articles of local interest. The old post office nearby
in Piazza Garibaldi—where you will find the custodians to both buildings—has been converted into an art gallery. ⊠ *Palazzo Caporale* ☎ *0835/
568315* ⊡ *€3 for both museum and art gallery* ⊙ *Sept.–May, daily
10–12:30 and 4–6; June–Aug., daily 10–12:30 and 4–7* ⊙ *Closed Wed.*

Terranova di Pollino

❹ *70 km (43 mi) south of Aliano, 125 km (78 mi) east of Matera.*

Founded in the 16th century as part of the Duchy of Noja, Terranova is
a quiet village—the end of the road for local buses—lying at the foothills
of Italy's largest nature preserve, the Pollino National Park. It is base camp
for hikes to sleepy Albanian hill communities and to the higher reaches
of the spectacular Pollino massif. Thanks to a relatively low population
density, wildlife thrives within the park, its best-known inhabitants being
the golden eagle and the endangered wolf—there were 34 at the latest
count, making up almost 10% of the population in all of Italy.

Where to Stay & Eat

★ ¢   ✕⊡ **Hotel Picchio Nero.** Situated just below the village of Terranova, this
hotel combines rustic simplicity and excellent fare ($–$$). At the helm

is the energetic Pino Golia, a welcoming, attentive host who has set up this first-class base for mountain hikers and dispenses copious information on local trails and history. The rooms are wood-paneled in Alpine style and look out onto soothing woods and valleys. The name *picchio nero* means "black woodpecker," one of the Pollino's conservation flagship species. ⊠ *Via Mulino 1, 85030* ☎ *0973/93170* 🖷 *0973/93181* ⊕ *www. picchionero.com* 🖵 *23 rooms, 2 family suites* 🛆 *Restaurant, bar; no a/c* 🖃 *AE, DC, MC, V* ⛟ *BP.*

Maratea

▶ ❺ *103 km (64 mi) southwest of Aliano, 217 km (135 mi) south of Naples.*

When encountering Maratea for the first time, you can be forgiven for thinking you've somehow arrived at the French Riviera. The high, twisty road resembles nothing so much as a corniche, complete with glimpses of a turquoise sea below. Divided by the craggy rocks into various separate localities—Maratea, Maratea Porto, Maratea Marina—the sequence ends above the main inland village, a tumble of cobblestone streets where the ruins of a much older settlement can be seen (Maratea Antica). At the summit of the hill stands a dramatic, gigantic Christ, a floating white ghost in the night sky reminiscent of the one in Rio de Janeiro. There's no shortage of secluded sandy strips in between the rocky headlands, which can get crowded in August. A summer minibus service connects all the different points once or twice an hour.

Where to Stay & Eat

$$ ✕ **Taverna Rovita.** Housed in a former convent with exposed beams, this restaurant in the heart of the old town offers a menu based on traditional recipes, but the food here is in a different league from that of Maratea's other eateries. The antipasti, for a start, are varied and abundant, and the homemade pasta comes with a selection of rich sauces that changes according to the season. Choose a locally caught fish for the main course. ⊠ *Via Rovita 13* ☎ *0973/876588* 🖃 *AE, DC, MC, V* ⊘ *Closed Nov.–Feb. and Tues. in Oct. and Mar.–May.*

$$–$$$ ✕🖾 **Villa Cheta.** Immersed in Mediterranean greenery, this large historic villa in the seaside village of Acquafredda is strategically close to the beach (access by elevator). Rooms are spruce and stylish without being overfurnished, while dining out on the restaurant's garden terrace ($$) against the backdrop of Basilicata's rugged coastline is simply *favoloso.* ⊠ *Acquafredda Maratea, 85041* ☎ *0973/878134* 🖷 *0973/878135* ⊕ *www.villacheta.it* 🖵 *23 rooms* 🛆 *Restaurant, minibars, beach, bar* 🖃 *AE, DC, MC, V* ⊘ *Closed Dec.–Mar. 15* ⛟ *MAP.*

CALABRIA

Italy's southernmost mainland region has seen more than its fair share of oppression, poverty, and natural disaster, but the region of Magna Graecia, mountains, and *mare* (sea) also claims more than its share of fantastic scenery and great beaches. The accent here is on the landscape, the sea, and the constantly changing dialogue between the two. Don't expect much in the way of sophistication in this least trodden of regions, but do remain open to the simple pleasures to be found—the country food, the friendliness, the disarming hospitality of the people. Aside from coast and culture, there are also some sights worth going out of your way for, from the vividly colored murals of Diamante to the ruins of Magna Graecia at Locri. The drive on the southbound A3 highway alone is a breathtaking experience, the more so as you approach Sicily, whose image grows tantalizingly nearer as the road wraps around the coastline once challenged by Odysseus. This is the road you should take for the big picture—but don't forget to stop for a bit to get a closer view of this fascinating land.

Diamante

❻ *51 km (32 mi) south of Maratea, 225 km (140 mi) south of Naples.*

One of the most fashionable of the string of small resorts lining Calabria's north Tyrrhenian coast, Diamante makes a good stop for its whitewashed maze of narrow alleys, brightly adorned with a startling variety of large-scale murals. The work of local artists, the murals—which range from cartoons to poems to serious portraits, and from tasteful to downright ugly—give a sense of wandering through a huge open-air art gallery. Flanking the broad, palm-lined seaside promenade are sparkling beaches to the north and south.

Where to Stay & Eat

$–$$ ✕ **Taverna del Pescatore.** One of a pair of good moderately priced fish restaurants down at the seafront by Diamante's small harbor (the other is Lo Scoglio), this is the less formal and more welcoming of the two, with spartan but bright decor. Naturally, fish predominates—whatever's hauled in is cooked in a variety of ways. Phone first to secure a table outside. ⊠ *Via Calvario 2* ☎ *0985/81482* ▤ *MC, V* ☉ *Closed Tues. Oct.–May.*

$$$ 🏨 **Grand Hotel San Michele.** A survivor from a vanishing age, the San Michele occupies a belle epoque–style, cliff-top former hunting lodge near the village of Cetraro, 20 km (12 mi) south of Diamante on SS18. Mingling Mediterranean charm with old-style elegance, the hotel is set within extensive gardens, and an elevator takes you down to the private beach at the base of the cliff. As in most hotels on Calabria's coast, substantial bargains are available on room rates outside July and August. ⊠ *Località Bosco 8/9, 87022 Cetraro* ☎ *0982/91012* ▤ *0982/ 91430* ⊕ *www.sanmichele.it* ☞ *72 rooms, 6 suites* ♻ *Restaurant, 9-hole golf course, tennis court, beach, bar, convention center, car rental* ▤ *AE, DC, MC, V* ☉ *Closed Nov.* ⦿ *BP.*

Cosenza

❼ *75 km (48 mi) south of Diamante, 185 km (115 mi) north of Reggio di Calabria.*

Cosenza, Calabria's biggest city, has a steep, stair-laden *centro storico* (historic city center) that truly hails from another age. Wrought-iron balconies overlook narrow alleyways with old-fashion storefronts and bars that have barely been touched by centuries of development. Flung haphazardly—and beautifully—across the top and side of a steep hill ringed by mountains, and watched over by a great, crumbling medieval castle, Cosenza also provides the best gateway for the Sila, whose steep walls rear up to the town's eastern side. Though Cosenza's outskirts are largely modern and ugly, culinary and photographic gems await in the rolling farmland nearby and the mountains to the east.

Crowning the Pancrazio hill above the old city, with views across to the Sila mountains, **Castello Svevo** is largely in ruins, having suffered successive earthquakes and a lightning strike that ignited gunpowder stored within. The castle takes its name from the great Swabian emperor Frederick II (1194–1250), who added two octagonal towers, though it dates back originally to the Normans, who fortified the hill against their Saracen foes. Occasional exhibitions and concerts are staged here in summer. ⊠ *Porta Piana.* 🎫 *Free* 🕙 *Daily 8 AM–8 PM.*

Cosenza's noblest square, **Piazza XV Marzo** (commonly called Piazza della Prefettura), houses government buildings as well as the elegant **Teatro Rendano.** From the square, the **Villa Comunale** (public garden) provides plenty of shaded benches for a rest.

need a break?	In the heart of the centro storico, the charming and historic **Gran Caffè Renzelli** (⊠ Corso Telesio 46 ☎ 0984/46814) makes a fine spot for a pause in your perambulations. At tables inside or out (there is a no-smoking room as well as an outside terrace), you can enjoy *varchiglia* (a dry almond cake) along with a host of sweet and wonderful coffee-liqueur combinations, each served with cream in a tall glass. Join in the *chiacchiere al caffè* (talks over coffee), echoing the discussions of the literary salon that once met here.

Cosenza's original **Duomo** was probably built in the middle of the 11th century but was destroyed by the earthquake of 1184. A new cathedral was consecrated in the presence of Emperor Frederick II in 1222. After many baroque additions, later alterations have restored some of the Provençal Gothic style. Inside, look for the lovely tomb of Isabella of Aragon, who died after falling from her horse en route to France in 1271. ⊠ *Piazza del Duomo,* ☎ *0984/77864* 🕙 *Daily 7:30–noon and 3:30–7.*

Where to Stay & Eat

¢–$$ ✕ **Da Giocondo.** In the new part of town, but near the centro storico, you can sample simple homemade dishes in a modern yet homey setting. Go for the local, freshly picked mushrooms from the Sila as an antipasto, followed by *rigatoni alla silana* (pasta with tomato, basil, peppers, and caciocavallo cheese), washed down with local Cirò wine. ⊠ *Via Piave 52* ☎ *0984/29810* ▤ *AE, DC, MC, V* 🕙 *No dinner Sun.*

¢–$ ✕ **L'Arco Vecchio.** This tavern-restaurant, right in the middle of the old town along the path up to the castle, appropriately under the famous Arch of Ciaccio, serves traditional Calabrian dishes in a warm, elegant vaulted room. Try the excellent *lagane e ceci* (homemade pasta with chickpeas). ⊠ *Piazza Archi di Ciaccio 21* ☎ *0984/72564* ▤ *AE, DC, MC, V* 🕙 *Closed Sun. and 2 wks in Aug.*

★ ¢ ✕ **Wine Bar DOC.** Representing the contemporary edge of Cosenza, this postmodern feat of interior decorating oozes fusion, whimsically plopping spreads of tempting traditional Calabrian salumi and a superlative collection of wines amid a whirl of glass and exposed stone, all tucked into the cozy arches of an ancient palazzo. All the trendiest locals come out not just for the voluminous wine list, which showcases Calabria's absolute best, but also for the wonderful smoked meats, cheeses, and inventive pasta dishes. Come to eat or just to drink. ⊠ *Vico San Tommaso 13, off Corso Telesio* ☎ *0984/73110* ☰ *AE, DC, MC, V* ☉ *Closed Mon. No lunch.*

\$ 🏨 **Royal.** Though lacking in character, this modern hotel in the new part of town is handy for buses departing for the Sila. The public spaces have a classical style with columns and Persian carpets on the marble floor. The restaurant specializes in local Calabrian dishes. ⊠ *Via Molinella 24/e, 87100* ☎ *0984/412165* 🖷 *0984/412461* ⊕ *www.hotelroyalsas.it* ⇴ *44 rooms* ♺ *Restaurant, bar, meeting room* ☰ *AE, DC, MC, V* ⏐◎⏐ *BP.*

¢ 🏨 **Excelsior.** This 1900 building is gradually being restored. The public areas are imposing, retaining their fin-de-siècle feel, while the spacious guest rooms are adequate if uninspiring. It's close to the shops of Cosenza's main drag, Corso Mazzini, and an easy walk across the Busento river from the centro storico. ⊠ *Piazza Matteotti 14, 87100* ☎ *0984/74383* 🖷 *0984/74384* ⊕ *www.italiaabc.it/a/excelsior* ⇴ *40 rooms* ♺ *Restaurant, bar, meeting room* ☰ *AE, DC, MC, V* ⏐◎⏐ *BP.*

Camigliatello

❽ *36 km (22 mi) east of Cosenza.*

Lined with chalets, Camigliatello, between Crotone and Cosenza, is one of the Sila Massif's major resort towns. Most of the Sila is not mountainous at all; it is, rather, an extensive, sparsely populated plateau with areas of thick forest. Unfortunately, the region has been exploited by construction and fuel industries, resulting in considerable deforestation. However, since 1968, when the area was designated a national park (Parco Nazionale della Calabria), strict rules have limited the felling of timber, and forests are now regenerating. There are well-marked trails through pine and beech woods, and ample opportunities for horseback riding. Fall and winter see droves of locals hunting mushrooms and gathering chestnuts, while ski slopes near Camigliatello also draw crowds. A couple of miles east of town, Lago Cecita makes a good starting point for exploring **La Fossiata**, a lovely wooded conservation area within the park.

Where to Stay

\$ 🏨 **Tasso.** On the edge of Camigliatello, less than 1 km (½ mi) from the ski slopes, this hotel is in a peaceful, picturesque location. Don't be put off by its oddly futuristic 1970s look—it's well equipped, with plenty of space for evening entertainment, including live music, and relaxation after a day of hiking or skiing. The restaurant has a terrace shaded by a walnut tree, and all rooms have balconies. ⊠ *Via degli Impianti Sportivi, Spezzano della Sila, 87058* ☎ *0984/578113* ⊕ *www. hoteltasso.it* ⇴ *82 rooms* ♺ *Restaurant, bar, lounge, nightclub, recreation room, meeting room, free parking; no a/c* ☰ *AE, DC, MC, V* ☉ *Closed Mar.–May and Nov.* ⏐◎⏐ *BP.*

Sports & the Outdoors

HIKING &
WALKING

One of the best hikes around Camigliatello is the **Strada delle Vette** (Peaks Road), a 13-km (8-mi) route that links the Sila's highest mountains. For maps and itineraries, contact the **Camigliatello tourist office** (⊠ Via Roma 5 ☎ 0984/578243).

HORSEBACK
RIDING

With plenty of trails winding through woods and around lakes, horseback riding is one of Sila's year-round attractions. Contact **Maneggio Sila** (⊠ Via Molarotta, 3 km [2 mi] outside Camigliatello ☎ 0984/578031 9 AM–1 PM).

SKIING

The slopes in the area are small and sometimes quite crowded. The best place to rent equipment is at the ski lift. Call for rental information and **slope conditions** (☎ 0984/578037).

Crotone

❾ *105 km (65 mi) east of Cosenza, 150 km (94 mi) northeast of Locri.*

Occupying the main bulge along Calabria's Ionian coastline, Crotone was founded by Achaeans from the Greek mainland in about 708 BC and soon became one of the great cities in Magna Graecia. Though the drab modern town has obliterated most of the ancient settlement, a remarkable gold ★ hoard was found at the **Santuario di Hera Lacinia** on a promontory 11 km (7 mi) to the south, known as Capo Colonna for the single remaining column from the temple of Hera. The area has free access during daylight hours and is well worth a visit, especially in April and May, when it is awash with wildflowers. At this writing, a museum was being built at the sanctuary to house some of the finds, but for the moment the treasure— including Hera's gold crown with intertwined fig and myrtle leaves—is staying put at the **Museo Archeologico Nazionale** close to the seafront castle in Crotone. ⊠ *Via Risorgimento 14* ☎ *096/223082* 🎫 €2 ⊙ *Daily 9–7:30. Closed 1st and 3rd Mon. of month.*

Pizzo

❿ *148 km (92 mi) south of Diamante, 107 km (66 mi) north of Reggio di Calabria.*

Built up along the slope of a steep promontory overlooking the coast and a fishing port, Pizzo has a good selection of seafood restaurants and a small cliff-top Aragonese castle (built in 1486) near the center of town. Here the French general Joachim Murat (1767–1815) was imprisoned, tried, and shot in October 1815, after a bungled attempt to rouse the people against the Bourbons and reclaim the throne of Naples given him by his brother-in-law Napoléon.

While in Pizzo, sample the renowned *gelato di Pizzo,* a rich, creamy delight available in many flavors at any of the outdoor bars in the central Piazza della Repubblica.

The **Chiesetta di Piedigrotta,** a little over a mile north of Pizzo's castle, at the bottom of a flight of steps leading down to the beach, is a 17th-century church implausibly hewn out of rock by shipwrecked Neapolitan sailors in thanks for their rescue. They filled it with statues of biblical and historical figures, and the collection today includes a bizarre ensemble showing Fidel Castro kneeling before Pope John XXIII (1881–1963) and President John F. Kennedy (1917–63). ⊠ *Via Nazionale* ⊙ *Daily 9–1 and 3–7:30.*

Where to Stay

$ ▦ **Hotel Murat.** Here's a good central choice for accommodation if you decide to overnight in Pizzo. Right on the town's main square, a stone's throw from the castle and perched overlooking the water, the Murat has comfortable rooms, of which the ones on the sides are biggest and have the best views (ask for 201 or 207). ⊠ *Piazza della Repubblica 41, 89812* ☎ *0963/534201* 🖷 *0963/534469* ⇆ *12 rooms* △ *Restaurant, bar* ▭ *AE, DC, MC, V* ⦿ *BP.*

Tropea

⓫ *28 km (17 mi) southwest of Pizzo, 107 km (66 mi) north of Reggio di Calabria.*

Ringed by cliffs and wonderful sandy beaches, the Tropea promontory is still undiscovered by the big tour operators. The main town, Tropea, easily wins the contest for prettiest town on Calabria's Tyrrhenian coast, its old palazzi built in simple golden stone on an elevation above the sea. On a clear day the seaward views from the waterfront promenade extend to embrace Stromboli's cone and at least four of the other Aeolians—the islands can be visited by motorboats that depart daily from Tropea in summer. Accommodations are good, and beach addicts will not be disappointed by the choice of magnificent sandy bays within easy reach of here. Some of the best are south at Capo Vaticano and north at Briatico.

In Tropea's harmonious warren of lanes, seek out the old Norman **Cattedrale**, whose interior displays a couple of unexploded U.S. bombs from World War II, with a grateful prayer to the Madonna attached to each. ⊠ *Piazza Sedile* ⊙ *Daily 7–noon and 4–7.*

From the belvedere at the bottom of the main square, Piazza Ercole, the church and Benedictine monastery of **Santa Maria della Isola** glistens on a rocky promontory above an aquamarine sea. Stroll out to visit the church on a path lined with fishermen's caves. Dating back to medieval times, the church was remodeled in the Gothic style, then given another facelift after an earthquake in 1905. The interior has an 18th-century nativity and some fragments of medieval tombs. ⊠ *Santa Maria della Isola* ⊙ *Daily 7–noon and 4–7.*

Where to Stay & Eat

$$ ✕ **Pimm's.** Since its glory days in the 1960s, this underground restaurant in Tropea's historic center has offered the town's top dining experience. Seafood is the best choice, with such specialties as pasta with sea urchins, smoked swordfish, and stuffed squid. The splendid sea views are an extra enticement. ⊠ *Corso Vittorio Emanuele 2* ☎ *0963/666105* ▭ *AE, DC, MC, V* ⊙ *Closed Nov. 15–Dec. 15; closed Mon.*

$$–$$$ Rocca Nettuno. Perched on the cliffs a 10-minute walk south of Tropea's town center, this deceptively large complex is one of the few hotels open throughout the year. Rooms are reasonably spacious and almost all have balconies. Some of the best—and quietest—are immersed in greenery near the cliff top. There is an all-inclusive package in summer months that includes a dine-around option so you can enjoy meals in town, too. ⊠ *Via Annunziata* ☎ *0963/998111* 🖷 *0963/603513* ⊕ *www.roccanettuno.com* ⤶ *264 rooms* ⚭ *2 restaurants, pizzeria, minibars, tennis court, massage, sauna, beach, 2 bars, theater* 🖃 *AE, DC, MC, V* ⦿| *FAP.*

Bagnara Calabra

⑫ *11 km (7 mi) south of Palmi, 36 km (22 mi) north of Reggio di Calabria.*

Fishing is in the blood of the local villagers in Bagnara Calabra, particularly when in pursuit of swordfish, for which the town has long enjoyed widespread fame. Casual trattorias make this a great lunch stop.

Where to Eat

$–$$ × **Taverna Kerkira.** Centrally located on Bagnara's main street, this ca-
Fodor'sChoice   sual restaurant emphasizes food above all else. The chef's mother hails
★   from Corfu, and dishes therefore represent creative Greek spins on Calabrian classics. Antipasti feature fish you'll encounter in few other places, such as delicately marinated, sashimilike *carpaccio di alalonga* (raw Tyrrhenian tunny with olive oil and soy sauce). *Farfalle* are prepared with Greek yogurt, lemon zest, cucumber, and a hint of mullet— a sublime creation. The chef also excels at *pesce spada* (swordfish)—try it breaded and baked with mint, vinegar, and parmigiano. ⊠ *Corso Vittorio Emanuele 217* ☎ *0966/372260* 🖃 *AE, DC, MC, V* ⦿ *Closed Mon. and Tues., Aug. 15–Sept. 15, and Dec. 21–Jan. 10.*

Reggio di Calabria

⑬ *26 km (16 mi) south of Scilla, 499 km (311 mi) south of Naples.*

Reggio di Calabria, the city on Italy's toe tip, is the jumping-off point for Messina- and Sicily-bound ferries, and was laid low by the same catastrophic earthquake that struck Messina in 1908. This raw city is one of Italy's most active ports, where you'll find every category of container ship and smokestack, but there's also a pleasant lido lined with palm fronds and urban beaches.

Reggio has one of southern Italy's most important archaeological mu-
★   seums, the **Museo Nazionale della Magna Grecia.** Prize exhibits here are two statues, known as the **Bronzi di Riace,** happened upon by an amateur deep-sea diver off Calabria's Ionian coast in 1972. Flaunting physiques that gym enthusiasts would die for, the pair are thought to date from the 5th century BC and have been attributed to both Pheidias and Polykleitos. It's possible that they were taken by the Romans as trophies from the site of Delphi and then shipwrecked on their return to Italy. Coins and votive tablets are among the numerous other treasures

from Magna Graecia contained in the museum. ⊠ *Piazza de Nava, Corso Garibaldi* ☎ *0965/812255* 🎫 *€5* ⊙ *Daily 9–7:30. Closed 1st and 3rd Mon. of month.*

Where to Stay

$$$ 🏨 **Miramare.** On the seafront midway between the port and the station, Miramare has one of the best locations in Reggio. It has been restored to evoke the charm of the early 20th century, yet has all modern facilities. ⊠ *Via Fata Morgana 1, 89127* ☎ *0965/812444* 🖷 *0965/812450* ⊕ *www.reggiocalabriahotels.it* 🛏 *96 rooms* ⚐ *Restaurant, bar, parking (fee)* ⊟ *AE, DC, V* ⧫○⧫ *BP.*

$$ 🏨 **Palace Masoanri's.** Right behind the Museo Nazionale, under the same ownership as the fancier Miramare, this modern hotel sits on a quiet side street with seaward views. Rooms are uninspiring though adequate for a night or two, and many have views over the straits. ⊠ *Via Vittorio Veneto 95, 89121* ☎ *0965/26433* 🖷 *0965/26436* ⊕ *www.reggiocalabriahotels.it* 🛏 *64 rooms* ⚐ *Bar, meeting room, parking (fee)* ⊟ *AE, DC, MC, V* ⧫○⧫ *BP.*

Aspromonte

⑭ *Gambarie: 42 km (26 mi) northeast of Reggio di Calabria.*

Rising to the east of Reggio di Calabria, Aspromonte is the name of the sprawling massif that dominates mainland Italy's southern tip. Long the haunt of brigands and the refuge of modern-day kidnappers—for whom industrialists, not tourists, are the usual targets—this thickly forested range reaches nearly 6,560 feet. In summer it makes a cool respite from the heat of the coast, offering endless opportunities for hiking and shady picnicking. On a clear day you can see right across to Mt. Etna, 60 km (36 mi) south. To get here going north from Reggio, turn inland off the autostrada or coast road at Gallico, 12 km (7 mi) north of town; driving east from Reggio on S184, turn left onto the S183 at Melito di Porto Salvo. Ask at **Reggio's tourist office** (⊠ Corso Garibaldi 329 ☎ 0965/892012) for Aspromonte walking itineraries.

en route   The fast S106 hugs Calabria's Ionian coast, leading south out of Reggio di Calabria and curving around Aspromonte to your left. Having rounded Capo Spartivento, the road proceeds north. If you don't want to continue farther north, turn left onto the S112dir, shortly before Bovalino and 14 km (9 mi) before reaching Locri. This winding mountain road takes you around the rugged northern slopes of Aspromonte, a highly scenic but rigorously winding route.

Locri

⑮ *100 km (62 mi) east of Reggio di Calabria.*

South of the seaside town of Locri, visit the excavations of **Locri Epizefiri,** where one of the most important of Magna Graecia's city-states stood. Founded around the 7th century BC, Locri became a regional power when—apparently assisted by Castor and Pollux—10,000 Locrians defeated an army of 130,000 from Kroton on the banks of the Sagra River, 25 km (16 mi) north. Founding colonies and gathering fame in the spheres of horse-breeding and music, Locri was responsible for the first written code of law in the Hellenic world. The walls of the city, parts of which are still visible, measured some 8 km (5 mi) in circumference, and the ruins within are scattered over a vast area. The museum is on the main coast road (S106) and the remains of a 5th-century BC Ionic temple are settled just behind it. ☎ 0964/390023 ▦ *Museum and site €2* ☉ *Site daily 9–1 hr before sunset, museum daily 9–7:30; museum and archaeological zone closed 1st and 3rd Mon. of month.*

Gerace

⑯ *10 km (6 mi) west of Locri, 110 km (68 mi) east of Reggio di Calabria.*

When the Saracens plundered Locri in the 7th century AD, the survivors fled inland to found Gerace, on an impregnable site that was later occupied and strengthened by the Normans. It's worth the short detour to visit this redoubt, its ruined castle tottering precariously on a jagged outcrop. Gerace's **Duomo** was founded in 1045 by Robert Guiscard (circa 1015–85), enlarged by Frederick II two centuries later, and is still the biggest church in Calabria today. Its simple, well-preserved interior has 20 columns of granite and marble, each different, and the 10th on the right, in verd antique (a green marble), changes tone according to the weather. ✉ *Piazza Vittorio Emanuele* ☎ *0964/356010* ☉ *Mar.–June and Aug. and Sept., daily 9:30–1 and 3–7; July, Tues.–Sun. 9–1 and 3–7; Oct.–Feb., daily 9:30–1 and 3–7.*

Where to Stay

$$ 🏨 **La Casa di Gianna.** Up a quiet alley in Gerace's old town, this refurbished palazzo adds an unusual touch of class to lodging standards in this part of Calabria. No expense has been spared with furnishings—polished parquet floors, quality ceramic tiles, and fine upholstery—and the staff is large enough to run a hotel 10 times the size. ✉ *Via Paolo Frasca 4, 89040* ☎ *0964/355024* 🖷 *0964/355081* ⊕ *www. lacasadigianna.it* 🛏 *9 rooms, 1 suite* ⚘ *Restaurant, minibars, bar* ▤ *AE, DC, MC, V* ◎ *BP.*

Stilo

⑰ *50 km (31 mi) north of Locri, 138 km (86 mi) northeast of Reggio di Calabria.*

Grandly positioned on the side of the rugged Monte Consolino, the village of Stilo is known for being the birthplace and home of the philosopher Tommaso Campanella (1568–1639), whose magnum opus was the socialistic *La Città del Sole* (*The City of the Sun*, 1602)—for which he spent 26 years as prisoner of the Spanish Inquisition. A tangible reason to visit the village is the tiny 10th-century Byzantine temple **La Cattólica.** Standing on a ledge above the town, this tiled and three-turreted building is believed to be the best preserved of its kind. ✉ *Via Cattólica* ▦ *Free* ☉ *Daily 9–7.*

Where to Stay

$$ 🏨 **San Giorgio.** Tucked away off Stilo's main Via Campanella, this hotel is housed in a 17th-century cardinal's palace, Palazzo Lamberti, and decked out in the style of that period, with elegantly furnished guest rooms. There are exhilarating views seaward from the garden. Half or full board is required—the food is acceptable, and there's nowhere else in town to eat anyway. ✉ *Via Citarelli 8, 89049* 🖀🖀*0964/775047* 📞*10 rooms* ⚅*Restaurant, pool, bar; no a/c in some rooms* ⊘ *Closed Oct. 20–Mar.* ⏊*MAP.*

> **en route** From Stilo you can take the S110 inland—a long twisty road that goes through the high Serra region, covered with a thick mantle of chestnut forest. There are terrific views to be enjoyed over the Ionian coast, and you can continue across the peninsula to Calabria's Tyrrhenian littoral, emerging at Pizzo. The total road distance between Stilo and Pizzo is around 80 km (50 mi).

BASILICATA & CALABRIA A TO Z

To research prices, get advice from other travelers, and book travel arrangements, visit www.fodors.com.

AIRPORTS

Twenty-seven kilometers (17 mi) north of Pizzo, Aeroporto di Lamezia caters to international charters and domestic flights, with connections to Milan, Bologna, and Rome; airlines servicing the airport are Alitalia and Air One. Reggio di Calabria's Aeroporto Tito Minniti handles Alitalia domestic flights only, with five departures daily to Rome, two to Milan. If heading straight for Matera or the Basilicata side of the Pollino massif via the UK, look into flights to Bari with Ryan Air or British Airways.

🚹 Airport Information **Aeroporto Bari Palese** 🖀 080/5835200 ⊕ www.seap-puglia. it. **Aeroporto di Lamezia** 🖀 0968/51766 or 0968/51205 ⊕ www.sacal.it. **Aeroporto Tito Minniti** 🖀 8488/65641 Alitalia ⊕ www.sogas.it. **Air One** 🖀 800/900966 ⊕ www. air-one.it. **Alitalia** 🖀 8488/65641. **British Airways** 🖀 0845/7733377 ⊕ www. britishairways.com. **RyanAir** 🖀 0871/2460000 from the UK ⊕ www.ryanair.com.

BOAT & FERRY TRAVEL

Hydrofoils, ferries, and fast ferries ply the Straits of Messina once or twice hourly from Reggio di Calabria and from Villa San Giovanni, day and night (reduced service in winter). Crossings take about 20 minutes from Reggio, about 40 minutes from Villa. Hydrofoils also run from Reggio to Sicily's Aeolian Islands. In Reggio contact SNAV and FS; in Villa, FS and Caronte.

🚹 Boat & Ferry Information **Caronte** 🖀 0965/793111. **FS** 🖀 0965/863545. **SNAV** 🖀 0965/29568 ⊕ www.snav.it.

BUS TRAVEL

Matera is linked with Bari and Metaponto by frequent buses operated by Ferrovie Appulo-Lucane, and with Taranto by SITA buses. In Calabria various bus companies make the north–south run with stops along both coasts; Ferrovie della Calabria operates many of the local services. In Reggio di Calabria, contact Lirosi for buses to Rome, leaving three times daily. From Reggio di Calabria, Salzone runs to Scilla, and Federico to Locri and Stilo.

Bus Information **Federico** ☎ 0965/590212. **Ferrovie Appulo-Lucane** ☎ 0835/332861. **Ferrovie della Calabria** ☎ 0984/36851. **Lirosi** ☎ 0966/575552. **Salzone** ☎ 0965/751586. **SITA** ☎ 0835/835007.

CAR RENTAL

You can rent cars at the Lamezia and Reggio di Calabria airports, at downtown locations in Matera, and at the Cosenza train station.

Local Agencies **Avis** ⊠ Vico XX Settembre 8, Matera ☎ 0835/336632 ⊠ Aeroporto Tito Minniti, Reggio di Calabria ☎ 0965/643023 ⊕ www.avisworld.com. **Damasco** ⊠ Vico XX Settembre 12, Matera ☎ 0835/334605. **Hertz** ⊠ Aeroporto dello Stretto, Reggio di Calabria ☎ 0965/643093 ⊕ www.hertz.it. **Maggiore-National** ⊠ Aeroporto dello Stretto, Reggio di Calabria ☎ 0965/643148 ⊕ www.maggiore.it.

CAR TRAVEL

Metaponto is a major road and rail junction for routes along the coast and inland. To get to Metaponto by car from Puglia's Taranto, take the S106 southwest for 45 km (28 mi). From Puglia's Bari, take the S96 south for 44 km (28 mi) to Altamura, then the S99 south 19 km (12 mi) to Matera. The A3 Autostrada del Sole runs between Salerno and Reggio di Calabria, with exits for Crotone (the Sila Massif), Pizzo, Rosarno (for Tropea), Palmi, and Scilla; it takes an inland route as far as Falerna, then tracks the Tyrrhenian coast south (except for the bulge of the Tropea promontory). Take the S18 for coastal destinations—or for a better view— on the Tyrrhenian side, and likewise the S106 (which is uncongested and fast) for the Ionian. To drive from Basilicata's Metaponto to Matera, take the S175 northwest for 45 km (28 mi). You can cross the Strait of Messina from Villa San Giovanni or Reggio.

EMERGENCY   ACI Emergency Service offers 24-hour roadside assistance.
SERVICES   **ACI dispatchers** ☎ 803/116.

EMERGENCIES

In Reggio di Calabria, the pharmacies Curia and Caridi are open at night. Elsewhere, late-night pharmacies are open on a rotating basis; information on current schedules is posted on any pharmacy door.

Police, Ambulance, Fire ☎ 113. **Hospital** ☎ 0965/8501 in Reggio di Calabria, 0835/2431 in Matera. **Curia** ⊠ Corso Garibaldi 455 ☎ 0965/332332. **Caridi** ⊠ Corso Garibaldi 327 ☎ 0965/24013.

LANGUAGE

The dialects of Basilicata and Calabria, which vary from village to village, are impenetrable to anyone with a knowledge of only textbook Italian. A further complication is the presence of Albanian-speaking locals in upland areas, especially around the Pollino massif. However, all— especially the younger generations—will speak Italian and you may find a considerable number of older people, returned émigrés from the United States or Canada, who are happy to show off their rusty English.

MAIL & SHIPPING

Post Offices **Cosenza** ⊠ Via Vittorio Veneto. **Matera** ⊠ Via Vittorio Veneto. **Reggio** ⊠ Via Miraglia.

SAFETY

LOCAL SCAMS The area is not noticeably more crime-ridden than any other Italian region, as far as foreign visitors are concerned. Car crime is probably the biggest threat: don't leave anything visible in your car overnight, and never leave your car unlocked.

WOMEN IN The south is more old-fashioned about independent women than other
BASILICATA & parts of Italy. But things have improved dramatically, and women can
CALABRIA expect nothing more menacing than stares from men.

TOURS

Foderaro organizes weekly bus tours of Reggio di Calabria, Scilla, Locri, and Gerace and boat tours to the Aeolian Islands. For English-language tours of Matera's sassi, consult the Matera tourist office for operators.

🚩 Fees & Schedules **Foderaro** ✉ Via Mazzini 185, Catanzaro 88100 ☎ 0961/726006 ⊕ www.foderaro.it.

TRAIN TRAVEL

The main north–south FS (Italian State Railways) line has hourly services from Reggio north to Pizzo, Diamante, and Maratea, continuing on as far as Salerno, Naples, and Rome. There are nine daily Intercity or Eurostar trains linking Reggio di Calabria with Naples (4–5 hours) and Rome (6–7 hours). All FS trains also stop at Villa San Giovanni (for connections to Sicily), a 20-minute ride from Reggio. Two fast Eurostar trains run daily between Metaponto and Naples (3¾ hours) and Rome (5½–6 hours), and three others connect Metaponto and Salerno (2¾–3½ hours), from which there are frequent connections to Naples and Rome. There are two connections to Milan, fastest time 11½ hours.

Within the region, the main FS line from Taranto stops in Metaponto, from which there are regular departures to Matera on Ferrovie Appulo-Lucane (FAL) trains. The FAL rail line links Matera to Altamura in Apulia (for connections to Bari) and to Ferrandina (for connections to Metaponto or Potenza). South of Metaponto, FS trains run into Calabria, either following the Ionian coast as far as Reggio di Calabria or swerving inland to Cosenza and the Tyrrhenian coast at Paola. Main FS services run along both coasts but can be crowded along the Tyrrhenian. Call for information on times.

🚩 Train Information **Ferrovie Appulo-Lucane** ☎ 0835/332861 ⊕ www.fal-srl.it. **FS (Italian State Railways)** ☎ 892021 ⊕ www.trenitalia.com.

TRAVEL AGENCIES

🚩 Local Agent Referrals **Simonetta** ✉ Corso Garibaldi 521, Reggio di Calabria ☎ 0965/331444.

VISITOR INFORMATION

🚩 Tourist Information **Camigliatello** ✉ Via Roma 5, 87052 ☎ 0984/578243. **Cosenza** ✉ Via P. Rossi, 87100 ☎ 0984/390595. **Maratea** ✉ Piazza del Gesù 32, 85046 ☎ 0973/876908. **Matera** ✉ Via de Viti de Marco 9, off Via Roma, 75100 ☎ 0835/331983. **Pizzo** ✉ Piazza della Repubblica, 88026 ☎ 0963/531310. **Reggio di Calabria** ✉ Corso Garibaldi 329, 89100 ☎ 0965/892012. **Tropea** ✉ Piazza Ercole, 88038 ☎ 0963/61475.

SICILY

16

Updated by
Robin S.
Goldstein

SICILY HAS BECKONED SEAFARING WANDERERS since the trials of Odysseus were first sung in Homer's *Odyssey*—perhaps the world's first travel guide. Strategically poised between Europe and Africa, this mystical land of three corners and a fiery volcano once hosted two of the most enlightened capitals of the West—one Greek, in Siracusa, and one Arab-Norman, in Palermo. The island has been a melting pot of every great civilization on the Mediterranean: Greek and Roman; then Arab and Norman; and finally French, Spanish, and Italian. Today the ancient ports of call peacefully fuse the remains of sackings past, with graceful Byzantine mosaics rubbing elbows with baroque flights of fancy—all piled atop stalwart Greek columns. Between their buildings blond-haired, blue-eyed descendants of Normans walk alongside the sultry, dark-eyed Mediterraneans more commonly considered typical of the region. The island shows something of all the cultures that have shaped its artistic heritage, a rich tapestry of art and architecture that includes massive Romanesque cathedrals, two of the best-preserved Greek temples in the world, Roman amphitheaters, and the delicate wrought-iron balconies of baroque palaces.

In the *Odyssey,* Sicily represented the unknown end of the world, yet the region eventually became a center of it under the Greeks and Normans, who recognized a paradise in its deep blue skies and temperate climate, its lush vegetation and rich marine life. Add to this paradise Sicily's unique cuisine—another harmony of elements, mingling Arab and Greek spices with Spanish and French influences using some of the world's tastiest seafood—along with the island's big, warm, fruity wines, and you can understand why those who arrived here were often reluctant to leave.

In modern times the traditional graciousness and nobility of the Sicilian people have continued to survive side by side with the destructive influences of the Mafia under Sicily's semi-autonomous government, although increasingly organized law enforcement suggests that the Mafia's grip on the island is slowly being loosened. Alongside some of the most exquisite architecture in the world lie the shabby, half-built products of some of the worst speculation imaginable. In recent years coastal Sicily, like much of the Mediterranean coast, has experienced a boom in tourism and a surge in condominium development. The chic boutiques purveying lace and linen in jet-set resort towns like Taormina give no clue of the lingering poverty in which their wares are produced. And yet, in Sicily's wind-swept heartland, a region that tourists have barely begun to explore, rolling vineyards, olive groves, and lovingly kept dirt roads leading to family farmhouses still tie Sicilians to land and tradition, forming a connected happiness that economic measures could not possibly describe.

It's not uncommon in small towns for visitors to receive invitations to a local's house for dinner. It doesn't matter if you don't speak Italian or speak only a little: they usually aren't offended if your pronunciation isn't perfect. One of the reasons for this, no doubt, is the fact that many Sicilians or their close relatives have themselves been strangers in foreign lands, and empathy goes a long way.

16

Numbers in the text correspond to numbers in the margin and on the Sicily, Palermo, Agrigento, and Siracusa maps.

If you have
3 days

A three-day visit to the island shouldn't require a car if you base yourself in 🖼 **Palermo** ❶–⓫ ▶. In this hub of Norman Sicily the highlights include the **Palazzo Reale** ❶ and the **Museo Archeologico Regionale** ❿, as well as a handful of churches. Take the bus out to **Monreale** ⓬ to admire the splendid cathedral, and compare it with the slightly earlier mosaic-laden monument at 🖼 **Cefalù** ⓭. Spend your last day exploring this seaside resort.

If you have
5 days

There are two distinct approaches to a five-day itinerary in Sicily, the first focusing on the island's western half, the second on the east. For the western itinerary, spend your first two nights in 🖼 **Palermo** ❶–⓫ ▶; then head west, dropping in on the half-finished temple of **Segesta** ⓯ and making 🖼 **Erice** ⓰ your next overnight stop. From Erice, follow the island's curve to the cliffside ruins of **Selinunte** ⓴ and leave much of the day for the Greek temple site at 🖼 **Agrigento** ㉑–㉗, where you can spend your fourth night. On your last day strike north on the S640 to meet the A19 autostrada near Caltanisetta, which will bring you back up to the Tyrrhenian coast. Get your shut-eye in 🖼 **Cefalù** ⓭ before turning westward back to Palermo. The eastern itinerary starts with one day in 🖼 **Palermo** ❶–⓫; on the second day head southeast, lunch at **Enna** ㊶, and then travel up A18 to 🖼 **Taormina** ㊾, where you'll spend your second night in the shadow of **Mt. Etna** ㊼. Spend your third day in town or at the volcano before heading south to the Greek wonders of 🖼 **Siracusa** ㉘–㊵. On the fourth day head southwest on the SS115 to 🖼 **Agrigento** ㉑–㉗.

If you have
9 days

Begin by following the western five-day itinerary above, but at Agrigento make for lofty and mysterious **Enna** ㊶; then spend the afternoon viewing the mosaics of the Roman villa at Casale, near **Piazza Armerina** ㊷. If you have time, stop off to see the Museo della Ceramica at **Caltagirone** ㊸ before continuing on the S124 to 🖼 **Siracusa** ㉘–㊵ for a day's exploring and a night's rest. Next, head to **Acireale** ㊽, perhaps stopping for a fish lunch there before landing for two nights at 🖼 **Taormina** ㊾. From here it's a brief drive or intense, rewarding walk up to the village of **Castelmola** ㊿, with memorable views over Taormina and **Mt. Etna** ㊼, where an excursion is worthwhile. From Taormina drive up the coast to **Messina** �999 and its Museo Regionale, before crossing—either from Messina or Milazzo, on the north coast—to the Aeolian archipelago, where 🖼 **Lipari** ⓼ has the biggest selection of accommodations and a superb Museo Archeologico. From here you can opt to explore the remaining six islands or return to the Sicilian mainland for your last night at 🖼 **Cefalù** ⓭.

Exploring Sicily

The rewards of a rental car are great in Sicily: the island is about 180 km (112 mi) north to south and 270 km (168 mi) across, filled with places of interest—sometimes out of the way. With a car at your disposal you can see both the interior and the coastline without the headaches of the notoriously spotty public transportation. The Aeolian Islands are connected by *aliscafi* (hydrofoils) and ferries.

About the Hotels & Restaurants

Sicilians are thrilled to share their culinary richness—you'll rarely find an eating establishment that isn't welcoming to outsiders. When you let the waiter or proprietor choose your meal for you, based on the season, you'll taste the best the island has to offer, and also earn their respect. Meals in Sicily tend to happen a bit later than on the mainland, especially lunch (rarely before 1:30 PM) and on weekends.

Sicily is Italy's largest region, with some of the most remote countryside. The good-quality hotels tend to be limited to the major cities and resorts of Palermo, Taormina, Siracusa, and Agrigento. There are some other superb establishments, such as converted villas with sea views and well-equipped modern hotels, but it's best not to expect to come across some enchanting oasis in the middle of nowhere. Recently there has been an explosion in the development of *agriturismo* lodgings (rural bed-and-breakfasts), many of them quite basic, but others providing the same facilities found in hotels.

WHAT IT COSTS In euros					
	$$$$	**$$$**	**$$**	**$**	**¢**
RESTAURANTS	over €22	€16–€22	€11–€16	€7–€11	under €7
HOTELS	over €220	€160–€220	€110–€160	€70–€110	under €70

Restaurant prices are for a second course (*secondo piatto*). Hotel prices are for two people in a standard double room in high season, including tax and service.

Timing

Sicily comes into its own in spring, but you're not alone in knowing this. Taormina and Erice attract a flood of visitors around Easter, and any visit scheduled for this time should be backed up by solid advance bookings. Many sights like inland Segesta are at their best in the clear spring light, and are far enough off the beaten track to ensure a fairly hassle-free time. August is hot and crowded, and beaches are clogged with vacationers. Come in September or October and you'll find acres of beach space. As with Easter, Christmas and New Year's draw visitors to the island, and reservations should always be made as early as possible. Other festivals, such as Agrigento's almond festival in February and the Carnevale in Acireale, can also mean a dearth of vacancies.

PALERMO

Once the intellectual capital of southern Europe, Palermo has always been at the crossroads of civilization. Favorably situated on a crescent-shape bay at the foot of Monte Pellegrino, it has attracted almost every people and culture touching the Mediterranean world. To Palermo's credit, it has absorbed these diverse cultures into a unique personality that is at once Arab and Christian, Byzantine and Roman, Norman and Ital-

Ceramics, Crafts & Carts

Sicily is one of the leaders in the Italian ceramics industry, with important factories at Caltagirone, in the interior, and Santo Stefano di Camastra, along the northern coast between Messina and Cefalù. Colorful Sicilian folk pottery can still be bought at bargain prices. Place mats, tablecloths, napkins, and clothing decorated with fine petit point are good buys in Cefalù, Taormina, and Erice, but they are nonetheless not cheap. Collectors have been combing Sicily for years for pieces of the colorful *carretti siciliani* (Sicilian carts). Before the automobile, these were the major form of transportation in Sicily, decorated in primary colors and in primitive styles.

16

Marionette Theater

Almost every major city in Sicily has a theater giving performances of the world-famous Sicilian *pupi* (marionettes). Adults as well as children will enjoy the colorful shows, the most popular of which are in Palermo, Acireale, and Taormina. Stories center on heroes from the Norman fables, distressed damsels, and Saracen invaders. Even if you can't understand Italian, the action is fast and furious, so it's easy to figure out what's going on.

Sweet Sicily

Desserts from Sicily are famous, none more than the wonderful cannoli, whose delicate pastry shell and just-sweet-enough ricotta barely resemble their foreign impostors. The traditional Easter cake is the *cassata siciliana,* a rich sponge cake with candied fruit and marzipan. From behind bakery windows and glass cases beam tiny marzipan sweets, bizarrely fashioned into brightly colored apples, cherries, hamburgers, and even prosciutto. Do as the locals do and dip your summer morning brioche—the best in Italy—into a cup of brilliantly refreshing coffee granita. The world's first ice cream is said to have been made by the Romans from the snow on the slopes of Mt. Etna, and the practice of producing top-quality gelato, and eating it in great quantities, is still prevalent throughout the island.

---

ian. The city's heritage encompasses all of Sicily's varied ages, but its distinctive aspect is its Arab-Norman identity, an improbable marriage that, mixed in with Byzantine and Jewish elements, created some resplendent works of art. These are most notable in the churches, from small jewels such as San Giovanni degli Eremiti to larger-scale works such as the cathedral. No less noteworthy than the architecture is Palermo's chaotic vitality, on display at some of Italy's most vibrant outdoor markets, public squares, street bazaars, and food vendors, and above all in its grand, discordant symphony of motorists, motor bikers, and pedestrians that triumphantly climaxes in the new town center each evening with Italy's most spectacular *passeggiata* (the leisurely social stroll along the principal thoroughfare).

Palermo was first colonized by Phoenician traders in the 6th century BC, but it was their descendants, the Carthaginians, who built the important fortress here that caught the covetous eye of the Romans. After the First

Punic War the Romans took control of the city in the 3rd century BC. Following several invasions by the Vandals, Sicily was settled by Arabs, who made the country an emirate and established Palermo as a showpiece capital that rivaled both Cordoba and Cairo in the splendor of its architecture. Nestled in the fertile Conca d'Oro (Golden Conch) plain, full of orange, lemon, and carob groves and enclosed by limestone hills, Palermo became a magical world of palaces and mosques, minarets and palm trees.

It was so attractive and sophisticated a city that the Norman ruler Roger de Hauteville (1031–1101) decided to conquer it and make it his capital (1072). The Norman occupation of Sicily resulted in the Palermo's golden age (1072–1194), a remarkable period of enlightenment and learning in which the arts flourished. The city of Palermo, which in the 11th century counted more than 300,000 inhabitants, became the European center for the Norman court and one of the most important ports for trade between East and West. Eventually the Normans were replaced by the Swabian ruler Frederick II (1194–1250), the Holy Roman Emperor, and incorporated into the Kingdom of the Two Sicilies. You will also see plenty of evidence in Palermo of the baroque art and architecture of the long Spanish rule. The Aragonese viceroys also brought the Spanish Inquisition to Palermo, which some historians believe helped foster the protective secret societies that evolved into today's Mafia.

Exploring Palermo

Sicily's capital is a multilayered, vigorous metropolis; approach it with an open mind, and you'll find it an enriching city, with a strong historical profile. You're likely to encounter some frustrating instances of inefficiency and, depending on the season, stifling heat. If you have a car, park it in a garage as soon as you can, and don't take it out until you are ready to depart.

Palermo is easily explored on foot, though you may choose to spend a morning taking a bus tour to help you get oriented. The Quattro Canti, or Four Corners, is the hub that separates the four sections of the old city: La Kalsa (the old Arab section) to the southeast, Albergheria to the southwest, Capo to the northwest, and Vucciria to the northeast. Each of these is a tumult of activity during the day, though at night the narrow alleys empty out and are best avoided altogether in favor of the more animated avenues of the new city north of Teatro Massimo. Sights you will want to see by day are scattered along three major streets: Corso Vittorio Emanuele, Via Maqueda, and Via Roma. The tourist information office in Piazza Castelnuovo will give you a map and a valuable handout that lists opening and closing times, which sometimes change with the seasons.

a good tour

Start at the **Palazzo Reale** ❶ �L, at the far west end of Corso Vittorio Emanuele, to see the mosaics in the Cappella Palatina and the royal apartments. Walk down Via dei Benedettini, following the five pink domes of **San Giovanni degli Eremiti** ❷. Back east on the Corso stands Palermo's **Cattedrale** ❸, a cacophony of Arab, Norman, and Gothic influences. Head east, stopping for a glance at the baroque balconies in Piazza Bologni to your right, and continue until you reach the intersection of Corso Vittorio Emanuele and Via Maqueda, the **Quattro Canti** ❹. Just east off Quat-

Palermo

tro Canti is Piazza Pretoria, adjacent to which Piazza Bellini holds a trio of eminent churches: the baroque **Santa Caterina** ⑤ and, up the stairs, **San Cataldo** ⑥ and **La Martorana** ⑦, which form a delightful Norman complex. Cross Via Roma into the Arab Kalsa neighborhood and follow Via Santa Anna to Piazza dei Vespri, turning left onto Vicolo dei Corriere to Piazza San Francesco d'Assisi, a great place to stop for a snack at the historic Focacceria San Francesco on Via Paternostro. Head across the piazza, down Via Merlo, and across to Via Alloro. Continuing east to **Palazzo Abatellis** ⑧ and its Galleria Regionale, holding a fine collection of medieval and Renaissance art. If you like puppets, take Via Alloro east and go northwest (left) on Via Butera to the **Museo delle Marionette** ⑨. Then take either Bus 104 or 105 back along Corso Vittorio Emanuele to transfer to 101 heading north along Via Roma to the **Museo Archeologico Regionale** ⑩. Cut through Via Bara all'Olivella to Piazza Verdi and the **Teatro Massimo** ⑪, and finally, if it's between the hours of 6 PM and 9 PM, head north along Via Ruggero Settimo to take your place in the larger-than-life evening passeggiata, a teeming mass of humanity in Piazza R. Settimo in front of the Teatro Politeama.

TIMING   Allow the better part of a day for this tour, with lunch around the Quattro Canti.

What to See

★ ③ **Cattedrale** (Cathedral). This church is a lesson in Palermitan eclecticism—originally Norman (1182), then Catalan Gothic (14th–15th century), then fitted out with a baroque and neoclassical interior (18th century). Its turrets, towers, dome, and arches come together in the kind of meeting of diverse elements that King Roger II (1095–1154), whose tomb is inside along with that of Frederick II, fostered during his reign. The back of the apse is gracefully decorated with interlacing Arab arches inlaid with limestone and black volcanic tufa. ⊠ *Corso Vittorio Emanuele, Capo* ☎ *091/334376* ⊡ *Crypt €1* ☉ *Church Mon.–Sat. 7–7, Sun. 8–1:30 and 4–7; crypt Mon.–Sat. 9:30–5:30.*

⑦ **La Martorana.** Distinguished by an elegant Norman campanile, this church was erected in 1143 but had its interior altered considerably during the baroque period. High along the western wall, however, is some of the oldest and best-preserved mosaic artwork of the Norman period. Near the entrance is an interesting mosaic of King Roger II being crowned by Christ. In it Roger is dressed in a bejeweled Byzantine stole, reflecting the Norman court's penchant for all things Byzantine. Archangels along the ceiling wear the same stole wrapped around their shoulders and arms. ⊠ *Piazza Bellini 3, Kalsa* ☎ *091/6161692* ☉ *Mon.–Sat. 8:30–1 and 3:30–5:30, Sun. 8:30–1.*

⑩ **Museo Archeologico Regionale** (Regional Museum of Archaeology). Especially interesting pieces in this small but excellent collection are the examples of prehistoric cave drawings and a marvelously reconstructed Doric frieze from the Greek temple at Selinunte. The frieze reveals the high level of artistic culture attained by the Greek colonists in Sicily some 2,500 years ago. ⊠ *Piazza Olivella 24, Via Roma, Olivella* ☎ *091/ 6116805* ⊡ *€4.50* ☉ *Tues.–Sat. 8:30–6:45, Sun. and Mon. 8:30–1.*

🌙 ❾ **Museo delle Marionette** (Marionette Museum). The traditional Sicilian *pupi,* with their glittering armor and fierce expressions, have become a symbol of Norman Sicily. Plots center on the chivalric legends of the troubadours, who, before the puppet theater, kept alive tales of Norman heroes in Sicily such as Orlando Furioso and William the Bad (1120–66). There are weekly performances here. ⊠ *Via Butera 1, Kalsa* ☎ *091/328060* ⊕ *www.museomarionettepalermo.it* 💷 *€3* ⊙ *Weekdays 9–1 and 4–7* ⊙ *Closed Aug. 13–26.*

❽ **Palazzo Abatellis.** Housed in this late-15th-century Catalan Gothic palace with Renaissance elements is the **Galleria Regionale.** Among its treasures are an *Annunciation* (1474) by Sicily's prominent Renaissance master Antonello da Messina (1430–79) and an arresting fresco by an unknown painter, titled *The Triumph of Death,* a macabre depiction of the plague years. ⊠ *Via Alloro 4, Kalsa* ☎ *091/6164317* 💷 *€4.50; additional €3.50 for guided tour* ⊙ *Mon.–Sat. 9–1 and 2:30–7:30, Sun. 9–1.*

▶ ❶ **Palazzo Reale** (Royal Palace). This historic palace, also called Palazzo dei Normanni (Norman Palace), was for centuries the seat of Sicily's semi-autonomous rulers. Because it now houses the Sicilian Parliament, little is viewable by the public. However, the **Cappella Palatina** (Palatine Chapel) remains open, built by Roger II in 1132 and a dazzling example of the unique harmony of artistic elements produced under the Normans. Here the skill of French and Sicilian masons was brought to bear on the decorative purity of Arab ornamentation and the splendor of 11th-century Greek Byzantine mosaics. The interior is covered with glittering mosaics and capped by a splendid 10th-century Arab honeycomb stalactite wooden ceiling. Biblical stories blend happily with scenes of Arab life—look for one showing a picnic in a harem—and Norman court pageantry.

The building is an interesting mesh of abutting 10th-century Norman and 17th-century Spanish structures. Upstairs are the royal apartments, including the **Sala di Re Ruggero** (King Roger's Hall), decorated with medieval murals of hunting scenes—an earlier (1120) secular counterpoint to the religious themes seen elsewhere. Tour guides escort you around these halls once used by one of the most splendid courts in Europe. French, Latin, and Arabic were spoken here, and Arab astronomers and poets exchanged ideas with Latin and Greek scholars in one of the most interesting marriages of culture in the Western world. ⊠ *Piazza Indipendenza, Albergheria* ☎ *091/7054317 palace, 091/7054732 chapel* 💷 *Free* ⊙ *Chapel: weekdays 9–11:45 and 3–4:45, weekends 9–11:45. Apartments: Mon., Fri., and Sat. 9–11:45.*

Piazza Pretoria. The square's centerpiece, a lavishly decorated fountain with 500 separate pieces of sculpture and an abundance of nude figures, so shocked some Palermitans when it was unveiled in 1575 that it got the nickname "Fountain of Shame." Extensive renovation and cleaning were completed in December 2003. It's even more of a sight when illuminated at night.

❹ **Quattro Canti.** The Four Corners is the intersection of Corso Vittorio Emanuele and Via Maqueda. Four rather exhaust-blackened baroque palaces from Spanish rule meet at concave corners, each with its own fountain and representations of a Spanish ruler, patron saint, and one of the four seasons.

★ ❻ **San Cataldo.** Three striking Saracenic scarlet domes mark this church, built in 1154 during the Norman occupation of Palermo. The church now belongs to the Knights of the Holy Sepulchre, and the spare but intense stone interior is rarely open to the public. ⊠ *Piazza Bellini 3, Albergheria.*

❷ **San Giovanni degli Eremiti.** Distinguished by its five reddish-orange domes and stripped-clean interior, this 12th-century church was built by the Normans on the site of an earlier mosque—one of 200 that once stood in Palermo. The emirs ruled Palermo for nearly two centuries and brought to it their passion for lush gardens and fountains. One is reminded of this while sitting in San Giovanni's delightful cloister of twin half columns, surrounded by palm trees, jasmine, oleander, and citrus trees. ⊠ *Via dei Benedettini, Albergheria* ☎ *091/6515019* 🎟 *€4.50* ☉ *Mon.–Sat. 9–7, Sun. 9–1.*

❺ **Santa Caterina.** The walls of this splendid baroque church (1596) in Piazza Bellini are covered with decorative 17th-century inlays of precious marble. ⊠ *Piazza Bellini, Kalsa* ☎ *091/6162488* ☉ *Open by appointment; reserve a day in advance.*

⓫ **Teatro Massimo.** Construction of this formidable neoclassical theater was started in 1875 by Giovanni Battista Basile and completed by his son Ernesto in 1897. A fire in 1974 rendered the theater inoperable, but it reopened with great fanfare in 1997, and its interior is now as glorious as ever. Claimed to be Italy's largest, the theater was featured in scenes in *The Godfather Part III*. Visits are by 25-minute guided tour only; English-speaking guides are available. ⊠ *Piazza Verdi 9, at the top of Via Maqueda* ☎ *091/6090831* ⊕ *www.teatromassimo.it* 🎟 *€3* ☉ *Tues.–Sat. 10–3:30, except during rehearsals.*

| off the beaten path | **CONVENTO DEI CAPPUCCINI** – Have you ever seen thousands of dead bodies all in a row? The spookiest sight in all of Sicily, this 16th-century catacomb houses more than 8,000 corpses of men, women, and young children, many mummified and preserved, hanging on the walls. Many of the fully clothed corpses wear priests' smocks (most of the dead were Capuchin monks). The Capuchins were founders and proprietors of the bizarre establishment from 1559 to 1880. It's memorable and not for the faint of heart; children (and adults) might be frightened or disturbed. ⊠ *Piazza Cappuccini north of Palazzo Reale* ☎ *091/212633* 🎟 *€2* ☉ *Daily 9–noon and 3–5.* |

Where to Stay & Eat

$$–$$$ ✕ **Il Mulinazzo.** Palermitans drive 45 minutes to savor modern and
Fodor's Choice startling combinations in chef Nino Graziano's traditional country
★ house, probably Sicily's best restaurant. Fava-bean puree (*macco*), a staple of the rural poor, is playfully paired with scampi and finished with ricotta, *speck* (cured ham), peppercorns, and fried basil leaf. A delicate fillet of pork is encrusted with pistachios and served with chocolate sauce,

ON THE MENU

SICILIAN CUISINE IS ONE of the oldest in existence, going back to Siracusan cooking competitions in 600 BC. The Sicilians even have a reasonable claim to the invention of pasta; maccheroni (long, thin pasta tubes) may well be today's purest survivor of the original. Today's cuisine represents Sicily's unique cultural mix, imaginatively combining fish, fruits, vegetables, and nuts with Italian pastas and Arab and North African ingredients such as couscous.

In Sicily, naturally, you'll enjoy some of the freshest seafood in all of Italy. Pasta con le sarde (an emblematic dish that goes back to the Saracen conquerors, with fresh sardines, olive oil, raisins, pine nuts, and wild fennel) is different at every restaurant. Grilled tonno (tuna) and triglie (red mullet) are reliable coastal staples. King, however, is pesce spada (swordfish), best enjoyed marinated (marinato), smoked (affumicato), or as the traditional involtini di pesce spada (swordfish roulades). Delicate ricci (sea urchins) are a specialty, as is spaghetti alla Norma (with a sauce of tomato, fried eggplant, ricotta, and basil). Meanwhile, the Sicilian bitter almond (mandorla), the pride of Agrigento, plays into everything from risotto alle mandorle to incomparable almond granita, an absolute must in summer.

Long neglected, Sicilian reds and whites are some of the most up-and-coming in the wine world, but still the bargains of Italy. The earthy nero d'avola grape bolsters many of Sicily's traditionally sunny, expansive reds, but lately it's often cut with cabernet or merlot. Meanwhile, the islands of Lipari and Pantelleria offer sweet, golden dessert wines, Malvasia and Passito. Marsala remains Sicily's most famous dessert wine. Look for anything from the world-renowned Planeta.

---

rice fritters, cinnamon applesauce, and swirls of raspberry. The wine list is excellent, and prices are reasonable—even for the spectacular tasting menu. Coming from Palermo, the restaurant is on the right side of SS 121 after 17 km (11 mi). It's after the Villafrati exit and a car dealership; the tiny sign is easy to miss. ⊠ *SS121, Località Bolognetta Nord, Villafrati* ☎ *091/8724870* ⊟ *AE, DC, MC, V* ⊗ *Closed Mon., 2 wks in Jan., and 2 wks in July. No dinner Sun.*

★ **$$–$$$** ✕ **Il Ristorantino.** A few miles into suburban Palermo—an easy taxi ride from the center—Pippo Anastasio, one of the true personalities of Sicilian cooking, has created one of the most modern restaurants in all of Sicily. Here, *pesce spada* (swordfish) reaches its loftiest heights, served simply marinated with olive oil, lemon, herb butter, and toast; meanwhile, Pippo's flights of fancy include *astice* (lobster) tortellini with cherry tomatoes, *bottarga* (cured tuna roe) and hot pepper. Dark wood contrasts with recessed lighting and stylized wall panels to create a design fusion that echoes the creativity of the menu. ⊠ *Piazzale Alcide De Gasperi 19, Resuttana* ☎ *091/512861* ⊟ *AE, DC, MC, V* ⊗ *Closed Mon., 1 wk in Jan., and Aug.*

$$–$$$ ✕ **Osteria dei Vespri.** This temple to modern Sicilian cuisine is foodie paradise in the *centro storico* (historic city center). Try the superb antipasto

6 variazioni di crudo dal mare (six variations of raw delicacies from the sea). Local fish is simply presented in dishes like tartare of bluefish with vinaigrette, and culinary skill is showcased in *casareccia* (homemade pasta) with tuna ragù. The wine list is one of the best in Palermo. ✉ *Piazza Croce dei Vespri 6, Kalsa* ☎ *091/6171631* ▬ *AE, DC, MC, V* ⊘ *Closed Sun. and 2 wks in Aug.*

$$ ✕ **Capricci di Sicilia.** It's said that this spot, in the heart of Palermo next to the Teatro Politeama, is the best place in town for *cassata siciliana* (ice cream with sponge cake, candied fruit, and marzipan). The atmosphere is a bit impersonal, but you'll find only typical Sicilian specialties here, such as tuna with garlic and mint, sardine *polpette* (minced sardine balls), or spaghetti with a ragù of sausage and fresh ricotta. ✉ *Via Pignatelli 6, Piazza Luigi Sturzo, Vucciria* ☎ *091/327777* ▬ *AE, DC, MC, V* ⊘ *Closed Mon.*

$$ ✕ **Gusto Divino.** Vaulted stone archways, exposed brick, and rows of fine bottles of Sicilian wine set the scene for nouveau Sicilian cuisine served to a chic business and university crowd. A well-thought-out list of Sicilian and Italian wines accompanies an ever-changing menu with novelties like linguine *con bottarga di tonno* (linguine with cured tuna roe and lemon zest). Pistachio features prominently in dishes. For dessert, don't miss one of Palermo's best versions of the classic *torta sette veli* (seven-layer chocolate cake), made with seven kinds of chocolate. ✉ *Corso Pisani 30, Albergheria* ☎ *091/6457001* ▬ *AE, DC, MC, V* ⊘ *Closed Sun. and Nov.*

$–$$ ✕ **Strascinu.** The specialty in this informal and busy restaurant on the outskirts of the city center is pasta *con le sarde* (with sardines), the region's ubiquitous Arab-Sicilian dish. Amphoras, Sicilian ceramics, and even a miniature, electrically operated puppet theater enliven the rustic decor, and there's a large garden with gazebos. ✉ *Viale Regione Siciliana 2286, Circumvallazione* ☎ *091/401292* ▬ *AE, DC, MC, V* ⊘ *Closed Aug. 8–18.*

★ $ ✕ **Casa del Brodo.** On the edge of the Vucciria and dating back to 1890, this restaurant—its two small rooms usually crowded with a mix of tourists and locals—is one of Palermo's oldest. You can't go wrong with Sicilian classics like pasta *alle sarde* (with fresh sardines, raisins, and pine nuts), *carni bollite* (boiled meats), or *zuppa di pesce* (fish stew). The risotto with mushrooms or asparagus is also a standout. ✉ *Corso Vittorio Emanuele 175, Vucciria* ☎ *091/321655* ▬ *AE, DC, MC, V* ⊘ *Closed Tues. in winter, Sun. in summer.*

★ ¢ ✕ **Antica Focacceria San Francesco.** This neighborhood bakery with turn-of-the-20th-century wooden cabinets, marble-top tables, and cast-iron ovens is an institution. It serves the snacks that locals love—and from which you can make an inexpensive meal. The big pan on the counter holds the delicious regional specialty *pani cu' la meusa* (boiled, sliced calf's spleen with Parmesan-like cacciocavallo cheese and salt). The squeamish can opt for the *panelle* (chickpea flour fritters), the fantastic *fritto misto* (assorted fried appetizers), or an enormous *arancino* (breaded, deep-fried ball of rice with tomato and meat or vegetable filling). ✉ *Via Paternostro 58, Kalsa* ☎ *091/320264* ▬ *AE, DC, MC, V* ⊘ *Closed Tues. in winter.*

¢ ✕ **Pani Ca Meusa.** This supremely local institution facing Palermo's old fishing port has had only one item on the menu—and one legendary manager-cum–sandwich maker—for more than 50 years. Calf's spleen sandwich, the joint's namesake, is sprinkled with a bit of salt and some lemon and served with or without cheese to a buzzing crowd of Palermo's battle-wearied elders. In our book, it beats the Focacceria San Francesco for the title of best in town. There's no seating, though—only counters. ⊠ *Via Cala 62, Kalsa* ☎ *No phone* ⚲ *Reservations not accepted* ▤ *No credit cards* ⊘ *Closed Sun. and Mon., and unpredictable other days.*

$$$$ 🏨 **Villa Igiea.** A short taxi ride through some rough-looking districts of Palermo takes you to this historic oasis of luxury and comfort in its own tropical garden at the edge of the bay. A meander through the grounds reveals such relics as an ancient Greek temple at the water's edge. Large rooms are furnished individually, the nicest with an Italian art nouveau flavor. Spacious lobbies and public rooms unfold onto a terrace and restaurant. There's hourly shuttle service to the city center. ⊠ *Salita Belmonte 43, Acquasanta, 3 km (2 mi) north of Palermo, 90142* ☎ *091/6312111* 🖶 *091/547654* ⊕ *www.cormorano.net/sgas/villaigiea/home.htm* ☞ *101 rooms, 12 suites* ⚲ *Restaurant, minibars, tennis court, pool, gym, bar, free parking* ▤ *AE, DC, MC, V* ⦿ *BP.*

★ $$$–$$$$ 🏨 **Centrale Palace Hotel.** Ideally located a stone's throw from Palermo's main historic sites, the Centrale is the only hotel in the heart of the centro storico that was once a stately private palace. Built in 1717 and painstakingly renovated in 1996, the hotel weaves old-world charm with modern comfort like few establishments on the island. All rooms and salons are tastefully furnished, and a 2003 expansion that added 40 new rooms and 6 spacious junior suites fits seamlessly into the mix. The young, welcoming staff provide professional service. The rooftop restaurant serves creative Sicilian cuisine. ⊠ *Corso Vittorio Emanuele 327, Vicciria, 90134* ☎ *091/336666* 🖶 *091/334881* ⊕ *www.centralepalacehotel.it* ☞ *104 rooms* ⚲ *Restaurant, minibars, cable TV, bar, free parking* ▤ *AE, DC, MC, V* ⦿ *BP.*

$$$ 🏨 **Grand Hotel et des Palmes.** This grande dame's fabled charm glows once more. The public rooms decorated in the classico style suggest the elegant life of Palermo society before World War I, when it was marked by tea dances and formal balls. Richard Wagner finished writing the opera *Parsifal* during a stay here. Guest rooms are filled with antiques and heavy fabrics. The "superior" rooms are more recently renovated. ⊠ *Via Roma 398, Vicciria, 90139* ☎ *091/6028111* 🖶 *091/331545* ⊕ *www.cormorano. net/sgas/despalmes/* ☞ *183 rooms, 6 suites* ⚲ *Restaurant, minibars, bar, cable TV, meeting rooms, parking (fee)* ▤ *AE, DC, MC, V* ⦿ *BP.*

$$$ 🏨 **Hotel Principe di Villafranca.** Not far from Palermo's glitzy shopping district, this hotel creates the feel of a luxurious private home with fine Sicilian antiques, imperial striped silks, creamy marble floors, and vaulted ceilings. It's easy to get comfortable in the understated surroundings: relax in the library with an aperitif or savor an authentic meal in the rustic adjoining Ristorante Firriato, which drizzles its dishes with a sublime, homemade balsamic vinegar. Rooms are elegant, with fine linens and more antiques. Ask for a room on the street side; back rooms can actually be noisier. ⊠ *Via G. Turrisi Colonna 4, Libertà, 90141* ☎ *091/6118523* 🖶 *091/588705* ⊕ *www.principedivillafranca.it* ☞ *30*

rooms, 4 suites ♨ *Restaurant, café, gym, library, Internet, meeting room, free parking* ▤ *AE, DC, MC, V* ⏻ *BP.*

$$$ 🏨 **Massimo Plaza Hotel.** This hotel has one of Palermo's best locations—right opposite the renovated Teatro Massimo. It is small and select, its few rooms spacious, comfortably furnished, and well insulated from the noise on Via Maqueda. Service is personal and polite, with Continental breakfast served in your room with the newspaper of your choice. Book in advance for one of the seven rooms that have theater views. ✉ *Via Maqueda 437, Vucciria, 90133* ☎ *091/325657* 🖨 *091/325711* ⊕ *www.massimoplazahotel.com* ⮑ *15 rooms* ♨ *Minibars, cable TV, bar, parking (fee)* ▤ *AE, DC, MC, V* ⏻ *BP.*

$$–$$$ 🏨 **Mondello Palace.** This is the leading hotel at the Mondello resort, making the best use of its location near the beach just north of Palermo. The private beach has cabins and changing rooms for the use of hotel guests. The rooms are large, with luxury baths, and most have balconies. In summer this is indisputably the place to be. ✉ *Viale Principe di Scalea, Mondello Lido, 90139* ☎ *091/450001* 🖨 *091/450657* ⮑ *83 rooms, 9 suites* ♨ *Restaurant, minibars, pool, gym, beach, windsurfing, boating, bar, free parking, some pets allowed* ▤ *AE, DC, MC, V* ⏻ *BP.*

¢ 🏨 **Hotel Moderno.** This third-floor hotel is a slice of patient old Palermo, right down to the 1930s technology at the reception desk. A slightly shabby, mirrored reception area and bar give way to simple but clean and comfortable rooms, some with balconies overlooking Via Roma. The location couldn't be better. Singles are a particularly good deal, at close to half the double room rate. ✉ *Via Roma 276, corner of Via Napoli, Vucciria, 90139* ☎ *091/588683* 🖨 *091/588260* ⮑ *38 rooms* ♨ *Bar, parking (fee)* ▤ *AE, DC, MC, V* ⏻ *BP.*

Nightlife & the Arts

The Arts

CONCERTS & OPERA **Teatro Massimo** (✉ Piazza Verdi, at the top of Via Maqueda, Vucciria ☎ 091/6053111 ⊕ www.teatromassimo.it), modeled after the Pantheon in Rome, is truly larger than life—it's the biggest theater in Italy. Concerts and operas are presented throughout the year. Live out your *Godfather* fantasies; an opera at the Massimo is an unforgettable Sicilian experience. The shamelessly grandiose neoclassical **Teatro Politeama Garibaldi** (✉ Piazza Ruggero Settimo, Libertà ☎ 091/6053315) stages a winter season of opera and orchestral works.

FESTIVALS The **Festa di Santa Rosalia** street fair is held July 9–15 in honor of the city's patron saint. Fireworks light up the evenings. **Epiphany** (January 6) is celebrated with Byzantine rites and a procession of townspeople in local costume through the streets of Piana degli Albanesi, 24 km (15 mi) south of Palermo. The village is named for the Albanian immigrants who first settled there, bringing with them the Byzantine Catholic rite.

PUPPET SHOWS Palermo's tradition of puppet theater holds an appeal for children and adults alike. Street artists often perform outside the Teatro Massimo in summer. The **Figli d'Arte Cuticchio Association** (✉ Via Bara all'Olivella 95, Kalsa ☎ 091/323400 ⊕ www.figlidartecuticchio.com 💶 €6) hosts performances every weekend at 6:30, Sept.–May.

Nightlife

Each night between 6 and 9 PM, all of Palermo's youth gather to shop, socialize, flirt, and plan the evening's affairs in an epic passeggiata along Via Ruggero Settimo (a northern extension of Via Maqueda) and filling Piazza Ruggero Settimo in front of Teatro Politeama. Some trendy bars also line Via Principe del Belmonte, intersecting with Via Roma and Via Ruggero Settimo.

BARS & CAFÉS **Kursaal Kalhesa** (⊠ Foro Umberto I 21, Kalsa ☎ 091/6161282) is one of the most fascinating places to drink or socialize down by the port and the Porta Felice. An energetic, eclectic crowd of Palermitan youth takes in lively jazz, coffee, and drinks inside an ancient city wall with spectacular 100-foot ceilings and an idyllic courtyard—it's truly representative of the New Palermo. There's live music (primarily jazz) Thursday night. Excellent, if pricey, Sicilian food with an Arab touch is served in the adjacent restaurant. Kursaal Kalhesa is closed Sunday night and Monday.

Enoteca Picone (⊠ Via Marconi 36, Libertà ☎ 091/331300 ⊕ www. enotecapicone.it ☉ Closed Mon.) is the best wine bar (and wineshop) in town, with a fantastic selection of Sicilian and national wines by the glass and bottle.

Parco Letterario Giuseppe Tomasi di Lampedusa (⊠ Vicolo della Neve all'Alloro 25, near the Piazza Marina, Kalsa ☎ 091/6160796 ⊕ www. parcotomasi.it) is a cultural center, wine bar, cafè, language school, and historic-tour operator. Down by the port in the deep heart of the Kalsa, the center, open Tuesday–Sunday 9 AM–1 AM, offers courses in Italian for foreigners, excellent local wines, a student social scene, and art shows; its little library (and just about everything else) focuses not just on Palermitan history but on the life and times of the center's namesake, Lampedusa, author of the canonical *Il Gattopardo* (*The Leopard*).

NIGHTCLUBS Most nightclubs and discotheques are scattered around the northern, newer end of town. In summer the nightlife scene shifts to **Mondello,** Palermo's seaside satellite on the other side of Monte Pellegrino. **Bar Costa** (⊠ Via G. D'Annunzio 15, Libertà ☎ 091/334835) overflows with Italian bar-style treats, coffee, and so on; they also ship their famous delicacies abroad. **Mikalsa** (⊠ Via Torremuzza 27, Kalsa ☎ 339/3146466 ⊕ www.mikalsa.it/) is a hip, coolly lighted nightspot with Sicily's best selection of Belgian beers. **Kandisky Florio** (⊠ Discesa Tonnara 4, Arenella suburbs ☎ 091/6375611) is a disco-bar-restaurant strikingly situated in a restored tuna factory.

The Outdoors

At the sandy beach of Mondello, sailing and windsurfing facilities and instruction are available through **Albaria** (⊠ Viale Regina Elena 89/a ☎ 091/453595).

Sicily's most important center for scuba diving and other water sports is on the island of **Ustica**, north of Palermo. Its rugged coast is dotted with grottoes that are washed by crystal-clear waters and filled with an incredible variety of interesting marine life. In July Ustica hosts the International Meeting of Marine Fishing, which attracts sportsmen as well as marine biologists from all over the world.

Shopping

Most shops are open 9–1 and 4 or 4:30–7:30 or 8 and closed Sunday; in addition, most food shops close Wednesday afternoon, and other shops normally close Monday morning. One main shopping area is around the **Politeama** and **Libertà**. A second nerve center for shoppers is the pair of parallel streets connecting modern Palermo with the train station, **Via Roma** and **Via Maqueda**, where boutiques and shoe shops become increasingly upmarket as you move from the **Quattro Canti** past Teatro Massimo to **Via Ruggero Settimo.**

North of Piazza Castelnuovo, **Via della Libertà** and the streets around it represent the luxury end of the scale, with some of Palermo's best-known stores. **Libreria Kalós** (⊠ Via XX Settembre 56B, Libertà ☎ 091/322380) publishes some of the finest books on Sicilian art and architecture. **Laboratoriao Italiano di Patricia Italiano** (⊠ Via Principe di Villafranca 42, Libertà ☎ 091/320282), in the heart of the new town, offers a large selection of ceramics at reasonable prices. More quality ceramics, stoneware, and tiling can be found at **De Simone** (⊠ Via Gaetano Daiti 13B Libertà ☎ 091/584876). On the corner of Via Principe di Belmonte, heavy fabric, fringe, and tassel seekers will find solace inside **Giuseppe Gramuglia** (⊠ Via Roma 412–414 Vucciria ☎ 091/583262).

For men's shirts and suits, try the elegant but friendly **Barbisio** (⊠ Corso Vittorio Emanuele 284–298, half a block from the Quattro Canti ☎ 091/329992). The classy **Carieri & Carieri** (⊠ Via E. Parisi 4 Libertà ☎ 091-321846) has a more extensive selection. **Pasticceria Alba** (⊠ Piazza Don Bosco 7/c, Libertà ☎ 091/309016 ☉ Closed Mon.) is where you'll find all the favorite Sicilian pastries such as cannoli and *cassata siciliana* (ice cream with sponge cake, candied fruit, and marzipan). It's at the top of Via della Libertà, near the entrance to La Favorita Park. The charming I **Peccatucci di Mamma Andrea** (Mamma Andrea's Small Sins; ⊠ Via Prinicipe di Scordia, 67, near Piazza Florio Vucciria ☎ 091/334835 ☉ Closed Mon.) offers a plethora of mouthwatering original creations, including jams, preserves, candies, liqueurs, honey, and Sicilian treats like superb *frutta di Martorana* (fruits and other shapes made out of almond paste).

Markets

If you're interested in truly connecting with local life while searching for souvenirs, a visit to one of Palermo's many bustling markets is essential. It's easy to see how the **Vucciria Market** got its name, which translates in dialect as "voices" or "hubbub." Palermo's most established outdoor market in the heart of the centro storico is a maze of side streets around Piazza San Domenico, where hawkers deliver incessant chants from behind stands brimming with mounds of olives, blood oranges, wild fennel, and long-stem artichokes. One of them will be going at the trunk of a swordfish with a cleaver while across the way another holds up a giant squid or dangles an octopus. Morning is the best time to see the market in full swing.

Between Via Roma and Via Maqueda the many *bancherelle* (market stalls) on Via Bandiera sell everything from socks to imitation designer handbags. Or wind your way through the Albergheria district and the historic **Ballarò Market,** where the Saracens did their shopping in the 11th century—joined by the Normans in the 12th. The market remains faithful to seasonal change as well as the original Arab commerce of fruit, vegetables, and grain.

MONREALE & THE TYRRHENIAN COAST

Sicily's northern shore, the Tyrrhenian coast, is mostly a succession of small holiday towns interspersed with stretches of sand. It's often difficult to find a calm spot here among the thousands of other tourists and locals in high summer, though the scene quiets down considerably after August. The biggest attraction is the old town of Cefalù, with one of Sicily's most remarkable medieval cathedrals, encrusted with mosaics. The coast on either side is dotted with ancient archaeological remains and Arab-Norman buildings. You need venture only a couple of miles south of Cefalù to explore the Monti Madonie national park, which contains the highest peak in Sicily after Mt. Etna—Pizzo Carbonara, at 6,500 feet. Piano della Battaglia has a fully equipped ski resort with lifts. The area has a very un-Sicilian aspect, with Swiss-type chalets, hiking paths, and even alpine churches.

From Palermo it's an easy drive or bus ride to Monreale, whose cathedral provides an instructive comparison to the one at Cefalù, built around the same time. The glittering mosaics here are among the finest in the whole Mediterranean. Fans of military architecture and great views should make the short drive inland to the castle of Cáccamo, site of a formidable Norman castle midway between Palermo and Cefalù.

Monreale

⑫ *10 km (6 mi) southwest of Palermo.*

★ Monreale's splendid **Duomo** is lavishly executed with mosaics depicting events from the Old and New Testaments. After the Norman conquest of Sicily the new princes showcased their ambitions through monumental building projects. William II (1154–89) built the church complex with a cloister and palace between 1174 and 1185, employing Byzantine craftsmen. The result was a glorious fusion of Eastern and Western influences, widely regarded as the finest example of Norman architecture in Sicily.

The major attraction is the 68,220 square feet of glittering gold mosaics decorating the cathedral interior. Christ Pantocrator dominates the apse area; the nave contains narratives of the Creation; and scenes from the life of Christ adorn the walls of the aisles and the transept. The painted wooden ceiling dates from 1816 to 1837. A small pair of binoculars will make it easier to read the Latin inscriptions. The roof commands a great view (a reward for climbing 172 stairs).

Bonnano Pisano's **bronze doors**, completed in 1186, depict 42 biblical scenes and are considered among the most important of medieval artifacts. Barisano da Trani's 42 panels on the north door, dating from 1179, present saints and evangelists. ⊠ *Piazza del Duomo* ☎ *091/6404413* 💲 *Free* ⊙ *Daily 8–6.*

The lovely **cloister** of the abbey adjacent to the Duomo was built at the same time as the church but enlarged in the 14th century. The beautiful enclosure is surrounded by 216 double columns, every other one decorated in a unique glass mosaic pattern. Note the intricate carvings on the bases and the capitals. Afterward, don't forget to walk behind the cloister to the **belvedere,** with stunning panoramic views over the Conca d'Oro (Golden Conch) valley toward Palermo. ⊠ *Piazza del Duomo* ☎ *091/6404403* 🖅 *€4.15* ☉ *Mon.–Sat. 9–6:30, Sun. 9–1.*

Where to Eat

$–$$ ✕ **La Botte.** It's worth the short drive or inexpensive taxi fare from Monreale to reach this restaurant, a good value for well-prepared local specialties. Dine alfresco on daily specials such as *pennette agli odori* (little penne with tomato, garlic, parsley, basil, mint, and oregano) or regular favorites including *involtini* (meat or fish roulades). Local wines are a good accompaniment. ⊠ *Contrada Lenzitti 20, S 186* ☎ *091/414051* 🖃 *AE, DC, MC, V* ☉ *Closed Mon. and June 20–Sept. 20. No dinner Sun.*

Cefalù

★ ⑬ *38 km (24 mi) northeast of Termini Imerese, 70 km (42 mi) east of Palermo.*

Cefalù is a classically appealing Sicilian old town built on a spur jutting out into the sea. It's dominated by a massive rock—*la rocca*—and a 12th-century Romanesque **Duomo,** one of the finest Norman cathedrals in Italy. Ruggero II began it in 1131 as an offering of thanks for having been saved here from a shipwreck. Its mosaics rival those of Monreale; whereas Monreale's Byzantine Pantocratic Christ figure is an austere and powerful image, emphasizing Christ's divinity, the Cefalù Christ is softer, more compassionate, and more human. The traffic going in and out of Cefalù town can be heavy in summer; you may want to take the 50-minute train ride from Palermo instead of driving. At the Duomo you must be suitably attired—no shorts or beachwear are permitted. ⊠ *Piazza Duomo* ☎ *0921/421293* ☉ *Daily 8–noon and 3:30–sunset.*

Where to Stay & Eat

$–$$$ ✕ **Al Porticciolo.** Nicola Mendolia's restaurant is comfortable, casual, and faithfully focused on the food. Dark, heavy, wooden tables create a comfortable environment filled with a mix of jovial locals and businesspeople. You might start with the *calamaretti piccoli fritti* (fried baby squid and octopus) and then follow with one of the chef's specials, which change weekly. Regardless, a refreshing *sgroppino* (whipped lemon sorbet with spumante) should end the meal. ⊠ *Via C. Ortolani di Bordonaro 66* ☎ *0921/921981* 🖃 *AE, DC, MC, V* ☉ *Closed Wed. and 2 wks in Nov.*

$–$$ ✕ **Gabbiano.** "Seagull" is an appropriate name for a beachside seafood restaurant with a nautical theme. House specialties are *involtini di pesce spada* (swordfish roulades) and spaghetti marinara. ⊠ *Via Lungomare Giardina 17* ☎ *0921/421495* 🖃 *AE, DC, MC, V* ☉ *Closed Jan., weekdays Feb., and Wed. except July and Aug.*

$–$$ ✕ **La Brace.** This bistro-style restaurant near the cathedral has been serving upscale dishes in a lively setting since 1977. Graceful ceiling vaults and rustic walls give it an informal air. A Dutchman, Dietmar Beckers, and an Indonesian, Thea de Haan, pride themselves on creatively reworking local ingredients. Look for dishes like *vitello in salsa agrodolce* *al mango ed uva sultanina* (veal cutlet in mango sweet-and-sour sauce with grapes), and save room for one of the parfaits. Prices are quite good given the quality. ✉ *Via XXV Novembre 10* ☎ *0921/423570* ▭ *AE, DC, MC, V* ☉ *Closed Mon., and Dec. 15–Jan. 15. No lunch Tues.*

$$–$$$$ 🏨 **Kalura.** Caldura, 2 km (1.3 mi) east along the coast, is the site of this modern hotel on a small promontory that's hard to reach without a car; it's only a few minutes by taxi from Cefalù, however. Sports facilities keep you from getting too sedentary, and the private beach is ideal for swimming. Rooms are bright and cheerful. Half board is required during high season (July and August). ✉ *Via V. Cavallaro 13, Località Caldura 90015,* ☎ *0921/421354* 📠 *0921/423122* ⊕ *www.kalura.it* 🛏 *65 rooms* 🍴 *Restaurant, tennis court, pool, beach, bar* ▭ *AE, DC, MC, V* 🍴 *MAP.*

★ $–$$$ 🏨 **Baia del Capitano.** This whitewashed hotel with large rooms and great amenities is in the peaceful district of Mazzaforno, about 5 km (3 mi) outside town. The ranch-style building is less than 30 years old, but it blends in with the rural surroundings. The colorful gardens extending to the surrounding olive groves are an ideal setting for reading or an afternoon siesta in the shade. A good sandy beach is a short walk away. ✉ *Contrada Mazzaforno, Mazzaforno 90015* ☎ *0921/420003* 📠 *0921/420163* ⊕ *www.baiadelcapitano.it* 🛏 *46 rooms* 🍴 *Restaurant, tennis court, pool, beach, Ping-Pong, bar, playground* ▭ *AE, DC, MC, V* ☉ *Closed Nov.–Mar.* 🍴 *MAP.*

Santo Stefano di Camastra

⑭ *33 km (20 mi) east of Cefalù, 152 km (95 mi) east of Messina.*

When the original village of Santo Stefano di Camastra was destroyed in a landslide in 1682, the local duke, Giuseppe Lanza, rebuilt it on the coast according to strict military principles—a geometric street grid and artery roads connecting the center with the periphery. Today Santo Stefano is filled with the vividly colored pottery for which the town has an international reputation. For a comprehensive pottery education, drop in on the **Museo della Ceramica** in the center of town. ✉ *Via Palazzo* ☎ *0921/331110* 🎟 *Free* ☉ *June–Sept., weekdays 9–1 and 4–8; Oct.–May, weekdays 9–1 and 3:30–7:30.*

Shopping

The Franco family has a long tradition of creating ceramic objets d'art by borrowing styles from past eras. Thus, Renaissance Madonnas rub shoulders with florid baroque vases, all richly colored and skillfully finished. Call ahead to visit their ceramic laboratory or the two **Ceramiche Franco** outlets, as the stores don't have set hours. (✉ *Via Nazionale 8* ☎ *0921/337222, 347/6004506 for reservations* ✉ *Via Vittoria 4* ☎ *0921/339925).*

WESTERN COAST TO AGRIGENTO
LAND OF TEMPLES

Western Sicily has a remote air, less developed than the eastern coast, and bearing traces of the North African culture that for centuries exerted a strong influence on this end of the island. Influences are most tangible in the coastal towns of Trapani and Marsala, and the outlying island of Pantelleria, nearer to the Tunisian coast than the Sicilian. In contrast, the cobbled streets of the hilltop town of Erice, outside Trapani, retain a strong medieval complexion, giving the town the air of a last outpost gazing out over the Mediterranean. The Greek presence is still strong, however, in the splendidly isolated site of Segesta and the cluster of cliffside ruined temples at Selinunte. The crowning glory of this region is the concentration of Greek temples at Agrigento, occupying a fabulous position on a height between the modern city and the sea.

Segesta

⑮ *30 km (19 mi) east of Trapani, 85 km (53 mi) southwest of Palermo.*

★ Segesta is the site of a **Tempio Dorico** (Doric temple) that's one of Sicily's most impressive, constructed on the side of a windswept barren hill overlooking a valley of wild fennel. Virtually intact today, the temple is considered by some to be finer in its proportions and setting than any other Doric temple left standing. The temple was actually started in the 5th century BC by the Elymian people, who some believe were refugees from Troy. At the very least, evidence indicates that they were non-Greeks; for example, they often sided with the Carthaginians. However, the style is in many ways Greek. The temple was never finished; the walls and roof never materialized, and the columns were never fluted. Just over 1 km (½ mi) away, near the top of the hill, are the remains of a fine **amphitheater,** with impressive views, especially at sunset, of nearby Monte Erice and the sea. ☎ 0924/952356 ⌨ €4.50 ☉ *Daily 9–1 hr before sunset.*

Erice

⑯ *35 km (22 mi) west of Segesta, 112 km (70 mi) west of Palermo.*

Erice is perched 2,450 feet above sea level, an enchanting medieval mountaintop aerie of castles and palaces, fountains, and cobblestone streets. Shaped like an equilateral triangle, the town was the ancient landmark Eryx, dedicated to the fertility goddess whom the Phoenicians called Astarte, the Greeks Aphrodite, and the Romans Venus. When the Normans arrived they built a castle on Monte San Giuliano, where today you'll find a lovely public park with benches and belvederes from which there are striking views of Trapani, the Egadi Islands, and, on a *very* clear day, Cape Bon and the Tunisian coast. Because of Erice's elevation, clouds conceal much of the view for most of the winter. Sturdy shoes and something warm to wear are recommended.

Fans of Sicilian sweets will make a beeline for **Pasticceria Grammatico** (⌂ Via Vittorio Emanuele 14 ☎ 0923/869390), run by Maria Grammatico, a former nun who gained international fame with *Bitter Almonds,* her life story co-written with Mary Taylor Simeti. Molded into striking shapes, including dolls and animals, her almond-paste creations are works of art. The balcony from the tearoom upstairs has wonderful views. At **Pasticceria del Convento** (⌂ Via Guarnotta 1 ☎ 0923/869777), Maria Grammatico's sister sells similar delectable treats.

Where to Stay & Eat

$–$$ ✕ **Monte San Giuliano.** Hidden within the labyrinth of lanes that makes up Erice, this restaurant near the main piazza has a satisfying traditional feel. Sit out on the tree-lined stone patio and sample spicy Arab-influenced seafood couscous, risotto with *rucola* (arugula) and swordfish, or delicious grilled tuna. Wash it all down with a good white Donnafugata, from the Rallo vineyards at Marsala. ⊠ *Vicolo San Rocco 7* ☎ *0923/869595* ⊟ *AE, DC, MC, V* ⊗ *Closed Mon., 2 wks mid-Jan., and 1st 2 wks Nov.*

$$ ✕🏨 **Elimo.** Located on one of Erice's main cobblestone streets, this intimate hotel has spacious rooms, the majority of which offer superb views (ask for one) overlooking the towns' characteristic rooftops and the vast valley below. The plasticky room doors and mix of antiques add a quirky aspect. Fresh ingredients and local meats are staples on the menu at Elimo's large, spectacularly picture-windowed restaurant ($–$$$), which boasts the same views. ⊠ *Via Vittorio Emanuele 75, 91016* ☎ *0923/ 869377* 🖷 *0923/869252* 🛏 *21 rooms* ⚙ *Restaurant, minibars, bar, lounge/library* ⊟ *AE, DC, MC, V* ⑩ *BP.*

$$ ✕🏨 **Moderno.** This modern, delightful hotel is decorated with local crafts and has a lovely terrace and a well-known restaurant ($–$$) serving seafood pasta and homemade desserts. In winter the lobby fireplace is always blazing. Some rooms, along with a large lounge and bar, are located directly across the street from the main hotel. ⊠ *Via Vittorio Emanuele 63, 91016* ☎ *0923/869300* 🖷 *0923/869139* ⊕ *www. pippocatalano.it* 🛏 *40 rooms* ⚙ *Restaurant, minibars, bar.* ⊟ *AE, DC, MC, V* ⑩ *BP.*

$ 🏨 **Ermione.** Nearly every room in this simple 1960s hotel offers lovely views of the Tyrrhenian Sea, although the tiled bathrooms and old-style Sicilian furniture are showing their age. The hotel is located 1 km (½ mi) from the centro storico of Erice with a restaurant serving well-executed basics to a healthy mix of locals and tourists. ⊠ *Via Pineta Comunale 43, 91016* ☎ *0923/869138* 🖷 *0923/869587* ⊕ *www. ermionehotel.com* 🛏 *46 rooms* ⚙ *Restaurant, bar, free parking* ⊟ *AE, DC, MC, V* ⑩ *MAP.*

The Outdoors

Capo San Vito, 40 km (25 mi) from Erice, is a long sandy beach on a promontory overlooking a bay in the Gulf of Castellammare. The town there, San Vito Lo Capo, is famous for its North African couscous, made with fish instead of meat. In late September it hosts the five-day **Cus Cus Fest,** a serious international couscous competition and festival with live music and plenty of free tastings.

Trapani

⑰ *30 km (18 mi) west of Segesta, 107 km (67 mi) west of Palermo.*

The modern town of Trapani, directly below Erice, is the departure point for ferries to the Egadi Islands and the island of Pantelleria, near the African coast. This rugged western end of Sicily is reminiscent of the many spaghetti Westerns that were filmed here.

The historic center is a well-kept secret. The lanes near Corso Italia hold a handful of churches worth wandering into. **Santa Maria di Gesù** (⊠ *Via*

San Pietro) has Gothic and Renaissance doors and a Madonna by Andrea della Robbia (1435–1525). **Sant'Agostino** (⊠ Piazzetta Saturno), behind the town hall, has a 14th-century rose window.

Where to Stay & Eat

$–$$ ✕ **P&G.** Opposite the Villa Margherita public gardens near the train station, this small restaurant has a quiet, dignified air and attentive service. The local pasta, *busiate,* is cooked with swordfish and eggplant, and the couscous features fish in summer (on Friday and Saturday and upon advance request) and meat in winter. A mixed grill of meats in a zesty orange sauce will revive any appetite suffering from fish fatigue. Reservations are a good idea on weekends. ⊠ *Via Spalti 1* ☎ *0923/547701* ▭ *MC, V* ⊗ *Closed Sun. and Aug.*

¢ ✕▥ **Ai Lumi.** If you can get past the abundance of the antipasto buffet, this appealing and attentive *tavernetta* (cozy tavern) with a medieval door and salami hanging from the ceiling serves hearty traditional soups and a variety of tasty fish and meat dishes. The bed-and-breakfast ($) located upstairs offers a variety of rooms with modern furnishings but a local Trapani feel, and mini-apartments at very good prices. The facilities are comfortable and the location couldn't be any more central. ⊠ *Corso Vittoria Emanuele 71/75, 91100* ☎ *0923/872418 or 347/ 8566570* ⊕ *www.ailumi.it* ⇆ *14 rooms* ▭ *DC, MC, V* ⊗ *Closed 20 days in June.*

Pantelleria

⑱ *100 km (62 mi) southwest of Sicily, 6 hrs by ferry from Trapani.*

Pantelleria, near the Tunisian coast, is one of Sicily's most evocative islands, although some find its starkness unappealing. If you're travel-weary and need a place to hole up for a few days in blissfully calm surroundings, however, this makes an ideal spot, its few hotels and restaurants catering to your basic needs. Many opt to rent accommodations in the traditional *dammuso* houses, with stout walls and domes for maximum coolness in the fierce summer heat. The hilly terrain offers plenty to explore, either on foot or astride a rented moped. Its volcanic formations, scant patches of forest, prehistoric tombs, and dramatic seascapes constitute an otherworldly landscape. From its grapes—the *zibibbo*—the locals make an amber-colored dessert wine called *Passito,* with a special process that involves drying the grapes. Daily ferries and, in summer, hydrofoils, connect the island with Trapani.

Marsala

⑲ *30 km (18 mi) south of Trapani, 140 km (87 mi) southwest of Palermo.*

The quiet seaside town of Marsala was once the main Carthaginian base in Sicily, from which Carthage fought for supremacy over the island against Greece and Rome. Nowadays it's more readily associated with the world-famous, richly colored sweet wine named after the town. In 1773 a British merchant named John Woodhouse happened upon Marsala and discovered that the wine here was as good as the port the British had long imported from Portugal. Two other wine merchants, Whitaker and

Ingram, rushed in, and by 1800 Marsala was exporting its wine all over the British Empire.

A sense of Marsala's past as a Carthaginian stronghold is captured by the well-preserved Punic warship displayed in the town's **Museo Archeologico Baglio Anselmi,** along with some of the amphoras and other artifacts recovered from the wreck. The vessel, which was probably sunk during the great sea battle that ended the First Punic War in 241 BC, was dredged up from the mud near the Egadi Islands in the 1970s and is now installed under a climate-controlled plastic tent. ⊠ *Lungomare Boéo 30* ☎ *0923/952535* 🎫 *€2* ⊙ *Mon., Tues., and Thurs. 9–2, Wed. and Fri.–Sun. 9–2 and 4–7.*

need a break?

The spacious *enoteca* (wine shop) **Divino Rosso** (⊠ Via XI Maggio (Largo A. Di Girolamo 1) ☎ 0923/711770) has a good selection of local wines, along with a brief but appealing food menu.

One of Sicily's foremost wine producers, the 150-year-old **Donnafugata Winery** is open for tours of their Cantina (reservations required) right in downtown Marsala. It's an interesting look at the winemaking process in Sicily, and it ends with a tasting of several whites and reds and a chance to buy wine as well; don't miss the famous Ben Ryè Passito di Pantelleria, a sweet dessert wine made from dried grapes, with intense notes of apricot. ⊠ *Via Lipari 18* ☎ *0923/724200* ⊕ *www.donnafugata. it* 🎫 *Free* ⊙ *Mon.–Sat. 9–4, by appointment only.*

off the beaten path

MAZARA DEL VALLO – Easily accessible at the end of the A29 highway, Mazara del Vallo is a typical time-frozen Sicilian port town with a beautiful baroque old center and pleasant palm-lined *lungomare* (promenade) running along the ocean. Some of the precious few tourists who venture to Mazara come to seek a glimpse of the Dancing Satyr, a precious Hellenistic bronze representing one of the mythological figures of the orgiastic group of Dionysus, Greek god of wine. Discovered in 1998 deep in the Mediterranean Sea by Mazara fishermen, the statue had probably been part of the cargo of a shipwrecked vessel sailing between Sicily and Cape Bon between the 3rd and 2nd century BC. It is on permanent display at **Museo Del Satiro** (⊠ Piazza Plebiscito, near the port 🎫 €4.50 ⊙ Daily 9–2 and 3–7:30). Besides the museum, Mazara buzzes with beachy activity in summer but is fairly sleepy in winter. It's a very relaxing place for a night's stopover or for lunch at one of the many seafood places and pizzerias lining the boardwalk or in the centro storico. The old port is a raw, colorful graveyard for rusty tugboats and fishing vessels.

Selinunte

❷⓿ *88 km (55 mi) southeast of Marsala, 114 km (71 mi) south of Palermo.*

Near the town of Castelvetrano, numerous **Greek temple ruins** perch on a plateau overlooking an expanse of the Mediterranean at Selinunte (or Selinus). The city was one of the most superb colonies of ancient Greece. The original complex held seven temples scattered over two sites separated by a harbor. Of the seven, only one—reconstructed in 1958—stands. Founded in the 7th century BC, Selinunte became the rich and prosperous rival of Segesta, which in 409 BC turned to the Carthaginians for help. The Carthaginians sent an army commanded by Hannibal to destroy the city. The temples were demolished, the city was razed, and 16,000 of Selinunte's inhabitants were slaughtered. The remains of Selinunte are in many ways unchanged from the day of its sacking—burn marks still scar the Greek columns, and much of the site still lies in rubble at its exact position of collapse at the hands of the Carthaginian attack. Selinunte is named after a local variety of wild parsley (*Apium graveolens* or *petroselinum*) that in spring grows in profusion among the ruined columns and overturned capitals. ☎ 0924/46277 🖭 €4.50 ☉ Daily 9–1 hr before sunset.

Agrigento

100 km (60 mi) southeast of Selinunte, 126 km (79 mi) south of Palermo.

In Agrigento you will be treated to what many experts consider the world's best-preserved remains of classical Greece. The natural defenses of Akragas, the city's Greek name, depended on its secure and quite lovely position between two rivers on a floodplain, a short distance from the sea. Settled in 582 BC, Akragas grew wealthy through trade with Carthage, just across the Mediterranean. Despite attacks from the Carthaginians at the end of the 5th century BC, the city survived through the Roman era, the Middle Ages (when it came under Arab and Norman rule), and into the modern age. Famous sons include the ancient Greek philosopher Empedocles (circa 490–430 BC) and the Italian playwright Luigi Pirandello (1867–1936).

Fodor's Choice
★ Whether you first come upon the **Valle dei Templi** (Valley of the Temples) in the early morning light, bathed by golden floodlights at night, or at their very best in February, when the valley is awash in the fragrant blossoms of thousands of almond trees, it's easy to see why Agrigento was celebrated by Pindar as "the most beautiful city built by mortal men." One ticket covers all temples, and none of the plaques is particularly helpful. ☒ *Zona Archeologica, Via dei Templi* ☎ 0922/497221 🖭 €4.50, €6 including museum ☉ Daily 8:30–7, later in summer.

㉑ The eight pillars of the **Tempio di Ercole** (Temple of Hercules) make up Agrigento's oldest temple complex, dating from the 6th century BC. Partially reconstructed in 1922, it reveals the remains of a large Doric temple that originally had 38 columns. Like all the area temples, it faces east. The Museo Archeologico Nazionale contains some of the marble warrior figures that once decorated its pediment.

㉒ The beautiful **Tempio della Concordia** (Concord), up the hill from the Temple of Hercules, is perhaps the best-preserved Greek temple in existence. The structure dates from about 430 BC, and owes its exceptional state of preservation to the fact that it was converted into a Christian church in the 6th century and was extensively restored in the 18th. Thirty-two Doric columns surround its large interior. It's a tradition in Agrigento for couples to visit the temple on their wedding day. To the left

**Valle dei Templi,
Agrigento**

of the temple is a Paleochristian **necropolis.** Early Christian tombs were both cut into the rock and dug into underground catacombs.

㉓ The **Tempio di Giunone** (Juno), east on the Via Sacra from the Temple of Concord, commands an exquisite view of the valley, especially at sunset. It's similar to but smaller than the Concordia and dates from about 450 BC. Traces of a fire that probably occurred during the Carthaginian attack in 406 BC, which destroyed the ancient town, can be seen on the walls of the cellar. Thirty of the original 34 columns still stand, of which 16 still retain their capitals.

㉔ Though never completed, the **Tempio di Giove** (Jupiter) was considered the eighth wonder of the world. The temple was probably built in gratitude for victory over Carthage and was constructed by prisoners captured in that war. Basically Doric in style, it did not have the usual colonnade of freestanding columns but rather a series of half columns attached to a solid wall. Inside the excavation you can see a cast (not the original) of one of the 38 colossal Atlas-like figures, or telamones, that supported the temple's massive roof. This design is unique among known Doric temples, and with a length of more than 330 feet the building is the largest-known classical temple. It's the first site that you'll encounter in the western archaeological zone of the Valle dei Templi, across the parking lot from the Tempio di Ercole. Note that it usually closes at 5.

㉕ The four columns supporting part of an entablature of the **Tempio di Castore e Polluce** (Castor and Pollux) have become emblematic of Agrigento, but, in fact, the reconstruction of 1836 haphazardly put together elements from diverse buildings. Right opposite, facing north, the **Santuario delle Divinità Ctonie** (Sanctuary of the Chthonic Divinities) has cultic altars and eight small temples dedicated to Demeter, Persephone, and other Underworld deities. In the vicinity are two columns of a temple dedicated to Hephaestus (Vulcan).

㉖ At the end of Via dei Templi, where it turns left and becomes Via Petrarca, stands the **Museo Archeologico Nazionale.** An impressive collection of antiquities from the site includes vases, votives, everyday objects, weapons, statues, and models of the temples. Visit the museum after you've seen the temples. ☒ *Contrada San Nicola* ☎ *0922/401565* 🖮 *€4.50, €6 including temples* ☉ *Sun. and Mon. 9–1, Tues.–Sat. 9–7.*

㉗ The **Hellenistic and Roman Quarter,** across the road from the archaeological museum, consists of four parallel streets, running north–south, that have been uncovered, along with the foundations of some houses from the Roman settlement (2nd century BC). Some of these streets still have their original mosaic pavements.

There's little reason to go up the hill from Valle dei Templi to the rather dreary modern city of Agrigento, where stacks of 1960s abominations sit in contrast to the Valley of the Temples below—except to ring the doorbell at the **Convento di Santo Spirito** and try the almond cakes and the *kus-kus* (sweet cake), made of pistachio nuts and chocolate, that the nuns prepare. There are no regular hours. ☒ *Salita di Santo Spirito, off Via Porcello* ☎ *No phone.*

Where to Stay & Eat

$$–$$$ ✕ **Trattoria dei Templi.** Near the archaeological area, between olive and almond groves, this simple restaurant can get very busy in the early evening, when it becomes too dark for temple exploring. The menu has all the classic Sicilian dishes, including spaghetti *ai ricci* (with sea urchin) in season, and plenty of grilled fish. The antipasti are exceptional. ☒ *Via Panoramica dei Templi 15* ☎ *0922/403110* ▤ *AE, DC, MC, V* ☉ *Closed Fri. Sept.–June, Sun. in July and Aug., and June 31–July 10.*

$–$$$ ✕ **Kokalos.** On a hillside opposite the temple ridge, 6 km (3½ mi) to the southeast near the Villagio Mosè, this large restaurant in an old village house has beautiful views over the temples. As well as serving local specialties, Kokalos includes a pizzeria and enoteca. ☒ *Via Cavaleri Magazzeni 3, Villagio Mosè* ☎ *0922/606427* ▤ *AE, DC, MC, V.*

$–$$$ ✕ **Le Caprice.** The high points of this popular restaurant in the temple area are the overflowing trays of antipasti and abundant plates of seafood, including a good swordfish involtini. The wine list is relatively extensive. ☒ *Via Panoramica dei Templi 51* ☎ *0922/26469* ▤ *AE, DC, MC, V* ☉ *Closed Fri. and 1st 2 wks in July.*

$$$$ 🏨 **Foresteria Baglio della Luna.** Fiery sunsets and moonlight cast a glow over this hotel in the valley below the temples, a couple of miles from

PRIZZI'S HONOR

BURIED IN THE HEART *of Mafia country (14 miles west of Lercara Friddi, which gave the world the mobster Lucky Luciano) Prizzi, population 6,000, is a fairy-tale aerie, a floating apparition of twisting stone alleyways and brown rooftops gently dusting the peak of a 3,267-foot mountain. Its medieval layout and architecture—surreally frozen in another age—and dreamy views of the surrounding countryside, perhaps best seen at sunset, make it well worth a stop along the way between Palermo and Agrigento. Prizzi was founded by the Greeks in about 480 BC, and was alternately conquered by the Byzantines (8th century AD) and Saracens (9th century AD), the latter of whom built three lofty castles and created a "cult of water" with an elaborate network of drinking troughs. Christian conquest came in the 11th century.*

The name "Prizzi" became known to the outside world through 1985's wryly comic mobster movie Prizzi's Honor, but the town feels as far removed as is imaginable from Hollywood glamour and glitz. There's little in the way of significant art or monuments, and the secrets of the Mafia presence lie out of reach to visitors, buried in inaccessible crevices of local culture. But you can spend hours wandering in and out of the maze of steeply sloped alleyways, with tiny, still-inhabited houses built into the rock, eventually giving way to the remains of the three castles and the mountain's dazzling peak, from which, on a clear day, you can view the sea of Sciacca to one side and the cone of Mt. Etna to the other.

Be forewarned, the remote town is always breezy and generally cold. Coming from Palermo, follow the signs to Sciacca; both Prizzi and Corleone are on the way.

town and easily accessible by taxi. A tower dating from the 8th century is central to the stone farmhouse complex, set around a peaceful geranium- and ivy-filled courtyard and a garden beyond. Standard rooms, some with views of the temples, are cozy but nothing fancy, with mellow walls and wooden furniture. The intimate, rustic restaurant serves an excellent risotto with scampi and good local wines. Note that the dirt road up to the hotel is unmarked. ⊠ *Contrada Maddalusa, Valle dei Templi, 92100* ☎ *0922/511061* 🖷 *0922/598802* ⊕ *www.venere. com/it/agrigento/bagliodellaluna* ➳ *22 rooms, 3 suites* ♨ *Restaurant, minibars, bar* 🖃 *AE, DC, MC, V* ⦿❙ *BP.*

\$\$\$–\$\$\$\$ 🏨 **Villa Athena.** There is much demand for this former villa, the only hotel right in the midst of the archaeological zone, so make reservations as early as possible. The price reflects its privileged position, as the hotel itself, although pleasant, is not outstanding. Many rooms have terraces overlooking the large gardens and the swimming pool. The temples are an easy walk away, and there's a convivial atmosphere in the bar, where a multinational crowd swaps stories. The restaurant is also excellent, though pricey, and a destination in itself. ⊠ *Via dei Templi 53, 92100* ☎ *0922/596288* 🖷 *0922/402180* ⊕ *www.athenahotels.com* ➳ *40 rooms* ♨ *Restaurant, minibars, indoor pool, bar, Internet* 🖃 *AE, DC, MC, V* ⦿❙ *BP.*

$$ ▦ **Tre Torri.** Stay here if you are sports-minded and bent on exploring the countryside around Agrigento. Bicycle tours and nature walks can be arranged or a boat booked for fishing trips and water sports. Public areas are spacious, and the modern rooms simply furnished. The hotel's location, Villagio Mosè, 5 km (3 mi) southeast of town, is on a regular bus route. Book on the Internet for a 10% discount. ✉ *Villagio Mosè, 92100* ☎ *0922/606733* ᵬ *0922/607839* ⊕ *www.htretorri.com* ⤴ *118 rooms* ⟁ *Restaurant, outdoor pool, gym, sauna, bar, meeting room* ▭ *AE, DC, MC, V* ��○⧽ *BP.*

Nightlife & the Arts
During the first half of February, Agrigento hosts a **Festa delle Mandorle,** (Almond Blossom Festival), with international folk dances, a costumed parade, and the sale of marzipan and other sweets made from almonds.

SIRACUSA

Siracusa (known to English-speakers as Syracuse), old and new, is a wonder to behold. One of the great ancient capitals of Western civilization, the city was founded in 734 BC by Greek colonists from Corinth and soon grew to rival, and even surpass, Athens in splendor and power; Siracusa became the largest, wealthiest city-state in the West and a bulwark of Greek civilization. Although the city lived under tyranny, rulers such as Dionysius filled their courts with Greeks of the highest artistic stature—among them Pindar, Aeschylus, and Archimedes. The Athenians did not welcome the rise of Siracusa and set out to conquer Sicily, but the natives outsmarted them in what was one of the greatest naval battles of ancient history (413 BC). Siracusa continued to prosper until it was conquered two centuries later by the Romans.

Siracusa still has some of the finest examples of baroque art and architecture; dramatic Greek and Roman ruins; and a Duomo that is the stuff of legend, a microcosm of the city's entire history in one edifice. The modern city also offers a wonderful lively baroque old town worthy of extensive exploration, pleasant piazzas, outdoor cafés and bars, and a wide assortment of excellent seafood. There are essentially two areas to explore in Siracusa: the Parco Archeologico, on the mainland; and the island of Ortygia, the ancient city first inhabited by the Greeks, which juts out into the Ionian sea and is connected to the mainland by two small bridges.

Exploring Siracusa

Siracusa's old nucleus of Ortygia is a compact area, a pleasure to amble around without getting unduly tired. In contrast, mainland Siracusa is a grid of wider avenues. At the northern end of Corso Gelone, above Viale Paolo Orsi, the orderly grid gives way to the ancient quarter of Neapolis, where the sprawling Parco Archeologico is accessible from Viale Teracati (an extension of Corso Gelone). East of Viale Teracati, about a 10-minute walk from the Parco Archeologico, the district of Tyche holds the archaeological museum and the church and catacombs of San Giovanni, both off Viale Teocrito (drive or take a taxi or city bus from Ortygia). Coming from the train station, it's a 15-minute trudge to Ortygia along Via Francesco Crispi and Corso Umberto.

Parco Archeologico & Museo Archeologico

a good walk

Start your tour of mainland Siracusa at the **Parco Archeologico** ㉘ ☞ (entrance from Largo Anfiteatro). Before reaching the ticket booth, pause briefly at the meager remains of the Ara di Ierone. Beyond the ticket office, the extensive Latomia del Paradiso stretches out on the right, and the Archaeological Park's pièce de résistance lies to the left: the awesome expanse of the Teatro Greco. Leave by the same way you entered, making a diversion before the park's exit (you'll need to show your entry ticket) to view the elliptical Anfiteatro Romano. From Largo Anfiteatro, head east along the busy Viale Teocrito, where after a few minutes you'll pass the **Museo Archeologico** ㉙. A few steps beyond is the much smaller but still intriguing **Museo del Papiro** ㉚. From here retrace your steps along Viale Teocrito before turning right up Via San Giovanni to visit the church of San Giovanni and the **Catacombe di San Giovanni** ㉛ beneath. From here drive or take one of the frequent city buses down Corso Gelone and Corso Umberto for the old city.

TIMING Allow at least a full day for this tour, which can be quite taxing. The Parco Archeologico has little or no shade, so early morning and late afternoon are the best times to visit on hot days.

What to See

㉛ **Catacombe di San Giovanni.** Not far from the Archaeological Park, off Viale Teocrito, the catacombs below the church of San Giovanni are one of the earliest-known Christian sites in the city. Inside the crypt of San Marciano is an altar where St. Paul preached on his way through Sicily to Rome. The frescoes in this small chapel are still bright and fresh, though some dating from the 4th century AD show their age. ⊠ *Piazza San Giovanni, Archeological Zone* ☎ *0931/66571* ☞ *€3.10* ☉ *Tues.–Sun. 9–12:30 and 2:30–5:30; longer hrs in summer.*

㉙ **Museo Archeologico.** The impressive collection of Siracusa's splendid archaeological museum is organized by region around a central atrium and ranges from Neolithic pottery to fine Greek statues and vases. You will want to compare the *Landolina Venus*—a headless, stout goddess of love who rises out of the sea in measured modesty (she is a 1st-century AD Roman copy of the Greek original)—with the much earlier (300 BC) elegant Greek statue of Hercules in Section C. Of a completely different style is a marvelous fanged Gorgon, its tongue sticking out, that once adorned the cornice of the Temple of Athena to ward off evildoers. One exhibit depicts the Temple of Apollo, the oldest Doric temple in Sicily, on the island of Ortygia. ⊠ *Viale Teocrito, Archeological Zone* ☎ *0931/464022* ☞ *€4.50, €6 including Archaeological Park, €8 including Museo Bellomo* ☉ *Tues.–Sat. 9–1 and 3–7, Sun. 9–1.*

㉚ **Museo del Papiro.** Close to Siracusa's Museo Archeologico, the Papyrus Museum demonstrates how papyruses are prepared from reeds and then painted—an ancient tradition in the city. Siracusa, it seems, has the only climate outside the Nile Valley in which the papyrus plant—from which the word "paper" comes—thrives. ⊠ *Viale Teocrito 66, Archeological Zone* ☎ *0931/61616* ☞ *Free* ☉ *Tues.–Sun. 9–1.*

Siracusa

*Ionian
Sea*

ORTYGIA

*Ionian
Sea*

Porto Grande

KEY
► Start of walk
🛈 Tourist information

0 ___ 3/4 mile
0 ___ 1 km

► **28** **Parco Archeologico** (Archaeological Park). Siracusa is most famous for its dramatic set of Greek and Roman ruins. Though the various ruins can be visited separately, you'll certainly want to see them all, along with the Museo Archeologico. If the park is closed, go up Viale G. Rizzo from Viale Teracati to the belvedere overlooking the ruins, which are flood-lighted at night. ⊠ *Viale Teocrito* 🕾 *0931/66206* 🖃 *€4.50 for all sites, €6 including Museo Archeologico* ☉ *Oct.–Mar., daily 9–4; Apr.–Sept., daily 9–5; last tickets sold 1 hr before closing.*

Before the park's ticket booth is the gigantic **Ara di Ierone** (Altar of Hieron), which was once used by the Greeks for spectacular sacrifices involving hundreds of animals. The first attraction in the park is the **Latomia del Paradiso,** a lush tropical garden full of palm and citrus trees. This series of quarries served as prisons for the defeated Athenians, who were enslaved; the quarries once rang with the sound of their chisels and hammers. At one end is the famous Orecchio di Dionisio, with an ear-shape entrance and unusual acoustics inside, as you'll discover if you clap your hands. The legend is that Dionysius used to listen in at the top of the quarry to hear what the slaves were plotting below.

★ The **Teatro Greco** (Greek Theater) is the chief monument in the Archaeological Park—and indeed one of Sicily's greatest classical sites and the most complete Greek theater surviving from antiquity. Climb to the top of the seating area (which could accommodate 15,000) for a fine view: all the seats converge upon a single point—the stage—which has the natural scenery and the sky as its background. Hewn out of the hillside rock in the 5th century BC, the theater saw the premieres of the plays of Aeschylus. Greek tragedies are still performed here in May and June of even-numbered years. Above and behind the theater runs the Via dei Sepulcri, in which streams of running water flow through a series of Greek sepulchres.

The well-preserved and striking **Anfiteatro Romano** (Roman Amphitheater) reveals much about the differences between the Greek and Roman personalities. Where drama in the Greek theater was a kind of religious ritual, the Roman amphitheater emphasized the spectacle of combative sports and the circus. This arena is one of the largest of its kind and was built around the 2nd century AD. The corridor where gladiators and beasts entered the ring is still intact, and the seats, some of which still bear the occupants' names, were hauled in and constructed on the site from huge slabs of limestone.

need a break?

For some great Sicilian cakes and ice cream on your way to the Archaeological Park, visit the bar-cum-*pasticceria* **Leonardi** (⊠ Viale Teocrito 123, Archeological Zone ☎ 0931/61411). It's popular with the locals, so you may have to line up for your cakes in holiday times. It's closed Wednesday.

Ortygia Island

a good walk

The central part of Siracusa is a modern city, with Corso Gelone its main shopping street. At its southern end, Corso Umberto leads to the Ortygia Island bridge, which crosses a harbor lined with fish restaurants. Begin at Piazza Pancali, the square where you arrive after crossing the bridge. Behind the piazza stand the scanty remains of the **Tempio di Apollo** ㉜ ▶. Proceed from here to **Piazza Archimede** ㉝, from which it's a brief walk to **Piazza del Duomo** ㉞, the main square of the old town and site of Siracusa's ancient and splendid **Duomo** ㉟. Other impressive buildings to see in the piazza include the **Palazzo Beneventano del Bosco** ㊱ and the church of **Santa Lucia alla Badia** ㊲; the Palazzo Bellomo, housing the **Museo Bellomo** ㊳, is just around the corner. After you've had your fill of this, stroll onto the waterfront where several bars cluster around the lovely **Fonte Aretusa** ㊴, a perfect spot for a break. Walking along the seafront promenade to the southern tip of Ortygia will bring you to the **Castello Maniace** ㊵. Ortygia's backstreets are largely composed of elegant baroque palazzi, whose uniformity is the result of the major reconstruction that took place following an earthquake in 1693, at a time when this style of baroque was de rigueur. Be sure to wander along Via della Maestranza, the main lateral street of the island, or Via Veneto, on the eastern side, where you'll notice the bulbous wrought-iron balconies said to have been fashioned to accommodate ladies' billowing skirts, and facades embellished with mermaids and gargoyles—and don't miss the stucco decoration on Palazzo Lantieri, on Via Roma (off Piazza Archimede).

TIMING   You'll need the better part of a day to do justice to Ortygia. Obviously, the more detours you make—and there are distractions aplenty here—the longer you'll spend. The Duomo alone can take an hour or so to see properly, and you could easily spend two more hours in the Museo Bellomo. There's no dearth of inviting bars and restaurants to break up your tour.

What to See

40 Castello Maniace. The southern tip of Ortygia island is occupied by a castle built by Frederick II (1194–1250), now an army barracks, from which there are fine views of the sea.

35 Duomo. Siracusa's Duomo is an archive of island history, beginning
Fodor's Choice   with the bottom-most excavations that have unearthed remnants of Sicily's
★   distant past, when the Siculi inhabitants worshipped their deities here. During the 5th century BC (the same time as Agrigento's Temple of Concord was built), the Greeks built a temple to Athena over it, and in the 7th century Siracusa's first Christian cathedral was built on top of the Greek structure. The massive columns of the original Greek temple were incorporated into the present structure and are clearly visible, embedded in the exterior wall along Via Minerva. The Greek columns were also used to dramatic advantage inside, where on one side they form chapels connected by elegant wrought-iron gates. The baroque facade, added in 1700, displays a harmonious rhythm of concaves and convexes. In front, the piazza is encircled by pink and white oleanders and elegant buildings ornamented with filigree grillwork. ⊠ *Piazza del Duomo, Ortygia* ☎ *0931/65328* ☉ *Daily 8–noon and 4–7:30.*

39 Fonte Aretusa. Just off the promenade along the harbor you'll find the Fountain of Arethusa, a freshwater spring next to the sea. This anomaly is explained by a Greek legend that tells how the nymph Arethusa was changed into a fountain by the goddess Artemis (Diana) when she tried to escape the advances of the river god Alpheus. She fled from Greece, into the sea, with Alpheus in close pursuit, and emerged in Sicily at this spring. It's said if you throw a cup into the Alpheus River in Greece it will emerge here at this fountain, which is home to a few tired ducks and some dull-colored carp—but no cups. If you want to stand right by the fountain, you need to gain admission through the aquarium; otherwise look down on it from Largo Aretusa.

38 Museo Bellomo. Siracusa's principal museum of art is inside Palazzo Bellomo, a lovely Catalan Gothic building with mullioned windows and an elegant exterior staircase. Among the paintings and sculptures are a *Santa Lucia* by Caravaggio (1573–1610) and a damaged but still brilliant *Annunciation* by Antonello da Messina. There are also exhibits of Sicilian nativity figures, silver, furniture, ceramics, and religious vestments. ⊠ *Via Capodieci 14, Ortygia* ☎ *0931/69511* 🎫 *€2.50* ☉ *Tues.–Sat. 9–6:30, Sun. 9–2:30.*

36 Palazzo Beneventano del Bosco. On a corner of the Piazza del Duomo, this elegant palazzo is a private residence, but you can take a peek at the impressive interior courtyard, ending in a grand winding staircase. ⊠ *Piazza del Duomo, Ortygia.*

33 **Piazza Archimede.** The center of this piazza has a baroque fountain, the *Fontana di Diana,* festooned with fainting sea nymphs and dancing jets of water. Look for the Chiaramonte-style **Palazzo Montalto,** an arched-window gem just off the piazza on Via Montalto.

34 **Piazza del Duomo.** In the heart of Ortygia, this ranks as one of Italy's most beautiful piazzas, its elongated space lined with Sicilian baroque treasures and outdoor cafés.

37 **Santa Lucia alla Badia.** This baroque church stands at one end of Piazza del Duomo and features an engaging wrought-iron balcony and pleasant facade. It opens only for a week each year preceding Christmas ⊠ *Piazza del Duomo, Ortygia* ☺ *Closed Dec. 21–13.*

▶ **32** **Tempio di Apollo.** Scattered through the piazza just across the bridge to Ortygia you'll find the ruins of a temple dedicated to Apollo, a model of which is in the Museo Archeologico. In fact, little of this noble Doric temple still remains except for some crumbled walls and shattered columns; the window in the south wall belongs to a Norman church that was built much later on the same spot. ⊠ *Piazza Pancali, Ortygia.*

Where to Stay & Eat

★ **$$-$$$** ✕ **Don Camillo.** Bursting with locals in the know, this renowned Ortygia restaurant is set in a gracious series of delicately arched rooms lined with wine bottles and sepia-tone images of Old Siracusa. Uniformly outstanding local dishes include the sublime spaghetti *delle Sirene,* with delicate ricci, shrimp, and butter; and the bolder *pennette alle pesce spada* (pasta tubes with swordfish, raisins, tomato, pine nuts, basil, and Marsala). End with a spicy cheese plate counterbalanced by Sicilian honey and sweet Marsala wine. ⊠ *Via Maestranza 96, Ortygia* ☎ *0931/ 67133* ▤ *AE, DC, MC, V* ☺ *Closed Sun., first 15 days in Nov. and first 15 days in July.*

$-$$$ ✕ **Fermento.** This hip wine bar–restaurant–Internet café is truly one of Sicily's most enchanting settings in which to dine or drink: warm lighting, dark vaulted stone, candles everywhere, a dim buzz, and Sicilian wines served in huge, beautiful tasting glasses. The menu really revolves around wine, with an excellent (if pricey) selection of local classics. Stick to the pasta dishes and creative salads rather than the meats. ⊠ *Via Crocifisso 44/46, Ortygia* ☎ *0931/60762* ▤ *AE, DC, MC, V* ☺ *Closed Tues.*

$-$$ ✕ **Ionico.** Enjoy seaside dining in the coastal Santa Lucia district. The Ionico has a terrace and veranda for alfresco meals, and the interior is plastered with diverse historical relics and has a cheerful open hearth for the winter. Chef-proprietor Roberto Giudice cooks meals to order or will suggest a specialty from a selection of market-fresh ingredients. Try the pasta *con acciughe e il pan grattato* (in an anchovy sauce). ⊠ *Riviera Dionisio il Grande 194, Santa Lucia* ☎ *0931/65540* ▤ *AE, DC, MC, V* ☺ *Closed Tues.*

$ ✕ **Archimede.** The *antipasto misto* (mixed antipasto) should whet your appetite for the predominantly seafood menu of this small establishment. Risotto di mare and pesce spada are specialties. Sample the *involtini all'Archimede* (roulades stuffed with fish and bread crumbs) or the *tagli-*

atelli all'Archimede (a fish and pasta dish). ✉ *Via Gemmellaro 8, Ortygia* ☎ *0931/69701* 🖃 *AE, DC, MC, V* ⊘ *Closed Sun.*

¢–$ ✕ **La Siciliana.** This is an ideal spot for an inexpensive pizza and a cool beer or white wine. There are more than 54 varieties of pizza, from the most exotic to the local fried variety served only in the evening, *Siciliana*, a crusty and flavorful calzone stuffed with *tuma* (fresh, unsalted cheese), anchovies, and black pepper. Other choices on the menu include pasta and fish. ✉ *Via Savoia 17, Ortygia* ☎ *0931/68944* 🖃 *DC, MC, V.*

$$$$ 🏨 **Grand Hotel.** An elegant, fantasy-inspired design prevails at this venerable institution, which has enjoyed a prime position overlooking the Porto Grande since 1898. A modern seascape sets a dreamy tone in the lobby, which is decked out in periwinkle leather club chairs, antiques, gilt mirrors, and marble inlaid floors lined with lights. Guest rooms have fine wood floors, modern fixtures, and stained-glass windows. The roof-garden restaurant has superb views over the harbor and seafront of Ortygia as well as excellent food. A shuttle service is provided to the hotel's private beach nearby. ✉ *Viale Mazzini 12, Porto Grande, 96100* ☎ *0931/464600* 🖨 *0931/464611* ⊕ *www.grandhotelsr.it* ⤸ *39 rooms, 19 suites* ☄ *Restaurant, minibars, beach, bar, meeting room, free parking* 🖃 *AE, DC, MC, V* ❙❙❙ *BP.*

$$$ 🏨 **Grand Hotel Villa Politi.** This grand 18th-century villa has been frequented by European royalty and various VIPs, including Winston Churchill. Now equipped with modern luxuries, it still retains its charm and elegance. The hotel is located near the archaeological zone but set back from the road in the ancient extensive gardens of the Latomie dei Cappuccini, overlooking a small archaeological site. High-quality service and all the trimmings are the standard. ✉ *Via M. Politi Laudien 2, Archeological Zone, 96100* ☎ *0931/412121* 🖨 *0931/36061* ⊕ *www.villapoliti.com* ⤸ *92 rooms, 4 suites, 4 deluxe suites* ☄ *2 restaurants, in-room safes, minibars, cable TV, pool, bar, free parking* 🖃 *AE, DC, MC, V* ❙❙❙ *BP.*

$$ 🏨 **Domus Mariae.** You can see the sea at the end of the corridor as you enter this hotel on Ortygia's eastern shore. In an unusual twist, it's run by nuns of the Ursuline order, who help to make the mood placid and peaceful. Don't expect monastic conditions, however; refined furnishings distinguish the public rooms, and guest rooms—six with sea views and others with great Ortygia street balconies—are bright, modern, and comfortable. The hotel's small, modest restaurant downstairs also serves truly superlative local food—walnut-radicchio risotto and the salad of citrus and seared eggplant both shine. ✉ *Via Vittorio Veneto 76, Ortygia, 96100* ☎🖨 *0931/24854 or 0931/24858* ⊕ *www.sistemia.it/domusmariae* ⤸ *12 rooms.* ☄ *Restaurant, bar, free parking* 🖃 *AE, DC, MC, V* ❙❙❙ *BP.*

$–$$ 🏨 **Park Hotel Helios.** This unpretentious hotel is in a quiet part of town north of the archaeological zone. Rooms are spacious and warmly lighted, the foyer bedecked with potted palms and Persian rugs. Outside are a barbecue and a play area for children. ✉ *Via Filisto 80, Archeological Zone, 96100* ☎ *0931/812366* 🖨 *0931/38096* ⤸ *143 rooms* ☄ *Restaurant, pool, sauna, playground, meeting room, free parking* 🖃 *AE, DC, MC, V.*

¢ 🏨 **Airone.** In a pretty old palazzo in the heart of Ortygia, this bed-and-breakfast (liberally interpreted—breakfast is included at a nearby bar) caters mostly to backpackers and young people who have the stamina

FodorśChoice
★

to brave the four-story climb up the stairs. The location is prime; rooms are spotless and spacious, some overlooking the coastline. Service is friendly and hassle-free (you get your own keys to the building), and the price can't be beat. ⊠ *Via Maestranza 111, 96100* 🕾🖶 *0931/69005* ⊕ *www.bedandbreakfastsicily.com* ⇋ *9 rooms* ⌂ *Lounge, parking (fee)* ▭ *No credit cards* ⊺◎⨉ *BP.*

Nightlife

On the edge of Ortygia, the **Ulysses Irish Pub** (⊠ Vicolo al Forte Vigliena 3/15 Ortygia 🕾 0931/465615) is a raucous home base for expats, suburbanites, and locals. Popular and filled with locals, **Il Bagatto** (⊠ Piazza S. Giuseppe 1 Ortygia 🕾 0931/464076) is in the heart of Ortygia.

Shopping

Siracusa's specialty is papyrus paper. But beware—most of what you buy is commercially produced, hard, and of inferior quality to the handmade paper, which feels like fabric. One of the best of the few places to buy the genuine article is **Galleria Bellomo** (⊠ Via Capodieci 15, Ortygia 🕾 0931/61340), opposite the Museo Bellomo. It's run by an artist who sells cards and paintings and will also give a demonstration of how to make the paper.

EASTERN SICILY
ON THE ROAD TO TAORMINA

Sicily's interior is for the most part underpopulated and untrammeled, though the Imperial Roman Villa at Casale, outside Piazza Armerina, gives precious evidence from an epoch gone by. Don't miss misty Enna, the Navel of Sicily, or Caltagirone, a ceramics center of renown. Halfway up the eastern coast, Catania packs the vivacity of Palermo, if not the artistic wealth; the city makes a good base for exploring lofty Mt. Etna, as does Taormina. Messina's scant attractions include its unparalleled position opposite the mountains of Calabria and one of the island's best museum collections.

Enna

🕗 *105 km (63 mi) northeast of Agrigento, 136 km (85 mi) southeast of Palermo.*

Deep in Sicily's interior, the fortress city of Enna commands exceptional views of the surrounding rolling plains, and, in the distance, Mt. Etna. Virtually unknown by tourists and relatively untouched by industrialization, this sleepy mountaintop city (altitude 2,844 feet) charms and prospers in a distinctly old-fashion, provincial and Sicilian way. Enna makes a good stopover for the night or just for lunch, as it's right along the autostrada between Palermo and Catania (and thus Siracusa).

The narrow, winding streets are dominated at one end by the impressive cliff-hanging **Castello di Lombardia,** built by Frederick II, easily visible as you approach town. (The castle isn't open to the public.)

In town, head straight for Via Roma, which leads to **Piazza Vittorio Emanuele,** the center of Enna's shopping scene and evening passeggiata. The attached **Piazza Crispi,** dominated by the shell of the grand old Hotel Belvedere, affords breathtaking panoramas of the hillside and smoking Etna looming in the distance.

The mysterious **Torre di Federico II** stands above the lower part of town. This octagonal tower, of unknown purpose, has been celebrated for millennia as marking the exact geometric center of the island—thus the tower's, and city's, nickname, Umbilicus Siciliae (Navel of Sicily); and indeed, the top of the tower just might be the only vantage point in all Sicily from which all three corners are ever visible.

Where to Stay & Eat

$–$$ ✕ **Centrale.** This casual place has served meals since 1889. The bright walls of an old palazzo are adorned with Sicilian pottery, and an outdoor terrace soothes diners in summer. The varied menu features local preparations such as *coppole di cacchio* (peppers stuffed with spaghetti, potato, and basil), grilled pork chops, and a good choice of Sicilian wines. ⊠ *Piazza VI Dicembre 9* ☎ *0935/500963* ▭ *AE, DC, MC, V* ⊘ *Closed Sat.*

¢ ✕ **La Botte.** Although the menu pays homage to tradition—*orrecchiette alla Norma* (small, ear-shape pasta with an eggplant and tomato sauce) is a Sicilian classic—some tasty dishes like the *papardelle alla botte* (wide noodles with meat sauce) qualify as more modern fare. Order from the wine list or let the friendly staff fill your carafe with the good local vintage from *la botte* (the barrel). ⊠ *Via Roma 488* ☎ *0935/502331* ▭ *AE, DC, MC, V* ⊘ *Closed Tues., fixed lunch menu Mon. and Wed.*

$ ▦ **Hotel Sicilia.** Sicily's interior has few decent accommodations, so if overnighting you'll have little choice but to stay at the Sicilia. Centrally located, the place is institutional-feeling and monopoly-priced, but its bright rooms (some with excellent views) are reliably clean and adequate. Reserve ahead for one with a bathtub (number 10), air-conditioning, or a view over the town and hillside rather than onto the piazza. ⊠ *Piazza Napoleone Colajanni 7, 94100* ☎ *0935/500850* ▤ *0935/500488* ⊕ *www.hotelsiciliaenna.it* ⇗ *60 rooms* ⚲ *Minibars, bar, parking; no a/c in some rooms* ▭ *AE, DC, MC, V* ⦿⦿ *BP.*

Nightlife

After dark, **Wine Bar Up** (⊠ Piazza Garibaldi ☎ 0935/501111), upstairs from Caffè Italia, is a hip place to stop for a drink.

Piazza Armerina

㊷ *120 km (75 mi) west of Catania.*

A quick look around Piazza Armerina is rewarding—the fanciful town has a feel of provincial warmth, and the crumbling yellow stone architecture with Sicily's trademark bulbous balconies creates quite an effect. The greatest draw, however, lies just down the road.

Fodor'sChoice The exceptionally well-preserved **Imperial Roman Villa** in Casale, 4 km
★ (2½ mi) from Piazza Armerina, is thought to have been a hunting lodge of the emperor Maximianus Heraclius (4th century AD). The excavations were not begun until 1950, and the wall decorations and vaulting

have been lost. However, some of the best mosaics of the Roman world cover more than 12,000 square feet under a shelter that hints at the layout of the original buildings. The mosaics were probably made by North African artisans, because they are similar to those in the Tunis Bardo Museum. The entrance was through a triumphal arch that led into an atrium surrounded by a portico of columns. Through this the *thermae*, or bathhouse, is reached. It's colorfully decorated with mosaic nymphs, a Neptune, and slaves massaging bathers. The peristyle leads to the main villa, where in the Salone del Circo you look down on mosaics illustrating Roman circus sports. Room 38 even reveals a touch of eroticism—surely only scratching the surface of the bacchanalian festivities that Maximilian conjured up. ⊠ *Casale* ☎ *0935/680036* ▧ *€4* ⊙ *Weekdays 9–1:30 and 3–1 hr before sunset, weekends 9–1 hr before sunset.*

Caltagirone

43 *30 km (18 mi) southeast of Piazza Armerina, 60 km (37 mi) southwest of Catania.*

Built over three hills, this charming baroque town is a center of Sicily's ceramics industry. Here you will find majolica balustrades, tile-decorated windowsills, and a monumental tile staircase of 142 steps—each decorated with a different pattern—leading up to the neglected **Santa Maria del Monte.** On the feast of San Giacomo (July 24), the staircase is illuminated with candles that form a tapestry design over the steps. It is the result of months of work preparing the 4,000 *coppi,* or cylinders of colored paper that hold oil lamps. At 9:30 PM on July 24, a squad of hundreds of boys springs into action to light the lamps, so that the staircase flares up all at once. ⊙ *Daily 7–noon and 4–7.*

Shopping
Of the numerous ceramic shops in Caltagirone's old center, **Branciforti** (⊠ Scala Santa Maria del Monte 3 ☎ 0933/24427 ⊕ www.ceramichebranciforti.it), right on Caltagirone's fabled ceramic steps, is one of the best, selling eye-catching work with deep shades of blue and swirling arabesques.

Palazzolo Acreide

44 *60 km (40 mi) southeast of Caltagirone, 40 km (25 mi) west of Siracusa.*

This small inland town is best known for its archaeological zone, the ancient Greek Akrai, founded by the Siracusans in 664 BC. The zone contains the foundations of a temple dedicated to Aphrodite and a well-preserved theater, whereas the town itself is unspectacularly baroque.

Ragusa

45 *25 km (15 mi) southwest of Palazzolo Acreide.*

Ragusa and Modica are the two chief cities in Sicily's smallest and sleepiest province, and the centers of a region known as Iblea. The dry, rocky, gentle countryside filled with canyons and grassy knolls is a unique landscape in Sicily. Iblea's trademark squat stone walls divide swaths of land in a manner reminiscent of the high English countryside—but summers are decidedly Sicilian, with dry heat so intense that life grinds to a standstill for several hours each day. This remote province hums along to its own tune, clinging to local customs, cuisines, and traditions in aloof disregard even for the rest of Sicily.

Ragusa is known for some great local red wines and its wonderful Ragusano DOP cheese (a creamy, doughy, flavorful version of caciocavallo, made by hand every step of the way). It's a modern city with a beautiful old town called **Ibla,** which was completely rebuilt after the devastating earthquake of 1693. A tumble of buildings perched on a hilltop and suspended between a deep ravine and a sloping valley, Ibla's tiny squares and narrow lanes make for pleasant meandering. The **Basilica di San Giorgio,** designed by Rosario Gagliardi of Noto in 1738, is one of the finest examples of Sicilian Baroque.

Catania

46 *60 km (37 mi) north of Siracusa, 94 km (59 mi) south of Messina.*

The chief wonder of Catania, Sicily's second city, is that it is there at all. Its successive populations were deported by one Greek tyrant, sold into slavery by another, and driven out by the Carthaginians. Every time the city got back on its feet it was struck by a new calamity: plague decimated the population in the Middle Ages, a mile-wide stream of lava from Mt. Etna swallowed most of the city in 1669, and 25 years later a disastrous earthquake forced the Catanese to begin again.

Three centuries later, the lava remains: scores of buildings constructed from solidified black lava stone. But today Catania is also in the midst of yet another resurrection—this time from crime, filth, and urban decay. Although the city remains loud and full of traffic, positive signs of gentrification are everywhere. Chic *osterie* (wine bars), designer bistros, and trendy ethnic home-furnishings shops have popped up all over town. Even more impressive are the vibrant nightlife, theater, dance, and live music to which the town now sways year-round.

Every evening, **Via Etnea** is host to one of Sicily's most enthusiastic passeggiate, in which Catanese of all ages take part. The street is closed to traffic until 10 PM and is strewn with cafés, clothing, jewelry, and shoe stores.

Many of Catania's buildings are constructed from solidified lava, and the black lava stone and showcase of baroque buildings have given the city a singular appearance. Nowhere is this clearer than in the centro storico. At the heart of Piazza del Duomo stands an elephant carved out of lava balancing an Egyptian obelisk. The photogenic elephant—the city's informal mascot—faces the Giovanni Vaccarini–designed facade of the Duomo, **Cattedrale di Sant'Agata,** inside of which composer Vincenzo Bellini is buried. Also of note are the three apses of lava that survive from the original Norman structure and a fresco from 1675 in the sacristy that portrays Catania's submission to Etna's attack. ⊠ *Bottom end of Via Etnea* ☎ *095/320044* ⊘ *Daily 8–noon and 4:30–7.*

Catania's greatest native son was the composer Vincenzo Bellini (1801–35), whose operas have thrilled audiences since their premieres in the first half of the 19th century. His home, now the **Museo Bellini-ano,** preserves memorabilia of the man and his work. ⊠ *Piazza San Francesco 3* ☎ *095/7150535* ⊠ *Free* ☉ *Mon., Wed., Fri., and Sun. 9–1, Tues. and Thurs. 9–1 and 3–6.*

need a break? Of the numerous pastry shops along Via Etnea, **Al Caprice** (⊠ Via Etnea 32 ☎ 095/320840) offers the greatest variety of homemade goodies and edible gifts, plus hot and cold snacks.

The selection of almond-based delights from **I Dolci di Nonna Vincenza** (⊠ Piazza San Placido 7, Palazzo Biscari ☎ 095/7151844 ⊕ www.dolcinonnavincenza.it) may be slight, but everything is fresh and phenomenally good. In response to demand, Nonna Vincenza ships abroad and even has an outlet in the Catania airport.

Where to Stay & Eat

$–$$ ✕ **Costa Azzurra.** At this seafood restaurant in the Ognina district, reserve a table on the veranda by the edge of the sea with good views of the harbor. The fritto misto can be ordered as an antipasto or a main course, and the pesce spada steak is a simple classic, served grilled with a large slice of lemon. ⊠ *Via De Cristofaro 4, Ognina, north of the center, on the way to the Taormina road* ☎ *095/497889* ⊟ *AE, DC, MC, V* ☉ *Closed Mon. and last 2 wks in Aug.*

★ **$–$$** ✕ **La Siciliana.** A meal at one of Sicily's finest eateries more than justifies the short taxi ride to La Siciliana, 3 km (1½ miles) from the center of Catania. Salvo La Rosa and sons serve a memorable array of seafood and meat dishes, exquisite homemade desserts, and a choice of more than 220 wines. The restaurant specializes in the ancient dish *ripiddu nivicatu* ("black" risotto with cuttlefish ink and fresh ricotta cheese) as well as *le sarde a beccafico* (stuffed sardines), and calamari *ripieni alla griglia* (grilled stuffed calamari). ⊠ *Viale Marco Polo 52* ☎ *095/376400* ⊕ *www.lasiciliana.it* ⊟ *AE, DC, MC, V* ☉ *Closed Mon. No dinner Sun.*

$$$–$$$$ ⊞ **Excelsior.** Ask for a room facing Piazza Verga, a neat tree-lined square in this quiet but central district of Catania. The relatively new Excelsior has air-conditioning and sound-insulated windows in all rooms, which are impeccably furnished with a careful balance of old and new motifs. The American Bar should provide solace if you're feeling nostalgic for a Manhattan. ⊠ *Piazza Verga 39, 95129* ☎ *095/7476111* ⊟ *095/537015* ⊕ *www.excelsiorcatania.thi.it* ⊃ *158 rooms, 13 suites, 5 junior suites* ⚷ *Restaurant, gym, steam room, bar, parking (fee)* ⊟ *AE, DC, MC, V* ⧖ *BP.*

$$ ⊞ **Savona.** This is a conveniently located and very modern hotel a stone's throw from Piazza del Duomo. The rooms are spacious, solidly furnished, and well equipped. Reception can help with parking suggestions. ⊠ *Via Vittorio Emanuele 210, 95124* ☎ *095/326982* ⊕ *www.hotelsavona.it* ⊃ *30 rooms* ⚷ *In-room safes, minibars, bar* ⊟ *MC, V* ⧖ *BP.*

Nightlife & the Arts

The opera season at the **Teatro Bellini** (⊠ Piazza Bellini, Catania ☎ 095/7150921 ⊕ www.teatromassimobellini.it), October to June, attracts top singers and productions to the birthplace of the great composer. Guided tours of the theater's lavish interior, built in 1890, run daily from 8:30 to 10:30.

International jazz acts bypass Palermo for Catania's live music scene, the best in Sicily. Check out **Teatro ABC** (⊠ Pietro Mascagni 92 ☎ 095/535382 ⊕ www.brassgroup.com). For more local fare, **La Bettola dei Cavalieri** (⊠ Piazza Federico di Svevia 20 ☎ 3405977489) has great jazz with an Italian bent. **La Chiave** (⊠ Via Landolina 64 ☎ 3479480910 ⊕ www.lachiave.it) features blues on Thursday and jazz on Sunday.

Mount Etna

47 *30 km (19 mi) north of Catania, 60 km (37 mi) south of Messina.*

Fodor'sChoice
★

Mt. Etna is one of the world's major active volcanoes and is the largest and highest in Europe—the cone of the crater rises to 10,902 feet above sea level. Plato sailed in just to catch a glimpse in 387 BC; in the 9th century AD, the oldest gelato of all was shaved off of its snowy slopes; and in the 21st century the volcano still claims annual headlines. Etna has erupted 11 times in the past 30 or so years, most spectacularly in 1971, 1983, 2001, and 2002, when in each case rivers of molten lava destroyed the two highest stations of the cable car that rises from the town of Sapienza. Although each eruption is predictably declared a "tragedy" by the media owing to the economic losses, Etna almost never threatens human life. Travel in the proximity of the crater depends on Mt. Etna's temperament, but you can walk up and down the enormous lava dunes and wander over its moonlike surface of dead craters. The rings of vegetation change markedly as you rise, with vineyards and pine trees gradually giving way to growths of broom and lichen. Catania and Taormina are the departure points for excursions around—but not always to the top of—Mt. Etna. Buses leave from Catania's train station in early morning.

Although the 2002 eruptions destroyed the gondola, you can still climb Etna with a **mandatory guide** (☎ 095/914141) from Rifugio Sapienza, altitude 6,266 feet. The cost is approximately €40–€50 per person for the two- to three-hour round-trip, including jeep and guide. For more personalized guided tours, contact the **Gruppo Guide Alpine Etna** (☎ 095/7914755).

Closer to the ground, an alternative view of the volcano can be had from the **Circumetnea railroad** (⊠ Via Caronda 352, Catania ☎ 095/541243 ☉ Closed Sun.), which runs near the volcano's base. The private railway almost circles Mt. Etna, running 114 km (71 mi) between Riposto and Catania—the towns are 30 km (19 mi) apart by the coast road. The line is small, slow, and only single-track, but offers some dramatic vistas of the volcano and goes through lava fields. The round-trip takes about five hours, there are about 10 departures a day, and tickets cost €11 round-trip.

For a bird's-eye view of Mt. Etna, you may be tempted to try paragliding or hang gliding; contact **No Limits Etna Center** (⊠ Via Milano 6/a, Catania ☎ 095/7212747 🖷 095/387313 ⊕ www.etnacenter.net). For nonpilots there are tandem flights and microlight trips, as well as courses of varying lengths. The company also organizes free climbing, caving, and diving expeditions.

Where to Stay

★ **$$$$** ✕▣ **Hotel Villa Paradiso Dell'Etna.** This 1920s hotel 10 km (6 mi) from Catania was a haunt for artists before General Rommel took over during World War II. When the tide turned in the war, it became a military hospital. Today, after a painstaking renovation, Paradiso Dell'Etna once again lives up to its name. Resembling an elegant private villa housing mementos of a memorable past, the hotel offers four exceptional suites and 30 sumptuous rooms, each filled with tasteful 19th-century Sicilian antiques and all the modern accessories befitting a four-star hotel. ⊠ *Via per Viagrande 37 (S.G. La Punta), 95030* ☎ *095/7512409* 🖷 *095/7413861* 🌐 *www.paradisoetna.it* 🛏 *30 rooms, 4 suites* 🗘 *Restaurant, minibars, pool, gym, bar, free parking* ▭ *AE, DC, MC, V* ¶◯¶ *BP.*

Acireale

48 *16 km (10 mi) north of Catania.*

Acireale sits amid a clutter of rocky pinnacles and lush lemon groves. The craggy coast is known as the Riviera dei Ciclopi, after the legend narrated in the *Odyssey* in which the blinded cyclops Polyphemus hurled boulders at the retreating Ulysses, thus creating spires of rock, or *faraglioni* (pillars of rock rising dramatically out of the sea). Tourism has barely taken off here, so it's a good destination if you feel the need to put some distance between yourself and the busloads of tourists in Taormina. And though the beaches are rocky, there's good swimming here, too.

During Carnival celebrations, considered the best in Sicily, streets are jammed with thousands of fancy-dressed revelers and floats dripping with flowers and gaudy papier-mâché models.

Begin your visit to Acireale with a stroll down to the public gardens, **Villa Belvedere,** at the end of the main Corso Umberto, for superb coastal views. There's a good vista from **Belvedere di Santa Caterina,** near the Terme, visited by Lord Byron (1788–1824) during his Italian wanderings.

With its cupola and twin turrets, Acireale's **Duomo** is an extravagant baroque construction dating back to the 17th century. In the chapel to the right of the altar, look for the 17th-century silver statue of Santa Venera, patron saint of Acireale, made by Mario D'Angelo, and the early 18th-century frescoes by Antonio Filocamo. ⊠ *Piazza Duomo* ☎ *095/601797* 🕙 *Daily 8–noon and 4–7.*

need a break? Acireale is renowned in Sicily for its marzipan, made into fruit shapes and delicious biscuits. You'll find the tasty treat in the many pasticcerias around town. **El Dorado** (⊠ Corso Umberto 5 ☎ 095/601464) serves delicious ice creams, and the *granita di mandorla* (almond granita), available in summer, invites a firsthand acquaintance. **Castorina** (⊠ Piazza del Duomo 20 ☎ 095/601546) sells marzipan candies (and cute gift boxes for them).

A unique creation at **Belvedere** (⊠ Corso Umberto 230 ☎ 095/894164) is the *nucatole,* a large cookie made with heaping quantities of chocolate, Nutella, nuts, and other wholesome ingredients.

The sulfur-rich volcanic waters from Mt. Etna found at **Terme di Acireale** were first enjoyed by the Greeks. In the 2nd century AD Acireale's patron saint, Venera, was martyred, after which the waters were accorded miraculous powers. After 1873, when the Santa Venera bathing establishment with its park was created, the baths attracted a stream of celebrated visitors, including Wagner. Book in advance to use the baths and have mud treatments and massages (multiday treatment packages are available). Nonpatrons can wander the gardens for free. ⊠ *Via delle Terme 47* ☎ *095/601508* 🖷 *095/606468* ⊕ *www.terme-acireale.com* 🖾 *Gardens free* ⊙ *Treatments by appointment, daily 7–1. Gardens daily 9–8.*

Where to Stay & Eat

$$–$$$ ✕ **Al Molino.** Right next to the old water mill on the *lungomare* (promenade) in Santa Maria la Scala, this stylish local haunt is devoted to seafood, from the antipasto and pasta to the main course. Follow local tradition and finish the meal with a lemon sorbet. ⊠ *Via Molino 104, Santa Maria la Scala* ☎ *095/7648116* ▭ *AE, MC, V* ⊙ *Closed Wed. and Jan.*

$–$$ ✕ **La Grotta.** This conventional-looking trattoria is a front for a dining room within a cave with an actual rock-face wall. Try the *insalata di mare* (a selection of delicately steamed fish served with lemon and olive oil) or fish grilled over charcoal. Chef-proprietor Carmelo Strano's menu is small, but there isn't a dud among the selections offered. ⊠ *Via Scalo Grande 46* ☎ *095/7648153* ⌂ *Reservations essential* ▭ *AE, DC, MC, V* ⊙ *Closed Tues. and mid-Oct.–early Nov.*

$$ 🏨 **Aloha D'Oro.** The best bet in Acireale, with two pools, proximity to both the sea and downtown, and a good restaurant/pizzeria, is Aloha. The 1960s Mediterranean-style stone structure is on the edge of the La Timpa nature reserve. A private walking path takes you down through the lemon and caper groves to the rocky beach. The hotel caters to a largely Italian crowd. Ask for one of the 33 rooms in zona 100, as they are farthest from the street, closest to the sea, and offer the best views. ⊠ *Via Gasperi 10, 95024* ☎ *095/7687001* 🖷 *095/606984* ⊕ *www.hotel-aloha.com* ⥲ *120 rooms* ⌂ *Restaurant, minibars, 2 pools* ▭ *AE, DC, MC, V* ⫿⊘⫿ *BP.*

Nightlife & the Arts

Acireale is known for its puppet theater, a Sicilian tradition that has all but died out in other parts of the island, with the exception of Palermo. See shows at **Coop E. Macri** (⊠ Corso Umberto 11 ☎ 095/606272). The **Teatro dell'Opera dei Pupi** (⊠ Via Nazionale 95, Turi Grasso ☎ 095/7648035 ⊕ www.teatropupimacri.it) has puppet shows and a puppet exhibit.

Shopping

At **Bottega d'Arte** (⊠ Via Vittorio Emanuele 88 ☎ 095/606805 or 095/601987 ⊙ Closed Sun.) you can see the local artist Salvatore Chiarenza at work carving wood statues and traditional carts, as his father and grandfather did before him. He also makes brass and wooden puppets.

Taormina

49 *43 km (27 mi) southwest of Messina, 50 km (31 mi) north of Catania.*

The natural beauty of the medieval mountaintop town of Taormina is so great that even its considerable overdevelopment has not spoiled its grandeur. The view of the sea and Mt. Etna from its jagged cactus-covered cliffs is as close to perfection as a panorama can get, especially on clear days, when the snowcapped volcano's white puffs of smoke rise against the blue sky. Writers have extolled Taormina's beauty almost since its founding in the 6th century BC by Greeks from Naples; Goethe and D. H. Lawrence were among its more recent well-known enthusiasts.

The Greeks put a premium on finding impressive locations to stage their dramas, and Taormina's **Teatro Greco** occupies one of the finest of theater sites. It was built during the 3rd century BC and rebuilt by the Romans during the 2nd century AD. Its acoustics are exceptional: even today a stage whisper can be heard in the last rows. In summer Taormina hosts an arts festival of music and dance events and a film festival; many performances are held in the Teatro Greco. ⊠ *Via Teatro Greco* ☎ *0942/232220* 💶 *€4.50* ☉ *Daily 9–1 hr before sunset.*

Taormina's many 14th- and 15th-century palaces have been carefully preserved. Especially beautiful is the **Palazzo Corvaja** (⊠ Largo Santa Caterina ☎ 0942/23243), with characteristic black-lava and white-limestone inlays. Today it houses the tourist office and the **Museo di Arte e Storia Popolare,** which has a collection of cribs, carts, puppets, and folk art. ⊠ *Palazzo Corvaja* 💶 *€2.60* ☉ *Tues.–Sun. 9–1 and 4–8.*

By footpath or car you can approach the medieval **Castello Saraceno** (⊠ Monte Tauro), enticingly perched on an adjoining cliff above town, but you cannot continue all the way to the castle itself.

From the main Corso Umberto, stroll down Via Bagnoli Croce to the **Parco Duca di Cesarò,** the lovely public gardens designed by Florence Trevelyan Cacciola, a Scottish lady "invited" to leave England following a romantic liaison with the future Edward VII (1841–1910). Arriving in Taormina in 1889, she married a local professor and devoted herself to the gardens, filling them with Mediterranean plants, ornamental pavilions (known as the beehives), and fountains. Stop by the panoramic bar, which has stunning views.

need a break?
A marzipan devotee should not leave Taormina without trying one of the gooey sweets—maybe in the guise of the ubiquitous *fico d'India* (prickly pear)—at **Pasticceria Etna** (⊠ Corso Umberto 112 ☎ 0942/24735 🖶 0942/21279). Locals swear by the cannoli, and the owner gleefully ships them abroad.

Where to Stay & Eat

$$$–$$$$ ✕ **La Giara.** Named after a giant Roman vase discovered underneath the bar, this is one of Taormina's oldest restaurants, elegant and classical in style, and enhanced by columns of Syracuse stone sculpted by local master stonecutters. The kitchen blends upscale modern techniques

with the simple flavors of traditional specialties. Try the *involtini di cernia al finocchietto selvatico* (stuffed grouper with wild fennel). You can extend your evening by taking an after-dinner drink at the popular piano bar. ✉ *Vico La Floresta 1* ☎ *0942/23360* 🖃 *AE, DC, MC, V* ☾ *No lunch. Closed Mon. and Nov.–Apr.*

$$–$$$ ✕ **Granduca.** There's an antiques shop in the entrance of this tastefully decorated restaurant, where cane chairs and luxurious plants jostle for space among the objets d'art. Your attention, however, will be principally occupied by the riveting views from the terrace. In summer you can eat outside at their pizzeria in the floral gardens. Try such well-executed dishes as fettuccine *al Granduca* (with a creamy vegetable sauce). ✉ *Corso Umberto 172* ☎ *0942/24983* 🖃 *AE, DC, MC, V* ☾ *Closed Tues., Nov., and 3 wks Feb.–Mar.*

$$ ✕ **La Dracena.** Just behind the castle, this place takes its name from the dragon tree in the garden, and is ideal for an alfresco meal. The *mezzelune* (half-open ravioli) and dishes with zucchini are very good. ✉ *Via Michele Amari 4* ☎ *0942/23491* 🖃 *AE, DC, MC, V* ☾ *Closed Mon. and mid-Jan.–mid-Mar.*

★ $–$$ ✕ **L'Arco dei Cappuccini.** Just off the radar screen of the main tourist strip (near Porta Messina, off Via Costanino Patricio) lies this clean, diminutive restaurant with white tablecloths. Outdoor seating and an upstairs kitchen help make room for a few more tables—good evidence that the locals are well aware that both the price and the quality cannot be beat anywhere else in town. Indulge in *sopressa di polipo* (steamed octopus carpaccio), gnocchi *con pistacchi* (with pistachio cream sauce), or the fresh catch of the day. ✉ *Via Cappuccini 7* ☎ *0942/24893* ⌔ *Reservations essential* 🖃 *AE, DC, MC, V* ☾ *Closed Wed. and Nov.–Easter.*

$$$$ 🏨 **Grand Hotel Timeo and Villa Flora.** The deluxe Timeo wears a graceful patina that suggests it's been here—in a princely perch overlooking the town and just below the Teatro Greco—untouched since the dolce vita days. A splash of baroque mixes with the Mediterranean flavor in the lobby, with wooden floors, tile- and brickwork, and vaulting. Wrought-iron and wicker chairs surround marble tables in the original bar from 1873 (made of gesso) and on the adjoining palatial patio. Rooms are decorated with fine earth-tone linens and drapes, Oriental rugs, gilt-framed prints, and exquisite moldings on butter-color walls. The hotel was restored in 1998, followed by the acquisition of the neighboring Villa Flora and its 31 rooms in 2001. A new pool and fitness center are the most recent additions. ✉ *Via Teatro Greco 59, 98039* ☎ *0942/23801* 🖷 *0942/628501* ⊕ *www.framonhotels.com* 🛏 *84 rooms* ⚭ *Restaurant, room service, in-room safes, minibars, pool, gym, bar, convention center* 🖃 *AE, DC, MC, V* ⎮❂⎮ *MAP.*

$$$$ 🏨 **San Domenico Palace.** Sweeping views from this converted 15th-century

Fodor's Choice Dominican monastery will linger in your mind long after you're gone. And
★ the sensuous gardens—full of red trumpet flowers, bougainvillea, and lemons—afford a dramatic vista of the castle, the sea, and Mt. Etna. Luxury and comfort are bywords in this deluxe hotel, which is considered by some to be one of the best in Europe. In spite of the ultramodern amenities, the San Domenico's Renaissance flavor is preserved by two exquisite cloisters, convent rooms, and the chapel, now a banquet and conference

facility. ✉ *Piazza San Domenico 5, 98039* ☎ *0942/613111* 🖷 *0942/ 625506* ⊕ *www.sandomenico.thi.it* 🛏 *93 rooms, 15 suites* ⚒ *2 restaurants, minibars, pool, gym, bar, free parking* ▭ *AE, DC, MC, V* ⑩ *BP.*

\$\$\$–\$\$\$\$ 🏨 **Romantik Villa Ducale.** Formerly the summer residence of a local aristocrat, this stupendously sited villa, a 10- to 15-minute walk from the center of Taormina, has been converted into a luxurious hotel by his great-grandson. Individually styled rooms furnished with antiques and an intimate wood-paneled library create an atmosphere at once homelike and romantic, and the vast roof terrace, where a fantastic breakfast is served, takes full advantage of the wide panorama embracing Etna and the bay below. In summer a free shuttle bus connects the hotel with the area's best beaches. ✉ *Via L. da Vinci 60, 98039* ☎ *0942/28153* 🖷 *0942/28710* ⊕ *www.hotelvilladucale.it* 🛏 *15 rooms, 1 suite* ⚒ *Minibars, bar* ▭ *AE, DC, MC, V* ⊘ *Closed Nov. 26–Feb. 27* ⑩ *BP.*

\$\$\$ 🏨 **Hotel Villa Paradiso.** On the edge of the old quarter, overlooking the lovely public gardens and facing the sea, this smaller hotel is not as well known as some of the blockbusters nearby, but with views of Etna from many rooms, delightful service, and a good restaurant, it's only a matter of time. Proprietor Salvatore Martorana will gladly share stories of Taormina in Goethe's day over an *aperitivo*. A regular hotel bus service runs to the beach. ✉ *Via Roma 2, 98039* ☎ *0942/23921* 🖷 *0942/ 625800* ⊕ *www.hotelvillaparadisotaormina.com* 🛏 *20 rooms, 17 junior suites* ⚒ *Restaurant, minibars, cable TV, tennis courts, library* ▭ *AE, DC, MC, V* ⑩ *BP.*

\$\$ 🏨 **Arathena Rocks Hotel.** Here's a good choice if you want to stay near the sea. Giardini Naxos makes a great base. In summer it's just as lively as Taormina, and the broad sandy beach nearby is a bonus. The hotel stands at one end of the bay, right on the cape where Greek settlers first landed in Sicily. There's a large pool, around which Sicilian singers and musicians entertain you every other night in summer. A twice-daily free bus service links the hotel to Taormina. ✉ *Via Calcide Eubea 55, 98035 Giardini Naxos* ☎ *0942/51349* 🖷 *0942/51690* 🛏 *49 rooms* ⊕ *www. hotelarathena.com* ⚒ *Restaurant, pool, bar, Internet; no a/c in some rooms* ▭ *AE, DC, MC, V* ⊘ *Closed Nov.–Easter* ⑩ *BP.*

\$\$ 🏨 **Villa Fiorita.** This converted private home near the Teatro Greco has excellent northerly coastal views from nearly every room. Rooms vary in size and furnishings, but most are bright, breezy, and colorful, with large windows and balconies (do ask). Prices are reasonable considering the compact swimming pool and garden. The elevator is at the top of 65 steps. ✉ *Via Pirandello 39, 98039* ☎ *0942/24122* 🖷 *0942/ 625967* ⊕ *www.villafioritahotel.com* 🛏 *24 rooms, 1 suite* ⚒ *In-room safes, pool, bar* ▭ *AE, MC, V* ⑩ *BP.*

The Arts

FESTIVALS   The Teatro Greco and the Palazzo dei Congressi, near the entrance to the theater, are the main venues for the summer festival dubbed **Taormina Arte** (☎ 0942/21142 ⊕ www.taormina-arte.com) held each year from May to September and encompassing classical music, ballet, theater, and the famous **film festival** (⊕ www.taorminafilmfest.it) in June or July.

Castelmola

 5 km (3 mi) west of Taormina, 65 km (40 mi) south of Messina.

If your passion for heights hasn't been quelled, visit Castelmola, the tiny town above Taormina with a spectacular 360-degree panorama. Local bars make their own refreshing almond wine.

 en route — The 50-km (30-mi) stretch of road between Taormina and Messina is flanked by lush vegetation and seascapes. Inlets are punctuated by gigantic, oddly shaped rocks. It was along this coast, legend says, that the giant cyclops hurled his boulders down on Ulysses and his terrified men as they fled to the sea in Homer's *Odyssey*.

Messina

43 km (27 mi) northeast of Taormina, 94 km (59 mi) northeast of Catania.

Messina's ancient history lists a series of disasters, but the city nevertheless managed to develop a fine university and a thriving cultural environment. At 5 o'clock in the morning on December 28, 1908, Messina changed from a flourishing metropolis of 120,000 to a heap of rubble, shaken to pieces by an earthquake that turned into a tidal wave and left 80,000 dead and the city almost completely leveled. As you approach the sickle-shaped bay, across which ferries connect Sicily to the mainland, you won't notice any outward indication of the disaster, except for the modern countenance of a 3,000-year-old city. The somewhat flat look is a precaution of seismic planning: tall buildings are not permitted.

The reconstruction of Messina's Norman and Romanesque **Duomo**, originally built by the Norman king Roger II in 1197, has retained much of the original plan, including a handsome crown of Norman battlements, an enormous apse, and a splendid wood-beam ceiling. The adjoining **bell tower**—of a much later date—contains one of the largest and most complex mechanical clocks in the world, constructed in 1933 with a host of gilded automatons, including a roaring lion, that spring into action every day at the stroke of noon. ✉ *Piazza del Duomo* ☎ *090/675175* ⊙ *Daily 8–12:30 and 4–7.*

Where to Stay & Eat

$–$$$ ✕ **Da Piero.** An institution in Messina for decades, this central restaurant (four blocks up from Piazza Cairoli) trades on its well-deserved reputation for classic Sicilian dishes, particularly seafood. In season, try the *involtini di pesce spada* (stuffed swordfish); the exquisite calamari are good at any time. Marsala sipped with one of the rich homemade desserts makes for a grand finale. ✉ *Via Ghibellina 121* ☎ *090/718365* ▭ *AE, DC, MC, V* ⊙ *Closed Sun. and Aug.*

$$$ ▥ **Grand Hotel Liberty.** Across the piazza from the train station, this hotel—at the top end of Messina's offerings—is a cool haven from the bustle of the surrounding streets. The entrance and public rooms are sumptuously fitted out in a white-marble neoclassical style with a meticulous attention to detail, whereas bedrooms are plainer but comfortably equipped. ✉ *Via I Settembre 15, 98123* ☎ *090/6409436* 🖷 *090/6409340* ⊕ *www.framon-hotels.com* 🖵 *52 rooms* ⚲ *Restaurant, minibars, bar, meeting rooms* ▤ *AE, DC, MC, V* ⧯ *BP.*

THE AEOLIAN ISLANDS

Off Sicily's northeast coast lies an archipelago of seven spectacular islands of volcanic origin. The Isole Eolie (Aeolian Islands), also known as the Isole Lipari (Lipari Islands), were named after Aeolus, the Greek god of the winds, who is said to keep all the earth's winds stuffed in a bag in his cave here. The Aeolians are a world of grottoes and clear-water caves carved by waves through the centuries. Superb snorkeling and scuba diving abound in the clearest and cleanest of Italy's waters. Of course the beautiful people of high society discovered the archipelago years ago—here Roberto Rossellini courted his star and future wife Ingrid Bergman in 1950—and you should not expect complete isolation, at least on the main islands. August, in particular, can get unpleasantly overcrowded, and lodging and travel should always be booked as early as possible.

Lipari provides the widest range of accommodations and is a good jumping-off point for day trips to the other islands. Most exclusive are Vulcano and Panarea, the former noted for its black sands and stupendous sunsets (and prices), as well as the acrid smell of its sulfur emissions, whereas the latter is, according to some, the prettiest. Most remarkable is Stromboli (pronounced with the accent on the first syllable) with its constant eruptions, and remotest are Filicudi and Alicudi, where electricity was introduced only in the 1980s. Access to the islands is via ferry and hydrofoil from Sicily (usually Messina) or Naples. The bars in the Aeolian Islands, and especially those on Lipari, are known for their granitas of fresh strawberries, melon, peaches, and other fruits. Many Sicilians, especially on the Aeolians and in Messina, Taormina, and Catania, begin the hot summer days with a granita *di caffè* (a coffee ice topped with whipped cream), into which they dunk their breakfast rolls. You can get one any time of day.

Lipari

52 *37 km (23 mi) north of Milazzo, 2 hrs 10 mins by ferry, 1 hr by hydrofoil; Milazzo: 41 km (25 mi) west of Messina.*

The largest and most developed of the Aeolians, Lipari welcomes you with distinctive pastel-color houses. Fields of spiky agaves dot the northernmost tip of the island, Acquacalda, indented with pumice and obsidian quarries. In the west is San Calogero, where you can explore hot springs and mud baths. From the red lava base of the island rises a plateau crowned with a 16th-century castle and a 17th-century cathedral.

★ The vast, multibuilding **Museo Eoliano** is one of the best archaeological museums in Europe, with an intelligently arranged collection of prehistoric finds—some dating as far back as 4000 BC—from various sites in the archipelago. ✉ *Via Castello* ☎ *090/9880174* 🖅 *€4.50* ☉ *Daily 9–1 and 3–7.*

Where to Stay & Eat

★ **$$–$$$** ✕⊡ **Il Filippino.** The views from the flower-strewn outdoor terrace of this restaurant in the upper town are a fitting complement to the superb fare. Founded in 1910, the restaurant is rightly rated one of the archipelago's best. Top choice is seafood: the zuppa di pesce and the antipasto platter of smoked and marinated fish are absolute musts. Leave some room for the local version of cassata, accompanied by sweet Malvasia wine from Salina. The restaurant also runs Residence Albergo Mendolita ($$), a comfortable bed-and-breakfast 300 yards away. ⊠ *Piazza Municipio* ☎ *090/9811002, 090/9812374 Mendolita* 🖶 *090/9814879* ⊕ *www.bernardigroup.it* 🛏 *18 rooms, 1 suite* ⚙ *Minibars, in-room safes* ☰ *AE, DC, MC, V* ⊙ *Closed Mon. in Oct.–Mar. and Nov. 10–Dec. 20.*

$$$–$$$$ ⊡ **Gattopardo Park Hotel.** Bright bougainvillea and fiery hibiscus set the tone in this grand villa, and its restaurant has sweeping views of the sea. Guest quarters are in the 19th-century main villa or in whitewashed bungalows in the surrounding tranquil parkland. Public rooms have wood-beamed ceilings and rustic-style furnishings. A minibus shuttles between the hotel and Spiagge Bianche. There are also trips around the island, boat excursions to Vulcano and Stromboli, and folklore evenings. Half board is required in summer; weekly discounts are available. ⊠ *Via Diana, 98055* ☎ *090/9811035* 🖶 *090/9880207* ⊕ *www.netnet.it/hotel/gattopardo* 🛏 *53 rooms* ⚙ *Restaurant, bar* ☰ *MC, V* ⊙ *Closed Nov.–Mar.* ⦿ *MAP.*

$$–$$$ ⊡ **Villa Augustus.** Tucked away off a side street in the center of Lipari's old town, this is a peaceful enclave where a simple homey spirit prevails, with friendly service and a discreet attention to detail. In addition to a palm-shaded backyard garden, there's a roof-garden offering good sea views. Apartment-style rooms are bright and spacious. You'll have to arrive during daytime hours, as the hotel is managed by only one person. ⊠ *Vico Ausonia 16, 98055* ☎ *090/9811232* 🖶 *090/9812233* ⊕ *www.villaaugustus.it* 🛏 *34 rooms* ⚙ *Gym, piano bar, meeting room* ☰ *AE, DC, MC, V* ⊙ *Closed Nov.–Feb.* ⦿ *BP.*

Vulcano

❸ *18 km (11 mi) northwest of Lipari, 25 mins by ferry, 10 mins by hydrofoil; 55 km (34 mi) northwest of Milazzo.*

True to its name—and the origin of the term—Vulcano has a profusion of fumaroles sending up jets of hot vapor, but the volcano here has long been dormant. Many come to soak in the strong-smelling sulfur baths whose odors will greet you, when the wind is in the right direction, long before you disembark. The island has some of the archipelago's best beaches, though the volcanic black sand can be off-putting at first. You can ascend to the crater (1,266 feet above sea level) on muleback for a wonderful view or take boat rides into the grottoes around the base. From Capo Grillo there is a view of all the Aeolians.

Where to Stay

★ **$$$–$$$$** ⊡ **Les Sables Noires.** Named for the black sands of the beach in front, this luxury hotel is superbly sited on the beautiful Porto di Ponente. The cool modern furnishings and inviting pool (for those unwilling to lounge on the private beach) induce a sybaritic mood, and the white-walled guest rooms are also tasteful and spacious. The restaurant, naturally, looks out over the bay: sunsets are framed by the towering faraglioni. Week-long stays are required in high season. ⊠ *Porto di Ponente, 98050* ☎ *090/9850* 🖷 *090/9852454* ⊕ *www.framon-hotels.com* ⬐ *48 rooms* ☖ *Restaurant, pool, beach, bar* ⊟ *AE, DC, MC, V* ⊘ *Closed mid-Oct.–mid-Apr.* ⅠⓄⅠ *BP.*

Salina

54 *15 km (9 mi) north of Lipari, 50 mins by ferry, 20 mins by hydrofoil; 52 km (38 mi) northwest of Milazzo.*

The second largest of the Aeolian Islands, Salina is also the most fertile—which accounts for its excellent Malvasia dessert wine. Excursions go up Mt. Fossa delle Felci, which rises to more than 3,000 feet. Salina is also the highest of the islands, and the vineyards and fishing villages along its slopes add to its allure. Malvasia wine here is locally produced, unlike that found on other islands. Salina has reasonably priced accommodations and restaurants—and fewer crowds than Lipari.

Where to Stay

$–$$ 🏨 **Bellavista.** This is a quiet hotel in a quiet location, even though it's right next to the port. Rooms are simply furnished and cheerfully decorated with bright materials and ceramic tiles. Almost all have sea views, which can be enjoyed from the balconies. The management provides a list of things to do while on Salina and can organize boat excursions and transport around the island, though you may well opt for the *dolce far niente* (idle life). ⊠ *Via Risorgimento, Santa Marina Salina, 98050* 🖷🖷 *090/9843009; 090/9281558 in winter* ⬐ *13 rooms* ⊟ *No credit cards* ⊘ *Closed Nov.–Mar.*

Panarea

55 *18 km (11 mi) north of Lipari, 2 hrs by ferry, 25–50 mins by hydrofoil; 55 km (33 mi) north of Milazzo.*

Panarea has some of the most dramatic scenery of the islands: wild caves carved out of the rock and dazzling flora. The exceptionally clear water and the richness of life on the sea floor make Panarea especially suitable for underwater exploration, though there is little in the way of beaches. The outlying rocks and islets make a gorgeous sight, and you can enjoy the panorama on an easy excursion to the small Bronze Age village at Capo Milazzese.

Where to Stay

$$$$ 🏨 **La Raya.** This discreet, expensive hotel is perfectly in keeping with the elite style of Panarea, most exclusive of the Aeolian islands. Public rooms, including bars, a broad terrace, and an open-air restaurant, are built into a hillside right on the port; the residential area is a 10-minute walk inland, though the rooms still enjoy the serene prospect of the sea and Stromboli from their balconies. The decor is elegant and understated, with Moorish-type hangings and low divans helping to create a tone of serene luxury. Families with young children are asked to book elsewhere.

✉ *San Pietro, 98050* ☎🖶 *090/983103* ⊕ *www.hotelraya.it* ⤶ *30 rooms* ⚹ *Restaurant, minibars, bar, nightclub* ▭ *AE, DC, MC, V* ☉ *Closed mid-Oct.–mid-Apr.* ⊦◎⊦ *BP.*

Stromboli

56 *40 km (25 mi) north of Lipari, 3 hrs 45 mins by ferry, 65–90 mins by hydrofoil; 63 km (40 mi) north of Milazzo.*

This northernmost of the Aeolians (also accessible from Naples) consists entirely of the cone of an active volcano. The view from the sea—especially at night, as an endless stream of glowing red-hot lava flows into the water—is unforgettable. Stromboli is in a constant state of mild dissatisfaction, and every now and then its anger flares up, so authorities insist that you climb to the top (about 3,031 feet above sea level) only with a guide. The round-trip—climb, pause, and descent—usually starting around 6 PM, takes about four hours; the lava is much more impressive after dark. Some choose to camp overnight atop the volcano—again, a guide is essential. You will find a small selection of reasonably priced hotels and restaurants in the main town, and a choice of lively clubs and cafés for the younger set. In addition to the island tour, excursions include boat trips around the naturally battlemented isle of Strombolicchio.

Numerous tour operators are available for Stromboli, among them **Società Navigazione Pippo** (☎ 090/986135 or 0338/9857883). Rates are around €20 per person for four hours.

Alicudi

57 *65 km (40 mi) west of Lipari, 3 hrs 25 mins–3 hrs 50 mins by ferry, 60–95 mins by hydrofoil; 102 km (68 mi) northwest of Milazzo.*

The farthest outpost of the Aeolians remains sparsely inhabited, wild, and at peace. Here and on Filicudi there is a tiny selection of accommodations, but you can rent rooms cheaply. Only the coming and going of hydrofoils (which run only occasionally, especially October–April) disturbs the rhythm of life here, and the only noise is the occasional braying of donkeys.

Filicudi

58 *30 km (16 mi) west of Salina (30–60 mins by hydrofoil); 82 km (54 mi) northwest of Milazzo.*

Just a dot in the sea, Filicudi is famous for its unusual volcanic rock formations and the enchanting **Grotta del Bue Marino** (Grotto of the Sea Ox). The crumbled remains of a prehistoric village are at Capo Graziano. The island, which is spectacular for walking and hiking and is still a truly undiscovered, restful haven, has a handful of hotels and pensions, and some families put up guests. Car ferries are available only in summer.

Where to Stay

★ **$$** ▦ **La Canna.** Set on a height above the tiny port, this pension commands fabulous views of sky and sea from its flower-filled terrace. It's wonderful to wake up to the utter tranquillity that characterizes any stay on this island. Rooms are small but adequate, kept clean and tidy by the friendly family staff. The cooking is quite good, usually centered around the day's catch (half or full board required in peak season). Arrange to be collected at the port. ⊠ *Via Rosa 43, 98050* ☎ *090/9889956* 🖷 *090/9889966* ⊕ *www.lacannahotel.it* ➩ *10 rooms* ⌂ *Restaurant, in-room safes, bar* ▭ *MC, V* ⧫〇◀ *MAP.*

SICILY A TO Z

To research prices, get advice from other travelers, and book travel arrangements, visit www.fodors.com.

AIRPORTS

Sicily can be reached from all major cities via Rome, Milan, or Naples on Alitalia. Meridiana, Air One, and Volare also connect Catania and Palermo to other cities all over Italy, and Alitalia operates periodic connections to Cagliari, Sardinia. Planes land at Aeroporto Falcone-Borsellino (also known as Aeroporto Punta Raisi), 32 km (19 mi) west of Palermo at Punta Raisi, or Catania's Aeroporto Fontanarossa, 5 km (3 mi) south of city center, the main airport on Sicily's eastern side. There are also direct flights to Sicily from London on Meridiana and from Munich on Lufthansa. Note that flights from Sicily to points elsewhere, especially one-way flights, can be bought much cheaper from travel agencies in Italy than internationally, or through Web sites.

�Ⓘ Airport Information **Aeroporto Fontanarossa** ☎ 095/7239111 ⊕ www.aeroporto. catania.it. **Aeroporto Punta Raisi** ☎ 091/591698 ⊕ www.gesap.it.

TRANSFERS Prestia & Comandè buses run every half hour between Palermo's Punta Raisi airport and the city center (Piazza Castelnuovo and the central station); tickets cost €4.65. Taxis charge around €35 for the same 45-minute trip. To get directly to the train station, take the hourly train leaving from the airport. There are also less frequent bus connections directly to and from Agrigento and Trapani on Sal and Segesta lines, respectively. Catania's Fontanarossa airport (closed frequently because of volcanic dust from Etna) is served by Alibus, which leaves about every 20 minutes from the airport and the central train station, with stops at Piazza Stesicoro, on Via Etnea, the Duomo, etc. The journey takes around 25 minutes; tickets cost €1. Taxis cost around €20.

🔳 Taxis & Shuttles **Alibus** ☎ 095/7360450. **Prestia & Comandè** ☎ 091/580457.

BOAT & FERRY TRAVEL

Frequent car ferries cross the strait between Villa San Giovanni in Calabria and Messina on the island. The crossing usually takes about a half hour, but during the summer months there can be considerable delays. Overnight car ferries operated by Tirrenia run daily all year between Naples and Palermo. Tirrenia also runs regular service between Palermo and Cagliari, Sardinia, and between Trapani and Tunisia (in winter, frequency can be as low as once per week). SNAV has a daytime service (April–October) by faster catamarans, which also carry vehicles. Passenger-only hydrofoils also cross the strait from Reggio di Calabria to Messina in about 15 minutes. Grimaldi Lines' Grandi Navi Veloci run beautiful cruise ship–like ferries to Genoa (a 20-hour trip) year-round. The Aeolian Islands are reachable by hydrofoil from Naples, Messina, Palermo, and Milazzo. From Milazzo you can get ferry service to the islands. Call SNAV or Siremar, the other major ferry company serving the Aeolians.

▣ Boat & Ferry Information Grandi Navi Veloci ☎ 091/587404 in Palermo ⊕ www1.gnv.it. **Siremar** ☎ 081/5800340. **SNAV** ☎ 091/6118525 Palermo, 081/7612348 Naples ⊕ www.snav.it. **Tirrenia** ☎ 081/7201111 Naples, 091/6021111 Palermo ⊕ www.gruppotirrenia.it.

BUS TRAVEL

Air-conditioned coaches connect major and minor cities and are often faster and more convenient than local trains but slightly more expensive. Various companies serve the different routes. SAIS runs frequently between Palermo and Catania, Messina, and Siracusa, in each case arriving at and departing from near the train stations. Cuffaro runs between Palermo and Agrigento. On the south and east coasts and in the interior, SAIS connects the main centers, including Catania, Agrigento, Enna, Taormina, and Siracusa. Etna Trasporti operates between Catania, Caltagirone, Piazza Armerina, and Taormina. Interbus serves the routes between Messina, Taormina, Catania, and Siracusa.

▣ Bus Information Cuffaro ☎ 091/6161510. **Etna Trasporti** ☎ 095/530396. **Interbus** ☎ 095/532716. **SAIS** ☎ 091/6166028 Palermo, 095/536168, 095/536201 Catania.

CAR RENTAL

Renting a car is the best way to get around Sicily. Trains are unreliable and slow, and buses, though faster and air-conditioned in summer, can be subject to delays and strikes. Cars can be rented at airports and downtown locations in every major city.

▣ Local Agencies Avis ⊠ Aeroporto Fontanarossa, Catania ☎ 095/340500 ⊠ Piazza S. Calogero 11, Agrigento ☎ 0922/26353 ⊠ Aeroporto Punta Raisi, Palermo ☎ 091/591684 ⊠ Via F. Crispi 113/115/117, Palermo ☎ 091/586940. **Hertz** ⊠ Aeroporto Fontanarossa, Catania ☎ 095/341595 ⊠ Via Toselli 16/c, Catania ☎ 095/322560 ⊠ Efeso Viaggi, Via Imera 209, Agrigento ☎ 0922/556090 ⊠ Aeroporto Punta Raisi, Palermo ☎ 091/213112 ⊠ Via Messina 7/e, Palermo ☎ 091/331668. **Maggiore** ⊠ Aeroporto Fontanarossa, Catania ☎ 095/340594 ⊠ Piazza Verga 48, Catania ☎ 095/536927 ⊠ Aeroporto Punta Raisi, Palermo ☎ 091/591681 ⊠ Stazione Marittima, Palermo ☎ 091/6810801.

CAR TRAVEL

This is the ideal way to explore Sicily. Modern highways circle and bisect the island, making all main cities easily reachable. A20 (supplemented by S113 at points) connects Messina and Palermo; Messina and Catania are linked by A18; running through the interior, from Catania to west of Cefalù, is A19; threading west from Palermo, A29 runs to Trapani and the airport, with a leg stretching down to Mazara del Vallo. The *superstrada* (highway) SS115 runs along the southern coast, and connecting superstrade lace the island.

You will likely hear stories about the dangers of driving in Sicily. Some are true, and others less so. In the big cities—especially Palermo, Catania, and Messina—streets are a honking mess, with lane markings and traffic lights taken as mere suggestions; you can avoid the chaos by leaving your car in a garage. However, once outside the urban areas autostrade, superstrade, and regional state roads turn into a driving enthusiast's dream—they are winding, sparsely populated, and well paved and maintained, and they usually reveal a new, stunning view around every bend.

RULES OF THE ROAD Sicilians, especially in Palermo, are among the country's most aggressive drivers. Traffic lights are taken with a grain of salt, and many large intersections are just games of chicken—you'll sit all day if you don't lurch out at some point. Do keep your eye out for all-important yield signs, which can be easy to miss but often take the place of stop signs or stoplights. People within earshot routinely double-park—if you're blocked in, don't worry, just start honking and the owner will come move his car (and then, of course, take your space).

EMBASSIES & CONSULATES
🚩 United Kingdom **U.K. Consulate** ✉ Via Cavour 121, Palermo ☎ 091/326412.

EMERGENCIES
🚩 **Ambulance, Police, Fire** ☎ 113. **Hospital** ☎ 091/288141, 095/7591111 Palermo.

INTERNET
🚩 Internet Shops **Internet Shop** ✉ Via Napoli 32/34, Kalsa, Palermo ☎ 091/320697). **Aboriginal Internet Cafe** ✉ Via S. Spinuzza 51, Teatro Massimo area, Palermo ☎ 091/6622229.

LANGUAGE
The Sicilian language is still strong on the island and varies enormously from town to town and from village to village. It sounds nothing like standard Italian; however, most Sicilians will speak to strangers (and do business) in standard Italian.

MAIL & SHIPPING
OVERNIGHT SERVICES In Palermo the local courier used by UPS is Randazzo. The local FedEx courier in Palermo is SDA. To call for pickups or information from either Federal Express or UPS, use their national service numbers.
🚩 Major Services **Federal Express** ☎ 800/123800 or 02/2188444. **Randazzo** ✉ Via Sturzo 260, Zona Industriale, Carini ☎ 091/868-0200. **SDA** ✉ Via Pablo Picasso, Palermo ☎ 800/016027. **UPS** ☎ 02/25088001.
🚩 Post Offices **Palermo** ✉ Via Roma 322, Kalsa ☎ 091/7531111. **Siracusa** ✉ Piazza delle Poste, Ortygia ☎ 0931/489111.

OUTDOORS & SPORTS
There is a surfeit of beaches in Sicily, but many of them are too rocky, too crowded, or too dirty to be enjoyed for long. Tours in the Sicilian national parks are organized by Biosport/The Sauron. Walking expeditions by the day or week, as well as canoeing and biking in the Etna, Nebrodi, Madonie, and Peloritani parks, can all be arranged.
🚩 Tour Operator **Biosport/The Sauron** ✉ Via Acireale, 98100 Messina ☎ 090/2282800 🖷 090/2282890 ⊕ www.thesauron.com.

SAFETY
Don't be paranoid about safety in Sicily, but do be careful. In the cities, particularly Palermo and Catania, it's not recommended to wander around unpopulated streets, especially at night, and you should never flaunt expensive watches, jewelry, and the like. Women traveling alone should keep out of deserted areas at all times. Watch your bags constantly (it's best to securely strap your handbag across your chest), especially at airports. Leav-

ing valuables visible in your car while you go sightseeing is inviting trouble (and it's best if your luggage is out of sight completely). Take precautions; then enjoy the company of the Sicilians. You will find them friendly and often willing to go out of their way to help you.

TOURS

Tours of Palermo and Monreale are provided by the Italian tour operator CST on Friday afternoon and Saturday morning, with pickups from your hotel or a central location such as outside the Politeama theater. Contact the agency to confirm details. CST also arranges tours of Taormina and Etna, bookable from their office in Taormina, as well as to Piazza Armerina, Agrigento, and western Sicily, or you can join a seven-day tour of all Sicily's major sights in a comfortable air-conditioned coach with an English-speaking guide, with weekly departures from either Palermo or Catania; the cost includes all meals and accommodations in luxury hotels.

🖬 Fees & Schedules **CST** ⊠ Via E. Amari 124, Palermo ☎ 091/7439655 ⊕ www.compagniasicilianaturismo.it ⊠ Corso Umberto 101, Taormina ☎ 0942/24189.

TRAIN TRAVEL

There are direct express trains from Milan and Rome to Palermo, Catania, and Siracusa. The Rome–Palermo and Rome–Siracusa trips take at least 10 hours. After Naples, the run is mostly along the coast, so try to book a window seat on the right if you're not on an overnight train. At Villa San Giovanni, in Calabria, the train is separated and loaded onto a ferryboat to cross the strait to Messina.

Main lines connect Messina, Taormina, Siracusa, and Palermo. Secondary lines are generally very slow and unreliable. The Messina–Palermo run, along the northern coast, is especially scenic. Call FS for information.

🖬 Train Information **FS** (Italian State Railways) ☎ 892021 ⊕ www.trenitalia.it.

VISITOR INFORMATION

🖬 Tourist Information **Acireale** ⊠ Via Oreste Scionti 15, 95024 ☎ 095/892129 ⊕ www.acirealeturismo.it. **Agrigento** ⊠ Viale della Vittoria 225, 92100 ☎ 0922/401352 ⊠ Via Cesare Battisti 15, 92100 ☎ 0922/20454. **Caltagirone** ⊠ Via V. Libertini 3, 95041 ☎ 0933/53809 ⊕ www.comune.caltagirone.ct.it. **Caltanisetta** ⊠ Corso Vittorio Emanuele 109, 93100 ☎ 0934/530411 ⊕ www.aapit.cl.it. **Catania** ⊠ Via Cimarosa 10, 95124 ☎ 095/7306222 ⊕ www.apt.catania.it ⊠ Stazione Centrale, 95129 ☎ 095/7306255 ⊠ Aeroporto Fontanarossa, 95121 ☎ 095/7306266. **Cefalù** ⊠ Corso Ruggero 77, 90015 ☎ 0921/421050 ⊕ www.cefalu-tour.pa.it. **Enna** ⊠ Via Roma 411, 94100 ☎ 0935/528228 ⊕ www.apt-enna.com. **Erice** ⊠ Via Conte Pepoli 56, 91016 ☎ 0923/869388. **Lipari** ⊠ Corso Vittorio Emanuele 202, 98055 ☎ 090/9880095. **Marsala** ⊠ Via XI Maggio 100, 91025 ☎ 0923/714097. **Messina** ⊠ Piazza della Repubblica, 98122 ☎ 090/672944 ⊠ Via Calabria 301bis, 98123 ☎ 090/674236 ⊕ www.azienturismomessina.it. **Monreale** ⊠ Piazza Duomo, 90046 ☎ 091/6564570. **Noto** ⊠ Piazzale XVI Maggio, 96017 ☎ 0931/836744. **Palermo** ⊠ Piazza Castelnuovo 35, 90141 ☎091/583847 ⊕www.aapit.pa.it ⊠ Stazione Centrale, Piazza Giulio Cesare, 90141 ☎091/6165914 ⊠ Aeroporto Punta Raisi, 90045 ☎ 091/591698. **Piazza Armerina** ⊠ Via Cavour 15, 94015 ☎ 0935/680201. **Siracusa** ⊠ Via San Sebastiano 43, 96100 ☎ 0931/481200 ⊕ www.apt-siracusa.it ⊠ Via Maestranza 33, 96100 ☎ 0931/464255. **Taormina** ⊠ Palazzo Corvaja, Largo Santa Caterina, 98039 ☎ 0942/23243 ⊕ www.gate2taormina.com. **Trapani** ⊠ Piazza Saturno, 91100 ☎ 0923/29000 ⊕ www.apt.trapani.it.

SARDINIA

17

Updated by
Robin S.
Goldstein

AN UNCUT JEWEL OF AN ISLAND, Sardinia remains unique and enigmatic. The mysterious stone *nuraghi* (ancient defensive structures) hint at the lifestyles of prehistoric settlers, and summer settlers of a more modern variety sail their yachts to the sparkling beaches of the Costa Smeralda to find modern luxury. But most of Sardinia's rugged land remains shepherd's country, silent and stark. Beautiful in its severity, Sardinia is a true getaway.

Known as Sardegna in Italian, the island is the second largest in the Mediterranean, just smaller than Sicily. Although it's less than an hour by air and only several hours by boat—180 km (112 mi)—from the mainland, large-scale tourism does not affect Sardinia except in July and August, when Italians take its beautiful coasts and clean waters by storm. The interior is *never* crowded; Italian tourists come more for the sea than for the rugged and deserted mountain scenery.

A Phoenician stronghold in ancient times and later a Spanish dominion, Sardinia doesn't seem typically Italian in its color and flavor. It was a bit too far from imperial and papal Rome, and from the palaces of the Savoy dynasty, to have been transformed by the events that forged the national character. Yet Giuseppe Garibaldi, the charismatic national hero who led his troops in fervid campaigns to unify Italy in the mid-19th century, chose to spend his last years in relative isolation on the small island of Caprera, just off the coast of Sardinia. Later political thinkers such as Gramsci and Cossiga, and such radical parties as the still-strong Partito Sardo d'Azione, have advocated Sardinian independence. It is one of the few regions that retains semi-autonomous political status.

The island's rugged landscape closely resembles that of Corsica, 16 km (10 mi) across the windswept Strait of Bonifacio to the north. A dense bush, or *macchia,* barely penetrable in some districts, covers large areas. The terrain is rough, like the short, sturdy shepherds you see in the highlands—impassive figures engaged in one of the few gainful occupations the stony land allows. Shaggy flocks of sheep and goats, bells around their necks, are familiar features in the Sardinian landscape, just as their meat and pecorino cheese are staples of the hearty cuisine of the island's interior. Aside from the chic opulence of the Costa Smeralda, there's little sophistication in Sardinia, but the cost of living on the island is typically higher than on the *continente,* as Sardinians refer to the rest of Italy. The sprawling cities of Cagliari and Sassari have a distinctly provincial air, which can betray their longstanding prominence in Italian intellectual life.

Sardinians are courteous but remote, often favoring their forbidding native language over Italian. In hamlets, women swathed in black shawls and long, full skirts look with suspicion upon strangers passing through. Like mainland Italians, the Sardinians are of varied origin. On the northwest coast, fine traceries of ironwork around a balcony underscore the Spanish influence. In the northeast, the inhabitants have Genoese or Pisan ancestry, and the headlands display the ruined fortresses of the ancient Pisan duchy of Malaspina on the Italian mainland. As you ex-

Numbers in the text correspond to numbers in the margin and on the Sardinia and Cagliari maps.

If you have
3 days

Unless you're planning a summer beach getaway, you would do well to confine the first two days of your visit to ⊡ **Cagliari** ❶–❻ ⌐. In Sardinia's capital look for Italianate architecture, churches of all styles, and the **Museo Archeologico** ❶, with the island's best antiquities collection. If you do not have your own transport, you can use taxis or buses to make easy day trips from Cagliari. Make a half-day excursion on the second day to **Pula** ❼; here great beaches rim the coast, and just outside is Nora, a Carthaginian and Roman archaeological site. On your third day head first to **Su Nuraxi** ⓫, the island's most imposing nuraghic monument, then stop at **Oristano** ⓭ for lunch before continuing on to ⊡ **Alghero** ⓱, a walled town with a Catalan heritage. Stay here for the third night; it's about three hours back to Cagliari on the northwest coast.

If you have
5 days

Follow the itinerary above for the first three days. On Day 4, visit Capo Caccia and its stunning cave, the Grotta di Nettuno near ⊡ **Alghero** ⓱. Then, choose between luxury and adventure. For the former, head to the Costa Smeralda in the afternoon and spend the fourth and fifth nights in one of the hotels in or near ⊡ **Porto Cervo** ㉒, about three hours to the northeast. For adventure (and a more economical option), make ⊡ **Nuoro** ⓯ your base from which to explore the rugged interior of the island. Don't spend much time in town; instead veer south into the Barbagia region.

If you have
7 days

Spend your first two days exploring ⊡ **Cagliari** ❶–❻ ⌐ and the beaches near Villasimius. On your third day go southwest from Cagliari, stopping at the ancient remains outside **Pula** ❼, and follow the western coast on the Strada Carlo Felice (S131) as far as the village of **Sant'Antioco** ❽. Here a 20-minute ferry ride takes you to the island of ⊡ **San Pietro** ❾ for the night. The next day continue up toward Oristano, making an inland detour to **Su Nuraxi** ⓫, outside the town of Barumini. Wildlife enthusiasts should jaunt north of Barumini to the **Giara di Gesturi** ⓬. On your fourth night, stay in ⊡ **Oristano** ⓭, which merits a cursory walk-through and a glimpse of the Carthaginian ruins at **Tharros** ⓮, just outside town. On Day 5 travel northeast to **Nuoro** ⓯ and its museum of folk culture before striking into the Barbagia region, where tortuous roads wind their way over a wild terrain. If you prefer coastal attractions, spend no more than half a day exploring the region, then head west from Nuoro on road 129 to Bosa, where you turn right and travel through hilly scrub country to ⊡ **Alghero** ⓱, on the northwest coast. Spend your fifth night here. The next day, check out Capo Caccia and the Grotta di Nettuno, or drive northeast across a coastline fringed with low cliffs, inlets, and small bays, stopping to appreciate the seaside resorts, including **Castelsardo** ⓳. Stay the night at the fishing village of ⊡ **Santa Teresa di Gallura** ⓴, surrounded by fine beaches and well-equipped hotels. Spend your last day on the sun-kissed beaches of one of Europe's premier summer holiday destinations, the Costa Smeralda. Its most exclusive address is ⊡ **Porto Cervo** ㉒, the place for a final splurge before taking a ferry or plane back to the mainland from Olbia.

17

plore the southern coast, you come upon the physiognomies, customs, dialects, place names, and holy buildings of the Turks, Moors, Phoenicians, Austrians, and mainland Italians. If there are any pure Sardinians—or Sards—left, perhaps they can be found in the south-central mountains, south of Nuoro, under the 6,000-foot crests of the Gennargentu Massif, in the rugged country still ironically called Barbagia, "Land of Strangers."

Exploring Sardinia

The island is about 260 km (162 mi) long from north to south and takes three to four hours to drive on the main roads; it's roughly 120 km (75 mi) across. By car is the best way to see the island's most interesting sights. Make an effort to take smaller roads for better views and a more rural experience. Avoid night driving and beware of fog in the rugged, mountainous interior. The main highway linking Cagliari with Sassari was begun in 1820 by the Savoy ruler Carlo Felice; designated S131, but still referred to as the Strada Carlo Felice by the islanders, it runs through the fertile Campidano Plain, bordered by rhododendrons for virtually all of the 216 km (134 mi) between the two cities. There's little traffic on the roads; trains and buses—and people in general—move at a gentle pace. Public transportation schedules are unreliable and service is slow, but a leisurely train ride through the countryside can be charming.

About the Restaurants & Hotels

Restaurants are generally more rustic than those on the mainland; most serve hearty Sardinian cooking, plus unremarkable versions of the Italian staples. Best are roast meats of every kind, from pig to lamb to goat to horse, in the interior; excellent seafood along the coast; and cured meats and cheese everywhere. Leave yourself in the hands of the chef and choose the plate of the day—that way you might just end up with a sublime plate of roast suckling pig rather than a subpar penne *all'arrabbiata*.

The island's most luxurious and expensive hotels are on the Costa Smeralda. They have magnificent facilities but close from fall to spring; many are too remote to be good touring bases. Other, equally attractive coastal areas have seen a spate of resort hotels and villa colonies sprouting up; they, too, close from October through April, which narrows the choice of hotels considerably in other months. Even newer hotels may seem a little old-fashion, and hotels of any vintage are hard to find inland. Small-town hotels have basic accommodations, restrained but genuine hospitality, and low rates.

WHAT IT COSTS In euros				
$$$$	**$$$**	**$$**	**$**	**¢**
RESTAURANTS over €22	€16–€22	€11–€16	€7–€11	under €7
HOTELS over €220	€160–€220	€110–€160	€70–€110	under €70

Restaurant prices are for a second course *(secondo piatto)*. Hotel prices are for two people in a standard double room in high season, including tax and service.

Beaches For their fine sand and lack of crowds, Sardinia's beaches are among the best in the Mediterranean; its waters are among the cleanest, with the exception of those in the immediate vicinity of Cagliari, Arbatax, and Porto Torres. The beach resorts of the Costa Smeralda, on the northeastern tip of the island, are exclusive and expensive, but elsewhere on the island you can find beach areas and varied prices. Cala di Luna and Cala Sisine conceal beautiful beaches among the rocky cliffs between Baunei and Dorgali, on the eastern coast, accessible only by boat from Cala Gonone or Arbatax. For more accessible beaches with more amenities, go to Santa Margherita di Pula, where there are several hotels; to Villasimius and the Costa Rei, on the southeastern coast; or to the sandy coves sheltered by wind-carved granite boulders on the northern coast in the Gallura district and the archipelago of La Maddalena.

17

Festivals Sardinia's remoteness is tangible in its numerous festivals. Ostensibly, they're for religious occasions, but often they are imbued with an almost pagan feel. The main festivals are at Cagliari (Festa di Sant'Efisio, May 1), Sassari (Ascension Day, the 40th day after Easter; La Cavalcata, penultimate Sunday of May, and I Candelieri, August 14), and Nuoro (the next to last Sunday in August). Some of the best are the smaller festivals in the mountain villages of the interior; in Fonni, in the heart of the Barbagia, locals celebrate the Festa di San Giovanni, held June 24, in traditional costume.

Horseback Riding Spaghetti Westerns were once filmed in Sardinia, and it's easy to imagine why: the rugged, mountainous terrain of the inland is the perfect frontier for an adventure on horseback. Riding the steep barren hills of the Barbagia you may catch a glimpse of the wild dwarf horse, which is native though endangered. On the flat coastal area the riding is easier but the scenery is still magnificent. Group itineraries and horse rentals can be arranged.

Setting Sail Sailing enthusiasts tack for Sardinia and its craggy coast full of wildly beautiful inlets accessible only by sea. You can watch the very rich engage in one of their favorite sports—yachting—at the posh resorts of the Costa Smeralda each August, when a number of regattas are held. Berthing and provisions facilities are available on all coasts, though concentrated in the area around the Costa Smeralda and La Maddalena areas in the northeast. The harbormaster, or *capitano di porto,* can issue permits for anchorage.

Shopping Sardinia is crafts heaven. Locally produced goods include bright woolen shawls and rugs, hand-carved wooden objects, gold filigree jewelry in traditional designs, coral jewelry, and, above all, handwoven baskets in all shapes and sizes. The best places to go for crafts are the various government-sponsored ISOLA centers in Cagliari, Sassari, Castelsardo, and Nuoro.

Timing

If you can help it, avoid Sardinia in steamy August, when the island's coast is swamped not only with tourists from the mainland but the Sards, too, taking their annual break. May and September are much quieter and still temperate. Sudden storms can be a hazard, but these blow over quickly. The sea remains warm enough for swimming well into October. The mountainous interior is probably at its best in spring, when the woods and valleys are alive with color and burgeoning growth. For the gradations of color, fall is also a good time. From November through February the *maestrale* (winter winds) are fierce and rain and clouds are common over high ground—and most of Sardinia is mountainous—and it snows most years in the Barbagia region. In the south the weather rarely turns cold, but winter is not beach weather. Additionally, many resorts are closed from October to April, limiting lodging possibilities.

CAGLIARI & THE SOUTHERN COAST

Sardinia's southern coast is a stunning succession of wild rocky inlets and pristine beaches. Though blissfully uncommercialized for the most part, the coast does have pockets of development that have sprouted as tourism has found a niche. Swaths of eucalyptus and lush pine groves artfully conceal hotels at Santa Margherita di Pula, one of Sardinia's most luxurious holiday enclaves. Pula is an inland town within easy reach of both good beaches and what is Sardinia's most important archaeological site, the Carthaginian and Roman city of Nora. South and west of Santa Margherita, the protected coast contains few beaches but does have jaw-dropping vistas unspoiled by construction.

Northeast of Pula is Sardinia's capital and largest city, Cagliari (pronounced *Cahl*-yah-ree), with the island's principal art and archaeology museums as well as an old cathedral and medieval towers that have lofty views of the surrounding sea, lagoons, and mountains.

East of Cagliari the coast is no less scenic, though it's more built up, especially around the resort of Villasimius, which is within a short distance of some first-class sandy beaches.

Cagliari

268 km (166 mi) south of Olbia.

The island's capital has steep streets and impressive Italianate architecture and churches in differing styles. Cagliari is characterized by its busy commercial center and waterfront with broad avenues, as well as by the typically narrow streets of the old hilltop citadel (called, simply, *Castello*). Much of the old town had fallen into disrepair, but it is currently the focus of a revitalization effort. Medieval Spanish conquerors from Aragon as well as Pisans and Piemontese all left their marks, and grand, decaying castles, floodlit by night, overlook the old center's winding streets and bustling port from far above.

CloseUp

ON THE MENU

SARDINIAN CUISINE *is sharply divided between hearty, meat-based dishes from the interior and Mediterranean seafood fare with Catalan and North African influences along the coast. Meat dishes are usually veal, roast agnello (lamb) and agnellino (baby lamb), or porcheddu (roast suckling pig, most often available during Eastertime). Cavallo (horsemeat), or the more general carne equino, is also a common specialty of Sardinia; it's generally served in the form of a bistecca (thin steak), which can be a bit chewy, but when properly grilled, also intensely flavored and delicious. Even homemade pastas might be topped with a wild boar sauce. Finally, Italy's original, and best, pecorino cheese, made from sheep's milk, comes from the rugged slopes of the interior.*

Langouste or aragosta (lobster) is a seafood specialty of the northern coast that can get pricey. Looking for the unusual? Try the ricci (sea urchins), which, unlike the Japanese uni, are served atop pasta. Bottarga, another prized Sardinian product, is a dried, cured tuna roe that's best when shaved off a block directly onto spaghetti or with butter on crostini (thin slices of toasted bread). Foreign conquerors left their legacies of bouillabaisse (known here as zimino), paella, and cuscus (couscous), also called cashkà.

Native pastas include malloreddus (small shells of bran pasta sometimes flavored with saffron), culurgiones (the Sardinian version of ravioli), and maccarones de busa (thick pasta twists). And crispy bread called pane carasau (carta di musica in Italian) is typical island fare. Prized around Italy, and around the world, is Sardinia's amaro di corbezzolo, a honey with a bouquet and taste primordially foresty, slightly bitter, and dazzlingly complex. It's made by bees that suck nectar from a plant known as arbutus, the tree strawberry.

▶ ❶ Begin your visit at the **Museo Archeologico** within the walls of the castle that the Pisans erected in the early 1300s to ward off attacks by the Aragonese and Catalans from what is now Spain. Among the intriguing artifacts are bronze statuettes from the tombs and dwellings of Sardinia's earliest inhabitants, who remain a prehistoric enigma. Ancient writers called them the nuraghic people, from the name of their curious stone dwellings, the nuraghi, which are unique to Sardinia. Archaeologists date most of the nuraghi from about 1300–1200 BC, the same time the ancient Israelites were establishing themselves in Canaan. In the 3rd century BC the Romans, following on the heels of Carthaginian invaders, conquered the island. ✉ *Cittadella dei Musei, Piazza Arsenale* ☎ *070/655911* 🎫 *€4* ☉ *Tues.–Fri. and Sun. 9–8, Sat. 9 AM–11 PM.*

❷ The 1305 **Torre di San Pancrazio**, part of the imposing medieval Pisan defenses, is just outside Cagliari's archaeological museum, and it marks the edge of the Castello district. You can climb up the tower for a fabulous panorama of the city and its surroundings. Curiously enough, the tower's back wall is missing, which allows you to see the series of wooden stairs and landings inside without climbing a step. ✉ *Piazza Indipendenza* ☎ *070/41108* 🎫 *Free* ☉ *Tues.–Sun. 9–1 and 3:30–7:30.*

❸ Torre dell'Elefante, twin to the tower of San Pancrazio, stands at the seaward end of Cagliari's bastions. Built in 1307, it was used as a prison in the 1800s. ⊠ *Via Università* ☎ *070/659674* ⌫ *Free* ☉ *Tues.–Sun. 9–1 and 3:30–7:30.*

❹ Cattedrale di Santa Maria, also known as the **Duomo,** was originally constructed in the 17th century, but the look was changed during construction in the mid-1930s. The tiers of columns on the facade resemble those of medieval Romanesque Pisan churches, but only the central portal is an authentic relic of that era. ⊠ *Piazza Palazzo, off Via Martini* ☎ *070/ 663837* ☉ *Daily 8–noon and 4–8.*

On the narrow streets of the **Castello,** the quarter below the Duomo, humble dwellings still open directly onto the sidewalk and the wash is hung out to dry on elaborate wrought-iron balconies. ⊹ *Climb up Terrazza Umberto I.*

❺ The Bastion of St. Remy, or **Terrazza Umberto I,** is a monumental neoclassical staircase and arcade added in the 19th century to the bastion built by the Spaniards 400 years earlier. It has long been covered by graffiti and attracts some seamy activity, but a massive, long-term restoration is under way. ⊠ *Piazza Costituzione.*

❻ The **Anfiteatro Romano** dates from the 2nd century AD. The well-preserved amphitheater arena—complete with underground passages and a beasts' pit—is evidence of the importance of this Roman outpost. ⊠ *Viale Fra Ignazio* ☎ *070/652956* ⌫ *Free* ☉ *Daily 10–1 and 3–6.*

Where to Stay & Eat

$$$–$$$$
Fodor'sChoice
★

✕ **S'Apposentu.** Informed by his studies in Corsica and mainland France, young chef Roberto Petza has quietly created a new model of Sardinian cuisine, one deeply entrenched in the ingredients of his native island. Petza's otherworldly creations might include a stunning plate of *lasagnette* (thin, flat noodles) with San Gavino saffron, sausage, and local ricotta; spectacular Sardinian *agnellino* (baby lamb); or roast pigeon with a sauce made from white vernaccia wine and *mirto,* a local digestive. The stage is a soaring, ultramodern space—even the place settings are cutting-edge—that is lovingly set in Cagliari's opera house, the Teatro Lirico. ⊠ *Teatro Lirico di Cagliari, Via Sant'Alenixedda* ☎ *070/4082315* ⊕ *www.sapposentu.it* ⌫ *Reservations essential* ☐ *AE, DC, MC, V* ☉ *Closed Mon. No dinner Sun.*

$$$
✕ **Dal Corsaro.** This formal restaurant near the port is one of the island's most recommended eating places, so make reservations. The interior is refined, the welcome cordial. The menu includes fish and meat, with such dishes as seafood antipasto and *porcheddu* (roast suckling pig). At various unpredictable times each year—always including August—the restaurant opens a branch at the seaside. ⊠ *Viale Regina Margherita 28* ☎ *070/664318,* ⌨ *Marina Piccola* ☎ *070/370295* ⌫ *Reservations essential* ☐ *AE, DC, MC, V* ☉ *Closed Sun. and Dec. 23–Jan. 10.*

$$
▥ **Panorama.** With its unprepossessing exterior, this hotel just outside downtown Cagliari is geared to the business class. Rooms are spacious and comfortable with modern, functional furniture. Try to reserve one on the higher of the nine floors and enjoy the view over the harbor and bay.

There's also a bar with—appropriately enough—a panoramic view on the top floor. ⊠ *Viale Armando Diaz 231, 09126* ☎ *070/307691* 🖷 *070/305413* ⊕ *www.hotelpanorama.it* ➲ *64 rooms, 28 suites* ⟡ *Restaurant, minibars, pool, bar, meeting room* ▭ *AE, DC, MC, V* ⟦◯⟧ *BP.*

¢ 🖾 **AeR Bundes Jack.** Despite the unprepossessing entrance under the arcades of Via Roma, this central *secondo piano* (third-floor) pensione is cozy, with inward-facing rooms and simple furnishings. The port is directly opposite, the bus and train stations steps away, and Via Roma itself presents an entertaining parade of shops and sit-down bars. Expect polite, friendly service. And yes, there's an elevator. ⊠ *Via Roma 75, 09100* ☎🖷 *070/657970* ➲ *14 rooms, 7 with bath* ⟡ *Bar* ▭ *No credit cards* ⟦◯⟧ *BP.*

Nightlife & the Arts

Cagliari's university stages concerts throughout the academic year; contact the tourist office for information.

FESTIVALS Thousands of costumed villagers, many of them on horseback, parade
Fodor'sChoice through town during Sardinia's greatest annual festival, the **Festa di Sant'**
★ **Efisio** (May 1–4). It's part of a four-day procession between Cagliari and Pula, and it's a good chance to take part in a centuries-old event.

CAFÉS   The coolest café-bar in all of Sardinia might just be the **Libarium Nostrum** (✉ Bastioni di Santa Croce ☎ 070/650943), a dim, bohemian Castello haunt full of nooks, crannies, wood beams, and castle walls. The gilded **Antico Caffè** (✉ Piazza Costituzione ☎ 070/650943) is a good place for a coffee or a cocktail, salads and sandwiches. It's been downtown at the corner of Via Garibaldi and Regina Margherita since 1855.

Shopping

Cagliari's two best shopping streets, full of boutiques, clothing stores, and such, are Via Manno and Via Garibaldi, just up from the port. **ISOLA** (✉ Via Bacaredda 176 ☎ 070/492756 ✉ Via Santa Croce 34 ☎ 070/651488) is a government-sponsored exhibition of artisan crafts; most of the work is for sale.

Sports

The **Lega Navale Italiana** (✉ Marina Piccola ☎ 070/303794 ⊕ www.leganavale.it) has information on the island's sailing facilities.

off the beaten path

SAN SPERATE – Walls throughout this small town 20 km (12 mi) north of Cagliari have been brightened with *murales* (murals) by local artists and some well-known Italian painters. The murals were begun in 1968 and continue to be expanded upon today, transforming the entire town into an open-air art gallery.

Villasimius

50 km (31 mi) east of Cagliari, 296 km (184 mi) south of Olbia.

The eastern route takes you through some dismal industrial suburbs on the road that leads to the scenic coast and beaches of Capo Boi and Capo Carbonara. Villasimius ranks as the chief resort here; the beautiful beaches lie a couple of miles north of town, on the golden sands of the Costa Rei.

Pula

❼ *29 km (18 mi) southwest of Cagliari, 314 km (195 mi) southwest of Olbia.*

Resort villages sprawl along the coast southwest of the capital, which has its share of fine scenery and good beaches. On the marshy shoreline between Cagliari's Aeroporto di Elmas and Pula, huge flocks of flamingos are a common sight. From Cagliari, first follow the S195 toward Teulada, then take the turnoff for Pula at Km 27.

The small **Museo Archeologico Comunale** has archaeological finds from excavations of a site at Nora, including amphoras, anchors, and inscribed stones, mostly dredged up from the sea. ✉ *Corso Vittorio Emanuele 67* ☎ *070/9209610* 🎫 *€3.60, €5 including Nora* ☉ *Daily 9–7.*

★ The narrow promontory outside Pula, **Nora**, was the site of a Phoenician, then Carthaginian, and later a Roman settlement. An old Roman road passes the moss-covered ruins of temples, an amphitheater, and a small Roman theater. Nora was a prime location—the Phoenicians scouted for good harbors, cliffs to shelter their craft from the wind, and an elevation from which they could defend themselves against attack. Extensive excavations have shed light on life in this ancient city from the 8th century BC onward. You can make out the channels through which hot air rose to warm the Roman baths; watch for the difference between the simple mosaic pavements laid by the Carthaginians and the more elaborate designs of the Romans. If the sea is calm, look under the clear waters along the shore for more ruins of the ancient city, submerged by earthquakes, rough seas, and erosion. You can take a guided tour, which begins on the hour. ✢ *3 km (2 mi) south of Pula* ☎ *070/9209138* 🎫 *€3.60, €5 including Museo Archeologico Comunale* ☉ *Daily 9–7:30.*

Sant'Efisio, the little Romanesque church at the base of the Nora promontory, plays a part in one of the island's most colorful annual events. A four-day procession during the Festa di Sant'Efisio accompanies a statue of the saint all the way from Cagliari and back again, culminating in a huge parade down Cagliari's main avenue. If you're in Sardinia from May 1 to May 4, don't miss it. ✢ *3 km (2 mi) south of Pula* ☎ *070/ 9208473* ☉ *Apr.–Sept., Sat. 3–6, Sun. 9:30–1 and 3–7:30; Oct.–Mar., Sun. 9:30–noon and 3–5.*

Where to Stay

Lodging and beaches that cater to the summer crowds visiting Pula and Nora are concentrated 4 km (2½ mi) south of Pula, a little more than 1½ km (1 mi) south of Nora, in a conglomeration of hotels that makes up the town of Santa Margherita di Pula.

$$$$ 🏨 **Flamingo.** Eucalyptus trees surround the main building and the six two-story cottages of this shady beachside resort hotel. Balconied rooms are light and airy, overlooking park or sea. Sports facilities abound, and the outdoor pool is open late into the night—a welcome treat in the balmy summer. ⊠ *Santa Margherita di Pula, 09010, 4 km (2½ mi) south of Pula* ☎ *070/9208361* 📠 *070/9208359* ⊕ *www.hotelflamingo.it* ⤺ *134 rooms* ⟁ *Restaurant, minibars, miniature golf, tennis court, pool, beach, dive shop, windsurfing, piano bar, dance club* ▭ *AE* ☉ *Closed Oct. 18–Apr. 18* �🍽 *BP.*

Sports

The 18-hole **Is Molas** (⊠ Santa Margherita di Pula ☎ 070/9241014 ⊕ www. ismolas.it) has won tributes from Tom Watson and Jack Nicklaus.

Sant'Antioco

❽ *75 km (47 mi) west of Pula, 100 km (62 mi) west of Cagliari.*

Off Sardinia's southwest coast is the sleepy island of Sant'Antioco—the most hectic activity seems to be the silent repairing of nets by local fishermen who have already pulled in their daily catch. It has become a popular holiday spot because of good beaches. The island has been connected to the mainland since Roman times by a still-standing causeway (the modern causeway that you traverse runs parallel).

Before leaving the main town, also called Sant'Antioco, take time to visit the **zona archeologica** at the top of the old section, which has terrific views of the Sardinian mainland. Here you can see a Punic necropolis and a burial site scattered with urns that contained the cremated remains of stillborn children. Admission includes a guided tour and entry to the on-site ethnographic and archaeological museums. ⊠ *Sant'Antioco* 🎫 *€5* ⊗ *Apr.–Sept., daily 9–1 and 3:30–7; Oct.–Mar., daily 9–1 and 3–6.*

Also of note on the island is the tiny fishing village of **Calasetta.** Its name literally means "silk cove," and it was from a villa outside this town that generations of an Armenian silk-trading family once supported much of the island's economy. ✛ *10 km (6 mi) northeast of Sant'Antioco town.*

off the beaten path

CARBONIA – If your curiosity prods you to seek more esoteric places, you could explore the towns in the hills inland from Sant'Antioco. In this rugged, once booming mining country stands Carbonia, a town built by Mussolini in 1938 to serve as an administrative center for the coal miners and their families. With its time-frozen fascist architecture—ordered rows of houses around a core of monumental public buildings on the broad Piazza Roma—it has been called an urban UFO set down in the Sardinian landscape. The Dopolavoro, in the piazza, was a fascist institution that organized coal workers' free time for them. Managers lived closest to the city center, while laborers lived in the shantytowns on the outskirts. For better or worse, Carbonia's coal industry was short-lived, and the enormous mines are long since abandoned; just outside of town you can hear the wind whistle through their ghostly shells among rows of still-inhabited public housing projects. ✛ *S126 and S78, 14 km (9 mi) northeast of Sant'Antioco.*

MONTE SIRAI – Here you'll find the remains of Sardinia's most important Carthaginian military stronghold, impregnably sited atop a hill providing views inland and far out to sea. ⊠ *On S126, 1 km (½ mi) north of Carbonia* 🕾 *0781/64044* ⊗ *Daily 9–dusk* 🎫 *€2.60.*

IGLESIAS – This is an authentic Sardinian town with a medieval cathedral. Traveling east past Domusnovas on the Cagliari–Iglesias highway, you can detour and drive right through an immense cave, the **Grotta di San Giovanni.** ✛ *34 km (21 mi) northeast of Sant'Antioco.*

San Pietro

❾ *5 km (3 mi) northwest of Sant'Antioco.*

A ferry at the small northern port of Calasetta connects Sant'Antioco with Carloforte, the main town on the smaller island of San Pietro. This classic little Italian port village and its surrounding coastline are a favorite of wealthy Cagliarians, many of whom have built weekend cottages here. The best views are from Capo Sandalo, on San Pietro's rugged western coast, but head to the island's southern tip for the beaches. During daylight hours the ferry departs every 20 minutes in summer and every 30 in winter—the trip takes 20 minutes.

Where to Stay

$ ⬚ **Hieracon.** Whitewashed modern rooms are offered by the art nouveau lodging that sits on the harbor in Carloforte. A small courtyard garden has a few palm trees near bungalow-style apartments. Try to get a front-facing room for a harbor view, though there may be some traffic noise. Avoid rooms at the top, which have low ceilings and no view. The central location means that you're a short walk from some good restaurants. ⊠ *Via Cavour 63, 09014 Carloforte* ☎ *0781/854028* 🖷 *0781/854893* 🛏 *17 rooms, 7 apartments* ⚖ *Restaurant, some kitchenettes, minibars, bar* ⊟ *AE, MC, V* ◉| *BP.*

Costa Verde

⑩ *35 km (22 mi) northwest of San Pietro, 80 km (50 mi) northwest of Cagliari.*

If you've come to Sardinia in search of untrammeled wilderness and sweeping sands as far as the eye can see, then this deserted coast is the place to find them. Hidden away in the forgotten northwest corner of Cagliari province, the Costa Verde is accessible only by a bumpy, unpaved track. The effort is worth it. The dune-backed sands shelter rare grasses and birdlife, as well as providing magnificent swimming.

You can approach the coast either from the town of Guspini, on the straggling S126, or from a turnoff a couple of miles farther south, which leads through the abandoned mining town of **Ingurtosu.** It's a strange, ghostly cluster of chimneys and workers' dwellings, forlorn amid the encroaching scrubland. Drive down the dirt track another 10 km (6 mi) or so, through woods of juniper, to reach the sea.

Where to Stay

★ **$$** ⬚ **Hotel Le Dune.** A remote oasis on the beach, this hotel was formerly a depot for the minerals dug out from the surrounding hills; you can still see the remains of wagons, rails, and other mining bric-a-brac scattered about, which adds to the desolate allure. Bamboo furnishings give simple guest rooms a light, spacious feel. Eleven of the rooms have their own sitting areas. Though facilities are minimal, they include a good cocktail bar, where you can contemplate the limitless sands stretching out on either side. For exploring, guided tours are available on request. ⊠ *Via Bau, 09031 Ingurtosu* ☎ *0709/77130* 🖷 *0709/77230* 🛏 *32 rooms* ⚖ *Restaurant, minibars, pool, bar, travel services; no room TVs* ⊟ *AE, DC, MC, V* ◉| *MAP.*

SU NURAXI TO THE COSTA SMERALDA

A more traditional—and wild—Sardinia awaits the traveler who ventures into the island's mountainous interior. The Taviani brothers, noted Italian filmmakers, made the hinterland of the Barbagia region, where traditional Sardinian customs are maintained in remote hilltop villages, the subject of the extraordinary film *Padre Padrone* (1977). Inland Sardinians are hardy souls, used to living in a climate that is as unforgiving in winter as it is intolerable in summer. Old traditions, including the vendetta, are firmly rooted in the social fabric of this mountainous land, which is barren and beautiful. Here, rare species of wildlife share the rocky uplands with sturdy medieval churches and the mysterious *nuraghi* (ancient stone defensive structures) left by prehistoric people. You may want to make your base Oristano, on the west coast and the medieval center of Sardinian nationalism.

As you move northward, the timeless beauty of the landscape begins to show greater signs of 20th-century development. The sunny resort of Alghero, the Spanish-influenced port on the west coast, is one of the island's premier holiday spots. Costa Smeralda, the luxury resort complex on the northeast corner of Sardinia, is as prestigious a summer getaway as any in Italy.

Su Nuraxi

⑪ *64 km (40 mi) northeast of Ingurtosu on the Costa Verde, 60 km (37*
Fodor'sChoice *mi) north of Cagliari.*
★

It's worth a detour to see the fascinating nuraghe of Su Nuraxi, off the main road outside the quiet little town of Barumini. You could spend hours clambering over an extraordinary—if partly eroded—structure of concentric rings of stone walls, chambers, passages, wells, a beehive tower, and the small surrounding village with the ruins of homes and streets.

The nuraghi, which were built beginning in the 16th century BC—the middle Bronze Age—vary from single defensive towers to multitower complexes sheltering whole communities, prehistoric versions of medieval walled towns and the forts of the American West. The uses of the nuraghi remain mysterious, largely because their construction predates written or pictorial history. Though this particular type of construction is unique to Sardinia, similar buildings dating from the same era are found in other parts of the Mediterranean, such as Cyprus and the Balearic islands off Spain. Of the 7,000 nuraghi on Sardinia, Su Nuraxi is the most impressive. A guided tour is required for viewing; one starts about every half hour. ✉ *1 km (½ mi) west of Barumini* ☎ *0337/813087* ✉ *€5* ☉ *Apr.–Sept., daily 9–7:30; Oct.–Mar., daily 9–5.*

Giara di Gesturi

⑫ *8 km (5 mi) north of Barumini, 68 km (42 mi) northwest of Cagliari.*

On the 45-square-km (28-square-mi) basalt plateau of Giara di Gesturi roams some of the island's more exotic wildlife, including a species of wild dwarf horse. Another rare species in the Giara is the mouflon, a wild sheep distinguishable from its domesticated counterpart by its long, curving horns and skittishness. Long hunted for their horns, the mouflon are now an endangered species, with only a few surviving on Sardinia and Corsica. The plateau is ✛ *Off S197, north of Gesturi.*

Oristano

⑬ *25 km (16 mi) north of Giara di Gesturi, 93 km (58 mi) northwest of Cagliari.*

Oristano, on the west coast, shone in the Middle Ages when it was capital of the Giudicato of Arborea, an independent duchy led by Sardinia's own Joan of Arc–type heroine, Eleanora di Arborea (circa 1340–1402). Oristano is now the scene of livestock fairs and a rousing series of horse races, called Sa Sartiglia, marking the end of February's Carnival. Otherwise, the city's beautiful but small colonial center exudes a distinct serenity, and Oristano's evening *passeggiata* (predinner stroll), which almost always teems with vivacious young children, has an unambitious friendliness about it.

off the beaten path

CABRAS – Ten kilometers (6 mi) northwest of Oristano you can see extensive marshlands where fishermen pole round-bottomed rush boats through shallow ponds teeming with eels and crayfish. Cabras is also home to the Torre di San Giovanni di Sinis, a striking 16th-century ruin of a perfectly cylindrical fortified tower atop a hill overlooking the water.

Where to Stay & Eat

★ **$$$** ✕ **Cocco e Dessì.** Chef Antonino Sanna's food is just as modern as his restaurant's bilevel interior and chrome bar. Try fusion flights of fancy such as crabs stuffed with sesame almond toffee and fish ravioli with escargot and scampi broth. There's an excellent tasting menu, and the prices are refreshingly reasonable, given that it's one of the most sophisticated restaurants in Sardinia. ⊠ *Via Tirso 31* ☎ *0783/300720* ⊕ *www.coccoedessi.it* ⌂ *Reservations essential* ▤ *AE, DC, MC, V* ⊙ *Closed Mon. No dinner Sun.*

$ ✕ **Trattoria Gino.** This extremely central trattoria has been run by the same family, under different names, for nearly a century. Authentic local seafood dishes include the *antipasto mare* (mixed seafood appetizer) and the delicious spaghetti *ai ricci* (with sea urchin). The lobster is a memorable splurge. Light walls lined with bottles of wine and simple rows of tables deck out the single room, and service is friendly and attentive. It's a popular spot for locals and an ideal lunch stop. ⊠ *Via Tirso 13* ☎ *0783/71428* ▤ *MC, V* ⊙ *Closed Sun., 1 wk in Jan., and 3 wks in Aug.*

$ ▦ **I.S.A. Hotel.** Oristano's best and most central downtown hotel has a clean and elegant (if a bit dated) lobby with chandeliers. Rooms, too, are well kept and comfortable, with simple white walls and wood furnishings, and excellent bathrooms. Nothing at the I.S.A. blows you away, but Oristano does everything in moderation, and the town's hotels are no exception. ⊠ *Piazza Mariano 50, 09170* ☎ *0783/360101* ➥ *49 rooms* ⌂ *Restaurant, minibars, bar, meeting room* ▤ *AE, DC, MC, V* ⊚ *BP.*

Nightlife & the Arts

☾ The **Sartiglia** festival, on the last Sunday of February's Carnival season, includes rich costumes and a ritual joust. Each summer the town holds an **arts and crafts exhibition** (Tourist office ✉ Via Cagliari 278 ☎ 0783/74191), with local foods and wines given prominence.

Tharros

⓮ *20 km (12 mi) west of Oristano, 113 km (70 mi) northwest of Cagliari.*

The site of the Carthaginian and Roman city of Tharros (Cabras in Italian), like Nora to the south, was chosen because it commanded the best views of the harbor and could provide an easy escape route if inland tribes threatened. Today the roadside ruins afford a scenic view over the Sinis Peninsula. Four Corinthian columns still stand, and there are baths and fragments of mosaics from the Roman city. As at Nora, there is much more submerged under water. ✉ *San Giovanni di Sinis* 🎟 *€4* ☉ *Daily 9–1 hr before sunset.*

At the **Museo Civico di Cabras** you can view many of the better-preserved urns and other artifacts that have been recovered from the ruins at Tharros. ✉ *Via Tharros 121* 🎟 *€2.60* ☉ *June–Aug., daily 9–1 and 4–8, Sept.–May, daily 9–1 and 3–7.*

| en route | On the way to Tharros you pass the ghost town of **San Salvatore**, revived briefly in the 1960s as a locale for spaghetti Westerns and since abandoned. The saloon from the movie set still stands. Among the dunes past San Salvatore are large **rush huts** formerly used by fishermen and now much in demand as back-to-nature vacation homes. The 5th-century church of **San Giovanni di Sinis**, on the Sinis Peninsula, is the oldest Christian church in Sardinia. |

Nuoro

⓯ *107 km (67 km) northeast of Tharros, 181 km (113 mi) north of Cagliari.*

The somewhat shabby provincial capital of Nuoro is on the edge of a gorge in the harsh mountainous area that culminates in Gennargentu, the island's highest massif (6,000 feet). Not much happens here; you can do some (relatively inexpensive) shopping amid strolling locals, or try the local Barbagia sausage, a sweet, fatty delight. The most interesting things in Nuoro are the views from the park on Sant'Onofrio Hill and the exhibits in the **Museo della Vita e delle Tradizioni Popolari Sarde** (Museum of Sardinian Life and Folklore), where you can see some domestic and agricultural implements, traditional jewelry, and local costumes draped on mannequins. ✉ *Via Mereu 56* ☎ *0784/242900* 🎟 *€2.60* ☉ *Mid-June–Sept., daily 9–8; Oct.–mid-June, daily 9–1 and 3–7.*

Make an excursion about 3 km (2 mi) east of Nuoro to **Monte Ortobene** (2,900 feet) for lofty views over the gulch below. Here you can also see up close the imposing statue of Christ the Redeemer overlooking the city. Picnic tables make this a handy spot for an alfresco lunch.

en route

Orgosolo, the old center of banditry halfway between Nuoro and Fonni, is still a poor and undeveloped village, but the houses have been daubed with murals vividly depicting political and cultural issues. The effect is startling and lively. The forest and grassy plain above the village make fine walking country. ⊹ *15 km (9 mi) south of Nuoro.*

Where to Stay & Eat

$$$ ✕▭ **Su Gologone.** Rooms here are impeccable private retreats, decked
Fodor'sChoice   out with traditional Sardinian fabrics, wood chests, paintings, and old
★   juniper wood beams on the ceilings. Staff members organize jeep and hiking expeditions. Stop in the rustic restaurant with its fireplace and wooden furnishings for an authentic Sardinian meal. Specialties include *maccarones de busa* (thick homemade pasta twists) and *culurgiones* (ravioli), *sebadas* (pockets of fried dough stuffed with cheese and lemon peel), and roast suckling pig. Much of the local Cannonau, a heady red wine, is made from grapes grown in the countryside around the inn. Su Gologone attracts droves of tourists, but for good reason. ⊠ *Località Su Gologone, 08025 Oliena, 20 km (12 mi) southeast of Nuoro* ☎ *0784/ 287512* 🖷 *0784/287668* ⊕ *www.sugologone.it* 🛏 *60 rooms, 8 suites* ⏧ *Restaurant, miniature golf, 2 tennis courts, pool, gym, massage, bicycles, bar, some pets allowed* ➟ *AE, DC, MC, V* ⊗ *Closed mid-Nov.–mid-Dec. and mid-Jan.–mid-Mar.* ¶◎¶ *MAP.*

★ **$** ▭ **Barbagia.** Rooms at this very simple, modern block-architecture hotel—more or less standard for provincial Nuoro—are more than comfortable, and those on the upper floor rooms have nice views out over the hills. The location is a bit out of the way, out by the stadium on the fringes of downtown. ⊠ *Via Aosta, 08100* ☎ *0784/35585* 🖷 *0784/ 232782* 🛏 *42 rooms* ⏧ *Restaurant, minibars, bar, lounge* ➟ *AE, DC, MC, V* ⊗ *Closed 1st 2 wks in Aug. and Dec. 22–Jan. 10.* ¶◎¶ *BP.*

Nightlife & the Arts

Nuoro's **Festa del Redentore** (Feast of the Redeemer) is held on the next-to-last Sunday in August. It's the best time to view the various traditional costumes of Sardinia's interior all in one place.

Shopping

Crafted for local festivals, wooden masks make unusual and festive souvenirs. The local shop of **ISOLA** (⊠ Via Monsignor Bua 10 ☎0784/31507) is in the middle of the old town.

Fonni

⑯ *30 km (19 mi) south of Nuoro, 137 km (85 mi) south of Olbia.*

In the heart of the Barbagia region, Fonni, with walls covered in murals, is the highest town on the island. This mountainous district, including Monte Spada and the Bruncu Spina refuge on the Gennargentu Massif, is Sardinia's most primitive. Life in some villages seems not to have changed much since the Middle Ages. Here a rigidly patriarchal society perpetuates the unrelenting practice of vendetta. Although as a tourist you may be looked at with curiosity, a smile goes a long way.

SARDINIA BY RAIL

*If you have the stamina, take the rickety old train on a leg of the journey that runs on a single-gauge track between Cagliari and Arbatax, midway up the east coast (involving a change at Mandas). The line has been operating since 1893; it takes about seven hours to cover the approximately 250 km (155 mi) of track. The train rattles up into the Barbagia district through some breathtaking mountain scenery, then eases down into the desert landscape inland from Arbatax, where the trip ends on the dock next to the fishing boats. The daily (early-morning) departures are run by the **Trenino Verde della Sardegna** (☎ 070/343112 or 0800/460220 ⊕ www.treninoverde. com), and the ticket costs around €15. In Tortoli, just outside Arbatax, **Dolce Casa** (✉ Via Sarcidano 3 ☎ 0782/624235, 44/07803452748 off-season in Britain 🖶 0782/623484) is a modest hotel run by an English-speaking couple. It's the best lodging option in the area, though it's open June–September only.*

High mountain roads wind and loop through the landscape; towns are small and undistinguished, their social fabric formed in complete isolation. On feast days elaborate regional costumes are taken out of mothballs and worn as an explicit statement of community identity.

Where to Eat

¢ ✕ **Barbagia.** The best place downtown for a midday meal is also one of the most friendly to foreigners—a prize in this aloof village. The cheerful owners usher you into a rustic room full of nicely made-up tables, the obligatory TV in the corner, and not much else. Try the assortment of local *salumi* (cured meats), the maccarones de busa, and the typical grilled *bistecca di cavallo* (horsemeat steak), which is excellent. ✉ *Via Umberto 106* ☎ *0784/58329* ▭ *No credit cards* ☉ *Closed Mon.*

Nightlife & the Arts

You can see one of the most characteristic of the Barbagia's celebrations in local costume during the **Festa di San Giovanni**, held June 24 in Fonni.

Shopping

Special candies are made from honey and nougat and sold in hilltop Tonara, southwest of Fonni. In the mountain village of Aritzo, about 45 km (28 mi) south of Fonni, high up in the Barbagia, you can find handcrafted wooden utensils and furniture.

en route   Head back to Nuoro, and from there take the S129 west about 65 km (40 mi) to coastal Bosa, where you turn north into hilly and arid scrub country, with an abundance of cactus and juniper. Pines and olive trees shelter low buildings from the steady winds that make these parts ideal for sailing. About the only cash crop here is cork from the cork trees dotting the landscape. Yet in the low valleys and along the riverbeds, masses of oleanders bloom in June and July, creating avenues of color.

Alghero

⑰   *135 km (84 mi) northwest of Fonni, 137 km (85 mi) southwest of Olbia.*

Among the larger centers on the northwest coast is Alghero, a pretty walled resort town with a distinctly Spanish flavor. It was built and inhabited in the 14th century by the Aragonese and Catalans, who constructed seaside ramparts and sturdy towers encompassing an inviting nucleus of narrow, winding streets with whitewashed palazzi. Rich wrought-iron scrollwork decorates balconies and screened windows; a Spanish motif appears in stone portals and in bell towers. The native language spoken here is a version of Catalan, not Italian, although you probably have to attend one of the masses conducted in Algherese to hear it.

The **Torre San Giovanni,** an old tower fortress, can be climbed for good views from the terrace. Stop at the interesting city history display on the computer terminals inside the tower. There's also a rotating set of exhibits and a miniature model of Alghero's old town. ✉ *Via Mateotti 12* ☎ *079/9731605* 🎟 *€2.50.*

West of Alghero are broad sandy beaches and the spectacular heights of **Capo Caccia,** an imposing limestone headland to the west. At the base of the sheer cliff the pounding sea has carved an entrance to the vast
★ ☉ **Grotta di Nettuno,** a fantastic cavern filled with water pools, stalactites, and stalagmites. You must visit with a guide; tours start on the hour. By land, you reach the entrance at the base of the cliff by descending the more than 600 dizzying steps of the aptly named *escala del cabirol* (mountain goat's stairway). ✚ *13 km (8 mi) west of Alghero* ☎ *079/ 946540* 🎟 *€8* ☉ *Apr.–Sept., daily 9–7; Oct., daily 10–5; Nov., daily 10–4; Jan.–Mar., daily 9–2.*

Taking a **boat tour** from Alghero to see the grotto takes 2½ hours and is much less exhausting than approaching on foot, but is not possible in winter or when seas are rough. Tours depart on the hour from June through September, less frequently off-season. ✉ *Navisarda* ☎ *079/950603* 🎟 *€18* ☉ *Apr., May, and Oct., daily 9–3; June–Sept., daily 9–5.*

Where to Stay & Eat

★ **$$$–$$$$** ✕ **Andreini.** Traverse the loftiest heights of Sardinian elegance at an expensive, opulent, ambitious—yet somehow cozy—restaurant. The place is set to the nines: candles, tablecloths, and waiters abound; the service and wine list are just so. The food is equally romantic; a great tasting menu highlights the Andreini brothers' artful use of local ingredients like pecorino cheese and wild fennel. Creations might include homemade cuttlefish-ink tagliatelle with asparagus or wild boar with Cannonau wine sauce. The weekday three-course "business lunch" is a good value. ✉ *Via Arduino 45* ☎ *079/982098* ⚘ *Reservations essential* ▤ *AE, DC, MC, V* ☉ *Closed Mon.*

$–$$ ✕ **Da Pietro.** A menu that includes *bucatini all'algherese* (hollow, spaghettilike pasta with a sauce of clams, capers, tomatoes, and olives) and baked fish with a white-wine sauce keeps this seafood restaurant bustling below its vaulted ceilings. Look for Da Pietro in the old town near Largo San Francesco. ⊠ *Via Ambrogio Machin 20* ☎ *079/979645* ☰ *AE, DC, MC, V* ⊗ *Closed Wed. and Dec. 15–27.*

★ $$$$ ▦ **Villa Las Tronas.** Gardens surround a narrow drive that separates this hotel's little island from the road, imparting a regal sense of seclusion to what was once a royal mansion. Belle epoque interiors have ornate gilt chairs or canopy-draped beds. The Villa is on a rocky promontory—above the sea but still near the center—and there are great views from most rooms. Service is elegant and impeccable, from the reception to the restaurant. It's open year-round, a rarity in these parts. ⊠ *Lungomare Valencia 1, 07041* ☎ *079/981818* 🖷 *079/981044* ⊕ *www.hvlt. com* 📾 *20 rooms, 5 suites* ⊘ *Restaurant, pool, gym, beach, bicycles, meeting room, some pets allowed* ☰ *AE, DC, MC, V* ¶◎¶ *MAP.*

$$–$$$ ▦ **Carlos V.** On the shore boulevard opposite the Villa Las Tronas, this modern hotel (pronounced Carlos Quinto) offers an array of gardens, terraces, and a big pool overlooking the sea. Don't settle for a slightly cheaper room facing the back; the pleasure here is all in the magnificent view from your balcony. Low-season rates are a bargain. ⊠ *Lungomare Valencia 24, 07041* ☎ *079/979501* 🖷 *079/980298* ⊕ *www. hotelcarlosv.it* 📾 *110 rooms* ⊘ *Restaurant, cable TV, miniature golf, 2 tennis courts, 2 pools, playground, business services, meeting rooms* ☰ *AE, DC, MC, V* ¶◎¶ *BP.*

¢–$ ▦ **San Francesco.** The convent that was once attached to the church of San Francesco has been reinvented as a hotel. The rooms are grouped around the 14th-century cloister and, though somewhat cramped, are modern and quiet. It's quite central, in Alghero's Spanish quarter. ⊠ *Via Machin 2, 07041* ☎🖷 *079/980330* ✑ *hotsfran@tin.it* 📾 *20 rooms* ⊘ *Bar, meeting room* ☰ *MC, V* ⊗ *Closed Nov.–mid-Dec.* ¶◎¶ *BP.*

Shopping

Coral and gold jewelry purveyors dot Alghero's old quarter. A great place to buy wine is **Bacco e Tabacco** (⊠ Via Roma 91 ☎ 079/9735030 ⊕ www.baccoetabacco.it), which also ships all over the world.

Nightlife

The **Caffè Costantino** (⊠ Piazza Civica 30 ☎ 079/976154) is sumptuous and elegant, with yellow flowered walls, chandeliers, classical music, and a warm crowd of distinguished, well-dressed Algherese. Stop in for a glass of local wine or just a coffee; it's open until midnight.

Baraonda (⊠ Piazza Umberto 75 ☎ 079/975922), a marvelous local wine bar, carries specialty liqueurs and grappas from all over Sardinia.

The hip **Tunnel 21** (⊠ Via G. Ferret 37) bar, inside an ancient tunnel, is striking and open late into the night.

Sassari

⑱ *34 km (21 mi) northeast of Alghero, 212 km (132 mi) north of Cagliari.*

Inland Sassari is an important university town and administrative center, notable for its ornate old cathedral, its good archaeological museum, and a history of intellectualism and bohemian student culture. Look for downtown vendors of *fainè*, a pizzalike chickpea-flour pancake glistening with olive oil, which is a Genovese and Sassarese specialty. Sassari is the hub of several highways and secondary roads leading to various coastal resorts, among them Stintino and Castelsardo.

Sassari's excellent **Museo Sanna** has the best archaeological collection outside Cagliari, spanning nuraghic, Carthaginian, and Roman histories, including well-preserved bronze statues and household objects from the second millennia BC. Summer hours vary from one year to the next. ⊠ *Via Roma at Via Asproni* ☎ *079/272203* 🎟 *€2* ☉ *Tues.–Sun. 9–8.*

Where to Eat

¢–$ ✕ **L'Assassino.** Get a true taste of great local Sassarese cooking—and many of the other obscure Sardinian specialties you might have been looking for but not yet found. Horse, donkey, and roast pig figure prominently on the menu; best of all is a *cena sarda,* a 10-dish tasting menu with *porcetto* (roast suckling pig), also spelled *porcheddu*. The service is friendly, and the room warm and cozy. Food is, unusually, served all afternoon long. ⊠ *Vicolo Ospizio Cappuccini 1, near Via Rosello* ☎ *079/235401* 🖃 *AE, DC, MC, V* ☉ *Closed Sun.*

Shopping

Sassari has Sardinia's main **ISOLA** (⊠ Giardini Pubblici ☎ 079/230101), a craft exhibition center in the public gardens next to Viale Mancini built specifically as a showcase for gifts and souvenirs.

Castelsardo

⑲ *32 km (20 mi) northeast of Sassari, 100 km (62 mi) west of Olbia.*

The walled seaside citadel of Castelsardo is a delight for basket lovers. Roadside stands and shops in the old town sell rugs and wrought iron, as well as baskets. Take the children to see the appropriately shaped ☾ **Roccia dell'Elefante** (Elephant Rock) on the road into Castelsardo; it was hollowed out by primitive man to become a *domus de janas* (literally, "fairy house," in fact a Neolithic burial chamber).

Santa Teresa di Gallura

⑳ *68 km (42 mi) northeast of Castelsardo, 65 km (41 mi) northwest of Olbia.*

At the northern tip of Sardinia, Santa Teresa di Gallura retains the relaxed, carefree air of a fishing village-turned-resort.

Where to Stay & Eat

¢ ✕🏨 **Canne al Vento.** Step into a family-run hotel and restaurant that is a quiet, cheerful haven. Despite a bland exterior, the place has a defiantly rustic feel, with a bamboo-roofed restaurant and the odd ornamental wagon wheel. Rooms are sparsely furnished but cool and comfortable. The restaurant ($$$) specializes in authentic island cuisine, for example *zuppa cuata* (bread, cheese, and tomato soup), porcheddu, and seafood. ⊠ *Via Nazionale 23, 07028* ☎ *0789/754219* 📠 *0789/754948* 🛏 *22 rooms* ☾ *Restaurant, minibars; no a/c* 🖃 *AE, DC, MC, V* ☉ *Closed Oct.–Mar. Restaurant closed Mon.* ❚❀❙ *BP.*

$$$–$$$$ ⊞ **Grand Hotel Corallaro.** This hotel has luxury accommodations in a panoramic spot right by the beach, a brief walk from the town center. Rooms are functional and some have balconies. Public rooms are much grander, furnished with wicker chairs, and there are terraces and lawns where you can sip preprandial drinks. Half or full board is required in high season; low-season discounts are sizeable. ⊠ *Località Rena Bianca, 07028* ☎ *0789/755475* 🖷 *0789/755431* ⊕ *www.hotelcorallaro.it* 🖙 *82 rooms* ⚲ *Restaurant, indoor pool, gym, Turkish baths* ▤ *MC, V* ⊘ *Closed mid-Oct.–Easter* ⦿ *MAP.*

La Maddalena

❷❶ *30 km (19 mi) east of Santa Teresa di Gallura, 45 km (20 mi) northwest of Olbia.*

From the port of Palau you can visit the archipelago of La Maddalena, seven granite islands embellished with lush green scrub and wind-bent pines. Car ferries make the 3-km (2-mi) trip about every half hour or so.

Pilgrims pay homage to **Garibaldi's tomb** (1807–82) on the grounds of his hideaway on Isola Caprera. Take the ferry to Isola Maddalena and then the bridge to Isola Caprera. ✛ *7 km (4½ mi) east of Isola Maddalena* ☎ *0789/727162* 🎫 *€2* ⊘ *Daily 9–1:30.*

Porto Cervo

★ ❷❷ *35 km (22 mi) southeast of La Maddalena, 30 km (19 mi) north of Olbia.*

Sardinia's northeastern coast is fringed with low cliffs, inlets, and small bays. This has become an upscale vacationland, with glossy resorts such as Baia Sardinia and Porto Rotondo just outside the confines of the famed Costa Smeralda, developed by the Aga Khan (born 1936), who in 1965 accidentally discovered the coast's charms—and potential—when his yacht took shelter here from a storm. In the late '60s and '70s, the Costa Smeralda, with its heart in Porto Cervo, was *the* place to summer. The attractions remain geared to those who can measure themselves by the yardstick of Khan's fabled riches. Italian Prime Minister Silvio Berlusconi certainly does: the lucky (or unlucky) might catch a passing glimpse of the 40-room villa of the increasingly unpopular prime minister now referred to by many Italians as the *distante signoria* (roughly translated as "distant lord of the manor"). Italy's most expensive hotels are here, and the world's most magnificent yachts anchor in the waters of Porto Cervo.

All along the coast, carefully tended lush vegetation surrounds vacation villages and discreet villas that have sprung up over the past decade in spurious architectural styles best described as bogus Mediterranean. The trend has been to keep this an enclave of the very rich. Outside the peak season, however, prices plunge and the majesty of the natural surroundings shines through, justifying all the hype and the Emerald Coast's fame as one of the truly romantic corners of the Mediterranean.

Where to Stay

$$$$ ⛶ **Cala di Volpe.** Long a magnet for the beautiful people, this hyper-glamorous establishment, now part of the Starwood Luxury Collection, was built to resemble an ancient Sardinian village. The rustic-elegant interior has wood-beam ceilings, terra-cotta floors, Sardinian arts-and-crafts decorations, and porticoes overlooking the sea. The Presidential Suite in the highest tower has a private pool. Prices are so high that you may think you've got the exchange rate wrong by a factor of 10—this is one of the most expensive hotels in the world. ⊠ *Cala di Volpe, 07020* ☎ *0789/976111* 🖷 *0789/976617* ⊕ *www.luxurycollection.com* ⌨ *107 rooms, 14 suites* ⚫ *2 restaurants, room service, in-room dataports, in-room safes, cable TV with movies, in-room VCRs, putting green, 3 tennis courts, pool, wading pool, spa, beach, boating, waterskiing, 3 bars, shops, babysitting, laundry service, concierge, business services, convention center, airport shuttle, car rental* ⊟ *AE, DC, MC, V* ⊗ *Closed Nov.–mid-Apr.* ⦿ *MAP.*

$$$$ ⛶ **Cervo Hotel.** Low Mediterranean buildings surround a large pool and garden in the heart of the Costa Smeralda's Porto Cervo. Colorful painted wood furniture and slipcovered pieces fill up the large rooms; most have a terrace. The five tennis courts are well-lighted at night. High-season prices are through the roof, but in winter, prices fall to as low as one-tenth the summer rate. This Starwood Sheraton hotel complex is next to the marina and *piazzetta* (small piazza)—a popular spot to see and be seen. ⊠ *Waterfront, 07020* ☎ *0789/931111* 🖷 *0789/931613* ⊕ *www.sheraton.com* ⌨ *86 rooms, 6 suites* ⚫ *5 restaurants, room service, minibars, cable TV with movies, 5 tennis courts, 3 pools (1 indoor), gym, beach, boating, waterskiing, squash, 4 bars, piano bar, babysitting, concierge, business services, convention center, travel services* ⊟ *AE, DC, MC, V* ⦿ *MAP.*

$$$ ⛶ **Nibaru.** Pinkish-red brick buildings with tiled roofs stand in a secluded inlet amid lush gardens—not bad for a hotel that enjoys all the best features of the Costa Smeralda at comparatively low rates. Guest rooms are just a few yards from the sea and some superb swimming spots and also within easy access of the Pevero Golf Club and the tennis courts of Porto Cervo. Even closer is Nibaru's lagoonlike outdoor pool. ⊠ *Località Cala di Volpe, 07020* ☎ *0789/96038* 🖷 *0789/96474* ⊕ *www. hotelnibaru.it* ⌨ *50 rooms, 2 suites* ⚫ *Minibars, pool, bar* ⊟ *AE, DC, MC, V* ⊗ *Closed mid-Oct.–mid-Apr.* ⦿ *BP.*

Sports & the Outdoors

The world-class, 18-hole **Pevero Golf Course** (⊠ Bay of Pevero ☎ 0789/958020) was designed by Robert Trent Jones.

The **Yacht Club Costa Smeralda** (⊠ Via della Marina ☎ 0789/902200 ⊕ www.yccs.it) provides use of its pool, restaurant, bar, and guest rooms to those with memberships at other yacht clubs.

Olbia

㉓ *30 km (19 mi) south of Porto Cervo, 106 km (66 mi) north of Nuoro.*

Set amid the resorts of Sardinia's northeastern coast, Olbia is a lively little seaport and port of call for mainland ferries at the head of a long, wide bay. The little basilica of **San Simplicio,** a short walk behind the main Corso Umberto, is worth searching out if you have any spare time in Olbia. The simple granite structure dates from the 11th century, part of the great Pisan church-building program, using pillars and columns recycled from Roman buildings. ⊠ *Via San Simplicio* ☎ *0789/23358* ⊙ *Daily 6:30–12:30 and 4–7.*

Where to Stay & Eat

$–$$ ✕ **Barbagia.** Traditional dishes from Sardinia's wild interior fuse with local ingredients here. Antipasti might be a refreshing salad of sliced tomato and fresh cheese (called *sa t'amata chi sa frughe*). Then try maccarones de busa with a wild boar sauce; you might also find roast lamb and suckling pig in season. A good selection of pizza is served for dinner only. This is a classic downtown gathering place with a simple, bright array of tables. ⊠ *Via Galvani 94* ☎ *0789/51640* ▤ *AE, DC, MC, V* ⊙ *Closed Wed. Oct.–June.*

$$ ⊡ **Martini.** Plush, modern, and businesslike, Martini occupies an eye-catching site on the shore of a lagoon north of town. The hotel has lounge chairs on the roof with views of the port. Most of the classic bedrooms also benefit from the excellent vista. It's a 20-minute walk or easy taxi ride from the port and center, and is thankfully detached from the early-morning and late-night comings and goings of ferries. ⊠ *Via G. D'Annunzio 21, 07026* ☎ *0789/26066 or 0789/24545* 🖷 *0789/26418* ⇔ *66 rooms* ♦ *Bar, minibars, meeting room* ▤ *AE, DC, MC, V* ⦿ *BP.*

Golfo Aranci

㉔ *19 km (12 mi) northeast of Olbia.*

At the mouth of the Gulf of Olbia, Golfo Aranci is a small-scale resort and major arrival point for ferries from the mainland. The craggy headland west of town has been left undeveloped as a nature reserve, and there are some inviting beaches within an easy drive.

SARDINIA A TO Z

To research prices, get advice from other travelers, and book travel arrangements, visit www.fodors.com.

AIR TRAVEL

Flying is by far the fastest and easiest way to get to the island. Sardinia's major airport is in Cagliari, with smaller ones at Alghero and Olbia, the latter providing access to the Costa Smeralda. Alitalia connects Cagliari with Rome and Palermo. Meridiana runs service between Cagliari and Paris, Bologna, Naples, Pisa, Venice, and Verona; between Olbia and Bologna, Milan, Pisa, and Rome; and has a Cagliari-Olbia service. Air One, in conjunction with Air Littoral, connects Alghero with Rome, Milan, and Nice; Olbia with Nice; and Cagliari with Milan and Strasbourg, France. RyanAir, the British low-cost carrier, has flights between London and Alghero, and also serves Olbia. A Rome–Cagliari flight takes about 40 minutes.

🛈 Airlines & Contacts Air One ☎ 06/488800 in Rome, 848/848880 elsewhere in Italy ⊕ www.air-one.it. **Alitalia** ☎ 800/223–5730 in U.S., 020/7602–7111 in London, 0990/448–259 in U.K., 06/65641 in Rome, 848/865641 elsewhere in Italy ⊕ www.alitalia.it. **Meridiana** ☎ 06/6529005 in Rome, 119/111333 elsewhere in Italy ⊕ www.meridiana.it. **RyanAir** ☎ 199/114114 in Italy, 0870/1–569–569 in U.K. ⊕ www.ryanair.com.

AIRPORTS

Cagliari's Aeroporto di Elmas is about 6 km (4 mi) west of town center, and there is regular bus service from the airport to Piazza Matteotti, in front of the train station. Alghero's Aeroporto Fertilia is 13 km (8 mi) from the city. A bus links the airport with the bus station in the center of town. Aeroporto Costa Smeralda is 4 km (2½ mi) southeast of Olbia, linked by local bus to Olbia.

🛈 Airport Information Aeroporto Costa Smeralda ☎ 0789/52634 ⊕ www.geasar.com. **Aeroporto di Elmas** ☎ 070/2128263 ⊕ www.aeroportodicagliari.com. **Aeroporto Fertilia** ☎ 079/935282 or 079/935033 ⊕ www.algheroaeroporto.it.

BOAT & FERRY TRAVEL

Large modern ferries run by Tirrenia Lines, Moby Lines, and the Ferrovie dell Statto (FS, Italian State Railways) connect Sardinia (ports at Porto Torres, Olbia, Arbatax, and Cagliari) with the mainland. These ferries are a popular mode of transport. Naples-Cagliari is Tirrenia's most popular route, but Tirrenia also connects La Spezia and Genoa with Porto Torres, Olbia, Arbatax, and Cagliari; Civitavecchia with Olbia, Arbatax, and Cagliari; Fiumicino with Golfo Aranci and Arbatax; and Cagliari with Palermo, Trapani, and Tunis. Moby Lines transports passengers and cars between Livorno and Olbia and between Civitavecchia and Olbia. FS ferries carry trains as well as passengers and cars; they sail from Civitavecchia to Golfo Aranci, near Olbia. Grimaldi's Grandi Navi Veloci run very comfortable ferries that resemble cruise ships between Genoa, Porto Torres, and Olbia, and French SNCM ferries also transport passengers to and from Marseille, France.

FARES & SCHEDULES The ferry ride on Tirrenia from Naples to Cagliari takes about 17 hours and costs approximately €60–€90 for first-class passage in mid- or high season with a berth. The Civitavecchia–Olbia/Golfo Aranci run (€27–€60) takes about eight hours and there are overnight sailings, or take a more expensive high-speed ferry (summer only), which takes just four to six hours but costs more and gets booked up weeks ahead during the peak of the season in mid-August. Normal ferry service is scheduled two or three times a week, and high-speed ferries depart one to four times daily.

🛈 Boat & Ferry Information FS ☎ 1478/88088 ⊕ www.fs-on-line.it. **Grandi Navi Veloci** ☎ 0789/200126 in Olbia, 079/51604 in Porto Torres ⊕ www.gnv.it. **Moby Lines** ☎ 06/42011455 or 0586/826824 ⊕ www.mobylines.it. **SNCM** ☎ 02/66117104, 33/0891701801 in France ⊕ www.sncm.fr. **Tirrenia** ☎ 1478/99000, 081/3172999 from cellular phones and outside Italy ⊕ www.tirrenia.it.

BUS TRAVEL

Cagliari is linked with the other towns of Sardinia by a network of buses. Local destinations are served by ARST. Major cities, excluding Olbia, are served by PANI. The heart of the Sardinian bus system is the Stazione Autolinee, across the square from the main tourist office in Cagliari. City buses in Cagliari and Sassari operate on the same system as those on the mainland: buy your ticket first, at a tobacco shop or machine, and cancel it by punching it in the machine on the bus. Fares are €0.65 per ride.

🚹 Bus Information **ARST** ☎ 070/4098324 or 1678/65042. **PANI** ☎ 070/652326. **Stazione Autolinee** ✉ Piazza Matteotti, Cagliari ☎ 070/4098324.

CAR RENTAL

🚹 Agencies **Avis** ✉ Aeroporto di Fertilia, Alghero ☎ 079/935064 ✉ Piazza Sulis 9, Alghero ☎ 079/979577 ✉ Via Roma, Cagliari ☎ 070/668128 ✉ Aeroporto di Elmas, Cagliari ☎ 070/240081 ✉ Aeroporto Costa Smeralda, Olbia ☎ 0789/69540 ✉ Via Mazzini 2, Sassari ☎ 079/235547 ⊕ www.avis.com. **Hertz** ✉ Aeroporto di Fertilia, Alghero ☎ 079/935054 ✉ Piazza Matteotti 8, Cagliari ☎ 070/651078 ✉ Aeroporto di Elmas, Cagliari ☎ 070/240037 ✉ Aeroporto Costa Smeralda, Olbia ☎ 0789/66024 ✉ Via Regina Elena 34, Olbia ☎ 0789/66024 ⊕ www.hertz.com. **Maggiore** ✉ Via Sassari 87, Alghero ☎ 079/979375 ✉ Aeroporto di Fertilia, Alghero ☎ 079/935045 ✉ Viale Monastir 116, Cagliari ☎ 070/273692 ✉ Aeroporto di Elmas, Cagliari ☎ 070/240069 ✉ Via D'Annunzio, Olbia ☎ 0789/22131 ✉ Aeroporto Costa Smeralda, Olbia ☎ 0789/69457 ✉ Piazza Santa Maria 6, Sassari ☎ 079/235507 ⊕ www.maggiore.it.

CAR TRAVEL

The best way to get around Sardinia is to drive. Cars may be taken on board most of the ferry lines connecting Sardinia with the mainland. The north–south S131 (Strada Carlo Felice) is a major highway, but something less than an *autostrada*, connecting Cagliari, Oristano, Sassari, and Porto Torres. The S131dir (not to be confused with the S131) and S129 connect the Strada Carlo Felice with Nuoro and the Barbagia. The S597 connects Sassari and Olbia.

ROAD CONDITIONS Roads are generally in good condition, but bear in mind that roadside facilities are infrequent, especially in the east. Try to avoid driving at night, when mountain roads are particularly hazardous and slow; and especially in winter, beware the fog when traversing the mountains at night (or even by day).

EMERGENCIES

Late-night pharmacies are open on a rotating basis; information on current schedules is pinned up on any pharmacy door or can be obtained by calling 192.

ACI provides 24-hour roadside assistance for emergencies.

🚹 **ACI** ☎ 803/116. **Ambulance** ✉ Cagliari ☎ 070/4092901. **Hospital** Ospedale Civile San Michele ✉ Via Peretti, Cagliari ☎ 070/543266. **Police** ☎ 112 or 113.

LANGUAGE

Although the Sard language is incomprehensible to mainland Italians, let alone to foreigners, most locals can switch from Sardinian to perfect Italian with ease. In the main tourist areas, most people you deal with will have a smattering of English—but often less than elsewhere in Italy.

MAIL & SHIPPING

⬛ Post Offices **Cagliari** ⊠ Piazza del Carmine, 09100 ☎ 070/663356. **Sassari** ⊠ Via Brigata Sassari, 07100 ☎ 079/231609.

TOURS

Cagliari travel agency gives tours of Sardinia. The Associazione Nazionale di Turismo Equestre can provide information on horseback riding tours along the coast or into the heart of the island. The Centro Vacanze Ala Birdi organizes riding vacations.

⬛ Horseback Riding Tours **Associazione Nazionale di Turismo Equestre** ⊠ Via Carso 35/a, Sassari ☎ 079/299889. **Cagliari** Viaggi Orrù ⊠ Via Roma 95, Cagliari ☎ 070/659858 ⊕ www.viaggiorru.it. **Centro Vacanze Ala Birdi** ⊠ Arborea, near Oristano ☎ 0783/80500 ⊕ www.alabirdi-arborea.it.

TRAIN TRAVEL

The Stazione Centrale in Cagliari is next to the bus station on Piazza Matteotti. There are fairly good connections between Olbia, Cagliari, Sassari, and Oristano. You can reach Nuoro via Macomer; Alghero is reached via Sassari. Service on the few other local lines is infrequent and slow. The fastest train between Olbia and Cagliari takes more than four hours. Local trains connect Golfo Aranci, the Ferrovie dello Stato (Italian State Railways, or Trenitalia) port for the train ferry, with Olbia (20 minutes) and Sassari with Alghero (35 minutes).

⬛ Train Information **Ferrovie dello Stato** ☎ 848/888088 ⊕ www.trenitalia.com.

VISITOR INFORMATION

The official Sardinia Web site has information for many island towns.

⬛ Tourist Information **Alghero** ⊠ Piazza Porta Terra 9, 07041 ☎ 079/979054. **Cagliari** ⊠ Piazza Mateotti, 09100 ☎ 070/669255 ⊠ Aeroporto di Elmas ☎ 070/240200. **Golfo Aranci** ⊠ City Hall, 07026 ☎ 0789/21672 June–Aug. **Nuoro** ⊠ Piazza Italia 19, 08100 ☎ 0784/30083. **Olbia** ⊠ Via Catello Piro 1, 07026 ☎ 0789/21453 ⊠ Aeroporto Costa Smeralda ☎ 0789/21453. **Oristano** ⊠ Via Cagliari 278, 09170 ☎ 0783/36831. **Sardinia** ⊕ www.regione.sardegna.it. **Sassari** ⊠ Viale Caprera 36, 07100 ☎ 079/299544.

UNDERSTANDING ITALY

THE PALMS OF SICILY

Excerpted from *Bella Tuscany: The Sweet Life in Italy* (1999), by Frances Mayes

'M NOT OFF THE PLANE IN PALERMO five minutes before I have an arancino in my hand, ready to taste the signature dish of Sicily. Ed has gone to find the rental car office and I head to the bar right in the center of the airport. There they are, a line of the deep-fried risotto balls formed into the size and shape of oranges. "What's inside?" I ask.

A man with those amazing black, Sicilian deep-as-wells eyes points to the round ones. "Ragà, signora. And the oval ones— besciamella e prosciutto." His eyes fascinate me as much as the arancini. All through the airport I've seen the same Byzantine, hidden, historical eyes. At the bar, savoring the crisp creamy texture of the rice, I'm watching a parade of these intensely Italian-looking Italians. Women with gobs of dark curls cascading and flowing, slender men who seem to glide instead of walk. Tiny girls with miniature gobs of the same dark curls, and old men formed by stoop labor, carrying their hats in their hands. Crowds surge to meet planes coming in from Rome, which is only an hour away. They're all waving and shouting greetings to deplaning Sicilians who probably have been gone a few days, judging from their carry-on bags. Ed comes back, bearing keys. He, too, polishes off an arancino and orders an espresso. He looks startled when he sees how small it is, barely a spoonful, with rich crema. One taste and he's transported.

The waiter sees his surprise. He's about 5'3". He looks up at Ed, almost a foot taller. "The farther south you go, signore, the smaller and the stronger."

Ed laughs, "È fantastico." He wheels our bag out to the green Fiat and zooms out of the garage.

Along the coastal road to Palermo, we glimpse the sea and cubical north African–style houses in a rocky landscape. The instant we enter Palermo, we're in wild traffic, careening traffic, traffic moving too fast for us to locate where we are going. Lanes disappear, avenue names keep changing, we turn and turn in mazes of one-way streets. "That barista should have said 'smaller, stronger, and faster,' " Ed shouts. At a light, he rolls down the window and calls desperately to a man revving his motorcycle in anticipation of the green, "Per favore, which way to Hotel Villa Igiea?"

"Follow me," he shouts back and he's off, spiraling among cars and glancing back now and then to see if we're behind him. Somehow we are. Ed seems to be in his wake, just going. At highway speeds on city streets, cars are neck-and-neck. On all four sides, we are two inches from other bite-sized cars. If someone braked, we'd be in a hundred-car pile-up. But no one brakes. At an intersection, the motorcyclist points to the left then waves. He swerves right so hard his ear almost touches the ground. We're tossed into a roundabout, spun, and emptied suddenly onto a quiet street. And there's the hotel. We creep into the parking lot and stop.

"Let's don't get in this car again until we leave. That was absolutely the worst."

"Suits me," Ed agrees. He's still gripping the wheel. "Let's take taxis. Everywhere. This is more like the running of the bulls than driving." We grab our bag, lock the Fiat, and don't look at the car again until we check out.

* * *

HE TAXI ARRIVES quickly and we launch into the bumper-car traffic. Yes, it's always like this, the driver tells us. No, there aren't many accidents. Why? He shrugs, everybody is used to it. We sit back, and he's right, we begin to feel the double-time rhythm of driving here. Drivers look alert, as though engaging in a contact sport. He drops us in the center near an esplanade closed to traffic. Out of the street's chaos, we're greeted by the scent of flowers. Vendors are selling freesias in all the Easter colors, purple, yellow, and white. Instead of the puny bouquets I buy at home, these are sold in armfuls, wrapped in a ruff of brazen pink foil and trailing ribbons.

Not wanting to take time for lunch, we sample sfincione, pizza with big bread crumbs on top, then keep going—palms, outdoor tables filled with people, small shops of luxurious bags and shoes, waiters with trays aloft carrying pastries and espresso.

Pastries! Every pasticceria displays an astonishing variety. We're used to drier Tuscan pastries; these are mounded with cream. A woman arranges her shop window with realistic marzipan pineapples, bananas, prickly pears, lemons, cherries, and, for the Easter season, lambs complete with curls. Inside, her cases display almond cakes, wild strawberry tarts, biscotti, and, of course, cannoli, but in all sizes, from thumb-sized to a giant as large as a leg of lamb. Two bakers pause in the kitchen doorway and all the customers step back as they gingerly balance and step. They bring out a three-foot tree made from small cannoli, a stiff pyramid like a French croquembouche at Christmas. Sfince, rice fritters filled with ricotta, cinnamon, candied oranges or strawberries, honor San Giuseppe, whose onomastico, name day, is March 19, when Italians also celebrate Father's Day.

The freezers glow with sorbetti—pistachio, lemon, watermelon, cinnamon, jasmine, almond, as well as the usual fruits. Most children seem to prefer gelato, not in a cup or cone, but stuffed inside a brioche. Just looking at the almond cake is almost enough satisfaction, but we instead split one of the crisp cannoli lined with chocolate and heavenly, creamy ricotta. No harm done; we're planning to walk for the rest of the afternoon.

* * *

ON THE FIRST DAY in a new place, it's good to wander, absorb colors, textures, and scents, see who lives here, and find the rhythm of the day. We'll crank into tourist mode later, making sure we don't miss the great sights. Dazed by actually coming to Palermo, by the flight, the espresso, and the day, we just take the appealing street, turning back if it begins to look dicey. Palms are everywhere. I wish I could take one back to Bramasole to replace the one December's freeze probably killed. Not only do I love palms because they mean tropical air, I love the image Wallace Stevens made: "the palm at the end of the mind." To imagine the end of the mind and to see not a blank wall or a roadblock or an abyss but a tall swaying palm seems felicitous to me.

We come upon a botanical park, dusty and empty except for cacti, carob, mulberry, agave, and shrubs with primitive, broad leaves. The palm looks native but was brought by Arabs in the ninth century along with their fountains, spices, arabesques, ice cream, mosaics, and domes. Palms and domes—gold, pomegranate, aqua, verdigris—characterize Palermo. How bold to color the five domes of San Giovanni degli Eremiti a burnt red. Inside, aromatic citrus blossoms and jasmine suffuse a cloister garden, a secretive respite from the tortured road outside.

On the map, we see that the Palazzo dei Normanni is nearby and decide to go in the famous Cappella Palatina today. The subjects of the mosaics, the guidebook says, seem to have been chosen with reference to the Holy Spirit and the theology of light. I'm intrigued, since these two concepts seem identical in my mind.

Originally built by those busy Arabs in the ninth century, the palace was expanded by the Normans in the twelfth century and established as the residence for their kings. Later residents and royalty left their bits and pieces, and today the styles have so long overlapped that the architecture simply looks like itself. Byzantine Greeks began the mosaic decoration in the twelfth century. Tessera by tessera, it must have taken them forever; every Bible story I ever heard glitters around this room. The floors, too, are mosaic or inlaid marble in designs like Oriental rugs.

The Holy Spirit and theology of light are only a layer. A lot is going on. It's like Palermo—each square inch occupied with life. I love the word "tesserae." It seems to shower silver and gold on its own. There's the whole Adam and Eve saga, the flood, there's Jacob wrestling with the angel, and in the dome and apse, Christ. In the dome he's surrounded by fore-shortened angels, each in intricate clothes. Christ offers a blessing in the apse. In both mosaics, he has long, long fingers. Looking through my opera glasses, I focus for a long time on his right hand, just this one small moment in the entire chapel— the hand held up, the thumb holding down the next-to-last finger, the other three straight, all formed with delicacy and subtle coloration. Late afternoon sun has a weak hold on the walls but still the gold around him sings with burnished amber light.

The rest of the Palazzo is closed. Walking back toward the center of Palermo, we pass rubble-filled lots still unrestored since World War II bombings. We look in open storefronts where hideous junk is sold and step off crowded sidewalks with fry-stations selling chickpea fritters. People are out gathering last minute food for dinner. About their business, the people look contained, silent, often weary. When they meet an acquaintance their faces break into vibrant expression. In the taxi back to the hotel, we hardly notice the near-death encounters.

The first two restaurants Ed selects for dinner are nixed by the hotel desk clerk. Dangerous areas, he tells us, making the motion of someone slicing a throat. He takes a ballpoint and scribbles out whole areas of our map. "What about this one?" Ed asks, pointing in our Italian restaurant guide to the highly regarded, unpronounceable N'grasciata. "And what does that mean?"

"In local dialect that means 'dirty' but don't be alarmed, just a way of speaking."

Speaking of what? I think. Dirty means dirty. "Your highest recommendation?"

"Sì, authentic. They have their own fishing boat. You won't see tourists there. I will call and they will expect you."

We're dropped off at a plain place which is even plainer inside. No tablecloths, a TV somewhere, no decor, no menu, harsh lighting and the buzz of bugs hitting the zapper. The waiter starts bringing out the food. I'm crazy about the panelli, chickpea fritters, and the platter of fried artichokes. Then comes pasta with pomarola, that intense, decocted tomato sauce, and baby octopus. I'm not so sure about this dish. I chew for a long time. The platter comes round again and Ed has more. We're offered another pasta, this one bucatini with sardines, currants, and fennel. The next dish is a grilled orata, which my dictionary translates as "gilthead," surrounded by fried frutta di mare—just various fish. I'm slowing down. I like a little bit of fish, not a lot. Ed loves anything that comes from the sea and is so obviously relishing the food that the waiter starts to hover, commenting on each morsel. He's pouring wine to the brim of the glass. His dolorous eyes look like Jesus' in the mosaic dome. His long fingers have tufts of black curly hair on each digit, and a matt of hair escapes the collar of his shirt. He has the long, four-inch-wide face I associate with newspaper photos of hijackers.

I revive briefly for the spicy melanzane— here's a touch of the Arabic, eggplant with cinnamon and pine nuts—but balk at the appearance of the stuffed squid (all those suction cups on the arms) and the sea bream sausage. Is he bringing us everything in the kitchen? Next comes a plate of fried potatoes. "Signora," our waiter says. "Signora." He can't believe that I have stopped eating. He pulls up a chair and sits down. "You must."

I smile and shake my head. Impossible. He rolls those dolorous eyes to heaven. "Ho paura," I'm afraid, I try to joke, pointing at the squid. He takes me literally and eats a bite himself to prove there's no cause for alarm. Still, I shake my head no. He takes my fork, gently grabs a handful of my hair and starts to feed me. I am so astonished I open my mouth and eat. I really hate the texture, like tenderized erasers.

As an afterthought, he brings out involtini, veal rolled around a layer of herbs and cheese, but even Ed has stopped by now. He's thanking the waiter. "The best fish in Palermo," he tells him.

"How do you know?" I ask him on the way out. The waiter bares his teeth in a big grin. No, he looks more like a wolf than Jesus.

"It had to be. That was a down-home place."

* * *

W E'RE OUT EARLY. In the Vucciria quarter, the market is stupendous. I've been to markets in France, Spain, Peru, San Francisco, all over Italy. This is the market. For the senses, ecstasy and assault. Because Palm Sunday is this weekend, perhaps it is more of an assault than usual. Lines of lambs, gutted and dripping, eyeballs bulging, hang by their feet. Their little hooves and tails look so sad. Their little guts look so horrifying. The rainbows of shining fish on ice, the mounds of shrimp still wiggling their antennae, painted carts of lemons, jewel-colored candied fruits, bins of olives, nuts, seeds—everything is presided over by dealers who shout, sing, cajole, joke, curse, barter, bad-

ger. They're loud and raucous. Could it be true, as I've read, that the Mafia runs the heroin trade out of here? A vendor holds out a basket of eels that look like live sterling silver. He gyrates his hips to emphasize their movement. This feels more like a carnival than the more decorous Tuscan markets we're used to. I wish for a kitchen so I could gather some of the lustrous eggplants and clumps of field greens. My stomach is growling so loud it sounds like a tiny horse neighing. Cooks here are in paradise. I'll never eat lamb again.

Ed refuses to go to the Catacombe dei Cappuccini, where 8,000 desiccated corpses are on exhibit. I have already bought a postcard of a red-haired girl under glass for decades, her delicate nostrils still stuffed with cotton, a ribbon in her hair. We have visited the same sort of place in Guanajuato, Mexico. I was fascinated; he was revolted. We decide on the Museo Archeologico, and we don't come out until it closes. I find this one of the best museums I've ever visited—so much of what interests me is gathered in this old convent. Phoenician anchors and amphoras dredged from the sea lie around the courtyard. Mysterious stelae painted with portraits were found on ancient grave sites in Marsala. Etruscan treasures, some with traces of paint, from the tombs at Chiusi, near us in Tuscany, somehow have ended up in Sicily. Here we get to see the sixth- and fifth-century BC metopes (panels of the temple frieze) removed from the Greek site at Selinunte, one of the most important Greek sites on the island. We find Demeter, the Cretan bull; Perseus, Hercules, and Athena star in various triumphs. Hera marries Zeus, and Actaeon becomes a stag. Seeing the familiar mythic players as they actually were on temples brings the legends closer to my imagination. These images come from the time when they were real to people, not just characters from the history of myth—an astounding telescoping of distance. The enormous scale, too, prepares us for the dimensions of the ruins we'll see.

We can't look at all 12,000 of the votive figures also excavated at Selinunte but we look until we can't look anymore. That only leaves rooms and rooms of Roman sculpture, Greek vases, and more and more. We meander through, stopped by painted fragments from Pompeii, a fantastic third century BC bronze ram, and a blur of mosaic pavements. Then, out. Onto the plain sidewalk, dazed and dazzled by what we've seen.

* * *

S THE FREESIAS BEGIN TO WILT IN OUR ROOM, we decide to start our tour of the island tomorrow morning. We have a glass of blood orange juice on our balcony. All we can hear is the rattle of palms below us in the breeze and the jingle of rigging on the sailboats in the bay.

"Do you want to come back?" I ask.

"Yes. We haven't seen whole areas of Palermo."

"It's hard to get a sense of the place. So layered, so crude, so complex—a daunting city."

"My core impression is of a chaos everyone here has learned how to survive."

* * *

UT I SUDDENLY REMEMBER a story a woman I met in Milwaukee told me about someone she knew. "This Midwestern soldier in World War II was on a ship which was bombed by retreating Germans in the harbor of Palermo," I tell Ed. "He survived even though almost everyone else was killed. I swam to shore and was stranded here. I think the Germans were retreating by then. One night he went to the opera—he'd never been before. At the end, he was so moved by the music he started to cry. All the horrors caught up with him. He just stood there during the applause and afterwards, openly crying. The audience started to file out. A man looked at him, paused, and touched him on the head, as though he were bestowing a benediction. As all the people passed him, each one stopped and touched him on the head.

"That's one of the best things I've ever heard. So that's Palermo."

Each succeeding conqueror of Sicily—Greeks, Carthaginians, Romans, Arabs, Normans, and all the rest—must have brought pocketfuls of wildflower seeds. The countryside in primavera is solidly in flower, rivers of yellow, purple cascading around rocks, roadsides lined with tiny blue-eyed blooms, and almond orchards whose long grasses are overtaken by white daisies. We made an easy exit, considering. We were only lost half an hour. Even though Ed was intimidated by traffic in Palermo, once we were out on the open road, I noticed his new skills, learned from the back seat of the taxis. He's relaxing into the concept that lanes do not exist much; the road is an open field for getting where you're going. The white line is the center of an imaginary lane to be used as needed.

Driving along the coast and meandering inland, the Mar Tirreno seven shades of blue out one window, and rampantly flowering hills out the other, it is easy to see why all those conquering hordes wanted this island. The landscape is everywhere various or dramatic. Anytime the perfume of orange and lemon groves wafts in the window, the human body has to feel suffused with a languorous well-being.

Soon we come to the turn-off for Segesta, first of the many Greek temples we hope to see in Sicily—the number rivals Greece itself. The Doric temple rises, just off the highway, where it has loomed on the hillside since the fifth century BC, which is close to forever. Along the climbing path, we see gigantic fennel growing, ten feet, even more. I always wondered how Prometheus took fire back to the Greeks in a fennel stalk. In these you could stash quite a few coals. In the process, maybe he invented grilled fennel.

The guidebook says of Segesta: "It is peripteral and hexastyle with 36 unfluted columns (9 m high, 2 m wide at base) on a stylobate 58 m by 23 m. The high entablature and the pediments are intact. The bosses used for maneuvering the blocks of the stylobate into position remain. Refinements include the curvature of the entablature and the abaci." Well, yes, but it's beautiful.

So is the equally ancient theater a short hike away. Greece was the first country I ever wanted to see. My longing was produced by a total immersion in Lord Byron when I was a senior in high school. In college, my friend Rena and I took a course in Greek drama. We wrote for brochures from Greek freighters and decided to drop out and see the world. We wanted to book passage on *Hellenic Destiny,* until our parents said absolutely not. I've never yet been to Greece. A few years ago I saw the magnificent temples at Paestum in the south of Italy and the longing was reawakened. "The mountains look on Marathon / and Marathon looks on the sea / and musing there an hour alone, / I dreamed that Greece might still be free." Something like that—it seems to scan into iambic tetrameter.

Like Paestum, Segesta is stripped down to pure silence, its skeletal purity etched against the sky. No one is here, though there were several people in the gift shop. We're alone with history and swallows swooping from their nests.

* * *

'M GLAD I DON'T HAVE TO take a test on Agrigento. For an American used to a comparatively straightforward history, all the Italian past seems hopelessly convoluted. The saga of the Greek ruins multiplies this complexity. Agrigento, since its Greek founding in the sixth century BC has been tossed among Carthaginians, Romans, Swabians, Arabians, Bourbons and Spaniards. Subjected to a name change during Mussolini's zeal to Italianize all things, the old name Akragas became Agrigento. I've seen the same zeal on the plaque outside where John Keats lived in Rome, cut off from his love and dying from tuberculosis. He's called Giovanni Keats, which somehow makes him seem more vulnerable than ever.

Akragas/Agrigento was Luigi Pirandello's birthplace. Traveling in Sicily casts his plays and stories, with their quirky sense of reality, in quite a natural light. The coexistence of the Greek ruins, the contemporary ruins, the tentacles of the Mafia, and the mundane day-to-day would skew my sense of time and place, too. The sun, Pirandello wrote, can break stones. Even in March, we feel the driving force on our heads as we walk in the Valley of the Temples.

All over a valley of almond trees and wildflowers stand a mind-boggling array of remains from an ancient town, from temples to sewer pipes. You could stay for days and not see everything. Unlike other sites, this one is quite populated with visitors. The Temple of Concordia is the best-preserved temple we've seen. Patch up the roof and the populace could commune with Castor and Pollux, to whom it probably was dedicated.

Five days ago I knew almost nothing about these ruins. Now the ancient dust covers my feet through my sandals; I have seen the unlikely survival of these buildings through rolls and rolls of time. These temples, men selling woven palm fronds for Palm Sunday, schoolchildren hiding among the columns, awed travelers like us with dripping gelato—all under the intense Sicilian sky. I'm thrilled. Just as I think that, Ed says, "This is a thrill of a lifetime."

Meandering, we stop at a cypress-guarded cemetery near Modica. Extravagant tombs are elaborately carved miniature houses laid along miniature streets. Here's the exuberance of Modica's art of the Baroque in microcosm. Through the grates or gates, the little chapels open to linen-draped altars with framed portraits of the dead and potted plants or vases of flowers. At thresholds, a few cats sun on the warmed marble. A woman is scrubbing, as she would her own stoop. With a corner of her apron, she polishes the round photo of a World War I soldier. A young girl weeds the hump of earth over a recent grave in the plain old ground. These dead cool off slowly; someone still tends flowers on plots where the inhabitants have lain for fifty years.

Cortona's cemetery, too, reflects the town, although not as grandly. A walled city of the dead situated just below the live city, it glows at night from the votive lights on each grave. Looking down from the Piazza del Duomo, it's hard not to imagine the dead up and about, visiting each other as their relatives still do right up the hill. The dead here probably would want more elaborate theatrical entertainments.

* * *

NEXT ON OUR ROUTE, AVOLA retains some charm. One-room-wide Baroque houses line the streets. Could we take home at least a dozen of the gorgeous children in their white smocks? On the corners men with hand-held scales scoop cockles from a mound on the sidewalk. Open trucks selling vegetables attract crowds of women with baskets. We keep turning down tiny roads to the sea. We can't find the beaches we expect—the unspoiled littoral dream of the island's limpid waters—only bleak beach towns, closed and depressing out of season.

It's only in Siracusa that I finally fall in love. In my Greek phase in college, I took Greek and Roman History, Greek and Roman Drama, Greek Etymology. At that point, my grandfather, who was sending me to college, drew a line. "I am not paying for you to stick your head in the clouds. You should get a certificate for teaching so you have something to fall back on." The message being, if your husband—whom you have gone to college to acquire, and no Yankees, please—dies or runs off.

Meanwhile, I was loving Aeschylus, the severe consequences of passion, pure-as-milk marble sculptures, the explorative spirit of the Greeks. Siracusa, therefore, is tremendously exciting to visit. Mighty Siracusa, ancient of ancients. Second to Athens in the classical world. We opt for a super-luxurious hotel on the connecting island of Ortigia, with a room surrounded by views of the water. We're suddenly not tired exactly, but saturated. We spend the afternoon in the huge bed, order coffee sent up, pull back the curtains and watch the fishing boats nosing—isn't that a Greek blue—into the harbor.

After siesta, we find Ortigia in high gear for Easter. Bars display chocolate eggs two feet tall, wrapped in purple cellophane and ribbons. Some are open on one side to reveal a marzipan Christ on the cross. Others have a surprise inside. I'd love to buy marzipan doves, lambs in baskets, chocolate hens. The lambs are like stuffed animals, large, decorated from nose to tail with fanciful marzipan curls. At the Antica Dolceria, they've gone into marzipan frenzy: Noah's ark complete with animals, the Greek temples, olives, pencils. Marzipan—called pasta reale—we realize is a serious folk art form. For me, three bites will suffice; maybe you have to have been born in Sicily to be able to eat more.

Ortigia is fantastic. The vague, intuitive sense of oppression I've felt in Sicily entirely lifts. Is the Mafia not in control here? People seem more lighthearted, playful, and swaggering. They look you in the eye, as people do in the rest of Italy. In the late afternoon, we walk all over the small island. It has its own Greek ruins just lying in a grassy plot at an intersection. An inscription carved into steps identifies the site as a temple to Apollo. Dense ficus trees along a walkway bordering the water are home to thousands of birds singing their evening doxology. Views across the water, Baroque iron balconies, Venetian Gothic windows, boarded up palazzi, and intricate medieval streets—layers and layers of architecture and time. Suddenly the streets intersect and widen at the Piazza del Duomo. The Baroque facade and entrance of the church in no way prepares you for the stunning surprise inside. Along one wall, the building incorporates a row of twelve majestic columns from the fifth-century BC Tempio di Atene. At evening, spikes of sunlight fall across the piazza, lighting the faces of those having an aperitivo at outdoor tables. Ordinary people, with the sun, like the sheen of gold mosaics, transforming their faces.

* * *

W E'RE READY TO PUT IN a full day on foot. In the museum on Ortigia, Caravaggio's painting of the burial of Santa Lucia, a local martyr in 304, who cut out her own eyes when a suitor admired them, occasioned a lecture from the guard worthy of any docent. And where are we from? Ah, he has a cousin in California; we should meet him when we return. Ed loves Annunciation paintings and the peeling one by da Messina enthralls him. Small local museums are my favorite kind. They stay close to the source, usually, and deepen a tourist-level connection with a place.

We walk across the bridge and through a park then through a honeycomb of streets.

The Museo Archeologico in Siracusa proper is world class. Intelligently arranged and exhibited, the art and craft of succeeding waves of life in this area are displayed. Beginning with prehistory we trace the history through one stunning room after another. Artifacts, statues, lion faces from the temple in ruins in Ortigia, Greek ex-votos, and an amazing bronze horse—oh, so much.

The amphitheater in Siracusa—what fabulous siting. The stone cup of the hill was chopped out into natural seating, a 300-degree arrangement focusing on a stage. Corridors were carved out for gladiators to enter and exit. In summer, the Greek plays are still performed here. What fun it would be to act in one. The ruins we've seen are the major ones; hundreds of other temples, foundations, baths, and unknown stones cover the island. This must be the ideal time to see them because hardly anyone is around. The solitude of these places sharpens the experience of happening upon them, the sense of discovery that for me lies at the heart of travel.

Frances Mayes is also the author of the best-selling Under the Tuscan Sun: At Home in Italy *(1996) and* In Tuscany *(2000), with photographs by Bob Krist. Her books are available from Broadway Books and in audio from Bantam, Doubleday, Dell.*

THE ARTLESS ART
OF ITALIAN COOKING

YOU ARE STAYING WITH FRIENDS in their villa in a windswept olive orchard above Florence. After a day in town—a morning at the Palazzo Pitti, afternoon in the Brancacci Chapel—you have returned to rest. In the garden, you find your hostess lifting heavy tomatoes into a basket, the acrid smell of their skins wafting up in the gentle September heat. You pick basil and tug figs from a tree that warms its back against the 14th-century kitchen wall. Inside, you watch while your hostess rinses the greens in the quarried stone sink. The tomatoes are still sun-warm when she scoops them, chopped, into a blender with the basil and a stream of olive oil; she pours the mixture into a faience bowl over steaming pasta. You eat at the kitchen table, pour wine from a crockery pitcher, and wipe your bowl with torn chunks of flour-flecked bread. Over the greens your hostess drizzles more olive oil and a bit of rock salt pinched from an open bowl. The figs melt in your mouth like chocolate. A scalding syrup of Arabic coffee streams from the *macchinetta*, and you're ready for a midnight survey of the olive groves.

Simple, earthy, at once wholesome and sensual, as sophisticated in its purity as the most complex cuisine, as inspired in its aesthetics as the art and architecture of its culture, Italian cooking strikes a chord that resonates today as it did in the Medici courts. Its enduring appeal can be traced to an ancient principle: respect for the essence of the thing itself—nothing more, nothing less. Like Michelangelo freeing the prisoners that dwelt within the stone—innate, organic—an Italian chef seems intuitively to seek out the crux of the thing he is about to cook and flatter it, subtly, with the purest of complements. To lay a translucent sheet of prosciutto—earthy, gamey, faintly redolent of brine—across the juicy pulchritude of a melon wedge is a stroke of insight into the nature of two ingredients as profound as the imaginings of Galileo.

Considering the pizzas, lasagnas, and red-drenched spaghetti that still pass for Italian food in many places abroad, it's no surprise that visitors to Italy are often struck by the austerity of the true Italian dishes put before them. The pasta is only lightly accented, not drowning in an industrial ladle-full of strong, soupy sauce. And although there may have been a parade of vegetable antipasti, the salad itself bears no resemblance to the smorgasbord of Anglo-American salad bars—it's a simple mix of greens, a drizzle of oil, a spritz, perhaps, of red-wine vinegar. If you've just come from Germanic countries, you'll notice a lack of Maggi, the bottled brown "flavor enhancer" that singes the tongue with monosodium glutamate, on the table. If you've come from Belgium, you'll miss the sauceboat of Hollandaise. And if you've come from France, you may shrug dismissively at the isolated ingredients you're served, saying as other Frenchmen before you, "But this is not really a true *cuisine. . . .*"

Ah, but it is. Shunning the complexities of heavy French sauces and avoiding the elaborate farce, Italian cuisine—having unloaded the aspirations of *alta cucina* onto its northern neighbors when Catherine de' Medici moved (chefs and all) to Paris—stands alone, proud, purist, unaffected.

The Italians' pride comes in part from a confidence in their raw ingredients, an earthiness that informs the appreciation of every citizen-connoisseur, from the roughest peasant in workers' blue to the vintner in shoulder-tied cashmere: they are in touch with land and sea. In the country, your host can tell you the source of every ingredient on the table, from the neighbor's potted goose to the porcini gathered in the beech grove yesterday. In the city, the market replaces the country network, and aggressive shopping will trace the genealogy of every mushroom, every artichoke, every wooden scoop of olives. And in balconies overhanging the seashore, the squid floating in their rich, blue-black ink were bought from a fisherman on the beach at dawn.

The spectrum of Italian regional cooking is as broadly varied as Italy's terrain, and cuisine and countryside are intimately allied. Emerging into sunlight from the Great St. Bernard pass into the Valle d'Aosta, the Piedmont, the hills of Lombardy, you'll find wood-lined Alpine trattorias offering rib-sticking gnocchi and air-dried beef, bubbling pots of *bagna cauda* (hot dipping sauce of olive oil and garlic), slabs of polenta, hearty walnut *torta* (cake). The pearl-spotted rice of Arborio, in the Po Valley, fuels an extraordinary array of risottos in Milan, where chefs shun olive oil in favor of the region's rich butter. Descend to Alba and savor the earthy perfume of truffles, the muscular Barolo wines. Cross over into Liguria and the cuisine changes as abruptly as the landscape: wild herbs, greens, and ground nuts flavor a panoply of sauces (consider the famous pesto, flavored with a "Riviera" basil rarely found elsewhere), served as condiments to meat as often as over pasta. The succulent pink pork of a Parma ham, the golden butterfat in a Reggiano cheese are nurtured on the same fertile soil of Emilia-Romagna, both the culinary and agricultural heart of Italy, and the *bistecca* of Tuscany comes from Chianina beef, pampered on local prairie grass and slaughtered at a tender age. Head south for sun-plumped eggplant, and quasi-tropical artichokes—in Rome, fried in delicate batter; in Calabria, stuffed with meat and sharp Pecorino from its hillside sheep herds. The chickpeas in Sicilian dishes remind you you're nearly in North Africa. And, of course, on this slender leg of land you are never far from the sea, and the harvest of its *frutti di mare* graces nearly every region—but none more than the islands and tide-washed shores of the south.

* * *

CAREENING IN YOUR RENTAL CAR down the western coast, clinging to the waterfront through sea-shanty villages that cantilever over the roaring surf, you feel a morning lag: your breakfast of *latte macchiato* and sugary *cornetto* has worn away. A real espresso would hit the spot; you hurtle down a web of switchbacks and pull into a seaside inn. You sip aromatic coffee and watch the waves. An hour passes in reverie—an aperitif, perhaps? Another hour over the Martini rosso, and you give in to the impulse, adjourning to the dining room. The odor of wood smoke drifts from the kitchen. A nutty risotto with a blush of tomato precedes a vast platter—austere, unembellished—of smoke-grilled fish, still sizzling, lightly brushed with oil, and glittering with rock salt. At the table beside yours, when the platter arrives, the woman rises and fillets the fish dexterously, serving her husband and sons.

There's a wholesomeness in the way Italians eat that is charming and contagious. If American foodies pick and kvetch and French gastronomes worship, Italians plunge into their meal with frank joy, earnest appreciation, and ebullient conversation. Yet they do not overindulge: portions are light, the drinking gentle, late suppers spartan with concern for digestion uppermost. It's as if the voice of Mamma still whispers moderation in their ear. They may, on the other hand, take disproportionate pleasure in watching guests eat, in surrounding them with congenial company, in pouncing on the bill. (This wholesome spirit even carries into the very bars: unlike the dark, louche atmosphere of Anglo lounges and pubs, in Italy you'll drink your *amaro* in a fluorescent-lit coffee bar without a whiff of sin in the air.)

Yet for all their straightforwardness, Italians are utterly at ease with their heritage, steeped from birth in the art and architecture that surrounds them. Without a hint of the grandiose, they'll construct a still life of figs and Bosc pears worthy of Caravaggio; a butcher will drape iridescent pheasants and quail, heads dangling, with the panache of a couturier. Consider the artless beauty of ruby-raw beef on an emerald bed of arugula, named for the preferred colors of the Venetian painter Carpaccio; pure white porcelain on damask; a mosaic of olives and pimientos in blown glass; a flash of folkloric pottery on a polished plank of oak.

In fact, it must be said: a large part of the pleasure of Italian dining is dining in Italy. We have all eaten in Italian restaurants elsewhere. The food can be superb, the ingredients authentic, the pottery and linens imported by hand. Yet who can conjure the blood-red ochre crumbling to gold on a Roman wall, the indigo and pastel hues of fishing boats rocking in a marina, the snow flurry of sugar papers on a café floor? These impart the essence that—as much as the basil on your bruschetta—flavors your Italian dining experience.

Inside the great walls of Lucca, you are lunching—slowly, copiously, and at length—in the shade of a vaulted portico. Strips of roasted eggplant and pepper steeped in garlic and oil; tortelloni stuffed with squab in a pool of butter and sage; roasted veal laced with green peppercorns; blackberries in thick cream. The bottle of Brunello di Montalcino, alas, is drained. It has been a perfect morning, walking the ramparts, and you have found the perfect restaurant: a Raphaelesque perspective of arcades and archways, pillars, porches, and loges spreads before you. The shadows and lines are strong in the afternoon sun; you admire from your seat in the cross breeze. It's only slowly that you realize that this Merchant/Ivory moment has a sound track, so organic to the scene you hadn't noticed—but now you feel goose bumps rising on your neck. It is Puccini: a young woman is singing, beautifully, from a groined arcade across the square, accompanied by a portable tape player.

". . . Ma quando vien lo sgelo . . . il primo sole è mio . . ."

Your coffee goes cold, untouched until the song, the moment, are over—and, in all its multifaceted magnificence, your Italian meal as well.

—Nancy Coons

THE PASSIONATE EYE: ITALIAN ART THROUGH THE AGES

TALIAN ART FLOWS as naturally as its wine, its sunshine, and its amore, and it has been springing from the Italian spirit for nearly as long. Perhaps nowhere else in the world has such a vital creative impulse flourished so bountifully within the noble sweep of the classical tradition. Perhaps no other country's cultural life has been so inextricably interwoven with its history.

And yet, Italy lives comfortably in the midst of all her accumulated treasures. She accepts them casually and affectionately, as she does her children and her flowers. True, some of her precious store has been gathered into world-famous museums, but Italians know best and love most intimately the art that surrounds their daily activity. They go to church among thousand-year-old mosaics, buy their groceries in a shop open since the time of Columbus, picnic on the steps of a temple that was old when Christ was born, and attend the opera in the same theaters where Rossini and Verdi saw their works premiered. Italy wears her heritage with a light and touching grace. She must: it is the very fabric of her life. For travelers from other countries, however, Italian art remains unique, extraordinary, worthy of worship. Here we offer a short history, focusing on Italy's greatest artistic achievement, the Renaissance—often called the nursery of Western art. The discoveries of 14th- and 15th-century Italian artists making it possible to render a realistic image of a person or an object determined the course of Western art right up until the late 19th century.

Art in the Middle Ages

The eastern half of the Roman Empire, based in Constantinople (Byzantium), was powerful long after the fall of Rome in AD 476: Italy remained influenced—and at times ruled—by the Byzantines. The artis-

tic revolution began when artists started to rebel against the Byzantine ethic, which dictated that art be exclusively Christian and that its aim be to arouse a sensation of mystical awe and reverence. This ethic forbade frivolous pagan portraits, bacchanalian orgy scenes, or delicate landscapes, as painted and sculpted by the Romans. Instead, biblical stories were depicted in richly colored mosaics—rows of figures against a gold background. (You can see some of the finest examples of this art at Ravenna, once the Western capital of the Empire, on the Adriatic coast.) Even altarpieces, painted on wood, followed the same model—stiff figures surrounded by gold, with no attempt made at an illusion of reality.

In the 13th century, the era of St. Francis and of a new humanitarian approach to Christianity, artists in Tuscany began to portray real people in real settings. Cimabue was the first to feel his way in this direction, but it was Giotto who broke decisively with the Byzantine style. Even if his sense of perspective is nowhere near correct and his figures still had typically Byzantine slanting eyes, he painted palpably solid people who, presumably, experienced real emotions.

By the end of the 14th century, the International Gothic Style (which had arrived from France) had made further progress toward realism, but more with depictions of plants, animals, and clothes than of the human figure. And, as you can see from Gentile da Fabriano's *Adoration of the Magi,* housed in the Galleria degli Uffizi in Florence, it was mainly a decorative art, much like a Byzantine mosaic.

Italian architecture during the Middle Ages followed a number of different trends. In the south, the solid Norman Romanesque style was dominant; towns such as Siena and Pisa in central Italy had their own Romanesque style, more graceful than its northern European counterparts. Like northern Romanesque, it was dominated by simple geometric forms, but buildings were covered with decorative toylike patterns done in multicolored marble. In northern Italy, building was in a more solemn red brick.

In Tuscany, the 13th century was a time of great political and economic growth, and there was a desire to celebrate the new wealth and power in the region's buildings. This is why such civic centers as the Palazzo Vecchio in Florence are so big and fortresslike. Florence's cathedral, the Duomo, was built on a colossal scale mainly in order to outdo the Pisans and the Sienese, Florence's rivals. All these Tuscan cathedrals are in the Italian version of Gothic, a style that originated in France and found its expression there in tall, soaring, light-and-airy verticality, intended to elevate the soul. The spiritual aspect of Gothic never really caught on in Italy, where the top priority for a church was to be grander and more imposing than the neighboring cities' churches.

Art in the Renaissance

The Renaissance, or "rebirth," did not evolve simply from a set of newfound artistic skills; the movement represented a revolution in attitudes whereby each individual was thought to play a specific role in the divine scheme of things. By fulfilling this role, it was believed, the individual gained a new dignity. It was no coincidence that this revolution took place in Florence, which in the 15th century was an influential, wealthy, highly evolved city-state. Artists here had the leisure, prestige, and self-confidence to develop their talent and produce works that would reflect this new dignity and strength as well as their own prowess. The sculptor Donatello, for example, wanted to astound rather than please with his defiant warts-and-all likenesses and their intense, heroic gazes. In painting, Masaccio's figures have a similarly assured air.

Art had changed gears in the early Renaissance: the Classical Age was now the model for a noble, moving, and realistic art. Artists studied ancient Roman ruins to learn about proportion and balance. They evolved the new science of perspective and took it to its limits with sometimes bizarre results, as in Uccello's dizzily receding *Deluge* (in Florence's church Santa Maria Novella) or his carousel-like *Battle of San Romano* (in the Uffizi in Florence). One of the most frequently used perspective techniques was foreshortening, or making an object seem smaller and more contracted, to create the illusion of distance. From this technique emerged the *sotto in su* effect—literally, "from below upward," meaning that the action in the picture takes place above you, with figures, buildings, and landscapes correspondingly foreshortened. It's a visual trick that must have delighted visitors who walked into, for example, Mantegna's Camera degli Sposi in Mantua and saw what appeared to be people curiously looking down at them through a gap in the ceiling.

The concept of the universal man was epitomized by the artist who was at home with an array of disciplines, including the science of perspective, Greek, Latin, anatomy, sculpture, poetry, architecture, philosophy—even engineering, as in the case of Leonardo da Vinci, the universal man par excellence. Not surprisingly, there was a change in attitude toward artists: whereas previously they had been considered workmen trained to carry out commissions, now they were seen as giant personalities, immensely skillful and with highly individual styles.

The new skills and realistic effects of Florentine painting rapidly found a sympathetic response among Venetian painters. Gentile Bellini and Antonio Carpaccio, just two of the many whose work fills the Accademia, took to covering their canvases with crowd scenes, buildings, canals, processions, dogs, ships, parrots, and chimneys. These were generally narrative paintings, telling the story of a saint's life or simply depicting everyday scenes.

It was the emphasis on color, though, that made Venetian art Venetian, and it was the late-15th-century masters of color, preeminently Giovanni Bellini and Giorgione, who began to use it as a means of evoking atmosphere. How different Giorgione's *Tempest* (in the Accademia) would be with a sunny blue sky instead of the ominous grays and dark greens that fill the background! For the first time, the atmosphere, not the figures, became the central focus of painting.

In architecture the Gothic excesses of the 13th century were toned down in the 14th, while the 15th ushered in a completely new approach. The humanist ideal was expressed through classical Roman design. In Florence, Brunelleschi used Roman columns for the basilica of San Lorenzo and Roman round arches—as opposed to pointed Gothic ones—for his Spedale degli Innocenti (Foundling Hospital), which is generally considered the first truly classical building of the Renaissance. Leon Battista Alberti's treatise on ideal proportion was even more influential as a manifesto of the Renaissance movement. Suddenly, architects had become erudite scholars and architecture far more earnest.

High Renaissance & Mannerism

Florence in the late 15th century and Rome in the early 16th (following its sacking in 1527) underwent a traumatic political and religious upheaval that naturally came to be reflected in art. Classical proportion and realism no longer seemed enough. The heroic style suddenly looked hollow and outdated. Tuscan artists such as Pontormo and Rosso Fiorentino found expression for their unease in discordant colors, elongated forms, tortured looks in staring eyes. Giambologna carved his *Hercules and the Centaur* (in Florence's Bargello) at the most agonizing moment of their battle, when Hercules bends the Centaur's back

to the point where it is about to snap. This is Mannerism, a style in which optimism and self-confidence are gone. What remains is a self-conscious, stylized virtuosity, the effect of which is neither to please (like Gothic) nor to impress (like Renaissance art) but to disquiet. Even Bronzino's portraits are cold, unsmiling, and far removed from the relaxed mood of the Renaissance portrait. By the 1530s an artistic exodus from Florence had taken place, and the city's golden age was over.

Venice, meanwhile, was following its own path. Titian's painting was a more virtuoso version of Bellini's and Giorgione's poetic style, but Titian later shifted the emphasis back to figures, rather than atmosphere, as the central focus of his paintings. Titian's younger contemporaries in Venice—Veronese, Tintoretto, and Bassano—wanted to make names for themselves. They started working on huge canvases—which gave them more freedom of movement—playing all sorts of visual games: juggling with viewpoints and perspective and using dazzlingly bright colors. This visual trickery parallels the self-conscious artifice of Florentine painting of the same period, but the exuberance of these Venetian painters, and the emotional quality of their work, remained significantly more vital than the arid works of central Italy toward the end of the 16th century.

Mannerism found a fairly precise equivalent in architecture. In Florence the rebellious younger generation (Michelangelo, Ammanati, Vasari) used the same architectural vocabulary as the Renaissance architects but distorted it deliberately and bizarrely in a way that would have made Alberti's hair stand on end. Michelangelo's staircase at the Biblioteca Laurenziana in Florence, for example, spills down like a gush of stone water, filling almost the entire floor space of the vestibule. Likewise, the inside walls are treated as if they were facades, though with columns and niches disproportionately large.

Andrea del Palladio, whose theories and elegant palaces were to be immensely influential on architecture elsewhere in Europe and as far north as England, was one of the greatest architects of the period.

The 17th & 18th Centuries

In the second half of the 16th century, Italy was caught up in the Counter-Reformation. This movement was a reaction against the Protestant Reformation of the Christian church that was sweeping through Europe. The Counter-Reformation enlisted art as an instrument for the diffusion of the Catholic faith. Artists were discouraged from expressing themselves as freely as they had before and from creating anything not of a religious nature. But within this framework they were able to evolve a style that appealed to the senses.

The Baroque—an emotional and heroic style that lasted through most of the 17th century—was propaganda art, designed to overwhelm the masses through its visual illusion, dramatic lighting, strong colors, and violent movement. There was an element of seduction in this propaganda: the repressive religiosity of the Counter-Reformation went hand in hand with a barely disguised eroticism. The best-known example of this ambiguity is Bernini's sculpture of the *Ecstasy of Saint Teresa* in Rome, in which the saint sinks back in what could be a swoon of either pain or pleasure, while a smiling angel stands over her holding an arrow. Both the painting and architecture of this period make extensive use of sensuous curves.

The cradle of the Baroque was Rome, where Pietro da Cortona and Bernini channeled their genius into spectacular theatrical frescoes, sculptures, palaces, and churches. Rome had become the artistic center of Italy. Florence was artistically dead by this time, and Venice was producing only hack imitations of Titian's and Tintoretto's paintings.

In the 18th century Venice came back into its own and Rome was practically finished as an artistic center. Venetian artists adopted the soft, overripe version of Baroque—known as rococo—that had originated in France. Free from the spiritual ideals that motivated the Baroque style, rococo celebrated sensuousness (and sensuality) for its own sake. Although Venice was nearing the last stages of its political decline, there was still immense wealth in the city, mostly in the hands of families who wished to make the world know about it—and what better way than through vast, dazzling rococo canvases, reassuringly stylized and removed from reality? The revival began with Sebastiano Ricci and was expertly elaborated on by Tiepolo. But it could never have taken place had there not been a return to the city's great artistic traditions. Late-16th-century color technique and expertise were drawn on and fused with what had been learned from the Baroque to create the magical, decadent world of the Venetian rococo.

This was the final flowering of Venetian painting. The death of Francesco Guardi in 1793, compounded by the fall of the Republic of Venice in 1797, marked the effective end of the city's artistic life. Neoclassicism found no champion here, except for the sculptor Canova, who, in any case, did his finest work after he left Venice.

Today the great tradition of Italian art is widely diffused, perhaps diluted, but it is certainly too early to write its obituary. That has been done periodically over the past 20 centuries, inevitably to the chagrin of the mistaken commentator. In the midst of the burgeoning vitality, which charms and occasionally maddens the visitor, the arts are not long to be neglected. Italians live the tradition too deeply.

—Sheila Brownlee

ARTISTICALLY SPEAKING: A GLOSSARY

You can increase your enjoyment of Italy's artistic treasures by knowing a few art and architecture terms.

Apse: A semicircular terminus found behind the altar in a church.

Atrium: The courtyard in front of the entrance to an ancient Roman villa or an early church.

Badia: Abbey.

Baldacchino: A canopy—often made of stone—above a church altar, supported by columns.

Baptistery: A separate structure or area in a church where rites of baptism are held.

Baroque: A 17th-century European art movement in which dramatic, elaborate ornamentation was used to stir viewers' emotions. The most famous Italian baroque artists were Carracci and Bernini.

Basilica: A rectangular Roman public building divided into aisles by rows of columns. Many early churches were built on the basilican plan, but the term is also applied to some churches without specific reference to architecture.

Belvedere: A lookout point; the word means "beautiful view."

Campanile: A bell tower of a church.

Capital: The crowning section of a column, usually decorated with Doric, Ionic, or Corinthian ornament.

Chiaroscuro: Literally "light/dark"; used to describe the distribution of light and shade in a painting, either with a marked contrast or a muted tonal gradation.

Cinquecento: Literally, "five hundred," used in Italian to refer to the 16th century.

Cupola: Dome.

Duomo: Cathedral.

Fresco: A wall-painting technique, used in Roman times and again in the early Renaissance, in which pigment was applied to wet plaster.

Gothic: Medieval architectural and ornamental style featuring pointed arches, high interior vaulting, and flying buttresses to emphasize height and, symbolically, an ascent to heaven.

Grotesques: Decorations of fanciful human and animal forms, embellished with flowers; first used in Nero's Golden House and rediscovered during the Renaissance.

Loggia: Roofed balcony or gallery.

Maestà: The Virgin and Child enthroned in majesty, often surrounded by angels, saints, or prophets.

Mannerism: Style of the mid-16th century in which artists—such as Pontormo and Rosso Fiorentino—sought to replace the warm, humanizing ideals of Leonardo and Raphael with super-elegant, emotionally cold forms. Portraits in the Mannerist style feature lively colors and often strangely contorted bodies.

Nave: The central aisle of a church.

Palazzo: A palace or, more generally, any large building.

Perspective: The illusion of three-dimensional space that was achieved in the early 15th century with the discovery that all parallel lines running in one direction appear to meet at a single point on the horizon known as the vanishing point.

Piano nobile: The main floor of a palace (the first floor above ground level).

Pietà: Literally "piety"; refers to an image of the Virgin Mary holding the crucified body of Christ on her lap.

Predella: A series of small paintings found below the main section of an altarpiece.

Putti: Cherubs, cupids, or other images of infant boys in painting.

Quattrocento: Literally "four hundred"; refers to the 15th century.

Renaissance: Major school of Italian art, literature, and philosophy (14th century–16th century) that fused innovations in realism with the rediscovery of the great heritage of classical antiquity. After Giotto introduced a new naturalism into painting in the early 14th century, Florentine artists of the early and mid-15th century such as Masaccio and Fra Filippo Lippi paved the way for the later 15th-century realism of Botticelli and Ghirlandaio. The movement particularly flourished in Florence and Venice, but most other Italian cities were participants as well. Some scholars believe that the movement culminated in Rome with the High Renaissance (circa 1490–1520) and the masterpieces of Leonardo, Raphael, and Michelangelo.

Rococo: Light, dainty 18th-century art and architectural style created in reaction to Baroque. Tiepolo is the leading painter of the style.

Romanesque: Architectural style of the 11th and 12th centuries that reworked ancient Roman forms, particularly barrel and groin vaults. Stark, severe, and magisterial, Romanesque basilicas are among Italy's most awe-inspiring churches.

Triptych: A three-panel painting executed on wood.

Trompe l'oeil: An artistic technique employed to "fool the eye" into believing that the object or scene depicted is actually real.

BOOKS & MOVIES

Books

Italian history, art, and culture have been examined in countless English-language books. Their profusion is a testament both to the wonders of Italy and to the challenge of defining what exactly "Italian" is. *The Italians,* by Luigi Barzini, dates from 1964 but remains a valuable effort toward this end; its lively analysis of the national character is both enlightening and frustrating in ways that make reading it a genuinely Italian experience.

Before, during, and after a visit to Italy, it's a pleasure to compare notes with your fellow travelers. Classics in the travel-essay genre, often mixing firsthand experience and selected history, include Jan Morris's *World of Venice,* Mary McCarthy's *Venice Observed* and *The Stones of Florence,* Eleanor Clark's *Rome and a Villa,* and James Lees-Milne's *Roman Mornings* and *Venetian Mornings.* Stepping further back in time, you can sample perceptive musings about Italy in Henry James's *Italian Hours* and Edith Wharton's *Italian Backgrounds* and *Italian Villas and their Gardens.*

Some English-speaking visitors have chosen to settle in Italy long-term, and the resulting expatriate memoirs make up their own literary subgenre. In *A Tuscan Childhood,* Kinta Beevor lovingly recounts growing up in a castle near Carrara between the two world wars. Iris Origo's *War in Val d'Orcia,* covering the years 1943–1944, is a moving document of life in wartime. Matthew Spender's *Within Tuscany: Reflections on a Time and Place* and Lisa St. Aubin de Terán's *A Valley in Italy: The Many Seasons of a Villa in Umbria* are both rewarding reads. Shirley Hazzard deftly chronicles her 1960s friendship with English writer Graham Greene in *Greene on Capri,* and in the process reveals much about the island. Tim Parks's *Italian Neighbors* tells with candor and good humor of the contemporary expatriate life in Verona.

For a general historical and art history framework, Harry Hearder's *Italy, A Short History* cuts right to the chase, with 2,000 years covered in less than 300 pages. For in-depth classical history, there's nothing quite like Edward Gibbon's *Decline and Fall of the Roman Empire,* an 18th-century masterpiece (available in abridged form) that has withstood the test of time. If you're more interested in recent events, consult Paul Ginsborg's *Italy and Its Discontents: 1980–2001* or Peter Robb's *Midnight in Sicily,* the latter a mix of memoir and 20th-century history concerning the beauties and brutalities of the *mezzogiorno.* Ann Cornelisen's *Women of the Shadows* gives another perspective on southern Italy, portraying the lives of peasant women in the years following World War II.

Michael Levey's clear and concise treatments of the Renaissance, *Early Renaissance* and *High Renaissance,* are good introductions to the most vaunted of artistic periods. Two wonderfully written and beautifully illustrated volumes on the subject are John T. Paoletti and Gary M. Radke's *Art in Renaissance Italy* and Evelyn Welch's eloquent *Art and Society in Italy 1350–1500. The Civilization of the Renaissance in Italy,* by 19th-century Swiss historian Jacob Burckhardt, is the classic study of the culture and politics of the time.

You can learn about the Renaissance and what comes after from those who actually lived it in *The Autobiography of Benvenuto Cellini,* Giorgio Vasari's *Lives of the Artists,* and Machiavelli's *The Prince,* and some recent studies of famous Renaissance and baroque figures offer fine opportunities to enter into lives lived centuries ago. Ross King has followed up his successful *Brunelleschi's Dome* with a tale about Michelangelo and Pope Julius II in *Michelangelo and the Pope's Ceiling.* R. W. B. Lewis fleshes out the details of perhaps Italy's most famous poet in *Dante;* also worth a look in the Penguin Lives series is Sherwin Nuland's *Leonardo da Vinci.* A more scholarly but eminently readable biography is *Leon Battista Alberti: Master Builder of the Italian Renaissance,* by Princeton Renaissance historian Anthony Grafton. Though the title is somewhat of a misnomer (as it's more about the father), Dava Sobel's *Galileo's Daughter* artfully brings to life the brilliant astronomer and his devotion to his family, particularly his first-born, Suor Maria Celeste. Christopher Hibbert's *House of Medici* details the rise and fall of Florence's first family. Andrea di Robilant deftly chronicles the romance of one of his ancestors in *A Venetian Affair: A True Story of Impossible Love in the 18th Century.*

For aficionados of Rome's artistic treasures, Georgina Masson's *Companion Guide to Rome* is a must. Eloquent writing and important scholarship are found in the works of such celebrated art historians as Richard Krautheimer, John Pope-Hennessy, John Shearman, Irving Lavin, Charles de Tolnay, and André Chastel. *Inside Rome,* from Phaidon Press, is a picture book that gives you a tantalizing peek into the sumptuous palaces, galleries, private homes, athletic clubs, and even historic coffeehouses of the eternal city. Fodor's *Holy Rome: A Millennium Guide to the Christian Sights* traces Christianity in Rome, as it can be seen today, through gorgeous photography, thematic essays, easy-to-follow itineraries, and biographical sketches. To some observers, the most beautiful book about the most beautiful city in the world is Richard de Combray's *Venice, Frail Barrier.*

Fiction often imparts a greater sense of a place than straight history books: Jacqueline Park reconstructs a forbidden love affair in 15th-century Ferrara between a nobleman and a Jewish woman in *The Secret Life of Grazia dei Rossi.* Margaret Forster provides a firsthand account of the life of the Brownings (Robert and Elizabeth Barrett) in Italy as seen through the eyes of a servant in *Lady's Maid.* Umberto

Eco's *The Name of the Rose* is a gripping murder mystery that will leave you with tremendous insight into monastic life in medieval Italy. Susan Sontag's *Volcano Lover,* set in 18th-century Naples, is about Sir William Hamilton, his wife, Emma, and Lord Nelson. *The Leopard,* by Giuseppe di Lampedusa, is a compelling portrait of Sicily during the political upheavals of the 1860s. Historical fiction set in the pre–World World II era includes Giorgio Bassani's quietly moving *Garden of the Finzi-Continis,* which tells of the lives of an upper-class Jewish family from Ferrara.

Other classics of 20th-century Italian fiction available in translation include *History: A Novel,* by Elsa Morante, *The Woman of Rome,* by Alberto Moravia, and *Zeno's Conscience,* by Italo Svevo. Lovers of detective stories will be highly entertained by the antics of Aurelio Zen, Michael Dibdin's bumbling detective. It's best to read them in order, as he builds on characters and situations; each novel is set in an Italian city. The series commences in Perugia with *Ratking.* Iain Pears writes about Italian art heists in his colorful novels; *Giotto's Hand* is a good place to start.

If you truly want to understand the Italian psyche, learn about the national passion for *calcio* (soccer). Joe McGinness offers some fine insights on the subject as he tags along with a team from Seria B in *The Miracle of Castel di Sangro.* Tim Parks made his own soccer odyssey with the Verona club and recorded his experiences in *A Season with Verona.*

To catch glimpses of the Tuscan landscape, pick up Harold Acton's *Great Houses of Tuscany: The Tuscan Villas* or Carey More's *Views from a Tuscan Vineyard.* The glories of historic Italian gardens are caught in the ravishing photographs of Judith Chatfield's *Gardens of the Italian Lakes,* Ethne Clark's *Gardens of Tuscany,* and Nicolas Saphiena's *Gardens of Naples.* Also worth a look is Joan Marble's *Notes from an Italian Garden.*

Fodor's own Escape Guides illuminate two of Italy's special regions in photos and prose. In the pages of *Escape to Tuscany*, stay at the convent where *The English Patient* was filmed and go ballooning over Chianti's vineyards, and in *Escape to the Amalfi Coast*, witness that area's impossible array of blues.

Although every year there are more and more cookbooks on Italian food, Waverley Root's *Food of Italy*, published in 1977, is still a handy (if not infallible) reference. Cooking inspiration may be found in Ada Boni's *The Talisman Italian Cook Book*, the Italian equivalent of the *Joy of Cooking*. Marcella Hazan's *Essentials of Italian Cooking* may be the definitive work in English. And finally, consult Burton Anderson's *Best Italian Wines* to help guide you through wine lists.

Movies

Italy has been the setting for numerous English-language films. The Academy Award–winning melodrama *The English Patient* (1996) makes ample use of the Italian landscape. *Tea with Mussolini* (1999) is Franco Zeffirelli's love letter to a group of Anglophone women who helped raise a character very much like the director himself in pre–World War II Tuscany. In *Under the Tuscan Sun*, the movie based on Frances Mayes's real-life fairy tale for smart women, the real star is the scenery. *The Talented Mr. Ripley* (1999), based on a Patricia Highsmith novel, is set in the sumptuous Italy of the 1950s. Indispensable and not at all dated are *A Room with a View* (1986), the Merchant/Ivory adaptation of the E. M. Forster novel, and *Enchanted April* (1991), which depicts the awakening spirits of four English women in Italy.

The Italian film industry has been prolific and often excellent. The acknowledged master is Federico Fellini, creator of the classics *Nights of Cabiria*, *La Strada*, and *La Dolce Vita*, among many others. Also counted among the leading Italian directors are Vittorio De Sica (*The Bicycle Thief*, *Umberto D.*), Luchino Visconti (*Ossessioni*, *Rocco and His Brothers*), and Roberto Rossellini (*Open City*, starring the incomparable Anna Magnani). More recently, *Cinema Paradiso* (1990), *Il Postino* (*The Postman*, 1995), and *La Vita è Bella* (*Life Is Beautiful*, 1997) have been international hits. Popular and critically acclaimed Italian films of the past few years include *La Finestra di Fronte* (*The Window across the Street*, 2002), *Ricordati di Me* (*Remember Me*, 2002), and *Io Non Ho Paura* (*I'm Not Scared*, 2003).

CHRONOLOGY

ca. 800 BC Rise of Etruscan city-states.

753 Traditional date for the founding of Rome.

750 Greek city-states begin to colonize Sicily and southern Italy.

600 Latin language becomes dominant in Etruscan League; Rome becomes established urban center.

510 Foundation of the Roman republic; expulsion of Etruscans from Roman territory.

410 Rome adopts the 12 Tables of Law, based on Greek models.

343 Roman conquest of Greek colonies in Campania.

312 Completion of Via Appia (Appian Way) to the south of Rome; an extensive Roman road system begins to develop.

264–241 First Punic War (with Carthage): increased naval power helps Rome gain control of southern Italy and then Sicily.

218–200 Second Punic War: Hannibal's attempted conquest of Italy, using elephants, is eventually crushed.

150 Roman Forum begins to take shape as the principal civic center in Italy.

146 Third Punic War: Rome razes city of Carthage and emerges as the dominant Mediterranean force.

133 Rome rules entire Mediterranean Basin except Egypt.

49 Julius Caesar conquers Gaul.

45 Civil war leaves Julius Caesar as sole ruler; Caesar's Forum is established.

44 Julius Caesar is assassinated.

31 The Battle of Actium resolves the power struggle that continued after Caesar's death; Octavian becomes sole ruler.

27 Rome's Imperial Age begins; Octavian (now named Augustus) becomes the first emperor and is later deified. The Augustan Age is celebrated in the works of Virgil (70 BC–AD 19), Ovid (43 BC–AD 17), Livy (59 BC–AD 17), and Horace (65–8 BC).

14 AD Augustus dies.

29 Jesus is crucified in the Roman colony of Judea.

43 Rome invades Britain.

50 Rome is the largest city in the world, with a population of a million.

65 Emperor Nero begins the persecution of Christians in the Empire; Saints Peter and Paul are executed.

70–80 Vespasian builds the Colosseum.

98–117   Trajan's military successes are celebrated with his Baths (98), Forum (110), and Column (113); the Roman Empire reaches its apogee.

ca. 150–200   Christianity gains a foothold within the Empire, with the help of the theological writings of Clement, Tertullian, and Origen.

165   A smallpox epidemic ravages the Empire.

212   Roman citizenship is conferred on all nonslaves in the Empire.

238   The first wave of Germanic invasions penetrates Italy.

293   Diocletian reorganizes the Empire into West and East.

313   The Edict of Milan grants toleration of Christianity within the Empire.

330   Constantine founds a new Imperial capital (Constantinople) in the East.

410   Rome is sacked by Visigoths.

476   The last Roman emperor, Romulus Augustus, is deposed. The Roman Empire falls.

552   Eastern emperor Justinian (527–565) recovers control of Italy.

570   Lombards gain control of much of Italy, including Rome.

590   Papal power expands under Gregory the Great.

610   Heraldius revives the Eastern Empire, thereafter known as the Byzantine Empire.

774   Frankish ruler Charlemagne (742–814) invades Italy under papal authority and is crowned Holy Roman Emperor by Pope Leo III (800).

ca. 800–900   The breakup of Charlemagne's (Carolingian) realm leads to the rise of Italian city-states.

811   Venice is founded by mainlanders escaping Barbarian invasions.

1054   The Schism develops between Greek (Orthodox) and Latin churches.

ca. 1060   Europe's first university is founded in Bologna.

1077   Pope Gregory VII leads the Holy See into conflict with the Germanic Holy Roman Empire.

1152–90   Frederick I (Barbarossa) is crowned Holy Roman Emperor (1155); punitive expeditions by his forces (Ghibellines) are countered by the Guelphs, supporters of the powerful Papal States in central Italy. Guelph-Ghibelline conflict becomes a feature of medieval life.

1204   Crusaders, led by Venetian doge Dandolo, capture Constantinople.

1257   The first of four wars is declared between Genoa and Venice; at stake is maritime control of the eastern Mediterranean.

1262   Florentine bankers issue Europe's first bills of exchange.

1264   Charles I of Anjou invades Italy, intervening in the continuing Guelph-Ghibelline conflict.

1275	Marco Polo (1254–1324) reaches the Orient.
1290–1375	Tuscan literary giants Dante Alighieri (1265–1321), Francesco Petrarch (1304–74), and Giovanni Boccaccio (1313–75) give written imprimatur to modern Italian language.
1309	The pope moves to Avignon in France, under the protection of French kings.
1355	Venetian doge Marino Falier is executed for treason.
1376	The pope returns to Rome, but rival Avignonese popes stand in opposition, creating the Great Schism until 1417.
1380	Venice finally disposes of the Genovese threat in the Battle of Chioggia.
1402	The last German intervention into Italy is repulsed by the Lombards.
1443	Brunelleschi's (1377–1446) cupola is completed on Florence's Duomo.
1447	Nicholas V founds the Vatican Library and inaugurates an era of papal enrichment of the arts.
1469–92	Lorenzo "Il Magnifico" (1449–92), the Medici patron of the arts, rules in Florence.
1498	Girolamo Savonarola (1452–98), the fanatical Dominican friar, is executed for heresy after leading Florence into a drive for moral purification, typified by his burning of books and ephemera in the "Bonfire of Vanities."
1499	Leonardo da Vinci's (1452–1519) *Last Supper* is completed in Milan.
1508	Michelangelo (1475–1564) begins work on the Cappella Sistina.
1509	Raphael (1483–1520) begins work on his Stanze in the Vatican.
1513	Machiavelli's (1469–1527) *The Prince* is published.
1521	The pope excommunicates Martin Luther (1483–1546) of Germany, precipitating the Protestant Reformation.
1545–63	The Council of Trent formulates the Roman Catholic response to the Protestant Reformation.
1546	Andrea Palladio (1508–80), architectural genius, wins his first commission in Vicenza.
1571	The combined navies of Venice, Spain, and the Papacy defeat the Turks in the Battle of Lepanto.
1626	The Basilica di San Pietro is completed in Rome.
1633	Galileo Galilei (1564–1642) faces the Inquisition.
1652	Sant'Agnese in Agone church, Borromini's (1599–1667) baroque masterpiece, is completed in Rome.
1667	The Piazza di San Pietro, designed by Bernini (1598–1680), is completed.
ca. 1700	Opera develops as an art form in Italy.

1720–90 The Great Age of the Grand Tour: northern Europeans visit Italy and start the vogue for classical studies. Among the famous visitors are Edward Gibbon (1758), Jacques-Louis David (1775), and Johann Wolfgang von Goethe (1786).

1778 Teatro alla Scala is completed in Milan.

1796 Napoléon begins his Italian campaigns, annexing Rome and imprisoning Pope Pius VI four years later.

1815 Austria controls much of Italy after Napoléon's downfall.

1848 Revolutionary troops under *Risorgimento* (Unification) leaders Giuseppe Mazzini (1805–72) and Giuseppe Garibaldi (1807–82) establish a republic in Rome.

1849 French troops crush rebellion and restore Pope Pius IX.

1860 Garibaldi and his "Thousand" defeat the Bourbon rulers in Sicily and Naples.

1870 Rome is finally captured by Risorgimento troops and is declared capital of Italy by King Vittorio Emanuele II.

1900 King Umberto I is assassinated by an anarchist; he is succeeded by King Vittorio Emanuele III.

1915 Italy enters World War I on the side of the Allies.

1922 Fascist "black shirts" under Benito Mussolini (1883–1945) march on Rome; Mussolini becomes prime minister and later "Il Duce" (literally "leader") of Italy.

1929 The Lateran Treaty: Mussolini recognizes Vatican City as a sovereign state, and the Church recognizes Rome as the capital of Italy.

1940–44 In World War II, Italy fights on the side of the Axis powers until its capitulation (1943), when Mussolini flees Rome. Italian partisans and Allied troops from the landings at Anzio (January 1944) win victory at Cassino (March 1944) and force the eventual withdrawal of German troops from Italy.

1957 The Treaty of Rome is signed, and Italy becomes a founding member of the European Economic Community.

1966 November flood damages many of Florence's artistic treasures.

1968–79 The growth of left-wing activities leads to the formation of the Red Brigades and provokes right-wing reactions. Bombings and kidnappings culminate in the abduction and murder of Prime Minister Aldo Moro (1916–78).

1980 Southern Italy is hit by a severe earthquake.

1991 Waves of refugees from neighboring Albania flood southern ports on the Adriatic. Mt. Etna erupts, spewing forth a lava stream that threatens the Sicilian town of Zafferana.

1992 The Christian Democrat Party, in power throughout the postwar period, loses its hold on a relative majority in Parliament.

1993 Italians vote for sweeping reforms after the Tangentopoli (Bribe City) scandal exposes widespread political corruption, including politicians' collusion with organized crime. A bomb outside the Galleria degli Uffizi in Florence kills five but spares the museum's most precious artwork; authorities blame the Cosa Nostra, flexing its muscles in the face of a crackdown.

1994 A center-right coalition wins in spring elections, and media magnate Silvio Berlusconi becomes premier—only to be deposed within a year. Italian politics seem to be evolving into the equivalent of a two-party system.

1995 Newly appointed Lamberto Dini takes hold of the government's rudder and, as president of the Council of Ministers, institutes major reforms and replaces old-line politicians.

1996 A league of center-left parties wins national elections and puts together a government coalition that sees the Democratic Party of the Left (PDS), the former Communist party, into power for the first time ever in Italy.

1997 Political stability and an austerity program put Italy on track toward the European Monetary Union and adoption of the single euro currency. Though only a copy, the statue of Roman emperor Marcus Aurelius is returned to its pedestal on the Campidoglio as a symbol of Rome's historic grandeur. A series of earthquakes hits the mountainous interior of central Italy, severely damaging villages and some historic towns. In Assisi, portions of the vault of the Basilica di San Francesco crumble, destroying frescoes by Cimabue.

1998 In February a U.S. Navy jet fighter on a low-flying training mission through the Italian Alps cuts a ski gondola cable, killing 20 people. Romano Prodi's center-left government, widely praised for its economic policies and lack of scandals, is brought down by a no-confidence vote in October, after the Reformed-Communist Party (PCI) withdraws its support for Prodi. The center-left regroups and forms a new government under Massimo D'Alema, leader of the former Communist Party, who in large part continues Prodi's policies. The pope visits Cuba. More than a million people see the Shroud of Turin, on display for just a few months.

1999 Italy serves as a principal base for NATO air raids against Serbia. Rome continues preparations for the Jubilee celebrations in 2000 with an array of public works projects. The International Olympic Committee chooses Turin to host the 2006 Winter Olympics.

2000 The Jubilee of the third millennium is proclaimed by Pope John Paul II. Millions of pilgrims flock to Rome.

2001 Media mogul Silvio Berlusconi is elected prime minister for the second time.

2002 The lira is supplanted by the euro as the currency of the land. Padre Pio (1887–1968), a revered Franciscan from Puglia and the first priest in church history to receive the stigmata, is canonized.

ITALIAN VOCABULARY

English	Italian	Pronunciation

Basics

English	Italian	Pronunciation
Yes/no	Sí/No	see/no
Please	Per favore	pear fa-**vo**-ray
Yes, please	Sí grazie	see **grah**-tsee-ay
Thank you	Grazie	**grah**-tsee-ay
You're welcome	Prego	**pray**-go
Excuse me, sorry	Scusi	**skoo**-zee
Sorry!	Mi dispiace!	mee dis-spee-**ah**-chay
Good morning/ afternoon	Buongiorno	bwohn-**jor**-no
Good evening	Buona sera	**bwoh**-na **say**-ra
Good bye	Arrivederci	a-ree-vah-**dare**-chee
Mr. (Sir)	Signore	see-**nyo**-ray
Mrs. (Ma'am)	Signora	see-**nyo**-ra
Miss	Signorina	see-nyo-**ree**-na
Pleased to meet you	Piacere	pee-ah-**chair**-ray
How are you?	Come sta?	**ko**-may **stah**
Very well, thanks	Bene, grazie	**ben**-ay **grah**-tsee-ay
And you?	E lei?	ay **lay**-ee
Hello (phone)	Pronto?	**proan**-to

Numbers

English	Italian	Pronunciation
one	uno	**oo**-no
two	due	**doo**-ay
three	tre	tray
four	quattro	**kwah**-tro
five	cinque	**cheen**-kway
six	sei	say
seven	sette	**set**-ay
eight	otto	**oh**-to
nine	nove	**no**-vay
ten	dieci	dee-**eh**-chee
eleven	undici	**oon**-dee-chee
twelve	dodici	**doe**-dee-chee
thirteen	tredici	**tray**-dee-chee

fourteen	quattordici	kwa-**tore**-dee-chee
fifteen	quindici	**kwin**-dee-chee
sixteen	sedici	**say**-dee-chee
seventeen	diciassette	dee-cha-**set**-ay
eighteen	diciotto	dee-**cho**-to
nineteen	diciannove	dee-cha-**no**-vay
twenty	venti	**vain**-tee
twenty-one	ventuno	vain-**too**-no
twenty-two	ventidue	vain-tee-**doo**-ay
thirty	trenta	**train**-ta
forty	quaranta	kwa-**rahn**-ta
fifty	cinquanta	cheen-**kwahn**-ta
sixty	sessanta	seh-**sahn**-ta
seventy	settanta	seh-**tahn**-ta
eighty	ottanta	o-**tahn**-ta
ninety	novanta	no-**vahn**-ta
one hundred	cento	**chen**-to
one thousand	mille	**mee**-lay
ten thousand	diecimila	dee-eh-chee-**mee**-la

Useful Phrases

Do you speak English?	Parla inglese?	**par**-la een-**glay**-zay
I don't speak Italian	Non parlo italiano	non **par**-lo ee-tal-**yah**-no
I don't understand	Non capisco	non ka-**peess**-ko
Can you please repeat?	Può ripetere?	pwo ree-**pet**-ay-ray
Slowly!	Lentamente!	**len**-ta-men-tay
I don't know	Non lo so	non lo **so**
I'm American/ British	Sono americano(a)	**so**-no a-may-ree-**kah**-no(a)
	Sono inglese	**so**-no een-**glay**-zay
What's your name?	Come si chiama?	**ko**-may see kee-**ah**-ma
My name is . . .	Mi chiamo . . .	mee kee-**ah**-mo
What time is it?	Che ore sono?	kay **o**-ray **so**-no
How?	Come?	**ko**-may
When?	Quando?	**kwan**-doe
Yesterday/today/ tomorrow	Ieri/oggi/domani	**yer**-ee/**o**-jee/ do-**mah**-nee

This morning/ ternoon	Stamattina/Oggi pomeriggio	sta-ma-**tee**-na/**o**-jee af-po-mer-**ee**-jo
Tonight	Stasera	sta-**ser**-a
What?	Che cosa?	kay **ko**-za
What is it?	Che cos'è?	kay ko-**zay**
Why?	Perché?	pear-**kay**
Who?	Chi?	kee
Where is . . .	Dov'è . . .	doe-**veh**
the bus stop?	la fermata dell'autobus?	la fer-**mah**-ta del ow-toe-**booss**
the train station?	la stazione?	la sta-tsee-**oh**-nay
the subway station?	la metropolitana?	la may-tro-po-lee-**tah**-na
the terminal?	il terminale?	eel ter-mee-**nah**-lay
the post office?	l'ufficio postale?	loo-**fee**-cho po-**stah**-lay
the bank?	la banca?	la **bahn**-ka
the . . . hotel?	l'hotel . . .?	lo-**tel**
the store?	il negozio?	eel nay-**go**-tsee-o
the cashier?	la cassa?	la **kah**-sa
the . . . museum?	il museo . . .?	eel moo-**zay**-o
the hospital?	l'ospedale?	lo-spay-**dah**-lay
the first aid station?	il pronto soccorso?	eel **pron**-to so-**kor**-so
the elevator?	l'ascensore?	la-shen-**so**-ray
a telephone?	un telefono?	oon tay-**lay**-fo-no
Where are the restrooms?	Dov'è il bagno?	do-**vay** eel **bahn**-yo
Here/there	Qui/là	kwee/la
Left/right	A sinistra/a destra	a see-**neess**-tra/a **des**-tra
Straight ahead	Avanti dritto	a-**vahn**-tee **dree**-to
Is it near/far?	È vicino/lontano?	ay vee-**chee**-no/lon-**tah**-no
I'd like . . .	Vorrei . . .	vo-**ray**
a room	una camera	**oo**-na **kah**-may-ra
the key	la chiave	la kee-**ah**-vay
a newspaper	un giornale	oon jor-**nah**-lay
a stamp	un francobollo	oon frahn-ko-**bo**-lo
I'd like to buy . . .	Vorrei comprare . . .	vo-**ray** kom-**prah**-ray
a cigar	un sigaro	oon see-**gah**-ro
cigarettes	delle sigarette	**day**-lay see-ga-**ret**-ay
some matches	dei fiammiferi	**day**-ee **fee**-ah-mee-fer-ee
some soap	una saponetta	**oo**-na sa-po-**net**-a
a city plan	una pianta della città	**oo**-na **pyahn**-ta day-la chee-**tah**

a road map of . . .	una carta stradale di . . .	**oo**-na **cart**-a stra-**dah**-lay dee
a country map	una carta geografica	**oo**-na **cart**-a jay-o-**grah**-fee-ka
a magazine	una rivista	**oo**-na ree-**veess**-ta
envelopes	delle buste	**day**-lay **booss**-tay
writing paper	della carta da lettere	**day**-la **cart**-a da **let**-air-ay
a postcard	una cartolina	**oo**-na car-toe-**lee**-na
a guidebook	una guida turistica	**oo**-na **gwee**-da too-**reess**-tee-ka

How much is it?	Quanto costa?	**kwahn**-toe **coast**-a
It's expensive/ cheap	È caro/economico	ay **car**-o/ay-ko-**no**-mee-ko
A little/a lot	Poco/tanto	**po**-ko/**tahn**-to
More/less	Più/meno	pee-**oo**/**may**-no
Enough/too (much)	Abbastanza/troppo	a-bas-**tahn**-sa/**tro**-po
I am sick	Sto male	sto **mah**-lay
Call a doctor	Chiama un dottore	kee-**ah**-mah oon doe-**toe**-ray
Help!	Aiuto!	a-**yoo**-toe
Stop!	Alt!	ahlt
Fire!	Al fuoco!	ahl **fwo**-ko
Caution/Look out!	Attenzione!	a-ten-**syon**-ay

Dining Out

A bottle of . . .	Una bottiglia di . . .	**oo**-na bo-**tee**-lee-ah dee
A cup of . . .	Una tazza di . . .	**oo**-na **tah**-tsa dee
A glass of . . .	Un bicchiere di . . .	oon bee-key-**air**-ay dee
Bill/check	Il conto	eel **cone**-toe
Bread	Il pane	eel **pah**-nay
Breakfast	La prima colazione	la **pree**-ma ko-la-**tsee**-oh-nay
Cocktail/aperitif	L'aperitivo	la-pay-ree-**tee**-vo
Dinner	La cena	la **chen**-a
Fixed-price menu	Menù a prezzo fisso	may-**noo** a **pret**-so **fee**-so
Fork	La forchetta	la for-**ket**-a
I am diabetic	Ho il diabete	o eel dee-a-**bay**-tay
I am vegetarian	Sono vegetariano/a	**so**-no vay-jay-ta-ree-**ah**-no/a
I'd like . . .	Vorrei . . .	vo-**ray**

I'd like to order	Vorrei ordinare	vo-**ray** or-dee-**nah**-ray
Is service included?	Il servizio è incluso?	eel ser-**vee**-tzee-o ay een-**kloo**-zo
It's good/bad	È buono/cattivo	ay **bwo**-no/ka-**tee**-vo
It's hot/cold	È caldo/freddo	ay **kahl**-doe/**fred**-o
Knife	Il coltello	eel kol-**tel**-o
Lunch	Il pranzo	eel **prahnt**-so
Menu	Il menù	eel may-**noo**
Napkin	Il tovagliolo	eel toe-va-lee-**oh**-lo
Please give me . . .	Mi dia . . .	mee **dee**-a
Salt	Il sale	eel **sah**-lay
Spoon	Il cucchiaio	eel koo-kee-**ah**-yo
Sugar	Lo zucchero	lo **tsoo**-ker-o
Waiter/Waitress	Cameriere/ cameriera	ka-mare-**yer**-ay/ ka-mare-**yer**-a
Wine list	La lista dei vini	la **lee**-sta **day**-ee **vee**-nee

MENU GUIDE

English	Italian
Set menu	Menù a prezzo fisso
Dish of the day	Piatto del giorno
Specialty of the house	Specialità della casa
Local specialties	Specialità locali
Extra charge	Extra . . .
In season	Di stagione
Cover charge/Service charge	Coperto/Servizio

Breakfast

Butter	Burro
Croissant	Cornetto
Eggs	Uova
Honey	Miele
Jam/Marmalade	Marmellata
Roll	Panino
Toast	Pane tostato

Starters

Assorted cold cuts	Affettati misti
Assorted seafood	Antipasto di pesce
Assorted appetizers	Antipasto misto
Toasted rounds of bread, fried or toasted in oil	Crostini/Crostoni
Diced-potato and vegetable salad with mayonnaise	Insalata russa
Eggplant parmigiana	Melanzane alla parmigiana
Fried mozzarella sandwich	Mozzarella in carrozza
Ham and melon	Prosciutto e melone
Cooked sausages and cured meats	Salumi cotti
Filled pastry shells	Vol-au-vents

Soups

"Angel hair," thin noodle soup	Capelli d'angelo
Cream of . . .	Crema di . . .
Pasta-and-bean soup	Pasta e fagioli
Egg-drop and parmesan cheese soup	Stracciatella

Pasta, Rice, and Pizza

Filled pasta	Agnolotti/ravioli/tortellini
Potato dumplings	Gnocchi

Semolina dumplings	Gnocchi alla romana
Pasta	Pasta
with four cheeses	*al quattro formaggi*
with basil/cheese/pine nuts/ garlic sauce	*al pesto*
with tomato-based meat sauce	*al ragù*
with tomato sauce	*al sugo* or *al pomodoro*
with butter	*in bianco* or *al burro*
with egg, parmesan cheese, and pepper	*alla carbonara*
green (spinach-based) pasta	*verde*
Rice	Riso
Rice dish	Risotto
with mushrooms	*ai funghi*
with saffron	*alla milanese*
Noodles	Tagliatelle
Pizza	Pizza
Pizza with seafood, cheese, artichokes, and ham in four different sections	Pizza quattro stagioni
Pizza with tomato and mozzarella	Pizza margherita
Pizza with oil, garlic, and oregano	Pizza marinara

Fish and Seafood

Anchovies	Acciughe
Bass	Persico
Carp	Carpa
Clams	Vongole
Cod	Merluzzo
Crab	Granchio
Eel	Anguilla
Lobster	Aragosta
Mackerel	Sgombro
Mullet	Triglia
Mussels	Cozze
Octopus	Polpo
Oysters	Ostriche
Pike	Luccio
Prawns	Gamberoni
Salmon	Salmone
Shrimp	Scampi
Shrimps	Gamberetti
Sole	Sogliola
Squid	Calamari
Swordfish	Pescespada

| Trout | Trota |
| Tuna | Tonno |

Methods of Preparation

Baked	Al forno
Cold, with vinegar sauce	In carpione
Fish stew	Zuppa di pesce
Fried	Fritto
Grilled (usually charcoal)	Alla griglia
Seafood salad	In insalata
Smoked	Affumicato
Stuffed	Ripieno

Meat

Boar	Cinghiale
Brain	Cervella
Braised meat with wine	Brasato
Chop	Costoletta
Duck	Anatra
Lamb	Agnello
Baby lamb	Abbacchio
Liver	Fegato
Pheasant	Fagiano
Pork roast	Arista
Rabbit	Coniglio
Steak	Bistecca
Sliced raw steak with sauce	Carpaccio
Mixed boiled meat	Bollito misto

Methods of Preparation

Battered with eggs and crumbs and fried	. . . alla milanese
Grilled	. . . ai ferri
Grilled (usually charcoal)	. . . alla griglia
Raw, with lemon/egg sauce	. . . alla tartara
Roasted	. . . arrosto
Very rare	. . . al sangue
Well done	. . . ben cotta
With ham and cheese	. . . alla valdostana
With parmesan cheese and tomatoes	. . . alla parmigiana

Vegetables

Artichokes	Carciofi
Asparagus	Asparagi
Beans	Fagioli

Brussels sprouts	Cavolini di Bruxelles
Cabbage	Cavolo
Carrots	Carote
Cauliflower	Cavolfiore
Cucumber	Cetriolo
Eggplants	Melanzane
Green beans	Fagiolini
Leeks	Porri
Lentils	Lenticchie
Lettuce	Lattuga
Mushrooms	Funghi
Onions	Cipolle
Peas	Piselli
Peppers	Peperoni
Potatoes	Patate
Roasted potatoes	*Patate arroste*
Boiled potatoes	*Patate bollite*
Fried potatoes	*Patate fritte*
Small, roasted potatoes	*Patatine novelle*
Mashed potatoes	*Purè di patate*
Radishes	Rapanelli
Salad	Insalata
vegetable	*mista*
green	*verde*
Spinach	Spinaci
Tomatoes	Pomodori
Zucchini	Zucchini

Sauces, Herbs, and Spices

Basil	Basilico
Bay leaf	Lauro
Chervil	Cerfoglio
Dill	Aneto
Garlic	Aglio
Hot dip with anchovies (for vegetables)	Bagna cauda
Marjoram	Maggiorana
Mayonnaise	Maionese
Mustard	Mostarda *or* senape
Oil	Olio
Parsley-based sauce	Salsa verde
Pepper	Pepe
Rosemary	Rosmarino
Tartar sauce	Salsa tartara
Vinegar	Aceto
White sauce	Besciamella

Cheeses

Fresh:	Caprino fresco
	Mascarpone
	Mozzarella
	Ricotta
Mild:	Caciotta
	Caprino
	Fontina
	Grana
	Provola
	Provolone dolce
	Robiola
	Scamorza
Sharp:	Asiago
	Gorgonzola
	Groviera
	Pecorino
	Provolone piccante
	Taleggio
	Toma

Fruits and Nuts

Almonds	Mandorle
Apple	Mela
Apricot	Albicocca
Blackberries	More
Black currant	Ribes nero
Blueberries	Mirtilli
Cherries	Ciliege
Chestnuts	Castagne
Coconut	Noce di cocco
Dates	Datteri
Figs	Fichi
Green grapes	Uva bianca
Black grapes	Uva nera
Grapefruit	Pompelmo
Hazelnuts	Nocciole
Lemon	Limone
Melon	Melone
Nectarine	Nocepesca
Orange	Arancia
Pear	Pera
Peach	Pesca
Pineapple	Ananas
Plum	Prugna/Susina
Prune	Prugna secca

Raisins	Uva passa
Raspberries	Lamponi
Red currant	Ribes
Strawberries	Fragole
Tangerine	Mandarino
Walnuts	Noci
Watermelon	Anguria/Cocomero
Dried fruit	Frutta secca
Fresh fruit	Frutta fresca
Fruit salad	Macedonia di frutta

Desserts

Custard filed pastry, with candied fruit	Cannoli
Ricotta filled pastry shells with sugar glaze	Cannoli alla siciliana
Ice cream with candied fruit	Cassata
Ricotta filed cake with sugar glaze	Cassata siciliana
Chocolate	Cioccolato
Cup of ice cream	Coppa gelato
Caramel custard	Crème caramel
Pie	Crostata
Fruit pie	Crostata di frutta
Ice cream	Gelato
Flaked pastry	Millefoglie
Chestnuts and whipped-cream cake	Montebianco
Whipped cream	Panna montata
Pastries	Paste
Sherbet	Sorbetto
Chocolate-coated ice cream	Tartufo
Fruit tart	Torta di frutta
Apple tart	Torta di mele
Ice-cream cake	Torta gelata
Vanilla	Vaniglia
Egg-based cream with sugar and Marsala wine	Zabaione
Ice-cream filled cake	Zuccotto

Alcoholic Drinks

On the rocks	Con ghiaccio
Straight	Liscio
With soda	Con seltz
Beer	Birra
light/dark	*chiara/scura*

Bitter cordial	Amaro
Brandy	Cognac
Cordial	Liquore
Aniseed cordial	Sambuca
Martini	Cocktail Martini
Port	Porto
Vermouth	Vermut/Martini
Wine	Vino
blush	*rosé*
dry	*secco*
full-bodied	*corposo*
light	*leggero*
red	*rosso*
sparkling	*spumante*
sweet	*dolce*
very dry	*brut*
white	*bianco*
Light wine	Vinello
Bottle	Bottiglia
Carafe	Caraffa
Flask	Fiasco

Nonalcoholic Drinks

Mineral water	Acqua minerale
carbonated	*gassata*
still	*non gassata*
Tap water	Acqua naturale
Tonic water	Acqua tonica
Coffee with steamed milk	Cappuccino
Espresso	Caffè espresso
with milk	*macchiato*
decaffeinated	*decaffeinato*
lighter espresso	*lungo*
with cordial	*corretto*
Fruit juice	Succo di frutta
Lemonade	Limonata
Milk	Latte
Orangeade	Aranciata
Tea	Tè
with milk/lemon	*col latte/col limone*
iced	*freddo*

INDEX